T0325729

Compact Data Structures

A Practical Approach

Compact data structures help represent data in reduced space while allowing querying, navigating, and operating it in compressed form. They are essential tools for efficiently handling massive amounts of data by exploiting the memory hierarchy. They also reduce the resources needed in distributed deployments and make better use of the limited memory in low-end devices.

The field has developed rapidly, reaching a level of maturity that allows practitioners and researchers in application areas to benefit from the use of compact data structures. This first comprehensive book on the topic focuses on the structures that are most relevant for practical use. Readers will learn how the structures work, how to choose the right ones for their application scenario, and how to implement them. Researchers and students in the area will find in the book a definitive guide to the state of the art in compact data structures.

Gonzalo Navarro is Professor of Computer Science at the University of Chile. He has worked for 20 years on the relation between compression and data structures. He has directed or participated in numerous large projects on web research, information retrieval, compressed data structures, and bioinformatics. He is the Editor in Chief of the *ACM Journal of Experimental Algorithmics* and also a member of the editorial board of the journals *Information Retrieval* and *Information Systems*. His publications include the book *Flexible Pattern Matching in Strings* (with M. Raffinot), 20 book chapters, more than 100 journal papers and 200 conference papers; he has also chaired eight international conferences.

Compact Data Structures

A Practical Approach

Gonzalo Navarro

Department of Computer Science,
University of Chile

CAMBRIDGE
UNIVERSITY PRESS

Shaftesbury Road, Cambridge CB2 8EA, United Kingdom

One Liberty Plaza, 20th Floor, New York, NY 10006, USA

477 Williamstown Road, Port Melbourne, VIC 3207, Australia

314–321, 3rd Floor, Plot 3, Splendor Forum, Jasola District Centre, New Delhi – 110025, India

103 Penang Road, #05–06/07, Visioncrest Commercial, Singapore 238467

Cambridge University Press is part of Cambridge University Press & Assessment, a department of the University of Cambridge.

We share the University's mission to contribute to society through the pursuit of education, learning and research at the highest international levels of excellence.

www.cambridge.org
Information on this title: www.cambridge.org/9781107152380

First published 2016

A catalogue record for this publication is available from the British Library

Library of Congress Cataloging-in-Publication data
Names: Navarro, Gonzalo, 1969– author.
Title: Compact data structures : a practical approach / Gonzalo Navarro, Universidad de Chile.
Description: New York, NY : University of Cambridge, [2016] | Includes bibliographical references and index.
Identifiers: LCCN 2016023641 | ISBN 9781107152380 (hardback : alk. paper)
Subjects: LCSH: Data structures (Computer science) | Computer algorithms.
Classification: LCC QA76.9.D35 N38 2016 | DDC 005.7/3–dc23
LC record available at https://lccn.loc.gov/2016023641

ISBN   978-1-107-15238-0   Hardback

A Aylén, Facundo y Martina, que aún me creen.
A Betina, que aún me soporta.
A mi padre, a mi hermana, y a la memoria de mi madre.

Contents

List of Algorithms

Foreword

This is a delightful book on data structures that are both time and space efficient. Space as well as time efficiency is crucial in modern information systems. Even if we have extra space somewhere, it is unlikely to be close to the processors. The space used by most such systems is overwhelmingly for structural indexing, such as B-trees, hash tables, and various cross-references, rather than for "raw data." Indeed data, such as text, take far too much space in raw form and must be compressed. A system that keeps both data and indices in a compact form has a major advantage.

Hence the title of the book. Gonzalo Navarro uses the term "compact data structures" to describe a newly emerging research area. It has developed from two distinct but interrelated topics. The older is that of text compression, dating back to the work of Shannon, Fano, and Huffman (among others) in the late 1940s and early 1950s (although text compression as such was not their main concern). Through the last half of the 20th century, as the size of the text to be processed increased and computing platforms became more powerful, algorithmics and information theory became much more sophisticated. The goal of data compression, at least until the year 2000 or so, simply meant compressing information as well as possible and then decompressing each time it was needed. A hallmark of compact data structures is working with text in compressed form saving both decompression time and space. The newer contributing area evolved in the 1990s after the work of Jacobson and is generally referred to as "succinct data structures." The idea is to represent a combinatorial object, such as a graph, tree, or sparse bit vector, in a number of bits that differs from the information theory lower bound by only a lower order term. So, for example, a binary tree on n nodes takes only $2n + o(n)$ bits. The trick is to perform the necessary operations, e.g., find child, parent, or subtree size, in constant time.

Compact data structures take into account both "data" and "structures" and are a little more tolerant of "best effort" than one might be with exact details of information theoretic lower bounds. Here the subtitle, "A Practical Approach," comes into play. The emphasis is on methods that are reasonable to implement and appropriate for today's (and tomorrow's) data sizes, rather than on the asymptotics that one sees with the "theoretical approach."

Reading the book, I was taken with the thorough coverage of the topic and the clarity of presentation. Finding, easily, specific results was, well, easy, as suits the experienced researcher in the field. On the other hand, the careful exposition of key concepts, with elucidating examples, makes it ideal as a graduate text or for the researcher from a tangentially related area. The book covers the historical and mathematical background along with the key developments of the 1990s and early years of the current century, which form its core. Text indexing has been a major driving force for the area, and techniques for it are nicely covered. The final two chapters point to long-term challenges and recent advances. Updates to compact data structures have been a problem for as long as the topic has been studied. The treatment here is not only state of the art but will undoubtedly be a major influence on further improvements to dynamic structures, a key aspect of improving their applicability. The final chapter focuses on encodings, working with repetitive text, and issues of the memory hierarchy. The book will be a key reference and guiding light in the field for years to come.

J. Ian Munro
University of Waterloo

Acknowledgments

I am indebted to Joshimar Córdova and Simon Gog, who took the time to exhaustively read large portions of the book. They made a number of useful comments and killed many dangerous bugs. Several other students and colleagues read parts of the book and also made useful suggestions: Travis Gagie, Patricio Huepe, Roberto Konow, Susana Ladra, Veli Mäkinen, Miguel Ángel Martínez-Prieto, Ian Munro, and Alberto Ordóñez. Others, like Yakov Nekrich, Rajeev Raman, and Kunihiko Sadakane, saved me hours of searching by providing instant answers to my questions. Last but not least, Renato Cerro carefully polished my English grammar. It is most likely that some bugs remain, for which I am the only one to blame.

Ian Munro enthusiastically agreed to write the Foreword of the book. My thanks, again, to a pioneer of this beautiful area.

I would also like to thank my family for bearing with me along this two-year-long effort. It has been much more fun for me than for them.

Finally, I wish to thank the Department of Computer Science at the University of Chile for giving me the opportunity of a life dedicated to academia in a friendly and supportive environment.

CHAPTER 1
Introduction

1.1 Why Compact Data Structures?

Google's stated mission, "to organize the world's information and make it universally accessible and useful," could not better capture the immense ambition of modern society for gathering all kinds of data and putting them to use to improve our lives. We are collecting not only huge amounts of data from the physical world (astronomical, climatological, geographical, biological), but also human-generated data (voice, pictures, music, video, books, news, Web contents, emails, blogs, tweets) and society-based behavioral data (markets, shopping, traffic, clicks, Web navigation, likes, friendship networks).

Our hunger for more and more information is flooding our lives with data. Technology is improving and our ability to store data is growing fast, but the data we are collecting also grow fast – in many cases faster than our storage capacities. While our ability to store the data in secondary or perhaps tertiary storage does not yet seem to be compromised, performing the desired processing of these data in the main memory of computers is becoming more and more difficult. Since accessing a datum in main memory is about 10^5 times faster than on disk, operating in main memory is crucial for carrying out many data-processing applications.

In many cases, the problem is not so much the size of the actual data, but that of the *data structures* that must be built on the data in order to efficiently carry out the desired processing or queries. In some cases the data structures are one or two orders of magnitude larger than the data! For example, the DNA of a human genome, of about 3.3 billion bases, requires slightly less than 800 megabytes if we use only 2 bits per base (A, C, G, T), which fits in the main memory of any desktop PC. However, the suffix tree, a powerful data structure used to efficiently perform sequence analysis on the genome, requires at least 10 bytes per base, that is, more than 30 gigabytes.

The main techniques to cope with the growing size of data over recent years can be classified into three families:

1

Efficient secondary-memory algorithms. While accessing a random datum from disk
is comparatively very slow, subsequent data are read much faster, only 100 times
slower than from main memory. Therefore, algorithms that minimize the random
accesses to the data can perform reasonably well on disk. Not every problem,
however, admits a good disk-based solution.

Streaming algorithms. In these algorithms one goes to the extreme of allowing only
one or a small number of sequential passes over the data, storing intermediate
values on a comparatively small main memory. When only one pass over the data
is allowed, the algorithm can handle situations in which the data cannot even be
stored on disk, because they either are too large or flow too fast. In many cases
streaming algorithms aim at computing approximate information from the data.

Distributed algorithms. These are parallel algorithms that work on a number of computers connected through a local-area network. Network transfer speeds are around
10 times slower than those of disks. However, some algorithms are amenable to
parallelization in a way that the data can be partitioned over the processors and
little transfer of data is needed.

Each of these approaches pays a price in terms of performance or accuracy, and
neither one is always applicable. There are also cases where memory is limited and a
large secondary memory is not at hand: routers, smartphones, smartwatches, sensors,
and a large number of low-end embedded devices that are more and more frequently
seen everywhere (indeed, they are the stars of the promised Internet of Things).

A topic that is strongly related to the problem of managing large volumes of data
is *compression*, which seeks a way of representing data using less space. Compression
builds on Information Theory, which studies the minimum space necessary to represent
the data.

Most compression algorithms require decompressing all of the data from the beginning before we can access a random datum. Therefore, compression generally serves
as a space-saving *archival* method: the data can be *stored* using less space but must be
fully decompressed before being used again. Compression is not useful for managing
more data in main memory, except if we need only to process the data sequentially.

Compact data structures aim precisely at this challenge. A compact data structure
maintains the data, and the desired extra data structures over it, in a form that not only
uses less space, but is able to access and query the data *in compact form*, that is, without
decompressing them. Thus, a compact data structure allows us to fit and efficiently
query, navigate, and manipulate much larger datasets in main memory than what would
be possible if we used the data represented in plain form and classical data structures
on top.

Compact data structures lie at the intersection of Data Structures and Information
Theory. One looks at data representations that not only need space close to the minimum possible (as in compression) but also require that those representations allow
one to efficiently carry out some operations on the data. In terms of information, data
structures are fully *redundant*: they can be reconstructed from the data itself. However,
they are built for efficiency reasons: once they are built from the data, data structures
speed up operations significantly. When designing compact data structures, one strug-
gles with this tradeoff: supporting the desired operations as efficiently as possible while

increasing the space as little as possible. In some.lucky cases, a compact data structure reaches almost the minimum possible space to represent the data and provides a rich functionality that encompasses what is provided by a number of independent data structures. General trees and text collections are probably the two most striking success stories of compact data structures (and they have been combined to store the human genome *and* its suffix tree in less than 4 gigabytes!).

Compact data structures usually require more steps than classical data structures to complete the same operations. However, if these operations are carried out on a faster memory, the net result is a faster (and smaller) representation. This can occur at any level of the memory hierarchy; for example, a compact data structure may be faster because it fits in cache when the classical one does not. The most dramatic improvement, however, is seen when the compact data structure fits in main memory while the classical one needs to be handled on disk (even if it is a solid-state device). In some cases, such as limited-memory devices, compact data structures may be the only approach to operate on larger datasets.

The other techniques we have described can also benefit from the use of compact data structures. For example, distributed algorithms may use fewer computers to carry out the same task, as their aggregated memory is virtually enlarged. This reduces hardware, communication, and energy costs. Secondary-memory algorithms may also benefit from a virtually larger main memory by reducing the amount of disk transfers. Streaming algorithms may store more accurate estimations within the same main memory budget.

1.2 Why This Book?

The starting point of the formal study of compact data structures can be traced back to the 1988 Ph.D. thesis of Jacobson, although earlier works, in retrospect, can also be said to belong to this area. Since then, the study of these structures has flourished, and research articles appear routinely in most conferences and journals on algorithms, compression, and databases. Various software repositories offer mature libraries implementing generic or problem-specific compact data structures. There are also indications of the increasing use of compact data structures inside the products of Google, Facebook, and others.

We believe that compact data structures have reached a level of maturity that deserves a book to introduce them. There are already established compact data structures to represent bitvectors, sequences, permutations, trees, grids, binary relations, graphs, tries, text collections, and others. Surprisingly, there are no other books on this topic as far as we know, and for many relevant structures there are no survey articles.

This book aims to introduce the reader to the fascinating algorithmic world of the compact data structures, with a strong emphasis on practicality. Most of the structures we present have been implemented and found to be reasonably easy to code and efficient in space and time. A few of the structures we present have not yet been implemented, but based on our experience we believe they will be practical as well. We have obtained the material from the large universe of published results and from our own experience, carefully choosing the results that should be most relevant to a practitioner. Each chapter finishes with a list of selected references to guide the reader who wants to go further.

On the other hand, we do not leave aside the theory, which is essential for a solid understanding of why and how the data structures work, and thus for applying and extending them to face new challenges. We gently introduce the reader to the beauty of the algorithmics and the mathematics that are behind the study of compact data structures. Only a basic background is expected from the reader. From algorithmics, knowledge of sorting, binary search, dynamic programming, graph traversals, hashing, lists, stacks, queues, priority queues, trees, and $\mathcal{O}$-notation suffices (we will briefly review this notation later in this chapter). This material corresponds to a first course on algorithms and data structures. From mathematics, understanding of induction, basic combinatorics, probability, summations, and limits, that is, a first-year university course on algebra or discrete mathematics, is sufficient.

We expect this book to be useful for advanced undergraduate students, graduate students, researchers, and professionals interested in algorithmic topics. Hopefully you will enjoy the reading as much as I have enjoyed writing it.

1.3 Organization

The book is divided into 13 chapters. Each chapter builds on previous ones to introduce a new concept and includes a section on applications and a bibliographic discussion at the end. Applications are smaller or more specific problems where the described data structures provide useful solutions. Most can be safely skipped if the reader has no time, but we expect them to be inspiring. The bibliography contains annotated references pointing to the best sources of the material described in the chapter (which not always are the first publications), the most relevant historic landmarks in the development of the results, and open problems. This section is generally denser and can be safely skipped by readers not interested in going deeper, especially into the theoretical aspects.

Pseudocode is included for most of the procedures we describe. The pseudocode is presented in an algorithmic language, not in any specific programming language. For example, well-known variables are taken as global without notice, widely known procedures such as a binary search are not detailed, and tedious but obvious details are omitted (with notice). This lets us focus on the important aspects that we want the pseudocode to clear up; our intention is not that the pseudocode is a cut-and-paste text to get the structures running without understanding them. We refrain from making various programming-level optimizations to the pseudocode to favor clarity; any good programmer should be able to considerably speed up a verbatim implementation of the pseudocodes without altering their logic.

After this introductory chapter, Chapter 2 introduces the concepts of Information Theory and compression needed to follow the book. In particular, we introduce the concepts of worst-case, Shannon, and empirical entropy and their relations. This is the most mathematical part of the book. We also introduce Huffman codes and codes suitable for small integers.

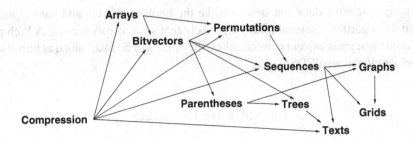

Figure 1.1. The most important dependencies among Chapters 2–11.

The subsequent chapters describe compact data structures for different problems. Each compact data structure stores some kind of data and supports a well-defined set of operations. Chapter 3 considers arrays, which support the operations of reading and writing values at arbitrary positions. Chapter 4 describes bitvectors, arrays of bits that in addition support a couple of bit-counting operations. Chapter 5 covers representations of permutations that support both the application of the permutation and its inverse as well as powers of the permutation. Chapter 6 considers sequences of symbols, which, apart from accessing the sequence, support a couple of symbol-counting operations. Chapter 7 addresses hierarchical structures described with balanced sequences of parentheses and operations to navigate them. Chapter 8 deals with the representation of general trees, which support a large number of query and navigation operations. Chapter 9 considers graph representations, both general ones and for some specific families such as planar graphs, allowing navigation toward neighbors. Chapter 10 considers discrete two-dimensional grids of points, with operations for counting and reporting points in a query rectangle. Chapter 11 shows how text collections can be represented so that pattern search queries are supported.

As said, each chapter builds upon the structures described previously, although most of them can be read independently with only a conceptual understanding of what the operations on previous structures mean. Figure 1.1 shows the most important dependencies for understanding why previous structures reach the claimed space and time performance.

These chapters are dedicated to *static* data structures, that is, those that are built once and then serve many queries. These are the most developed and generally the most efficient ones. We pay attention to construction time and, especially, construction space, ensuring that structures that take little space can also be built within little extra memory, or that the construction is disk-friendly. Structures that support updates are called *dynamic* and are considered in Chapter 12.

The book concludes in Chapter 13, which surveys some current research topics on compact data structures: encoding data structures, indexes for repetitive text collections, and data structures for secondary storage. Those areas are not general or mature enough to be included in previous chapters, yet they are very promising and will probably be the focus of much research in the upcoming years. The chapter then also serves as a guide to current research topics in this area.

Although we have done our best to make the book error-free, and have manually verified the algorithms several times, it is likely that some errors remain. A Web page with comments, updates, and corrections on the book will be maintained at http://www .dcc.uchile.cl/gnavarro/CDSbook.

1.4 Software Resources

Although this book focuses on understanding the compact data structures so that the readers can implement them by themselves, it is worth noting that there are several open-source software repositories with mature implementations, both for general and for problem-specific compact data structures. These are valuable both for practitioners that need a structure implemented efficiently, well tested, and ready to be used, and for students and researchers that wish to build further structures on top of them. In both cases, understanding why and how each structure works is essential to making the right decisions on which structure to use for which problem, how to parameterize it, and what can be expected from it.

Probably the most general, professional, exhaustive, and well tested of all these libraries is Simon Gog's *Succinct Data Structure Library (SDSL)*, available at https:// github.com/simongog/sdsl-lite. It contains C++ implementations of compact data structures for bitvectors, arrays, sequences, text indexes, trees, range minimum queries, and suffix trees, among others. The library includes tools to verify correctness and measure efficiency along with tutorials and examples.

Another generic library is Francisco Claude's *Library of Compact Data Structures (LIBCDS)*, available at https://github.com/fclaude/libcds. It contains optimized and well-tested C++ implementations of bitvectors, sequences, permutations, and others. A tutorial on how to use the library and how it works is included.

Sebastiano Vigna's *Sux* library, available at http://sux.di.unimi.it, contains high-quality C++ and/or Java implementations of various compact data structures, including bitvectors, arrays with cells of varying lengths, and (general and monotone) minimal perfect hashing. Other projects accessible from there include sophisticated tools to manage inverted indexes and Web graphs in compressed form.

Giuseppe Ottaviano's *Succinct* library provides efficient C++ implementations of bitvectors, arrays of fixed and variable-length cells, range minimum queries, and others. It is available at https://github.com/ot/succinct.

Finally, Nicola Prezza's *Dynamic* library provides C++ implementations of various data structures supporting insertions of new elements: partial sums, bitvectors, sparse arrays, strings, and text indexes. It is available at https://github.com/nicolaprezza/ DYNAMIC.

The authors of many of these libraries have explored much deeper practical aspects of the implementation, including cache efficiency, address translation, word alignments, machine instructions for long computer words, instruction pipelining, and other issues beyond the scope of this book.

Many other authors of articles on practical compact data structures for specific problems have left their implementations publicly available or are willing to share them upon request. There are too many to list here, but browsing the personal pages of the authors, or requesting the code, is probably a fast way to obtain a good implementation.

1.5 Mathematics and Notation

This final technical section is a reminder of the mathematics behind the $\mathcal{O}$-notation, which we use to describe the time performance of algorithms and the space usage of data structures. We also introduce other notation used throughout the book.

$\mathcal{O}$-notation. This notation is used to describe the asymptotic growth of functions (for example, the cost of an algorithm as a function of the size of the input) in a way that considers only sufficiently large values of the argument (hence the name "asymptotic") and ignores constant factors.

Formally, $\mathcal{O}(f(n))$ is the set of all functions $g(n)$ for which there exist constants $c > 0$ and $n_0 > 0$ such that, for all $n > n_0$, it holds $|g(n)| \leq c \cdot |f(n)|$. We say that $g(n)$ is $\mathcal{O}(f(n))$, meaning that $g(n) \in \mathcal{O}(f(n))$. Thus, for example, $3n^2 + 6n - 3$ is $\mathcal{O}(n^2)$ and also $\mathcal{O}(n^3)$, but it is not $\mathcal{O}(n \log n)$. In particular, $\mathcal{O}(1)$ is used to denote a function that is always below some constant. For example, the cost of an algorithm that, independently of the input size, performs 3 accesses to tables and terminates is $\mathcal{O}(1)$. An algorithm taking $\mathcal{O}(1)$ time is said to be constant-time.

It is also common to abuse the notation and write $g(n) = \mathcal{O}(f(n))$ to mean $g(n) \in \mathcal{O}(f(n))$, and even to write, say, $g(n) < 2n + \mathcal{O}(\log n)$, meaning that $g(n)$ is smaller than $2n$ plus a function that is $\mathcal{O}(\log n)$. Sometimes we will write, for example, $g(n) = 2n - \mathcal{O}(\log n)$, to stress that $g(n) \leq 2n$ and the function that separates $g(n)$ from $2n$ is $\mathcal{O}(\log n)$.

Several other notations are related to $\mathcal{O}$. Mostly for lower bounds, we write $g(n) \in \Omega(f(n))$, meaning that there exist constants $c > 0$ and $n_0 > 0$ such that, for all $n > n_0$, it holds $|g(n)| \geq c \cdot |f(n)|$. Alternatively, we can define $g(n) \in \Omega(f(n))$ iff $f(n) \in \mathcal{O}(g(n))$. We say that $g(n)$ is $\Theta(f(n))$ to mean that $g(n)$ is $\mathcal{O}(f(n))$ and also $\Omega(f(n))$. This means that both functions grow, asymptotically, at the same speed, except for a constant factor.

To denote functions that are asymptotically negligible compared to $f(n)$, we use $g(n) = o(f(n))$, which means that $\lim_{n \to \infty} \frac{g(n)}{f(n)} = 0$. For example, saying that a data structure uses $2n + o(n)$ bits means that it uses $2n$ plus a number of bits that grows sublinearly with n, such as $2n + \mathcal{O}(n/\log n)$. The notation $o(1)$ denotes a function that tends to zero as n tends to infinity, for example, $\log \log n / \log n = o(1)$. Finally, the opposite of the $o(\cdot)$ notation is $\omega(\cdot)$, where $g(n) = \omega(f(n))$ iff $f(n) = o(g(n))$. In particular, $\omega(1)$ denotes a function that tends to infinity (no matter how slowly) when n tends to infinity. For example, $\log \log n = \omega(1)$.

When several variables are used, as in $o(n \log \sigma)$, it must be clear to which the $o(\cdot)$ notation refers. For example, $n \log \log \sigma$ is $o(n \log \sigma)$ if the variable is σ, or if the variable is n but σ grows with n (i.e., $\sigma = \omega(1)$ as a function of n). Otherwise, if we refer to n but σ is a constant, then $n \log \log \sigma$ is not $o(n \log \sigma)$.

These notations are also used on decreasing functions of n, to describe error margins. For example, we may approximate the harmonic number $H_n = \sum_{k=1}^{n} \frac{1}{k} = \ln$

$n + \gamma + \frac{1}{2n} - \frac{1}{12n^2} + \frac{1}{120n^4} - \ldots$, where $\gamma \approx 0.577$ is a constant, with any of the following formulas, having a decreasing level of detail:[1]

$$H_n = \ln n + \gamma + \frac{1}{2n} + \mathcal{O}\left(\frac{1}{n^2}\right)$$

$$= \ln n + \gamma + \mathcal{O}\left(\frac{1}{n}\right)$$

$$= \ln n + \mathcal{O}(1)$$

$$= \mathcal{O}(\log n),$$

depending on the degree of accuracy we want. We can also use $o(\cdot)$ to give less details about the error level, for example,

$$H_n = \ln n + \gamma + \frac{1}{2n} + o\left(\frac{1}{n}\right)$$

$$= \ln n + \gamma + o(1)$$

$$= \ln n + o(\log n).$$

We can also write the error in relative form, for example,

$$H_n = \ln n + \gamma + \frac{1}{2n} \cdot \left(1 + \mathcal{O}\left(\frac{1}{n}\right)\right)$$

$$= \ln n \cdot \left(1 + \mathcal{O}\left(\frac{1}{\log n}\right)\right)$$

$$= \ln n \cdot (1 + o(1)).$$

When using the notation to denote errors, the inequality $\frac{1}{1+x} = 1 - x + x^2 - \ldots = 1 - \mathcal{O}(x)$, for any $0 < x < 1$, allows us to write $\frac{1}{1+o(1)} = 1 + o(1)$, which is useful for moving error terms from the denominator to the numerator.

Logarithm. This is a very important function in Information Theory, as it is the key to describing the entropy, or amount of information, in an object. When the entropy (or information) is described in bits, the logarithm must be to the base 2. We use log to denote the logarithm to the base 2. When we use a logarithm to some other base b, we write $\log_b$. As shown, the natural logarithm is written as ln. Of course, the base of the logarithm makes no difference inside $\mathcal{O}$-formulas (unless it is in the exponent!).

The inequality $\frac{x}{1+x} \leq \ln(1 + x) \leq x$ is useful in many cases, in particular in combination with the $\mathcal{O}$-notation. For example,

$$\ln(n(1 + o(1))) = \ln n + \ln(1 + o(1)) \leq \ln n + o(1).$$

It also holds

$$\ln(n(1 + o(1))) \geq \ln n + \frac{o(1)}{1 + o(1)} = \ln n + o(1).$$

---

[1] In the first line, we use the fact that the tail of the series converges to $\frac{c}{n^2}$, for some constant c.

Therefore, $\ln(n(1 + o(1))) = \ln n + o(1)$. More generally, if $f(n) = o(1)$, and b is any constant, we can write $\log_b(n(1 + f(n))) = \log_b n + \mathcal{O}(f(n))$. For example, $\log(n + \log n) = \log n + \mathcal{O}(\log n/n)$.

Model of computation. We consider realistic computers, with a computer word of w bits, where we can carry out in constant time all the basic arithmetic $(+, -, \cdot, /,$ mod, ceilings and floors, etc.) and logic operations (bitwise *and, or, not, xor,* bit shifts, etc.). In modern computers w is almost always 32 or 64, but several architectures allow for larger words to be handled natively, reaching, for example, 128, 256, or 512 bits.

When connecting with theory, this essentially corresponds to the RAM model of computation, where we do not pay attention to restrictions in some branches of the RAM model that are unrealistic on modern computers (for example, some variants disallow multiplication and division). In the RAM model, it is usually assumed that the computer word has $w = \Theta(\log n)$ bits, where n is the size of the data in memory. This logarithmic model of growth of the computer word is appropriate in practice, as w has been growing approximately as the logarithm of the size of main memories. It is also reasonable to expect that we can store any memory address in a constant number of words (and in constant time).

For simplicity and practicality, we will use the assumption $w \geq \log n$, which means that with one computer word we can address any data element. While the assumption $w = \mathcal{O}(\log n)$ may also be justified (we may argue that the data should be large enough for the compact storage problem to be of interest), this is not always the case. For example, the dynamic structures (Chapter 12) may grow and shrink over time. Therefore, we will not rely on this assumption. Thus, for example, we will say that the cost of an algorithm that inspects n bits by chunks of w bits, processing each chunk in constant time, is $\mathcal{O}(n/w) = \mathcal{O}(n/\log n) = o(n)$. Instead, we will not take an $\mathcal{O}(w)$-time algorithm to be $\mathcal{O}(\log n)$.

Strings, sequences, and intervals. In most cases, our arrays start at position 1. With $[a, b]$ we denote the set $\{a, a + 1, a + 2, \ldots, b\}$, unless we explicitly imply it is a real interval. For example, $A[1, n]$ denotes an array of n elements $A[1], A[2], \ldots, A[n]$. A *string* is an array of elements drawn from a finite universe, called the *alphabet*. Alphabets are usually denoted $\Sigma = [1, \sigma]$, where σ is some integer, meaning that $\Sigma = \{1, 2, \ldots, \sigma\}$. The alphabet elements are called *symbols, characters,* or *letters*. The *length* of the string $S[1, n]$ is $|S| = n$. The set of all the strings of length n over alphabet Σ is denoted Σ^n, and the set of all the strings of any length over Σ is denoted $\Sigma^* = \cup_{n \geq 0} \Sigma^n$. Strings and sequences are basically synonyms in this book; however, substring and subsequence are different concepts. Given a string $S[1, n]$, a *substring* $S[i, j]$ is, precisely, the array $S[i], S[i + 1], \ldots, S[j]$. Particular cases of substrings are *prefixes*, of the form $S[1, j]$, and *suffixes*, of the form $S[i, n]$. When $i > j$, $S[i, j]$ denotes the empty string ε, that is, the only string of length zero. A *subsequence* is more general than a substring: it can be any $S[i_1] . S[i_2] \ldots S[i_r]$ for $i_1 < i_2 < \ldots < i_r$, where we use the dot to denote concatenation of symbols (we might also simply write one symbol after the other, or mix strings and symbols in a concatenation). Sometimes we will also use $\langle a, b \rangle$ to denote the same as $[a, b]$ or write sequences as $\langle a_1, a_2, \ldots, a_n \rangle$. Finally, given a string $S[1, n]$, S^{rev} denotes the reversed string, $S[n] . S[n - 1] \ldots S[2] . S[1]$.

1.6 Bibliographic Notes

Growth of information and computing power. Google's mission is stated in http://www.google.com/about/company.

There are many sources that describe the amount of information the world is gathering. For example, a 2011 study from *International Data Corporation (IDC)* found that we are generating a few zettabytes per year (a zettabyte is 2^{70}, or roughly 10^{21}, bytes), and that data are more than doubling per year, outperforming Moore's law (which governs the growth of hardware capacities).[2] A related discussion from 2013, arguing that we are much better at storing than at using all these data, can be read in *Datamation*.[3] For a shocking and graphical message, the 2012 poster of *Domo* is also telling.[4]

There are also many sources about the differences in performance between CPU, caches, main memory, and secondary storage, as well as how these have evolved over the years. In particular, we used the book of Hennessy and Patterson (2012, Chap. 1) for the rough numbers shown here.

Examples of books about the mentioned algorithmic approaches to solve the problem of data growth are, among many others, Vitter (2008) for secondary-memory algorithms, Muthukrishnan (2005) for streaming algorithms, and Roosta (1999) for distributed algorithms.

Suffix trees. The book by Gusfield (1997) provides a good introduction to suffix trees in the context of bioinformatics. Modern books pay more attention to space issues and make use of some of the compact data structures we describe here (Ohlebusch, 2013; Mäkinen *et al.*, 2015). Our size estimates for compressed suffix trees are taken from the Ph.D. thesis of Gog (2011).

Compact data structures. Despite some previous isolated results, the Ph.D. thesis of Jacobson (1988) is generally taken as the starting point of the systematic study of compact data structures. Jacobson coined the term *succinct data structure* to denote a data structure that uses $\log N + o(\log N)$ bits, where N is the total number of different objects that can be encoded. For example, succinct data structures for arrays of n bits must use $n + o(n)$ bits, since $N = 2^n$. To exclude mere data compressors, succinct data structures are sometimes required to support queries in constant time (Munro, 1996).

In this book we use the term *compact data structure*, which refers to the broader class of data structures that aim at using little space and query time. Other related terms are used in the literature (not always consistently) to refer to particular subclasses of data structures (Ferragina and Manzini, 2005; Gál and Miltersen, 2007; Fischer and Heun, 2011; Raman, 2015): *compressed* or *opportunistic* data structures are those using $\mathcal{H} + o(\log N)$ bits, where $\mathcal{H}$ is the entropy of the data under some compression model (such as the bit array representations we describe in Section 4.1.1); data structures using $\mathcal{H} + o(\mathcal{H})$ bits are sometimes called *fully compressed* (for example, the Huffman-shaped wavelet trees of Section 6.2.4 are almost fully compressed). A data structure that adds

---

[2] http://www.emc.com/about/news/press/2011/20110628-01.htm.
[3] http://www.datamation.com/applications/big-data-analytics-overview.html.
[4] http://www.domo.com/blog/2012/06/how-much-data-is-created-every-minute.

$o(\log N)$ bits and operates on any raw data representation that offers basic access (such as the rank and select structures for bitvectors in Sections 4.2 and 4.3) is sometimes called a *succinct index* or a *systematic* data structure. Many indexes supporting different functionalities may coexist over the same raw data, adding up to $\log N + o(\log N)$ bits. A *non-systematic* or *encoding* data structure, instead, needs to encode the data in a particular format, which may be unsuitable for another non-systematic data structure (like the wavelet trees of Section 6.2); in exchange it may use less space than the best systematic data structure (see Section 4.7 for the case of bitvectors). A data structure that uses $o(\log N)$ bits and does not need to access to the data at all is also called *non-systematic* or an *encoding*, in the sense that it does not access the raw data. Such small encodings are special, however, because they cannot possibly reproduce the original data; they answer only some types of queries on it (an example is given in Section 7.4.1; then we study encodings with more detail in Section 13.1).

The second edition of the *Encyclopedia of Algorithms* (Kao, 2016) contains good short surveys on many of the structures we discuss in the book.

Required knowledge. Good books on algorithms, which serve as a complement to follow this book, are by Cormen *et al.* (2009), Sedgewick and Wayne (2011), and Aho *et al.* (1974), among too many others to cite here. The last one (Aho *et al.*, 1974) is also a good reference for the RAM model of computation. Authoritative sources on algorithmics (yet possibly harder to read for the novice) are the monumental works of Knuth (1998) and Mehlhorn (1984). Books on algorithms generally cover analysis and $\mathcal{O}$-notation as well. Rawlins (1992) has a nice book that is more focused on analysis. The books by Graham *et al.* (1994) and by Sedgewick and Flajolet (2013) give a deeper treatment, and the handbook by Abramowitz and Stegun (1964) is an outstanding reference. Cover and Thomas (2006) offer an excellent book on Information Theory and compression fundamentals; we will cover the required concepts in Chapter 2.

Implementations. Some of the compact data structure libraries we have described have associated publications, for example, Gog's (Gog and Petri, 2014) and Ottaviano's (Grossi and Ottaviano, 2013). Another recent publication (Agarwal *et al.*, 2015) reports on *Succinct*, a distributed string store for column-oriented databases that supports updates and sophisticated string searches, achieving high performance through the use of compact data structures. No public code is reported for the latter, however.

A couple of recent articles hint at the interest inside Google for the development of compact tries (Chapter 8) for speech recognition in Android devices (Lei *et al.*, 2013) and for machine translation (Sorensen and Allauzen, 2011). A related implementation, called MARISA tries, is available at https://code.google.com/p/marisa-trie.

Facebook's *Folly* library (https://github.com/facebook/folly) now contains an implementation of Elias-Fano codes (Chapter 3).[5]

An example of the use of compressed text indexes (Chapter 11) in bioinformatic applications is the Burrows-Wheeler Aligner (BWA) software (Li and Durbin, 2010), available from http://bio-bwa.sourceforge.net.

---

[5] https://github.com/facebook/folly/blob/master/folly/experimental/EliasFanoCoding.h

Bibliography

Abramowitz, M. and Stegun, I. A. (1964). *Handbook of Mathematical Functions with Formulas, Graphs, and Mathematical Tables*. Dover, 9th edition.

Agarwal, R., Khandelwal, A., and Stoica, I. (2015). Succinct: Enabling queries on compressed data. In *Proc. 12th USENIX Symposium on Networked Systems Design and Implementation (NSDI)*, pages 337–350.

Aho, A. V., Hopcroft, J. E., and Ullman, J. D. (1974). *The Design and Analysis of Computer Algorithms*. Addison-Wesley.

Cormen, T. H., Leiserson, C. E., Rivest, R. L., and Stein, C. (2009). *Introduction to Algorithms*. MIT Press, 3rd edition.

Cover, T. and Thomas, J. (2006). *Elements of Information Theory*. Wiley, 2nd edition.

Ferragina, P. and Manzini, G. (2005). Indexing compressed texts. *Journal of the ACM*, **52**(4), 552–581.

Fischer, J. and Heun, V. (2011). Space-efficient preprocessing schemes for range minimum queries on static arrays. *SIAM Journal on Computing*, **40**(2), 465–492.

Gál, A. and Miltersen, P. B. (2007). The cell probe complexity of succinct data structures. *Theoretical Computer Science*, **379**(3), 405–417.

Gog, S. (2011). *Compressed Suffix Trees: Design, Construction, and Applications*. Ph.D. thesis, Ulm University, Germany.

Gog, S. and Petri, M. (2014). Optimized succinct data structures for massive data. *Software Practice and Experience*, **44**(11), 1287–1314.

Graham, R. L., Knuth, D. E., and Patashnik, O. (1994). *Concrete Mathematics – A Foundation for Computer Science*. Addison-Wesley, 2nd edition.

Grossi, R. and Ottaviano, G. (2013). Design of practical succinct data structures for large data collections. In *Proc. 12th International Symposium on Experimental Algorithms (SEA)*, LNCS 7933, pages 5–17.

Gusfield, D. (1997). *Algorithms on Strings, Trees and Sequences: Computer Science and Computational Biology*. Cambridge University Press.

Hennessy, J. L. and Patterson, D. A. (2012). *Computer Architecture: A Quantitative Approach*. Morgan Kauffman, 5th edition.

Jacobson, G. (1988). *Succinct Data Structures*. Ph.D. thesis, Carnegie Mellon University.

Kao, M.-Y., editor (2016). *Encyclopedia of Algorithms*. Springer, 2nd edition.

Knuth, D. E. (1998). *The Art of Computer Programming, volume 3: Sorting and Searching*. Addison-Wesley, 2nd edition.

Lei, X., Senior, A., Gruenstein, A., and Sorensen, J. (2013). Accurate and compact large vocabulary speech recognition on mobile devices. In *Proc. 14th Annual Conference of the International Speech Communication Association (INTERSPEECH)*, pages 662–665.

Li, H. and Durbin, R. (2010). Fast and accurate long-read alignment with Burrows-Wheeler transform. *Bioinformatics*, **26**(5), 589–595.

Mäkinen, V., Belazzougui, D., Cunial, F., and Tomescu, A. I. (2015). *Genome-Scale Algorithm Design*. Cambridge University Press.

Mehlhorn, K. (1984). *Data Structures and Algorithms 1: Sorting and Searching*. EATCS Monographs on Theoretical Computer Science. Springer-Verlag.

Munro, J. I. (1996). Tables. In *Proc. 16th Conference on Foundations of Software Technology and Theoretical Computer Science (FSTTCS)*, LNCS 1180, pages 37–42.

Muthukrishnan, S. (2005). *Data Streams: Algorithms and Applications*. Now Publishers.

Ohlebusch, E. (2013). *Bioinformatics Algorithms: Sequence Analysis, Genome Rearrangements, and Phylogenetic Reconstruction*. Oldenbusch Verlag.

Raman, R. (2015). Encoding data structures. In *Proc. 9th International Workshop on Algorithms and Computation (WALCOM)*, LNCS 8973, pages 1–7.

Rawlins, G. J. E. (1992). *Compared to What? An Introduction to the Analysis of Algorithms*. Computer Science Press.

Roosta, S. H. (1999). *Parallel Processing and Parallel Algorithms: Theory and Computation*. Springer.

Sedgewick, R. and Flajolet, P. (2013). *An Introduction to the Analysis of Algorithms*. Addison-Wesley-Longman, 2nd edition.

Sedgewick, R. and Wayne, K. (2011). *Algorithms*. Addison-Wesley, 4th edition.

Sorensen, J. and Allauzen, C. (2011). Unary data structures for language models. In *Proc. 12th Annual Conference of the International Speech Communication Association (INTERSPEECH)*, pages 1425–1428.

Vitter, J. S. (2008). *Algorithms and Data Structures for External Memory*. Now Publishers.

CHAPTER 2

Entropy and Coding

In this chapter we cover some minimal notions of Information Theory and Data Compression required to understand the compact data structures we present in the book. We offer further pointers at the end of the chapter.

In broad terms, the *entropy* is the minimum number of bits needed to unambiguously identify an object from a set. The entropy is then a lower bound to the space used by the compressed representation of an object. The holy grail of compressed data structures is to use essentially the space needed to identify the objects, but choosing a representation that makes it easy to answer queries on them.

2.1 Worst-Case Entropy

The most basic notion of entropy is that it is the minimum number of bits required by identifiers, called *codes*, if we assign a unique code to each element of a set $\mathcal{U}$ and all the codes are of the same length.

This is called the *worst-case* entropy of $\mathcal{U}$ and is denoted $\mathcal{H}_{\mathrm{wc}}(\mathcal{U})$. It is easy to see that

$$\mathcal{H}_{\mathrm{wc}}(\mathcal{U}) = \log |\mathcal{U}|$$

bits (recall that log is the logarithm in base 2): If we used codes of length $\ell < \mathcal{H}_{\mathrm{wc}}(\mathcal{U})$, we would have only $2^{\ell} < 2^{\mathcal{H}_{\mathrm{wc}}(\mathcal{U})} = 2^{\log |\mathcal{U}|} = |\mathcal{U}|$ distinct codes, which would be insufficient for giving a distinct code to each element in $\mathcal{U}$.

Therefore, if all the codes have the same length, this length must be at least $\lceil \mathcal{H}_{\mathrm{wc}}(\mathcal{U}) \rceil$ bits. If they are of different lengths, then the *longest* ones still must use at least $\lceil \mathcal{H}_{\mathrm{wc}}(\mathcal{U}) \rceil$ bits. This explains the adjective "worst-case."

For example, the worst-case entropy of all the sequences of n bits is $\log(2^n) = n$ bits, whereas the worst-case entropy of all the strings of length n over alphabet $\Sigma = [1, \sigma]$ is $\log(\sigma^n) = n \log \sigma$ bits. That is, one needs that many bits to encode *any possible* sequence of n symbols.

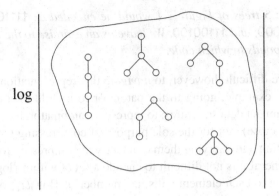

log

Figure 2.1. The worst-case entropy of $\mathcal{T}_4$, the general ordinal trees of 4 nodes.

As a more exciting example, consider the worst-case entropy of the set of all the general ordinal trees of n nodes, $\mathcal{T}_n$. In an ordinal tree, each node has an arbitrary number of children and distinguishes their order. It is known that the number of general ordinal trees is

$$|\mathcal{T}_n| = \frac{1}{n}\binom{2n-2}{n-1},$$

which is the $(n-1)$th Catalan number. By using Stirling's approximation to the factorial, $n! = \sqrt{2\pi n}\left(\frac{n}{e}\right)^n\left(1 + \mathcal{O}\left(\frac{1}{n}\right)\right)$, we have

$$|\mathcal{T}_n| = \frac{(2n-2)!}{n!(n-1)!} = \frac{(2n-2)^{2n-2}e^n e^{n-1}}{e^{2n-2}n^n(n-1)^{n-1}\sqrt{\pi n}}\left(1 + \mathcal{O}\left(\frac{1}{n}\right)\right) = \frac{4^n}{n^{3/2}}\cdot\Theta(1),$$

and therefore

$$\mathcal{H}_{\mathrm{wc}}(\mathcal{T}_n) = \log|\mathcal{T}_n| = 2n - \Theta(\log n)$$

is the minimum number of bits into which any general ordinal tree of n nodes can be encoded.

Example 2.1 *Figure 2.1 illustrates the worst-case entropy of $\mathcal{T}_4$. This is $\mathcal{H}_{\mathrm{wc}}(\mathcal{T}_4) = \log\left(\frac{1}{4}\binom{6}{3}\right) = \log 5 \approx 2.322$.*

Unlike the examples of bit sequences and strings, the classical representations of trees are very far from this number; actually they use at least n *pointers*. Since such pointers must distinguish among the n different nodes, by the same reasoning on the entropy they must use at least $\log n$ bits. Therefore, classical representations of trees use at least $n \log n$ bits, whereas $2n$ bits should be sufficient to represent any tree of n nodes.

Indeed, it is not very difficult to encode a general tree using $2n$ bits: traverse the tree in depth-first-order, writing a 1 upon arriving at a node, and a 0 when leaving it in the recursion. It is an easy exercise to see that one can recover the tree from the resulting stream of $2n$ 1s and 0s.

Example 2.2 *The 5 trees of Figure 2.1 would be encoded as* 11110000, 11010100, 11101000, 11011000, *and* 11100100. *We leave as an exercise to the reader to identify which tree corresponds to which code.*

It is much more difficult, however, to *navigate* this representation in constant time per operation; for example, going to the parent or to a child of a node. This is the whole point of compact data structures: to represent combinatorial objects within their entropy space (or close), not for the sole purpose of compressing them, but also with the aim of navigating and querying them efficiently in compressed form.

Note that in general it is not difficult to encode a set $\mathcal{U}$ within $\lceil \log |\mathcal{U}| \rceil$ bits. It is a matter of assigning to each element a distinct number of $\lceil \log |\mathcal{U}| \rceil$ bits. The problem with such a code is practicality: It might not be simple to convert the code back into the element unless one has a table of $|\mathcal{U}|$ cells that stores the mapping. This can be practical (and we will use it) when $\mathcal{U}$ is small and we have to encode many such elements, but otherwise we need to consider codes that are easier to handle.

Example 2.3 *We can encode the* $|\mathcal{T}_4| = 5$ *trees of* $\mathcal{T}_4$ *with codes of length* $\lceil \log(|\mathcal{T}_4|) \rceil = 3$, *for example,* $\{000, 001, 010, 011, 100\}$.

Note that in this example we use only 3 bits to encode the elements of $\mathcal{T}_4$, whereas in Example 2.2 we used $2n = 8$. We showed that $\mathcal{H}_{wc}(\mathcal{T}_n) = 2n - \Theta(\log n)$, so for large trees, using $2n$ bits comes close to optimal (or, in technical terms, using $2n$ bits is *asymptotically optimal*). For small trees of $n = 4$ nodes, the $\Theta(\log n)$ factor is still significant. In Chapters 7 and 8 we show that we can navigate the representation of Example 2.2 in constant time, using $o(n)$ bits in addition to the $2n$.

2.2 Shannon Entropy

In classical Information Theory, one assumes that there is an infinite source that emits elements $u \in \mathcal{U}$ with *probabilities* $\Pr(u)$. By using codes of varying lengths of $\ell(u)$ bits (shorter codes for the more probable elements), one can reduce the *average* length of the codes:

$$\overline{\ell} = \sum_{u \in \mathcal{U}} \Pr(u) \cdot \ell(u).$$

Then a natural question is how to assign codes that minimize the average code length. A fundamental result of Information Theory is that the minimum possible average code length for codes that can be univocally decoded is

$$\mathcal{H}(\Pr) = \sum_{u \in \mathcal{U}} \Pr(u) \cdot \log \frac{1}{\Pr(u)},$$

which is called the *Shannon entropy* of the *probability distribution* $\Pr : \mathcal{U} \to [0.0, 1.0]$. The measure $\mathcal{H}(\Pr)$ can be interpreted as how many bits *of information* are contained in each element emitted by the source. The more biased the probability distribution, the more "predictable," or the less "surprising," the output of the source is, and the less information is carried by its elements. In particular, if one probability tends to 1.0 and all the others tend to 0.0, then $\mathcal{H}(\text{Pr})$ tends to 0.[1]

Example 2.4 *A service in the Sahara desert announces the weather condition every day, which is an element in {sun, rain, snow}. The Shannon entropy, or amount of surprise, from such a source is close to zero. If the service is in, say, New York, the source will be less predictable and thus contain more information, and its Shannon entropy will be higher.*

The formula of $\mathcal{H}(\text{Pr})$ also suggests that an optimal code for u should be $\log \frac{1}{\text{Pr}(u)}$ bits long. Actually, it can be proved that no other choice of code lengths reaches the optimal average code length $\mathcal{H}(\text{Pr})$. This means that, as anticipated, more probable elements should receive shorter codes. Note that, no matter how we assign the codes to reduce the *average* code length, the length of the *longest* code is still at least $\lceil \mathcal{H}_{\text{wc}}(\mathcal{U}) \rceil$.

Example 2.5 *Assume that the 5 trees of $\mathcal{T}_4$ arise with probabilities {0.6, 0.3, 0.05, 0.025, 0.025}. Their Shannon entropy is then $\mathcal{H} = 0.6 \cdot \log \frac{1}{0.6} + 0.3 \cdot \log \frac{1}{0.3} + 0.05 \cdot \log \frac{1}{0.05} + 2 \times 0.025 \cdot \log \frac{1}{0.025} \approx 1.445 < \log 5 = \mathcal{H}_{\text{wc}}(\mathcal{T}_4)$. Thus we could encode the trees using, on average, less than $\mathcal{H}_{\text{wc}}$ bits per tree. For example, we could assign 0 to the first tree, 10 to the second, 110 to the third, 1110 to the fourth, and 1111 to the fifth. The average code length is then $0.6 \cdot 1 + 0.3 \cdot 2 + 0.05 \cdot 3 + 2 \times 0.025 \cdot 4 = 1.550$ bits. This is larger than $\mathcal{H}$ but smaller than $\mathcal{H}_{\text{wc}}$. On the other hand, our longest code length is $4 \geq \lceil \mathcal{H}_{\text{wc}} \rceil$.*

When all the probabilities are equal, $\text{Pr}(u) = \frac{1}{|\mathcal{U}|}$, the Shannon entropy is maximized, reaching precisely $\log |\mathcal{U}|$, and the optimum is to use codes of about the same length for all the elements. Then the set is said to be *incompressible*. In this case, the Shannon entropy coincides with our measure of worst-case entropy, $\mathcal{H}_{\text{wc}}(\mathcal{U})$.

Example 2.6 *Assume that the 5 trees of $\mathcal{T}_4$ arise with probabilities 0.2 each. Then the Shannon entropy is $\mathcal{H} = 5 \times 0.2 \cdot \log \frac{1}{0.2} = \log 5 = \mathcal{H}_{\text{wc}}$. Still we could use codes of average length less than $\lceil \log 5 \rceil = 3$, for example, {00, 01, 10, 110, 111}, with average code length $3 \times 0.2 \cdot 2 + 2 \times 0.2 \cdot 3 = 2.4$, which is larger than $\mathcal{H}_{\text{wc}} \approx 2.322$ but smaller than $3 = \lceil \mathcal{H}_{\text{wc}} \rceil$. The longest code, however, is of length $3 = \lceil \mathcal{H}_{\text{wc}} \rceil$.*

2.3 Empirical Entropy

Consider the particular case $\mathcal{U} = \{0, 1\}$, that is, where our infinite source emits bits. Assume that bit 1 is emitted with probability p and bit 0 with probability $1 - p$. The Shannon entropy of this source, also called binary entropy, is then

$$\mathcal{H}(p) = p \log \frac{1}{p} + (1 - p) \log \frac{1}{1 - p}.$$

Figure 2.2 shows $\mathcal{H}(p)$ as a function of the probability p. As expected, $\mathcal{H}(0.0) = \mathcal{H}(1.0) = 0$, that is, the entropy (or information, or surprise) is zero when one element

---

[1] We take the usual analytical limit $0 \cdot \log \frac{1}{0} = \lim_{x \to 0} x \cdot \log \frac{1}{x} = 0$.

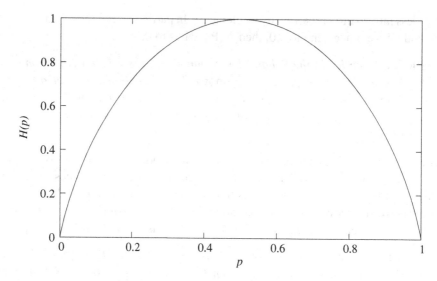

Figure 2.2. The binary entropy function $\mathcal{H}(p)$.

has probability 1.0 and the other 0.0. Also, $\mathcal{H}(0.5) = 1$, that is, the entropy reaches its maximum (in this case, 1 bit per bit) when the elements are emitted with the same probability.

The concept of Shannon entropy also applies when the elements are *sequences* of those bits emitted by the source. Assume that the source emits each bit independently of the rest (this is called a "memoryless" or "zero-order" source). If we take chunks of n bits and call them our elements, then we have $\mathcal{U} = \{0, 1\}^n$, and the Shannon entropy of the sequences is $n\mathcal{H}(p)$ (more generally, the entropy of two independent events is the sum of their entropies).

When the source emits symbols from a more general alphabet $\Sigma = [1, \sigma]$, where symbol s has probability p_s, the Shannon entropy of the source becomes

$$\mathcal{H}(\langle p_1, \ldots, p_\sigma \rangle) = \sum_{1 \leq s \leq \sigma} p_s \log \frac{1}{p_s}$$

bits. Again, we have $\mathcal{H} = 0$ when some p_s is 1.0 and all the rest are 0.0, and $\mathcal{H} = \log \sigma$ when $p_s = \frac{1}{\sigma}$ for all s. A sequence of n elements from Σ, belonging to $\mathcal{U} = \Sigma^n$, that is, a string of length n, has Shannon entropy $n\mathcal{H}(\langle p_1, \ldots, p_\sigma \rangle)$.

In this section we show how the Shannon entropy can be used to define an entropy notion for individual sequences without assuming they come from a certain source.

2.3.1 Bit Sequences

Assume we have a *concrete* bit sequence, $B[1, n]$, that we wish to compress somehow. Here we do not have an ideal model of a known source that emits bits, we have only B. We may have a good reason to expect that B has more 0s than 1s, however, or more 1s than 0s. Therefore, we may try to compress B using that property. That is, we will *assume* that B has been generated by a zero-order source that emits 0s and 1s. Let m be the number of 1s in B. Then it makes sense to assume that the source emits 1s with probability $p = \frac{m}{n}$. This leads to the concept of *zero-order empirical entropy*:

$$\mathcal{H}_0(B) = \mathcal{H}\left(\frac{m}{n}\right) = \frac{m}{n}\log\frac{n}{m} + \frac{n-m}{n}\log\frac{n}{n-m}.$$

The empirical entropy is thus the Shannon entropy of a source that emits 1s with the *observed* probability of the 1s in B. It can be shown that if B indeed comes from a zero-order source with probability p, then it has $m \approx p \cdot n$ 1s with very high probability.

The practical meaning of the zero-order empirical entropy is that, if a compressor attempts to compress B by using some fixed code $C(1)$ for the 1 (which can even use a fractional number of bits; see Section 2.6.4) and some fixed code $C(0)$ for the 0, then it cannot compress B to less than $n\mathcal{H}_0(B)$ bits. Otherwise we would have $m|C(1)| + (n-m)|C(0)| < n\mathcal{H}_0(B)$. Calling $p = \frac{m}{n}$, this would give $p|C(1)| + (1-p)|C(0)| < \mathcal{H}_0(B) = \mathcal{H}(p)$, which means that this code would break the lower bound of the Shannon entropy.

A Connection with Worst-Case Entropy

It is interesting that the concepts of zero-order empirical entropy and of worst-case entropy are closely related, despite their different origins. Consider the set $\mathcal{B}_{n,m}$ of all the bit sequences of length n with m 1s. Then $|\mathcal{B}_{n,m}| = \binom{n}{m}$, and its worst-case entropy is

$$\mathcal{H}_{wc}(\mathcal{B}_{n,m}) = \log\binom{n}{m} = n\log n - m\log m - (n-m)\log(n-m) - \mathcal{O}(\log n)$$

$$= n\left(\frac{m}{n}\log\frac{n}{m} + \frac{n-m}{n}\log\frac{n}{n-m}\right) - \mathcal{O}(\log n)$$

$$= n\mathcal{H}_0(B) - \mathcal{O}(\log n),$$

where we used Stirling's approximation in the first line and expanded $n\log n = m\log n + (n-m)\log n$ in the second.

Therefore, the zero-order empirical entropy can be understood simply in terms of how many different bit sequences there are with m 1s. We saw in Section 2.1 that the worst-case entropy of bit sequences of length n is n bits. However, if $m \ll n$, the subset $\mathcal{B}_{n,m}$ of the sparse bit sequences that have only m 1s is much smaller, and thus it can be encoded with $n\mathcal{H}(\frac{m}{n})$ bits. Note that the zero-order empirical entropy is the same for any sequence in $\mathcal{B}_{n,m}$ and thus refers to a worst-case encoding of the set.

Example 2.7 *Consider $\mathcal{B}_{100,20}$, the class of bit sequences of length 100 with 20 1s. Its worst-case entropy is $\mathcal{H}_{wc}(\mathcal{B}_{100,20}) = \log\binom{100}{20} \approx 68.861$ bits. The zero-order empirical entropy of any $B \in \mathcal{B}_{100,20}$ is $\mathcal{H}_0(B) = \mathcal{H}(\frac{20}{100}) = \frac{20}{100}\log\frac{100}{20} + \frac{80}{100}\log\frac{100}{80} \approx 0.72193$, thus $n\mathcal{H}_0(B) \approx 72.193$ bits. Note that $\mathcal{H}_0(B)$ is slightly larger than $\mathcal{H}_{wc}(\mathcal{B}_{100,20})$, by an $\mathcal{O}(\log n)$ factor.*

On the other hand, consider the class of "balanced" bit sequences, which have as many 0s as 1s, $\mathcal{B}_{n,n/2}$. This set is of size $|\mathcal{B}_{n,n/2}| = \binom{n}{n/2} = \frac{2^n}{\sqrt{n}} \cdot \Theta(1)$, and therefore its worst-case entropy is $\mathcal{H}_{wc}(\mathcal{B}_{n,n/2}) = n - \Theta(\log n)$. Then this class is incompressible in terms of worst-case entropy because it is not much smaller than the whole class of sequences of n bits. In terms of zero-order empirical entropy, it cannot be compressed to less than $n\mathcal{H}(\frac{1}{2}) = n$ bits.

Note that a balanced sequence can be perfectly compressible for other reasons. For example, the 0s might tend to appear before the 1s. The limitation above arises because we are assuming that the only source of compressibility of B is the frequency of its 1s. That is, once again, we are assuming that B is generated from a zero-order source of bits. Depending on the application, one must find out the reasons why the objects at hand might be compressible and use an according model (there are some exceptions, such as the general ordinal trees, where even the worst-case entropy is a quite good model).

Finally, sometimes we will use the following bound:

$$
\begin{aligned}
n\mathcal{H}_0(B) &= n\left(\frac{m}{n}\log\frac{n}{m} + \frac{n-m}{n}\log\frac{n}{n-m}\right) \\
&= m\log\frac{n}{m} + (n-m)\log\left(1 + \frac{m}{n-m}\right) \\
&\leq m\log\frac{n}{m} + (n-m)\frac{1}{\ln 2}\frac{m}{n-m} = m\log\frac{n}{m} + \mathcal{O}(m),
\end{aligned}
$$

where in the last line we used $\log(1+x) = \frac{\ln(1+x)}{\ln 2}$ and $\ln(1+x) \leq x$.

2.3.2 Sequences of Symbols

The zero-order empirical entropy of a string $S[1, n]$, where each symbol s appears n_s times in S, is also defined in terms of the Shannon entropy of its observed probabilities:

$$
\mathcal{H}_0(S) = \mathcal{H}\left(\left\langle\frac{n_1}{n}, \ldots, \frac{n_\sigma}{n}\right\rangle\right) = \sum_{1\leq s\leq\sigma}\frac{n_s}{n}\log\frac{n}{n_s}.
$$

Example 2.8 *Let $S =$ abracadabra. Then $n = 11$, $n_a = 5$, $n_b = n_r = 2$, and $n_c = n_d = 1$. The zero-order empirical entropy of S is $\mathcal{H}_0(S) = \frac{5}{11}\cdot\log\frac{11}{5} + 2\times\frac{2}{11}\cdot\log\frac{11}{2} + 2\times\frac{1}{11}\cdot\log\frac{11}{1} \approx 2.040$. Therefore, one could compress S to $n\mathcal{H}_0(S) \approx 22.44$ bits, less than the $n\log\sigma = 11\cdot\log 5 \approx 25.54$ bits of the worst-case entropy of the strings of length $n = 11$ and alphabet of size $\sigma = 5$.*

Once again, this explains why texts may be compressible even when their worst-case entropy (Section 2.1) is $n\log\sigma$ bits. If, for example, their symbol frequencies are far from uniform, then they can be compressed up to $n\mathcal{H}(\langle\frac{n_1}{n}, \ldots, \frac{n_\sigma}{n}\rangle)$ bits, simply because there are fewer strings with those frequencies, and then fewer bits are needed to identify which string is at hand:

$$
\log\binom{n}{n_1, \ldots, n_\sigma} = n\mathcal{H}\left(\left\langle\frac{n_1}{n}, \ldots, \frac{n_\sigma}{n}\right\rangle\right) - \mathcal{O}(\sigma\log n).
$$

A subtle point for the curious reader: The $\mathcal{O}(\sigma\log n)$ extra bits of the Shannon entropy allow us to encode *any* $S[1, n]$, obtaining $n\mathcal{H}(\langle\frac{n_1}{n}, \ldots, \frac{n_\sigma}{n}\rangle)$ bits on average if the source has those frequencies. Instead, within $\log\binom{n}{n_1,\ldots,n_\sigma}$ bits we can encode *only* the sequences that have exactly those frequencies. The reason why both entropies are so close is that long sequences emitted with a probabilistic distribution concentrate sharply around the mean.

2.4 High-Order Entropy

While the mere frequency of the symbols $\Sigma = [1, \sigma]$ can be an important source of compressibility for a sequence S, it is not the only one. For example, if one tokenizes the words in an English text, zero-order compression typically reduces the text to about 25% of its size. However, good compressors can reach less than 15% by exploiting the so-called *high-order entropy* or *kth-order entropy*. This is a measure of the information carried by a symbol given that we know the k symbols that precede it in S. Indeed, one can better guess what the next word is in an English text if one knows some words preceding it. The lower the surprise, the lower the entropy.

In terms of the Shannon entropy, sources "with memory" remember the last k symbols emitted, and the probability of each emitted symbol may depend on this memory (this is a particular case of a Markov chain). The probability of s given that $s_1 \ldots s_k$ was just emitted is $\Pr(s|s_1 \ldots s_k)$. Then, when $s_1 \ldots s_k$ has just been emitted, the entropy of the next symbol is

$$\mathcal{H}([s_1 \ldots s_k]) = \mathcal{H}(\langle \Pr(1|s_1 \ldots s_k), \ldots, \Pr(\sigma|s_1 \ldots s_k) \rangle),$$

and the Shannon entropy of the probabilistic distribution is

$$\mathcal{H}(\Pr) = \sum_{s_1 \ldots s_k} \Pr(s_1 \ldots s_k) \, \mathcal{H}([s_1 \ldots s_k]).$$

Here $\Pr(s_1 \ldots s_k)$ is the probability of emitting $s_1 \ldots s_k$, which can be computed from the conditional probabilities.

Example 2.9 *Consider again the source of weather conditions of New York, in Example 2.4. This is for sure not a memoryless source. Let us consider a first-order model for it, where the weather of a day depends (only) on that of the previous day. Assume*

$$\begin{aligned}
&\Pr(\text{sun}|\text{sun}) = 0.5, &&\Pr(\text{rain}|\text{sun}) = 0.25, &&\Pr(\text{snow}|\text{sun}) = 0.25, \\
&\Pr(\text{sun}|\text{rain}) = 0.3, &&\Pr(\text{rain}|\text{rain}) = 0.6, &&\Pr(\text{snow}|\text{rain}) = 0.1, \\
&\Pr(\text{sun}|\text{snow}) = 0.2, &&\Pr(\text{rain}|\text{snow}) = 0.2, &&\Pr(\text{snow}|\text{snow}) = 0.6.
\end{aligned}$$

For example, since

$$\Pr(\text{sun}) = \Pr(\text{sun}|\text{sun})\Pr(\text{sun}) + \Pr(\text{sun}|\text{rain})\Pr(\text{rain}) + \Pr(\text{sun}|\text{snow})\Pr(\text{snow}),$$

and similarly for $\Pr(\text{rain})$ *and* $\Pr(\text{snow})$, *we can obtain from the system of three equations the global probabilities* $\Pr(\text{sun}) \approx 0.34$, $\Pr(\text{rain}) \approx 0.36$, $\Pr(\text{snow}) \approx 0.30$. *The Shannon entropy of a source with these global probabilities is* $\mathcal{H}(\langle 0.34, 0.36, 0.30 \rangle) \approx 1.581$ *bits. However, the Shannon entropy of the first-order model is lower,* $\mathcal{H}(\Pr) = \Pr(\text{sun}) \cdot \mathcal{H}(\langle 0.5, 0.25, 0.25 \rangle) + \Pr(\text{rain}) \cdot \mathcal{H}(\langle 0.3, 0.6, 0.1 \rangle) + \Pr(\text{snow}) \cdot \mathcal{H}(\langle 0.2, 0.2, 0.6 \rangle) \approx 1.387$.

When considering concrete sequences $S[1, n]$, we can compute the *empirical kth-order entropy* of S by considering the frequencies of the symbols depending on the preceding k symbols:

$$\mathcal{H}_k(S) = \sum_{C = s_1 \ldots s_k} \frac{|S_C|}{n} \cdot \mathcal{H}_0(S_C),$$

where S_C is a string formed by collecting the symbol that follows each occurrence of the context $C = s_1 \ldots s_k$ in S. A moment of thought shows that $\mathcal{H}_k(S)$ is equal to $\mathcal{H}(\text{Pr})$ if we replace $\text{Pr}(s|s_1 \ldots s_k)$ by the relative number of times s appears after the context $s_1 \ldots s_k$ (or, which is the same, in $S_{s_1 \ldots s_k}$), and $\text{Pr}(s_1 \ldots s_k)$ by the relative frequency of the string $s_1 \ldots s_k$ in S.

Example 2.10 *Consider again the string* $S = \texttt{abracadabra}$ *of Example 2.8, and* $k = 1$. *Then* $S_\texttt{a} = \texttt{bcdb\$}$ *(we have added an artificial terminator* \$ *to S for technical convenience),* $S_\texttt{b} = \texttt{rr}$, $S_\texttt{c} = \texttt{a}$, $S_\texttt{d} = \texttt{a}$, *and* $S_\texttt{r} = \texttt{aa}$. *Then* $\mathcal{H}_0(S_\texttt{a}) \approx 1.922$ *and* $\mathcal{H}_0(S_\texttt{b}) = \mathcal{H}_0(S_\texttt{c}) = \mathcal{H}_0(S_\texttt{d}) = \mathcal{H}_0(S_\texttt{r}) = 0$. *The first-order empirical entropy of S is thus* $\mathcal{H}_1(S) = \frac{5}{11}\mathcal{H}_0(S_\texttt{a}) + \frac{2}{11}\mathcal{H}_0(S_\texttt{b}) + \frac{1}{11}\mathcal{H}_0(S_\texttt{c}) + \frac{1}{11}\mathcal{H}_0(S_\texttt{d}) + \frac{2}{11}\mathcal{H}_0(S_\texttt{r}) \approx$ *0.874, much less than its zero-order entropy computed in Example 2.8.*

Extending the concept of zero-order empirical entropy, $n\mathcal{H}_k(S)$ is a lower bound to the number of bits that any encoding of S can achieve if the code of each symbol can be a function of itself and the k symbols preceding it in S. As before, any compressor breaking that barrier would also be able to compress symbols coming from the corresponding kth-order source into less than its Shannon entropy.

As expected, it holds $\log \sigma \geq \mathcal{H}_0(S) \geq \mathcal{H}_1(S) \geq \ldots \geq \mathcal{H}_{k-1}(S) \geq \mathcal{H}_k(S)$ for any k. Note that, for sufficiently large k values (at most for $k = n - 1$, and usually much sooner), it holds $\mathcal{H}_k(S) = 0$ because all the contexts of length k appear only once in S. At this point, the model becomes useless as a lower bound for compressors. Even before reaching $\mathcal{H}_k(S) = 0$, compressors cannot achieve $n\mathcal{H}_k(S)$ bits in practice for very high k values, because they must store the set of σ^{k+1} probabilities, or, equivalently, the set of σ^{k+1} codes,[2] so that the decompressor can reconstruct S. In theory, it is common to assume that S can be compressed up to $n\mathcal{H}_k(S) + o(n)$ bits for any $k + 1 \leq \alpha \log_\sigma n$ and any constant $0 < \alpha < 1$, because in this case one can store σ^{k+1} numbers in $[1, n]$ (such as frequencies) within $\sigma^{k+1} \log n \leq n^\alpha \log n = o(n)$ bits.

2.5 Coding

The entropy tells us the minimum average code length we can achieve, and even suggests giving each symbol s a code with length $\log \frac{1}{\text{Pr}(s)}$ to reach that optimum. To obtain kth-order entropy, we must use a different set of codes for each different previous context. However, in either case the entropy measure does not tell how to build a suitable set of codes.

An *encoding* is an injective function $\mathcal{C} : \Sigma \to \{0, 1\}^*$ that assigns a distinct sequence of bits $\mathcal{C}(s)$ to each symbol $s \in \Sigma$. Encodings are also simply called *codes*, overloading the meaning of the individual code assigned to a symbol. Since we will

---

[2] Similarly, adaptive compressors must record σ^{k+1} escape symbols somewhere along the compressed file.

encode a sequence of symbols of Σ by means of concatenating their codes, even injective functions may be unsuitable, because they may lead to concatenations that cannot be unambiguously decoded.

Example 2.11 *Assume our set of codes is $C(s_1) = 0$, $C(s_2) = 1$, $C(s_3) = 00$. Then the concatenation $C(s_1) \cdot C(s_3) = 000$, looks exactly the same as $C(s_3) \cdot C(s_1) = 000$, and thus we cannot know which one of the two sequences was encoded.*

An encoding is said to be *unambiguous* if, given a concatenation of bits, there is no ambiguity regarding the original sequence that was encoded. Said another way, if we define a new code C' on sequences of symbols of Σ, $C' : \Sigma^* \to \{0, 1\}^*$, so that $C'(s_1 \ldots s_k) = C(s_1) \ldots C(s_k)$, then code C is unambiguous iff C' is an injective function.

Example 2.12 *Assume our set of codes is $C(s_1) = 1$, $C(s_2) = 10$, $C(s_3) = 00$. This code is unambiguous: if a bit sequence starts with 0, then it must start with $C(s_3) = 00$ and we can continue. Otherwise it starts with a 1, and we must see how many 0s are there up to the next 1 or the end of the sequence. If there are 2z 0s (for some $z \geq 0$), then it was $C(s_1) = 1$ followed by z occurrences of $C(s_3) = 00$. If there are $2z + 1$ 0s, then it was $C(s_2) = 10$ followed by z occurrences of $C(s_3) = 00$.*

The example shows a shortcoming of unambiguous codes: It might not be possible to decode the next symbol s in constant time or even in time proportional to $|C(s)|$. It is more useful that an encoding also be *instantaneous*, that is, that we have sufficient information to determine s as soon as we read the last bit of $C(s)$. Apart from the obvious efficiency advantage, instantaneous codes can be easily embedded in other streams, because they do not depend on their context to be decoded.

It can be shown that instantaneous codes are precisely the so-called *prefix-free codes* or just *prefix codes*. A code C is a prefix code if no code $C(s)$ is a prefix of any other code $C(s')$. Clearly, with a prefix code there cannot be ambiguity with respect to whether we are seeing the final bit of a code or rather the middle of a longer code. Somewhat surprisingly, unambiguous codes that are not prefix codes are useless: there is always a prefix code that is at least as good as any given unambiguous code.

Example 2.13 *We can find a prefix code where code lengths are the same as those assigned in Example 2.12: $C(s_1) = 1$, $C(s_2) = 01$, $C(s_3) = 00$. Now we can determine the symbol that is encoded next in a bit sequence as soon as we read the last bit of its code.*

The reason is the so-called *Kraft-McMillan inequality*: Any unambiguous code C (and thus any prefix code C), satisfies

$$\sum_{s \in \Sigma} 2^{-\ell(s)} \leq 1,$$

where $\ell(s) = |C(s)|$, and on the other hand, a prefix code (and thus an unambiguous code) with lengths $\ell(s)$ always exists if the above inequality holds. Hence, given an unambiguous code C, it satisfies the inequality, and thus there is a prefix code with the same code lengths.

Algorithm 2.1: Building a prefix code over $\Sigma = [1, \sigma]$, given the desired lengths. Assumes for simplicity that the codes fit in a computer word.

    Input : $S[1, \sigma]$, with $S[i].s$ a distinct symbol and $S[i].\ell$ its desired code length.
    Output: Array S (reordered) with a new field computed, $S[i].code$, an integer
               whose $S[i].\ell$ lowest bits are a prefix code for $S[i].s$ (reading from most
               to least significant bit).

1 Sort $S[1, \sigma]$ by increasing $S[i].\ell$ values
2 $S[1].code \leftarrow 0$
3 **for** $i \leftarrow 2$ **to** σ **do**
4 | $S[i].code \leftarrow (S[i-1].code + 1) \cdot 2^{S[i].\ell - S[i-1].\ell}$

This leads to a simple way of assigning reasonably good codes, called the *Shannon-Fano codes*. Given that the optimal code length is $\log \frac{1}{\Pr(s)}$, assign code length $\ell(s) = \left\lceil \log \frac{1}{\Pr(s)} \right\rceil$. Then it holds

$$\sum_{s \in \Sigma} 2^{-\ell(s)} = \sum_{s \in \Sigma} 2^{-\left\lceil \log \frac{1}{\Pr(s)} \right\rceil} \leq \sum_{s \in \Sigma} 2^{-\log \frac{1}{\Pr(s)}} = \sum_{s \in \Sigma} \Pr(s) = 1,$$

and thus, by the Kraft-McMillan inequality, there is a prefix code with those lengths. Actually, it is not difficult to find: Process the lengths from shortest to longest, giving to each code the next available binary number of the appropriate length, where "available" means we have not yet used the number or a prefix of it. More precisely, if the sorted lengths are $\ell_1, \ldots, \ell_\sigma$, then the first code is 0^{ℓ_1} (ℓ_1 0s), and the code for s_{i+1} is obtained by summing 1 to the ℓ_i-bit number assigned to s_i, and then appending $\ell_{i+1} - \ell_i$ 0s to it. The Kraft-McMillan inequality guarantees that we will always find a free number of the desired length for the next code. Algorithm 2.1 gives the pseudocode, returning the assigned codes as integer values (for example, code 000110 is stored as the number 6, which cannot lead to confusion because we also know the code length).

A Shannon-Fano code obtains an average code length that is less than 1 bit over the Shannon entropy. This is because the average code length is

$$\bar{\ell} = \sum_{s \in \Sigma} \Pr(s) \cdot \left\lceil \log \frac{1}{\Pr(s)} \right\rceil < \sum_{s \in \Sigma} \Pr(s) \cdot \left(\log \frac{1}{\Pr(s)} + 1 \right) = \mathcal{H}(\Pr) + 1.$$

Example 2.14 *Consider the set $\mathcal{T}_4$ with the probabilities given in Example 2.5,* $\{0.6, 0.3, 0.05, 0.025, 0.025\}$, *which had Shannon entropy* $\mathcal{H} \approx 1.445$. *The Shannon-Fano code gives lengths* $\lceil \log \frac{1}{0.6} \rceil = 1$ *for the first tree,* $\lceil \log \frac{1}{0.3} \rceil = 2$ *for the second,* $\lceil \log \frac{1}{0.05} \rceil = 5$ *for the third, and* $\lceil \log \frac{1}{0.025} \rceil = 6$ *for the last two. Then we start assigning code* 0 *to the first tree. For the second, the first available code of length 2 is* 10, *obtained by summing 1 to 0 and appending* $2 - 1 = 1$ *0s to it. For the third, we obtain* 11000 *by adding 1 to* 10, *getting* 11, *and then appending* $5 - 2 = 3$ *0s. For the fourth and fifth we have codes* 110010 *and* 110011. *The average length of this code is* $0.6 \cdot 1 + 0.3 \cdot 2 + 0.05 \cdot 5 + 2 \times 0.025 \cdot 6 = 1.75$ *bits. This is less than* $\mathcal{H} + 1$, *but we found a better code in Example 2.5.*

The example shows that, although Shannon-Fano codes always spend less than 1 bit over the entropy, they are not necessarily optimal. The next section shows how to build optimal codes.

2.6 Huffman Codes

Huffman devised an algorithm that, given a probability distribution $\Pr : \Sigma \rightarrow [0.0, 1.0]$, obtains a prefix code of minimum average length. Thus, Huffman is optimal among the codes that assign an integral number of bits to each symbol. In particular, it is no worse than Shannon-Fano codes, and so the number of bits it outputs is between $n\mathcal{H}(\Pr)$ and $n(\mathcal{H}(\Pr) + 1)$, wasting less than 1 bit per symbol. Similarly, if $\Pr$ are the relative symbol frequencies in a string $S[1, n]$, then Huffman codes compress S to less than $n(\mathcal{H}_0(S) + 1)$ bits.

2.6.1 Construction

The Huffman algorithm progressively converts a set of $|\Sigma|$ nodes into a binary tree. At every moment, it maintains a set of binary trees. The leaves of the trees correspond to the symbols $s \in \Sigma$, and each tree has a *weight* equal to the sum of the probabilities of the symbols at its leaves. The algorithm starts with $|\Sigma|$ trees, each being a leaf node corresponding to a distinct symbol $s \in \Sigma$, with weight $\Pr(s)$. Then $|\Sigma| - 1$ tree merging steps are carried out, finishing with a single tree of weight 1.0 and with all the $|\Sigma|$ leaves.

The merging step always chooses two trees T_1 and T_2 of minimum weight and joins them by creating a new root, whose left and right children are T_1 and T_2, and whose weight is the sum of the weights of T_1 and T_2.

The single tree resulting from the algorithm is called the *Huffman tree*. If we interpret going left as the bit 0 and going right as the bit 1, then the path from the root to the leaf of each $s \in \Sigma$ spells out its code $C(s)$. The Huffman tree minimizes the average code length, $\sum_{s \in \Sigma} \Pr(s) \cdot \ell(s)$.

Example 2.15 *Figure 2.3 illustrates the Huffman algorithm on the probabilities of Example 2.8:* $\Pr(\mathtt{a}) = \frac{5}{11}$, $\Pr(\mathtt{b}) = \Pr(\mathtt{r}) = \frac{2}{11}$, *and* $\Pr(\mathtt{c}) = \Pr(\mathtt{d}) = \frac{1}{11}$. *The final Huffman tree on the left assigns the codes* $C(\mathtt{a}) = 0$, $C(\mathtt{b}) = 110$, $C(\mathtt{r}) = 111$, $C(\mathtt{c}) = 100$, *and* $C(\mathtt{d}) = 101$. *The average code length is* $\frac{5}{11} \cdot 1 + 2 \times \frac{2}{11} \cdot 3 + 2 \times \frac{1}{11} \cdot 3 \approx 2.091$, *very close to* $\mathcal{H}(\Pr) = \mathcal{H}_0(S) \approx 2.040$. *A Shannon-Fano code obtains a higher average code length,* ≈ 2.727 *bits.*

On the bottom right we show another valid Huffman tree that is obtained by breaking ties in another way (we leave as an exercise to the reader to determine the corresponding merging order). Its average code length is also $\frac{5}{11} \cdot 1 + \frac{2}{11} \cdot 2 + \frac{2}{11} \cdot 3 + 2 \times \frac{1}{11} \cdot 4 \approx 2.091$.

The Huffman algorithm runs in time $\mathcal{O}(|\Sigma| \log |\Sigma|)$. This can be obtained, for example, by maintaining the trees in a priority queue to extract the next two minimum weights. Algorithm 2.2 shows another way. We first sort the weights into a linked list L and then repeatedly remove the first (i.e., lightest) two trees of the list in order to

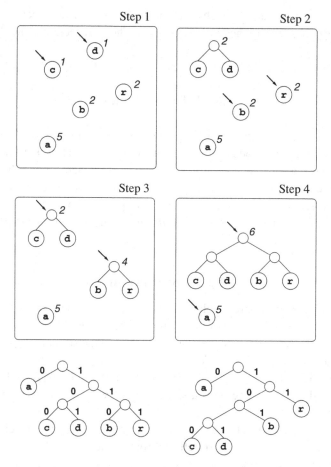

Figure 2.3. The Huffman algorithm on 5 symbols. Instead of probabilities we show their frequencies, in italics and close to the tree roots. The arrows show the trees chosen at each step. The final Huffman tree on the left shows the codes assigned. The one on the right is another valid Huffman tree obtained by choosing other trees to merge when there are ties.

merge them into a new tree. The insertion point I for this new tree always advances in L toward the higher weights (because the new merged tree is never lighter than the previous). Thus, although each search for the new insertion point I scans L linearly (lines 8–9), only one traversal of L is carried out along the whole construction. The total cost after sorting then amortizes to $\mathcal{O}(|\Sigma|)$, because L has fewer than $2|\Sigma|$ nodes.

The sorting by frequencies can be done in time $\mathcal{O}(|\Sigma| \log |\Sigma|)$ as usual, or if the weights are frequencies in a string $S[1, n]$, one can use RadixSort to obtain $\mathcal{O}(|\Sigma| + n)$ time. This can be useful when Σ is large compared to n.

2.6.2 Encoding and Decoding

Once the Huffman tree is built, we simply traverse it recursively to obtain the code for each symbol, and store the codes in an array indexed by $s \in \Sigma$. Encoding is then easily done symbol by symbol.

Algorithm 2.2: Building a Huffman tree over the alphabet $\Sigma = [1, \sigma]$. The list L can be allocated as an array $L[1, 2\sigma - 1]$.

---

1 **Proc** *HuffmanTree(S)*

  Input : $S[1, \sigma]$, with $S[i].s$ a distinct symbol and $S[i].f$ its frequency (or weight).

  Output: Huffman tree with internal node fields l (left) and r (right) and leaf field s (symbol).

2 | Sort $S[1, \sigma]$ by increasing $S[i].f$ values

3 | Create list L linked by field $L.next$, with its ith node

4 | $L.s \leftarrow S[i].s, L.f \leftarrow S[i].f, L.l \leftarrow$ null, $L.r \leftarrow$ null

5 | $I \leftarrow L$ (the first list node)

6 | **while** $L.next \neq$ null **do**

7 | Create list node $N.l \leftarrow L, N.r \leftarrow L.next, N.f \leftarrow N.l.f + N.r.f$

8 | **while** $I.next \neq$ null **and** $I.next.f \leq N.f$ **do**

9 | $I \leftarrow I.next$

10 | $N.next \leftarrow I.next$

11 | $I.next \leftarrow N$

12 | $L \leftarrow L.next.next$

13 | **return** L (regarded as a tree; fields *next* are to be ignored)

Although the longest Huffman code can be of length $|\Sigma| - 1$, it turns out that its length is also limited by $\lfloor \log_\phi \frac{1}{p_{min}} \rfloor$, where p_{min} is the minimum probability in Pr and $\phi = (1 + \sqrt{5})/2 \approx 1.618$ is the golden ratio. In particular, if the probabilities are obtained from the observed frequencies in a sequence of n symbols, then $p_{min} \geq \frac{1}{n}$, and the maximum possible Huffman code length is $\log_\phi n$. Thus, a 32-bit word can for sure hold the code of any file of size up to $n = \phi^{32} > 2^{22}$ (4 megabytes, if we assume one byte per symbol); this rises to 16 terabytes with 64-bit words. Thus, a few computer words suffice in all the conceivable cases to manipulate Huffman codes and write them to the output in constant time (Chapter 3 offers more details on handling the bits inside computer words). Thus, encoding takes $\mathcal{O}(n)$ time. This is also true in theory, as in the RAM model of computation $\mathcal{O}(\log n)$ bits can be manipulated in $\mathcal{O}(1)$ time.

For decoding, we can use the Huffman tree. We read the successive bits of the stream and move from the root to a leaf according to the bits read. When we arrive at a leaf, we output its corresponding symbol and return to the tree root. Therefore, the total decoding time is proportional to the bit length of the compressed sequence, $\mathcal{O}(n(\mathcal{H}(\text{Pr}) + 1))$. Given that the codes are of length $\mathcal{O}(\log n)$, it also holds that any symbol is decoded in $\mathcal{O}(\log n)$ time. We see next how to speed this up.

2.6.3 Canonical Huffman Codes

Example 2.15 shows that there are several valid (and optimal) Huffman trees: there may not only be ties in the weights when choosing the two trees to merge, but we can also exchange the left and right children of any node.

From all the possible Huffman trees, the so-called *canonical Huffman tree* is usually preferred because it enables more efficient decoding. In this tree, the leaf depths are nondecreasing when read left to right. The Huffman tree we built on the bottom left of Figure 2.3 happens to be canonical, whereas that on the bottom right is not.[3]

Building a canonical Huffman tree is simple. We use Algorithm 2.2 just to determine the Huffman code lengths, $\ell(s)$ (that is, the depth of the leaf labeled s), but ignore the actual codes produced by the algorithm. We then assign codes, from shortest to longest, choosing the next available binary number of $\ell(s)$ bits, as done in Algorithm 2.1 for the Shannon-Fano codes.

Canonical Huffman trees also allow for a compact representation using $|\Sigma| \log |\Sigma| + \mathcal{O}(\log^2 n)$ bits, using three arrays:

1. $L[1, |\Sigma|]$ stores the symbols of Σ in left-to-right leaf order.
2. $F[1, h]$, where $h = \mathcal{O}(\log n)$ is the Huffman tree height, stores $F[\ell] = i$ iff $L[i]$ is the first symbol whose code is of length ℓ. If there are no symbols of length ℓ, then $F[\ell] = F[\ell + 1]$.
3. $C[1, h]$ stores in $C[\ell]$ the Huffman code of $L[F[\ell]]$, that is, the first code of length ℓ. The code is stored in the ℓ lowest bits of the number $C[\ell]$. If there are no codes of length ℓ, then $C[\ell] = C[\ell + 1]/2$ (that is, the first code of length $\ell + 1$ without its last 0; this value will not be used for encoding, but instead to drive a binary search).

Algorithm 2.3 shows how to build this representation, by generating the Huffman tree shape with Algorithm 2.2, then collecting the symbols and depths from the Huffman tree leaves in array S, then using Algorithm 2.1 to generate the codes, and finally building the arrays L, F, and C.

We show how this structure can be used for efficient decoding. From the incoming bit sequence to decode, we take the first h bits and place them at the lowest h bits of a number N. Now we have to find the ℓ such that $C[\ell] \cdot 2^{h-\ell} \leq N < C[\ell + 1] \cdot 2^{h-\ell-1}$, which is found by binary search in time $\mathcal{O}(\log h) = \mathcal{O}(\log \log n)$. We know that the next code is of length ℓ, so we discard the $h - \ell$ lowest bits of N by doing $N \leftarrow \lfloor N/2^{h-\ell} \rfloor$, and output the symbol $L[F[\ell] + N - C[\ell]]$. We then advance in the input stream by ℓ bits and are ready for the next code. Algorithm 2.4 gives the pseudocode.

Example 2.16 *Consider the canonical code* $C(\mathtt{a}) = 00$, $C(\mathtt{b}) = 010$, $C(\mathtt{c}) = 011$, $C(\mathtt{d}) = 100$, $C(\mathtt{e}) = 10100$, $C(\mathtt{f}) = 10101, \ldots, C(\mathtt{p}) = 11111$. *Then we have* $L[1, 16] = \langle \mathtt{a}, \ldots, \mathtt{p} \rangle$, $h = 5$, $F[1, 5] = \langle 1, 1, 2, 5, 5 \rangle$, *and* $C[1, 5] = \langle 0, 00, 010,$ $1010, 10100 \rangle = \langle 0, 0, 2, 10, 20 \rangle$. *This is illustrated in Figure 2.4.*

Now assume we have to decode 1000010101. *We read the first* $h = 5$ *bits,* $N = 10000 = 16$. *It is between* $C[3] \cdot 2^{5-3} = 2 \cdot 2^2 = 8$ *and* $C[4] \cdot 2^{5-4} - 1 = 10 \cdot 2^1 - 1 = 19$, *therefore the length of the first code is* 3. *Thus we set* $N \leftarrow \lfloor 16/2^{5-3} \rfloor = 4$, *and the code is* $L[F[3] + 4 - C[3]] = L[4] = \mathtt{d}$. *We advance* $\ell = 3$ *positions in the input.*

---

[3] Some definitions assume that the consecutive codes of the same length must correspond to increasing symbols of Σ, but we do not require this.

Algorithm 2.3: Building a Canonical Huffman code representation.

> **Input** : $S[1, \sigma]$, with $S[i].s$ a distinct symbol and $S[i].f$ its frequency (or weight).
> **Output**: Arrays L, F, and C representing a Canonical Huffman code for S. Uses
> fields ℓ and $code$ in the cells of S.

1 $T \leftarrow HuffmanTree(S)$ (Algorithm 2.2)
2 $computeLengths(S, T, 0, 1)$
3 Run Algorithm 2.1 on S (it also sorts S by increasing ℓ values)
4 **for** $i \leftarrow 1$ **to** σ **do** $L[i] \leftarrow S[i].s$
5 $h \leftarrow S[\sigma].\ell$
6 **for** $l \leftarrow 1$ **to** h **do** $F[l] \leftarrow 0$
7 **for** $i \leftarrow \sigma$ **downto** 1 **do**
8 $\quad F[S[i].\ell] \leftarrow i$
9 $\quad C[S[i].\ell] \leftarrow S[i].code$
10 **for** $l \leftarrow h - 1$ **downto** 1 **do**
11 $\quad$ **if** $F[l] = 0$ **then**
12 $\quad\quad F[l] \leftarrow F[l + 1]$
13 $\quad\quad C[l] \leftarrow C[l + 1]/2$

14 **Proc** $computeLengths(S, T, d, i)$
> **Input** : Huffman subtree rooted at node T, of depth d, table S and position i.
> **Output**: Records the symbols $S[i].s$ and lengths $S[i].\ell$, consecutively starting
> from i, for the leaves below T. Returns the next free position i.

15 $\quad$ **if** $T.l =$ null **then** (T is a leaf)
16 $\quad\quad S[i].s \leftarrow T.s; S[i].\ell \leftarrow d$
17 $\quad\quad i \leftarrow i + 1$
18 $\quad$ **else**
19 $\quad\quad i \leftarrow computeLengths(S, T.l, d + 1, i)$
20 $\quad\quad i \leftarrow computeLengths(S, T.r, d + 1, i)$
21 $\quad$ **return** i

Algorithm 2.4: Reading a symbol with a Canonical Huffman code.

> **Input** : $L[1, \sigma]$, $F[1, h]$, and $C[1, h]$ representing a Canonical Huffman code.
> **Output**: The next symbol decoded from a bit stream.

1 $N \leftarrow$ next h bits from the stream
2 Find ℓ such that $C[\ell] \cdot 2^{h-\ell} \leq N < C[\ell + 1] \cdot 2^{h-\ell-1}$ by binary search
3 $N \leftarrow \lfloor N/2^{h-\ell} \rfloor$
4 Advance ℓ bits in the input stream
5 **return** $L[F[\ell] + N - C[\ell]]$

---

i	$L[i]$	code	len	code $\cdot 2^{h-len}$	len	$F[len]$	$C[len]$	$C[len] \cdot 2^{h-len}$
1	a	00	2	00000 = 0	1	1	0	0
2	b	010	3	01000 = 8	2	1	00	0
3	c	011	3	01100 = 12	3	2	010	8
4	d	100	3	10000 = 16	4	5	1010	20
5	e	10100	5	10100 = 20	5	5	10100	20
6	f	10101	5	10101 = 21				
...	...	...	...	...				
16	p	11111	5	11111 = 31				

Figure 2.4. The representation of the Canonical Huffman code of Example 2.16. We show the code on the left and its representation on the right. Under column $code \cdot 2^{h-len}$ we show in gray how the codes are completed up to length h. On the right, under column $C[len]$, we show in gray the codes that are extrapolated because no code of that length exists. The last column shows the data where the binary search for decoding is carried out.

Now we read the next $h = 5$ bits, $N = 00101 = 5$. It is between $C[2] \cdot 2^{5-2} = 0$ and $C[3] \cdot 2^{5-3} - 1 = 7$, so the length of the next code is $\ell = 2$. We set $N \leftarrow \lfloor 5/2^{5-2} \rfloor = 0$, and the code is $L[F[2] + 0 - C[2]] = L[1] = $ a. We advance $\ell = 2$ positions in the input.

Finally, we read the next $h = 5$ bits, $N = 10101 = 21$. It is $\geq C[5] \cdot 2^0 = 20$, thus $\ell = 5$ and N does not change. The code is $L[F[5] + 21 - C[5]] = L[6] = $ f. We advance $\ell = 5$ positions and the input is consumed.

Though not evident in this example, the algorithm may request up to $h - 1$ nonexistent bits from the end of the stream. Those can be filled arbitrarily.

Thus, using canonical Huffman codes, we can decompress a sequence of n encoded symbols in time $\mathcal{O}(n \log \log n)$. This is usually faster than a bitwise decoding, unless the alphabet is small or the codes are very short on average.

2.6.4 Better than Huffman

As said, Huffman codes are optimal, but only if we assign an integral number of bits to each code. It is possible to do better than Huffman if one assigns a *fractional* number of bits per code. This is not as weird as it sounds: consider encoding *trits*, symbols in $\{0, 1, 2\}$. We can encode 3 trits (which have $3^3 = 27$ possible values) in 5 bits (which have 32 combinations), thus using $\frac{5}{3} \approx 1.667 > \log 3 \approx 1.585$ bits per trit. The trick is to encode several symbols together. A more principled approach is *arithmetic coding*, which uses less than 2 extra bits *for the whole sequence*, that is, it encodes the sequence in less than $n\mathcal{H}(\Pr) + 2$ bits. For compact data structures, however, arithmetic coding is less convenient, because it is not possible to access a symbol of the sequence without decoding from the beginning. In general, we will use Huffman as our gold standard, although in some cases we will use the trick of encoding several symbols together.

2.7 Variable-Length Codes for Integers

Huffman codes are the best possible among those giving the same code to the same symbol. Sometimes, however, they can be inconvenient because of the size of Σ: Even with a canonical code, we have spent $|\Sigma| \log |\Sigma|$ bits to store L, which in some applications can be large compared to the $n(\mathcal{H}(\text{Pr}) + 1)$ bits of the compressed data. For some particular cases, we can design *fixed* codes, which do not depend on the sequence to compress but work well on the typical sequences in which we are interested.

A good example is the need to compress a sequence of natural numbers when usually most of them are small. In this case, we can choose a fixed code that favors small numbers. We next show some of the most popular ones. Note that all these codes are prefix codes. From now on we assume we want to encode a natural number $x > 0$ and call $|x|$ its length in bits. If we want to encode the 0 as well (or up to some negative value), we may shift the values to encode.

Unary Codes

The unary code is convenient when x is extremely small:

$$u(x) = 0^{x-1} . 1,$$

where 0^{x-1} means $x - 1$ bits 0. The unary code of x uses $|u(x)| = x$ bits. For example, $u(1) = 1$, $u(2) = 01$, $u(3) = 001$, $u(4) = 0001$, and so on. It is also customary to use the reverse bits, $1^{x-1} . 0$.

Gamma (γ) Codes

This code is convenient when x is small. The γ-code of x is

$$\gamma(x) = 0^{|x|-1} . [x]_{|x|} = u(|x|) . [x]_{|x|-1},$$

where $[x]_\ell$ stands for the ℓ least significant bits of x. Gamma codes can also be understood in terms of unary codes: We encode in unary the length $|x|$ of x and then encode the number x (without its highest bit) in binary.

For example, $\gamma(1) = \gamma(1) = 1$, $\gamma(2) = \gamma(10) = 010$, $\gamma(3) = \gamma(11) = 011$, $\gamma(4) = \gamma(100) = 00100$, and so on. It holds

$$|\gamma(x)| = 2|x| - 1 = 2\lfloor \log x \rfloor + 1 = \mathcal{O}(\log x),$$

so gamma codes become shorter than unary codes for $x \geq 6$.

To decode $\gamma(x)$, we read z 0s until finding a 1, and then read that 1 and the following z bits to form the value of x. This can be done in $\mathcal{O}(z) = \mathcal{O}(|x|) = \mathcal{O}(\log x)$ time, which can be good enough because we choose to use γ-codes when most x values are small. Still, we can do better. If we assume that we are encoding numbers x that fit in the computer word, then the first part of $\gamma(x)$, $u(|x|)$, also fits in a computer word, and thus the problem of finding z reduces to finding the highest 1 in a computer word. This is directly supported in many architectures (more details are given near the end of Section 4.5.2). If it is not, we can precompute a table that, for every nonzero chunk of b bits, tells where the highest 1 is. Then we need at most $\lceil |x|/b \rceil$ table accesses to find the highest 1. The table has 2^b entries of $\log b$ bits. For example, with $b = 16$ we require only 32 kilobytes of memory and can decode any 32-bit number in 1 or 2 accesses. Since most numbers are small when γ-codes are used, it might be even better to use $b = 8$, so the global table is tiny and will normally reside in cache.

Delta (δ) Codes

When numbers are too large for γ-codes to be efficient, we can use δ-codes:

$$\delta(x) = \gamma(|x|) \cdot [x]_{|x|-1},$$

that is, we γ-encode the length of x and then encode x without its highest bit. For example, $\delta(1) = \delta(1) = 1$, $\delta(2) = \delta(10) = 0100$, $\delta(3) = \delta(11) = 0101$, $\delta(4) = \delta(100) = 01100$, and so on. It holds

$$|\delta(x)| = |\gamma(|x|)| + |x| - 1 = |x| + 2||x|| - 2 = |x| + 2\lfloor \log |x| \rfloor$$
$$= \log x + \mathcal{O}(\log \log x).$$

The δ-codes are shorter than γ-codes for $x \geq 32$ (and of the same length for $16 \leq x \leq 31$). The δ-codes can be decoded in $\mathcal{O}(1)$ time if γ-codes can. In case a global table is used, it is very small because it must decode numbers up to length $\mathcal{O}(\log |x|) = \mathcal{O}(\log \log x)$. For example, a table of 64 entries suffices to decode any 64-bit number with one access.

Rice Codes

Rice codes choose one parameter ℓ for the whole sequence. Let $y = \lfloor x/2^\ell \rfloor$. The Rice code for x is then

$$Rice(x) = u(y + 1) \cdot [x]_\ell,$$

that is, the ℓ lowest bits of x are encoded preceded by the highest bits, which are encoded in unary. Note that $[x]_\ell$ will use ℓ bits even if x has fewer than ℓ significant bits, padding with 0s on the left if necessary.

By appropriately choosing ℓ, Rice codes can yield better compression than γ-codes or δ-codes and are the favorite encoders for inverted indexes. Rice codes are a particular case of Golomb codes, which are more complicated and can yield slightly better compression.

Variable Byte (VByte) Codes

These codes usually require more space than the previous ones and are useful only for larger numbers. Their aim is to speed up decoding by ensuring that only byte-aligned data are read. The number x is cut into 7-bit chunks, $x = x_1 \cdot x_2 \ldots x_k$. Each chunk is then stored in the lowest bits of a byte, whose highest bit is 0 for $x_1, \ldots, x_{k-1}$, and 1 for x_k.

To read x, we start with $y \leftarrow 0$ and read bytes $b_1, b_2, \ldots, b_k$, until we read a byte $b_k \geq 128$. Each time we read a byte $b_i < 128$, we do $y \leftarrow (y + b_i) \cdot 2^7$. When we read b_k, the final value is $x = y + b_k - 128$. In practice, numbers fit in a few bytes, and this decoding process is faster than the previous ones.

Simple-9 and PforDelta

These codes are aimed at retaining the good space performance of bitwise codes and the good time performance of bytewise codes. They encode and decode a short sequence of numbers (not each one individually) and read whole computer words from the input. In general, they achieve excellent performance and can be easily decoded in constant time.

Simple-9 encodes as many numbers as possible in a 32-bit word. The highest 4 bits of the word indicate how many numbers are encoded. If the next 28 values to encode are 1 or 2, then we can use one bit for each. Otherwise, if the next 14 values are up to 4, then we can use 2 bits for each. If not, but the next 9 numbers are up to 8, then we can use 3 bits for each (wasting a bit), and so on. There are in total 9 possibilities (i.e., encoding the next $\lfloor 28/m \rfloor$ values using $m = 1, 2, 3, 4, 5, 7, 9, 14$, or 28 bits per value). Numbers over 28 bits cannot be encoded. The variant Simple-16 introduces more cases, combining different lengths, to use all the 16 4-bit combinations.

PforDelta, instead, encodes a fixed amount of numbers at a time (typically 128), using for all of them the number of bits needed for the largest one. A fraction of the largest numbers (usually 10%) is encoded separately, and the other 90% is used to calculate how many bits are needed per number.

Algorithm 2.5 gives the encoding procedures for most of the described codes. It assumes the code fits in an integer variable (c). To compute $|x| = \lfloor \log x \rfloor + 1$ we must find its highest 1, as explained. In **vbyte**, we assume that the highest bytes will be read first. In **simple9**, x is an array and we must encode from $x[k]$, leaving k at the next position to encode; function $code(m)$ encodes the chosen value of m using 4 bits.

2.8 Jensen's Inequality

A tool that is frequently used to analyze compression methods is Jensen's inequality. It establishes that, if $f(x)$ is a concave function (that is, $f(\frac{x+y}{2}) \geq \frac{f(x)+f(y)}{2}$ for all x and y, like the logarithm), then

$$f\left(\frac{\sum_i a_i x_i}{\sum_i a_i}\right) \geq \frac{\sum_i a_i f(x_i)}{\sum_i a_i},$$

for any values x_i and positive weights a_i. Equality is reached only if all the x_i values are equal or f is linear. In particular, if we have m values $x_1, \ldots, x_m$ and the weights are all equal, $a_i = \frac{1}{m}$, this gives

$$f\left(\frac{\sum_i x_i}{m}\right) \geq \frac{\sum_i f(x_i)}{m}.$$

Roughly said, the function of the average is larger than the average of the functions. We will use Jensen's inequality many times in the book.

Differential Encoding of Increasing Numbers

Assume we have increasing numbers $0 = y_0 < y_1 < y_2 < \ldots < y_m = n$. As a way to compress them, we store them differentially: we encode $x_1, \ldots, x_m$, where $x_i = y_i - y_{i-1}$. If m is not much smaller than n, then most x_i values will be small, and we can apply the encoding methods just seen. For example, assume we use δ-codes. The total

---

Algorithm 2.5: Various integer encodings.

Input : x, the number to be encoded, Rice parameter ℓ, and Simple9 position k.
Output: $\langle c, b \rangle$ so that the code consists of the b lowest bits of integer c.

1 **Proc** unary (x)
2 | **return** $\langle 1, x \rangle$

3 **Proc** gamma (x)
4 | **return** $\langle x, 2 \cdot |x| - 1 \rangle$

5 **Proc** delta (x)
6 | $\langle c', b' \rangle \leftarrow$ gamma$(|x|)$
7 | **return** $\langle x + 2^{|x|-1}(c' - 1), |x| + b' - 1 \rangle$

8 **Proc** rice (x, ℓ)
9 | $y \leftarrow \lfloor x/2^{\ell} \rfloor$
10 | **return** $\langle (x \bmod 2^{\ell}) + 2^{\ell}, \ell + y + 1 \rangle$

11 **Proc** vbyte (x)
12 | $c \leftarrow 0; b \leftarrow 0$
13 | **while** $x \geq 128$ **do**
14 | | $c \leftarrow c + 2^b \cdot (x \bmod 128)$
15 | | $b \leftarrow b + 8$
16 | | $x \leftarrow \lfloor x/128 \rfloor$
17 | **return** $\langle c + 2^b \cdot (x + 128), b + 8 \rangle$

18 **Proc** simple9 (x, k)
19 | $m \leftarrow |x[k]|$
20 | $p \leftarrow 1; c \leftarrow 0$
21 | **while** $(p + 1) \cdot \max(m, |x[k + p]|) \leq 28$ **do**
22 | | $m \leftarrow \max(m, |x[k + p]|)$
23 | | $p \leftarrow p + 1;$
24 | **while** $p \cdot (m + 1) \leq 28$ **do** $m \leftarrow m + 1$
25 | **while** $p > 0$ **do**
26 | | $c \leftarrow c \cdot 2^m + x[k]$
27 | | $k \leftarrow k + 1; p \leftarrow p - 1$
28 | **return** $\langle c + 2^{28} \cdot code(m), 32 \rangle$

---

size of the encoding will then be

$$\sum_i |\delta(x_i)| = \sum_i |x_i| + 2\lfloor \log |x_i| \rfloor = \sum_i \lfloor \log x_i \rfloor + 1 + 2\lfloor \log(\lfloor \log x_i \rfloor + 1) \rfloor$$

$$= \sum_i \log x_i + 2 \log \log x_i + \mathcal{O}(1)$$

$$\leq m \log \frac{n}{m} + 2m \log \log \frac{n}{m} + \mathcal{O}(m),$$

where we have applied Jensen's inequality twice in the last line, on the concave functions $\log x$ and $\log \log x$, and $a_i = 1/m$.

This also yields our first encoding for a bit sequence $B[1, n]$ with m 1s that gets close to its zero-order entropy, $n\mathcal{H}_0(B) = m \log \frac{n}{m} + \mathcal{O}(m)$ (recall the end of Section 2.3.1): We call y_i the positions of the 1s and δ-encode the gaps x_i between them. Note that Huffman coding is useless in principle to compress a bit sequence, as it needs at least one bit per bit. We will see, however, successful encodings in Chapter 4, by encoding the bits in groups.

Concatenations of Strings

Another consequence of Jensen's inequality we will use later is the following. Let S_1 and S_2 be two strings of lengths n_1 and n_2, respectively, and $S = S_1 . S_2$ be their concatenation, of length $n = n_1 + n_2$. Then $n_1 \mathcal{H}_0(S_1) + n_2 \mathcal{H}_0(S_2) \leq n\mathcal{H}_0(S)$. To see this, let us call $n_{s,1}$, $n_{s,2}$, and n_s the number of occurrences of symbol s in S_1, S_2, and S, respectively. Then we have

$$n_1 \mathcal{H}_0(S_1) + n_2 \mathcal{H}_0(S_2) = \sum_{s \in \Sigma} n_{s,1} \log \frac{n_1}{n_{s,1}} + \sum_{s \in \Sigma} n_{s,2} \log \frac{n_2}{n_{s,2}}$$

$$= \sum_{s \in \Sigma} \left(n_{s,1} \log \frac{n_1}{n_{s,1}} + n_{s,2} \log \frac{n_2}{n_{s,2}} \right) \leq \sum_{s \in \Sigma} n_s \log \frac{n}{n_s} = n\mathcal{H}_0(S).$$

To obtain the inequality we have used Jensen's formula on each $s \in \Sigma$, with $i \in \{1, 2\}$, $a_i = n_{s,i}$, $x_i = \frac{n_i}{n_{s,i}}$, and $f = \log$.

2.9 Application: Positional Inverted Indexes

A (positional) inverted index is a data structure that provides fast word searches on a natural language text T. For each distinct word s of the text, the index stores the list of the positions where s appears in the text, in increasing order. Let n be the number of words in T, and n_s the number of times word s appears in T. Then the positions stored by the list of word s form a sequence $0 < p_1 < p_2 < \ldots < p_{n_s} \leq n$. If we encode the differences using δ-codes as in Section 2.8, the total space used by the list is $n_s \log \frac{n}{n_s} + 2n_s \log \log \frac{n}{n_s} + \mathcal{O}(n_s)$ bits. Summing this space over all the words s in the text, we obtain

$$\sum_s n_s \log \frac{n}{n_s} + 2n_s \log \log \frac{n}{n_s} + \mathcal{O}(n_s) \leq n\mathcal{H}_0(T) + 2n \log \mathcal{H}_0(T) + \mathcal{O}(n)$$

bits, where $\mathcal{H}_0(T) = \sum_s \frac{n_s}{n} \log \frac{n}{n_s}$ is the zero-order empirical entropy of T if regarded as a sequence of words. The intriguing part of the inequality is the second term, $2n \log \mathcal{H}_0(T)$. It comes from $\sum_s 2n_s \log \log \frac{n}{n_s}$, by applying Jensen's inequality with $f = \log$, $a_s = n_s$, and $x_s = \log \frac{n}{n_s}$.

Note that $n\mathcal{H}_0(T)$ is basically the space reached by a Huffman compression of T if we take the words as the basic symbols. As said, such a Huffman compression reduces T to about 25% of its plain representation on typical English texts. The fact that the positional inverted index can be compressed as much as T should not be surprising: the index can be regarded as an alternative representation of T, as T can be reconstructed from the lists.

In both cases, the actual words must be stored separately, but the vocabulary is usually small compared to the text size. An empirical law known as Heaps' law states that the number of distinct words in a text of n words grows as $\mathcal{O}(n^\beta)$, where $0 < \beta < 1$ is a constant that depends on the text type (and is in practice close to 0.5).

2.10 Summary

The worst-case entropy of a set $\mathcal{U}$ is $\log |\mathcal{U}|$, the minimum number of bits needed to distinguish an element in the worst case. When each $u \in \mathcal{U}$ is assigned a probability p_u, then Information Theory establishes that the minimum average code length is $\mathcal{H} = \sum_{u \in \mathcal{U}} p_u \log \frac{1}{p_u}$. To compress specific sequences one can use their empirical entropy, which estimates p_u from the frequencies in the sequence. Optimal coding methods like Huffman reach a code length below $\mathcal{H} + 1$ bits per element. On large or infinite sets like the natural numbers one may use fixed codes that optimize the space usage for certain common distributions.

2.11 Bibliographic Notes

In this chapter we focused on *semi-static* compression. This means that first we compute the probabilities of the symbols, then we build the codes, and finally we encode the symbols, all using the same codes. Instead of these steps, *adaptive* compression gathers and updates the probabilities as it compresses the sequence, performing only one pass. Although dynamic compression is convenient in many cases, semi-static compression is more appropriate for the compact data structures we use in this book.

An excellent book on Information Theory is by Cover and Thomas (2006). It covers entropy and coding, although it does not focus on the practical aspects of efficient coding. This is well covered in many books on compression (Storer, 1988; Bell *et al.*, 1990; Witten *et al.*, 1999; Moffat and Turpin, 2002; Solomon, 2007; Salomon *et al.*, 2013). While these describe most of the topics we have covered, some parts of the chapter deserve further references.

Worst-case entropy. Computing worst-case entropies is a matter of counting the number of combinatorial objects of a certain kind. There are excellent books on this topic (Sedgewick and Flajolet, 2013; Graham *et al.*, 1994).

Shannon and empirical entropy. Modern Information Theory started with the seminal work of Shannon (1948), presented more in depth in the book by Shannon and Weaver (1949). Gagie (2006) gives more insights on the limits of the kth-order empirical entropy measure.

Huffman codes. Huffman (1952) found the well-known algorithm to build an optimal prefix code. Schwartz and Kallick (1964) introduced canonical Huffman codes. Katona and Nemetz (1976) showed that a symbol with probability p is assigned a Huffman codeword of length at most $\lfloor \log_\phi(1/p) \rfloor$. Liddell and Moffat (2006) describe some further improvements over the fast decoding method we have presented. Arithmetic coding was presented by Witten *et al.* (1987).

The handling of large alphabets in the Huffman algorithm was considered recently (Gagie *et al.*, 2015). They represent canonical codes in $\mathcal{O}(\sigma \log \log n)$ bits. Decoding can be done in constant time per symbol (in theory), while in practice it remains $\mathcal{O}(\log \log n)$.

Variable-length codes. Apart from the classical codes, covered in books, VByte was proposed by Williams and Zobel (1999), Simple by Anh and Moffat (2005), and PforDelta by Zukowski *et al.* (2006). Others we have not mentioned are Zeta codes (Boldi and Vigna, 2005), VSEncoding (Silvestri and Venturini, 2010), and QMX (Trotman, 2014).

Inverted indexes. The book by Witten *et al.* (1999) focuses on the application of codes for inverted indexes on text databases. More recent books that cover this topic are by Büttcher *et al.* (2010) and Baeza-Yates and Ribeiro-Neto (2011). Heaps (1978) stated the law that describes the vocabulary growth. We will revisit inverted indexes several times in the book.

Bibliography

Anh, V. N. and Moffat, A. (2005). Inverted index compression using word-aligned binary codes. *Information Retrieval*, **8**, 151–166.

Baeza-Yates, R. and Ribeiro-Neto, B. (2011). *Modern Information Retrieval*. Addison-Wesley, 2nd edition.

Bell, T. C., Cleary, J., and Witten, I. H. (1990). *Text compression*. Prentice Hall.

Boldi, P. and Vigna, S. (2005). Codes for the World Wide Web. *Internet Mathematics*, **2**(4), 407–429.

Büttcher, S., Clarke, C. L. A., and Cormack, G. V. (2010). *Information Retrieval: Implementing and Evaluating Search Engines*. MIT Press.

Cover, T. and Thomas, J. (2006). *Elements of Information Theory*. Wiley, 2nd edition.

Gagie, T. (2006). Large alphabets and incompressibility. *Information Processing Letters*, **99**(6), 246–251.

Gagie, T., Navarro, G., Nekrich, Y., and Ordóñez, A. (2015). Efficient and compact representations of prefix codes. *IEEE Transactions on Information Theory*, **61**(9), 4999–5011.

Graham, R. L., Knuth, D. E., and Patashnik, O. (1994). *Concrete Mathematics – A Foundation for Computer Science*. Addison-Wesley, 2nd edition.

Heaps, H. (1978). *Information Retrieval: Theoretical and Computational Aspects*. Academic Press.

Huffman, D. A. (1952). A method for the construction of minimum-redundancy codes. *Proceedings of the Institute of Electrical and Radio Engineers*, **40**(9), 1098–1101.

Katona, G. O. H. and Nemetz, T. O. H. (1976). Huffman codes and self-information. *IEEE Transactions on Information Theory*, **22**(3), 337–340.

Liddell, M. and Moffat, A. (2006). Decoding prefix codes. *Software Practice and Experience*, **36**(15), 1687–1710.

Moffat, A. and Turpin, A. (2002). *Compression and Coding Algorithms*. Springer.

Salomon, D., Motta, G., and Bryant, D. (2013). *Data Compression: The Complete Reference*. Springer.

Schwartz, E. S. and Kallick, B. (1964). Generating a canonical prefix encoding. *Communications of the ACM*, **7**, 166–169.

Sedgewick, R. and Flajolet, P. (2013). *An Introduction to the Analysis of Algorithms*. Addison-Wesley-Longman, 2nd edition.

Shannon, C. E. (1948). A mathematical theory of communication. *Bell Systems Technical Journal*, **27**, 398–403.

Shannon, C. E. and Weaver, W. (1949). *A Mathematical Theory of Communication*. University of Illinois Press.

Silvestri, F. and Venturini, R. (2010). VSEncoding: efficient coding and fast decoding of integer lists via dynamic programming. In *Proc. 19th ACM Conference on Information and Knowledge Management (CIKM)*, pages 1219–1228.

Solomon, D. (2007). *Variable-Length Codes for Data Compression*. Springer-Verlag.

Storer, J. (1988). *Data Compression: Methods and Theory*. Addison-Wesley.

Trotman, A. (2014). Compression, SIMD, and postings lists. In *Proc. 19th Australasian Document Computing Symposium (ADCS)*, page 50.

Williams, H. E. and Zobel, J. (1999). Compressing integers for fast file access. *The Computer Journal*, **42**, 193–201.

Witten, I. H., Neal, R. M., and Cleary, J. G. (1987). Arithmetic coding for data compression. *Communications of the ACM*, **30**, 520–540.

Witten, I. H., Moffat, A., and Bell, T. C. (1999). *Managing Gigabytes: Compressing and Indexing Documents and Images*. Van Nostrand Reinhold, 2nd edition.

Zukowski, M., Heman, S., Nes, N., and Boncz, P. (2006). Super-scalar RAM-CPU cache compression. In *Proc. 22nd International Conference on Data Engineering (ICDE)*, page 59.

CHAPTER 3
Arrays

An *array* $A[1, n]$ is a sequence of elements that can be read and written at arbitrary positions. That is, the array is an abstract data type that supports the operations:

read(A, i): returns $A[i]$, for any $1 \leq i \leq n$.
write(A, i, x): sets $A[i] \leftarrow x$, for any $1 \leq i \leq n$ and any x.

Unlike the classical array programming construct, we are interested in space-efficient array representations, which hopefully store only the useful bits of each number $A[i]$. In some cases the array values are uniform and it is reasonable to use the same number of bits for all. In others, the numbers are very different and we prefer to allocate a variable number of bits for each.

Example 3.1 *If we are storing the number of days per month worked by employees, then 5 bits are sufficient, and usually necessary too. On the other hand, if we store the number of children of employees, although in principle the number is not bounded, 1–3 bits will be sufficient for most of them. It is not space-efficient to allocate the maximum number of bits for everyone.*

As seen in Chapter 2, variable-length elements also appear frequently as a result of compression, and compression will generally not work if we allocate the maximum number of bits to every element. In Chapter 2 we described ways to encode the variable-length elements so that the sequences can be decoded from the beginning. In this chapter we are more ambitious: to support **read** on arrays efficiently, we need to directly extract the bits corresponding to any arbitrary element.

In this chapter we discuss how to store arrays in compact form, using ideally only the bits needed for each element, while providing efficient **read** operations. We will also provide efficient **write** operations on arrays of fixed-length cells. On variable-length cells, a **write** operation may change the length of the cell, which introduces other complications that will be dealt with later (in Chapter 12). The chapter starts with very basic folklore techniques to handle elements of fixed and variable size. Then we show how to compute range sums on arrays. At the end we show applications such as constant-time array initialization and more sophisticated variable-length encodings.

In general, we will assume that the elements use a small number of bits, which fit in a computer word of w bits and thus can be manipulated in constant time. We call "integer" the numeric data type offered by the language using w bits.

3.1 Elements of Fixed Size

Assume that every element in A is stored in ℓ bits. A simple solution such as allocating $A[1, n]$ as an array of integers may waste a lot of space, $w \cdot n$ bits, where just $\ell \cdot n$ would suffice (recall that we assume $\ell \leq w$, and that usually $\ell \ll w$). Although it might be possible to allocate an array of so-called "short integers," typically using $16n$ bits, or bytes, using $8n$ bits, it might be that none of them is close to the right number of bits actually needed.

Example 3.2 *In Example 3.1, when encoding days in a month using 5 bits, even using an array of bytes would waste $8/5 - 1 = 60\%$ of extra space!*

Structure

To use the right amount of space, we allocate an array of integers $W[1, \lceil \ell n/w \rceil]$, which is sufficient to encode n elements of ℓ bits.[1] We regard these ℓn bits stored in W as a virtual bit array $B[1, \ell n]$. We will store each $A[i]$ at $B[(i-1)\ell + 1, i\ell]$, placing the most significant bits first: the bit $B[j]$ is stored at the rth most significant bit of $W[\lceil j/w \rceil]$, where $r = ((j-1) \bmod w) + 1$.

Example 3.3 *Figure 3.1 illustrates this arrangement, on a toy array $A[1, 10]$ of days worked in the month by $n = 10$ employees, with $\ell = 5$. The grayed blocks will be used later.*

In this structure, we can read a single bit $B[j]$ with the formula

$$B[j] = \lfloor W[\lceil j/w \rceil] / 2^{w-r} \rfloor \bmod 2.$$

We can also convert some $B[j] = 0$ to 1 by adding 2^{w-r} to $W[\lceil j/w \rceil]$, and convert $B[j] = 1$ to 0 by subtracting 2^{w-r}. See Algorithm 3.1.

Read Operation

To provide constant-time access to $A[i]$, we must extract a whole chunk of the form $B[j', j]$ from W, with $j - j' + 1 \leq w$. First, assume that $\lceil j'/w \rceil = \lceil j/w \rceil$, that is, $B[j', j]$ is contained in the single word $W[\lceil j/w \rceil]$. In this case, letting $r = ((j-1) \bmod w) + 1$, $B[j', j]$ is obtained as

$$B[j', j] = \lfloor W[\lceil j/w \rceil] / 2^{w-r} \rfloor \bmod 2^{j-j'+1}.$$

This is shown schematically on the left of Figure 3.2.

---

[1] The only reason to use an array of integers instead of, say, bytes, or short or long integers, is that programming languages typically assign the basic integer type to the unit of memory that is most efficiently handled by the target computer.

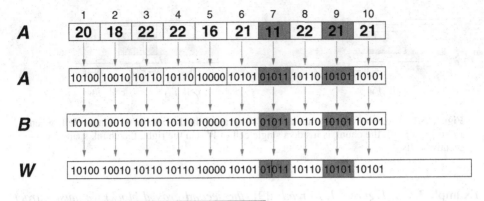

Figure 3.1. Storing an array A of $n = 10$ elements, each using $\ell = 5$ bits. In the second row we visualize the bits of the numbers. Bit array B is formed by concatenating those 5-bit chunks. Array W partitions those bits into new chunks of $w = 32$ bits. Finally, W can be seen as an array of $\lceil \ell n/w \rceil = 2$ numbers. The shaded blocks illustrate operations read($A, 7$) and read($A, 9$).

Algorithm 3.1: Reading and writing on bit arrays.

---

1 **Proc** bitread(B, j)

 Input : Bit array $B[1, n]$ (seen as the integer array $W[1, \lceil n/w \rceil]$) and the
     position j to read.

 Output: Returns $B[j]$.

2   $r \leftarrow ((j - 1) \bmod w) + 1$
3   **return** $\lfloor W[\lceil j/w \rceil]/2^{w-r} \rfloor \bmod 2$

4 **Proc** bitset(B, j)

 Input : Bit array $B[1, n]$ (seen as the integer array $W[1, \lceil n/w \rceil]$), and the
     position j to set.

 Output: Sets $B[j] \leftarrow 1$.

5   $r \leftarrow ((j - 1) \bmod w) + 1$
6   **if** $\lfloor W[\lceil j/w \rceil]/2^{w-r} \rfloor \bmod 2 = 0$ **then**
7    $\lfloor W[\lceil j/w \rceil] \leftarrow W[\lceil j/w \rceil] + 2^{w-r}$

8 **Proc** bitclear(B, j)

 Input : Bit array $B[1, n]$ (seen as the integer array $W[1, \lceil n/w \rceil]$), and the
     position j to clear.

 Output: Sets $B[j] \leftarrow 0$.

9   $r \leftarrow ((j - 1) \bmod w) + 1$
10   **if** $\lfloor W[\lceil j/w \rceil]/2^{w-r} \rfloor \bmod 2 = 1$ **then**
11    $\lfloor W[\lceil j/w \rceil] \leftarrow W[\lceil j/w \rceil] - 2^{w-r}$

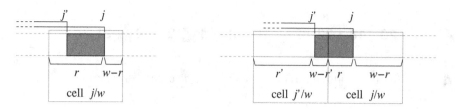

Figure 3.2. Accessing the bit chunks $B[j', j']$ (grayed) in the cells of W. On the left, when $\lceil j'/w \rceil = \lceil j/w \rceil$, the chunk is inside a single cell of W. On the right, the chunk spans 2 consecutive cells.

Example 3.4 *In Figure 3.1, to read $A[9]$ (the second grayed block) we must extract* $B[(9-1)\ell + 1, 9\ell] = B[41, 45] = B[j', j]$. *Thus $r = 13$, $\lceil j'/w \rceil = \lceil j/w \rceil = 2$, and* $A[9] = \lfloor W[2]/2^{19} \rfloor \bmod 2^5 = 21$.

Instead, if $\lceil j/w \rceil = \lceil j'/w \rceil + 1$, then $B[j', j]$ spans 2 words in W. In this case we also compute $r' = (j' - 1) \bmod w$, and it holds

$$B[j', j] = \lfloor W[\lceil j/w \rceil]\,/\,2^{w-r} \rfloor + (W[\lceil j'/w \rceil]\ \bmod\ 2^{w-r'}) \cdot 2^r,$$

as is shown schematically on the right of Figure 3.2.

Example 3.5 *In Figure 3.1, to read $A[7]$ (the first grayed block) we must extract $B[(7-1)\ell + 1, 7\ell] = B[31, 35] = B[j', j]$. Thus $\lceil j'/w \rceil = 1$ and $\lceil j/w \rceil = 2$, so we compute $r' = 30$ and $r = 3$. Now $A[7] = \lfloor W[2]/2^{29} \rfloor + (W[1] \bmod 2^2) \cdot 2^3 = 3 + 1 \cdot 8 = 11$.*

Therefore, we can read any $A[i]$ in constant time using $\mathsf{read}(A, i) = A[i] = B[(i-1)\ell + 1, i\ell]$ and the formulas above to extract it from W. The result can be directly interpreted as the integer $A[i]$.

A common speedup method, when $\ell \ll w$, is to avoid that cells of A cross the border between cells of W, so that the simpler formula always applies. This may require wasting up to $\ell - 1$ bits in each cell of W, so that if a cell of A crosses the border, it is made to start at the beginning of the next cell.

Write Operation

To perform $\mathsf{write}(A, i, x)$, we must set $B[(i-1)\ell + 1, i\ell] = B[j', j] \leftarrow x$, for a number x of $j - j' + 1$ bits. We first clear (that is, set to zero) the area $B[j', j]$, and then place x in it. If $\lceil j/w \rceil = \lceil j'/w \rceil$, we clear the area with

$$W[\lceil j/w \rceil] \leftarrow W[\lceil j/w \rceil] - (\lfloor W[\lceil j/w \rceil]\,/\,2^{w-r} \rfloor \bmod 2^{j-j'+1}) \cdot 2^{w-r},$$

and then we set the cleared area to x as follows (see Figure 3.2 again):

$$W[\lceil j/w \rceil] \leftarrow W[\lceil j/w \rceil] + x \cdot 2^{w-r}.$$

On the other hand, if $\lceil j/w \rceil = \lceil j'/w \rceil + 1$, the area to clear spans 2 words, and then we must place the corresponding parts of x:

$$W[\lceil j/w \rceil] \leftarrow W[\lceil j/w \rceil] \bmod 2^{w-r} + (x \bmod 2^r) \cdot 2^{w-r}$$
$$W[\lceil j'/w \rceil] \leftarrow W[\lceil j'/w \rceil] - (W[\lceil j'/w \rceil] \bmod 2^{w-r}) + \lfloor x/2^r \rfloor.$$

Algorithm 3.2 summarizes the operations. Throughout the book we will also use **bitsread** and **bitswrite** to operate on single computer words, as if they were arrays of length 1.

Programming

We mapped A to W via a bitvector B, and using the highest bit first, for pedagogical reasons. This leads to the arrangement on the left of Figure 3.3, which is easier to visualize. Many programmers prefer the arrangement on the right of the figure, because it leads to slightly cleaner formulas. In addition, we limited ourselves to classical mathematical operations on the integers for maximum generality, but in many programming languages there are operators that can translate our formulas into faster operations on the computer.

For example, in C language, and similar ones like C++ or Java, where the arrays start at zero (that is, $B[0, \ell n - 1]$ and $W[0, \lceil \ell n/w \rceil - 1]$), if we use the arrangement on the right of Figure 3.3, the formula to read $B[j]$ can be written as[2]

$$(\texttt{W[j/w]} \texttt{ >> } (\texttt{j \% w})) \texttt{ \& } 1,$$

where we assume the arrays contain unsigned integers. Independently of the current value of $B[j]$, we can set $B[j] \leftarrow 1$ with

$$\texttt{W[j/w]} \texttt{ |= } 1 \texttt{ << } (\texttt{j \% w}),$$

and we set $B[j] \leftarrow 0$ with

$$\texttt{W[j/w]} \texttt{ \&= } \sim(1 \texttt{ << } (\texttt{j \% w})).$$

Similarly, $A[i]$ corresponds to $B[j', j] = B[i\ell, (i+1)\ell - 1]$. When $B[j', j]$ falls within a single word, we can read it with the formula

$$(\texttt{W[j/w]} \texttt{ >> } (\texttt{j' \% w})) \texttt{ \& } ((1 \texttt{ << } (\texttt{j-j'+1})) \texttt{ - } 1),$$

and set it to x using

$$\texttt{W[j/w]} \texttt{ \&= } \sim(((1 \texttt{ << } (\texttt{j-j'+1})) \texttt{ - } 1) \texttt{ << } (\texttt{j' \% w}))$$
$$\texttt{W[j/w]} \texttt{ |= } \texttt{x} \texttt{ << } (\texttt{j' \% w}).$$

When $B[j', j]$ spans 2 words, we can read it using

$$(\texttt{W[j'/w]} \texttt{ >> } (\texttt{j' \% w})) \texttt{ |}$$
$$(\texttt{W[j/w]} \texttt{ \& } ((1 \texttt{ << } ((\texttt{j+1) \% w})) \texttt{ - } 1)) \texttt{ << } (\texttt{w - } (\texttt{j' \% w})),$$

---

[2] We can rewrite 'j % w' as 'j & (w-1)', since the operator & is faster than the modulus %. However, the formula is less clear and most decent compilers do the change automatically during the optimization phase.

Algorithm 3.2: Read and write on arrays of cells of fixed length ℓ. We will also use bitsread and bitswrite as operating on the bit array B.

---

1 **Proc** bitsread(W, j', j)

     Input : Array W (representing a bit array B) and range $B[j', j]$ to read.

     Output: Returns $B[j', j]$ as an integer.

2   **if** $j' > j$ **then return** 0

3    $r \leftarrow ((j - 1) \bmod w) + 1$

4   **if** $\lceil j/w \rceil = \lceil j'/w \rceil$ **then return** $\lfloor W[\lceil j/w \rceil] / 2^{w-r} \rfloor \bmod 2^{j-j'+1}$

5    $r' \leftarrow (j' - 1) \bmod w$

6   **return** $\lfloor W[\lceil j/w \rceil] / 2^{w-r} \rfloor + (W[\lceil j'/w \rceil] \bmod 2^{w-r'}) \cdot 2^r$

7 **Proc** read(A, i)

     Input : Array A of ℓ-bit cells (seen as the integer array W), and the position i

               to read.

     Output: Returns $A[i]$.

8   **return** bitsread(W, $(i - 1)\ell + 1$, $i\ell$)

9 **Proc** bitswrite(W, j', j, x)

     Input : Array W (representing a bit array B), and range $B[j', j]$ where we

               must write the element x (of length $|x| \le j - j' + 1$).

     Output: Assigns $B[j', j] \leftarrow x$.

10   **if** $j' > j$ **then return**

11   $r \leftarrow ((j - 1) \bmod w) + 1$

12   **if** $\lceil j/w \rceil = \lceil j'/w \rceil$ **then**

13      $W[\lceil j/w \rceil] \leftarrow W[\lceil j/w \rceil] - (\lfloor W[\lceil j/w \rceil]/2^{w-r} \rfloor \bmod 2^{j-j'+1}) \cdot 2^{w-r}$

14      $W[\lceil j/w \rceil] \leftarrow W[\lceil j/w \rceil] + x \cdot 2^{w-r}$

15   **else**

16      $r' \leftarrow (j' - 1) \bmod w$

17      $W[\lceil j/w \rceil] \leftarrow W[\lceil j/w \rceil] \bmod 2^{w-r} + (x \bmod 2^r) \cdot 2^{w-r}$

18      $W[\lceil j'/w \rceil] \leftarrow W[\lceil j'/w \rceil] - (W[\lceil j'/w \rceil] \bmod 2^{w-r'}) + \lfloor x/2^r \rfloor$

19 **Proc** write(A, i, x)

     Input : Array A of ℓ-bit cells (seen as the integer array W), and the position i

               where we must write the element x.

     Output: Assigns $A[i] \leftarrow x$.

20   bitswrite(W, $(i - 1)\ell + 1$, $i\ell$, x)

---

and set it to x with

```
W[j'/w] = (W[j'/w] & ((1 << (j' % w)) - 1)) | (x << (j' % w))
 W[j/w] = (W[j/w] & ~((1 << ((j+1) % w)) - 1))
          | (x >> (w - (j' % w))).
```

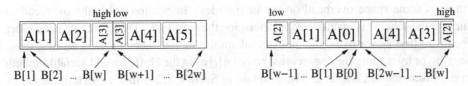

Figure 3.3. Deploying the chunks $A[i] = B[(i-1)\ell + 1, i\ell]$ on the integer array W, where the third cell of A is split into high and low parts. The method we have described is on the left. On the right, an arrangement that is more popular among programmers (and with arrays starting at 0). In both cases, the highest bits in each cell of A and W are drawn to the left.

All the pseudocodes in the rest of the book can be made compatible with this arrangement by just changing Algorithms 3.1 and 3.2.

Using Fractions of Bits

We have assumed so far that each element $A[i]$ uses an integral number ℓ of bits. This may be wasteful when the numbers belong to a small interval whose size is not a power of 2. For example, consider storing trits (recall Section 2.6.4), which take values in $\{0, 1, 2\}$. If we use 2 bits per value, then an array $A[1, n]$ of trits requires $2n$ bits. However, it should be sufficient with $n \log 3 \approx 1.585n$ bits.

The arithmetic formulas we have developed to store ℓ-bit numbers are easily extended to store numbers that take values in $[0, d - 1]$, where we assume that $d \ll 2^w$. We can encode $k = \lfloor w/\log d \rfloor$ values of A in a single computer word: the values $x_1, \ldots, x_k$ are regarded as the d-base digits of the number $X = \sum_{i=1}^{k} x_i \cdot d^{k-i}$. Since $X < d^k = 2^{k \log d} \le 2^w$, we can store X in a single word of array W.

Therefore, we implement read(A, i) by computing $j = \lceil i/k \rceil$ and $r = ((i - 1) \bmod k) + 1$, and then

$$A[i] = \lfloor W[j] / d^{k-r} \rfloor \bmod d.$$

To implement write(A, i, x), we first clear the area in W and then write x in it:

$$W[j] \leftarrow W[j] - (\lfloor W[j] / d^{k-r} \rfloor \bmod d) \cdot d^{k-r} + x \cdot d^{k-r}.$$

Note that each value of A is encoded inside a single word of W. Since we write k numbers in w bits, the number of bits used per value is $w/k = \frac{w}{\lfloor w/\log d \rfloor} < \frac{w}{w/\log d - 1} = \frac{w}{w - \log d} \cdot \log d$, that is, only slightly more than $\log d$ bits if $d \ll 2^w$.

Example 3.6 *Consider storing trits. We can pack $k = \lfloor 32/\log 3 \rfloor = 20$ trits in a 32-bit word, by interpreting them as a number of 20 digits in base 3. The number is in the range $[0, 3^{20} - 1]$, which fits in 32 bits. To recover the rth value inside a word $W[j]$, we compute $\lfloor W[j]/3^{20-r} \rfloor \bmod 3$. Each trit then occupies $\frac{32}{20} = 1.6$ bits, close to $\log 3 \approx 1.585$.*

3.2 Elements of Variable Size

Now we consider the case where each element $A[i]$ uses a different number of bits, ℓ_i. We aim to use as close to ℓ_i bits as possible to store $A[i]$, but each storage technique imposes some space overhead on top of the ideal. In Section 3.2.1, the overhead of the storage scheme is insufficient to determine the lengths ℓ_i. Therefore, we need other means to find ℓ_i, for example, an external source such as another array storing those lengths, or by reading the consecutive bits of $A[i]$ as in the Huffman and variable-length codes discussed in Chapter 2. The structure of Section 3.2.2, instead, determines ℓ_i by itself and thus allows storing each $A[i]$ with the minimum possible number of bits.

The basic idea is, just as in Section 3.1, to concatenate one entry after another on a bit array $B[1, N]$, with $N = \sum_{i=1}^{n} \ell_i$, and then represent B as an array of integers W. We can then use the same mechanisms described in that section to read any desired element. The main obstacle is that the entry $A[i]$ is not at $B[(i-1)\ell + 1, i\ell]$ as in Section 3.1, but at $B[1 + \sum_{t=1}^{i-1} \ell_t, \sum_{t=1}^{i} \ell_t]$. Therefore, we need efficient ways to compute these sums.

3.2.1 Sampled Pointers

Let us logically (not physically) cut A into consecutive *blocks* of k elements, for some parameter k. Then, apart from W, we store an array $P[1, \lceil n/k \rceil]$ of *pointers* to B, so that $P[j]$ stores the position where $A[(j-1)k + 1]$ starts in B. Therefore, the position where $A[i]$ starts in B is

$$p = P[\lceil i/k \rceil] + \sum_{t=(\lceil i/k \rceil - 1)k+1}^{i-1} \ell_t.$$

To find p, we read one cell of P and then compute fewer than k values ℓ_t. Finally, once p is identified, we know that $A[i]$ is stored in $B[p, p + \ell_i - 1]$. The total space used for P is $w\lceil n/k \rceil$ bits, thus parameter k allows trading space for time. This technique performs reasonably well, depending heavily on the speed to compute the lengths ℓ_t.

Example 3.7 *Figure 3.4 illustrates this arrangement on an array $A[1, 10]$ of the number of children of $n = 10$ employees, with $k = 4$. In this case, the numbers (plus 1) are γ-coded (see Section 2.7), and the lengths are obtained by decoding the numbers themselves. To obtain $A[7]$ (grayed), we start decoding from position $P[\lceil 7/k \rceil] = P[2] = 9$ of B ($P[2]$ is grayed), and we must decode 2 values, $A[(\lceil 7/k \rceil - 1)k + 1, 7 - 1] = A[5, 6]$, before reaching the desired one. We decode $6 = \gamma(00110)$ and then $2 = \gamma(010)$. Finally, we decode the desired value, $4 = \gamma(00100)$, thus $A[7] = 4 - 1 = 3$. The areas we traversed in B are also grayed.*

As seen in Section 2.7, we do not need to fully decode $A[5, 6]$, but just to read as much as needed from the codes in order to skip them. In γ-codes, it is sufficient to find the first 1 to know how much to skip.

It is easy to build B and P on a single pass over the array A. If A does not fit in main memory, it can be read from disk by small buffers, so that the main memory required for the construction is basically that of the final representation, B plus P. Even this compressed representation can be written by buffers to disk, so that it can be built on a computer with less memory than the one that will finally hold the data structure.

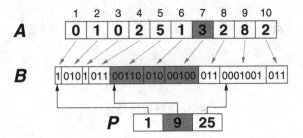

Figure 3.4. Storing an array A with $n = 10$ elements. The numbers (plus 1) are γ-coded, and we concatenate the codes in bit array B. On the bottom, array P points to 1 element out of $k = 4$, so it contains $\lceil n/k \rceil = 3$ entries. The block shades illustrate operation read$(A, 7)$.

3.2.2 Dense Pointers

If we wish to obtain constant time in our sampled pointers, we can set $k = 1$, so that P points to all the elements in A. This is generally a bad idea because then P uses wn bits, which is already larger than the space used by the data. In that case, it is better to simply store the data using full integers!

This can be alleviated by choosing a slightly larger constant k. A better tradeoff, however, is obtained by using a two-level scheme of pointers. In addition to using the sampled array of pointers P as before, with a parameter k, we use another array, $P'[1, n]$. In $P'[i]$ we store the offset in B from the beginning of the block to the starting position of $A[i]$, that is,

$$P'[i] = \sum_{t=(\lceil i/k \rceil - 1)k+1}^{i-1} \ell_t.$$

Therefore, $A[i]$ will start in B at position $p = P[\lceil i/k \rceil] + P'[i]$. Said another way, what we used to compute in time $\mathcal{O}(k)$ is now precomputed in $P'[i]$.

We note that this encoding already contains the information on the length $\ell_i = (P[\lceil (i+1)/k \rceil] + P'[i+1]) - (P[\lceil i/k \rceil] + P'[i])$, and therefore we do not need to store the lengths elsewhere or use the prefix-free encodings of Chapter 2. We can simply write the $|x| = \lfloor \log x \rfloor + 1$ bits needed to encode x. Even better, we can shift the values so that the smallest number in A is mapped to 1, and then encode only the $|x| - 1$ lowest bits of x (as the highest bit must be 1). In particular, number 1 will be encoded with zero bits.

Example 3.8 *Figure 3.5 illustrates the scheme, on the same array of Figure 3.4. To read $A[7]$, we add up $P[\lceil 7/k \rceil] = P[2] = 3$ and $P'[7] = 3$, and thus decode B from position $3 + 3 = 6$. The next code starts at $P[\lceil (7 + 1)/k \rceil] + P'[7 + 1] = P[2] + P'[8] = 3 + 5 = 8$. Thus we extract $B[6, 7] = $ 00. Adding the highest bit we obtain 100 = 4, and thus the answer is $A[7] = 4 - 1 = 3$.*

Once again, this structure is easily built with a sequential pass on A, and the process uses a negligible amount of main memory.

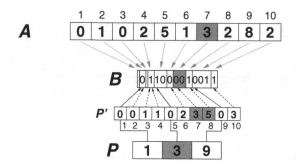

Figure 3.5. Storing the same array of Figure 3.4, now using dense pointers. The numbers (plus 1 in this case) can now be written with the exact number of bits needed (even one less) instead of using γ-codes. Array P' points to all the elements, but it stores values relative to the last pointer of P. The shaded blocks illustrate operation read($A, 7$).

Space

Let $\ell_{\max} = \max_{i=1}^{n} \ell_i \leq w$. The maximum value that can then be stored in a cell of P' is $(k-1)\ell_{\max}$. By storing P' as an array of fixed-size cells (Section 3.1), we use $n\lceil \log((k-1)\ell_{\max})\rceil$ bits, whereas P still requires $w\lceil n/k \rceil$ bits. The sum is optimized roughly for $k = w \cdot \ln 2$, where the space is below $(0.92 + \log(w\ell_{\max}))n = \mathcal{O}(n \log w)$ bits.

If w is much larger than $\log N$, we can store P as an array of cells of $\log N$ bits, instead of w-bit integers. Then the space is $(0.92 + \log(\ell_{\max} \log N))n = \mathcal{O}((\log \log n + \log \ell_{\max})n)$, since $N \leq n\,\ell_{\max}$.

When the numbers are short, the space overhead of this structure is considerable, because it includes at least $\log \log n$ bits per number. However, it may be acceptable when storing larger numbers. To compare it with the sampled pointers of Section 3.2.1, assume that scheme is used with δ-codes (Section 2.7). It also uses $w\lceil n/k \rceil$ bits for P, but instead of array P', its overhead comes from the $2\lfloor \log |x| \rfloor + 1$ bits used by δ-codes on top of the $|x| - 1$ bits we use to encode each value $A[i] = x$. By Jensen's inequality (Section 2.8), the δ-code overheads add up at most to $(1 + 2\log(N/n))n \leq (1 + \log \ell_{\max} + \log(N/n))n$. This is better than the overhead of dense pointers when the values are generally short (that is, N is not much larger than n).

Other more sophisticated variable-length arrangements will be described in Sections 3.4.2 and 3.4.3. Yet another competitive alternative will be described later, in Section 6.4.5.

3.3 Partial Sums

The techniques we have developed are applicable to a closely related problem called *partial sums*. Imagine we have an array $A[1, n]$ of relatively small nonnegative numbers and wish to answer two kinds of queries on it:

sum(A, i): returns $\sum_{j=1}^{i} A[j]$, with sum($A, 0$) = 0.
search(A, j): returns $\min\{i \geq 0, \text{sum}(A, i) \geq j\}$, or $n + 1$ if $j > \text{sum}(A, n)$.

It is easy to solve this problem by creating an array $S[i] = \mathsf{sum}(A, i)$, so that $\mathsf{sum}(A, i)$ is solved in constant time and $\mathsf{search}(A, j)$ in $\mathcal{O}(\log n)$ time by a binary search on S. The problem is that S requires much more space than A. If the numbers in A require ℓ bits, those in S may require $\log(2^\ell n) = \ell + \log n$ bits, thus adding $n \log n$ bits of space.

Let us use the sampling technique of Section 3.2.1 to store A (encoding its entries as desired). In addition to the sampled pointers P, we will store a sampled array $S[0, \lfloor n/k \rfloor]$, so that $S[i] = \mathsf{sum}(A, ik)$. Then we compute

$$\mathsf{sum}(A, i) = S[\lfloor i/k \rfloor] + \sum_{t=\lfloor i/k \rfloor k+1}^{i} A[t].$$

This requires reading less than k cells from A. Then the space overhead of S is $w \lceil n/k \rceil$ bits and the time to compute sum is $\mathcal{O}(k)$. Those accesses are consecutive, so the technique is fast in practice. It is convenient to use the same k for S and for the sampled array P of Section 3.2.1. If the values $A[i]$ are not very different from each other, we can even use fixed-length cells as in Section 3.1, and then array P is not necessary.

Note that we can also use sum to compute range sums on A, that is, $\sum_{t=i'}^{i} A[t] = \mathsf{sum}(A, i) - \mathsf{sum}(A, i' - 1)$.

To solve $\mathsf{search}(A, j)$, we first run a binary search on the sampled sums S to find the i such that $S[i] \leq j < S[i + 1]$, and then scan A from position $t = ik$ onwards, until it holds $S[i] + \sum_{r=ik+1}^{t} A[r] \geq j$. Then we return $\mathsf{search}(A, j) = t$. The time is then $\mathcal{O}(\log n + k)$. For example, we can have $\mathcal{O}(w)$ time for sum and search with n extra bits of space.

When the elements of A are bits, the operations sum and search correspond to the operations rank and select studied in Chapter 4. In the case of bits, these operations can be implemented in $\mathcal{O}(1)$ time and $o(n)$ bits on top of A. Moreover, in Section 4.5.1 we will use rank and select on bitvectors to improve some results on general partial sums.

3.4 Applications

3.4.1 Constant-Time Array Initialization

We will apply our compact storage of bit arrays to solve a common programming problem. Assume we have an array $A[1, n]$ of ℓ-bit entries where only a small fraction of them will be written and then the array will be discarded, but we need to initialize all the cells of A. The effort to initialize A may then be too large compared to the little use we will make of it.

Example 3.9 *A Boolean query $(X$ and $Y)$ or Z on a relational database can be run as follows. Set an array $A[k] = 0$ for all $1 \leq k \leq n$. Then set $A[x] = 1$ for the rows x matching X. Now, for each row y matching Y, increase $A[y]$ by 1 and report y if $A[y] = 2$. Finally, for each row z matching Z, report z if $A[z] \neq 2$ (to avoid reporting duplicates). The problem with such a scheme is that, even if the queries X, Y, and Z do* *not return many answers, we have to initialize $A[k]$ for all the n rows, which may be very costly.*

One solution to this problem is to avoid allocating A at all and just manage its m written cells using a binary search tree or a hash table. This is good when m is very small and still may impose a considerable overhead to access the array. We will present a solution that is generally faster and is better than initializing the array when m is up to 10% of n, in practice.

Initializable Arrays

An elegant solution to the problem is to use the so-called *initializable arrays*. These are arrays of cells of fixed length as in Section 3.1 but include a further operation

initialize(A, v): sets $A[k] \leftarrow v$ for all k,

that is supported in *constant time*. The operations **read** and **write** on initializable arrays will be called **iread** and **iwrite**.

A classical solution to this challenge is as follows. Use a second array $D[1, n]$ and a stack $S[1, s]$ (whose size is initially $s = 0$ and will become $s = m$). The following invariant will be maintained:

$$A[i] \text{ has been written} \iff 1 \leq D[i] \leq s \land S[D[i]] = i.$$

Then setting $s \leftarrow 0$ is sufficient to establish the invariant when we create the array upon operation initialize(A, v). Note that arrays D and S are allocated but not written at all, just like A.

To carry out **iwrite**(A, i, x), we first set $A[i] \leftarrow x$. Now, if $A[i]$ had not been already written, we must restore the invariant. We use the formula above to determine if $A[i]$ was written before. If it was not, then we restore the invariant by increasing $s \leftarrow s + 1$ and setting $D[i] \leftarrow s$ and $S[s] \leftarrow i$.

For the operation **iread**(A, i) we do as follows: If $A[i]$ was written, we must return $A[i]$, and if not, we must return v. Once again, the formula above tells how to check if $A[i]$ was written.

The correctness of this scheme is easily seen. If $A[i]$ has been written, then at some time we stored $D[i] = s$ and $S[s] = i$ for some s, and thus cell i will pass the check. If $A[i]$ has not been written yet, then value $D[i]$ can be arbitrary. If $D[i] < 1$ or $D[i] > s$, then we immediately note it. But it is still possible that $D[i]$ points, by chance, at a cell in $S[1, s]$. However, $S[D[i]]$ was allocated for some other $D[j]$ when $A[j]$ was written, and then $S[D[i]] = S[D[j]]$ must point to j, not to i. Thus, cell i will fail the check.

Note that we can easily reinitialize all the values of A to (the same or another) value v, by simply setting $s \leftarrow 0$ again (and remembering the current value of v). We can also "un-write" a written $A[i]$ by setting $S[D[i]] \leftarrow S[s]$, $D[S[s]] \leftarrow D[i]$, and $s \leftarrow s - 1$. This is useful for maintaining S small if we handle a varying but small set of active cells in A. Finally, we can use S to traverse all the written cells in A efficiently.

Example 3.10 *In the same scenario of Example 3.9, consider the query (X and not Y) or Z. We can then initialize $A[k] \leftarrow 0$ for all k, write $A[x] \leftarrow 1$ for those x that match X, then un-write $A[y]$ for those y that match Y, and finally write $A[z] \leftarrow 1$ for those z that match Z. Now we traverse and report all the written cells in*

A. Note that setting A[y] ← 0 instead of un-writing A[y] is not so efficient, because in the last traversal using S we may process many cells that are written but contain a 0.

Reducing Space

The problem with the presented scheme is that it needs to allocate up to $2n$ additional integers, or $2wn$ additional bits, for the arrays D and S, and this can be very large compared to the ℓn bits needed by A itself.

A way to reduce space is to use a bit array $B[1, n]$ so that $B[i] = 1$ iff $A[i]$ has been written. This bit array simplifies determining whether $A[i]$ has been written. It is easily maintained by initializing $B[k] ← 0$ for all $1 \le k \le n$ in the beginning, and then setting $B[i] ← 1$ when writing $A[i]$ and $B[i] ← 0$ when un-writing it (if desired).

Of course, the problem translates into initializing $B[1, n]$ in constant time! Consider that we store B in an array $W[1, \lceil n/w \rceil]$ as in Section 3.1. Instead of using an initializable bit array B, we will use an initializable array W, which has significantly fewer cells, with the techniques just described.

We then initialize B by setting $W[k] ← 0$ for $1 \le k \le \lceil n/w \rceil$ in constant time, using initialize$(W, 0)$. We can re-initialize B at any time in the same way. To implement iread(B, i), we first obtain $z ← $ iread$(W, \lceil i/w \rceil)$ from the initializable array W, and then bitread(z, r), with $r = ((i - 1) \bmod w) + 1$, gives us $B[i]$. Similarly, to implement iwrite(B, i, x) (with $x = 0$ or 1) we read $z ← $ iread$(W, \lceil i/w \rceil)$, perform bitset(z, r) or bitclear(z, r) depending on x, and then execute iwrite$(W, \lceil i/w \rceil, z)$. We can also automatically un-write cells of W every time an operation $B[i] ← 0$ leaves $W[\lceil i/w \rceil] = 0$. Algorithm 3.3 implements this variant of initializable arrays directly, without resorting to the classic solution on W. It stores the current value of v in a variable v_0.

Example 3.11 *Figure 3.6 illustrates this arrangement on an array representing $n = 40$ elements during the resolution of the query of Example 3.9. The cells 5, 25, and 28 match X and Y, whereas cell 29 matches only X.*

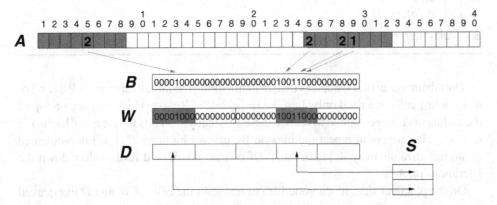

Figure 3.6. Storing an array A of $n = 40$ elements, using computer words of $w = 8$ bits for illustration. Bit array B is virtual; its contents are stored in the initializable array W. The cells of W that are initialized are grayed, and the graying is projected onto the corresponding cells in A.

Algorithm 3.3: Manipulating initializable arrays.

---

1 **Proc** initialize(A, n, v)

 Input : Integer array $A[1, n]$ and default value v.

 Output: Computes its initializable representation B, D, S, s, and v_0.

2 $v_0 \leftarrow v$

3 Allocate bit array $B[1, n]$ (as the integer array $W[1, \lceil n/w \rceil]$)

4 Allocate integer arrays $D[1, \lceil n/w \rceil]$ and $S[1, \lceil n/w \rceil]$

5 $s \leftarrow 0$

6 **Proc** iread(A, i)

 Input : Array A (seen as A itself plus arrays B, D, S, s, and v_0), and position i

    to read.

 Output: Returns $A[i]$.

7 $p \leftarrow \lceil i/w \rceil$

8 **if** $1 \leq D[p] \leq s$ **and** $S[D[p]] = p$ **and** bitread(B, i) $= 1$ **then**

9   **return** read(A, i) (Algorithm 3.2)

10 **else**

11   **return** v_0

12 **Proc** iwrite(A, i, x)

 Input : Array A (seen as A itself plus arrays B, D, S, s, and v_0; B is also seen

    as W), and position i where we must write the element x.

 Output: Assigns $A[i] \leftarrow x$.

13 write(A, i, x) (Algorithm 3.2)

14 $p \leftarrow \lceil i/w \rceil$

15 **if** $D[p] < 1$ **or** $D[p] > s$ **or** $S[D[p]] \neq p$ **then**

16   $s \leftarrow s + 1$

17   $D[p] \leftarrow s$

18   $S[s] \leftarrow p$

19   $W[p] \leftarrow 0$

20 bitset(B, i)

The advantage of this scheme is that, in maintaining the initializable array $W[1, n']$ of $n' = \lceil n/w \rceil$ cells, we need only $3wn' = 3w\lceil n/w \rceil < 3(n + w)$ bits of space on top of the ℓn bits of A. If we wanted to reduce these (basically)[3] $3n$ bits to just $n + \mathcal{O}(n/w) = n + o(n)$ bits, we could repeat the idea on W, using a bit array $B'[1, n']$ implemented on an initializable array $W'[1, \lceil n'/w \rceil]$. Of course, this would further slow down the operations on A.

On the practical side, it is a good idea to maintain the cells of W and D interleaved in memory, so that any cell of W and its corresponding cell of D are accessed at the cost of a single cache miss. With this scheme, the cost to access A is 1–4 cache misses. Thus, if the number of accesses to A is more than a certain percentage of n (around 10% in practice), an explicit initialization might be a better choice.

---

[3] We will generally ignore those negligible effects due to ceilings.

In the particular case that $A[1, n]$ is a bit array (that is, $\ell = 1$), we do not need the intermediary bit array B. We directly store $A[1, n]$ in $W[1, \lceil n/w \rceil]$. We run initialize$(A, 0)$ as initialize$(W, 0)$, and initialize$(A, 1)$ as initialize$(W, 2^w - 1)$. We run iread(A, i) by extracting the appropriate bit from $z \leftarrow$ iread$(W, \lceil i/w \rceil)$ and iwrite(A, i, x) by first reading $z \leftarrow$ iread$(W, \lceil i/w \rceil)$, then updating the appropriate bit in z, and finally doing iwrite$(W, \lceil i/w \rceil, z)$. If W is stored interleaved with D, then the only time overhead in practice is that of accessing S. This scheme can be extended to the case $\ell > 1$, but its space overhead is $2\ell n$ bits, which for any $\ell > 1$ is more than the $3n$ bits of the basic arrangement. Finally, note that the case of Example 3.10 is even more extreme, because we do not need $A = W$ at all, just D and S.

3.4.2 Direct Access Codes

Our technique for efficiently computing partial sums enables a more sophisticated variable-length code that allows extracting any element $A[i]$ in time proportional to $\ell_i = |A[i]|$.

Structure

Consider an entry $A[i]$ of length ℓ_i. We will cut the ℓ_i bits into $d_i = \lceil \ell_i/b \rceil$ short *pieces* of b bits each. Each of the pieces, except the last, will be prepended with a bit 1, whereas the last will be prepended with a 0. The encoding of $A[i]$ can then be written as

$$m_{i,1} \cdot p_{i,1} \cdot m_{i,2} \cdot p_{i,2} \cdots m_{i,d_i} \cdot p_{i,d_i},$$

where $p_{i,j}$ are the pieces and $m_{i,j}$ are the bits prepended to the pieces. The pieces contain the bits of $A[i]$ from highest to lowest, that is, $A[i]$ is equal to the concatenation $p_{i,1} \cdot p_{i,2} \cdots p_{i,d_i}$, except possibly for some unused highest bits of $p_{i,1}$ (which are set to 0). The mark bits are $m_{i,r} = 1$ if $r < d_i$ and $m_{i,d_i} = 0$. Note that this is analogous to the VByte encoding discussed in Section 2.7 (which corresponds to using $b = 7$, and to signaling the last piece of a code with a 1 instead of a 0).

The encodings for $A[1], A[2], \ldots, A[n]$ will be stored in a layered way. The first layer stores two arrays:

$$A_1 = p_{1,1} \cdot p_{2,1} \cdots p_{n,1},$$
$$M_1 = m_{1,1} \cdot m_{2,1} \cdots m_{n,1}.$$

That is, A_1 stores the first piece of all the elements in A, and M_1 stores all the first marking bits.

Since all the pieces in A_1 and M_1 are of fixed length (b and 1, respectively), we can use the technique of Section 3.1 to pack A_1 in bn bits and M_1 in n bits, and extract any desired $p_{i,1}$ and $m_{i,1}$ in constant time.

Let $i_1 < i_2 < \ldots$ be the elements in A using more than 1 piece. Our second layer then consists of the following two arrays:

$$A_2 = p_{i_1,2} \cdot p_{i_2,2} \cdots,$$
$$M_2 = m_{i_1,2} \cdot m_{i_2,2} \cdots$$

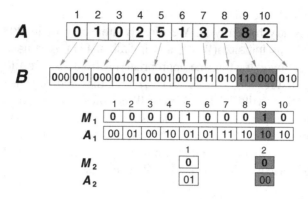

Figure 3.7. Storing the same array of Figure 3.4, now using direct access codes with piece length $b = 2$. In array B we write each variable-length number in pieces of length b, and add the marking bits (in bold) to the beginning of each piece. On the bottom we arrange the same pieces and marking bits in a layered way, so that the ith number is extracted from the ith column. The grayed blocks illustrate operation read($A, 9$).

That is, A_2 stores the second pieces of all the elements in A that have 2 or more pieces, and M_2 stores all the corresponding marking bits. This decomposition continues for $m = \lceil \ell_{\max}/b \rceil$ layers, which suffices to represent the longest numbers.

Example 3.12 *Figure 3.7 exemplifies this arrangement, again on the same array of Figure 3.4, with $b = 2$. The grayed blocks will be used later.*

Read Operation

To access $A[i]$, we start reading $A_1[i]$ and $M_1[i]$. If $M_1[i] = 0$, it means that $A[i] = A_1[i]$ and the **read** operation is complete. If, instead, $M_1[i] = 1$, then $A_1[i]$ is only the first piece of a longer element, which continues in A_2. The problem lies in knowing which is the position i' that corresponds to i in A_2. It is not hard to see that

$$i' = \sum_{j=1}^{i} M_1[j] = \mathsf{sum}(M_1, i),$$

or, equivalently, i' is the number of 1s in $M_1[1, i]$. Therefore, we preprocess the bit arrays M_r for partial sum queries (Section 3.3).

Once we obtain i' from i, we read $A_2[i']$ and $M_2[i']$. If $M_2[i'] = 0$, it means that $A[i]$ spans 2 pieces, which we have already read, thus we can return $A[i] = A_1[i] \cdot 2^b + A_2[i']$. Otherwise, $M_2[i'] = 1$ and we must continue with $A_3[i'']$ and $M_3[i'']$, for $i'' = \mathsf{sum}(M_2, i')$, and so on. Algorithm 3.4 gives the pseudocode.

Example 3.13 *Figure 3.7 shows the process to read $A[9]$ (grayed). We start reading $A_1[9] = 10 = 2$. Since $M_1[9] = 1$, the code continues in A_2. We compute the new position as $i' = \mathsf{sum}(M_1, 9) = 2$. Now we read $A_2[2] = 00 = 0$. Since $M_2[2] = 0$, the code finishes here, and thus $A[9] = 2 \cdot 2^2 + 0 = 8$.*

Algorithm 3.4: Reading from a direct access code representation. The read instructions in lines 2 and 7 are those of Algorithm 3.2.

---

1 **Proc** read(A, i)

    Input : Integer array A (seen as arrays A_r, bitvectors M_r, and piece length b) and position i to read.

    Output: Returns the value $A[i]$.

2     $v \leftarrow$ read(A_1, i)

3     $r \leftarrow 1$

4   **while** bitread(M_r, i) = 1 **do**

5         $i \leftarrow$ sum(M_r, i) (Section 3.3)

6         $r \leftarrow r + 1$

7         $v \leftarrow v \cdot 2^b +$ read(A_r, i)

8   **return** v

Construction

Algorithm 3.5 gives the pseudocode to create a direct access code representation in time $\mathcal{O}(n\,\ell_{\max}/b)$, using just the space to store the input array A and its final representation. If necessary, the construction can be implemented using only $\mathcal{O}(\ell_{\max}/b)$ small buffers in main memory, by reading array A from disk by buffers, and writing arrays A_r and M_r by buffers as well.

Time and Space

To read $A[i]$ we compute $\mathcal{O}(\ell_i/b)$ partial sums, that is, shorter elements are extracted faster. This is generally good because, when the varying lengths come from a compression scheme, there must be more short than long elements if the compression has been successful. If we access the positions uniformly at random, the average number of sum computations is $\mathcal{O}(N/(nb))$, since $\sum_{i=1}^{n} \ell_i = N$.

On the other hand, the space wasted is up to $b - 1$ bits per element in the pieces $p_{i,1}$, plus one bit per piece in the M_r arrays. Let us ignore for simplicity the extra space to compute the partial sums on M_r. The first part adds to $bn - n$ bits. The second is $\sum_{i=1}^{n} \lceil \ell_i/b \rceil < N/b + n$ bits. Adding both, we obtain the upper bound $bn + N/b$. This is optimized for $b = \sqrt{N/n}$, yielding a total wasted space of $2n\sqrt{N/n}$. This is worse than the space overhead of δ-coding we obtained for the sparse pointers at the end of Section 3.2.2, but is still acceptable if the numbers are not very small (the space overhead per data bit is $\mathcal{O}(\sqrt{n/N})$). Using this value of b, the average time to read a value is $\mathcal{O}(\sqrt{N/n})$ computations of sum.

Using the technique of Section 3.3 on the bit arrays M_r, each sum operation takes time $\mathcal{O}(k)$ and poses a space overhead of $(N/b + n)(w/k)$ bits. For example, with $k = w$, we use $N/b + n$ extra bits and compute each sum operation in time $\mathcal{O}(w)$, which is very fast because it accesses only the w bits of a single word of the array W_r where M_r is stored. In Section 4.2.1 we introduce the operation *popcount*, which counts the number of 1s in a machine word in constant time. Then operation access(A, i) with

---

Algorithm 3.5: Creating direct access codes from an array.

Input : The integer array $A[1, n]$ to be represented and the piece length b.
Output: Computes the number of levels m and arrays A_r and M_r, of lengths $N[r]$,
for $1 \leq r \leq m$.

1 $m \leftarrow 0$
2 **for** $i \leftarrow 1$ **to** n **do**
3   **if** $\lceil |A[i]|/b \rceil > m$ **then**
4        $m \leftarrow \lceil |A[i]|/b \rceil$

5 Allocate array $N[1, m]$ of integers
6 **for** $r \leftarrow 1$ **to** m **do**
7      $N[r] \leftarrow 0$

8 **for** $i \leftarrow 1$ **to** n **do**
9      $N[\lceil |A[i]|/b \rceil] \leftarrow N[\lceil |A[i]|/b \rceil] + 1$

10 **for** $r \leftarrow m$ **downto** 1 **do**
11   **if** $r < m$ **then**
12       $N[r] \leftarrow N[r] + N[r+1]$
13   Allocate array $A_r[1, N[r]]$ of b-bit cells (see Section 3.1)
14   Allocate array $M_r[1, N[r]]$ of 1-bit cells (see Section 3.1)

15 **for** $r \leftarrow 1$ **to** m **do**
16     $N[r] \leftarrow 0$

17 **for** $i \leftarrow 1$ **to** n **do**
18     $\ell \leftarrow \lceil |A[i]|/b \rceil$
19   **for** $r \leftarrow 1$ **to** ℓ **do**
20       $N[r] \leftarrow N[r] + 1$
21   write$(A_r, N[r], \lfloor A[i]/2^{(\ell-r)b} \rfloor \bmod 2^b)$
22   **if** $r < \ell$ **then**
23   bitset$(M_r, N[r])$
24   **else**
25   bitclear$(M_r, N[r])$

26 Preprocess all the arrays M_r for sum queries (Section 3.3)

---

direct access codes takes time $\mathcal{O}(1 + |A[i]|/b)$ if we use the formula

$$\mathsf{sum}(M_r, i) = S_r[\lfloor i/w \rfloor] + popcount(M_r[\lfloor i/w \rfloor w + 1, i]),$$

where S_r stores the sampled sums of M_r, and all the bits read from M_r are in the cell $W_r[\lfloor i/w \rfloor] + 1$. In Section 4.2.2 we obtain constant time for an operation called rank_1, which turns out to be equivalent to sum on bit arrays. This operation requires only $0.2(N/b + n)$ extra bits to obtain constant time with $w = 64$, for example, so the rank-based solution is even more attractive.

Optimal Space

Although for simplicity we used the same b value for all the arrays A_r, we can choose a different cell width b_r for each array, aiming to optimize the space usage. The optimal values for b_r can be easily computed via dynamic programming. Let S_ℓ be the least total space we can achieve in order to encode the numbers in $A[1, n]$ that use more than ℓ bits (i.e., such that $|A[i]| > \ell$), devoid of their highest ℓ bits (i.e., $A[i] \bmod 2^{|A[i]|-\ell}$). Let m be the maximum length $|A[i]|$ of a number in array A. Further, let n_ℓ be the number of values in A with more than ℓ bits. Thus $n_0 = n$, $n_m = 0$, and $S_m = 0$, since there are no numbers with more than m bits to represent. For any $0 \le \ell < m$, it holds

$$S_\ell = \min_{1 \le b \le m-\ell} (b+1)n_\ell + S_{\ell+b},$$

which accounts for each choice of using b bits for the first array A_r (and 1 bit for M_r), and then representing the rest of the values that have further bits.

Thus, the optimum space is S_0, which is computed in time $\mathcal{O}(m^2)$ by going from S_m to S_0. Note that since A stores integers, $\mathcal{O}(m^2)$ is just $\mathcal{O}(w^2)$.

Attaining the optimum space may lead to the use of many arrays A_r, which affects the time to read the numbers. It is also possible to optimize the space subject to the condition of using at most t levels A_r, $1 \le r \le t$. For this, let $S_{\ell,r}$ be the least space as before, but subject to using at most r further levels. Then $S_{m,r} = 0$ for all r, and $S_{\ell,1} = (m - \ell + 1)n_\ell$ for all $\ell < m$ (since we are forced to use one further level). For the other values, it holds

$$S_{\ell,r} = \min_{1 \le b \le m-\ell} (b+1)n_\ell + S_{\ell+b,r-1},$$

and we look for $S_{0,t}$. This is computed in time $\mathcal{O}(m^2 t) = \mathcal{O}(w^3)$ (since there cannot be more than $t = m = \mathcal{O}(w)$ levels). Algorithm 3.6 gives the pseudocode for this computation. The resulting array, $L[1, t]$, must be stored together with A_r and M_r.

Note that we can avoid storing the last bit array M_t, as we know that there are no further layers (this requires a slight change to Algorithm 3.4 as well). To include this saving in the optimization, we initialize $S_{\ell,1} = (m - \ell)n_\ell$.

3.4.3 Elias-Fano Codes

Operation **search** on partial sums enables another sophisticated variable-length encoding, which is better suited to small values of N/n. In parallel to the bit array B that contains the elements of A, we store another bit array M, so that $M[j] = 1$ when an element of A starts at $B[j]$. Then the position where $A[i]$ starts in B is the position of the ith 1 in M (and it ends just before the position of the $(i + 1)$th 1 in M). The operation of finding the ith 1 in M is, precisely, **search**(M, i). The numbers x can be stored in B using $|x| - 1$ bits as before, but we cannot have zero-length codes. Therefore, the numbers must be shifted so that they start at 2.

Example 3.14 *Figure 3.8 shows the Elias-Fano coding of the same array of Figure 3.4 (adding 2 to the numbers so that the 0 can be represented). To access $A[7]$ (grayed), we*

Algorithm 3.6: Finding optimal piece lengths for direct access codes.

Input : Integer array $A[1, n]$ and maximum number t of levels allowed.
Output: Computes the optimal number of levels t and the piece lengths $L[1, t]$.

1 $m \leftarrow 0$
2 **for** $i \leftarrow 1$ **to** n **do**
3 | **if** $|A[i]| > m$ **then** $m \leftarrow |A[i]|$

4 Allocate arrays $S[0, m][1, t]$, $B[0, m][1, t]$, and $N[0, m]$ of integers
5 **for** $\ell \leftarrow 0$ **to** m **do** $N[\ell] \leftarrow 0$
6 **for** $i \leftarrow 1$ **to** n **do**
7 | $N[|A[i]| - 1] \leftarrow N[|A[i]| - 1] + 1$

8 **for** $\ell \leftarrow m - 1$ **downto** 0 **do**
9 | $N[\ell] \leftarrow N[\ell] + N[\ell + 1]$

10 **for** $r \leftarrow 1$ **to** t **do** $S[m, r] \leftarrow 0$
11 **for** $\ell \leftarrow 0$ **to** $m - 1$ **do**
12 | $S[\ell, 1] \leftarrow (m - \ell + 1) \cdot N[\ell]$
13 | $B[\ell, 1] \leftarrow m - \ell + 1$

14 **for** $r \leftarrow 2$ **to** t **do**
15 | **for** $\ell \leftarrow 0$ **to** $m - 1$ **do**
16 | | $S[\ell, r] \leftarrow +\infty$
17 | | **for** $b \leftarrow 1$ **to** $m - \ell$ **do**
18 | | | $c \leftarrow (b + 1) \cdot N[\ell] + S[\ell + b, r - 1]$
19 | | | **if** $c < S[\ell, r]$ **then**
20 | | | | $S[\ell, r] \leftarrow c$
21 | | | | $B[\ell, r] \leftarrow b$

22 Allocate array $L[1, t]$
23 $\ell \leftarrow 0; r \leftarrow 0$
24 **while** $\ell < m$ **do**
25 | $r \leftarrow r + 1$
26 | $L[r] \leftarrow B[\ell, t - r + 1]$
27 | $\ell \leftarrow \ell + L[r]$

28 $t \leftarrow r$
29 Free S, B, and N

---

read $B[\mathsf{search}(M, 7), \mathsf{search}(M, 8) - 1] = B[9, 10] = 01$. *Now we add the highest bit to obtain* $101 = 5$, *and then* $A[7] = 5 - 2 = 3$.

Elias-Fano codes are an attractive choice when most of the numbers to represent are very small, since its space is equivalent to γ-coding the numbers (Section 2.7): each number x uses $2(|x| - 1)$ bits, for a total of $2(N - n)$ bits. Our implementation of search yields at least $\mathcal{O}(\log n)$ time to read a number with this encoding. In Section 4.3 we show that search on bit arrays is equivalent to operation select_1 on bitvectors

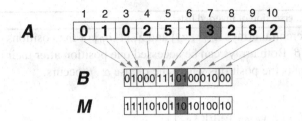

Figure 3.8. Storing the same array of Figure 3.4 using Elias-Fano codes. The numbers are shifted by 2 so that the value 0 can be encoded. The grayed blocks illustrate operation read(A, 7).

and give constant-time implementations of select_1 using $o(|M|)$ extra bits of space. Another implementation, in Section 4.4, stores M in $n \log(N/n) + 2n + o(n)$ bits of space, still supporting select_1 in constant time.

3.4.4 Differential Encodings and Inverted Indexes

In Section 2.9 we used the variable-length encodings of Section 2.7 to represent a list of increasing numbers $0 = y_0 < y_1 < y_2 < \ldots < y_m = n$ using m differences $x_i = y_i - y_{i-1}$. This encoding allowed us to decode the list from the beginning, but it does not support the access to a particular element y_i without decoding the whole list. To support operation read(Y, i) on the (virtual) array $Y[i] = y_i$ we need to compute $y_i = \sum_{j=1}^{i} x_j$, that is, operation sum(X, i) on the (actual) array $X[1, m]$. In the case of an inverted index, which was the application considered in Section 2.9, operation sum gives us direct access to the position of the ith occurrence of a word in the text.

Operation search(X, i) is also useful for inverted indexes. The positional indexes described in Section 2.9 can be used to find a phrase of two words, $\alpha . \beta$. The answers are the positions p in the text so that p appears in the list of α and $p + 1$ in the list of β. To find those positions, we start at positions $p_\alpha = p_\beta = 1$ of the arrays Y_α and Y_β. If $Y_\alpha[p_\alpha] + 1 = Y_\beta[p_\beta]$, then we report $Y_\alpha[p_\alpha]$ and increase both p_α and p_β by 1 (recall that we compute $Y_{\alpha/\beta}[i]$ as sum($X_{\alpha/\beta}$, i)). Otherwise we advance the pointers: if $Y_\alpha[p_\alpha] < Y_\beta[p_\beta]$, we advance p_α to the first position that is useful for the current value of p_β: $p_\alpha \leftarrow$ search(X_α, $Y_\beta[p_\beta] - 1$). Similarly, if $Y_\alpha[p_\alpha] \geq Y_\beta[p_\beta]$, we set $p_\beta \leftarrow$ search(X_β, $Y_\alpha[p_\alpha] + 1$). Then we restart the loop.

Algorithm 3.7 shows the pseudocode. The related calls to search followed by sum, in lines 5–6 and 8–9, are implemented more efficiently as a single operation that finds both p and y.

The sampling scheme we use to support partial sums on the arrays X, and the way we intersect the inverted lists using operation search, underlies all the current techniques for intersecting inverted lists in main memory. The Elias-Fano codes described in Section 3.4.3 have also proved to be effective in this application.

3.4.5 Compressed Text Collections

Assume we have a collection of text documents in English. We concatenate all the documents into a single text $T[1, n]$ of n *words*. As mentioned in Section 2.4, the

---

Algorithm 3.7: Intersection of inverted lists.

Input : Differential arrays $X_\alpha[1, n_\alpha]$ and $X_\beta[1, n_\beta]$ of the positions of words α and β. Both arrays can be accessed one position after their end.

Output: Outputs the positions where the phrase $\alpha . \beta$ occurs.

---

1   $p_\alpha \leftarrow 1; p_\beta \leftarrow 1$
2   $y_\alpha \leftarrow \mathsf{read}(X_\alpha, 1); y_\beta \leftarrow \mathsf{read}(X_\beta, 1)$
3   **while** $p_\alpha \leq n_\alpha$ **and** $p_\beta \leq n_\beta$ **do**
4   **if** $y_\alpha < y_\beta - 1$ **then**
5       $p_\alpha \leftarrow \mathsf{search}(X_\alpha, y_\beta - 1)$
6       $y_\alpha \leftarrow \mathsf{sum}(X_\alpha, p_\alpha)$
7   **else if** $y_\alpha \geq y_\beta$ **then**
8       $p_\beta \leftarrow \mathsf{search}(X_\beta, y_\alpha + 1)$
9       $y_\beta \leftarrow \mathsf{sum}(X_\beta, p_\beta)$
10   **else**
11   **output** y_α
12       $p_\alpha \leftarrow p_\alpha + 1; p_\beta \leftarrow p_\beta + 1$
13       $y_\alpha \leftarrow y_\alpha + \mathsf{read}(X_\alpha, p_\alpha)$
14       $y_\beta \leftarrow y_\beta + \mathsf{read}(X_\beta, p_\beta)$

---

wordwise zero-order entropy of English allows us to reduce the text to about 25% of its original size. This is achieved, for example, by counting the frequencies of the distinct words in the text and building a Huffman code for them (Section 2.6). Then, if $h(t)$ is the bitwise Huffman code of word t, the compressed text is $h(T[1]) . h(T[2]) \ldots h(T[n])$. The size of the Huffman tree itself is $o(n)$, because of the Heaps' law stated in Section 2.9.

Thus, our compressed text T is encoded in at most $n(\mathcal{H}_0(T) + 1) + o(n)$ bits, where $\mathcal{H}_0(T)$ refers to the wordwise entropy. This is good for compression purposes, but a compressed text collection should offer direct access to any fragment of the original text. In particular, we wish to be able to print any range $T[i, j]$ of $j - i + 1$ words of T without having to decompress it from the beginning.

We can use the techniques of Section 3.2 to provide direct access to T. Apart from the sampled pointers of Section 3.2.1, which can be used in combination with the Huffman codes, we can the dense pointers of Section 3.2.2, which contain sufficient information to determine the length of the code. In this case we do not need Huffman codes anymore. We can simply sort the distinct words of T from most to least frequent and use the number $i - 1 \geq 0$, of $\lceil \log i \rceil$ bits, as the identifier of the ith word. Note that these $\lceil \log i \rceil$-bit codes form the best possible encoding (that is, an injective mapping from words to bit sequences; see Section 2.5): exchanging two codes, or using numbers out of $[0, v - 1]$ for a vocabulary of v words, cannot reduce the average code length. Therefore, the average length of these codes can be less than that of Huffman codes. This is possible because the codes are not unambiguous. Yet we can decode them in combination with the information on their length.

As the average number of bits in a vocabulary word is not so small, the direct access codes of Section 3.4.2 are a good choice to encode the numbers $i - 1$. While the numbers $i - 1$ themselves are not prefix-free, their direct access codes $m_{i,1} \cdot p_{i,1} \ldots m_{i,d_i} \cdot p_{i,d_i}$ are: a shorter code $m_{j,1} \cdot p_{j,1} \ldots m_{j,d_j} \cdot p_{j,d_j}$, with $d_j < d_i$, cannot be a prefix of the longer one because $m_{i,d_j} = 0$ and $m_{j,d_j} = 1$. Thus the space of a direct access code representation of the numbers $i - 1$ cannot be less than that of Huffman codes. In practice, the overhead of direct access codes is only slightly larger than the optimal overhead of encoding the numbers in prefix-free form. For that small difference in space, direct access to the text collection is obtained. This solution is faster than using sampled pointers.

3.5 Summary

An array $A[1, n]$ where all the cells use ℓ bits can be stored in ℓn bits so that any position can be read and written very efficiently. When the cells have variable lengths, it is possible to use the sum of the exact number of bits needed by each cell, N, plus some space overhead to enable reading of arbitrary positions. The overhead per element can be w/k bits and the read time be $\mathcal{O}(k)$ (sampled pointers), or the overhead can be $\mathcal{O}(\log(N/n))$ bits and the read time be $\mathcal{O}(1)$ (Elias-Fano codes), or the overhead can be $\mathcal{O}(\sqrt{N/n})$ bits and the average read time be $\mathcal{O}(\sqrt{N/n})$ (direct access codes). The best choice in practice depends on the data and the access pattern. The techniques are extended to compute partial sums, where one can solve sum and search in $\mathcal{O}(w)$ time using just n bits over the raw data. All the structures are easily built in linear time and without using more than the final space they need. Arrays of fixed or variable length cells find application as a basic component of most compact data structures.

3.6 Bibliographic Notes

Standard techniques. The techniques to store arrays in fixed-width cells are folklore programming methods, as well as the sampled pointers to access variable-size cells. The dense pointers of Section 3.2.2 have been described, for example, by Raman *et al.* (2007) and by Ferragina and Venturini (2007), but the general idea can be traced back to the earliest articles on compact data structures, for example, that of Jacobson (1989). This may have even appeared before in different forms.

Initializable arrays. Initializable arrays have been described several times. The earliest mention may be an exercise by Aho *et al.* (1974, Ex. 2.12). They are later fully described by Mehlhorn (1984, Sec. III.8.1) and Bentley (1989, Column 1). The version using $3n$ bits is proposed in a recent survey (Navarro, 2014), and it is experimentally studied by Fredriksson and Kilpeläinen (2016). They found that the classical structure is useful only if we use up to 1% of the array, whereas the one using $3n$ bits is useful up to 10%.

Direct access codes. The direct access codes were proposed by Brisaboa *et al.* (2013). They showed experimentally the superiority of this encoding over the other techniques described in this chapter (including Elias-Fano and the combination of sampled pointers with many of the encodings described in Chapter 2), at least when the average code length is not too small. They also found that the sampled pointers work better for partial sums, when several consecutive values must be accessed.

Elias-Fano codes. Elias-Fano codes date back to Fano (1971) and Elias (1974). They outperform direct access codes on sequences of small numbers, such as differentially encoded inverted indexes of various kinds. Recently, further improvements were obtained by combining Elias-Fano with other codes, so that different parts of the array are encoded in different ways (Ottaviano and Venturini, 2014; Kärkkäinen *et al.*, 2014).

Inverted indexes and compressed texts. In-memory intersection algorithms for compressed inverted lists, considering various sampling methods, became popular with the availability of larger main memories (Strohman and Croft, 2007; Culpepper and Moffat, 2010; Transier and Sanders, 2010). Brisaboa *et al.* (2013) studied the idea described in Section 3.4.5.

Bibliography

Aho, A. V., Hopcroft, J. E., and Ullman, J. D. (1974). *The Design and Analysis of Computer Algorithms*. Addison-Wesley.

Bentley, J. (1989). *Programming Pearls*. Addison-Wesley.

Brisaboa, N. R., Ladra, S., and Navarro, G. (2013). DACs: Bringing direct access to variable-length codes. *Information Processing and Management*, **49**(1), 392–404.

Culpepper, J. S. and Moffat, A. (2010). Efficient set intersection for inverted indexing. *ACM Transactions on Information Systems*, **29**(1), article 1.

Elias, P. (1974). Efficient storage and retrieval by content and address of static files. *Journal of the ACM*, **21**, 246–260.

Fano, R. (1971). On the number of bits required to implement an associative memory. Memo 61, Computer Structures Group, Project MAC, Massachusetts.

Ferragina, P. and Venturini, R. (2007). A simple storage scheme for strings achieving entropy bounds. *Theoretical Computer Science*, **371**(1), 115–121.

Fredriksson, K. and Kilpeläinen, P. (2016). Practically efficient array initialization. *Software Practice and Experience*, **46**(4), 435–467.

Jacobson, G. (1989). Space-efficient static trees and graphs. In *Proc. 30th IEEE Symposium on Foundations of Computer Science (FOCS)*, pages 549–554.

Kärkkäinen, J., Kempa, D., and Puglisi, S. J. (2014). Hybrid compression of bitvectors for the FM-index. In *Proc. 24th Data Compression Conference (DCC)*, pages 302–311.

Mehlhorn, K. (1984). *Data Structures and Algorithms 1: Sorting and Searching*. EATCS Monographs on Theoretical Computer Science. Springer-Verlag.

Navarro, G. (2014). Spaces, trees and colors: The algorithmic landscape of document retrieval on sequences. *ACM Computing Surveys*, **46**(4), article 52.

Ottaviano, G. and Venturini, R. (2014). Partitioned Elias-Fano indexes. In *Proc. 37th International Conference on Research and Development in Information Retrieval (SIGIR)*, pages 273–282.

Raman, R., Raman, V., and Rao, S. S. (2007). Succinct indexable dictionaries with applications to encoding *k*-ary trees, prefix sums and multisets. *ACM Transactions on Algorithms*, **3**(4), article 43.

Strohman, T. and Croft, B. (2007). Efficient document retrieval in main memory. In *Proc. 30th Annual International Conference on Research and Development in Information Retrieval (SIGIR)*, pages 175–182.

Transier, F. and Sanders, P. (2010). Engineering basic algorithms of an in-memory text search engine. *ACM Transactions on Information Systems*, **29**(1), article 2.

CHAPTER 4

Bitvectors

A *bitvector* is a bit array $B[1, n]$ that supports the following operations:

access(B, i): returns the bit $B[i]$, for any $1 \leq i \leq n$.

rank$_v(B, i)$: returns the number of occurrences of bit $v \in \{0, 1\}$ in $B[1, i]$, for any $0 \leq i \leq n$; in particular rank$_v(B, 0) = 0$. If omitted, we assume $v = 1$.

select$_v(B, j)$: returns the position in B of the jth occurrence of bit $v \in \{0, 1\}$, for any $j \geq 0$; we assume select$_v(B, 0) = 0$ and select$_v(B, j) = n + 1$ if $j >$ rank$_v(B, n)$. If omitted, we assume $v = 1$.

Bitvectors are fundamental in the implementation of most compact data structures. Therefore, an efficient implementation is of utmost importance.

While **access** is equivalent to operation **read** on bit arrays, **rank** and **select** correspond to the **sum** and **search** operations of partial sums (Section 3.3), if we interpret the bits 0 and 1 as the numbers 0 and 1, respectively. We will take advantage of the fact that the array elements are bits to provide improved solutions for **rank** and **select**. These results will then be used to improve the **sum** and **search** solutions seen in Section 3.3.

In addition, we put more emphasis on the compression of bitvectors than when we studied arrays. Many applications give rise to *unbalanced* bitvectors, that is, with far fewer 1s than 0s, or vice versa, and thus with low empirical zero-order entropy (recall Chapter 2). We will compress bitvectors B to $n\mathcal{H}_0(B) + o(n)$ bits, using those $o(n)$ extra bits to support the operations. We will also achieve high-order entropy, $n\mathcal{H}_k(B) + o(n)$ bits.

Note that bit arrays were not compressible with the techniques of Chapter 3, because cells were encoded individually, and thus we needed at least one bit for the 0 and one for the 1. This made n bits a lower bound to the space we used to encode the bit array $B[1, n]$. The key to obtain compression in this chapter is to encode blocks of bits as a single unit. Then we will develop $o(n)$-bit structures that can be added on top of the bit array or the compressed representation of B to support **rank** and **select**. We will also study a completely different representation that is convenient for very sparse bitvectors (that is, with few 1s).

We will consider only static bitvectors, which cannot be modified once built. Unlike bit arrays, where operation write was easy to implement in constant time, maintaining rank and select support upon updates is costlier. We consider dynamic bitvectors in Chapter 12.

4.1 Access

In Section 3.1 we saw how to store a bit array $B[1, n]$ in an array of integers $W[1, \lceil n/w \rceil]$, so that we use basically n bits and support $\text{read}(A, i)$ in constant time. This translates directly into operation $\text{access}(B, i) = \text{read}(B, i)$. In this section we focus on providing the same support on compressed representations of B.

4.1.1 Zero-Order Compression

In many cases of interest, B contains many more 0s than 1s, or vice versa. In those cases, we can *encode* B in a different form, so that we use space close to its *zero-order empirical entropy*, $n\mathcal{H}_0(B)$ bits, and still perform the operations in constant time. In Chapter 2 we showed that $n\mathcal{H}_0(B) \approx n$ when there are about as many 0s as 1s, therefore the technique we describe here is not useful in that case: it would actually increase the space and the time. Instead, it significantly reduces the space on unbalanced bitvectors.

Structure

Let us (conceptually) divide B into blocks of b bits, where b is a parameter. Each block $B_i = B[(i-1)b+1, ib]$, is said to be of *class* c_i, where c_i is the number of 1s in B_i.

Note that different classes have different numbers of elements. Precisely, class c contains $\binom{b}{c}$ elements, that is, the number of ways we can choose the positions of the c 1s among the b positions in the block.

Example 4.1 *If $b = 4$, then class 0 has only one element, {0000}. Class 1 has 4 elements, {0001, 0010, 0100, 1000}. Class 2 has 6 elements, {0011, 0101, 0110, 1001, 1010, 1100}. Then the numbers decrease again: class 3 has 4 elements and class 4 has 1 element.*

We will describe each block B_i using a pair (c_i, o_i), where o_i is called the *offset*. The offset is a number that identifies which block is B_i among those of its class c_i, that is,

$$0 \le o_i < \binom{b}{c_i}.$$

Example 4.2 *For $b = 4$ and class 1, we can assign number 0 to the block 0001, 1 to 0010, 2 to 0100, and 3 to 1000, and therefore the offset is between 0 and $3 = \binom{4}{1} - 1$. For class 2, we can assign 0 to 0011, 1 to 0101, 2 to 0110, 3 to 1001, 4 to 1010, and 5 to 1100. Thus the offset is between 0 and $5 = \binom{4}{2} - 1$. For class 3, we can assign number 0 to the block 0111, 1 to 1011, 2 to 1101, and 3 to 1110, and then the offset is between 0 and $3 = \binom{4}{3} - 1$.*

Our compressed representation of B is formed by an array $C[1, \lceil n/b \rceil]$, where $C[i] = c_i$, and an array $O[1, \lceil n/b \rceil]$, with $O[i] = o_i$. For this encoding to obtain compression we must use, for each number o_i, the exact number of bits needed to represent an offset of class c_i, that is,

$$|o_i| = L[c_i] = \left\lceil \log \binom{b}{c_i} \right\rceil,$$

where we have introduced a small array $L[0, b]$, so that $L[c]$ gives the number of bits used to encode an offset of class c.

Encoding and Decoding

We have left open the way to assign offsets to the elements of a class. We will assign them in increasing numeric order of the block values, seen as integers. Note that there are $\binom{b-1}{c}$ blocks starting with 0, which will precede the $\binom{b-1}{c-1}$ blocks starting with 1. This leads to a simple way to convert a block content B_i to an offset o_i and back. To convert $\beta = B_i$, of class $c = c_i$, into o_i, start with $o_i = 0$ and check the first bit of β. If $\beta = 1 . \beta'$, then increase o_i by $\binom{b-1}{c}$, to "skip over" all those offsets for blocks that start with a 0, and continue with $\beta \leftarrow \beta', c \leftarrow c - 1$, and $b \leftarrow b - 1$. If, instead, $\beta = 0 . \beta'$, then leave o_i and c unchanged and continue with $\beta \leftarrow \beta'$ and $b \leftarrow b - 1$.

Example 4.3 *To encode $\beta = 0100$, we start with $b = 4$, $c = 1$, and $o_i = 0$. Since the first bit of β is a 0, we continue with $\beta = 100$, $b = 3$, and $c = 1$. Now, the first bit of β is a 1, so we set $o_i \leftarrow o_i + \binom{b-1}{c} = 0 + \binom{2}{1} = 2$, and continue with $\beta = 00$, $b = 2$, and $c = 0$. This is the final value of o_i, since the rest of the bits in β are 0s.*

As a more contrived example, consider encoding $\beta = 1011$. We start with $b = 4$, $c = 3$, and $o_i = 0$. Since the first bit of β is a 1, we set $o_i \leftarrow o_i + \binom{3}{3} = 1$, and continue with $\beta = 011$, $b = 3$, and $c = 2$. Since the first bit is a 0, we go on with $\beta = 11$, $b = 2$, and $c = 2$. The first bit of β is now a 1, so we set $o_i \leftarrow o_i + \binom{1}{2} = 1$ (note that $\binom{x}{y} = 0$ if $x < y$). Thus the final step is for $\beta = 1$, $b = 1$, and $c = 1$. The first bit of β is a 1, so we set $o_i \leftarrow o_i + \binom{0}{1} = 1$ and finish with this offset. This shows that o_i also has its final value when $b = c$.

On the other hand, to recover the block $\beta = B_i$ of length b corresponding to a class $c = c_i$ and an offset $o = o_i$, we run the reverse process. If $o < \binom{b-1}{c}$, then β starts with a 0, and we continue with $b \leftarrow b - 1$ to obtain the following bits. If, instead, $o \geq \binom{b-1}{c}$, then β starts with a 1, and the rest of the bits are obtained from $o \leftarrow o - \binom{b-1}{c}$, $b \leftarrow b - 1$, and $c \leftarrow c - 1$.

Example 4.4 *Let us decode the blocks of Example 4.3. If we start with $o = 2$, $b = 4$ and $c = 1$, we first check that $o < \binom{b-1}{c} = \binom{3}{1} = 3$, so β starts with a 0, and we continue with $o = 2$, $b = 3$ and $c = 1$. Now $o \geq \binom{2}{1} = 2$, so β continues with a 1, and we go on with $o \leftarrow o - 2 = 0$, $b = 2$ and $c = 0$. The rest of the bits of β are similarly found to be 0, so $\beta = 0100$.*

For the second case, consider decoding $o = 1$, $b = 4$, and $c = 3$. We first check that $o \geq \binom{3}{3} = 1$, so β starts with a 1, and we continue with $o \leftarrow o - 1 = 0$, $b = 3$, and $c = 2$. Now $o < \binom{2}{2} = 1$, so β continues with a 0, and we go on with $o = 0$, $b = 2$ and

---

Algorithm 4.1: Encoding and decoding bit blocks as pairs (c, o).

---

1 **Proc** *encode*(B, b)
    Input : An integer (seen as a bit array $B[1, b]$). Table K is global.
    Output: Returns the pair (c, o) that encodes B.

2    $c \leftarrow 0$
3   **for** $j \leftarrow 1$ **to** b **do**
4   **if** bitread$(B, j) = 1$ **then**
5          $c \leftarrow c + 1$

6    $o \leftarrow 0$
7    $c' \leftarrow c$
8    $j \leftarrow 1$
9   **while** $0 < c' \leq b - j$ **do**
10   **if** bitread$(B, j) = 1$ **then**
11        $o \leftarrow o + K[b - j, c']$
12        $c' \leftarrow c' - 1$
13      $j \leftarrow j + 1$
14   **return** (c, o)

15 **Proc** *decode*(c, o, b)
    Input : A pair (c, o) and b.
    Output: Returns the bit array $B[1, b]$ (an integer) corresponding to (c, o).

16    $B \leftarrow 0$ (seen as an integer)
17    $j \leftarrow 1$
18   **while** $c > 0$ **do**
19   **if** $o \geq K[b - j, c]$ **then**
20   bitset(B, j)
21        $o \leftarrow o - K[b - j, c]$
22        $c \leftarrow c - 1$
23      $j \leftarrow j + 1$
24   **return** B

$c = 2$. Since $o \geq \binom{1}{2} = 0$, β continues with a 1. In the last step, we have $o = 0$, $b = 1$ and $c = 1$, where $o \geq \binom{0}{1} = 0$, so the last bit of β is a 1. We conclude that $\beta = $ 1011.

To run this process efficiently, we precompute all the combinatorials $K[i, j] = \binom{i}{j}$ for all $0 \leq i, j \leq b$, which requires only b^2 integers of space. With this table, encoding and decoding is carried out in $\mathcal{O}(b)$ time. Algorithm 4.1 gives the pseudocode.

Space Usage

Before showing how to provide efficient access to this encoding, let us motivate it by showing that it actually compresses B.

First, we have the array of classes, $C[1, \lceil n/b \rceil]$. Since each cell of C requires $\lceil \log(b+1) \rceil$ bits, the whole array can be encoded in

$$\lceil n/b \rceil \cdot \lceil \log(b+1) \rceil = (n/b) \log b + \mathcal{O}(n/b)$$

bits. Thus, as we choose a larger value for b, C uses less space but, as we have seen, decoding a block becomes slower.

The most interesting part, however, is the analysis of the number of bits required for array O. Since each o_i uses $|o_i| = \left\lceil \log \binom{b}{c_i} \right\rceil$ bits, the bits in O add up to

$$\sum_{i=1}^{\lceil n/b \rceil} \left\lceil \log \binom{b}{c_i} \right\rceil < \sum_{i=1}^{\lceil n/b \rceil} \log \binom{b}{c_i} + \lceil n/b \rceil$$

$$= \log \prod_{i=1}^{\lceil n/b \rceil} \binom{b}{c_i} + \lceil n/b \rceil \leq \log \binom{n}{m} + \lceil n/b \rceil \leq n \mathcal{H}_0(B) + \lceil n/b \rceil,$$

where $m = \sum_{i=1}^{\lceil n/b \rceil} c_i$ is the total number of 1s in B. In the first step, we simply removed the ceilings. In the second step we used $\log a + \log b = \log(ab)$. The third step is the most difficult. It takes into account that $\binom{b}{c} \cdot \binom{b}{c'} \leq \binom{2b}{c+c'}$. To see this, note that $\binom{2b}{c+c'}$ is the number of ways to choose $c + c'$ positions among $2b$ positions. Instead, $\binom{b}{c} \cdot \binom{b}{c'}$ counts the number of ways to choose c positions among the first b positions multiplied by the number of ways to choose c' among the second b positions. Certainly, all those ways are counted in $\binom{2b}{c+c'}$, among many others. The final step uses the definition of zero-order empirical entropy (see Section 2.3.1).

Therefore, the total space used, considering C, O, L, and K, is $n \mathcal{H}_0(B) + (n/b) \log b + \mathcal{O}(n/b + wb^2)$ bits.

Efficient Access

Array C is implemented using fixed cells of $\lceil \log(b+1) \rceil$ bits. Using the technique of Section 3.1, we access any $C[i]$ in constant time. The cells of array O, instead, are of variable size. We use the arrangement of Section 3.2.1, storing in an array $P[1, \lceil n/(bk) \rceil]$ pointers to the starting positions of 1 out of k cells of O. This arrangement is particularly efficient in our case, because the length $\ell_t = |O[t]|$ can be computed efficiently as $\ell_t = L[C[t]]$, without the need to access O at all. Therefore, to compute the starting position of a cell $O[i]$, we require only up to k cache-friendly accesses to array C, which supports very fast **read** operations, and L, which is small. Adding the time to decode the offset $O[i]$ into the block B_i, it turns out that any block B_i is obtained in $\mathcal{O}(k+b)$ time. The extra space used by P to provide this access time is $w \lceil n/(bk) \rceil$ bits. Algorithm 4.2 shows the pseudocode.

Example 4.5 *Figure 4.1 illustrates this encoding, with toy values $b = k = 4$. Array R will be used later. We illustrate the process of accessing $B[31]$ (grayed): We start traversing O from position $P[\lceil 31/(bk) \rceil] = P[2] = 8$ and C from position $C[(\lceil 31/(bk) \rceil - 1)k + 1] = 5$. We do not really access O, just update its offset as we traverse (the grayed area of) C: Since $L[C[5]] = L[0] = 0$, we stay at $O[8]$; then $L[C[6]] = L[2] = 3$, so we skip to $O[11]$, then $L[C[7]] = L[0] = 0$, so we stay at $O[11]$.*

Algorithm 4.2: Answering access on compressed bitvectors. The last two lines can be optimized to decode only up to the desired bit.

---

1 **Proc** access(B, i)

   Input : Bitvector B (seen as arrays C, O, P, and L, and parameters b and k, with O seen in turn as W) and position i.

   Output: Returns $B[i]$.

2 $\quad i_s \leftarrow \lceil i/(kb) \rceil$

3 $\quad p \leftarrow P[i_s]$

4 $\quad$ **for** $t \leftarrow (i_s - 1)k + 1$ **to** $\lceil i/b \rceil - 1$ **do**

5 $\quad\quad \lfloor\; p \leftarrow p + L[\text{read}(C, t)]$

6 $\quad c \leftarrow \text{read}(C, \lceil i/b \rceil)$

7 $\quad o \leftarrow \text{bitsread}(W, p, p + L[c] - 1)$

8 $\quad blk \leftarrow decode(c, o, b)$ (Algorithm 4.1)

9 $\quad$ **return** bitread($blk, ((i - 1) \bmod b) + 1)$

Now that we arrived at $C[\lceil 31/b \rceil] = C[8]$, we read the next $L[C[8]] = L[3] = 2$ bits from $O[11, 12] = 01$ (grayed in O). We carry out the decoding process on $o = 01 = 1$, which is of class $c = C[8] = 3$ and of length $b = 4$. This yields $B_8 = 1011$ (see Example 4.4). Finally, we return $B_8[((31 - 1) \bmod b) + 1] = B_8[3] = 1$.

Practical Considerations

The two parameters, b and k, yield a space-time tradeoff. In practice, the value of b is limited by our ability to perform fast numeric computations on the blocks of b bits,

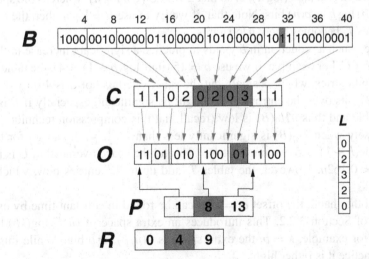

Figure 4.1. Storing a compressible bitvector B with arrays C and O, using $b = 4$. Note that some entries of array O are of length zero. On the bottom, we show the arrays P of Section 3.2.1 and R of Section 4.2.3, using a sampling of $k = 4$. From those pointers one advances block by block on O, using the information on C and L. The block shades illustrate operation access($B, 31$).

when decoding offsets (note that $|o_i|$ can be as large as $\left\lceil \log \binom{b}{b/2} \right\rceil \approx b$). It is a good idea to choose $b + 1$ as a power of 2, so that the $\lceil \log(b+1) \rceil$ bits of the cells of C are fully used. For example, as 64-bit arithmetic is well supported in most computers, we might use $b = 63$, so that $\log(b+1) = 6$. The space overhead of C is thus $6n/63 < 0.095n$, that is, below 0.1 bits over the entropy. This overhead can be reduced further if efficient arithmetic operations can be performed on words of more than 64 bits, for example, using wide integers in a particular architecture, or a good package for multiword arithmetic (see the bibliographic references at the end of the chapter).

As can be seen in Algorithm 4.2, the k accesses to C are done on a contiguous area of the array. For reasonable values of k, we expect the method to require 3 cache misses, for the access to P, the first access to C, and the access to O (arrays L and K are very small and will most likely reside in cache).

For example, if we choose $b = k = w - 1$, the time will be $\mathcal{O}(w)$ and the space will be $n\mathcal{H}_0(B) + (n/w)\log w + \mathcal{O}(n/w + w^3) = n\mathcal{H}_0(B) + o(n)$ bits. Recall from the end of Section 2.3.1 that this can also be written as $m \log \frac{n}{m} + \mathcal{O}(m) + o(n)$.

Constant Time

Two points in our **access** process are not constant time: the $\mathcal{O}(k)$ time to find $O[i]$ and the $\mathcal{O}(b)$ time to decode it into a block content.

The decoding of an offset o_i can be done in constant time by storing a table T_c for each class c, so that $T_c[o]$ stores the b bits corresponding to the block of class c with offset o. Since each table T_c has $\binom{b}{c}$ entries, the total number of entries across all the tables T_c is $\sum_{c=0}^{b} \binom{b}{c} = 2^b$, each using b bits.

Keeping this space low poses a new, stricter, restriction on b. In theory, this is not a problem: we can set $b = (\log n)/2$, so that $2^b b = \mathcal{O}(\sqrt{n} \log n)$, whereas the space of C is still $(n/b)\log b = o(n)$ bits. Note that, if we try to use $b = \log n$, then the overhead of the tables T_c becomes huge: $n \log n$ bits.

However, such a reduction in b yields in practice a significant increase in the overhead of array C. For example, if we use $b = 15$ (thus $\log(b+1) = 4$), the tables T_c add up to 32,768 entries, which is small, but the space overhead of C is $4n/15 < 0.267n$, that is, 0.27 bits over the entropy. This might be significant, especially if B is highly compressible and thus $n\mathcal{H}_0(B)$ is low (recall that this compression technique is relevant precisely when $\mathcal{H}_0(B)$ is significantly less than 1). If we try to go for the next value of $\log(b+1) = 5$, we must set $b = 31$, and the space overhead of C is reduced to $5n/31 < 0.162n$. However, the tables T_c add up to 2^{31} entries now, which is too much.

On the other hand, the offset $o_i = O[i]$ can be found in constant time by using the technique of Section 3.2.2. This introduces an extra space of $(n/b)\log(kb)$ bits. By choosing, for example, $k = b$, the extra space is $2(n/b)\log b$ bits. While this is still $o(n)$, in practice it is rather high.

As a conclusion, it is possible to have constant-time access with the compressed bitvector representation, but it is not advisable in practice: in most cases, the extra space it entails defeats the goal of compressing the bitvector. Still, the $\mathcal{O}(w)$-time variant is fast: As explained, it generally incurs a constant number of cache misses, and thus it can be taken as a good practical implementation of the fully constant-time version of the structure.

4.1.2 High-Order Compression

The machinery we developed in Section 4.1.1 can be used for other kinds of compression. We describe one that can compress B into $n\mathcal{H}_k(B) + o(n)$ bits, for any $k = o(\log n)$. In practice, it requires the use of small-sized blocks (such as $b = (\log n)/2$), and therefore its space overhead is relatively large. It is also slower in practice. For this reason, it can be recommended only when the high-order entropy of B is much lower than its zero-order entropy.

The idea is to collect all the *different* blocks B_i of B, and compute the *frequency* of each different block, that is, the number of times it appears as a block in B. Let us call $D_1, D_2, \ldots$ the different blocks. We compute a Huffman code (recall Section 2.6) on the blocks $D_1, D_2, \ldots$, according to their frequencies, obtaining codes $h(D_1), h(D_2), \ldots$. The bitvector B is then encoded as an array $H[1, \lceil n/b \rceil]$, where $H[i] = h(B_i)$, the Huffman code of the block B_i. Note that H is not an array of integers, but of variable-length bit sequences.

We provide access to this representation with the mechanism of Section 3.2.1. This time, in order to skip over k values of H, we must decode the entries $H[t]$ until reaching the desired one, which is also decoded. Since the longest Huffman code uses $\mathcal{O}(\log(n/b))$ bits (Section 2.6.2), using canonical Huffman codes we can decode each block in $\mathcal{O}(\log\log n)$ time (recall Section 2.6.3). Therefore, the access time is $\mathcal{O}(k \log\log n)$.[1]

Example 4.6 *Figure 4.2 shows an example of this encoding with $k = b = 4$. To access $B[27]$ (grayed), we start decoding H from $P[\lceil 27/(bk) \rceil] = P[2] = 11$. The decoded area of H is grayed. After decoding the third code, $0000 = D_1 = h^{-1}(00)$, we extract the bit $D_1[((27 - 1) \bmod b) + 1] = D_1[3] = 0$.*

Note that array H contains a Huffman coding of the blocks of B. If we used the same block sizes in Section 4.1.1, then the concatenation $C[i] . O[i]$ would be a prefix code for block B_i, and two blocks with the same content would receive the same code. Since Huffman is optimal under these conditions, the encoding in this section is never larger than that of Section 4.1.1.

Furthermore, as mentioned, the space obtained by this encoding is $n\mathcal{H}_k(B) + o(n)$ bits, for any $k = o(\log n)$. This is a consequence of compressing blocks of $b = \Theta(\log n)$ bits. To see this, note that we could encode each block of b symbols by storing the first k bits in plain form and then writing the output of a semi-static arithmetic coder (Section 2.6.4) built on the global kth-order frequencies, for the other $b - k$ bits of the block. This yields at most $n\mathcal{H}_k(B) + (k + 2)\lceil n/b \rceil = n\mathcal{H}_k(B) + o(n)$ bits in total.

---

[1] We could speed this up to $\mathcal{O}(k + \log\log n)$ by storing an array C' similar to C, where $C'[i] = |H[i]|$. Array C' would then require $\mathcal{O}((n/b)\log\log(n/b)) = o(n)$ further bits. Unlike in Section 4.1.1, however, this array is not necessary, because Huffman codes can be decoded without its help. Alternatively, we show soon how Huffman codes can be improved if we know their length $C'[i]$.

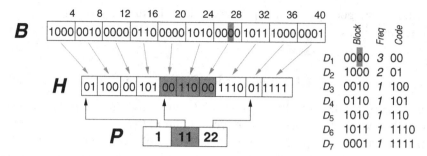

Figure 4.2. Storing a compressible bitvector B with array H, using $b = 4$. On the right we show the Huffman code used for the blocks. On the bottom, the array P of Section 3.2.1 using a sampling of $k = 4$. From those pointers one advances block by block on H, by decoding each one. The block shades illustrate operation **access**$(B, 27)$.

Since each distinct block receives a unique code, by the same argument of the previous paragraph, Huffman encoding of the blocks achieves the same size or less.

Note that the Huffman model requires up to 2^b entries (that is, all the possible different blocks), and therefore we have to choose a small b to guarantee that the model does not grow beyond control. For example, with $b = (\log n)/2$ we limit the model size to $\mathcal{O}(\sqrt{n}\log n)$ bits, which is pretty small, but with $b = \log n$ it can reach $\mathcal{O}(n \log n)$ bits. In practice, since the encoding of Section 4.1.1 is able to use a larger b value, it is more efficient than this one unless $\mathcal{H}_k(B)$ is significantly smaller than $\mathcal{H}_0(B)$.

Constant Time

By using the arrangement of Section 3.2.2, we obtain constant-time access to H, and then we can decode $H[i]$ into B_i directly. Since the maximum length of a cell is $\mathcal{O}(\log(n/b))$, the extra space is $\mathcal{O}((n/b) \log(k \log(n/b)))$ bits, which is made $o(n)$ by choosing $k = b = (\log n)/2$. Once again, this is a very significant space overhead in practice.

On the other hand, having direct access to any code allows for improved compression, because Huffman codes are no longer necessary. Since the access process tells us the length $\ell_i = |H[i]|$, the codes need not be prefix-free (or even unambiguous). Rather, we can sort the distinct blocks $D_1, D_2, \ldots$ by decreasing frequency and assign them the codes ε (the empty string), 0, 1, 00, 01, 10, 11, 000, etc. In addition, this allows for obtaining the index j corresponding to the code of block D_j in constant time: $j = 2^{\ell_i} + H[i]$. A table storing the block content D_j corresponding to each index j completes the decoding.

Example 4.7 *With the same example of Figure 4.2, we would assign ε to D_1, 0 to D_2, 1 to D_3, 00 to D_4, 01 to D_5, 10 to D_6, and 11 to D_7. Then the encoded sequence would be shortened to $H = $ 01000110011. For example, to decode 11, we compute $2^{|11|} + 11 = 2^2 + 3 = 7$.*

Note that this is the same encoding we used in Section 3.4.5, where we instead combined it with direct access codes.

4.2 Rank

We now show how to support operation $\mathsf{rank}_1(B, i)$, which is the default meaning of $\mathsf{rank}(B, i)$. We do not need to worry about $\mathsf{rank}_0(B, i)$ because $\mathsf{rank}_0(B, i) = i - \mathsf{rank}_1(B, i)$. We start considering a simple bit array representation of B, to which we will add a structure of $o(n)$ bits that supports rank. Later we combine the results with the compressed bitvector representations seen in Section 4.1.

A trivial solution would be to create an array of integers $R[1, n]$, where we store $R[i] = \mathsf{rank}_1(B, i)$. The problem is that array R would occupy n integers, many times more than the n bits used by the bit array B itself!

A less trivial solution is to note that $\mathsf{rank}_1(B, i) = \mathsf{sum}(B, i)$ if we regard B as an array of 1-bit numbers, and use the partial sums solution of Section 3.3. This would yield, for example, n bits of extra space and $\mathcal{O}(w)$ time for rank.

In this section we show that better solutions are possible, because the numbers we sum up are bits. We will reach constant time with $o(n)$ bits on top of B.

4.2.1 Sparse Sampling

Instead of storing array R for *all* the values of i, we will store it only for the values that are multiples of $s = k \cdot w$, for some parameter k. That is, we store $R[0, \lfloor n/s \rfloor]$, with

$$R[i] = \mathsf{rank}_1(B, is).$$

Since each of the cells of R occupies w bits, we have at most $n/k + w$ bits allocated for R (we will generally ignore the last w bits).

In order to compute $\mathsf{rank}_1(B, i)$, we add up two values:

1. $R[\lfloor i/s \rfloor]$, which contains the number of 1s in $B[1, \lfloor i/s \rfloor s]$;
2. the number of 1s in $B[\lfloor i/s \rfloor s + 1, i]$.

Since we store B using an array of integers $W[1, \lceil n/w \rceil]$ (recall Section 3.1), the second point corresponds to counting the number of 1s in the words $W[\lfloor i/s \rfloor k + 1, \lfloor i/w \rfloor]$, plus the number of 1s in the first $i \bmod w$ bits of $W[\lfloor i/w \rfloor + 1]$. For this last word, in Section 3.1 we saw how to efficiently isolate the desired bits in a word. Therefore, our problem reduces to counting the number of 1s in a word fast.

This problem is called *population counting* or just *popcount*. Many modern architectures implement popcount directly, and many languages provide a primitive that uses the architecture-supported operation if available, or an efficient implementation otherwise. One such method, in C and for a word `bits`, works in time $\mathcal{O}(popcount(\mathtt{bits}))$:

```c
c = 0;
while (bits)
    { bits &= bits-1; c++; }
return c;
```

Another formula that generally does fewer operations is, for $w = 32$,

```c
bits = bits - ((bits >> 1) & 0x55555555);
bits = (bits & 0x33333333) + ((bits >> 2) & 0x33333333);
return ((bits + (bits >> 4) & 0x0F0F0F0F) * 0x01010101) >> 24;
```

Algorithm 4.3: Answering rank with sparse sampling.

---

1 **Proc** rank(B, i)

> **Input** : Bitvector B (seen as arrays W and R and parameter k) and position i.
> **Output**: Returns $\text{rank}_1(B, i)$.

2    $i_s \leftarrow \lfloor i/(kw) \rfloor$

3    $i_w \leftarrow \lfloor i/w \rfloor$

4    $r \leftarrow R[i_s]$

5   **for** $t \leftarrow i_s \cdot k + 1$ **to** i_w **do**

6      $\lfloor\; r \leftarrow r + popcount(W[t])$

7   **return** $r + popcount(\text{bitsread}(W[i_w + 1], 1, i \bmod w))$

Its 64-bit version is obtained by duplicating all the hexadecimal constants (for example, 0x0F0F0F0F becomes 0x0F0F0F0F0F0F0F0F) and changing the 24 at the end to 56.

Algorithm 4.3 gives the method to compute rank_1. In total, we perform up to k memory accesses (one in R and less than k in W) and use $(1 + 1/k)n$ bits (n for W and n/k for R). This allows us to get space arbitrarily close to n bits, but at increasing time cost.

Note that the solution is very similar to the one given in Section 3.3 for operation sum. Here we achieve a w-fold speedup (for summing bits) because of the wordwise popcount operation. In Section 3.3, we summed up the numbers one by one, which is reasonable if they are relatively large. In Section 4.5.1 we will use our newer tools to provide faster sum and search operations.

Practical Considerations

The k cells read from W are contiguous in memory, and therefore most of them will be cache hits. If the array W is not shared with other components of the software, we can also avoid the cache miss incurred when accessing R, by storing R and W interleaved: the word $R[i]$ is placed just before $W[ik + 1]$.

For example, with $k = w = 64$, the space of $W + R$ is just $1.016n$ bits, and operation rank is fast and practical. If the architecture has efficient popcounting operations on wide integers (which can go from $w' = 128$ to $w' = 512$ in modern processors), then we can store entries of R every $k \cdot w'$ bits, not $k \cdot w$ (but R still stores plain integers of w bits). Then the total space for R becomes $w\lceil n/(kw') \rceil$ bits, while the cost of rank does not change.

In general, however, with the sampling technique we described, it is not possible to obtain constant time with $n + o(n)$ bits. This requires a more complex scheme, which we describe next.

4.2.2 Constant Time

To achieve $n + o(n)$ bits of space with a constant number of memory accesses, we resort to a hierarchical scheme: B is divided into *superblocks* of $s = w \cdot k$ bits, and

---

Algorithm 4.4: Answering rank with dense sampling.

---

1 **Proc** rank(B, i)

> **Input** : Bitvector B (seen as arrays W, R, and R' and parameter k) and
> position i.
>
> **Output**: Returns rank$_1(B, i)$.

2    $i_w \leftarrow \lfloor i/w \rfloor$

3   **return** $R[\lfloor i/(kw) \rfloor] + \text{read}(R', i_w)$

4          $+ popcount(\text{bitsread}(W[i_w + 1], 1, i \bmod w))$

---

each superblock is divided into *blocks* of w bits (this division is only conceptual). We store the same array $R[0, \lfloor n/s \rfloor]$ of Section 4.2.1, which gives the rank values at the beginnings of superblocks. We also store a new array $R'[0, \lfloor n/w \rfloor]$ that gives the rank values at the beginnings of blocks, but relative to their superblock. That is,

$$R'[i] = \text{rank}_1(B, iw) - R[\lfloor iw/s \rfloor]$$

counts the number of 1s up to the ith block, from the beginning of its superblock. Now, to compute rank$_1(B, i)$, we add up three values:

1. $R[\lfloor i/s \rfloor]$, which contains the number of 1s in $B[1, \lfloor i/s \rfloor s]$;
2. $R'[\lfloor i/w \rfloor]$, which contains the number of 1s in $B[\lfloor i/s \rfloor s + 1, \lfloor i/w \rfloor w]$;
3. the number of 1s in $B[\lfloor i/w \rfloor w + 1, i]$, that is, the number of 1s in the first $i \bmod w$ bits of $W[\lfloor i/w \rfloor + 1]$.

Algorithm 4.4 shows the pseudocode. Array R' is stored with fixed-length cells.

Example 4.8 *Figure 4.3 shows an example of this data structure, with $k = w = 4$. To compute* rank($B, 31$) *we add up the contents of $R[\lfloor 31/(kw) \rfloor] = R[1] = 4$ (grayed) and $R'[\lfloor 31/w \rfloor] = R'[7] = 2$ (grayed). Then we popcount the first $31 \bmod 4 = 3$ bits of block $B[29, 32]$ (also grayed) to obtain the final answer, $4 + 2 + 2 = 8$.*

Compared to Section 4.2.1, we have now precomputed most of the values that must be summed after $B[\lfloor i/s \rfloor s + 1]$. The key that distinguishes this from simply using $k = 1$ in Section 4.2.1 is that the values stored in R' are smaller than those in R (they are between 0 and $s - w$), and therefore they can be stored in fewer bits: $1 + \lfloor \log(s - w) \rfloor$ is sufficient.

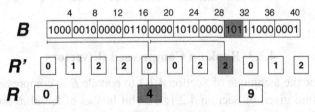

Figure 4.3. The constant-time rank scheme, with $k = w = 4$. Array R stores 1 accumulated rank every kw bits and R' stores 1 (relative) accumulated rank every w bits. The block shades and lines illustrate operation rank($B, 31$).

The space on top of W is thus $w\lceil n/s\rceil + \lceil \log s\rceil \lceil n/w\rceil = n/k + n\log(kw)/w$ $+\mathcal{O}(n/w)$ bits. This can be made $o(n)$ by choosing, say, $k = w$. Then the space becomes $2(n/w)\log w + \mathcal{O}(n/w) = \mathcal{O}(n\log\log n/\log n) = o(n)$ bits.

In theory, the formula we gave for popcounting is not constant-time because it grows loglogarithmically with w (for example, it would require one more step for $w > 256$, and this will be sufficient up to $w \le 2^{16}$). A way to obtain truly constant time is to precompute in a table all the popcounts for all the possible blocks of $(\log n)/2$ bits. This table requires $\mathcal{O}(\sqrt{n}\log\log n) = o(n)$ bits and allows popcounting a block of $\mathcal{O}(\log n)$ bits in constant time. Then we take $\log n$ as the computer word length and still obtain $o(n)$ bits of space. In modern architectures, using such a table is slightly slower than the formula we have given, thus we leave this remark only to prevent theoretical concerns.

Note that this two-level scheme to achieve constant time and $o(n)$ bits of extra space is similar to the one used in Section 3.2.2 to locate a variable-length block in constant time. While the overhead of this arrangement is not very low, it is perfectly acceptable when speed is important and the relative impact of B in the overall space usage of a data structure is low. A good example of this situation is the use of bitvectors M_r in the implementation of direct access codes (Section 3.4.2): We can replace $\mathsf{sum}(M_r, i)$ by $\mathsf{rank}_1(M_r, i)$ in line 5 of Algorithm 3.4, so that the time to read a number of ℓ bits is $\mathcal{O}(1 + \ell/b)$.

Practical Considerations

Arranging the block and superblock lengths so that we read memory positions that are word- or byte- aligned makes a significant difference in performance. For example, if we set $s = 256$, we can store R' as an array of $\lceil n/w\rceil$ bytes. The total space used by $W + R' + R$ will be $n + 8n/w + wn/256$. For both $w = 32$ and $w = 64$, this is $1.375n$. The space overhead can be reduced by using yet another level, with super-superblocks of length 2^{16}. Thus we have a new array S that uses $wn/2^{16}$ bits, but the superblock array R now stores short integers of 16 bits. The total space is below $1.313n$ bits for $w = 32$ and $1.189n$ bits for $w = 64$. Once again, this can be further reduced if the processor performs fast popcount on words of $w' > w$ bits.

To reduce cache misses, we can store R interleaved with R', that is, each entry of R is followed by its k corresponding entries in R'. This makes it most likely that the entries we read in R and R' fit in the same cache line. For example, with $w = 64$, we can choose $k = 8$ and store two w-bit words per superblock: one word with the value of R, and another packing the 7 9-bit R' values of that superblock (the first is always zero and thus omitted), which is sufficient since $2^9 = kw$. The space used is $1.250n$. As in Section 4.2.1, we can also interleave these arrays with the cells of W, if it can be modified.

4.2.3 Rank on Compressed Bitvectors

We can combine the technique of Section 4.1.1 to encode B in compressed form, with the rank structure given in Section 4.2.1: The bit blocks of length b are represented in the arrays C of classes and O of offsets. We define $s = b \cdot k$ for a parameter k, and store the array $P[1, \lceil n/s\rceil]$ of sampled pointers to O, as well as the array $R[0, \lfloor n/s\rfloor]$ giving the rank values just before the sampled positions.

Algorithm 4.5: Answering rank with sparse sampling on compressed bitvectors. The last two lines can be optimized to decode/popcount only the first bits.

---

1 **Proc** rank(B, i)

  Input : Bitvector B (seen as arrays C, O, P, R, and L, and parameters b and k,
       with O seen in turn as W) and position i.

  Output: Returns $\text{rank}_1(B, i)$.

2 $i_s \leftarrow \lceil i/(kb) \rceil$

3 **if** $i \bmod kb = 0$ **then return** $R[i_s]$

4 $p \leftarrow P[i_s]$

5 $r \leftarrow R[i_s - 1]$

6 **for** $t \leftarrow (i_s - 1)k + 1$ **to** $\lfloor i/b \rfloor$ **do**

7   $c \leftarrow \text{read}(C, t)$

8   $p \leftarrow p + L[c]$

9   $r \leftarrow r + c$

10 **if** $i \bmod b = 0$ **then return** r

11 $c \leftarrow \text{read}(C, \lceil i/b \rceil)$

12 $o \leftarrow \text{bitsread}(W, p, p + L[c] - 1)$

13 $blk \leftarrow decode(c, o, b)$ (Algorithm 4.1)

14 **return** $r + popcount(\text{bitsread}(blk, 1, i \bmod b))$

A fortunate consequence of having the vector C readily available is that, to solve $\text{rank}_1(B, i)$, we do not need to decode and popcount all the blocks B_t from the last block pointed from P to the one that contains i. Instead, we start at $p = P[\lceil i/s \rceil]$ and $r = R[\lfloor i/s \rfloor]$ and accumulate $p \leftarrow p + L[C[t]]$ and $r \leftarrow r + C[t]$, until reaching the block B_t where position i lies. Then the block is extracted from position p, and popcounted up to position $i \bmod b$. We return the accumulated value of r plus the local popcount of the block. In fact, we can regard R as a structure supporting partial sums on C (Section 3.3). Algorithm 4.5 gives the pseudocode.

For example, by using $k = b = w$, the space is $n\mathcal{H}_0(B) + \mathcal{O}((n/w)\log w) = n\mathcal{H}_0(B) + o(n)$: We have at most $n\mathcal{H}_0(B) + n/w$ bits in array O, $(n/w)\log w$ bits in C, and n/w bits in P (the sampled pointers to O) and in R (the sampled rank accumulators), apart from other very small arrays. For example, with computer words of $w = 64$ bits, the structure poses around $0.125n$ bits of space overhead over the entropy. Although it takes $\mathcal{O}(k + b) = \mathcal{O}(w)$ time, operation rank is fast and practical.

Example 4.9 *Figure 4.1 also shows the corresponding array $R[0, 2]$, aligned to $P[1, 3]$. We continue Example 4.5, now computing* rank$(B, 31)$. *We start with the precomputed rank $r = R[\lfloor 31/(bk) \rfloor] = R[1] = 4$. As we traverse C and O (without really accessing O), we use the classes in C to increase the partial rank value in $r = 4$. We start, like for* access, *at $C[(\lceil 31/(bk) \rceil - 1)k + 1] = 5$. Since $C[5] = 0$, we stay with rank 4. Since $C[6] = 2$, we increase the rank to $4 + 2 = 6$. Since $C[7] = 0$, we stay with rank 6. Finally, we extract $B_8 = 1011$ as in Example 4.5, and popcount the range $B_8[1, 31 \bmod 4] = B_8[1, 3] = 101$, which has 2 1s, thus the final value is* rank$(B, 31) = 6 + 2 = 8$.

If constant time is desired, we can combine the techniques of Sections 3.2.2 and 4.2.2. This still requires $n\mathcal{H}_0(B) + o(n)$ bits, but the space overhead is significantly higher in practice. It is also possible to obtain high-order compression with the technique of Section 4.1.2, but unless we store array R' for constant-time rank, we need to decode and popcount every block B_t from the last sampled one, and therefore the process is slower.

4.3 Select

Operation select_v is, in a sense, the inverse of rank_v: $\mathsf{rank}_v(B, \mathsf{select}_v(B, j)) = j$. Since $\mathsf{rank}_v(B, i)$ is a nondecreasing function of i, $\mathsf{select}_v(B, j)$ can be solved by a binary search on the interval $[1, n]$ to find the leftmost position i where $\mathsf{rank}_v(B, i) = j$. Then $i = \mathsf{select}_v(B, j)$. This is a simple way to add the select functionality to any rank-capable implementation of bitvectors, when the performance of select is not crucial, or when n is not very large. The solution uses no space and works both for $v = 0$ and $v = 1$.

In practice, if B is stored as a bit array on $W[1, \lceil n/w \rceil]$ and the data structure for rank is the array R of Section 4.2.1, it is better to first run a binary search on R, and then sequentially popcount the words of W looking for the one where rank j is reached or exceeded. Finally, we scan this word bitwise to find the exact position i. In case the bitvector is compressed with classes and offsets (Section 4.2.3), we scan the classes $C[t]$ instead of popcounting. If there is a second level of precomputed ranks in array R' (Section 4.2.2), then we scan the cells of R' instead of popcounting. We can also use binary search on R', although this is convenient only if the superblocks contain many blocks.

This binary-search-based implementation takes time $\mathcal{O}(k + w)$, or just $\mathcal{O}(\log n)$ on top of a constant-time rank implementation. When a faster solution is needed, we must store specific data structures for select_v. In general, the solutions for select are slower and use more space than those for rank. Moreover, unlike the case of rank_v, the structures for select_0 will not be useful for select_1 and vice versa. We will describe the structures for select_1 (called select by default), and these must be replicated for select_0 if needed.

Let $B[1, n]$ have m 1s. A basic constant-time solution for select is to store the m answers to the queries in an array $S[j] = \mathsf{select}(B, j)$. This array uses $m \log n$ bits, which is acceptable only if the bitvector is very sparse (i.e., $m \ll n$). The more sophisticated solutions we explore in the sequel start from this basic arrangement and seek to reduce its space.

4.3.1 A Simple Heuristic

A simple tradeoff between a binary-search based select using no space and a constant-time select using $m \log n$ bits is to store a sampled set of answers. Fix a sampling step s and store array $S[0, \lceil m/s \rceil]$, so that

$$S[p] = \mathsf{select}(B, ps + 1),$$

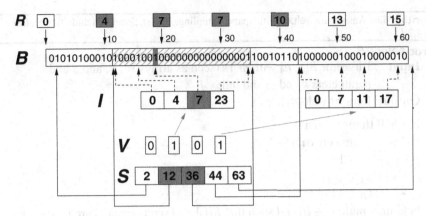

Figure 4.4. The data structures for **select** on a bitvector B of $n = 62$ bits and $m = 16$ 1s using $s = 4$. We show array $S[0, \lceil m/s \rceil] = S[0, 4]$ of Section 4.3.1, which helps narrow the binary searches. We also show the bitvector $V[1, 4]$ and the array I of Section 4.3.2, where the long blocks (2 and 4, where V is 1) have a corresponding chunk in I where the positions of their s 1s are recorded. Only the short blocks (1 and 3) are binary searched when V and I are used. On the top we include the array R of **rank**, with sampling step 10. The various block shades illustrate operation $\text{select}_1(B, 7)$.

where the last cell is $S[\lceil m/s \rceil] = n + 1$. This requires $w(1 + \lceil m/s \rceil)$ bits of space and reduces the search for $\text{select}(B, j)$ to the range $B[S[\lceil j/s \rceil - 1], S[\lceil j/s \rceil] - 1]$. Within this area, we run a binary search helped by the array R and, depending on the case, R' or C, as explained. The search can switch to sequential if the area to search turns out to be short.

Example 4.10 *Figure 4.4 shows a bitvector of length $n = 62$ and $m = 16$ 1s, where we chose sampling step $s = 4$. The bitvector V and array I will be used later. To solve* $\text{select}_1(B, 7)$ *we run a binary search on the area* $B[S[\lceil 7/s \rceil - 1], S[\lceil 7/s \rceil] - 1] = B[S[1], S[2] - 1] = B[12, 35]$, *which is hatched in B. This binary search is done on (the grayed cells of) the array R of Section 4.2, and then the final block of R is sequentially scanned. We find the 7th 1 of B in $B[19] = 1$, so* $\text{select}_1(B, 7) = 19$ *(shaded in B).*

If we choose, for example, $s = w^2$, then the space of S is $\mathcal{O}(wm/s) = \mathcal{O}(m/w) = o(m)$ bits. In addition, if the 1s are uniformly distributed in B, then the area between two consecutive values of S is of length sn/m. If we run the binary search on R, whose blocks are of kw bits, then the binary search time is $\mathcal{O}\left(\log \frac{sn}{mkw}\right) = \mathcal{O}\left(\log \frac{w}{k} + \log \frac{n}{m}\right)$. This is $\mathcal{O}\left(\log \frac{n}{m}\right)$ if $k = \Omega(w)$ (as seen at the end of Section 4.2.1, values like $k = w$ are typical, to have low space overhead for R). In some cases, however, the 1s are not uniformly distributed, and this heuristic may take up to $\mathcal{O}(\log n)$ time if it has to run the binary search on a very long area between two consecutive values of S.

In addition to this time, which counts mostly cache misses, the search ends with a cache-friendly scan of $\mathcal{O}(k)$ words of W (or cells of C) and the $\mathcal{O}(w)$ time to find the precise bit in the final word. These two steps have little impact in practice.

Algorithm 4.6 gives the pseudocode for the case of B stored in plain form, in combination with the sparse **rank** sampling of Section 4.2.1.

Algorithm 4.6: Answering **select** with sparse sampling. The structures include those of Section 4.2.1.

---

1 **Proc** select(B, j)

    Input : Bitvector $B[1, n]$ with m **1**s (seen as arrays W, R, and S and
              parameters k and s) and index j.

    Output: Returns select$_1(B, j)$.

2   **if** $j = 0$ **then return** 0

3   **if** $j > m$ **then return** $n + 1$

4     $p \leftarrow \lceil j/s \rceil - 1$

5     $i_1 \leftarrow \lfloor S[p]/(kw) \rfloor$

6     $i_2 \leftarrow \lfloor (S[p+1] - 1)/(kw) \rfloor$

7   Find maximum $i_s \in [i_1, i_2]$ such that $R[i_s] \leq j$ with binary search

8     $r \leftarrow R[i_s]$

9     $i_w \leftarrow i_s \cdot k$

10   **while** $r + popcount(W[i_w + 1]) < j$ **do**

11         $i_w \leftarrow i_w + 1$

12         $r \leftarrow r + popcount(W[i_w])$

13   **for** $i \leftarrow 1$ **to** w **do**

14   **if** bitread$(W[i_w + 1], i) = 1$ **then**

15             $r \leftarrow r + 1$

16   **if** $r = j$ **then**

17   **return** $i_w \cdot w + i$

4.3.2 An $\mathcal{O}(\log \log n)$ Time Solution

It is possible to combine the ideas of binary search and precomputed answers in a way that guarantees $\mathcal{O}(\log \log n)$ time, with $\mathcal{O}(n/\log n) = o(n)$ bits of space. Let us define *variable-length blocks* in B as the ranges between consecutive entries of S. All the blocks contain exactly s **1**s, and our binary search in the previous section operated on one such block. Note this fortunate combination: (1) if a block is short, then the binary search on it will be fast; (2) if it is long, then it is sparse, and the space needed to directly store all the **select** answers inside the block is low compared to its length.

Precisely, a block will be called *long* if it is longer than $s \cdot \log^2 n$, and if not, it will be called *short*. A bitvector $V[1, \lceil m/s \rceil]$ will indicate with $V[p] = 1$ that the block $B[S[p-1], S[p] - 1]$ is long. We will store all the s answers to **select** inside long blocks, in an array $I[1, *]$ of fixed cells of $\lceil \log n \rceil$ bits. Therefore, to solve **select**(B, j), we first compute the block $p = \lceil j/s \rceil$. If $V[p] = 1$, then j falls in a long block, and the answer inside it is precomputed, precisely in

$$I[s \cdot (\mathsf{rank}(V, p) - 1) + ((j - 1) \mod s) + 1].$$

Otherwise we continue as in Algorithm 4.6. Since I uses $s\lceil \log n \rceil$ bits per long block, and there cannot be more than $n/(s \log^2 n)$ long blocks overall, the space used by I is at most $n/\log n = o(n)$ bits. Bitvector V is even shorter, and it should be preprocessed for constant-time rank queries (Section 4.2.2).

Now the binary search is limited to within short blocks, which are at most $s \log^2 n$ in length. To obtain the desired complexity, let us choose $s = \log^2 n \log \log n$. We must also use the two-level rank sampling of Section 4.2.2, setting the sampling of array R to s and that of array R' to $\log n \log \log n$. The space then stays in $\mathcal{O}(n/\log n)$ bits.

The binary search on R spans $\log^2 n$ cells and thus takes time $\mathcal{O}(\log \log n)$. We also run a binary search in R', on the resulting superblock of R. This again takes $\mathcal{O}(\log \log n)$ time because there are $\log n$ blocks per superblock. The final block is also scanned in time $\mathcal{O}(\log \log n)$, if we advance by popcounting on chunks of $\log n$ bits until we exceed the desired rank. The precise bit is found in constant time in the final chunk of $\log n$ bits by precomputing a table that extends the one described in Section 4.2.2: for any chunk X of $(\log n)/2$ bits and any j, it stores $\mathsf{select}(X, j)$. Then one or two applications of the table on the last $\log n$ bits suffice to find the answer.

As before, it is better in practice to use multiples of w instead of $\log n$, and to process bitwise the last word in the block.

Example 4.11 *Consider the same bitvector B of Example 4.10. Figure 4.4 shows the corresponding bitvector V and array I, where we assume that blocks with more than $4s = 16$ bits are long. To solve the same query $\mathsf{select}_1(B, 7)$, we compute the block number $p = \lceil 7/s \rceil = 2$, and since $V[2] = 1$, the block is long and the answer is explicitly stored. Indeed, $\mathsf{select}_1(B, 7) = S[p - 1] + I[s \cdot (\mathsf{rank}(V, p) - 1) + ((7 - 1) \bmod s) + 1] = S[1] + I[4 \cdot 0 + 3] = 12 + 7 = 19$.*

Algorithm 4.7 shows how the required structures are built in two $\mathcal{O}(n)$-time passes over B. Note that we first allocate a safe amount of space and then truncate the arrays, to avoid further passes (the arrays only use $o(n)$ bits, so the safe allocation is not a serious problem). If necessary, the structures can be built using a negligible amount of main memory, by reading bitvector B from disk by small buffers (twice) and also writing arrays R, S, V, and I to disk by buffers (S needs to be reread again from disk).

4.3.3 Constant Time

To achieve constant time, we can repeat the idea of Section 4.3.2 inside short blocks. Take $s = \log^2 n$ and cut blocks into *miniblocks* of $s' = (\log \log n)^2$ entries. Miniblocks spanning more than $s'(\log \log n)^2$ bits will be called long, otherwise they will be short. We can store all the s' answers inside long miniblocks. Since we are also inside a short block, the answers require only $s' \cdot \log(s \log^2 n) = \mathcal{O}((\log \log n)^3)$ bits, and since there are no more than $n/(s'(\log \log n)^2) = \mathcal{O}(n/(\log \log n)^4)$ long miniblocks, the total space incurred is $\mathcal{O}(n/\log \log n) = o(n)$ bits.

Short miniblocks are of length $\mathcal{O}((\log \log n)^4) = o(\log n)$ bits, and therefore the search inside them can be carried out in constant time using the same precomputed table that handles every possible chunk of $(\log n)/2$ bits.

It should not be surprising that this solution, while achieving constant time and $o(n)$ extra bits, incurs in high extra space. This is expected from the $\mathcal{O}(n/\log \log n)$ extra space complexity. Still, using this space is worthy when speed is crucial and the space of

---

Algorithm 4.7: Building the select structures.

Input : Bit array $B[1, n]$, parameters k and s.
Output: Builds the structures S, V, and I on B.

1 Allocate array $S[0, \lceil n/s \rceil]$ of integers
2 $r \leftarrow 0$
3 **for** $i \leftarrow 1$ **to** n **do**
4   **if** bitread$(B, i) = 1$ **then**
5        $r \leftarrow r + 1$
6   **if** $r \bmod s = 1$ **then**
7           $S[(r - 1)/s] \leftarrow i$

8 $t \leftarrow \lceil r/s \rceil$
9 $S[t] \leftarrow n + 1$
10 Truncate S at $S[0, t]$
11 Allocate bit array $V[1, t]$
12 Allocate array $I[1, \lceil n/(s \log^2 n) \rceil \cdot s]$ of $\lceil \log n \rceil$-bit elements
13 $j \leftarrow 0$
14 **for** $p \leftarrow 1$ **to** t **do**
15   **if** $S[p] - S[p - 1] \leq s \cdot \log^2 n$ **then**
16   bitclear(V, p)
17   **else**
18   bitset(V, p)
19   **for** $i \leftarrow S[p - 1]$ **to** $S[p] - 1$ **do**
20   **if** bitread$(B, i) = 1$ **then**
21             $j \leftarrow j + 1$
22   write$(I, j, i - S[p - 1])$

23 Truncate I to $I[1, j]$
24 Preprocess V for rank queries (Section 4.2.2)

---

the bitvector in the whole data structure is not so significant. We see one such case in the next section. Another example, depending on the case, might be supporting constant-time decoding of entries in the Elias-Fano representation of Section 3.4.3.

Some intermediate solutions have also been implemented with success, for example, storing the S array for miniblocks, but not I and V. That is, we use the heuristic solution at the level of miniblocks, where the cost of a bad case is not so high. This incurs in practice in a space overhead of $0.15\,n$–$0.25\,n$ bits and performs only 2–3 times slower than rank.

4.4 Very Sparse Bitvectors

All the solutions seen up to now have a space overhead of $o(n)$ bits. This can be too high when m is much smaller than n. Instead, our simple constant-time solution for select$_1$ that stores all the answers in $m\lceil \log n\rceil$ bits shows that the select problem is easy on sparse bitvectors. In this section we build a more sophisticated version of this idea, reaching constant-time select$_1$ within $m\log\frac{n}{m} + \mathcal{O}(m) = n\mathcal{H}_0(B) + \mathcal{O}(m)$ bits. It is impossible to have constant-time rank within this space, but we will obtain time $\mathcal{O}\left(\min\left(\log m, \log\frac{n}{m}\right)\right)$.

4.4.1 Constant-Time Select

Let us consider again the full array $S[1, m]$ where $S[j] = \mathsf{select}(B, j)$. We choose a parameter $r = \left\lfloor \log\frac{n}{m}\right\rfloor$ and split these m numbers in two parts: $S[j] = h_j \cdot l_j$, where l_j are the lowest r bits of $S[j]$ and h_j are the $\lceil \log n\rceil - r$ highest bits. That is, $l_j = S[j]$ mod 2^r, $h_j = \lfloor S[j]/2^r\rfloor$, and $S[j] = h_j \cdot 2^r + l_j$. We store the numbers l_j directly in an array of r-bit values $L[1, m]$, so that $L[j] = l_j$. This array is stored with the technique of Section 3.1, thus it uses $mr = m\left\lfloor \log\frac{n}{m}\right\rfloor$ bits.

The highest bits h_j will instead be represented using a bitvector H. This bitvector will be all 0s, except for 1s set at $H[h_j + j]$, for all $1 \le j \le m$. Note that the sequence h_j is nondecreasing, thus $h_j + j$ is strictly increasing. The highest bit set in H is at $h_m + m$. Since $S[m] \le n$, we have $h_m + m \le n/2^r + m = n/2^{\lfloor \log\frac{n}{m}\rfloor} + m < n/2^{\log\frac{n}{m}-1} + m \le 2n/\frac{n}{m} + m = 3m$. Thus bitvector H is at most $3m$ in length. We build the structure for constant-time select (Section 4.3.3) on H, which adds $o(m)$ bits.

Now, by construction, it holds $h_j = \mathsf{select}_1(H, j) - j$, and therefore, we can compute any

$$\mathsf{select}_1(S, j) = S[j] = h_j \cdot 2^r + l_j = (\mathsf{select}_1(H, j) - j) \cdot 2^r + L[j]$$

in constant time. The total space is $m\left\lfloor \log\frac{n}{m}\right\rfloor + 3m + o(m) = m\log\frac{n}{m} + \mathcal{O}(m)$ bits. A finer analysis shows that the space is $m\log\frac{n}{m} + 2m + o(m)$ bits.

Example 4.12 *Consider the same bitvector B of Example 4.10. Figure 4.5 shows its representation using L and H, with $r = 2$. To solve the same query* $\mathsf{select}_1(B, 7)$, *we recover* $h_7 = \mathsf{select}_1(H, 7) - 7 = 11 - 7 = 4$. *Then* $\mathsf{select}_1(B, 7) = h_7 \cdot 2^2 + L[7] = 4 \cdot 4 + 3 = 19$. *The involved cells are grayed in each array.*

4.4.2 Solving Rank

The solution for rank is not as direct as for select. A simple way to compute $\mathsf{rank}_1(B, i)$ is to run a binary search on the $\mathsf{select}_1(B, j)$ values, to find the maximum j such that $\mathsf{select}_1(B, j) \le i$, and then $\mathsf{rank}_1(B, i) = j$. Since we have constant-time select$_1$, this binary search takes $\mathcal{O}(\log m)$ time. For $m \ge \sqrt{n}$, however, it is possible to improve the time to $\mathcal{O}(\log\frac{n}{m})$. The solution we describe next takes time $\mathcal{O}\left(\min\left(\log m, \log\frac{n}{m}\right)\right)$ and is more efficient in all cases than a plain binary search on select$_1$ queries.

Note that bitvector H, where we have set 1s at positions $h_j + j$, can be interpreted as follows: consider the numbers $h_1, h_2, \ldots, h_m$ in order. If we have an area $h_j = h_{j+1} = \ldots = h_{j+t}$, this means that $S[j], S[j + 1], \ldots, S[j + t]$ belong to the same *chunk* of

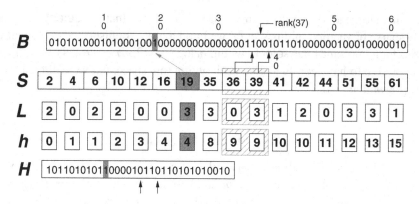

Figure 4.5. Representing a bitvector B with array L and bitvector H, using $r = 2$. Arrays S and h are shown for clarity, but only L and H are stored. Grayed blocks and arrows illustrate operation $\mathsf{select}_1(B, 7)$, whereas hatched blocks and black arrows illustrate operation $\mathsf{rank}_1(B, 37)$.

size 2^r in B, namely $B[h_j \cdot 2^r, (h_j + 1) \cdot 2^r - 1]$. The positions

$$h_j + j, h_{j+1} + (j+1), \dots, h_{j+t} + (j+t),$$

$$= h_j + j, (h_j + j) + 1, \dots, (h_j + j) + t$$

form a contiguous block of 1s in H. When we finally move on to $h_{j+t+1} > h_j$, we will set the next 1 in $h_{j+t+1} + (j + t + 1) > (h_j + j) + (t + 1)$ and a 0 will appear at $H[(h_j + j) + (t + 1)]$. Therefore, each 0 in H indicates that we have moved on to the next chunk in B, whereas each 1 indicates a 1 in B that falls in the current chunk. This can also be seen as H storing, in unary (as $1^x 0$), the number x of 1s inside the consecutive chunks of B.

Example 4.13 *Consider again Figure 4.5, where the chunks are of length $2^r = 4$ except the first. The first chunk is $B[1, 3] = \mathsf{010}$, which contains one 1, and thus H starts with $\mathsf{10}$ ($h_1 = 0$). The second chunk is $B[4, 7] = \mathsf{1010}$, which contains two 1s, and thus H continues with $\mathsf{110}$ ($h_2 = h_3 = 1$). The third chunk, $B[8, 11] = \mathsf{0010}$, has one 1, so H continues with $\mathsf{10}$ ($h_4 = 2$).*

Bitvector H gives us sufficient information to narrow the binary search for $\mathsf{rank}_1(B, i)$ to within the chunk of i. This chunk is $s = \lfloor i/2^r \rfloor$. We compute $p = \mathsf{select}_0(H, s) - s$ and $p' = \mathsf{select}_0(H, s + 1) - (s + 1)$. Then p is the number of 1s in $B[1, s \cdot 2^r - 1]$, and p' is the number of 1s in $B[1, (s + 1) \cdot 2^r - 1]$. Since $s \cdot 2^r \le i < (s + 1) \cdot 2^r$, it must be that $p \le \mathsf{rank}(B, i) \le p'$. Moreover, we know that $h_{p+1} = \dots = h_{p'} = s$, and thus $L[p + 1, p']$ is increasing. Therefore, the answer is found through a binary search on $L[p + 1, p']$ for the value $i \bmod 2^r$.

Since the size of the interval is 2^r, the binary search takes $\mathcal{O}(\log 2^r) = \mathcal{O}\left(\log \frac{n}{m}\right)$ time. On the other hand, the interval cannot be larger than the whole array L, and thus the binary search time is also upper bounded by $\mathcal{O}(\log m)$. This binary search is very fast, because it requires accesses to the fixed-size cells of array L. In practice, the interval $L[p + 1, p']$ can be so short that a sequential search may perform better than a binary search.

Note that, to support rank, bitvector H must also have the structures to support $select_0$ (those of Section 4.3.3 again, now for the 0s).

Example 4.14 *Consider solving* $rank_1(B, 37)$ *in Figure 4.5. We first compute the chunk* $s = \lfloor 37/4 \rfloor = 9$ *where position 37 lies. Now we compute* $p = select_0(H, s) - s = 17 - 9 = 8$ *and* $p' = select_0(H, s + 1) - (s + 1) = 20 - 10 = 10$. *Thus the area* $h_{p+1} = \ldots = h_{p'} = 9$ *is* $h_9 = h_{10} = 9$, *and we run a binary search on* $L[9, 10] = \langle 0, 3 \rangle$ *for 37 mod 4 = 1. We find that we must include up to* $L[9]$, *thus the answer is* $rank_1(B, 37) = 9$. *The involved data is indicated with black arrows and hatched areas in the figure.*

Algorithm 4.8 shows the procedures for $select_1$ and $rank_1$. A procedure for $access(B, i)$ is obtained by changing what $rank(B, i)$ returns in line 9, so that it returns 1 if $j > p$ and $L[j] = i \bmod 2^r$, and 0 otherwise.

Finally, $select_0(B, j')$ can be solved in $\mathcal{O}(\log m)$ time through a binary search on the constant-time $select_1$ queries: if $select_1(B, j) = i$, then there are $i - j$ 0s in $B[1, i]$. We run a binary search on the interval $j \in [1, m]$, so that if $select_1(B, j) = i$ and $i - j < j'$, then the binary search goes right, otherwise it goes left. Finally we find a j such that $select_1(B, j) = i_1$, $select_1(B, j + 1) = i_2$, and $i_1 - j < j' \leq i_2 - (j + 1)$. Then $select_0(B, j') = j + j'$.

Algorithm 4.9 gives the pseudocode for the construction of the data structures. The construction takes $\mathcal{O}(n)$ time (it could take $\mathcal{O}(m)$ time if we were given the positions of the m 1s). As before, it is not difficult to carry it out using a negligible amount of main memory, by buffering B, H, and L.

Algorithm 4.8: Answering select and rank on very sparse bitvectors. Bitvector H uses the select structures of Section 4.3.3. Assume $L[0] = 0$.

1 **Proc** select(B, j)
  Input : Bitvector $B[1, n]$ with m 1s (seen as bitvector H, array L, and parameter r) and index j.
  Output: Returns $select_1(B, j)$.

2   **if** $j > m$ **then return** $n + 1$
3   **return** $(select_1(H, j) - j) \cdot 2^r + read(L, j)$

4 **Proc** rank(B, i)
  Input : Bitvector B (seen as bitvector H, array L, and r) and index i.
  Output: Returns $rank_1(B, i)$.

5    $s \leftarrow \lfloor i/2^r \rfloor$
6    $p \leftarrow select_0(H, s) - s$
7    $p' \leftarrow select_0(H, s + 1) - (s + 1)$
8   Find maximum $j \in [p + 1, p']$ such that $read(L, j) \leq i \bmod 2^r$
      by binary search (set $j = p$ if $p = p'$ or $read(L, p + 1) > i \bmod 2^r$)
9   **return** j

Algorithm 4.9: Building rank and select structures for very sparse bitvectors.

Input : Bit array $B[1, n]$, also seen as array W.
Output: Computes r and structures H and L for B.

1 $m \leftarrow 0$
2 **for** $i \leftarrow 1$ **to** $\lceil n/w \rceil$ **do**
3 $\quad \lfloor\ m \leftarrow m + popcount(W[i])$
4 $r \leftarrow \lfloor \log \frac{n}{m} \rfloor$
5 Allocate bitvector $H[1, m + \lfloor n/2^r \rfloor]$
6 Allocate array $L[1, m]$ of cells of fixed length r
7 **for** $j \leftarrow 1$ **to** $m + \lfloor n/2^r \rfloor$ **do**
8 $\quad \lfloor\ $ bitclear(H, i) (can be initialized wordwise)
9 $j \leftarrow 0$
10 **for** $i \leftarrow 1$ **to** n **do**
11 $\quad $ **if** bitread$(B, i) = 1$ **then**
12 $\quad\quad \mid\ j \leftarrow j + 1$
13 $\quad\quad \mid\ $ write$(L, j, i \bmod 2^r)$
14 $\quad\quad \lfloor\ $ bitset$(H, \lfloor i/2^r \rfloor + j)$

15 Preprocess H for select$_0$ and select$_1$ queries (Section 4.3.3)

4.4.3 Bitvectors with Runs

In some cases the bitvector B does not contain a very different amount of 1s and 0s, but they are clustered together in m runs of 1s and $m \pm 1$ runs of 0s. An example are bilevel images and fax transmissions.

This is a different reason for the bitvector to be compressible, which is not captured by the zero-order entropy. The first-order entropy, $\mathcal{H}_1(B)$, will certainly be low, but the mechanisms we have seen to reach this entropy measure involve a significant $o(n)$ term in the space. We show a simple reduction from bitvectors with a few runs to sparse bitvectors that allows us apply the techniques in this section.

Let $B[1, n] = 0^{z_1} 1^{o_1} 0^{z_2} 1^{o_2} \ldots 0^{z_m} 1^{o_m} 0^{z_{m+1}}$, where all z_i and o_i are positive with the possible exceptions of z_1 and z_{m+1}. Then we represent B with two bitvectors,

$$Z = 1\, 0^{z_1 - 1}\, 1\, 0^{z_2 - 1} \ldots 1\, 0^{z_m - 1}\, 1,$$

$$O = 1\, 0^{o_1 - 1}\, 1\, 0^{o_2 - 1} \ldots 1\, 0^{o_m - 1}\, 1,$$

to mark the lengths of the runs of 0s and 1s, respectively. If $z_1 = 0$, then the block $1\, 0^{z_1 - 1}$ is omitted. Note that, if m is small, then both O and Z are sparse and thus can be represented in $2m \log \frac{n}{m} + \mathcal{O}(m)$ bits.

To compute select$_1(B, j)$, we find the position in B of $O[j]$. The position belongs to the run number $r = $ rank$_1(O, j)$. Then there are r runs of zeros before it, whose lengths add up to select$_1(Z, r + 1) - 1$. Therefore, it holds

$$\mathsf{select}_1(B, j) = \begin{cases} j + \mathsf{select}_1(Z, \mathsf{rank}_1(O, j) + 1) - 1, & \text{if } z_1 > 0, \\ j + \mathsf{select}_1(Z, \mathsf{rank}_1(O, j)) - 1, & \text{if } z_1 = 0. \end{cases}$$

With an analogous reasoning we obtain

$$\mathsf{select}_0(B, j) = \begin{cases} j + \mathsf{select}_1(O, \mathsf{rank}_1(Z, j)) - 1, & \text{if } z_1 > 0, \\ j + \mathsf{select}_1(O, \mathsf{rank}_1(Z, j) + 1) - 1, & \text{if } z_1 = 0. \end{cases}$$

To compute $\mathsf{rank}_1(B, i)$, we use binary search to find the largest j such that $\mathsf{select}_1(Z, j) + \mathsf{select}_1(O, j) - 1 \le i$. Assume $z_1 > 0$. Then, if $i < \mathsf{select}_1(Z, j + 1) + \mathsf{select}_1(O, j) - 1$ (or Z does not have $j + 1$ 1s), then i falls inside the jth run of 0s and $\mathsf{rank}_1(B, i) = \mathsf{select}_1(O, j) - 1$. Otherwise i falls inside the jth run of 1s and $\mathsf{rank}_1(B, i) = i - \mathsf{select}_1(Z, j + 1) + 1$. We leave the case $z_1 = 0$ as an exercise to the reader. Note that in this process we also obtain the information to answer $\mathsf{access}(B, i)$.

Example 4.15 *Bitvector* $B[1, 20] = 00001111111100101111$ *has* $m = 3$ *runs of* 0s *(of lengths* $z_1 = 4$, $z_2 = 2$, *and* $z_3 = 1$) *and* $m = 3$ *runs of* 1s *(of lengths* $o_1 = 8$, $o_2 = 1$, *and* $o_3 = 4$). *It is then represented by bitvectors* $Z = 1000101$ *and* $O = 1000000011000$ *(note that* $z_{m+1} = z_4 = 0$, *because* B *does not end with* 0s).

Let us solve $\mathsf{select}_1(B, 3)$. *Since* $z_1 > 0$, *this is* $3 + \mathsf{select}_1(Z, \mathsf{rank}_1(O, 3) + 1) - 1 = 3 + \mathsf{select}_1(Z, 1 + 1) - 1 = 3 + 5 - 1 = 7$. *Similarly, to solve* $\mathsf{select}_0(B, 6)$ *we return* $6 + \mathsf{select}_1(O, \mathsf{rank}_1(Z, 6)) - 1 = 6 + \mathsf{select}_1(O, 2) - 1 = 6 + 9 - 1 = 14$.

Now consider $\mathsf{rank}_1(B, 14)$. *Since* $\mathsf{select}_1(Z, 2) + \mathsf{select}_1(O, 2) - 1 = 5 + 9 - 1 = 13 \le 14$ *but* $\mathsf{select}_1(Z, 3) + \mathsf{select}_1(O, 3) - 1 > 14$, *we have* $j = 2$. *Now, since* $\mathsf{select}_1(Z, 3) + \mathsf{select}_1(O, 2) - 1 = 7 + 9 - 1 = 15 > 14$, *we know that* $B[14]$ *falls inside the* jth *(second) run of* 0s. *Then the answer is* $\mathsf{select}_1(O, 2) - 1 = 9 - 1 = 8$.

Finally, consider $\mathsf{rank}_1(B, 10)$. *Since* $\mathsf{select}_1(Z, 1) + \mathsf{select}_1(O, 1) - 1 = 1 + 1 - 1 = 1 \le 10$ *but* $\mathsf{select}_1(Z, 2) + \mathsf{select}_1(O, 2) - 1 > 10$, *we have* $j = 1$. *Now, since* $\mathsf{select}_1(Z, 2) + \mathsf{select}_1(O, 1) - 1 = 5 + 1 - 1 = 5 \le 10$, *we know that* $B[10]$ *falls iside the* jth *(first) run of* 1s. *Therefore, the answer is* $10 - \mathsf{select}_1(Z, 2) + 1 = 10 - 5 + 1 = 6$.

The select queries on B take time $\mathcal{O}(\min(\log m, \log \frac{n}{m}))$, coming from the rank queries on Z and O, whereas rank and access queries on B take $\mathcal{O}(\log m)$ time, coming from the binary search.

4.5 Applications

4.5.1 Partial Sums Revisited

In Section 3.3 we added sum and search operations to arrays, thus supporting partial sum functionality. The use of rank and select leads to new solutions for this problem.

Fixed-Length Numbers

Consider an array $A[1, n]$ of numbers of fixed length ℓ. We can use the scheme of Section 3.1 to store them in ℓn bits, and with the method of Section 3.3 we solve sum and search in time $\mathcal{O}(\log n)$ and $\mathcal{O}(n)$ extra bits. By using a small table that stores the sum of every chunk of $\lfloor (\log n)/(2\ell) \rfloor$ numbers, packed in ℓ bits each, we can speed up the time for **sum** to $\mathcal{O}(\ell)$. The time for **search**, however, still involves a binary search and thus does not improve.

We can, instead, use the structure of Section 4.4. Assume for now that $A[i] > 0$ for all i. We set up a bitvector $B[1, U]$, where $U = \text{sum}(A, n)$. The bitvector will have all 0s, except that $B[\text{sum}(A, i)] = 1$ for all $1 \leq i \leq n$. The following equivalences are then immediate:

$$\text{sum}(A, i) = \text{select}_1(B, i),$$

$$\text{search}(A, j) = \text{rank}_1(B, j - 1) + 1,$$

$$\text{read}(A, i) = \text{sum}(A, i) - \text{sum}(A, i - 1).$$

Therefore, **sum** and **read** on $A[i]$ are supported in constant time, whereas **search** is supported in $\mathcal{O}\left(\log \frac{U}{n}\right) = \mathcal{O}(\ell)$ time (since $U \leq n \cdot 2^\ell$). The space of this representation of A is $n \log \frac{U}{n} + 2n + o(n) \leq \ell n + 2n + o(n)$ bits, close to that of the simple scheme.

As a practical note, observe that we can make array L of Section 4.4 store exactly the lower $\ell \geq \lfloor \log \frac{U}{n} \rfloor$ bits of the positions of the 1s. This reaches the given space bound and makes $L[1, n]$ coincide with an explicit representation of the array $A[1, n]$. Thus, $\text{read}(A, i)$ is done much more efficiently by directly accessing $L[i] = A[i]$. Then bitvector H can be regarded as an extra data structure that provides **sum** and **search** operations on top of A.

If A contains zeros, we can instead encode the values $A[i] + i$ in a bitvector $B[1, U + n]$. The space stays in $n \log \frac{U+n}{n} + \mathcal{O}(n) \leq \ell n + \mathcal{O}(n)$ bits. The operations are translated as follows:

$$\text{sum}(A, i) = \text{select}_1(B, i) - i,$$

$$\text{search}(A, j) = \text{select}_0(B, j) - j + 1,$$

$$\text{read}(A, i) = \text{sum}(A, i) - \text{sum}(A, i - 1).$$

Note that the interpretation of B is analogous to that of bitvector H in Section 4.4: every 1 in B represents a new cell of A that is completed, and every 0 represents an increment of 1 with respect to the previous cell. Thus the formula for $\text{search}(A, j)$ counts how many cells (1s) were processed before we performed j increments (0s).

While the times for **sum** and **read** stay basically identical to the previous solution, operation select_0 requires $\mathcal{O}(\log n)$ time in Section 4.4, and thus **search** becomes significantly slower.

A variant that retains the same space and time complexities of the basic solution, and poses only a small penalty in practice, is to set up a bitvector $Z[1, n]$ where $Z[i] = 1$ iff $A[i] > 0$. The positive values of A are then written on an array $A'[1, \text{rank}(Z, n)]$, and we use the basic representation on A' (where all the elements are positive). Then we have the following translation:

$$\text{sum}(A, i) = \text{sum}(A', \text{rank}(Z, i)),$$

$$\text{search}(A, j) = \text{select}(Z, \text{search}(A', j)),$$

$$\text{read}(A, i) = \begin{cases} 0, & \text{if } Z[i] = 0, \\ \text{read}(A', \text{rank}(Z, i)), & \text{if } Z[i] = 1. \end{cases}$$

By giving constant-time rank and select support to Z, this solution adds at most $n + o(n)$ bits on top of the basic solution, and constant-time overhead.

Variable-Length Numbers

Now consider that each element $A[i]$ uses ℓ_i bits of space, with $N = \sum_{i=1}^{n} \ell_i$. We can use exactly the same arrangement as for fixed-length numbers. This time, however, the space of the array L is not N bits, but rather

$$n \log \frac{U}{n} \geq n \log \frac{\sum_{i=1}^{n} 2^{\ell_i - 1}}{n} \geq n \frac{\sum_{i=1}^{n} \log 2^{\ell_i - 1}}{n} = \sum_{i=1}^{n} \ell_i - 1 = N - n.$$

Here we used Jensen's inequality (Section 2.8), which becomes an equality only when all the ℓ_is are equal. While in many cases the space of this representation is acceptable, it may be significantly larger than the minimum of N bits if the numbers are of very different length. For example, if $n/2$ numbers use k bits and $n/2$ use 1 bit, then $N = n(k+1)/2$, but this representation uses at least $n(k-2)$ bits, almost twice the space.

Positional Inverted Indexes Again

When we described positional inverted indexes in Section 2.9, we used a worst-case space analysis of the form $n \log \frac{U}{n}$. Therefore, the fact that our new representation of variable-length values reaches the worst case does not affect that analysis. The differentially encoded list for word s, say, D_s, had n_s numbers adding up to n, therefore our new representation requires $n_s \log \frac{n}{n_s} + \mathcal{O}(n_s)$ bits. Added over all the lists D_s, this gives $n\mathcal{H}_0(T) + \mathcal{O}(n)$ bits, better than the result of the (pessimistic) analysis using δ-codes obtained in Section 2.9. Moreover, now we have constant-time access to the ith occurrence of word s in T ($\mathsf{sum}(D_s, i)$) and can find the position in D_s where the sum exceeds some threshold j ($\mathsf{search}(D_s, j)$) in time $\mathcal{O}\left(\log \frac{n}{n_s}\right)$. This speeds up the list intersection algorithm described in Section 3.4.4.

4.5.2 Predecessors and Successors

A problem closely related to rank and select is the *predecessor* problem (and its symmetric *successor* problem). Given a set of values $-\infty = x_0 < x_1 < \ldots < x_m < x_{m+1} = +\infty$, the predecessor problem is to build a data structure that, given a query y, finds $\mathsf{pred}(y) = x_k$ such that $x_k \leq y < x_{k+1}$. Similarly, the successor of y is $\mathsf{succ}(y) = x_k$ such that $x_{k-1} < y \leq x_k$.

If we have a bitvector $B[1, n = x_m]$ where only $B[x_i] = 1$ for all $1 \leq i \leq m$, then we can reduce pred and succ to analogous operations on bitvectors:

$$\mathsf{pred}(B, y) = \mathsf{select}(B, \mathsf{rank}(B, y)),$$

$$\mathsf{succ}(B, y) = \mathsf{select}(B, \mathsf{rank}(B, y - 1) + 1).$$

Therefore, any solution for bitvectors becomes a solution for the predecessor and successor problems. In general, in the predecessor problem, m is assumed to be much smaller than n. The bitvector solutions we have seen in this chapter obtain constant time only if we use $\Omega(n \log \log n / \log n)$ bits of space, which can be too much in this scenario. Our solution for very sparse bitvectors (Section 4.4) removes that $o(n)$ term from the space, but predecessor/successor queries require $\mathcal{O}(\log m)$ or $\mathcal{O}\left(\log \frac{n}{m}\right)$ time. This is not the best time that can be achieved for this problem (see the bibliographic notes), but the solution is practical and uses little space.

Even if one is willing to use $o(n)$ extra bits, our constant-time solution for **select** uses $\mathcal{O}(n/\log\log n)$ bits, which is rather high. Instead, a practical solution for **pred** (and, analogously, **succ**) is possible within $\mathcal{O}(n\log\log n/\log n)$ bits and in constant time.

The idea is in the same spirit of Section 4.2.2, defining superblocks of length $s = w^2$ and blocks of length $b = w$ in B. Array $R[1, \lceil n/s\rceil]$ now stores $R[j] = \text{pred}(B, (j-1)s)$, whereas array $R'[1, \lceil n/b\rceil]$ stores $R'[j] = \min((j-1)b - \text{pred}(B, (j-1)b), s)$. A query $\text{pred}(B, i)$ is then solved in three steps:

1. We clear the bits to the right of i in the block where i lies, $B[(\lceil i/b\rceil - 1)b + 1, \lceil i/b\rceil b]$. If the result is not the integer 0, then the answer is the position of the rightmost remaining 1.
2. Otherwise the predecessor is before position $(\lceil i/b\rceil - 1)b + 1$, so $\text{pred}(B, i) = \text{pred}(B, (\lceil i/b\rceil - 1)b)$. We then read $d = R'[\lceil i/b\rceil]$. If $d < s$, then the cell of R' contains a valid position, and the predecessor is at $(\lceil i/b\rceil - 1)b - d$.
3. Otherwise the predecessor is more than s positions away from $(\lceil i/b\rceil - 1)b + 1$, and therefore it is before $(\lceil i/s\rceil - 1)s + 1$, thus $\text{pred}(B, i) = \text{pred}(B, (\lceil i/s\rceil - 1)s)$. The answer is then directly stored at $R[\lceil i/s\rceil]$.

The remaining issue is how to find the rightmost 1 in a computer word (and the leftmost 1, to implement **succ**). Depending on how we are interpreting the order of the bits (recall the discussion at the end of Section 3.1), these correspond to finding the least or the most significant 1 in a word. A trick to find the position of the least significant bit, in C and for a 64-bit word `bits`, is as follows:

```
int decode[64] = {
       0, 1,56, 2,57,49,28, 3,61,58,42,50,38,29,17, 4,
      62,47,59,36,45,43,51,22,53,39,33,30,24,18,12, 5,
      63,55,48,27,60,41,37,16,46,35,44,21,52,32,23,11,
      54,26,40,15,34,20,31,10,25,14,19, 9,13, 8, 7, 6 };
return decode[(0x03f79d71b4ca8b09 * (bits & -bits))>>58]);
```

Unfortunately, a similar trick to find the highest bit is unknown, but as it corresponds to the binary logarithm of the number, many architectures offer a direct primitive to compute it. Standard libraries and compilers generally offer a call that uses the hardware instruction or a good implementation (it is called `fls` in FreeBSD, for example). A typical solution is to cast the number to floating-point format using a hardware instruction and then reading the bits that encode the exponent.

As usual, if all this fails, we can use small precomputed tables that work by chunks of $(\log n)/2$ bits (recall the decoding of γ-codes in Section 2.7).

Since **pred** and **succ** refer to finding the preceding or following 1 in a bitvector, they will also be written as pred_1 and succ_1, and we will refer to the corresponding 0-based versions as pred_0 and succ_0. Those can be solved analogously, by complementing the bits when building the tables or performing the bit tricks.

4.5.3 Dictionaries, Sets, and Hashing

The *dictionary* is one of the most fundamental abstract data types. It stores a set $\mathcal{K}$ of *n keys* with associated *values*. The keys are usually basic data types such as integers, floats, or strings, whereas the values can be any kind of data. The dictionary should answer two kinds of queries:

find(x): Returns whether $x \in \mathcal{K}$.
retrieve(x): Returns the value associated with x if $x \in \mathcal{K}$, or null otherwise.

The abstract data type that supports only operation find is called *set*. A common technique to handle sets and dictionaries is *hashing*. Hashing builds a function $h : \mathcal{X} \to [1, m]$ that maps a universe $\mathcal{X}$ onto a range of integers $[1, m]$, where m is usually much smaller than $|\mathcal{X}|$ (which can even be infinite). Then a classical solution for the dictionary problem is to find a suitable hash function that maps the data type $\mathcal{X}$ of the keys onto some range $[1, m]$, and to maintain an array $A[1, m]$ that stores in $A[h(x)]$ the data associated with each key $x \in \mathcal{K}$. The unused cells of A store a null value to signal that those keys are not in $\mathcal{K}$. If we want only set functionality, the array A is replaced by a bit array $B[1, m]$, so that $B[h(x)] = 1$ iff $x \in \mathcal{K}$.

The main problem in hashing are the *collisions*, that is, pairs $x \neq y$ for which $h(x) = h(y)$. Since usually $m < |\mathcal{X}|$, collisions are unavoidable. Thus the goal is to make them as unlikely as possible. A good hash function, without being actually random, behaves as uniformly random on $[1, m]$, so that the probability of a collision is about $\frac{1}{m}$.

The so-called families of *universal hash functions* guarantee that, if one chooses a function h at random from the family, it holds $\Pr(h(x) = h(y)) \leq \frac{1}{m}$ for any $x \neq y$. Therefore, h behaves as a uniform random variable. A simple such family is $h(x) = 1 + ((ax + b) \bmod p) \bmod m$ for a prime $p > m$, $1 \leq a < p$ and $0 \leq b < p$ (each choice of a and b gives an element of the family).

In *closed hashing* the collisions $h(x) = h(y)$ are resolved by putting x or y in another position of A. Assume x occupies the place $A[h(x)]$ and we want to insert y at the same position $A[h(y)]$. Then a second function $r(\cdot)$ is used, so that we probe the positions $h(y) + r(y)$, $h(y) + 2r(y)$, $h(y) + 3r(y)$, and so on (subtracting m when the position exceeds m), until a free slot in A is found. If we choose m to be a prime and $r(y) < m$, then this procedure will find a free slot if there is one. Upon an operation find or retrieve, we must traverse the same sequence of slots until we find y, or a null slot, at some $h(y) + k \cdot r(y)$. In the first case the datum is at $A[h(y) + k \cdot r(y)]$, whereas in the second case y is not in $\mathcal{K}$. The search cost is then $\mathcal{O}(k)$.

Collisions may defeat the main purpose of hashing: constant-time access. If m is very close to n, then we use less space for A, but the time to locate y grows beyond control: if we assume the probed positions are uniformly distributed, then the average value of k is $\frac{1}{\alpha} \ln \frac{1}{1-\alpha}$, where $\alpha = \frac{n}{m} \leq 1$ is called the *load factor*. Therefore, for good performance one needs to use m sufficiently larger than n; a value of $m > 1.25\,n$ (or $\alpha < 0.8$) is generally advised. As m grows, the hashing becomes faster, but the array A becomes larger as well.

Let us call s the number of bits needed to represent a key and its associated data. The size of $A[1, m]$ is thus $sm = \frac{1}{\alpha}sn$. If the set of keys is static, we can use bitvectors to reduce this space. Set up a bitvector $B[1, m]$ so that $B[i] = 1$ iff $A[i]$ is not null, and give it constant-time rank support (Section 4.2.2). Then compact the array A into $A'[1, n]$, so that $A'[\text{rank}_1(B, i)] = A[i]$ for each $B[i] = 1$. Now, $A[i]$ is null iff $B[i] = 0$, and if not null, then the value $A[i]$ is in $A'[\text{rank}_1(B, i)]$. This retains constant time and practicality, and reduces the space to $sn + m + o(m) = (s + \frac{1}{\alpha} + o(1))n$ bits. Therefore, the impact of α on the space is greatly reduced, and we can use a lower α value to reduce the number k of probes and improve performance.

Perfect Hash Functions

The possibility of collisions forces us to store the keys as part of the satellite data. That is, the s bits include $\log |\mathcal{X}|$ bits to store the key,[2] so as to compare the key of x with that of the element stored at $A[h(x)]$. In fact, any hashing scheme answering find and retrieve must use at least the $s'n$ bits of satellite data (where $s' \leq s$ does not account for the key) plus $\log \binom{|\mathcal{X}|}{n} = n \log \frac{|\mathcal{X}|}{n} + \mathcal{O}(n)$ bits to specify which elements of $\mathcal{X}$ are in $\mathcal{K}$.

When the set $\mathcal{K}$ of keys is static, it is possible to go one step further and design a *perfect hash function*, which has no collisions and thus offers $\mathcal{O}(1)$ worst-case time for find and retrieve. Operation find(x) then just checks if x coincides with the key stored at $A[h(x)]$: If x is not at $A[h(x)]$, then it is not in $\mathcal{K}$. If it is, operation retrieve(x) retrieves its satellite data from $A[h(x)]$.

In some cases, we want to query only for keys $x \in \mathcal{K}$, thus find is not needed and retrieve can be implemented without storing the keys in the satellite data (we just return $A[h(x)]$ with no checks). This lets us break the barrier of the $\log \binom{|\mathcal{X}|}{n}$ bits of storage. We describe a procedure to generate a perfect hash function that uses only $2.46n + o(n)$ bits, independently of the size of $\mathcal{X}$, plus the $s'n$ bits of satellite data.

Construction. We choose three hash functions from a universal family that maps $\mathcal{X}$ to the following intervals:

$$h_0(x) \in [0, m/3 - 1],$$

$$h_1(x) \in [m/3, 2m/3 - 1], \text{ and}$$

$$h_2(x) \in [2m/3, m - 1],$$

where $m = \lceil (c\,n)/3 \rceil \cdot 3$ for some constant $c > 1.23$ (slightly larger is enough).

Each element $x \in \mathcal{K}$ will be identified with a triple $e_x = (h_0(x), h_1(x), h_2(x))$. For each value $v \in [0, m - 1]$ we build l_v, a list of the triples where v is mentioned. Let n_v be the length of l_v. Each triple e_x also points to its three nodes in lists $l_{h_0(x)}$, $l_{h_1(x)}$, and $l_{h_2(x)}$.

Now we want to sort the triples in such a way that each new triple has a value v that is mentioned for the first time. We will do this by generating the reverse order, where each new triple has a value that is mentioned for the last time. Initially, we insert the v values for which $n_v > 0$ in a priority queue, sorted from lowest to highest n_v. We repeatedly extract the next v value from the queue. If $n_v > 1$, our functions $h_i(x)$ are not good, and we must start the whole process again (the value $m \approx 1.23n$ ensures that this will happen only a constant number of times, with very high probability). Instead,

---

[2] If $\mathcal{X}$ is infinite some variable-length encoding is used, think for example of string keys.

if $n_v = 1$, then the only triple $e_x \in l_v$ is the last one that mentions v in this process. We push e_x in a stack S. We also take the other two elements v' and v'' in e_x and remove e_x from $l_{v'}$ and $l_{v''}$, also decreasing $n_{v'}$ and $n_{v''}$ by 1 (this may change the position of v' and v'' in the priority queue; a value whose counter $n_{v'}$ or $n_{v''}$ reaches zero must be removed from the queue).

Once the process finishes, we have the triples sorted in S so that in each e_x there is a v that is mentioned for the first time (this is because the elements are extracted from S in reverse order). Now we initialize arrays $G[v] \leftarrow 3$ and $V[v] \leftarrow 0$ for all $v \in [0, m-1]$. Array G will be the final output of the algorithm, whereas V is used to indicate which values have been visited. Non-visited values v will always have $G[v] = 3$. Now we pop elements e_x from S. For $e_x = (v_0, v_1, v_2)$, let v_j be the first of the three with $V[v_j] = 0$ (and thus $G[v_j] = 3$). We then set

$$G[v_j] \leftarrow (j - G[v_0] - G[v_1] - G[v_2]) \bmod 3,$$

and also set $V[v_i] \leftarrow 1$ for $i = 0, 1, 2$ (note that, if any of those v_i was not already visited, then $G[v_i]$ will always stay in 3).

Algorithm 4.10 shows how we try to build G given tentative hash functions h_i : $\mathcal{K} \rightarrow [0, m/3 - 1]$. It takes $\mathcal{O}(n)$ time (the priority queue operations can be implemented in constant time because its values are in $[1, n]$ and the keys decrease by 1 each time). With high probability (and on average) we iterate $\mathcal{O}(1)$ times on this procedure until finding suitable hash functions h_i.

Hashing. Given the way we assign $G[v]$, it holds that $(G[v_0] + G[v_1] + G[v_2])$ mod $3 = j$ if j was the chosen value when we processed $e_x = (v_0, v_1, v_2)$. Our perfect hash function for x will then be $h(x) = v_j = h_j(x)$, which by our construction will be unique over all the values x (because each e_x chooses a v_j that appears for the first time). That is, we compute

$$h(x) = h_j(x), \quad \text{with } j = (G[h_0(x)] + G[h_1(x)] + G[h_2(x)]) \bmod 3.$$

This will yield a value in $[0, m-1] \approx [0, 1.23\,n]$, while using $2m \approx 2.46n$ bits of space (since $G[v] \in [0, 3]$, we use 2 bits per value).

Example 4.16 *Figure 4.6 illustrates the construction of a minimal perfect hash function. Let us assume $m = 12$ and take $h_0(x) = 5x$ mod 7, $h_1(x) = 7x$ mod 13, and $h_2 = 9x$ mod 17 (we will take them modulo $m/3 = 4$ and add $m/3 = 4$ and $2m/3 = 8$ to h_1 and h_2, respectively). We hash the set $\mathcal{K} = \{100, 200, 300, 400, 500\}$, obtaining the corresponding triples $(3, 7, 8), (2, 5, 11), (2, 7, 10), (1, 5, 9), (1, 7, 8)$. The multiplicities of the values mentioned in the triples, from lowest to highest, are $n_3 = 1$, $n_9 = 1, n_{10} = 1, n_{11} = 1, n_1 = 2, n_2 = 2, n_5 = 2, n_8 = 2, n_7 = 3$. Now let us process them by increasing n_v.*

We take $n_3 = 1$ and then append triple $(3, 7, 8)$ in front of S. We update $n_7 \leftarrow 2$ and $n_8 \leftarrow 1$. Now we take $n_8 = 1$ and then append triple $(1, 7, 8)$ in front of S. We update $n_1 \leftarrow 1$ and $n_7 \leftarrow 1$. We take $n_1 = 1$ and then append triple $(1, 5, 9)$ in front of S. We update $n_5 \leftarrow 1$ and $n_9 \leftarrow 0$ (value 9 is then removed from the queue). Now we take $n_5 = 1$ and append triple $(2, 5, 11)$ in front of S. We update $n_2 \leftarrow 1$ and $n_{11} \leftarrow 0$ (node 11 abandons the queue). Finally, we take $n_2 = 1$ and append the last triple, $(2, 7, 10)$,

---

Algorithm 4.10: Building a perfect hash function. Uses operations *push/pop* on stack S, and *insert/extractMin* on priority queue Q.

Input : Universal hash functions $h_0, h_1, h_2 : \mathcal{X} \to [0, m/3 - 1]$
Output: Returns $G[1, n]$ built from the hash functions, or null if it fails.

1 Allocate arrays $L[0, m - 1]$ of lists and $N[0, m - 1]$ of numbers
2 **for** $v \leftarrow 0$ **to** $m - 1$ **do** $L[v] \leftarrow$ null; $N[v] \leftarrow 0$
3 **for** $x \in \mathcal{K}$ **do**
4 $\quad$ $(v_0, v_1, v_2) \leftarrow (h_0(x), m/3 + h_1(x), 2m/3 + h_2(x))$
5 $\quad$ Allocate a node e with fields *vals* and *ptrs*
6 $\quad$ **for** $j \leftarrow 0$ **to** 2 **do**
7 $\quad\quad$ Allocate list node p_j and link it in $L[v_j]$; $N[v_j] \leftarrow N[v_j] + 1$
8 $\quad\quad$ $p_j.triple \leftarrow e$
9 $\quad$ $e.vals \leftarrow (v_0, v_1, v_2)$; $e.ptrs \leftarrow (p_0, p_1, p_2)$
10 Allocate priority queue $Q[1,m]$ of values v sorted by increasing $N[v]$
11 **for** $v \leftarrow 0$ **to** $m - 1$ **do**
12 $\quad$ **if** $N[v] > 0$ **then** $insert(Q, v)$
13 Allocate stack $S[1, n]$ of triples
14 **while** Q *is not empty* **do**
15 $\quad$ $v \leftarrow extractMin(Q)$
16 $\quad$ **if** $N[v] > 1$ **then return** null (also free N, L, Q, and S)
17 $\quad$ $p \leftarrow L[v]$ (the only value in the list); $e \leftarrow p.triple$
18 $\quad$ $(v_0, v_1, v_2) \leftarrow e.vals$; $push(S, (v_0, v_1, v_2))$
19 $\quad$ **for** $j \leftarrow 0$ **to** 2 **do**
20 $\quad\quad$ Unlink $e.ptrs[j]$ from $L[v_j]$ and free it
21 $\quad\quad$ $N[v_j] \leftarrow N[v_j] - 1$ (update position of v_j in Q)
22 $\quad\quad$ **if** $N[v_j] = 0$ **then** $extractMin(Q)$ (removes v_j)
23 $\quad$ Free node e
24 Allocate array $G[0, m - 1]$ over $[0, 3]$ and bit array $V[0, m - 1]$
25 **for** $v \leftarrow 0$ **to** $m - 1$ **do** $G[v] \leftarrow 3$; $V[v] \leftarrow 0$
26 **for** $i \leftarrow 1$ **to** n **do**
27 $\quad$ $(v_0, v_1, v_2) \leftarrow pop(S)$
28 $\quad$ $j \leftarrow$ minimum in $\{0, 1, 2\}$ with $V[v_j] = 0$ (there is one)
29 $\quad$ $G[v_j] \leftarrow (j - G[v_0] - G[v_1] - G[v_2]) \bmod 3$
30 $\quad$ **for** $j \leftarrow 0$ **to** 2 **do** $V[v_j] \leftarrow 1$
31 Free N, L, Q, S, and V; **return** G

---

in front of S. The remaining counters become 0, the queue becomes empty, and we stop.

The sorted list is then $(2, 7, 10), (2, 5, 11), (1, 5, 9), (1, 7, 8), (3, 7, 8)$. We now initialize $G[0, 11] = 3$ and start processing the tuples (we omit the management of V to detect visited nodes).

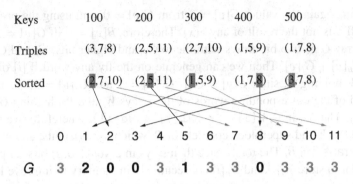

Figure 4.6. Building a minimal perfect hash function. On the top we show the original keys, and then how they are mapped to triples. The triples are then sorted so that there is a new value (grayed) in each triple when read left to right. Now the sorted triples are processed to form G. The grayed value sets a new cell in G (black arrow and black numbers in G) and marks the other 2 as visited (gray arrows, only shown when they mark new elements). The unassigned values in G retain their original value 3 (in gray).

For the first, $(2, 7, 10)$, the first non-visited value is $v_0 = 2$, so we assign $G[2] \leftarrow (0 - G[2] - G[7] - G[10]) \bmod 3 = 0$. The second tuple is $(2, 5, 11)$. Its first non-visited value is $v_1 = 5$, so we assign $G[5] \leftarrow (1 - G[2] - G[5] - G[11]) \bmod 3 = 1$. The third tuple is $(1, 5, 9)$. Its first non-visited value is $v_0 = 1$, so we assign $G[1] \leftarrow (0 - G[1] - G[5] - G[9]) \bmod 3 = 2$. The fourth tuple is $(1, 7, 8)$. Its first non-visited value is $v_2 = 8$, so we assign $G[8] \leftarrow (2 - G[1] - G[7] - G[8]) \bmod 3 = 0$. The last tuple is $(3, 7, 8)$. Its first non-visited value is $v_0 = 3$, so we assign $G[3] \leftarrow (0 - G[3] - G[7] - G[8]) \bmod 3 = 0$. Now we have our final output, shown in the figure.

Let us hash the values in $\mathcal{K}$ to verify that there are no collisions. For example, to compute $h(100)$ we find $j = (G[h_0(100)] + G[h_1(100)] + G[h_2(100)]) \bmod 3 = (G[3] + G[7] + G[8]) \bmod 3 = (0 + 3 + 0) \bmod 3 = 0$. Therefore, $h(100) = h_0(100) = 3$ (recall that we take h_j modulo $m/3 = 4$ and add the appropriate shifts). Similarly, $h(200) = 5$, $h(300) = 2$, $h(400) = 1$, $h(500) = 8$.

Finally, we can further reduce the $2.46n$ bits of G to about $(1.23 \cdot \log 3)n$ by rewriting any $G[v] = 3$ as $G[v] = 0$ (which makes no difference in the hashing formula), and then take advantage that G contains values in $\{0, 1, 2\}$, that is, trits. As shown in Example 3.6, we can pack 20 trits in a 32-bit word (or 40 trits in 64 bits). Then G occupies $(1.23 \cdot \frac{32}{20})n = 1.968n < 2n$ bits (we can choose $m = 1.25n > 1.23n$ to enjoy a faster construction, and then the space is exactly $2n$ bits).

Note, however, that the space for satellite data is $s'm$ bits, not $s'n$ as promised. In some cases we do not have any satellite data (for example, we may use perfect hashing to generate short unique identifiers for complex objects), and then this arrangement is convenient. However, if $s' > 2$, it is better to resort to the technique we describe next, which uses $2.46n + s'n + o(n)$ bits.

Minimal Perfect Hashing

Perfect hash functions with $m = n$ are called *minimal*. To make our construction minimal, we can use rank_1 on a bitvector $B[0, m-1]$ as before, thus raising the space to $(2n + m) + o(n) \approx 3.23n + o(n)$ bits. This can be reduced back to $2.46n + o(n)$ by distinguishing again the values $G[v] = 3$ from $G[v] = 0$, and using the property that $G[v] = 3$ iff v is not the result of any $h(x)$. Therefore, $B[v] = 0$ iff $G[v] = 3$. We can store the array G as two bit arrays with the lower and higher bits, G_l and G_h, so that $G[v] = 2G_h[v] + G_l[v]$. Then we can generate on the fly any word $W[i]$ of the integer array W holding B: since $B[v] = 0$ iff $G_h[v] = 1$ and $G_l[v] = 1$, we negate the bitwise-and of the corresponding words of the arrays W_l and W_h holding G_l and G_h, respectively. That is, in C, `W[i] = ~(Wl[i] & Wh[i])`. Therefore, we only need to store the block and superblock counters of B, which use $o(n)$ bits, and not B itself, to compute rank_1 on B. The total space then stays in $2.46n + o(n)$ bits. In practice, it is convenient to store $W_l[i]$ and $W_h[i]$ consecutively in memory to improve locality of reference.

Alternatively, we can represent $B[0, m-1]$ explicitly, so that we know that $G[v] = 3$ if $B[v] = 0$, and otherwise the value is packed in $G'[\mathsf{rank}_1(B, v)]$, in the shorter array $G'[1, n]$ of the values that are not 3. Since those values are in $\{0, 1, 2\}$, we can use the technique already described to pack G' in $\frac{32}{20}n = 1.6n$ bits. If we use a compressed bitvector for B, it uses $m\mathcal{H}_0(B) + o(m) = m\mathcal{H}(1.23^{-1}) + o(m) < 0.86n + o(n)$ bits. The total is again $2.46n + o(n)$ bits.

Monotone Minimal Perfect Hashing

Assume the universe is an integer range, $\mathcal{X} = [1, u]$, and we want our perfect hash function to also preserve the order between the keys, that is, $h(x) < h(y)$ if $x < y$. The data can then be interpreted as a bitvector $B[1, u]$ with n 1s, where we must support queries $\mathsf{rank}_1(B, i)$ only if $i \in \mathcal{K}$, but we cannot do $\mathsf{rank}(B, i)$ if $B[i] = 0$, and cannot even tell the value of $B[i]$. As this query support is insufficient to recover B, we can store these hash functions in less than $\log \binom{u}{n}$ bits.

A trivial way to add monotonicity on top of minimal perfect hashing is to associate the position of each key as satellite information. This requires, however, $n \log n$ additional bits. Let us show how to reduce this space.

We choose a subset $\mathcal{K}' \subset \mathcal{K}$ taking every $(\log n)$th element, thus $|\mathcal{K}'| = n/\log n$. We then divide $\mathcal{K}$ into the resulting $n/\log n$ ranges $\mathcal{K}_1, \mathcal{K}_2, \ldots$, and build a small trivial monotone minimal perfect hash function for each range of $\log n$ keys. Since we need to store only the position j inside the range (the global position, for range i, is $(i-1)\log n + j$), this requires in total $n \log \log n$ bits for the satellite data, plus $\mathcal{O}(n)$ bits for the minimal perfect hash functions themselves.

The remaining problem is how to find the range corresponding to a given key x. Let k_i be the smallest element in $\mathcal{K}_i$. Then x must be sought in $\mathcal{K}_i$ if $k_i \leq x < k_{i+1}$. Let ℓ_i be the number of highest bits shared by all the elements in $\mathcal{K}_i$, and let p_i be the number formed with the ℓ_i highest bits of k_i. Then x can belong to $\mathcal{K}_i$ only if it shares its ℓ_i highest bits with k_i.

We store a minimal perfect hash function for all the values in $\mathcal{K}$, associating their corresponding ℓ_i value as satellite data. This takes other $n \log \log u + \mathcal{O}(n)$ bits of space, since $\ell_i \leq \log u$. This function is then used to obtain the ℓ_i value corresponding to the search key x.

Note that no two pairs (p_i, ℓ_i) and (p_j, ℓ_j) can be equal. To see this, assume $(p_i, \ell_i) = (p_j, \ell_j)$ for $i < j$. Notice that there must be a key starting with $p_i . 0$ and another starting with $p_i . 1$ in $\mathcal{K}_i$; otherwise the keys would share at least $\ell_i + 1$ highest bits. But the same must happen in $\mathcal{K}_j$, which is not possible because there can be no numbers starting with $p_i . 0$ in $\mathcal{K}_j$, since all its values are larger than those in $\mathcal{K}_i$ and there are already elements starting with $p_i . 1$ in $\mathcal{K}_i$.

This means that we can obtain distinct numbers of fixed length $\log u + \log \log u$, by encoding the numbers ℓ_i in $\log \log u$ bits, concatenating the ℓ_i bits of p_i, and then padding with 0s. Those $n / \log n$ distinct numbers are then stored in another minimal perfect hash function, which gives the corresponding range identifier i as satellite data. Since it stores only $n / \log n$ values, the total space is $\mathcal{O}(n)$ bits. Given x, and knowing its corresponding ℓ_i value, we encode its ℓ_i highest bits as described and find its corresponding range number i with this hash function. Then we find x in $\mathcal{K}_i$ as explained.

Example 4.17 *Let us build a monotone minimal perfect hash function for the keys* $\mathcal{K} = \{100, 200, \ldots, 900\}$. *Let us make ranges of 3 elements, so we have* $\mathcal{K}_1 = \{100, 200, 300\}$, $\mathcal{K}_2 = \{400, 500, 600\}$, *and* $\mathcal{K}_3 = \{700, 800, 900\}$.

Our first substructure is a minimal perfect hash function for each $\mathcal{K}_i$, *associating as satellite data the relative position of each element in* $\mathcal{K}_i$. *For example, in* $\mathcal{K}_3$, *we associate 700 with 1, 800 with 2, and 900 with 3.*

Regarded as 10-bit numbers, the values are

$\mathcal{K}_1$			$\mathcal{K}_2$			$\mathcal{K}_3$		
100	=	0001100100	400	=	0110010000	700	=	1010111100
200	=	0011001000	500	=	0111110100	800	=	1100100000
300	=	0100101100	600	=	1001011000	900	=	1110000100

so the numbers in $\mathcal{K}_1$ *share the prefix* 0, *of length 1, those in* $\mathcal{K}_2$ *share the prefix* ε, *of length 0, and those in* $\mathcal{K}_3$ *share the prefix* 1, *of length 1. Therefore, we store a global minimal perfect hash function for* $\mathcal{K}$, *associating length 1 to the values 100, 200, 300, 700, 800, and 900, and length 0 to the values 400, 500, and 600.*

Finally, since the lengths can be represented in one bit and the shared prefixes are also of at most one bit, we concatenate one bit for the length and one for the prefix, obtaining 10 = 2 *for* $\mathcal{K}_1$, 00 = 0 *for* $\mathcal{K}_2$ *(could also have been* 01*), and* 11 = 3 *for* $\mathcal{K}_3$. *Therefore, we store a small minimal perfect hash function associating the subsets with the numbers: we associate 1 (meaning* $\mathcal{K}_1$*) to* 2 = 10, *2 (meaning* $\mathcal{K}_2$*) to* 0 = 00, *and 3 (meaning* $\mathcal{K}_3$*) to* 3 = 11.

Now let us query for the key 700 = 1010111100. *We use the global hash function to find that its associated length is 1. Concatenating the length (using one bit) and its highest bit, we get* 11 = 3. *The last hash table gives us the value 3 associated with the key* 3 = 11, *so we know 700 belongs to* $\mathcal{K}_3$. *Next we query the monotone minimal perfect hash function of* $\mathcal{K}_3$, *where 700 is associated the value 1. But since we are in* $\mathcal{K}_3$, *we must add to it the* $3 \cdot 2$ *elements in* $\mathcal{K}_1$ *and* $\mathcal{K}_2$, *thus the final result is* $1 + 3 \cdot 2 = 7$.

Thus, we have monotone minimal perfect hashing in $\mathcal{O}(n \log \log u)$ bits and $\mathcal{O}(1)$ time. In the bibliographic notes we point to other results. Note that this technique cannot be used to find the predecessor of x (Section 4.5.2), because it works only if $x \in \mathcal{K}$.

4.6 Summary

With $o(n)$ bits of space on top of a bit array $B[1, n]$, we can support **access**, **rank**, and **select** operations in constant time. In practice, the $o(n)$ bits can be about $0.03\,n$ for **rank** (reaching $0.06\,n$ to include **select**) and the operations require a few cache misses (not always guaranteed for **select**). For faster operations, about $0.15\,n$–$0.25\,n$ bits are needed for each of **rank**, select_0, and select_1. Still, **select** is always 2–3 times slower slower than **rank** in practice. It is also possible to compress B to $n\mathcal{H}_0(B) + o(n)$ bits and retain those constant times, where the $o(n)$ bits are below $0.1\,n$ in practice (plus the desired overhead for **rank** and **select**). When the number m of 1s in B is much smaller than n, an alternative using $n\mathcal{H}_0(B) + \mathcal{O}(m)$ bits poses a much lower overhead over the entropy. It supports select_1 in constant time and **access** and **rank** in time $\mathcal{O}\big(\log \frac{n}{m}\big)$. All the structures reviewed are easily built in linear time and within the final space they need. Apart from representations of partial sums, predecessor/successor structures, and hashing, bitvectors underlie virtually every data structure we will see throughout the book.

4.7 Bibliographic Notes

Plain bitvectors. Jacobson (1989) initiated the study of **rank** and **select** operations on bitvectors stored in plain form (that is, as bit arrays). Although he expressed the operation times in terms of number of bit accesses, his solution for **rank** is actually constant-time on the RAM model and corresponds to what we describe in Section 4.2.2. González *et al.* (2005) studied the simpler solution we describe in Section 4.2.1 to reduce the space overhead. Okanohara and Sadakane (2007) proposed the three-level directory we describe in Section 4.2.2, reducing the space of their "dense arrays" to $0.19\,n$ bits. Vigna (2008) and Gog and Petri (2014) proposed the idea of interleaving the arrays, obtaining $0.25\,n$ bits.

The popcount techniques we described are collected by Knuth (2009, Sec. 7.1.3), who gives the 64-bit version together with many other useful bit manipulation techniques. These include the solution we give to find the least significant 1 in a word.

Clark (1996) obtained the first constant-time solution for **select** queries. The variant we describe in Section 4.3.3 is close to Clark's proposal (he does not use bitvector V but rather leaves free unused space in I). Gog and Petri (2014) proposed the idea we sketch at the end of that section about not storing I for the miniblocks. This turns out to be very efficient in practice. González *et al.* (2005) showed that the binary search solution of Section 4.3.1 performs reasonably well for short bitvectors (up to around $n = 2^{20}$). Vigna (2008) called "hinted binary search" the idea of Section 4.3.2 and studied several other efficient combinations for 64-bit architectures.

It has also been shown how to combine the extra structures of **rank** and **select**, by exploiting their complementarity, in order to considerably reduce their space (Navarro and Providel, 2012; Zhou *et al.*, 2013).

Compressed bitvectors. The compression to zero-order entropy of Sections 4.1.1 and 4.2.3 builds on ideas started by Pagh (2001) and completed by Raman *et al.* (2007). Their version yields constant time. Claude and Navarro (2008) studied the practical variant that uses sampled pointers, but stored a precomputed table to decode the blocks, and thus paid the high space overhead due to short blocks. Navarro and Providel (2012) proposed the version that reconstructs the block from its offset on the fly, and Gog and Petri (2014) studied practical improvements over it. The recurrence to map between blocks and offsets is much older; see, for example, Davisson (1966).

Extensions for multiword arithmetic exist for various architectures; see http://en.wikipedia.org/wiki/Streaming_SIMD_Extensions for a popular one. An excellent package to do multiword arithmetic by software is the *GNU Multiple Precision Arithmetic Library (GMP)* at http://gmplib.org.

The idea of Section 4.1.2 for high-order compression was described by Ferragina and Venturini (2007) for general strings, supporting **access** in constant time. Adding **rank** and **select** for bitvectors, as well as considering a Huffman coding and sampled pointers, are natural variations. Beskers and Fischer (2014) studied practical implementations of this idea.

Very sparse bitvectors. The structure of Section 4.4 was presented by Okanohara and Sadakane (2007), based on much older proposals by Fano (1971) and Elias (1974). Okanohara and Sadakane called it "sparse arrays"; they also introduced other ideas to store sparse bitvectors. They used other structures to represent bitvector H in sparse arrays, and thus their time complexities look different from the ones we obtained. Gog and Petri (2014) presented improved implementations of these sparse arrays. Kärkkäinen et al. (2014) studied combined formats where distinct areas of the bitvectors are encoded differently. Our representation for bitvectors with runs in Section 4.4.3 was proposed by Delpratt et al. (2006, Sec. 3.2). Foschini et al. (2006) explored several other practical implementations of bitvectors with runs.

Space lower bounds. Apart from the n data bits, the constant-time solutions we described use $\mathcal{O}(n \log \log n / \log n)$ bits for **rank** and $\mathcal{O}(n / \log \log n)$ bits for **select**. Golynski (2007) proved that, if the bitvector B is stored in plain form, so that we can access any word-size block of B in constant time, then $\Omega(n \log \log n / \log n)$ bits are necessary to have constant-time operations. He also achieved $\mathcal{O}(n \log \log n / \log n)$ extra bits of space for constant-time **select**, but the solution is far from practical. Later Golynski et al. (2007) achieved constant time for the operations using $n\mathcal{H}_0(B) + \mathcal{O}(n \log \log n / \log^2 n)$ bits, thus showing that the lower bound can be broken by storing B in a convenient form. Pătraşcu (2008) further improved this result, obtaining $n\mathcal{H}_0(B) + \mathcal{O}(n / \log^c n)$ bits while answering **rank** and **select** in time $\mathcal{O}(c)$, for any constant c. Pătraşcu and Viola (2010) then proved that this space is essentially optimal, which means that **rank** queries cannot run in constant time within $n\mathcal{H}_0(B) + \mathcal{O}(m)$ bits when the number of 1s is $m = o(n / \log^c n)$ for every constant c. Finer tradeoffs considering the number of 1s in B have also been studied (Golynski, 2007; Golynski et al., 2007; Grossi et al., 2009; Golynski et al., 2014).

Raman et al. (2007) also considered a weaker scenario where $\text{rank}(B, i)$ is computed only if $B[i] = 1$ (a null value is returned otherwise), and $\text{select}_1(B, j)$ is supported, but not $\text{select}_0(B, j)$. These operations can be supported in constant time using only $n\mathcal{H}_0(B) + o(m) + \mathcal{O}(\log \log n)$ bits.

Partial sums. Maintaining partial sums over n numbers of ℓ bits is usually studied in the dynamic scenario, where changes to the numbers are allowed. A result that applies in the static case is an $\Omega(\sqrt{\log n / \log \log n})$ time lower bound for **search** when $\ell n + o(\ell n)$ bits of space are used (Hon *et al.*, 2011). They also present a structure matching this lower bound for **search** and with constant time for **sum** within this space. The dynamic case will be discussed in length in Section 12.9.

Predecessor queries. Beame and Fich (2002) proved that constant time for predecessors is not possible within $\mathcal{O}(m \operatorname{polylog} n)$ space. Gupta *et al.* (2007) explored some schemes where $m \log \frac{n}{m}(1 + o(1))$ bits are used and the optimal times for the predecessor problem are reached for **rank** queries. This structure is sensitive to the distribution of the 1s in the bitvector, and it would obtain $N + o(N)$ bits of space in the variable-length partial sums of Section 4.5.1. In fact, *all* the binary searches we have made on arrays of n elements of numbers in $[1, N]$ can be sped up, in theory, by sampling one element out of $\log^2 N$ and inserting them into a predecessor data structure like a bounded ordered dictionary (Mehlhorn and Näher, 1990), which will take $\mathcal{O}(n / \log N)$ bits of space. The predecessor structure finds the pair of sampled values that enclose the answer in $\mathcal{O}(\log \log N)$ time, and a final binary search in the $\log^2 N$ elements between the sampled values completes the search in another $\mathcal{O}(\log \log N)$ time. Good practical implementations of this data structure exist (Dementiev *et al.*, 2004; Nash and Gregg, 2008), yet the difference with a binary search is not so significant on the smaller sampled universes we are considering.

Hashing. Hashing is a classical topic in algorithms and is presented in most textbooks, such as those by Motwani and Raghavan (1995) or Cormen *et al.* (2009). Universal hashing was proposed by Carter and Wegman (1979) and perfect hashing by Fredman *et al.* (1984). A structure supporting queries **find** in constant time and asymptotically optimal space was introduced by Brodnik and Munro (1999). If we give away operation **find**, and aim only to return a unique value for keys in the set, then it is possible to use $\mathcal{O}(n)$ bits, as we have shown. The minimum space needed to store a minimal perfect hash function is $n / \ln 2 \approx 1.44n$ bits (Fredman *et al.*, 1984). Our presentation closely follows the description of Botelho *et al.* (2013), which uses around $2.7n$ bits (we showed how to use slightly less, while still being practical). The idea is related to a previous article (Chazelle *et al.*, 2004), where it is described less clearly, as a by-product. The best current implementation of minimal perfect hash functions achieves nearly $2n$ bits (Belazzougui *et al.*, 2009) and uses bitvectors to achieve minimality.

The most efficient implementations of monotone minimal perfect hash functions are those by Belazzougui *et al.* (2011). They obtain $\mathcal{O}(n \log \log u)$ bits of space while hashing in constant time in the way we have shown. With a more sophisticated mechanism, they reduce the space to $\mathcal{O}(n \log \log \log u)$ bits, although the hashing time raises to $\mathcal{O}(\log \log u)$. It is not known if one can achieve $\mathcal{O}(n)$ bits of space with monotonicity.

Bibliography

Beame, P. and Fich, F. E. (2002). Optimal bounds for the predecessor problem and related problems. *Journal of Computer and System Sciences*, **65**(1), 38–72.

Belazzougui, D., Botelho, F. C., and Dietzfelbinger, M. (2009). Hash, displace, and compress. In *17th Annual European Symposium on Algorithms (ESA)*, LNCS 5757, pages 682–693.

Belazzougui, D., Boldi, P., Pagh, R., and Vigna, S. (2011). Theory and practice of monotone minimal perfect hashing. *ACM Journal of Experimental Algorithmics*, **16**(3), article 2.

Beskers, K. and Fischer, J. (2014). High-order entropy compressed bit vectors with rank/select. *Algorithms*, **7**, 608–620.

Botelho, F. C., Pagh, R., and Ziviani, N. (2013). Practical perfect hashing in nearly optimal space. *Information Systems*, **38**(1), 108–131.

Brodnik, A. and Munro, J. I. (1999). Membership in constant time and almost-minimum space. *SIAM Journal on Computing*, **28**(5), 1627–1640.

Carter, L. and Wegman, M. N. (1979). Universal classes of hash functions. *Journal of Computer and System Sciences*, **18**(2), 143–154.

Chazelle, B., Kilian, J., Rubinfeld, R., and Tal, A. (2004). The Bloomier filter: an efficient data structure for static support lookup tables. In *Proc. 15th Annual ACM-SIAM Symposium on Discrete Algorithms (SODA)*, pages 30–39.

Clark, D. R. (1996). *Compact PAT Trees*. Ph.D. thesis, University of Waterloo, Canada.

Claude, F. and Navarro, G. (2008). Practical rank/select queries over arbitrary sequences. In *Proc. 15th International Symposium on String Processing and Information Retrieval (SPIRE)*, LNCS 5280, pages 176–187.

Cormen, T. H., Leiserson, C. E., Rivest, R. L., and Stein, C. (2009). *Introduction to Algorithms*. MIT Press, 3rd edition.

Davisson, L. D. (1966). Comments on 'Sequence time coding for data compression.' *Proceedings of the IEEE (Corresp.)*, **54**, 2010.

Delpratt, O., Rahman, N., and Raman, R. (2006). Engineering the LOUDS succinct tree representation. In *Proc. 5th International Workshop on Experimental Algorithms (WEA)*, LNCS 4007, pages 134–145.

Dementiev, R., Kettner, L., Mehnert, J., and Sanders, P. (2004). Engineering a sorted list data structure for 32 bit key. In *Proc. 6th Workshop on Algorithm Engineering and Experiments (ALENEX)*, pages 142–151.

Elias, P. (1974). Efficient storage and retrieval by content and address of static files. *Journal of the ACM*, **21**, 246–260.

Fano, R. (1971). On the number of bits required to implement an associative memory. Memo 61, Computer Structures Group, Project MAC, Massachusetts.

Ferragina, P. and Venturini, R. (2007). A simple storage scheme for strings achieving entropy bounds. *Theoretical Computer Science*, **371**(1), 115–121.

Foschini, L., Grossi, R., Gupta, A., and Vitter, J. S. (2006). When indexing equals compression: Experiments with compressing suffix arrays and applications. *ACM Transactions on Algorithms*, **2**(4), 611–639.

Fredman, M. L., Komlós, J., and Szemerédi, E. (1984). Storing a sparse table with $O(1)$ worst case access time. *Journal of the ACM*, **31**(3), 538–544.

Gog, S. and Petri, M. (2014). Optimized succinct data structures for massive data. *Software Practice and Experience*, **44**(11), 1287–1314.

Golynski, A. (2007). Optimal lower bounds for rank and select indexes. *Theoretical Computer Science*, **387**(3), 348–359.

Golynski, A., Grossi, R., Gupta, A., Raman, R., and Rao, S. S. (2007). On the size of succinct indices. In *Proc. 15th Annual European Symposium on Algorithms (ESA)*, LNCS 4698, pages 371–382.

Golynski, A., Orlandi, A., Raman, R., and Rao, S. S. (2014). Optimal indexes for sparse bit vectors. *Algorithmica*, **69**(4), 906–924.

González, R., Grabowski, S., Mäkinen, V., and Navarro, G. (2005). Practical implementation of rank and select queries. In *Proc. Posters of 4th Workshop on Efficient and Experimental Algorithms (WEA)*, pages 27–38.

Grossi, R., Orlandi, A., Raman, R., and Rao, S. S. (2009). More haste, less waste: Lowering the redundancy in fully indexable dictionaries. In *Proc. 26th International Symposium on Theoretical Aspects of Computer Science (STACS)*, LIPIcs 3, pages 517–528.

Gupta, A., Hon, W.-K., Shah, R., and Vitter, J. S. (2007). Compressed data structures: Dictionaries and data-aware measures. *Theoretical Computer Science*, **387**(3), 313–331.

Hon, W.-K., Sadakane, K., and Sung, W.-K. (2011). Succinct data structures for searchable partial sums with optimal worst-case performance. *Theoretical Computer Science*, **412**(39), 5176–5186.

Jacobson, G. (1989). Space-efficient static trees and graphs. In *Proc. 30th IEEE Symposium on Foundations of Computer Science (FOCS)*, pages 549–554.

Kärkkäinen, J., Kempa, D., and Puglisi, S. J. (2014). Hybrid compression of bitvectors for the FM-index. In *Proc. 24th Data Compression Conference (DCC)*, pages 302–311.

Knuth, D. E. (2009). *The Art of Computer Programming, volume 4: Fascicle 1: Bitwise Tricks & Techniques; Binary Decision Diagrams*. Addison-Wesley Professional.

Mehlhorn, K. and Näher, S. (1990). Bounded ordered dictionaries in $O(\log \log N)$ time and $O(n)$ space. *Information Processing Letters*, **35**(4), 183–189.

Motwani, R. and Raghavan, P. (1995). *Randomized Algorithms*. Cambridge University Press.

Nash, N. and Gregg, D. (2008). Comparing integer data structures for 32 and 64 bit keys. In *Proc. 10th Workshop on Algorithm Engineering and Experiments (ALENEX)*, LNCS 5038, pages 28–42.

Navarro, G. and Providel, E. (2012). Fast, small, simple rank/select on bitmaps. In *Proc. 11th International Symposium on Experimental Algorithms (SEA)*, LNCS 7276, pages 295–306.

Okanohara, D. and Sadakane, K. (2007). Practical entropy-compressed rank/select dictionary. In *Proc. 9th Workshop on Algorithm Engineering and Experiments (ALENEX)*, pages 60–70.

Pagh, R. (2001). Low redundancy in static dictionaries with constant query time. *SIAM Journal of Computing*, **31**(2), 353–363.

Pătraşcu, M. (2008). Succincter. In *Proc. 49th Annual IEEE Symposium on Foundations of Computer Science (FOCS)*, pages 305–313.

Pătraşcu, M. and Viola, E. (2010). Cell-probe lower bounds for succinct partial sums. In *Proc. 21st Annual ACM-SIAM Symposium on Discrete Algorithms (SODA)*, pages 117–122.

Raman, R., Raman, V., and Rao, S. S. (2007). Succinct indexable dictionaries with applications to encoding k-ary trees, prefix sums and multisets. *ACM Transactions on Algorithms*, **3**(4), article 43.

Vigna, S. (2008). Broadword implementation of rank/select queries. In *Proc. 7th International Workshop on Experimental Algorithms (WEA)*, LNCS 5038, pages 154–168.

Zhou, D., Andersen, D. G., and Kaminsky, M. (2013). Space-efficient, high-performance rank and select structures on uncompressed bit sequences. In *Proc. 12th International Symposium on Experimental Algorithms (SEA)*, LNCS 7933, pages 151–163.

CHAPTER 5

Permutations

A *permutation* π of $[1, n]$ is a reordering of the values $\{1, 2, \ldots, n\}$. It can be regarded as an array $\pi[1, n]$ where each value $1 \le i \le n$ appears exactly once. Permutations are useful as internal components of many data structures; we will see an example in Section 6.1.

There are $n!$ permutations of $[1, n]$, and therefore their worst-case entropy (Section 2.1) is $\log n!$. Using Stirling's approximation to the factorial, this is

$$\log n! = \log\left(\sqrt{2\pi n}(n/e)^n (1 + \mathcal{O}(1/n))\right) = n \log n - \Theta(n)$$

bits. This means that a basic array representation with cells of $\lceil \log n \rceil$ bits (Section 3.1) is close to being optimal. Such an array representation provides, in constant time, the basic computation of $\pi(i)$ for any i. In many cases, however, we need to support some extended functionality:

$\pi^{-1}(i)$: The inverse permutation of i, that is, the number j such that $\pi(j) = i$.
$\pi^k(i)$: The iterated application of π over i, that is, $\pi(\pi(\ldots \pi(i)\ldots))$ k times. We allow k to be negative, meaning the iterated application of π^{-1}.

Both π^{-1} or any π^k, for any fixed k, are permutations themselves and thus can be supported in constant time by explicitly storing the corresponding array. This requires $n\lceil \log n \rceil$ bits for each desired k. In this chapter we will show a data structure that, using $(1 + \epsilon)n \log n + \mathcal{O}(n)$ bits, for any $\epsilon > 0$, supports all of the above operations, simultaneously, in time $\mathcal{O}(1/\epsilon)$.

Then we will consider families of compressible permutations, which appear in various applications of interest. In particular, we will show how a permutation π that can be split into ρ ascending runs can be represented in $n \log \rho(1 + o(1))$ bits (and less), so that any $\pi(i)$ and $\pi^{-1}(i)$ can be computed in time $\mathcal{O}(\log \rho)$.

5.1 Inverse Permutations

A simple way to compute $\pi^{-1}(i)$ is to call $i_0 = i$ and compute $i_1 = \pi(i_0) = \pi(i)$, $i_2 = \pi(i_1) = \pi(\pi(i))$, $i_3 = \pi(i_2) = \pi(\pi(\pi(i)))$, and so on, until $i_k = \pi(i_{k-1}) = \pi^k(i) = i$.

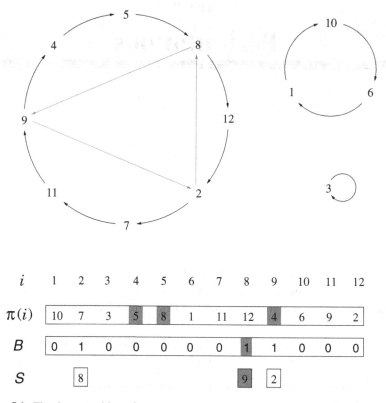

Figure 5.1. The decomposition of a permutation π of size $n = 12$ into its 3 cycles, and the shortcut data structure for $t = 3$. The shortcuts are illustrated as gray arrows. The grayed blocks illustrate operation $\pi^{-1}(5)$.

This must eventually occur in any permutation. At this point we have found $\pi^{-1}(i) = i_{k-1}$, in time $\mathcal{O}(k)$.

The problem with such a method is that k can be as large as n (consider the permutation $\pi(i) = (i \bmod n) + 1$). Even on a random permutation, the expected value of k is $\Theta(n/\log n)$, so this method is unlikely to be practical. However, it can be converted into a simple solution with guaranteed time performance.

The values $i = i_0 \to i_1 \to i_2 \to i_3 \to \ldots \to i_{k-1} \to i_k \to i_0$ form what is called a *cycle* of π. One can partition any permutation into its cycles, which is called the *cycle decomposition* of the permutation. There may be from one cycle of length n (as in the permutation example above) to n cycles of length 1 (as in $\pi(i) = i$). In our method, the cost to find $\pi^{-1}(i)$ is the length of the cycle where i belongs.

Example 5.1 *Figure 5.1 shows how the permutation $\pi = (10\ 7\ 3\ 5\ 8\ 1\ 11\ 12\ 4\ 6\ 9\ 2)$ is decomposed into 3 cycles. The gray arrows and blocks, and the arrays B and S, will be used soon.*

To speed up this process, we will introduce the idea of *shortcuts*. Let $t \geq 1$ be an integer parameter. Shortcuts will then ensure that the process of finding $\pi^{-1}(i)$ performs no more than t steps. To ensure this, every t steps along cycles of length $> t$, we will introduce an extra arrow (grayed in Figure 5.1) that maps i to $\pi^{-t}(i)$. If the cycle length is not a multiple of t, then a final shortcut, shorter than t, is added to enforce the limit of t steps.

The process of computing $\pi^{-1}(i)$ is now as follows. Set $j \leftarrow i$ and repeat the following steps: If $\pi(j) = i$, then the answer is j. Otherwise, if there exists a shortcut mapping j to s, then make $j \leftarrow s$; otherwise make $j \leftarrow \pi(j)$. Take only the first shortcut along the process.

Example 5.2 *In Figure 5.1 we create shortcuts (shown as gray arrows) for $t = 3$. Note the shorter shortcut $2 \rightarrow 8$. Now consider computing $\pi^{-1}(5)$. We start with $j = 5$. Since there is no shortcut associated with 5, we make $j \leftarrow \pi(5) = 8$. Now there is a shortcut mapping 8 to 9, so we make $j \leftarrow 9$. There is another shortcut mapping 9 to 2, but we take only the first shortcut in the process, so we ignore it and make $j \leftarrow \pi(9) = 4$. Now it holds $\pi(4) = 5 = i$, thus we return $\pi^{-1}(5) = 4$. The traversed cells of π are grayed in the figure.*

The structures to represent the shortcut are a bitvector $B[1, n]$, where $B[i] = 1$ iff there is a shortcut leaving from i, and an array S to store the targets of the shortcuts: if $B[i] = 1$, then the target of the shortcut leaving i is $S[\text{rank}(B, i)]$. Along the process we need to read only positions $B[j]$ and will compute rank at most once. We can use the constant-time rank structure (Section 4.2.2) or the sparse sampling (Section 4.2.1) to compute rank in time $\mathcal{O}(t)$. Therefore, shortcuts are tested in constant time and followed in time at most $\mathcal{O}(t)$, and thus the process to compute any $\pi^{-1}(i)$ takes time $\mathcal{O}(t)$. Algorithm 5.1 shows the pseudocode.

A cycle of length $\ell > t$ will have $\lceil \ell/t \rceil$ shortcuts, therefore S contains no more than $\frac{2n}{t+1}$ cells and thus requires at most $\frac{2}{t+1} n \lceil \log n \rceil$ bits (in a worst case where all the cycles are of length $t + 1$). The size of B is $n + o(n)$ bits, and we also store π in $n \lceil \log n \rceil$ bits. By calling $\epsilon = \frac{2}{t+1}$, we have $(1 + \epsilon)n \log n + \mathcal{O}(n)$ total bits of space and $\mathcal{O}(1/\epsilon)$ time.

Algorithm 5.1: Answering π^{-1} with shortcuts. Boolean variable s indicates whether we can follow a shortcut.

1 **Proc** inverse(π, i)

> **Input** : Permutation π (seen as arrays π and S, bitvector B, and parameter t) and position i.
> **Output**: Returns $\pi^{-1}(i)$.

2    $j \leftarrow i$

3    $s \leftarrow$ **true**

4   **while** read(π, j) $\neq i$ **do**

5   **if** s and bitread(B, j) $= 1$ **then**

6        $j \leftarrow$ read(S, rank(B, j))

7        $s \leftarrow$ **false**

8   **else**

9        $j \leftarrow$ read(π, j)

10   **return** j

Note that ϵ can be made $o(1)$. For example, $\epsilon = \frac{1}{\log n}$ achieves $\mathcal{O}(\log n)$ time and $n \log n + \mathcal{O}(n)$ bits of space, which is asymptotically optimal with respect to the worst-case entropy of permutations. But we can also get, for example, $\mathcal{O}(\log \log n)$ time, still within $n \log n(1 + o(1))$ bits of space.

Construction

The data structure we have described can be built in linear time, with the help of an additional bit array $V[1, n]$ that is initially all 0s (Section 3.1). We scan $\pi(i)$ sequentially from $i = 1$ to $i = n$. Each time we find $V[i] = 0$, we stop the sequential scan and start traversing this new, still unexplored, cycle. We set $V[i] \leftarrow 1$, $V[\pi(i)] \leftarrow 1$, $V[\pi(\pi(i))] \leftarrow 1$, and so on until we find that we have arrived at the original value $i = \pi^k(i)$ and thus uncovered a new cycle of length k. Now we restart our sequential scanning from $i \leftarrow i + 1$. In this process, each cell is visited twice: once in the sequential scan and once while uncovering its cycle. Note that cycles are not retraversed once we have found their leftmost position in π and marked all of their positions in V.

Along this process we also create $B[1, n]$ as a bit array, initially with all 0s. As we traverse the elements $\pi^k(i)$ of the cycles of length over t, each time k is a multiple of t, we set $B[\pi^k(i)] \leftarrow 1$. When we finally arrive at $\pi^k(i) = i$, we set one more 1 in $B[i]$.

Once the traversal is complete, we convert B into a bitvector with **rank** support (Section 4.2.2) and allocate the array $S[1, \mathrm{rank}(B, n)]$. Now we repeat the process of finding the cycles, but this time we remember the last cycle position j that was the source of a shortcut: We start with $j \leftarrow i$ and iterate on $\pi^k(i)$. Each time we find $B[\pi^k(i)] = 1$, we set $S[\mathrm{rank}(B, \pi^k(i))] \leftarrow j$ and $j \leftarrow \pi^k(i)$. We also set the final shortcut.

Finally, we free the space of V, whose n bits are the only superfluous space we used for the construction. The whole construction time is $\mathcal{O}(n)$. Algorithm 5.2 shows the pseudocode.

5.2 Powers of Permutations

Now we consider the problem of efficiently computing any π^k, for positive or negative k. The idea is to write the cycle decomposition of π explicitly, so that value $\pi(i)$ is next to i, and thus from the value i we know the value $\pi^k(i)$ in constant time.

Let $C_1, C_2, \ldots, C_c$ be the cycle decomposition of π, and $\ell_i = |C_i|$. Then we define a new permutation $\tau = C_1 . C_2 \ldots C_c$, and a bitvector $D = 0^{\ell_1-1}10^{\ell_2-1}1 \ldots 0^{\ell_c-1}1$. Let $\tau(j) = i$. Then the cycle in which i participates starts at $p = \mathrm{pred}(D, j - 1) + 1$ and ends just before $s = \mathrm{succ}(D, j) + 1$ (in Section 4.5.2 we saw efficient ways to implement these operations in constant time). Therefore, the position in τ where $\pi^k(i)$ appears is

$$p' = p + ((j + k - p) \bmod (s - p)),$$

and then it holds $\pi^k(i) = \tau(p')$.

Example 5.3 *Figure 5.2 shows the permutation τ of the cycles of the permutation π of Example 5.2. To compute $\pi^{20}(12)$, we start computing $j = \tau^{-1}(12) = 3$ (grayed).*

Algorithm 5.2: Building the shortcut structure.

Input : Permutation π (seen as an array $\pi[1, n]$) and parameter t.
Output: Builds structures S and B for π.

1 Allocate bitvectors $V[1, n]$ and $B[1, n]$
2 **for** $i \leftarrow 1$ **to** n **do**
3 $\quad$ bitclear(V, i); bitclear(B, i) (can be initialized wordwise)
4 **for** $i \leftarrow 1$ **to** n **do**
5 $\quad$ **if** bitread(V, i) = 0 **then**
6 $\quad\quad$ bitset(V, i)
7 $\quad\quad$ $j \leftarrow$ read(π, i); $k \leftarrow 1$
8 $\quad\quad$ **while** $j \neq i$ **do**
9 $\quad\quad\quad$ **if** k mod $t = 0$ **then**
10 $\quad\quad\quad\quad$ bitset(B, j)
11 $\quad\quad\quad$ bitset(V, j)
12 $\quad\quad\quad$ $j \leftarrow$ read(π, j); $k \leftarrow k + 1$
13 $\quad\quad$ **if** $k > t$ **then**
14 $\quad\quad\quad$ bitset(B, i)

15 Preprocess B for rank queries (Section 4.2.2)
16 Allocate array $S[1, \text{rank}(B, n)]$ with cells of length $\lceil \log n \rceil$
17 **for** $i \leftarrow 1$ **to** n **do**
18 $\quad$ **if** bitread(V, i) = 1 **then**
19 $\quad\quad$ bitclear(V, i); $j \leftarrow$ read(π, i)
20 $\quad\quad$ **while** bitread(V, j) = 1 **do**
21 $\quad\quad\quad$ **if** access(B, j) = 1 **then**
22 $\quad\quad\quad\quad$ write(S, rank(B, j), i)
23 $\quad\quad\quad\quad$ $i \leftarrow j$
24 $\quad\quad\quad$ bitclear(V, j); $j \leftarrow$ read(π, j)
25 $\quad\quad$ **if** access(B, j) = 1 **then**
26 $\quad\quad\quad$ write(S, rank(B, j), i)
27 $\quad\quad$ $i \leftarrow j$

28 Free V

Now we compute the limits of the cycle where 12 *lies:* $p = \text{pred}(3 - 1) + 1 = 1$ *and* $s = \text{succ}(3) + 1 = 9$. *Then the number corresponding to* $\pi^{20}(12)$ *is at position* $p + ((j + k - p) \bmod (s - p)) = 1 + ((3 + 20 - 1) \bmod (9 - 1)) = 7$ *in* τ. *Therefore, the answer is* $\tau(7) = 9$.

Similarly, consider $\pi^{-20}(1)$. *Then* $j = \tau^{-1}(1) = 11$. *Its cycle starts at* $p = \text{pred}(11 - 1) + 1 = 9$ *and ends just before* $s = \text{succ}(11) + 1 = 12$. *The number corresponding to* $\pi^{-20}(1)$ *is at position* $p + ((j + k - p) \bmod (s - p)) = 9 + ((11 - 20 - 9) \bmod (12 - 9)) = 9$ *in* τ, *and thus the answer is* $\tau(9) = 10$.

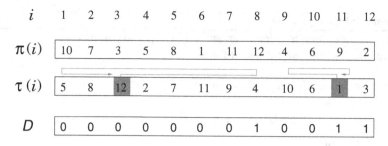

Figure 5.2. The permutation τ of the cycles of our permutation π of Figure 5.1, and the corresponding bitvector D. We show the way we run around the cycle to compute $\pi^{20}(12)$ and $\pi^{-20}(1)$.

Therefore, all we need in order to compute powers of π (including $\pi^1 = \pi$ itself and π^{-1}) is to represent permutation τ so that we can compute both $\tau(i)$ and $\tau^{-1}(i)$. With the technique of Section 5.1, we represent τ in $(1 + \epsilon)n \log n + \mathcal{O}(n)$ bits, so that we can compute any π^k in time $\mathcal{O}(1/\epsilon)$. Note that this time, even computing $\pi(i)$ requires time $\mathcal{O}(1/\epsilon)$, whereas in Section 5.1 it required a simple array access. Algorithm 5.3 shows the pseudocode.

Construction

The same linear-time process to detect the cycles described in Section 5.1 can be used to build τ and D together, in linear time: as we discover the cycles, we append their positions to τ and the corresponding bits to D (a 1 at the end of each cycle and a 0 otherwise). Once τ is built, we can discard π, if desired. Now we apply the construction of Section 5.1 to τ and build the pred and succ structures on D. Note that this time we need $2n \log n + \mathcal{O}(n)$ bits to build the representation, as we build τ and D while we maintain π.

5.3 Compressible Permutations

As seen in the beginning of this chapter, the worst-case entropy of permutations is $n \log n - \Theta(n)$ bits, and thus the representations seen up to now are almost worst-case

---

Algorithm 5.3: Answering π^k with the cycle decomposition of π. Value k can be positive or negative.

---

1 **Proc** power(π, i, k)
> **Input** : Permutation π (seen as permutation τ and bitvector D), position i, and power k.
> **Output**: Returns $\pi^k(i)$.

2 $\quad j \leftarrow$ inverse(τ, i)
3 $\quad p \leftarrow$ pred$(D, j - 1) + 1$
4 $\quad s \leftarrow$ succ$(D, j) + 1$
5 $\quad$ **return** read$(\tau, p + ((j + k - p) \bmod (s - p)))$

optimal. However, in various cases the permutations belong to some specific subset that, for being small, turns out to be compressible. In this section we will consider, in particular, the set of permutations that can be split into a small set of increasing contiguous subsequences.

We will say that a *run* of a permutation π is a maximal range $\pi[i, j]$ such that $\pi(i) < \pi(i+1) < \pi(i+2) < \ldots < \pi(j)$. Then π can be decomposed in a unique way into runs, whose number will be called ρ. Furthermore, we call $n_1, n_2, \ldots, n_\rho$ the lengths of those runs, and define

$$\mathcal{H}(\pi) = \sum_{i=1}^{\rho} n_i \log \frac{n}{n_i}$$

as the *entropy* of π (we could, analogously, consider maximal decreasing runs $\pi(i) > \pi(i+1) > \pi(i+2) > \ldots > \pi(j)$, and even combinations of increasing and decreasing runs, but we will stick to this concrete case). By Jensen's inequality (Section 2.8), it follows that $\mathcal{H}(\pi) \leq n \log \rho \leq n \log n$.

Intuitively, permutations with fewer runs have lower entropy, and their entropy is even lower if the runs are of very different lengths. An interesting fact is that the entropy of a permutation is related to the effort needed to *sort* it using the *MergeSort* algorithm. This algorithm can be thought of as hierarchically merging the runs of π until obtaining a single run.

Example 5.4 *Consider the permutation* $\pi = (3\ 9\ 2\ 5\ 6\ 7\ 10\ 11\ 13\ 15\ 14\ 16\ 12\ 1\ 4\ 8)$. *It has length* $n = 16$ *and* $\rho = 5$ *runs of lengths* $n_1 = 2$ $(3\ 9)$, $n_2 = 8$ $(2\ 5\ 6\ 7\ 10\ 11\ 13\ 15)$, $n_3 = 2$ $(14\ 16)$, $n_4 = 1$ (12), *and* $n_5 = 3$ $(1\ 4\ 8)$, *thus its entropy is* $\mathcal{H}(\pi) = 2 \cdot \log \frac{16}{2} + 8 \cdot \log \frac{16}{8} + 2 \cdot \log \frac{16}{2} + 1 \cdot \log \frac{16}{1} + 3 \cdot \log \frac{16}{3} \approx 31.245 \approx 16 \cdot 1.953 < 16 \cdot 2.322 \approx n \log \rho < 16 \cdot 4 = 64 = n \log n$. *A basic Merge-Sort algorithm moves* $n \lceil \log n \rceil = 64$ *numbers from one array to another to sort it. Instead, Figure 5.3 shows a different way to sort it by moving only* $32 = 16 \cdot 2$ *numbers (note that merging two increasing lists of lengths* n' *and* n'' *requires* $n' + n''$ *moves).*

The example shows, on one hand, that there is no need to use a perfect balanced merging tree for MergeSort to work, but any binary merging tree can be used. On the other hand, one can see that, if the ith run is of length n_i and is at depth ℓ_i in the merging tree, then the run will induce $n_i \ell_i$ moves along the whole MergeSort process. Therefore, the optimal tree is the one minimizing $\sum_i n_i \ell_i$, and thus the optimal merging tree is precisely the Huffman tree of the frequencies $\langle \frac{n_1}{n}, \frac{n_2}{n}, \ldots, \frac{n_\rho}{n} \rangle$ (Section 2.6). Furthermore, the number of moves performed by a MergeSort guided by the Huffman tree is between $\mathcal{H}(\pi)$ and $\mathcal{H}(\pi) + n$, since $\mathcal{H}(\pi)$ corresponds to the zero-order entropy of Section 2.3. In Figure 5.3 we actually chose a Huffman tree.

The technique of detecting the ρ runs in a linear-time pass, building the Huffman tree, and finally sorting the array guided by the tree takes total time $\mathcal{O}(\mathcal{H}(\pi) + n + \rho \log \rho)$, and it can be applied on any array of elements with a total order. Of course, sorting is trivial in the particular case of permutations (just write $1, 2, \ldots, n$). What is interesting in the case of permutations π is that this modified MergeSort algorithm leads to a *representation* of π that uses $\sum_i n_i \ell_i$ bits. Assume that at each node of the merging tree we store a bitvector where, in the process of merging

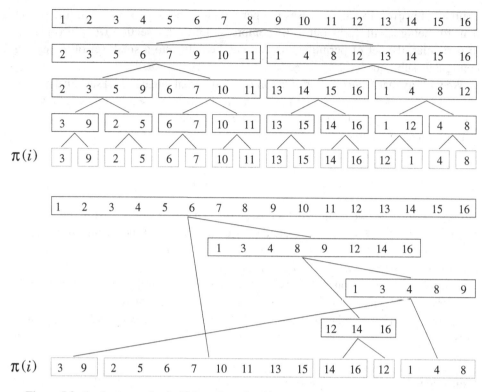

Figure 5.3. On the top, a classical MergeSort algorithm on a permutation π. Each stage reads two runs and merges them into a new run above them, therefore the total work is proportional to the sum of the black rectangles. After $\lceil \log n \rceil$ stages, requiring n moves each, the permutation is sorted. On the bottom, the same permutation is sorted with a different MergeSort-like strategy, merging shorter runs first and needing far fewer moves.

the two children, we append a 0 when we take a value from the left, and a 1 when we take one from the right.

Example 5.5 *The permutation of Example 5.4 is represented with the data shown in Figure 5.4, which is drawn after Figure 5.3 by replacing the numbers with bits that tell whether the number came from the left or from the right. The gray numbers in the leaves are shown for clarity, but they can be deduced from the rest of the data.*

With this information, we can compute any $\pi(i)$ and $\pi^{-1}(i)$. Let us first consider $\pi^{-1}(i)$. We start at position $j \leftarrow i$ at the root node u. Recall that u represents the sorted permutation $\pi(j) = j$, so we want to find where its array position j comes from in the merging. Let B_u be the bitvector stored at node u. Then, if $B_u[j] = 0$, the number j comes in the merging from its left child, and it is at position $j \leftarrow \mathsf{rank}_0(B_u, j)$ in that child. Otherwise $B_u[j] = 1$, and then j comes from the right child of u, where it is at position $j \leftarrow \mathsf{rank}_1(B_u, j)$. We continue recursively from the corresponding child of u, until reaching a leaf v. At this point, $\pi^{-1}(i)$ corresponds to local offset j in v, which must be converted into a global offset.

Instead, $\pi(i)$ is computed bottom-up. Let v be the leaf node to which i belongs and j be its local offset within v. Now, if v is the left child of its parent u, then the offset within u is $j \leftarrow \mathsf{select}_0(B_u, j)$. Otherwise v is the right child of u, and then its position

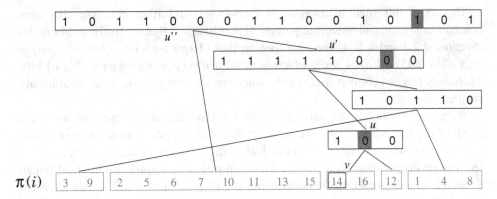

Figure 5.4. The data structure built after the Huffman tree on Figure 5.3. It contains sufficient data to represent the permutation π (drawn in gray). Grayed blocks illustrate operations $\pi(11)$ and $\pi^{-1}(14)$.

in u is $j \leftarrow \mathsf{select}_1(B_u, j)$. Now we continue from u recursively until the root, where we finally have $j = \pi(i)$.

Example 5.6 *Consider again Figures 5.3 (bottom) and 5.4, and let us compute $\pi(11)$. Position 11 corresponds to offset $j = 1$ at the leaf v that contains $(14\ 16)$, which is drawn in third left-to-right position (the position is inside a black square). Since v is a left child of its parent u (which is the node representing $(12\ 14\ 16)$), its position within u is $j \leftarrow \mathsf{select}_0(B_u, 1) = \mathsf{select}_0(100, 1) = 2$. Now this node is the left child of its parent node u' (which is the right child of the root), and thus its position in u' is $j \leftarrow \mathsf{select}_0(B_{u'}, 2) = \mathsf{select}_0(11111000, 2) = 7$. Finally, u' is the right child of the root u'', and thus its position at the root is $j \leftarrow \mathsf{select}_1(B_{u''}, 7) = \mathsf{select}_1(1011000110010101, 7) = 14$. Thus the answer is $\pi(11) = 14$. All the involved bits are in grayed blocks.*

Let us now do the reverse process to compute $\pi^{-1}(i)$ for $i = 14$. We start at the root node, u'', with $j = 14$. Since $B_{u''}[14] = 1$, we conclude that i comes from the right child u' of u'', where it is at position $j \leftarrow \mathsf{rank}_1(B_{u''}, 14) = 7$. Now, since $B_{u'}[7] = 0$, it follows that i comes from the left child u of u', where it is at position $j \leftarrow \mathsf{rank}_0(B_{u'}, 7) = 2$. Finally, since $B_u[2] = 0$, we know that i comes from the left child v of u, at position $j \leftarrow \mathsf{rank}_0(B_u, 2) = 1$. Then $i = 14$ comes from the first position in v. Since the elements of v start at position 11 in the sequence, the answer is $\pi^{-1}(14) = 11 + 1 - 1 = 11$.

The example shows that we need the following information in addition to the bitvectors B stored at the nodes:

1. The Huffman tree, with pointers to the children and to the parent of each node.
2. A bitvector $G[1, n]$, with the ith 1 set at the position in π where the ith run starts. In our example, we have $G[1, 16] = 1010000000101100$. We prepare G for constant-time rank queries, using the compressed structure of Section 4.2.3. This requires $\rho \log \frac{n}{\rho} + \mathcal{O}(\rho) + o(n) = \mathcal{O}(\rho \log n) + o(n)$ bits of space.
3. An array $L[1, \rho]$ storing in $L[i]$ a pointer to the leaf of the Huffman tree where the ith run is represented.
4. At each leaf, the starting position *pos* of its run in π.

This extra information amounts to $\mathcal{O}(\rho w) + o(n)$ further bits. We also need constant-time rank and select support on all the bitvectors B of the Huffman tree nodes (Sections 4.2.2 and 4.3.3). The total space is thus $(\mathcal{H}(\pi) + n)(1 + o(1)) + \mathcal{O}(\rho w) = \mathcal{H}(\pi)(1 + o(1)) + \mathcal{O}(n + \rho w)$, which is at most $n \log \rho + o(n \log \rho) + \mathcal{O}(\rho w)$ bits. Therefore, this structure is useful only when the number of runs, ρ, is significantly smaller than n.

With this information, we solve $\pi^{-1}(i)$ and $\pi(i)$ queries in time proportional to the depth of the leaf where i lies: We solve $\pi^{-1}(i)$ with a traversal from the root to that leaf, and $\pi(i)$ with a traversal from that leaf, $L[\text{rank}_1(G, i)]$, to the tree root. Since no leaf can be deeper than $\mathcal{O}(\log n)$ in a Huffman tree with frequencies in $[1, n]$ (recall Section 2.6.2), the total time for both queries is $\mathcal{O}(\log n)$. Algorithm 5.4 gives the pseudocode for queries.

Algorithm 5.4: Answering read and inverse on compressible permutations. The tree fields are l (left child), r (right child), and p (parent).

---

1 **Proc** inverse(π, i)

    Input   : Permutation π (seen as Huffman tree T with bitvectors B in internal nodes and positions *pos* in leaves) and position i.

    Output: Returns $\pi^{-1}(i)$.

2    $v \leftarrow T.root$

3   **while** v *is not a leaf* **do**

4   **if** access$(v.B, i) = 0$ **then**

5          $i \leftarrow \text{rank}_0(v.B, i)$

6          $v \leftarrow v.l$

7   **else**

8          $i \leftarrow \text{rank}_1(v.B, i)$

9          $v \leftarrow v.r$

10   **return** $v.pos + i - 1$

11 **Proc** read(π, i)

    Input   : Permutation π (seen as Huffman tree T with bitvectors B in internal nodes and positions *pos* in leaves, bitvector G and array L), and position i.

    Output: Returns $\pi(i)$.

12   $v \leftarrow L[\text{rank}(G, i)]$

13   $i \leftarrow i - v.pos + 1$

14   **while** $v \neq T.root$ **do**

15   **if** $v = v.p.l$ **then**

16          $i \leftarrow \text{select}_0(v.p.B, i)$

17   **else**

18          $i \leftarrow \text{select}_1(v.p.B, i)$

19       $v \leftarrow v.p$

20   **return** i

Algorithm 5.5: Building the compressed permutation representation. Frees the original array.

Input : A permutation π, seen as an array $\pi[1, n]$.

Output: Builds its compressed representation with Huffman tree T, bitvector G, array L, and value ρ.

1 Allocate bitvector $G[1, n]$
2 $\rho \leftarrow 1$
3 bitset(G, 1)
4 **for** $i \leftarrow 2$ **to** n **do**
5   **if** $\pi[i] < \pi[i - 1]$ **then**
6   bitset(G, i)
7          $\rho \leftarrow \rho + 1$
8   **else**
9   bitclear(G, i)

10 Prepare G for rank queries (Section 4.2.3)
11 Allocate array $S[1, \rho]$ with fields s (symbols) and f (weights); in turn s is formed by fields $s.i$ (run start position) and $s.p$ (run id)
12 $p \leftarrow 1$
13 $S[1].s.i \leftarrow 1$; $S[1].s.p \leftarrow 1$
14 **for** $i \leftarrow 2$ **to** n **do**
15   **if** $\pi[i] < \pi[i - 1]$ **then**
16          $S[p].f \leftarrow i - S[p].s.i$
17          $p \leftarrow p + 1$
18          $S[p].s.i \leftarrow i$; $S[p].s.p \leftarrow p$

19 $S[p].f \leftarrow n + 1 - S[p].s.i$
20 $T \leftarrow HuffmanTree(S)$ (Algorithm 2.2)
21 Free S
22 Allocate array $L[1, \rho]$ of pointers
23 $CreateLeaves(\pi, T.root, L)$ (Algorithm 5.6)
24 Free π
25 $CreateBitvectors(T.root)$ (Algorithm 5.6)
26 Free $T.root.A$

Construction

After detecting the ρ runs and their lengths in a single scan over π, the Huffman algorithm builds the tree in time $\mathcal{O}(\rho \log \rho)$ (Section 2.6). Now we simulate MergeSort, so as to build the bitvectors in total time $\mathcal{O}(\mathcal{H}(\pi) + n)$. The other elements of the structure are easily built in time $\mathcal{O}(\rho)$, so the total construction time is $\mathcal{O}(\mathcal{H}(\pi) + n + \rho \log \rho) = \mathcal{O}(n \log \rho)$.

Algorithms 5.5 and 5.6 give the details. We allocate an extra array $v.A$ to merge the children of v, and retain it until v is merged with its sibling. Since we first create the arrays $v.A$ for the leaves and then remove π, the space needed for the construction is $2n \log n + \mathcal{O}(\rho w)$ bits. However, we can build the structures using 3 small buffers of main memory, since all the temporary arrays $v.A$ can be generated on disk and merged by buffers.

Algorithm 5.6: Building the compressed permutation representation: additional functions. Apart from the symbols $v.s$ at the leaves, we use the weights $v.f$ left in all the nodes by Algorithm 2.2.

---

1 **Proc** *CreateLeaves*(π, v, L)

   Input : A permutation array $\pi[1, n]$, Huffman tree node v, and leaf array L.
   Output: Builds the A arrays and *pos* fields for the leaves below v. It also fills
   the array L and the fields $v.p$.

2 | **if** $v.l =$ null **then** (v is a leaf)
3 | | $v.pos \leftarrow v.s.i$
4 | | $L[v.s.p] \leftarrow v$
5 | | Allocate array $v.A[1, v.f]$ of integers
6 | | **for** $i \leftarrow 1$ **to** $v.f$ **do**
7 | | | $v.A[i] \leftarrow \pi[v.pos + i - 1]$

8 | **else**
9 | | *CreateLeaves*$(\pi, v.l, L)$; *CreateLeaves*$(\pi, v.r, L)$
10 | | **if** $v.f = n$ **then** $v.p \leftarrow$ null (v is the tree root)
11 | | $v.l.p \leftarrow v; v.r.p \leftarrow v$

12 **Proc** *CreateBitvectors*(v)

   Input : A Huffman tree node v.
   Output: Builds the bitvectors B for the internal nodes below v.

13 | **if** $v.l =$ null **then return** (v is a leaf)
14 | *CreateBitvectors*$(v.l)$; *CreateBitvectors*$(v.r)$
15 | Allocate bitvector $v.B[1, v.f]$ and array $v.A[1, v.f]$ of integers
16 | $pl \leftarrow 1; pr \leftarrow 1$
17 | **for** $i \leftarrow 1$ **to** $v.f$ **do**
18 | | **if** $pl \le v.l.f$ **and** ($pr > v.r.f$ **or** $v.l.A[pl] < v.r.A[pr]$) **then**
19 | | | $v.A[i] \leftarrow v.l.A[pl]$
20 | | | bitclear$(v.B, i)$
21 | | | $pl \leftarrow pl + 1$
22 | | **else**
23 | | | $v.A[i] \leftarrow v.r.A[pr]$
24 | | | bitset$(v.B, i)$
25 | | | $pr \leftarrow pr + 1$
26 | Free $v.l.A$ and $v.r.A$
27 | Prepare $v.B$ for **rank** and **select** queries (Sections 4.2.2 and 4.3.3)

Reducing Query Time

If the argument i of queries $\pi(i)$ and $\pi^{-1}(i)$ distributes uniformly in $[1, n]$, then the average query time is $\mathcal{O}(1 + \mathcal{H}(\pi)/n)$, the average length of a Huffman code in the tree of π (or, which is the same, the average distance from the root to a leaf, considering the weights of the leaves). This is at most $\mathcal{O}(\log \rho)$ and becomes faster as the permutation is more compressible. The worst case, however, is $\mathcal{O}(\min(\rho, \log n))$, the maximum possible height of the Huffman tree. We could have $\mathcal{O}(\log \rho)$ worst case by using a balanced tree of the runs, but then we would lose the compression to zero-order entropy.

It is possible to retain almost the same compressed space and construction time while limiting the depth of the Huffman tree (and thus the worst-case query times) to $\mathcal{O}(\log \rho)$. A simple technique is to artificially increase all the frequencies below a threshold f, to f. The right threshold value $1 \leq f \leq n$ to obtain a desired tree height $c \cdot \log \rho$ (for some $c > 1$) can be found with a binary search. Since thresholding does not disorder the frequencies, these need to be sorted only once, and then the Huffman tree can be rebuilt in $\mathcal{O}(\rho)$ time (Section 2.6.1) for each tested value of f. Thus the total construction time increases to $\mathcal{O}(\rho \log n)$.

When limiting the depth to $\mathcal{O}(\log \rho)$, the space increases by just $\mathcal{O}(n/\rho)$ bits in most cases. This can be guaranteed if we use optimal length-restricted Huffman codes; we offer pointers in the bibliographic discussion.

In Section 6.4.1 we will show how sequence representations can be used to further reduce the time for queries while retaining compression.

5.4 Applications

5.4.1 Two-Dimensional Points

Let $(x_1, y_1), \ldots, (x_n, y_n)$ be points on a discrete grid $[1, u] \times [1, u]$ (the coordinates can also be fixed-precision real numbers that we properly scale to the integer interval $[1, u]$). We wish to store the points so that they can be accessed in x-order or in y-order, simultaneously.

A basic storage scheme of the coordinates as fixed-length arrays $X[1, n]$ and $Y[1, n]$, so that $(x_i, y_i) = (X[i], Y[i])$, requires $2n\lceil \log u \rceil$ bits, without any particular order. We could sort the points in, say, x-order, so that the ith point in x-order is $(X[i], Y[i])$.

Note that in this case, we have $X[i] \leq X[i + 1]$. If we instead store $X'[1] = X[1]$ and $X'[i + 1] = X[i + 1] - X[i]$, we can use the variable-length representation for partial sums described in Section 4.5.1, so that we can recover $X[i] = \sum_{j=1}^{i} X'[j]$ in constant time (and fast in practice). The total space of this representation will be $n \log \frac{n+u}{n} + \mathcal{O}(n) = n \log \frac{u}{n} + \mathcal{O}(n)$ bits.

If we store the Y vector as a plain array, then the total space has been reduced to $n \log u + n \log \frac{u}{n} + \mathcal{O}(n) = n \log \frac{u^2}{n} + \mathcal{O}(n)$ bits, and we still recover any point in x-coordinate order in constant time. Note that this space is asymptotically optimal, because there are $\binom{u^2 + n - 1}{n}$ ways to choose n points from a discrete grid of size $u \times u$ (permitting repetitions),[1] and

$$\log \binom{u^2 + n - 1}{n} = n \log \frac{u^2 + n}{n} - \mathcal{O}(\log(u + n)) \geq n \log \frac{u^2}{n} - \mathcal{O}(\log(u + n)).$$

But we still do not allow retrieving the points in y-order. To do this, we also sort the array Y and represent it in the same way of X. Now the total space is reduced

---

[1]   In general, the number of ways to choose b objects among a choices without allowing repetitions is $\binom{a}{b}$, whereas allowing repetitions it is $\binom{a+b-1}{b}$. Here the choices are the $u \cdot u$ possible positions, and the objects are the n points.

to $2n \log \frac{u}{n} + \mathcal{O}(n)$ bits, but we have lost the connection between the two coordinates of the same point. That is, for example, for both the point sets $\{(1, 1), (2, 2)\}$ and $\{(1, 2), (2, 1)\}$, we have the same representation, $X = \langle 1, 2 \rangle$ and $Y = \langle 1, 2 \rangle$.

To recover the mapping between an x-coordinate $X[i]$ and its corresponding y-coordinate $Y[j]$ after having sorted X and Y, we use a permutation π, where $\pi(i) = j$. Therefore, the ith point in x-order is $(X[i], Y[\pi(i)])$ (where both arrays are represented as described), and the ith point in y-order is $(X[\pi^{-1}(i)], Y[i])$. If the permutation π is represented as in Section 5.1, then the total space of this representation is $2n \log \frac{u}{n} + \mathcal{O}(n) + (1 + \epsilon)n \log n < (1 + \epsilon)n \log \frac{u^2}{n} + \mathcal{O}(n)$ bits, and we have constant-time access to the points in both orderings. More precisely, the time is $\mathcal{O}(1)$ in x-order and $\mathcal{O}(1/\epsilon)$ in y-order, or vice versa, as desired. If we accept $\mathcal{O}(\log n)$ access time to the points in y-order, then we can set $\epsilon = \frac{1}{\log n}$ and the space becomes asymptotically optimal, $n \log \frac{u^2}{n} + \mathcal{O}(n)$ bits.

Example 5.7 *Consider the point set* $\{(40, 17), (111, 13), (13, 50), (40, 47)\}$, *with* $n = 4$ *and* $u = 111$. *Then we represent* $X[1, 4] = \langle 13, 40, 40, 111 \rangle$, $Y[1, 4] = \langle 13, 17, 47, 50 \rangle$, *and* $\pi = (4\ 2\ 3\ 1)$. *Therefore, for example, the first point in x-order is* $(X[1], Y[\pi(1)]) = (X[1], Y[4]) = (13, 50)$, *whereas the first point in y-order is* $(X[\pi^{-1}(1)], Y[1]) = (X[4], Y[1]) = (111, 13)$. *Now the arrays X and Y can be stored differentially, as* $X'[1, 4] = \langle 13, 27, 0, 71 \rangle$ *and* $Y'[1, 4] = \langle 13, 4, 30, 3 \rangle$.

5.4.2 Inverted Indexes Revisited

Consider a text $T[1, n]$ of n words and wordwise zero-order empirical entropy $\mathcal{H}_0(T)$. In Section 3.4.5 we showed how to store T in nearly $n\mathcal{H}_0(T)$ bits so that any word $T[i]$ could be retrieved in time $\mathcal{O}(\log n)$ (or possibly less, depending on the parameter b). Then in Section 4.5.1 we showed how its positional inverted index can be represented in $n\mathcal{H}_0(T) + \mathcal{O}(n)$ bits, so that the position of the ith occurrence of any word is retrieved in constant time.

Therefore, a text database where we want to support fast location of words and extraction of text snippets (or any kind of access to the text), needs at least $2n\mathcal{H}_0(T) + \mathcal{O}(n)$ bits. This space is clearly redundant, as both the text and the inverted index represent the same information (one can be built from the other).

A clean way to exploit this redundancy is to regard the concatenation of the inverted lists of all the words as a permutation π on $[1, n]$, given that each position of $T[1, n]$ appears in exactly one list. Moreover this permutation is compressible because the list of word s forms an increasing contiguous subsequence of length n_s, the number of times s appears in T. This means that, even if we do not consider that longer runs could be formed by chance,

$$\mathcal{H}(\pi) = \sum_s n_s \log \frac{n}{n_s} = n\mathcal{H}_0(T).$$

Therefore, the technique of Section 5.3 represents π in $\mathcal{H}(\pi)(1 + o(1)) + \mathcal{O}(n + \rho \log \rho)$ bits, where ρ is the alphabet size. As mentioned in Section 2.9, in practice it holds $\rho = \mathcal{O}(n^\beta)$ for some constant $0 < \beta < 1$, and thus the total space is just $n\mathcal{H}_0(T)(1 + o(1)) + \mathcal{O}(n)$ bits. In addition, we will use a bitvector $D[1, n]$ that marks with a 1 the positions of π where each new inverted list starts. The space of this bitvector, with constant-time rank and select support, is within the $\mathcal{O}(n)$ bits already considered. For a small price in time, however, it is better to represent it with the technique of Section 4.4.

Then, the ith occurrence of text word s is at position $\pi(\text{select}(D, s) + i - 1)$, and the number of occurrences of s in T is $\text{select}(D, s + 1) - \text{select}(D, s)$. Conversely, the word at $T[i]$ is $\text{rank}(D, \pi^{-1}(i))$. Note that we are mapping words to the interval $s \in [1, \rho]$; an array storing the actual content of each word is also needed, just as with any other scheme. Overall the space usage is now essentially that of the zero-order empirical wordwise entropy of T, and we have access to both T and its inverted index, in time $\mathcal{O}(\log \rho) = \mathcal{O}(\log n)$. Thus the price of the space reduction is some loss of speed in access.

Example 5.8 *Consider the text $T[1, 6] =$ "to be or not to be". Then the positional inverted list for* "to" *is* $\langle 1, 5 \rangle$, *for* "be" *is* $\langle 2, 6 \rangle$, *for* "or" *is* $\langle 3 \rangle$, *and for* "not" *is* $\langle 4 \rangle$. *If we concatenate them, we get* $\pi = (1\ 5\ 2\ 6\ 3\ 4)$, *which actually has less than* $\rho = 4$ *runs, just by chance. The beginnings of the lists are marked in* $D[1, 6] = 101011$. *Now, for example, the second occurrence* ($i = 2$) *of the word* "be" *in T, to which we have assigned the identifier $s = 2$, is at position* $\pi(\text{select}(D, 2) + 2 - 1) = \pi(3 + 2 - 1) = 6$. *On the other hand, the content of $T[3]$ is the word number* $s = \text{rank}(D, \pi^{-1}(3)) = \text{rank}(D, 5) = 3$, *that is,* "or".

5.5 Summary

A permutation π of $[1, n]$ can be represented in $(1 + \epsilon)n \log n$ bits so that $\pi(i)$ is answered in constant time and $\pi^{-1}(i)$ in time $\mathcal{O}(1/\epsilon)$. A related arrangement computes any positive or negative power, $\pi^k(i)$, in time $\mathcal{O}(1/\epsilon)$, but then even $\pi(i)$ takes time $\mathcal{O}(1/\epsilon)$. The construction is linear-time. If π has ρ runs with entropy of the run lengths $\mathcal{H}(\pi)$, then it can be represented in essentially $\mathcal{H}(\pi) \leq n \log \rho$ bits, so that any $\pi(i)$ and $\pi^{-1}(i)$ can be computed in average time $\mathcal{O}(1 + \mathcal{H}(\pi)/n)$ and worst-case time $\mathcal{O}(\log \rho)$. The construction time in this case is proportional to the number of bits in the representation. Permutations appear in many compact data structures, most prominently for representing sequences (Chapter 6).

5.6 Bibliographic Notes

Inverses and powers. All the results of Sections 5.1 and 5.2 were found by Munro *et al.* (2012). Apart from the tradeoff based on parameter t, they introduce a more complicated scheme that achieves $\mathcal{O}(\log n / \log \log n)$ time within $\log n! + o(n)$ bits; the time and space are slightly better than what we obtain using parameter $t = \log n$. They also proved that their space/time tradeoff is essentially optimal (see also Golynski (2009)). In addition to permutations, they consider more general functions $f : [1, n] \to [1, n]$, providing the same functionality. We will present this extension in Section 8.5.7.

Compressible permutations. The results of Section 5.3 are from Barbay and Navarro (2013), who also explore several other measures of compressibility of permutations. The earlier idea of running MergeSort in time $\mathcal{O}(n \log \rho)$ dates back to Knuth (1998). Several authors studied and surveyed various measures of "presortedness" of arrays and permutations (Munro and Spira, 1976; Mannila, 1985; Moffat and Petersson, 1992; Levcopoulos and Petersson, 1994). Faster compressed representations of permutations can be obtained using data structures for sequences (Barbay *et al.*, 2014); some will be discussed in the applications of Chapter 6.

Limited-length Huffman. An algorithm to find the optimal Huffman-like tree with a maximum height h was given by Larmore and Hirschberg (1990), who reduce the construction to the coin collector's problem. Their algorithm takes $\mathcal{O}(h\rho) = \mathcal{O}(\rho \log n)$ time and is practical. Milidiú and Laber (2001) gave an $\mathcal{O}(\rho)$-time approximation and proved that only ϵn bits are added to $\mathcal{H}(\pi)$ to obtain $h = \lceil \log \rho \rceil + \lceil \log_\phi(1/\epsilon) \rceil + 1$ (where $\phi = \frac{1+\sqrt{5}}{2} \approx 1.618$ is the golden ratio). Thus we can limit the depth to $\mathcal{O}(\log \rho)$ by adding just $\mathcal{O}(n/\rho)$ bits of redundancy. The penalties are usually much smaller in practice (Gagie *et al.*, 2015).

The simpler technique we used is inspired by the bounds of Katona and Nemetz (1976) (see also Buro (1993)), who showed that if a symbol has frequency $p \cdot n$, then any Huffman code assigns it a codeword of length at most $\lfloor \log_\phi(1/p) \rfloor$, and thus h is at most $\lfloor \log_\phi(n/f) \rfloor$, where f is the smallest frequency. Gagie *et al.* (2015) evaluate these and other approximations and heuristics, concluding that this simple method works in practice almost like the optimal one (Larmore and Hirschberg, 1990) and much better than the guaranteed approximation of Milidiú and Laber. Witten *et al.* (1999, Ch. 9) also describe a close variant of this simple method.

Inverted indexes. The application of Section 5.4.2 is described by Barbay and Navarro (2013).

Bibliography

Barbay, J. and Navarro, G. (2013). On compressing permutations and adaptive sorting. *Theoretical Computer Science*, **513**, 109–123.

Barbay, J., Claude, F., Gagie, T., Navarro, G., and Nekrich, Y. (2014). Efficient fully-compressed sequence representations. *Algorithmica*, **69**(1), 232–268.

Buro, M. (1993). On the maximum length of Huffman codes. *Information Processing Letters*, **45**(5), 219–223.

Gagie, T., Navarro, G., Nekrich, Y., and Ordóñez, A. (2015). Efficient and compact representations of prefix codes. *IEEE Transactions on Information Theory*, **61**(9), 4999–5011.

Golynski, A. (2009). Cell probe lower bounds for succinct data structures. In *Proc. 20th Annual ACM-SIAM Symposium on Discrete Algorithms (SODA)*, pages 625–634.

Katona, G. O. H. and Nemetz, T. O. H. (1976). Huffman codes and self-information. *IEEE Transactions on Information Theory*, **22**(3), 337–340.

Knuth, D. E. (1998). *The Art of Computer Programming, volume 3: Sorting and Searching*. Addison-Wesley, 2nd edition.

Larmore, L. L. and Hirschberg, D. S. (1990). A fast algorithm for optimal length-limited Huffman codes. *Journal of the ACM*, **37**(3), 464–473.

Levcopoulos, C. and Petersson, O. (1994). Sorting shuffled monotone sequences. *Information and Computation*, **112**(1), 37–50.

Mannila, H. (1985). Measures of presortedness and optimal sorting algorithms. *IEEE Transactions on Computers*, **34**, 318–325.

Milidiú, R. L. and Laber, E. S. (2001). Bounding the inefficiency of length-restricted prefix codes. *Algorithmica*, **31**(4), 513–529.

Moffat, A. and Petersson, O. (1992). An overview of adaptive sorting. *Australian Computer Journal*, **24**(2), 70–77.

Munro, J. I. and Spira, P. M. (1976). Sorting and searching in multisets. *SIAM Journal on Computing*, **5**(1), 1–8.

Munro, J. I., Raman, R., Raman, V., and Rao, S. S. (2012). Succinct representations of permutations and functions. *Theoretical Computer Science*, **438**, 74–88.

Witten, I. H., Moffat, A., and Bell, T. C. (1999). *Managing Gigabytes: Compressing and Indexing Documents and Images*. Van Nostrand Reinhold, 2nd edition.

CHAPTER 6

Sequences

We will call *sequence* $S[1, n]$ a generalization of bitvectors whose elements $S[i]$ belong to an *alphabet* $\Sigma = [1, \sigma]$. Each element of Σ is called a *symbol*. The abstract data type supports the same operations as bitvectors:

access(S, i): returns the symbol $S[i]$, for any $1 \le i \le n$.

rank$_c(S, i)$: returns the number of occurrences of symbol $c \in \Sigma$ in $S[1, i]$, for any $0 \le i \le n$; in particular rank$_c(S, 0) = 0$.

select$_c(S, j)$: returns the position in S of the jth occurrence of symbol $c \in \Sigma$, for any $j \ge 0$; we assume select$_c(S, 0) = 0$ and select$_c(S, j) = n + 1$ if $j > $ rank$_c(S, n)$.

The size of the alphabet varies widely across applications. For example it can be as small as 4 on DNA sequences, or as large as several million, in the case of the vocabulary of a text collection or the number of nodes in a graph (Section 9.1.2 shows how graphs can be represented as sequences).

We will build on our ability to handle bitvectors, developed in Chapter 4, and in the use of permutations, Chapter 5, to support these operations on sequences. Handling sequences is more challenging than bitvectors. To illustrate this point, let us attempt a simple solution and see its shortcomings. Suppose we set up σ bitvectors $B_c[1, n]$, for $c \in \Sigma$, so that $B_c[i] = 1$ iff $S[i] = c$. Then we have the easy translation

$$\text{rank}_c(S, i) = \text{rank}_1(B_c, i),$$

$$\text{select}_c(S, j) = \text{select}_1(B_c, j).$$

The problem with this solution is the space. If we use, for example, the solutions of Chapter 4 that guarantee constant time for rank and select on bitvectors within $n + o(n)$ bits, then the total space of this solution will be $n\sigma + o(n\sigma)$, which is way too much (consider that $S[1, n]$ can be stored as an array in $n\lceil \log \sigma \rceil$ bits!). Even if we use the compressed bitvector representations that support constant-time rank and select, the term $o(n\sigma)$ in the space remains, and it can easily become dominant (it is at least $\Omega(n\sigma \log \log n / \log n)$ if constant times are desired).

Instead, given that there will be only n 1s across the σ bitvectors B_c, we can use the representation for very sparse bitvectors of Section 4.4. In this case, if we call n_c the number of occurrences of c in S, the total space will be

$$\sum_{c \in \Sigma} n_c \log \frac{n}{n_c} + \mathcal{O}(n_c) = n\mathcal{H}_0(S) + \mathcal{O}(n)$$

bits, which is much more acceptable (recall Section 2.3.2). Then the times of the operations will be $\mathcal{O}\left(\log \min \left(n_c, \frac{n}{n_c}\right)\right) = \mathcal{O}(\log n)$ for $\mathsf{rank}_c(S, i)$ and $\mathcal{O}(1)$ for $\mathsf{select}_c(S, j)$.

This solution, however, does not efficiently support the most basic operation, $\mathsf{access}(S, i)$. This can be solved only by probing each bitvector B_c until finding $B_c[i] = 1$ and then returning c, which takes $\mathcal{O}(\sigma \log n)$ time. Alternatively, we can in addition represent $S[1, n]$ as a compressed array, extending the technique of Section 4.1.2 to symbols of $\log \sigma$ bits (thus using blocks of $b = (\log_\sigma n)/2$ symbols). This requires $n\mathcal{H}_0(S) + o(n \log \sigma)$ bits and supports $\mathsf{access}(S, i)$ in time $\mathcal{O}(1)$.

Overall, while the operation times could be acceptable, the space of this solution is $2n\mathcal{H}_0(S) + o(n \log \sigma) + \mathcal{O}(n)$ bits, at least twice what could be hoped for. Along this chapter we show how to achieve more convenient space/time tradeoffs and more elegant solutions.

For simplicity, we will assume that $\sigma = \mathcal{O}(n)$, that is, the alphabet is not excessively large compared to the sequence length. We must otherwise add a mechanism to map Σ to the symbols that actually appear in S (such as a very sparse bitvector, Section 4.4, or a dictionary, Section 4.5.3).

6.1 Using Permutations

In this section we introduce a solution that is convenient for large alphabets. It uses $n \log \sigma + n \cdot o(\log \sigma)$ bits of space, and supports access and rank in $\mathcal{O}(\log \log \sigma)$ time and select in $\mathcal{O}(1)$ time. While this structure is not a compressed representation of S, it will be a key component to compress S to its zero-order empirical entropy in Section 6.3.

Let us divide $S[1, n]$ into $\lceil n/\sigma \rceil$ *chunks* S_k of length σ, that is,

$$S[1, n] = S_1[1, \sigma] . S_2[1, \sigma] \ldots S_{\lceil n/\sigma \rceil}[1, \sigma]$$

(where for simplicity we assume that the last chunk is of length σ too). The solution has two parts: the first solves the operations up to the granularity of the chunk, whereas the second completes the information by querying the corresponding chunk.

6.1.1 Chunk-Level Granularity

The chunk-level granularity of the answers is provided by σ bitvectors $A_c, c \in \Sigma$, which add up to $2n$ bits. Precisely,

$$A_c = 1^{\mathsf{rank}_c(S_1, \sigma)} 0 \, 1^{\mathsf{rank}_c(S_2, \sigma)} 0 \ldots 1^{\mathsf{rank}_c(S_{\lceil n/\sigma \rceil}, \sigma)}.$$

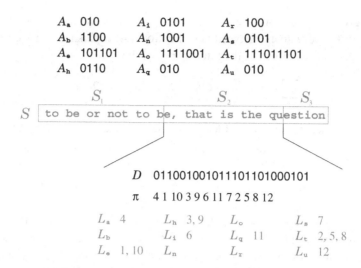

Figure 6.1. A string S of length $n = 30$ (ignore whitespaces and commas) over an alphabet of $\sigma = 12$ symbols, split into $\lceil n/\sigma \rceil = 3$ chunks S_1, S_2, and S_3. The grayed structures are conceptual and not represented. On top of S we show the bitvectors A_c that solve the queries up to the chunk-level granularity, and on the bottom the bitvector D and permutation π that represent the chunk S_2.

Essentially, A_c records, in unary, the number of occurrences of symbol c inside each of the chunks. Each bitvector A_c has n_c 1s and $\lceil n/\sigma \rceil - 1$ 0s, which adds up to less than $2n$ in total (basically n 1s and n 0s).

Example 6.1 *Figure 6.1 shows the string $S =$ "to be or not to be, that is the question" of length $n = 30$ over an alphabet of size $\sigma = 12$ (ignoring whitespaces and commas). For legibility, we write the letters in S as* a, b, e, h, i, n, o, q, r, s, t, u, *but these are interpreted as the numbers 1 to 12. The string S is divided into $\lceil n/\sigma \rceil = 3$ chunks of length $\sigma = 12$, the last one being shorter. The corresponding bitvectors A_c are shown on top of the string. The structures D and π that represent chunk S_2 will be used later.*

The operations on S are then translated into operations on bitvectors A_c and chunks S_k as follows, where $k = \lceil i/\sigma \rceil$ is the chunk where $S[i]$ belongs:

$$\mathsf{access}(S, i) = \mathsf{access}(S_k, ((i - 1) \bmod \sigma) + 1),$$

$$\mathsf{rank}_c(S, i) = \mathsf{select}_0(A_c, k - 1) - (k - 1) + \mathsf{rank}_c(S_k, ((i - 1) \bmod \sigma) + 1),$$

$$\mathsf{select}_c(S, j) = (s - j) \cdot \sigma + \mathsf{select}_c(S_{s-j+1}, s - \mathsf{pred}_0(A_c, s)),$$

$$\text{where } s = \mathsf{select}_1(A_c, j).$$

Let us explain the formulas. In the case of $\mathsf{access}(S, i)$, we simply compute the chunk number k where $S[i]$ lies and access the corresponding offset within chunk S_k. For $\mathsf{rank}_c(S, i)$, we compute with $\mathsf{rank}_1(A_c, \mathsf{select}_0(A_c, k - 1)) = \mathsf{select}_0(A_c, k - 1) - (k - 1)$ the number of 1s in A_c before chunk k, that is, the number of occurrences of c before S_k. Then we add the number of occurrences of c in S_k up to $S[i]$. Finally, for $\mathsf{select}_c(S, j)$, we start finding the jth occurrence of c in A_c, $s = \mathsf{select}_1(A_c, j)$. Then $s - j + 1$ is the number of the chunk where the answer lies. We add the offset of this chunk, $(s - j) \cdot \sigma$, to the position of the desired c within chunk S_{s-j+1}. The local index

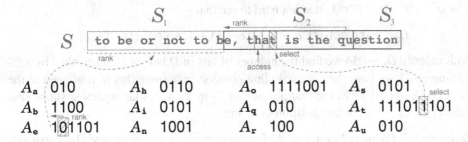

Figure 6.2. The chunk-level granularity operations illustrated on the A_c bitvectors of Figure 6.1. Operation access$(S, 15)$ is shown in open gray blocks, and rank$_e(S, 23)$ and select$_t(S, 5)$ in blocks hatched in different directions. The dashed lines refer to the chunk-level granularity and the solid lines to the within-chunk operations.

of the desired c is the number of 1s from the beginning of the chunk $s - j + 1$ in A_c up to s, that is, $s - \text{pred}_0(A_c, s)$.

Example 6.2 *Figure 6.2 illustrates the operations on the structure of Figure 6.1. To solve query* access$(S, 15)$, *we compute the chunk number* $k = \lceil 15/\sigma \rceil = 2$ *where 15 lies, and reduce the problem to query* access$(S_k, ((15 - 1) \bmod \sigma) + 1) =$ access$(S_2, 3) = $ h *on chunk* S_2.

To solve query rank$_e(S, 23)$, *we compute the chunk number* $k = \lceil 23/\sigma \rceil = 2$ *where 23 lies, and then find the number of times* e *occurs before* $S_k = S_2$, *that is,* select$_0(A_e, k - 1) - (k - 1) = 2 - 1 = 1$. *To this, we add* rank$_e(S_k, ((23 - 1) \bmod \sigma) + 1) = $ rank$_e(S_2, 11) = 2$, *the number of times* e *appears in* S_2 *up to global position 23. Thus the final answer is* $1 + 2 = 3$.

Finally, to solve select$_t(S, 5)$, *we first compute* $s = $ select$_1(A_t, 5) = 6$, *the position in* A_t *of the desired occurrence of* t. *This is in the block* $s - 5 + 1 = 2$, *thus we skip* $(s - 5) \cdot \sigma = 12$ *positions in* S, *and then find in the block* $S_{s-5+1} = S_2$ *the occurrence of* t *number* $s - \text{pred}_0(A_t, s) = 6 - 4 = 2$, *that is, we answer* $12 + $ select$_t(S_2, 2) = 12 + 5 = 17$.

Therefore, with the $2n + o(n)$ bits used by the bitvectors A_c with constant-time select$_{0/1}$ and pred$_0$ (Sections 4.3.3 and 4.5.2), we reduce in $\mathcal{O}(1)$ time the operations on S to the same operations within a chunk.

As a technicality, note that we need σ pointers to the bitvectors A_c. If σ is so large that this becomes an issue, we can concatenate $A = A_1 . A_2 \ldots A_\sigma$, and easily translate the operations used on A_c to operations on the single bitvector A. We leave this as an exercise to the reader.

6.1.2 Operations within a Chunk

A chunk $C[1, \sigma]$ will be represented as the permutation induced by its inverted index, exactly as in Section 5.4.2, but using the symbols of Σ instead of the words, and representing the permutation without compression, as in Section 5.1. Let L_c be the sequence of the positions of symbol c in C, in increasing order. Then consider the permutation $\pi = L_1 . L_2 \ldots L_\sigma$ on $[1, \sigma]$. Unlike in Section 5.4.2, there may be empty lists L_c, precisely when c does not appear in C. Therefore, the bitvector D used to mark the starting positions of the lists L_c in π must be slightly modified to handle empty lists:

$D = 0^{|L_1|}1\,0^{|L_2|}1\ldots0^{|L_\sigma|}1$. It is not hard to see that

$$L_c = \pi[\text{select}_1(D, c-1) - (c-1) + 1, \text{select}_1(D, c) - c]:$$

With $\text{select}_1(D, c-1)$ we find the number of bits in D before L_c starts, then by subtracting $c-1$ we have the corresponding position in π (note that π is aligned to the 0s in D). Adding 1 gives the first position of L_c in π. A similar argument shows that $\text{select}_1(D, c) - c$ is the last position of L_c in π.

Example 6.3 *Figure 6.1 shows, in the bottom part, the structures π and D corresponding to the second chunk, S_2, of the string of Example 6.1. It also shows the conceptual inverted lists L_c (some of which are empty). For example, the list $L_{t=11}$ is in the range* $\pi[\text{select}_1(D, 11-1) - (11-1) + 1, \text{select}_1(D, 11) - 11] = \pi[9, 11] = (2\ 5\ 8)$.

We now have the following equivalences:

$$\text{select}_c(C, j) = \pi(\text{select}_1(D, c-1) - (c-1) + j),$$

$$\text{access}(C, i) = \text{select}_0(D, j) - j + 1, \text{ where } j = \pi^{-1}(i).$$

Let us explain these equations. Query $\text{select}_c(C, j) = L_c[j]$ is the simplest. We already saw that $\text{select}_1(D, c-1) - (c-1)$ is the last position in π preceding L_c. Then by adding j we have the position of $L_c[j]$. For $\text{access}(C, i)$, $j = \pi^{-1}(i)$ tells us where the position i is mentioned in π, that is, in the concatenation of the inverted lists L_c. Now we need to find out which list j is in. To do this, $\text{select}_0(D, j)$ finds the position corresponding to $\pi(j)$ in D, and subtracting $j-1$ we find the c value of the list L_c we are in.

The most complicated operation is $\text{rank}_c(C, i)$. The answer is the largest j such that $L_c[j] \le i$, thus we run a binary search for the largest k such that $\pi(k) \le i$ in the area $k \in [\text{select}_1(D, c-1) - (c-1) + 1, \text{select}_1(D, c) - c]$, that is, the area of L_c in π (note that π is increasing in this area). While this requires in the worst case $\mathcal{O}(\log \sigma)$ accesses to π, this is $\mathcal{O}(1)$ on average if the symbols are uniformly distributed in C. In practice, the range is usually so small that a sequential search is preferable.

Example 6.4 *Figure 6.3 continues the example of Figure 6.2, showing the internal representation of the chunk $C = S_2$. We now complete the queries of Example 6.2, each of which is illustrated in gray in Figure 6.3.*

For $\text{access}(S_2)$ we first compute $j = \pi^{-1}(3) = 4$, the position where 3 appears in π. Now, to find the list L_c to which this corresponds, we compute $\text{select}_0(D, j) - j + 1 = 7 - 4 + 1 = 4$. Thus the result is the letter $4 = $ h.

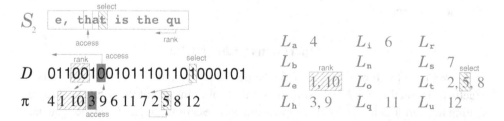

Figure 6.3. The representation of the chunk S_2 of Figure 6.1, illustrating the operations of Example 6.4. We illustrate operation $\text{access}(S_2, 3)$ with open or solid gray blocks, and $\text{rank}_e(S_2, 11)$ and $\text{select}_t(S_2, 2)$ with blocks hatched in different directions.

To find $\mathsf{rank}_{\mathsf{e}=3}(S_2, 11)$, *we run a binary search for the number* 11 *in the area* $\pi[\mathsf{select}_1(D, \mathsf{e} - 1) - (\mathsf{e} - 1) + 1, \mathsf{select}_1(D, \mathsf{e}) - \mathsf{e}] = \pi[\mathsf{select}_1(D, 2) - 2 + 1,$ $\mathsf{select}_1(D, 3) - 3] = \pi[2, 3] = (1\ 10)$, *finding that the last position* ≤ 11 *is* $\pi(3)$. *The answer is then the local offset of* $\pi(3)$ *in* $\pi[2, 3]$, *that is,* 2.

Finally, to solve $\mathsf{select}_{\mathsf{t}=11}(S_2, 2) = L_{\mathsf{t}}[2]$, *we first compute the position of* $L_{\mathsf{t}}[j]$ *in* π, $\mathsf{select}_1(D, \mathsf{t} - 1) - (\mathsf{t} - 1) + j = \mathsf{select}_1(D, 10) - 10 + 2 = 18 - 10 + 2 = 10$, *and then return* $\pi(10) = 5$.

Algorithm 6.1 shows the pseudocode for the three operations. The permutation π and the bitvector D of chunk k are called π_k and D_k, respectively.

Algorithm 6.1: Answering access, rank, and select with the permutation-based structure.

---

1 **Proc** access(S, i)

    Input : Sequence S (seen as bitvectors A_c and chunks S_k, in turn seen as
             permutations π_k and bitvectors D_k) and position i.

    Output: Returns access(S, i).

2    $k \leftarrow \lceil i/\sigma \rceil$

3    $i' \leftarrow ((i - 1) \bmod \sigma) + 1$

4    $j \leftarrow \mathsf{inverse}(\pi_k, i')$ (Algorithm 5.1)

5   **return** $\mathsf{select}_0(D_k, j) - j + 1$

6 **Proc** rank$_c$(S, i)

    Input : Sequence S (seen as bitvectors A_c and chunks S_k, in turn seen as
             permutations π_k and bitvectors D_k), symbol c, and position i.

    Output: Returns rank$_c$(S, i).

7   **if** $i = 0$ **then return** 0

8    $k \leftarrow \lceil i/\sigma \rceil$

9    $i' \leftarrow ((i - 1) \bmod \sigma) + 1$

10   $sL \leftarrow \mathsf{select}_1(D_k, c - 1) - (c - 1)$

11   $eL \leftarrow \mathsf{select}_1(D_k, c) - c$

12   Binary search $[sL + 1, eL]$ for the largest j such that
      $\mathsf{read}(\pi_k, j) \leq i'$ (set $j = sL$ if $\mathsf{read}(\pi_k, sL + 1) > i'$)

13   **return** $\mathsf{select}_0(A_c, k - 1) - (k - 1) + (j - sL)$

14 **Proc** select$_c$(S, j)

    Input : Sequence S (seen as bitvectors A_c and chunks S_k, in turn seen as
             permutations π_k and bitvectors D_k), symbol c, and index j.

    Output: Returns select$_c$(S, j).

15   **if** $j = 0$ **then return** 0

16   $s \leftarrow \mathsf{select}_1(A_c, j)$

17   **if** $s > |A_c|$ **then return** $n + 1$

18   $j' \leftarrow s - \mathsf{pred}_0(A_c, s)$

19   $sL \leftarrow \mathsf{select}_1(D_{s-j+1}, c - 1) - (c - 1)$

20   **return** $(s - j) \cdot \sigma + \mathsf{read}(\pi_{s-j+1}, sL + j')$

Algorithm 6.2: Building the permutation-based representation.

> **Input**   : Sequence $S[1, n]$ over alphabet $[1, \sigma]$.
> **Output**: Builds the permutation representation of S: A_c and S_k (as π_k and D_k).

1 Allocate array $F[0, \sigma]$ of integers
2 **for** $c \leftarrow 1$ **to** σ **do** $F[c] \leftarrow 0$
3 **for** $i \leftarrow 1$ **to** n **do**
4 $\quad \lfloor \; F[S[i]] \leftarrow F[S[i]] + 1$

5 **for** $c \leftarrow 1$ **to** σ **do**
6 $\quad$ Allocate bit array $A_c[1, F[c] + \lceil n/\sigma \rceil - 1]$
7 $\quad \lfloor \; F[c] \leftarrow 0$

8 **for** $k \leftarrow 1$ **to** $\lceil n/\sigma \rceil$ **do**
9 $\quad$ **for** $i \leftarrow (k-1)\sigma + 1$ **to** $\min(k\sigma, n)$ **do**
10 $\quad\quad$ $F[S[i]] \leftarrow F[S[i]] + 1$
11 $\quad\quad \lfloor$ bitset$(A_{S[i]}, F[S[i]])$
12 $\quad$ **for** $c \leftarrow 1$ **to** σ **do**
13 $\quad\quad$ $F[c] \leftarrow F[c] + 1$
14 $\quad\quad \lfloor$ bitclear$(A_c, F[c])$

15 **for** $k \leftarrow 1$ **to** $\lceil n/\sigma \rceil$ **do**
16 $\quad$ **for** $c \leftarrow 0$ **to** σ **do** $F[c] \leftarrow 0$
17 $\quad$ $\ell \leftarrow \min(k\sigma, n) - (k-1)\sigma$
18 $\quad$ Allocate array $\pi_k[1, \ell]$ of $\lceil \log \sigma \rceil$-bit values
19 $\quad$ Allocate bit array $D_k[1, \ell + \sigma]$
20 $\quad$ **for** $i \leftarrow (k-1)\sigma + 1$ **to** $\min(k\sigma, n)$ **do**
21 $\quad\quad \lfloor \; F[S[i]] \leftarrow F[S[i]] + 1$
22 $\quad$ **for** $c \leftarrow 1$ **to** σ **do**
23 $\quad\quad$ $F[c] \leftarrow F[c] + F[c-1]$
24 $\quad\quad \lfloor$ bitset$(D_k, F[c] + c)$
25 $\quad$ **for** $i \leftarrow (k-1)\sigma + 1$ **to** $\min(k\sigma, n)$ **do**
26 $\quad\quad$ $F[S[i] - 1] \leftarrow F[S[i] - 1] + 1$
27 $\quad\quad$ write$(\pi_k, F[S[i] - 1], i - (k-1)\sigma)$
28 $\quad\quad \lfloor$ bitclear$(D_k, F[S[i] - 1] + S[i] - 1)$

29 Free F and (if desired) S
30 Preprocess all A_c for $\mathsf{select}_{0/1}$ and pred_0 queries
31 Preprocess all D_k for $\mathsf{select}_{0/1}$ queries
32 Preprocess all π_k for read and $\mathsf{inverse}$ queries

---

6.1.3 Construction

The construction is described in Algorithm 6.2. Lines 1–14 build the bitvectors A_c and lines 15–28 build the structures π_k and D_k of the chunks. The construction clearly runs in time $\mathcal{O}(n)$ if we use the technique of Section 5.1 to represent the permutations π_k. The memory space needed is that of S and the final structures, plus just $\mathcal{O}(\sigma \log \sigma)$ bits.

By reading S twice from disk by small buffers, we can also generate the bitvectors A_c by small buffers, needing only the main memory space for σ such buffers (or we can make σ/σ' passes if we can hold only σ' buffers). In a second pass, we read S from disk once more and build each chunk using just $\mathcal{O}(\sigma \log \sigma)$ bits of main memory.

6.1.4 Space and Time

The bitvector D_k of each chunk k contains σ 1s and σ 0s, and therefore all the bitvectors D_k add up to $2n + o(n)$ bits, considering the support for constant-time **select**. Added to the $2n + o(n)$ bits of the bitvectors A_c, we have $4n + o(n)$ bits plus the space to store all the permutations π_k.

If we use the representation of Section 5.1 for π_k, we use $(1 + \epsilon)\sigma \log \sigma + \mathcal{O}(\sigma)$ bits per chunk, adding up to a total space of $(1 + \epsilon)n \log \sigma + \mathcal{O}(n)$ bits. With this representation, we have **access**(S, i) in time $\mathcal{O}(1/\epsilon)$, **select**$_c(S, j)$ in time $\mathcal{O}(1)$, and **rank**$_c(S, i)$ in time $\mathcal{O}(\log \sigma)$. By choosing, for example, $1/\epsilon = \log \sigma$, we have all the operations in $\mathcal{O}(\log \sigma)$ time, and a total space of $n \log \sigma + \mathcal{O}(n)$ bits.

We can also speed up **access** to time $\mathcal{O}(\log \log \sigma)$ by choosing $1/\epsilon = \log \log \sigma$. This raises the space to $n \log \sigma + \mathcal{O}\left(\frac{n \log \sigma}{\log \log \sigma}\right) = n \log \sigma + n \cdot o(\log \sigma)$ bits. Note that the last term is not sublinear in n,[1] which makes explicit the fact that this structure is not convenient for small alphabets. Concretely, the $4n$-bit overhead can be very significant when σ is small.

Guaranteeing $\mathcal{O}(\log \log \sigma)$ *Time for* rank

As explained, **rank**$_c(S, i)$ can be solved in time $\mathcal{O}(\log \sigma)$ via binary search, and in practice it can be even faster. We show now how to ensure $\mathcal{O}(\log \log \sigma)$ time for **rank**$_c(S, i)$ queries. This solution will rarely be faster than a sequential or binary search (and thus it should be used only in special cases), but it allows us to claim $\mathcal{O}(\log \log \sigma)$ time complexity for **rank**$_c(S, i)$: it can be made $\mathcal{O}(\log \log \sigma)$ if desired, and it is actually better in practice. The rest of this section can thus be safely skipped by practice-oriented readers.

We consider a block size $b = \log^2 \sigma$ and sample the lists L_c whose length is $|L_c| > b$, taking every bth value. We insert those sampled values into a predecessor data structure (Section 4.5.2). Then the binary search for i' in L_c (line 12 of Algorithm 6.1) will be replaced by a predecessor search to find the predecessor sample of i', and then a binary search in the block of L_c between that sample and the next. The predecessor will be found in $\mathcal{O}(\log \log \sigma)$ time, and the binary search also takes time $\mathcal{O}(\log b) = \mathcal{O}(\log \log \sigma)$.

For space reasons, we cannot use the predecessor structures described in Section 4.5.2. A suitable one, instead, is described next. It requires $\mathcal{O}(t \log \sigma)$ bits to manage t elements in $[1, \sigma]$. In our case, added over all the lists L_c of the chunk, we have at most $t = \sigma/\log^2 \sigma$, and thus the structure uses $\mathcal{O}(\sigma/\log \sigma)$ bits per chunk and $\mathcal{O}(n/\log \sigma)$ bits overall.

The structure, $\mathcal{P}$, on a universe $[0, \sigma - 1]$, is recursive. It cuts the universe into $\sqrt{\sigma}$ sub-universe ranges of length $\sqrt{\sigma}$ and contains a sub-structure *bottom*$(\cdot)$ on each

---

[1] That is, it is not $o(n \log \sigma)$ as a function of n. For example, if $\sigma = \mathcal{O}(1)$, then $o(n \log \sigma) = o(n)$, but $n \cdot o(\log \sigma) = \Theta(n)$.

nonempty sub-universe (of the form $[0, \sqrt{\sigma} - 1]$). Each element $x = x_h \cdot x_l$, where x_h and x_l are the highest and lowest $(\log \sigma)/2$ bits of x, is stored as the element x_l in the sub-structure $bottom(x_h)$. In addition, another sub-structure top on the universe $[0, \sqrt{\sigma} - 1]$ stores the indexes of the sub-universes that are nonempty. Each structure also knows its minimum and maximum elements, min and max. Structures top and $bottom(\cdot)$ are recursively deployed until they contain $\log \sigma$ elements, at which point they can be handled by binary search.

To find the predecessor of $y = y_h \cdot y_l$, we first see if $y_h \in top$, and if so, if $bottom(y_h).min \le y$. If so, we recursively find the predecessor x_l of y_l in sub-structure $bottom(y_h)$ and answer $y_h \cdot x_l$. Otherwise the predecessor of y is not in its sub-universe. In this case, the answer is the maximum element of the largest nonempty sub-universe before y_h, that is, we (recursively) find the predecessor x_h of $y_h - 1$ in top and return $x_h \cdot bottom(x_h).max$. The recursive query process takes time $\mathcal{O}(\log \log \sigma)$, as we halve $\log \sigma$ in each step.

To maintain the total space within $\mathcal{O}(t \log \sigma)$ bits, we represent $\mathcal{P}$ as follows. The main data structure is a perfect hash table (Section 4.5.3) where the non-empty sub-universes x_h are stored, with the sub-structures $bottom(x_h)$ associated with them as satellite data. Thus we find in constant time whether $y_h \in top$ and, if so, its corresponding sub-structure $bottom(y_h)$. The element $\mathcal{P}.max$ is not additionally stored in $\mathcal{P}$ (this implies a minor change in the search algorithm we gave: start by checking if $y \ge \mathcal{P}.max$ and if so return $\mathcal{P}.max$), and this holds recursively for all the sub-structures. Thus each element $x = x_h \cdot x_l$ we store in $\mathcal{P}$ either is the maximum in $bottom(x_h)$ or not. If it is, we charge it for the space of storing in top the key x_h and the satellite data $bottom(x_h)$, but x_l is not inserted in $bottom(x_h)$. Otherwise we count its insertion in $bottom(x_h)$, but not in top, as some other $x' = x_h \cdot x_l'$ will be charged for that. Therefore, each element x is charged for $\mathcal{O}(\log \sigma)$ bits in only 1 structure, and the total space is $\mathcal{O}(t \log \sigma)$ bits as promised. The construction is $\mathcal{O}(t)$ expected time, due to the perfect hash tables.

6.2 Wavelet Trees

In the beginning of this chapter we showed the inconveniences of a solution that stores one bitvector per symbol. The wavelet tree is another approach to address those problems. Instead of a "plain" structure with one bitvector B_c telling the positions where each individual symbol c appears in S, the wavelet tree uses a *hierarchical* partitioning of the alphabet. That is, for the first step, we divide the alphabet symbols $[1, \sigma]$ into two roughly equal parts, $[1, \lceil \sigma/2 \rceil]$ and $[\lceil \sigma/2 \rceil + 1, \sigma]$, and create a bitvector $B_{\langle 1, \sigma \rangle}[1, n]$ where $B_{\langle 1, \sigma \rangle}[i] = 0$ iff $S[i] \in [1, \lceil \sigma/2 \rceil]$. That is, $B_{\langle 1, \sigma \rangle}$ acts exactly as B_c but for a class of symbols. This division then continues recursively.

6.2.1 Structure

The bitvector $B_{\langle 1, \sigma \rangle}$ is used to partition the sequence S into two subsequences: one contains, in order, the symbols $S[i] \in [1, \lceil \sigma/2 \rceil]$, and another contains, in order, the symbols $S[i] \in [\lceil \sigma/2 \rceil + 1, \sigma]$. We call the former sequence $S_{\langle 1, \lceil \sigma/2 \rceil \rangle}$ and the latter

$S_{(\lceil\sigma/2\rceil+1,\sigma)}$. In general, $S_{(a,b)}$ will denote the subsequence of S formed by the symbols that are between a and b; therefore $S = S_{(1,\sigma)}$. Note the following important relations:

$$S_{(1,\lceil\sigma/2\rceil)}[\mathsf{rank}_0(B_{(1,\sigma)}, i)] = S_{(1,\sigma)}[i], \text{ if } B_{(1,\sigma)}[i] = 0,$$

$$S_{(\lceil\sigma/2\rceil+1,\sigma)}[\mathsf{rank}_1(B_{(1,\sigma)}, i)] = S_{(1,\sigma)}[i], \text{ if } B_{(1,\sigma)}[i] = 1.$$

Now we recursively repeat the process on the subsequences $S_{(1,\lceil\sigma/2\rceil)}$ and $S_{(\lceil\sigma/2\rceil+1,\sigma)}$. In the first case, we divide the alphabet range $[1, \lceil\sigma/2\rceil]$ into two roughly equal parts, $[1, \lceil\sigma/4\rceil]$ and $[\lceil\sigma/4\rceil+1, \lceil\sigma/2\rceil]$, marking in a bitvector $B_{(1,\lceil\sigma/2\rceil)}$ whether each symbol of $S_{(1,\lceil\sigma/2\rceil)}$ belongs to $[1, \lceil\sigma/4\rceil]$ or to $[\lceil\sigma/4\rceil+1, \lceil\sigma/2\rceil]$. The corresponding subsequences of $S_{(1,\lceil\sigma/2\rceil)}$ are $S_{(1,\lceil\sigma/4\rceil)}$ and $S_{(\lceil\sigma/4\rceil+1,\lceil\sigma/2\rceil)}$, respectively. Analogously, we divide the alphabet range $[\lceil\sigma/2\rceil+1, \sigma]$ into $[\lceil\sigma/2\rceil+1, \lceil3\sigma/4\rceil]$ and $[\lceil3\sigma/4\rceil+1, \sigma]$. This recursive partitioning continues until the subsequences we obtain are of the form $S_{(c,c)}$, that is, they contain only one symbol.

The wavelet tree is a binary tree where the root corresponds to $S_{(1,\sigma)}$, the σ leaves correspond to $S_{(c,c)}$, and the two children of an internal node corresponding to $S_{(a,b)}$ represent $S_{(a,\lfloor(a+b)/2\rfloor)}$ (left child) and $S_{(\lfloor(a+b)/2\rfloor+1,b)}$ (right child). Note that we have used limits of the form $\lceil i \cdot \sigma/2^\ell\rceil$ in the first levels for simplicity, but these do not coincide with the general formula for larger values of ℓ, and cause troubles near the leaves.

Example 6.5 *Figure 6.4 shows a wavelet tree for the sequence $S =$* "to be or not to be, that is the question" *of Example 6.2 (recall that white-spaces and commas are ignored). Here $\langle 1, \sigma\rangle =$* a, b, e, h, i, n, o, q, r, s, t, u, *which we interpret as the numbers 1 to 12. The left child of the root corresponds to $S_{(1,\lceil\sigma/2\rceil)} = S_{(1,6)} = S_{a,b,e,h,i,n} =$* "benbehaiheein". *This is the sequence of the letters in $S = S_{(1,\sigma)}$ that belong to $[1, \lceil\sigma/2\rceil] = [1, 6]$. Those letters are at the positions marked with a 0 in $B_{(1,12)}$. For example, $S_{(1,12)}[21] = $* h *belongs to $[1, 6]$, and thus $B_{(1,12)}[21] = 0$. That* h *at $S_{(1,12)}[21]$ is mapped to $S_{(1,6)}[9] = $* h, *because $\mathsf{rank}_0(B_{(1,12)}, 21) = 9$. Arrows and shading will be used later.*

A notable property of this arrangement is that the bitvectors $B_{(a,b)}$ contain sufficient information to retrieve any $S[i]$, and thus they are a valid representation of S. The key idea is that, if $S_{(a,b)}[i] \leq \lfloor(a+b)/2\rfloor$, then this symbol appears in $S_{(a,\lfloor(a+b)/2\rfloor)}$, precisely at position $\mathsf{rank}_0(B_{(a,b)}, i)$. That is, it holds $S_{(a,\lfloor(a+b)/2\rfloor)}[\mathsf{rank}_0(B_{(a,b)}, i)] = S_{(a,b)}[i]$. Similarly, if $S_{(a,b)}[i] > \lfloor(a+b)/2\rfloor$, then this symbol appears in $S_{(\lfloor(a+b)/2\rfloor+1,b)}$, at position $\mathsf{rank}_1(B_{(a,b)}, i)$. Therefore, we can track a desired symbol $S[i] = c$ from the root of the wavelet tree to the leaf corresponding to $S_{(c,c)}$.

More operationally, suppose we want to solve $\mathsf{access}(S, i) = S[i]$. If $B_{(1,\sigma)}[i] = 0$, then we know that $S[i] \in [1, \lceil\sigma/2\rceil]$, and therefore $S[i]$ appears in $S_{(1,\lceil\sigma/2\rceil)}$, the sequence represented by the left child of the root. At this node, the position is $\mathsf{rank}_0(B_{(1,\sigma)}, i)$. If, instead, $B_{(1,\sigma)}[i] = 1$, then $S[i] \in [\lceil\sigma/2\rceil+1, \sigma]$ and $S[i]$ appears in $S_{(\lceil\sigma/2\rceil+1,\sigma)}$, the sequence represented at the right child of the root. At this node, the position where $S[i]$ appears is $\mathsf{rank}_1(B_{(1,\sigma)}, i)$. In general, we start at the root node with $[a, b] = [1, \sigma]$ and examine $B_{(a,b)}[i]$. If it is a 0, we move to the left child of the node, set $i \leftarrow \mathsf{rank}_0(B_{(a,b)}, i)$, and $[a, b] \leftarrow [a, \lfloor(a+b)/2\rfloor]$. If it is instead a 1, we move to the right child of the node, set $i \leftarrow \mathsf{rank}_1(B_{(a,b)}, i)$, and $[a, b] \leftarrow [\lfloor(a+b)/2\rfloor+1, b]$.

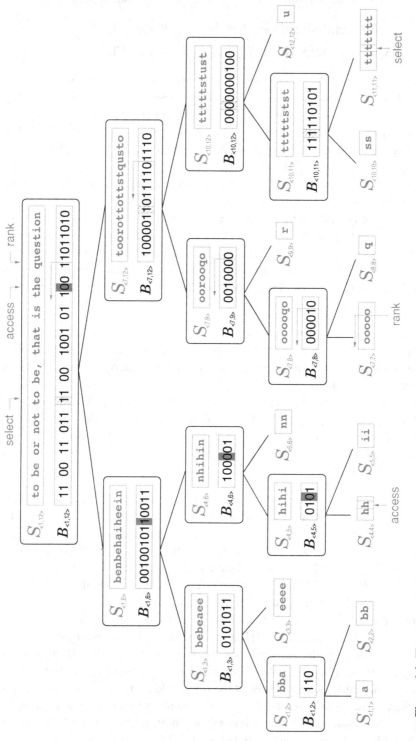

Figure 6.4. The representation of the same sequence of Example 6.2 using a wavelet tree. We show in black the elements that are actually represented (tree topology and bitvectors $B_{(a,b)}$), and in gray the elements that are only conceptual (leaves and sequences $S_{(a,b)}$). The various shaded blocks and arrows illustrate operations $\mathsf{access}(S, 21)$, $\mathsf{rank}_\mathsf{o}(S, 23)$, and $\mathsf{select}_\mathsf{t}(S, 3)$.

Algorithm 6.3: Answering access and rank with wavelet trees. The fields in the tree nodes are left child l, right child r, and bitvector B.

---

1 **Proc** access(S, i)
    Input : Sequence S (seen as wavelet tree T) and position i.
    Output: Returns access(S, i).
2     $v \leftarrow T.root$
3     $[a, b] \leftarrow [1, \sigma]$
4   **while** $a \neq b$ **do**
5   **if** access$(v.B, i) = 0$ **then**
6             $i \leftarrow \text{rank}_0(v.B, i)$
7             $v \leftarrow v.l$
8             $b \leftarrow \lfloor (a + b)/2 \rfloor$
9   **else**
10            $i \leftarrow \text{rank}_1(v.B, i)$
11            $v \leftarrow v.r$
12            $a \leftarrow \lfloor (a + b)/2 \rfloor + 1$
13   **return** a

14 **Proc** rank$_c(S, i)$
    Input : Sequence S (seen as wavelet tree T), symbol c, and position i.
    Output: Returns rank$_c(S, i)$.
15    $v \leftarrow T.root$
16    $[a, b] \leftarrow [1, \sigma]$
17   **while** $a \neq b$ **do**
18   **if** $c \leq \lfloor (a + b)/2 \rfloor$ **then**
19            $i \leftarrow \text{rank}_0(v.B, i)$
20            $v \leftarrow v.l$
21            $b \leftarrow \lfloor (a + b)/2 \rfloor$
22   **else**
23            $i \leftarrow \text{rank}_1(v.B, i)$
24            $v \leftarrow v.r$
25            $a \leftarrow \lfloor (a + b)/2 \rfloor + 1$
26   **return** i

When we arrive at a leaf, corresponding to $S_{\langle c,c \rangle}$, we return c. Moreover, note that the final value of i is the number of c's up to the one we have accessed, rank$_{S[i]}(S, i)$. Algorithm 6.3 gives the pseudocode.

Example 6.6 *Let us compute* access$(S, 21) = S[21]$ *in the wavelet tree of Example 6.5. The accessed bitvector positions are shown in solid gray blocks in Figure 6.4. Since we find that* $B_{\langle 1,12 \rangle}[21] = 0$ *at the wavelet tree root, we know that the answer belongs to* $[1, 6]$ *and thus continue the search from the left child of the* *root. Moreover, the symbol is at $S_{\langle 1,6 \rangle}[\text{rank}_0(B_{\langle 1,12 \rangle}, 21)] = S_{\langle 1,6 \rangle}[9]$, so we access $B_{\langle 1,6 \rangle}[9] = 1$. Therefore, our symbol is in $[4, 6]$, and thus we have to move to the right child. We know that our symbol is at $S_{\langle 4,6 \rangle}[\text{rank}_1(B_{\langle 1,6 \rangle}, 9)] = S_{\langle 4,6 \rangle}[4]$. Now we have that $B_{\langle 4,6 \rangle}[4] = 0$, so we know that the symbol belongs to $[4, 5]$ and thus we go to the left child. In this child, our symbol is at $S_{\langle 4,5 \rangle}[\text{rank}_0(B_{\langle 4,6 \rangle}, 4)] = S_{\langle 4,5 \rangle}[3]$. Now we read $B_{\langle 4,5 \rangle}[3] = 0$, therefore our symbol belongs to $[4, 4]$, and we finish, answering 4 (that is, h).*

The height of the wavelet tree is $\lceil \log \sigma \rceil$, and thus the **access**(S, i) method we have described takes time $\mathcal{O}(\log \sigma)$ if we use constant-time **rank** on the bitvectors (Section 4.2.2). As for the space, note that all the bitvectors $B_{\langle a,b \rangle}$ at the same depth form a partition of $[1, \sigma]$ and thus add up to n bits. Therefore, the total number of bits in the wavelet tree is $n \lceil \log \sigma \rceil$, essentially the same space used to represent S in plain form. If we add the tree pointers, the pointers to the bitvectors, and the extra space to provide constant-time **rank** queries, the total space becomes $n \log \sigma + o(n \log \sigma) + \mathcal{O}(\sigma w)$ bits.

6.2.2 Solving Rank and Select

We have shown that our mechanism to solve $S[i] = \textbf{access}(S, i)$ also provides the number of occurrences of $S[i]$ in $S[1, i]$, that is, $\text{rank}_{S[i]}(S, i)$. This idea can be generalized to solve any query $\text{rank}_c(S, i)$. The only difference is that, instead of moving from the root toward the leaf corresponding to $S[i]$, we move toward the leaf of c.

We start at the root, representing the sequence $S_{\langle a,b \rangle} = S_{\langle 1,\sigma \rangle}$. If $c \leq \lfloor (a + b)/2 \rfloor$, we know that the leaf of c descends from the left child of the node, thus we move to the left child, set $i \leftarrow \text{rank}_0(B_{\langle a,b \rangle}, i)$, and $[a, b] \leftarrow [a, \lfloor (a + b)/2 \rfloor]$. Otherwise the leaf c descends from the right child, thus we move to the right child, set $i \leftarrow \text{rank}_1(B_{\langle a,b \rangle}, i)$, and $[a, b] \leftarrow [\lfloor (a + b)/2 \rfloor + 1, b]$. In both cases we maintain the invariant that the number of occurrences of c in $S_{\langle a,b \rangle}[1, i]$ is the answer to the query. When we finally arrive at the leaf of c, the sequence is $S_{\langle c,c \rangle}$, and thus the current value of i is the answer. Note that this time we do not descend by considering the value of $B_{\langle a,b \rangle}[i]$, but rather on the side of the interval where c is. Algorithm 6.3 gives the pseudocode. Just as for **access**, the time is $\mathcal{O}(\log \sigma)$.

Example 6.7 *Let us compute* $\text{rank}_{\text{o}=7}(S, 23)$ *in the wavelet tree of Example 6.5. The positions considered are shown with leftward gray arrows in Figure 6.4. At the wavelet tree root, we find that* $\text{o} \in [7, 12]$, *the second half of the interval* $[a, b] = [1, \sigma] = [1, 12]$. *Thus we move to the right child of the root and recompute* $i \leftarrow \text{rank}_1(B_{\langle 1,12 \rangle}, 23) = 13$. *In the right child, corresponding to* $S_{\langle 7,12 \rangle}$, *we find that* $\text{o} \in [7, 9]$, *the first half of the interval* $[7, 12]$, *and thus we continue on the left child of the node, which represents* $S_{\langle 7,9 \rangle}$. *We recompute* $i \leftarrow \text{rank}_0(B_{\langle 7,12 \rangle}, 13) = 6$. *In the node of* $S_{\langle 7,9 \rangle}$, *we find that* $\text{o} \in [7, 8]$, *the left half of the interval* $[7, 9]$. *So we move to the left child, which represents* $S_{\langle 7,8 \rangle}$, *recomputing* $i \leftarrow \text{rank}_0(B_{\langle 7,9 \rangle}, 6) = 5$. *Finally, since* $\text{o} \in [7, 7]$, *the left half of* $[7, 8]$, *we move to the left child of the node, which is the leaf corresponding to* $S_{\langle 7,7 \rangle}$, *and recompute* $i \leftarrow \text{rank}_0(B_{\langle 7,8 \rangle}, 5) = 4$. *Since we are in a leaf, we return 4, the current value of* i.

By essentially the reverse process we can compute $\mathsf{select}_c(S, j)$. The idea is now to track *upwards* the jth occurrence of c in S. At the leaf node of c, we know that this corresponds to $S_{\langle c,c \rangle}[j]$. Now we must track that position up to the root, where we will find the position of that c in S. In general, we are at a position $S_{\langle a,b \rangle}[j]$ and need to find the corresponding position in the parent of the node of $S_{\langle a,b \rangle}$. Let us call $S_{\langle a',b' \rangle}$ the sequence corresponding to the parent of the current node. If the current node is the left child of its parent, then we know that the positions of $S_{\langle a,b \rangle}$ correspond to 0s in $B_{\langle a',b' \rangle}$, therefore we move to the parent node and recompute $j \leftarrow \mathsf{select}_0(B_{\langle a',b' \rangle}, j)$. Otherwise the current node is the right child of its parent, so the corresponding position in the parent node is $j \leftarrow \mathsf{select}_1(B_{\langle a',b' \rangle}, j)$. When we reach the root node, we return j.

Example 6.8 *Let us compute* $\mathsf{select}_{\mathsf{t}=\mathsf{11}}(S, 3)$. *Figure 6.4 illustrates the upward path in gray hatched blocks. We start in the leaf corresponding to* $S_{\langle 11,11 \rangle}$ *(since* $\mathsf{t} = 11$*), precisely at the position* $S_{\langle 11,11 \rangle}[3]$. *Since this leaf is the right child of its parent, which corresponds to* $S_{\langle 10,11 \rangle}$, *we move to the parent and update* $j \leftarrow \mathsf{select}_1(B_{\langle 10,11 \rangle}, 3) = 3$. *This node is the left child of its parent, which corresponds to* $S_{\langle 10,12 \rangle}$, *thus we move to this parent and update* $j \leftarrow \mathsf{select}_0(B_{\langle 10,12 \rangle}, 3) = 3$. *In turn, this node is the right child of its parent, which corresponds to* $S_{\langle 7,12 \rangle}$, *so we move to the parent and update* $j \leftarrow \mathsf{select}_1(B_{\langle 7,12 \rangle}, 3) = 7$. *Note that* $S_{\langle 7,12 \rangle}[7] = \mathsf{t}$ *is the same* t *of* $S_{\langle 7,7 \rangle}[3]$. *Finally, this node is the right child of the root, which corresponds to* $S_{\langle 1,12 \rangle}$, *and thus the final value is* $j \leftarrow \mathsf{select}_1(B_{\langle 1,12 \rangle}, 7) = 10$. *Thus we return 10, the position of the 3rd occurrence of* t *in* S.

If we add the data structures to support select queries in constant time on the bitvectors $B_{\langle a,b \rangle}$ (Section 4.3.3), the time for this query is also $\mathcal{O}(\log \sigma)$. Note that the upward traversal seems to require upward pointers in the tree, plus σ pointers from each symbol c to the leaf corresponding to $S_{\langle c,c \rangle}$. This still maintains the extra space in $\mathcal{O}(\sigma w)$ bits, but it can be avoided by finding the leaf recursively from the root, as for $\mathsf{rank}_c(S, i)$, and then all the nodes in the upward path from $S_{\langle c,c \rangle}$ are available during the return from the recursion. Algorithm 6.4 details the select procedure.

Practical Considerations

Using constant-time rank and select structures on the bitvectors yields a total wavelet tree space of $n \log \sigma + o(n \log \sigma)$ bits, and supports the wavelet tree queries in $\mathcal{O}(\log \sigma)$ time. However, we observed in Section 4.3.3 that obtaining constant-time select on bitvectors may require a significant amount of extra space (even if sublinear in theory), and in this case the space of the bitvectors dominates that of the whole structure. We instead showed in Sections 4.3.2 and 4.3.3 that it was possible to obtain $\mathcal{O}(\log \log n)$ select time with practical space overheads, and described some realizations with 15%–25% space overhead (which must be paid twice since we need both select_0 and select_1). Their times are in practice better than the truly constant-time solutions. For these reasons we will continue assuming that the complexity for select on bitvectors is constant: it can be made truly constant if desired, and in practice it is better (although it is always slower than rank in practice).

Adding the 25% space overhead of practical rank solutions (Section 4.2.2), very fast rank and select requires in practice 55%–75% extra space on top of the $n \log \sigma$ bits.

Algorithm 6.4: Answering **select** with wavelet trees. The fields in the tree nodes are left child l, right child r, and bitvector B.

---

1 **Proc select$_c$(S, j)**
    Input : Sequence S (seen as wavelet tree T), symbol c, and index j.
    Output: Returns select$_c$(S, j).
2   **return** $select(T.root, 1, \sigma, c, j)$

3 **Proc** $select(v, a, b, c, j)$
    Input : Wavelet tree node v, its range $[a, b]$, symbol c, and index j.
    Output: Returns select$_c$(S_v, j), S_v being the subsequence of S represented at
             node v.
4   **if** $a = b$ **then**
5   **return** j
6   **if** $c \leq \lfloor (a + b)/2 \rfloor$ **then**
7         $j \leftarrow select(v.l, a, \lfloor (a + b)/2 \rfloor, c, j)$
8   **return** select$_0$($v.B$, j)
9   **else**
10        $j \leftarrow select(v.r, \lfloor (a + b)/2 \rfloor + 1, b, c, j)$
11   **return** select$_1$($v.B$, j)

Depending on the relevance of the time versus space performance, solutions for **rank** and **select** with much lower space overhead, even if $\mathcal{O}(\log n)$ time, can be preferable (see Sections 4.2.1 and 4.3.1).

6.2.3 Construction

The wavelet tree can be built in time $\mathcal{O}(n \log \sigma)$, by generating each bitvector $B_{\langle a,b \rangle}$ and then partitioning $S_{\langle a,b \rangle}$ into $S_{\langle a, \lfloor (a+b)/2 \rfloor \rangle}$ and $S_{\langle \lfloor (a+b)/2 \rfloor + 1, b \rangle}$. Once partitioned, we can free or reuse the space of the old $S_{\langle a,b \rangle}$. Then we recursively build the subtrees on the sequences $S_{\langle a, \lfloor (a+b)/2 \rfloor \rangle}$ and $S_{\langle \lfloor (a+b)/2 \rfloor + 1, b \rangle}$. Algorithm 6.5 shows the details. The total extra space needed, apart from S and the final wavelet tree built, is $n \log \sigma$ bits. The wavelet tree bitvectors $B_{\langle a,b \rangle}$ can be stored on disk as they are built, to free main memory space.

If the $n \log \sigma$ bits of extra space are a problem, a technique that reduces them to just n bits can be applied. It has the same time complexity, but it is slower in practice. The idea is, in each call of *build*, to partition S in-place into S_l and S_r instead of allocating new space for them. We first compute z and build B, preprocessing it for constant-time **rank** queries. This will be used as a device to compute the final position of any $S[i]$: If $B[i] = 0$, its final position after the partitioning is rank$_0$(B, i), otherwise it is $z +$ rank$_1$(B, i). Once we write all the symbols $S[i]$ to their final positions, it holds $S_l = S[1, z]$ and $S_r = S[z + 1, n]$, and we can make the recursive calls.

To partition S, we carry out a process similar to the one described in Section 5.1 to build a permutation. We set up a bit array $V[1, n]$, initially with all 0s. If $V[i] = 1$, this

---

Algorithm 6.5: Building a wavelet tree. Frees the original string.

Input : Sequence $S[1, n]$ over alphabet $[1, \sigma]$.
Output: Builds the wavelet tree T of S.

1 $T \leftarrow build(S, n, 1, \sigma)$

2 **Proc** $build(S, n, a, b)$
    Input : String $S[1, n]$ on alphabet $[a, b]$.
    Output: Returns a wavelet tree for S. Frees S.

3   **if** $a = b$ **then**
4   Free S
5   **return** null

6   Allocate tree node v
7      $m \leftarrow \lfloor (a + b)/2 \rfloor$
8      $z \leftarrow 0$
9   **for** $i \leftarrow 1$ **to** n **do**
10   **if** $S[i] \le m$ **then**
11             $z \leftarrow z + 1$

12   Allocate strings $S_l[1, z]$ and $S_r[1, n - z]$
13   Allocate bit array $v.B[1, n]$
14     $z \leftarrow 0$
15   **for** $i \leftarrow 1$ **to** n **do**
16   **if** $S[i] \le m$ **then**
17   bitclear($v.B, i$)
18             $z \leftarrow z + 1$
19             $S_l[z] \leftarrow S[i]$
20   **else**
21   bitset($v.B, i$)
22             $S_r[i - z] \leftarrow S[i]$

23   Free S
24     $v.l \leftarrow build(S_l, z, a, m)$
25     $v.r \leftarrow build(S_r, n - z, m + 1, b)$
26   Preprocess $v.B$ for **rank** and **select** queries
27   **return** v

---

will mean that $S[i]$ contains its final value after partitioning. We traverse $S[i]$ from $i = 1$ to $i = n$, looking for cells $V[i] = 0$. When we find one, we set $j \leftarrow i$ and start a cycle where we read $c = S[j]$, compute the final position k for c as explained, swap $c \leftrightarrow S[k]$, set $V[k] \leftarrow 1$, and continue with $j \leftarrow k$, until we return to the original position $j = i$. Note that we are following the cycle of the virtual permutation where we write each symbol $S[j]$ at its correct position and then have to find the right place for the symbol that was previously at that position. The process takes $\mathcal{O}(n)$ time. If desired, we can write the bitvector B to disk after partitioning S, so that the main memory space needed is just $2n + o(n)$ bits apart from S.

Alternatively, we can make a more intensive use of the disk and use the original algorithm. By maintaining the intermediate strings $S_{\langle a,b \rangle}$ and bitvectors $B_{\langle a,b \rangle}$ on disk and processing them by small buffers, the wavelet tree can be built using just $\mathcal{O}(\sigma w)$ bits (for the tree pointers) and a few buffers in main memory.

6.2.4 Compressed Wavelet Trees

The wavelet tree uses $n \log \sigma + o(n \log \sigma) + \mathcal{O}(\sigma w)$ bits and performs **access**, **rank**, and **select** in time $\mathcal{O}(\log \sigma)$. Thus it seems to use about the same space as the structure of Section 6.1, while being slower. An important difference is that wavelet trees are significantly smaller when the alphabet size is small or moderate, since they do not have the $\mathcal{O}(n)$ bits of space overhead. In asymptotic terms, if $\sigma = \mathcal{O}(1)$, the wavelet tree occupies $n \log \sigma + o(n)$ bits, whereas the structure of Section 6.1 stays in $n \log \sigma + \mathcal{O}(n)$. Also, the difference between the wavelet tree time complexities of $\mathcal{O}(\log \sigma)$ and the complexities of the form $\mathcal{O}(\log \log \sigma)$ obtained in Section 6.1 are noticeable only for not so small values of σ.

In this section we explore another advantage of wavelet trees: their ability to be compressed to the zero-order entropy of S while retaining the same times for the operations or better.

Compressing the Bitvectors

An immediate way to compress the wavelet tree is to use compressed representations for its bitvectors $B_{\langle a,b \rangle}$. Assume that we use the representation of Section 4.1.1, with **rank** and **select** support (again, assume for simplicity that these operations take constant time, which can be achieved if necessary but it might require significant extra space on wavelet trees). Let $n_{\langle a,b \rangle} = |S_{\langle a,b \rangle}|$ for all $\langle a, b \rangle$, and $m = \lfloor (a+b)/2 \rfloor$. The space of this representation for $B_{\langle a,b \rangle}$ is then

$$n_{\langle a,m \rangle} \log \frac{n_{\langle a,b \rangle}}{n_{\langle a,m \rangle}} + n_{\langle m+1,b \rangle} \log \frac{n_{\langle a,b \rangle}}{n_{\langle m+1,b \rangle}} + o(n_{\langle a,b \rangle}),$$

where we will omit the $o(n_{\langle a,b \rangle})$ redundancy term for now. Assume, inductively, that the subsequences $S_{\langle a,m \rangle}$ and $S_{\langle m+1,b \rangle}$, corresponding to the children of $S_{\langle a,b \rangle}$ in the wavelet tree, are already represented in $n_{\langle a,m \rangle} \mathcal{H}_0(S_{\langle a,m \rangle})$ and $n_{\langle m+1,b \rangle} \mathcal{H}_0(S_{\langle m+1,b \rangle})$ bits, respectively, again ignoring the redundancies. Then the space used for the subtrees of the two children of the node is

$$n_{\langle a,m \rangle} \mathcal{H}_0(S_{\langle a,m \rangle}) + n_{\langle m+1,b \rangle} \mathcal{H}_0(S_{\langle m+1,b \rangle})$$

$$= \sum_{c=a}^{m} n_c \log \frac{n_{\langle a,m \rangle}}{n_c} + \sum_{c=m+1}^{b} n_c \log \frac{n_{\langle m+1,b \rangle}}{n_c},$$

where $n_c = n_{\langle c,c \rangle}$ is the number of occurrences of c in S. If we add up the compressed space for $B_{\langle a,b \rangle}$ and that of the subtrees of the children of the node, considering that $n_{\langle a,m \rangle} = \sum_{c=a}^{m} n_c$ and $n_{\langle m+1,b \rangle} = \sum_{c=m+1}^{b} n_c$, we obtain

$$\sum_{c=a}^{b} n_c \log \frac{n_{\langle a,b \rangle}}{n_c} = n_{\langle a,b \rangle} \mathcal{H}_0(S_{\langle a,b \rangle}).$$

Since we use no bitvectors at the leaves, their space is indeed $n_{\langle c,c \rangle} \mathcal{H}_0(S_{\langle c,c \rangle}) = 0$ bits, thus the base of the induction holds, and by the calculations above, it holds for all the nodes of the wavelet tree. In particular, it holds at the root node, showing that the space used by all the compressed bitvectors is $n\mathcal{H}_0(S)$ bits. To this we must add the redundancy, which is $o(|B_{\langle a,b \rangle}|)$ for any bitvector $B_{\langle a,b \rangle}$; therefore the total redundancy is $o(n \log \sigma)$ bits.

Overall using compressed bitvectors reduces the total space to $n\mathcal{H}_0(S) + o(n \log \sigma) + \mathcal{O}(\sigma w)$ bits, and retains the time for the operations.

Huffman-Shaped Wavelet Trees

In practice, operating on compressed bitvectors is slower than on plain ones. An alternative to obtain nearly zero-order compressed space while using plain bitvectors is to give a Huffman shape (Section 2.6) to the wavelet tree, instead of using a balanced tree of height $\lceil \log \sigma \rceil$.

We first gather the frequencies n_c of each symbol c in S. Now we apply Algorithm 2.2 to obtain the Huffman tree. Finally, we attach bitvectors B_v to each node v of the Huffman tree, analogous to the bitvectors $B_{\langle a,b \rangle}$ of the balanced wavelet trees. This time, the bits of the bitvectors B_v correspond to the bits of the Huffman codes of the symbols.

Consider the root node v, representing the string $S_v = S$. The bitvector $B_v[1, n]$ has $B_v[i] = 0$ iff the first bit of the Huffman code of symbol $S[i]$ is 0. The left child of the root, v_l, will represent the string S_{v_l} formed by all the symbols in S whose Huffman code starts with a 0. The right child, v_r, will correspond to the string S_{v_r} of the symbols of S whose Huffman code starts with a 1. Once again, if $B_v[i] = 0$ then $S_{v_l}[\text{rank}_0(S_v, i)] = S_v[i]$, otherwise $S_{v_r}[\text{rank}_1(S_v, i)] = S_v[i]$. The bitvectors B_{v_l} and B_{v_r} will separate the symbols of S_{v_l} and S_{v_r} according to the second bit of their Huffman code, and so on.

To count the total number of bits in all the bitvectors B_v, consider the leaf corresponding to a symbol c, at depth $|h(c)|$, representing $S_{\langle c,c \rangle}$ of length n_c (recall that $h(c)$ is the bitwise Huffman code of symbol c). Each of the n_c occurrences of c in $S_{\langle c,c \rangle}$ induces one bit in each bitvector B_v from the root to the parent of the leaf, that is, precisely $|h(c)|$ bits in total. Therefore, the n_c occurrences induce $n_c \cdot |h(c)|$ bits. Added over the leaves for all the symbols c, we have exactly the same number of bits output by Huffman-compressing S, that is, $\sum_c n_c \cdot |h(c)| < n(\mathcal{H}_0(S) + 1)$. If we add the space for rank and select on the bitvectors, plus the tree pointers and the Huffman model, the total space is $n(\mathcal{H}_0(S) + 1)(1 + o(1)) + \mathcal{O}(\sigma w)$ bits.

Example 6.9 *Figure 6.5 shows a Huffman-shaped wavelet tree for the same sequence of Example 6.2. The total number of bits in the bitvectors is 99, the same of the Huffman encoding of S. We illustrate in gray blocks the bits induced by S[21] = h, 0111 from root to leaf, which are the same bits emitted by the compressor when it encodes h.*

The operations on a Huffman-shaped wavelet tree proceed exactly as in a plain balanced wavelet tree. For access(S, i), we traverse the tree from the root to the leaf of $S[i]$, in $|h(S[i])|$ steps, and obtain precisely $h(S[i])$, which must then be mapped to $S[i]$ using the Huffman model (we can store the symbols at the wavelet tree leaves, for example). For rank$_c(S, i)$, we must use the bits of the code $h(c)$ in order to descend to the leaf of c, in $|h(c)|$ steps. Finally, for select$_c(S, j)$ we can have a pointer to the leaf

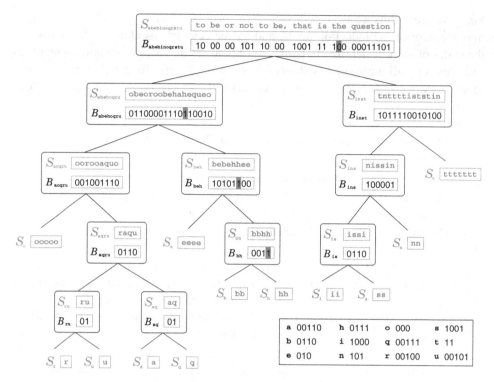

Figure 6.5. The representation of the same sequence of Example 6.2 using a Huffman-shaped wavelet tree. We show in black the elements that are actually represented (tree topology and bitvectors B_v) and in gray the elements that are only conceptual (leaves and sequences S_v). In addition, we must store the mapping from each symbol to its Huffman code (shown on the bottom right). The grayed blocks illustrate the bits induced by $S[21] = \mathbf{h}$.

of c and move upwards from there (or, as explained, move downwards to the leaf and then upwards), also in $|h(c)|$ steps.

Compared to using compressed bitvectors, a Huffman-shaped wavelet tree requires up to n extra bits (yet in practice this is much less), but it reduces the $o(n \log \sigma)$ bits of space overhead to just $o(n(\mathcal{H}_0(S) + 1))$, that is, it also compresses the redundancy. In addition, it is usually faster because it uses plain bitvectors.

If space is the main concern, we can even combine compressed bitvectors with Huffman shape. This reduces the space to $n\mathcal{H}_0(S) + o(n(\mathcal{H}_0(S) + 1)) + \mathcal{O}(\sigma w)$ bits.

Time Complexities

Since the maximum length of a Huffman code is $\mathcal{O}(\log n)$ (Section 2.6.2), this is the worst-case time for operations **access**, **rank**, and **select**. On the other hand, if we choose i uniformly at random in $[1, n]$ and perform **access**(S, i), or **rank**$_c(S, j)$ or **select**$_c(S, j)$ with $c = S[i]$, then the average time for the operations is $\mathcal{O}\left(\frac{1}{n} \sum_c n_c |h(c)|\right) = \mathcal{O}(1 + \mathcal{H}_0(S))$, which is less than $\mathcal{O}(\log \sigma)$ on compressible sequences. That is, operations can be even *faster* than on a balanced wavelet tree using plain bitvectors.

We can also maintain the same average time performance while ensuring that the worst case of the operations is within $\mathcal{O}(\log \sigma)$, by limiting the depth of the Huffman tree as done in Section 5.3. As mentioned in that section, this adds only $\mathcal{O}(n/\sigma)$ bits of redundancy.

In fact, the Huffman-shaped wavelet trees and the Huffman trees used to compress permutations are closely related. Consider the inverted index of S, where the vocabulary is $[1, \sigma]$. This index can be regarded as a permutation π, just as in Section 5.4.2. Then the Huffman-shaped wavelet tree of S is structurally identical[2] to the Huffman tree used to represent π in compressed form. The procedure for $\pi^{-1}(i)$ is similar to that for **access**, and the one for $\pi(i)$ is analogous to that for **select**. Compare Algorithm 5.4 with Algorithms 6.3 and 6.4. This connection will be exploited more in depth in Section 6.4.1.

Construction

The time to build a Huffman-shaped wavelet tree is $\mathcal{O}(\sigma \log \sigma)$ for the Huffman algorithm, and then $\mathcal{O}(n(\mathcal{H}_0(S) + 1))$ if we apply the same construction algorithm as for balanced wavelet trees (now splitting S_v according to the next highest bit of the Huffman code of each symbol). That is, the construction on compressible sequences is faster than that of the balanced wavelet tree. The same techniques to reduce the main memory usage during construction can be applied when building Huffman-shaped wavelet trees.

6.2.5 Wavelet Matrices

The wavelet tree uses a space close to the plain or the compressed size of the sequence S it represents, except for a term of the form $\mathcal{O}(\sigma w)$ bits. In the balanced wavelet tree, this space is due to the pointers: each tree node has 2 pointers to its children and a pointer to its bitvector $B_{\langle a,b \rangle}$, leading to 3σ pointers (the leaves are not represented). In the Huffman-shaped wavelet tree, we have in addition a symbol table storing 1 word per symbol with its Huffman code.[3] When the alphabet size is small, this extra space poses no problem at all and this is the way wavelet trees should be implemented.

There are cases, however, where the alphabet size is significant compared to n, and an alternative representation is necessary (one may say that the technique of Section 6.1 is to be preferred in this case, but wavelet trees have other uses, as we will see, for example, in Chapter 10).

For a balanced wavelet tree, a reasonable idea is to concatenate all the bitvectors $B_{\langle a,b \rangle}$ at each level ℓ into a single bitvector B_ℓ. The tree topology can then be discarded. This results in some problems, however. First, we must be able to identify, along our wavelet tree traversals, the *range* in B_ℓ that corresponds to the bitvector $B_{\langle a,b \rangle}$ of our current node (at depth ℓ). Second, as can be seen in Figure 6.4, the deepest bitvector B_ℓ may have "holes" due to leaves that are at depth $\lceil \log \sigma \rceil - 1$.

---

[2] Except for some longer runs that can be formed by chance.

[3] We also store the source symbol that corresponds to each leaf. This can be stored for free as a pointer to the symbol table instead of the otherwise null pointer of the tree. When a child points inside the table, we know it is a leaf and which symbol it represents.

The wavelet matrix is an arrangement that solves these problems while retaining almost the same speed of pointer-based wavelet trees. In the wavelet matrix, the bitvectors $B_\ell[1, n]$, for $\ell \in [1, \lceil \log \sigma \rceil]$, are made contiguous (no holes) by concatenating the bitvectors $B_{\langle a,b \rangle}$ in a particular order: all the nodes at level ℓ that are left children will be put before all the nodes that are right children. Within left or right children, the original ordering of the previous level is retained.

Let $z_\ell = \mathsf{rank}_0(B_\ell, n)$ be the number of 0s at each level. These numbers will be precomputed and stored with the wavelet matrix. At the first level, $B_1 = B_{\langle 1, \sigma \rangle}$ coincides with the bitvector at the wavelet tree root. The corresponding sequence of the first level is also $S_1 = S_{\langle 1, \sigma \rangle} = S$. Then the sequence S_2 is a reshuffling of S_1, as follows. If $B_1[i] = 0$, then $S_2[\mathsf{rank}_0(B_1, i)] = S_1[i]$, otherwise $S_2[z_1 + \mathsf{rank}_1(B_1, i)] = S_1[i]$. That is, *all* the 0s in B_1 go to the left in S_2, and *all* the 1s go to the right.

Note that S_2 is simply the concatenation of $S_{\langle 1, \lceil \sigma/2 \rceil \rangle}$ and $S_{\langle \lceil \sigma/2 \rceil+1, \sigma \rangle}$, that is, the strings at the left and right children of the wavelet tree root. Similarly, $B_2 = B_{\langle 1, \lceil \sigma/2 \rceil \rangle} \cdot B_{\langle \lceil \sigma/2 \rceil+1, \sigma \rangle}$. That is, for $i \in [1, z_1]$, we set $B_2[i] = 0$ iff $S_2[i] \in [1, \lceil \sigma/4 \rceil]$, whereas in $i \in [z_1 + 1, n]$ we set $B_2[i] = 0$ iff $S_2[i] \in [\lceil \sigma/2 \rceil + 1, \lceil 3\sigma/4 \rceil]$.

However, the wavelet tree nodes are shuffled in a different way starting with level 3. Now we have that $S_3[\mathsf{rank}_0(B_2, i)] = S_2[i]$ if $B_2[i] = 0$ and $S_3[z_2 + \mathsf{rank}_1(B_2, i)] = S_2[i]$ if $B_2[i] = 1$. Therefore, $S_3 = S_{\langle 1, \lceil \sigma/4 \rceil \rangle} \cdot S_{\langle \lceil \sigma/2 \rceil+1, \lceil 3\sigma/4 \rceil \rangle} \cdot S_{\langle \lceil \sigma/4 \rceil+1, \lceil \sigma/2 \rceil \rangle} \cdot S_{\langle \lceil 3\sigma/4 \rceil+1, \sigma \rangle}$ shuffles the wavelet tree nodes of level 3: first the 2 left children, then the 2 right children.

From the wavelet matrix, we can easily compute $\mathsf{access}(S, i) = S[i]$ in $\mathcal{O}(\log \sigma)$ time, as follows. Start at level $\ell = 1$, where we know that $S[i] \in [a, b] = [1, \sigma]$. Now, in general, if $B_\ell[i] = 0$, then set $i \leftarrow \mathsf{rank}_0(B_\ell, i)$ and $[a, b] \leftarrow [a, \lfloor (a+b)/2 \rfloor]$. If, instead, $B_\ell[i] = 1$, then set $i \leftarrow z_\ell + \mathsf{rank}_1(B_\ell, i)$ and $[a, b] \leftarrow [\lfloor (a+b)/2 \rfloor + 1, b]$. Then we go on to level $\ell + 1$. When $a = b$ we know that the answer is a (or b). Thus we perform as many rank operations as on a standard wavelet tree.

Example 6.10 *Figure 6.6 shows the wavelet matrix for the sequence of Example 6.2. Note that S_1 is the same $S_{\langle 1, 12 \rangle}$ of Figure 6.4, and S_2 is the concatenation of $S_{\langle 1, 6 \rangle}$ and $S_{\langle 7, 12 \rangle}$. The other sequences also correspond to the sequences of each level, yet they are shuffled. Note that the last level is incomplete: because of the way we partition the alphabet, all the leaves that are not in the last level are right children, thus they are put on the right of the last bitvector and no holes appear in the sequence.*

The figure also shows, with grayed blocks, the computation of $S[21] = \mathsf{access}(S, 21)$. We start at $B_1[21] = 0$, thus we know that $S[21] \in [1, 6]$ and that the position is mapped to $i \leftarrow \mathsf{rank}_0(B_1, 21) = 9$ in S_2. Now we have $B_2[9] = 1$, so we know that $S[21] \in [4, 6]$ and that it is in S_3 at position $i \leftarrow z_2 + \mathsf{rank}_1(B_2, 9) = 14 + 4 = 18$. Since $B_3[18] = 0$, we know that $S[21] \in [4, 5]$ and that it is in S_4 at position $i \leftarrow \mathsf{rank}_0(B_3, 18) = 12$. Since $B_4[12] = 0$, we know that $S[21] \in [4, 4]$, thus $S[21] = 4 = \mathtt{h}$. Indeed, $S[21]$ is at $S_5[\mathsf{rank}_0(B_4, 12)] = S_5[8] = \mathtt{h}$.

For $\mathsf{rank}_c(S, i)$ we also need to keep track of the position where the bitvector $B_{\langle a,b \rangle}$ starts in B_ℓ. In fact, it is simpler to keep the previous position. In the beginning this position is $p \leftarrow 0$. We start at level $\ell = 1$ with $[a, b] = [1, \sigma]$. In general, if $c \le \lfloor (a+b)/2 \rfloor$, we move left: we update $i \leftarrow \mathsf{rank}_0(B_\ell, i)$, $[a, b] \leftarrow [a, \lfloor (a+b)/2 \rfloor]$, and $p \leftarrow \mathsf{rank}_0(B_\ell, p)$. If instead $c > \lfloor (a+b)/2 \rfloor$, we move right: we update $i \leftarrow$

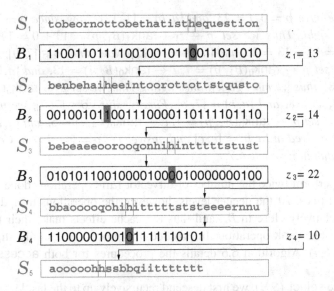

Figure 6.6. The representation of the same sequence of Example 6.2 using a wavelet matrix. We show in black the elements that are actually represented (bitvectors B_ℓ and values z_ℓ), and in gray the elements that are only conceptual (sequences S_ℓ). Open and solid gray blocks illustrate operation access(S, 21).

$z_\ell + \mathsf{rank}_1(B_\ell, i)$, $[a, b] \leftarrow [\lfloor (a + b)/2 \rfloor + 1, b]$, and $p \leftarrow z_\ell + \mathsf{rank}_1(B_\ell, p)$. When we finally reach $[a, b] = [c, c]$, we return $i - p$.

Example 6.11 *The operation* $\mathsf{rank}_{\circ=7}(S, 23)$ *is illustrated in Figure 6.7 with gray downward diagonal arrows. The leftmost arrows point to p and the rightmost ones*

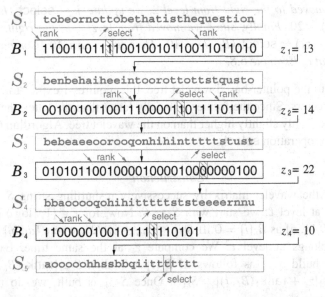

Figure 6.7. Illustration of the operations of Examples 6.11 and 6.12 on the wavelet matrix of Figure 6.6: $\mathsf{rank}_\circ(S, 23)$ is shown with downward arrows, whereas $\mathsf{select}_t(S, 3)$ is shown with hatched blocks and upward arrows.

to i. In B_1 we have $p = 0$, $i = 23$, and $[a, b] = [1, 12]$. Now, since $\circ = 7 \in [7, 12]$, we must go right. Thus we set $p \leftarrow z_1 + \mathsf{rank}_1(B_1, p) = 13 + 0 = 13$, $i \leftarrow z_1 + \mathsf{rank}_1(B_1, i) = 13 + 13 = 26$, and $[a, b] = [7, 12]$. Now, since $\circ \in [7, 9]$, we must go left. Thus we set $p \leftarrow \mathsf{rank}_0(B_2, p) = 7$, $i \leftarrow \mathsf{rank}_0(B_2, i) = 13$, and $[a, b] = [7, 9]$. Now $\circ \in [7, 8]$, thus we must go left once again. Thus we set $p \leftarrow \mathsf{rank}_0(B_3, p) = 3$, $i \leftarrow \mathsf{rank}_0(B_3, i) = 8$, and $[a, b] = [7, 8]$. Finally, since $\circ \in [7, 7]$, we must go left again. Thus we set $p \leftarrow \mathsf{rank}_0(B_4, p) = 1$, $i \leftarrow \mathsf{rank}_0(B_4, i) = 5$, and $[a, b] = [7, 7]$. Now we have arrived at $[a, b] = [c, c]$ and answer $i - p = 5 - 1 = 4$. Compare this process with that in Example 6.7.

Thus, we perform twice the number of bitvector **rank** operations done on pointer-based wavelet trees. At the deeper levels, however, the operations to update p and i tend to fall relatively close in B_ℓ, and thus the cache effects make their time closer to that of just one **rank** operation. In practice, the process takes only slightly more than **access**(S, i). Algorithm 6.6 details the procedures for both **access** and **rank** queries.

To compute **select**$_c(S, j)$, we first descend recursively up to the last level in order to find p, as done for **rank**$_c(S, i)$. At the end of the recursion, we set $j \leftarrow p + j$. When we return from the recursion, if we had gone left, we now set $j \leftarrow \mathsf{select}_0(B_\ell, j)$, whereas if we had gone right, we now set $j \leftarrow \mathsf{select}_1(B_\ell, j - z_\ell)$. When we complete this calculation on the bitvector B_1, j contains the answer.

Example 6.12 *Figure 6.7 also illustrates operation* **select**$_t(S, 3)$, *with gray upward diagonal arrows. We start at the top just as for* **rank**$_t$, *ending up in level $\ell = 5$ with $p = 15$. Thus we start with $j \leftarrow p + 3 = 18$. Since we went right when moving from $\ell = 4$ to $\ell = 5$, we go up and update $j \leftarrow \mathsf{select}_1(B_4, j - z_4) = \mathsf{select}_1(B_4, 8) = 16$. Now, since we moved left from level 3, we update $j \leftarrow \mathsf{select}_0(B_3, j) = \mathsf{select}_0(B_3, 16) = 23$. Since we moved to the right from level 2, we update $j \leftarrow \mathsf{select}_1(B_2, j - z_2) = \mathsf{select}_1(B_2, 9) = 20$. Finally, since we moved from level 1 to the right, we set $j \leftarrow \mathsf{select}_1(B_1, j - z_1) = \mathsf{select}_1(B_1, 7) = 10$. Thus we return 10. Compare this processes with that of Example 6.8.*

Compared to the pointer-based wavelet tree, this requires 1 extra **rank** per original **select** on bitvectors. Since the former is usually faster than the latter, the time on the wavelet matrix is only slightly higher than on the wavelet tree. Algorithm 6.7 gives the pseudocode for operation **select**.

Construction

We can build the wavelet matrix by successively reshuffling string S. Let us call S_ℓ its version at level ℓ; we start with $S_1 = S$. Now, for $\ell \in [1, \lceil \log \sigma \rceil]$, we build the bitvector $B_\ell[1, n]$ as $B_\ell[i] = 0$ iff $S[i] \leq \lfloor (a_i + b_i)/2 \rfloor$, where $[a_i, b_i]$ is the range where $S[i]$ belongs at level ℓ. We compute z_ℓ at the same time. Except at the last level, we build $S_{\ell+1}$ as follows: if $B_\ell[i] = 0$, then $S_{\ell+1}[\mathsf{rank}_0(B_\ell, i)] = S_\ell[i]$; otherwise $S_{\ell+1}[z_\ell + \mathsf{rank}_1(B_\ell, i)] = S_\ell[i]$. Once $S_{\ell+1}$ is built, we do not need S_ℓ anymore.

Algorithm 6.8 details the construction. The symbols from different intervals $[a_i, b_i]$ are mixed in the same string S_ℓ. Instead of keeping track of those intervals, we map the

---

Algorithm 6.6: Answering access and rank with wavelet matrices.

---

1 **Proc** access(S, i)

    Input : Sequence S (seen as the bitvectors B_ℓ and numbers z_ℓ of the wavelet
                matrix) and position i.

    Output: Returns access(S, i).

2    $\ell \leftarrow 1$

3    $[a, b] \leftarrow [1, \sigma]$

4   **while** $a \neq b$ **do**

5   **if** access(B_ℓ, i) = 0 **then**

6            $i \leftarrow \mathsf{rank}_0(B_\ell, i)$

7            $b \leftarrow \lfloor(a + b)/2\rfloor$

8   **else**

9            $i \leftarrow z_\ell + \mathsf{rank}_1(B_\ell, i)$

10           $a \leftarrow \lfloor(a + b)/2\rfloor + 1$

11        $\ell \leftarrow \ell + 1$

12   **return** a

13 **Proc** rank$_c$(S, i)

    Input : Sequence S (seen as the bitvectors B_ℓ and numbers z_ℓ of the wavelet
                matrix), symbol c, and position i.

    Output: Returns rank$_c$(S, i).

14   $p \leftarrow 0$

15   $\ell \leftarrow 1$

16   $[a, b] \leftarrow [1, \sigma]$

17   **while** $a \neq b$ **do**

18   **if** $c \leq \lfloor(a + b)/2\rfloor$ **then**

19          $i \leftarrow \mathsf{rank}_0(B_\ell, i)$

20          $p \leftarrow \mathsf{rank}_0(B_\ell, p)$

21          $b \leftarrow \lfloor(a + b)/2\rfloor$

22   **else**

23          $i \leftarrow z_\ell + \mathsf{rank}_1(B_\ell, i)$

24          $p \leftarrow z_\ell + \mathsf{rank}_1(B_\ell, p)$

25          $a \leftarrow \lfloor(a + b)/2\rfloor + 1$

26       $\ell \leftarrow \ell + 1$

27   **return** $i - p$

---

symbols that go to the right to the interval $[1, *]$, so that all the symbols in S_ℓ belong to an interval of the form $[1, m]$, where m depends on ℓ. Ideally, to build $S_{\ell+1}$ we just have to take the symbols of S_ℓ and divide them into $[1, m/2]$ (which go left) and $[m/2 + 1, m]$ (which go right), mapping the latter to $[1, m/2]$ as well. However, odd values of m introduce slight complications. In the next paragraphs we show how to handle

---

Algorithm 6.7: Answering **select** with wavelet matrices.

---

1 **Proc** select$_c$(S, j)

   Input : Sequence S (seen as the bitvectors B_ℓ and numbers z_ℓ of the wavelet
             matrix), symbol c, and index j.
   Output: Returns select$_c$(S, j).

2 | **return** $select(1, 0, 1, \sigma, c, j)$

---

3 **Proc** $select(\ell, p, a, b, c, j)$

   Input : Wavelet matrix level ℓ, position p preceding the range $[a, b]$ where c
             belongs in S_ℓ, symbol c, and index j.
   Output: Returns the position in S_ℓ of the jth c of S.

4 | **if** $a = b$ **then**
5 | | **return** $p + j$
6 | **if** $c \leq \lfloor (a + b)/2 \rfloor$ **then**
7 | | $j \leftarrow select(\ell + 1, \mathsf{rank}_0(B_\ell, p), a, \lfloor (a + b)/2 \rfloor, c, j)$
8 | | **return** select$_0$(B_ℓ, j)
9 | **else**
10 | | $j \leftarrow select(\ell + 1, z_\ell + \mathsf{rank}_1(B_\ell, p), \lfloor (a + b)/2 \rfloor + 1, b, c, j)$
11 | | **return** select$_1$($B_\ell, j - z_\ell$)

---

this situation to simulate exactly what occurs when the intervals $[a_i, b_i]$ are split into $[a_i, \lfloor (a_i + b_i)/2 \rfloor]$ and $[\lfloor (a_i + b_i)/2 \rfloor + 1, b_i]$.

An interval $[a, b]$ will be mapped to $[1, m] = [1, b - a + 1]$. If m is even, then $b - a$ and $b + a$ are odd, thus the left subinterval of $[a, b]$ will be $[a, \lfloor (a + b)/2 \rfloor] = [a, (a + b - 1)/2] = [a, a + (b - a - 1)/2] = [a, a + m/2 - 1]$, and then it will be mapped to $[1, m/2]$. The right interval will thus be mapped to $[1, m - m/2] = [1, m/2]$. If, instead, m is odd, then $b - a$ and $b + a$ are even, thus the left subinterval of $[a, b]$ will be $[a, \lfloor (a + b)/2 \rfloor] = [a, (a + b)/2] = [a, a + (b - a)/2] = [a, a + (m - 1)/2]$, and then it will be mapped to $[1, (m + 1)/2]$. The right interval will then be mapped to $[1, m - (m + 1)/2] = [1, (m - 1)/2]$. Therefore, the way the intervals $[a_i, b_i]$ are divided depends only on $m = b_i - a_i + 1$, the left interval is always $[1, \lceil m/2 \rceil]$, and the right one is then $[1, m - \lceil m/2 \rceil]$.

At each level, there will be intervals of the form $[1, m]$ and $[1, m - 1]$. Let us call *longer* and *shorter* the symbols belonging to those intervals, respectively (this is independent of the lexicographic value of the symbols). The positions in S_ℓ of the shorter symbols will be marked in a bit array $M[1, n]$.

To see inductively that only intervals of the form $[1, m]$ and $[1, m - 1]$ exist in a level, note that this trivially holds for level 1 and assume it holds for level ℓ. Then, if m is even, the shorter symbols belong to the odd-sized interval $[1, m - 1]$. The longer symbols will be partitioned into intervals of size $[1, m/2]$, whereas the shorter ones will be partitioned into $[1, ((m - 1) + 1)/2] = [1, m/2]$ (left) and $[1, ((m - 1) - 1)/2] = [1, m/2 - 1]$ (right). Therefore, in the next level, the shorter symbols will be those

---

Algorithm 6.8: Building a wavelet matrix. Frees the original string.

Input : Sequence $S[1, n]$ over alphabet $[1, \sigma]$.
Output: Builds the wavelet matrix of S: bitvectors B_ℓ and numbers z_ℓ.

```
 1  Allocate bit arrays M[1, n] and M'[1, n], and string S'[1, n]
 2  for i ← 1 to n do bitclear(M, i) (can be initialized wordwise)
 3  m ← σ
 4  for ℓ ← 1 to ⌈log σ⌉ do
 5   │  z_ℓ ← 0
 6   │  Allocate bit array B_ℓ[1, n]
 7   │  for i ← 1 to n do
 8   │   │  if S[i] ≤ ⌈(m − bitread(M, i))/2⌉ then
 9   │   │   │  bitclear(B_ℓ, i)
10   │   │   │  z_ℓ ← z_ℓ + 1
11   │   │  else
12   │   │   │  bitset(B_ℓ, i)
13   │   │   │  S[i] ← S[i] − ⌈(m − bitread(M, i))/2⌉
14   │  Preprocess B_ℓ for rank and select queries
15   │  if ℓ < ⌈log σ⌉ then
16   │   │  pl ← 0; pr ← z_ℓ
17   │   │  for i ← 1 to n do
18   │   │   │  b ← bitread(B_ℓ, i)
19   │   │   │  if b = 0 then pl ← pl + 1; p ← pl
20   │   │   │  else pr ← pr + 1; p ← pr
21   │   │   │  S'[p] ← S[i]
22   │   │   │  if m mod 2 = b then write(M', p, b)
23   │   │   │  else write(M', p, bitread(M, i))
24   │   │   │  if ⌈m/2⌉ = 2 and bitread(M', p) = 1 then n ← n − 1
25   │   │  S ↔ S'; M ↔ M'
26   │   │  m ← ⌈m/2⌉
27  Free M, M', S, and S'
```

---

that are shorter in this level and belong to the right partition of $[1, m − 1]$. Instead, if m is odd, then the shorter symbols belong to the even-sized interval $[1, m − 1]$. The longer symbols will be partitioned into two intervals of size $[1, (m + 1)/2]$ (left) and $[1, (m − 1)/2] = [1, (m + 1)/2 − 1]$ (right). The shorter elements, instead, will be partitioned into two equal-sized intervals of length $[1, (m − 1)/2] = [1, (m + 1)/2 − 1]$. Therefore, in the next level the longer elements will be those that are currently longer and belong to the left partition. This logic is condensed in lines 22–23.

The construction process requires $\mathcal{O}(n \log \sigma)$ time, and the extra space, apart from S and the wavelet matrix, is $n \log \sigma + 2n$ bits. The same mechanism of Section 6.2.3 can be used to reduce this extra space to just $2n$ bits, and we can also send the bitvectors

B_ℓ to disk as soon as they are built, to reduce the main memory usage to the space of S plus $2n$ bits. We can also make a more intensive use of the disk, buffering S, M, and B_ℓ, as well as the left and right hands of S' and M', so that we build the structure using just a constant number of buffers in main memory. The final size of the wavelet matrix, including the support for **rank** and **select** on bitvectors, is $n \log \sigma + o(n \log \sigma)$ bits.

Instead of bit arrays M and M', we could use some mechanism to partition the alphabet that allows for a simpler calculation. For example, we can use the highest bit of the binary representation of the symbols in $[0, \sigma - 1]$. Then the algorithm can be simplified by removing the references to M and M' in lines 1, 8, 13, 25, and 27, and eliminating lines 2 and 22–24.

However, this may introduce up to n bits of redundancy when σ is slightly larger than a power of 2. For example, if $\Sigma = [0, 16]$, we would spend B_1 just to distinguish $[0, 15]$ from $[16, 16]$. The mechanism we have given, instead, partitions the alphabet as evenly as possible and makes good use of each bitvector B_ℓ. If the alphabet is $[0, 16]$ (in our case, $[1, 17]$), its last bitvector will be very short, thus saving space (this is what is taken care of in line 24 of Algorithm 6.8, where we avoid copying the characters c whose interval is $[c, c]$ to the next level).

Compression

Just as in Section 6.2.4, we can represent the bitvectors B_ℓ in compressed form. Since the bitvectors $B_{\langle a,b \rangle}$ appear as contiguous chunks inside bitvectors B_ℓ, we can maintain the same reasoning as when we concluded that the total space becomes $n\mathcal{H}_0(S) + o(n \log \sigma)$. The only difference is that some of the blocks of Section 4.1.1 may cross a boundary between bitvectors $B_{\langle a,b \rangle}$. Since there are at most $\sigma - 1$ block boundaries across all the bitvectors B_ℓ, this cannot induce more than $\mathcal{O}(\sigma \log n) = \mathcal{O}(\sigma w)$ further bits of space, and the effect is unnoticeable in practice.

Just as for pointer-based wavelet trees, we might wish to use Huffman-shaped wavelet matrices in order to obtain close to zero-order compression without using the slower compressed bitvectors. The problem is that in a levelwise deployment, the irregular shape of the Huffman tree would induce holes in the bitvectors B_ℓ, which would lead to incorrect results when tracking the symbols. Using canonical Huffman codes (Section 2.6.3) would leave all the holes to the left and solve the problem (except that we prefer them to the right, but this is easy to fix).

However, the wavelet matrix scrambles the order of the nodes within the same level and thus also reorders the holes. Since all the left children of level ℓ (i.e., those whose ℓth bit is a 0) are put in level $\ell + 1$ to the left of all the right children, and their previous order is otherwise retained, the symbols end up sorted in any level by the lexicographic order of their *reverse* codes: For $\ell = 1$ the codes, read left to right in the matrix, are 0 and 1. For $\ell = 2$, they are 00, 10, 01, and 11. For $\ell = 3$, they are 000, 100, 010, 110, 001, 101, 011, and 111. Even if canonical Huffman assigns contiguous numbers in the same level, holes may appear again with this rearrangement.

Example 6.13 *We modify canonical Huffman so that shorter codes go to the right, and apply it on the example of Figure 6.5. We obtain the following codes:*

a	00000	h	0011	o	101	s	0101
b	0010	i	0100	q	00001	t	11
e	011	n	100	r	00010	u	00011

Now consider a short sequence $S = $ ans (this is not the real sequence of Figure 6.5; the reader can work out the full example and will find similar problems). Then we have $S_1 = $ ans and $B_1 = 010$, $S_2 = $ asn and $B_2 = 010$, $S_3 = $ ans and $B_3 = 000$, $S_4 = $ as and $B_4 = 01$, $S_5 = $ a and $B_5 = 0$.

Let us now access $S[3] = $ s. We access $B_1[3] = 0$, then $B_2[2] = 1$, then $B_3[3] = 0$, and finally $B_4[3]$, which is out of bounds. The problem is that $B_3[2]$ was the last bit of the code of n, and thus it is not present in B_4. Thus, our calculation that tracks the position of s is wrong.

A solution to this problem relies on the Kraft-McMillan inequality (Section 2.5): Run the Huffman algorithm to obtain not a code for each symbol, but just the desired length. Any other code that gives those lengths to the symbols is also optimal (and is also a valid Huffman code). Moreover, if we assign the codes in increasing length order, in any prefix-free form, there will always be a place for our next code.

Let us call p_ℓ^{rev} the number p written in ℓ bits and then reversed. Let $\ell_1, \ell_2, \ldots, \ell_\sigma$ be the lengths assigned to the codes by the Huffman algorithm, in increasing order. A suitable assignment of codes then starts with a set of 2 available codes, $C = \langle 1, 0 \rangle$, sorted by decreasing numeric value of the *reversed* codes. Then we process the lengths ℓ_i from $i = 1$. For each length ℓ_i, we take the first code $c \in C$. If $|c| = \ell_i$, we assign the code c to the corresponding symbol, remove it from C, and move on to the next length. Otherwise it must be $|c| < \ell_i$. At this point we extend all the codes in C by 1 bit, so that each $c \in C$ is replaced by 2 codes, $c \, . \, 0$ and $c \, . \, 1$. To keep those codes sorted, we just need to first add all the codes $c \, . \, 1$ and then all the codes $c \, . \, 0$. The Kraft-McMillan inequality ensures that we exhaust C and the list of lengths at the same time, and the overall process requires linear time, $\mathcal{O}(\sigma)$, that is, constant time per Huffman tree node.

Example 6.14 *In Figure 6.5, the Huffman algorithm has assigned the code lengths 2 to t, 3 to e, n, and o, 4 to b, h, i, and s, and 5 to a, q, r, and u. Then we start with $C = \langle 1, 0 \rangle$. Since $|1| = 1 < \ell_1 = 2$, we extend all the symbols in C, obtaining $C = \langle 11, 01, 10, 00 \rangle$ (note that the codes are sorted by the numerical value of their reversed bit sequence). Now we extract 11 from C. Since $|11| = 2 = \ell_1$, we assign the code 11 to t and go on with $\ell_2 = 3$. Since the next code of C is shorter than ℓ_2, we extend all the codes, obtaining $C = \langle 011, 101, 001, 010, 100, 000 \rangle$. Now, the next 3 lengths are $\ell_2 = \ell_3 = \ell_4 = 3$, so we assign the next 3 codes: 011 to e, 101 to n, and 001 to o. The remaining codes are $C = \langle 010, 100, 000 \rangle$. Since $\ell_5 = 4$ is larger than the codes in C, we extend them and obtain $C = \langle 0101, 1001, 0001, 0100, 1000, 0000 \rangle$. Now we have the right length to assign codes 0101 to b, 1001 to h, 0001 to i, and 0100 to s. The remaining codes are $C = \langle 1000, 0000 \rangle$. Since the next length, $\ell_9 = 5$, is larger than the length of the first code of C, we expand them all to obtain $C = \langle 10001, 00001, 10000, 00000 \rangle$. We assign these 4 codes to a, q, r, and u. Figure 6.8*

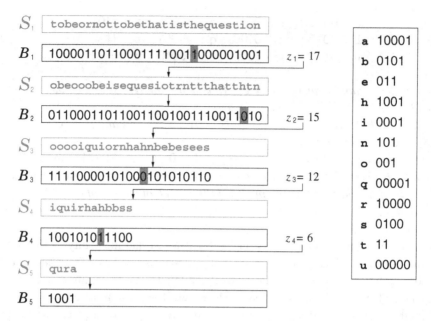

Figure 6.8. The representation of the sequence of Example 6.2 using a Huffman-shaped wavelet matrix. We show in black the elements that are actually represented (bitvectors B_ℓ and values z_ℓ) and in gray the elements that are only conceptual (sequences S_ℓ). We also show on the right the Huffman code found to be suitable for the wavelet matrix. The solid gray blocks illustrate operation access(S, 21).

shows the resulting wavelet matrix. The total number of bits in the bitvectors is 99, just as for the Huffman-shaped wavelet tree of Figure 6.5.

The resulting code is prefix-free and optimal, and all the holes in the wavelet matrix appear at the right of the bitvectors, so they can be ignored and we can use exactly the same algorithms as on the balanced wavelet matrix. The only difference is that we use the bits of the codes to decide whether to go left or right, as on Huffman-shaped wavelet trees. For operations $\mathsf{rank}_c(S, i)$ and $\mathsf{select}_c(S, j)$, we need to obtain the code of c. These codes are stored in a table $Encode[1, \sigma]$.

For access(S, i), we need to obtain the symbol corresponding to a code. For this we store tables $Decode_\ell$ for each length ℓ, where the Huffman codes of length ℓ are numerically sorted and associated with their source symbols. We run a binary search on $Decode_\ell$ for the code (of length ℓ) we have read, and find the corresponding source symbol in time $\mathcal{O}(\ell)$, since there can be only $\mathcal{O}(2^\ell)$ codes of length ℓ. This search does not affect the time complexity.

Algorithm 6.9 details the procedure to build the codes, and Algorithm 6.10 shows how to build the wavelet matrix from Huffman codes. The same techniques we have seen to reduce main memory usage can be applied.

Example 6.15 *Let us carry out operation* access(S, 21) *on the wavelet matrix of Figure 6.8. Since $B_1[21] = 1$, we set $i \leftarrow z_1 + \mathsf{rank}_1(B_1, 21) = 17 + 11 = 28$ and move to level 2. Since $B_2[28] = 0$, we set $i \leftarrow \mathsf{rank}_0(B_2, 28) = 14$ and move to level 3. Since $B_3[14] = 0$, we set $i \leftarrow \mathsf{rank}_0(B_3, 14) = 8$ and move to level 4. Since $B_4[8] = 1$,*

Algorithm 6.9: Building a suitable Huffman code for wavelet matrices. Assumes for simplicity that the codes fit in a computer word.

Input : Sequence $S[1, n]$ over alphabet $[1, \sigma]$.

Output: Builds Huffman codes $Code[1, \sigma]$ appropriate for wavelet matrices: the code of s consists of the $Code[s].\ell$ highest bits of $Code[s].c$.

1 Allocate array $C[1, \sigma]$ of integers
2 Allocate array $Code[1, \sigma]$ with fields c (a code) and ℓ (its length)
3 Allocate array $F[1, \sigma]$ with integer fields s (a symbol), f (a frequency), and ℓ (code length)
4 **for** $c \leftarrow 1$ **to** σ **do**
5     $F[c].s \leftarrow c; F[c].f \leftarrow 0$
6 **for** $i \leftarrow 1$ **to** n **do**
7     $F[S[i]].f \leftarrow F[S[i]].f + 1$
8 $T \leftarrow HuffmanTree(F)$ (Algorithm 2.2)
9 $computeLengths(F, T, 0, 1)$ (Algorithm 2.3)
10 Sort F by increasing value of field ℓ (the code length)
11 $C[1] \leftarrow 0; m \leftarrow 1; \ell \leftarrow 0$
12 **for** $j \leftarrow 1$ **to** σ **do**
13   **while** $F[j].\ell > \ell$ **do**
14   **for** $r \leftarrow j$ **to** m **do**
15           $C[m + r - j + 1] \leftarrow C[r]$
16   bitset$(C[r], w - \ell)$
17        $m \leftarrow 2 \cdot m - j + 1$
18        $\ell \leftarrow \ell + 1$
19     $Code[F[j].s].c \leftarrow C[j]; Code[F[j].s].\ell \leftarrow \ell$
20 Free F, T, and C

---

we set $i \leftarrow z_4 + \mathsf{rank}_1(B_4, 8) = 6 + 4 = 10$ *and move to level 5. Since* $|B_5| < 10$, *we have finished reading the code. The bits read (grayed) were* **1001**, *which is the code for* h.

Despite having removed the space of the pointers, Huffman-shaped wavelet matrices still have an extra space of $\mathcal{O}(\sigma w)$ bits to store the tables *Encode* and *Decode*. This can be reduced to just $\sigma w + \mathcal{O}(\sigma \log \log n + w \log n)$ bits by storing pointers to each table $Decode_\ell$, which records only the codes. The associated symbols are represented with a sequence $E[1, \sigma]$ over the alphabet $[1, \mathcal{O}(\log n)]$ of the code lengths, so that $E[c]$ is the code length of symbol c. By reassigning the codes of each length ℓ so that a numerically larger code corresponds to a lexicographically larger symbol, it holds that $Encode[c] = Decode_\ell[\mathsf{rank}_\ell(E, c)]$, where $\ell = E[c]$, and the symbol corresponding to the code found at $Decode_\ell[i]$ is $\mathsf{select}_\ell(E, i)$. With the representation of Section 6.1, E uses $\sigma \log \log n(1 + o(1))$ bits. It encodes in time $\mathcal{O}(\log \log \log n)$ and decodes in time $\mathcal{O}(1)$. In practice, a wavelet tree representation of E may be preferable for such a small alphabet.

Algorithm 6.10: Building a wavelet matrix from Huffman codes. Frees the original string.

Input : Sequence $S[1, n]$ over alphabet $[1, \sigma]$, and Huffman codes $Code[1, \sigma]$
from Algorithm 6.9.

Output: Builds the wavelet matrix of S: bitvectors B_ℓ and numbers z_ℓ.

1   Allocate string $S'[1, n]$
2   $\ell \leftarrow 1$
3   **while** $n > 0$ **do**
4     $z_\ell \leftarrow 0$
5   Allocate bit array $B_\ell[1, n]$
6   **for** $i \leftarrow 1$ **to** n **do**
7   **if** bitread$(Code[S[i]].c, w - \ell) = 0$ **then**
8   bitclear(B_ℓ, i)
9         $z_\ell \leftarrow z_\ell + 1$
10   **else**
11   bitset(B_ℓ, i)
12   Preprocess B_ℓ for **rank** and **select** queries
13     $pl \leftarrow 0; pr \leftarrow z_\ell$
14     $n' \leftarrow 0$
15   **for** $i \leftarrow 1$ **to** n **do**
16   **if** $Code[S[i]].\ell > \ell$ **then**
17         $n' \leftarrow n' + 1$
18   **if** bitread$(B_\ell, i) = 0$ **then**
19           $pl \leftarrow pl + 1; S'[pl] \leftarrow S[i]$
20   **else**
21           $pr \leftarrow pr + 1; S'[pr] \leftarrow S[i]$
22     $S \leftrightarrow S'$
23     $n \leftarrow n'$
24     $\ell \leftarrow \ell + 1$
25   Free S and S'

6.3 Alphabet Partitioning

The wavelet tree variants give a good solution for compressing S to its zero-order entropy while performing the three operations in time $\mathcal{O}(\log \sigma)$. This is higher than the $\mathcal{O}(\log \log \sigma)$ times obtained in Section 6.1 for large alphabets (for small alphabets, the difference in time complexities is not that significant). However, the representation of Section 6.1 is not compressed. In this section we show how both ideas can be combined using a technique called alphabet partitioning. The result will have the best of both worlds, for large alphabets: fast operation times and zero-order compression of S. This technique should not be used when the alphabet is relatively small, since in that case the space and time overheads will be significant.

Imagine that we sort the symbols $[1, \sigma]$ by decreasing frequency in S, and then group them into $1 + \lfloor \log \sigma \rfloor$ *classes* of symbols: class ℓ contains the 2^ℓth to the $(2^{\ell+1} - 1)$th most frequent symbols; that is, each class $\ell \geq 0$ contains the next 2^ℓ most frequent symbols.

Let $C(c)$ be the class to which symbol $c \in [1, \sigma]$ belongs. Then we define a sequence $K[1, n]$, where $K[i] = C(S[i])$ is the class of $S[i]$. In addition, we define sequences S_ℓ, so that S_ℓ contains all the symbols in S of class ℓ, in the same order they appear in S; that is, we have

$$S_\ell[\text{rank}_\ell(K, i)] = S[i], \quad \text{if } K[i] = \ell.$$

Note that the alphabet of S_ℓ is of size 2^ℓ. We will rename the symbols of class ℓ to the values in $[1, 2^\ell]$. To maintain this mapping, we store function C in a sequence $C[1, \sigma]$, so that $C[c] = C(c)$. Now, if $C[c] = \ell$, then c is of class ℓ and it is mapped to $\text{rank}_\ell(C, c)$ in S_ℓ; that is, the first $c \in [1, \sigma]$ of class ℓ (where $C[c] = \ell$) will be mapped to the value 1, the second symbol c of class ℓ to the value 2, and so on until 2^ℓ (note that array C is similar to the array E used at the end of Section 6.2.5). The sequence S_ℓ where we have mapped the symbols to $[1, 2^\ell]$ will be called L_ℓ.

Our data structure is then composed of the following elements:

1. The sequence $C[1, \sigma]$, implemented with a wavelet tree. The alphabet of this sequence is of size $1 + \lfloor \log \sigma \rfloor$, therefore it answers access, rank, and select queries in time $\mathcal{O}(\log \log \sigma)$.

2. The sequence $K[1, n]$ of classes, implemented with a wavelet tree. It also answers the queries in time $\mathcal{O}(\log \log \sigma)$.

3. The sequences L_ℓ, for $0 \leq \ell \leq \lfloor \log \sigma \rfloor$, where $L_\ell[i] = \text{rank}_\ell(C, S_\ell[i])$. These sequences are represented with the technique of Section 6.1, so they support select in $\mathcal{O}(1)$ time and access and rank in $\mathcal{O}(\log \log 2^\ell) = \mathcal{O}(\log \log \sigma)$ time.

Example 6.16 *Figure 6.9 illustrates the alphabet partitioned representation of the same sequence of Example 6.2 (recall that whitespaces and commas are ignored). On the right we show the symbols in decreasing order of frequency and the classes they are assigned to. Since there are $1 + \lfloor \log \sigma \rfloor = 4$ classes, we have 4 sequences L_ℓ. For example, since e $= 3$ and o $= 7$ are of class $\ell = 1$, it holds $C[3] = C[7] = 1$. Also, in L_1, the es of S_1 are mapped to $\text{rank}_\ell(C, e) = \text{rank}_1(C, 3) = 1$, and the os are mapped to $\text{rank}_\ell(C, o) = \text{rank}_1(C, 7) = 2$. Therefore, $S_1 = $ oeoooeeeo is represented as $L_1 = 212221112$. Finally, $K[i] = 1$ whenever $S[i] = $ e or $S[i] = $ o.*

Let us show how to support $\text{access}(S, i)$ on this representation. First, we find the class of $S[i]$ with $\ell \leftarrow \text{access}(K, i)$ and the position in L_ℓ where $S[i]$ has been mapped with $k \leftarrow \text{rank}_\ell(K, i)$. We then find the mapped value of $S[i]$ with $m \leftarrow \text{access}(L_\ell, k)$. Finally, we retrieve the actual value $S[i] = \text{select}_\ell(C, m)$. The total time is $\mathcal{O}(\log \log \sigma)$.

Let us now consider $\text{rank}_c(S, i)$. First, we find the class of c with $\ell \leftarrow \text{access}(C, c)$. The mapped value of c is then $m \leftarrow \text{rank}_\ell(C, c)$. Now we map the interval $S[1, i]$ to $L_\ell[1, k]$ where all the (mapped) occurrences of c must appear, with $k \leftarrow \text{rank}_\ell(K, i)$. Then the answer is the number of occurrences of m in $L_\ell[1, k]$, which we compute with $\text{rank}_m(L_\ell, k)$. The total time is $\mathcal{O}(\log \log \sigma)$.

Finally, let us consider $\text{select}_c(S, j)$. We find the class and the mapped value of c, $\ell \leftarrow \text{access}(C, c)$ and $m \leftarrow \text{rank}_\ell(C, c)$. Now the jth position of (the mapped) c

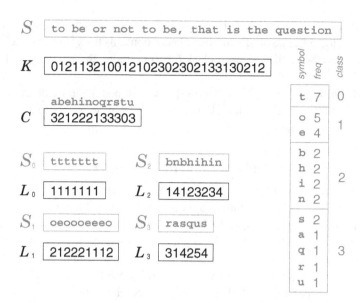

Figure 6.9. The representation of the sequence of Example 6.2 using alphabet partitioning. We show in black the elements that are actually represented (sequences K, C, and L_ℓ) and in gray the elements that are only conceptual.

in L_ℓ is found with $k \leftarrow \mathsf{select}_m(L_\ell, j)$. Finally, our answer is the position of $L_\ell[k]$ in S, $\mathsf{select}_\ell(K, k)$. The operation takes $\mathcal{O}(\log\log\sigma)$ time. Algorithm 6.11 provides the detail of the operations.

Example 6.17 *Let us solve* $\mathsf{access}(S, 13)$ *in this representation (see Figure 6.10). The class of $S[13]$ is $\ell = \mathsf{access}(K, 13) = 1$, thus $S[13]$ is represented in L_1, at position $k = \mathsf{rank}_1(K, 13) = 6$. Thus $m = \mathsf{access}(L_1, 6) = 1$ is the mapped value of $S[13]$; indeed $S_1[6] = S[13]$. Finally, we return* $\mathsf{select}_\ell(C, m) = \mathsf{select}_1(C, 1) = 3 = \mathsf{e}$.

To solve $\mathsf{rank}_{\mathsf{o}=7}(S, 23)$, *we find the class $\ell = \mathsf{access}(C, \mathsf{o}) = 1$ of o. The position $S[23]$ then corresponds to position $k = \mathsf{rank}_1(K, 23) = 7$ in L_1. The mapped value of o in L_1 is $m = \mathsf{rank}_1(C, \mathsf{o}) = 2$. The answer is then $\mathsf{rank}_m(L_\ell, k) = \mathsf{rank}_2(L_1, 7) = 4$.*

Finally, to solve $\mathsf{select}_{\mathsf{t}=11}(S, 3)$, *we find the class $\ell = \mathsf{access}(C, \mathsf{t}) = 0$ and the mapped value $m = \mathsf{rank}_0(C, \mathsf{t}) = 1$ of t. Thus the third occurrence of t in S corresponds to the third occurrence of 1 in L_0. This is at position $k = \mathsf{select}_m(L_\ell, 3) = \mathsf{select}_1(L_0, 3) = 3$ in L_0. The answer is then the position of the kth occurrence of 0 in K, $\mathsf{select}_\ell(K, k) = \mathsf{select}_0(K, 3) = 10$.*

Space and Construction

A wavelet tree representation of $C[1, \sigma]$ takes $\sigma\log\log\sigma\,(1 + o(1))$ bits. The wavelet tree of K must be given Huffman shape in order to exploit its compressibility. It turns out that the space of this wavelet tree, plus a plain representation of the sequences L_ℓ, add up to $n\mathcal{H}_0(S) + o(n\mathcal{H}_0(S)) + \mathcal{O}(n)$ bits. To see this, let $p(c)$ be the position of symbol c in the sequence of symbols sorted by decreasing frequency. Then it holds $n_c \leq n/p(c)$, where n_c is the number of occurrences of c in S, that is, the most frequent symbol appears at most n times, the second most frequent one appears at most $n/2$ times, the third most frequent one appears at most $n/3$ times, and so

---

Algorithm 6.11: Answering access, rank, and select with alphabet partitioning.

---

1 **Proc** access(S, i)
    Input : Sequence S (seen as sequences C, K, and L_ℓ) and position i.
    Output: Returns access(S, i).
2     $\ell \leftarrow$ access(K, i)
3     $k \leftarrow$ rank$_\ell(K, i)$
4     $m \leftarrow$ access(L_ℓ, k)
5   **return** select$_\ell(C, m)$

6 **Proc** rank$_c(S, i)$
    Input : Sequence S (seen as sequences C, K, and L_ℓ), symbol c, and position
           i.
    Output: Returns rank$_c(S, i)$.
7     $\ell \leftarrow$ access(C, c)
8     $m \leftarrow$ rank$_\ell(C, c)$
9     $k \leftarrow$ rank$_\ell(K, i)$
10   **return** rank$_m(L_\ell, k)$

11 **Proc** select$_c(S, j)$
    Input : Sequence S (seen as sequences C, K, and L_ℓ), symbol c, and index j.
    Output: Returns select$_c(S, j)$.
12     $\ell \leftarrow$ access(C, c)
13     $m \leftarrow$ rank$_\ell(C, c)$
14     $k \leftarrow$ select$_m(L_\ell, j)$
15   **return** select$_\ell(K, k)$

---

on. Since symbol c will belong to level $\ell = \lfloor \log p(c) \rfloor$, it will be represented in L_ℓ, which has an alphabet of size 2^ℓ. A plain representation (as in Section 6.1) will use essentially $\log 2^\ell = \ell \le \log p(c)$ bits for each of the n_c occurrences of c. Adding over all the symbols, we have $\sum_c n_c \log p(c) \le \sum_c n_c \log(n/n_c) = n\mathcal{H}_0(S)$ bits (recall

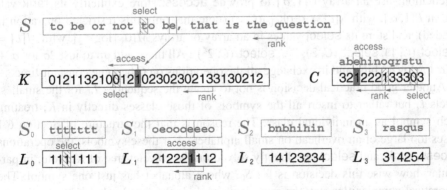

Figure 6.10. The operations of Example 6.17 on the structure of Figure 6.9. The operations related to access(S, 13) are shown with open or solid gray blocks, and those related to rank$_o(S, 23)$ and select$_t(S, 3)$ in blocks hatched in different directions.

Section 2.3.2). The redundancy of the data structure of Section 6.1 then adds up $o(n\mathcal{H}_0(S))$ further bits.

The sequence K stores the levels $\ell = \lfloor \log p(c) \rfloor$ of the symbols. We store it within $n(\mathcal{H}_0(K) + 1)(1 + o(1))$ bits. Since the empirical zero-order entropy of K is a lower bound to the space used by any encoder that always gives the same code to the same symbol, let us measure the space of encoding K using γ-codes (Section 2.7). Then we have

$$n\mathcal{H}_0(K) \leq \sum_{i=1}^{n} (2\lfloor \log \lfloor \log p(S[i]) \rfloor \rfloor + 1) \leq 2 \sum_{i=1}^{n} \log \log p(S[i]) + n$$

$$= 2 \sum_{c=1}^{\sigma} n_c \log \log p(c) + n \leq 2 \sum_{c=1}^{\sigma} n_c \log \log(n/n_c) + n$$

$$\leq 2n \log \mathcal{H}_0(S) + n = o(n\mathcal{H}_0(S)) + \mathcal{O}(n),$$

where in the first line we used the length of γ-codes, in the second the fact that $n_c \leq n/p(c)$, and in the third we applied Jensen's inequality as in Section 2.9. Calculation shows that this formula also absorbs the $\mathcal{O}(\sigma \log \log \sigma)$ bits of C; we give the pointers to the complete analysis in the bibliographic discussion.

An intuitive explanation of how it is possible that we obtain zero-order compression by simply dividing S into subsequences and using *uncompressed* representations for them is that the symbols that are grouped in any sequence L_ℓ have roughly the same frequency, and thus a plain representation is not far from a compressed one. That is, it is sufficient to group symbols of similar frequency to obtain compression, even if each group is represented in plain form (it is crucial to take advantage of the alphabet size, however, hence the mapping we use with C).

The construction of the structure poses no challenges and is dominated by the time for building the wavelet trees, $\mathcal{O}(n \log \log \sigma)$. The details are shown in Algorithm 6.12. By buffering sequences and bitvectors, one can run the construction within $\mathcal{O}(\sigma w)$ bits of main memory, plus one small buffer per class.

Practical Considerations

Unless σ is really large, it is wise to replace the wavelet tree of C with a faster representation: use an array $C[1, \sigma]$ to provide **access**, store explicitly its **rank** values in $R[1, \sigma]$, with $R[c] = \text{rank}_{C[c]}(C, c)$ (note that only this restricted operation is needed), and store its **select** values in an array of arrays $M[0, \lfloor \log \sigma \rfloor]$, with $M[\ell] = \langle \text{select}_\ell(C, 1), \text{select}_\ell(C, 2), \ldots, \text{select}_\ell(C, 2^\ell) \rangle$. All these add up to just $2\sigma \log \sigma + \mathcal{O}(\sigma \log \log \sigma)$ bits, and in exchange all the operations on C become constant-time.

Another good practical decision is not to create the sequences L_ℓ for the smallest levels ℓ, but rather to insert all the symbols of those classes directly in K, treating each symbol as an individual class. The reason is that the structure of Section 6.1 poses too large of an overhead on small alphabets. For these symbols, the operations **access**, **rank**, and **select** are directly solved on the wavelet tree of K. Note, in particular, how wise this decision is for S_0, whose alphabet has just one symbol. The theoretical complexities stay the same if we include the first $\log \log \sigma$ levels directly in K.

Algorithm 6.12: Building the alphabet partitioning representation.

Input : Sequence $S[1, n]$ over alphabet $[1, \sigma]$.
Output: Builds the alphabet partitioning representation of S: sequences C, K, and
L_ℓ.

---

1 Allocate array $F[1, \sigma]$ with fields s (a symbol) and f (a frequency)
2 **for** $c \leftarrow 1$ **to** σ **do**
3 $\quad\lfloor\ F[c].s \leftarrow c; F[c].f \leftarrow 0$
4 **for** $i \leftarrow 1$ **to** n **do**
5 $\quad\lfloor\ F[S[i]].f \leftarrow F[S[i]].f + 1$
6 Sort F by decreasing value of field f
7 Allocate string $C[1, \sigma]$ over alphabet $[0, \lfloor\log\sigma\rfloor]$
8 **for** $\ell \leftarrow 0$ **to** $\lfloor\log\sigma\rfloor$ **do**
9 $\quad\lfloor\ n_\ell \leftarrow 0$
10 **for** $j \leftarrow 1$ **to** σ **do**
11 $\quad\mid\ \ell \leftarrow \lfloor\log j\rfloor$
12 $\quad\mid\ C[F[j].s] \leftarrow \ell$
13 $\quad\lfloor\ n_\ell \leftarrow n_\ell + F[j].f$
14 Free F
15 Preprocess C as a wavelet tree (Algorithm 6.5)
16 Allocate string $K[1, n]$ over alphabet $[0, \lfloor\log\sigma\rfloor]$
17 **for** $\ell \leftarrow 0$ **to** $\lfloor\log\sigma\rfloor$ **do**
18 $\quad\mid$ Allocate string $L_\ell[1, n_\ell]$ over alphabet $[1, 2^\ell]$
19 $\quad\lfloor\ n_\ell \leftarrow 0$
20 **for** $i \leftarrow 1$ **to** n **do**
21 $\quad\mid\ \ell \leftarrow \mathsf{access}(C, S[i])$
22 $\quad\mid\ K[i] \leftarrow \ell$
23 $\quad\mid\ n_\ell \leftarrow n_\ell + 1$
24 $\quad\lfloor\ L_\ell[n_\ell] \leftarrow \mathsf{rank}_\ell(C, S[i])$
25 Preprocess K as a Huffman-shaped wavelet tree
26 Preprocess each L_ℓ as a permutation-based data structure (Algorithm 6.2)

6.4 Applications

6.4.1 Compressible Permutations Again

In Section 6.2.4 we pointed out the similarity between compressed wavelet trees and
the technique to represent compressible permutations given in Section 5.3. The relation
between permutations and sequences is indeed deeper, and independent of the wavelet
tree structure. In this section we show how to use the connection to obtain compressed
representations of permutations with loglogarithmic query times.

Let π be a permutation on $[1, n]$ with ρ runs of increasing values (recall
Section 5.3). The interval $[1, n]$ is then covered by those ranges, $[p_1 + 1, p_2]$, $[p_2 +
1, p_3]$, ..., $[p_\rho + 1, p_{\rho+1}]$, with $p_1 = 0$ and $p_{\rho+1} = n$.

Now consider the inverse permutation π^{-1}. All the elements belonging to the rth run of π are identified because they are values between $p_r + 1$ and p_{r+1}. Let us replace all those values by the run identifier r. The result is then a sequence $S[1, n]$ over the alphabet $[1, \rho]$.

Since the elements in $\pi(p_r + 1, p_{r+1})$ are increasing, the values $p_r + 1, p_r + 2, \ldots, p_{r+1}$ appear at increasing positions of π^{-1}, precisely at $\pi(p_r + 1) < \pi(p_r + 2) < \ldots < \pi(p_{r+1})$. Therefore, the jth occurrence of symbol r in S is at position $\pi(p_r + j)$, that is, $\pi(p_r + j) = \mathsf{select}_r(S, j)$. Conversely, taking π^{-1} on both sides of that equation, we have $p_r + j = \pi^{-1}(\mathsf{select}_r(S, j))$. Thus, if $i = \mathsf{select}_r(S, j)$, then $\pi^{-1}(i) = p_r + j$. It is easy to obtain r and j given i: $r = S[i]$ and $j = \mathsf{rank}_r(S, i)$.

Example 6.18 *Consider again the permutation of Example 5.4*

$$\pi = (3\ 9\ 2\ 5\ 6\ 7\ 10\ 11\ 13\ 15\ 14\ 16\ 12\ 1\ 4\ 8).$$

It has length $n = 16$ and $\rho = 5$ runs that start at positions $p_1 + 1 = 1$, $p_2 + 1 = 3$, $p_3 + 1 = 11$, $p_4 + 1 = 13$, $p_5 + 1 = 14$. Its inverse permutation is

$$\pi^{-1} = (14\ 3\ 1\ 15\ 4\ 5\ 6\ 16\ 2\ 7\ 8\ 13\ 9\ 11\ 10\ 12).$$

By replacing each element in π^{-1} by the run it belongs to, we obtain

$$S = 5\ 2\ 1\ 5\ 2\ 2\ 2\ 5\ 1\ 2\ 2\ 4\ 2\ 3\ 2\ 3.$$

Then, for example, it holds $\pi(7) = \pi(p_2 + 5) = \mathsf{select}_2(S, 5) = 10$. On the other hand, $\pi^{-1}(10) = p_2 + 5 = 7$ because $S[10] = 2$ and $\mathsf{rank}_2(S, 10) = 5$.

Assume we store a bitvector $D[1, n]$ with $D[p_r + 1] = 1$ and 0 elsewhere, so that we compute $p_r = \mathsf{select}(D, r) - 1$ in constant time (we also need constant-time rank on D). Sequence S can be represented using alphabet partitioning (Section 6.3), so that it uses $n\mathcal{H}_0(S)(1 + o(1)) + \mathcal{O}(n)$ bits. Since S contains $n_r = p_{r+1} - p_r$ occurrences of symbol r, it holds $n\mathcal{H}_0(S) = \mathcal{H}(\pi)$. Therefore, the total space is $\mathcal{H}(\pi)(1 + o(1)) + \mathcal{O}(n)$ bits. With this representation, we can compute any $\pi(i)$ or $\pi^{-1}(i)$ in time $\mathcal{O}(\log \log \rho)$. Algorithm 6.13 gives the pseudocode.

Algorithm 6.13: Answering read and inverse on compressible permutations using sequence representations.

---

1 **Proc** $\mathsf{read}(\pi, i)$
  Input : Permutation π (seen as sequence S and bitvector D) and position i.
  Output: Returns $\pi(i)$.

2 | $r \leftarrow \mathsf{rank}(D, i)$
3 | $j \leftarrow i - \mathsf{pred}(D, i) + 1$
4 | **return** $\mathsf{select}_r(S, j)$

5 **Proc** $\mathsf{inverse}(\pi, i)$
  Input : Permutation π (seen as sequence S and bitvector D), and position i.
  Output: Returns $\pi^{-1}(i)$.

6 | $r \leftarrow \mathsf{access}(S, i)$
7 | $j \leftarrow \mathsf{rank}_r(S, i)$
8 | **return** $\mathsf{select}(D, r) + j - 1$

6.4.2 Compressed Text Collections Revisited

In Section 3.4.5 we considered the problem of giving direct access to a text collection that is compressed to (about) its wordwise zero-order empirical entropy, $n\mathcal{H}_0(T)$. We showed that any arbitrary word could be accessed in time $\mathcal{O}(\log n)$. Then in Section 4.5.1 we showed that a positional inverted index on T could be stored in $n\mathcal{H}_0(T) + \mathcal{O}(n)$ bits, so that any occurrence of any word in T could be located in $\mathcal{O}(1)$ time. Later in Section 5.4.2, we showed that both structures (the text and its inverted index) could be unified in a single permutation formed by the concatenation of the inverted lists, so that T is basically the inverse of that permutation. Therefore, within $n\mathcal{H}_0(T)(1 + o(1)) + \mathcal{O}(n)$ bits, we could have access to any position in T and to any occurrence of any word in $\mathcal{O}(\log n)$ time. The slowdown was seen as a consequence of halving the space; now we show this is not the case.

Let us represent $T[1, n]$ as a sequence of values in $[1, \sigma]$, where σ is the size of the vocabulary of T (recall from Section 2.9 that $\sigma = \mathcal{O}(n^\beta)$ in practice, for some constant $0 < \beta < 1$). This is a large alphabet, which justifies the use of alphabet partitioning (Section 6.3). This representation uses $n\mathcal{H}_0(T)(1 + o(1)) + \mathcal{O}(n)$ bits, just as in Section 5.4.2. Now, in order to extract the ith word of T, we simply perform access(T, i), in time $\mathcal{O}(\log \log \sigma) = \mathcal{O}(\log \log n)$. On the other hand, the jth entry of the inverted list of word s is just select$_s(T, j)$, which is also computed in $\mathcal{O}(\log \log n)$ time.

Therefore, we have a representation for T and its inverted index that is as small as the compressed text and provides loglogarithmic time access to T and to its inverted index. In addition, this representation provides the operation rank$_s(T, i)$, which is useful for implementing the list intersection algorithm of Section 3.4.4. To find the positions of the phrase formed by the words s_1 and s_2, we follow the procedure described in Algorithm 6.14.[4]

6.4.3 Non-positional Inverted Indexes

A *non-positional inverted index* for a collection of text documents chooses a subset of relevant words to index (called *terms*) and records in which documents each term appears. Such an index can be represented as a sequence S, which is partitioned into segments $S[i_t, f_t]$ for each term t. Each such segment contains the list of the documents x where t appears. A bitvector B marks the beginning of those segments, with $B[i_t] = 1$ for all t.

The most basic queries in such an inverted index ask to find the number of documents where term t appears (called the *document frequency* of t) and to find the ith document where term t appears. These are easily computed as $f_t - i_t + 1$ and access$(S, i_t + i - 1)$, respectively, where $i_t = $ select(B, t) and $f_t = $ succ$(B, i_t + 1) - 1$.

Apart from this basic functionality, the most important operation in non-positional inverted indexes is to compute the intersection of two lists, which corresponds to the Boolean AND operation (that is, list the documents where both terms t and t' appear).

---

[4] This algorithm deviates slightly from Algorithm 3.7. In that case, advancing i_1 and i_2 by one unit was very cheap, thus the recommended sequence of operations is different.

Algorithm 6.14: Positional inverted list intersection over a sequence representation of the text.

Input : Sequence $T[1, n]$ with **rank** and **select** support, and words
$s_1, s_2 \in [1, \sigma]$.

Output: Finds the positions where s_1 occurs in T followed by s_2.

1   $i_1 \leftarrow 1$; $p_1 \leftarrow \mathsf{select}_{s_1}(T, 1)$
2   $i_2 \leftarrow 1$; $p_2 \leftarrow \mathsf{select}_{s_2}(T, 1)$
3   **while** $p_1 \leq n - 1$ **and** $p_2 \leq n$ **do**
4   **if** $p_1 < p_2 - 1$ **then**
5          $i_1 \leftarrow \mathsf{rank}_{s_1}(T, p_2 - 2) + 1$
6          $p_1 \leftarrow \mathsf{select}_{s_1}(T, i_1)$
7   **else if** $p_1 \geq p_2$ **then**
8          $i_2 \leftarrow \mathsf{rank}_{s_2}(T, p_1) + 1$
9          $p_2 \leftarrow \mathsf{select}_{s_2}(T, i_2)$
10   **else**
11   **output** position p_1
12         $i_1 \leftarrow i_1 + 1$
13         $p_1 \leftarrow \mathsf{select}_{s_1}(T, i_1)$

A wavelet tree representation of S can compute this intersection efficiently. Finding the documents x where both terms t and t' appear corresponds to finding the symbols x that appear in both $S[i_t, f_t]$ and $S[i_{t'}, f_{t'}]$. We start at the root of the wavelet tree with the intervals $[i_t, f_t]$ and $[i_{t'}, f_{t'}]$. The procedure at each node v is as follows. If one of the two intervals is empty (that is, $i_t > f_t$ or $i_{t'} > f_{t'}$), we stop the computation in this node. Otherwise we recursively continue to the left child of v, mapping the intervals $[i_t, f_t]$ and $[i_{t'}, f_{t'}]$ to the 0s they contain in B_v, and to the right child of v mapping the intervals to the 1s they contain in B_v. When we reach a leaf corresponding to document x and both ranges are nonempty, we report x.

Algorithm 6.15 carries out the intersection. It can be easily extended to intersect more than two terms, to compute the union (Boolean OR) of two or more terms, and to list the documents when at least k of the query terms appear, which generalizes operations AND and OR. Note that this functionality is not exclusive of inverted indexes: We can use wavelet trees to compute intersections or unions of elements in two ranges of a sequence of any kind.

Note that we can carry out this procedure on a wavelet tree or matrix, but not on the sequence representation of Section 6.1. An alternative to the wavelet trees or matrices is to represent each interval $S[i_t, f_t]$, of increasing document identifiers, with the partial sums technique of Section 3.4.4, which also supports intersections. Both intersection algorithms perform competitively, and the differential encodings of Section 3.4.4 are more space-efficient.

In exchange, the wavelet tree (or matrix) supports further functionality. For example, the documents need not be sorted in increasing order in $S[i_t, f_t]$. Instead, they can be stored in decreasing *relevance* order (a relevance measure can be, for example, the *term*

Algorithm 6.15: Non-positional inverted list intersection over a wavelet tree of the concatenated inverted lists.

Input : Concatenation of document lists S (seen as wavelet tree T over alphabet $[1, D]$) and two ranges $[i_t, f_t]$, $[i_{t'}, f_{t'}]$.

Output: Reports the symbols (documents) that occur in both ranges.

1 $inters(T.root, 1, D, i_t, f_t, i_{t'}, f_{t'})$

2 **Proc** $inters(v, a, b, i_t, f_t, i_{t'}, f_{t'})$

     Input : A node v of the wavelet tree of S representing the symbol range $[a, b]$, and sequence ranges $[i_t, f_t]$, $[i_{t'}, f_{t'}]$.

     Output: Reports the symbols (documents) that occur in both ranges below v.

3   **if** $i_t > f_t$ **or** $i_{t'} > f_{t'}$ **then**
4         $\lfloor$ **return**
5   **if** $a = b$ **then**
6         $\lfloor$ **output** a; **return**
7      $m \leftarrow \lfloor (a + b)/2 \rfloor$
8      $i \leftarrow \mathsf{rank}_0(v.B, i_t - 1) + 1; \ f \leftarrow \mathsf{rank}_0(v.B, f_t)$
9      $i' \leftarrow \mathsf{rank}_0(v.B, i_{t'} - 1) + 1; \ f' \leftarrow \mathsf{rank}_0(v.B, f_{t'})$
10    $inters(v.l, a, m, i, f, i', f')$
11    $inters(v.r, m + 1, b, i_t - i + 1, f_t - f, i_{t'} - i' + 1, f_{t'} - f')$

---

frequency, that is, the number of times t appears in d). This ordering permits traversing only a prefix of the segment $S[i_t, f_t]$ when only highly relevant documents are sought.

Another way to exploit the wavelet tree is to allow for query expansion, that is, to convert a query term t into a union of terms with the same or more general meaning. For example, terms can be ordered so that synonyms are contiguous, and therefore we can take a supersegment $S[i_s, f_s]$ that contains all the synonyms of t instead of just $S[i_t, f_t]$. The intersection algorithm works identically. Hierarchical clustering of terms, into more and more general meanings, is also possible, so that every cluster is mapped to a contiguous interval of terms. One can then decide at query time which is the proper supersegment for a term.

By using Algorithm 6.15 to intersect a segment $S[i_s, f_s]$ with itself, we obtain all the unique documents inside it. This can be used in more general contexts to obtain the d unique elements in a range. To analyze this algorithm, we can consider that we reach the d distinct leaves, at cost $\mathcal{O}(d \log D)$. However, not all the paths can be distinct. In the worst case, all the $2d$ nodes up to depth $\log d$ are traversed (in total time $\mathcal{O}(d)$), and then we traverse a distinct path of length $\log D - \log d$ from each node of depth d to a leaf. Thus the total cost is $\mathcal{O}(d(1 + \log(D/d)))$. Figure 6.11 illustrates the analysis.

6.4.4 Range Quantile Queries

Another illustration of the power of wavelet trees beyond the mere representation of sequences is their ability to solve a problem called range quantile queries. Given an

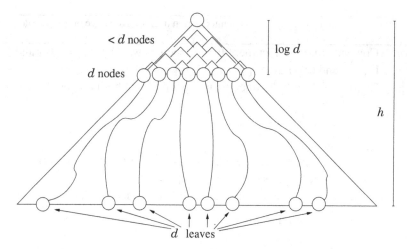

Figure 6.11. Schematic illustration of the number of nodes traversed for reaching d wavelet tree leaves, in the worst case.

array $A[1, n]$ of numbers in $[1, u]$, we look for a representation that efficiently solves the following query: given $[i, j]$ and $k \in [1, j - i + 1]$, return the kth largest value in $A[i, j]$.

Assume we represent A using a wavelet tree (it could also be a wavelet matrix). Let v be the wavelet tree root and $B_v[1, n]$ its bitvector. If $\ell = \mathsf{rank}_1(B_v, j) - \mathsf{rank}_1(B_v, i - 1) \geq k$, then there are k or more values in $A[i, j]$ that belong to the right child v_r of v, and these are larger than those that belong to the left child v_l. This means that the kth largest value in $A_v[i, j]$ is in A_{v_r}. Thus we move to node v_r and update the interval to $i \leftarrow \mathsf{rank}_1(B_v, i - 1) + 1$ and $j \leftarrow \mathsf{rank}_1(B_v, j)$. Otherwise there are fewer than k 1s in $B_v[i, j]$, and all those values are larger than the kth largest value. Therefore, the kth largest value in $A[i, j]$ is the $(k - \ell)$th largest value in A_{v_l}. Thus we must look for the answer on v_l, updating the range to $i \leftarrow \mathsf{rank}_0(B_v, i - 1) + 1$ and $j \leftarrow \mathsf{rank}_0(B_v, j)$, and updating $k \leftarrow k - \ell$. When we arrive at the leaf of number x, we know that x is the kth largest value in the range. Moreover x occurs $j - i + 1$ times in the original range. The total time for the query is $\mathcal{O}(\log u)$. Algorithm 6.16 shows the procedure.

6.4.5 Revisiting Arrays of Variable-Length Cells

In Section 3.2 we explored several alternatives to providing direct access to arrays $A[1, n]$ of variable-length cells storing numbers in $[1, u]$. The alphabet partitioning technique of Section 6.3 provides a practical mechanism to give direct access to any element in time $\mathcal{O}(\log \log u)$ and using $n \log \log u(1 + o(1))$ bits of extra space over the plain representation of the numbers.

The idea is to define a sequence $K[1, n]$ on alphabet $[0, \lfloor \log u \rfloor]$, so that $K[i] = \lfloor \log A[i] \rfloor$. Then, for each $\ell \in [1, \lfloor \log u \rfloor]$, we store an array A_ℓ with all the values $A[i] \in [2^\ell, 2^{\ell+1} - 1]$, devoided of their highest bit. That is, if $K[i] = \ell$, then $A_\ell[\mathsf{rank}_\ell(K, i)] = A[i] - 2^\ell$ (except for $\ell = 0$, where we directly know that $A[i] = 1$). By regarding K as a sequence of classes, this is exactly the idea of alphabet partitioning, now used in a simpler setting where we want only to provide operation $\mathsf{read}(A, i)$ on variable-length array elements.

Algorithm 6.16: Solving range quantile queries on wavelet trees.

Input : Array $A[1, n]$ of integers in $[1, u]$ (seen as wavelet tree T), range $[i, j]$
             and integer k.
Output: Returns the kth largest value in $A[i, j]$.

1 $v \leftarrow T.root$
2 $a \leftarrow 1; b \leftarrow u$
3 **while** $a < b$ **do**
4       $m \leftarrow \lfloor (a + b)/2 \rfloor$
5       $i' \leftarrow \mathsf{rank}_1(v.B, i - 1) + 1$
6       $j' \leftarrow \mathsf{rank}_1(v.B, j)$
7       $\ell \leftarrow j' - i' + 1$
8   **if** $\ell \geq k$ **then**
9          $i \leftarrow i'$
10         $j \leftarrow j'$
11         $v \leftarrow v.r$
12         $a \leftarrow m + 1$
13   **else**
14         $i \leftarrow i - i' + 1$
15         $j \leftarrow j - j'$
16         $v \leftarrow v.l$
17         $b \leftarrow m$
18         $k \leftarrow k - \ell$

19 **return** a (the value occurs $j - i + 1$ times in the range)

If we represent K with a wavelet tree and the arrays A_ℓ with cells of fixed length ℓ, then we need one **access** and **rank** operation on the wavelet tree (which can be combined into one) plus a fast access to an array A_ℓ, to solve **read**(A, i). This is competitive with direct access codes (Section 3.4.2) and Elias-Fano codes (Section 3.4.3). By giving Huffman shape to the wavelet tree of K, the prefix that identifies $|A[i]|$ is encoded within its zero-order entropy, which outperforms in space at least the γ-codes, δ-codes, Rice codes, and VByte codes of Section 2.7, for which we obtained direct access in Section 3.2.

Example 6.19 *Consider the array* $A[1, 10] = \langle 1, 2, 1, 3, 6, 2, 4, 3, 9, 3 \rangle$. *Then* $K = \langle 0, 1, 0, 1, 2, 1, 2, 1, 3, 1 \rangle, A_1 = \langle 0, 1, 0, 1, 1 \rangle, A_2 = \langle 2, 0 \rangle$, *and* $A_3 = \langle 1 \rangle$. *Then, to find* $A[4]$, *we see that its length is* $\ell = K[4] = 1$, *and therefore the value* $A[4] - 2^\ell = A[4] - 2$ *is stored at* $A_\ell[\mathsf{rank}_\ell(K, 4)] = A_1[2] = 1$, *therefore* $A[4] = 1 + 2 = 3$.

6.5 Summary

A sequence $S[1, n]$ over alphabet $[1, \sigma]$ can be represented in $n \log \sigma + n\, o(\log \sigma)$ bits (which includes an $\mathcal{O}(n)$ term) so that operation **select** is supported in time $\mathcal{O}(1)$ and **access** and **rank** in time $\mathcal{O}(\log \log \sigma)$. The construction takes linear time. By increasing the time of **select** to $\mathcal{O}(\log \log \sigma)$, the space can be reduced to $n\mathcal{H}_0(S)(1 + o(1)) + \mathcal{O}(n)$ bits. Construction time raises to $\mathcal{O}(n \log \log \sigma)$. These are good choices when the alphabet size σ is relatively large. When σ is not so large, a wavelet tree representation is preferable. It takes $n\mathcal{H}_0(S)(1 + o(1)) + \mathcal{O}(\sigma w)$ bits of space and supports all the operations in time $\mathcal{O}(\log \sigma)$. The wavelet tree is built in time $\mathcal{O}(n \log \sigma)$. Sequences are used to represent compressed permutations and functions; labeled trees, graphs, and binary relations (Chapters 8 and 9); and texts (Chapter 11).

Wavelet trees offer more functionality than just **access**, **rank**, and **select**, which is useful to represent grids (Chapter 10) and solve other problems on general sequences, such as range quantile queries. When this extended functionality is needed on large alphabets, wavelet matrices are useful: they retain the same complexities of wavelet trees but significantly reduce the constant that multiplies the $\mathcal{O}(\sigma w)$ term in the space.

6.6 Bibliographic Notes

Permutation-based representation. The permutation-based technique of Section 6.1 was proposed by Golynski *et al.* (2006). The predecessor structure we described to reduce the time of **rank** is by Mehlhorn and Näher (1990). As already mentioned in Section 4.7, practical implementations of this structure exist, but in most cases the difference with a binary search does not justify the added complexity on the small sampled universes that arise in this application.

Golynski *et al.* (2006) also explored the idea of representing π^{-1} explicitly and computing π as its inverse, which yields constant time for **access**, $\mathcal{O}(\log \log \sigma)$ time for **select**, and, using a slightly denser sampling for predecessors, $\mathcal{O}(\log \log \sigma \log \log \log \sigma)$ time for **rank**. Barbay *et al.* (2011) managed to reduce the space of this structure to $n\mathcal{H}_k(S) + n\, o(\log \sigma)$ for any $k = o(\log_\sigma n)$, with only slightly higher operation times. Grossi *et al.* (2010) retained this compressed space while improving the time complexities: $\mathcal{O}(\log \log \sigma)$ time for **rank** and either $\mathcal{O}(\log \log \sigma)$ time for **access** and $\mathcal{O}(1)$ time for **select**, or vice versa. The way to achieve kth order compression is to use an **access**-enabled compressed representation (like that of Ferragina and Venturini (2007); we described a variant for bitvectors in Section 4.1.2) and to add small extra structures to support **rank** and **select**. These variants are rather complex and have not been implemented.

Wavelet trees. Wavelet trees were introduced by Grossi *et al.* (2003), who also showed that the use of zero-order compressed bitvectors B on the tree nodes leads to zero-order compression of S, $n\mathcal{H}_0(S) + o(n \log \sigma)$ bits. Mäkinen and Navarro (2005) proposed giving Huffman shape to the wavelet trees to obtain $n(\mathcal{H}_0(S) + 1)(1 + o(1)) + \mathcal{O}(\sigma w)$ bits of space without the need to compress the bitvectors, and showed that this reduces the average query times under reasonable assumptions. Foschini *et al.* (2006) also explored the idea of changing the wavelet tree shape but with the purpose of adapting to the distribution of the queries. They mentioned that the wavelet tree space is largely independently of its shape if the bitvectors are compressed. Barbay and Navarro (2013) proved that the space becomes $n\mathcal{H}_0(S)(1 + o(1)) + \mathcal{O}(\sigma w)$ bits when compressed bitvectors and Huffman shape are combined.

Ferragina *et al.* (2007) introduced the multiary wavelet trees to reduce the operation times to $\mathcal{O}\left(1 + \frac{\log \sigma}{\log \log n}\right)$ while retaining $n\mathcal{H}_0(S) + o(n \log \sigma)$ bits of space. Their space was further reduced to $n\mathcal{H}_0(S) + o(n)$ bits by Golynski *et al.* (2008). Barbay and Navarro (2013) used multiary Huffman-shaped wavelet trees (using Huffman on a non-binary target alphabet) to obtain the same space and worst-case time of Golynski *et al.* (2008), but combined with a reduced $\mathcal{O}\left(1 + \frac{\mathcal{H}_0(S)}{\log \log n}\right)$ average-case time for the operations. In practice, however, multiary implementations have not yielded clear practical advantages (Bowe, 2010), except for a bytewise implementation that we mention later (Brisaboa *et al.*, 2012), which has worked well in a particular application.

All these wavelet tree implementations have an extra space of $\mathcal{O}(\sigma w)$ bits, used to represent the tree nodes and pointers to bitvectors. Mäkinen and Navarro (2007) showed how to simulate a balanced wavelet tree by concatenating all the bitvectors of each level, so that the extra space becomes just $\mathcal{O}(w \log \sigma)$ bits. Zero-order compression can still be achieved by compressing the bitvectors, and Zhang *et al.* (2008) also showed how (canonical) Huffman-shaped wavelet trees can be implemented without pointers. Gagie *et al.* (2015) showed that, in this case, the Huffman model can be stored in $\mathcal{O}(\sigma \log \log n)$ bits. In the chapter we do not describe these pointerless wavelet trees, but directly the wavelet matrix, proposed by Claude *et al.* (2015) to speed up pointerless wavelet trees. They also presented the Huffman-shaped wavelet matrices we described, although in this case the model occupies $\mathcal{O}(\sigma w)$ bits (with a small constant). The ideas we discussed to reduce this constant are also inspired by Gagie *et al.* (2015).

The space-efficient construction we describe is the simplest one studied by Claude *et al.* (2011). They present more sophisticated schemes using virtually no extra space and with the same $\mathcal{O}(n \log \sigma)$ time complexity (albeit slower in practice). Tischler (2011) describes other techniques. Time-efficient methods have been proposed as well: Munro *et al.* (2016) presented a construction running in time $\mathcal{O}(n \log \sigma / \sqrt{\log n})$; others explored practical multi-core constructions (Fuentes-Sepúlveda *et al.*, 2014; Shun, 2015; Labeit *et al.*, 2016).

Several surveys on wavelet trees explore their flexibility to solve problems not only on sequences, but also on discrete grids and in other scenarios (Ferragina *et al.*, 2009; Grossi *et al.*, 2011; Gagie *et al.*, 2012; Makris, 2012; Navarro, 2014). Grossi and Ottaviano (2012) used wavelet trees on strings in order to implement compressed tries (tries are described in Section 8.5.3).

Alphabet partitioning. The technique of Section 6.3 was introduced by Barbay *et al.* (2014). They use a more theoretically appealing version that obtains the same asymptotic time complexities of the technique of Section 6.1, while using $n\mathcal{H}_0(S) + o(n(\mathcal{H}_0(S) + 1))$ bits of space. In the practical part of the article they introduce and analyze the version we have presented, showing empirically that it performs better in practice.

Lower bounds and optimality. Belazzougui and Navarro (2015) proved a lower bound of $\Omega(\log \log_w \sigma)$ time for operation rank, on a RAM machine of w bits, for any structure using $\mathcal{O}\left(n\, w^{\mathcal{O}(1)}\right)$ space. They matched that time within compressed space, together with constant-time for **select** and any superconstant time for **access**, or vice versa. Golynski (2009) proved that in any representation with a redundancy of $o(n \log \sigma)$ bits, the product of the **access** and **select** times must be $\omega(\log_\sigma n)$. In particular, if the alphabet is large enough so that $\log \sigma = \Omega(\log n)$, we cannot have constant time for both operations simultaneously. When σ is polynomial in w, Belazzougui and Navarro (2015) achieve $n\mathcal{H}_0(S) + o(n)$ bits and constant time for all the operations.

These are currently the best results, and they are very close to optimal, although not as practical as the ones we have described in the chapter.

Compressible permutations Our application of alphabet partitioning to compressible permutations follows the description of Barbay *et al.* (2014). With the theoretically best current results on sequence representation (Belazzougui and Navarro, 2015), the space would be $\mathcal{H}(\pi)(1 + o(1)) + o(n)$ bits, the time for $\pi(i)$ would be $\mathcal{O}(1)$, and that for $\pi^{-1}(i)$ would be $\mathcal{O}\left(\log \log_w \rho\right)$. Barbay *et al.* (2014) describe other applications to representing functions on $[1, n]$ (which are more general than permutations), permutations with other kinds of regularities, and other structures.

Inverted indexes. Barbay *et al.* (2014) also describe the idea of Section 6.4.2. Brisaboa *et al.* (2012) optimized it for the case of natural language texts, by using multiary wavelet trees that store byte sequences B_v at the nodes. Arroyuelo *et al.* (2010) showed how this structure can simulate a non-positional inverted index. More recently, Arroyuelo *et al.* (2012a,b) studied the practicality of this approach compared to classical inverted indexes, in the context of distributed text search engines.

The use of wavelet trees for implementing flexible non-positional inverted indexes and other applications to information retrieval was studied by Gagie *et al.* (2012). Implementations of some of those ideas turned out to compete with classical schemes (Culpepper *et al.*, 2010; Konow and Navarro, 2012).

Other applications of wavelet trees. Gagie *et al.* (2009) proposed the use of wavelet trees to solve range quantile queries. The time achieved by this solution is close to the optimal $\mathcal{O}(\log k / \log \log n)$ (Chan and Wilkinson, 2013). Külekci (2014) proposed and experimentally studied the technique we describe in Section 6.4.5 for direct access on variable-length codes. A related idea (Baruch *et al.*, 2016) is to use canonical-Huffman-shaped wavelet trees and replace maximal perfect binary subtrees by arrays, since all the elements in those subtrees use the same number of bits.

Bibliography

Arroyuelo, D., González, S., and Oyarzún, M. (2010). Compressed self-indices supporting conjunctive queries on document collections. In *Proc. 17th International Symposium on String Processing and Information Retrieval (SPIRE)*, LNCS 6393, pages 43–54.

Arroyuelo, D., Gil-Costa, V., González, S., Marín, M., and Oyarzún, M. (2012a). Distributed search based on self-indexed compressed text. *Information Processing and Management*, **48**(5), 819–827.

Arroyuelo, D., González, S., Marín, M., Oyarzún, M., and Suel, T. (2012b). To index or not to index: time-space trade-offs in search engines with positional ranking functions. In *Proc. 35th*

International ACM Conference on Research and Development in Information Retrieval (SIGIR), pages 255–264.

Barbay, J. and Navarro, G. (2013). On compressing permutations and adaptive sorting. *Theoretical Computer Science*, **513**, 109–123.

Barbay, J., He, M., Munro, J. I., and Rao, S. S. (2011). Succinct indexes for strings, binary relations and multilabeled trees. *ACM Transactions on Algorithms*, **7**(4), article 52.

Barbay, J., Claude, F., Gagie, T., Navarro, G., and Nekrich, Y. (2014). Efficient fully-compressed sequence representations. *Algorithmica*, **69**(1), 232–268.

Baruch, G., Klein, S. T., and Shapira, D. (2016). A space efficient direct access data structure. In *Proc. 26th Data Compression Conference (DCC)*, pages 63–72.

Belazzougui, D. and Navarro, G. (2015). Optimal lower and upper bounds for representing sequences. *ACM Transactions on Algorithms*, **11**(4), article 31.

Bowe, A. (2010). *Multiary Wavelet Trees in Practice*. Honours thesis, RMIT University, Australia.

Brisaboa, N. R., Fariña, A., Ladra, S., and Navarro, G. (2012). Implicit indexing of natural language text by reorganizing bytecodes. *Information Retrieval*, **15**(6), 527–557.

Chan, T. and Wilkinson, B. (2013). Adaptive and approximate orthogonal range counting. In *Proc. 24th Annual ACM-SIAM Symposium on Discrete Algorithms (SODA)*, pages 241–251.

Claude, F., Nicholson, P., and Seco, D. (2011). Space efficient wavelet tree construction. In *Proc. 18th International Symposium on String Processing and Information Retrieval (SPIRE)*, LNCS 7024, pages 185–196.

Claude, F., Navarro, G., and Ordóñez, A. (2015). The wavelet matrix: An efficient wavelet tree for large alphabets. *Information Systems*, **47**, 15–32.

Culpepper, S., Navarro, G., Puglisi, S., and Turpin, A. (2010). Top-*k* ranked document search in general text databases. In *Proc. 18th Annual European Symposium on Algorithms (ESA B)*, LNCS 6347, pages 194–205 (part II).

Ferragina, P. and Venturini, R. (2007). A simple storage scheme for strings achieving entropy bounds. *Theoretical Computer Science*, **371**(1), 115–121.

Ferragina, P., Manzini, G., Mäkinen, V., and Navarro, G. (2007). Compressed representations of sequences and full-text indexes. *ACM Transactions on Algorithms*, **3**(2), article 20.

Ferragina, P., Giancarlo, R., and Manzini, G. (2009). The myriad virtues of wavelet trees. *Information and Computation*, **207**(8), 849–866.

Foschini, L., Grossi, R., Gupta, A., and Vitter, J. S. (2006). When indexing equals compression: Experiments with compressing suffix arrays and applications. *ACM Transactions on Algorithms*, **2**(4), 611–639.

Fuentes-Sepúlveda, J., Elejalde, E., Ferres, L., and Seco, D. (2014). Efficient wavelet tree construction and querying for multicore architectures. In *Proc. 13th International Symposium on Experimental Algorithms (SEA)*, LNCS 8504, pages 150–161.

Gagie, T., Puglisi, S. J., and Turpin, A. (2009). Range quantile queries: Another virtue of wavelet trees. In *Proc. 16th International Symposium on String Processing and Information Retrieval (SPIRE)*, LNCS 5721, pages 1–6.

Gagie, T., Navarro, G., and Puglisi, S. J. (2012). New algorithms on wavelet trees and applications to information retrieval. *Theoretical Computer Science*, **426-427**, 25–41.

Gagie, T., Navarro, G., Nekrich, Y., and Ordóñez, A. (2015). Efficient and compact representations of prefix codes. *IEEE Transactions on Information Theory*, **61**(9), 4999–5011.

Golynski, A. (2009). Cell probe lower bounds for succinct data structures. In *Proc. 20th Annual ACM-SIAM Symposium on Discrete Algorithms (SODA)*, pages 625–634.

Golynski, A., Munro, J. I., and Rao, S. S. (2006). Rank/select operations on large alphabets: a tool for text indexing. In *Proc. 17th ACM-SIAM Annual Symposium on Discrete Algorithms (SODA)*, pages 368–373.

Golynski, A., Raman, R., and Rao, S. S. (2008). On the redundancy of succinct data structures. In *Proc. 11th Scandinavian Workshop on Algorithm Theory (SWAT)*, LNCS 5124, pages 148–159.

Grossi, R. and Ottaviano, G. (2012). The wavelet trie: Maintaining an indexed sequence of strings in compressed space. In *Proc. 31st ACM Symposium on Principles of Database Systems (PODS)*, pages 203–214.

Grossi, R., Gupta, A., and Vitter, J. S. (2003). High-order entropy-compressed text indexes. In *Proc. 14th Annual ACM-SIAM Symposium on Discrete Algorithms (SODA)*, pages 841–850.

Grossi, R., Orlandi, A., and Raman, R. (2010). Optimal trade-offs for succinct string indexes. In *Proc. 37th International Colloquium on Algorithms, Languages and Programming (ICALP)*, pages 678–689.

Grossi, R., Vitter, J. S., and Xu, B. (2011). Wavelet trees: From theory to practice. In *Proc. 1st International Conference on Data Compression, Communications and Processing (CCP)*, pages 210–221.

Konow, R. and Navarro, G. (2012). Dual-sorted inverted lists in practice. In *Proc. 19th International Symposium on String Processing and Information Retrieval (SPIRE)*, LNCS 7608, pages 295–306.

Külekci, M. O. (2014). Enhanced variable-length codes: Improved compression with efficient random access. In *Proc. 24th Data Compression Conference (DCC)*, pages 362–371.

Labeit, J., Shun, J., and Blelloch, G. E. (2016). Parallel lightweight wavelet tree, suffix array and FM-index construction. In *Proc. 26th Data Compression Conference (DCC)*, pages 33–42.

Mäkinen, V. and Navarro, G. (2005). Succinct suffix arrays based on run-length encoding. *Nordic Journal of Computing*, **12**(1), 40–66.

Mäkinen, V. and Navarro, G. (2007). Rank and select revisited and extended. *Theoretical Computer Science*, **387**(3), 332–347.

Makris, C. (2012). Wavelet trees: A survey. *Computer Science and Information Systems*, **9**(2), 585–625.

Mehlhorn, K. and Näher, S. (1990). Bounded ordered dictionaries in $O(\log \log N)$ time and $O(n)$ space. *Information Processing Letters*, **35**(4), 183–189.

Munro, J. I., Nekrich, Y., and Vitter, J. S. (2016). Fast construction of wavelet trees. *Theoretical Computer Science*, **638**, 91–97.

Navarro, G. (2014). Wavelet trees for all. *Journal of Discrete Algorithms*, **25**, 2–20.

Shun, J. (2015). Parallel wavelet tree construction. In *Proc. 25th Data Compression Conference (DCC)*, pages 63–72.

Tischler, G. (2011). On wavelet tree construction. In *Proc. 22nd Annual Symposium on Combinatorial Pattern Matching (CPM)*, LNCS 6661, pages 208–218.

Zhang, Y., Pei, Z., Yang, J., and Liang, Y. (2008). Canonical Huffman code based full-text index. *Progress in Natural Science*, **18**(3), 325–330.

CHAPTER 7

Parentheses

In this chapter we focus on a data structure that might seem a bit abstract but has important applications that will become clear in Chapters 8 and 9. It is used to describe a hierarchy, or a containment relation, along a line.

A *balanced sequence of parentheses* is a bitvector $B[1, n]$, where the bit 1 is interpreted as an opening parenthesis, ' (', and the bit 0 is interpreted as a closing parenthesis, ') '. A balanced sequence satisfies the following:

- The sequence length n is even, and B is formed by $n/2$ *matching pairs* of parentheses: an opening parenthesis at $B[i]$ associated with a closing parenthesis at $B[j]$, for some $j > i$. Every such matching pair defines a *segment* $B[i, j]$.
- Any two such segments either are disjoint or one is contained in the other. Thus no two segments overlap, and their containment relation defines a hierarchy.

Example 7.1 *Figure 7.1 shows a balanced sequence of $n = 40$ parentheses (20 opening and 20 closing ones), and the hierarchy of segments it defines. The hatched region marks the segment between two matching parentheses: the one that opens at $B[9]$ and the one that closes at $B[22]$. This matching pair defines the segment $[9, 22]$, which contains segments like $[10, 19]$ and $[20, 21]$.*

A useful concept is the *excess* of B at position i:

$$\mathsf{excess}(B, i) = \mathsf{rank}_1(B, i) - \mathsf{rank}_0(B, i) = 2 \cdot \mathsf{rank}_1(B, i) - i,$$

that is, the number of opening minus closing parentheses in $B[1, i]$ (note that $\mathsf{excess}(B, 0) = 0$). This coincides with the number of segments that cover position $B[i]$ (if a segment terminates at $B[i]$, it is not counted in $\mathsf{excess}(B, i)$). An alternative definition of balancedness is that $\mathsf{excess}(B, i) \geq 0$ for all i, and $\mathsf{excess}(B, n) = 0$. Let us also define

$$\mathsf{excess}(B, i, j) = \mathsf{excess}(B, j) - \mathsf{excess}(B, i - 1).$$

Because the excess changes by ± 1 at consecutive positions, if $B[i]$ is an opening parenthesis, then there is a smallest $j > i$ such that $\mathsf{excess}(B, i, j) = 0$. That j is precisely

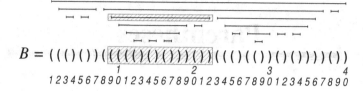

$$B = ((( )( )) ((\langle\langle\langle\langle( )\langle)\langle)\langle\rangle\rangle\rangle\langle\langle\rangle\rangle ((( )(( ))( )( )))) ( ))$$

1234567890 1234567890 1234567890 1234567890

Figure 7.1. A balanced sequence of parentheses and the segments corresponding to matching pairs of parentheses. Each starting of a segment is signaled with an opening parenthesis, and each ending of a segment with a closing parenthesis. We highlight the segment [9, 22].

the position of the closing parenthesis matching $B[i]$. Analogously, i is the largest value before j with $\mathsf{excess}(B, i, j) = 0$, and i is the opening parenthesis matching $B[j]$. We can then use excess to define the matching pairs of B.

Example 7.2 *In the segment highlighted in Figure 7.1, it holds* $\mathsf{excess}(9) = 3$, *and the excess is never less than 3 to the right of $B[9]$ until we reach* $\mathsf{excess}(22) = 2$. *Then* $\mathsf{excess}(9, 22) = 0$ *(note that $B[9, 22]$ is balanced).*

We define a number of operations on B, which will be useful for representing trees and graphs. We start with a few intuitive ones:

$\mathsf{close}(B, i)$: returns the position j of the closing parenthesis that matches the one that opens at $B[i] = `(`$.

$\mathsf{open}(B, j)$: returns the position i of the opening parenthesis that matches the one that closes at $B[j] = `)`$.

$\mathsf{enclose}(B, i)$: returns the rightmost position $k < i$ such that $[k, \mathsf{close}(B, k)]$ contains i. This is the smallest segment strictly containing position i.

Then the set of $n/2$ segments described by B can be written as

$$\{[i, \mathsf{close}(B, i)], \ B[i] = `(`\} = \{[\mathsf{open}(B, j), j], \ B[j] = `)`\}.$$

We will not directly solve these operations, but a more abstract set of operations that include the above ones as particular cases:

$$\mathsf{fwdsearch}(B, i, d) = \min\{j > i, \ \mathsf{excess}(B, j) = \mathsf{excess}(B, i) + d\} \cup \{n+1\},$$

$$\mathsf{bwdsearch}(B, i, d) = \max\{j < i, \ \mathsf{excess}(B, j) = \mathsf{excess}(B, i) + d\} \cup \{0\}.$$

These operations look for a desired relative excess d, in forward or backward direction from position i. One can easily verify the following identities:

$$\mathsf{close}(B, i) = \mathsf{fwdsearch}(B, i, -1),$$

$$\mathsf{open}(B, i) = \mathsf{bwdsearch}(B, i, 0) + 1,$$

$$\mathsf{enclose}(B, i) = \mathsf{bwdsearch}(B, i, -2) + 1.$$

Example 7.3 *Figure 7.2 illustrates the function* excess *and some basic operations that build on it. The opening parenthesis at $B[8]$ has* $\mathsf{excess}(8) = 2$. *Its matching parenthesis is at* $\mathsf{close}(8) = \mathsf{fwdsearch}(8, -1) = 37$, *the first position to the right with excess $2 - 1 = 1$. Conversely,* $\mathsf{open}(37) = \mathsf{bwdsearch}(37, 0) + 1 = 7 + 1 = 8$, *as 7 is the first position to the left of 37 with excess $1 + 0 = 1$. Those connections*

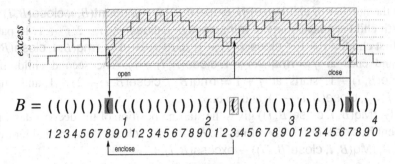

Figure 7.2. The function excess(B, i) of the parentheses of Figure 7.1. We also illustrate operations close($B, 8$), open($B, 37$), and enclose($B, 23$).

are shown in gray and with the double arrow on the parentheses (the relevant area of excess() *is hatched). On the other hand, the opening parenthesis at $B[23]$ (hatched) has* excess(23) $= 3$. *It holds* enclose(23) $=$ bwdsearch$(23, -2) + 1 = 7 + 1 = 8$, *our previous opening parenthesis, since 7 is the first opening parenthesis to the left of 23 with excess $3 - 2 = 1$.*

Although the full set of applications of these operations will be made clear in Chapters 8 and 9, some of those are already apparent: we have seen that the containment relations of the segments $[i, \text{close}(B, i)]$ defines a hierarchy. Then excess(B, i) is the nesting *depth* of the segment $[i, \text{close}(B, i)]$ in the hierarchy, enclose(B, i) gives the opening parenthesis of the *parent* of $[i, \text{close}(B, i)]$ in the hierarchy, and in general bwdsearch$(B, i, -d - 1)$ gives the opening parenthesis of the ancestor of $[i, \text{close}(B, i)]$ at distance d.

Example 7.4 *Consider the segments of Figure 7.1. The hatched segment $[9,$ close$(9)] = [9, 22]$ has nesting depth* excess$(9) = 3$. *Its parent in the hierarchy is the segment starting at* enclose$(9) = 8$, *that is, the segment $[8, $ close$(8)] = [8, 37]$. The grandparent of $[9, 22]$ is the segment starting at* bwdsearch$(9, -3) + 1 = 0 + 1 = 1$, *that is, the segment $[1, $ close$(1)] = [1, 40]$.*

For the application in Chapter 8, we will need a further set of more sophisticated operations. In their definition, we use excess($B, i \ldots j$) to denote the sequence $\langle \text{excess}(B, i), \text{excess}(B, i + 1), \ldots, \text{excess}(B, j) \rangle$.

$$\text{rmq}(B, i, j) = \text{leftmost position of a minimum in } \text{excess}(B, i \ldots j),$$

$$\text{rMq}(B, i, j) = \text{leftmost position of a maximum in } \text{excess}(B, i \ldots j),$$

$$\text{mincount}(B, i, j) = \text{times the minimum occurs in } \text{excess}(B, i \ldots j),$$

$$\text{minselect}(B, i, j, t) = \text{position of the } t\text{th minimum in } \text{excess}(B, i \ldots j).$$

These operations will be useful for navigating the hierarchy. For example, just as enclose(B, i) tells us which the parent segment of $[i, \text{close}(B, i)]$ is, these operations let us move toward its *children* segments. Recall that excess(B, k) $\geq$ excess(B, i) for $i \leq k \leq \text{close}(B, i) - 1$, and note that the children segments of $[i, \text{close}(B, i)]$ start at every position $k + 1 \leq \text{close}(B, i) - 1$ such that excess(B, k) $=$ excess(B, i), that is, after each minimum excess in $[i, \text{close}(B, i) - 2]$.

Then the number of children of $[i, \mathsf{close}(B, i)]$ is $\mathsf{mincount}(B, i, \mathsf{close}(B, i) - 2)$, and its tth child segment starts at $\mathsf{minselect}(B, i, \mathsf{close}(B, i) - 2, t) + 1$. In particular, the first child, if $i + 1 \leq \mathsf{close}(B, i) - 1$, starts at $i + 1 = \mathsf{rmq}(B, i, \mathsf{close}(B, i) - 2) + 1$ and ends at $j = \mathsf{rmq}(B, i + 1, \mathsf{close}(B, i) - 1)$. The second child, if $j + 1 \leq \mathsf{close}(B, i) - 1$, starts at $j + 1 = \mathsf{rmq}(B, j, \mathsf{close}(B, i) - 2) + 1$ and ends at $\mathsf{rmq}(B, j + 1, \mathsf{close}(B, i) - 1)$, and so on.

Finally, $\mathsf{rMq}(B, i, \mathsf{close}(B, i))$ gives the starting position of the deepest descendant of segment $[i, \mathsf{close}(B, i)]$. Therefore, the *height* of $[i, \mathsf{close}(B, i)]$ in the hierarchy is $\mathsf{excess}(B, \mathsf{rMq}(B, i, \mathsf{close}(B, i))) - \mathsf{excess}(B, i)$.

Example 7.5 *Consider again the sequence in Figure 7.2, and our segment* $[8, \mathsf{close}(8)] = [8, 37]$ *with grayed endpoints. It has two child segments,* $[9, 22]$ *and* $[23, 36]$. *The excess at 8,* $\mathsf{excess}(8) = 2$, *is reached again only at the children endpoints,* $\mathsf{excess}(22) = \mathsf{excess}(36) = 2$, *inside the segment* $[8 + 1, 37 - 1]$. *Thus the positions* $8 \leq k < \mathsf{close}(8) - 1 = 36$ *with* $\mathsf{excess}(k) = 2$ *are* $k = 8$ *and* $k = 22$, *and the children of* $[8, 37]$ *start at* $k + 1 = 9$ *and* $k + 1 = 23$. *Operation* $\mathsf{rmq}(8 + 1, \mathsf{close}(8) - 1) = \mathsf{rmq}(9, 36)$ *returns* 22, *the final position of the first child. The value* $\mathsf{mincount}(8, 35) = 2$ *indicates that* $[8, 37]$ *has two child segments. These are enumerated by* $\mathsf{minselect}(8, 35, 1) + 1 = 8 + 1 = 9$ *and* $\mathsf{minselect}(8, 35, 2) + 1 = 22 + 1 = 23$. *Finally, the height of segment* $[8, 37]$ *in the hierarchy is* $\mathsf{excess}(\mathsf{rMq}(8, 37)) - \mathsf{excess}(8) = \mathsf{excess}(12) - \mathsf{excess}(8) = 6 - 2 = 4$ *(as can be checked more directly in Figure 7.2).*

7.1 A Simple Implementation

Now we show how the operations on balanced parentheses can be implemented in $\mathcal{O}(\log n)$ time, while using only $o(n)$ bits on top of $B[1, n]$. This time will be reduced to $\mathcal{O}(\log \log n)$ in Section 7.2, with a more complex implementation. To simplify notation, we will drop the B from the arguments of the operations, assuming it by default.

The main data structure to support the operations is the so-called *range min-max tree (rmM-tree)*. We first describe this structure and then show how the operations are carried out on it. These will be divided into three homogeneous groups: (1) fwdsearch and bwdsearch, (2) rmq and related operations, and (3) rank and select-like operations.

7.1.1 Range Min-Max Trees

Given a sequence of n parentheses (or bits) $B[1, n]$, we choose a block size b. Then the range min-max tree or rmM-tree of B is a complete binary tree where the ith leaf *covers* $B[(i - 1)b + 1, ib]$, and each internal node covers the union of the areas covered by its two children. Depending on which operations we wish to support, rmM-tree nodes summarize different data on the area they cover. Most operations can be supported by storing just the total excess of, and the minimum excess reached in, the covered area of B. Other operations will require a few extra fields, in particular the maximum excess reached in the covered area (this is where the name "range min-max tree" comes from), or the number of times the minimum excess occurs.

Algorithm 7.1: Converting between leaf numbers and positions of the rmM-tree.

1 **Proc** *leafnum*(k)
   Input : A leaf number k. Uses r, the number of leaves.
   Output: Returns the position where the kth leaf is represented in the rmM-tree.

2 $\quad$ **if** $k \leq 2r - 2^{\lceil \log r \rceil}$ **then return** $2^{\lceil \log r \rceil} - 1 + k$
3 $\quad$ **else return** $2^{\lceil \log r \rceil} - 1 - r + k$

4 **Proc** *numleaf*(v)
   Input : A node position v in the rmM-tree. Uses r, the number of leaves.
   Output: Returns the left-to-right position of leaf v.

5 $\quad$ **if** $v \geq 2^{\lceil \log r \rceil}$ **then return** $v - 2^{\lceil \log r \rceil} + 1$
6 $\quad$ **else return** $v - 2^{\lceil \log r \rceil} + 1 + r$

Being a complete binary tree means that all the levels of the rmM-tree are full, except possibly the last one, whose nodes are all packed on the left. A complete binary tree can be stored in heap-like form without pointers. That is, an rmM-tree with $r = \lceil n/b \rceil$ leaves is represented in an array $R[1, 2r - 1]$ cells, so that the children of the cell $R[v]$ are at cells $R[2v]$ and $R[2v + 1]$. The parent of cell $R[v]$ is at cell $R[\lfloor v/2 \rfloor]$.

The rmM-tree is of height $h = \lceil \log r \rceil$. If r is a power of 2, then the last level of the rmM-tree is full (of leaves). Otherwise leaves 1 to $2r - 2^h$ are in the last level (grouped on the left), and the other $2^h - r$ leaves are in the previous level (grouped on the right). A node v is internal iff its children exist, that is, if $2v + 1 \leq 2r - 1$, or which is the same, if $v < r$; note that either both children exist or none do. For $k \leq 2r - 2^h$, the kth leaf is at $R[2^h - 1 + k]$, whereas for $k > 2r - 2^h$ the kth leaf is at $R[2^h - 1 - r + k]$. Conversely, if $R[v]$ is a leaf node, it is the kth leaf for $k = v - 2^h + 1$ if $2^h \leq v \leq 2r - 1$, otherwise it is $k = v - 2^h + 1 + r$. Those conversions are given in Algorithm 7.1.

Our data structure is thus made up of the bit array B and the rmM-tree R. The total space it uses is $n + \mathcal{O}((n/b) \log n)$ bits, assuming the rmM-tree stores a constant number of fields using $\log n$ bits each. We will consider the following fields (not all of which are needed for all the operations) for each rmM-tree node v covering $B[s, e]$:

$R[v].e$ is the total excess in $B[s, e]$:

$$R[v].e = \mathsf{excess}(e) - \mathsf{excess}(s - 1).$$

$R[v].m$ is the minimum local left-to-right excess in $B[s, e]$:

$$R[v].m = \min\{\mathsf{excess}(p) - \mathsf{excess}(s - 1), s \leq p \leq e\}.$$

$R[v].M$ is the maximum local left-to-right excess in $B[s, e]$:

$$R[v].M = \max\{\mathsf{excess}(p) - \mathsf{excess}(s - 1), s \leq p \leq e\}.$$

$R[v].n$ is the number of times the minimum excess occurs in $B[s, e]$:

$$R[v].n = |\{p, \ s \leq p \leq e, \mathsf{excess}(p) - \mathsf{excess}(s - 1) = R[v].m\}|.$$

Note that $R[v].m \leq 1$, $R[v].M \geq -1$, and $R[v].n \geq 1$ for any node v.

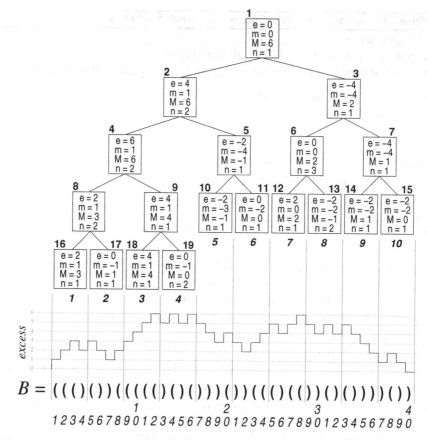

Figure 7.3. An rmM-tree with $b = 4$ built on the parentheses sequence of Figure 7.1. It has $r = 10$ leaves and $r - 1 = 9$ internal nodes. Its height is $h = \lceil \log 10 \rceil = 4$. From the 10 leaves, $2r - 2^h = 4$ are in the final, incomplete level, and the other 6 are in the previous one. The nodes are laid levelwise in array R, so the children of node v are $2v$ and $2v + 1$. The fields e, m, M, and n refer to the area of B covered by each node.

Example 7.6 *Figure 7.3 shows the rmM-tree with (toy) parameter $b = 4$ built on the parentheses sequence of Figure 7.1. Since $n = 40$ and $b = 4$, we have $r = \lceil n/b \rceil = 10$ leaves. The height of the rmM-tree is $h = \lceil \log 10 \rceil = 4$. The rmM-tree has $2r - 1 = 19$ nodes, whose positions in the array R are written on top of each square. Below the leaf nodes of the rmM-tree we annotate, in italics, the corresponding block of B (that is, the left-to-right leaf number). Leaves 1 to $2r - 2^h = 20 - 16 = 4$ are in the last level, grouped on the left, and the other $2^h - r = 16 - 10 = 6$ are in the previous level, grouped on the right. For $k \leq 2r - 2^h = 4$, the kth leaf is at $R[2^h - 1 + k] = R[15 + k]$, as can be verified for the leaf 1, at $R[16]$, to the leaf 4, at $R[19]$. For $k > 2r - 2^h = 4$, the kth leaf is at $R[2^h - 1 - r + k] = R[5 + k]$, as can be verified for the leaf 5, at $R[10]$, to the leaf 10, at $R[15]$. Conversely, leaves at positions $16 = 2^h \leq v \leq 2r - 1 = 19$ correspond to leaf numbers $k = v - 2^h + 1 = v - 15$, as can be verified for the positions $v = 16$ (corresponding to leaf number $16 - 15 = 1$) to $v = 20$ (corresponding to leaf number $19 - 5 = 4$). Leaves at positions $v < 2^h = 16$*

correspond to leaf numbers $k = v - 2^h + 1 + r = v - 5$, as it can be verified for the positions $v = 10$ (corresponding to leaf number $10 - 5 = 5$) to $v = 15$ (corresponding to leaf number $15 - 5 = 10$).

The figure also shows the values for each of the 4 fields we have defined.

Construction

The rmM-tree $R[1, 2r - 1]$ is easily built from $B[1, n]$ in linear time and without using any extra space. First, we traverse the blocks of B one by one and compute the fields e, m, M, and n of the r leaves. Then we traverse the internal nodes of R, from $R[r - 1]$ to $R[1]$, computing the fields of each node v in constant time from those of its children $2v$ and $2v + 1$ using the following recurrences, which are easy to see:

$$R[v].e = R[2v].e + R[2v + 1].e,$$

$$R[v].m = \min(R[2v].m, R[2v].e + R[2v + 1].m),$$

$$R[v].M = \max(R[2v].M, R[2v].e + R[2v + 1].M),$$

$$R[v].n = \begin{cases} R[2v].n & \text{if } R[2v].m < R[2v].e + R[2v + 1].m, \\ R[2v + 1].n & \text{if } R[2v].m > R[2v].e + R[2v + 1].m, \\ R[2v].n + R[2v + 1].n & \text{if } R[2v].m = R[2v].e + R[2v + 1].m. \end{cases}$$

The only delicate point is to realize that, since excess values are local to each area, when we have to translate a value that is local to the area covered by $R[2v + 1]$ to a value that is valid in the area covered by $R[v]$, we must add to it the excess $R[2v].e$.

Example 7.7 *We can verify the equations on some of the rmM-tree nodes of Figure 7.3. For example, node $v = 6$ is built from its children $2v = 12$ and $2v + 1 = 13$. Note that the node covers the area $B[25, 32] = ()(())()$, from which we see that $R[6].e = 0$, $R[6].m = 0$, $R[6].M = 2$, and $R[6].n = 3$. Indeed, $R[6].e = R[12].e + R[13].e = 2 - 2 = 0$, $R[6].m = \min(R[12].m, R[12].e + R[13].m) = \min(0, 2 - 2) = 0$, $R[6].M = \max(R[12].M, R[12].e + R[13].M) = \max(2, 2 - 1) = 2$ and, since $R[12].m = R[12].e + R[13].m$, we have $R[6].n = R[12].n + R[13].n = 1 + 2 = 3$.*

On the other hand, to build $R[7]$ from $R[14]$ and $R[15]$, since $R[7].m = -4$ is obtained from $R[14].e + R[15].m = -2 - 2 = -4$, we have $R[7].n = R[15].n = 1$. Instead, $R[7].M = 1$ is obtained from $R[14].M = 1$.

To speed up both construction and queries on the rmM-tree, we will precompute a small table that is independent of the rmM-tree. Let us choose $c = \lfloor (\log n)/2 \rfloor$ and build a table $C[0, 2^c - 1]$, that is, with at most $\sqrt{n}$ entries. Each entry $C[x]$ contains the fields e, m, M, and n, just like the cells of R. The fields of $C[x]$ are computed with respect to the c bits that form the number x, interpreted as parentheses. Table C is built in just $\mathcal{O}(\sqrt{n} \log n)$ time and uses $\mathcal{O}(\sqrt{n} w)$ bits of space if we use 1 computer word per field for simplicity. Algorithm 7.2 shows the construction.

With C, and ensuring that b is a multiple of c, we can speed up the construction of the leaves of the rmM-tree by processing them by chunks of c bits. Algorithm 7.3 shows the details. The leaves are then filled in time $\mathcal{O}(n/\log n)$, and the internal nodes require only $\mathcal{O}(n/b)$ additional time.

Algorithm 7.2: Building the C table for the rmM-trees.

Input : Chunk size c.

Output: Builds the C table for any rmM-tree.

1   Allocate array $C[0, 2^c - 1]$ with integer fields e, m, M, and n
2   **for** $x \leftarrow 0$ **to** $2^c - 1$ **do**
3     $C[x].e \leftarrow 0$; $C[x].m \leftarrow 2$; $C[x].M \leftarrow -2$; $C[x].n \leftarrow 0$
4   **for** $p \leftarrow 1$ **to** c **do**
5   **if** bitread$(x, p) = 1$ **then**
6         $C[x].e \leftarrow C[x].e + 1$
7   **else**
8         $C[x].e \leftarrow C[x].e - 1$
9   **if** $C[x].e > C[x].M$ **then**
10        $C[x].M \leftarrow C[x].e$
11   **if** $C[x].e < C[x].m$ **then**
12        $C[x].m \leftarrow C[x].e$
13        $C[x].n \leftarrow 1$
14   **else if** $C[x].e = C[x].m$ **then**
15        $C[x].n \leftarrow C[x].n + 1$

In Practice

By choosing $c = \Theta(\log n)$, $b = \Theta(\log^2 n)$, and storing fields of $\log n$ bits in R, we will obtain $\mathcal{O}(\log n)$ time for all the operations and $n + \mathcal{O}(n/\log n)$ bits of space. In practice, scanning blocks will be much faster if we set c to a convenient value like 8 or 16, so as to read byte- or short-aligned chunks of memory. In this case, the operation **bitsread** to extract a chunk can be replaced by directly reading a cell in the array W that holds the bit array B, by declaring W as an array of bytes or of shorts. In fact, if we read unaligned chunks, we can simplify Algorithm 7.4 and similar ones that use C, but reading aligned chunks is much faster.

The block size b should ideally be set to the size of a cache line; $b = 1024$ bits is a good choice. We then traverse a block with at most 128 accesses to table C if $c = 8$, or 64 if $c = 16$ (if $c = 8$, table C is very small and is probably always in cache). If we use 32-bit integers for the 4 rmM-tree fields, the space overhead is $2 \cdot 4 \cdot 32/1024 = 0.25$ bits per parenthesis, that is, a total space of $1.25n$ bits. Doubling b leads to $1.13n$ bits, which is very reasonable, and still blocks are scanned with 1–2 cache misses. Larger values of b further decrease the space overhead but increase the time to scan a block.

If this tradeoff is an issue, we can do better with a slightly more complex arrangement: Since the fields of R we use require only $\lceil \log(2\ell) \rceil = 1 + \lceil \log \ell \rceil$ bits for the nodes that cover an area of length ℓ,[1] most cells require much less than 32-bit integers. We can then save space by splitting R into more than one array. For example, we can use 16 bits for the lowest $15 - \lceil \log b \rceil$ levels of the rmM-tree and 32 bits for the

---

[1] The most demanding one is the field e, which goes from $-\ell$ to $+\ell$. We can reduce the range to $[-\ell, \ell - 1]$ by using field M: if $M = \ell$, we know that $e = \ell$ as well.

Algorithm 7.3: Building the rmM-tree.

Input : Parentheses sequence $B[1, n]$, table C, and parameters b and c (with c dividing b and $B[n + 1, n + b]$ padded with 1s for simplicity).

Output: Builds the rmM-tree R.

1   $r \leftarrow \lceil n/b \rceil$
2   Allocate array $R[1, 2r - 1]$ with integer fields e, m, M, and n
3   **for** $k \leftarrow 1$ **to** r **do** (first part: building the leaves)
4      $v \leftarrow leafnum(k)$
5      $R[v].e \leftarrow 0; R[v].m \leftarrow 2; R[v].M \leftarrow -2; R[v].n \leftarrow 0$
6   **for** $p \leftarrow (k - 1)b/c + 1$ **to** kb/c **do**
7         $x \leftarrow \mathsf{bitsread}(B, (p - 1)c + 1, pc)$
8   **if** $R[v].e + C[x].m < R[v].m$ **then**
9            $R[v].m \leftarrow R[v].e + C[x].m$
10           $R[v].n \leftarrow C[x].n$
11   **else if** $R[v].e + C[x].m = R[v].m$ **then**
12           $R[v].n \leftarrow R[v].n + C[x].n$
13   **if** $R[v].e + C[x].M > R[v].M$ **then**
14           $R[v].M \leftarrow R[v].e + C[x].M$
15         $R[v].e \leftarrow R[v].e + C[x].e$
16   **for** $v \leftarrow r - 1$ **downto** 1 **do** (second part: building the internal nodes)
17      $R[v].e \leftarrow R[2v].e + R[2v + 1].e$
18   **if** $R[2v].m < R[2v].e + R[2v + 1].m$ **then**
19         $R[v].m \leftarrow R[2v].m$
20         $R[v].n \leftarrow R[2v].n$
21   **else**
22         $R[v].m \leftarrow R[2v].e + R[2v + 1].m$
23   **if** $R[2v].m > R[2v].e + R[2v + 1].m$ **then**
24           $R[v].n \leftarrow R[2v + 1].n$
25   **else**
26           $R[v].n \leftarrow R[2v].n + R[2v + 1].n$
27      $R[v].M \leftarrow \max(R[2v].M, R[2v].e + R[2v + 1].M)$

---

higher levels. With $b = 1024 = 2^{10}$, the 5 lowest levels use 16 bits, and then the fraction of rmM-tree nodes using 32 bits is $1/2^5 = 1/32$. This reduces the number 32 in the above space calculations to $16 + 32/32 = 17$, yielding less than $1.13n$ bits in total. With $b = 2048$, we use about $1.07n$ bits.

7.1.2 Forward and Backward Searching

We now show how to compute the basic operations fwdsearch and bwdsearch, for $d < 0$. These require only the fields e and m of the rmM-tree and cover all the major uses of fwdsearch and bwdsearch (our solution also handles bwdsearch$(i, 0)$ if

$B[i] = 0$, as required to implement **open**(i)). The case $d > 0$ is solved analogously, but the field M is also required (we show the required changes for **fwdsearch** when solving operation **rMq**, in Section 7.1.3).

Assume we want to compute **fwdsearch**(i, d), that is, find the smallest $j > i$ such that **excess**$(j) = $ **excess**$(i) + d$, for some $d < 0$. We find j in up to 3 steps. First, we scan the block of $i + 1$. If we do not find j inside that block, we make use of the rmM-tree to find the block where j belongs. Finally, we scan that second block to find the exact position of j.

Scanning the Initial Block

We scan the block of $i + 1$, $B[s, e] = B[(\lceil (i + 1)/b \rceil - 1)b + 1, \lceil (i + 1)/b \rceil b]$, from $i + 1$ up to e, looking for the position j. A simple linear-time scan proceeds as follows: we start with $j \leftarrow i$ and $d' \leftarrow 0$, which will denote **excess**$(j) - $ **excess**(i), and examine the bits $B[j]$ for j from $i + 1$ to e. For each j we increase d' by 1 if $B[j] = 1$ and decrease it by 1 if $B[j] = 0$. If, for some $j > i$, we reach $d' = d$, then j is the answer to the query.

To speed up this process, the bitwise scanning proceeds only up to the next chunk-aligned position of $B[s, e]$. At that point we start a chunkwise scan. We consider the chunks p from $\lceil i/c \rceil + 1$ and at each point read the bits of the chunk into a number x. Now, if $d' + C[x].m > d$, then the excess d is not reached inside the chunk, so we update $d' \leftarrow d' + C[x].e$ and continue with the next chunk.

If we find a chunk x such that $d' + C[x].m \leq d$, then the minimum excess reached inside the chunk is $\leq d$. Since the excess changes by ± 1, excess d is actually reached inside the chunk. Then we process the chunk again, now bitwise, to find the exact position j.

Algorithm 7.4 shows how to scan a block. It takes time $\mathcal{O}(c + b/c)$.

Using the rmM-Tree

If we reach the end of the block without finding $d' = d$, we traverse the rmM-tree from the leaves to the root looking for the node that covers the answer to the query. First, we identify the leaf v corresponding to $B[s, e]$, $v = leafnum(\lceil (i + 1)/b \rceil)$. Now we find whether v is a right child of its parent, that is, if v is odd. If so, then we have already processed up to the end of the parent of v: we move to the parent by setting $v \leftarrow (v - 1)/2$ and continue.

If v is instead a left child of its parent, then we must determine whether **excess**$(i) + d$ is reached inside its right sibling, $v + 1$. We ask whether $d' + R[v + 1].m > d$. If so, we are sure that d is not reached within the area covered by $v + 1$, and thus it is not reached within the area covered by the parent of v. We update $d' \leftarrow d' + R[v + 1].e$ and go to the parent, $v \leftarrow v/2$.

If there exists an answer to the query, we will find at some point a right sibling $v + 1$ where the excess falls at or below d. At this point we start descending from $v \leftarrow v + 1$ to find the leftmost leaf where this occurs. As long as v has children (i.e., $v < r$), we check whether the excess falls at or below d within the left child, that is, we ask whether $d' + R[2v].m \leq d$. If it does, we move to the left child, $v \leftarrow 2v$. Otherwise we descend to the right child, updating $d' \leftarrow d' + R[2v].e$ and $v \leftarrow 2v + 1$.

The time of the upward and downward traversals is $\mathcal{O}(\log(n/b))$. A final twist allowed by the rmM-tree structure is that we can check if the node following v at

---

Algorithm 7.4: Scanning a block for fwdsearch(i, d). We assume $p = t + 1$ after the normal execution of the loop in lines 11–14.

---

1 **Proc** $fwdblock(B, i, d)$

    Input : Parentheses sequence $B[1, n]$, table C, block and chunk sizes b and c, and parameters i and $d < 0$.

    Output: Returns $\langle d', j \rangle$. If the position j is inside the block of $i + 1$, this is $\langle d, j \rangle$; otherwise d' is the excess from $i + 1$ to the end of the block, and j is just past the block.

2   (first stage: bitwise scan)

3     $f \leftarrow \lceil i/c \rceil$ (chunk to be scanned bitwise)

4     $t \leftarrow \lceil (i + 1)/b \rceil b/c$ (last chunk of the block)

5     $d' \leftarrow 0$

6   **for** $j \leftarrow i + 1$ **to** fc **do**

7   **if** bitread$(B, j) = 1$ **then** $d' \leftarrow d' + 1$

8   **else** $d' \leftarrow d' - 1$

9   **if** $d' = d$ **then return** $\langle d, j \rangle$

10   (second stage: chunkwise scan)

11   **for** $p \leftarrow f + 1$ **to** t **do**

12        $x \leftarrow$ bitsread$(B, (p - 1)c + 1, pc)$

13   **if** $d' + C[x].m \le d$ **then break**

14        $d' \leftarrow d' + C[x].e$

15   **if** $p > t$ **then return** $\langle d', tc + 1 \rangle$ (j is not in the block)

16   (third stage: bitwise scan again)

17   **for** $j \leftarrow (p - 1)c + 1$ **to** pc **do**

18   **if** bitread$(B, j) = 1$ **then** $d' \leftarrow d' + 1$

19   **else** $d' \leftarrow d' - 1$

20   **if** $d' = d$ **then return** $\langle d, j \rangle$

---

its same level (i.e., $v + 1$) contains the answer, even if it is not a sibling of v. Then we can switch to the downward traversal without going up to the common ancestor of both nodes. With this trick, the time decreases when the answer is close to i: we take $\mathcal{O}\left(\log \frac{\text{fwdsearch}(i,d)-i}{b}\right)$ time.

Scanning the Final Block

The process on the rmM-tree stops when we arrive at a leaf node v; let it be the kth leaf, for $k = numleaf(v)$. At this point we perform a second sequential scan, this time on the block $B[(k - 1)b + 1, kb]$ that corresponds to leaf k, looking for the precise answer j.

Algorithm 7.5 gives the pseudocode. The trick of $v + 1$ is implicit in line 7, where the check $v + 1 < 2^{\lceil \log(v+1) \rceil}$ ensures that v is not the rightmost node in its level[2] (if it is, we cannot access $v + 1$ and must instead return that there is no answer). The worst-case cost of this search is $\mathcal{O}(\log(n/b) + c + b/c)$. We can obtain $\mathcal{O}(\log n)$

---

[2] In C, this can be simplified to the test '`v & (v+1) != 0`'.

Algorithm 7.5: Computing fwdsearch(i, d). We assume $R[2r].m = n + 1$ to avoid border cases in line 7.

---

1 **Proc** fwdsearch(B, i, d)

     Input   : Parentheses sequence $B[1, n]$ and its rmM-tree $R[1, 2r - 1]$ for
                 $r = \lceil n/b \rceil$, and parameters i and $d < 0$.

     Output: Returns fwdsearch(i, d).

2   (sequential scan in the original block)

3     $\langle d', j \rangle \leftarrow fwdblock(B, i, d)$ (Algorithm 7.4)

4   **if** $d' = d$ **then return** j

5   (upward search in the rmM-tree)

6     $v \leftarrow leafnum(\lceil (i + 1)/b \rceil)$ (Algorithm 7.1)

7   **while** $v + 1 < 2^{\lceil \log(v+1) \rceil}$ **and** $d' + R[v + 1].m > d$ **do**

8   **if** $v \bmod 2 = 0$ **then**

9            $d' \leftarrow d' + R[v + 1].e$

10        $v \leftarrow \lfloor v/2 \rfloor$

11   **if** $v + 1 = 2^{\lceil \log(v+1) \rceil}$ **then return** $n + 1$ (not found)

12   (downward search in the rmM-tree)

13     $v \leftarrow v + 1$

14   **while** $v < r$ **do**

15   **if** $d' + R[2v].m \le d$ **then**

16            $v \leftarrow 2v$

17   **else**

18            $d' \leftarrow d' + R[2v].e$

19            $v \leftarrow 2v + 1$

20   (sequential scan in the final block)

21     $k \leftarrow numleaf(v)$ (Algorithm 7.1)

22     $\langle d', j \rangle \leftarrow fwdblock(B, (k - 1)b, d - d')$ (Algorithm 7.4)

23   **return** j

---

total time by using $b = c \log n$ (multiplied by any integer), which in addition yields little space: $n + \mathcal{O}(n/\log n) = n + o(n)$ bits.

Example 7.8 *Let us compute* close$(9) = $ fwdsearch$(9, -1)$ *to find the endpoint of the hatched segment in Figure 7.1. The answer should be position $B[22]$, as seen in the parentheses sequence. Figure 7.4 illustrates the process, showing the accessed data in black.*

We start scanning the leaf $k = 3$, where position $i + 1 = 10$ appears. When examining the parentheses of the rest of the block, $B[10, 12]$, we obtain relative excess $d' = 1, 2, 3$, not the desired $d = -1$. Therefore, we end the block with $d' = 3$. We have processed the area $B[10, 12]$.

Now we compute the position $R[v]$ of the leaf we have been examining, $v = 18$. We consider its next node, $v + 1 = 19$. Since $d' + R[19].m = 2 > d$, the excess d is not reached within $R[19]$, so we continue upwards. Since 18 is even, it is a left child of

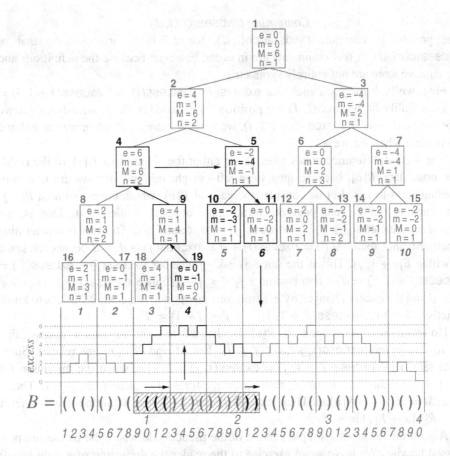

Figure 7.4. The process for fwdsearch(9, −1) on the structure of Figure 7.3. The data accessed are shown in black. We sequentially scan part of block 3, where the traversal starts, then move upwards on the rmM-tree through nodes 19, 9, and 4, then move downwards through nodes 5 and 11, and finally complete the query by sequentially scanning the block 6.

its parent, so we update $d' \leftarrow d' + R[19].e = 3$. We have now processed up to the end of $R[v + 1]$, $B[10, 16]$, without finding the answer; then we move to the parent in R, $v \leftarrow \lfloor v/2 \rfloor = 9$.

We now examine the node next to v, $v + 1 = 10$. Since $d' + R[10].m = 0 > d$, the excess d is not reached within $R[10]$, so we continue upwards. Since $v = 9$ is odd, it is a right child of its parent, and thus we have already processed up to the end of the block it covers, $B[10, 16]$. Then we just set $v \leftarrow \lfloor v/2 \rfloor = 4$ to reach its parent.

Now we examine the node next to v, $v + 1 = 5$. Since $d' + R[5].m = -1 \le d$, we know that d is reached inside $R[5]$. Therefore, we start the downward traversal from $v \leftarrow v + 1 = 5$.

The children of $v = 5$ are $2v = 10$ and $2v + 1 = 11$. We see if d is reached within $2v = 10$. Since $d' + R[10].m = 0 > d$, we know that d is not reached inside $2v$, so we skip it with $d' \leftarrow d' + R[10].e = 1$ and set $v \leftarrow 2v + 1 = 11$. We have processed $B[10, 20]$.

Finally, $v = 11$ is a leaf, so we compute the corresponding leaf number, $k = 6$, and perform a sequential scanning of $B[(k − 1)b + 1, kb] = B[21, 24]$, starting with $d' = 1$ and aiming to reach $d' = d = -1$. This is achieved at $j = 22$, which is the answer.

Computing bwdsearch(i, d)

The process to compute bwdsearch(i, d), for $d < 0$, is analogous to that of fwdsearch(i, d). A few comments are in order, however, because the definitions and the data we store are not entirely symmetric.

First, we look for $j < i$ such that excess(j) − excess(i) = −excess($j + 1, i$) = d. Thus, unlike fwdsearch(i, d), the position i is included in the count. Also, since we aim to find $d' = d = -$excess($j + 1, i$), we have to increase d' when we see a 0 and decrease it when we see a 1.

The second difference arises when using either the chunk data, $C[x]$, or the rmM-tree node data, $R[v]$, because they store left-to-right minima, and we are now proceeding right-to-left. Let us consider the case of $R[v]$, which covers an area $B[s, j]$ that ends at our current position j (the case of $C[x]$ is identical). That is, we have $d' = -$excess($j + 1, i$) = excess(j) − excess(i) > d. Our goal is to determine whether or not excess(j') = excess(i) + d = excess(j) − d' + d occurs for some j' within $B[s + 1, j]$. This is the same as asking whether excess(j) − excess(j') = excess($j' + 1, j$) = $d' - d$ for some $s \leq j' \leq j - 1$. Since excess($j + 1, j$) = 0 < $d' - d$ and the excess changes by ± 1 from one position to the next, it suffices to know whether $M = \max\{$excess($j' + 1, j$), $s \leq j' \leq j - 1\} \geq d' - d$.

However, what is stored in $R[v]$ is the left-to-right minimum excess, that is, $R[v].m = \min\{$excess(s, j'), $s \leq j' \leq j\}$. But M and $R[v].m$ are related. Since excess(s, j') + excess($j' + 1, j$) = excess(s, j) = $R[v].e$, when the minimum for $R[v].m$ is reached for some j', the maximum for M is reached for $j' + 1$. Therefore, $M = R[v].e - R[v].m$. Thus, excess(i) + d is reached within node v whenever $d' - R[v].e + R[v].m \leq d$.

Algorithm 7.6 gives a simple version of the pseudocode where the blocks are processed bitwise. We leave as an exercise to the reader the derivation of a right-to-left version of Algorithm 7.4 and to incorporate it to Algorithm 7.6 to speed it up to $\mathcal{O}(\log(n/b) + c + b/c)$ time, just as for fwdsearch.

7.1.3 Range Minima and Maxima

The operations rmq(i, j) and related ones (rMq, mincount, and minselect) are solved by considering the maximal rmM-tree nodes that cover the interval $B[i, j]$ and finding the positions with the minimum (or maximum) excess. A common routine for all these operations is to find the local left-to-right minimum (or maximum) excess value in a range $B[i, j]$.

Finding the Minimum Excess in $B[i, j]$, and rmq(i, j)

We start processing the block $B[s, e] = B[(\lceil i/b \rceil - 1)b + 1, \lceil i/b \rceil b]$ where position i belongs. We start with position $p \leftarrow i - 1$, local excess $d \leftarrow 0$, and minimum excess found $m \leftarrow 2$. Now we examine the bits $B[p]$ for p from i to e. For each p we increase d by 1 if $B[p] = 1$ and decrease it by 1 if $B[p] = 0$. If, at any moment, it holds $d < m$, we set $m \leftarrow d$. If $j \leq e$ (that is, the whole $B[i, j]$ is within a single block), we scan only up to position j and return the obtained value m. Algorithm 7.7 gives a version of this scanning that proceeds by chunks, thus it takes $\mathcal{O}(c + b/c)$ time.

Algorithm 7.6: A simple version of bwdsearch(i, d), where we scan the blocks bitwise for simplicity.

---

1 **Proc** bwdsearch(B, i, d)

   Input : Parentheses sequence $B[1, n]$ and its rmM-tree $R[1, 2r - 1]$ for
             $r = \lceil n/b \rceil$, and parameters i and $d < 0$ (or $d = 0$ and $B[i] = 0$).
   Output: Returns bwdsearch(i, d).

2 | (sequential scan in the original block)
3 | $k \leftarrow \lceil i/b \rceil$; $d' \leftarrow 0$
4 | **for** $j \leftarrow i$ **downto** $(k - 1)b + 1$ **do**
5 | | **if** bitread(B, j) = 1 **then** $d' \leftarrow d' - 1$
6 | | **else** $d' \leftarrow d' + 1$
7 | | **if** $d' = d$ **then** **return** $j - 1$

8 | (upward search in the rmM-tree)
9 | $v \leftarrow leafnum(k)$ (Algorithm 7.1)
10 | **while** $v < 2^{\lceil \log v \rceil}$ **and** $d' - R[v - 1].e + R[v - 1].m > d$ **do**
11 | | **if** $v \bmod 2 = 1$ **then**
12 | | | $d' \leftarrow d' - R[v - 1].e$
13 | | $v \leftarrow \lfloor v/2 \rfloor$

14 | **if** $v = 2^{\lceil \log v \rceil}$ **then** **return** 0 (not found)
15 | (downward search in the rmM-tree)
16 | $v \leftarrow v - 1$
17 | **while** $v < r$ **do**
18 | | **if** $d' - R[2v + 1].e + R[2v + 1].m \le d$ **then**
19 | | | $v \leftarrow 2v + 1$

20 | | **else**
21 | | | $d' \leftarrow d' - R[2v + 1].e$
22 | | | $v \leftarrow 2v$

23 | (sequential scan in the final block)
24 | $k \leftarrow numleaf(v)$ (Algorithm 7.1)
25 | **for** $j \leftarrow kb$ **downto** $(k - 1)b$ **do**
26 | | **if** $d' = d$ **then** **return** j
27 | | **if** bitread(B, j) = 1 **then** $d' \leftarrow d' - 1$
28 | | **else** $d' \leftarrow d' + 1$

If $j > e$, we traverse the rmM-tree from the leaves to the root, looking for the minimum value in $B[e + 1, j]$. First, we identify the leaf v corresponding to the block $B[s, e]$ we have traversed: $v = leafnum(\lceil i/b \rceil)$. Now we find whether v is a right child of its parent, that is, if v is odd. If so, we simply go to the parent of v, with $v \leftarrow (v - 1)/2$.

Instead, if v is a left child of its parent, its right sibling is $v + 1$. We determine whether the area covered by $R[v + 1]$ is contained in $B[i, j]$. If so, we can process $R[v + 1]$ in constant time: The minimum excess reached inside node $v + 1$ is $d + R[v + 1].m$,

---

Algorithm 7.7: Scanning a block for min(i, j).

---

1 **Proc** *minblock*(B, i, j)

 Input : Parentheses sequence $B[1, n]$, table C, chunk size c, and parameters i
     and j. Assumes i and j belong to the same block.

 Output: Returns $\langle m, d \rangle$, where m is the minimum local left-to-right excess in
     $B[i, j]$, and $d = \mathsf{excess}(i, j)$.

2 (first stage: bitwise scan)

3 $k \leftarrow \lceil (i - 1)/c \rceil + 1$ (first chunk to be scanned chunkwise)

4 $k' \leftarrow \lfloor j/c \rfloor$ (last chunk to be scanned chunkwise)

5 $d \leftarrow 0; m \leftarrow 2$

6 **for** $p \leftarrow i$ **to** $\min(j, (k - 1)c)$ **do**

7 **if** $\mathsf{bitread}(B, p) = 1$ **then** $d \leftarrow d + 1$

8 **else** $d \leftarrow d - 1$

9 **if** $d < m$ **then** $m \leftarrow d$

10 **if** $j \leq (k - 1)c$ **then return** $\langle m, d \rangle$

11 (second stage: chunkwise scan)

12 **for** $p \leftarrow k$ **to** k' **do**

13 $x \leftarrow \mathsf{bitsread}(B, (p - 1)c + 1, pc)$

14 **if** $d + C[x].m < m$ **then** $m \leftarrow d + C[x].m$

15 $d \leftarrow d + C[x].e$

16 (third stage: bitwise scan again)

17 **for** $p \leftarrow k'c + 1$ **to** j **do**

18 **if** $\mathsf{bitread}(B, p) = 1$ **then** $d \leftarrow d + 1$

19 **else** $d \leftarrow d - 1$

20 **if** $d < m$ **then** $m \leftarrow d$

21 **return** $\langle m, d \rangle$

---

thus if $d + R[v + 1].m < m$ we set $m \leftarrow d + R[v + 1].m$. In any case, we update $d \leftarrow d + R[v + 1].e$ and move to the parent of v, $v \leftarrow v/2$.

Once we finally find the node $v + 1$ that is not contained in $B[i, j]$, we traverse the rmM-tree downwards from $v \leftarrow v + 1$. We repeatedly test whether the left child of v, $2v$, is contained in $B[i, j]$. If it is not, we simply descend to it, $v \leftarrow 2v$. Otherwise we process the whole child $2v$: If $d + R[2v].m < m$, then we set $m \leftarrow d + R[2v].m$, and in any case we update $d \leftarrow d + R[2v].e$. Then we descend to $v \leftarrow 2v + 1$.

The downward traversal stops when we arrive at the leaf node containing position $j + 1$, the k'th leaf for $k' = \lceil (j + 1)/b \rceil$. Then we perform a final sequential scan on $B[(k' - 1)b + 1, j]$, inside the corresponding block. At each step, we increase d by 1 if $B[p] = 1$ and decrease it by 1 if $B[p] = 0$, and if $d < m$ we set $m \leftarrow d$. When we finish processing the position $p = j$, we have in m the minimum local excess in $B[i, j]$.

To determine whether an rmM-tree node u is contained in $B[i, j]$, we check whether it is an ancestor of the k'th leaf, which contains the first position $(j + 1)$ that should not be covered by u. Let $\ell = \textit{leafnum}(k')$ be the position of the leaf in R. Now, the depth of any node $R[v]$ is $\lfloor \log v \rfloor + 1$. Since the parent of any node v is $\lfloor v/2 \rfloor$, the ancestor of ℓ at the depth of u is $\lfloor \ell/2^{\lfloor \log \ell \rfloor - \lfloor \log u \rfloor} \rfloor$. Therefore, as we advance from $B[i]$ left-to-right, node u is contained in $B[i, j]$ iff $\lfloor \ell/2^{\lfloor \log \ell \rfloor - \lfloor \log u \rfloor} \rfloor \neq u$. This test involves a simple bit shift operation. It does not work, however, when u is deeper than leaf ℓ (which can happen when r is not a power of 2 and u is a leaf as well). This is easily detected because $u > \ell$.

Algorithm 7.8 gives the details. We again use the trick of moving to node $v + 1$ even when it is not a sibling of v (line 9). This ensures that the rmM-tree traversal costs $\mathcal{O}\left(\log \frac{j-i+1}{b}\right)$ time, thus improving on shorter intervals.

Algorithm 7.8: Computing the minimum excess in $B[i, j]$.

---

1 **Proc** $minexcess(B, i, j)$

    Input : Parentheses sequence $B[1, n]$ and its rmM-tree $R[1, 2r - 1]$ for
               $r = \lceil n/b \rceil$, and indexes i and j.

    Output: Returns m, the minimum local excess in $B[i, j]$.

2   (sequential scan in the original block)

3   $k \leftarrow \lceil i/b \rceil$

4   $\langle m, d \rangle \leftarrow minblock(B, i, \min(kb, j))$ (Algorithm 7.7)

5   **if** $j \leq kb$ **then return** m

6   (upward search in the rmM-tree)

7   $k' \leftarrow \lceil (j + 1)/b \rceil$

8   $v \leftarrow leafnum(k); \ell \leftarrow leafnum(k')$ (Algorithm 7.1)

9   **while** $v + 1 > \ell$ **or** $\lfloor \ell/2^{\lfloor \log \ell \rfloor - \lfloor \log(v+1) \rfloor} \rfloor \neq v + 1$ **do**

10   **if** $v \bmod 2 = 0$ **then**

11   **if** $d + R[v + 1].m < m$ **then** $m \leftarrow d + R[v + 1].m$

12         $d \leftarrow d + R[v + 1].e$

13     $v \leftarrow \lfloor v/2 \rfloor$

14   (downward search in the rmM-tree)

15   $v \leftarrow v + 1$

16   **while** $v < r$ **do**

17   **if** $d + R[v].m \geq m$ **then return** m

18   **if** $\lfloor \ell/2^{\lfloor \log \ell \rfloor - \lfloor \log(2v) \rfloor} \rfloor \neq 2v$ **then**

19   **if** $d + R[2v].m < m$ **then** $m \leftarrow d + R[2v].m$

20         $d \leftarrow d + R[2v].e$

21         $v \leftarrow 2v + 1$

22   **else** $v \leftarrow 2v$

23   **if** $d + R[v].m \geq m$ **then return** m

24   (sequential scan in the final block)

25   $\langle m', d' \rangle \leftarrow minblock(B, (k' - 1)b + 1, j)$ (Algorithm 7.7)

26   **if** $d + m' < m$ **then**

27     $m \leftarrow d + m'$

28   **return** m

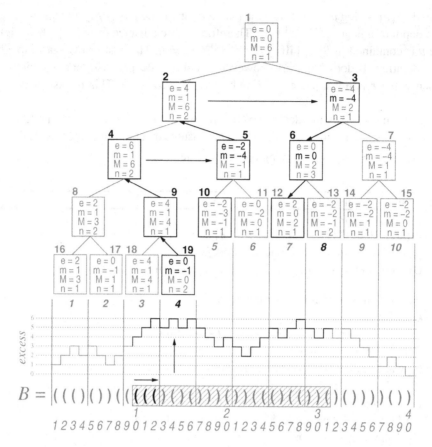

Figure 7.5. The process to find the minimum local excess in $B[10, 31]$ on the structure of Figure 7.3. The data accessed are shown in black. We sequentially scan part of block 3, where the traversal starts, then move upwards on the rmM-tree through nodes 19, 9, 4, and 2, and then move downwards through nodes 3 and 6. At this point we realize that we have already found the minimum and do not need to complete the traversal.

We also use another speedup in lines 17 and 23: even if the next node v exceeds $B[i, j]$, we can safely preempt the search for lower values of m if $d + R[v].m \geq m$. Thus we may not even reach the precise position j. Note also that we can easily avoid computing logarithms all the time in lines 9 and 18, given the way v is updated.

The sequential traversal of the leaves costs $\mathcal{O}(c + b/c)$. With the proper choices of c and b, the total time is $\mathcal{O}(\log n)$, as for previous operations.

Example 7.9 *Let us compute the minimum local excess in $B[10, 31]$. Figure 7.5 illustrates the process, showing in black the accessed data. The answer should be -1, which is reached at position $B[22]$, as seen in the excess zone.*

We start with $m = 2$ and $d = 0$. Upon processing $B[10]$, in block number 3, we obtain $d = 1$ and thus reduce m to 1. Processing $B[11, 12]$ does not bring any further reduction in m, and leaves us with $d = 3$. Now we start the process on the rmM-tree from leaf $v = leafnum(3) = 18$. The leaf that contains $j + 1 = 32$ is number $k' = 8$, corresponding in R to position $\ell = leafnum(8) = 13$. Node $v + 1 = 19$ is inside $B[i, j]$

because $v + 1 > \ell$. Since $d + R[19].m = 2 \geq m$, we do not find any new minimum inside $R[19]$. We update $d \leftarrow d + R[19].e = 3$ and go to the parent, $v \leftarrow \lfloor v/2 \rfloor = 9$.

The node next to v, $v + 1 = 10$, is inside $B[i, j]$ since $\lfloor \ell/2^{\lfloor \log \ell \rfloor - \lfloor \log(v+1) \rfloor} \rfloor = \lfloor 13/2^{3-3} \rfloor = 13 \neq 10$, so we continue our upward traversal. Since v is a right child, we only have to update $v \leftarrow 4$.

Now $v = 4$ is a left child, and its right sibling $v + 1 = 5$ is inside $B[i, j]$ because $\lfloor \ell/2^{\lfloor \log \ell \rfloor - \lfloor \log(v+1) \rfloor} \rfloor = \lfloor 13/2^{3-2} \rfloor = 6 \neq 5$ is the ancestor of ℓ at the depth of $v + 1$. Thus we process $v + 1 = 5$. Since $d + R[5].m = -1 < m$, we have found a new minimum, $m = -1$. We update $d \leftarrow d + R[5].e = 1$ and go to the parent, $v \leftarrow 2$.

The node next to v, $v + 1 = 3$, exceeds $B[i, j]$ because $\lfloor \ell/2^{\lfloor \log \ell \rfloor - \lfloor \log(v+1) \rfloor} \rfloor = \lfloor 13/2^{3-1} \rfloor = 3$, so $v + 1$ is the ancestor of ℓ at the depth of $v + 1$.

Therefore, we start the downward traversal from $v \leftarrow v + 1 = 3$. Since $d + R[3].m = -3$, there is a chance of reducing m inside v. The left child of v, $2v = 6$, also exceeds $B[i, j]$, so we set $v \leftarrow 2v$ and continue. We can now safely stop the search because $d + R[6].m = 1 \geq m$, so m cannot be reduced inside the node $v = 6$, and this node contains what remains of $B[i, j]$.

Once we determine the minimum excess m in $B[i, j]$, we are ready to carry out the operations rmq(i, j), mincount(i, j), and minselect(i, j, t). For rmq(i, j), we simply find m and then run fwdsearch$(i - 1, m)$, that is, we find the leftmost position $p \geq i$ where excess$(i, p) = m$.

Example 7.10 *Continuing with Example 7.9, the position $B[22]$ of the leftmost minimum in $B[10, 31]$, that is, rmq$(10, 31)$, is found with fwdsearch$(10 - 1, m) = 22$, precisely as done in Example 7.8. Note that fwdsearch enters into branches of the rmM-tree that were skipped by minexcess, thus it is not easy to merge both traversals. For example, we do not want to find the precise position $B[22]$ until we are sure that the minimum is -1 and not smaller.*

The other operations are slightly less direct and are described next.

Operation rMq(i, j)

Operation rMq(i, j) is totally analogous to rmq(i, j), using field M instead of m (therefore, we must store this field only if we need operation rMq). A procedure similar to Algorithm 7.8 computes M, the maximum excess in $B[i, j]$. Once we determine M, a method analogous to fwdsearch$(i - 1, M)$ finds the first position where excess M occurs. Note, however, that this method is not totally identical to those of Algorithms 7.4 and 7.5, because we are looking for an excess that is larger than excess(i), not smaller. Therefore, the condition "$\leq d$" in line 13 of Algorithm 7.4 must change to "$\geq d$." In Algorithm 7.5, the second condition in line 7 must change to "$d' + R[v + 1].M < d$" (ensuring $R[2r].M = 2n + 1$ to avoid border cases), and line 15 to "**if** $d' + R[2v].M \geq d$ **then**."

Operation mincount(i, j)

For mincount(i, j) and minselect(i, j, t), we need the field n of the rmM-tree nodes, thus this field should be stored only if we need to support these operations. A traversal

---

Algorithm 7.9: Computing mincount(i, j). Blocks are scanned bitwise for simplicity.

---

1 **Proc** mincount(B, i, j)

    Input : Parentheses sequence $B[1, n]$ and its rmM-tree $R[1, 2r - 1]$ for
          $r = \lceil n/b \rceil$, and indexes i and j.

    Output: Returns mincount(i, j).

2     $m \leftarrow minexcess(B, i, j)$ (Algorithm 7.8)

3     $k \leftarrow \lceil i/b \rceil$; $v \leftarrow leafnum(k)$

4     $t \leftarrow 0$; $d \leftarrow 0$

5   **for** $p \leftarrow i$ **to** $\min(j, kb)$ **do**

6   **if** bitread(B, j) = 1 **then** $d \leftarrow d + 1$

7   **else** $d \leftarrow d - 1$

8   **if** $d = m$ **then** $t \leftarrow t + 1$

9   **if** $j \le kb$ **then return** t

10    $k' \leftarrow \lceil (j + 1)/b \rceil$; $\ell \leftarrow leafnum(k')$

11   **while** $v + 1 > \ell$ **or** $\lfloor \ell/2^{\lfloor \log \ell \rfloor - \lfloor \log(v+1) \rfloor} \rfloor \neq v + 1$ **do**

12   **if** $v \bmod 2 = 0$ **then**

13   **if** $d + R[v + 1].m = m$ **then** $t \leftarrow t + R[v + 1].n$

14           $d \leftarrow d + R[v + 1].e$

15        $v \leftarrow \lfloor v/2 \rfloor$

16    $v \leftarrow v + 1$

17   **while** $v < r$ **do**

18   **if** $d + R[v].m > m$ **then return** t

19   **if** $\lfloor \ell/2^{\lfloor \log \ell \rfloor - \lfloor \log(2v) \rfloor} \rfloor \neq 2v$ **then**

20   **if** $d + R[2v].m = m$ **then** $t \leftarrow t + R[2v].n$

21           $d \leftarrow d + R[2v].e$

22           $v \leftarrow 2v + 1$

23   **else** $v \leftarrow 2v$

24   **if** $d + R[v].m > m$ **then return** t

25   **for** $p \leftarrow (k' - 1)b + 1$ **to** j **do**

26   **if** bitread(B, p) = 1 **then** $d \leftarrow d + 1$

27   **else** $d \leftarrow d - 1$

28   **if** $d = m$ **then** $t \leftarrow t + 1$

29   **return** t

---

similar to the one of Algorithm 7.8 is carried out, now accumulating the number of times the minimum appears.

Algorithm 7.9 shows the pseudocode, without using chunkwise operations for simplicity. Now we can preempt the search only when the minimum of the current node v is strictly larger than m. As an exercise to the reader, we leave adding the chunkwise mechanism and integrating it with Algorithm 7.8 to avoid traversing the nodes twice: simply restart the counter $t \leftarrow 0$ each time a new, smaller value for m is found.

Operation minselect(i, j, t)

Finally, operation minselect(i, j, t) proceeds as for mincount(i, j), but each time the counter is going to reach or exceed t, we move downward to find the leaf, and finally the exact position, where the tth occurrence of the minimum m is reached. Unlike mincount, operation minselect is not easily integrated in a single traversal with *minexcess*, since it could perform extra work to find the tth occurrence of a current minimum that is not the final minimum value m. Algorithm 7.10 gives the details, without using chunks for simplicity.

Algorithm 7.10: Computing minselect(i, j, t), with mincount(i, j) $\geq t$. Blocks are scanned bitwise for simplicity.

---

1 **Proc** minselect(B, i, j, t)

    Input : Parentheses sequence $B[1, n]$ and its rmM-tree $R[1, 2r - 1]$ for
            $r = \lceil n/b \rceil$, indexes i and j, and counter t.

    Output: Returns minselect(i, j, t).

2    $m \leftarrow minexcess(B, i, j)$ (Algorithm 7.8)

3    $d \leftarrow 0; k \leftarrow \lceil i/b \rceil; v \leftarrow leafnum(k)$

4   **for** $p \leftarrow i$ **to** $\min(j, kb)$ **do**

5   **if** bitread(B, j) $= 1$ **then** $d \leftarrow d + 1$ **else** $d \leftarrow d - 1$

6   **if** $d = m$ **then**

7           $t \leftarrow t - 1$; **if** $t = 0$ **then return** p

8    $k' \leftarrow \lceil j/b \rceil; \ell \leftarrow leafnum(k')$

9   **while** $v + 1 > \ell$ **or** $\lfloor \ell/2^{\lfloor \log \ell \rfloor - \lfloor \log(v+1) \rfloor} \rfloor \neq v + 1$ **do**

10   **if** $v \bmod 2 = 0$ **then**

11   **if** $d + R[v + 1].m = m$ **then**

12   **if** $t \leq R[v + 1].n$ **then break**

13            $t \leftarrow t - R[v + 1].n$

14         $d \leftarrow d + R[v + 1].e$

15      $v \leftarrow \lfloor v/2 \rfloor$

16    $v \leftarrow v + 1$

17   **while** $v < r$ **do**

18   **if** $\lfloor \ell/2^{\lfloor \log \ell \rfloor - \lfloor \log(2v) \rfloor} \rfloor = 2v$ **then** $v \leftarrow 2v$

19   **else if** $d + R[2v].m > m$ **then**

20         $d \leftarrow d + R[2v].e; v \leftarrow 2v + 1$

21   **else if** $t \leq R[2v].n$ **then** $v \leftarrow 2v$

22   **else**

23         $t \leftarrow t - R[2v].n$

24         $d \leftarrow d + R[2v].e; v \leftarrow 2v + 1$

25   **for** $p \leftarrow (k' - 1)b + 1$ **to** j **do**

26   **if** bitread(B, p) $= 1$ **then** $d \leftarrow d + 1$ **else** $d \leftarrow d - 1$

27   **if** $d = m$ **then**

28         $t \leftarrow t - 1$; **if** $t = 0$ **then return** p

---

7.1.4 Rank and Select Operations

Several operations in Chapters 8 and 9 will require performing binary rank and select (Chapter 4) on B but also some extensions of them. For example, we will be interested in detecting the deepest segments in a parentheses sequence. Note that such segments look like '()', or 10 if seen as bits. We will be interested in determining how many deepest segments are there up to a given point in B and in finding the position of the jth deepest segment in B. Those are analogous to the rank and select operations, now extended to consider the occurrences of short *predefined* sequences s:

$\text{rank}_s(B, i)$: returns the number of occurrences of bit string $s \in \{0, 1\}^*$ in $B[1, i]$, for any $0 \le i \le n$; in particular $\text{rank}_s(B, 0) = 0$. Note that the occurrence of s must end within $B[1, i]$.

$\text{select}_s(B, j)$: returns the first position of the jth occurrence of bit string $s \in \{0, 1\}^*$ in B, for any $j \ge 0$; we assume $\text{select}_s(B, 0) = 0$. For $j > \text{rank}_s(B, n)$ it holds $\text{select}_s(B, j) = n + 1$.

It is not hard to enhance the implementations used for dense bitvectors in Sections 4.2 and 4.3, so that one counts the occurrences of bit strings like 10. This requires only changing the precomputation of the tables R, R', S, etc., that should now count the number of occurrences of 10. Operation *popcount* should now be applied not directly over a word `bits`, but rather over (`bits >> 1`) `&` `~bits` (in C). Finally, some care has to be exercised to avoid missing occurrences of 10 that cross borders between words and blocks. All these changes are straightforward and are left as an exercise to the reader.

Since we aim for $\mathcal{O}(\log n)$ time and $\mathcal{O}(n/\log n)$ extra bits, we can use the rank structure of Section 4.2.1, which uses sparse sampling, and select can be solved without extra space, via binary search on the rank samples plus scanning. While rank is in practice faster than the operations on the rmM-tree, the times for this implementation of select are comparable.

An alternative to using the techniques of Chapter 4 is to integrate operations rank and select into the rmM-trees. For example, to support rank_{10} and select_{10} we should add a counter $R[v].l$ that tells the number of occurrences of 10 *ending* inside the area of B covered by node v (even if they do not start inside the area). Then $\text{rank}_{10}(i)$ is solved by adding up the l fields over the rmM-tree nodes that cover $B[1, i]$, as detailed in Algorithm 7.11. Operation $\text{select}_{10}(j)$ is solved similarly, by going toward the jth occurrence of 10; see Algorithm 7.12. The algorithms scan the block bitwise for simplicity.

7.2 Improving the Complexity

We have shown how to solve all the desired operations in time $\mathcal{O}(\log n)$. In practical terms, this complexity is quite good, especially if we consider that it consists of scanning contiguous areas of memory (the blocks) plus, if necessary, traversing the rmM-tree. Here the time is actually $\mathcal{O}(\log((j - i)/b))$, where i and j delimit the area of B we traverse to solve the operations.

Algorithm 7.11: Computing $rank_{10}(i)$ on B. We scan the block bitwise for simplicity.

---

1 **Proc** $rank_{10}(i)$
  Input : Parentheses sequence $B[1, n]$ and its rmM-tree $R[1, 2r - 1]$ for
    $r = \lceil n/b \rceil$, and index i.
  Output: Returns $rank_{10}(B, i)$.

2 **if** $i = 0$ **then return** 0
3 $k \leftarrow \lceil i/b \rceil$; $\ell \leftarrow leafnum(k)$
4 $l \leftarrow 0$; $v \leftarrow 1$
5 **while** $v < r$ **do**
6 | **if** $\lfloor \ell/2^{\lfloor \log \ell \rfloor - \lfloor \log(2v) \rfloor} \rfloor \neq 2v$ **then**
7 | | $l \leftarrow l + R[2v].l$
8 | | $v \leftarrow 2v + 1$
9 | **else** $v \leftarrow 2v$
10 **for** $p \leftarrow (k - 1)b + 1$ **to** i **do**
11 | **if** $bitsread(B, p - 1, p) = 10$ **then** $l \leftarrow l + 1$
12 **return** l

Nevertheless, for the more ambitious readers, we show in this section how we can ensure $\mathcal{O}(\log \log n)$ time for all the operations, while maintaining the $\mathcal{O}(n/\log n)$ extra space. This material is more sophisticated and will be presented precisely, but not up to the level of pseudocode.

Algorithm 7.12: Computing $select_{10}(j)$ on B. We scan the block bitwise for simplicity.

---

1 **Proc** $select_{10}(j)$
  Input : Parentheses sequence $B[1, n]$ and its rmM-tree $R[1, 2r - 1]$ for
    $r = \lceil n/b \rceil$, and value j.
  Output: Returns $select_{10}(B, j)$.

2 **if** $j = 0$ **then return** 0
3 $v \leftarrow 1$
4 **while** $v < r$ **do**
5 | **if** $R[2v].l < j$ **then**
6 | | $j \leftarrow j - R[2v].l$
7 | | $v \leftarrow 2v + 1$
8 | **else** $v \leftarrow 2v$
9 $k \leftarrow numleaf(v)$
10 **for** $p \leftarrow (k - 1)b + 1$ **to** kb **do**
11 | **if** $bitsread(B, p - 1, p) = 10$ **then**
12 | | $j \leftarrow j - 1$
13 | | **if** $j = 0$ **then return** p
14 **return** $n + 1$

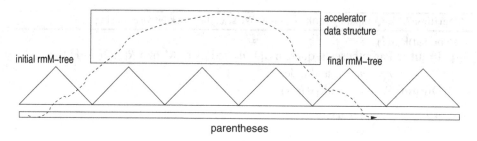

Figure 7.6. The general scheme to solve the operations in $\mathcal{O}(\log \log n)$ time.

The main idea is to cut the sequence $B[1, n]$ of parentheses into relatively large *buckets* of $\beta = \Theta(\log^3 n)$ parentheses (tens of thousands, in practice). Thus there are $n' = \lceil n/\beta \rceil$ buckets; note that $n' = \mathcal{O}(n/\log^3 n)$. For each bucket, we create the structure of Section 7.1. Operations inside the buckets will cost $\mathcal{O}(\log \beta) = \mathcal{O}(\log \log n)$ time. If an operation cannot be solved within its bucket, we resort to "accelerator" data structures to find the target bucket and complete the operation in it. Figure 7.6 illustrates the concept, which is analogous to how the blocks and the rmM-tree work. We will describe how each kind of query is solved and the new data structures it needs.

7.2.1 Queries inside Buckets

We will use a smaller block size $b = \Theta(\log n \log \log n)$. Note that, since the rmM-trees will now cover β parentheses, the fields e, m, M, and n will require only $\mathcal{O}(\log \beta) = \mathcal{O}(\log \log n)$ bits, and therefore the total space of the rmM-trees is $\mathcal{O}((n/b) \log \log n) = \mathcal{O}(n/\log n)$ bits.

We enhance the table C that was used to process the blocks by chunks of $c = (\log n)/2$ bits, so that we do not have to perform any operation bitwise. More precisely, we add another dimension with a value $1 \le l \le c$, so that $C[x][l]$ stores the fields e, m, M, and n corresponding to the lowest l bits of x (the original values $C[x]$ now correspond to $C[x][c]$). The size of C is still very small, $\mathcal{O}(\sqrt{n}\, w \log n)$ bits.

Now, if have to traverse $B[i, j]$, we process the first $l = c - ((i - 1) \bmod c)$ bits using $C[\cdot][l]$, then we use $C[\cdot][c]$ several times, and finally process the last $l' = j \bmod c$ bits using $C[\cdot][l']$ (let us ignore special cases where $j - i < c$ for simplicity). In this way the time to process any block is $\mathcal{O}(b/c) = \mathcal{O}(\log \log n)$. Operations inside the rmM-tree of a bucket will then cost $\mathcal{O}(\log \log n)$ for the starting block, $\mathcal{O}(\log \beta) = \mathcal{O}(\log \log n)$ for the rmM-tree and another $\mathcal{O}(\log \log n)$ for the final block.

In Practice

A practical choice is to set $\beta = 2^{15}$ and then use short integers to represent the rmM-tree fields. In this case, it is better to prescind of the field e and store absolute values (of the local rmM-tree) in the fields m and M. This simplifies the code and saves space (we saved more space by storing relative values when the rmM-tree spanned the whole sequence, at the end of Section 7.1.1, but now the fields are already short). Since $-2^{15} \le m \le 1$ and $-1 \le M \le 2^{15}$, 16 bits are sufficient to represent them. Thus, if we set

$c = 16$ and $b = 1024$, we can scan any block with at most 64 accesses to C. In practice, processing up to c bits sequentially is fast enough; extending table C is not necessary.

The space overhead of the rmM-trees, removing field e, is $(2 \cdot 3 \cdot 16/1024) < 0.1$ bits per parenthesis, better than that obtained in Section 7.1.1 with the more complex arrangement. The processing times of the blocks is similar.

The traversal of the rmM-tree is faster without the field e and fewer nodes are traversed: The rmM-tree has a height of $\log(\beta/b) = 5$, whereas the global rmM-tree with, for example, $n = 2^{30}$ and $b = 1024$, has a height of 20. In addition, traversing these small rmM-trees has better locality of reference than a global rmM-tree.

7.2.2 Forward and Backward Searching

A query fwdsearch(i, d) is first solved inside the bucket of i, $k^* = \lceil i/\beta \rceil$. If the answer is not found there, we finish at the end of bucket k^* with a new target $d < 0$ of excess difference (this is the original d minus excess$(i + 1, k^*\beta)$). By storing the absolute excess right before the beginning of each bucket in an array $e[1, n']$, $e[k] = $ excess$((k - 1)\beta)$, we can convert the relative excess sought, d, into an absolute one, $e = e[k^* + 1] + d$. Thus, our goal is to find the leftmost bucket $k' > k^*$ whose minimum absolute excess inside the bucket is $\leq e$. Once we find bucket k', we again convert the absolute excess into a relative one, $d' = e - e[k']$, and complete the search with a fwdsearch$(0, d')$ query inside bucket k'.

Similarly, we try to solve bwdsearch(i, d) first in bucket k^*, and if we fail, we convert the remaining excess difference $d < 0$ into the absolute $e = e[k^*] + d$, find the rightmost bucket $k' < k^*$ with minimum excess $\leq e$, convert e back into $d' = e - e[k' + 1]$, and answer bwdsearch(β, d') inside bucket k'.

Let $m[1, n']$ be an array such that $m[k]$ is the minimum global excess in bucket k. Our problem is reduced to finding the smallest $k' > k^*$ (or the largest $k' < k^*$, for a backward search) such that $m[k'] \leq e$. We will describe the solution for the forward search, as the backward search solution is symmetric.

Left-to-Right Minima Tree

Consider carrying out the search from some bucket k^*. If $m[k^* + 1] \leq e$, then the answer is $k^* + 1$. Otherwise we must continue the search. If $m[k^* + 2] \geq m[k^* + 1]$, then we are not interested in bucket $k^* + 2$, regardless of the value of e. Only the next bucket $k^* + g$ where $m[k^* + g] < m[k^* + 1]$ has a chance of being relevant for the search. Therefore, our first step will be to record, for each bucket, the next bucket that is relevant to it, in an array $next[1, n']$.

Array $next$ can be built in $\mathcal{O}(n')$ time as follows. We start with an empty stack and start traversing $m[n']$ to $m[1]$. When we are about to process $m[k]$, the stack will maintain the left-to-right minima in $m[k + 1, n']$. To process $m[k]$, we remove every element $\geq m[k]$ from the stack. If the stack becomes empty, we set $next[k] \leftarrow 0$, meaning there is no useful value for bucket k after it. Otherwise we set $next[k] \leftarrow k'$, where k' is the bucket at the top of the stack. This means that the next relevant value for bucket k is $m[k'] < m[k]$. Finally, we push k on the stack. It is easy to see that this process takes linear time, since each element is inserted once, and removed at most once, from the stack.

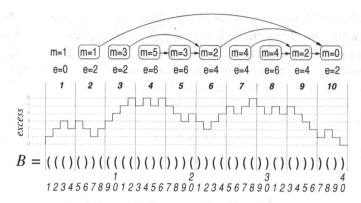

Figure 7.7. The bucket scheme with arrays e and m, for bucket size $\beta = 4$. Array *next* is illustrated with arrows. It defines the left-to-right minima tree on the buckets: each bucket points to the next one having a smaller m value.

Field *next* acts as the parent pointer of a tree of buckets. If we want to find the first bucket k' after k^* with $m[k'] \le e$, and if the answer is not $k^* + 1$, then we need to check only the $m[\cdot]$ values of the parent of $k^* + 1$, the parent of its parent, and so on.

Example 7.11 *Figure 7.7 illustrates the bucket scheme on the sequence of Figure 7.1, for a toy bucket size $\beta = 4$, with arrays e and m, and the tree resulting from array next[$\cdot$] (arrows point to the parents). Note that the first bucket does not participate in the tree since we always start searches from $k^* + 1$. Note also that since the lowest excess occurs at the last parenthesis, our tree always has a single root.*

To find the answer starting at some block, only its ancestors need to be reviewed. For example, if we start at block $k^* + 1 = 4$ with the absolute excess target $e = 1$, we need to review the minima of its ancestors, $\langle m[4], m[5], m[6], m[10] \rangle = \langle 5, 3, 2, 0 \rangle$, to find the first value ≤ 1 (it occurs in block 10). If we reverse the sequence, we have a classical predecessor problem: find the predecessor of $e = 1$ in the increasing sequence $\langle 0, 2, 3, 5 \rangle$.

We would like to have a predecessor structure (Section 4.5.2) for the $m[\cdot]$ values on each path of this tree; however, this could require quadratic space. We next describe a classical data structure that we will adapt to our problem.

Level Ancestor Queries

Given a tree node v and a distance d, this problem aims to find the ancestor at distance d from v. We will describe a structure to answer this query in constant time, on the tree defined by our *next* fields (interpreted as parent). Its space usage is $\mathcal{O}(n' \log n')$ words, which is $\mathcal{O}(n / \log n)$ bits.

In the process of determining the field *next*, we could also easily compute node depths in *depth*$[1, n']$, as *depth*$[k] = 1$ when *next*$[k] = 0$ and *depth*$[k] = 1 + $ *depth*$[next[k]]$ otherwise. We will also fill an array *leaf*$[1, n']$ telling which nodes are leaves: we set *leaf*$[k] = 1$ when we first insert k in the tree, and then *leaf*$[k] = 0$ when some k' with *next*$[k'] = k$ appears. Once the tree is built, we initialize a mark *mark*$[k] = 0$ for all buckets k. We then collect the r buckets k with *leaf*$[k] = 1$ and sort them by decreasing *depth*$[k]$ value.

Therefore, if we take the first element from the sorted array, the result is the deepest leaf k in the tree. We obtain its whole path toward the root using the *next* field, and set a field $mark[k'] = 1$ for all those k' in that path. The result is that we have extracted the longest leaf-to-root path from the tree. We write this sequence of buckets in an array $V[1][1, depth[k]]$.

Imagine that we remove this longest path from the tree. The result is a disconnected set of subtrees. We will keep extracting longest root-to-leaf paths from those subtrees. To do this, we keep taking the next leaf k of maximum depth from the sorted array. This time, however, we will extract and mark the ancestors of k until we find a marked bucket, which means that we have reached the root k' of the connected component of the tree. There will be another difference: Let ℓ be the length of the path we extracted. We will also take the next ℓ ancestors of k', even if they are already marked and thus already written somewhere else in V. We write the whole extracted path in $V[2][1, 2\ell]$ (of course, we may extract less than 2ℓ nodes if we reach the actual root of the tree). The position where a bucket k is written in B for the first time (when it becomes marked) will be called its *primary copy*, and any other place where it is written in V will be called a *secondary copy*.

We continue with this process until the sorted array becomes empty. The result is a set $V[1, r]$ of arrays. The total length of all the arrays in V is no more than $2n'$, since at least the first half of each extracted path is formed by primary copies.

We will store an array $jump[1, n'][0, \lfloor \log n' \rfloor]$, so that $jump[k][a] = \langle i, j \rangle$ such that $V[i][j]$ holds the primary copy of the ancestor of k at distance 2^a, if it exists. This array, the biggest in the data structure, uses $\mathcal{O}(n' \log n')$ cells. To build it, we first create an array $pos[1, n']$, used only for construction, where $pos[k] = \langle i, j \rangle$ iff $V[i][j]$ holds the primary copy of k. This array is easily filled while V is written. We then fill $jump$ for increasing values of a, using $jump[k][0] = pos[next[k]]$ and $jump[k][a + 1] = jump[V[jump[k][a]]][a]$.

Example 7.12 *Figure 7.8 illustrates the construction and properties of the data structure, for the tree corresponding to Figure 7.7. On the top left, we have the tree of buckets (node identifiers are bucket numbers). The node depths are written in italics besides the lower-right corner of each node, and the leaves are hatched. The array of $r = 5$ leaves, sorted by decreasing depth, is $\langle 4, 8, 3, 7, 2 \rangle$ (breaking ties arbitrarily). We take the first element of the array, leaf 4, and extract its path to the root (circled in a dashed line).*

On the top right, we have written the nodes of this longest path in $V[1]$ and marked in gray the nodes of the extracted path. The black nodes form a disconnected set of subtrees. We take the second element of the sorted array, leaf 8. Its path toward the root of its connected component is circled.

On the bottom left, we have written in $V[2]$ this new extracted path. It contains a first part of (black) primary copies of nodes (8 and 9) of length $\ell = 2$, and then other ℓ consecutive ancestors (in gray) as secondary copies. There is only 1 more element, not $\ell = 2$, because we reached the tree root. Now we choose the next leaf of the sorted array, 3.

On the bottom right, we completed the process and created $r = 5$ rows in V. Each element has exactly 1 primary copy and zero or more secondary copies, but there are

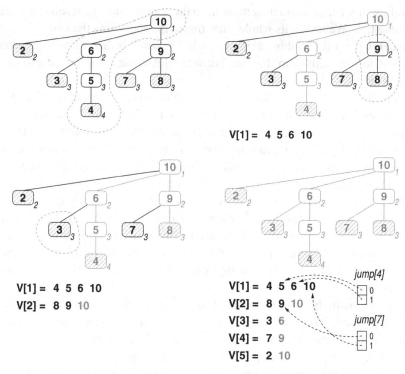

$$V[1] = 4\ 5\ 6\ 10$$

$$V[1] = 4\ 5\ 6\ 10$$
$$V[2] = 8\ 9\ 10$$

$$V[1] = 4\ 5\ 6\ 10$$
$$V[2] = 8\ 9\ 10$$
$$V[3] = 3\ 6$$
$$V[4] = 7\ 9$$
$$V[5] = 2\ 10$$

Figure 7.8. Four steps in the construction of the level ancestor queries structure for the implicit left-to-right minima tree of Figure 7.7. In each step, a longest leaf-to-root path is extracted, grayed, and written as a new row $V[i]$. This creates several disconnected subtrees. Grayed numbers on the rows $V[i]$ are secondary copies of elements, which are past the actual path extracted. On the bottom-right we also show some entries of the *jump* structure.

no more than $2n'$ elements in the V arrays. We illustrate a couple of jump entries; they point to the primary copies of the elements.

Once we have V and *jump* computed, we can find the ancestor of v at distance d as follows. First, we find $\langle i, j \rangle = jump[v][\lfloor \log d \rfloor]$. Let $V[i][j] = v'$. Thus v' is the ancestor of v at distance $d' = 2^{\lfloor \log d \rfloor} \le d$. This means that v' is of height at least d', and therefore, when its primary copy was written in $V[i][j]$, array $V[i]$ had started with the deepest leaf in the subtree of v' and reached v' in position $j \ge d'$. Thus the ℓ value of $V[i]$ is at least d'. This means that at least other $\ell \ge d'$ ancestors of v' are copied after its primary copy $V[i][j]$ (unless the tree root is reached). The answer to the query is the ancestor of v' at distance $d - d' < d'$, and since this must be written after $V[i][j]$, we simply return $V[i][j + d - d']$.

Example 7.13 *In the structure of Figure 7.8, let us compute the ancestor at distance $d = 3$ of node $v = 4$. We compute $a = \lfloor \log d \rfloor = 1$ and $d' = 2^a = 2$. The ancestor at distance $d' = 2$ of $v = 4$ is found at $jump[v][a] = jump[4][1] = \langle 1, 3 \rangle$, meaning that it is at $V[1][3] = 6$. Now we know that the answer can be directly found at $V[1][3 + d - d'] = V[1][4] = 10$.*

As a second example, consider the node $v = 7$ and distance $d = 2$. Although we have $d' = 2^{\lfloor \log d \rfloor} = 2 = d$ and thus the answer is directly at $V[jump[7][1]] = 10$, let us do the exercise of using a secondary entry. We use $d' = 1$ and $jump[7][0] = \langle 2, 2 \rangle$ (we can do this in this very special case because d' is still $\geq d/2$). Since this is a primary copy at $V[2][2]$, we know there are at least 2 other entries written after $V[2][2]$ (or we reach the root, as in this case). Thus we can use $V[2][2 + d - d'] = V[2][3] = 10$.

In practice, all the arrays $V[i]$ can be concatenated into one, so the pointers from *jump* are a single integer.

Including Weights

Our problem is, however, slightly more complicated than finding the ancestor at distance d. Each node k has a value $m[k]$. These form a decreasing sequence as we move toward the root. We are given a target value e and want to find the nearest ancestor k' of k for which $m[k'] \leq e$.

Let us consider a row $V[i][1, l] = \langle k_1, k_2, \ldots, k_l \rangle$ and build a predecessor data structure on the sequence $m[k_l] < \ldots < m[k_2] < m[k_1]$. We can then solve our problem as follows. We start with the node v corresponding to the first bucket of our search. We then run a binary search for e in the values $m[V[jump[v][a]]]$, for $0 \leq a \leq \lfloor \log n' \rfloor$. This will find, in $\mathcal{O}(\log \log n)$ time, a node $v' = V[jump[v][a]]$ such that $m[v']$ is larger than or equal to e but $m[V[jump[v][a + 1]]] < e$, so we know we have made it more than half the way toward the objective. Let us call $\langle i, j \rangle = jump[v][a]$ this entry. With the same argument as for level ancestor queries, we know that the answer to the query is in $V[i]$, somewhere starting from j. Therefore, we look for the predecessor of e in $V[i]$, in a structure built for its $m[\cdot]$ values.

Example 7.14 *Consider the row $V[1]$ in Figure 7.8. It contains the nodes $\langle 4, 5, 6, 10 \rangle$, whose $m[\cdot]$ values (recall Example 7.11) are $\langle 5, 3, 2, 0 \rangle$. Now, to find the excess $e = 1$ starting from bucket $v = k^* + 1 = 4$, we first perform a binary search on $jump[4][0, 1]$, finding $jump[4][1] = \langle 1, 3 \rangle$ as the farthest node in $jump[4]$ with $m[\cdot]$ value still larger than e (indeed, $V[1][3] = 6$ and $m[6] = 2 > 1 = e$). We also know that the answer must be in $V[1]$, somewhere to the right of $V[1][3]$. Therefore, we can perform a predecessor search on the array $\langle 0, 2, 3, 5 \rangle$ (the $m[\cdot]$ values reversed) to find that $m[10] = 0$ is the bucket where the excess $e = 1$ is reached.*

The predecessor structure can be as simple as a sparse bitvector B_i for each vector $V[i]$, with 1s at all the l positions $V[i][j] + 1$. The bucket of e is then $V[i][l - \text{rank}(B_i, e + 1) + 1]$. Since the m values in $V[i]$ cannot decrease by more than β from one position to the next, the consecutive 1s in B_i cannot be more than β positions apart. Thus the rightmost of the l 1s in B_i is at position $l\beta$. With the representation of Section 4.4, B_i requires $l \log \beta + \mathcal{O}(l) = \mathcal{O}(l \log \log n)$ bits, adding up to $\mathcal{O}(n' \log \log n) = o(n/ \log^2 n)$ bits in total. It answers rank in time $\mathcal{O}(\log \beta) = \mathcal{O}(\log \log n)$.

Note that it is not necessary to build B_i on rows $V[i][1, l]$ for which $l = \mathcal{O}(\log n)$; those can just be binary searched. Alternatively, we can build the structure for all the rows, and then discard the explicit table V, since we can use select to recover any individual cell $V[i][j]$ in constant time.

7.2.3 Range Minima and Maxima

Operations $\mathsf{rmq}(i, j)$ and relatives are solved as in Section 7.1.3 if i and j fall within the same bucket. Otherwise the minimum can be in the bucket of i, $k_1 = \lceil i/\beta \rceil$, in the bucket of j, $k_2 = \lceil j/\beta \rceil$, or in an intermediate bucket (if there are any). Therefore, we find the minimum in the range $[i - (k_1 - 1)\beta, \beta]$ of the bucket k_1, μ_1, and convert it to a global excess, $\mu_1 + e[k_1]$. We also find the minimum in the range $[1, j - (k_2 - 1)\beta]$ of the bucket k_2, μ_2, and also convert it to a global excess, $\mu_2 + e[k_2]$. Finally, we find the minimum in the buckets $k_1 + 1$ to $k_2 - 1$, μ_3. Then the global minimum in $[i, j]$ is $\mu = \min(\mu_1 + e[k_1], \mu_2 + e[k_2], \mu_3)$.

Therefore, we need only a mechanism to find the minimum within the whole buckets $k = k_1 + 1$ to $k' = k_2 - 1$, that is, finding the minimum in $m[k, k']$. This is called a *range minimum query* on general arrays of numbers.

Range Minimum Queries

We describe a structure that takes $\mathcal{O}(n' \log n')$ words, that is, $\mathcal{O}(n/\log n)$ bits, and returns the minimum of $m[k, k']$ in constant time.

Assume n' is a power of 2 for simplicity (for example, $m[\cdot]$ can be extended to the next power of 2 with fake values $+\infty$), and consider a perfect binary tree T on top of this extended array $m[\cdot]$. Just like the rmM-tree of Section 7.1.1, the nodes of T with height h cover disjoint areas of length 2^h of $m[\cdot]$: the root, with height $h = \log n'$, covers the whole $m[\cdot]$, its two children cover the intervals $m[1, n'/2]$ and $m[n'/2 + 1, n']$, and so on. The nodes v of T are numbered in heap-like order, that is, the root is 1, and the left and right children of node v are $2v$ and $2v + 1$.

For each node v of T covering $m[s, e]$, we store an array L with the left-to-right minima in $m[s, e]$ if v is a right child, or an array R with the right-to-left minima in $m[s, e]$ if v is a left child: for all $0 \le p \le e - s$, we store

$$L[v][p] = \min\{m[s], \ldots, m[s + p]\} = \min(L[v][p - 1], m[s + p]) \text{ or}$$

$$R[v][p] = \min\{m[e - p], \ldots, m[e]\} = \min(R[v][p - 1], m[e - p]),$$

where the rightmost formulas show how to fill each cell in constant time. Since T has height $\log n'$, and all the $L[v]$ and $R[v]$ cells at each height h add up to $\mathcal{O}(n')$ cells, the total cells and construction time are $\mathcal{O}(n' \log n')$.

Now, to find the minimum in $m[k, k']$, we find the lowest node of T, v^*, that covers the interval $[k, k']$. To do this in constant time, we find the most significant bit where the numbers $k - 1$ and $k' - 1$ differ. Say it is the hth bit counting from the right. Then v^* is of height h, and it is the ℓth left-to-right node at that height, for $\ell = \lceil k/2^h \rceil$. Therefore, $v^* = n'/2^h + \ell - 1$, and the interval it covers is $m[s, e] = m[(\ell - 1)2^h + 1, \ell \, 2^h]$.

The desired bit can be found by computing the bitwise-xor of $k - 1$ and $k' - 1$ and then finding the most significant bit of the result. Both operations have a direct implementation in most processors (see Section 4.5.2); otherwise they can be carried out with a couple of applications of small precomputed tables of $\sqrt{n'}$ entries that handle any sequence of $(\log n')/2$ bits.

Once we know that v^* splits $[k, k']$, we know that its left child $2v^*$ covers $m[s, p]$ and its right child $2v^* + 1$ covers $m[p + 1, e]$, for $p = (s + e - 1)/2$. Then the minimum of $m[k, k']$ is either the minimum of $m[k, p]$ or the minimum of $m[p + 1, k']$. The former

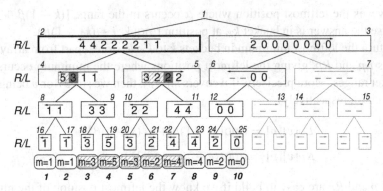

Figure 7.9. The tree T built for range minimum queries on the array $m[\cdot]$ of Figure 7.7. Each level stores left-to-right (L) or right-to-left (R) minima on the area it covers; note that array R is stored backwards. The hatched areas illustrate query $\mathsf{rmq}(3, 7)$, which is solved at the children of node 2, which is the lowest common ancestor of leaves 3 and 7. The range for $\mathsf{rmq}(3, 7)$ spans a suffix of the area covered by the left child, node 4 (it is seen as a prefix of its array R) and a prefix of the area covered by the right child, node 5 (it is seen as a prefix of its array L). The minima in both prefixes are grayed, and the answer is the smaller of the two, value 2.

is $R[2v^*][p - k]$, and the latter is $L[2v^* + 1][k' - p - 1]$. We choose the minimum of both and return it.

Example 7.15 *Figure 7.9 shows the structure built on the $m[\cdot]$ array of Example 7.11. We have grayed the areas that are added to extend $n' = 10$ to the next power of 2, $n' = 16$ (we may avoid actually storing that fake data). Each node of the tree has array L or R. Array L gives the left-to-right minima found as we traverse the area it covers; array R gives the right-to-left minima in reverse order. Slanted numbers on the top of each node indicate their position in the levelwise enumeration of the nodes.*

Let us find the minimum from $k = 3$ to $k' = 7$. The numbers $k - 1 = 2 = \mathsf{0010}$ and $k' - 1 = 6 = \mathsf{0110}$ differ in their third bit (that is, the most significant bit where they differ is the third, counting from the right), thus $h = 3$. This is the height of node v^*, which is the ℓth left-to-right node at that height, for $\ell = \lceil k/2^h \rceil = \lceil 3/8 \rceil = 1$. Therefore, $v^* = n'/2^h + \ell - 1 = 16/8 + 1 - 1 = 2$ (node v^* is drawn with a bold border).

Node $v^* = 2$ covers $m[s, e] = m[1, 8]$. Its left child, node $2v^* = 4$, covers $m[s, p] = m[1, 4]$, and its right child, node $2v^* + 1 = 5$, covers $m[p + 1, e] = m[5, 8]$. Then the minimum of $m[3, 7]$ is either the minimum of $m[k, p] = m[3, 4]$ or the minimum of $m[p + 1, k'] = m[5, 7]$. The former is $R[2v^*][p - k] = R[4][1] = 3$, and the latter is $L[2v^* + 1][k' - p - 1] = L[5][2] = 2$ (arrays L and R are numbered from 0). The minimum is then 2, the smaller of $R[4][1]$ and $L[5][2]$.

Solving $\mathsf{rmq}(i, j)$ *and* $\mathsf{rMq}(i, j)$

Recall our scheme of partitioning the search for the minimum global excess in range $[i, j]$ into buckets k_1, k_2, and the range between $k = k_1 + 1$ and $k' = k_2 - 1$. After determining that the minimum is μ, we can easily solve $\mathsf{rmq}(i, j)$ as follows. First, we see if $\mu = \mu_1 + e[k_1]$. If it is, then we return $\mathsf{rmq}(i - (k_1 - 1)\beta, \beta)$ in bucket k_1, as the leftmost occurrence of μ lies there. Otherwise, if μ is reached in the buckets k to k', the answer is the leftmost position where μ occurs in the range $[(k-1)\beta+1, k'\beta]$. Otherwise the answer is in bucket k_2, at position $\mathsf{rmq}(1, j - (k_2 - 1)\beta)$.

To return the leftmost minimum in buckets k to k' we store, apart from arrays L and R, arrays Lp and Rp, giving the leftmost positions where the minimum occurs inside the bucket ranges. More precisely, if v covers $m[s, e]$, then we store (for v being a right or a left child, respectively)

$$Lp[v][p] = \mathsf{rmq}((s-1)\beta+1, (s+p)\beta) \text{ or}$$

$$Rp[v][p] = \mathsf{rmq}((e-p-1)\beta+1, e\beta).$$

Arrays Lp and Rp are easy to build if we know the leftmost position of the minimum in each bucket, which are computed in an $\mathcal{O}(n)$-time pass over B.

Thus, after we find node v^* splitting $[k, k']$ into ranges $[k, p]$ at $2v^*$ and $[p+1, k']$ at $2v^* + 1$, we do as follows: if $R[2v^*][p-k] \leq L[2v^*+1][k'-p-1]$, we return $Rp[2v^*][p-k]$, otherwise we return $Lp[2v^*+1][k'-p-1]$.

Example 7.16 *In Figure 7.9, the array $Rp[4][0, 3]$ for node 4 is $\langle 13, 9, 7, 1 \rangle$, and the array $Lp[5][0, 3]$ for node 5 is $\langle 19, 22, 22, 22 \rangle$ (see also Figure 7.7, since those are positions in B). In the query of Example 7.15, we chose $L[5][2] = 2$, thus the leftmost position is $Lp[5][2] = 22$. This is, indeed, $\mathsf{rmq}((k-1)\beta+1, k'\beta) = \mathsf{rmq}(9, 28)$.*

Operation $\mathsf{rMq}(i, j)$ is solved with analogous structures for the maxima. Note that arrays L and R are redundant once we have Lp and Rp, because $L[v][p] = m[\lceil Lp[v][p]/\beta \rceil]$ and $R[v][p] = m[\lceil Rp[v][p]/\beta \rceil]$; the same occurs for the maxima and array $M[\cdot]$.

Solving $\mathsf{mincount}(i, j)$

For $\mathsf{mincount}(i, j)$, we first compute the minima μ, μ_1, μ_2, and μ_3, and then return $t_1 + t_2 + t_3$, which are computed as follows. First, if $\mu < \mu_1 + e[k_1]$, then $t_1 = 0$, otherwise we compute $t_1 = \mathsf{mincount}(i - (k_1 - 1)\beta, \beta)$ inside the bucket k_1. Second, if $\mu < \mu_2 + e[k_2]$, then $t_2 = 0$, otherwise we compute $t_2 = \mathsf{mincount}(1, j - (k_2 - 1)\beta)$ inside the bucket k_2. Finally, if $\mu < \mu_3$, then $t_3 = 0$, otherwise t_3 is the number of times the minimum of $m[k, k']$ occurs inside buckets k to k'.

To find this latter number we also store arrays Ln and Rn giving the number of times the minima occur in the area considered by each cell, that is, if v covers $m[s, e]$, we store (for right or left children, respectively)

$$Ln[v][p] = \mathsf{mincount}((s-1)\beta+1, (s+p)\beta) \text{ or}$$

$$Rn[v][p] = \mathsf{mincount}((e-p-1)\beta+1, e\beta).$$

These arrays are easily built if we know the number of times the minimum occurs in each bucket, which can be computed in an $\mathcal{O}(n)$-time pass over B.

Thus, after finding v^* and p, we do as follows: if $R[2v^*][p-k] < L[2v^*+1][k'-p-1]$, then $t_3 = Rn[2v^*][p-k]$; if $L[2v^*+1][k'-p-1] < R[2v^*][p-k]$, then $t_3 = Ln[2v^*+1][k'-p-1]$; and otherwise $t_3 = Ln[2v^*+1][k'-p-1] + Rn[2v^*][p-k]$ since both sides have the same minimum.

Example 7.17 *In Figure 7.9, the array* $Rn[4][0, 3]$ *for node 4 is* $\langle 2, 1, 1, 2 \rangle$, *and the array* $Ln[5][0, 3]$ *for node 5 is* $\langle 1, 1, 1, 1 \rangle$ *(see also Figure 7.7). In the query of Example 7.15, we chose* $L[5][2] = 2 < 3 = R[4][1]$, *thus the number of times the minimum 2 appears in the range is* $Ln[5][2] = 1$. *This is, indeed,* $\mathsf{mincount}((k-1)\beta + 1, k'\beta) = \mathsf{mincount}(9, 28)$.

Solving $\mathsf{minselect}(i, j, t)$

Finally, to solve $\mathsf{minselect}(i, j, t)$ we first compute the value t_1 of $\mathsf{mincount}(i, j)$. Then, if $t \le t_1$, we just return $\mathsf{minselect}(i - (k_1 - 1)\beta, \beta, t)$ inside bucket k_1, otherwise we set $t \leftarrow t - t_1$.

Now we compute t_3 of $\mathsf{mincount}(i, j)$ and check whether $t \le t_3$, in which case we return the tth occurrence of the minimum in $[(k-1)\beta + 1, k'\beta]$. Otherwise we set $t \leftarrow t - t_3$ and return $\mathsf{minselect}(1, j - (k_2 - 1)\beta, t)$ inside bucket k_2.

Therefore, we need to find the tth occurrence of the minimum of $m[k, k']$ inside the range $[(k-1)\beta + 1, k'\beta]$. Note that arrays Ln and Rn already have the information on the number of times the minimum occurs inside their areas. Assume we have computed v^* and p. Then, if $\mu = R[2v^*][p - k]$, we must consider the $Rn[2v^*][p - k]$ occurrences of μ in $m[k, p]$. If $t \le Rn[2v^*][p - k]$, we return the tth occurrence of μ in buckets k to p, otherwise we set $t \leftarrow t - Rn[2v^*][p - k]$. If the answer is not in R, we return the tth occurrence of μ in buckets $p + 1$ to k'.

Consider finding the tth occurrence of μ in buckets k to p; the other case is symmetric and uses L instead of R. We have $R[2v^*][p - k] = \mu$, that is, the minimum in buckets k to p is μ. It also holds $R[2v^*][p - k - 1] = \mu$ if the minimum in buckets $k + 1$ to p is μ, $R[2v^*][p - k - 2] = \mu$ if the minimum in buckets $k + 2$ to p is μ, and so on, until we reach some $R[2v^*][p - k - g - 1] > \mu$, meaning that μ does not appear anymore in buckets $k + g + 1$ to p (it may be that $g = p - k$ if μ is the minimum up to bucket p). Then the numbers

$$Rn[2v^*][p - k] - Rn[2v^*][p - k - 1],$$

$$Rn[2v^*][p - k] - Rn[2v^*][p - k - 2], \dots,$$

$$Rn[2v^*][p - k] - Rn[2v^*][p - k - g],$$

$$Rn[2v^*][p - k]$$

form a nondecreasing sequence that gives the number of times μ appears in buckets k, k to $k + 1$, k to $k + 2$, and so on until k to $k + g - 1$ and finally k to p. We are interested in finding the point $0 \le q < g$ such that

$$Rn[2v^*][p - k] - Rn[2v^*][p - k - q] < t \le Rn[2v^*][p - k] - Rn[2v^*][p - k - q - 1],$$

or else $q = g$, because this means that the tth occurrence of μ is within the bucket $k + q$, and we can find it with

$$\mathsf{minselect}(1, \beta, t - (Rn[2v^*][p - k] - Rn[2v^*][p - k - q]))$$

inside that bucket.

Therefore, given an area of values $R[2v^*][p - k - g] = \dots = R[2v^*][p - k] = \mu$, what is needed is to build a predecessor data structure on the nondecreasing values

$Rn[2v^*][p - k - g], \ldots, Rn[2v^*][p - k]$ so as to find the predecessor of $Rn[2v^*][p - k] - t$. Just as in Section 7.2.2, it holds that successive values in Rn within an area with the same μ differ at most by β, and thus we can find predecessors in time $\mathcal{O}(\log \log n)$. This time, however, there may be repeated values in Rn. These can be handled analogously as done in Section 4.5.1 for partial sums: Mark in a bitvector B only the distinct values in the area of Rn, and for each new 1 in B append $0^{d-1}1$ to a bitvector Z, where d is the number of times that value appears in the area of Rn. Then we compute $r = \mathsf{rank}(B, x)$, the number of distinct values up to x in B, and $\mathsf{select}(Z, r)$ is the total number of values, that is, the predecessor of x.

Example 7.18 *As a very small example, in Figure 7.9, the array $Rn[4][0, 3]$ for node 4 is $\langle 2, 1, 1, 2 \rangle$, and the corresponding array $R[4][0, 3]$ is $\langle 5, 3, 1, 1 \rangle$. The entries $R[4][2, 3]$ have the same minimum value, 1. These correspond to the first 2 blocks, where $m = 1$ is reached once in each. Accordingly, the number of occurrences of this minimum in $Rn[4][2, 3]$ is $\langle 1, 2 \rangle$. If we have to solve $\mathsf{minselect}(i, j, t)$ within this area, we want to find the bucket in this list where t is reached, so that we can then enter the bucket to find the precise position.*

7.2.4 Rank and Select Operations

The various basic and extended rank and select operations are not solved through any rmM-tree, but instead are implemented directly over B using the techniques of Chapter 4, as described in Section 7.1.4. To obtain $\mathcal{O}(\log \log n)$ time for those operations while still using $\mathcal{O}(n/ \log n)$ extra bits of space, we can implement rank and select as in Section 4.3.2.

7.3 Multi-Parenthesis Sequences

Sequences of parentheses can be generalized to having σ *types* of parentheses. This can describe a set of superimposed hierarchies. Seen separately, each type of parenthesis defines a hierarchy. Their union may or may not, depending on the application, form a global hierarchy.

Example 7.19 *A multi-parentheses sequence with $\sigma = 3$ types, forming a single hierarchy, is '[([ ] { ( ) }) { }]'. An example forming independent hierarchies is '([ ) { [( ] })] [ ]'.*

A useful representation of a multi-parentheses sequence $P[1, n]$ (over alphabet $[1, 2\sigma]$, to account for the opening and closing parenthesis of each type) consists of

1. a sequence $S[1, n]$ on alphabet $[1, \sigma]$ (Chapter 6);
2. simple parenthesis sequences $B_t[1, n_t]$, one for each $t \in [1, \sigma]$, with $\sum_{t=1}^{\sigma} n_t = n$;
3. optionally, a simple global parentheses sequence $B[1, n]$.

In S we encode the types of the parentheses, but not if they are opening or closing; this is encoded separately in B. The sequences B_t encode the parentheses of B that are of type t, $B_t[i] = B[\mathsf{select}_t(S, i)]$. The total space is $n \log \sigma + 2n$ bits, plus a sublinear part to support rank and select on S and navigation on the parentheses of B and all the B_t. If some types are more frequent than others, then compressed representations of S will save space.

The purpose of B is to allow navigation on the whole hierarchy without regard for the types of the parentheses, in case all the types integrate into a single hierarchy. If this is not the case, or we do not need the global navigation, then B can be dropped. The sequence S and the parenthesis sequences B_t are sufficient for navigating each hierarchy separately and for switching from one to the other. In this case the total space becomes $n \log \sigma + n = n \log(2\sigma)$ bits, the same as a plain storage of $P[1, n]$.

The sequence S is used as a common domain to switch to any desired hierarchy. For example, given the global position $P[i]$ of some opening parenthesis, we can find the smallest segment of type $t \in [1, \sigma]$ containing it: We start with $p \leftarrow \mathsf{rank}_t(S, i)$, which gives the position in B_t of the last parenthesis of type t in $P[1, i]$. If $B_t[p] = 1$, then this is the correct starting point of the segment. We compute $q = \mathsf{close}(B_t, p)$ and return the global segment $[\mathsf{select}_t(S, p), \mathsf{select}_t(S, q)]$. Instead, if $B_t[p] = 0$, we have found a closing parenthesis. It is easy to see that the correct answer is the smallest segment enclosing p in B_t. Therefore, we adjust $p \leftarrow \mathsf{enclose}(B_t, \mathsf{open}(B_t, p)) = \mathsf{bwdsearch}(B_t, p, -1) + 1$, and then find q and map to S as before. Note that we have made no use of B.

Example 7.20 *Let* $P[1, 12] = $ '[([ ] { ( ) }) { }]'. *Let us use the symbols* p, s, *and* c *for parentheses, square, and curly brackets, respectively. Then our representation of* P *is* $S = $ spsscppcpccs, $B = (((( ) (()))( ))$, *and the sequences* $B_p = (())$, $B_s = [[]]$, *and* $B_c = \{\}\{\}$ *(we respect their types for clarity, but all are actually bitvectors).*

To find the lowest parenthesis ($t = $ p) *that contains* $P[5]$, *we find* $p \leftarrow \mathsf{rank}_p(S, 5) = 1$. *Since* $B_p[p] = 1$, *the segment in* B_p *is the one starting at* $p = 1$ *and ending at* $q = \mathsf{close}(B_p, p) = 4$. *Now we map the segment* $[p, q] = [1, 4]$ *to* S, *returning* $[\mathsf{select}_p(S, p), \mathsf{select}_p(S, q)] = [2, 9]$.

The same query for $t = $ s *and* $i = 7$ *yields* $p \leftarrow \mathsf{rank}_s(S, 7) = 3$, *but now* $B_s[p] = 0$. *Therefore, we adjust* $p \leftarrow \mathsf{enclose}(B_s, \mathsf{open}(B_s, 3)) = \mathsf{enclose}(B_s, 2) = 1$. *Then we find* $q \leftarrow \mathsf{close}(B_s, p) = 4$ *and map the answer to* S, *returning* $[\mathsf{select}_s(S, p), \mathsf{select}_s(S, q)] = [1, 12]$.

Algorithm 7.13 summarizes the procedure. Other navigation operations are easily implemented, for example, finding the first descendant of a certain type (in case there is a global hierarchy). In Section 9.4 we will use multi-parentheses to represent planar graphs.

7.3.1 Nearest Marked Ancestors

An important application of multi-parenthesis sequences is the following. We have some segments that are marked, and in addition to the normal navigation of the hierarchy, we might need to move to the nearest marked ancestor of a segment.

This is directly solved with Algorithm 7.13. In this case, we have all the hierarchy in B, and the sequence S of the types is also binary, with $S[i] = 1$ iff the parenthesis $B[i]$

Algorithm 7.13: Finding the smallest segment of a type containing a position.

---

1 **Proc** *encloseType*(P, t, i)

    Input : Multi-parentheses sequence $P[1, n]$ (seen as sequence S, and bitvectors B and B_t), type t, and the position i of an opening parenthesis in P.

    Output: Returns the smallest segment of type t in P that contains $P[i]$.

2     $p \leftarrow \mathsf{rank}_t(S, i)$

3   **if** $B_t[p] = 0$ **then**

4         $p \leftarrow \mathsf{bwdsearch}(B_t, p, -1) + 1$

5     $q \leftarrow \mathsf{close}(B_t, p)$

6   **return** $[\mathsf{select}_t(S, p), \mathsf{select}_t(S, q)]$

---

is marked. In addition, we have the sequences B_0 of the unmarked parentheses and B_1 of the marked ones. Since we are not navigating over the unmarked segments, we may drop B_0, retaining only B for normal navigation and S and B_1 for moving to marked ancestors.

If we have m marked segments, the total space is $2n + m + o(n)$ bits. If m is very small compared with n, we may represent S as a compressed bitvector (Chapter 4), which yields $n + m \log(n/m) + \mathcal{O}(m) + o(n)$ bits in total.

7.4 Applications

As stated in the beginning of this chapter, balanced parentheses are a basic abstract structure whose most important applications are in the representation of trees (Chapter 8) and graphs (Chapter 9). Nevertheless, we describe a couple of other applications here.

7.4.1 Succinct Range Minimum Queries

In Section 7.2.3 we studied the problem of, given an array $A[1, n]$ of arbitrary numbers, returning the leftmost position of a minimum in any range $A[i, j]$. The solution we used required $\mathcal{O}(n \log n)$ words of space (this was not a problem because we used it on a small array). Using parentheses these queries, which we call $\mathsf{rmq}_A(i, j)$, can be solved using just $2n + o(n)$ bits *without accessing A at all*. That is, we could even delete A and the data structure would still be able to answer queries $\mathsf{rmq}_A(i, j)$.

The main structure to achieve this is the left-to-right minima tree of Section 7.2.2, built on A. Note that, if we start from the node that represents i and move upwards from the node, we reach nodes v with progressively smaller values that are to the right of i, while all the skipped values are larger than that of v. At some point, however, we move from a node v to a node u that is to the right of j. Then the smallest value in $[i, j]$ was that of the last node v.

Example 7.21 *Figure 7.10 shows an array $A[1, 21]$ and its left-to-right minima tree (the segments and parentheses will be used soon). To find $\mathsf{rmq}_A(5, 10)$, we start from*

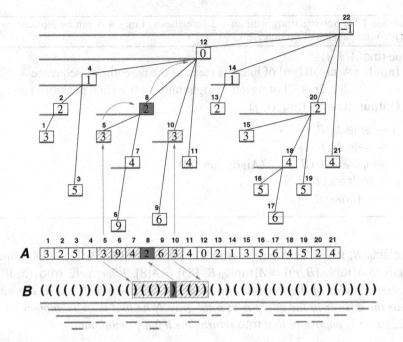

Figure 7.10. An array A, its left-to-right minima tree, and its parentheses representation B. The parentheses represent the hierarchy of segments (in gray, on the bottom) resulting from the subtree inclusion (the segments are also shown covering the subtree areas). Arrows and shades illustrate the process to solve operation $\mathsf{rmq}(5, 10)$: the rmq on A is projected onto an rmq on the excess in B, therefore array A is not really needed. The areas in A and B, as well as the extreme nodes in the tree, are hatched. The answer to the query is grayed.

the node of 5 and climb to its successive ancestors. The parent of node 5 is the node 8. Then the parent of node 8 is the node 12, but this is after the right limit, 10. Thus, the minimum in $A[5, 10]$ is at $A[8]$.

Therefore, we can answer $\mathsf{rmq}_A(i, j)$ without consulting A at all; just the topology of the left-to-right minima tree suffices. To obtain the promised $2n + o(n)$ bits, we represent the hierarchy of this tree (of $n + 1$ nodes) with $n + 1$ segments: the segment of node v covers all the cells in the subtree rooted at v. This is a contiguous area that ends precisely at the cell of v. Therefore, the node representing $A[i]$ corresponds to the ith endpoint of a segment, left to right.

The containment relation between segments will be represented with parentheses, in a bitvector $B[1, 2n + 2]$. Therefore, the cells $A[i]$ and $A[j]$ correspond to the ith and jth closing parentheses, at positions $p = \mathsf{select}_0(B, i)$ and $q = \mathsf{select}_0(B, j)$, respectively. The highest ancestor of the node of i that is not to the right of j corresponds to the highest segment that ends within $[p, q]$. Its endpoint is then $r = \mathsf{rmq}(B, p, q)$, and thus its position in A is $\mathsf{rank}_0(B, r)$. Algorithm 7.14 gives the pseudocode.

Example 7.22 *Consider the parentheses in Figure 7.10 and the associated segments in gray. The segment corresponding to $A[5]$ ends at the closing parenthesis in $B[p]$, where $p = \mathsf{select}_0(B, 5) = 13$. The segment of $A[10]$ ends at $B[q]$, for*

Algorithm 7.14: Solving rmq_A with $2n + 2$ parentheses. Lines 4–5 can be replaced by the $\text{rmq}(p, q)$ computation of Section 7.2.3.

---

1 **Proc** $\text{rmq}(A, i, j)$

    Input : Array $A[1, n]$ of integers (seen as the parentheses sequence
                $B[1, 2n + 2]$ of its left-to-right minima tree) and positions i and j.
    Output: Returns $\text{rmq}_A(i, j)$.

2      $p \leftarrow \text{select}_0(B, i)$
3      $q \leftarrow \text{select}_0(B, j)$
4      $m \leftarrow \textit{minexcess}(B, p, q)$ (Algorithm 7.8)
5      $r \leftarrow \text{fwdsearch}(B, p - 1, m)$
6   **return** $\text{rank}_0(B, r)$

$q = \text{select}_0(B, 10) = 22$. *Now* $r = \text{rmq}(B, p, q) = \text{rmq}(B, 13, 22) = 18$, *which corresponds to* $A[\text{rank}_0(B, r)] = A[\text{rank}_0(B, 18)] = A[8]$. *Effectively,* $\text{rmq}_A(5, 10) = 8$. *The extreme nodes of the tree and the range of the query in A and B are hatched, whereas the answer to the query is in solid gray. Note that there is another minimum at $B[22]$, so it is important that* rmq *returns the leftmost minimum.*

It is tempting to replace the technique taking $\mathcal{O}(n \log n)$ words used in Section 7.2.3 by our new rmq_A that requires only $2n + o(n)$ bits. Note, however, that this succinct solution makes use of the rmq operation on the parentheses, and this in turn uses, precisely, that rmq_A solution of Section 7.2.3 (this causes no space problems because it is applied on $\mathcal{O}(n/\log^3 n)$ elements).

Construction

We can build the parentheses representation on top of the left-to-right minima tree built in Section 7.2.2, where we represented it via parent pointers (using the field *next*). This time, as construction space is more relevant, we overwrite the cells of A to avoid using any extra space. We do not generate the parent pointers; we instead write the $2n + 2$ parentheses directly, from right to left. The stack of the left-to-right minima is maintained using the rightmost cells of A. Algorithm 7.15 gives the details.

7.4.2 XML Documents

Our second application is the representation of XML documents. In XML a text collection is hierarchically structured with the use of *tags*. Tags are marks in the text, which come in the form of an opening tag (written `<tag>`) and a closing tag (written `</tag>`). Tags can nest, but cannot overlap (that is, there cannot be something like `<t1> <t2> </t1> </t2>`). There are also tags that occupy a single position, `<tag/>`, which are usually interpreted as `<tag></tag>`. Tags may have "attributes," which can be interpreted as special tags inside the content of the original tag.

We will use parentheses and bitvectors to solve the following problem: given a position in the text file, which is the structural node it belongs? Let us regard the XML text as a sequence of n tokens, t of which are tags. A bitvector $B[1, n]$ will mark with 1s

---

Algorithm 7.15: Building the parentheses representation of the left-to-right minima hierarchy. The rightmost part of A is rewritten to be used as a stack with the current left-to-right minima.

Input : Array $A[1, n]$ of integers.
Output: Builds $B[2n + 2]$, the parentheses representation of the left-to-right minima tree hierarchy of A.

1 $s \leftarrow n + 1$ (top of stack in A)
2 Allocate bitvector $B[1, 2n + 2]$
3 $B[2n + 2] \leftarrow 0$
4 $j \leftarrow 2n + 1$ (where to write in B)
5 **for** $i \leftarrow n$ **downto** 1 **do**
6   **while** $s \le n$ **and** $A[i] \le A[s]$ **do**
7           $s \leftarrow s + 1$
8           $B[j] \leftarrow 1; j \leftarrow j - 1$
9       $s \leftarrow s - 1$
10      $A[s] \leftarrow A[i]$
11      $B[j] \leftarrow 0; j \leftarrow j - 1$
12 **while** $j > 0$ **do**
13      $B[j] \leftarrow 1; j \leftarrow j - 1$

---

the tag positions, and aligned to its 1s, a parentheses sequence $P[1, t]$ will describe the nesting structure of the tags.

Example 7.23 *Figure 7.11 shows parts of a book example, where words and tags are tokens. On the left of the tags we show the resulting hierarchical segment structure. The bitvector at their left marks the beginnings and endings of the segments (that is, positions of tags) with 1s, and the positions of the other words with 0s. Aligned to the 1s, the parentheses describe the hierarchy of segments. Arrows and blocks will be used soon.*

Now, given a text position i, we can find the previous tag with $m \leftarrow \mathsf{pred}(B, i)$. The corresponding position in P is $p \leftarrow \mathsf{rank}(B, m) = \mathsf{rank}(B, i)$ (that is, we do not need to compute m). If $P[p]$ is an opening parenthesis, then it is the opening position of the innermost segment that contains position i. Otherwise the segment is $p \leftarrow \mathsf{enclose}(P, \mathsf{open}(P, p)) = \mathsf{bwdsearch}(P, p, -1) + 1$. In both cases the starting position of the segment in the text is $\mathsf{select}(B, p)$.

Example 7.24 *Let i be the position of the grayed word* Kraft *in Figure 7.11. Then positions m and p are grayed in B and P, and we find that the word is inside the name of the theorem, which starts at position $i - 2$ (also grayed).*

Instead, let i be the position of the hatched word countably. *Initial positions m and p are hatched in B and P. However, since $P[p]$ is a closing parenthesis, we change it to $p = \mathsf{enclose}(P, \mathsf{open}(P, p))$, which corresponds to the start of the theorem structure (also hatched).*

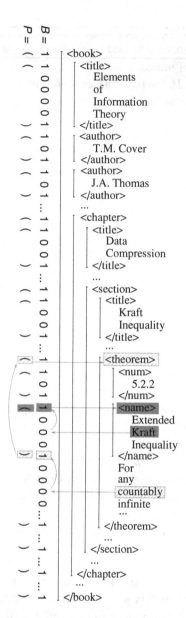

Figure 7.11. Part of the XML structure of a book. Shades and arrows illustrate the process of finding the smallest structure containing the words Kraft and countably.

Note the similarity of this solution with that for nearest marked ancestors (Section 7.3.1). In fact, we can use Algorithm 7.13 verbatim with $t = 1$, $S = B$, and $B_1 = P$. General multi-parenthesis sequences can also be used to distinguish different types of XML tags. For example, some tags may indicate how the text below them must be displayed (as in the HTML tags that indicate type, size and color of the font, and so on).[3] If we have to display a text excerpt without processing the document from the

---

[3] HTML is an instantiation of XML used to format Web pages, where there is a set of tags with predefined meaning.

beginning, we may ask for all the successive nearest ancestors in the HTML hierarchy that are of the type that affects the formatting.

7.5 Summary

A balanced sequence of n parentheses is a bitvector that describes hierarchical or containment relations along a line. Various operations that navigate the hierarchy toward parents and children can be implemented using $n + o(n)$ bits and taking $\mathcal{O}(\log n)$ time, or even $\mathcal{O}(\log \log n)$ with a more sophisticated implementation. The construction requires linear time and $o(n)$ bits on top of the parentheses sequence. Sequences of multiple parenthesis types can also be handled. Parentheses permit implementing range minimum queries in $2n + o(n)$ bits; many other uses will be seen in Chapters 8 and 9.

7.6 Bibliographic Notes

Basic operations. Jacobson (1989) initiated the study of the representation of balanced parentheses, in order to navigate trees and graphs using the operations **open**, **close**, and **enclose** (plus **rank** and **select**). Munro and Raman (2001) then improved the space to asymptotically optimal and the operation times to constant. Geary *et al.* (2006) introduced a simpler solution for those operations, which is implementable. In all cases, the idea is to define *pioneer* parentheses as those whose matching parenthesis is *far* (i.e., in another block, after cutting the sequence into blocks). By storing matching information about pioneers, the operations are reduced to within-block searches. A further level of smaller blocks reduces the searches to an interval of size $\mathcal{O}(\log n)$, which can be scanned in constant time using global precomputed tables. Recently, Vigna (2013) started the study of fast solutions to these queries by resorting to bit manipulations instead of precomputed tables. Note that, with these few operations, we cannot move directly to the tth child or to the dth ancestor of a segment, for example.

Fully functional parentheses. Navarro and Sadakane (2014) proposed the range min-max tree and used it to solve all the operations we describe in Section 7.1 in a unified form. Many of those operations required separate sublinear structures in previous work (Chiang *et al.*, 2005; Sadakane, 2007; Lu and Yeh, 2008; Munro *et al.*, 2012). While Navarro and Sadakane also describe a constant-time solution, we have opted for their simple $\mathcal{O}(\log n)$-time variant, which is easy to implement. The $\mathcal{O}(\log \log n)$ time structures we describe in Section 7.2 (Córdova and Navarro, 2016) are inspired by the constant-time solution, but here we strived for simplicity of implementation. Arroyuelo *et al.* (2010) showed that already the $\mathcal{O}(\log n)$-time variant is faster, in practice, than other implementable constant-time representations (Geary *et al.*, 2006) in various realistic application scenarios, and Córdova and Navarro (2016) show that the variant of Section 7.2 yields further improvements. Section 8.7 gives more details.

Multi-parentheses. Chuang *et al.* (1998) used multi-parenthesis sequences to encode planar graphs. Several others followed that path (Munro and Raman, 2001; Chiang *et al.*, 2005; Gavoille and Hanusse, 2008; Barbay *et al.*, 2012). Section 9.7 gives more details. The solution for nearest marked ancestors is explicitly described by Russo *et al.* (2011, Lemma 4.4).

Level-ancestor queries. The classical level-ancestor data structure we describe in Section 7.2.2 is based on the presentation by Bender and Farach-Colton (2004), although previous solutions exist (Berkman and Vishkin, 1994). The way we include weights follows Navarro and Sadakane (2014), who also introduce the left-to-right minima trees. These were independently discovered by Fischer and Heun (2011), who called them 2d-min-heaps. They gave a linear-time construction that, unlike the one we describe in Section 7.4.1, does not overwrite A and uses $n + o(n)$ extra bits.

Range-minimum queries. The rmq_A structure we used in Section 7.2.3 for an array of integers is not the most classical one. It is due to Yuan and Atallah (2010), and we chose it because it reduces the problem to two non-overlapping intervals; thus it is possible to add up the number of occurrences of the minima in each interval, for example. With this structure, our description is much simpler than the original one (Navarro and Sadakane, 2014), but it is unclear if we could speed it up to constant time.

The rmq_A problem has a fascinating history related to the lowest common ancestor (lca) problem on trees, that is, the lowest node that is an ancestor of two given tree nodes. Gabow *et al.* (1984) showed that rmq_A could be reduced to an lca problem on the *Cartesian tree* (Vuillemin, 1980) of the array. The Cartesian tree of $A[1, n]$ is a binary tree defined as follows: The root is the leftmost position p of a minimum in $A[1, n]$. Its left child is, recursively, the Cartesian tree of $A[1, p - 1]$, and its right child is the Cartesian tree of $A[p + 1, n]$. The Cartesian tree of an empty interval is the null pointer. In the Cartesian tree, the inorder number of a node corresponds to the position of A it represents, and the leftmost minimum in $A[i, j]$ is the inorder number of the lca of the nodes with inorders i and j. Figure 7.12 shows the Cartesian tree for

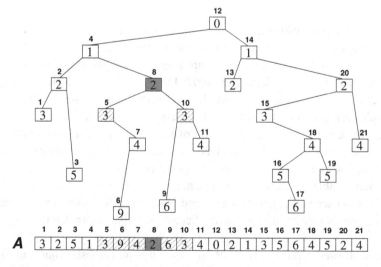

Figure 7.12. The Cartesian tree of the array of Figure 7.10, with the same areas and nodes shaded.

our example of Figure 7.10. The left-to-right minima tree we used in Section 7.4.1 is indeed the result of converting the (binary) Cartesian tree into a general tree. We will describe this transformation in detail in Section 8.2.1.

Berkman and Vishkin (1993), in turn, showed how to reduce the lca problem on any tree to an rmq_A problem (on the depths of the nodes in an Eulerian traversal of the tree), where consecutive entries in the array differ by ± 1. Bender *et al.* (2005) gave a simple solution to this restricted rmq_A problem in constant time and $\mathcal{O}(n)$ words of space. Following this path, any general rmq_A problem can be solved in constant time and linear space. Access to the original array A is still needed.

The first succinct solution for rmq without accessing A required $4n + o(n)$ bits: Sadakane (2007) presented an lca solution working only on the leaves of a suffix tree (Section 11.5). To use it on a Cartesian tree, one would have to add $n - 1$ artificial leaves, thus leading to the $4n$-bit space. The final $2n$-bit solution, by Fischer and Heun (2011), uses a parentheses representation of the left-to-right minima tree analogous to the one we describe in Section 7.4.1 (which they called 2d-min-heaps, as explained). However, the one we have presented is simpler and faster in practice (Ferrada and Navarro, 2016).

XML and HTML. The XML and HTML standards (Section 7.4.2) are described in http://www.w3.org/XML and http://www.w3.org/html. The example book we chose in Figure 7.11 is that of Cover and Thomas (2006).

Bibliography

Arroyuelo, D., Cánovas, R., Navarro, G., and Sadakane, K. (2010). Succinct trees in practice. In *Proc. 12th Workshop on Algorithm Engineering and Experiments (ALENEX)*, pages 84–97.

Barbay, J., Castelli Aleardi, L., He, M., and Munro, J. I. (2012). Succinct representation of labeled graphs. *Algorithmica*, **62**(1–2), 224–257.

Bender, M. and Farach-Colton, M. (2004). The level ancestor problem simplified. *Theoretical Computer Science*, **321**(1), 5–12.

Bender, M. A., Farach-Colton, M., Pemmasani, G., Skiena, S., and Sumazin, P. (2005). Lowest common ancestors in trees and directed acyclic graphs. *Journal of Algorithms*, **57**(2), 75–94.

Berkman, O. and Vishkin, U. (1993). Recursive star-tree parallel data structure. *SIAM Journal on Computing*, **22**(2), 221–242.

Berkman, O. and Vishkin, U. (1994). Finding level-ancestors in trees. *Journal of Computer and System Sciences*, **48**(2), 214–230.

Chiang, Y. T., Lin, C. C., and Lu, H.-I. (2005). Orderly spanning trees with applications. *SIAM Journal on Computing*, **34**(4), 924–945.

Chuang, R. C.-N., Garg, A., He, X., Kao, M.-Y., and Lu, H.-I. (1998). Compact encodings of planar graphs via canonical orderings and multiple parentheses. In *Proc. 25th International Colloquium on Automata, Languages and Programming (ICALP)*, LNCS 1443, pages 118–129.

Córdova, J. and Navarro, G. (2016). Simple and efficient fully-functional succinct trees. *CoRR*, **abs/1601.06939**. http://arxiv.org/abs/1601.06939.

Cover, T. and Thomas, J. (2006). *Elements of Information Theory*. Wiley, 2nd edition.

Ferrada, H. and Navarro, G. (2016). Improved range minimum queries. In *Proc. 26th Data Compression Conference (DCC)*, pages 516–525.

Fischer, J. and Heun, V. (2011). Space-efficient preprocessing schemes for range minimum queries on static arrays. *SIAM Journal on Computing*, **40**(2), 465–492.

Gabow, H. N., Bentley, J. L., and Tarjan, R. E. (1984). Scaling and related techniques for geometry problems. In *Proc. 16th ACM Symposium on Theory of Computing (STOC)*, pages 135–143.

Gavoille, C. and Hanusse, N. (2008). On compact encoding of pagenumber. *Discrete Mathematics and Theoretical Computer Science*, **10**(3), 23–24.

Geary, R. F., Rahman, N., Raman, R., and Raman, V. (2006). A simple optimal representation for balanced parentheses. *Theoretical Computer Science*, **368**(3), 231–246.

Jacobson, G. (1989). Space-efficient static trees and graphs. In *Proc. 30th IEEE Symposium on Foundations of Computer Science (FOCS)*, pages 549–554.

Lu, H.-I. and Yeh, C. (2008). Balanced parentheses strike back. *ACM Transactions on Algorithms*, **4**(3), 1–13.

Munro, J. I. and Raman, V. (2001). Succinct representation of balanced parentheses and static trees. *SIAM Journal on Computing*, **31**(3), 762–776.

Munro, J. I., Raman, R., Raman, V., and Rao, S. S. (2012). Succinct representations of permutations and functions. *Theoretical Computer Science*, **438**, 74–88.

Navarro, G. and Sadakane, K. (2014). Fully-functional static and dynamic succinct trees. *ACM Transactions on Algorithms*, **10**(3), article 16.

Russo, L. M. S., Navarro, G., and Oliveira, A. (2011). Fully-compressed suffix trees. *ACM Transactions on Algorithms*, **7**(4), article 53.

Sadakane, K. (2007). Compressed suffix trees with full functionality. *Theory of Computing Systems*, **41**(4), 589–607.

Vigna, S. (2013). Broadword implementation of parenthesis queries. *CoRR*, **abs/1301.5468**. http://arxiv.org/abs/1301.5468.

Vuillemin, J. (1980). A unifying look at data structures. *Communications of the ACM*, **23**(4), 229–239.

Yuan, H. and Atallah, M. J. (2010). Data structures for range minimum queries in multidimensional arrays. In *Proc. 21st Annual ACM-SIAM Symposium on Discrete Algorithms (SODA)*, pages 150–160.

CHAPTER 8

Trees

Trees are one of the most pervasive data structures in Computer Science. They are also one of the most striking success stories of compact data structures: We can represent a tree of n nodes using basically $2n$ bits instead of $\mathcal{O}(n)$ pointers (or machine words). Moreover, the compact representations have much richer functionality than most classical representations.

Let us distinguish two types of trees: *ordinal* and *cardinal*. Ordinal trees allow for an arbitrary number of children per node but distinguish only their order. For example, the parse tree of a program or the structure of an XML document are ordinal trees. Cardinal trees, instead, have a fixed set $[1, \sigma]$ of types of children, and each node might have one or no child of each type. The most common example of a cardinal tree is the binary tree, where each node may have a left and may have a right child. Having only a left child is not the same as having only a right child; an ordinal tree cannot make this distinction. Other examples are digital trees or tries (see Section 8.5.3), which have an alphabet $[1, \sigma]$ and there can be at most one child for each alphabet symbol.

In addition, trees can be *labeled*, meaning that edges have an associated label from an alphabet $[1, \sigma]$. For example, an XML tree can be regarded as a labeled tree if we associate the tag names with their corresponding edges. Unlike a trie, a labeled tree node may have several children with the same label, and they can appear in any order. Thus, a cardinal tree can be regarded as a special type of labeled tree. An alternative model labels the nodes, not the edges. The two models are not very different, as we can assign the label of the node to the edge that leads to it (making an exception for the root). Thus, we will consider only labels at the edges.

We will mainly consider ordinal trees in this chapter and show how the solutions are extended to cardinal and labeled trees. In Chapter 2 we showed that $2n - \Theta(\log n)$ bits are necessary to represent the topology of every possible ordinal tree of n nodes. On the other hand, classical pointer-based implementations of ordinal trees use at least n pointers (each non-root node is pointed by exactly one tree edge, and there is a pointer to the root). These n pointers require at least $n \log n$ bits (as each pointer must distinguish between the n target nodes) and typically use nw bits, with one word per pointer. We will instead show that $2n + o(n)$ bits are sufficient for representing any ordinal tree topology in a way that it is still efficiently navigable. Our representations are static; dynamism is deferred to Chapter 12.

The mere size obtained by these compact representations is not their most striking aspect. In fact, carefully engineered static representations using pointers of varying length can approach this size: Deploy the nodes linearly on a sequence, starting with the root and recursively writing the subtrees of its children, one after the other. Thus, the first child of each node is encoded right after it, and the node stores only a forward offset (in bits) to its next sibling. If the distance to its next sibling is d, then the whole subtree of the node can be encoded with $\lceil \log d \rceil$-bit pointers, and so on, recursively.

As said, this representation may achieve surprisingly little space and allows us to navigate to the first child and next sibling of a node in constant time. However, this navigation is rather limited. A classical representation may have an array of children to allow moving directly to the tth child, a pointer to the parent to move upwards, and so on. However, each new constant-time query or navigation operation we wish to support, like moving to an arbitrary ancestor of the node, moving to the first leaf in its subtree, knowing its subtree size, its preorder value, and so on, requires adding more and more fields to the node, thereby increasing the space. While many such operations can be supported using linear space (i.e., $\mathcal{O}(n)$ words), the constants quickly become large. Instead, the representations we will describe support, within $2n + o(n)$ bits, a large number of queries and navigation operations. See Table 8.1, which will be our guide.

We start with a simple levelwise representation of trees, LOUDS, that uses **rank** and **select** on bitvectors (Chapter 4) to provide a small number of operations, yet sufficient for many applications. When this functionality suffices, LOUDS is faster and smaller in practice than the other representations we study. We also show how binary and cardinal trees can be supported with LOUDS. Later, we describe a more powerful representation based on balanced parentheses, BP, and show how a large number of tree operations can be translated into a few primitives on parentheses (Chapter 7). We also revisit the binary trees under the BP representation. Finally, we introduce a different way to use the balanced parentheses, DFUDS, with a different mapping from tree operations to operations on parentheses. DFUDS is more efficient than BP for descending to the ith child, which is an important operation in various applications, but it does not support depth-related operations. We also show how cardinal trees are efficiently supported with DFUDS. At the end, we cover labeled trees, which arise in various applications and work best on LOUDS and DFUDS representations.

8.1 LOUDS: A Simple Representation

The representation called *Level-Order Unary Degree Sequence (LOUDS)*, is fully described by its name. Consider a bitvector $B[1, 2n + 1]$ where we first write 10 (which will avoid some border cases) and then traverse the tree level by level, starting from the root. For each new node v with c children, we append $1^c 0$ to B. We will call these $c + 1$ bits the *description* of node v. Thus, B clearly has $n + 1$ 0s, as we write one per node plus the initial one. It also has exactly n 1s, as we write one per edge plus the initial one.

Table 8.1. Operations on ordinal trees, separated in groups. The last group is for labeled trees. For simplicity, we take the tree T as implicit in the arguments of the operations.

Operation	Meaning
root()	The root node
fchild(v)	The first child of node v, if it exists
lchild(v)	The last child of node v, if it exists
nsibling(v)	The next sibling of node v, if it exists
psibling(v)	The previous sibling of node v, if it exists
parent(v)	The parent of node v, if it exists
isleaf(v)	Whether v is a leaf node
nodemap(v)	A unique identifier in $[1, n]$ for v, called its *index*
nodeselect(i)	The node v with index i
depth(v)	Depth of node v; the depth of the root is 1
height(v)	Height of node v; the height of a leaf is 0
deepestnode(v)	A deepest node in the subtree of node v
subtree(v)	Number of nodes in the subtree of v, counting v
isancestor(u, v)	Whether u is an ancestor of v (or v itself)
levelancestor(v, d)	The ancestor at distance d from v ($d=1$ is parent(v))
preorder(v)	Preorder value of v (first v, then each subtree)
preorderselect(i)	Node v with preorder i
postorder(v)	Postorder value of v (first each subtree, then v)
postorderselect(i)	Node v with postorder i
children(v)	Number of children of node v
child(v, t)	The tth child of node v, if it exists
childrank(v)	The t such that node v is the tth child of its parent
lca(u, v)	The lowest common ancestor of nodes u and v
leafnum(v)	The number of leaves in the subtree of node v
leafrank(v)	The number of leaves to the left of node v, plus 1
leafselect(i)	The ith left-to-right leaf node in the tree
childrenlabeled(v, l)	Number of children of node v via edges labeled l
labeledchild(v, l, t)	The tth left-to-right child of v by an edge labeled l
childlabel(v)	The label of the edge that leads to node v

We will preprocess B for binary **rank** and **select** queries on bitvectors (Chapter 4). Since B has almost as many 0s as 1s, we do not attempt to compress it with the techniques of Section 4.1; the variants designed for plain bitvectors are preferable. The LOUDS representation is just the bitvector B, and it supports the first and third group of operations of Table 8.1 within a constant amount of **rank** and **select** operations on B.

In a classical representation, nodes are identified with a pointer to their position in memory. In a LOUDS representation (and in all the others we will describe), they are identified by a position in B, from where their operations are easily performed. In LOUDS, in particular, the identifier of a node will be the first position of its description.

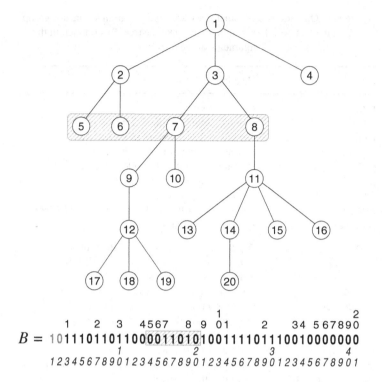

$$B = \texttt{10111011011000011010100111101110010000000}$$

Figure 8.1. An ordinal tree and its LOUDS representation, bitvector B. The numbers inside the nodes are the indexes given by operation **nodemap**. Those are also shown on top of each node in the bitvector. Below the bitvector we show its positions: the identifier of a node is the position where its description starts. The first 2 bits of B, in gray, do not correspond to any node. We highlight all the tree nodes at level 3, and their contiguous deployment in B.

Operations

The operation **nodemap** assigns to each node an *index* in $[1, n]$, and **nodeselect** maps indexes to nodes. These operations are useful for associating satellite data with nodes in a compact array of n cells. Since each node has exactly one 0 at the end, we use $\mathsf{nodemap}(v) = \mathsf{rank}_0(B, v - 1)$ and $\mathsf{nodeselect}(i) = \mathsf{select}_0(B, i) + 1$.

Example 8.1 *Figure 8.1 shows an ordinal tree and its LOUDS representation. Inside the nodes we write the indexes assigned by operation* **nodemap**. *Note that this corresponds to the levelwise order in which the nodes are deployed in LOUDS (the figure highlights a level of the tree and the contiguous area where it is deployed in the bitvector). The tree has $n = 20$ nodes, thus bitvector B has $2n + 1 = 41$ bits, 21 0s and 20 1s. Below the bitvector we write its positions; these act as node identifiers for all the operations. Thus the root node is 3, its identifier is* $\mathsf{nodemap}(3) = \mathsf{rank}_0(B, 3 - 1) = 1$, *and its description is $B[3, 6] = 1110$ because it has 3 children. The node with identifier 5 is* $\mathsf{nodeselect}(5) = \mathsf{select}_0(B, 5) + 1 = 14$, *and its description is $B[14] = 0$.*

Some other operations from Table 8.1 are also easy in LOUDS: $\mathsf{root}() = 3$ and $\mathsf{isleaf}(v)$ iff $B[v] = 0$ (the description of a leaf is simply a 0). Further, the number of children of v is $\mathsf{children}(v) = \mathsf{succ}_0(B, v) - v$. As explained in Section 4.5.2, succ

and pred can be implemented with rank and select, but faster implementations are possible.[1]

The remaining operations of the first and third group are easily built on top of child, parent, and childrank. The key to finding the tth child of v is to realize that, in B, the same nodes are enumerated twice, in the same order: The 0s enumerate the nodes as we traverse them, whereas the 1s enumerate the nodes as we traverse their parents (that is, the 1s enumerate the children of the nodes). Therefore, the tth 0 terminates the description of a node u that is a child of the node v in whose description appears the $(t-1)$th 1 (the shift is because the first node has no parent). This correspondence between 0s and 1s implies the following identities:

$$\mathsf{child}(v,t) = \mathsf{select}_0(B, \mathsf{rank}_1(B, v-1+t)) + 1,$$

$$\mathsf{parent}(v) = \mathsf{pred}_0(B, j) + 1, \text{ where } j = \mathsf{select}_1(B, \mathsf{rank}_0(B, v-1)),$$

$$\mathsf{childrank}(v) = j - \mathsf{pred}_0(B, j), \text{ for the same } j,$$

where j maps the node to its corresponding 1 in B, and then pred_0 finds the starting position of the parent (that is, where that run of 1s starts).

With these operations, we have that $\mathsf{fchild}(v) = \mathsf{child}(v,1)$, $\mathsf{lchild}(v) = \mathsf{child}(v, \mathsf{children}(v))$, $\mathsf{psibling}(v) = \mathsf{child}(\mathsf{parent}(v), \mathsf{childrank}(v) - 1)$ and, analogously, $\mathsf{nsibling}(v) = \mathsf{child}(\mathsf{parent}(v), \mathsf{childrank}(v) + 1)$. However, when we know that the operations can be applied, it is much faster to use $\mathsf{psibling}(v) = \mathsf{pred}_0(B, v-2) + 1$ and $\mathsf{nsibling}(v) = \mathsf{succ}_0(B, v) + 1$.

Algorithm 8.1 summarizes all the LOUDS operations we have described. Where necessary, we indicate the check that should be performed if we are not sure that the operation can be applied (for example, fchild on a leaf, psibling on a first child, and so on). In those cases one may return 0, indicating a null node. Note that in some operations like $\mathsf{psibling}(v)$ and $\mathsf{nsibling}(v)$, the check can be more expensive than the operation itself, and it may be unnecessary (for example, we might know the position of v among its siblings).

Example 8.2 *Figure 8.2 illustrates some operations on the representation of Figure 8.1. Node 10 has index* $\mathsf{nodemap}(10) = \mathsf{rank}_0(B, 10-1) = 3$, *and the node with index 3 is* $\mathsf{nodeselect}(3) = \mathsf{select}_0(B, 3) + 1 = 10$ *(this is shown in gray and with an arrow in the figure). Node 29 (the one with index 12) has* $\mathsf{children}(29) = \mathsf{succ}_0(B, 29) - 29 = 32 - 29 = 3$ *children (shown hatched), and its second one is* $\mathsf{child}(29, 2) = \mathsf{select}_0(B, \mathsf{rank}_1(B, 29-1+2)) + 1 = \mathsf{select}_0(B, 18) + 1 = 39$, *the node with index 18. For* $\mathsf{parent}(39)$, *we compute* $j = \mathsf{select}_1(B, \mathsf{rank}_0(B, 39-1)) = 30$, *and then* $\mathsf{parent}(39) = \mathsf{pred}_0(B, 30) + 1 = 29$, *the node with index 12. Node 39 is also the second child of its parent 29, because* $\mathsf{childrank}(39) = j - \mathsf{pred}_0(B, j) = 30 - 28 = 2$. *These relations are shown with double arrows in the*

---

[1] In this case, unless the tree has huge arities, a sequential chunkwise scan for the next or previous 0 is the best choice. Note that the techniques to find the highest or lowest 1 in a computer word bits seen in Section 4.5.2 can also be applied to find the highest or lowest 0 for succ_0 and pred_0, by inverting the bits of the word. In C, for example, this can be obtained with $\sim$bits; otherwise $2^w - 1 - $ bits has the same effect.

Algorithm 8.1: Computing the ordinal tree operations using LOUDS.

Input : Ordinal tree T (seen as LOUDS bitvector B), node v (a position in B), and indexes i and t.

1 **Proc** root(T)
2 $\quad$ **return** 3

3 **Proc** fchild(T, v) — *assuming* access$(B, v) = 1$
4 $\quad$ **return** child$(T, v, 1)$

5 **Proc** lchild(T, v) — *assuming* access$(B, v) = 1$
6 $\quad$ **return** child$(T, v, \text{children}(T, v))$

7 **Proc** nsibling(T, v) — *assuming* $B[\text{select}_1(B, \text{rank}_0(B, v-1)) + 1] = 1$
8 $\quad$ **return** $\text{succ}_0(B, v) + 1$

9 **Proc** psibling(T, v) — *assuming* $B[\text{select}_1(B, \text{rank}_0(B, v-1)) - 1)] = 1$
10 $\quad$ **return** $\text{pred}_0(B, v-2) + 1$

11 **Proc** parent(T, v) — *assuming* $v \neq 3$
12 $\quad$ $j \leftarrow \text{select}_1(B, \text{rank}_0(B, v-1))$
13 $\quad$ **return** $\text{pred}_0(B, j) + 1$

14 **Proc** isleaf(T, v)
15 $\quad$ **return** access$(B, v) = 0$

16 **Proc** nodemap(T, v)
17 $\quad$ **return** $\text{rank}_0(B, v-1)$

18 **Proc** nodeselect(T, i)
19 $\quad$ **return** $\text{select}_0(B, i) + 1$

20 **Proc** children(T, v)
21 $\quad$ **return** $\text{succ}_0(B, v) - v$

22 **Proc** child(T, v, t) — *assuming* $t \leq \text{children}(T, v)$
23 $\quad$ **return** $\text{select}_0(B, \text{rank}_1(B, v-1+t)) + 1$

24 **Proc** childrank(T, v) — *assuming* $v \neq 3$
25 $\quad$ $j \leftarrow \text{select}_1(B, \text{rank}_0(B, v-1))$
26 $\quad$ **return** $j - \text{pred}_0(B, j)$

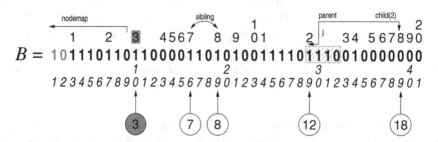

Figure 8.2. Illustration of the operations of Example 8.2 on the LOUDS representation of Figure 8.1.

Algorithm 8.2: Computing lca(u, v) on the LOUDS representation.

Input : Ordinal tree T (seen as LOUDS bitvector B), nodes u and v (positions in B).

Output: Returns lca(u, v).

1 **while** $u \neq v$ **do**
2   **if** $u > v$ **then**
3       $\lfloor u \leftarrow$ parent(T, u)
4   **else**
5       $\lfloor v \leftarrow$ parent(T, v)

6 **return** u

---

figure. The next sibling of node 16 *(with index* 7*) is* nsibling(16) = $\text{succ}_0(B, 16) + 1 = $ 19 *(with index* 8*) and the previous sibling of node* 19 *is* psibling(19) = $\text{pred}_0(B, 19 - 2) + 1 = 16$. *This is illustrated with a double curved arrow in the figure.*

Though LOUDS cannot solve other operations of Table 8.1 with a constant number of **rank** and **select** operations, a reasonably efficient technique can be used to compute one of the most complex ones, lca(u, v). The idea is to climb from u and v toward their ancestors until finding the meeting point in the paths. To make sure we meet at the right point, we can take the parent of the deeper of the two nodes at each step. Although LOUDS cannot efficiently compute the depth of a node, it holds that if $u > v$ (seen as bitvector positions), then depth(u) $\geq$ depth(v). Therefore, the procedure in Algorithm 8.2 can be applied. Also, when d is not large or when v is not too deep, operations isancestor(u, v), levelancestor(v, d) and depth(v) can be reasonably solved via successive **parent** operations.

Construction

The construction of the LOUDS representation of a tree that is given with a pointer representation makes use of a queue, where we initially put the root node and then repeatedly extract the first node, append $1^c 0$ to B, where c is the number of children of the node, and enqueue its c children. This is repeated until the queue becomes empty. The process takes linear time and at most nw bits of space for the queue, in addition to the original tree.

In many cases, it is possible to do better in terms of extra space, by reusing the same tree pointers. For example, assume the tree T is structured with two pointers in each node v: v.*first* points to the first child of v and v.*next* to its next sibling. We can then reuse the *next* fields to implement the queue as a linked list without using any extra space: since the children of a new node to enqueue are already linked by field *next*, we only have to make the *next* field of the last node in the queue point to the first node in the children list of the new node. It is even possible to recover the original pointer-based tree after the process (or we can free the tree nodes as we process them). Algorithm 8.3 shows the details. The bitvector B we generate can be immediately buffered and written to disk if necessary, therefore all we need is for the original tree T to fit in main memory.

Algorithm 8.3: Building the LOUDS representation from a pointer-based tree, without using any extra space. Lines 6 and 14–17 restore the tree; otherwise we can just free the node p after line 13.

Input : Ordinal tree T of n nodes, with fields *first* (first child) and *next* (next sibling).

Output: Builds the LOUDS representation $B[1, 2n + 1]$ of T.

1 $Q \leftarrow T.root$ (queue head)
2 $L \leftarrow T.root$ (queue tail)
3 Allocate bit array $B[1, 2n + 1]$
4 bitset$(B, 1)$; bitclear$(B, 2)$
5 $i \leftarrow 3$ (where we append bits in B)
6 $j \leftarrow 1$ (where the 1 of the node we are processing now is)
7 **while** $Q \neq$ null **do**
8 $\quad$ $L.next \leftarrow Q.first$
9 $\quad$ **while** $L.next \neq$ null **do**
10 $\quad\quad$ bitset(B, i); $i \leftarrow i + 1$
11 $\quad\quad$ $L \leftarrow L.next$
12 $\quad$ bitclear(B, i); $i \leftarrow i + 1$
13 $\quad$ $p \leftarrow Q$; $Q \leftarrow Q.next$
14 $\quad$ **if** bitread$(B, j + 1) = 0$ **then**
15 $\quad\quad$ $p.next \leftarrow$ null
16 $\quad\quad$ $j \leftarrow j + 1$
17 $\quad$ $j \leftarrow j + 1$
18 Preprocess B for **rank** and **select** queries (Chapter 4)

Alternatively, if T is on disk, we need to sort the nodes in levelwise order, and then we can read the nodes and write the bits of B by buffers, without need of a queue.

Time and Space in Practice

If we use the constant-time **rank** and **select** implementations of Sections 4.2.2 and 4.3.3 for B, the supported LOUDS operations take constant time. This comes at a significant extra space on top of the $2n$ bits of B. Since we have to implement the solutions for **rank**, **select**$_0$, and **select**$_1$, the total space may be around $3.6n$ bits. This may be acceptable in applications where the space of the tree topology is a small fraction of the total space of the data structures, and retaining fast operation times is important.

To reduce this space, we can use instead slower implementations of **rank** and **select**. For example, we can guarantee $\mathcal{O}(\log \log n)$ time (Section 4.3.2). Using the more practical variants of this idea, mentioned at the end of that section, the space is around $2.65n$ bits.

To reduce space further, we can use the heuristic techniques described in Sections 4.2.1 and 4.3.1. The time complexities then grow to $\mathcal{O}(\log n)$, but the space can be as low as $2.1n$ bits with acceptable performance. The implementation of the BP and DFUDS representations, which build on the parentheses of Chapter 7, is generally slower, and therefore even this low-memory variant of LOUDS is competitive in time with those representations. Its drawback is, as explained, its limited functionality.

8.1.1 Binary and Cardinal Trees

The LOUDS representation adapts well to cardinal trees. Let T be a cardinal tree on $[1, \sigma]$. Instead of using $1^c 0$ to represent a node with c children, we will represent nodes using σ bits, so that the kth bit tells whether the child of type k is present or not. In the case of binary trees, for example, leaves will be represented with 00, nodes with both children with 11, nodes with only a left child with 10, and nodes with only a right child with 01.

While different from the LOUDS representation of ordinal trees, we will still call LOUDS this cardinal tree representation, because it shares the same spirit.

Space

A cardinal tree with n nodes will require exactly σn bits, in the form of a bitvector $B[1, \sigma n]$. The number of cardinal trees is $|T_n^\sigma| = \binom{\sigma n + 1}{n}/(\sigma n + 1)$, and thus their worst-case entropy (Section 2.1) is

$$\mathcal{H}_{wc}(T_n^\sigma) = \log \frac{\binom{\sigma n + 1}{n}}{\sigma n + 1} = \left(\sigma \log \frac{\sigma}{\sigma - 1} + \log(\sigma - 1) \right) n - \mathcal{O}(\log n).$$

For example, for binary trees ($\sigma = 2$) our representation uses $2n$ bits, which asymptotically matches the lower bound $\mathcal{H}_{wc}(T_n^2) = 2n - \mathcal{O}(\log n)$. However, this does not happen for $\sigma = 3$, where we use $3n$ bits while the lower bound is $\mathcal{H}_{wc}(T_n^3) = (3\log(3/2) + 1)n - \mathcal{O}(\log n) < 2.755n$. As σ increases, the space of σn bits gets farther from the lower bound $\mathcal{H}_{wc}(T_n^\sigma) = n \log \sigma + \mathcal{O}(n)$. A simple way to match this lower bound is to use a compressed representation for bitvector B (Section 4.1). Since $B[1, \sigma n]$ has only $n - 1$ 1s (one per non-root node), we reach $n \log \sigma + \mathcal{O}(n\sigma \log \log n / \log n)$ bits of space, which is asymptotically optimal for small $\sigma = \mathcal{O}(\log n / \log \log n)$. Within this space, we can support rank in constant time and select in time $\mathcal{O}(\log \log n)$ (Sections 4.2.3 and 4.3.2).

For larger σ, we can use the representation for very sparse bitvectors (Section 4.4), which gives the asymptotically optimal space of $n \log \sigma + \mathcal{O}(n)$ bits. It supports rank in time $\mathcal{O}(\log \sigma)$ and select$_1$ in constant time. Section 8.4, however, will offer generally better techniques for handling these larger arities.

Operations

The given representation has various interesting properties. First, since the ith node in levelwise order starts at position $\sigma(i - 1) + 1$ in B, we can simplify and consider that i is the node identifier, thus removing the need of operations nodemap and nodeselect. Like in the ordinal trees, the 1s that signal the nodes at the description of their parents are also deployed in levelwise order: the ith 1 refers to the node described at position $\sigma \cdot i + 1$. Then node v (which, remember, is a levelwise index) has its lth child iff $B[\sigma(v - 1) + l] = 1$, and in this case it holds labeledchild$(v, l) =$

Algorithm 8.4: Computing the cardinal tree operations using LOUDS.

Input : Cardinal tree T on $[1, \sigma]$ (seen as LOUDS bitvector $B[1, \sigma n]$), node v, indexes i and t, and label l.

1 **Proc** root(T)
2 | **return** 1

3 **Proc** fchild(T, v) — *assuming* children(T, v) > 0
4 | **return** $\text{rank}_1(B, \sigma(v-1)) + 2$

5 **Proc** lchild(T, v) — *assuming* children(T, v) > 0
6 | **return** $\text{rank}_1(B, \sigma v) + 1$

7 **Proc** nsibling(T, v) — *assuming* $\lceil \text{succ}_1(B, j+1)/\sigma \rceil = \lceil j/\sigma \rceil$,
                          where $j = \text{select}_1(B, v-1)$
8 | **return** $v + 1$

9 **Proc** psibling(T, v) — *assuming* $\lceil \text{pred}_1(B, j-1)/\sigma \rceil = \lceil j/\sigma \rceil$, *same* j
10 | **return** $v - 1$

11 **Proc** parent(T, v) — *assuming* $v \neq 1$
12 | **return** $\lceil \text{select}_1(B, v-1)/\sigma \rceil$

13 **Proc** isleaf(T, v)
14 | **return** $\text{bitsread}(B, \sigma(v-1)+1, \sigma v) = 0^\sigma$

15 **Proc** children(T, v)
16 | **return** $popcount(\text{bitsread}(B, \sigma(v-1)+1, \sigma v))$

17 **Proc** child(T, v, t) — *assuming* $t \leq$ children(T, v)
18 | **return** $\text{rank}_1(B, \sigma(v-1)) + t + 1$

19 **Proc** childrank(T, v) — *assuming* $v \neq 1$
20 | $j \leftarrow \text{select}_1(B, v-1)$
21 | **return** $popcount(\text{bitsread}(B, (\lceil j/\sigma \rceil - 1)\sigma + 1, j))$

22 **Proc** childrenlabeled(T, v, l)
23 | **return** $B[\sigma(v-1)+l] = 1$

24 **Proc** labeledchild(T, v, l) — *assuming* childrenlabeled(T, v, l)
25 | **return** $\text{rank}_1(B, \sigma(v-1)+l) + 1$

26 **Proc** childlabel(T, v) — *assuming* $v \neq 1$
27 | **return** $((\text{select}_1(B, v-1) - 1) \bmod \sigma) + 1$

$\text{rank}_1(B, \sigma(v-1)+l) + 1$. Note that we are using the labeled tree terminology to refer to cardinal trees, assuming labeledchild(v, l) = labeledchild($v, l, 1$), which is the only choice in cardinal trees. We also take childrenlabeled(v, l) as a Boolean that tells whether the child labeled l exists or not. The parent of v is parent(v) = $\lceil j/\sigma \rceil$, where $j = \text{select}_1(B, v-1)$, and the position from where v descends from its parent is childlabel(v) = $((j-1) \bmod \sigma) + 1$.

We can also perform the classical ordinal navigation operations. Node v has children(v) = $\text{rank}_1(B, \sigma v) - \text{rank}_1(B, \sigma(v-1))$ children, and it holds isleaf(v)

Algorithm 8.5: Computing basic binary tree operations using LOUDS. We explicitly check if the operations can be applied.

Input : Binary tree T (seen as LOUDS bitvector $B[1, 2n]$) and node v.

1 **Proc** root(T)
2 $\quad$ **return** 1

3 **Proc** parent(T, v)
4 $\quad$ **if** $v = 1$ **then** **return** 0 (null)
5 $\quad$ **return** $\lceil$select$_1(B, v - 1)/2\rceil$

6 **Proc** isleaf(T, v)
7 $\quad$ **return** bitsread($B, 2v - 1, 2v$) = 00

8 **Proc** leftchild(T, v)
9 $\quad$ **if** access($B, 2v - 1$) = 0 **then return** 0 (null)
10 $\quad$ **return** rank$_1(B, 2v - 1) + 1$

11 **Proc** rightchild(T, v)
12 $\quad$ **if** access($B, 2v$) = 0 **then return** 0 (null)
13 $\quad$ **return** rank$_1(B, 2v) + 1$

14 **Proc** childlabel(T, v)
15 $\quad$ **if** $v = 1$ **then** **return** 0
16 $\quad$ **return** ((select$_1(B, v - 1) - 1$) mod 2) + 1

---

iff children(v) = 0.[2] The tth existing child of v, if it exists, is child(v, t) = rank$_1(B, \sigma(v - 1)) + t + 1$, and then fchild($v$) = rank$_1(B, \sigma(v - 1)) + 2$ and lchild(v) = rank$_1(B, \sigma v) + 1$. We have childrank(v) = rank$_1(B, j)$ − rank$_1(B, (\lceil j/\sigma \rceil - 1)\sigma)$ = $popcount(B[(\lceil j/\sigma \rceil - 1)\sigma + 1, j])$, where j is computed as for parent. The other operations are even simpler: nsibling(v) = $v + 1$ and psibling(v) = $v - 1$. Algorithm 8.4 summarizes all the operations. We indicate the check that should be performed to ensure that the operation can be applied. Operation lca(u, v) can be solved exactly as in Algorithm 8.2.

Algorithm 8.5 shows how the operations simplify in the case of binary trees. We remove various cardinal tree operations that make little sense on binary trees. Also, for clarity we use operations leftchild(v) and rightchild(v) instead of labeledchild($v, 1$) and labeledchild($v, 2$). In this case, we explicitly check whether the operations can be applied, returning the null tree identifier 0 if they cannot. This makes operation childrenlabeled(v, l) unnecessary.

Example 8.3 *Figure 8.3 shows a binary tree and its LOUDS representation as a cardinal tree. Inside nodes we write their indexes (which are now taken as the node identifiers). The tree has $n = 12$ nodes, thus bitvector B has $2n = 24$ bits. Below the bitvector we write its positions. For example, the description of node 3 (grayed) starts at $B[2 \cdot (3 - 1) + 1] = B[5]$. Since $B[5, 6] = 01$, node 3 has only a right child. This right*

---

[2] Unless σ is very large, it is better to compute children(v) = $popcount(B[\sigma(v - 1) + 1, \sigma v])$ and isleaf(v) iff $B[\sigma(v - 1) + 1, \sigma v] = 0^\sigma$ (refer to Section 4.2.1).

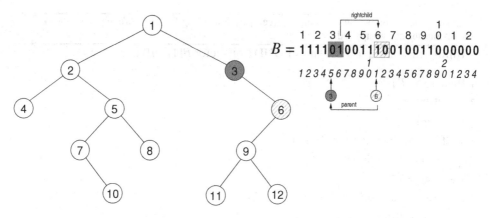

Figure 8.3. A binary tree and its LOUDS representation (bitvector B only). The same conventions of Figure 8.1 are used. On the right we illustrate the relations between node 3 (grayed) and its right child, node 6 (hatched).

child is rightchild$(3) =$ rank$_1(B, 2 \cdot 3) + 1 = 6$ *(hatched). We know that 6 is a right child of its parent because* childlabel$(6) = ((\text{select}_1(B, 6 - 1) - 1) \bmod 2) + 1 = (5 \bmod 2) + 1 = 2$. *Also, the parent of node 6 is* parent$(6) = \lceil \text{select}_1(B, 6 - 1)/2 \rceil = \lceil 6/2 \rceil = 3$. *These operations are also illustrated in the figure.*

Construction

Assume we have a classical representation of the cardinal tree where each node v contains an array of its σ possible children, $v.children$. Then, after enqueueing the root of T, we take each node v from the queue. We append σ bits to B, for $1 \le t \le \sigma$: a 1 if $v.children[t] \neq$ null or a 0 if it is null. The non-null children are also enqueued. This builds B in linear time. If we free each array of children as we enqueue its non-null elements, we do not require more space than that of the original tree.

We can also operate with the tree nodes sorted levelwise on disk, if we store the array of children together with each node. Then the tree can be read by small buffers and B can also be written by buffers, without the need of a queue.

8.2 Balanced Parentheses

A key idea to obtain a wider functionality is to represent the tree with the balanced parentheses studied in Chapter 7. We will start with the most intuitive idea; Section 8.3 will show a different one. In both cases all the tree functionality will be reduced to the small set of primitives we studied for balanced parentheses.

We will represent an ordinal tree T of n nodes as a balanced sequence of parentheses (BP) $B[1, 2n]$ as follows. We traverse the tree in depth-first search order. When we arrive at a node for the first time, we append an opening parenthesis to B, whose position will become the identifier of the node. When we finally leave the subtree of a node, we append a closing parenthesis to B. The resulting parentheses sequence, in terms of Chapter 7, represents the subtree-containment hierarchy of the nodes.

Algorithm 8.6 shows the procedure. It takes linear time and uses only the extra space of the recursion, which is proportional to the tree height. This is only problematic if

---

Algorithm 8.6: Building the BP representation from a pointer-based ordinal tree, using only extra space for the recursion stack. If we want to free the tree space, we can free v in line 9.

Input : Ordinal tree T of n nodes, with fields *first* (first child) and *next* (next sibling).

Output: Builds the BP representation $B[1, 2n]$ of T.

1 Allocate bitvector $B[1, 2n]$
2 *build*$(T.root, 1)$
3 Preprocess B for parenthesis queries (Chapter 7)

4 **Proc** *build*(v, i)

    Input : Tree node v and offset i where to write it in B.

    Output: Writes the subtree of v in B starting from position i and returns the new position to where to keep writing.

5   **while** $v \neq$ null **do**
6   bitset(B, i); $i \leftarrow i + 1$
7         $i \leftarrow$ *build*$(v.first, i)$
8   bitclear(B, i); $i \leftarrow i + 1$
9         $v \leftarrow v.next$
10   **return** i

---

the tree height is very significant. Unlike in Algorithm 8.3, we do not know of a way to avoid this extra space.

Basic Operations

The key property of the BP representation is that any subtree of T is mapped to a contiguous region in the bitvector B. This facilitates a number of operations that were difficult in LOUDS.

Example 8.4 *Figure 8.4 revisits Example 7.2, now interpreting the parentheses as the BP representation of the tree from Figure 8.1. Recall that we interpret the opening parentheses as 1s and the closing ones as 0s. The indexes of the nodes now reflect their preorder enumeration. The tree has $n = 20$ nodes, and thus B has 20 1s and 20 0s. The hatched region marks the subtree rooted at the node with index 6, and it corresponds with the contiguous hatched region marked in the parentheses.*

Figure 8.5 is similar to Figure 7.2, but now it shows the connection with the tree nodes. The node with index 5 has its opening parenthesis at $B[8]$ (grayed), thus its identifier is 8 and it spans the area $B[8, \mathsf{close}(B, 8)] = B[8, 37]$. The node with index 13 is at $B[23]$ (hatched). It holds $\mathsf{enclose}(B, 23) = 8$, the node with index 5, as node 8 is the parent of node 23.

Many of the operations of Table 8.1 can be easily rewritten in terms of basic parenthesis primitives. The first child of v is simply $v + 1$, and its next sibling is the position following $\mathsf{close}(B, v)$. The previous sibling of v is $\mathsf{open}(B, v - 1)$, that is, the position of the opening parenthesis that matches the one that closes at $B[v - 1]$. The parent of v

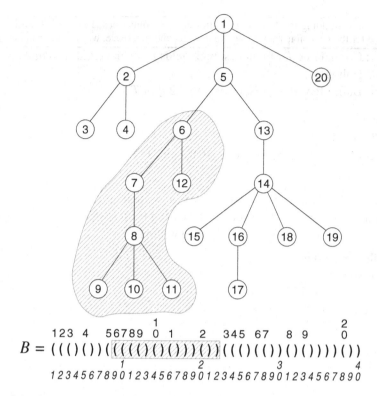

Figure 8.4. The same ordinal tree of Figure 8.1 and its BP representation. The parentheses coincide with those representing segments in Figure 7.1, which then describe the subtree-containment hierarchy in this tree. The subtree of the node with index 6 is hatched in the tree and in the parentheses.

is simply $\mathsf{enclose}(B, v)$, as already noted, and, in general, the ancestor at distance d is $\mathsf{bwdsearch}(B, v, -d - 1) + 1$. Leaves look like $()$, thus v is a leaf iff $B[v + 1] = 0$. The preorder of v is simply the number of opening parentheses up to v, and postorder is similar if we consider the closing parentheses. The depth of v is simply the excess up to v (parentheses opened and not yet closed). The number of nodes in the subtree of v

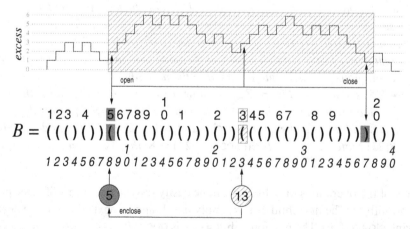

Figure 8.5. Basic BP operations on the BP representation of the tree of Figure 8.4. The node 8 (with preorder index 5) is grayed. The end of its subtree is found with $\mathsf{close}(8) = 37$ (and also $\mathsf{open}(37) = 8$). It is the parent of node 23 (with preorder index 13) because $\mathsf{enclose}(23) = 8$.

Algorithm 8.7: Computing the simple BP operations on ordinal trees.

Input : Ordinal tree T (seen as BP bitvector B), nodes u and v, indexes i and d.

1 **Proc** root(T)
2 | **return** 1

3 **Proc** fchild(T, v) — *assuming* $B[v + 1] = 1$
4 | **return** $v + 1$

5 **Proc** lchild(T, v) — *assuming* $B[v + 1] = 1$
6 | **return** open(B, close(B, v) − 1)

7 **Proc** nsibling(T, v) — *assuming* $B[$close(B, v) + 1$] = 1$
8 | **return** close(B, v) + 1

9 **Proc** psibling(T, v) — *assuming* $v > 1$ **and** $B[v − 1] = 0$
10 | **return** open($B, v − 1$)

11 **Proc** parent(T, v) — *assuming* $v \neq 1$
12 | **return** enclose(B, v)

13 **Proc** isleaf(T, v)
14 | **return** access($B, v + 1$) = 0

15 **Proc** nodemap(T, v) = preorder(T, v)
16 | **return** rank$_1(B, v)$

17 **Proc** nodeselect(T, i) = preorderselect(T, i)
18 | **return** select$_1(B, i)$

19 **Proc** postorder(T, v)
20 | **return** rank$_0(B,$ close(B, v))

21 **Proc** postorderselect(T, i)
22 | **return** open($B,$ select$_0(B, i)$)

23 **Proc** depth(T, v)
24 | **return** $2 \cdot$ rank$_1(B, v) − v$

25 **Proc** subtree(T, v)
26 | **return** (close(B, v) − $v + 1$)/2

27 **Proc** isancestor(T, u, v)
28 | **return** $u \leq v \leq$ close(B, u)

29 **Proc** levelancestor(T, v, d)
30 | **return** bwdsearch($B, v, −d − 1$) + 1

---

is half the number of parentheses between v and close(B, v). Finally, u is an ancestor of v iff v is between u and close(B, u). Algorithm 8.7 gives the details. Where necessary, we indicate the check that should be performed to ensure that the operation can be applied.

Example 8.5 *Consider again the representation in Figure 8.4. The node with index (and preorder) 7 is* nodeselect(7) = select$_1(B, 7) = 10$. *Its first child* *is* $\mathsf{fchild}(10) = 10 + 1 = 11$, *whose label is* $\mathsf{nodemap}(11) = \mathsf{rank}_1(B, 11) = 8$ *(this is also its preorder number). The next sibling of* 10 *is* $\mathsf{nsibling}(10) = \mathsf{close}(B, 10) + 1 = 19 + 1 = 20$, *the node with preorder* 12. *The parent of node* 20 *is* $\mathsf{parent}(20) = \mathsf{enclose}(B, 20) = 9$, *the node with preorder* 6. *The postorder of node* 9 *is* $\mathsf{postorder}(9) = \mathsf{rank}_0(B, \mathsf{close}(B, 9)) = \mathsf{rank}_0(B, 22) = 10$. *Its depth is* $\mathsf{depth}(9) = 2 \cdot \mathsf{rank}_1(B, 9) - 9 = 2 \cdot 6 - 9 = 3$. *The size of its subtree is* $\mathsf{subtree}(9) = (\mathsf{close}(B, 9) - 9 + 1)/2 = (22 - 9 + 1)/2 = 7$. *It is an ancestor of node* 11 *since* $9 \le 11 \le \mathsf{close}(B, 9) = 22$. *Finally, the ancestor at distance* 2 *from node* 20 *is* $\mathsf{levelancestor}(20, 2) = \mathsf{bwdsearch}(B, 20, -2 - 1) + 1 = 8$, *whose preorder is* 5.

Operations on Leaves

The operations related to leaves are addressed as follows. Since leaves appear in B as $() = 10$, we translate $\mathsf{leafrank}(v) = \mathsf{rank}_{10}(B, v) + 1$, $\mathsf{leafnum}(v) = \mathsf{leafrank}(\mathsf{close}(B, v)) - \mathsf{leafrank}(v)$, and $\mathsf{leafselect}(i) = \mathsf{select}_{10}(B, i)$. We already considered those extended $\mathsf{rank/select}$ primitives in Section 7.1.4.

Remaining Operations

Operations height, $\mathsf{deepestnode}$, $\mathsf{children}$, child, $\mathsf{childrank}$, and lca require the more sophisticated primitives we studied in Chapter 7, which count and locate minimum and maximum excess positions in a range. The deepest node below v is the one reaching the maximum depth (or excess), between v and $\mathsf{close}(B, v)$, thus $\mathsf{deepestnode}(v) = \mathsf{rMq}(B, v, \mathsf{close}(B, v))$, and the difference of depths between v and $\mathsf{deepestnode}(v)$ is $\mathsf{height}(v)$. As for the children, note that each minimum in $\mathsf{excess}(B, v, \mathsf{close}(B, v) - 2)$ corresponds to the position that precedes a new child of v. Therefore, the number of children is $\mathsf{mincount}(B, v, \mathsf{close}(B, v) - 2)$, and the tth child starts at $\mathsf{minselect}(B, v, \mathsf{close}(B, v) - 2, t) + 1$. Finally, $\mathsf{childrank}(v)$ is the number of times the minimum excess occurs from the parent of v to v.

These operations are also sufficient to compute $\mathsf{lca}(u, v)$. Assume $u < v$. Let $x = \mathsf{lca}(u, v)$. Then u and v descend from x by different children (if they descended by the same child, x would not be the lca). The lowest excess between the starting points u and v is at the parenthesis that closes the child of x that is an ancestor of u, or that closes another child of x that lies between u and v. Thus, $\mathsf{lca}(u, v)$ is obtained by adding 1 to that value, to get the next sibling, and taking the parent, which is x. If u is an ancestor of v, the minimum excess occurs at u itself, and the general procedure works as well. Algorithm 8.8 gives the details.

Example 8.6 *Figure 8.6 illustrates some operations on the representation of Figure 8.4. At the top, we show* rMq *and* height. *The node labeled* 13 *is* $\mathsf{nodeselect}(13) = 23$ *(its subtree is shown hatched on the parentheses). Its deepest node is* $\mathsf{rMq}(B, 23, \mathsf{close}(B, 23)) = \mathsf{rMq}(B, 23, 36) = 28$, *the node with index* 17 *(grayed). Thus,* $\mathsf{height}(23) = \mathsf{depth}(28) - \mathsf{depth}(23) = 6 - 3 = 3$.

Operations $\mathsf{children}$, child, *and* $\mathsf{childrank}$ *are illustrated in the middle of Figure 8.6. The node* 8, *with preorder* 5 *(its subtree is hatched on the parentheses), contains* $\mathsf{children}(8) = \mathsf{mincount}(B, 8, \mathsf{close}(B, 8) - 2) = \mathsf{mincount}(B, 8, 35) = 2$ *minima (at positions* 8 *and* 22*). The hatched area of* excess *shows the range*

Algorithm 8.8: Computing the more complex BP operations on ordinal trees.

Input : Ordinal tree T (seen as BP bitvector B), nodes u and v, indexes i and t.

1 **Proc** height(T, v)
2 $\quad$ **return** depth$(T, \text{deepestnode}(T, v)) - \text{depth}(T, v)$

3 **Proc** deepestnode(T, v)
4 $\quad$ **return** rMq$(B, v, \text{close}(B, v))$

5 **Proc** children(T, v)
6 $\quad$ **return** mincount$(B, v, \text{close}(B, v) - 2)$

7 **Proc** child(T, v, t) — *assuming* $t \leq$ children(T, v)
8 $\quad$ **return** minselect$(B, v, \text{close}(B, v) - 2, t) + 1$

9 **Proc** childrank(T, v) — *assuming* $v \neq 1$
10 $\quad$ **return** mincount$(B, \text{enclose}(B, v), v)$

11 **Proc** lca(T, u, v)
12 $\quad$ **if** $u > v$ **then** $u \leftrightarrow v$
13 $\quad$ **return** enclose$(B, \text{rmq}(B, u, v) + 1)$

14 **Proc** leafnum(T, v)
15 $\quad$ **return** leafrank$(T, \text{close}(B, v)) - \text{leafrank}(T, v)$

16 **Proc** leafrank(T, v)
17 $\quad$ **return** rank$_{10}(B, v) + 1$

18 **Proc** leafselect(T, i)
19 $\quad$ **return** select$_{10}(B, i)$

$[8, \text{close}(B, 8) - 2] = [8, 35]$, *where the minima are to be found. Then its first child is* child$(8, 1) = \text{minselect}(B, 8, 35, 1) + 1 = 8 + 1 = 9$ *(with preorder 6), and the second is* child$(8, 2) = \text{minselect}(B, 8, 35, 2) + 1 = 22 + 1 = 23$*. Indeed,* childrank$(23) = \text{mincount}(B, \text{enclose}(B, 23), 23) = \text{mincount}(B, 8, 23) = 2$*.*

Finally, the bottom part of Figure 8.6 illustrates the lca *operation. Consider nodes 11 and 24, with preorders 8 and 14, respectively (in gray). The area* $[11, 24]$ *between them is hatched both on the parentheses and in the excess zone. We compute their lowest common ancestor as* lca$(11, 24) = \text{enclose}(B, \text{rmq}(B, 11, 24) + 1) = \text{enclose}(B, 22 + 1) = \text{enclose}(B, 23) = 8$*.*

Time and Space in Practice

With the simple parentheses representation of Section 7.1, all the BP operations can be carried out in time $\mathcal{O}(\log n)$ within $2n + \mathcal{O}(n/\log n)$ bits of space. In practice, considering the calculations at the end of Section 7.1.1 and a lightweight rank/select support on B (Sections 4.2.1 and 4.3.1), the space can be around $2.35n$ bits and the operation times can be close to those of the slowest LOUDS implementation discussed at the end of Section 8.1. The times do not really grow noticeably with n in most cases (we recall that $\mathcal{O}(\log n)$ is a crude upper bound). Of course, the BP representation has a wider functionality than LOUDS.

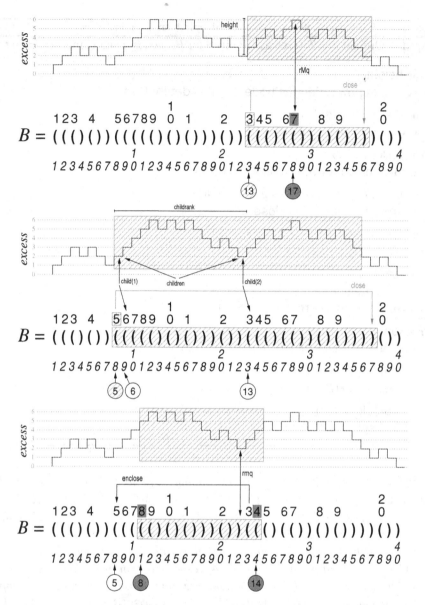

Figure 8.6. The operations from Example 8.6 on the BP representation of the tree in Figure 8.4.

The basic primitives **fwdsearch** and **bwdsearch** require only the fields e and m of the rmM-tree. If we store only these fields and the **rank/select** support for B, the space decreases to $2.23n$ bits and we can already support all the operations in Algorithm 8.7.

The more complex implementation of Section 7.2 yields faster operations within the same space.

8.2.1 Binary Trees Revisited

In Section 8.1.1 we showed how to represent binary trees in asymptotically optimal space, so that a number of operations could be supported. We show here an alternative representation that, although it uses a bit more space and is a bit slower in practice, supports additional operations: subtree, isancestor, preorder, preorderselect, lca, the operations on leaves, and a new useful ordering for binary trees:

$$\text{inorder}(v) = \text{inorder value of node } v,$$

$$\text{inorderselect}(i) = \text{node } v \text{ with inorder } i.$$

The inorder corresponds to enumerating the nodes left-to-right: first the left subtree, then the node, then the right subtree. For example, in a binary search tree, an inorder enumeration yields the keys in increasing order.

If we represented a binary tree directly as a general ordinal tree, we could not distinguish between a node with just a left child and a node with just a right child. A way to get around this problem would be to consider that the null pointers of the binary tree are the leaves. That is, for example, a node with no children would look as $(()())$, a node with only a left child with no children would look as $((()())())$, and with only a right child with no children, $(()(()()))$. The problem is that a binary tree with n nodes would require $4n + 2$ bits.

Structure

To use only $2n$ bits, we will apply a classical bijection between binary trees T of n nodes and general trees G of $n + 1$ nodes. This is defined as follows: G has a new root node, and the children of the root of G are the nodes in the rightmost path of T. Each node of the rightmost path becomes, in G, the root of the recursive transformation of its left subtree in T. With this transformation, the postorder numbering of the nodes in G corresponds to the inorder numbering of the nodes in T.[3]

Example 8.7 *Figure 8.7 illustrates the transformation of the binary tree of Figure 8.3 into a general tree. Note that the numbers inside the nodes correspond both to inorder numbers of the binary tree and to postorder numbers of the general tree.*

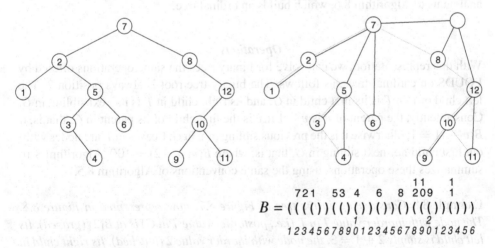

Figure 8.7. On the left, the binary tree of Figure 8.3 with inorder numbering of the nodes. On the right, its transformation into a general tree and its BP representation (the binary tree edges are kept as dotted lines for illustration purposes). The inorder numbers have become postorder numbers.

---

[3] This is the relation between the (binary) Cartesian tree of Figure 7.12 and the (general) left-to-right minima tree of Figure 7.10.

Algorithm 8.9: Building the BP representation from a pointer-based binary tree with fields l and r, using only extra space for the recursion stack. If we want to free the tree space, we can free v in line 11.

Input : Binary tree T of n nodes, with fields l (left) and r (right).

Output: Builds the BP representation $B[1, 2n + 2]$ of the general tree that corresponds to T.

1 Allocate bitvector $B[1, 2n + 2]$
2 bitset($B, 1$)
3 $build(T.root, 2)$
4 bitclear($B, 2n + 2$)
5 Preprocess B for parenthesis queries (Chapter 7)

6 **Proc** $build(v, i)$
  Input : Tree node v and offset i where to write it in B.
  Output: Writes the subtree of v in B starting from position i and returns the new position to where to keep writing.
7   **while** $v \neq$ null **do**
8   bitset(B, i); $i \leftarrow i + 1$
9    $i \leftarrow build(v.l, i)$
10   bitclear(B, i); $i \leftarrow i + 1$
11   $v \leftarrow v.r$
12 **return** i

The balanced parentheses representation of G requires only $2n + 2$ bits. Algorithm 8.9 shows how to generate it directly from the binary tree. Note that it is analogous to Algorithm 8.6, which builds an ordinal tree.

Operations

With this representation, we can solve for binary trees the same operations offered by LOUDS on cardinal trees, as follows. The binary tree root is always position 2. The left child of v in T is its first child in G, and its right child in T is its next sibling in G. Consequently, the parent of v is $v - 1$ if v is the first child of its parent in G, that is, if $B[v - 1] = 1$; otherwise it is the previous sibling of v in G. Leaves in T are nodes without first child nor next sibling in G, that is, where $B[v, v + 2] = 100$. Algorithm 8.10 summarizes these operations, using the same conventions of Algorithm 8.5.

Example 8.8 *Consider again the tree of Figure 8.7, now represented in Figure 8.8. The node with inorder value 7 in T (i.e., postorder value 7 in G) is at $B[2]$ (grayed). Its left child is simply $2 + 1 = 3$, the node with inorder value 2 (hatched). Its right child in T is its next sibling in G,* nsibling$(G, 2) =$ close$(B, 2) + 1 = 15 + 1 = 16$, *the node with inorder 8 in T (hatched in the other direction). Analogously, the parent of node 3 (with inorder 2) is 2 (with inorder 7) because $B[3 - 1] = B[2] = 1$, so 3 is a left child of its parent. Instead, the parent of node 16 (with inorder 8) is* psibling$(G, 16) =$

Algorithm 8.10: Computing basic binary tree operations using BP. We explicitly check if the operations can be applied.

Input : Binary tree T (seen as a general ordinal tree G and its BP bitvector B)
   and node v.

1 **Proc** root(T)
2 $\quad\lfloor$ **return** 2

3 **Proc** parent(T, v)
4 $\quad$ **if** $v = 2$ **then return** 0 (null)
5 $\quad$ **if** access($B, v - 1$) = 1 **then**
6 $\quad\quad\lfloor$ **return** $v - 1$
7 $\quad$ **else**
8 $\quad\quad\lfloor$ **return** open($B, v - 1$)

9 **Proc** isleaf(T, v)
10 $\quad\lfloor$ **return** bitsread($B, v + 1, v + 2$) = 00

11 **Proc** leftchild(T, v)
12 $\quad$ **if** access($B, v + 1$) = 0 **then return** 0 (null)
13 $\quad$ **return** $v + 1$

14 **Proc** rightchild(T, v)
15 $\quad$ $c \leftarrow$ close(B, v)
16 $\quad$ **if** access($B, c + 1$) = 0 **then return** 0 (null)
17 $\quad$ **return** $c + 1$

18 **Proc** childlabel(T, v)
19 $\quad$ **if** access($B, v - 1$) = 1 **then**
20 $\quad\quad\lfloor$ **return** 1 (i.e., v is a left child)
21 $\quad$ **else**
22 $\quad\quad\lfloor$ **return** 2 (i.e., v is a right child)

---

open($B, 16 - 1$) = 2 *(with inorder 7), because* $B[16 - 1] = B[15] = 0$, *so 16 is the right child of its parent.*

As promised, we can solve several other operations that cannot be carried out efficiently on the LOUDS representation of binary trees. First, as mentioned, the inorder

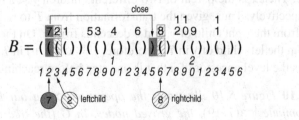

Figure 8.8. The operations of Example 8.8 on the binary tree representation of Figure 8.7. Node 2 (with inorder index 7) is grayed, and its left and right children (3 and 16, with inorders 2 and 8) are hatched in different directions.

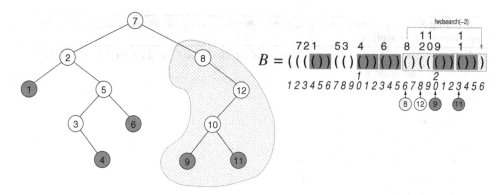

Figure 8.9. The operations of Example 8.9 on the binary tree representation of Figure 8.7. We show the leaves in gray and the subtree of the node with inorder 8 hatched.

in T corresponds to the postorder in G. An important property is that the subtree of v in T corresponds to the contiguous area that goes from v to the closing parenthesis of the parent of v in G, close(B, enclose(B, v)) = fwdsearch(B, v, -2). Therefore, we can compute the subtree size of v by counting those parentheses and dividing by 2. Similarly, u is an ancestor of v if v falls within that region.

The operations on leaves are easily carried out using this property again and the fact that leaves look like $()$ = 100 in B and are deployed in the same order as in G. Operations leafrank and leafselect are reduced to (extended) primitives rank$_{100}$ and select$_{100}$ in B, whereas operation leafnum counts (using leafrank) the number of leaves in the range from v to fwdsearch(B, v, -2).

Example 8.9 *Consider once again our binary tree, now in Figure 8.9. We hatched the subtree of the node with inorder 8. This node is at $B[16]$ in the parentheses representation. Its subtree is formed by the nodes with inorders 8 to 12. These are deployed in the area $B[16,$ fwdsearch(B, 16, -2)$] = B[16, 26]$. The number of nodes in this subtree is thus $(26 - 16)/2 = 5$. The node with inorder 12 (at $B[18]$) descends from 16 because $16 \le 18 \le 26$.*

We have also grayed the leaves and their descriptions. The node 16 contains 2 leaves in its subtree, since leafnum(16) = leafrank(fwdsearch(B, 16, -2)) $-$leafrank(16) = leafrank(26) $-$ leafrank(16) $= 5 - 3 = 2$.

Finally, the operation lca(u, v) is solved as follows. After enforcing $u < v$ and discarding the case where v descends from u in G, we compute $x =$ lca(G, u, v) in the general tree. Then x is the parent of two different children $y < z$ that are ancestors of u and v, respectively. Thus, given the transformation from T to G, it follows that in T, z descends from the right child of y, and v descends from z. On the other hand, u must descend from the left child of y in T. Therefore, $y =$ lca(u, v) in T. The node y can be computed as the level ancestor of u that is one step before reaching x.

Example 8.10 *Figure 8.10 illustrates the operation lca in our binary tree (on the left). We compute lca(7, 19), the grayed nodes. In G (the tree on the right), their lca is x (horizontally hatched). Thus u descends from child y of x and v descends from child z of x. Nodes y and z are diagonally hatched in different directions in*

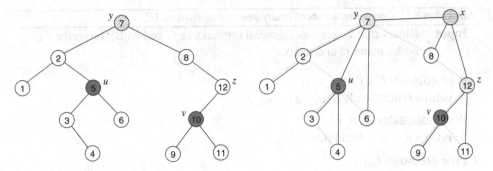

Figure 8.10. The lca operation of Example 8.10 on the binary tree representation of Figure 8.7. The lca of nodes u and v is y in the binary tree (left), but x in the general tree (right). Node y is the child of x in the way to u.

G. *Then, in T, u descends from the left child of y and v descends from z, which in turn descends from the right child of y. Therefore, in T it holds* $\text{lca}(u, v) = y$ *(doubly hatched in T). Since* $\text{depth}(u) - \text{depth}(x) = 3 - 1 = 2$ *in G, we find the answer as* $y = \text{levelancestor}(u, 2 - 1)$ *in G.*

Algorithm 8.11 gives the pseudocode for the advanced operations. As before, we have left out some operations on cardinal trees that are trivial or redundant on binary trees, like fchild, lchild, nsibling, psibling, children, child, and childrank. We can identify nodemap and nodeselect with inorder and inorderselect, respectively. We can also solve preorder and preorderselect, as they differ by 1 in T and G.

Instead, we are unable to compute operation depth and all the related ones: height, deepestnode, levelancestor, postorder, and postorderselect (note that $\text{postorder}(v) = \text{preorder}(v) + \text{subtree}(v) - \text{depth}(v)$, thus if we had postorder we would have depth). Those operations could still be supported if we used the mechanism we described to convert T into a general ordinal tree G of $2n + 1$ nodes (and thus using $4n + 2$ bits).

Note that we have optimized the implementation of lca, using the fact that the rmq primitive used to compute x in G will indeed find the leftmost minimum, which is the closing parenthesis of the desired node y. Still, the operation is slightly more complicated than when we found the lca in the Cartesian tree using rmq on its parentheses representation (recall Section 7.4.1 and Figure 7.12). The reason is that, in that case, the operation was defined on the inorder values of the nodes (which are associated with closing parentheses in G). Then the final open and the checks in Algorithm 8.11 were not needed.

8.3 DFUDS Representation

Although the BP representation of Section 8.2 solves all the operations of Table 8.1, it needs to resort to more complex operations on parentheses (which demand more space in practice, as discussed) for operations children, child, and childrank, which are very basic when we traverse the tree toward specific children. Actually, these operations were much simpler on the weaker LOUDS representation seen in Section 8.1.

Algorithm 8.11: Computing advanced binary tree operations using BP.

Input : Binary tree T (seen as a general ordinal tree G and its BP bitvector B)
nodes u and v, and index i.

1 **Proc** subtree(T, v)
2 | **return** (fwdsearch($B, v, -2$) $- v$)$/2$

3 **Proc** isancestor(T, u, v)
4 | **return** $u \leq v \leq$ fwdsearch($B, u, -2$)

5 **Proc** preorder(T, v)
6 | **return** preorder(G, v) $- 1$

7 **Proc** preorderselect(T, i)
8 | **return** preorderselect($G, i + 1$)

9 **Proc** inorder(T, v)
10 | **return** postorder(G, v)

11 **Proc** inorderselect(T, v)
12 | **return** postorderselect(G, v)

13 **Proc** lca(T, u, v)
14 | **if** $u > v$ **then** $u \leftrightarrow v$
15 | **if** isancestor(G, u, v) **then return** u
16 | **return** open(B, rmq(B, u, v))

17 **Proc** leafnum(T, v)
18 | **return** leafrank(T, fwdsearch($B, v, -2$)) $-$ leafrank(T, v)

19 **Proc** leafrank(T, v)
20 | **return** rank$_{100}$(B, v) $+ 1$

21 **Proc** leafselect(T, i)
22 | **return** select$_{100}$(B, i)

The *Depth-First Unary Degree Sequence (DFUDS)* representation is a combination of LOUDS and BP that almost obtains the best of both worlds: a coverage of operations wider than LOUDS combined with traversal toward specific children simpler than BP. In exchange, DFUDS loses operation **depth** and related ones.

Structure

The DFUDS representation of an ordinal tree T is defined as follows: Start with a bitvector B with the first bits $B[1, 3] = 110$ (this is to avoid special cases later) and then traverse T in preorder. For each new node v, with c children, append its description $1^c 0$ to B. The final size of B is $2n + 2$ bits. While a recursive construction is very simple, Algorithm 8.12 shows how this can be done without using any extra space for the stack. This time, unlike in Algorithm 8.3, we are unable to retain the original pointer-based tree, so we can only free it. If the tree has to be maintained, the recursive implementation can still be used if the tree is not too high.

Algorithm 8.12: Building the DFUDS representation from a pointer-based tree, without using any extra space and freeing the tree as we traverse it.

Input : Ordinal tree T of n nodes, with fields *first* (first child) and *next* (next sibling).

Output: Builds the DFUDS representation $B[1, 2n + 2]$ of T.

1 $Q \leftarrow T.root$ (queue head)
2 Allocate bitvector $B[1, 2n + 2]$
3 bitswrite($B, 1, 3, 110$)
4 $i \leftarrow 4$ (where to write in B)
5 **while** $Q \neq$ null **do**
6 | $F \leftarrow Q.first$
7 | $N \leftarrow Q.next$
8 | Free Q
9 | **if** $F =$ null **then**
10 | | $Q \leftarrow N$
11 | **else**
12 | | $Q \leftarrow F$
13 | | bitset(B, i); $i \leftarrow i + 1$
14 | | **while** $F.next \neq$ null **do**
15 | | | bitset(B, i); $i \leftarrow i + 1$
16 | | | $F \leftarrow F.next$
17 | | $F.next \leftarrow N$
18 | bitclear(B, i); $i \leftarrow i + 1$
19 Preprocess B for parenthesis queries (Chapter 7)

Example 8.11 *Figure 8.11 shows the DFUDS representation of an ordinal tree, writing bits as parentheses. The nodes are numbered in preorder, and their deployment in B is indicated with the numbers on top. For example, since the root has 3 children, the first node in B is written as* ((($. *The node with preorder 4 is a leaf, and its representation is simply* ')'. *Note that, with the first 3 parentheses added to B, the sequence becomes balanced.*

An important property of the DFUDS representation is that, like BP and unlike LOUDS, all the nodes in the subtree of v are contiguous in B, starting at v. However, the area cannot be delimited simply by a close(B, v) operation. The precise nature of the DFUDS structure is expressed by the following property: *The net excess inside any subtree of T is* -1.

This can be seen inductively, as follows. The leaves are represented simply by a closing parenthesis, so their excess is -1. Now consider a node v with c children. Then v is deployed as c opening parentheses followed by a closing parenthesis, which adds up to excess $c - 1$. Then v is followed by the subtrees that represent its c children. Assume inductively that each such subtree has an excess of -1; then the total excess is

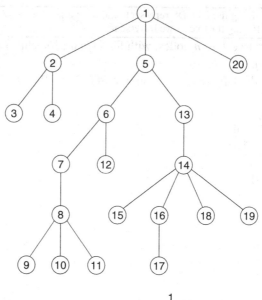

$$B = (\,(\,)\,(\,(\,(\,)\,(\,(\,)\,)\,)\,)\,(\,)\,(\,(\,)\,(\,)\,(\,(\,(\,)\,)\,)\,)\,)\,(\,)\,(\,(\,(\,(\,)\,)\,(\,)\,)\,)\,)$$

Figure 8.11. The ordinal tree of Figure 8.1 and its DFUDS representation. Nodes are traversed in preorder and ' $(^c)$ ' is written for each node with c children. The first 3 parentheses (grayed) are artificial.

$c - 1 - c = -1$. Therefore, prepending a single opening parenthesis makes the whole sequence balanced.

Operations

The net excess property is useful for navigation. Consider the description of a node v with c children, at $B[v, v + c] = 1^c\,0$. Then the first child of v starts at $B[v + c + 1]$. Note that the opening parenthesis at $B[v + c - 1]$ matches the closing parenthesis at $B[v + c]$, thus the first child of v starts at $\mathsf{close}(B, v + c - 1) + 1$. Since the subtree of the first child of v has an excess of -1, its last parenthesis (which is always a closing one) is $\mathsf{close}(B, v + c - 2)$, thus the second child of v starts at $\mathsf{close}(B, v + c - 2) + 1$. In general, the tth child of v starts at $\mathsf{close}(B, v + c - t) + 1$, thus $\mathsf{child}(v, t) = \mathsf{close}(B, \mathsf{succ}_0(B, v) - t) + 1$. Figure 8.12 illustrates these relations. It also holds $\mathsf{children}(v) = \mathsf{succ}_0(B, v) - v$ and thus $\mathsf{isleaf}(v)$ iff $B[v] = 0$. Operations fchild, lchild, $\mathsf{nsibling}$, and $\mathsf{psibling}$ are easy particular cases of child.

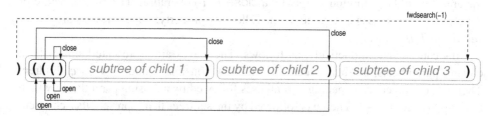

Figure 8.12. The DFUDS scheme, showing how the parent/child relations are identified and how the end of the subtree is found with $\mathsf{fwdsearch}$.

Equivalently, to find the parent of v, we know that the closing parenthesis at $B[v-1]$ is matched by an opening parenthesis in the description of the parent of v, thus $\mathsf{parent}(v) = \mathsf{pred}_0(B, \mathsf{open}(B, v-1)) + 1$ and $\mathsf{childrank}(v) = \mathsf{succ}_0(B, \mathsf{open}(B, v-1)) - \mathsf{open}(B, v-1)$.

The fact that the excess in any subtree is -1 gives also the tool to delimit the area of the subtree of v. It is $[v, \mathsf{fwdsearch}(B, v-1, -1)]$. This immediately yields the formulas to compute **subtree** and **isancestor**.

Nodes are enumerated in preorder, and each node terminates with a 0. Thus we can easily compute $\mathsf{preorder}(v) = \mathsf{rank}_0(B, v-1)$ and $\mathsf{preorderselect}(i) = \mathsf{select}_0(B, i) + 1$ (recall that B starts with a spurious 110, which is convenient now). Also, since leaves are represented as a single closing parenthesis, and (like every node) are preceded by another closing parenthesis, we can look for $)) = 00$ to spot the leaves. That is, $\mathsf{leafrank}(v) = \mathsf{rank}_{00}(B, v-1) + 1$ and $\mathsf{leafselect}(i) = \mathsf{select}_{00}(B, i) + 1$. Finally, as usual, $\mathsf{leafnum}(v) = \mathsf{leafrank}(\mathsf{fwdsearch}(B, v-1, -1) + 1) - \mathsf{leafrank}(v)$ counts the leaves from v to the end of its subtree.

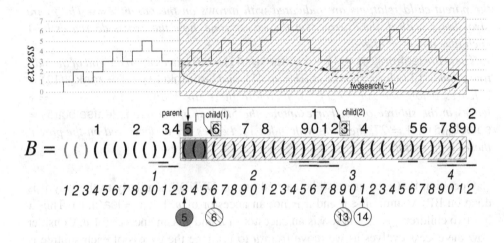

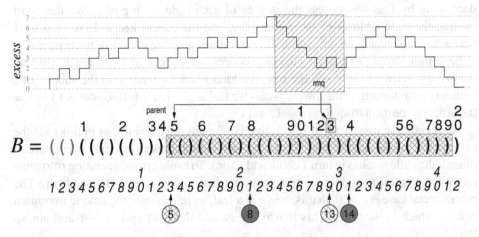

Figure 8.13. Illustration of operations on the DFUDS representation of the tree from Figure 8.11. On the top, the operations from Example 8.12. On the bottom, the operation $\mathsf{lca}(21, 31)$ (the nodes with indexes 8 and 14).

Example 8.12 *Figure 8.13 (top) illustrates some basic operations. The node with index 5 starts at position* $\mathsf{preorderselect}(B,5) = \mathsf{select}_0(B,5)+1 = 13$ *in B (its description is grayed in the figure), and conversely, the preorder of 13 is* $\mathsf{preorder}(13) = \mathsf{rank}_0(B,13-1) = 5$*. This node closes at* $\mathsf{fwdsearch}(B,13-1,-1) = 41$ *(the area is hatched on the parentheses and in the excess zone, and the computation of* $\mathsf{fwdsearch}$ *is shown with a solid arrow on the excess zone). Therefore, its subtree contains* $\mathsf{subtree}(13) = (41-13)/2+1 = 15$ *nodes, and node 31, with index 14, is in its subtree (that is,* $\mathsf{isancestor}(13,31)$ *holds) because* $13 \leq 31 \leq 41$*.*

This node has $\mathsf{children}(13) = \mathsf{succ}_0(B,13) - 13 = 15 - 13 = 2$ *children. Its first child is* $\mathsf{child}(13,1) = \mathsf{close}(B,\mathsf{succ}_0(B,13)-1)+1 = \mathsf{close}(B,14)+1 = 16$*, the node with index 6. The second child of 13 is* $\mathsf{child}(13,2) = \mathsf{close}(B,\mathsf{succ}_0(B,13)-2)+1 = \mathsf{close}(B,13)+1 = 29$*, the node with index 13. Indeed, the parent of node 29 is* $\mathsf{parent}(29) = \mathsf{pred}_0(B,\mathsf{open}(B,29-1))+1 = \mathsf{pred}_0(B,13)+1 = 13$*. Moreover, node 29 is the second child of its parent because* $\mathsf{childrank}(29) = \mathsf{succ}_0(B,\mathsf{open}(B,29-1)) - \mathsf{open}(B,29-1) = \mathsf{succ}_0(B,13) - 13 = 15 - 13 = 2$*. Children are hatched (in the other direction), and the parent-child relations are indicated with arrows on the parentheses. The figure also shows, with dashed arrows on the excess zone, how the excess decreases by 1 each time a new child ends.*

There are $\mathsf{leafrank}(41+1) - 1 = \mathsf{rank}_{00}(41) = 10$ *leaves up to the end of the subtree of node 13 (whose subtree finishes at 41), and* $\mathsf{leafrank}(13) - 1 = \mathsf{rank}_{00}(12) = 2$ *leaves before the subtree of 13, therefore there are* $\mathsf{leafnum}(13) = 10 - 2 = 8$ *leaves in the subtree of 13. For example, the 5th leaf of the tree is* $\mathsf{leafselect}(5) = \mathsf{select}_{00}(5)+1 = 27$*, the node with index 11. Leaves are underscored on the parentheses representation.*

Operation $\mathsf{lca}(u,v)$ can also be carried out on DFUDS, similarly to the way it is done on BP. Assume $u < v$ and u is not an ancestor of v. Let $x = \mathsf{lca}(u,v)$. Thus x has two children $y < z$, where y is an ancestor of u and z is an ancestor of v. Consider how the excess evolves as we move from u to v. Since the excess of each subtree is -1, we reach excess -1 when we traverse the whole subtree of u. The excess keeps decreasing by 1 as we process the subtree of each right sibling of u. We then start reading the right siblings of the parent of u, and the excess keeps decreasing by 1 for each complete subtree traversed. This continues until we complete the traversal of y. Each right sibling of y makes the excess decrease further, until we reach z, where the excess increases (by $c - 1$ if z has c children) and we reach v in the subtree of z without ever returning to the lowest excess we had at $z - 1$. Therefore, $\mathsf{lca}(u,v) = x = \mathsf{parent}(z) = \mathsf{parent}(\mathsf{rmq}(B,u,v-1)+1)$.

A special case may occur if $c = 1$, that is, if z has only 1 child, as in this case the excess after processing the first 10 of z is again the minimum (this may occur several times if the child of z has in turn 1 child, and so on). To avoid errors, operation rmq must return the first left-to-right minimum position (this is how we have defined rmq). The other special case is $c = 0$, that is, $z = v$ is a leaf, as in this case the unique minimum is at v, which is incorrect. This is why we extend the rmq up to $v - 1$ and not up to v.

Finally, by starting the rmq area at the 0 that finishes the description of u, $\mathsf{succ}_0(u)$, the formula turns out to work well also when u is an ancestor of v, as in this case the minimum is at the closing parenthesis that precedes the child of u from where v descends.

Example 8.13 *The bottom part of Figure 8.13 illustrates the computation of* lca(21, 31), *the grayed nodes with index 8 and 14, respectively, in Figure 8.11. The first left-to-right minimum of* excess(succ$_0$(B, 21), 31 $-$ 1) $=$ excess(B, 24, 30) *(hatched area in the excess zone) occurs at* rmq(B, 24, 30) $=$ 28, *the position preceding* $z = 29$, *with index 13 (hatched in the other direction). Note that, since z has only one child, there exists a second minimum at position 30, which is not the right one. Now we know that z is a child of* $x = 13 =$ lca(21, 31) *(the node with index 5), and the answer is found, precisely, with* $x =$ parent(z). *The parentheses area of x is doubly hatched.*

As anticipated, operation depth is not supported by the DFUDS representation. The same happens with the other related operations: height, deepestnode, levelancestor, postorder, and postorderselect.

Algorithms 8.13 and 8.14 detail the operations, dividing them into basic and advanced, respectively (though none is particularly complex on DFUDS, except possibly lca). When necessary, we indicate the check that should be performed if we are not

---

Algorithm 8.13: Computing the simple DFUDS operations on ordinal trees.

Input : Ordinal tree T (seen as DFUDS bitvector B), nodes u and v, and index i.

1 **Proc** root(T)
2 $\quad\mid\quad$ **return** 4

3 **Proc** fchild(T, v) — *assuming $B[v] = 1$*
4 $\quad\mid\quad$ **return** succ$_0$(B, v) $+ 1$

5 **Proc** lchild(T, v) — *assuming $B[v] = 1$*
6 $\quad\mid\quad$ **return** close(B, v) $+ 1$

7 **Proc** nsibling(T, v) — *assuming $B[\text{open}(B, v - 1) - 1] = 1$*
8 $\quad\mid\quad$ **return** fwdsearch($B, v - 1, -1$) $+ 1$

9 **Proc** psibling(T, v) — *assuming $B[v - 2, v - 1] \neq 10$*
10 $\quad\mid\quad$ **return** close(B, open($B, v - 1$) $+ 1$) $+ 1$

11 **Proc** parent(T, v) — *assuming $v \neq 4$*
12 $\quad\mid\quad$ **return** pred$_0$(B, open($B, v - 1$)) $+ 1$

13 **Proc** isleaf(T, v)
14 $\quad\mid\quad$ **return** access(B, v) $= 0$

15 **Proc** nodemap(T, v) $=$ preorder(T, v)
16 $\quad\mid\quad$ **return** rank$_0$($B, v - 1$)

17 **Proc** nodeselect(T, i) $=$ preorderselect(T, i)
18 $\quad\mid\quad$ **return** select$_0$(B, i) $+ 1$

19 **Proc** subtree(T, v)
20 $\quad\mid\quad$ **return** (fwdsearch($B, v - 1, -1$) $- v$)/2 $+ 1$

21 **Proc** isancestor(T, u, v)
22 $\quad\mid\quad$ **return** $u \leq v \leq$ fwdsearch($B, u - 1, -1$)

Algorithm 8.14: Computing the more complex DFUDS operations on ordinal trees.

Input : Ordinal tree T (seen as DFUDS bitvector B), nodes u and v, and indexes
i and t.

1 **Proc** children(T, v)
2   **return** $\text{succ}_0(B, v) - v$

3 **Proc** child(T, v, t) — *assuming* $t \leq$ children(T, v)
4   **return** $\text{close}(B, \text{succ}_0(B, v) - t) + 1$

5 **Proc** childrank(T, v) — *assuming* $v \neq 4$
6    $p \leftarrow \text{open}(B, v - 1)$
7   **return** $\text{succ}_0(B, p) - p$

8 **Proc** lca(T, u, v)
9   **if** $u > v$ **then** $u \leftrightarrow v$
10   **return** parent$(B, \text{rmq}(B, \text{succ}_0(B, u), v - 1) + 1)$

11 **Proc** leafnum(T, v)
12   **return** leafrank$(T, \text{fwdsearch}(B, v - 1, -1) + 1) -$ leafrank(T, v)

13 **Proc** leafrank(T, v)
14   **return** $\text{rank}_{00}(B, v - 1) + 1$

15 **Proc** leafselect(T, i)
16   **return** $\text{select}_{00}(B, i) + 1$

---

sure that the operation can be applied. Note that only lca needs primitive rmq, whereas all the others use only **fwdsearch**, **bwdsearch**, **rank**, and **select**. The fields M and n of the rmM-trees are not used.

8.3.1 Cardinal Trees Revisited

In Section 8.1.1 we showed how to adapt LOUDS to represent cardinal trees of arity σ using σn bits, and that the space could be reduced to $n \log \sigma + \mathcal{O}(n)$ bits while supporting the operations in time $\mathcal{O}(\log \sigma)$.

The operations supported in Algorithm 8.4 are those of LOUDS and of labeled trees. If we are willing to spend other $2n + o(n)$ bits, we can add a DFUDS representation of the tree topology (regarding it as an ordinal tree) and support all the ordinal DFUDS functionality over it.

The structure consists of (1) the DFUDS representation of the corresponding ordinal tree, and (2) a bitvector $S[1, \sigma n]$ where, for each node v with preorder p, $S[\sigma(p - 1) + 1, \sigma p]$ contains the σ bits that tell which of the σ possible children of v exist; that is, S is the same as the bitvector B of Section 8.1.1 but now stored in preorder.

Then, in addition to the ordinal tree operations of DFUDS, we support the labeled tree operations by relating the node in the DFUDS representation to its children in S, and following procedures similar to those in Algorithm 8.4. Those are detailed in Algorithm 8.15. Unless σ is very large, it is better to replace lines 6 and 11 with

---

Algorithm 8.15: Computing the additional cardinal tree operations on DFUDS.

Input : Cardinal tree T (seen as DFUDS bitvector $B[1, 2n + 2]$ and the
bitvector $S[1, \sigma n]$), node v, and label l.

1 **Proc** childrenlabeled(T, v, l)
2     $p \leftarrow$ preorder(T, v)
3   **return** $S[\sigma(p - 1) + l] = 1$

4 **Proc** labeledchild(T, v, l) — *assuming* childrenlabeled(T, v, l)
5     $p \leftarrow$ preorder(T, v)
6     $t \leftarrow$ rank$_1(S, \sigma(p - 1) + l) -$ rank$_1(S, \sigma(p - 1))$
7   **return** child(T, v, t)

8 **Proc** childlabel(T, v) — *assuming* $v \neq 4$
9     $p \leftarrow$ preorder($T,$ parent(v))
10    $j \leftarrow$ childrank(T, v)
11   **return** select$_1(S,$ rank$_1(S, \sigma(p - 1)) + j) - \sigma(p - 1)$

---

sequential scanning. When σ is large, however, labeled trees offer more efficient solutions; we consider them next.

8.4 Labeled Trees

Up to now we have considered ordinal and cardinal trees. Cardinal trees with labels $[1, \sigma]$ can be seen as a particular case of general labeled trees, restricted to having at most one child labeled with any $l \in [1, \sigma]$, and with the children sorted by their label. The solutions for cardinal trees we have seen up to now either are fast (constant-time operations) but require σn bits of space (which is acceptable only for very small σ), or use reasonable space ($n \log \sigma + \mathcal{O}(n)$ bits) but operation times are $\mathcal{O}(\log \sigma)$.

In this section we introduce a more general technique that can handle arbitrary labels; that is, each node may have zero or more children with any given label, and labels may appear in any order. The structure uses $n \log \sigma + o(n \log \sigma) + \mathcal{O}(n)$ bits, and operation times decrease to $\mathcal{O}(\log \log \sigma)$. Alternatively, we can keep $n \log \sigma$ bits and $\mathcal{O}(\log \sigma)$ operation times, but with an extremely simple implementation. The structure also supports other operations with labels that are not possible with the cardinal tree representations seen up to now.

Structure

Consider a LOUDS or DFUDS bitvector B representing the topology of a tree T with n nodes, without regard for the labels. We add a sequence (Chapter 6) $S[1, n]$ formed as follows: We traverse the nodes $v \in T$ in left-to-right order of their deployment in B (that is, levelwise ordering for LOUDS and preorder for DFUDS). For each node v with $c =$ children(v) children, we append to S the labels of the edges that connect v with each of the c children, in order, that is, we append childlabel(child($v, 1$)) to childlabel(child(v, c)).

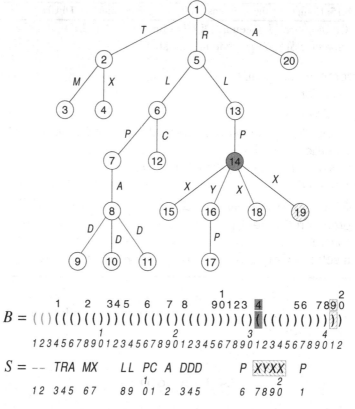

$$B = \text{(())}((\text{()}(\text{())})(\text{()}((\text{()})(\text{()}((\text{())})))()(((\text{())})(\text{())})))$$

$S = \text{-- TRA MX \quad LL PC A DDD \qquad P XYXX \quad P}$

Figure 8.14. A labeled tree with the same topology of that of Figure 8.11, its DFUDS representation B, and the string S storing the labels. The spaces in S are introduced to align the labels of the c children of each node with the c opening parentheses of its description. The grayed node is 31 (with index 14). The labels of its children, **XYXX**, are hatched in S, and the third child labeled **X**, 41 (with index 19) is hatched in the other direction.

It is easy to see that the positions in S correspond to the 1s in B. Therefore, given a node v (that is, a position in B), the labels of its c children can be found at $S[s+1, s+c]$, where $s = \mathsf{rank}_1(B, v-1)$.[4]

Example 8.14 *Figure 8.14 shows a labeled tree, the DFUDS representation of its topology, and the corresponding string S with the labels. Note that the first 2 cells of S are unused, because they correspond to fake 1s in B.*

The positions in S are associated with the 1s in B. For example, the node $v = 4$, with index 1 and described at $B[4, 7] = ((($, corresponds to $S[3, 5] = $ "TRA", which contains the labels of the $c = 3$ children of the node v. This is correct since $s = \mathsf{rank}_1(B, v-1) = 2$ and thus $S[s+1, s+c] = S[3, 5]$. Shadings will be used later.

---

[4] To account for the fake 1 added in the beginning of LOUDS deployment, or the two 1s in the beginning of DFUDS, we should subtract 1 or 2 from s, but we avoid this for simplicity. The only consequence is 1 or 2 unused positions in the beginning of S.

Operations

This representation allows for an efficient implementation of the labeled tree operations, if we choose a sequence representation from Chapter 6 for S. The number of children labeled l is $\mathsf{childrenlabeled}(v, l) = \mathsf{rank}_l(S, s + c) - \mathsf{rank}_l(S, s)$. The tth left-to-right child labeled l, if it exists, is $\mathsf{labeledchild}(v, l, t) = \mathsf{child}(v, j)$, where $j = \mathsf{select}_l(S, \mathsf{rank}_l(S, s) + t) - s$. Note that j is the position of the tth occurrence of l inside the area of the children of v in S. Once we know j, we simply descend to the jth ordinal child of v. Conversely, to find the label by which v descends from its parent we first find $u = \mathsf{parent}(v)$ and $j = \mathsf{childrank}(v)$. Then, since v is the jth child of its parent u, we have $\mathsf{childlabel}(v) = \mathsf{access}(S, \mathsf{rank}_1(B, u - 1) + j)$. Note that parent and $\mathsf{childrank}$ can be computed with a single method, faster than calling both operations independently.

Example 8.15 *Let us consider Figure 8.14 again. Take the node $v = 31$, with index 14 (grayed). Since $s = \mathsf{rank}_1(B, 31 - 1) = 16$ and v has $c = \mathsf{children}(31) = 4$ children, the labels of those children are written in $S[s + 1, s + c] = S[17, 20] = XYXX$ (hatched). Thus, for example, we have $\mathsf{childrenlabeled}(31, X) = \mathsf{rank}_X(S, 20) - \mathsf{rank}_X(S, 16) = 4 - 1 = 3$.*

The third child labeled X is $\mathsf{labeledchild}(31, X, 3) = \mathsf{child}(31, j)$, with $j = \mathsf{select}_X(S, \mathsf{rank}_X(S, 16) + 3) - 16 = \mathsf{select}_X(S, 4) - 16 = 20 - 16 = 4$. Thus, the answer is $u = \mathsf{child}(31, 4) = 41$, the node with index 19 (hatched in the other direction). Conversely, to find $\mathsf{childlabel}(41)$, the label by which 41 descends, we find its parent $v = \mathsf{parent}(41) = 31$ and $j = \mathsf{childrank}(41) = 4$. Now we find the label written in $\mathsf{access}(S, \mathsf{rank}_1(B, 31 - 1) + 4) = S[16 + 4] = S[20] = X$.

Note that these operations work regardless of whether or not we are using a LOUDS or a DFUDS representation for the ordinal topology of T. This gives us the freedom to choose a simpler representation supporting fewer operations (LOUDS) or a more complex one supporting a more complete set (DFUDS). Algorithm 8.16 gives the pseudocode.

In Practice

Unless the tree arity is very large, it is convenient to represent S as a simple array, without any $\mathsf{rank}/\mathsf{select}$ support, and solve $\mathsf{childrenlabeled}$ and $\mathsf{labeledchild}$ by a simple linear scan on the corresponding area of S.

We can also use this representation for cardinal trees. In this case, if we maintain the children sorted by label, we can support $\mathsf{childrenlabeled}$ and $\mathsf{labeledchild}$ in time $O(\log \sigma)$ by just a binary search on the children of the node, and $\mathsf{childlabel}$ needs a simple constant-time access to S.

Next we consider what complexities can be obtained with more elaborated sequence representations, but these are justified only if the arities (or σ, in the case of cardinal trees) are very large.

Space and Time

If we use wavelet trees (Section 6.2) to represent S, times will be $O(\log \sigma)$ for the three operations in Algorithm 8.16 (this holds for general labeled trees,

---

Algorithm 8.16: Computing the labeled tree operations on LOUDS or DFUDS.

Input : Labeled tree T (seen as a LOUDS or DFUDS bitvector B and the sequence $S[1, n + 1]$), node v, label l, and index t.

1 **Proc** childrenlabeled(T, v, l)
2    $\quad s \leftarrow \mathsf{rank}_1(B, v - 1)$
3    $\quad c \leftarrow \mathsf{children}(T, v)$
4    $\quad$ **return** $\mathsf{rank}_l(S, s + c) - \mathsf{rank}_l(S, s)$

5 **Proc** labeledchild(T, v, l, t) — *assuming* $t \leq$ childrenlabeled(T, v, l)
6    $\quad s \leftarrow \mathsf{rank}_1(B, v - 1)$
7    $\quad j \leftarrow \mathsf{select}_l(S, \mathsf{rank}_l(S, s) + t) - s$
8    $\quad$ **return** child(v, j)

9 **Proc** childlabel(T, v) — *assuming* $v \neq$ root()
10    $\quad u \leftarrow \mathsf{parent}(v)$
11    $\quad j \leftarrow \mathsf{childrank}(v)$
12    $\quad s \leftarrow \mathsf{rank}_1(B, u - 1)$
13    $\quad$ **return** access($S, s + j$)

---

independently of the arity of the nodes). For larger alphabets, we might use alphabet partitioning (Section 6.3), where operation times decrease to $\mathcal{O}(\log \log \sigma)$. In these two representations, the space of B plus S is close to the zero-order entropy of S, $n\mathcal{H}_0(S) + o(n \log \sigma) + \mathcal{O}(n)$ bits (recall Chapter 2). If the alphabet is large and we are not interested in the compressibility of S, we can achieve the same $\mathcal{O}(\log \log \sigma)$ times and $n \log \sigma + o(n \log \sigma) + \mathcal{O}(n)$ bits of space with the simpler technique of Section 6.1.

If we use LOUDS for the tree, this is a case where it may be justified to use constant-time **rank/select** support, since the space for S is likely to dominate. Then the time complexity is dominated by the operations on S.

In the case of DFUDS, if we use the simple parentheses representation of Section 7.1, its $\mathcal{O}(\log n)$ times dominate the complexities associated with S. Instead, by using the $\mathcal{O}(\log \log n)$ time implementation of Section 7.2 and $\mathcal{O}(\log \log \sigma)$ time operations on S, the total complexity is $\mathcal{O}(\log \log n)$ (we assume $\sigma < n$, which is reasonable as there are only $n - 1$ labels in the tree).

Extended Operations

Having all the labels explicitly in a sequence S allows for other operations not considered in our original set. Consider the combination with a DFUDS representation. We can find the number of times a label l occurs in the subtree of v, by first computing the position $j = \mathsf{fwdsearch}(B, v - 1, -1)$ where the subtree of v finishes in B, then delimiting the positions $s = \mathsf{rank}_1(B, v - 1)$ and $e = \mathsf{rank}_1(B, j)$ of the subtree in S, and finally counting the number of occurrences of l with $\mathsf{rank}_l(S, e) - \mathsf{rank}_l(S, s)$.

An important related operation is to retrieve the ith occurrence of l in the subtree of v, in preorder. This poses a problem for our representation because the labels in S do not appear in preorder. Instead, we could store the symbols in S sorted by preorder of the target nodes, that is, associated with the 0s of the DFUDS representation: the

$$
\begin{array}{c}
\hspace{3.5cm} 1 \hspace{3.2cm} 2 \\
1 \quad 2 \quad 345 \quad 6 \quad 7 \; 8 \quad 90123 \; 4 \hspace{1.2cm} 56 \; 7890 \\
B = (\,(\,)\,(\,(\,(\,)\,(\,(\,)\,)\,)\,(\,(\,)\,(\,(\,)\,(\,)\,(\,(\,(\,)\,)\,)\,)\,)\,(\,)\,(\,(\,(\,(\,)\,)\,(\,)\,(\,)\,)\,)\,) \\
1 \hspace{2.4cm} 2 \hspace{1.8cm} 3 \hspace{2cm} 4 \\
123456789012345678901234567890123456789012
\end{array}
$$

$$
\begin{array}{c}
S = \hspace{1.5cm} - \quad TMX \quad R \quad L \; P \quad\;\; ADDDC \; L \hspace{1cm} PX \; YPXXA \\
\hspace{6cm} 1 \hspace{2.5cm} 2 \\
1 \quad\; 234 \quad 5 \quad 6 \; 7 \quad\; 89012 \; 3 \hspace{1cm} 45 \; 67890
\end{array}
$$

Figure 8.15. The representation of the same tree of Figure 8.14, now associating the labels with the closing parenthesis positions in DFUDS. Grayed and shaded areas illustrate Example 8.16.

label of the edge leading to node v is stored at $S[\mathsf{preorder}(v)] = S[\mathsf{rank}_0(B, v - 1)]$. In this case we would delimit the subtree of v in S with $s = \mathsf{preorder}(v)$ and $e = s + \mathsf{subtree}(v) - 1$. Then the counting formula $\mathsf{rank}_l(S, e) - \mathsf{rank}_l(S, s)$ works verbatim; note that the edge associated with v itself is not in its subtree, but it rather labels the edge that leads to v. To retrieve the ith occurrence of l in the subtree of v, we find its preorder position with $p = \mathsf{select}_l(S, \mathsf{rank}_l(S, s) + i)$, and then the answer is $\mathsf{preorderselect}(p)$.

The problem with this choice is that the operations of Algorithm 8.16 do not work anymore and cannot be efficiently implemented, since the labels of the children of a node v are not contiguous in S. The only exception is $\mathsf{childlabel}(T, v) = \mathsf{access}(S, \mathsf{preorder}(v))$.

The same happens if we combine S with a BP representation (Section 8.2): We can write the label of the edge leading to a node v at $S[\mathsf{preorder}(v)]$, and the extended operations we have described would work as well, but also the operations of Algorithm 8.16 would not work, except $\mathsf{childlabel}$.

If these extended operations are more important than those of Algorithm 8.16, then we can use this preorder-based deployment of S in DFUDS or BP, and carry out the operations $\mathsf{childrenlabeled}$ and $\mathsf{labeledchild}$ by sequentially or binary searching all the children of the node.

Example 8.16 *Figure 8.15 shows the same tree of Figure 8.14, now associating the labels with the closing parentheses of B. For example, we can determine the number of labels P below the subtree of node 29 (with index 13, grayed and with its subtree hatched) by first determining $\mathsf{subtree}(29) = 7$ and then counting the number of occurrences of P in $S[\mathsf{preorder}(29) + 1, \mathsf{preorder}(29) + \mathsf{subtree}(29) - 1] = S[14, 19]$, by computing $\mathsf{rank}_P(S, 19) - \mathsf{rank}_P(S, 13) = 3 - 1 = 2$.*

Now, to find the second P in the subtree, we first find its position in S, $p = \mathsf{select}_P(S, \mathsf{rank}_P(S, 13) + 2) = \mathsf{select}_P(S, 3) = 17$, and then return $\mathsf{preorderselect}(T, 17) = 39$ (that is, precisely, the node with index 17; it is hatched in the other direction).

8.5 Applications

Trees have many applications in Computer Science. In this section we explore a few that make use of the different representations and operations we have studied for ordinal, cardinal, binary, and labeled trees.

8.5.1 Routing in Minimum Spanning Trees

We start with a simple application of ordinal trees. Let a connected graph $G = (V, E)$ describe the possible bidirectional connections to communicate between nodes, with costs associated with the edges. The minimum spanning tree (MST) is formed by the edges of E that connect G at minimum cost. The cost of the tree is the sum of the costs of its edges. There are various classical and well-known algorithms for finding minimum spanning trees.

Once built, the MST is useful for routing. There exists a unique path through the MST edges between every pair of nodes in V, and we can use the MST to find this path efficiently.

We can regard the MST as an ordinal tree, by arbitrarily choosing a root and fixing the order between the children of every node. Then we can maintain it in $2n + o(n)$ bits with any of the representations seen in this chapter, where $n = |V|$ is the number of nodes in G.

The key observation is that the route from a node u to another node v consists in moving from u to $\mathsf{lca}(u, v)$, and then from $\mathsf{lca}(u, v)$ to v.

Example 8.17 *Figure 8.16 illustrates an MST on the left, and one of the possible ordinal trees representing it, on the right. We have chosen node* d *to be the tree root, but any other choice would work. If we want to travel from node* j *to* h, *we must follow the grayed path. This path can be found in the ordinal tree by traversing from* j *to* c $= \mathsf{lca}($j, h$)$, *and then from* c *to* h.

This property enables our representations to efficiently answer various questions about routes.

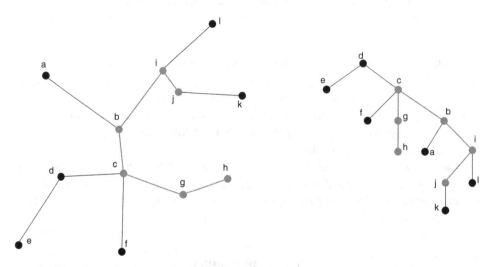

Figure 8.16. An MST on the left, and a possible ordinal tree that represents it on the right. A path between nodes h and j is shown in gray. On any ordinal tree, the path always goes from one node to the lca of the two nodes, and then from the lca to the other node.

Route Length

The length of the route from u to v is easily computed as

$$(\text{depth}(u) - \text{depth}(\text{lca}(u, v))) + (\text{depth}(v) - \text{depth}(\text{lca}(u, v)))$$
$$= \text{depth}(u) + \text{depth}(v) - 2 \cdot \text{depth}(\text{lca}(u, v)).$$

A BP representation is necessary to compute this formula, because we cannot efficiently compute depth with LOUDS or DFUDS.

Enumerating the Path

The list of the nodes to traverse in order to move from u to v can be obtained as follows. First, compute $x \leftarrow \text{lca}(u, v)$. Next start at $y \leftarrow u$ and repeat the process of outputting y and setting $y \leftarrow \text{parent}(y)$, until we reach $y = x$. Now output x and repeat the process from $y \leftarrow v$. This second time, however, we must output the nodes in reverse order (from x to v); therefore we need to first push the nodes in a stack and then extract and output them.

The use of a stack can be avoided by using the following, slightly slower, process: For d from $\text{depth}(v) - \text{depth}(x) - 1$ to 1, output $\text{levelancestor}(v, d)$, and finally output v.

For this second method, we also need the BP representation, because a depth computation is involved. The first method, instead, can be carried out using either BP or DFUDS. Interestingly, it can be carried out more efficiently using a LOUDS representation and without actually computing lca (or, more precisely, finding it as a by-product of the enumeration). The idea is inspired by Algorithm 8.2, where we computed $\text{lca}(u, v)$ by climbing from both nodes, alternatingly, toward their common ancestor. See Algorithm 8.17.

Algorithm 8.17: Enumerating the path from u to v with LOUDS. Uses operations *push* and *pop* on stack S; *pop* returns the element removed.

Input : Ordinal tree T (seen as LOUDS bitvector B), nodes u and v.
Output: Outputs the path from u to v.

1 $S \leftarrow$ empty stack
2 **while** $u \neq v$ **do**
3   **if** $u > v$ **then**
4   **output** u
5          $u \leftarrow \text{parent}(T, u)$
6   **else**
7          $push(S, v)$
8          $v \leftarrow \text{parent}(T, v)$
9 **output** u
10 **while** S *is not empty* **do**
11   **output** $pop(S)$

Path Membership

We can also ask whether the path from u to v needs to go through a node z. Once $x = \mathsf{lca}(u, v)$ is determined, this question becomes

$$\mathsf{isancestor}(x, z) \wedge (\mathsf{isancestor}(z, u) \vee \mathsf{isancestor}(z, v)).$$

This is efficiently implemented in BP or DFUDS by computing the position z' where the subtree of z ends (i.e., $z' = \mathsf{close}(z)$ in BP or $z' = \mathsf{fwdsearch}(z - 1, -1)$ in DFUDS). Then z is in the path from u to v iff $z = x$ or $[z, z']$ contains exactly one of u and v.

We note, however, that our $2n + o(n)$ bits is not the optimal space for this problem, because in the MST we would not need to distinguish a tree root or the order of children. That is, rather than an ordinal tree, we could represent an acyclic connected undirected graph. The number of such graphs is $\mathcal{O}(\alpha^n/n^{5/2})$, where $\alpha < 2.956$, and therefore $n \log \alpha - \mathcal{O}(\log n) < 1.564n - \mathcal{O}(\log n)$ bits are sufficient to describe any such structure.

8.5.2 Grammar Compression

A *context-free grammar*, or just a grammar for us, is a set $\mathcal{R}$ of rewriting rules of a certain type that generate a set of strings. There is a set Σ of *terminal* symbols, which form the strings that will be generated, and a set $\mathcal{V}$ of *nonterminal* symbols, which represent sets of strings. The rules are of the form

$$A \rightarrow B_1 B_2 \ldots B_k,$$

where $A \in \mathcal{V}$ is a nonterminal and $B_i \in \mathcal{V} \cup \Sigma$ are terminals or nonterminals. This means that whenever we see an A, we can replace it by the sequence $B_1 B_2 \ldots B_k$. The case $k = 0$ is written $A \rightarrow \varepsilon$ and means A can be removed. The grammar has an *initial symbol* $S \in \mathcal{V}$. The rewriting rules are applied starting with S until we obtain a string of all terminals. Each such string is said to be *generated* by the grammar.

Grammars are useful to describe *languages*, that is, sets of strings like all the correct programs in a programming language, all the correct XML documents, all the correct arithmetic formulas, and so on. Parsers, that is, programs that recognize the structure of the strings in those languages, can almost be automatically derived from grammars and are key in the development of compilers and interpreters, XML processors, and so on.

Example 8.18 *The grammar formed by the two rules*

$$S \rightarrow (S) S$$

$$S \rightarrow \varepsilon$$

generates all the sequences of balanced parentheses (Chapter 7). For example, by successive replacements of S using these two rules, we can generate $\underline{S} \Rightarrow (\underline{S}) S \Rightarrow ((\underline{S}) S) S \Rightarrow (( ) \underline{S}) S \Rightarrow (( )) \underline{S} \Rightarrow (( )) (\underline{S}) S \Rightarrow (( )) ( ) \underline{S} \Rightarrow (( )) ( )$, where we have underlined the occurrence of S that is replaced in each iteration.

T how can a clam cram in a clean cream can

$$R \begin{cases} A \rightarrow \_c & E \rightarrow AB \\ B \rightarrow an & F \rightarrow \_a \\ C \rightarrow am & G \rightarrow Ar \\ D \rightarrow Al & H \rightarrow FD \end{cases}$$

C S → howEHCGC_inHeBGeCE

Figure 8.17. The Re-Pair compression of a popular tongue twister. In the rules, we use the underscore to denote the whitespace for legibility.

In this section we are interested in another use of grammars, called *grammar compression*: Given a text string $T[1, n]$, we derive from T a set of rules R so that from its initial symbol S we can derive T and only T. If T is repetitive, then R is small and acts as a compressed representation of T.

While finding the smallest grammar that generates a given text T is NP-complete, an excellent heuristic is called *Re-Pair*. Re-Pair looks for the most frequent pair of symbols in T, say, ab, creates a rule $A \rightarrow ab$, and replaces every occurrence of ab in T by the nonterminal A. It now iterates (the new most frequent pair may include nonterminals), generating new rules, until every pair appears once. To the set of rules R obtained, Re-Pair adds a new one, $S \rightarrow C$, where C is the sequence resulting from T after all the replacements. Re-Pair can be implemented in linear time and space.

Example 8.19 *Figure 8.17 shows the Re-Pair compression of a string. Compression is not very effective in this case, but the resulting grammar is sufficiently illustrative for our purposes. We generated 8 nonterminals, A to H, plus the initial symbol S that derives C.*

Note that there is exactly one rule per nonterminal. Calling $\sigma = |\Sigma|$, $r = |R|$ and $c = |C|$, the space to represent the grammar is $(2r + c) \log(\sigma + r)$. If the aim is just compression, then the rules can be represented in a space-efficient form that needs full decompression before we can use it to obtain T. Instead, we aim to use the grammar as a *compressed data structure* that represents the text T. Here the aim is to never decompress T, but rather maintain its grammar and efficiently extract any substring $T[i, j]$ on demand. In this case we need a readily accessible representation of R and C.

A bitvector $P[1, n]$, marking with 1s the positions where each symbol of C begins in T, is useful for determining the portion of C that must be extracted to display $T[i, j]$: Let $s = \mathsf{rank}(P, i - 1)$ and $e = \mathsf{rank}(P, j + 1)$. Then we have to extract (1) a (possibly empty) suffix of $C[s]$, (2) the complete string generated by $C[s + 1, e - 1]$, and (3) a (possibly empty) prefix of $C[e]$. If $s = e$, then $T[i, j]$ is totally contained in $C[s = e]$. If we store P using very sparse bitvectors (Section 4.4), it requires $c \log(n/c) + \mathcal{O}(c)$ bits of space, proportional to the grammar size.

Therefore, the basic problem is to expand a symbol $C[p]$. If $C[p] = a$ is a terminal, then we output a. Otherwise there exists a rule $C[p] \rightarrow BC$, and we recursively expand B and then C. By storing R as an array of pairs of $\lceil \log r \rceil$-bit numbers, where the tth array position corresponds to the nonterminal number t, we easily carry out the expansion in optimal time. If we make the grammar balanced (i.e., of height $\mathcal{O}(\log n)$), we can also extract a suffix or a prefix of length ℓ from $C[p]$ in time $\mathcal{O}(\ell + \log n)$. By also storing the length to which each nonterminal expands, we can obtain the same time to obtain ℓ symbols from the middle of $C[p]$. Overall any $T[i, j]$ can be extracted in time $\mathcal{O}(j - i + \log n)$.

Grammar compression works best when the text is very repetitive. In this case the largest part of the representation is the set of rules $\mathcal{R}$, because many rules are generated and a very small C results. A natural question is whether it is actually necessary to spend $2r \log(\sigma + r)$ bits on $\mathcal{R}$. The answer is no, we can do with just $r \log r + \mathcal{O}(\sigma + r)$ bits by using ordinal trees and permutations (Chapter 5). Note that σ is usually insignificant compared to r, thus the reduction in space is by about a half. We are not counting the $r \log n$ bits to store the length to which each nonterminal expands, as they might be sampled to trade space for time.

The idea is as follows. Regard $\mathcal{R}$ as a directed acyclic graph (DAG) where the nodes are $\Sigma \cup \mathcal{V}$, and each rule $A \to BC$ induces an edge from A to B and another from A to C. Those will be called left and right edges, respectively. Now, if we take only the left edges of the DAG, and interpret an edge $A \to B$ as B being the *parent* of A, then we obtain a set of trees, since each node can have at most one parent (that is, terminals have no rules and each nonterminal A has exactly one rule with exactly one left term B). We add a special root as the parent of all the nodes without a parent, and call $\mathcal{T}_L$ the resulting tree. Similarly, we form a tree $\mathcal{T}_R$ with the right edges. Now, given a nonterminal $A \to BC$, B is the parent of A in $\mathcal{T}_L$ and C is the parent of A in $\mathcal{T}_R$.

Example 8.20 *Figure 8.18 illustrates the decomposition of the rules of Figure 8.17 into two trees. For example, we know that* $\mathsf{D} \to \mathsf{A}\mathsf{I}$ *because the parent of* D *in* $\mathcal{T}_L$ *is* A *and the parent of* D *in* $\mathcal{T}_R$ *is* I.

Let us renumber the terminals and nonterminals so as to identify them with their nodemap value in $\mathcal{T}_L$. Nonterminals can be freely renamed, but terminals cannot. Since terminals are the children of the special root, we can sort them so as to respect their order in Σ, thus retaining their identity.

In addition, we store a permutation π in $[1, \sigma + r + 1]$, so that $\pi(A) = $ nodemap$(\mathcal{T}_R, v_R)$, where $v_R \in \mathcal{T}_R$ corresponds to symbol A; that is, π translates node identifiers in $\mathcal{T}_L$ to node identifiers in $\mathcal{T}_R$. Permutation π is stored using the technique of Section 5.1, so that it uses $(\sigma + r) \log(\sigma + r) + \mathcal{O}(\sigma + r)$ bits of space and can compute any value $\pi^{-1}(j)$ in time $\mathcal{O}(\log(\sigma + r))$.

Now, given a nonterminal symbol A to expand, where A is a nodemap value of $\mathcal{T}_L$, we proceed as follows. We compute $v = $ nodeselect$(\mathcal{T}_L, A)$. If parent$(\mathcal{T}_L, v) = $ root$(\mathcal{T}_L)$, then A is indeed a terminal symbol, more precisely, childrank$(\mathcal{T}_L, v)$. Otherwise A is a nonterminal $A \to BC$, and we must obtain B and C. The left one is easily obtained as $B = $ nodemap$(\mathcal{T}_L, $ parent$(\mathcal{T}_L, v))$. The right one requires more work, as we have to switch to $\mathcal{T}_R$ and back: $C = \pi^{-1}($nodemap$(\mathcal{T}_R, $ parent$(\mathcal{T}_R, $ nodeselect$(\mathcal{T}_R, \pi(A))))).$

LOUDS is the best choice for representing $\mathcal{T}_L$ and $\mathcal{T}_R$, for various reasons. First, we need only the operations **parent, root, childrank, nodemap,** and **nodeselect,** all of which are supported in LOUDS, more efficiently than in BP or DFUDS. Second,

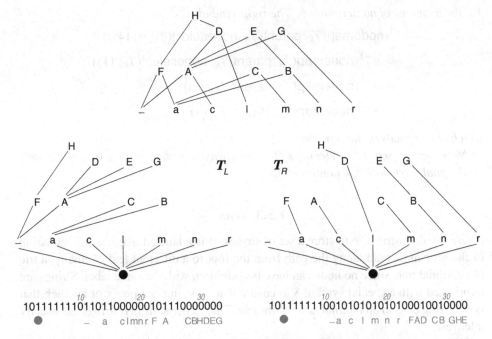

Figure 8.18. At the top, the rules of Figure 8.17 in DAG form. On the bottom, its representation as trees $\mathcal{T}_L$ and $\mathcal{T}_R$ (drawn upwards). For each rule $A \to BC$, B is the parent of A in $\mathcal{T}_L$ and C is the parent of A in $\mathcal{T}_R$. Below each tree we show its LOUDS deployment. To maintain the correct order of terminals, we flip the trees upside down instead of rotating them.

LOUDS will give the terminals the first **nodemap** values, which makes it easy to distinguish them from nonterminals (v is a terminal iff **nodemap**$(v) \leq \sigma + 1$), and we can build permutation π only on the range of nonterminal identifiers, needing $r \log r + \mathcal{O}(\sigma + r)$ bits in total.

As a result, extracting a rule requires $\mathcal{O}(\log r)$ time, but the rules require about half the space, which can be a very significant reduction.

Example 8.21 *The LOUDS representations of the trees in Figure 8.18 are shown at the bottom. Note that we have added the spurious initial bits* **10**. *The gray sequences below the bits also show the* **nodemap** *(levelwise) order in the symbols. Thus the permutation π that maps the order in $\mathcal{T}_L$ to the order in $\mathcal{T}_R$ (considering that position 1 is the tree root) is*

$$\pi = \langle 1, 2, 3, 4, 5, 6, 7, 8, 9, 10, 12, 13, 15, 11, 16, 14 \rangle.$$

Finally, the bitvector that marks where the symbols of C begin in T is

$$P = 1111000100001010010111100001101001101000.$$

Let us extract the rule $\mathsf{D} \to \mathsf{AI}$. *The identifier of* D *is 14, its levelwise position in $\mathcal{T}_L$. First, we find the node of* D *in $\mathcal{T}_L$ with* $v = \mathsf{nodeselect}(\mathcal{T}_L, 14) = 31$. *Now, the left symbol to which* D *rewrites is* $\mathsf{nodemap}(\mathcal{T}_L, \mathsf{parent}(\mathcal{T}_L, 31)) = \mathsf{nodemap}(\mathcal{T}_L, 24) =$

10, *the identifier of nonterminal* **A**. *The right symbol is*

$$\pi^{-1}(\text{nodemap}(\mathcal{T}_R, \text{parent}(\mathcal{T}_R, \text{nodeselect}(\mathcal{T}_R, \pi(14)))))$$

$$= \pi^{-1}(\text{nodemap}(\mathcal{T}_R, \text{parent}(\mathcal{T}_R, \text{nodeselect}(\mathcal{T}_R, 11))))$$

$$= \pi^{-1}(\text{nodemap}(\mathcal{T}_R, \text{parent}(\mathcal{T}_R, 26)))$$

$$= \pi^{-1}(\text{nodemap}(\mathcal{T}_R, 16)) = \pi^{-1}(5) = 5,$$

which corresponds to the terminal I.

Note that the first $\sigma + 1$ *elements of* π *are always the identity, thus we build* π *only on the final r symbols, the nonterminals.*

8.5.3 Tries

A *trie* is a data structure to store a set of strings. It is a labeled tree where each string of the set can be read along the path from the root to a different leaf. Actually, a trie is a cardinal tree, since no node can have two children with the same label. Strings are terminated with a special symbol $ to ensure that no string is a prefix of another, that is, no string ends in an internal node of the trie. Thus, a trie storing n strings has exactly n leaves.

To save space, nodes with a single descendant leaf are recursively converted into a leaf. The removed characters are then stored in a string associated with the leaf.

Example 8.22 *At the top of Figure 8.19 we show the trie formed by the* 20 *most common names given in Chile to girls born in 2010. The other elements of the figure will be used later.*

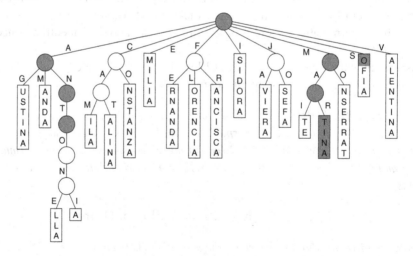

$B = (\;(\;)\;(\;(\;(\;(\;(\;(\;(\;(\;(\;)\;(\;(\;(\;)\;)\;)\;(\;)\;(\;)\;(\;)\;(\;(\;)\;)\;)\;(\;(\;)\;(\;(\;)\;)\;)\;)\;)\;(\;(\;(\;)\;)\;)\;)\;(\;)\;)\;)\;(\;(\;)\;(\;(\;)\;)\;)\;)\;)$

$S =$ ACEFIJMSV GMN   T O N EI   AO MT   ELR   AO   AO IR

$L =$ USTINAANDALLAAILAALINANSTANZAMILIARNANDAORENCIAANCISCASIDORAVIERASEFATETINANSERRATOFIAALENTINA

$M =$ 10000001000010001010001000001000000010000010000010000001000000010000010000010000100100010000000100001000000000

Figure 8.19. A trie of 20 strings. The blocks associated with leaves store the rest of the strings, with terminators $ omitted. Grayed nodes and strings illustrate Example 8.23. Below the trie, our compact representation.

The basic operation of the trie is to determine whether a string, called the *search pattern* $P[1, m]$, is in the set. We descend from the root following the characters of P (P is terminated with $), until either the current node has no child labeled with the desired character (thus P is not in the set) or we arrive at a leaf. At this point, if P is present in the set, it is in this leaf. Thus, we compare the rest of P with the string stored in the leaf. Note that the search time depends only on m and not on n.

A more powerful operation enabled by tries is the so-called *prefix search*, that is, given a search pattern $P[1, m]$, determine the number of strings prefixed by P, or enumerate them. The search is very similar to the basic one, with the difference that we do not append the $ to P. If we reach a node that has no child labeled by the corresponding character $P[i]$, then P does not prefix any string in the set. If we reach a leaf, then P may prefix only the string of that leaf, thus we must check if the rest of P still prefixes the string stored in the leaf. This time, a third termination condition is possible: We may scan all of P and still be at an internal node v. Then the number of leaves descending from v is the number of strings prefixed by P, and we can list them using a full traversal from v.

Example 8.23 *In the set of Example 8.22 we may wonder whether* $P =$ SOLEDAD *was a top-20 common name. We descend by the* S *and reach the leaf corresponding to* SOFIA. *When comparing the rest of P,* OLEDAD, *with the string stored in the leaf,* OFIA, *we find a mismatch, thus* SOLEDAD *was not a top-20 common name.*

If we ask the same question about $P =$ ANAIS, *we descend by the label* A, *then by* N, *and then find no child descending by label* A, *thus* ANAIS *was not a top-20 common name either.*

If we look for $P =$ MARTINA, *we descend by the* M, *by the* A, *by the* R, *and reach a leaf where the stored string,* TINA, *matches the rest of P; thus* MARTINA *was a top-20 common name.*

If we look for common names starting with $P =$ AN, *we descend by the* A, *by the* N, *and exhaust P at the corresponding node. This node has 2 descendant leaves, corresponding to* ANTONELLA *and* ANTONIA.

All the traversals described are grayed in the trie of Figure 8.19. We have omitted the terminator $ in patterns and strings for simplicity.

If the labels of the children of each trie node are sorted left-to-right, then the rank of the first and last leaves descending from v give the lexicographic interval of the strings prefixed by P in the set. Also, for patterns P not in the set, we can compute their string predecessor and successor: Once the desired child of v labeled $P[i]$ is not present, we can look for the previous/next child, and then systematically descend toward its last/first child until reaching a leaf. This leaf is the predecessor/successor of P in the set.

A Compact Representation

Tries are very powerful data structures yet frequently blamed for their high space usage. With the labeled tree representations we have developed in this chapter, a set of n strings of total length ℓ (counting terminators $) can be represented with at most $\ell(\log \sigma + 2) + o(\ell)$ bits, where σ is the alphabet size. This is very close to the $\ell \log \sigma$ bits needed to store the strings alone (actually, our structure could store less than ℓ characters, if the strings share paths).

Let the trie have t nodes. We will use a DFUDS representation for the tree topology, $B[1, 2t + 2]$ and associate it with a string $S[1, t]$ containing the edge labels. The edges are associated with the 1s of the DFUDS bitvector, so as to allow efficient downward traversal of the trie. The strings in the leaves will be concatenated, left to right, in another string $L[1, l]$, without the separators $. A bitvector $M[1, l + n]$ will store their consecutive lengths $l_1, l_2, \ldots$ in L, as $M = 10^{l_1} 10^{l_2} \ldots$. The total space is $(t + l) \log \sigma + 2t + l + n + o(t + l + n) \leq \ell(\log \sigma + 2) + o(\ell)$ bits, since $t + l + n \leq \ell + 1$ (we leave checking this, by induction on the tree structure, as an exercise to the reader).

Example 8.24 *At the bottom of Figure 8.19 we show the compact representation for that trie.*

The strings will be identified with their corresponding leaf node rank, 1 to n. String $s \in [1, n]$ will correspond to leaf $v = \mathsf{leafselect}(s)$. The string content is obtained in two phases. The prefix of s that is in the edge labels is obtained in reverse order, by repeatedly computing $\mathsf{childlabel}(v)$ and moving to the parent, $v \leftarrow \mathsf{parent}(v)$, until reaching the root. The remaining suffix of s is $\mathit{suff}(s) = L[\mathsf{select}(M, s) - s + 1, \mathsf{select}(M, s + 1) - (s + 1)]$.

To search for a $-terminated pattern $P[1, m]$, we start at $v \leftarrow \mathsf{root}()$ and, for increasing i, repeat $v \leftarrow \mathsf{labeledchild}(v, P[i])$, until either the desired child is not found (so P is not in the set) or we reach a leaf node v after examining $P[1, i]$. Now we compute the leaf identifier, $s = \mathsf{leafrank}(v)$, and compare $P[i + 1, m - 1]$ with $\mathit{suff}(s)$. If they are equal, then P is the string with identifier s, otherwise P is not in the set.

Algorithm 8.18 gives the pseudocode for extracting a string and searching for a pattern. If we use a simple DFUDS representation taking $\mathcal{O}(\log n)$ time per operation, and implement $\mathsf{labeledchild}$ by a simple binary search on the range of labels in S corresponding to the children of v, then a string of length l is extracted in time $\mathcal{O}(l \log n)$ and pattern $P[1, m]$ is searched for in time $\mathcal{O}(m \log n)$. To reduce the complexities, we can use the more complex $\mathcal{O}(\log \log n)$ time parentheses implementation for DFUDS and add a $\mathsf{rank/select}$ data structure on S to reach $\mathcal{O}(\log \log \sigma)$ time for $\mathsf{labeledchild}$. The times then become $\mathcal{O}(l \log \log n)$ and $\mathcal{O}(m \log \log n)$, respectively.

If we perform a prefix search and terminate in a node v, then the number of strings prefixed by P is $\mathsf{leafnum}(v)$, and their lexicographic range in the set is $[\mathsf{leafrank}(v), \mathsf{leafrank}(v) + \mathsf{leafnum}(v) - 1]$. To enumerate the strings, we perform a depth-first traversal from v, maintaining the symbols of the current path in a stack, and printing the whole stack plus the string stored in each leaf we reach.

To find the predecessor/successor of a pattern P not in the set, we reach the node v where we cannot descend further, run a binary search for the edge that precedes/follows the missing one, descend to the child of v by that edge, and then continue descending using $\mathsf{lchild/fchild}$ until reaching a leaf.

Autocompletion Search

Many search systems suggest ways to complete the string as one types. This is called autocompletion. The suggested strings come from a predefined set and are generally ranked in some way. The autocompletion then suggests the highest-ranked matching string.

Algorithm 8.18: Extraction and pattern search in tries.

---

1 **Proc** *extract*(*s*)
  Input : Trie (seen as DFUDS tree *T*, sequence *S*, string *L*, and bitvector *M*).
  Output: Outputs the string with identifier *s*.

2 | *v* ← leafselect(*T*, *s*)
3 | **if** childlabel(*T*, *v*) = $ **then**
4 | | *show*(parent(*T*, *v*))
5 | **else**
6 | | *show*(*v*)
7 | | **output** *L*[select(*M*, *s*) − *s* + 1, select(*M*, *s* + 1) − (*s* + 1)]

8 **Proc** *show*(*v*)
  Input : Trie node *v*.
  Output: Outputs the path labels from the root to *v*.

9 | **if** *v* ≠ root(*T*) **then**
10 | | *show*(parent(*T*, *v*))
11 | | **output** childlabel(*T*, *v*)

12 **Proc** *search*(*P*)
  Input : Trie (seen as DFUDS tree *T*, sequence *S*, string *L*, and bitvector *M*),
        and search pattern *P*[1, *m*] terminated in $.
  Output: Returns the string identifier corresponding to *P*, or 0 if *P* is not in the
        set.

13 | *v* ← root(*T*)
14 | *i* ← 0
15 | **while not** isleaf(*T*, *v*) **do**
16 | | *i* ← *i* + 1
17 | | *v* ← labeledchild(*T*, *v*, *P*[*i*])
18 | | **if** *v* = 0 **then** (null, so there was no child labeled *P*[*i*])
19 | | | **return** 0
20 | *s* ← leafrank(*T*, *v*)
21 | **if** *P*[*i*+1, *m*−1] = *L*[select(*M*, *s*)−*s*+1, select(*M*, *s*+1)−(*s*+1)] **then**
22 | | **return** *s*
23 | **return** 0

This can be readily implemented in combination with our tries as follows. The identifiers of the leaves are in the range [1, *n*]. Consider an array *A*[1, *n*] where the ranks of the *n* strings are written, in the left-to-right order of leaves (the lower the number, the higher the preference). Now build on *A* the rmq_A data structure of Section 7.4.1, which uses $2n + o(n)$ bits and does not require *A* to be stored.

With such a small extra space on top of our compact trie structures, we can offer efficient autocompletion searches: As the user types in the successive letters of a search pattern P, we descend in the trie. Let v be the current trie node. The string we offer for autocompleting the search is then $s = \mathsf{rmq}_A(\mathsf{leafrank}(v), \mathsf{leafrank}(v) + \mathsf{leafnum}(v) - 1)$. We call $extract(s)$ of Algorithm 8.18 to extract its characters and display them.

Example 8.25 *In an application for the Civil Registry, where the names of the new-borns are registered, we offer autocompletion search based on how frequent the name is this year. The array of ranks corresponding to the strings of Figure 8.19 is* $A = \langle 16, 18, 6, 7, 19, 9, 11, 8, 10, 3, 15, 5, 12, 17, 13, 14, 1, 20, 2, 4 \rangle$. *Then we build the 2n-bit structure of Section 7.4.1 on A and discard A.*

Imagine now the user types **A**. *We descend to the first child of the root, compute the leaf interval* [1, 4], *and then* $s = \mathsf{rmq}_A(1, 4) = 3$ *is our best bet on what the user wants to type. Thus we offer the autocompletion* **ANTONELLA**. *But the user does not take it and types instead an* **M**. *Thus we descend to the second child of the current node, whose leaf interval is* [2, 2]. *Thus we offer the only possible autocompletion of* **AM**, **AMANDA**.

Patricia Trees

Consider again the trie of Figure 8.19. There is a path of 3 consecutive nodes with only one child, labeled **T**, **O**, **N**, which occurs because **ANTONELLA** and **ANTONIA** share a long prefix. If we could ensure that no such "unary" nodes exist, then, since the trie has n leaves, it would have at most $n - 1$ internal nodes. Then the space usage of the trie topology would decrease to at most $4n + o(n)$ bits.

Patricia trees remove these unary nodes in tries. The idea is that any path of unary nodes is collapsed into a single edge, now labeled by the concatenation of those edge labels. From this concatenation, Patricia trees store only the first letter and the length. In our example, the path would be labeled by **TON**, but we would store only $(\mathsf{T}, 3)$.

The search in a Patricia tree proceeds as follows. We start with $i \leftarrow 1$ at the node $v \leftarrow \mathsf{root}()$. Now we descend to $v \leftarrow \mathsf{labeledchild}(v, P[i])$, if possible (otherwise P is not in the set, as usual). Let $(P[i], g)$ be the symbol and length associated with the edge traversed. Then we set $i \leftarrow i + g$, and continue. This terminates when either we do not find the desired label, or we arrive at a leaf, or i exceeds m, the pattern length, in an internal node.

If we reach a leaf, since we have skipped some characters of P, we are not sure that the traversed prefix of P actually matches the string at this leaf. Therefore, we must compare *the whole P* with the string. For this reason, we must store the complete strings at the leaves, not only their suffix as before. Note that the search cost is still proportional to m.

Instead, if we reach $i > m$ at an internal node v, we know that the last symbol of P, \$, cannot label the edges toward v, so P does not appear in the set. The situation is different if we are doing a prefix search for P, which in this case is not terminated with \$. It could be that P finishes in the middle of the edge toward v, but again we do not know if the skipped characters of P match those that lead to v. However, all the leaves that descend from v share the same prefix up to v, therefore, P matches the prefix up to v iff it matches the first m characters of *any* string in a leaf descending from v. Thus, we take, say, the leftmost leaf, and compare its first m characters with P. If they match, then P prefixes all the strings at the leaves that descend from v; otherwise P prefixes no string.

A compact implementation of a Patricia tree must associate the 1s of the DFUDS representation with two label sequences. One is S, as before. The other is a sequence of *skips*, G, where we store the second component of the edges (the number of characters to skip). There are up to $2n - 1$ skip values and each can be as large as ℓ, but in fact all of them can only add up to ℓ (the skip values toward leaves are irrelevant and can be set to 1). Thus, it is best to use a variable-length representation that allows for direct access, so as to use $\mathcal{O}(n \log(\ell/n))$ bits. Sections 3.2 and 6.4.5 give several solutions that offer direct access on variable-length numbers.

Finally, to help reduce the space, the bitvector M marking the initial positions of the strings in L can be represented in compressed form, as in the partial-sums solutions of Section 4.5.1. In this case, it also uses $\mathcal{O}(n \log(\ell/n))$ bits. Overall the total space of a Patricia tree representation is $\ell \log \sigma + \mathcal{O}(n \log(\ell \sigma /n))$ bits.

Actually, Patricia trees go one step further. Since fewer than $2n$ nodes are created independently of the lengths of the strings, they convert the alphabet to binary; that is, a string of length l is regarded as a binary string of length $l \log \sigma$. This increases the number of internal nodes to exactly $n - 1$, increases the length of the skips by a factor of $\log \sigma$ (thus, the representation of G grows by an additive factor of $\mathcal{O}(n \log \log \sigma)$ bits), and increases the search time in the trie up to $m \log \sigma$ steps. The advantage is that, in a classical scenario, binary trees are easier to handle without wasting too much space. In our case the advantage of such a decision is unclear, especially because we wish to support operations **leafrank**, **leafnum**, and **leafselect**, which are not efficiently handled in the LOUDS representation of binary trees. Instead, we should use the BP representation, which is no faster than DFUDS.

A First Approach to Suffix Trees

In general, even in non-binary form, it is not clear that the overhead of converting a trie into a Patricia tree pays off. The possible reduction in space due to the elimination of unary nodes may be outweighed by the need to store the skips, more characters in L, and a longer M.

However, one instance where its use is advisable is when implementing *suffix trees*. In a first and simple approach, a suffix tree is a trie containing all the suffixes of a text $T[1, n]$. This text is terminated with $T[n] = \$$, which is assumed to be lexicographically smaller than all the other symbols.

When the strings to be stored in the trie are all the suffixes of a single string $T[1, n]$, they add up to length $\ell = n(n + 1)/2 = \mathcal{O}(n^2)$, but the text T can be used as a replacement of the sequence L and bitvector M: We need to store, for each trie leaf, only the starting position of the corresponding suffix in T. The array of those positions in leaf order, $A[1, n]$, is called the *suffix array* of T. If the children of the nodes are sorted by increasing label, then the leaves list the suffixes of T in lexicographic order, and $A[1, n]$ can be simply regarded as a reordering of the suffixes of T in lexicographic order.

The suffix tree is a useful tool to find the occurrences of patterns $P[1, m]$ in T in time proportional to m rather than to n. To search for P in T, we use prefix search in the trie. We want to spot all the substrings of T equal to P. But every substring $T[i, j]$ is the prefix of suffix $T[i, n]$. Therefore, we want to find all the suffixes of T that are

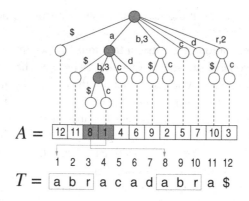

Figure 8.20. A suffix tree and array of a text. Skip lengths equal to 1 are omitted in the edge labels. The grayed elements illustrate the search for $P = \mathsf{abr}$, whose occurrences in the text are highlighted.

prefixed by P. If our search ends up at a node v, corresponding to a leaf range $[s, e]$, we have that $A[s, e]$ contains the starting positions of all the occurrences of P in T. If, during the search, we need to access the string corresponding to the leaf index s, it is at $T[A[s], n]$.

Example 8.26 *Figure 8.20 shows a text* $T[1, 12] = \mathsf{abracadabra\$}$, *its suffix array* $A[1, 12]$, *and the suffix tree on top of it, where only the skip values larger than* 1 *are explicit.*

For example, to find the occurrences of $P[1, 3] = \mathsf{abr}$ *in* T, *we start at the root node with* $i = 1$. *We descend by the edge labeled* $P[1] = \mathsf{a}$, *whose skip value is* 1, *so we set* $i \leftarrow i + 1 = 2$. *Now we descend by the edge labeled* $P[i] = P[2] = \mathsf{b}$, *reaching the lowest grayed node,* v. *The skip value of this edge is* 3, *so we set* $i \leftarrow i + 3 = 5$. *But* $m = 3 < 5$, *so there are no more characters to read from* P. *Now we go to the leftmost leaf of* v. *Since the range of leaves below* v *is* [leafrank(v), leafrank(v) + leafnum$(v) - 1$] $= [3, 4]$ *(grayed), the leftmost leaf of* v *is leaf number* 3. *Thus we read* $A[3] = 8$ *and compare* $P[1, m] = P[1, 3]$ *with* $T[A[3], A[3] + m - 1] = T[8, 10]$. *Since they match,* P *appears in* T. *The number of times it appears is the size of the range of leaves below* v, $4 - 3 + 1 = 2$. *The positions where* P *appears are listed in* $A[3, 4] = \langle 8, 1 \rangle$ *(shown in gray rectangles on the text).*

Thus, our suffix tree representation requires $n \log \sigma$ bits for T, $n \log n$ bits for the suffix array A, up to $4n + o(n)$ bits for the trie topology, and up to $2n \log \sigma$ bits for the sequence S of edge labels. The skips need not be stored: if we have matched $P[1, i]$ and reached node u, and now descend to node v by symbol $P[i + 1]$, then let $A[s, e] = A[$leafrank(v), leafrank(v) + leafnum$(v) - 1]$ be the range of the suffixes covered by v. Then $P[1, i] = T[A[k], A[k] + i - 1]$ for every $s \le k \le e$. Further, $T[A[s] + i, n]$ and $T[A[e] + i, n]$ coincide in their first g symbols, where g is precisely the skip value labeling the edge from u to v. Since we are interested only in values of g up to $m - i$, we compute the longest shared prefix between $T[A[s] + i, A[s] + m - 1]$ and $T[A[e] + i, A[e] + m - 1]$, and its length is the skip value. Note that we can compare those symbols right away with $P[i + 1, i + g]$, instead of waiting until reaching a leaf.

Example 8.27 *In Example 8.26 we could have found the skip* 3, *when going down by* $P[2] = $ b, *by computing the longest prefix shared between* $T[A[3] + 1, n] = T[9, 12] = $ bra$ *and* $T[A[4] + 1, n] = T[2, 12] = $ bracadabra$, *since the interval covered by the node* v *is* $A[3, 4]$.

In total, we perform $\mathcal{O}(m)$ steps to search for P, and the structure uses $n \log n + \mathcal{O}(n \log \sigma)$ bits. In Chapter 11 we will show how this space can be significantly reduced. Suffix trees enable other powerful operations that we will also explore in Chapter 11. For example, if we wish to know the length of the prefix shared by two suffixes $T[i, n]$ and $T[j, n]$, we find the positions in A with values i and j, that is, $A^{-1}[i]$ and $A^{-1}[j]$ (for example, regarding A as a permutation and taking the inverse), find the corresponding suffix tree leaves $u = $ leafselect$(A^{-1}[i])$ and $v = $ leafselect$(A^{-1}[j])$, and compute $x = $ lca(u, v). Now, the sum of the skip lengths from the root to x (which we will be able to compute efficiently) is the length of the prefix shared. As another example, we can find the longest string that is repeated in T (in our example, abra), by traversing the whole suffix tree in depth-first order and recording the internal node with maximum sum of skips from the root (in Figure 8.20, this is the lowest grayed node, with value 4).

8.5.4 LZ78 Compression

A popular compression technique, used inside formats like GIF, is Lempel-Ziv 1978, or simply LZ78. It is not as effective as other compression formats, but in exchange, any text substring $T[i, j]$ can be extracted in optimal time $\mathcal{O}(j - i + 1)$ from the compressed text.

The LZ78 compression algorithm processes $T[1, n]$ from left to right and cuts it into z substrings, called *phrases*. This process is called the *parsing* of T. As the text is parsed, each new phrase is extended as much as possible to the right as long as it matches some previous phrase, and then the next character (the mismatched one) is also included. Note that not every previous substring of T can be used to form a new phrase; only a whole previous phrase can be used.

To parse the text efficiently, the algorithm builds the so-called *LZ78 trie*, which stores all the phrases built up to now. Since each phrase is formed by concatenating a previous phrase with a final character, it holds that the prefix of any phrase is also a phrase. The set of phrases is thus said to be *prefix-closed*. This means that *every node* of the LZ78 trie represents a phrase, thus at the end it has z nodes plus the root. Moreover, all the phrases are distinct (we append $ to T to ensure this for the final phrase as well).

We associate each trie node with its corresponding phrase number. Thus, the parsing is carried out as follows. In the beginning, the LZ78 trie has only the root node, with phrase number 0. Now, in general, if we have already processed $T[1, i - 1]$ and created phrases 1 to $k - 1$, we descend in the LZ78 trie by $T[i]$, $T[i + 1]$, $T[i + 2]$, and so on, until we reach a trie node v from where it is not possible to descend by $T[i + t]$. Then, the kth phrase is $T[i, i + t]$. We add a new child of v descending by character $T[i + t]$, and give it the phrase identifier k. In the compressed file, we write the kth pair: $\langle p, T[i + t] \rangle$, where p is the phrase number of node v.

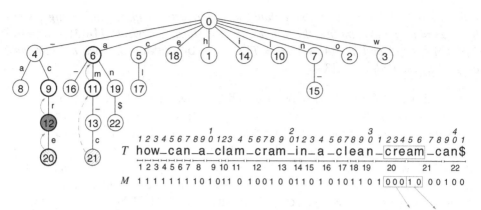

Figure 8.21. A text T and its LZ78 parsing into $z = 22$ phrases. The space is shown as an underscore for legibility. On top of T we show the LZ78 trie, with phrase numbers inside the nodes. Below the text and the trie we show the sequence of pairs that encode T. The gray node is that of phrase number 12, coded as $\langle 9, r \rangle$ because it is the child by an edge labeled r of the node representing phrase 9. Phrase 12 represents the text _cr, which can be read in the labels from the root of the trie to its node. We also show the compact representation of the trie, composed of M, N, B, and S. The arrows and the nodes with bold borders and/or hatched illustrate Example 8.30. Their corresponding elements in T and in the compact structures are also highlighted.

Example 8.28 *Figure 8.21 shows the LZ78 parsing of the same text of Figure 8.17, into $z = 22$ phrases. At the top we show the LZ78 trie, with the phrase number inside each node. At the bottom right of the trie we show how the parsing cuts T into phrases. Below the trie and the text we can see the sequence of pairs, where each phrase is coded as its parent phrase in the trie and the new character. The other elements of the figure will be explained later.*

The sequence of pairs requires $z(\log z + \log \sigma)$ bits of space. Once the text is compressed into z pairs $\langle p(k), c(k) \rangle$, $1 \leq k \leq z$, we can decompress any phrase $\langle p(k), c(k) \rangle$ as follows: If $p(k) = 0$, the phrase contains just character $c(k)$, which we output. We otherwise recursively expand the referenced phrase, number $p(k)$ (i.e., $\langle p(p(k)), c(p(k)) \rangle$), and then we output $c(k)$. Decompression of the whole file proceeds by sequentially decompressing all the pairs left to right.

Example 8.29 *Let us decompress the phrase number 12, $\langle p(12), c(12) \rangle = \langle 9, r \rangle$ in Example 8.28 (the corresponding node is grayed in the trie of Figure 8.21). Since $9 \neq 0$, we first decompress the phrase number 9, $\langle 4, c \rangle$. Since $4 \neq 0$, we first decompress the phrase number 4, $\langle 0, \_ \rangle$. Now we output '_', then return to phrase 9 and output 'c', and finally return to phrase 12 and output 'r'. Overall we output _ c r, the whole content of phrase number 12.*

Note that the LZ78 trie is dynamic, as it undergoes insertions along the compression process. Therefore, the static representations we have described in Section 8.5.3 do not directly apply. At decompression time, the trie is static and is represented implicitly in the compressed file, in the form of the parent pointers p of the pairs $\langle p, c \rangle$. This format is clearly convenient for efficient decompression of the whole file.

A Compact Data Structure

Instead of just decompressing the whole text, we could aim for a compact data structure that represents T and supports extraction of any substring $T[i, j]$, as we did with grammar compression in Section 8.5.2. With this aim, we represent the (final) LZ78 trie explicitly, in the form of a BP sequence of parentheses $B[1, 2z + 2]$ for the topology, the sequence of edge labels $S[1, z]$, associated with the preorders of the nodes, and the array $N[1, z]$, where $N[k]$ is the preorder of the node associated with the phrase number k. Overall the structures B, S, and N require $z(\log z + \log \sigma + 2) + o(z)$ bits of space, close to that of the bare sequence of pairs.

To support fast extraction of $T[i, j]$, we also store a bitvector $M[1, n]$, where $M[p] = 1$ iff a phrase starts at text position p. Since M has z 1s, it can be represented as a very sparse bitvector (Section 4.4) in $z \log(n/z) + \mathcal{O}(z)$ bits, which raises the total space requirement to $z(\log n + \log \sigma) + \mathcal{O}(z)$ bits.

Then the extraction of a substring $T[i, j]$ proceeds as follows. We find the phrase where j belongs with $k = \mathsf{rank}(M, j)$. The LZ78 trie node of phrase k is $v = \mathsf{preorderselect}(N[k])$. We do not want to extract the whole phrase k; we want to avoid its last $d = \mathsf{succ}(M, j + 1) - (j + 1)$ characters. Thus, we move to $v \leftarrow \mathsf{levelancestor}(v, d)$, and from there on we extract all the characters from v to the root, or until we have extracted $j - i + 1$ characters. If we reach the root and still have not extracted $j - i + 1$ characters, we restart from $v = \mathsf{preorderselect}(N[k - 1])$ (now $\mathsf{levelancestor}$ is not needed) and so on. Algorithm 8.19 depicts the procedure.

Example 8.30 *Figure 8.21 also shows our compact representation. Let us extract $T[i, j] = T[32, 36] = \mathsf{cream}$ (shown in gray in T and M, where it spans two phrases). Position $j = 36$ is at phrase number $k \leftarrow \mathsf{rank}(M, 36) = 21$. It appears in the LZ78 trie at the node v with preorder number $N[21] = 11$ (v is hatched in the trie and in B). Since $j = 36$ is at distance $\mathsf{succ}(M, 36 + 1) - (36 + 1) = 39 - 37 = 2$ of the end of phrase $k = 21$, we perform $v \leftarrow \mathsf{levelancestor}(v, 2)$, resulting in the node representing phrase 11 (a dashed arrow leads from the hatched node to it). This node and all the others participating in the extraction have bold borders; they are also highlighted in B. From this node, we obtain $S[\mathsf{preorder}(v)] = S[9] = \mathsf{m}$ and go to its parent $v \leftarrow \mathsf{parent}(v)$ (the node representing phrase 6). Once again we obtain $S[\mathsf{preorder}(v)] = S[7] = \mathsf{a}$ and go to its parent $v \leftarrow \mathsf{parent}(v)$. As this is the root, we have exhausted this phrase.*

Now we take the previous phrase, $k = 20$, represented by the node v with preorder $N[20] = 6$ (hatched in the other direction). Next we repeat $S[\mathsf{preorder}(v)] = S[6] = \mathsf{e}$, $v \leftarrow \mathsf{parent}(v)$, $S[\mathsf{preorder}(v)] = S[5] = \mathsf{r}$, $v \leftarrow \mathsf{parent}(v)$, and $S[\mathsf{preorder}(v)] = S[4] = \mathsf{c}$. At this point we have extracted $\ell = j - i + 1 = 5$ characters and can stop. We have filled $L[1, 5] = \mathsf{cream}$.

Algorithm 8.19: Extraction of a text substring from its LZ78 representation. Assume $N[0] = 1$ to avoid border cases.

---

1 **Proc** *extract*(i, j)

    Input : LZ78 trie of text T (seen as BP tree $\mathcal{T}$, string S, fixed-length cells
            array N, and bitvector M).

    Output: Writes $T[i, j]$ in string $L[1, j - i + 1]$.

2    $k \leftarrow \mathsf{rank}(M, j)$

3    $v \leftarrow \mathsf{preorderselect}(\mathcal{T}, \mathsf{read}(N, k))$

4    $d \leftarrow \mathsf{succ}(M, j + 1) - (j + 1)$

5    $v \leftarrow \mathsf{levelancestor}(\mathcal{T}, v, d)$

6    $\ell \leftarrow j - i + 1$

7   Allocate string $L[1, \ell]$

8   **while** $\ell > 0$ **do**

9   **while** $\ell > 0$ **and** $v \neq \mathsf{root}(\mathcal{T})$ **do**

10          $L[\ell] \leftarrow S[\mathsf{preorder}(\mathcal{T}, v)]$

11          $\ell \leftarrow \ell - 1$

12          $v \leftarrow \mathsf{parent}(\mathcal{T}, v)$

13       $k \leftarrow k - 1$

14       $v \leftarrow \mathsf{preorderselect}(\mathcal{T}, \mathsf{read}(N, k))$

We chose the BP representation because we need the operation **levelancestor** and do not need to traverse the trie downwards, where BP would be slower. As described, the extraction time is $\mathcal{O}(\log(n/z) + (j - i + 1) \log \log z)$. This can be converted to optimal, in theory, by using heavier data structures. We offer the references at the end of the chapter.

8.5.5 XML and XPath

Let us revisit the representation of XML documents mentioned in Section 7.4.2. This time we are concerned with querying the XML structure itself.

Several languages are used to query and manipulate XML-structured document collections. The best known one is *XPath*, on top of which more complex ones like *XQuery* are built. We do not aim for a full exposition of the XPath language; we just point out that efficiently solving XPath queries requires solving searches of the following types, among others:

1. Traverse the topology in any direction: parent, first child, next sibling, last child, previous sibling, and ith child.
2. Determine ancestorship between two nodes, or which one is after the other in preorder.
3. Find the first/last node descending from v with tag t, in preorder.
4. Find the next/previous node after/before v, in preorder, with tag t.
5. Find the first/last child of node v with tag t.

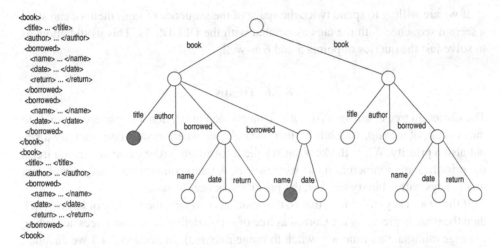

```
<book>
  <title> ... </title>
  <author> ... </author>
  <borrowed>
    <name> ... </name>
    <date> ... </date>
    <return> ... </return>
  </borrowed>
  <borrowed>
    <name> ... </name>
    <date> ... </date>
  </borrowed>
</book>
<book>
  <title> ... </title>
  <author> ... </author>
  <borrowed>
    <name> ... </name>
    <date> ... </date>
    <return> ... </return>
  </borrowed>
</book>
```

Figure 8.22. An XML collection and its tree representation. Gray nodes illustrate Example 8.31.

6. Find the next/previous sibling of node v with tag t.
7. Find the closest ancestor of node v with tag t.

Other queries are related to the text content, which are not considered here. For the above queries, a representation that can be a good compromise is a DFUDS topology with the tag labels associated with the 0s of the bitvector. Therefore, all the operations on the topology (point 1), including ith child, can be solved efficiently, and also the queries about ancestorship or preordering (point 2). The queries of points 3 and 4 are solved with **rank/select** operations on the sequence of tags S (plus using the topology to know where the subtree of v ends). The queries of points 5 and 6 require a sequential traversal over the children of v. Finally, the query of point 7 can be solved only by sequentially visiting the ancestors of v. A BP representation would be almost equally convenient, except for directly going to the ith child (this is not, however, a very frequent operation in XPath).

Example 8.31 *Figure 8.22 shows an excerpt of the XML structure for handling a library. Each book stores its title and author, plus a list of borrowing events. Each such event records the name of the borrower, the date the book was taken out, and the return date. Books not yet returned have no return record.*

Assume we want to know the titles of books not yet returned and the name of the last borrower. A strategy could be: for each book, *(1) find the last* name *label that descends from the* book *node and get its content, (2) go up to its parent, (3) if it has a child labeled* return, *then skip steps 4–6, (4) go up to the parent (the* book *node), (5) descend to the* title *child, getting its content as well, (6) output* name *and* title, *and (7) go on to the next sibling of the* book *node. The nodes output in our example are grayed in the figure.*

Note that a more efficient strategy could be implemented if the non-returned borrowing records included a tag indicating so. We could then jump over the books and search directly for those tags.

If we are willing to spend twice the space of the sequence of tags, then we can store a second sequence with the tags associated with the DFUDS 1s. This would allow us to solve fast the queries of points 5 and 6 as well.

8.5.6 Treaps

The Cartesian tree of an array $A[1, n]$ we mentioned in Section 7.6 also corresponds to the concept of a *treap*, which is a binary search tree where nodes have not only a key but also a priority. While the keys satisfy the left-to-right order of binary search trees, the priorities are nonincreasing as we descend. A treap combines a binary search tree on the keys with a binary heap on the priorities, hence its name.

If the search keys are 1 to n, that is, the positions in A, and the priority of key i is $A[i]$, then the treap is precisely the Cartesian tree of A (we defined Cartesian trees according to range minima; this time we switch to range maxima). In Section 7.4.1 we encoded the topology of this Cartesian tree (as explained also in Sections 7.6 and 8.2.1) using $2n + o(n)$ bits. This is sufficient if the keys are $[1, n]$ and the precise priority values are unimportant (we want only to obtain the highest-priority key in a range).

Imagine, however, that the keys $x_1 < x_2 < \ldots < x_n$ belong to some universe $[1, U]$ and that the priorities $p_1, p_2, \ldots, p_n$ belong to another universe $[1, V]$, and we have to store them as well. Further, our query gives a range $[x_l, x_r]$ in the universe $[1, U]$ and must retrieve all the values $x_i \in [x_l, x_r]$ whose priority is larger than some $p \in [1, V]$.

The keys can be represented efficiently using variable-length codes of the differences $x_i - x_{i-1}$: we can store them within $\mathcal{O}(n \log(U/n))$ bits and can retrieve any x_i in constant time as a partial sum, using the techniques of Section 4.5.1. Further, we use the **search** operation to find the range $A[i, j]$ of the keys contained in $[x_l, x_r]$ in time $\mathcal{O}(\log \min(U/n, n))$.

To extract all the values in $A[i, j]$ with priority larger than p, we use the rMq_A structure of Section 7.4.1 (we renamed it as rMq_A to remind us that it extracts range maxima, not minima). We first compute $m \leftarrow \mathsf{rMq}_A(i, j)$. If $A[m] \leq p$ we finish, because there are no priorities larger than p in $A[i, j]$. Otherwise we output the key x_m and continue recursively on $A[i, m - 1]$ and $A[m + 1, j]$. This continues until an interval is empty or its maximum priority does not exceed p. Since we output an element each time we perform two recursive calls, the total amount of work is proportional to the number of elements we output, e. Using the fast parentheses implementation of Section 7.2, the total time is $\mathcal{O}(\log \min(U/n, n) + e \log \log n)$.

A problem with this scheme is that we must store A, that is, the priorities, in plain form. Next we propose an alternative representation where both keys and priorities can be stored differentially because of the treap properties (yet the differences will be slightly larger than before).

Let x_v and p_v be the key and priority, respectively, of the Cartesian tree node v. We store them differentially in arrays $X[1, n]$ and $P[1, n]$, indexed by preorder values. The key at $X[\mathsf{preorder}(v)]$ is represented differentially with respect to the key of its parent $u = \mathsf{parent}(v)$: if v is a left child, then we represent $X[\mathsf{preorder}(v)] = x_u - x_v$, otherwise $X[\mathsf{preorder}(v)] = x_v - x_u$. Instead, the priority is always represented as $P[\mathsf{preorder}(v)] = p_u - p_v$. For the root node v, with $\mathsf{preorder}(v) = 1$, we store $X[1] = x_v$ and $P[1] = p_v$.

Algorithm 8.20: Reporting the largest values in a range using a treap.

Input : Treap on $A[1, n]$ (seen as binary Cartesian tree T and arrays X and P),
range $[x_l, x_r]$, and priority p.
Output: Outputs all $x_i \in [x_l, x_r]$ where $A[i] > p$.

1 $explore(\text{root}(T), \text{access}(X, 1), \text{access}(P, 1), x_l, x_r, p)$

2 **Proc** $explore(v, x, q, x_l, x_r, p)$
     Input : Treap node v with key x and priority q, range $[x_l, x_r]$ and priority p.
     Output: Outputs all the keys in $[x_l, x_r]$ under v with priority over p.

3   **if** $q \leq p$ **then return**
4   **if** $x_l \leq x \leq x_r$ **then output** x
5   **if** $x_l < x$ **then**
6         $u \leftarrow \text{leftchild}(T, v)$
7         $x_u \leftarrow x - \text{access}(X, \text{preorder}(T, u))$
8         $q_u \leftarrow q - \text{access}(P, \text{preorder}(T, u))$
9         $explore(u, x_u, q_u, x_l, x_r, p)$
10   **if** $x_r > x$ **then**
11        $u \leftarrow \text{rightchild}(T, v)$
12        $x_u \leftarrow x + \text{access}(X, \text{preorder}(T, u))$
13        $q_u \leftarrow q - \text{access}(P, \text{preorder}(T, u))$
14        $explore(u, x_u, q_u, x_l, x_r, p)$

Example 8.32 *The differential arrays corresponding to a treap encoding of the Cartesian tree of Figure 7.12 are as follows:*

$$X = \langle 12, 8, 2, 1, 1, 4, 3, 2, 1, 2, 1, 1, 2, 1, 6, 5, 3, 2, 1, 1, 1 \rangle,$$

$$P = \langle 0, 1, 1, 1, 3, 1, 1, 1, 5, 1, 3, 1, 1, 1, 1, 1, 1, 1, 1, 1, 2 \rangle.$$

The arrays X and P are then represented using any technique for variable-length cells (Sections 3.2 and 6.4.5) without the need for partial sums. We perform all the searches from the root and thus always know the key and priority of the current node, using it to compute those of the left or right child as we descend. Then we can solve the query using the simple method of Algorithm 8.20.

While the algorithm offers no good worst-case guarantees, if the treap height is $\mathcal{O}(\log n)$ (which is the expected height if the priorities form a random permutation in A, for example), then the number of nodes traversed is $\mathcal{O}(e + \log n)$. In this case the query time is $\mathcal{O}((\log n + e) \log \log n)$, only slightly higher than with the original representation. In exchange, we do not need to compute partial sums to obtain the keys and priorities, but just access on variable-length cells.

As for the storage, we compress both keys and priorities, not only keys, but the gaps are larger because the values are not totally sorted. Still, most of the numbers belong to the lowest part of the tree, where their differences are small. Note that, if desired, we

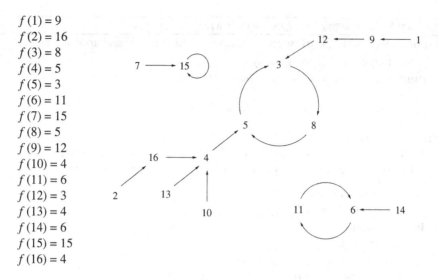

$f(1) = 9$
$f(2) = 16$
$f(3) = 8$
$f(4) = 5$
$f(5) = 3$
$f(6) = 11$
$f(7) = 15$
$f(8) = 5$
$f(9) = 12$
$f(10) = 4$
$f(11) = 6$
$f(12) = 3$
$f(13) = 4$
$f(14) = 6$
$f(15) = 15$
$f(16) = 4$

Figure 8.23. On the left, an integer function, and on the right, its graph representation. An arrow $i \rightarrow j$ means $f(i) = j$.

can still store the keys as left-to-right differences in X and extract them using partial sums; the key of x_v is $\mathsf{sum}(X, \mathsf{inorder}(v))$.

8.5.7 Integer Functions

The permutations on $[1, n]$ studied in Chapter 5 are particular cases of *integer functions* $f : [1, n] \rightarrow [1, n]$. Since there are n^n functions in the domain $[1, n]$, their worst-case entropy is exactly $n \log n$ bits, and therefore storing the function as a simple array $F[1, n]$ with fixed-length cells $F[i] = f(i)$ is essentially optimal. However, this representation only supports computing any $f(i)$ in constant time. We are interested in a representation that, just as for permutations (Section 5.2), can efficiently compute $f^k(i)$ for any integer k (positive or negative; we discuss the negative case soon).

The key idea is to consider a graph with the nodes $i \in [1, n]$, and set a directed edge from every node i to its corresponding target $f(i)$. The result will be a set of $c \geq 1$ cycles (as in permutations) and possibly a tree sprouting from each node in those cycles.

Example 8.33 *Figure 8.23 shows a function* $f : [1, 16] \rightarrow [1, 16]$ *and its representation as a graph. In this case,* $c = 3$ *cycles are formed.*

We represent this structure as an ordinal tree T of $n + c + 1$ nodes. The root of T has c children, one per cycle, in any order (thus T has c nodes of depth 2). The node corresponding to the ith cycle, of length ℓ_i, has ℓ_i children, one per node involved in the cycle. The left-to-right order of these ℓ_i children must correspond to the cycle order (starting at some point in the cycle). Thus T has $\ell = \sum_{i=1}^{c} \ell_i$ nodes at depth 3. Finally, the subtree of each of those depth-3 nodes corresponds to the subtree sprouting from it in the graph (the order among siblings is unimportant).

We represent the topology of T with BP, using $2(n + c) + o(n)$ bits. In addition, we use a bitvector $B[1, n + c + 1]$ where $B[i] = 1$ iff the tree node with preorder i

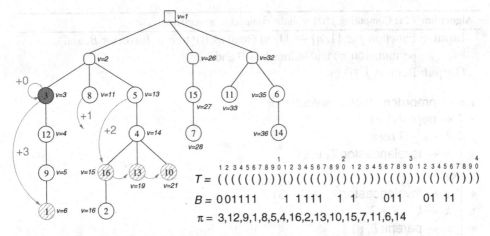

Figure 8.24. On the left, the tree describing the graph of Figure 8.23. On the bottom right, the compact representation of this information. There is one child of the root per cycle, whose children are the cycle elements. From each of them, we represent the tree that sprouts from that element in the cycle. Grayed elements illustrate Example 8.36.

is of depth 3 or more (that is, it corresponds to an actual node in the graph). This requires $3(n+c) + o(n)$ bits in total, which is between $3n + o(n)$ and $6n + o(n)$. Our final component is a permutation π on $[1, n]$, which collects the domain elements represented in T in preorder. Since not all the tree nodes correspond to domain values (only those of depth 3 or more), the actual preorder of the node representing value i in T is $\mathsf{select}(B, \pi^{-1}(i))$. Conversely, a tree node with preorder p and depth 3 or more corresponds to the domain value $\pi(\mathsf{rank}(B, p))$.

Example 8.34 *Figure 8.24 shows the tree representation of the function f of Figure 8.23 (the grayed nodes and arrows will be used later). For example, to find the node corresponding to $i = 4$, we start computing $j \leftarrow \pi^{-1}(4) = 7$. Then the preorder of the node of i is $p \leftarrow \mathsf{select}(B, 7) = 9$. The BP tree node with preorder p is $v \leftarrow \mathsf{preorderselect}(9) = 14$.*

Conversely, the node $v = 14$ has preorder $p \leftarrow \mathsf{preorder}(14) = 9$. It corresponds to the jth 1 in B, for $j \leftarrow \mathsf{rank}(B, 9) = 7$. Therefore, the corresponding number is $i \leftarrow \pi(7) = 4$.

To compute $f(i)$, we first find the node v corresponding to i. If $\mathsf{depth}(v) > 3$, then v belongs to the trees of the original graph. Thus the desired node is simply $u \leftarrow \mathsf{parent}(v)$, and $f(i)$ is found by mapping u back to its position in π. Instead, if $\mathsf{depth}(v) = 3$, then v belongs to the cycle formed by all of its siblings. In this case, we must find its next sibling, if it exists; otherwise we want its first sibling: compute $u \leftarrow \mathsf{nsibling}(v)$, and if $u = \text{null}$, then compute instead $u \leftarrow \mathsf{fchild}(\mathsf{parent}(v))$.

Example 8.35 *Let us compute $f(4)$ with this representation. In Example 8.34 we found that its node is $v = 14$. Since $\mathsf{depth}(v) = 4 > 3$, the desired node is $u \leftarrow \mathsf{parent}(v) = 13$. Its preorder value is $q \leftarrow \mathsf{preorder}(u) = 8$, and its position in π is $r \leftarrow \mathsf{rank}(B, 8) = 6$. Therefore, $f(4) = \pi(6) = 5$.*

Algorithm 8.21: Computing $f^k(i)$ with the compact representation.

Input : Function $f : [1, n] \to [1, n]$ (seen as BP tree T, bitvector B, and
permutation π) and values $k > 0$ and i.
Output: Returns $f^k(i)$.

1 $v \gets$ preorderselect(T, select(B, $\pi^{-1}(i)$))
2 $d \gets$ depth(T, v)
3 **if** $d - k \geq 3$ **then**
4 $\quad\lfloor\ u \gets$ levelancestor(T, v, k)

5 **else**
6 $\quad v \gets$ levelancestor($T, v, d - 3$)
7 $\quad k \gets k - d + 3$
8 $\quad u \gets$ parent(T, v)
9 $\quad c \gets 1 + ((\text{childrank}(T, v) + k - 1) \bmod \text{children}(T, u))$
10 $\quad\lfloor\ u \gets$ child(T, u, c)

11 **return** $\pi(\text{rank}(B, \text{preorder}(T, u)))$

Now let us compute $f(5)$, where 5 corresponds to node $v = 13$. Since depth(v) = 3,
the desired node is $u \gets$ nsibling(v) = null. Thus we cycle and take the first sib-
ling: $u \gets$ fchild(parent(v)) = fchild(2) = 3. We continue with $q \gets$ preorder(u) =
3, $r \gets$ rank($B, 3$) = 1, and then obtain $f(5) = \pi(1) = 3$.

In order to compute $f^k(i)$, for $k > 0$, we generalize the above procedure as follows. We obtain the node v corresponding to i. If depth(v) $- k \geq 3$, we compute
$u =$ levelancestor(v, k) and then transform u back to its domain value. Otherwise,
with k applications of f on i we start traversing the cycle. We first reach the cycle,
by computing $v \gets$ levelancestor(v, depth(v) $- 3$) and $k \gets k -$ depth(v) $+ 3$. Now
we compute the child rank of the correct sibling, $u \gets$ parent(v) and $c \gets 1 +$
((childrank(v) $+ k - 1$) mod children(u)). Finally, we compute $u \gets$ child(u, c) and
transform u back into a domain value.

Algorithm 8.21 shows the pseudocode. If we use $\mathcal{O}(n)$ bits to implement π^{-1}
(Section 5.1), then the total space is $n \log n + \mathcal{O}(n)$ bits, and the time to compute
any $f^k(i)$ is $\mathcal{O}(\log n)$. This can be sped up by letting the permutation use more space:
using $n \log n + \mathcal{O}(n \log \log n) = n \log n(1 + o(1))$ bits and using the faster parentheses
implementation of Section 7.2, $f^k(i)$ can be computed in time $\mathcal{O}(\log \log n)$.

The Inverse Function

Unless f is a bijection in $[1, n]$ (in which case it is a permutation), $f^{-k}(i)$ for positive
k is interpreted as the set of all those $j \in [1, n]$ such that $f^k(j) = i$. First, assume that
i is mapped to a tree node v with depth(v) > 3. Then the answers are all the descendants of v with depth depth(v) $+ k$. The first such descendant is found with $u \gets$
fwdsearch(v, k), and the next ones by iterating with $u \gets$ fwdsearch(close(u), 1).
This finds the next node to the right at the same depth of u, even if it is not a sibling
of u. This process finishes when we find that $u >$ close(v), which means that we have
traversed all the desired nodes in the subtree of v.

Algorithm 8.22: Computing $f^{-k}(i)$ with the compact representation. For simplicity, the parenthesis operations interpret T as the BP sequence.

Input : Function $f : [1, n] \rightarrow [1, n]$ (seen as BP tree T, bitvector B, and permutation π) and values $k > 0$ and i.
Output: Outputs the set $f^{-k}(i)$.

1   $v \leftarrow \mathsf{preorderselect}(T, \mathsf{select}(B, \pi^{-1}(i)))$
2   $list(v, k)$
3   **if** $\mathsf{depth}(T, v) = 3$ **then**
4     $u \leftarrow \mathsf{parent}(v)$
5   **while** $k > 0$ **do**
6       $v \leftarrow \mathsf{psibling}(T, v)$
7   **if** $v = \mathsf{null}$ **then** $v \leftarrow \mathsf{lchild}(T, u)$
8       $k \leftarrow k - 1$
9   **if** $k > 0$ **then** $list(v, k)$
10   **output** $\pi(\mathsf{rank}(B, \mathsf{preorder}(T, v)))$ (instead of $list(v, 0)$)

11 **Proc** $list(v, k)$
    Input : A node v of T and a distance k.
    Output: Outputs all the descendants of v at distance k.
12    $x \leftarrow \mathsf{fwdsearch}(T, v, k)$
13   **while** $x \leq \mathsf{close}(T, v)$ **do**
14   **output** $\pi(\mathsf{rank}(B, \mathsf{preorder}(T, x)))$
15      $x \leftarrow \mathsf{fwdsearch}(T, \mathsf{close}(T, x), 1)$

If $\mathsf{depth}(v) = 3$, the procedure is more complicated because we may enter other subtrees across the cycle of v and even the subtree of v again (with another depth k). We must iterate on the previous procedure k times: we move (cyclically) to the previous siblings of v and find the descendants at depth $\mathsf{depth}(v) + k - 1 = 3 + k - 1$, $\mathsf{depth}(v) + k - 2 = 3 + k - 2$, and so on. The procedure guarantees that no repeated results are reported. The cost to compute π^{-1} is paid once, and then each step costs only the associated tree traversals. For example, using $n \log n + \mathcal{O}(n)$ bits and the parentheses implementation of Section 7.2, the total time is $\mathcal{O}\big(\log n + (k + |f^{-k}(i)|) \log \log n\big)$. Algorithm 8.22 gives the details.

Example 8.36 *Let us compute $f^{-k}(3)$ for $k = 3$. The process is illustrated in gray in Figure 8.24. From Figure 8.23, we can see that the values j such that $f^3(j) = i = 3$ are $f^{-3}(3) = \{1, 16, 13, 10, 3\}$. To find them, we first map $i = 3$ to the node $v = 3$ (grayed) and carry out $list(v, 3)$ from Algorithm 8.22. The first descendant of v at distance $k = 3$ is $x \leftarrow \mathsf{fwdsearch}(v, 3) = 6$. Since $x = 6 \leq 10 = \mathsf{close}(v)$, x is a correct descendant, and we report its value, 1. Now we move to the next node at the same depth of x, $x \leftarrow \mathsf{fwdsearch}(\mathsf{close}(x), 1) = \mathsf{fwdsearch}(7, 1) = 16$. But since $x = 16 > 10 = \mathsf{close}(v)$, this node does not descend from v and we return from $list(v, 3)$.*

We now take $v \leftarrow$ psibling$(v) =$ null, and therefore change it to $v \leftarrow$ lchild$(u) = 13$, where $u =$ parent$(v) = 2$. We decrease $k \leftarrow k - 1 = 2$ and call list$(v, 2)$, to list the descendants of v at distance 2. We start by computing $x \leftarrow$ fwdsearch$(v, 2) = 15$, and since $x = 15 \le 24 =$ close(v), we report the number of x, 16. Now we take the next node at the same depth, $x \leftarrow$ fwdsearch$($close$(x), 1) =$ fwdsearch$(18, 1) = 19$. Since $x = 19 \le 24 =$ close(v), we report the number of x, 13. We take the next node, $x \leftarrow$ fwdsearch$($close$(x), 1) =$ fwdsearch$(20, 1) = 21$. Since $x = 21 \le 24 =$ close(v), we report the number 10. When we try to take the next node of the same depth, fwdsearch$($close$(x), 1) =$ fwdsearch$(22, 1) = 41 >$ close(v) (because there are no other nodes at this depth) and we finish with list$(v, 2)$.

Now we take $v \leftarrow$ psibling$(v) = 11$ and decrease $k \leftarrow k - 1 = 1$. This node has no descendants at distance 1, so nothing is reported (list$(v, 1)$ starts by computing $x \leftarrow$ fwdsearch$(v, 1) = 14 > 12 =$ close(v), so it returns).

Finally, we take $v \leftarrow$ psibling$(v) = 3$ and decrease $k \leftarrow k - 1 = 0$. Since $k = 0$ we report the number 3 corresponding to the current node v and finish.

The operations of finding the next or previous node at the same level were not considered in our basic set of Table 8.1:

$$\text{levelnext}(v) = \text{first node to the right of } v \text{ with its same depth,}$$

$$\text{levelprev}(v) = \text{first node to the left of } v \text{ with its same depth.}$$

They are easily solved with levelnext$(v) =$ fwdsearch$($close$(v), 1)$ (as said) and levelprev$(v) =$ open$($bwdsearch$(v, 0) + 1)$.

Faster Inverse Function

For large k values, the procedure for $f^{-k}(i)$ is not so efficient, because it takes $\Omega(k \log \log n)$ time. Consider $f^{-100}(3)$ in our example: we will cycle through the siblings of v without finding nodes to report for many large k values, until k reaches the height of the siblings of v. For the more ambitious readers, we show how this spurious time can be avoided.

Let $u =$ parent(v) and $a =$ children(u). Consider a sibling $v_t =$ psibling$^t(v)$ (taking psibling as cyclic to maintain the notation simple) and $h_t =$ height(v_t). Then v_t has nodes to report in its subtree if $h_t \ge k - t$. However, if k is large, we will again find $v_{a+t} = v_t$, and this time there will be nodes to report in its subtree if $h_t \ge k - t - a$. In general, across several rounds, we will report all the nodes descending from v_t at distances $k - t$, $k - t - a$, $k - t - 2a$, and so on until the maximum $s \ge 0$ such that $k - t - sa > 0$ (separately we handle the case where we report node v_t itself, i.e., $k - t - sa = 0$, as in line 10 of Algorithm 8.22). That is, the least distance toward the nodes to report in the subtree of v_t is $d_t = 1 + ((k - t - 1) \bmod a)$. Therefore, we are interested only in the nodes v_t where $h_t \ge d_t$, for $t \in [0, \min(k, a) - 1]$. For each such node v_t, we invoke $list(v_t, d_t + sa)$ for $s = 0, 1, \ldots$ until $d_t + sa > h_t$.

The final problem is how to identify the proper nodes v_t without scanning them all. The general idea, without considering cycling on the siblings and large values of k, is that we want to work on v_t only if $h_t \ge k - t$, that is, $h_t + t \ge k$. We will perform range maximum queries on the values $h_t + t$, so as to extract them from largest to smallest, processing them until we extract one that is smaller than k, and then we can stop. Now we enter into details, because cycling through children introduces some discontinuities in the ranges.

Let us consider two subranges in $t \in [0, \min(k, a) - 1]$. One goes from $t = 0$ to $t = k' - 1$, with $k' = 1 + ((k - 1) \bmod a)$ and the other from $t = k'$ to $t = a - 1$. In the first subrange, we have $d_t = 1 + ((k - t - 1) \bmod a) = k' - t$. That is, the limits are of the form $h_t \geq d_t = k' - t$, or $h_t + t \geq k'$. The second subrange $[k', \min(k, a) - 1]$, if not empty, has $d_{k'} = 1 + ((k - k' - 1) \bmod a) = a$, and then any other d_t is $d_t = 1 + ((k - t - 1) \bmod a) = d_{k'} - (t - k') = a - (t - k')$. That is, the limits are of the form $h_t \geq d_t = a - (t - k')$, or $h_t + t \geq a + k'$.

Therefore, we proceed separately in up to two ranges (the second may be empty): $t \in [0, k' - 1]$ and $t \in [k', \min(a, k) - 1]$. In the first range, we have to process every v_t with $h_t + t \geq k'$, and in the second, every v_t with $h_t + t \geq a + k'$. In each of those ranges $t \in [l, r]$, we must identify those $h_t + t \geq \kappa$, for some constant κ (k' or $a + k'$). In addition, one of those ranges may move cyclically in the siblings of v: let $c_v = \mathsf{childrank}(v)$, then if $[c_v - 1, c_v] \subseteq [l, r]$, we split $[l, r]$ into $[l, c_v - 1]$ and $[c_v, r]$. Thus we may have one to three ranges.

Let us consider any such range. To efficiently find those $t \in [l, r]$ such that $h_t + t \geq \kappa$, we define a virtual array $U[1, \ell]$ where $U[i] = \mathsf{height}(x_i) - i$ and x_i is the ith left-to-right node at depth 3 in T. We build on U a succinct range maximum query structure rMq_U analogous to the one built for minima in Section 7.4.1. Only the rMq_U structure is stored, which requires $2\ell + o(\ell) \leq 2n + o(n)$ further bits. We spend other $n + c + o(n + c)$ bits for a bitvector B_3 analogous to B, which marks with a 1 the nodes at depth 3 in preorder. Now, at query time, we map the interval $t \in [l, r]$ to the child range $[c_1, c_2] = [c_v - r, c_v - l]$ if $c_v - r > 0$, and $[c_1, c_2] = [c_v - r + a, c_v - l + a]$ otherwise. This interval is mapped to $U[p, q]$, where $p = \mathsf{rank}(B_3, \mathsf{preorder}(\mathsf{child}(u, c_1)))$ and $q = p + r - l$. In $U[p, q]$ we have all the values $h_t + t$ shifted by some constant (note that t runs to the left in the list of siblings, whereas the i in the definition of U runs to the right, hence the opposite signs).

We now carry out a process similar to the one described in Section 8.5.6. Let $m \leftarrow \mathsf{rMq}_U(p, q)$. Then m corresponds to $\mathsf{child}(u, c_1 + m - p)$, which is v_t for $t = l + (q - m)$. If $h_t + t < \kappa$, or equivalently, $h_t < d_t$, or equivalently, $\mathsf{height}(v_t) < 1 + ((k - t - 1) \bmod a)$, then there are no nodes to report below v_t, neither below any other sibling in $[c_1, c_2]$, as v_t maximizes $h_t + t$ in this range. Therefore, the whole process of the interval $U[p, q]$ can stop. If, instead, we have $h_t \geq d_t$, then we process v_t for all its relevant distances and continue recursively with the subintervals $U[p, m - 1]$ and $U[m + 1, q]$.

This process ensures that we work proportionally to the number of useful nodes v_t, which is amortized by the reported descendants of those useful nodes. Then the time is, finally, $\mathcal{O}(\log n + |f^{-k}(i)| \log \log n)$.

As a practical consideration, note that we can reorder the subtrees of all the nodes v at depth 3 so that their longest path is always the leftmost one. This simplifies the operations $\mathsf{height}(v) = \mathsf{succ}_0(B, v) - v - 1$ and also, if $k \leq \mathsf{height}(v)$, then $\mathsf{fwdsearch}(v, k) = v + k$.

8.6 Summary

The topology of an ordinal tree of n nodes can be represented in $2n + o(n)$ bits, which is asymptotically optimal. Several representations are possible, all of which are built in linear time. LOUDS is the simplest and most efficient, but the operations supported are limited (much less limited than most classical representations, however). BP offers the maximum functionality. DFUDS is faster when moving to specific children, which is the most important operation in various cases, but it cannot compute node depths and related operations. LOUDS can carry out its operations in $\mathcal{O}(\log\log n)$ time and even $\mathcal{O}(1)$ by spending a bit more extra space. BP and DFUDS resort to operations on balanced parentheses, which can be implemented in $\mathcal{O}(\log n)$ time and even $\mathcal{O}(\log\log n)$ with more sophisticated structures. Labeled trees can be represented by adding a string of labels and combining the topology operations with queries on the sequence. Various representations are successfully adapted to the particular case of cardinal and binary trees. Important applications of trees are the representation of tries and suffix trees (Chapter 11), and k^2-trees for graphs and grids (Chapters 9 and 10).

8.7 Bibliographic Notes

Raman and Rao (2013) have written a short survey that briefly covers all the succinct tree representations. More bibliographic discussion (with some overlap) related to the implementation of the primitives on parentheses can be found in Section 7.6.

Early representations. Katajainen and Mäkinen (1990) survey several early binary tree representations using basically $2n$ bits, but these require linear-time scans to simulate tree navigation operations. Clark and Munro (1996) proposed one of the early tree representations that efficiently implemented some operations, but it still lacked fundamental ones like parent. Its space was low but not optimal: $3n + o(n)$ bits.

LOUDS. The study of tree representations using optimal space and time was initiated by Jacobson (1989), who proposed the LOUDS representation. The operations reached constant time once the $\mathcal{O}(1)$-time structures for binary rank and select appeared (Clark, 1996). Delpratt *et al.* (2006) reported on an implementation of LOUDS.

BP. Jacobson (1989) also explored representations based on balanced parentheses, but the space was $10n + o(n)$ bits, far from optimal. Munro and Raman (2001) improved the space to $2n + o(n)$ bits and the times to constant. Their representation supports all the operations that can be translated into open, close, enclose, $rank_1$, $rank_0$, $select_1$, and $select_0$. Geary *et al.* (2006a) introduced a simpler constant-time solution for open, close, and enclose.

Several of the remaining operations of Table 8.1 were added on top of this representation, each requiring constant time but additional $o(n)$-bit structures: children (Chiang *et al.*, 2005), lca (Sadakane, 2007), levelancestor (Munro *et al.*, 2012), child, childrank, and height (Lu and Yeh, 2008).

DFUDS. Benoit *et al.* (2005) introduced the DFUDS format. Its main merit was to support constant-time child and related operations very easily, as well as labeled operations by associating the labels with the 1s of the corresponding nodes (their proposal for cardinal trees achieves, in theory, constant time for those labeled operations as well). The operations childrank, depth, levelancestor, and lca were added later (Geary *et al.*, 2006b; Jansson *et al.*, 2012), all in constant time but each requiring different $o(n)$-bit data structures. We have not covered the operations related to depth in the chapter, because they are complicated and require significant extra space in practice (they are not supported with the parenthesis primitives we considered). Our lca formula is simplified from the original (Jansson *et al.*, 2012).

Fully functional representation. Navarro and Sadakane (2014) proposed the solution that builds mostly on operations fwdsearch, bwdsearch, rmq, and variants. Arroyuelo *et al.* (2010) showed that even the simple $\mathcal{O}(\log n)$-time implementation is faster in practice than other implementable constant-time representations (Geary *et al.*, 2006a) and that the times are almost constant in various realistic application scenarios. They also showed that LOUDS is smaller and faster than the parenthesis-based representations (although its functionality is more limited). In practice, the operations are carried out within a few microseconds. The rmM-tree based representations of BP and DFUDS use about $2.4n$ bits, whereas LOUDS could outperform them while using up to $2.1n$ bits (the solution given in Algorithm 8.2 is also from Arroyuelo *et al.* (2010)). Finally, they showed that engineered representations like that described in the beginning of this chapter are space-competitive, although their functionality is much more limited. Some of the implementations have been extended to the dynamic scenario with good results (Joannou and Raman, 2012).

Tree covering. Yet another representation, not described in this chapter, is called *tree covering (TC)*. It was first proposed by Geary *et al.* (2006b). Its set of operations was then expanded by He *et al.* (2012) and simplified by Farzan and Munro (2014). The final result supports all the operations of Table 8.1 and a few more, yet it is complex and seems not to have been implemented. The main idea is to cut the tree into mini-trees and these into micro-trees. The connections between mini-trees can be represented with pointers, and those between micro-trees can also be represented with pointers local to their mini-tree. Global precomputed tables answer queries in constant time inside micro-trees, and several other $o(n)$-bit structures are used to complete the operations in constant time. Farzan and Munro (2014) go further and show that they can emulate any representation, be it BP, DFUDS, or TC, producing any $\log n$ bits of either representation in constant time. Thus, by adding appropriate $o(n)$-bit tables, one can have any desired BP, DFUDS, or TC functionality within the same $2n + o(n)$ bits.

Cardinal trees. Jacobson (1989) extended the LOUDS representation to cardinal trees, as we have described them. Benoit *et al.* (2005) showed how to combine the DFUDS topology representation with a bitvector in order to support the labeled operations in constant time within $n \log \sigma + 2n + o(n)$ bits. Raman *et al.* (2007) used their compressed bitvector representations to reduce the space of this DFUDS representation, making it asymptotically optimal at the cost of losing a few operations.

The bijection between binary and general trees was already used by Munro and Raman (2001) to support the basic binary tree operations within asymptotically optimal space. The operation lca in binary trees using this mapping is implicit in the work of Fischer and Heun (2011). Farzan and Munro (2014) introduced a TC representation of binary (and cardinal) trees that uses asymptotically optimal space and supports these and many other operations, including depth, height, levelancestor, levelprev, and levelnext. Operations inorder and inorderselect were later added to this set (Davoodi *et al.*, 2014).

The bound on the number of cardinal trees over alphabet $[1, \sigma]$ can be found, for example, in the book of Graham *et al.* (1994).

Labeled trees. He *et al.* (2014) recently introduced a representation of labeled trees that is more powerful than the one described in Section 8.4, but it also requires more space in practice. Operations such as finding the nearest ancestor labeled t (which we mention in Section 8.5.5) can be efficiently implemented. Basically, one ordinal unlabeled tree is extracted from the main tree for each label, and then labeled tree operations are carried out with the main and the extracted tree corresponding to the involved label. The space they need is $n \log \sigma + \mathcal{O}(n)$ bits. Tsur (2014) showed how to support some of those extended operations in $n \log \sigma + 2n + o(n)$ bits.

Further compression. Jansson *et al.* (2012) proposed a representation where some trees can be compressed to less than $2n$ bits. The idea is to interpret the DFUDS descriptions $1^c 0$ as the unary representation of numbers c. The bitvector is then replaced by an array of variable-length elements that statistically encode those numbers. This array may use less than $2n$ bits if certain arities appear more frequently than others. For example, on binary search trees resulting from inserting random permutations, the entropy of the node arities is $(\frac{1}{3} + \log 3)n \approx 1.919n$, and therefore this representation would use $1.919n + o(n)$ bits. The same space is achieved in this case by Davoodi *et al.* (2014) in their TC representation of binary trees. In both cases, however, the structures include heavy sublinear-sized structures, so it is unclear if improvements of this kind would show up in practice.

Minimum spanning trees. The asymptotic number of acyclic connected undirected graphs was found by Otter (1948). A representation using $1.564n + o(n)$ bits was given by Farzan and Munro (2014), as a consequence of their uniform paradigm for encoding trees.

Grammar compression. A good reference for grammar compression is Kieffer and Yang (2000), who also prove that this method converges to the statistical entropy of the source. Finding the smallest grammar that generates a given text T is NP-complete (Storer, 1977; Storer and Szymanski, 1982; Charikar *et al.*, 2005), which justifies the use of good heuristics such as Re-Pair (Larsson and Moffat, 2000).

Tabei *et al.* (2013) introduced the compact grammar representation using two trees we describe in Section 8.5.2. González *et al.* (2014) propose a heuristic alternative that performs well in practice. Bille *et al.* (2015) showed how to extract any $T[i, j]$ from a grammar-compressed representation in time $\mathcal{O}(j - i + \log n)$; what we showed is a simplified version for balanced grammars (Claude and Navarro, 2010). This $\mathcal{O}(\log n)$ time for **access** is not far from optimal on grammar-compressed sequences (Verbin and Yu, 2013). One may wonder if such a representation can also support **rank** and **select** operations. Belazzougui *et al.* (2015) recently obtained $\mathcal{O}(\log n)$ time for those but multiplying the space by σ, the alphabet size, and $\mathcal{O}(\log n / \log \log n)$ time using even more space. They also show that it is unlikely that those times can be improved. Navarro and Ordóñez (2014) studied a practical alternative.

Bille *et al.* (2015) also show that the bitvector B representing a tree topology can be grammar-compressed, while the operations can still be done in time $\mathcal{O}(\log n)$. This form of compression is useful when the trees have many repeated subtrees, as shown in practical applications (Navarro and Ordóñez, 2016).

Tries. Tries were introduced by Fredkin (1960), and Patricia trees by Morrison (1968). Suffix trees were introduced by Weiner (1973) and suffix arrays by Manber and Myers (1993). These structures are well covered in more recent books as well (Crochemore and Rytter, 2002; Adjeroh *et al.*, 2008). The compact suffix tree we described is a simplification of that of Munro *et al.* (2001). We warn, however, that our presentation of suffix trees in this chapter is very preliminary and lacks important functionalities commonly associated with suffix trees. A more complete treatment of compressed suffix trees and arrays will be given in Chapter 11.

Grossi and Ottaviano (2014) introduced more sophisticated ways to represent tries in compact form. A thorough empirical study (Martínez-Prieto *et al.*, 2016) shows that these are very competitive with the state of the art for representing large string dictionaries.

The set of 20 most common names were obtained from the site of the Civil Registry of Chile, see http://www.registrocivil.cl/Servicios/Estadisticas/Archivos/NombresComunes/damas.html.

LZ78. The LZ78 compression format was introduced by Ziv and Lempel (1978), and it is well described in many compression books, such as Bell *et al.* (1990). Sadakane and Grossi (2006) proposed the technique to extract any $T[i, j]$ in optimal time. This was later used in a text index based on LZ78 compression (Arroyuelo *et al.*, 2012).

XML and XPath. The description of the XML and XPath standards are available at http://www.w3.org/XML and http://www.w3.org/TR/xpath, respectively. A system that solves a large subset of XPath using ideas similar to those we presented on a compact XML representation (and also the extended operations in Section 8.4) is SXSI (Arroyuelo *et al.*, 2015).

Treaps. Treaps have been studied in relation to randomized binary search trees (Seidel and Aragon, 1996), but in the static case they are equivalent to Cartesian trees (Vuillemin, 1980). The strategy for finding the values larger than a constant using range maximum queries appears in Muthukrishnan (2002), for example. Teuhola (2011) and Claude *et al.* (2014) proposed the mechanism to encode the keys differentially with respect to the parent node. Konow *et al.* (2013) proposed to encode the priorities at the same time and used treaps to represent inverted indexes for ranked conjunctive and disjunctive queries. For that problem, the rmq-based methods are unsuitable for implementing the algorithms that are enabled with treaps.

Integer functions. The solution for integer functions we describe in Section 8.5.7 is slightly simplified from Munro *et al.* (2012). They use a different solution for working only on the useful nodes when computing $f^{-1}(i)$, which uses $2\sum_{i=1}^{\ell}(1 + \text{height}(x_i))$ bits; ours uses only 2ℓ bits.

Bibliography

Adjeroh, D., Bell, T., and Mukherjee, A. (2008). *The Burrows-Wheeler Transform: Data Compression, Suffix Arrays, and Pattern Matching*. Springer.

Arroyuelo, D., Cánovas, R., Navarro, G., and Sadakane, K. (2010). Succinct trees in practice. In *Proc. 12th Workshop on Algorithm Engineering and Experiments (ALENEX)*, pages 84–97.

Arroyuelo, D., Navarro, G., and Sadakane, K. (2012). Stronger Lempel-Ziv based compressed text indexing. *Algorithmica*, **62**(1), 54–101.

Arroyuelo, D., Claude, F., Maneth, S., Mäkinen, V., Navarro, G., Nguyễn, K., Sirén, J., and Välimäki, N. (2015). Fast in-memory XPath search using compressed indexes. *Software Practice and Experience*, **45**(3), 399–434.

Belazzougui, D., Puglisi, S. J., and Tabei, Y. (2015). Access, rank, select in grammar-compressed strings. In *Proc. 23rd Annual European Symposium on Algorithms (ESA)*, LNCS 9294, pages 142–154.

Bell, T. C., Cleary, J., and Witten, I. H. (1990). *Text Compression*. Prentice Hall.

Benoit, D., Demaine, E. D., Munro, J. I., Raman, R., Raman, V., and Rao, S. S. (2005). Representing trees of higher degree. *Algorithmica*, **43**(4), 275–292.

Bille, P., Landau, G. M., Raman, R., Sadakane, K., Rao, S. S., and Weimann, O. (2015). Random access to grammar-compressed strings and trees. *SIAM Journal on Computing*, **44**(3), 513–539.

Charikar, M., Lehman, E., Liu, D., Panigrahy, R., Prabhakaran, M., Sahai, A., and Shelat, A. (2005). The smallest grammar problem. *IEEE Transactions on Information Theory*, **51**(7), 2554–2576.

Chiang, Y. T., Lin, C. C., and Lu, H.-I. (2005). Orderly spanning trees with applications. *SIAM Journal on Computing*, **34**(4), 924–945.

Clark, D. R. (1996). *Compact PAT Trees*. Ph.D. thesis, University of Waterloo, Canada.

Clark, D. R. and Munro, J. I. (1996). Efficient suffix trees on secondary storage. In *Proc. 7th Annual ACM-SIAM Symposium on Discrete Algorithms (SODA)*, pages 383–391.

Claude, F. and Navarro, G. (2010). Self-indexed grammar-based compression. *Fundamenta Informaticae*, **111**(3), 313–337.

Claude, F., Nicholson, P. K., and Seco, D. (2014). On the compression of search trees. *Information Processing and Management*, **50**(2), 272–283.

Crochemore, M. and Rytter, W. (2002). *Jewels of Stringology*. World Scientific.

Davoodi, P., Navarro, G., Raman, R., and Rao, S. S. (2014). Encoding range minima and range top-2 queries. *Philosophical Transactions of the Royal Society A*, **372**(20130131).

Delpratt, O., Rahman, N., and Raman, R. (2006). Engineering the LOUDS succinct tree representation. In *Proc. 5th International Workshop on Experimental Algorithms (WEA)*, LNCS 4007, pages 134–145.

Farzan, A. and Munro, J. I. (2014). A uniform paradigm to succinctly encode various families of trees. *Algorithmica*, **68**(1), 16–40.

Fischer, J. and Heun, V. (2011). Space-efficient preprocessing schemes for range minimum queries on static arrays. *SIAM Journal on Computing*, **40**(2), 465–492.

Fredkin, E. (1960). Trie memory. *Communications of the ACM*, **3**, 490–500.

Geary, R. F., Rahman, N., Raman, R., and Raman, V. (2006a). A simple optimal representation for balanced parentheses. *Theoretical Computer Science*, **368**(3), 231–246.

Geary, R. F., Raman, R., and Raman, V. (2006b). Succinct ordinal trees with level-ancestor queries. *ACM Transactions on Algorithms*, **2**(4), 510–534.

González, R., Navarro, G., and Ferrada, H. (2014). Locally compressed suffix arrays. *ACM Journal of Experimental Algorithmics*, **19**(1), article 1.

Graham, R. L., Knuth, D. E., and Patashnik, O. (1994). *Concrete Mathematics – A Foundation for Computer Science*. Addison-Wesley, 2nd edition.

Grossi, R. and Ottaviano, G. (2014). Fast compressed tries through path decompositions. *ACM Journal of Experimental Algorithmics*, **19**(3), article 4.

He, M., Munro, J. I., and Rao, S. S. (2012). Succinct ordinal trees based on tree covering. *ACM Transactions on Algorithms*, **8**(4), article 42.

He, M., Munro, J. I., and Zhou, G. (2014). A framework for succinct labeled ordinal trees over large alphabets. *Algorithmica*, **70**(4), 696–717.

Jacobson, G. (1989). Space-efficient static trees and graphs. In *Proc. 30th IEEE Symposium on Foundations of Computer Science (FOCS)*, pages 549–554.

Jansson, J., Sadakane, K., and Sung, W.-K. (2012). Ultra-succinct representation of ordered trees with applications. *Journal of Computer and System Sciences*, **78**(2), 619–631.

Joannou, S. and Raman, R. (2012). Dynamizing succinct tree representations. In *Proc. 11th International Symposium on Experimental Algorithms (SEA)*, LNCS 7276, pages 224–235.

Katajainen, J. and Mäkinen, E. (1990). Tree compression and optimization with applications. *International Journal of Foundations of Computer Science*, **1**(4), 425–448.

Kieffer, J. C. and Yang, E.-H. (2000). Grammar-based codes: A new class of universal lossless source codes. *IEEE Transactions on Information Theory*, **46**(3), 737–754.

Konow, R., Navarro, G., Clarke, C. L. A., and López-Ortiz, A. (2013). Faster and smaller inverted indices with treaps. In *Proc. 36th Annual International ACM Conference on Research and Development in Information Retrieval (SIGIR)*, pages 193–202.

Larsson, J. and Moffat, A. (2000). Off-line dictionary-based compression. *Proceedings of the IEEE*, **88**(11), 1722–1732.

Lu, H.-I. and Yeh, C. (2008). Balanced parentheses strike back. *ACM Transactions on Algorithms*, **4**(3), 1–13.

Manber, U. and Myers, G. (1993). Suffix arrays: a new method for on-line string searches. *SIAM Journal on Computing*, **22**(5), 935–948.

Martínez-Prieto, M. A., Brisaboa, N., Cánovas, R., Claude, F., and Navarro, G. (2016). Practical compressed string dictionaries. *Information Systems*, **56**, 73–108.

Morrison, D. (1968). PATRICIA – practical algorithm to retrieve information coded in alphanumeric. *Journal of the ACM*, **15**(4), 514–534.

Munro, J. I. and Raman, V. (2001). Succinct representation of balanced parentheses and static trees. *SIAM Journal on Computing*, **31**(3), 762–776.

Munro, J. I., Raman, V., and Rao, S. S. (2001). Space efficient suffix trees. *Journal of Algorithms*, **39**(2), 205–222.

Munro, J. I., Raman, R., Raman, V., and Rao, S. S. (2012). Succinct representations of permutations and functions. *Theoretical Computer Science*, **438**, 74–88.

Muthukrishnan, S. (2002). Efficient algorithms for document retrieval problems. In *Proc. 13th Annual ACM-SIAM Symposium on Discrete Algorithms (SODA)*, pages 657–666.

Navarro, G. and Ordóñez, A. (2014). Grammar compressed sequences with rank/select support. In *Proc. 21st International Symposium on String Processing and Information Retrieval (SPIRE)*, LNCS 8799, pages 31–44.

Navarro, G. and Ordóñez, A. (2016). Faster compressed suffix trees for repetitive text collections. *Journal of Experimental Algorithmics*, **21**(1), article 1.8.

Navarro, G. and Sadakane, K. (2014). Fully-functional static and dynamic succinct trees. *ACM Transactions on Algorithms*, **10**(3), article 16.

Otter, R. (1948). The number of trees. *Annals of Mathematics*, **49**, 583–599.

Raman, R. and Rao, S. S. (2013). Succinct representations of ordinal trees. In *Space-Efficient Data Structures, Streams, and Algorithms*, LNCS 8066, pages 319–332. Springer.

Raman, R., Raman, V., and Rao, S. S. (2007). Succinct indexable dictionaries with applications to encoding k-ary trees, prefix sums and multisets. *ACM Transactions on Algorithms*, **3**(4), article 43.

Sadakane, K. (2007). Compressed suffix trees with full functionality. *Theory of Computing Systems*, **41**(4), 589–607.

Sadakane, K. and Grossi, R. (2006). Squeezing succinct data structures into entropy bounds. In *Proc. 17th Annual ACM-SIAM Symposium on Discrete Algorithms (SODA)*, pages 1230–1239.

Seidel, R. and Aragon, C. R. (1996). Randomized search trees. *Algorithmica*, **16**(4/5), 464–497.

Storer, J. A. (1977). NP-completeness results concerning data compression. Technical Report 234, Department of Electrical Engineering and Computer Science, Princeton University.

Storer, J. A. and Szymanski, T. G. (1982). Data compression via textual substitution. *Journal of the ACM*, **29**(4), 928–951.

Tabei, Y., Takabatake, Y., and Sakamoto, H. (2013). A succinct grammar compression. In *Proc. 24th Annual Symposium on Combinatorial Pattern Matching (CPM)*, LNCS 7922, pages 235–246.

Teuhola, J. (2011). Interpolative coding of integer sequences supporting log-time random access. *Information Processing and Management*, **47**(5), 742–761.

Tsur, D. (2014). Succinct representation of labeled trees. *Theoretical Computer Science*, **562**, 320–329.

Verbin, E. and Yu, W. (2013). Data structure lower bounds on random access to grammar-compressed strings. In *Proc. 24th Annual Symposium on Combinatorial Pattern Matching (CPM)*, LNCS 7922, pages 247–258.

Vuillemin, J. (1980). A unifying look at data structures. *Communications of the ACM*, **23**(4), 229–239.

Weiner, P. (1973). Linear pattern matching algorithm. In *Proc. 14th Annual IEEE Symposium on Switching and Automata Theory*, pages 1–11.

Ziv, J. and Lempel, A. (1978). Compression of individual sequences via variable length coding. *IEEE Transactions on Information Theory*, **24**(5), 530–536.

CHAPTER 9
Graphs

Graphs are pervasive in Computer Science, as they are useful for modeling many scenarios: the Web, social networks, road networks, communication networks, electric networks, protein interactions, meshes, triangulations, and in general any model where objects can be connected or related in some way. A graph is essentially a set of *nodes* or *vertices* connected pairwise by *arcs* or *edges*. In *directed* graphs, the edges have a direction (that is, they go from a *source* node v to a *target* node u; we say that u is *adjacent* to v). An example is the "following" relation in Twitter or the network of flights in an airline. In *undirected* graphs, the edges are symmetric and *connect* v and u. An example is the "friends" relation in Facebook or the cities that are connected by (two-way) roads. Graphs are visualized with nodes as circles and arcs as arrows (directed) or lines (undirected) between them. In this chapter we will assume for simplicity that there cannot be more than one edge between two nodes (in directed graphs, there can be one edge in each direction between two nodes). However, many of the structures we describe can be extended to handle edge multiplicity.

A directed graph is denoted $G = (V, E)$, where V is the set of vertices and $E \subseteq V \times V$ is the set of edges. We use $n = |V|$ and $e = |E|$. In this chapter we aim at supporting the following operations on directed graphs G:

adj(G, v, u): tells whether there is an edge from v to u, that is, $(v, u) \in E$.
neigh(G, v): returns the list of neighbors of v, that is, $\{u, (v, u) \in E\}$.
rneigh(G, v): returns the list of reverse neighbors of v, that is, $\{u, (u, v) \in E\}$.
outdegree(G, v): returns the number of neighbors of v, |neigh(G, v)|.
indegree(G, v): returns the number of reverse neighbors of v, |rneigh(G, v)|.

In many representations, one also has direct access to the individual elements neigh$(G, v)[j]$ and rneigh$(G, v)[j]$.

On undirected graphs, we also represent the edges as ordered pairs in E. If $(v, u) \in E$, we implicitly assume that $(u, v) \in E$; only one of the two should be explicitly listed in E. In these graphs we only implement the operations adj$(G, v, u) = $ adj(G, u, v), neigh$(G, v) = $ rneigh(G, v), and degree$(G, v) = $ |neigh(G, v)| = |rneigh(G, v)|, because there is no concept of direction in the edges.

Let us assume $V = [1, n]$ for simplicity. A basic way to represent a directed graph G is to store the *adjacency list*[1] of each node $v \in V$, which enumerates neigh(G, v). We store an array $N[1, e] = N(1).N(2)\ldots N(n)$, where $N(v) = $ neigh(G, v), as well as an array $V[1, n + 1]$ where $V[v]$ points to the beginning of $N(v)$ in N and $V[n + 1] = e +$ 1. This representation uses, essentially, $e \log n + n \log e$ bits, and supports operations

$$\text{outdegree}(G, v) = V[v + 1] - V[v],$$

$$\text{neigh}(G, v)[j] = N[V[v] + j - 1]$$

in constant time. If the nodes are sorted inside each sublist $N(v)$, we can also compute adj(G, v, u) in time $\mathcal{O}(\log \text{outdegree}(G, v)) = \mathcal{O}(\log n)$ through a binary search for u in $N(v) = N[V[v], V[v + 1] - 1]$.

A first question is how space-efficient is this representation. The worst-case entropy (Section 2.1) of the set of all the directed graphs of n nodes and e edges is

$$\log \binom{n^2}{e} = e \log \frac{n^2}{e} + \mathcal{O}(e)$$

bits, because $\binom{n^2}{e}$ counts the ways of choosing e distinct pairs from $V \times V$. This shows that the basic adjacency list representation uses reasonable space in general. It always holds $e \le n^2$, and in most graphs of interest it also holds $e = \Omega(n)$ and $e = o(n^2)$. A reasonable assumption in many practical cases is $e = n^{1+\alpha}$ for some constant (and typically small) $0 < \alpha < 1$. In this case, the worst-case entropy is $(1 - \alpha)e \log n + \mathcal{O}(e)$ bits, whereas the standard representation uses $e \log n + o(e)$ bits.

The representation is not so convenient for undirected graphs, however, because if $(u, v) \in E$, we have to add v to the list of $N(u)$ and u to the list of $N(v)$, in order to efficiently solve neigh queries. Therefore, an undirected graph with n nodes and e edges requires $2e \log n + n \log(2e)$ bits of space. The number of bits needed to represent undirected graphs is

$$\log \binom{\binom{n+1}{2}}{e} = e \log \frac{n^2}{e} + \mathcal{O}(e),$$

because we have to choose e edges among the $\binom{n}{2} + n = \binom{n+1}{2}$ undirected choices ($\binom{n}{2}$ choices $(u, v) = (v, u)$ with $u \ne v$ plus n choices (v, v)). Therefore, the representation takes roughly twice the necessary space.

This representation also has a weakness on directed graphs: it does not efficiently support the operations indegree and, especially, rneigh. While the former could be answered by storing other $n \log n$ bits with the indegrees of all the nodes, to answer rneigh fast we need to double the space by representing the transpose of G as well, that is, $G'(V, E')$ where $E' = \{(u, v), (v, u) \in E\}$. Then we have rneigh$(G, v) = $ neigh(G', v).

An alternative classical graph representation is the *adjacency matrix*, a binary matrix $M[1, n][1, n]$ where $M[v][u] = 1$ iff adj(G, v, u). Apart from adj, however, every other operation costs $\mathcal{O}(n)$ time. In addition, the matrix can be recommended only for very dense graphs, because it uses n^2 bits of space. Undirected graphs can save half the space in this representation, by storing only the $\binom{n+1}{2} = \frac{n(n+1)}{2}$ bits of the upper

---

[1] Also called *adjacency array* when any element can be accessed directly.

triangular matrix: edge (v, u) is stored as $M[\min(v, u)][\max(v, u)] = 1$. Still, this space is acceptable only if the graph is very dense.

Considering the worst-case entropy of the directed graphs, we cannot expect to find a representation that is much smaller than classical adjacency lists. We will, however, provide more functionality within similar space, in particular the operations we have defined. In the case of undirected graphs, where the classical representation uses twice the necessary space, we will support the desired operations within half their space, that is, close to the worst-case entropy. We will also consider restricted classes of graphs that are important in practice and where much better representations are possible. In particular, we will show how to take advantage of clustering in the graphs and how to represent planar graphs within $\mathcal{O}(n)$ bits.

9.1 General Graphs

9.1.1 Using Bitvectors

A simple idea to better represent the adjacency matrix is to regard it as a sequence of n bitvectors $M[v][1, n]$. Since there will be e 1s in total, we can use sparse bitvector representations to improve the space usage when e is far from n^2. The use of bitvectors will, in addition, enhance the matrix functionality.

Consider the very sparse bitvectors of Section 4.4. Then the representation of row $M[v]$, which has $e_v = \mathsf{outdegree}(G, v)$ 1s, requires $e_v \log \frac{n}{e_v} + \mathcal{O}(e_v)$ bits. Added over all the bitvectors, this gives $\sum_{v \in V} e_v \log \frac{n}{e_v} + \mathcal{O}(e)$. By Jensen's inequality (Section 2.8), this is at most $e \log \frac{n^2}{e} + \mathcal{O}(e)$ (reached when all $e_v = e/n$), which asymptotically matches the worst-case entropy. Actually, the space can be less if the distribution of outdegrees is skewed.

With this representation, we easily support the operations

$$\mathsf{adj}(G, v, u) \text{ iff } \mathsf{access}(M[v], u) = 1,$$

$$\mathsf{neigh}(G, v)[j] = \mathsf{select}_1(M[v], j),$$

$$\mathsf{outdegree}(G, v) = \mathsf{rank}_1(M[v], n),$$

the first and the third ones in time $\mathcal{O}(\log n)$, and neigh in time $\mathcal{O}(1)$. Still, we cannot efficiently support queries rneigh unless we double the space with the transposed graph. In the case of undirected graphs, we must also represent every edge twice.

This representation is in theory interesting for directed graphs, because it asymptotically reaches the worst-case entropy. However, it is rarely a good choice in practice. As mentioned, the classical adjacency list representation is not much larger in most graphs of interest, and it is simpler and faster. Our main focus will be the use of compact data structures to provide all the desired functionality within basically the same space of classical adjacency list representations.

9.1.2 Using Sequences

Consider the following structure. We use the permutation-based representation of sequences (Section 6.1) for N, and replace V by a bitvector $B[1, e + n] = 1\,0^{e_1}1\,0^{e_2}1 \ldots 0^{e_n}$. For B, we use a representation giving constant-time rank and select

(Chapter 4). We can then compute

$$\text{outdegree}(G, v) = \text{select}(B, v + 1) - \text{select}(B, v) - 1,$$

$$\text{neigh}(G, v)[j] = \text{access}(N, \text{select}(B, v) - v + j),$$

$$\text{adj}(G, v, u) \quad \text{iff} \quad \text{rank}_u(N, \text{select}(B, v + 1) - (v + 1))$$

$$-\text{rank}_u(N, \text{select}(B, v) - v) = 1,$$

the first in constant time and the others in time $\mathcal{O}(\log \log n)$. The first two formulas are immediate once we note that $N(v)$ starts at position $\text{select}(B, v) - v + 1$ in array N. The last formula counts how many times u is mentioned in the list $N(v)$, which should be 1 or 0.

This representation can be slightly slower and is more complicated than a plain array implementation of N and V, and uses essentially the same space, $e \log n(1 + o(1)) + \mathcal{O}(n)$ bits. It has, however, an important advantage. Consider the operation $\text{rank}_v(N, e)$. It tells how many times v appears in all the adjacency lists, that is, $\text{indegree}(G, v)$. More importantly, it solves $\text{rneigh}(G, v)[j]$ efficiently: with $p = \text{select}_v(N, j)$ we find the jth place where v is mentioned in an adjacency list. Then $u = \text{select}_0(B, p) - p$ is the node in whose list v is mentioned for the jth time. That is, we have

$$\text{indegree}(G, v) = \text{rank}_v(N, e),$$

$$\text{rneigh}(G, v)[j] = \text{select}_0(B, \text{select}_v(N, j)) - \text{select}_v(N, j),$$

the former in time $\mathcal{O}(\log \log n)$ and the latter in constant time, without using further space.

Example 9.1 *Figure 9.1 shows a directed graph, its classical representation (arrays N and V) and its new representation (sequence N and bitvector B). The outdegree of node 2 is* $\text{outdegree}(2) = \text{select}(B, 3) - \text{select}(B, 2) - 1 = 8 - 5 - 1 = 2$. *Its*

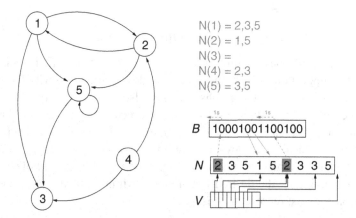

Figure 9.1. A graph on the left, and its representations on the right. In gray we show the adjacency lists $N(v)$. A classical representation of the graph is formed by the array N (the adjacency lists concatenated) plus the array V pointing to the beginning of each list $N(v)$ in array N. In our representation, N is converted into a sequence and V is replaced by the bitvector B. Gray arrows and blocks illustrate operations $\text{neigh}(2)$ and $\text{rneigh}(2)$.

Algorithm 9.1: Computing operations on general directed graphs.

Input : Directed graph G (seen as sequence N and bitvector B), nodes v and u, and index j.

1 **Proc** adj(G, v, u)
2    $b \leftarrow$ select(B, v)
3    $r_1 \leftarrow$ rank$_u(N, b - v)$
4    $r_2 \leftarrow$ rank$_u(N,$ succ($B, b + 1) - (v + 1))$
5   **return** $r_2 - r_1 = 1$

6 **Proc** neigh(G, v, j) — *assuming $j \leq$* outdegree(G, v)
7   **return** access($N,$ select($B, v) - v + j$)

8 **Proc** rneigh(G, v, j) — *assuming $j \leq$* indegree(G, v)
9    $p \leftarrow$ select$_v(N, j)$
10   **return** select$_0(B, p) - p$

11 **Proc** outdegree(G, v)
12    $b \leftarrow$ select(B, v)
13   **return** succ($B, b + 1) - b - 1$

14 **Proc** indegree(G, v)
15   **return** rank$_v(N, e)$

---

first neighbor is neigh(2)[1] = access($N,$ select($B, 2) - 2 + 1$) = access($N, 4$) = 1 *and its second neighbor is* neigh(2)[2] = access($N,$ select($B, 2) - 2 + 2$) = access($N, 5$) = 5 *(see the solid gray arrows). Its indegree is* indegree(2) = rank$_2(N, 9) = 2$. *To find its first reverse neighbor we compute* $p \leftarrow$ select$_2(N, 1) = 1$, *then the neighbor is* rneigh(2)[1] = select$_0(B, p) - p = 2 - 1 = 1$. *For the second, we compute* $p \leftarrow$ select$_2(N, 2) = 6$, *and then* rneigh(2)[2] = select$_0(B, p) - p = 10 - 6 = 4$. *The process is shown with grayed blocks in N and gray dashed arrows to B.*

   In conclusion, within the same space, this representation offers more functionality, such as permitting the backward navigation of the edges. Algorithm 9.1 gives the pseudocode. Note that, if we build the structure on the transpose of G, each neighbor of v is accessed in constant time and each reverse neighbor in time $\mathcal{O}(\log \log n)$.

   If we are willing to have $\mathcal{O}(\log \log n)$ time for both the direct and the reverse neighbors, then we can use alphabet partitioning (Section 6.3) and reduce the space to $e\mathcal{H}_0(N)(1 + o(1)) + \mathcal{O}(e + n)$ bits. The entropy of N is related to the skewed distribution of indegrees in G. For example, if few nodes are targets of many edges and most are targets of a few, as is the case on the Web and in Twitter, then $\mathcal{H}_0(N)$ can be low. Recall that the compression obtained in Section 9.1.1 was related to the outdegrees, which are less skewed in those applications.

Algorithm 9.2: Computing operations on general undirected graphs.

Input : Undirected graph G (seen as sequence N, bitvector B and bit array S), nodes v and u, and index j.

1 **Proc** adj(G, v, u)
2   **if** $v = u$ **then** **return** bitread(S, v) = 1
3    $b \leftarrow$ select(B, v)
4    $r_1 \leftarrow$ rank$_u$($N, b - v$)
5    $r_2 \leftarrow$ rank$_u$(N, succ($B, b + 1$) $- (v + 1)$)
6   **if** $r_2 - r_1 = 1$ **then** **return true**
7    $b \leftarrow$ select(B, u)
8    $r_1 \leftarrow$ rank$_v$($N, b - u$)
9    $r_2 \leftarrow$ rank$_v$(N, succ($B, b + 1$) $- (u + 1)$)
10   **return** $r_2 - r_1 = 1$

11 **Proc** neigh(G, v, j) — *assuming* $j \leq$ degree(G, v)
12   **if** bitread(S, v) = 1 **then**
13   **if** $j = 1$ **then** **return** v
14   **else** $j \leftarrow j - 1$
15    $b \leftarrow$ select(B, v)
16    $d \leftarrow$ succ($B, b + 1$) $- b - 1$
17   **if** $j \leq d$ **then**
18   **return** access($N, b + j$)
19    $p \leftarrow$ select$_v$($N, j - d$)
20   **return** select$_0$(B, p) $- p$

21 **Proc** degree(G, v)
22   **if** bitread(S, v) = 1 **then** $s \leftarrow 1$ **else** $s \leftarrow 0$
23    $b \leftarrow$ select(B, v)
24   **return** $s + ($succ($B, b + 1$) $- b - 1) +$ rank$_v$(N, e)

9.1.3 Undirected Graphs

Another advantage of this structure is that it can represent undirected graphs without doubling the space. Each edge (v, u) is represented once, without also inserting (u, v). When asked to retrieve the neighbors of v, we retrieve both its direct and reverse neighbors. More precisely, to solve neigh(G, v)$[j]$, we retrieve the jth direct neighbor if $j \leq e_v =$ outdegree(G, v), and otherwise retrieve the $(j - e_v)$th reverse neighbor. If there are self-loops (v, v), we must handle them, for example, by representing them separately in a bit array $S[1, n]$ with $S[v] = 1$ iff $(v, v) \in E$. Thus, for undirected graphs, this representation effectively uses half the space of the classical adjacency lists and offers the same functionality. Algorithm 9.2 gives the pseudocode.

Example 9.2 *Figure 9.2 shows an undirected graph, with its classical representation (arrays N and V) and its compact representation (a sequence N of half the*

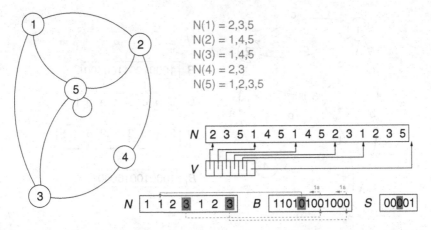

Figure 9.2. An undirected graph on the left, and its representation on the right. In gray we show the adjacency lists $N(v)$, where each edge is represented twice. A classical representation is formed by the top arrays N and V, where N is the concatenation of the lists $N(v)$ and V points to the beginnings of the lists $N(v)$ in array N. On the bottom, we show a compact representation based on a shorter sequence N (storing only the edges (v, u) with $v > u$), the bitvector B that replaces V, and the bit array S that marks nodes v with self-loops (v, v). Gray blocks and arrows illustrate the query $\mathsf{neigh}(3)$.

length and the bit sequences B and S). In the sequence we chose to represent, from $\{(u, v), (v, u)\}$, the pair (v, u) with $v > u$. There are in total $e = 7$ edges excluding self-loops. Node 3 has no self-loop since $S[3] = 0$. Then it has $\mathsf{degree}(3) = (\mathsf{select}(B, 3 + 1) - \mathsf{select}(B, 3) - 1) + \mathsf{rank}_3(N, 7) = (6 - 4 - 1) + 2 = 3$ neighbors. The first one is obtained with $\mathsf{neigh}(2)[1] = \mathsf{access}(N, \mathsf{select}(B, 3) - 3 + 1) = \mathsf{access}(N, 2) = 1$ (see the grayed block in B and the gray solid arrow). The second and the third are obtained as reverse neighbors (see grayed blocks in N and gray dashed arrows): $p \leftarrow \mathsf{select}_3(N, 1) = 4$, and then the second neighbor is $\mathsf{neigh}(2)[2] = \mathsf{select}_0(B, p) - p = 4$; $p \leftarrow \mathsf{select}_3(N, 2) = 7$ and the third neighbor is $\mathsf{neigh}(2)[3] = \mathsf{select}_0(B, p) - p = 5$.

9.1.4 Labeled Graphs

In some cases the graph edges have labels drawn from an alphabet $[1, \lambda]$. Then edges can be thought of as triples (v, u, l), where l is the label of the edge. This adds $e \log \lambda$ bits to the worst-case entropy.

Storing the labels within this space is not challenging: we can have an array $L[1, e]$ where $L[i]$ contains the label of the edge corresponding to $N[i]$. It is then easy to attach the corresponding label to each retrieved edge. However, if we represent L as a sequence, we enable other more sophisticated queries. We would like to have, apart from the usual queries on G, the ability to answer the same queries on each graph $G_l(V, E_l)$ formed by the edges labeled l in G, that is, $E_l = \{(v, u), (v, u, l) \in E\}$. Let us call those queries adj_l, neigh_l, rneigh_l, $\mathsf{outdegree}_l$, and $\mathsf{indegree}_l$.

Storing L as a sequence allows us to answer $\mathsf{outdegree}_l(G, v) = r_2 - r_1$, where $r_2 \leftarrow \mathsf{rank}_l(L, \mathsf{select}(B, v + 1) - (v + 1))$ and $r_1 \leftarrow \mathsf{rank}_l(L, \mathsf{select}(B, v) -$

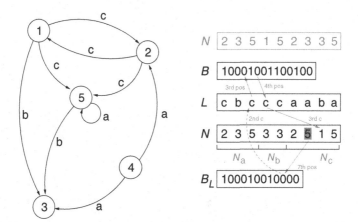

Figure 9.3. A labeled directed graph on the left, and its compact representation on the right. A simple representation would be the sequence N in gray (at the top) and the bitvector B, as with unlabeled graphs, plus the sequence L storing the labels. In the improved representation, N is rearranged so that all the edges labeled **a**, **b**, and **c** are stored contiguously (in black). Bitvector B_L marks the limits of those areas, N_a, N_b, and N_c. The gray solid arrows illustrate the query neigh(2)[1]. The gray block and dashed arrows illustrate rneigh(5)[2].

v). Then $\text{neigh}_l(G, v)[j]$ is $\text{access}(N, \text{select}_l(L, r_1 + j))$. It is not so easy to support the other queries, however.

Another arrangement of the data uses basically the same space and supports all those queries and more, with the exception of $\text{adj}(G, v, u)$. It is inspired by the representation of Section 6.3. We maintain L and B, but store N in a different order, grouped by labels. Let N_l be the sequence corresponding to G_l. Then we redefine $N = N_1 . N_2 \ldots N_\lambda$. We also store a bitvector $B_L = 1\,0^{|N_1|}1\,0^{|N_2|}1 \ldots 0^{|N_\lambda|}$ to mark the lengths of the concatenated sequences in N and give it constant-time rank and select support. The total space is then $e(\log n + \log \lambda)(1 + o(1)) + \mathcal{O}(n + \lambda)$ bits.

Example 9.3 *In Figure 9.3 we have added labels to the graph of Figure 9.1. On the right we show its improved compact representation. We show how the lists N_l are concatenated into the new sequence N. The set of labels is $[1, \lambda]$ for $\lambda = 3$, so let us interpret $a = 1$, $b = 2$, and $c = 3$. Arrows and shades will be used soon.*

Bitvector B delimits the lists in the original order, whereas B_L delimits the area of each label in the new order. Sequence L stores the labels of the edges in the original order and N stores their target nodes in the new order. A key property of the new order is that it maintains the original order of the edges within any label l. We can then solve the queries as follows. Queries $\text{outdegree}(G, v)$ and $\text{indegree}(G, v)$ are computed as before using B and N, respectively (this still works on N with the new ordering of the edges). For $\text{neigh}(G, v)[j]$, we know that the label of the edge is $l \leftarrow L[p]$, where $p \leftarrow \text{select}(B, v) - v + j$. The target node is then at

$$N[\text{select}(B_L, l) - l + \text{rank}_l(L, p)].$$

This is because the edges labeled l start in N at position $\text{select}(B_L, l) - l + 1$, and our edge, which is at position p in the original order, is the kth one with label l, for

$k = \mathsf{rank}_l(L, p)$. Since the order of edges stays the same in the new order, then p is mapped to the position in N given by the formula.

For $\mathsf{rneigh}(G, v)[j]$, we find the jth occurrence of v in N as before, $p \leftarrow \mathsf{select}_v(N, j)$ (this is not the same order in which rneigh returns the neighbors in the original arrangement, but this order can be chosen arbitrarily). The label of this edge is $l \leftarrow \mathsf{select}_0(B_L, p) - p$, whose area in N starts at $q \leftarrow \mathsf{select}(B_L, l) - l + 1$. This is then the $(p - q + 1)$th edge labeled l, and therefore its position in L is $s \leftarrow \mathsf{select}_l(L, p - q + 1)$. Finally, the target node is $\mathsf{select}_0(B, s) - s$, the node owning the list containing position s in L.

Operations neigh and rneigh now return a pair, where the second component is the label of the edge. Each neighbor is obtained by neigh in time $\mathcal{O}(\log\log n + \log\log \lambda) = \mathcal{O}(\log\log n)$.[2] Each reverse neighbor is listed in $\mathcal{O}(1)$ time. For $\mathsf{adj}(G, v, u)$, we can only try $\mathsf{adj}_l(G, v, u)$ label by label, thus the cost is $\mathcal{O}(\lambda \log\log n)$.

Example 9.4 *Consider the labeled graph in Figure 9.3. To find* $\mathsf{neigh}(2)[1]$, *we compute* $p \leftarrow \mathsf{select}(B, 2) - 2 + 1 = 4$. *Then the label of the edge is* $l \leftarrow L[p] = \mathsf{c} = 3$. *The target node of this edge is at* $N[\mathsf{select}(B_L, \mathsf{c}) - \mathsf{c} + \mathsf{rank}_\mathsf{c}(L, p)] = N[5 + 3] = N[8] = 1$. *Thus* $\mathsf{neigh}(2)[1] = (1, \mathsf{c})$. *The steps are illustrated with gray solid arrows.*

To obtain $\mathsf{rneigh}(5)[2]$, *we find* $p \leftarrow \mathsf{select}_5(N, 2) = 7$ *(the gray block). It corresponds to label* $l \leftarrow \mathsf{select}_0(B_L, 7) - 7 = 3 = \mathsf{c}$. *The area of* N_c *in* N *starts at* $q \leftarrow \mathsf{select}(B_L, \mathsf{c}) - \mathsf{c} + 1 = 6$. *Then the position of the edge in* L *is* $s \leftarrow \mathsf{select}_\mathsf{c}(L, p - q + 1) = \mathsf{select}_\mathsf{c}(L, 2) = 3$. *Finally, the target node is* $\mathsf{select}_0(B, s) - s = 4 - 3 = 1$. *Thus* $\mathsf{rneigh}(5)[2] = (1, \mathsf{c})$. *The steps are illustrated in gray dashed arrows.*

Let us now consider the labeled operations. The area of $\mathsf{neigh}_l(G, v)$ is computed with

$$p_1 = \mathsf{select}(B, v) - v, \qquad p_2 = \mathsf{select}(B, v + 1) - (v + 1),$$

which delimit the area $L[p_1 + 1, p_2]$ of $\mathsf{neigh}(v)$;

$$r_1 = \mathsf{select}(B_L, l) - l, \qquad r_2 = \mathsf{select}(B_L, l + 1) - (l + 1),$$

which delimit the area $N[r_1 + 1, r_2]$ of N_l; and

$$q_1 = \mathsf{rank}_l(L, p_1), \qquad q_2 = \mathsf{rank}_l(L, p_2),$$

which delimit the area $N[r_1 + q_1 + 1, r_1 + q_2]$ of $\mathsf{neigh}_l(v)$ in N. We then solve

$$\mathsf{outdegree}_l(G, v) = q_2 - q_1,$$

$$\mathsf{neigh}_l(G, v)[j] = N[r_1 + q_1 + j],$$

$$\mathsf{indegree}_l(G, v) = \mathsf{rank}_v(N, r_2) - \mathsf{rank}_v(N, r_1),$$

$$\mathsf{adj}_l(G, v, u) \text{ iff } \mathsf{rank}_u(N, r_1 + q_2) - \mathsf{rank}_u(N, r_1 + q_1) = 1,$$

and find the position of $\mathsf{rneigh}_l(G, v)[j]$ in N with $\mathsf{select}_v(N, \mathsf{rank}_v(N, r_1) + j)$, then mapping it to L as for rneigh.

---

[2] Here we assume that $\lambda \le e \le n^2$, that is, there are no more labels than edges.

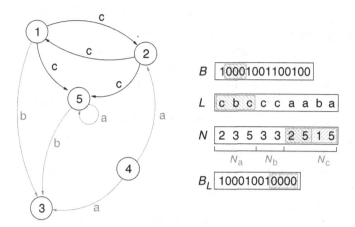

Figure 9.4. On the left, the labeled graph of Figure 9.3, where we leave in black only the edges of G_c. On the right, the areas computed in Example 9.5 on the compact representation, which refer to label c. The area of edges leaving from node 1 is hatched in B and L; that of edges labeled c is hatched in the other direction in N and B_L; and the area of edges labeled c and leaving from node 1 is doubly hatched in N.

Example 9.5 *Consider again the labeled graph of Figure 9.3. The area of* $\mathsf{neigh}_{c=3}(v)$ *for* $v = 1$ *is computed with* $p_1 \leftarrow \mathsf{select}(B, v) - v = 0$ *and* $p_2 \leftarrow \mathsf{select}(B, v + 1) - (v + 1) = 3$ *(then the area of* $\mathsf{neigh}(1)$ *is* $L[p_1 + 1, p_2] = L[1, 3])$, $r_1 \leftarrow \mathsf{select}(B_L, \mathsf{c}) - \mathsf{c} = 5$ *and* $r_2 \leftarrow \mathsf{select}(B_L, \mathsf{c} + 1) - (\mathsf{c} + 1) = 9$ *(then the area of* N_c *is* $N[r_1 + 1, r_2] = N[6, 9])$, *and* $q_1 \leftarrow \mathsf{rank}_\mathsf{c}(L, p_1) = 0$ *and* $q_2 \leftarrow \mathsf{rank}_\mathsf{c}(L, p_2) = 2$ *(then the area of* $\mathsf{neigh}_\mathsf{c}(v)$ *is* $N[r_1 + q_1 + 1, r_1 + q_2] = N[5 + 1, 5 + 2] = N[6, 7] = \langle 2, 5 \rangle)$. *These areas are hatched in Figure 9.4.*

Thus, we have $\mathsf{outdegree}_\mathsf{c}(v) = q_2 - q_1 = 2$, $\mathsf{neigh}_\mathsf{c}(v)[1] = N[r_1 + q_1 + 1] = N[6] = 2$, $\mathsf{neigh}_\mathsf{c}(v)[2] = N[r_1 + q_1 + 2] = N[7] = 5$, *and* $\mathsf{indegree}_\mathsf{c}(v) = \mathsf{rank}_v(N, r_2) - \mathsf{rank}_v(N, r_1) = 1$. *To find this reverse neighbor,* $\mathsf{rneigh}_\mathsf{c}(v)[1]$, *we compute* $t \leftarrow \mathsf{select}_v(N, \mathsf{rank}_v(N, r_1) + 1) = \mathsf{select}_v(N, 0 + 1) = 8$. *This is in* L *at position* $s \leftarrow \mathsf{select}_\mathsf{c}(L, t - r_1) = 4$, *which is the area of node* $\mathsf{select}_0(B, s) - s = 2$. *Thus* $\mathsf{rneigh}_\mathsf{c}(v)[1] = 2$. *Finally,* $\mathsf{adj}_\mathsf{c}(v, u)$ *for* $u = 2$ *is true since* $\mathsf{rank}_u(N, r_1 + q_2) - \mathsf{rank}_u(N, r_1 + q_1) = \mathsf{rank}_2(N, 7) - \mathsf{rank}_2(N, 5) = 1$.

Algorithms 9.3 and 9.4 give the pseudocode. Note that we have replaced a select_0 by a pred_1 in rneigh, which can be faster. We leave the task of deriving the undirected versions of the operations as an exercise to the reader.

Some further operations are possible. We can count all the edges labeled l in G with $\mathsf{rank}_l(L, e)$, and the jth such edge is at position $p \leftarrow \mathsf{select}_l(L, j)$; therefore it corresponds to the edge

$$(v, u) = (\mathsf{select}_0(B, p) - p, \mathsf{access}(N, \mathsf{select}(B_L, l) - l + \mathsf{rank}_l(L, p))).$$

Another query we can support is to list all the nodes v that are sources of edges labeled l. We start a cursor in L at position $c \leftarrow 0$ and obtain the first result by computing $p \leftarrow \mathsf{select}_l(L, 1)$. Thus we report the source node $v \leftarrow \mathsf{select}_0(B, p) - p$. To avoid listing the same node again if it is the source of another edge labeled l, we

---

Algorithm 9.3: Computing operations on labeled directed graphs. The code for indegree(G, v) and outdegree(G, v) is as in Algorithm 9.1.

Input : Labeled directed graph G (seen as sequences L and N and bitvectors B and B_L), nodes v and u, and index j.

1 **Proc** adj(G, v, u)
2   **for** $l \leftarrow 1$ **to** λ **do**
3   **if** adj(G, l, v, u) **then return true**
4   **return false**

5 **Proc** neigh(G, v, j) — *assuming $j \le$ outdegree(G, v)*
6     $p \leftarrow$ select(B, v) $- v + j$
7     $l \leftarrow$ access(L, p)
8     $q \leftarrow$ select(B_L, l) $- l$
9   **return** (access(N, $q +$ rank$_l$(L, p)), l)

10 **Proc** rneigh(G, v, j) — *assuming $j \le$ indegree(G, v)*
11     $p \leftarrow$ select$_v$(N, j)
12     $t \leftarrow$ select$_0$(B_L, p)
13     $l \leftarrow t - p$
14     $s \leftarrow$ select$_l$(L, $t -$ pred(B_L, t))
15   **return** (select$_0$(B, s) $- s$, l)

---

move the cursor forward to the end of its list, $c \leftarrow$ succ(B, $v + p$) $- (v + 1)$. Now the next result is obtained with $p \leftarrow$ select$_l$(L, $1 +$ rank$_l$(L, c)). We report the new node, advance the cursor, and so on.

For listing target nodes of edges labeled l, we should enumerate the distinct elements in N[select(B_L, l) $- l + 1$, select(B_L, $l + 1$) $- (l + 1)$], which can be done efficiently if N is represented with a wavelet tree (see the last part of Section 6.4.3).

9.1.5 Construction

For the bitvector-based representation of Section 9.1.1, we simply build the very sparse bitvector representation of each $N(v)$ and then free $N(v)$. Thus, we need at most $\mathcal{O}(n)$ bits on top of the initial representation.

For the sequence-based representation of Section 9.1.2, we use the construction of Algorithm 6.2. The sequence can be built chunk by chunk from the lists $N(v)$, simulating their concatenation N and freeing each list $N(v)$ as soon as it is included in the sequence. Since no list $N(v)$ is longer than n, the maximum extra space usage is $2n \log n + \mathcal{O}(n)$ bits, if we build a new chunk with a small part of a list $N(v)$ and a part of the next list $N(v + 1)$. Converting V into a bitvector takes other $\mathcal{O}(n + e)$ bits.

Algorithm 9.4: Computing label-specific operations on directed graphs.

Input : Labeled directed graph G (seen as sequences L and N and bitvectors B and B_L), nodes v and u, label l, and index j.

1 **Proc** adj(G, l, v, u)
2     $b \leftarrow$ select(B, v)
3     $p_1 \leftarrow b - v; p_2 \leftarrow$ succ$(B, b + 1) - (v + 1)$
4     $r \leftarrow$ select$(B_L, l) - l$
5     $q_1 \leftarrow$ rank$_l(L, p_1); q_2 \leftarrow$ rank$_l(L, p_2)$
6   **return** rank$_u(N, r + q_2) -$ rank$_u(N, r + q_1) = 1$

7 **Proc** neigh(G, l, v, j) — *assuming* $j \leq$ outdegree(G, l, v)
8     $p \leftarrow$ select$(B, v) - v$
9     $r \leftarrow$ select$(B_L, l) - l$
10     $q \leftarrow$ rank$_l(L, p)$
11   **return** access$(N, r + q + j)$

12 **Proc** rneigh(G, l, v, j) — *assuming* $j \leq$ indegree(G, l, v)
13     $r \leftarrow$ select$(B_L, l) - l$
14     $t \leftarrow$ select$_v(N,$ rank$_v(N, r) + j)$
15     $s \leftarrow$ select$_l(L, t - r)$
16   **return** select$_0(B, s) - s$

17 **Proc** outdegree(G, l, v)
18     $b \leftarrow$ select(B, v)
19     $p_1 \leftarrow b - v; p_2 \leftarrow$ succ$(B, b + 1) - (v + 1)$
20   **return** rank$_l(L, p_2) -$ rank$_l(L, p_1)$

21 **Proc** indegree(G, l, v)
22     $b \leftarrow$ select(B_L, l)
23     $r_1 \leftarrow b - l; r_2 \leftarrow$ succ$(B_L, b + 1) - (l + 1)$
24   **return** rank$_v(N, r_2) -$ rank$_v(N, r_1)$

In case of an undirected graph where the edges are duplicated, we may halve N on the way, by ignoring any edge where a higher-numbered node is pointed from a lower-numbered one.

Labeled graphs can be built with a simplification of Algorithm 6.12, where the classes are given by the edge labels: we precompute the starting points in N of each area N_l and process the edges (v, u, l) sorted by v: we add l at the end of the written part of L and u at the end of the written part of N_l.

In all cases, the adjacency lists can be read from disk as we build the bitvectors or chunks in main memory, thus we build the structures in memory within almost exactly the final space needed by the structure. We can also send the resulting structure to disk as the bitvectors or chunks are produced, if necessary.

9.2 Clustered Graphs

An important class of graphs that arises in many applications are the clustered graphs, where the nodes can be divided into a few subsets $V = V_1 \cup V_2 \cup \ldots \cup V_t$ so that most edges connect two nodes of some V_i. In this case it is possible to design graph representations that take advantage of the clustering. In this section we study one such representation, the k^2-tree, which performs well on Web graphs, social networks, and RDF stores.

9.2.1 K^2-Tree Structure

Assume n is a power of k, for some parameter k. Then a k^2-tree divides the adjacency matrix $M[1, n][1, n]$ into k^2 equal areas of the form

$$M\left[(n/k)(r - 1) + 1, (n/k)r\right]\left[(n/k)(c - 1) + 1, (n/k)c\right]$$

for rows $1 \le r \le k$ and columns $1 \le c \le k$. This partition is represented as the root of a k^2-ary cardinal tree, where children correspond to submatrices in column-major order. If any of the k^2 submatrices has no 1s, then the corresponding child of the node is absent. We then continue the decomposition recursively for each nonempty submatrix. We finish at the tree leaves, which represent single cells of M. The height of the k^2-tree is always $h = \log_k n$, but not all the branches reach the maximum depth $h + 1$.

The k^2-tree is, in essence, a succinct representation of this cardinal tree, using the LOUDS-based variant described in Section 8.1.1. The main difference is that leaves that are at depth $h + 1$ do not need to store their k^2 0s indicating they have no children, because we already know that they have the maximum possible depth.

In this representation, all the operations we will support need only rank and access on the LOUDS bitvector B: the root is node 1; the lth child of node p (for $l \in [1, k^2]$) exists iff childrenlabeled(p, l), that is, if $B[k^2(p - 1) + l] = 1$; and if so, it is node labeledchild$(p, l) = \text{rank}_1(B, k^2(p - 1) + l) + 1$. Note that we will not attempt to access the child of a node in the last level.

In order to represent a graph of n nodes, we will complete M with 0s up to $M[1, s][1, s]$, with $s = k^{\lceil \log_k n \rceil}$. Those spurious empty areas add little extra space in the k^2-tree, $\mathcal{O}(s) = \mathcal{O}(kn)$ bits, because they have no 1s. In general, the k^2-tree represents large empty submatrices within little space, which makes it a good choice when the graph is clustered and the nodes in each V_i have consecutive numbers in $[1, n]$. Note that, in this case, most of the 1s in the matrix lie around the main diagonal.

For simplicity we will generally assume that n is already a power of k in our discussions.

Example 9.6 *Figure 9.5 shows a graph of $n = 15$ nodes with some degree of clustering, its matrix $M[1, 16][1, 16]$, and its k^2-tree representation for $k = 2$. Below the tree, we show its LOUDS-based representation, where nodes at depth $1 + \log_k s = 1 + \log_2 16 = 5$ are known to be leaves. The grayed cells and nodes will be used later.*

For example, consider the first submatrix, $M[1, 8][1, 8]$, corresponding to the first child of the root. It has 4 submatrices, $M[1, 4][1, 4]$, $M[5, 8][1, 4]$, $M[1, 4][5, 8]$, and $M[5, 8][5, 8]$. Only the first 3 submatrices contain 1s, thus only the first 3 children

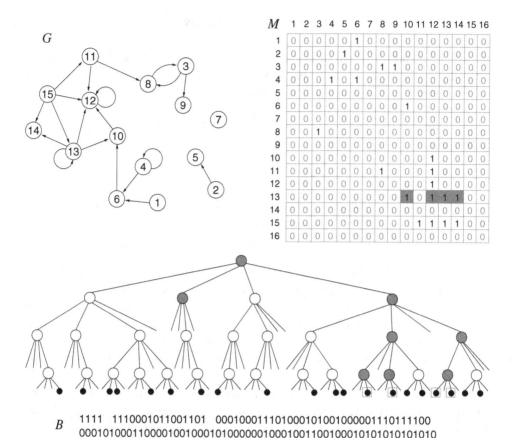

Figure 9.5. A graph of 15 nodes (top left) and its adjacency matrix M (top right). On the bottom, the corresponding k^2-tree representation, with its LOUDS bitvector B below, separating the levels with spaces and with the last level in another line. The small black circles are the nodes in the last level of the tree, which are known to be leaves because they have the maximum depth. The leaves at higher nodes are simply omitted (only the dangling edge is shown). Gray matrix cells and tree nodes, plus squares containing last-level leaves, illustrate the process to answer neigh(13).

of the node exist. Let us now consider the first submatrix. It is in turn divided into $M[1, 2][1, 2]$, $M[3, 4][1, 2]$, $M[1, 2][3, 4]$, and $M[3, 4][3, 4]$. Only the latter contains 1s, thus the corresponding node has only its fourth child. In turn, this child has only its fourth child, corresponding to the only 1 it contains, at cell $M[4, 4]$.

The bitvector at the bottom corresponds to a levelwise traversal of the tree. We have separated the bitvectors of each level with spaces for legibility. The last level, where we will not try to query for children, is shown on the second line.

9.2.2 Queries

The k^2-tree is a symmetric representation of the adjacency matrix, and as such it can extract with analogous procedures any neigh(G, v) or rneigh(G, v) list, by finding all the 1s along row v or column v, respectively. The idea is to compute the k children of

---

Algorithm 9.5: Operation adj on a k^2-tree.

Input : A graph G of n nodes and more than zero edges (seen as k^2-tree T) and nodes v and u.

```
 1  Proc adj(G, v, u)
 2      p ← root(T)
 3      s ← k^⌈log_k n⌉
 4      while s > 1 do
 5          l ← s/k
 6          r ← ⌈v/l⌉; c ← ⌈u/l⌉
 7          if not childrenlabeled(T, p, (c − 1)k + r) then
 8              return false
 9          p ← labeledchild(T, p, (c − 1)k + r)
10          s ← l
11          v ← v − l(r − 1); u ← u − l(c − 1)
12      return true
```

---

the root that intersect the desired row or column, and then continue recursively on all those that are nonempty. When we reach leaves, we report their 1s.

Algorithms 9.5 and 9.6 show the pseudocode. Note that, while operation adj is carried out in time $\mathcal{O}(h) = \mathcal{O}(\log_k n)$, operations neigh and rneigh have no better worst-case guarantee than $\mathcal{O}(n)$, and indegree and outdegree are not directly supported. On a clustered graph, however, neigh and rneigh enter into few submatrices and perform efficiently.

Example 9.7 *Figure 9.5 shows in gray the cells accessed, and the k^2-tree nodes traversed, to list* neigh(13). *Since row 13 intersects with only the second and fourth submatrices, $M[9, 16][1, 8]$ and $M[9, 16][9, 16]$, we traverse only the second and fourth children of the root. In the first of those, we are interested only in the sub-submatrices $M[13, 16][1, 4]$ and $M[13, 16][5, 8]$, both of which are empty (consequently, the second child of the root has no second nor fourth child). In the submatrix $M[9, 16][9, 16]$, corresponding to the fourth child of the root, we are interested in submatrices $M[13, 16][9, 12]$ and $M[13, 16][13, 16]$. Those correspond to the second and fourth children of that node. In these submatrices row 13 is in the upper band, thus we explore their first and third children. For example, in $M[13, 16][9, 12]$ we are interested in the first child, $M[13, 14][9, 10]$, and the third, $M[13, 14][11, 12]$. In the first of those, for example, we explore the first and third children, of which the third exists, $M[13, 10] = 1$, and is reported as a neighbor.*

Undirected Graphs

Since the k^2-tree can symmetrically extract direct and reverse neighbors, we can represent undirected graphs by just encoding the edges (v, u) so that $v \leq u$. Then, to solve neigh(G, v), we apply the same procedures neigh(G, v) and rneigh(G, v) of Algorithm 9.6. We only have to be careful to not report the edge (v, v) twice, if it exists.

Algorithm 9.6: Operations neigh and rneigh on a k^2-tree.

Input : A graph G of n nodes and more than zero edges (seen as k^2-tree T) and node v.

1 **Proc** neigh(G, v)
2     $creport(\text{root}(T), v, 1, k^{\lceil \log_k n \rceil})$

3 **Proc** $creport(p, r, c_0, s)$
    Input : Nonempty submatrix $M'[1, s][1, s]$ of M corresponding to tree node p, which starts at column c_0 of M, and local row r to report.
    Output: Outputs the columns $c_0 - 1 + c$ such that $M'[r, c] = 1$.

4   **if** $s = 1$ **then** output c_0
5   **else**
6        $l \leftarrow s/k$
7        $r_l \leftarrow \lceil r/l \rceil$
8        $r \leftarrow r - l(r_l - 1)$
9   **for** $c \leftarrow 1$ **to** k **do**
10   **if** childrenlabeled$(T, p, (c - 1)k + r_l)$ **then**
11              $creport(\text{labeledchild}(T, p, (c - 1)k + r_l), r, c_0 + (c - 1)l, l)$

12 **Proc** rneigh(G, v)
13     $rreport(\text{root}(T), v, 1, k^{\lceil \log_k n \rceil})$

14 **Proc** $rreport(p, c, r_0, s)$
    Input : Nonempty submatrix $M'[1, s][1, s]$ of M corresponding to tree node p, which starts at row r_0 of M, and local column c to report.
    Output: Outputs the rows $r_0 - 1 + r$ such that $M'[r, c] = 1$.

15   **if** $s = 1$ **then** output r_0
16   **else**
17        $l \leftarrow s/k$
18        $c_l \leftarrow \lceil c/l \rceil$
19        $c \leftarrow c - l(c_l - 1)$
20   **for** $r \leftarrow 1$ **to** k **do**
21   **if** childrenlabeled$(T, p, (c_l - 1)k + r)$ **then**
22              $rreport(\text{labeledchild}(T, p, (c_l - 1)k + r), c, r_0 + (r - 1)l, l)$

9.2.3 Reducing Space

In Section 8.1.1 we saw that a LOUDS-based representation of a cardinal tree over an alphabet of size k^2 has the problem of requiring k^2 bits for each node of the tree, and the use of compressed bitvectors (Section 4.4) was suggested to reduce the space.

In the worst case, if we have e edges in an $n \times n$ matrix, each point may induce a path of length $h = \log_k n = \log_{k^2} n^2$ in the tree, and each node in the path may use k^2 bits to represent its children. This maximum of $e\,k^2 \log_k n$ bits cannot be reached, however, because not all the paths can be fully different. Analogously as in the last part of Section 6.4.3 (recall Figure 6.11), the worst case is that all the nodes up to depth $\ell + 1$, with $\ell = \lfloor \log_{k^2} e \rfloor$, participate in some path, and from each such node there is a single distinct path of length $h - \ell$ toward a leaf. This yields a maximum of

$$\frac{(k^2)^{\ell+1} - 1}{k^2 - 1} + e\,(h - \ell) < e\left(\frac{k^2}{k^2 - 1} + 1 + \log_{k^2}\frac{n^2}{e}\right)$$

distinct nodes. If we represent B in plain form, then the nodes in the distinct paths of length $h - \ell$ cost k^2 bits each, which adds up to

$$e\left(\frac{k^2}{k^2 - 1} + k^2\left(1 + \log_{k^2}\frac{n^2}{e}\right)\right)$$

bits. If we represent B using very sparse bitvectors (Section 4.4), then the space becomes the number of nodes times $\log(k^2)$, that is, $\mathcal{O}\left(e\log\frac{n^2}{e} + e\log k\right)$ bits. This is of the same order of the worst-case entropy of directed graphs, plus an $\mathcal{O}(e\log k)$ additive penalty. To this, we must add up to $\mathcal{O}(kn)$ bits that are lost when we expand the grid dimensions to the next power of k^2. This analysis is rather pessimistic on clustered graphs, as demonstrated in practical applications.

The use of very sparse bitvectors may considerably slow down the operations, as they build mostly on operation rank, which is not so fast in this representation. An alternative to reduce space without much impact on the time is as follows. Since we know that the leaves in the last level will require no traversal operations, we can split bitvector B into two parts, $B = B_T . B_L$, where B_T is the part corresponding to nodes at depths 1 to h, and B_L is the part of the LOUDS representation corresponding to the level at depth $h + 1$. Only B_T needs to be a bitvector supporting operation rank; B_L can be a simple bit array supporting operation bitread (Chapter 3).

To obtain the best time performance, we represent B_T as a plain bitvector. This wastes more space as k grows, but on the other hand B_T becomes shorter in relation to B_L as k grows. Compressing B_L impacts much less on the time and reduces its space contribution from ek^2 to $2e\log k + \mathcal{O}(e)$ bits.

On the other hand, we can take advantage of the fact that B_L needs only bitread and that it comes in chunks of k^2 bits to design more compressed representations for it. For example, since there are at most 2^{k^2} distinct chunks (and usually much less when the graph is clustered), we can compress them statistically using Huffman codes (Section 2.6; the source symbols are bit arrays of length k^2). To allow for direct access to the ith chunk in B_L, we can use the techniques developed to store arrays of variable-sized elements (Sections 3.2 and 6.4.5).

Example 9.8 *The leaves of Figure 9.5 (second line of bits) contain the following chunks, in decreasing order of frequency:* 0001 *(4 times),* 0010 *(4 times),* 1010 *(3 times), and one occurrence of* 0100, 0110, 1000, *and* 0011. *A Huffman code for those frequencies assigns them codes* 00, 01, 10, 1100, 1101, 1110, *and* 1111, *respectively.*

Thus we replace the bitvector in the second line by the following sequence of variable-length codes: $B_L =$ 00 1100 1101 00 01 01 1110 00 00 1111 01 01 10 10 10. Thus, instead of $15 \cdot 4 = 60$, we reduce B_L to 38 bits.

Another way to reduce space and even improve the time is to use different k values at each level of the k^2-tree. For example, we can use a larger k value near the root, where all of the submatrices are likely to be nonempty, and let k decrease as we move toward the leaves. The leaves themselves may use a larger k again, if that is convenient to encode them statistically.

9.2.4 Construction

From the array $E[1, e]$ of edges we can construct the k^2-tree directly, as follows: (1) initialize a queue of submatrix ranges and associated range of E to process, the first one being the whole $M[1, s][1, s]$ and the whole array $E[1, e]$; (2) take each submatrix from the queue, say, of $s \times s$ with associated range $E[i, j]$, and partition $E[i, j]$ in-place, separating the edges (v, u) into k^2 sub-ranges according to the value of $(\lceil u/l \rceil - 1)k + \lceil v/l \rceil$, where $l = s/k$ and the coordinates are local to the submatrix; (3) append a 1 to the LOUDS bitvector of the tree for each nonempty range, and a 0 for each empty range, in the proper order; (4) enqueue the submatrices with nonempty sub-ranges if we are not processing the last level; (5) continue until the queue is empty.

The in-place partitioning of the edges into k^2 different values can be done in linear time with a simple variant of RadixSort. Since the construction requires sorting the e edges across $\log_k n$ levels, the total time required is $\mathcal{O}(e \log_k n)$. This construction needs extra space only for the queue (which can be efficiently maintained on disk, if necessary).

Algorithm 9.7 shows the details. Note that we first allocate a maximum possible space for bitvector B and then remove the unused part at the end. We can, instead, dynamically reallocate B as it grows. We can also improve our first upper bound with the more sophisticated formulas we have derived.

We do not consider how to produce an appropriate ordering of the nodes to yield a good clustering. This depends on the application; we give some references at the end of the chapter.

9.3 *K*-Page Graphs

In this section we study a family of undirected graphs that can be drawn without letting their edges cross, which is of interest in VLSI design. The most restricted class of the family is called *one-page* graphs, whose nodes can be arranged on a line and the edges drawn as arcs over the line, without crossings. That is, there is a way to interpret the nodes as numbers in $[1, n]$ so that there are no edges (v, u) and (v', u') with $v < v' < u < u'$. For simplicity, apart from assuming that no multiple edges may connect two nodes, we will disregard self-loops (v, v) (which can be handled with n additional bits or other means).

Algorithm 9.7: Building the k^2-tree. Uses operations *enqueue* and *dequeue* on queue Q. It first allocates the maximum possible space for B and then reduces it.

Input : Array $E[1, e]$ of edges ($E[i].v, E[i].u$), values n and k.
Output: Computes B, the k^2-tree for E.

1   $s \leftarrow k^{\lceil \log_k n \rceil}$
2   $Q \leftarrow \langle (1, n, s/k, 0, 0) \rangle$ (queue of tuples (i, j, l, r_0, c_0))
3   Allocate bitvector $B[1, ek^2 \log_k n]$ (the LOUDS representation)
4   $t \leftarrow 0$ (where we write in B)
5   **while** Q *is not empty* **do**
6     $(i, j, l, r_0, c_0) \leftarrow dequeue(Q)$
7   Sort $E[i, j]$ with key $(\lceil (E[\cdot].u - c_0)/l \rceil - 1)k + \lceil (E[\cdot].v - r_0)/l \rceil$
8     $p \leftarrow i$
9   **for** $c \leftarrow 1$ **to** k **do**
10   **for** $r \leftarrow 1$ **to** k **do**
11         $t \leftarrow t + 1$
12   **while** $p \le j$ **and** $\lceil (E[p].u - c_0)/l \rceil = c$
13   **and** $\lceil (E[p].v - r_0)/l \rceil = r$ **do**
14           $p \leftarrow p + 1$
15   **if** $p > i$ **then**
16   bitset(B, t)
17   **if** $l > 1$ **then**
18   enqueue($Q, (i, p - 1, l/k, r_0 + (r - 1)l, c_0 + (c - 1)l)$)
19           $i \leftarrow p$
20   **else** bitclear(B, t)

21 Reallocate B to use only t bits

More generally, the edges of a *k-page graph* $G = (V, E)$ can be decomposed into k disjoint subsets $E = E_1 \cup \ldots \cup E_k$, so that we choose one ordering for the nodes and each subgraph $G_k = (V, E_k)$ is a one-page graph using that common order.

The number of connected k-page graphs is at least $\frac{2^{kn-k^2}}{2k!}$; therefore their worst-case entropy is at least $kn - \mathcal{O}(k^2)$. Also, the densest possible k-page graphs have $e \le (k + 1)n - 3k$ edges. We will study representations of k-page graphs using $\mathcal{O}(kn)$ and $\mathcal{O}(e \log k)$ bits, which are based on the parenthesis and multi-parenthesis structures studied in Chapter 7.

9.3.1 One-Page Graphs

The nodes of a one-page graph form a containment structure: two edges (v, u) and (v', u'), for $v < u$ and $v' < u'$, define segments $[v, u]$ and $[v', u']$ that either are disjoint, or one is contained in the other. This containment structure allows for a representation using parentheses (Chapter 7).

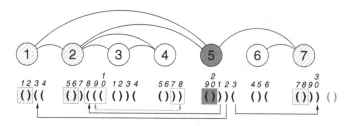

Figure 9.6. A one-page graph and its representation using parentheses. Node 5 is grayed and its neighbors are hatched. The black arrows show how the matching parentheses of the node connect it with its neighbors. Instead, the gray arrow between the appropriate areas of nodes 2 and 4 (inside open rectangles) shows the matching pair of parentheses that connects them.

Consider the following representation with a sequence $B[1, 2(n + e + 1)]$ of parentheses: We traverse the nodes from $v = 1$ to $v = n$. For each new node v, we (1) append '()' to B; (2) append as many ')'s as edges connect v with nodes $u < v$ (graphically, at its left); (3) append as many '('s as edges connect v with nodes $u > v$ (graphically, at its right). We complete the sequence with a final '()' to avoid special cases. In total, we write $2(n + e + 1)$ parentheses, and the representation is balanced: every edge is first seen as an opening parenthesis and later as a closing one.

Example 9.9 *Figure 9.6 shows a one-page graph and its parentheses representation on the bottom. Node 5 (grayed) is represented as '()' followed by ')' and by '('. The pair '()' identifies the node. The next two parentheses represent its two neighbors to the left, nodes 1 and 2. The last opening parenthesis represents its neighbor to the right, 7. Arrows show some matching parenthesis pairs, which will be used to identify the neighbors.*

Consider a node whose corresponding pair '()' starts at $B[v]$. Note that pairs '()' can be formed only when we encode the nodes. Thus, the left-to-right number of v is $1 + \mathsf{rank}_{10}(B, v)$. Conversely, the jth left-to-right node starts in B at $\mathsf{select}_{10}(B, j)$ (those extended $\mathsf{rank/select}$ operations were defined in Section 7.1.4). In the sequel we will use v as the node identifier. We can map those to indexes $[1, n]$ and back using $\mathsf{rank}_{10}/\mathsf{select}_{10}$.

To retrieve the neighbors of v, we must find the parentheses that match those that are written after v. We have $b = \mathsf{succ}_1(B, v + 2) - (v + 2)$ closing parentheses after v, which denote b backward arcs connecting v with nodes to the left. From position $v + 2 + b$, we have $f = \mathsf{succ}_0(B, v + 2 + b) - (v + 3 + b)$ opening parentheses. These denote forward arcs connecting v with nodes to the right (we subtract $v + 3 + b$ because succ_0 will also include the opening parenthesis of the pair '()' of the next node). Thus we can compute the number of neighbors of v as $\mathsf{degree}(G, v) = b + f$.

Now, to compute $\mathsf{neigh}(G, v)[j]$, we find the backward and the forward neighbors separately. For the backward neighbors, we take each position $v + 1 + j$, for $1 \le j \le b$, and compute $p \leftarrow \mathsf{open}(B, v + 1 + j)$. The node corresponding to that arc is thus $\mathsf{pred}_1(B, \mathsf{pred}_0(B, p))$. For the forward neighbors, we take each position $v + 1 + b + j$, for $1 \le j \le f$, and compute $p \leftarrow \mathsf{close}(B, v + 1 + b + j)$. The node corresponding to that arc is $\mathsf{pred}_1(B, p)$.

Example 9.10 *Consider again Figure 9.6 and node* 5. *Its position in* B *is* $v =$ $\mathsf{select}_{10}(5) = 19$. *We compute its number of backward neighbors as* $b = \mathsf{succ}_1(v + 2) - (v + 2) = \mathsf{succ}_1(21) - 21 = 2$. *Its number of forward neighbors is* $f = \mathsf{succ}_0(v + 2 + b) - (v + 3 + b) = \mathsf{succ}_0(23) - 24 = 1$.

The first backward neighbor, with $j = 1$, *is computed as* $p \leftarrow \mathsf{open}(v + 1 + j) = \mathsf{open}(21) = 8$, *and then the node is* $\mathsf{pred}_1(\mathsf{pred}_0(8)) = \mathsf{pred}_1(7) = 5$, *which has index* $1 + \mathsf{rank}_{10}(5) = 2$. *The second backward neighbor,* $j = 2$, *is found with* $p \leftarrow \mathsf{open}(v + 1 + j) = \mathsf{open}(22) = 3$, *and then the node is* $\mathsf{pred}_1(\mathsf{pred}_0(3)) = \mathsf{pred}_1(2) = 1$, *with index* $1 + \mathsf{rank}_{10}(1) = 1$. *The only forward neighbor,* $j = 1$, *is computed with* $p \leftarrow \mathsf{close}(v + 1 + b + j) = \mathsf{close}(23) = 30$, *and the node is* $\mathsf{pred}_1(30) = 27$, *which has index* $1 + \mathsf{rank}_{10}(27) = 7$.

Finally, we can determine whether $\mathsf{adj}(G, v, u)$ for $v < u$, as follows. Let b_v and f_v be the b and f values for node v, and b_u and f_u those corresponding to u. Then v and u are neighbors iff there is a pair of matching parentheses between $B[p, q] = B[v + 2 + b_v, v + 1 + b_v + f_v]$ (all of them opening) and $B[p', q'] = B[u + 2, u + 1 + b_u]$ (all of them closing). First, if $p > q$ or $p' > q'$ (i.e., $f_v = 0$ or $b_u = 0$), then v and u cannot be neighbors. Otherwise, if $\mathsf{close}(B, p) < p'$, then v and u are not neighbors, because the farthest-reaching edge from v arrives at a node before u. Otherwise, if $\mathsf{close}(B, p) \leq q'$, then v and u are neighbors, because they are connected by the edge leaving at $p = v + 2 + b_v$. Otherwise the edges of u are contained in $[p, \mathsf{close}(B, p)]$, as edges cannot cross, and therefore the backward edges from u can arrive only at positions after v. Thus, only the last closing parenthesis from u can connect it to v. Consequently, at this point, v and u are neighbors iff $\mathsf{open}(B, q') \leq q$.

Example 9.11 *Let us see that nodes* $v = 5$ *(with index 2) and* $u = 15$ *(with index 4) are connected in Figure 9.6. They have* $b_v = 1$, $f_v = 3$, $b_u = 2$, *and* $f_u = 0$; *therefore their ranges are* $[p, q] = [8, 10]$ *and* $[p', q'] = [17, 18]$. *These are shown in the figure with open rectangles. They pass the test* $p \leq q$ *(or* $f_v > 0$*) and* $p' \leq q'$ *(or* $b_u > 0$*), as well as* $\mathsf{close}(p) = 21 \geq 17 = p'$. *Yet this edge does not connect* v *and* u, *since* $\mathsf{close}(p) = 21 > 18 = q'$. *Thus, the only opportunity is that the last closing parenthesis of* u *connects it to* v. *This is actually the case, since* $\mathsf{open}(q') = \mathsf{open}(18) = 9 \leq 10 = q$. *The gray arrow in the figure connects the matching parentheses.*

Algorithm 9.8 gives the pseudocode. The queries require a constant number of parenthesis operations, thus with the implementation of Section 7.2, both $\mathsf{neigh}(G, v, j)$ and $\mathsf{adj}(G, v, u)$ take time $\mathcal{O}(\log \log n)$. Operation $\mathsf{degree}(G, v)$ requires only succ operations, which can be implemented in $\mathcal{O}(1)$ time with the technique of Section 4.5.2. The space of the structure is $2(n + e) + o(n)$ bits.

9.3.2 K-Page Graphs

For a k-page graph, we can repeat the one-page data structure for each subgraph $G_i = (V, E_i)$. The same nodes are listed in each structure, with the same order, thus we can easily identify nodes across the structures. Therefore, if G has n nodes and e edges, its representation takes $2(kn + e) + o(kn + e)$ bits. The one-page operations are easily generalized by carrying them out on each of the k pages and merging the results. We

---

Algorithm 9.8: Computing operations on one-page graphs.

Input : One-page graph G (seen as bitvector B), nodes v and u, and index j.

1 **Proc** adj(G, v, u)
2 | if $v > u$ then $u \leftrightarrow v$
3 | $l \leftarrow \mathsf{succ}_1(B, v + 2)$
4 | **return** $match(B, l, \mathsf{succ}_0(B, l) - 2, u + 2, \mathsf{succ}_1(B, u + 2) - 1)$

5 **Proc** $match(B, p, q, p', q')$
  | **Input** : Parentheses sequence B and ranges $[p, q]$ and $[p', q']$ with $q < p'$.
  | **Output**: Returns whether there is a matching pair of parentheses connecting
         $B[p, q]$ (all opening) and $B[p', q']$ (all closing).
6 | if $p > q$ or $p' > q'$ then **return false**
7 | $c \leftarrow \mathsf{close}(B, p)$
8 | if $c < p'$ then **return false**
9 | if $c \le q'$ then **return true**
10 | **return** $\mathsf{open}(B, q') \le q$

11 **Proc** neigh(G, v, j) — *assuming* $j \le$ degree(G, v)
12 | $b \leftarrow \mathsf{succ}_1(B, v + 2) - (v + 2)$
13 | if $j \le b$ then
14 | **return** $\mathsf{pred}_1(B, \mathsf{pred}_0(B, \mathsf{open}(B, v + 1 + j)))$
15 | **return** $\mathsf{pred}_1(B, \mathsf{close}(B, v + 1 + j))$

16 **Proc** degree(G, v)
17 | **return** $\mathsf{succ}_0(B, \mathsf{succ}_1(v + 2)) - (v + 3)$

---

need to apply select$_{10}$ to find the position of the node in each sequence; therefore the node identifiers will now be their index, and not their position in a particular sequence. By implementing **select** in constant time (Section 4.3.3), degree(G, v) takes $\mathcal{O}(k)$ time, adj(G, v, u) requires $\mathcal{O}(k \log \log n)$ time (as it uses primitives **open** and **close**), and generating neigh(G, v) requires time $\mathcal{O}(k + $ degree$(G, v) \log \log n)$.

Example 9.12 *Figure 9.7 extends the one-page graph of Figure 9.6 to a three-page graph, each with its corresponding parentheses sequence (the sequences P, B_*, and S below will be used later).*

To compute degree(v) *for* $v = 5$ *(grayed), we consider the three sequences. In the first, v corresponds to position $v_{\mathsf{p}} \leftarrow$ select$_{10}(v) = 19$. As in Example 9.10, we compute* $\mathsf{succ}_0(\mathsf{succ}_1(v_{\mathsf{p}} + 2)) = \mathsf{succ}_0(\mathsf{succ}_1(21)) = \mathsf{succ}_0(23) = 25$, *thus we have $25 - (v_{\mathsf{p}} + 3) = 3$ neighbors in the first page. In the second sequence, v corresponds to position $v_{\mathsf{p}} \leftarrow$ select$_{10}(v) = 15$. Then we compute* $\mathsf{succ}_0(\mathsf{succ}_1(v_{\mathsf{p}} + 2)) = \mathsf{succ}_0(\mathsf{succ}_1(17)) = \mathsf{succ}_0(17) = 18$, *thus we have $18 - (v_{\mathsf{p}} + 3) = 0$ neighbors in the second page. In the third sequence, v corresponds to position $v_{\mathsf{p}} \leftarrow$* select$_{10}(v) = 12$. *Then we compute* $\mathsf{succ}_0(\mathsf{succ}_1(v_{\mathsf{p}} + 2)) = \mathsf{succ}_0(\mathsf{succ}_1(14)) =$

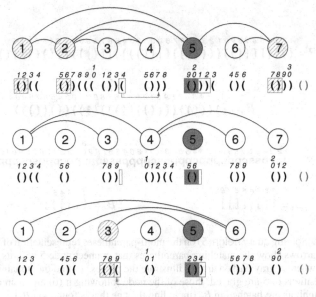

$$P = ()((([[\{(())((((\{()(]\{(())]][[(()))(\}()(]\}}())]$$

Figure 9.7. A 3-page graph and its representation using parentheses. Node 5 is grayed and its neighbors are hatched. The parentheses that could connect nodes 3 and 5 are inside open rectangles, and gray arrows show their relations in each sequence. On the bottom, the multi-parentheses sequence representing the same graph.

$\mathsf{succ}_0(15) = 16$, *thus we have* $16 - (v_p + 3) = 1$ *neighbor in the third page. Summing up,* $\mathsf{degree}(v) = 4$.

The neighbors of v are hatched. There are 3 in the first sequence, which are computed as in Example 9.10: 2, 1, and 7. In the second sequence there are no neighbors of v. In the third, we find the neighbor index 3 with the same procedure.

Finally, let us determine whether $\mathsf{adj}(v, u)$ *for* $v = 3$ *and* $u = 5$. *The corresponding areas of parentheses are enclosed in gray rectangles in each sequence. In the first, v corresponds to position* $v_p = 11$ *and u to* $u_p = 19$. *We compute* $b_v = 1$. *But since* $\mathsf{close}(v_p + 2 + b_v) = \mathsf{close}(14) = 17 < 21 = u_p + 2$ *(as shown by the gray arrow), v and u are not neighbors. In the second sequence, v corresponds to position* $v_p = 7$ *and u to* $u_p = 15$. *We compute* $f_v = 0$, *and therefore v and u are not connected. Finally, in the third sequence v corresponds to position* $v_p = 7$ *and u to* $u_p = 12$. *Now we compute* $b_v = 0$, $f_v = 1$, $b_u = 1$, *and* $f_u = 0$. *Since* $\mathsf{close}(v_p + 2 + b_v) = \mathsf{close}(9) = 14$ *is between* $u_p + 2 = 14$ *and* $u_p + 1 + b_u = 14$, *we find that v and u are indeed connected. A gray arrow shows this connection.*

Since k-page graphs have at most $e \leq (k + 1)n - 3k$ edges, the space of $2(kn + e)$ bits is at most $2n(2k + 1)$. This is about a factor of 4 away from the known lower bound of $kn - \mathcal{O}(k^2)$ on the worst-case entropy.

A Multi-parentheses Structure

When k is not very small, an alternative solution reduces the linear dependence on k. We encode all the data in a single multi-parentheses structure $P[1, 2(n + e)]$

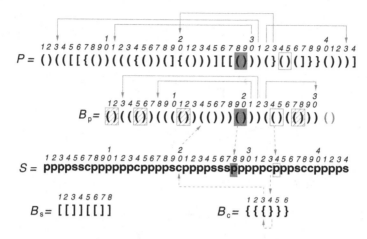

Figure 9.8. Solving query neigh(5) on the multi-parentheses representation of Figure 9.7. The gray solid arrows show the matching parentheses that connect node 5 with its neighbors in P and in B_p, whereas gray dashed arrows illustrate the process to find the remaining neighbor in B_c. The positions of 5 are grayed, those of the node following it (6) are in an open rectangle, and the neighbors are hatched in B_p (including the one that is found via B_c).

(Section 7.3), with k types of parentheses. In P, we encode (V, E_1) as usual, with one type of parentheses, and then each other (V, E_i) is encoded with parentheses of type i. For $i > 1$, we do not encode the pair ' ( ) ' for each node, but rather add the parentheses of type i somewhere after the corresponding type-1 node marks ' ( ) ' in P. Thus the subsequence of each type of parentheses is balanced. To represent P, we do not need the global parentheses sequence B of Section 7.3 (which would not be balanced anyway), just the subsequences B_i for $i \in [1, k]$ and the global sequence S of types. The spurious pair ' ( ) ' at the end is added only after B_1, not in P.

Example 9.13 *In the bottom part of Figure 9.7 we show the sequence P with $k = 3$ types of parentheses corresponding to our three-page graph. Its representation using sequences B_* and S is shown in Figure 9.8 (the subindices of B correspond to "parentheses," "square brackets," and "curly brackets").*

The parenthesis subsequences B_i require $2(n + e + 1)$ bits in total, whereas S can be encoded in $2(n + e) \log k$ bits. The total space is $2(n + e)(1 + \log k) + o((n + e) \log k)$ bits, which is less than the previous representation if, roughly, $\frac{e}{n} < \frac{k-1}{\log k} - 1$. On a sparse graph of $e = n$ edges, this representation can be smaller than the previous one for $k \geq 7$ or so. On the densest graphs, the previous representation always uses less space.

The use of S and B_i also enables faster query algorithms. To compute $\mathsf{degree}(G, v)$, we first identify the range of v in B_1: it spans $B_1[v_p, v'_p - 1]$, for $v_p \leftarrow \mathsf{select}_{10}(B_1, v)$ and $v'_p \leftarrow \mathsf{select}_{10}(B_1, v + 1)$. This range is mapped to S with $v_s \leftarrow \mathsf{select}_1(S, v_p)$ and $v'_s \leftarrow \mathsf{select}_1(S, v'_p)$. Then $\mathsf{degree}(G, v) = v'_s - v_s - 2$. If we use the sequence representation based on permutations (Section 6.1), then degree takes constant time.

To compute the list $\mathsf{neigh}(G, v)$, we first find v_p, v'_p, v_s, and v'_s. The neighbors in B_1 are computed in the same way they were computed for one-page graphs. For each other sequence B_i, we first obtain the range of parentheses of v in B_i, $[p_i, q_i] =$

[$\text{rank}_i(S, v_s) + 1$, $\text{rank}_i(S, v'_s)$]. Now, for each $r \in [p_i, q_i]$, we find the matching parenthesis: if $B_i[r] = 1$ then $t \leftarrow \text{close}(B_i, r)$, otherwise $t \leftarrow \text{open}(B_i, r)$. Now position t must be mapped again to B_1 in order to determine the corresponding node: $t_s \leftarrow \text{select}_i(S, t)$ and $t_p \leftarrow \text{rank}_1(S, t_s)$. Finally, the neighbor identifier is $\text{rank}_{10}(B_1, t_p)$.

The resulting complexity is not so good, however. With our sequence representation, $\text{neigh}(G, v)$ takes time $\mathcal{O}(k \log \log k + \text{degree}(G, v) \log \log n)$ (assuming $k \leq n$). This is worse than with the previous structure.

However, we can do better. If we use instead a wavelet tree representation for S (Section 6.2), then the complexity for degree raises to $\mathcal{O}(\log k)$, and for neigh it raises to $\mathcal{O}(k \log k + \text{degree}(G, v)(\log k + \log \log n))$. But the wavelet tree enables a different algorithm for neigh, where we traverse only the pages where v has neighbors. This reduces the time for neigh to $\mathcal{O}(\log k + \text{degree}(G, v)(\log k + \log \log n))$. The algorithm considers only the sequences B_i where symbol i appears in $S[v_s, v'_s]$. This was solved in the last part of Section 6.4.3. Algorithm 9.9 adapts that solution to our case.

Example 9.14 *Let us solve the same queries of Example 9.12 on the multi-parentheses representation P of the bottom of Figure 9.7. This is now shown in detail in Figure 9.8, with P at the top and the bitvectors B_* and sequence S on the bottom. For $v = 5$, $\text{degree}(v)$ computes $v_p \leftarrow \text{select}_{10}(B_1, v) = 19$ and $v'_p \leftarrow \text{select}_{10}(B_1, v + 1) = 24$. We then map those positions to S with $v_s \leftarrow \text{select}_{1=p}(S, v_p) = 28$ and $v'_s \leftarrow \text{select}_{1=p}(S, v'_p) = 34$. Thus, we return $\text{degree}(v) = v'_s - v_s - 2 = 4$ (we show the marker of node v in B_p and S in solid gray, and that of node $v + 1$ as an open rectangle).*

The figure illustrates the process to compute $\text{neigh}(v)$. The connections in P to the neighbors of v are shown with solid arrows, and the neighbors are hatched in B_p. For simplicity, we will consider the pages one by one instead of illustrating the procedure on the wavelet tree. We compute the limits in $B_1 = B_p$ and S as before. Then we know that v has $v'_p - v_p - 2 = 3$ neighbors in B_p. Those are obtained exactly as in Example 9.10.

Now we have to consider $B_2 = B_s$ and $B_3 = B_c$. For $i = 2 = s$, we compute the range corresponding to $S[v_s, v'_s] = S[28, 34]$ in B_s. This is $B_s[p_s, q_s] = B_s[\text{rank}_s(S, 28) + 1, \text{rank}_s(S, 34)] = B_s[7, 6]$. Since the range is empty, v has no neighbors in B_s. We repeat the procedure on $i = 3 = c$: the range $S[28, 34]$ is mapped to $B_c[p_c, q_c] = B_c[\text{rank}_c(S, 28) + 1, \text{rank}_c(S, 34)] = B_c[4, 4]$. Thus there is a neighbor to report, with $j = 1$. The process is illustrated with gray dashed arrows. It holds $B_c[p_c - 1 + j] = B_c[4] = 0$, thus its matching curly bracket is at $t \leftarrow \text{open}(B_c, 4) = 3$. Now we map $t = 3$ back to S with $t_s \leftarrow \text{select}_c(S, 3) = 20$, and then to B_p with $t_p \leftarrow \text{rank}_p(S, 20) = 14$. Thus, the index of the last neighbor of v is $\text{rank}_{10}(B_p, 14) = 3$.

The only procedure that retains, in the worst case, a linear dependence on k is that for $\text{adj}(G, v, u)$. We test it in B_1 as in the one-page case. For the other sequences B_i, we compute $[p_i, q_i]$ for v and $[p'_i, q'_i]$ for u, as in operation neigh. We restrict them to retain only the opening parentheses in $[p_i, q_i]$, $p_i \leftarrow \min(q_i + 1, \text{succ}_1(B_i, p_i))$, and only the closing parentheses in $[p'_i, q'_i]$, $q'_i \leftarrow \max(p'_i - 1, \text{pred}_0(B_i, q'_i))$. We then run $\text{match}(B_i, p_i, q_i, p'_i, q'_i)$ of Algorithm 9.8. We iterate on i until we find an edge that connects v and u in some B_i, or until we examine all the sequences without success. This costs $\mathcal{O}(k(\log k + \log \log n))$ time.

Algorithm 9.9: Computing degree and neigh on k-page graphs represented with multiparenthesis sequences.

Input : k-page graph G (seen as a multiparentheses sequence, represented with a wavelet tree S and bitvectors B_i) and node v.

1 **Proc** degree(G, v)
2    $v_p \leftarrow$ select$_{10}(B_1, v)$
3    $v'_p \leftarrow$ succ$_0(B_1,$ succ$_1(B_1, v_p + 2)) - 1$
4    $v_s \leftarrow$ select$_1(S, v_p)$; $v'_s \leftarrow$ select$_1(S, v'_p)$
5   **return** $v'_s - v_s - 2$

6 **Proc** neigh(G, v)
7    $v_p \leftarrow$ select$_{10}(B_1, v)$
8    $v'_p \leftarrow$ succ$_0(B_1,$ succ$_1(B_1, v_p + 2)) - 1$
9    $v_s \leftarrow$ select$_1(S, v_p)$; $v'_s \leftarrow$ select$_1(S, v'_p)$
10    $neigh(S.root, 1, k, v_s, v'_s - 1)$

11 **Proc** $neigh(v, a, b, p, q)$
    Input : Node v of wavelet tree of S containing alphabet range $[a, b]$ and interval $[p, q]$ of S_v.
    Output: Reports the corresponding neighbors in B_i for each $i \in [a, b]$ that appears in $S_v[p, q]$.
12   **if** $p > q$ **then return**
13   **if** $a = b$ **then**
14   **for** $j \leftarrow p$ **to** q **do**
15   **if** access(B_a, j) $= 0$ **then**
16             $t \leftarrow$ open(B_a, j)
17   **else** $t \leftarrow$ close(B_a, j)
18   **if** $a > 1$ **then**
19             $t \leftarrow$ rank$_1(S,$ select$_a(S, t))$
20   **output** rank$_{10}(B_a, t)$
21   **else**
22       $m \leftarrow \lfloor (a + b)/2 \rfloor$
23       $p_l \leftarrow$ rank$_0(v.B, p - 1) + 1$; $q_l \leftarrow$ rank$_0(v.B, q)$
24       $neigh(v.l, a, m, p_l, q_l)$
25       $neigh(v.r, m + 1, b, p - p_l + 1, q - q_l)$

A way to speed up this procedure in practice is to run it only on the sequences B_i such that i appears in both ranges of S (that of u and that of v). Those i values are obtained, on a wavelet tree, as in Algorithm 6.15. Note that, in line 6, it reports only the symbol a (our i), but it could also report the ranges $[i_t, f_t]$ and $[i'_t, f'_t]$, and these are our ranges $[p_i, q_i]$ and $[p'_i, q'_i]$. While it gives no improved worst-case guarantees, using this procedure is never slower (and is generally faster) than trying the symbols one by one. The details are in Algorithm 9.10.

Algorithm 9.10: Computing adj on k-page graphs. We assume that *inters* (Algorithm 6.15) reports not only a, but the triples $(a, [i_r, f_r], [i'_r, f'_r])$), and use it as an iterator.

Input : k-page graph G (seen as sequence S and bitvectors B_i, with S seen as a wavelet tree), nodes v and u.

1 **Proc** adj(G, v, u)
2   **if** $v > u$ **then** $u \leftrightarrow v$
3    $v_\mathsf{p} \leftarrow \mathsf{select}_{10}(B_1, v); u_\mathsf{p} \leftarrow \mathsf{select}_{10}(B_1, u)$
4    $v'_\mathsf{p} \leftarrow \mathsf{succ}_0(B_1, \mathsf{succ}_1(B_1, v_\mathsf{p} + 2)) - 1$
5    $u'_\mathsf{p} \leftarrow \mathsf{succ}_0(B_1, \mathsf{succ}_1(B_1, u_\mathsf{p} + 2)) - 1$
6    $v_\mathsf{s} \leftarrow \mathsf{select}_1(S, v_\mathsf{p}); v'_\mathsf{s} \leftarrow \mathsf{select}_1(S, v'_\mathsf{p})$
7    $u_\mathsf{s} \leftarrow \mathsf{select}_1(S, u_\mathsf{p}); u'_\mathsf{s} \leftarrow \mathsf{select}_1(S, u'_\mathsf{p})$
8   **for** $(i, [p_i, q_i], [p'_i, q'_i]) \leftarrow inters(S.root, 1, k, v_\mathsf{s}, v'_\mathsf{s} - 1, u_\mathsf{s}, u'_\mathsf{s} - 1)$ **do**
9      $p_i \leftarrow \min(q_i + 1, \mathsf{succ}_1(B_i, p_i))$
10      $q'_i \leftarrow \max(p'_i - 1, \mathsf{pred}_0(B_i, q'_i))$
11   **if** $match(B_i, p_i, q_i, p'_i, q'_i)$ (Algorithm 9.8) **then**
12   **return true**

13   **return false**

Example 9.15 *Let us solve* adj(v, u) *for $v = 3$ and $u = 5$, on the representation of Figure 9.8. We compute* $v_\mathsf{p} \leftarrow \mathsf{select}_{10}(B_1, v) = 11, v'_\mathsf{p} \leftarrow \mathsf{select}_{10}(B_1, v + 1) = 15,$ $u_\mathsf{p} \leftarrow \mathsf{select}_{10}(B_1, u) = 19,$ *and* $u'_\mathsf{p} \leftarrow \mathsf{select}_{10}(B_1, u + 1) = 24.$ *We then compute* $v_\mathsf{s} \leftarrow \mathsf{select}_{1=\mathsf{p}}(S, v_\mathsf{p}) = 15, v'_\mathsf{s} \leftarrow \mathsf{select}_{1=\mathsf{p}}(S, v'_\mathsf{p}) = 21, u_\mathsf{s} \leftarrow \mathsf{select}_{1=\mathsf{p}}(S, u_\mathsf{p}) = 28,$ *and* $v'_\mathsf{s} \leftarrow \mathsf{select}_{1=\mathsf{p}}(S, u'_\mathsf{p}) = 34.$

The intersection algorithm on the ranges $S[v_\mathsf{s}, v'_\mathsf{s} - 1] = S[15, 20]$ *and* $S[u_\mathsf{s}, u'_\mathsf{s} - 1] = S[28, 33]$ *yields results for the pages* $1 = \mathsf{p}$ *and* $3 = \mathsf{c}$. *The call for the first range gives the same result as it did for the one-page case: there is no connection in this page. For* B_c, *the intersection returns the ranges* $[p_\mathsf{c}, q_\mathsf{c}] = [3, 3]$ *for v and* $[p'_\mathsf{c}, q'_\mathsf{c}] = [4, 4]$ *for u. Restricting these intervals to the desired kind of parentheses does not change them. Finally, the procedure* match$()$ *indicates that these two ranges are connected.*

Faster adj *Queries for Large* k

A way to obtain time $\mathcal{O}(\log k(\log k + \log \log n))$ for query adj is as follows. We use a particular order for the parentheses corresponding to each node in P. We will still maintain together all the opening or closing parentheses of each type corresponding to each node, and the closing ones will come before the opening ones, but the ordering between types will be fixed as follows:

1. The closing parentheses of type i will appear before the closing ones of type j if the node connected by the rightmost parenthesis of type i is to the left of the one connected by the rightmost parenthesis of type j.
2. The opening parentheses of type i will appear before the opening ones of type j if the node connected by the leftmost parenthesis of type i is to the right of the one connected by the leftmost parenthesis of type j.

Note an important property of **adj** (already implicit in procedure *match* of Algorithm 9.8): If there is an arc of type i connecting v and u (for $v < u$), then either u is the rightmost node connected with v in page i, or v is the leftmost node connected with u in page i. Otherwise, if they match with the parenthesis pair at positions (p, q), then the pairs matching $p - 1$ (which would close after q) and $q + 1$ (which would open before p) would cross.

Therefore, it is sufficient to see if v is connected with u by the rightmost closing parenthesis of each type associated with u, or if u is connected with v by the leftmost opening parenthesis of each type associated with v. Further, since at most one parenthesis type will connect v and u, and the types of closing parentheses associated with u are sorted by the node they connect with their rightmost parenthesis, we can use binary search to find the rightmost closing parenthesis that may connect u with v. Similarly, we use binary search to find the leftmost parenthesis of v that may connect it with u. To make this binary search in $\mathcal{O}(\log k)$ steps, we store a bitvector $L[1, 2(n + e)]$ marking the first of each run of equal parentheses in P.

Example 9.16 *The sequence P of Figure 9.7 would be reordered to*

$$P = (\,)\{(([[(\,)\}\{((((\,)]\}\{((\,)]))[[(\,)))\}((\,)\}]((\,)])),$$

according to this method. For example, the (forward) arcs leaving node 1 are sorted so that we first write the curly bracket (as it reaches node 6), then the parentheses (as the leftmost one reaches node 5), and finally the square brackets (which reach nodes 3 and 4).

For example, the edge that connects $v = 2$ with $u = 5$ is of type 1, and it is the rightmost-reaching forward arc leaving node 2 in that page (it is not, instead, the leftmost-reaching backward arc leaving node 5). Thus, to solve $\mathsf{adj}(v, u)$ we could binary search the types of closing parentheses associated with node 5. The curly brackets do not qualify because the leftmost-reaching one connects u with node $3 > 2 = v$. The parentheses could connect u with v, but the leftmost-reaching backward edge leaving u does not; it connects u with node 1. Thus, we now examine the forward parentheses leaving node $v = 2$. The rightmost-reaching curly bracket connects v with node $6 > 5 = u$, so it is not useful. Finally, the rightmost-reaching parenthesis leaving v connects it with u.

It is likely that in practice this procedure is faster than the intersection-based one only for quite large values of k.

Sparse Graphs

An alternative structure that is more convenient for sparse graphs is obtained by removing the ' ( ) ' node marks from S and B_1 and using instead a new bitvector $R[1, 2e]$ that marks the starting positions of the nodes in S (if there are isolated nodes, these should be renumbered to appear at the end). Then the space becomes $2e(2 + \log k) + o(e \log k)$ bits, which is better than the one we have described whenever $e/n < 1 + \log k$. In addition, it solves **degree** in constant time using R.

9.3.3 Construction

Embedding a graph G into k pages, or determining that this is not possible, is NP-complete even for $k = 2$. If we are given the right node ordering, the problem is easy to solve for $k = 2$ pages, but it is still NP-complete in general. Instead, it is possible to find the right order in linear time for one-page graphs (i.e., $k = 1$). The algorithm is involved so we omit it; see the references at the end of the chapter.

If the order and the assignment of edges to pages is given, it is easy to compute the parentheses representation by first computing numbers of neighbors to the left and to the right in each page and then writing the parentheses.

9.4 Planar Graphs

Finally, we study a family of graphs that arises in important applications and admits very space-efficient representations. They arise, for example, in road networks, city maps, chip design, network routing, and polygon meshes used in computer graphics or surface modeling.

Planar graphs are connected undirected graphs that can be drawn on the plane without letting edges cross. A planar graph of n nodes and e edges that is drawn on the plane divides it into $f = e - n + 2$ regions called *faces*. One of those regions is infinite and is called the *external face*; the others are internal and have a finite area. A given planar graph can be drawn in different ways in the plane; in particular any face can be chosen to be the external one. In many cases, one is not interested in the exact positions assigned to the nodes on the plane, but in the topological relations defined by the mapping, that is, the list of edges that enclose each face and the edges that enclose the whole graph (which are the edges that "enclose the external face"; a planar graph can be drawn on a sphere and then the external face looks like any other face). A planar graph with its topological mapping to the plane defined is called a *planar map* or a *plane graph*.

Example 9.17 *Figure 9.9 shows two planar maps that represent the same planar graph. The two maps have the same external face, traversed by the nodes $\langle \mathsf{a}, \mathsf{b}, \mathsf{c}, \mathsf{d} \rangle$. They also share the face $\langle \mathsf{a}, \mathsf{c}, \mathsf{e} \rangle$, but the nodes are listed in different order if we traverse them, say, clockwise. On the other hand, they have faces where the nodes are not the same, for example, $\langle \mathsf{a}, \mathsf{c}, \mathsf{d} \rangle$ appears on the left but not on the right. Note that all the planar maps of the same planar graph must have the same number of faces, $f = e - n + 2$.*

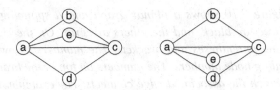

Figure 9.9. Two planar maps representing the same planar graph. Note that the faces are different, though there must be the same number of faces.

Planar graphs can be represented in much less space than general graphs. Not only do they have $e \leq 3n - 6$ edges, but the total number of n-node planar graphs is known to be between 27.22^n and 30.06^n, thus their worst-case entropy is between $4.76n$ and $4.91n$. Another entropy measure is known in terms of the number of edges of planar maps: there are $\frac{2(2e)!3^e}{e!(e+2)!}$ rooted connected planar maps of e edges (rooted means that an edge is distinguished and given a direction, so we may count the same map $2e$ times). Thus the worst-case entropy is $(2 + \log 3)e - \mathcal{O}(\log e) \geq 3.58e - \mathcal{O}(\log e)$. The exact entropy of planar graphs (without defining their mapping to the plane) is unknown, but it must be less than $3.58e$. We will study planar graph representations that use $\mathcal{O}(n) = \mathcal{O}(e)$ bits and efficiently support the operations adj, neigh, and degree. We will disregard multiple edges between two nodes and self-loops.

The one-page graphs studied in Section 9.3.1 correspond exactly to the *outerplanar* graphs, which are the planar graphs that can be drawn with all their nodes on the external face (these include all the trees). Graphs of 2 pages are also planar, but there are 3-page graphs that are not planar. On the other hand, every planar graph can be embedded in 4 pages in linear time. Since planar graphs have $e < 3n$ edges, the representation using $2(kn + e)$ bits we developed in Section 9.3.2 immediately yields a representation for planar graphs using at most $8n + 2e \leq 14n$ bits (ignoring sublinear terms), which answers all the queries in $\mathcal{O}(\log \log n)$ time. In this section we will show that this result can be improved considerably, to $2(n + e) \leq 4e$ bits, which is not far from the lower bound of $3.58e$ bits.

An important particular case of planar graphs are the planar *triangulations*, or *triangular graphs*. In a triangulation, every face is delimited by exactly 3 edges. Every triangulation of n nodes has exactly $e = 3n - 6$ edges. The number of triangulations is $\frac{2(4n+1)!}{(3n+2)!(n+1)!}$, therefore their worst-case entropy is $(8 - 3\log 3)n - \mathcal{O}(\log n) = (\frac{8}{3} - \log 3)e - \mathcal{O}(\log e) > 1.08e - \mathcal{O}(\log e)$. We will show that the structures we develop for planar graphs can use even less space, $2e$ bits, when the graph is a triangulation.

9.4.1 Orderly Spanning Trees

Let us build a *spanning tree* T of the graph $G(V, E)$, that is, a tree whose vertices are V and whose edges belong to E, and encode T with parentheses with the BP representation (Section 8.2). We identify the nodes of V with their preorder number in T. The $e - n + 1$ edges of E that are not in T are encoded as follows: Let (v, u) be such an edge, with $v < u$. Then we insert an opening (square) bracket right after close(v) and a closing bracket right after u.

Example 9.18 *Figure 9.10 shows a planar graph and a spanning tree. The edges belonging to the tree are black, and the others are gray. On the right, we show the representation using parentheses and brackets. The numbers below the parentheses are the corresponding node numbers. The numbers on top of the brackets indicate the other node with which the associated edge connects. For example, nodes 10 and 13 are connected, thus the corresponding matching pair of brackets opens after the ') ' of node 10 and closes after the ' (' of node 13.*

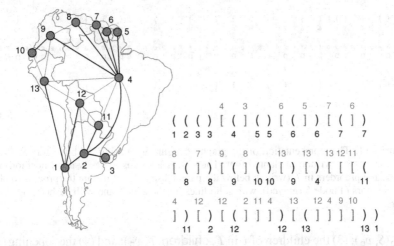

Figure 9.10. The planar graph induced by the map of South America and its spanning tree representation. The black parentheses describe the spanning tree using BP (we write the pre-order index of the nodes below the parentheses). The gray square brackets describe the other edges in E (we write the preorder index of the matched node on top of each square bracket).

If we build T carefully, it holds as in the example that (a) the sequence of brackets is balanced, and (b) after the construction, there is a matching pair of brackets between v and u iff there is an edge (v, u) in E (and not in T). For condition (a), all we need is that, whenever $v < u$, it also holds **close**(v) $< u$, that is, there cannot be an edge of E (and not in T) linking a node with an ancestor in T. While condition (a) is easy to handle, condition (b) is more subtle, and cannot be enforced on every graph (but it can on planar graphs). We will build a particular class of spanning trees called *orderly spanning trees*. These induce an ordering in **neigh**(G, v): in the counterclockwise (**ccw**) order of the neighbors of v, we will have (1) the parent p, then (2) the neighbors $u < v$ of v that are not in T, then (3) the children of v in T, and finally (4) the neighbors $u > v$ of v that are not in T.

Example 9.19 *The* **ccw** *order of the neighbors of node 4 (Brazil) in Figure 9.10 is (1) its parent in T, node 2; (2) its neighbors not in T with smaller numbers, node 3; (3) its children in T, nodes 5 to 9; and (4) its neighbors not in T with larger numbers, nodes 13, 12, and 11.*

Note that every pair of parentheses or brackets corresponds to an edge in E; therefore the resulting sequence is $P[1, 2e]$, with $2(n - 1)$ parentheses and $2(e - n + 1)$ brackets. Let us represent it, as before, as a string $S[1, 2e]$ and bitvectors B_p and B_s. Since there are only 2 types, S is also a bitvector, thus the total space is $4e + o(e)$ bits. Note that bitvector B_p is precisely the BP representation of T.

Solving Queries

For **degree**(G, v), we find $v_p \leftarrow$ **preorderselect**(T, v) = **select**$_1$(B_p, v) and then add up: (1) 1 for the parent of v in T if v is not the root; (2) the (closing) brackets that follow the opening parenthesis of v in P, $b \leftarrow$ **succ**$_p$($S, v_s + 1$) $- (v_s + 1)$ with $v_s \leftarrow$

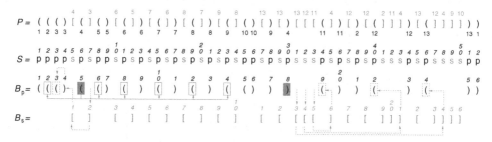

Figure 9.11. The representation of the graph of Figure 9.10 using the bitvectors S, B_p, and B_s. Positions are written in slanted font. The spaces allow us to easily align positions in S, B_p, B_s, and preorders in T (written below the parentehses). We illustrate the process to obtain the neighbors of node 5 (grayed), with solid lines for those in T and with dashed lines for the others.

$\mathsf{select}_p(S, v_p)$; (3) the children of v in T, $\mathsf{children}(T, v_p)$; and (4) the (opening) brackets that follow the closing parenthesis of v in P, $f \leftarrow \mathsf{succ}_p(S, v'_s + 1) - (v'_s + 1)$, where $v'_s \leftarrow \mathsf{select}_p(S, \mathsf{close}(B_p, v_p))$.

Example 9.20 *Figure 9.11 shows the representation of the graph in Figure 9.10 using S, B_p, and B_s. The neighbors of Brazil (with preorder index $v = 4$; its opening and closing parentheses are grayed) are shown with open rectangles, with an indication of how they are obtained (with solid lines for the edges in T and dashed for the others). To find their number, we first compute the position of v in B_p, $v_p \leftarrow \mathsf{preorderselect}(v) = 5$. Then, since v_p is not the root, we count its parent, node 2. We also count $\mathsf{children}(v_p) = 5$ (nodes 5 to 9). Now, to compute the number of preceding neighbors not in T, we find $v_s \leftarrow \mathsf{select}_p(S, v_p) = 6$. The number of preceding neighbors is then $b = \mathsf{succ}_p(S, v_s + 1) - (v_s + 1) = 8 - 7 = 1$ (node 3, as can be seen in $P[7]$). Finally, to compute the number of following neighbors not in T, we find $v'_p \leftarrow \mathsf{close}(B_p, v_p) = 18$ and $v'_s \leftarrow \mathsf{select}_p(S, v'_p) = 30$. Then the number of following neighbors is $f = \mathsf{succ}_p(S, v'_s + 1) - (v'_s + 1) = 34 - 31 = 3$ (nodes 13, 12, and 11, as can be seen in $P[31, 33]$). Overall Brazil has $1 + 5 + 1 + 3 = 10$ neighbors.*

To compute $\mathsf{neigh}(G, v)[j]$, we use the same variables as before. The first neighbor we report is $\mathsf{preorder}(T, \mathsf{parent}(T, v_p))$, if $v_p \neq \mathsf{root}(T)$. For the next b neighbors, we first compute

$$r \leftarrow \mathsf{rank}_p(S, \mathsf{select}_s(S, \mathsf{open}(B_s, \mathsf{rank}_s(S, v_s + j)))).$$

Then $B_p[r]$ is the closing parenthesis preceding the opening bracket that matches the jth bracket closing after node v. Thus we report the node index $\mathsf{preorder}(T, \mathsf{open}(B_p, r))$. The next $\mathsf{children}(T, v_p)$ neighbors we report are $\mathsf{preorder}(T, \mathsf{child}(T, v_p, j))$. The final f neighbors are found with the opening brackets after the parenthesis closing v:

$$r \leftarrow \mathsf{rank}_p(S, \mathsf{select}_s(S, \mathsf{close}(B_s, \mathsf{rank}_s(S, v'_s + j)))),$$

and we report $\mathsf{preorder}(T, r)$.

Example 9.21 *Let us enumerate some of the neighbors of Example 9.20. First, $\mathsf{parent}(v_p) = 2$ is node index $\mathsf{preorder}(2) = 2$. Second, its neighbor not in T and to the left is found from $S[v_s + 1] = S[7]$. We do $r \leftarrow \mathsf{rank}_p(S, \mathsf{select}_s(S, \mathsf{open}$*

$(B_s, \mathsf{rank}_s(S, 7)))) = \mathsf{rank}_p(S, \mathsf{select}_s(S, \mathsf{open}(B_s, 2))) = \mathsf{rank}_p(S, \mathsf{select}_s(S, 1)) = \mathsf{rank}_p(S, 5) = 4$. *The node to return then has its closing parenthesis at* $B_p[4]$. *We compute its index with* $\mathsf{preorder}(\mathsf{open}(B_p, 4)) = \mathsf{preorder}(3) = 3$. *Third, the children of* v_p *are* $\mathsf{child}(v_p, j) = \{6, 8, 10, 12, 14\}$, *corresponding to node indexes (taking preorder)* $\{5, 6, 7, 8, 9\}$. *Finally, let us compute one of its neighbors to the right. Those are found from* $S[v'_s + 1, v'_s + f] = S[31, 33]$. *Let us choose* $S[v'_s + 1] = S[31]$. *We do* $r \leftarrow \mathsf{rank}_p(S, \mathsf{select}_s(S, \mathsf{close}(B_s, \mathsf{rank}_s(S, 31)))) = \mathsf{rank}_p(S, \mathsf{select}_s(S, \mathsf{close}(B_s, 13))) = \mathsf{rank}_p(S, \mathsf{select}_s(S, 24)) = \mathsf{rank}_p(S, 48) = 24$. *Therefore, the neighbor index is* $\mathsf{preorder}(24) = 13$.

Finally, we can compute $\mathsf{adj}(G, v, u)$ as follows. Let $v < u$ and compute v_p, v'_s and $f_v = f$ as before for v. Compute analogously u_p, u_s and $b_u = b$ for u. Then, if $v_p = \mathsf{parent}(T, u_p)$, they are neighbors (the edge is in T). Otherwise we map $p_s \leftarrow \mathsf{rank}_s(S, v'_s) + 1$, $q_s \leftarrow p_s + f_v - 1$, $p'_s \leftarrow \mathsf{rank}_s(S, u_s) + 1$, and $q'_s \leftarrow p'_s + b_u - 1$. We then return $match(B_s, p_s, q_s, p'_s, q'_s)$, as usual. Algorithm 9.11 gives the details.

Example 9.22 *Let us perform a few* adj *computations on Figure 9.11. Does Argentina* ($v = 2$) *border Brazil* ($u = 4$)? *We do* $v_p \leftarrow \mathsf{preorderselect}(v) = 2$ *and* $u_p \leftarrow \mathsf{preorderselect}(u) = 5$; *then we verify that* $v_p = \mathsf{parent}(u_p)$, *so the answer to* $\mathsf{adj}(2, 4)$ *is yes (the edge is in* T).

Does Brazil ($v = 4$) *border Peru* ($u = 13$)? *We find that they do via examining the interval of forward arrows leaving* v *and the backward arrows leaving* u. *The former is obtained with* $S[v'_s + 1, v'_s + f_v] = S[31, 33]$ *and the latter with* $S[u_s + 1, u_s + b_u] = S[46 + 1, 46 + 4] = S[47, 50]$. *These two intervals are mapped to* $B_s[13, 15]$ *and* $B_s[23, 26]$, *respectively. Indeed, the matching pair of brackets* $(13, 24)$ *connects both intervals.*

Finally, does Brazil border Ecuador ($u = 10$)? *In this case,* u *does not have backward edges. If it had, they would not be after the interval* $B_s[13, 15]$ *of* v, *even when* $v < u$ *(this occurs because* v *is an ancestor, but not a parent, of* u). *Thus the answer to* $\mathsf{adj}(4, 10)$ *is no.*

Ordered Neighbors

The cw neighbor ordering is useful for planar graphs. For example, if we want to traverse a face F where (v, u) belongs, we can do as follows: find the position j of v in $\mathsf{neigh}(G, u)$, then move to $(v, u) \leftarrow (u, \mathsf{neigh}(G, u, j + 1))$, and repeat until returning to the original point. In this case, we traverse the face F where the direction from v to u enumerates its edges in clockwise order (cw). If we use $\mathsf{neigh}(G, u, j - 1)$ instead of $\mathsf{neigh}(G, u, j + 1)$, we traverse the other face F' where (v, u) belongs, in ccw order.

Figure 9.12 illustrates these traversals, and Algorithm 9.12 shows how to find the position j of v in $\mathsf{neigh}(G, u)$, by adapting the algorithm for $\mathsf{adj}(G, v, u)$. Algorithm 9.13 adds other operations that simplify navigating toward the different kinds of neighbors.

Further Space Reduction

As said, the space of this representation is just $4e + o(e)$ bits, close to the worst-case entropy of planar maps, $3.58e$. All the operations cost $\mathcal{O}(\log \log n)$ time. The 4-page-based representation, instead, uses $8n + 2e + o(n)$ bits, which is at least $\frac{14}{3}e > 4.66e$

Algorithm 9.11: Computing operations on planar graphs.

Input : Planar graph G (seen as bitvectors S, B_s, and B_p, the latter representing an ordinal tree T), nodes v and u (preorders in T), and index j.

```
 1 Proc adj(G, v, u)
 2 │  if v > u then u ↔ v
 3 │  v_p ← preorderselect(T, v); u_p ← preorderselect(T, u)
 4 │  if v_p = parent(T, u_p) then return true
 5 │  v'_p ← close(B_p, v_p)
 6 │  v'_s ← select_p(S, v'_p); f ← succ_p(S, v'_s + 1) − (v'_s + 1)
 7 │  u_s ← select_p(S, u_p); b ← succ_p(S, u_s + 1) − (u_s + 1)
 8 │  p_s ← v'_s − v'_p + 1; p'_s ← u_s − u_p + 1
 9 │  return match(B_s, p_s, p_s + f − 1, p'_s, p'_s + b − 1) (Algorithm 9.8)
```

```
10 Proc neigh(G, v, j) — assuming j ≤ degree(G, v)
11 │  v_p ← preorderselect(T, v)
12 │  if v ≠ 1 then
13 │  │  if j = 1 then return preorder(T, parent(T, v_p))
14 │  └  else j ← j − 1
15 │  v_s ← select_p(S, v_p); b ← succ_p(S, v_s + 1) − (v_s + 1)
16 │  if j ≤ b then
17 │  │  v_o ← open(B_s, v_s − v_p + j)
18 │  └  return preorder(T, open(B_p, select_s(S, v_o) − v_o))
19 │  else j ← j − b
20 │  if j ≤ children(T, v_p) then return preorder(T, child(T, v_p, j))
21 │  else j ← j − children(T, v_p)
22 │  v'_p ← close(B_p, v_p)
23 │  v_c ← close(B_s, select_p(S, v'_p) − v'_p + j)
24 └  return preorder(T, select_s(S, v_c) − v_c)
```

```
25 Proc degree(G, v)
26 │  v_p ← preorderselect(T, v)
27 │  if v = 1 then d ← 0 else d ← 1
28 │  v_s ← select_p(S, v_p); d ← d + succ_p(S, v_s + 1) − (v_s + 1)
29 │  d ← d + children(T, v_p)
30 │  v'_s ← select_p(S, close(B_p, v_p)); d ← d + succ_p(S, v'_s + 1) − (v'_s + 1)
31 └  return d
```

---

since $e < 3n$. In terms of n, this representation uses at most $4e \le 12n$ bits, whereas the 4-page-based one can use up to $14n$ bits.

We note that the comparison with $3.58e$ is not totally fair, however, since this is the entropy of planar maps. Instead, our orderly spanning tree technique can represent only planar graphs, because it may alter the mapping to the plane in order to obtain the spanning tree. This will be clear when we discuss its construction, in Section 9.4.3.

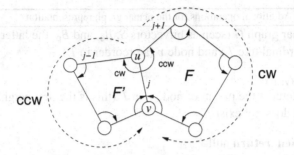

Figure 9.12. Traversing a face using the neighbor ordering. By finding the next neighbor in ccw order, we traverse the face in cw order, and vice versa.

This space can still be improved, at the price of some added complication. Note that, in P, the brackets that follow an opening parenthesis are closing, and the brackets that follow a closing parenthesis are opening. Therefore, in principle, sequence B_s is redundant. If the sequence could be dropped, the space would become $2(n + e) + o(n)$ bits. This is at most $8n$ since $e < 3n$.

Algorithm 9.12: Finding which neighbor of u is v on planar graphs. Assumes an orderly spanning tree was used to build the representation.

Input : Planar graph G (seen as bitvectors S, B_s, and B_p, the latter representing an ordinal tree T) and adjacent nodes v and u (preorders in T).

Output: Returns j such that $v = \mathsf{neigh}(G, u)[j]$.

1 **Proc** $findneigh(G, v, u)$
2 $\quad v_p \leftarrow \mathsf{preorderselect}(T, v);\ u_p \leftarrow \mathsf{preorderselect}(T, u)$
3 $\quad u_s \leftarrow \mathsf{select_p}(S, u_p);\ b_u \leftarrow \mathsf{succ_p}(S, u_s + 1) - (u_s + 1)$
4 $\quad$ **if** $v < u$ **then**
5 $\quad\quad$ **if** $v_p = \mathsf{parent}(T, u_p)$ **then return** 1
6 $\quad\quad v'_p \leftarrow \mathsf{close}(B_p, v_p);\ v'_s \leftarrow \mathsf{select_p}(S, v'_p)$
7 $\quad\quad p_s \leftarrow v'_s - v'_p;\ p'_s \leftarrow u_s - u_p$
8 $\quad\quad c \leftarrow \mathsf{close}(B_s, p_s + 1)$
9 $\quad\quad$ **if** $c \le p'_s + b_u$ **then return** $1 + (c - p'_s)$
10 $\quad\quad$ **else return** $1 + b_u$ (must be connected by the last '$]$' of u)
11 $\quad$ **else**
12 $\quad\quad$ **if** $u = 1$ **then** $d \leftarrow 0$ **else** $d \leftarrow 1$
13 $\quad\quad$ **if** $u_p = \mathsf{parent}(T, v_p)$ **then return** $d + b_u + \mathsf{childrank}(T, u_p, v_p)$
14 $\quad\quad u'_p \leftarrow \mathsf{close}(B_p, u_p);\ u'_s \leftarrow \mathsf{select_p}(S, u'_p)$
15 $\quad\quad v_s \leftarrow \mathsf{select_p}(S, v_p)$
16 $\quad\quad b_v \leftarrow \mathsf{succ_p}(S, v_s + 1) - (v_s + 1)$
17 $\quad\quad p_s \leftarrow u'_s - u'_p;\ p'_s \leftarrow v_s - v_p$
18 $\quad\quad o \leftarrow \mathsf{open}(B_s, p'_s + b_v)$
19 $\quad\quad$ **if** $o > p_s$ **then return** $1 + b_u + \mathsf{children}(T, u_p) + (o - p_s)$
20 $\quad\quad$ **else return** $1 + b_u + \mathsf{children}(T, u_p) + 1$
$\quad\quad$ (must be connected by the first '$[$' of u, which cannot be root)

Algorithm 9.13: Additional operations for the planar graph representation.

Input : Planar graph G (seen as bitvectors S, B_s, and B_p, the latter representing an ordinal tree T) and node v (a preorder in T).

1 **Proc** *parent*(G, v)

       Output: Returns the parent of node v in T (this is the first neighbor) or null if it does not exist

2   **if** $v = 1$ **then return** null
3     $v_p \leftarrow$ preorderselect(T, v)
4     $u_p \leftarrow$ parent(T, v_p)
5   **return** preorder(T, u_p)

6 **Proc** *backward*(G, v)

       Output: Returns the number of backward neighbors of node v (those start at position 2 in neigh(G, v), or at position 1 if v is the root of T)

7     $v_p \leftarrow$ preorderselect(T, v)
8     $v_s \leftarrow$ select$_p(S, v_p)$
9   **return** succ$_p(S, v_s + 1) - (v_s + 1)$

10 **Proc** *children*(G, v)

       Output: Returns the number of children of node v in T (those start after the backward neighbors in neigh(G, v))

11     $v_p \leftarrow$ preorderselect(T, v)
12   **return** children(T, v_p)

13 **Proc** *forward*(G, v)

       Output: Returns the number of forward neighbors of node v (those are the last in neigh(G, v))

14     $v_p \leftarrow$ preorderselect(T, v)
15     $v_p' \leftarrow$ close(B_p, v_p)
16     $v_s' \leftarrow$ select$_p(S, v_p')$
17   **return** succ$_p(S, v_s' + 1) - (v_s' + 1)$

The problem with dropping B_s is that, although we can reproduce the whole array in a left-to-right process, we cannot efficiently compute **open** and **close** queries on it without its explicit representation. We will manage to solve those queries using only S and B_p, by intervening the balanced parentheses representation of Chapter 7. More precisely, we will show (1) how to generate blocks of P in constant time using S and B_p and (2) how to compute all the **open** and **close** queries on the virtual sequence P.

For the first part, we aim to reproduce any block of $c = \lfloor (\log n)/4 \rfloor$ bits of P. The block $P[(j-1)c + 1, jc]$ can be inferred from $S[(j-1)c + 1, jc]$ and $B_p[p, p + c - 1]$, where $p = \mathsf{rank}_p(S, (j-1)c + 1)$. Thus we build a global precomputed table

$J[0, 2^c - 1][0, 2^c - 1]$, so that

$$J[S[(j - 1)c + 1, jc], B_p[p, p + c - 1]] = P[(j - 1)c + 1, jc].$$

The size of J is only $\mathcal{O}(\sqrt{n} \log n)$ bits.

Example 9.23 *Take the block $P[33, 40] = $ [( ]) [ ) [(, for $c = 8$, in Figure 9.11. It corresponds to $S[33, 40] = $ spspspsp. To produce the block from $S[33, 40]$, we need to know the value of the parentheses preceding the symbols s in $S[33, 40]$. Those are found by computing $p \leftarrow \mathsf{rank}_p(S, 33) = 18$, and then the parentheses of interest are $B_p[p, p + c - 1] = B_p[18, 25] = $) ( )) ( ) ( ). With $S[33, 40]$ and $B_p[18, 25]$ we can recover $P[33, 40]$: $S[33] = $ s must correspond to $P[33] = $ ' [' because the preceding parenthesis is $B_p[18] = $ ') ' (note that this parenthesis is at $P[30]$, out of the block $P[33, 40]$). Then $P[34] = B_p[19] = $ ' ('. Then $S[35] = $ s implies that $P[35] = $ '] ' because the preceding parenthesis is $P[34] = $ ' (', and so on. Note that only the parentheses in $B_p[18, 22]$ will be actually needed. This process is encoded in table J, in particular $J[$spspspsp,) ( )) ( ) ( )$] = J[10101010, 01001010] = J[170, 74] = $ [( ]) [ ) [(, where we have interpreted p $= 0$ and s $= 1$.*

For the second part, we must modify the rmM-tree of Sections 7.1 and 7.2 so that they are built on top of the virtual sequence $P[1, 2e]$. We define $\mathsf{excess}(P, i) = \mathsf{rank}_{[}(P, i) - \mathsf{rank}_{]}(P, i)$, that is, the excess of the brackets, ignoring the parentheses. Therefore, from i to $i + 1$, excess may decrease by 1, increase by 1, or stay the same. Thus we can use this formula to compute the fields e, m, M, and n in all the rmM-tree nodes. The algorithms for traversing this new rmM-tree, as well as the speedups of Section 7.2, work exactly in the same way. The main difference arises when we have to sequentially scan parts of P: we have to generate the blocks of P on the fly from S and B_p. Therefore, we can scan the blocks symbolwise, or we can use the blocks to feed a precomputed table similar to C (Algorithm 7.2), which takes a piece of S and a piece of B_p and stores the total, minimum, and maximum excess, as well as the number of occurrences of the minimum excess (these values can directly be stored in the corresponding cells of J).

Therefore, we retain the $\mathcal{O}(\log \log n)$ time for the queries, while representing any planar graph in $2(n + e) + o(n)$ bits. The implementation is more complex, but probably as fast as the basic one. Note that to traverse several consecutive blocks of P we need to do only one rank to map the first position to B_p. All the needed parentheses will be read from that position onwards.

9.4.2 Triangulations

The orderly spanning trees used for planar graphs in Section 9.4.1 satisfy additional properties when applied on a triangulation: except for the first, second, and last nodes in preorder, every node is connected via brackets with at least one preceding and at least one following neighbor. As a consequence, except for those 3 nodes, each opening parenthesis is followed by at least one closing bracket, and each closing parenthesis is followed by at least one opening bracket.

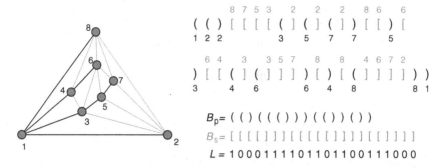

Figure 9.13. A triangulation represented with the multi-parentheses derived from a spanning tree. On the bottom, its representation using B_p and L.

Example 9.24 *The graph of Figure 9.10 is not a triangulation because the external face is limited by more than 3 edges. Figure 9.13 shows a triangulation and its representation using the spanning tree technique. Note that every parenthesis is followed by a bracket of the other direction, except for the nodes 1, 2, and 8: there are exactly 4 parentheses not satisfying the general rule. The arrays on the bottom right will be described shortly.*

Together with the fact that the direction of each bracket is the opposite of that of the preceding parenthesis, we can adapt the technique described at the end of Section 9.4.1 to reduce the total number of bits to $2e$.

We will not use $S[1, 2e]$ anymore. It will be sufficient to use B_p and B_s (which add up to $2e$ bits), if we represent B_s in a different way: Every run of k (equal) brackets in B_s will be replaced by 10^{k-1}. Let us call $L[1, 2(e - n + 1)]$ this bitvector. Thus our representation will be formed by B_p and L.

With this representation, we can map any (opening or closing) parenthesis position $B_p[v_p]$ to $v_l = L[\text{select}(L, v_p - 2)]$ (the -2 accounts for the first two parentheses, which have no brackets following them). The run of brackets ends at $\text{succ}(L, v_l + 1) - 1$. Similarly, any position v_l can be mapped back to $B_p[\text{rank}(L, v_l) + 2]$.

In addition we represent the $o(e)$-bit structures of the balanced parentheses for B_s, without representing B_s itself. The **open** and **close** queries on B_s will be solved with its rmM-tree (plus the accelerators of Section 7.2, if desired), and each needed block $B_s[(j - 1)c + 1, jc]$ will be generated on the fly using $B_p[\text{rank}(L, (j - 1)c + 1) + 2]$ onwards and $L[(j - 1)c + 1, jc]$, similarly as we did before with table J, but now replacing the bits of L by square brackets. This time we must consume a new parenthesis before processing each new bit set in L.

Example 9.25 *The array $P[1, 2e]$ is shown at the top of Figure 9.13. On the bottom, the bitvectors $B_p[1, 2(n - 1)]$, $B_s[1, 2(e - n + 1)]$, and $L[1, 2(e - n + 1)]$. We represent only B_p and L.*

The queries are solved almost as in Algorithm 9.11. We show the version for this representation in Algorithms 9.14 and 9.15. Overall we use only $2e + o(e)$ bits of space

---

Algorithm 9.14: Computing neigh and degree on triangular graphs.

Input : Triangular graph G (seen as bitvectors B_p and B_s, the former
representing an ordinal tree T and the latter represented with bitvector
L), node v (a preorder in T), and index j.

1 **Proc** neigh(G, v, j) — *assuming $j \leq$ degree(G, v)*
2     $v_p \leftarrow$ preorderselect(T, v)
3   **if** $v \neq 1$ **then**
4   **if** $j = 1$ **then return** preorder(T, parent(T, v_p))
5   **else** $j \leftarrow j - 1$
6   **if** $v_p > 2$ **then**
7        $v_l \leftarrow$ select($L, v_p - 2$)
8        $b \leftarrow$ succ($L, v_l + 1$) $- v_l$
9   **if** $j \leq b$ **then**
10           $r \leftarrow$ rank(L, open($B_s, v_l + j - 1$)) $+ 2$
11   **return** preorder(T, open(B_p, r))
12   **else** $j \leftarrow j - b$
13   **if** $j \leq$ children(T, v_p) **then return** preorder(T, child(T, v_p, j))
14   **else** $j \leftarrow j -$ children(T, v_p)
15     $v'_l \leftarrow$ select(L, close(B_p, v_p) $- 2$)
16     $r \leftarrow$ rank(L, close($B_s, v'_l + j - 1$)) $+ 2$
17   **return** preorder(T, r)

18 **Proc** degree(G, v)
19     $v_p \leftarrow$ preorderselect(T, v)
20   **if** $v = 1$ **then** $d \leftarrow 0$ **else** $d \leftarrow 1$
21   **if** $v_p > 2$ **then**
22        $v_l \leftarrow$ select($L, v_p - 2$)
23        $d \leftarrow d +$ succ($L, v_l + 1$) $- v_l$
24     $d \leftarrow d +$ children(T, v_p)
25   **if** $v \neq 1$ **and** $v \neq n$ **then**
26        $v'_p \leftarrow$ close(B_p, v_p)
27        $v'_l \leftarrow$ select($L, v'_p - 2$)
28        $d \leftarrow d +$ succ($L, v'_l + 1$) $- v'_l$
29   **return** d

---

and solve the queries in time $\mathcal{O}(\log \log n)$. Note, in addition, that the mapping operations are simpler than on planar graphs.

9.4.3 Construction

There exists a linear-time algorithm to embed planar graphs in $k = 4$ pages. We omit it because it is too involved for our scope; see the references at the end of the chapter.

Algorithm 9.15: Computing adj on triangular graphs.

Input : Triangular graph G (seen as bitvectors B_p and B_s, the former
representing an ordinal tree T and the latter represented with bitvector
L), nodes v and u (preorders in T), and index j.

1 **Proc** adj(G, v, u)
2   **if** $v > u$ **then** $u \leftrightarrow v$
3     $v_p \leftarrow$ preorderselect(T, v); $u_p \leftarrow$ preorderselect(T, u)
4   **if** $v_p =$ parent(T, u_p) **then return true**
5   **if** $v_p = 1$ **then return false**
6     $v'_p \leftarrow$ close(B_p, v_p)
7     $v_l \leftarrow$ select$(L, v'_p - 2)$; $u_l \leftarrow$ select$(L, u_p - 2)$
8   **return** $match(B_s, v_l,$ succ$(L, v_l + 1) - 1, u_l,$ succ$(L, u_l + 1) - 1)$
    (Algorithm 9.8)

Instead, we will describe the algorithm for generating an orderly spanning tree, so that
the best representations of planar graphs and triangulations can be derived from it. We
warn the reader that the algorithm is not simple. It can be skipped without missing how
the data structure works.

The algorithm requires the planar graph to be already mapped to the plane, that is,
that each node lists its neighbors in ccw order and that the list of nodes F_G forming
the external face is built. Such a mapping is computed in linear time as a by-product of
planarity testing algorithms; see the references at the end of the chapter.

To present the algorithm we need some definitions. First, given the external face of
G and two nodes r and v of it, cw(G, r, v) is the sequence of nodes $r, \ldots, v$ traversed
when going from r to v in clockwise order along F_G. Analogously, ccw(G, r, v) goes
from r to v in counterclockwise order. We also define prev(G, r) and next(G, r) as
the nodes preceding and following r, respectively, in counterclockwise order. Thus,
prev(G, r) is the second element of cw(G, r, v) and next(G, r) is the second element
of ccw(G, r, v). Given a face F of G and two nodes r and v on F, we may also speak
of ccw(F, r, v), cw(F, r, v), pred(F, v), and next(F, v), to refer to an ordered traversal
of the nodes in the boundary of F. We will also speak of considering the faces where
v belongs, in cw or ccw order, according to the cw or ccw traversal of the neighbors
of v (each face is defined by two consecutive neighbors).

Second, an *articulation point* of a connected graph G is a node whose removal disconnects G. Graphs without articulation points are called *biconnected*. A graph that
is not biconnected can be divided into its *biconnected components*, which have only
articulation points in common. If we interpret articulation points as connecting biconnected components, then the structure is acyclic: there is a unique path of articulation
points between two biconnected components.

Example 9.26 *Consider the graph in Figure 9.10, and let $r = 1$ and $v = 8$.*
Then cw$(G, 1, 8) = \langle 1, 13, 10, 9, 8 \rangle$ *and* ccw$(G, 1, 8) = \langle 1, 2, 3, 4, 5, 6, 7, 8 \rangle$. *Also*

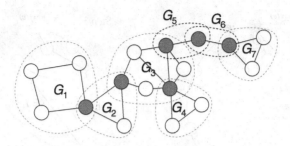

Figure 9.14. A graph with 7 biconnected components (circled in dashed lines). The articulation points are the nodes in gray.

$\mathsf{prev}(G, 1) = 13$, $\mathsf{next}(G, 1) = 2$, $\mathsf{prev}(G, 8) = 7$, and $\mathsf{next}(G, 8) = 9$. The external face of the graph can be listed with, for example, $F_G = \mathsf{ccw}(G, 1, 1) = \langle 1, 2, 3, 4, 5, 6, 7, 8, 9, 10, 13, 1 \rangle$.

Figure 9.14 shows a graph with 7 biconnected components, G_1 to G_7. They are connected through the articulation points (grayed). There is a single entry node (an articulation point) when entering to G_i from another G_j (the entry point may depend on j).

Building the Spanning Tree

The algorithm to generate the spanning tree assumes G is biconnected; we show later how to proceed otherwise. The algorithm is recursive, adding edges to a global spanning tree T. First we have to fix a "root" node r (which will be the root of the spanning tree) and a "leaf" node v (which will be a leaf of the spanning tree). Nodes r and v can be any two different nodes along F_G. A high-level description of the algorithm follows (most steps are illustrated in Figure 9.15):

1. If G contains only the edge (r, v), then add it to T and finish.

2. Find a parent node p for v. This will be the neighbor of v that is closest to r in $\mathsf{cw}(G, r, v)$. Note that p may be the same r. Figure 9.15 shows r, v, and p grayed in Step 2.

3. Remove v from G, as well as all the edges incident on v. Call G' the resulting graph (we do not maintain G and G' separately, but just use the names to refer to the old and new graphs). Add edge (p, v) to T. Figure 9.15 shows in gray the disappearing edges, in black the new edges in $F_{G'}$, and (p, v) with a gray dashed line, in Step 3.

4. This removal may create a set of articulation points in G'. Detect the biconnected components $G_1, G_2, \ldots$ of G'. For this, it is sufficient to traverse the segment $C = \mathsf{ccw}(G', \mathsf{prev}(G, v), \mathsf{next}(G, v))$, that is, the new edges added to $F_{G'}$ with respect to F_G. Figure 9.15 shows the articulation points in gray, and the biconnected components circled in dashed lines, in Step 4.

5. Proceed recursively on each of the biconnected components G_i. Define the new root r_i and leaf v_i for G_i as follows (Figure 9.15 shows nodes r_i grayed and nodes v_i hatched in Step 5):

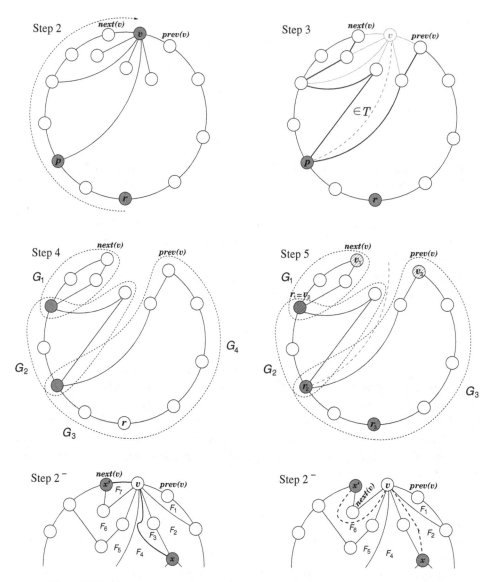

Figure 9.15. Various steps in the construction of the spanning tree of a planar graph.

(a) Let r_i be the node of G_i that is closest to r in G' (it holds $r_i = r$ if $r \in G_i$; this is the case of G_3 in Figure 9.15). Here closeness is always well defined because, if $r \notin G_i$, then there is a single path from r to G_i through articulation points; the last articulation point in this path is r_i.

(b) Since v and p are both on the external face of G, the edge (p, v) cuts G into two: the biconnected components are either to one side of (p, v) or to the other (Figure 9.15 shows again the dashed gray edge (p, v) in Step 5; then G_1 and G_2 are on the same side of $\mathsf{next}(G, v)$ and G_3 is on the same side of $\mathsf{prev}(G, v)$). In case $p = \mathsf{prev}(G, v)$, all the G_is are considered to be on the same side of $\mathsf{next}(G, v)$, and vice versa. We then choose v_i as follows.

(c) If G_i is on the side of $\mathsf{prev}(G, v)$, then define $S = \mathsf{ccw}(G, r, v) \cap$ $\mathsf{ccw}(G_i, \mathsf{next}(G_i, r_i), \mathsf{prev}(G_i, r_i))$. If $S = \emptyset$, then $v_i = \mathsf{next}(G_i, r_i)$; otherwise v_i is the last element of S.

(d) If G_i is on the side of $\mathsf{next}(G, v)$, then define $S = \mathsf{cw}(G, r, v) \cap$ $\mathsf{cw}(G_i, \mathsf{prev}(G_i, r_i), \mathsf{next}(G_i, r_i))$. If $S = \emptyset$, then $v_i = \mathsf{prev}(G_i, r_i)$; otherwise v_i is the last element of S.

As such, the algorithm already works in triangulations and triconnected graphs (that is, those that need the removal of two nodes to be disconnected). However, to make it work on other planar graphs, we need to alter the embedding in the plane in some cases. Intuitively, if we regard r as being on the bottom and v on the top of G, then prior to choosing p we move all the edges (v, x) that can be moved to rightward faces, as much as possible to the right. Then, after choosing p, we move all the edges (v, x) on faces to the right of (v, p) leftward, as much as possible (but still to the right of (v, p)).

2^-. Before step 2, consider the internal faces $F_1, \ldots, F_f$ where v belongs, in CW order from the one where $\mathsf{prev}(G, v)$ also belongs until the one where $\mathsf{next}(G, v)$ also belongs.

(a) For each node $x \in \mathsf{ccw}(F_i, v, v)$ that is also a neighbor of v, and the edge (v, x) is not in F_i but rather in faces F_j for $j > i$ (each edge belongs to two consecutive faces; one may be the external face), move the edge (v, x) toward the interior of face F_i.

In Step 2^- of Figure 9.15 we show 7 faces around v, numbered F_1 to F_7 in CW order. We find a node x (grayed) in F_2 that is a neighbor of v, but the edge (v, x) is in F_3 and F_4. Then, on the right of Step 2^-, this edge (now dashed) has been moved inside F_2. The same happens with x' (grayed) in F_6, where the edge (v, x') belongs to F_7. Note that moving this edge inside F_6 changes the external face of G, also modifying $\mathsf{next}(G, v)$. Faces F_3 and F_7 are eliminated, and two new faces inside the original F_2 and F_6 are created (to show interesting cases, the neighbors of v are not the same as in the previous steps).

2^+. After step 2, consider the internal faces $F'_1, \ldots, F'_g$ where v belongs, in CCW order from the last one where p also belongs until the one where $\mathsf{prev}(G, v)$ also belongs.

(a) For each node $x \in \mathsf{cw}(F'_i, v, v)$ that is also a neighbor of v, and the edge (v, x) is not in F'_i but rather in faces F'_j for $j > i$, move the edge (v, x) toward the interior of face F'_i.

In Step 2^- (right) of Figure 9.15, we now analyze the faces $F_4 = F'_1$ to $F_1 = F'_4$, and move the edge (v, x) back inside F_4.

We have assumed that G is initially biconnected. If it is not, the articulation points define a tree of biconnected components G_i. Thus we can generate the spanning tree T_i for each component and then T will be the union of the edges of all the trees T_i (articulation points v will have edges toward more than one T_i).

To build the parentheses layout, the final spanning tree T must be traversed in CCW order. That is, the children of the tree root r must be traversed in CCW order from $\mathsf{next}(G, r)$ to $\mathsf{prev}(G, r)$ (only some of the neighbors of r in G are children of r in T).

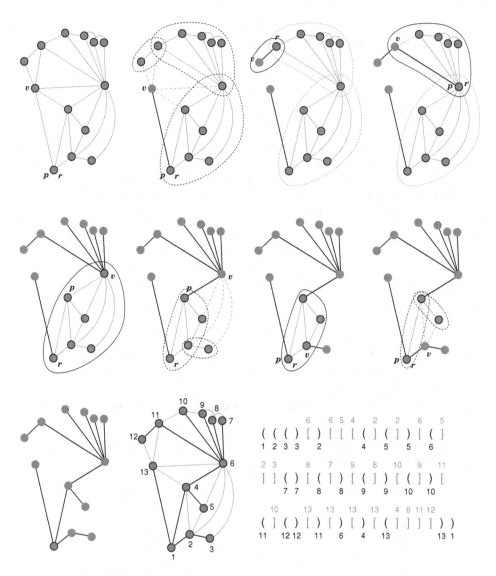

Figure 9.16. Running the orderly spanning tree construction algorithm on the graph of Figure 9.10.

Similarly, the children of an internal node v must be traversed in CCW order, starting from the parent p of v in T.

Example 9.27 *Figure 9.16 shows how the algorithm operates on the graph of Figure 9.10 if we start with $r = $ Chile and $v = $ Peru. We choose $p = r$. In the second plot, we mark in black the edge (p, v) that is added to T, draw with dashes the edges that are removed from G, and draw in gray the node v that is also removed. The biconnected components are circled in black dashed lines.*

In the third plot we solve a biconnected component (circled in a full black line) that has only one edge. In the fourth, we choose r, v, and p for the second biconnected component, adding the edge (v, p) to T.

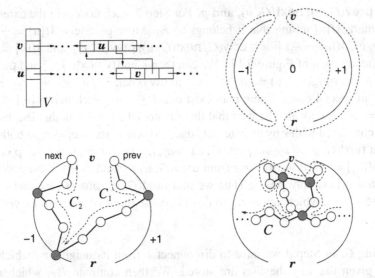

Figure 9.17. Several aspects of the linear-time construction of orderly spanning trees. On the top left, the doubly linked circular list structures holding the edges of G, where edges $(u, v) = (v, u)$ also point to each other. On the top right, the way $M[\cdot]$ values are assigned: $+1$ on $\mathrm{ccw}(G, r, v)$, -1 on $\mathrm{ccw}(G, \mathrm{next}(G, v), \mathrm{prev}(G, r))$, and 0 elsewhere. On the bottom left, the list C touching F_G at various points (grayed), all of which are then articulation points in G'. We distinguish the parts C_1 and C_2 of C with dashed arrows. On the bottom right, a part of C with some articulation points (grayed) not in F_G appearing after we remove the edges from v (grayed too). Those appear at least twice in a traversal of C (dashed arrow).

In the fifth plot (second row), we have processed the whole biconnected component similarly, and choose r, v, and p for the last component. In the sixth, we add the edge (p, v) to T, disconnect v from the graph, and find the two biconnected components that remain.

In the seventh plot, we have already solved the smallest component, of only one edge, and choose v and $p = r$ for the largest. In the eighth, we add (p, v) to T and leave two biconnected components of just one edge. Those are completed in the ninth plot, which has the final spanning tree T. At its right we show T inside G, with its ccw numbering of the nodes and the corresponding parentheses representation.

Note that the resulting tree is not the same that we had in Figure 9.10. In fact, that spanning tree is correct, but it is not generated by this algorithm for any initial choices of r and v. This shows that there may be other algorithms to obtain a correct spanning tree.

Linear Time Construction

We have first described the algorithm at a high level. Now we present the details of how it runs in $\mathcal{O}(e) = \mathcal{O}(n)$ time.

The list of neighbors u of each node v will be stored in ccw order as a circular doubly linked list. By following the list backwards we can also traverse the neighbors in cw order. The list element for edge (v, u) stores the identifier of node u (which belongs to $[1, n]$). We also cross-link the edges $(u, v) = (v, u)$ in the lists of v and u (so we can also obtain the identifier of v from an edge (v, u) of the list of v). An array $V[1, n]$ stores in $V[v]$ a pointer to the doubly linked list of v. Figure 9.17 (top left) illustrates the structure.

Finding prev(G, v), next(G, v), and p. For Step 2, each node u in the external face stores a mark $M[u]$ telling that it belongs to F_G. More precisely, $M[u] = +1$ if $u \in$ ccw(G, r, v), $M[u] = -1$ if $u \in$ ccw(G, next(G, v), prev(G, r)), and $M[u] = 0$ if $u \notin F_G$ (see the top right of Figure 9.17). We can then identify next(G, v) and prev(G, v) as follows. Let neigh(G, v) = $\langle u_1, \ldots, u_d \rangle$ in cw order. Let us add $u_{d+1} = u_1$ to this list to avoid special cases. There may exist one $1 \leq i \leq d$ such that $M[u_i] = -1$ and $M[u_{i+1}] = +1$. It may also happen that there is no $M[u_i] = -1$ in this list, but in this case v is connected with r by an external edge, so there is some $u_i = r$. In both cases it holds that next(G, v) = u_i and prev(G, v) = u_{i+1}. Also, in the first case, p is the first u_j with $M[u_j] = -1$ if we traverse from prev(G, v) to next(G, v) in cw order; in the second case it is simply $p = r$. Thus we find next(G, v), prev(G, v), and p in time $\mathcal{O}($degree(G, v)$)$, which amortizes to $\mathcal{O}(e)$ because those edges are removed from G in Step 3.

Generating C. In Step 3 we have to disconnect v from its neighbors, which is easily done given the way the lists are stored. We then compute $F_{G'}$, which replaces $\langle$prev(G, v), v, next(G, v)$\rangle$ by $C =$ ccw(G', prev(G, v), next(G, v)). We generate C as follows. First we identify v in the neighbor list of $u =$ prev(G, v) (using the cross-links, since we know the position of $u = u_{i+1}$ in the list of v), and then remove all the edges (v, x). Now we start from u, and take the neighbor u' of u that followed v in ccw order. Then, from the position of u in the neighbor list of u', we find the next neighbor of u' in ccw order, and so on until we reach next(G, v) (recall Figure 9.12). Each edge of C is thus found in constant time. Since each edge of E will belong to C at most once along the algorithm, the work $\mathcal{O}(|C|)$ amortizes to $\mathcal{O}(e)$.

Detecting articulation points. In Step 4 we must find the articulation points and biconnected components. In principle, all the articulation points can be found by traversing ccw(G', r, r) and detecting the nodes that are visited at least twice (see Figure 9.14). To do this in $\mathcal{O}(|C|)$ time, we avoid traversing the segments ccw(G, r, prev(G, v)) and ccw(G, next(G, v), r). Instead, we use the fact that, just like p, every node in C that is also in F_G is an articulation point (with the exception of the extremes prev(G, v) and next(G, v)), and that every articulation point in $F_{G'}$ must be in C.[3]

Therefore, all the nodes in F_G that became articulation points can be found simply by traversing C and checking which nodes are in F_G (i.e., $M[\cdot] \neq 0$). If we traverse C from prev(G, v) to next(G, v), we first find the elements in F_G that are in cw(G, prev(G, v), r) and then those that are in cw(G, prev(G, r), next(G, v)), in that order. We can easily split $C = C_1 . C_2$, so that C_2 starts at the first node u with $M[u] = -1$ (that is, u is the first node of C that is in cw(G, prev(G, r), next(G, v))). See the bottom left of Figure 9.17.

The articulation points in C that are not in F_G can also be found in $\mathcal{O}(|C|)$ time, by traversing C and detecting any node that is visited at least twice. See the bottom right

---

[3] With respect to F_G, the new contour $F_{G'}$ lost the edges (prev(G, v), v) and (v, next(G, v)), and gained C. There were no articulation points in G, so there were no repeated nodes when traversing F_G. Articulation points in G' are nodes that appear at least twice when traversing $F_{G'} \subseteq F_G \cup C$; therefore they must appear in C.

of Figure 9.17. The same vector M can be used for detecting the repeated nodes of C. Since the nodes $v \notin F_G$ have $M[v] = 0$, we set their values to $M[v] \neq 0$ as we visit them. Then the next node v we visit is an articulation point iff $M[v] \neq 0$ (either because it is repeated in C or because it was already in F_G). For the next steps, it is useful to mark $M[\cdot] \leftarrow +1$ on C_2 before reaching the node p, and $M[\cdot] \leftarrow -1$ elsewhere and in C_1.

Finding the biconnected components. In Step 5 we find the nodes r_i and v_i for each G_i and also build the (implicit) list F_{G_i}. This can be done together with the detection of the articulation points and the recursive calls within the biconnected components, as follows. We traverse C_1 starting from $\mathsf{prev}(G, v)$, detecting the articulation points u as explained. The first such node delimits a leaf G_i of the tree of biconnected components induced by articulation points. Thus we disconnect G_i from G' and recursively call the algorithm on G_i. This recursive call adds the corresponding edges to the global orderly spanning tree T and also removes all the edges in G_i. Once this is done, the leaf of the tree of biconnected components has been removed and we restart the traversal of C_1 from u, finding the subsequent components and solving each of them recursively. When we finish traversing C_1, we similarly traverse C_2 backwards from $\mathsf{next}(G, v)$, so that the articulation points in $\mathsf{ccw}(G, \mathsf{next}(G, v), \mathsf{prev}(G, r))$ are detected in that order.

Recursive calls. To disconnect G_i and prepare it for the recursive call, we create a copy of its articulation point u and call it r_i. We leave in r_i the neighbors that belong to G_i (which form a range of the neighbors of u), and remove them from u (u still belongs to G'). The range of edges that will belong to the list of r_i are those in the list of u between the last one visited in C and the current one by which we returned to u. To find them, we can traverse C backwards until finding u again, which still amortizes to $\mathcal{O}(|C|)$ because those edges will belong to G_i. Once the range of r_i is known, it can be disconnected in constant time from the list of u. The range of nodes in C that we have traversed now belongs to F_{G_i}, and will be marked as such in array M, as detailed next.

On C_1, we define v_i as the last node in $\mathsf{ccw}(G_i, r_i, r_i)$ that was in F_G (that is, with $M[\cdot] = +1$); if there is no such node, then v_i is $\mathsf{next}(G_i, r_i)$. Then we set $M[v_i] \leftarrow +1$, and $M[\cdot]$ is already -1 for all the nodes in the traversed part of C_1, due to the way we used M to detect repeated nodes. The nodes of F_{G_i} that were already in F_G, if any, are also left with their original value, $M[\cdot] = +1$ (thus they are implicitly included in F_{G_i}).

On C_2, we start defining v_i as the last node in $\mathsf{cw}(G_i, r_i, r_i)$ that was in F_G (that is, with $M[\cdot] = -1$); if there is no such node, v_i is $\mathsf{prev}(G_i, r_i)$. Then we set $M[v_i] \leftarrow +1$, $M[r_i] \leftarrow +1$, and $M[\cdot]$ is already $+1$ for all the nodes in the traversed part of C_2, again because of the way we used M. The nodes of F_{G_i} that were already in F_G, if any, are also left with their original value $M[\cdot] = -1$. When, along C_2, we find the node p, we are passing to the other side of the edge (v, p) and switch to computing $v_i \leftarrow \mathsf{next}(G_i, r_i)$. Again, all the $M[\cdot]$ values become correct once we set $M[v_i] \leftarrow +1$ and $M[r_i] \leftarrow +1$.

Note that there may be a final biconnected component left, rooted at r, which must be processed at the end, and whose v node is defined as on C_1. The $M[\cdot]$ values in the remaining part of C are already -1, and those in F_G are already $+1$, so no updates to M are necessary.

All the above work requires time $\mathcal{O}(|C|)$, which as explained amortizes to $\mathcal{O}(e)$, plus the recursive calls to solve biconnected components. As these have different v_i nodes each time, they are at most $\mathcal{O}(n)$. As we separately counted the work done inside the recursive calls apart from the calls themselves, this extra time is $\mathcal{O}(n)$.

Changing the mapping to the plane. Finally, we have the steps 2^- and 2^+. For these, we will first mark all the neighbors of v with $M[v] = +1$ (all the other involved nodes have a 0). Then we will consider each consecutive pair of neighbors of v, in order from prev(G, v) to next(G, v). Each pair $\langle u_i, u_{i+1} \rangle$ corresponds to a new face F, which must be traversed in ccw order with the technique we have already described. We unmark the pair of neighbors and traverse F until we find a marked element x or we return to v. In the first case, we have found an edge (v, x) to move inside F: we move x right after u_i in the list of neighbors of v, redefine x as its successor in the list of neighbors, and this completes the traversal of F. If we find v again, we are also done with F. We then continue with the next pair of neighbors. At the end, the (possibly) new nodes prev(G, v) and next(G, v) are marked in M as appropriate. The step 2^+ is similar.

Note that all the edges considered in these steps are those that connect v to its neighbors and those in C. Thus the work is $\mathcal{O}(\text{degree}(G, v) + |C|)$, which has already been shown to amortize to $\mathcal{O}(e)$.

Overall the time to build T is $\mathcal{O}(e)$, and the space is $8e + \mathcal{O}(n)$ words: $8e$ for the edge lists, n for V, $2n$ bits for M, and up to $\mathcal{O}(n)$ extra words for the recursion stack (although this is significant only in very special graphs).

Building the Compact Representation

To avoid using even more space for building T, we use the memory in a way that allows us see the original graph (before its edges were deleted along the process) and the edges that were added to T.

We allocate a single memory chunk E of $2e$ elements for all the doubly linked lists, reserving contiguous memory space for the list of every node. Each entry $V[v]$ points to the beginning of the area of the neighbors of v, which are stored left-to-right in ccw order. The pointers of the linked list are used normally, without regard for this arrangement. When edges are deleted, they are only disconnected from their list, but not physically moved. This creates a problem only when deleting the first edge of the list of a node v, at position $V[v]$, since the pointer from V is then invalid. Such invalid pointers are detected by setting the pointer to the previous element in the circular list to null, $V[v].prev \leftarrow$ null. When this condition is detected, we can instead use $V[v].next$ as the beginning of the list. To keep this working, we must ensure that, if $V[v].next$ is in turn deleted, we set $V[v].next \leftarrow V[v].next.next$. Therefore, from $V[v]$ we can always access the list at some valid position in constant time, without ever changing the value of $V[v]$.

When performing a recursive call on a graph G_i connected to G by an articulation point u, a new root node r_i must be created for G_i, taking a segment of the list of u (this list is also contiguous in memory, as it is a ccw range of neighbors of u). The range is easily disconnected from the list of u in constant time. After the recursive call on G, we must restore the invariant on $V[u].next$, in the case that the list of r_i started at $V[u]$. Note that, in the recursive calls on graphs G_i, the root r_i will be an extra node not in V, thus the pointer to its list of edges will be stored separately.

Once the whole process terminates, all the edges have been removed from G. However, since the list elements are never moved and $V[v]$ points to their beginning, we can still access the original neighbors of any v in CCW order, because they are laid contiguously between addresses $V[v]$ and $V[v+1] - 1$.

The way to add edges (p, v) to T exploits the fact that the edge is simultaneously deleted from G. Each time a node p is set as the parent of another node v in T (and (p, v) is deleted from G), we mark the target node v in the list of p as $-v$, to signal that v is a child of p in T. We separately store the global root r of G (and of T), as well as $\mathsf{prev}(G, r)$ and $\mathsf{next}(G, r)$.

Now, to build the parentheses representation, we traverse T starting from node r, outputting an opening parenthesis, traversing each child of r in CCW order from $\mathsf{next}(G, r)$ to $\mathsf{prev}(G, r)$, and then outputting the final closing parenthesis. The array M is used to mark already traversed nodes in T: traversed nodes v have $M[v] = +2$, so initially no node is marked as traversed. For each non-root node v we traverse, we mark $M[v] \leftarrow +2$. We then traverse its list counting the number b_v of backward edges (which point to traversed nodes that are not the parent of v), and the number of f_v of forward edges (which point to non-traversed nodes that are not children of v). We then output an opening parenthesis, output b_v closing brackets, recursively traverse the children of v in CCW order, if any (these are contiguous in the list), then output a closing parenthesis, and output f_v opening brackets.

Finally, we free V and E, and terminate, all in time $\mathcal{O}(e)$.

9.5 Applications

9.5.1 Binary Relations

A binary relation $\mathcal{B}$ on a set $\mathcal{S}$ of *subjects* and a set $\mathcal{O}$ of *objects* is any subset $\mathcal{B} \subseteq \mathcal{S} \times \mathcal{O}$. If we identify, for simplicity, $\mathcal{S} = [1, \sigma]$ and $\mathcal{O} = [1, n]$, then $\mathcal{B}$ can be regarded as a binary matrix of $\sigma \times n$ cells. We call $e = |\mathcal{B}|$ the number of pairs in $\mathcal{B}$. In addition, the relations can be labeled, so that each pair $(s, o) \in \mathcal{B}$ has a label attached from a set $\mathcal{L} = [1, \lambda]$.

Binary relations appear frequently when modeling data. Graphs are just a particular case, where $\mathcal{S} = \mathcal{O} = V$ and $\mathcal{B} = E$. An application of a more general relation are recommender systems, where users are related to products they have bought or rented and can indicate their level of satisfaction with the product (but they may choose to not leave an opinion as well). The level of satisfaction associated with each pair $(s, o) \in \mathcal{B}$ can be regarded as the label for that pair. This is used for recommending new products to a customer x. One simple rule is that, if another user y liked/disliked approximately the same products as x, then other products liked by y will probably be liked by x.

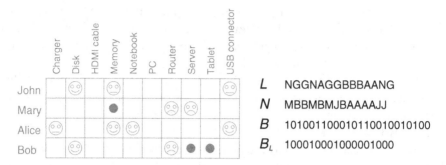

Figure 9.18. A binary relation and our representation. We show in gray the conceptual information and in black the actual representation.

While conceptually they are very different, binary relations can be represented as slight extensions of graphs. The main change is that the set of sources of edges needs not be the same as the set of targets of edges. However, our sequence representations for directed unlabeled or labeled graphs (Section 9.1) can be used verbatim, taking N as the concatenation of the sequence of subjects associated with each object. This representation requires $e \log \sigma (1 + o(1)) + \mathcal{O}(n)$ bits for unlabeled relations and $e(\log \sigma + \log \lambda)(1 + o(1)) + \mathcal{O}(n + \lambda)$ bits for labeled ones. Note that, since we have identified S with the matrix rows, N is collecting the matrix points column-wise, not row-wise as in Section 9.1. If there are more subjects than objects ($\sigma > n$), we may let N traverse the matrix row-wise as usual, to reduce the space to $e \log n(1 + o(1)) + \mathcal{O}(\sigma)$ bits.

Example 9.28 *Figure 9.18 illustrates a binary relation where 4 customers are related to 10 products they have bought. For brevity we identify customers and products with their initials. That is, the subjects are $S = \{J, M, A, B\}$, and the objects are $\mathcal{O} = \{C, D, H, M, N, P, R, S, T, U\}$. In some cases the customers have indicated if the product was good (G, smiley face), bad (B, angry face), or neutral (N, inexpressive face). Where no opinion was given, we use a solid circle (A). Those are the labels, $\mathcal{L} = \{A = 1, B = 2, G = 3, N = 4\}$. On the right, we show the labeled-graph-like representation of Section 9.1.4 for this matrix.*

By reducing them to queries on labeled graphs, we can answer questions such as: who bought a memory? (neigh query), what has Mary bought? (rneigh query), did Bob buy a router, and if so, did he like it? (adj query, solvable by testing each label in turn), what purchases were evaluated as being bad? (listing pairs labeled l), who was unhappy with the server? (neigh$_l$ query), which purchases did Alice like? (rneigh$_l$ query), and so on.

9.5.2 RDF Datasets

Another example of binary relations are the RDF (Resource Description Framework) stores. RDF stores maintain a set of subjects, a set of objects, and a set $\mathcal{P}$ of *predicates*. Subjects are related to objects via predicates, which is expressed with *triples* $(s, p, o) \in S \times \mathcal{P} \times \mathcal{O}$. For example, "employee e works at company c" can be represented as a triple $(e, \text{works at}, c)$. RDF stores are just sets of triples. The basic RDF queries are incomplete triples, like $(s, ?, o)$, $(?, p, o)$, $(?, p, ?)$, where one should return all the

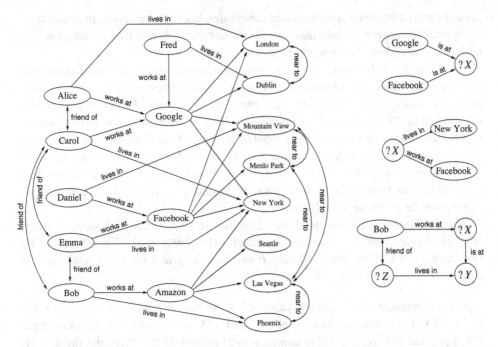

Figure 9.19. An RDF store about friend relations and workplaces (left) and some SPARQL queries on it (right). The unlabeled arrows correspond to the predicate is at.

triples in the store that match the query at the defined positions. For example, query (?, **works at**, c) returns all the triples (e, **works at**, c) in the store, for any employee e (that is, all the employees that work at company c).

A way to handle the triples is to regard the store as a binary relation $\mathcal{B} \subseteq \mathcal{S} \times \mathcal{O}$, where each pair ($s, o$) is associated with a set of labels, one per predicate p such that (s, p, o) is in the store. Then a slight extension of the representation of Section 9.5.1, to handle multiple labels, allows for several relevant queries on the database.

In this section we explore an alternative representation that takes advantage of the fact that the set $\mathcal{P}$ is usually small. We represent the RDF store as a set of binary relations $B_p \subseteq \mathcal{S} \times \mathcal{O}$, one per predicate $p \in \mathcal{P}$, so that (s, o) $\in B_p$ iff (s, p, o) $\in \mathcal{B}$. While this arrangement makes queries inefficient when the predicate is not set, it has other advantages. One is that the RDF data are usually clustered, and then storing each B_p with the k^2-tree of Section 9.2 uses much less space than the representation of Section 9.5.1.

A second advantage is that the symmetric nature of the k^2-tree allows for efficient *join queries* on the RDF data. The most popular query language for RDF is SPARQL, which specifies a graph of relations that must hold for triples to be retrieved. Each node in the query graph represents a subject or an object, and edges are labeled by the predicates that must relate them. Thus edges correspond to the triple-queries we have described, and solving the whole query requires joining the triple-queries by their common nodes.

Example 9.29 *On the left of Figure 9.19 we show an RDF store where objects and subjects can be persons, companies, and locations. The predicates are* friend of *between* *persons*, works at *between persons and companies*, is at *between companies and loca-tions*, lives in *between persons and locations, and* near to *between locations. Note how nodes may be objects for some predicates and subjects for others.*

On the right of the figure we show some queries. Assume Carol *and* Emma *want to move to the same city. One works at* Google *and the other at* Facebook. *The query at the top looks for locations they could move to. It is formed by two related triples,* (Google, is at, ?X) *and* (Facebook, is at, ?X). *Here ?X means that the first and second triples may contain any value X but it must be the same X for both. The query has three matches in the graph, for X =* London, *X =* Mountain View, *and X =* New York.

The second query finds persons that live in New York *and work at* Facebook. *It is formed by the triples* (?X, lives in, New York) *and* (?X, works at, Facebook). *This matches in the graph for X =* Emma.

The third query finds friends of Bob *that live in a city where the company where he works has a brand. It is formed by the triples* (Bob, works at, ?X), (?X, is at, ?Y), (?Z, lives in, ?Y), (Bob, friend of, ?Z). *It matches the graph for* ⟨X = Amazon, Y = New York, Z = Carol *or* Z = Emma⟩.

Let us consider the simplest cases of join: the object-object $(s, p, ?X)$ and $(s', p', ?X)$, the subject-object $(s, p, ?X)$ and $(?X, p', o)$, and the subject-subject $(?X, p, o)$ and $(?X, p', o')$. These can be solved efficiently by traversing the k^2-trees of the binary relations B_p and $B_{p'}$. In the first case, we must traverse the row s of B_p in synchronization with the row s' of $B_{p'}$, reporting every element found in the same column o. In the second case, we must traverse the row s of B_p and the column o of $B_{p'}$, reporting every offset g such that we find an element at column g in B_p and at row g in $B_{p'}$. The third case is analogous to the first.

Algorithms 9.16 and 9.17 show how the object-object and subject-object join operations, respectively, can be carried out on the k^2-tree (the case subject-subject is analogous). In the subject-object join, we must assume that $\mathcal{S} \cap \mathcal{O} \neq \emptyset$, that is, some elements act as subjects and objects depending on the triple. A prefix $[1, t]$ of both $[1, \sigma]$ and $[1, n]$ can be reserved for the identifiers of those objects (then we would need only to traverse that prefix of the matrices, but we do not exploit this in Algorithm 9.17). Several other variants can be handled as well, for example, if s, s', o, or o' are unspecified. Again, there are no relevant performance guarantees for these join operations, but they perform well in practice if the relations are sparse or clustered, since the k^2-tree can skip large areas where one of the two relations has no pairs.

These algorithms only solve queries formed by two edges with a coincident node. For more complex queries, intermediate results have to be intersected sequentially, which is more costly. A good strategy is to find edge pairs that yield small intermediate results and solve these using k^2-trees.

9.5.3 Planar Routing

Services such as finding routes to move from one place to another (in a city or a country) are frequently used from cellphones, so using little space and bandwidth for storing and transmitting data about streets and routes is important. Let us consider a simple setup for a city with intersections (nodes) and street segments connecting them (edges), where

---

Algorithm 9.16: Object-object join on RDF graphs using k^2-trees.

---

1 **Proc** $object\text{-}object(T_p, T_{p'}, s, s')$

    Input : Binary relations B_p and $B_{p'}$ of $N \times N$ with $N = k^{\lceil \log_k \max(n,\sigma) \rceil}$ (seen as
        k^2trees T_p and $T_{p'}$ with more than zero pairs), subjects s and s'.
    Output: Outputs matches X for join query $(s, p, ?X)$ and $(s', p', ?X)$.

2     $ooreport(\mathsf{root}(T_p), \mathsf{root}(T_{p'}), s, s', 1, N)$

3 **Proc** $ooreport(v, v', r, r', c_0, t)$

    Input : Nonempty submatrices $M[1, t][1, t]$ and $M'[1, t][1, t]$ of B_p and $B_{p'}$,
        corresponding to k^2-tree nodes v and v', both starting at column c_0 of
        B_p and $B_{p'}$, and local rows r and r' to intersect.
    Output: Outputs the columns $c_0 - 1 + c$ such that $M[r, c] = M'[r', c] = 1$.

4   **if** $t = 1$ **then output** c_0

5   **else**

6         $l \leftarrow t/k$

7         $r_l \leftarrow \lceil r/l \rceil$; $r'_l \leftarrow \lceil r'/l \rceil$

8         $r \leftarrow r - l(r_l - 1)$; $r' \leftarrow r' - l(r'_l - 1)$

9   **for** $c \leftarrow 1$ **to** k **do**

10   **if** $\mathsf{childrenlabeled}(T_p, v, (c - 1)k + r_l)$ **and**
            $\mathsf{childrenlabeled}(T_{p'}, v', (c - 1)k + r'_l)$ **then**

11                 $v_l \leftarrow \mathsf{labeledchild}(T_p, v, (c - 1)k + r_l)$

12                 $v'_l \leftarrow \mathsf{labeledchild}(T_{p'}, v', (c - 1)k + r'_l)$

13                 $ooreport(v_l, v'_l, r, r', c_0 + (c - 1)l, l)$

---

all the edges are bidirectional (which may be appropriate for pedestrian traversals), and no bridges or tunnels (which are usually very few and could be treated as exceptions).

As the resulting map is planar, we can represent it with the techniques of Section 9.4. A city with n intersections and e street segments can then be represented in just $2(n + e) + o(n)$ bits. For example, the street graph of Greater London had $n \approx 85,000$ intersections and $e \approx 115,000$ segments in 2010, thus we could represent the street topology within about 50 kilobytes. A classical representation, instead, would use $n + 2e$ words, that is, close to 1.2 megabytes in a 32-bit architecture.

In addition, we must store the coordinates of the intersections. If we use a precision of 10 meters, then each coordinate fits in 13 bits (because the city area fits within a square of 60×45 kilometers). This adds almost 270 kilobytes (note that this is the heaviest part in our compressed representation but only a minor increase for a classical representation).

Consider the problem of finding a path in the city from our current location (say, in an intersection node v) toward another intersection u with coordinates (x, y). This can be solved with classical single-source shortest-path algorithms, which in the particular case of planar graphs can be solved in $\mathcal{O}(n)$ worst-case time. However, those algorithms require storing significant extra data per node during their execution, which we wish to avoid, and do not take advantage of the fact that nodes have coordinates in the plane. In

---

Algorithm 9.17: Subject-object join on RDF graphs using k^2-trees.

---

1 **Proc** $subject\text{-}object(T_p, T_{p'}, s, o)$

    Input : Binary relations B_p and $B_{p'}$ of $N \times N$ with $N = k^{\lceil \log_k \max(n, \sigma) \rceil}$ (seen as
             k^2trees T_p and $T_{p'}$ with more than zero pairs), subject s and object o.
    Output: Outputs matches X for join query $(s, p, ?X)$ and $(?X, p', o)$.

2    $soreport(\mathsf{root}(T_p), \mathsf{root}(T_{p'}), s, o, 1, N)$

3 **Proc** $soreport(v, v', r, c, g_0, t)$

    Input : Nonempty submatrices $M[1, t][1, t]$ and $M'[1, t][1, t]$ of B_p and $B_{p'}$,
             corresponding to k^2-tree nodes v and v', starting at column g_0 of B_p
             and row g_0 of $B_{p'}$, local row r of B_p and column c of $B_{p'}$ to intersect.
    Output: Outputs the offsets $g_0 - 1 + g$ such that $M[r, g] = M'[g, c] = 1$.

4   **if** $t = 1$ **then** output g_0

5   **else**

6        $l \leftarrow t/k$

7        $r_l \leftarrow \lceil r/l \rceil; c_l \leftarrow \lceil c/l \rceil$

8        $r \leftarrow r - l(r_l - 1); c \leftarrow c - l(c_l - 1)$

9   **for** $g \leftarrow 1$ **to** k **do**

10   **if** childrenlabeled$(T_p, v, (g - 1)k + r_l)$ **and**
                childrenlabeled$(T_{p'}, v', (c_l - 1)k + g)$ **then**

11              $v_l \leftarrow$ labeledchild$(T_p, v, (g - 1)k + r_l)$

12              $v'_l \leftarrow$ labeledchild$(T_{p'}, v', (c_l - 1)k + g)$

13              $soreport(v_l, v'_l, r, c, g_0 + (g - 1)l, l)$

---

an online scenario, where a route is required while driving or walking, it is important to find a solution fast, even if it is not optimal.

A reasonable heuristic that uses no extra space is to start from v and repeatedly move toward the neighbor that most reduces the distance to u. It is actually better to maximize the ratio between the reduction in distance toward u and the length of the traversed segment. That is, if we are at a node v and move toward a neighbor v', then the relative benefit is $\frac{d(u,v) - d(u,v')}{d(v,v')}$. We choose the neighbor v' that maximizes this benefit. Algorithm 9.18 implements this strategy.

This algorithm does not guarantee to find the optimal path from v to u, but it can be used to obtain a reasonable path. The optimal algorithm can be run when the greedy algorithm does not find a satisfactory solution (say, when its cost is higher than $d(v, u)$ by a given factor). The algorithm, however, is rather weak in the sense that it stalls as soon as it needs to move away from the target in order to reach it (even if we let it move away, the algorithm may then return to the previous closer point, falling in a loop).

An even faster strategy, which may produce worse results, is to move toward the first neighbor that reduces the distance. This is called a *first-fit* strategy, as opposed to the *best-fit* one we have described.

Algorithm 9.18: Routing on a planar graph through the locally maximum benefit path. With $d(\cdot, \cdot)$ we denote the Euclidean distance.

Input : Planar graph G of nodes with coordinates, nodes v and u.

Output: Outputs a greedy path from v to u using the locally maximum benefit, stopping at u or when no move gives a positive benefit.

---

1 **while** $v \neq u$ **do**
2     $m \leftarrow 0$
3   **for** $i \leftarrow 1$ **to** $\text{degree}(G, v)$ **do**
4        $v' \leftarrow \text{neigh}(G, v, i)$
5        $b \leftarrow (d(v, u) - d(v', u))/d(v, v')$
6   **if** $b > m$ **then**
7           $m \leftarrow b; bv \leftarrow v'$

8   **if** $m = 0$ **then return**
9   **output** bv
10    $v \leftarrow bv$

Example 9.30 *Figure 9.20 shows the planar graph corresponding approximately to the Old Town of Stockholm. We have marked nodes v_i (gray) and u (black) and the paths (black) that would be followed by the greedy algorithm. The path from v_1 does not reach u, as it gets stuck at the hatched node t, from where every move drives one away from u. The path from v_2 does not even leave the source node, because the first move leads to a position slightly farther from u. The path from v_3 reaches u and is almost optimal.*

In dashed lines we show the result of the first-fit strategy, assuming we find the first neighbor in CCW order that improves our current position, and that in the beginning we start from the exterior face. From v_1 this finds a comparable strategy but requires computing 9 distances to u instead of the 21 computed by the best-first strategy. From v_2, it is equally helpless. For v_3 the first-fit strategy fails, whereas the best-fit one had found a good solution.

We will exploit the planar nature of the graph to apply a stronger heuristic. The idea is as follows. We draw an imaginary segment $\overline{uv}$ from u to v. Now we start traversing from v, along the face F from where the segment reaches v. We arbitrarily choose an orientation (CW or CCW) and traverse the internal contour of F from v until reaching an edge (s, t) that intersects the segment $\overline{uv}$. When this happens, we stay at the same source node s of the segment, but switch to the other face where (s, t) lies, and continue the traversal from there without crossing the segment.

This simple procedure is guaranteed to reach u. Just like the previous one, it does not need any extra memory. Algorithm 9.19 shows it in detail. To traverse the face we make use of the procedure $findneigh$ of Algorithm 9.12. Our current node in the face is s and the next one is t. To advance, $j \leftarrow findneigh(s, t)$ indicates that s is the jth neighbor of t, therefore the $(j + 1)$th neighbor of t follows it in CCW order. This corresponds to the CW traversal of the face (recall the discussion around Figure 9.12). When we detect that

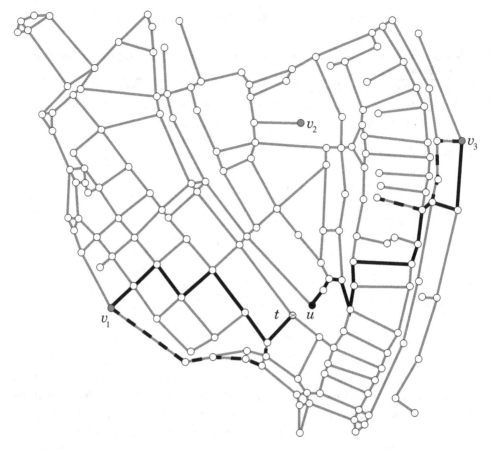

Figure 9.20. Greedy traversals on a street graph, from the gray nodes to the black one. The best-fit strategy is drawn as a black solid path, whereas the first-fit strategy is shown with a dashed path.

Algorithm 9.19: Routing on a planar graph through face traversals. We omit some details about geometry. We measure angles $_s\angle_u^{t'}$ in radians, as positive angles in CCW direction from u to t' around s. We assume two segments sharing an extreme node do not intersect.

Input : Planar graph G of nodes with coordinates, and nodes v and u.
Output: Outputs a path from v to u using CW face traversal.

1   $s \leftarrow v$
2   $a \leftarrow 2\pi$ (maximum positive angle, in CCW direction)
3   **for** $j \leftarrow 1$ **to** degree(G, v) **do**
4      $t' \leftarrow$ neigh(G, s, j)
5   **if** $_s\angle_u^{t'} < a$ **then**
6         $a \leftarrow {_s\angle_u^{t'}}$
7         $t \leftarrow t'$

8   **while** $s \neq u$ **do**
9   **while** $\overline{st}$ intersects $\overline{uv}$ **do**
10         $j \leftarrow (j \bmod$ degree$(G, t)) + 1$
11         $t \leftarrow$ neigh(G, s, j)
12   **output** t
13      $j \leftarrow (findneigh(G, s, t) \bmod$ degree$(G, t)) + 1$ (Algorithm 9.12)
14      $s \leftarrow t$
15      $t \leftarrow$ neigh(G, s, j)

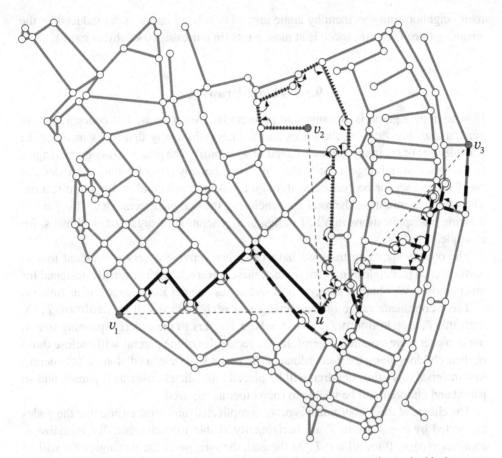

Figure 9.21. Face-based traversals on a street graph, from the gray nodes to the black one. The path from each gray node v_i is shown with a different style. Circular arrows show how the algorithm chooses the next edge, avoiding those that cross the segment (v_i, u) (those segments are shown with dashed lines).

the segment $\overline{st}$ intersects $\overline{uv}$, we switch to the neighboring face by simply increasing j without changing s.

Example 9.31 *Figure 9.21 shows how the same traversals of Example 9.30 are solved with this second algorithm, in thick lines of different type for the three source points. The algorithm always finds a solution, albeit not necessarily the optimal one. The path found from v_1 is indeed optimal. The paths from v_2 and v_3 reach some dead ends and trace back, but are reasonably good (we could remove those loops if we maintained the path instead of immediately reporting and forgetting the nodes).*

A potential problem for our face traversal is that the orderly spanning tree construction algorithm may alter the mapping of the streets to the plane in Steps 2^- and 2^+. As a consequence, a CCW traversal of the neighbors of the affected nodes may not correspond to an actual CCW traversal. Since this step does not affect many nodes and we know the positions of the intersections in the plane, a solution is to mark the nodes whose neighbor order has been affected by these steps, and in those cases traverse all their neighbors and sort them by angle instead of relying on the order induced by the spanning tree. The extra space is at most n bits (in our case, 10 kilobytes more).

9.5.4 Planar Drawings

How to draw a graph is an important problem in several areas. The concept is more general than just drawing the nodes and the edges in a way that looks nice. Let us consider one of the many variants, called *two-visibility*. The goal is to assign rectangles to the nodes, with integer coordinates, in a way that any pair of connected nodes can "see" each other (or be connected through a link) in horizontal or vertical direction. The goal is to minimize the total area enclosing the assigned rectangles. This kind of drawing has applications in VLSI design and generation of organizational maps, for example.

The orderly spanning trees we have described provide a very convenient tool to perform such rectangle alignment (in fact, these traversals were originally designed for this purpose). We obtain a placement of rectangles on an $n \times n$ integer grid as follows.

The x-coordinate range of the rectangle of each node v will be [leafrank(T, v), leafrank(T, v) + leafnum(T, v) − 1], where T refers to the orderly spanning tree in our compact representation. Therefore, the rectangles of the parents will enclose those of their children along the x-coordinate. The nodes will be placed along a CCW depth-first traversal of T, thus children will be placed immediately over their parent, and so parent and children will be visible to each other as required.

The choice of the y-coordinate is more complicated, and must ensure that the nodes connected by edges not in T are horizontally visible to each other. We initialize y-counters $y(v) \leftarrow 0$ for all $v \in T$. At the end, the y-range of the rectangle of v will be [$y(\text{parent}(T, v)) + 1, y(v)$], and for the root [$1, y(\text{root}(T))$]. As we traverse T in CCW depth-first order, we initialize $h \leftarrow y(\text{parent}(T, v))$ and, for each forward edge (v, u) (that is, not in T and pointing to a node that is after v in the traversal) in CW order, we increase h and set $y(u) \leftarrow \max(y(u), h)$, which ensures that u will reach a y-coordinate high enough to horizontally see v. The final value of $y(v)$ is $\max(y(\text{parent}(T, v)) + 1, y(v), h)$, which accounts respectively for starting after its parent, being tall enough to see its backward neighbors, and being tall enough to see its forward neighbors. The process is described in Algorithm 9.20.

Example 9.32 *Figure 9.22 shows the result of applying the algorithm on the graph of Figure 9.11. We show in gray that every pair of connected nodes can see each other. Let us follow a few steps.*

We start with the root 1, setting $y[1] \leftarrow 1$. Then its child 2, invoked with $y = 1$, sets $y[4] \leftarrow 2$, $y[5] \leftarrow 3$, and $y[6] \leftarrow 4$ for its forward neighbors, finally setting its definitive value at $y[2] \leftarrow \max(1, 0, 4) = 4$. Now node 3, the only child of 2, is invoked with $y = 4$. It sets $y[6] \leftarrow \max(4, 5) = 5$ for its only forward neighbor, and sets its definitive value at $y[3] \leftarrow \max(5, 0, 5) = 5$. Now, when we reach node 4, the second child of 1 and invoked with $y = 1$, $y[4] = 2$ is large enough to see its backward neighbor 2. It also sets $y[13] \leftarrow 2$ for its only forward neighbor, and finally sets $y[4] \leftarrow \max(2, 2, 2) = 2$.

Algorithm 9.20: Two-visibility drawing of a planar graph.

Input : Planar graph G of n nodes (seen as its orderly spanning tree T and the associated compact representation).

Output: Outputs one rectangle per node v, satisfying two-visibility.

1 Allocate array $y[1, n]$ of integers in $[1, n]$
2 **for** $v \leftarrow 1$ **to** n **do** $y[v] \leftarrow 0$
3 $traverse(1, 0)$
4 Free $y[1, n]$

5 **Proc** $traverse(v, y)$

   Input : Node v of G and the maximum y-coordinate of its parent, y.
   Output: Outputs one rectangle per node in the subtree of v, satisfying two-visibility.

6     $f \leftarrow forward(G, v)$ (Algorithm 9.13)
7     $h \leftarrow y$
8   **for** $j \leftarrow$ degree(G, v) **downto** degree$(G, v) - f + 1$ **do**
9        $h \leftarrow h + 1$
10       $u \leftarrow$ neigh(G, v, j)
11       $y[u] \leftarrow \max(y[u], h)$
12     $y[v] \leftarrow \max(y + 1, y[v], h)$
13     $v_\mathsf{p} \leftarrow$ preorderselect(T, v)
14     $x_1 \leftarrow$ leafrank(T, v_p)
15     $x_2 \leftarrow x_1 +$ leafnum$(T, v_\mathsf{p}) - 1$
16   **output** $(v, [x_1, x_2] \times [y + 1, y[v]])$
17   **for** $j \leftarrow 1$ **to** children(T, v_p) **do**
18       $traverse(\text{preorder}(T, \text{child}(T, v_\mathsf{p}, j)), y[v])$

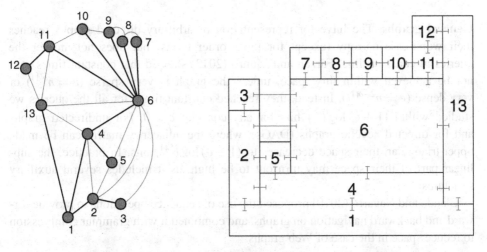

Figure 9.22. The two-visibility drawing of our example graph.

Its child, 5, is then invoked with y = 2. It has already y[5] = 3, which was set to ensure that it can see its backward neighbor 2. Now it sets y[6] ← max(5, 3) = 5, so y[6] is not changed. Thus its final value is settled as y[5] ← max(3, 3, 3) = 3. Now 6, the second child of 4, is invoked with y = 2, but it already has y[6] = 5 to ensure that it sees its backward neighbors 5, 2, and 3. It sets y[13] ← max(2, 3) = 3 to ensure that 13 will see it, then its value stays at y[6] ← max(3, 5, 3) = 5, and so on.

9.6 Summary

General directed and undirected graphs of n nodes and e edges can be encoded in space close to their worst-case entropy while supporting forward and backward navigation, plus adjacency and degree queries, in $\mathcal{O}(\log \log n)$ time per datum retrieved. Clustered graphs can be encoded within less space while supporting efficient navigation in practice, although most query times have no worst-case guarantees. K-page graphs can be encoded using $\mathcal{O}(kn)$ or $\mathcal{O}(e \log k)$ bits, which is proportional to their worst-case entropy. Planar graphs, where $e < 3n$, can be encoded in $\mathcal{O}(e)$ bits while supporting queries in $\mathcal{O}(\log \log n)$ time: one can use $2(n + e) + o(n) < 4e + o(e)$ bits, while the entropy is near $3.58e$. For the particular case of triangulations, the space can be reduced to $2e + o(n)$ bits, while the entropy is about $1.08e$. All the constructions take linear time, $\mathcal{O}(n + e)$, and $\mathcal{O}(n + e)$ words of extra space. Graphs can be extended to represent binary relations and grids (Chapter 10).

9.7 Bibliographic Notes

Graph theory is a large area in Discrete Mathematics and Computer Science. Several books focus on its algorithmic and data structuring aspects (Deo, 2004; Agnarsson and Greenlaw, 2006; Benjamin *et al.*, 2015).

General graphs. The bitvector representation of arbitrary directed graphs reaches their worst-case entropy (except for lower-order terms) but does not answer the queries in constant time. Farzan and Munro (2013) showed that constant times cannot be achieved within this space, unless the graph is very sparse ($e = n^{o(1)}$) or very dense ($e = n^{2-o(1)}$). Instead, they reached constant times for all the queries we studied within $(1 + \epsilon) \log \binom{n^2}{e}$ bits for any constant $\epsilon > 0$. For undirected graphs and for directed acyclic graphs (DAGs), where the adjacency matrix can be made upper-triangular, their space decreases to $(1 + \epsilon) \log \binom{\binom{n}{2}}{e}$ bits. In practice, the sublinear part of their space may turn out to be high, as it includes several auxiliary structures.

Claude and Navarro (2010) proposed the use of sequence operations to provide forward and backward navigation on graphs, and combined it with grammar compression to reduce space in the case of Web graphs.

Clustered graphs. The k^2-tree was introduced by Brisaboa *et al.* (2014) for the compact representation of Web graphs. A combination with a partition of the Web graph into domains made it even smaller and faster (Claude and Ladra, 2011). While in general the URL lexicographic ordering produces a good clustering of Web graphs, other orderings can obtain better results. A combination of the k^2-tree with those better clusterings (Hernández and Navarro, 2014) obtained 1–2 bits per edge on typical Web crawls.

Several other techniques are used to compress Web graphs, which exploit the clustering mostly to design efficient variable-length codes to compress the adjacency lists. An important project in this area is the WebGraph framework, hosted at http://webgraph.di.unimi.it, which contains state-of-the art compressed data structures and large test graphs. Many of the current best results have been derived from this project (Boldi and Vigna, 2004, 2005; Boldi *et al.*, 2009, 2011), but there are also some competitive alternatives (Apostolico and Drovandi, 2009; Grabowski and Bieniecki, 2014). While many of those techniques use less space than the k^2-tree, they handle only **neigh** queries. The ability of the k^2-tree to handle **rneigh** queries symmetrically makes it useful for various problems that require this sort of backward traversal. Backward traversal can also be enabled with those other techniques by representing the transposed graph as well, but then their space is not so competitive.

Social networks are much less compressible than Web graphs, but still it is possible to reach 8–13 bits per edge. In this case, k^2-trees combined with clustering methods (Hernández and Navarro, 2014) produce again very compact representations, among various other competitive alternatives (Chierichetti *et al.*, 2009; Maserrat and Pei, 2010; Boldi *et al.*, 2011; Claude and Ladra, 2011; Grabowski and Bieniecki, 2014). Since social networks do not have a natural node ordering like URLs, finding a good ordering is crucial. Clustering algorithms that have worked well for this problem are based on the use of shingles (Gibson *et al.*, 2005; Buehrer and Chellapilla, 2008), but clustering of graphs is a much broader topic (Schaeffer, 2007).

The in-place radix sort used for the k^2-tree construction is given as an exercise in various textbooks. Duvanenko (2009) describes it in detail.

K-page graphs. Bernhart and Kainen (1979) bounded the maximum number of edges in a k-page graph. The bound on the number of k-page graphs is from Gavoille and Hanusse (2008). Chung *et al.* (1987) proved the NP-completeness of embedding a graph into the least possible number of pages and reviewed related results. Mitchell (1979) gave a simplified linear-time embedding for one-page graphs.

Jacobson (1989) gave the first queryable representation for k-page graphs, using $9kn$ bits. This was improved by Munro and Raman (2001), whose representation is the one we show in the chapter. It uses $2(kn + e)$ bits and carries out **degree** and **adj** in $\mathcal{O}(k)$ time as well as **neigh**(G, v) in $\mathcal{O}(k + \textbf{degree}(G, v))$ time. Those times rely on constant-time queries on balanced parentheses. In our case those times are multiplied by $\mathcal{O}(\log \log n)$ to account for the practical representations of parenthesis sequences given in Chapter 7.

The representation we described based on sequences S and B_* is analogous to that of Gavoille and Hanusse (2008). They obtain the same $2e(2 + \log k)$ bits and also consider the case of multiple edges, disconnected graphs, and self-loops (v, v).

Planar graphs. The bounds on the number of planar graphs are taken from Boni-chon *et al.* (2006), yielding entropy 4.76n to 4.91n, and Tutte (1963, Eq. 5.1), yield-ing entropy 3.58e for planar maps. The exact entropy of planar graphs is unknown (Liskovets and Walsh, 1987).

Since any planar graph can be embedded in 4 pages, the k-page representation of Munro and Raman (2001) yields $8n + 2e$ bits for representing planar graphs. Yan-nakakis (1989) gave a (rather involved) linear-time algorithm to embed a planar graph in 4 pages and also showed that some planar graphs effectively need 4 pages.

We have omitted this construction in favor of the more efficient encodings obtained by canonical orderings. The concept of a canonical ordering was introduced for tri-angular graphs (de Fraysseix *et al.*, 1990) and then extended to triconnected graphs (Kant, 1996). Chuang *et al.* (1998) used it to generate canonical spanning trees, and Chiang *et al.* (2005) generalized them to orderly spanning trees, which can be built for any planar graph, triconnected or not. The latter are the ones we use in the chapter, although the construction is much simpler for triconnected graphs. The construction of the orderly spanning tree requires the planar graph to already have a mapping into the plane, that is, that its faces are identified (although the mapping can be changed by the spanning tree construction). Such an initial mapping can be found as a by-product of a planarity test algorithm. Hopcroft and Tarjan (1974) found the first of those algo-rithms; those of Boyer and Myrvold (2004) and de Fraysseix *et al.* (2006) are state of the art. Implementations are readily available, for example, in https://code.google.com/p/planarity.

Chiang *et al.* (2005) proposed the idea we describe for representing planar graphs based on orderly spanning trees in $2(n + e)$ bits. The previous work by Chuang *et al.* (1998) used more than $\frac{5}{3}e + 5n$ bits, which since $e \leq 3n$ is at least $2e + 4n$ (if the oper-ation **degree** is not supported, they use $\frac{4}{3}e + 5n \geq 2e + 3n$ bits). The techniques of Chuang *et al.* (1998) are not very different from the ones we presented. The difference is that, lacking the orderly spanning trees, they had to add fictitious edges to the graph to make it triconnected so as to use canonical spanning trees (on triconnected planar graphs, they reach $2(n + e)$ bits). In both cases they show how to handle multiple edges and other extensions, at some extra cost in the bit count.

Since we assume planar graphs are connected, those $2(n + e)$ bits are at most $4e$, which is close to Tutte's lower bound of 3.58e bits to represent a planar map with-out any query support (but this technique can represent any planar graph, not any pla-nar map). That lower bound was first matched with encodings that did not support queries (Keeler and Westbrook, 1995). Recently, Blelloch and Farzan (2010) matched it with structures using $o(n)$ bits over the entropy and supporting the queries we have considered in constant time. They also showed how to encode planar graphs (not pla-nar maps) within their worst-case entropy plus $o(n)$ bits, with constant query time, even when the precise entropy is not known. Those data structures are too complex to be presented in the chapter, and it is not clear if an implementation would be practical.

Triangulations. The bound on the number of planar triangulations, yielding entropy around 1.08e, is from Tutte (1962, Eq. 5.11).

A canonical ordering is simpler to obtain for triangulations than for general planar graphs. Moreover, one can cover all the edges with 3 spanning trees, so that the children and parents of each node v enumerate **neigh**(G, v) in **ccw** order. Those spanning trees are called realizers and date back to Schnyder (1990), who gave the first linear-time construction (see the excellent survey by Miura *et al.* (2005)). Yamanaka and Nakano (2010) proposed the $2e$-bit representation of triangulations we describe, improving upon previous similar ideas that obtained $n + 2e$ bits (Chiang *et al.*, 2005; Chuang *et al.*, 1998).

The lower bound of around $1.08e$ bits was first matched with encodings that did not support queries (He *et al.*, 2000), but later Castelli Aleardi *et al.* (2008) managed to encode triangulations within the entropy space plus $o(n)$ bits while supporting queries. They also obtained optimal space and time on triconnected graphs, which have worst-case entropy $2e$ (Tutte, 1963, Eq. 8.17). Their encoding, again, is too complex to be described in the chapter.

Extensions. Various other graph families of interest have been studied for efficient encoding. An important one is that of *separable graphs*, studied by Blandford *et al.* (2003). Those graphs can be separated into two nonempty parts of $\Theta(n)$ nodes by removing $\mathcal{O}(n^\epsilon)$ nodes from V, for a constant $0 < \epsilon < 1$. Recursively, those two parts must be separable as well (n then accounts for the size of the subgraphs). Various important graph families have small separators, for example, planar graphs fit with $\epsilon = 1/2$ and 3-dimensional meshes with $\epsilon = 2/3$.

Blandford *et al.* show that separable graphs have $\mathcal{O}(n)$ edges, and they present $\mathcal{O}(n)$-bit structures that support our queries in constant time. The main idea is to recursively partition the graph, renumbering the nodes in each partition, and using differential encoding for the adjacency lists. One problem with this approach is that it is not always easy to find the separators. Some approximations and heuristics work for general graphs, with better guarantees for some classes of graphs.

They show experimentally that real-life graphs also tend to have small separators, including Web graphs, meshes, circuits, street maps, and routing graphs. On those, they obtain around 4–6 bits per edge. In a more theoretical derivative, Blelloch and Farzan (2010) showed how to match the worst-case entropy of any chosen family of separable graphs, plus $o(n)$ bits. The key idea is to encode the set of all the small graphs up to a certain size using an identifier for each, and to use small precomputed tables to retrieve and query the graph represented by each identifier.

Some research also has been done on representing *partial orders*, which are transitively closed DAGs (that is, if $(x, y) \in E$ and $(y, z) \in E$, then $(x, z) \in E$). This can be seen as storing any DAG with the requirement of determining in constant time if one node is reachable from another. The so-called *width k* of the partial order (maximum number of nodes without order relation between any of them) determines how well it can be compressed: there are $n!\, 4^{n(k-1)}\, n^{\mathcal{O}(1)}$ such partial orders, so the worst-case entropy is $2kn + n \log n - \mathcal{O}(n)$ (Brightwell and Goodall, 1996). On the other hand, some representations using $2kn + (1 + \epsilon)n \log n + o(kn)$ bits solve reachability queries in constant time and several other queries in time $\mathcal{O}(k)$ (Farzan and Fischer, 2011). While partial orders may have small k depending on the application, a partial order chosen uniformly at random has $k = n/2 + o(n)$ with high probability (Kleitman and Rothschild, 1975). In such cases, their structure needs $n^2 + o(n^2)$ bits. The structure by Munro and Nicholson (2015), instead, always takes the asymptotically optimal $n^2/4 + o(n^2)$ bits and solves reachability queries in constant time. They also show how to solve **neigh** and **rneigh** queries optimally and extend their structure to support reachability queries on arbitrary directed graphs.

Other classes that have received some attention are bounded-genus graphs (Lu, 2002), which generalize planar graphs to those that can be embedded in more complex topological surfaces (the plane has genus zero); labeled graphs, which have labels on the edges or on the nodes (Barbay *et al.*, 2012; Ferragina *et al.*, 2015); graphs where adjacency can be determined with compact labeling schemes (Kannan *et al.*, 1992), which include graphs with limited arboricity, interval graphs, and c-decomposable graphs; and so on. A recent practical proposal is GLOUDS (Fischer and Peters, 2016), which extends the LOUDS format (Section 8.1) with extra information to represent trees that have a few extra edges; they report good results for $e \leq 5n$.

Binary relations and labeled graphs. The representation we introduce for binary relations with labels is based on that of Barbay *et al.* (2013), where many powerful operations are studied (more than those considered here). This is related to other previous theoretical proposals (Barbay *et al.*, 2007, 2011), which were also used to obtain results on labeled planar graphs (Barbay *et al.*, 2012).

RDF. The RDF standard is available at http://www.w3.org/RDF, and SPARQL is described at http://www.w3.org/TR/rdf-sparql-query. Compressed representations of RDF have been studied for some time (Fernández *et al.*, 2013), and the use of k^2-trees has been pursued recently (Álvarez-García *et al.*, 2015). Some extensions of k^2-trees to handle many predicates have also been studied (Álvarez-García *et al.*, 2014). The solution we described is a simplification of the proposal of Álvarez-García *et al.* (2015) based on "vertical partitioning" (i.e., use one relation per predicate). Other RDF storage systems such as *MonetDB* (http://www.monetdb.org), *RDF-3X* (http://code.google .com/p/rdf3x) or *Hexastore* (Weiss *et al.*, 2008) use much more space and are not much faster (sometimes they are much slower). In exchange, they offer further functionality, especially dynamism.

Street maps. The size of the graph of streets in London was obtained from Masucci *et al.* (2013). Shortest path algorithms can be run in linear time on planar graphs (Henzinger *et al.*, 1997), but as explained, they require storing a fair amount of extra data. The algorithm to traverse the faces toward the objective is called "Face-2" by Bose *et al.* (2001) and simplifies a previous algorithm by Kranakis *et al.* (1999) that has better guarantees but usually performs worse. These algorithms are related to another routing problem, where wireless networks on a region can connect when they are sufficiently close, and thus one looks for a distributed routing protocol that guarantees delivery. In this case, each node knows only its neighbors and the information on the network is not centralized. A related model, when the network is fixed, is that each node stores the next neighbor of the optimal path toward every other node. Then a compact representation uses only $8n + o(n)$ bits per node and can compute the next hop in $\mathcal{O}(\log^{2+\epsilon} n)$ time for any constant $\epsilon > 0$ (Gavoille and Hanusse, 1999). Lu (2010) reduced this space to $7.181n + o(n)$ bits by using orderly spanning trees.

Graph drawing. Planar graph drawing is a wide research topic, because planar graphs are used to represent many different situations such as VLSI design, software engineering and modeling tools, visual languages, algorithm animation, games, etc. There are whole books on the topic (Nishizeki and Rahman, 2004). Canonical orderings were originally introduced for the purpose of drawing planar graphs (de Fraysseix *et al.*, 1990; Schnyder, 1990; Kant, 1996; Miura *et al.*, 2005).

Other types of drawings are appropriate depending on what the graph represents. Two-visibility drawing applies in particular to VLSI design, to print components with only horizontal and vertical wires. The algorithm we describe is simplified from that in Chiang *et al.* (2005), who prove that a grid of $(n - 1) \times \lfloor \frac{2n+1}{3} \rfloor$ points is sufficient for holding the drawing generated by the algorithm, and that this is optimal in the worst case. Canonical orderings have also been used for other types of planar graph drawings such as floor planning (Liao *et al.*, 2003) and segment visibility (Zhang and He, 2005).

Bibliography

Agnarsson, G. and Greenlaw, R. (2006). *Graph Theory: Modeling, Applications, and Algorithms.* Pearson.

Álvarez-García, S., Brisaboa, N. R., de Bernardo, G., and Navarro, G. (2014). Interleaved k^2-tree: Indexing and navigating ternary relations. In *Proc. 24th Data Compression Conference (DCC)*, pages 342–351.

Álvarez-García, S., Brisaboa, N. R., Fernández, J., Martínez-Prieto, M., and Navarro, G. (2015). Compressed vertical partitioning for efficient RDF management. *Knowledge and Information Systems*, **44**(2), 439–474.

Apostolico, A. and Drovandi, G. (2009). Graph compression by BFS. *Algorithms*, **2**(3), 1031–1044.

Barbay, J., Golynski, A., Munro, J. I., and Rao, S. S. (2007). Adaptive searching in succinctly encoded binary relations and tree-structured documents. *Theoretical Computer Science*, **387**(3), 284–297.

Barbay, J., He, M., Munro, J. I., and Rao, S. S. (2011). Succinct indexes for strings, binary relations and multilabeled trees. *ACM Transactions on Algorithms*, **7**(4), article 52.

Barbay, J., Castelli Aleardi, L., He, M., and Munro, J. I. (2012). Succinct representation of labeled graphs. *Algorithmica*, **62**(1-2), 224–257.

Barbay, J., Claude, F., and Navarro, G. (2013). Compact binary relation representations with rich functionality. *Information and Computation*, **232**, 19–37.

Benjamin, A., Chartrand, G., and Zhang, P. (2015). *The Fascinating World of Graph Theory.* Princeton University Press.

Bernhart, F. and Kainen, P. C. (1979). The book thickness of a graph. *Journal of Combinatorial Theory, Series B*, **27**, 320–331.

Blandford, D. K., Blelloch, G. E., and Kash, I. A. (2003). Compact representations of separable graphs. In *Proc. 14th Annual ACM-SIAM Symposium on Discrete Algorithms (SODA)*, pages 679–688.

Blelloch, G. E. and Farzan, A. (2010). Succinct representations of separable graphs. In *Proc. 21st Annual Symposium on Combinatorial Pattern Matching (CPM)*, LNCS 6129, pages 138–150.

Boldi, P. and Vigna, S. (2004). The WebGraph framework I: Compression techniques. In *Proc. 13th International Conference on World Wide Web (WWW)*, pages 595–602.

Boldi, P. and Vigna, S. (2005). Codes for the World Wide Web. *Internet Mathematics*, **2**(4), 407–429.

Boldi, P., Santini, M., and Vigna, S. (2009). Permuting Web and social graphs. *Internet Mathematics*, **6**(3), 257–283.

Boldi, P., Rosa, M., Santini, M., and Vigna, S. (2011). Layered label propagation: A multiresolution coordinate-free ordering for compressing social networks. In *Proc. 20th International Conference on World Wide Web (WWW)*, pages 587–596.

Bonichon, N., Gavoille, C., Hanusse, N., Poulalhon, D., and Schaeffer, G. (2006). Planar graphs, via well-orderly maps and trees. *Graphs and Combinatorics*, **22**(2), 185–202.

Bose, P., Morin, P., Stojmenovic, I., and Urrutia, J. (2001). Routing with guaranteed delivery in ad hoc wireless networks. *Wireless Networks*, **7**(6), 609–616.

Boyer, J. M. and Myrvold, W. J. (2004). On the cutting edge: Simplified $O(n)$ planarity by edge addition. *Journal of Graph Algorithms and Applications*, **8**(3), 241–273.

Brightwell, G. and Goodall, S. (1996). The number of partial orders of fixed width. *Order*, **13**(4), 315–337.

Brisaboa, N. R., Ladra, S., and Navarro, G. (2014). Compact representation of Web graphs with extended functionality. *Information Systems*, **39**(1), 152–174.

Buehrer, G. and Chellapilla, K. (2008). A scalable pattern mining approach to Web graph compression with communities. In *Proc. 1st International Conference on Web Search and Web Data Mining (WSDM)*, pages 95–106.

Castelli Aleardi, L., Devillers, O., and Schaeffer, G. (2008). Succinct representations of planar maps. *Theoretical Computer Science*, **408**(2-3), 174–187.

Chiang, Y. T., Lin, C. C., and Lu, H.-I. (2005). Orderly spanning trees with applications. *SIAM Journal on Computing*, **34**(4), 924–945.

Chierichetti, F., Kumar, R., Lattanzi, S., Mitzenmacher, M., Panconesi, A., and Raghavan, P. (2009). On compressing social networks. In *Proc. 15th ACM International Conference on Knowledge Discovery and Data Mining (SIGKDD)*, pages 219–228.

Chuang, R. C.-N., Garg, A., He, X., Kao, M.-Y., and Lu, H.-I. (1998). Compact encodings of planar graphs via canonical orderings and multiple parentheses. In *Proc. 25th International Colloquium on Automata, Languages and Programming (ICALP)*, LNCS 1443, pages 118–129.

Chung, F. R. K., Leighton, F. T., and Rosenberg, A. L. (1987). Embedding graphs in books: A layout problem with applications to VLSI design. *SIAM Journal on Algebraic and Discrete Methods*, **8**(1), 33–58.

Claude, F. and Ladra, S. (2011). Practical representations for Web and social graphs. In *Proc. 20th ACM Conference on Information and Knowledge Management (CIKM)*, pages 1185–1190.

Claude, F. and Navarro, G. (2010). Extended compact Web graph representations. In T. Elomaa, H. Mannila, and P. Orponen, editors, *Algorithms and Applications (Ukkonen Festschrift)*, LNCS 6060, pages 77–91. Springer.

de Fraysseix, H., Pach, J., and Pollack, R. (1990). How to draw a planar graph on a grid. *Combinatorica*, **10**(1), 41–51.

de Fraysseix, H., Ossona de Mendez, P., and Rosenstiehl, P. (2006). Trémaux trees and planarity. *International Journal of Foundations of Computer Science*, **17**(5), 1017–1030.

Deo, N. (2004). *Graph Theory with Applications to Engineering and Computer Science*. Prentice-Hall of India.

Duvanenko, V. J. (2009). In-place hybrid N-bit-radix sort. *Dr. Dobb's Journal*. November.

Farzan, A. and Fischer, J. (2011). Compact representation of posets. In *Proc. 22nd International Symposium on Algorithms and Computation (ISAAC)*, LNCS 7074, pages 302–311.

Farzan, A. and Munro, J. I. (2013). Succinct encoding of arbitrary graphs. *Theoretical Computer Science*, **513**, 38–52.

Fernández, J. D., Martínez-Prieto, M. A., Gutiérrez, C., Polleres, A., and Arias, M. (2013). Binary RDF representation for publication and exchange (HDT). *Journal of Web Semantics*, **19**, 22–41.

Ferragina, P., Piccinno, F., and Venturini, R. (2015). Compressed indexes for string searching in labeled graphs. In *Proc. 24th International Conference on World Wide Web (WWW)*, pages 322–332.

Fischer, J. and Peters, D. (2016). GLOUDS: Representing tree-like graphs. *Journal of Discrete Algorithms*, **36**, 39–49.

Gavoille, C. and Hanusse, N. (1999). Compact routing tables for graphs of bounded genus. In *Proc. 26th International Colloquium on Automata, Languages and Programming (ICALP)*, LNCS 1644, pages 351–360.

Gavoille, C. and Hanusse, N. (2008). On compact encoding of pagenumber. *Discrete Mathematics and Theoretical Computer Science*, **10**(3), 23–24.

Gibson, D., Kumar, R., and Tomkins, A. (2005). Discovering large dense subgraphs in massive graphs. In *Proc. 31st International Conference on Very Large Data Bases (VLDB)*, pages 721–732.

Grabowski, S. and Bieniecki, W. (2014). Tight and simple Web graph compression for forward and reverse neighbor queries. *Discrete Applied Mathematics*, **163**, 298–306.

He, X., Kao, M. Y., and Lu, H.-I. (2000). A fast general methodology for information-theoretically optimal encodings of graphs. *SIAM Journal on Computing*, **30**, 838–846.

Henzinger, M. R., Klein, P. N., Rao, S., and Subramanian, S. (1997). Faster shortest-path algorithms for planar graphs. *Journal of Computer and Systems Sciences*, **55**(1), 3–23.

Hernández, C. and Navarro, G. (2014). Compressed representations for Web and social graphs. *Knowledge and Information Systems*, **40**(2), 279–313.

Hopcroft, J. and Tarjan, R. E. (1974). Efficient planarity testing. *Journal of the ACM*, **21**(4), 549–568.

Jacobson, G. (1989). Space-efficient static trees and graphs. In *Proc. 30th IEEE Symposium on Foundations of Computer Science (FOCS)*, pages 549–554.

Kannan, S., Naor, M., and Rudich, S. (1992). Implicit representation of graphs. *SIAM Journal on Discrete Mathematics*, **5**(4), 596–603.

Kant, G. (1996). Drawing planar graphs using the canonical ordering. *Algorithmica*, **16**(1), 4–32.

Keeler, K. and Westbrook, J. (1995). Short encodings of planar graphs and maps. *Discrete Applied Mathematics*, **58**, 239–252.

Kleitman, D. J. and Rothschild, B. L. (1975). Asymptotic enumeration of partial orders on a finite set. *Transactions of the American Mathematical Society*, **205**, 205–220.

Kranakis, E., Singh, H., and Urrutia, J. (1999). Compass routing on geometric networks. In *Proc. 11th Canadian Conference on Computational Geometry (CCCG)*.

Liao, C.-C., Lu, H.-I., and Yen, H.-C. (2003). Compact floor-planning via orderly spanning trees. *Journal of Algorithms*, **48**(2), 441–451.

Liskovets, V. A. and Walsh, T. R. (1987). Ten steps to counting planar graphs. *Congressus Numerantium*, **60**, 269–277.

Lu, H.-I. (2002). Linear-time compression of bounded-genus graphs into information-theoretically optimal number of bits. In *Proc. 13th Annual ACM-SIAM Symposium on Discrete Algorithms (SODA)*, pages 223–224.

Lu, H.-I. (2010). Improved compact routing tables for planar networks via orderly spanning trees. *SIAM Journal on Discrete Mathematics*, **23**(4), 2079–2092.

Maserrat, H. and Pei, J. (2010). Neighbor query friendly compression of social networks. In *Proc. 16th ACM International Conference on Knowledge Discovery and Data Mining (SIGKDD)*, pages 533–542.

Masucci, A. P., Stanilov, K., and Batty, M. (2013). Limited urban growth: London's street network dynamics since the 18th century. *PLoS ONE*, **8**(8), e69469.

Mitchell, S. L. (1979). Linear algorithms to recognize outerplanar and maximal outerplanar graphs. *Information Processing Letters*, **9**(5), 229–232.

Miura, K., Azuma, M., and Nishizeki, T. (2005). Canonical decomposition, realizer, Schnyder labeling and orderly spanning trees of plane graphs. *International Journal of Foundations of Computer Science*, **16**(1), 117–141.

Munro, J. I. and Nicholson, P. K. (2015). Succinct posets. *Algorithmica*. Early view, DOI 10.1007/s00453-015-0047-1.

Munro, J. I. and Raman, V. (2001). Succinct representation of balanced parentheses and static trees. *SIAM Journal on Computing*, **31**(3), 762–776.

Nishizeki, T. and Rahman, M. S. (2004). *Planar Graph Drawing*, volume 12 of *Lecture Notes on Computing*. World Scientific.

Schaeffer, S. E. (2007). Graph clustering. *Computer Science Review*, **1**(1), 27–64.

Schnyder, W. (1990). Embedding planar graphs on the grid. In *Proc. 1st Annual ACM-SIAM Symposium on Discrete Algorithms (SODA)*, pages 138–148.

Tutte, W. T. (1962). A census of planar triangulations. *Canadian Journal of Mathematics*, **14**, 21–38.

Tutte, W. T. (1963). A census of planar maps. *Canadian Journal of Mathematics*, **15**, 249–271.

Weiss, C., Karras, P., and Bernstein, A. (2008). Hexastore: Sextuple indexing for semantic Web data management. *Proceedings of the VLDB Endowment*, **1**(1), 1008–1019.

Yamanaka, K. and Nakano, S.-I. (2010). A compact encoding of plane triangulations with efficient query supports. *Information Processing Letters*, **110**(18-19), 803–809.

Yannakakis, M. (1989). Embedding planar graphs in four pages. *Journal of Computer and Systems Sciences*, **38**(1), 36–67.

Zhang, H. and He, X. (2005). Visibility representation of plane graphs via canonical ordering tree. *Information Processing Letters*, **96**(2), 41–48.

CHAPTER 10

Grids

A two-dimensional *grid* is a matrix of c columns and r rows, where each cell may or may not contain a *point*. We call n the total number of points in the grid. In the basic case, points have no associated data. We will also consider the case of *weighted points*, where the points have an associated integer priority (or weight) in the range $[1, u]$.

Grids arise naturally in applications related to geographic information systems (GIS), computational geometry, and multidimensional data in general, but also as internal components of other data structures that are not related to geometry. We have already seen applications in Chapter 9 (the adjacency matrix), where graph edges (v, u) were modeled essentially as points on a grid of size $|V| \times |V|$.

In this chapter we focus on a more geometric interpretation of grids, where queries refer to the points lying on a two-dimensional range of the grid. We consider the following queries on a grid G:

count(G, x_1, x_2, y_1, y_2): returns the number of points lying on the rectangle $[x_1, x_2] \times [y_1, y_2]$ of G, that is, within the column range $[x_1, x_2]$ and at the same time within the row range $[y_1, y_2]$.

report(G, x_1, x_2, y_1, y_2): reports the (x, y) coordinates of all the points lying on the range $[x_1, x_2] \times [y_1, y_2]$ of G.

top(G, x_1, x_2, y_1, y_2, m): reports m points (x, y) with highest priority in the range $[x_1, x_2] \times [y_1, y_2]$ of G, for the case of weighted points.

Algorithms to solve related problems, like determining whether a rectangular area is empty, or reporting points in some specific coordinate order, will be derived as modifications of these three queries. Although much less ample than the complex queries that may arise in computational geometry applications, the basic queries on axis-aligned areas cover the needs of a large number of applications and are amenable to efficient solutions.

In principle, representing n points on a $c \times r$ grid[1] has a worst-case entropy (Section 2.1) of $\log \binom{cr}{n} = n \log \frac{cr}{n} + \mathcal{O}(n)$ bits. For example, if $c = r = n$, this is $n \log n + \mathcal{O}(n)$ bits, which is about half the space needed to store the x and y coordinate of each point. In Section 5.4.1 we already saw how to obtain this space and retrieve the points in x- or y-coordinate order. However, it is difficult to efficiently answer our queries in that format.

We will study two main representations for grids. One uses the wavelet trees we introduced in Section 6.2, which yield a simple implementation that provides state-of-the-art results in terms of worst-case space and time. A second one uses the k^2-trees we introduced in Section 9.2. These do not offer good worst-case guarantees, but perform well in practice. Moreover, k^2-trees achieve much better space than wavelet trees when the points of the grid are clustered, as is the case in many applications.

10.1 Wavelet Trees

This structure, described in Section 6.2, can be used to represent a set of points. The first step is to convert the grid into a new one with n columns and exactly one point per column. Let us sort the points by x-coordinate (i.e., column) into $P = \langle (x_1, y_1), \ldots, (x_n, y_n) \rangle$ (that is, $x_i \leq x_{i+1}$ for all i). We then create a grid where point (x_i, y_i) is actually represented as (i, y_i). The mapping between the original coordinates and this more convenient grid is represented with a bitvector (Chapter 4) $B[1, c + n] = 1\,0^{n_1}1\,0^{n_2}\ldots 1\,0^{n_c}$, where n_v is the number of points with $x_i = v$ (it may be that $n_v = 0$). Note that we used a similar technique to represent a binary relation in Section 9.5.1.

Then the point (x, y) is translated to some x-coordinate falling between $\mathsf{select}_1(B, x) - x + 1$ and $\mathsf{select}_1(B, x + 1) - (x + 1)$. This slight ambiguity is not a problem, because queries should not distinguish between those ranges either: Any query about the range $[x_1, x_2] \times [y_1, y_2]$ is mapped to $[\mathsf{select}_1(B, x_1) - x_1 + 1, \mathsf{select}_1(B, x_2 + 1) - (x_2 + 1)] \times [y_1, y_2]$ in order to contain all the desired mapped points. On the other hand, any point (x, y) returned by the structure must be mapped back to $(\mathsf{select}_0(B, x) - x, y)$.

Example 10.1 *Figure 10.1 shows a grid of 12×16, with 16 points, and how its columns are mapped into a new grid with one column per point. The column range of query $[x_1, x_2] \times [y_1, y_2] = [2, 10] \times [3, 9]$ is mapped to $[\mathsf{select}_1(B, x_1) - x_1 + 1, \mathsf{select}_1(B, x_2 + 1) - (x_2 + 1)] = [3 - 2 + 1, 22 - 11] = [2, 11]$. Consider the point $(8, 3)$ found on the mapped grid. It corresponds to the point $(\mathsf{select}_0(B, 8) - 8, 3) = (6, 3)$ on the original grid.*

Once we have transformed the grid into an $n \times r$ grid with exactly one point (i, y_i) per column i, we can interpret it as a string $S[1, n]$, with $S[i] = y_i$. If we represent B as a compressed bitvector (Section 4.1.1), the space of S and B adds up to

---

[1]. In this chapter we will refer to the points and grid sizes in the format *(column, row)*, to match the most used notation (x, y) for the points.

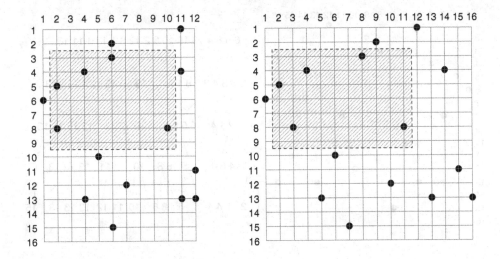

$$B = 10100110010100010111101000100$$

Figure 10.1. The columns of an original grid on the left, of 12×16, are mapped onto a new 16×16 grid, on the right, which has exactly one point per column. On the bottom we show the corresponding bitvector B. We highlight a query range $[2, 10] \times [3, 9]$ on the left, which is mapped to $[2, 11] \times [3, 9]$ on the right.

$n \log r + o(n \log r) + n \log \frac{c+n}{n} + o(c + n) = n \log \frac{cr}{n} + \mathcal{O}(n) + o(c + n \log r)$, matching the worst-case entropy up to lower-order terms.

From now on we can assume the mapping is done, and focus simply on answering queries on the range $[x_1, x_2] \times [y_1, y_2]$ in an $n \times r$ grid of n points, represented as the wavelet tree of string $S[1, n]$ over alphabet $[1, r]$. We can also assume that r is not larger than n, since otherwise we can also map the y-coordinates to eliminate empty rows.

Since the alphabet size is generally significant compared with the length of the string, a wavelet matrix (Section 6.2.5) is the appropriate representation for S. We will explain and exemplify the algorithms on wavelet trees, which is more intuitive since the y-coordinate grid ordering corresponds to the left-to-right wavelet tree node ordering. The pseudocodes, instead, will be described on the wavelet matrix, to help the reader implement them.

Example 10.2 *Figure 10.2 shows a grid and its wavelet tree representation. On the bottom, it shows the graphical interpretation of the first two levels of the wavelet tree decomposition: we partition the grid by y-coordinate zones. Note that, at the lowest level of the wavelet tree, we have the y-coordinates of all the points in increasing order.*

Construction

This representation is built in time $\mathcal{O}(c + n \log n)$ and just $3n + c$ bits of extra space on top of the initial array of coordinates (x_i, y_i). We first sort the pairs by increasing x-coordinate. We then traverse them, writing on $B[1, c + n]$ a 1 each time the x-coordinate increases and a 0 each time a new point is found with the current x-coordinate. Now we pack the y_i values in the first half of the array, and use the second half to store the

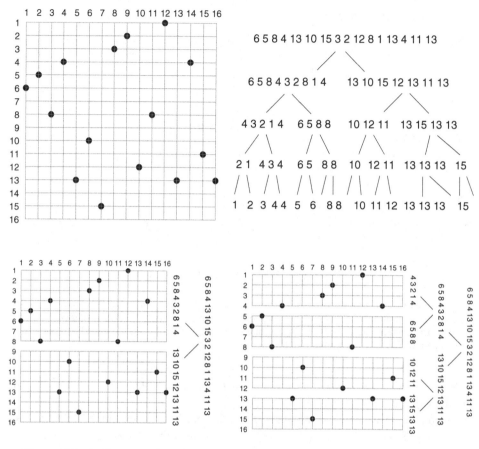

Figure 10.2. At the top, a 16×16 grid with one point per column (left) and its wavelet tree representation (right). At the bottom, we visualize the first two levels of the wavelet tree decomposition (left and right) on the grid.

resulting wavelet matrix. If we apply the wavelet matrix construction algorithm that requires $2n$ bits of extra space (Section 6.2.5), the total overhead is just $3n + c$ bits as promised. At the end, we free the y_i values and build the rank/select structures on B.

10.1.1 Counting

The counting problem can be regarded as follows: We want to know how many symbols from $S[x_1, x_2]$ belong to the range $[y_1, y_2]$. Consider the following general procedure on the nodes of the wavelet tree for S. Let a node v represent the symbol range $[a, b]$, and assume we want to know how many symbols in $S_v[x_1, x_2]$ lie in the range $[y_1, y_2]$. There are then four possibilities: (i) $x_1 > x_2$, in which case the answer is zero; (ii) $[a, b] \cap [y_1, y_2] = \emptyset$, in which case the answer is zero; (iii) $[a, b] \subseteq [y_1, y_2]$, in which case the answer is $x_2 - x_1 + 1$; and (iv) none of the above, in which case we must recurse on the two children of v. Algorithm 10.1 gives the procedure, implemented on the wavelet matrix of S.

Example 10.3 *Figure 10.3 illustrates the processing of a query* count$(2, 11, 3, 9)$ *on our example grid. We start at the root, v_0, with the interval $[x_1, x_2] = [2, 11]$. All the points of interest are in $S[2, 11] = 5, 8, 4, 13, 10, 15, 3, 2, 12, 8$ (but this string is not*

Algorithm 10.1: Answering count with a wavelet matrix.

1 **Proc** count(G, x_1, x_2, y_1, y_2)
     Input : An $n \times r$ grid G (seen as a sequence S, in turn seen as the bitvectors
                 B_ℓ and values z_ℓ of its wavelet matrix) and range $[x_1, x_2] \times [y_1, y_2]$.
     Output: Returns the number of points in the range.

2   **return** *count*($x_1, x_2, y_1, y_2, 1, 1, r$)

3 **Proc** *count*($x_1, x_2, y_1, y_2, \ell, a, b$)
     Input : Range $[x_1, x_2]$ of level ℓ, inside a segment of S_ℓ that represents
                 symbols in $[a, b]$ and symbol range $[y_1, y_2]$.
     Output: Returns the number of symbols in $S_\ell[x_1, x_2]$ belonging to $[y_1, y_2]$.

4   **if** $x_1 > x_2$ **then return** 0
5   **if** $[a, b] \cap [y_1, y_2] = \emptyset$ **then return** 0
6   **if** $[a, b] \subseteq [y_1, y_2]$ **then return** $x_2 - x_1 + 1$
7     $x_1^l \leftarrow \mathsf{rank}_0(B_\ell, x_1 - 1) + 1$
8     $x_2^l \leftarrow \mathsf{rank}_0(B_\ell, x_2)$
9     $x_1^r \leftarrow z_\ell + x_1 - x_1^l + 1$
10    $x_2^r \leftarrow z_\ell + x_2 - x_2^l$
11    $m \leftarrow \lfloor (a + b)/2 \rfloor$
12   **return** *count*($x_1^l, x_2^l, y_1, y_2, \ell + 1, a, m$) +
13   *count*($x_1^r, x_2^r, y_1, y_2, \ell + 1, m + 1, b$)

---

explicit). Since the symbol interval of the root is $[1, 16]$, *which is neither disjoint with
nor contained in* $[y_1, y_2] = [3, 9]$, *we follow both children recursively. In the left child,
v_1, the string interval becomes* $S_{v_1}[2, 7] = 5, 8, 4, 3, 2, 8$. *The symbol interval of* v_1
is $[1, 8]$, *again neither disjoint with nor contained in* $[3, 9]$. *Thus, we recurse on both*

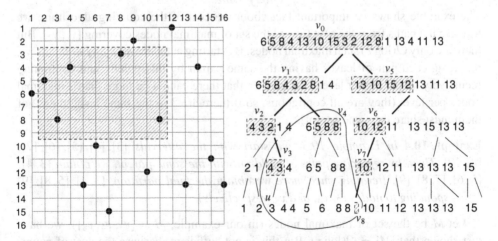

Figure 10.3. Counting the number of points in $[2, 11] \times [3, 9]$ (shaded) on the example grid
and its wavelet tree. The shaded regions in the wavelet tree strings show how the x-range is
subdivided across the nodes. The nodes v_3, v_4, and v_8 (enclosed in a curve) cover the y-range
of the query. The shaded regions in those nodes contain all the points in the query range.

children of v_1. On its left child, v_2, the string interval becomes $S_{v_2}[1, 3] = 4, 3, 2$. The symbol interval of v_2 is $[1, 4]$, so we continue on both children. The left child of v_2 has symbol interval $[1, 2]$, which is disjoint with the query interval $[3, 9]$, so this node is not explored. The right child of v_2, v_3, has string interval $S_{v_3}[1, 2] = 4, 3$ and symbol interval $[3, 4]$. Since the symbol interval is contained in the query interval $[3, 9]$, both points belong to the result and we count them, $2 - 1 + 1 = 2$.

Now let us return to the right child of v_1, v_4, with string interval $S_{v_4}[2, 4] = 5, 8, 8$. Its symbol interval is $[5, 8]$. Since this is contained in the query interval $[3, 9]$, we count all the $4 - 2 + 1 = 3$ points in this node.

We then continue with the right child of the root, v_5, with string interval $S_{v_5}[1, 4] = 13, 10, 15, 12$. Its symbol interval is $[9, 16]$, so we recurse in both children. Note that the right child of v_5 has symbol interval $[13, 16]$, which is disjoint with the query interval $[3, 9]$, thus this node is not explored. The left child of v_5, v_6, has string interval $S_{v_6}[1, 2] = 10, 12$ and symbol interval $[9, 12]$. We recurse on both children, but the right child has symbol interval $[11, 12]$, which is disjoint with the query interval $[3, 9]$ and thus not considered. The left child of v_6, v_7, has string interval $S_{v_7}[1, 1] = 10$ and symbol interval $[9, 10]$. We recurse on both children, but its right child has symbol interval $[10, 10]$, disjoint with $[3, 9]$, and thus it is not considered.

Finally, the left child of v_7, v_8, has string interval $S_{v_8}[1, 0]$, which is empty, and therefore we do not regard it further even if its symbol interval, $[9, 9]$, is not disjoint with that of the query.

Note that the final nodes we have considered for the counting are v_3, which covers symbol interval $[3, 4]$ and yielded 2 results; v_4, which covers symbol interval $[5, 8]$ and yielded 3 results; and v_8, which covers symbol interval $[9, 9]$ and yielded zero results. These 3 nodes are the maximal ones covering the y-coordinate interval of the query, $[y_1, y_2] = [3, 9]$ (this set is enclosed with a curve in the figure). The complete answer is $\mathsf{count}(2, 11, 3, 9) = 5$.

Query Time

The example shows an important fact about the cost of the counting algorithm: we traverse the paths from the root toward the set of maximal nodes covering $[y_1, y_2]$. But there are only $\mathcal{O}(\log r)$ such maximal nodes: By starting at the leaves $y_1, y_1 + 1, \ldots, y_2$, replacing each pair of leaves having the same parent by that parent, and continuing recursively on the higher levels, we can see that there cannot be more than 2 maximal nodes per level (they are all contiguous, so if there are 3 in the same level, then 2 of them must share the same parent).

Example 10.4 *In Example 10.3, we start with the intervals* $[3], [4], [5], [6], [7], [8], [9]$. *Then, by replacing pairs of children with the same parent, we obtain* $[3, 4], [5, 6], [7, 8], [9]$. *Iterating once more we obtain the final partition,* $[3, 4], [5, 8], [9]$ *(corresponding to nodes* v_3, v_4, *and* v_8, *respectively).*

Let M be the set of maximal nodes (in our example, $M = \{v_3, v_4, v_8\}$); we have just shown that $|M| = \mathcal{O}(\log r)$. But this is not sufficient, because the cost of counting is proportional to the total number of nodes in the paths from the root to the nodes in M. Let A be the set of the ancestors of the nodes in M (in our example, $A = \{v_0, v_1, v_2, v_5, v_6, v_7\}$). Note that the y-coordinate ranges of the nodes in A are not contained in $[y_1, y_2]$, but they intersect with $[y_1, y_2]$. Thus, similarly as before, there cannot be 3 nodes of A at a single level, since the middle one would then be included in $[y_1, y_2]$. Therefore, $|A| = \mathcal{O}(\log r)$ as well, and counting takes $\mathcal{O}(|M| + |A|) = \mathcal{O}(\log r)$ time (if $c < r$, we can transpose the grid and all the queries, to obtain time $\mathcal{O}(\log c)$).

Emptiness Queries

If we are interested only in determining whether the query range is empty of points, we can use the same procedure but stop as soon as we find any point, in line 6 of Algorithm 10.1. This is somewhat faster than a full counting, but the worst-case time does not change.

10.1.2 Reporting

For reporting, we follow the same procedure as for counting, but in line 6 of Algorithm 10.1, instead of simply returning the number $x_2 - x_1 + 1$ of points, we execute *outputx*(ℓ, i) and *outputy*(ℓ, a, b, i) for each i in $[x_1, x_2]$. These procedures are shown in Algorithm 10.2. To output the x-coordinate, we have to return upwards to the root of the wavelet tree, until finding the original position of the point in the root interval. To output the y-coordinate, we have to continue downwards until reaching the leaf interval, where we discover the row value. Therefore, each point is reported in $\mathcal{O}(\log r)$ time (again, we can switch coordinates to obtain $\mathcal{O}(\log c)$ time, if convenient).

Depending on the application, it might be that we only need to report one of the two coordinates. In practice, reporting the y-coordinates is faster, because we go downwards with **rank** operations, which are faster than the **select** operations needed to go upwards in the tree. Moreover, the number of nodes to traverse to report y-coordinates is generally lower, for two reasons.

The first reason is that, in specific queries (which are the most common in practice), the maximal wavelet tree nodes are close to the leaves. Let $q = y_2 - y_1 + 1$. Any wavelet tree node of height h covers 2^h nodes; therefore the maximal nodes covering the y-coordinate range have a maximum height of $\lceil \log q \rceil$. Thus, the maximum possible cost to report the y-coordinate of each point is $\mathcal{O}(\log q)$, which shows that shorter queries can report their points faster: they need $\mathcal{O}(\log r + occ \cdot \log q)$ time to report occ points.

The second reason is that it is possible to report the resulting y-coordinates faster than doing it one by one, as shown in procedure *outputally*(ℓ, a, b, x_1, x_2) of Algorithm 10.2. To appreciate the improvement, let v be a maximal node and m be the number leaves that descend from v and contain points to report. The cost of reporting these points is then the number of nodes in the paths from v to those m leaves. While the paths can be of length up to $\lceil \log q \rceil$, they cannot be completely disjoint, so the cost is less than $\mathcal{O}(m \log q)$. In the worst case, all the highest $2m$ descendants of v, at distance up to $\lceil \log m \rceil$ from v, can be traversed, and then each leaf must be individually tracked from a distinct descendant at distance $\lceil \log m \rceil$ from v, across $\lceil \log q \rceil - \lceil \log m \rceil$ levels. Thus, the total cost is no more than $\mathcal{O}(m(1 + \log(q/m)))$. We have already used this idea; recall Figure 6.11, where now $h = \log q$ and $d = m$.

Let q_i be the y-coordinate range below the ith maximal node (whose height is then $\log q_i$), and let m_i be the number of results below that node. Then $q = \sum_i q_i$

Algorithm 10.2: Procedures for report on a wavelet matrix.

---

1 **Proc** *outputx*(ℓ, i)
    Input : String S (seen as bitvectors B_ℓ and numbers z_ℓ of its wavelet matrix),
          level ℓ, and position i of S_ℓ.
    Output: Reports the position of $S_\ell[i]$ in S.

2   **while** $\ell > 1$ **do**
3         $\ell \leftarrow \ell - 1$
4   **if** $i \leq z_\ell$ **then** $i \leftarrow \mathsf{select}_0(B_\ell, i)$
5   **else** $i \leftarrow \mathsf{select}_1(B_\ell, i - z_\ell)$
6   **output** i

7 **Proc** *outputy*(ℓ, a, b, i)
    Input : String S (seen as bitvectors B_ℓ and numbers z_ℓ of its wavelet matrix),
          level ℓ, and position i of S_ℓ, which has symbol range $[a, b]$.
    Output: Outputs $S_\ell[i]$.

8   **while** $a \neq b$ **do**
9   **if** $\mathsf{access}(B_\ell, i) = 0$ **then**
10             $i \leftarrow \mathsf{rank}_0(B_\ell, i)$
11             $b \leftarrow \lfloor (a + b)/2 \rfloor$
12   **else**
13             $i \leftarrow z_\ell + \mathsf{rank}_1(B_\ell, i)$
14             $a \leftarrow \lfloor (a + b)/2 \rfloor + 1$
15         $\ell \leftarrow \ell + 1$
16   **output** a

17 **Proc** *outputally*(ℓ, a, b, x_1, x_2)
    Input : String S (seen as bitvectors B_ℓ and numbers z_ℓ of its wavelet matrix),
          level ℓ, and range $[x_1, x_2]$ of S_ℓ, with symbol range $[a, b]$.
    Output: Outputs the symbols in $S_\ell[x_1, x_2]$ in ascending symbol order.

18   **if** $x_1 > x_2$ **then return**
19   **if** $a = b$ **then output** $x_2 - x_1 + 1$ occurrences of a
20     $x_1^l \leftarrow \mathsf{rank}_0(B_\ell, x_1 - 1) + 1; x_2^l \leftarrow \mathsf{rank}_0(B_\ell, x_2)$
21     $x_1^r \leftarrow z_\ell + x_1 - x_1^l + 1; x_2^r \leftarrow z_\ell + x_2 - x_2^l$
22     $m \leftarrow \lfloor (a + b)/2 \rfloor$
23   *outputally*$(\ell + 1, a, m, x_1^l, x_2^l)$
24   *outputally*$(\ell + 1, m + 1, b, x_1^r, x_2^r)$

---

and $occ = \sum_i m_i$ is the total number of results. In the worst case there is only one result per leaf, thus $m_i \leq q_i$. Therefore, if $occ \geq q$, we may reach all the leaves, and the total cost is simply $\mathcal{O}(occ)$. Otherwise the total cost is $\mathcal{O}\left(\sum_i m_i \log(q_i/m_i)\right)$. By Jensen's inequality (Section 2.8), taking $a_i = m_i$, $x_i = q_i/m_i$, and $f = \log$, this is at most $\mathcal{O}\left(occ \log\left(\sum_i m_i(q_i/m_i)/occ\right)\right) = \mathcal{O}(occ \log(q/occ))$. To these costs we must add the $\mathcal{O}(\log r)$ time to find the maximal nodes. This shows that, in addition to the influence of the query area, queries that return more points can report each point faster.

10.1.3 Sorted Reporting

If we use *outputally* in line 6 of Algorithm 10.1, then the points will be reported in increasing y-coordinate order. If we use instead *outputy* for each of the $x_2 - x_1 + 1$ values, left to right, then the points will not be reported in a clear order. In certain cases we are interested in listing the points within $[x_1, x_2] \times [y_1, y_2]$ in x-coordinate order. If we want all the points in the range, then obtaining them all first and sorting them by the desired criterion afterwards is a reasonable choice. However, if we want to obtain them progressively, this solution is not efficient.

If we can obtain the leftmost point $(x, y) \in [x_1, x_2] \times [y_1, y_2]$, we can report it and then ask for the leftmost point in $[x + 1, x_2] \times [y_1, y_2]$, and so on. This works because there is exactly one point per column.[2] Therefore, finding the leftmost point in a range is sufficient for our purposes (finding the rightmost point will be analogous). We call this operation leftmost(G, x_1, x_2, y_1, y_2).

We might similarly want to report just the points with smallest y-coordinate in the range. This time the grid may have several points with the same minimum y-coordinate, and we must report them all. We call this operation highest(G, x_1, x_2, y_1, y_2).

Sorted by Columns

Let us start with the query leftmost(G, x_1, x_2, y_1, y_2). If we are at a wavelet tree node v corresponding to symbol range $[a, b]$, with string range $S_v[x_1, x_2]$, then there are four possibilities, as for counting: (i) $x_1 > x_2$, in which case there are no points to report; (ii) $[a, b] \cap [y_1, y_2] = \emptyset$, in which case there are no points to report; (iii) $[a, b] \subseteq [y_1, y_2]$, in which case all the points in $S_v[x_1, x_2]$ are valid, and hence the leftmost point is $S_v[x_1]$; and (iv) none of the above, in which case we must recurse on the two children of v. Once we have the leftmost answers from the left and right children, we map both to the range $S_v[x_1, x_2]$ and choose the leftmost of the two. Algorithm 10.3 gives the procedure, implemented on the wavelet matrix of S. Its complexity is similar to the procedure for counting, $\mathcal{O}(\log r)$.

Example 10.5 *Consider the query of Figure 10.3, now to return the leftmost point in the range. At the root node we have $S[2, 11]$ and go both left and right. Its left child, v_1, has range $S_{v_1}[2, 7]$ and also goes left and right. Its left child, v_2, has range $S_{v_2}[1, 3]$, and it has only a relevant right child, v_3. In v_3, with range $S_{v_3}[1, 2]$, we find that its symbol range $[3, 4]$ is totally contained in the query range $[3, 9]$, thus we return the leftmost value in its interval, $S_{v_3}[1]$. Its parent maps this position to $S_{v_2}[1]$ and returns it to v_1. The right child of v_1, v_4, with range $S_{v_4}[2, 4]$, has symbol range $[5, 8] \subseteq [3, 9]$, so it returns its leftmost position, $S_{v_4}[2]$. Now v_1 has received position $S_{v_2}[1]$ from its left child v_2, and position $S_{v_4}[2]$ from its right child v_4. It maps the first to $S_{v_1}[4]$ and the second to $S_{v_1}[2]$, thus it chooses the leftmost, $S_{v_1}[2]$, and returns it to the root. The*

---

[2] If the points were mapped from a grid where several share the same x-coordinate, then this method will report them one by one before considering others to the right.

Algorithm 10.3: Finding the leftmost point in a range with a wavelet matrix.

---

1 **Proc** leftmost(G, x_1, x_2, y_1, y_2)

    Input : An $n \times r$ grid G (seen as a sequence S, in turn seen as the bitvectors B_ℓ and values z_ℓ of its wavelet matrix) and range $[x_1, x_2] \times [y_1, y_2]$.

    Output: Returns the leftmost point in $[x_1, x_2] \times [y_1, y_2]$.

2     $x \leftarrow \textit{leftmost}(x_1, x_2, y_1, y_2, 1, 1, r)$

3   **return** $(x, \mathsf{access}(S, x))$ (or "range is empty" if $x = +\infty$)

4 **Proc** $\textit{leftmost}(x_1, x_2, y_1, y_2, \ell, a, b)$

    Input : Range $[x_1, x_2]$ of level ℓ, inside a segment of S_ℓ that represents symbols in $[a, b]$, and symbol range $[y_1, y_2]$.

    Output: Returns leftmost point of $S_\ell[x_1, x_2]$ belonging to $[y_1, y_2]$.

5   **if** $x_1 > x_2$ **then return** $+\infty$

6   **if** $[a, b] \cap [y_1, y_2] = \emptyset$ **then return** $+\infty$

7   **if** $[a, b] \subseteq [y_1, y_2]$ **then return** x_1

8     $x_1^l \leftarrow \mathsf{rank}_0(B_\ell, x_1 - 1) + 1; \; x_2^l \leftarrow \mathsf{rank}_0(B_\ell, x_2)$

9     $x_1^r \leftarrow z_\ell + x_1 - x_1^l + 1; \; x_2^r \leftarrow z_\ell + x_2 - x_2^l$

10     $m \leftarrow \lfloor (a + b)/2 \rfloor$

11     $x^l \leftarrow \textit{leftmost}(x_1^l, x_2^l, y_1, y_2, \ell + 1, a, m)$

12     $x^r \leftarrow \textit{leftmost}(x_1^r, x_2^r, y_1, y_2, \ell + 1, m + 1, b)$

13   **if** $x^l \neq +\infty$ **then** $x^l \leftarrow \mathsf{select}_0(B_\ell, x^l)$

14   **if** $x^r \neq +\infty$ **then** $x^r \leftarrow \mathsf{select}_1(B_\ell, x^r - z_\ell)$

15   **return** $\min(x^l, x^r)$

---

right child of the root does not report any point, so the root maps $S_{v_1}[2]$ to $S[2]$ and returns the point $(2, S[2]) = (2, 5)$, the final answer.

Sorted by Rows

The second query, highest(G, x_1, x_2, y_1, y_2), can be solved similarly to counting, except that we do not stop when we find a maximal node, but rather continue to the leftmost wavelet tree leaf that contains some valid point. Algorithm 10.4 shows the procedure. Note that the answer array A is allocated only once, and from there on it is only overwritten when we translate the x values to their positions in the parent node, so no serious allocation problems arise. The algorithm reports m points in time $\mathcal{O}((m + 1) \log r)$.

Example 10.6 *Consider returning the highest points in the query of Figure 10.3. We first descend to v_1, v_2, and v_3. Although v_3 is a maximal node covering the query range, we continue to its left node, which is the leaf u corresponding to $[a, b] = [3, 3]$. Here the range is $S_u[1, 1]$, so we return the answer set $A = \{(1, 3)\}$. Properly translated, this will be the final answer. The parent of u, v_3, translates A to $A = \{(2, 3)\}$ and does not consider its right child because it has already found an answer at its left child, which must be preferred (it is higher in the grid). The parent of v_3, v_2, translates the answer to $A = \{(2, 3)\}$ and returns it to its parent, v_1. This node translates the answer*

Algorithm 10.4: Finding the highest points (smallest y-coordinates) in a range with a wavelet matrix.

---

1 **Proc** highest(G, x_1, x_2, y_1, y_2)

> **Input** : An $n \times r$ grid G (seen as a sequence S, in turn seen as the bitvectors B_ℓ and values z_ℓ of its wavelet matrix) and range $[x_1, x_2] \times [y_1, y_2]$.
>
> **Output**: Returns the highest points in $[x_1, x_2] \times [y_1, y_2]$.

2 | **return** $highest(x_1, x_2, y_1, y_2, 1, 1, r)$

3 **Proc** $highest(x_1, x_2, y_1, y_2, \ell, a, b)$

> **Input** : Range $[x_1, x_2]$ of level ℓ, inside a segment of S_ℓ that represents symbols in $[a, b]$, and symbol range $[y_1, y_2]$.
>
> **Output**: Returns $\langle A, t \rangle$, where $A[1, t]$ contains the t points with minimum value in $S_\ell[x_1, x_2]$ that are within range $[y_1, y_2]$.

4 | **if** $x_1 > x_2$ **then return** $\langle$null$, 0 \rangle$

5 | **if** $[a, b] \cap [y_1, y_2] = \emptyset$ **then return** $\langle$null$, 0 \rangle$

6 | **if** $a = b$ **then**

7 | | Allocate array $A[1, x_2 - x_1 + 1]$ of points (x, y)

8 | | **for** $i \leftarrow 1$ **to** $x_2 - x_1 + 1$ **do**

9 | | | $A[i] \leftarrow (x_1 + i - 1, a)$

10 | | **return** $\langle A, x_2 - x_1 + 1 \rangle$

11 | $x_1^l \leftarrow \mathsf{rank}_0(B_\ell, x_1 - 1) + 1; x_2^l \leftarrow \mathsf{rank}_0(B_\ell, x_2)$

12 | $x_1^r \leftarrow z_\ell + x_1 - x_1^l + 1; x_2^r \leftarrow z_\ell + x_2 - x_2^l$

13 | $m \leftarrow \lfloor (a + b)/2 \rfloor$

14 | $\langle A, t \rangle \leftarrow highest(x_1^l, x_2^l, y_1, y_2, \ell + 1, a, m)$

15 | **if** $t \neq 0$ **then**

16 | | **for** $i \leftarrow 1$ **to** t **do**

17 | | | $A[i].x \leftarrow \mathsf{select}_0(B_\ell, A[i].x)$

18 | | **return** $\langle A, t \rangle$

19 | $\langle A, t \rangle \leftarrow highest(x_1^r, x_2^r, y_1, y_2, \ell + 1, m + 1, b)$

20 | **for** $i \leftarrow 1$ **to** t **do**

21 | | $A[i].x \leftarrow \mathsf{select}_1(B_\ell, A[i].x - z_\ell)$

22 | **return** $\langle A, t \rangle$

---

to $A = \{(5, 3)\}$ and again does not explore its right child, v_4. The parent of v_1 is the root node, where the answer is translated to $A = \{(8, 3)\}$, the final result. The right child, v_5, is not explored.

10.2 K^2-Trees

The *region quadtree* (which we will call just quadtree) is a well-known data structure in computational geometry. It is based on partitioning an $s \times s$ two-dimensional grid into 4 equal-sized quadrants:

$[1, \lfloor s/2 \rfloor] \times [1, \lfloor s/2 \rfloor]$	$[\lfloor s/2 \rfloor + 1, s] \times [1, \lfloor s/2 \rfloor]$
$[1, \lfloor s/2 \rfloor] \times [\lfloor s/2 \rfloor + 1, s]$	$[\lfloor s/2 \rfloor + 1, s] \times [\lfloor s/2 \rfloor + 1, s]$

This partition is represented as the root of a 4-ary cardinal tree. If one of the 4 quadrants has no points, then the corresponding child of the node is absent. We recurse on this decomposition for each nonempty quadrant until reaching the leaves, which represent single cells.

This definition enhances the fact that the quadtree is a particular case ($k = 2$) of the k^2-trees introduced in Section 9.2.1, which allow us to partition the grid into k^2 subgrids instead of only 4. We will interpret the k^2-tree children as traversing the matrix in row-major order (in Section 9.2.1 we used column-major, because the matrix cells were also written in the other way; this allows for the use of a single k^2-tree implementation for both purposes).

Example 10.7 *Figure 10.4 shows another $s \times s = 16 \times 16$ grid (now allowing zero or more points per column) and its k^2-tree representation, for $k = 2$ (that is, the tree is actually a quadtree representing the grid). The first children of the k^2-tree root describe, left to right, the quadrants $[1, 8] \times [1, 8]$, $[9, 16] \times [1, 8]$, $[1, 8] \times [9, 16]$, and $[9, 16] \times [9, 16]$.*

Below the quadtree, we show its LOUDS-based representation, where nodes at depth $1 + \log_k s = 1 + \log_2 16 = 5$ are known to be leaves. We separate the bitvectors of each level with spaces for legibility, and leave the last level in a second line. Shaded nodes and areas and bold edges will be used later.

Note that the first 3 quadrants of the grid are identical to the first 3 quadrants of the rotated matrix of Figure 9.5. Consequently, the subtrees of the first 3 root children are identical.

Space and Construction

In order to represent a grid of size $c \times r$, we will complete it with empty cells up to size $s \times s$, with $s = k^{\lceil \log_k \max(c,r) \rceil}$. As described in Section 9.2.3, this representation uses

$$n \left(\frac{k^2}{k^2 - 1} + k^2 \left(1 + \log_{k^2} \frac{s^2}{n} \right) \right)$$

bits. If we represent the k^2-tree bitvector as in Section 4.4, then the space becomes $\mathcal{O}\left(n \log \frac{s^2}{n} + n \log k\right)$ bits. This is the same order of the worst-case entropy of n points distributed on an $s \times s$ grid, plus an additive penalty of $\mathcal{O}(n \log k)$ bits. Still, this analysis is rather pessimistic on clustered grids. Other practical suggestions to improve the space given in Section 9.2.3 can be applied in the case of grids as well.

The construction is carried out from the array of n points (x_i, y_i) exactly as when building the graphs in Section 9.2.4. We have to modify only the fact that we now traverse the points in row-major order. That is, in Algorithm 9.7, take $E[p].u$ as the y-coordinate and $E[p].v$ as the x-coordinate.

10.2.1 Reporting

The k^2-tree cannot count the number of points in a range $[x_1, x_2] \times [y_1, y_2]$ without traversing them all, so we describe only the method for reporting. The idea is to compute which of the k^2 children of the root intersect with the query area, and then continue recursively on all those that are nonempty. When we reach leaves, we report them.

Algorithm 10.5 gives the pseudocode. Note how lines 8 and 9 handle the possibility that the query range contains the sub-grid, which must be the case in lines 4–5 (thus the only sub-grid point can be immediately reported without further tests). Finally, note that we do not waste any time on children sub-grids that do not intersect with the query.

Example 10.8 *Figure 10.4 also shows the k^2-tree nodes traversed to handle the query* report(3, 6, 4, 14) *on the grid. Since the query intersects with only the first quadrant,* $[1, 8] \times [1, 8]$, *and the third one,* $[1, 8] \times [9, 16]$, *we traverse only the first and third*

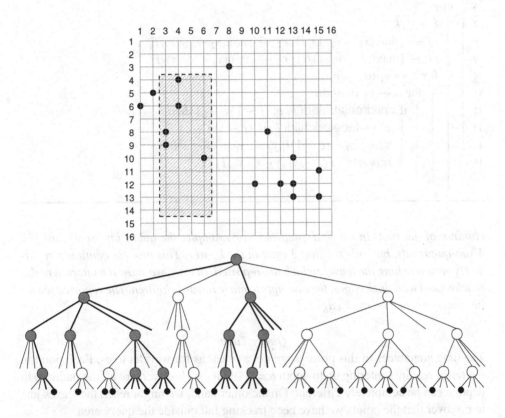

1111 1110001011001101 0001000111010001010010000011110111100
0001010001100001001000101000000100010001001000101000010001000

Figure 10.4. A grid of size 16×16 with 16 points, and its k^2-tree representation (LOUDS bitvector on the bottom, separating the levels with spaces and with the last level in another line). We show the query $[3, 6] \times [4, 14]$ and the k^2-tree nodes (grayed) and edges (thick) traversed to report the points inside it. The result is the 5 leaves (black nodes) reached by thick edges.

Algorithm 10.5: Procedure for report on a k^2-tree.

---

1 **Proc** report(G, x_1, x_2, y_1, y_2)

  Input : An $s \times s$ grid G (seen as k^2-tree T, with s a power of k) and range
             $[x_1, x_2] \times [y_1, y_2]$.

  Output: Outputs the points (x, y) in $[x_1, x_2] \times [y_1, y_2]$.

2 | $report(\text{root}(T), x_1, x_2, y_1, y_2, 0, 0, s)$

3 **Proc** $report(v, x_1, x_2, y_1, y_2, x_0, y_0, s)$

  Input : k^2-tree node v of nonempty sub-grid
             $[x_0 + 1, x_0 + s] \times [y_0 + 1, y_0 + s]$ and range $[x_1, x_2] \times [y_1, y_2]$
             intersecting with the sub-grid.

  Output: Outputs the sub-grid points (x, y) in $[x_1, x_2] \times [y_1, y_2]$.

4 | **if** $s = 1$ **then**

5 | | **output** $(x_0 + 1, y_0 + 1)$

6 | **else**

7 | | $l \leftarrow s/k$

8 | | $c_1 \leftarrow \lceil \max(x_1 - x_0, 1)/l \rceil$; $c_2 \leftarrow \lceil \min(x_2 - x_0, s)/l \rceil$

9 | | $r_1 \leftarrow \lceil \max(y_1 - y_0, 1)/l \rceil$; $r_2 \leftarrow \lceil \min(y_2 - y_0, s)/l \rceil$

10 | | **for** $r \leftarrow r_1$ **to** r_2 **do**

11 | | | **for** $c \leftarrow c_1$ **to** c_2 **do**

12 | | | | **if** childrenlabeled$(T, v, (r-1)k + c)$ **then**

13 | | | | | $v' \leftarrow$ labeledchild$(T, v, (r-1)k + c)$

14 | | | | | $x_0' \leftarrow x_0 + (c-1)l$; $y_0' \leftarrow y_0 + (r-1)l$

15 | | | | | $report(v', x_1, x_2, y_1, y_2, x_0', y_0', l)$

---

*children of the root. In the first quadrant, for example, the query intersects with the
4 sub-quadrants, but only the first 3 exist in the k^2-tree. This process continues recursively until reaching the leaves, which are reported. In gray, we show the internal nodes
reached and with thick edges, the attempts to move toward children. The reported leaves
are those reached by thick edges.*

Query Time

The time guarantees of this process are not as clear as for wavelet trees. Each point in
the range requires entering up to depth $h = 1 + \log_k s$. However, not all the paths up to
depth h can be completely different. On the other hand, we might reach the leaves just
to discover that the points we have been tracking fall outside the query area.

We can obtain an upper bound by separately counting two types of nodes in our
traversal: (1) nodes whose area is contained in the query, and (2) other nodes whose
area intersects with the query. The algorithm does not spend any time in nodes whose
area is disjoint with the query. Note also that only the nodes of type (2) can lead us to
no result, so we will count the nodes in (1) in terms of the results they yield and those
in (2) in terms of their total number.

Let $p = x_2 - x_1 + 1$, $q = y_2 - y_1 + 1$, and occ be the number of points to report. Then the nodes of type (1) are at most $occ \cdot \log_k s$, as each point to return requires traversing all of its ancestors (not all of them are of type (1), but we count them all). However, a more refined bound is possible. At level ℓ of the k^2-tree, the grid has been divided into sub-grids of $(s/k^{\ell-1}) \times (s/k^{\ell-1})$, and thus the query area can contain at most $(pq)/(s/k^{\ell-1})^2$ nodes of type (1). We may assume that all the nodes of type (1) up to level ℓ are traversed, and from there each individual point is tracked down up to the leaves, at level $h = 1 + \log_k s$. Therefore, the number of nodes of type (1) is at most

$$\sum_{l=1}^{\ell} \frac{pq}{(s/k^{l-1})^2} + occ \cdot (h - \ell) = \mathcal{O}\left(\frac{pq}{(s/k^{\ell-1})^2} + occ \cdot (h - \ell)\right).$$

As this is valid for any ℓ, we choose $\ell = 1 + \lfloor \log_k \left(s \cdot \sqrt{(occ + 1)/(pq)}\right)\rfloor$, which yields the bound $\mathcal{O}\left(occ \cdot (1 + \log_k(pq/occ))\right)$ for the nodes of type (1).

Each node v of type (1) will explore its k^2 children, one by one. The children u that contain points are also of type (1), and thus the cost of having considered u is charged to u itself, not to v. However, v may also contain many children that do not contain points (marked with 0 in the LOUDS representation), and those can only be charged to v. To reduce this cost, we may use succ_1 in the LOUDS region of the children of v to find only the children u that contain points. As the k^2 children distribute across k contiguous segments in the LOUDS layout, the cost that is charged to v decreases to $\mathcal{O}(k)$. Therefore, the time cost for all the nodes of type (1) is $\mathcal{O}\left(occ \cdot k(1 + \log_k(pq/occ))\right)$.

Now let us count all the nodes of type (2), as explained. Given the size of the nodes of level ℓ, there can be only $\mathcal{O}\left(1 + (p + q)/(s/k^{\ell-1})\right)$ of them that intersect with the border of the query area. When processing each such node v, we may perform k^2 probes to find children u of type (1) or (2). For children u of type (2), we charge the cost to u, but those of type (1) may have no points and thus must be charged to v as above. Again, we can use succ_1 on the children of v to reduce this cost to $\mathcal{O}(k)$ per node. Therefore, the time cost is $\mathcal{O}\left(k(1 + (p + q)/(s/k^{\ell-1}))\right)$. Summed over all the levels up to $h - 1$ (there are no nodes of type (2) at level h because the cells are of size 1), this yields a total cost of $\mathcal{O}(k \log_k s + p + q)$ for processing the nodes of type (2). Then the total query time is upper bounded by

$$\mathcal{O}\left(k \log_k s + p + q + occ \cdot k \left(1 + \log_k \frac{pq}{occ}\right)\right) = \mathcal{O}(p + q + (occ + 1)k \log_k s).$$

The more detailed formula shows that, as it happened with wavelet trees (Section 10.1.2), queries with smaller areas are solved faster, and the reporting time per occurrence decreases when the density of points in the area is higher. The shape of the area is also important, because the query time is proportional to its perimeter (this is a component of the cost that is not present in wavelet trees). For a square query of side q, the term $\mathcal{O}(q)$ is relevant only when the query area is large and has few points. Consider, however, a long and thin rectangular query such as $p = \mathcal{O}(1)$. Then the term $\mathcal{O}(q)$ is as high as if we scanned the query band sequentially, which is competitive only if the area has many points to report (indeed, all the query areas when we used k^2-trees in Section 9.2.1 had $p = 1$ or $q = 1$). Still, recall that these are pessimistic upper bounds; query times are significantly better when the points are clustered.

Finally, note that the query time worsens with k, which suggests that $k = 2$ is the best choice. As k grows, the k^2-tree gets shorter, but we may explore many empty cells as we go down. We can, however, obtain the best from both worlds by using different k values at different levels: we may use a larger k in the first levels, where most cells are nonempty, and let it decrease at deeper levels of the tree.

10.3 Weighted Points

When points have associated weights (or relevances, or priorities), an additional query becomes of interest: $\mathsf{top}(G, x_1, x_2, y_1, y_2, m)$ returns m heaviest points in $[x_1, x_2] \times [y_1, y_2]$, breaking ties arbitrarily among points of equal weight. The ways to solve this query depend on the structure we are using to represent the grid.

10.3.1 Wavelet Trees

In addition to the (conceptual) string S_v associated with each wavelet tree node v, consider the string P_v containing the priorities of the corresponding points (priorities are numbers in $[1, u]$). We will not store P_v explicitly, just a range maximum query data structure for it, as described in Section 7.4.1 for range minima (here we will denote rMq the analogous operation for range maxima). Therefore, in addition to the $|S_v| + o(|S_v|)$ bits of the bitvector B_v associated with node v, we will store $2|S_v| + o(|S_v|)$ bits for the rMq data structure of P_v. Thus the total space becomes $3n \log r + o(n \log r)$ bits (plus the bitvector for mapping coordinates, if needed). In addition, we will store an array $P[1, n]$ with the explicit priorities of the points sorted by y-coordinate (i.e., aligned to the wavelet tree leaves). This adds other $n \log u$ bits to the space. Recall that in practice we use a wavelet matrix, so there is one rMq structure per level ℓ, for the conceptual array P_ℓ that is aligned to the string S_ℓ.

Queries

With this structure, we can obtain the highest-priority point in any range $S_v[x_1^v, x_2^v]$, using $x_*^v = \mathsf{rMq}_{P_v}(x_1^v, x_2^v)$. We can then track down the position of x_*^v until reaching the leaves, to obtain the actual priority p^v of the point from the array P. Note that, if we have the $\mathcal{O}(\log r)$ maximal wavelet tree nodes covering the query range, then the first answer to the top query should be the maximum of the maxima of those $\mathcal{O}(\log r)$ intervals $P_v[x_1^v, x_2^v]$, say, $x_*^u = \mathsf{rMq}_{P_u}(x_1^u, x_2^u)$. The second maximum can be the maximum of any of the other intervals $P_v[x_1^v, x_2^v]$ of maximal nodes, or it can be the next maximum of the interval $P_u[x_1^u, x_2^u]$. The latter is either $\mathsf{rMq}_{P_u}(x_1^u, x_*^u - 1)$ or $\mathsf{rMq}_{P_u}(x_*^u + 1, x_2^u)$.

This leads to the following method for solving $\mathsf{top}(x_1, x_2, y_1, y_2, m)$ queries: (1) find the $\mathcal{O}(\log r)$ maximal wavelet tree nodes covering $[y_1, y_2]$, with the corresponding area $[x_1^v, x_2^v]$ of each maximal node v; (2) for each such v, compute $x_*^v = \mathsf{rMq}_{P_v}(x_1^v, x_2^v)$, find its actual priority p^v and y-coordinate y^v by tracking it to the leaves, and insert those tuples $(v, x_1^v, x_2^v, x_*^v, y^v, p^v)$ into a max-priority queue sorted by component p^v; (3) extract the maximum-priority tuple of the queue, $(u, x_1^u, x_2^u, x_*^u, y^u, p^u)$, and report the pair (y^u, p^u); (4) split the interval $[x_1^u, x_2^u]$ into $[x_1^u, x_*^u - 1]$ and $[x_*^u + 1, x_2^u]$, find their rMqs, and insert both in the queue (except empty intervals) as in step (2); (5) repeat step (3) until reporting m points. If we also want to report the x coordinates, we can do

---

Algorithm 10.6: Answering top with a wavelet matrix. Uses operations *insert* and *extractMax* on priority queue Q.

---

1 **Proc** top$(G, x_1, x_2, y_1, y_2, m)$

    Input : An $n \times r$ weighted grid G (seen as a sequence S, in turn seen as the bitvectors B_ℓ and values z_ℓ of its wavelet matrix, the rMq structures on arrays P_ℓ, and array P), range $[x_1, x_2] \times [y_1, y_2]$, and value m.

    Output: Outputs m highest-priority points in $[x_1, x_2] \times [y_1, y_2]$.

2      $Q \leftarrow$ empty max-queue of tuples $(\ell, a, b, x_1, x_2, x_*, y, p)$ sorted by p

3   *populate*$(Q, x_1, x_2, y_1, y_2, 1, 1, r)$

4   **for** $i \leftarrow 1$ **to** m **do**

5          $(\ell, a, b, x_1, x_2, x_*, y, p) \leftarrow$ *extractMax*(Q) (stop if Q is empty)

6   **output** (y, p) (trace x_* upwards to output the x-coordinate)

7   **if** $x_1 < x_*$ **then** *addcandidate*$(Q, x_1, x_* - 1, \ell, a, b)$

8   **if** $x_* < x_2$ **then** *addcandidate*$(Q, x_* + 1, x_2, \ell, a, b)$

9 **Proc** *populate*$(Q, x_1, x_2, y_1, y_2, \ell, a, b)$

    Input : Priority queue Q, range $[x_1, x_2]$ of level ℓ, inside a segment of S_ℓ that represents symbols in $[a, b]$, and symbol range $[y_1, y_2]$.

    Output: Inserts in Q the tuples for the maximal segments covering the query.

10   **if** $x_1 > x_2$ **or** $[a, b] \cap [y_1, y_2] = \emptyset$ **then** **return**

11   **if** $[a, b] \subseteq [y_1, y_2]$ **then** *addcandidate*$(Q, x_1, x_2, \ell, a, b)$

12   **else**

13          $x_1^l \leftarrow \mathsf{rank}_0(B_\ell, x_1 - 1) + 1; x_2^l \leftarrow \mathsf{rank}_0(B_\ell, x_2)$

14          $x_1^r \leftarrow z_\ell + x_1 - x_1^l + 1; x_2^r \leftarrow z_\ell + x_2 - x_2^l$

15   *populate*$(Q, x_1^l, x_2^l, y_1, y_2, \ell + 1, a, \lfloor (a+b)/2 \rfloor)$

16   *populate*$(Q, x_1^r, x_2^r, y_1, y_2, \ell + 1, \lfloor (a+b)/2 \rfloor + 1, b)$

17 **Proc** *addcandidate*$(Q, x_1, x_2, \ell, a, b)$

    Input : Priority queue Q, and range $S_\ell[x_1, x_2]$ over symbols in $[a, b]$.

    Output: Inserts the tuple of $S_\ell[x_1, x_2]$ in Q.

18      $x_* \leftarrow \mathsf{rMq}_{P_\ell}(x_1, x_2); x' \leftarrow x_*; y_a \leftarrow a; y_b \leftarrow b; l \leftarrow \ell$

19   **while** $y_a < y_b$ **do**

20   **if** $\mathsf{access}(B_l, x') = 0$ **then**

21              $x' \leftarrow \mathsf{rank}_0(B_l, x'); y_b \leftarrow \lfloor (y_a + y_b)/2 \rfloor$

22   **else** $x' \leftarrow z_l + \mathsf{rank}_1(B_l, x'); y_a \leftarrow \lfloor (y_a + y_b)/2 \rfloor + 1$

23          $l \leftarrow l + 1$

24   *insert*$(Q, (\ell, a, b, x_1, x_2, x_*, y_a, \mathsf{read}(P, x')))$

---

it in step (3) by tracking the position x_*^v upwards to the root. Algorithm 10.6 gives the details.

Example 10.9 *Figure 10.5 shows a version of the grid of Figure 10.3, where we have given priorities to the points (priorities are written on the grid instead of the black circles). Below each (conceptual) string S_v in the wavelet tree, we show the corresponding*

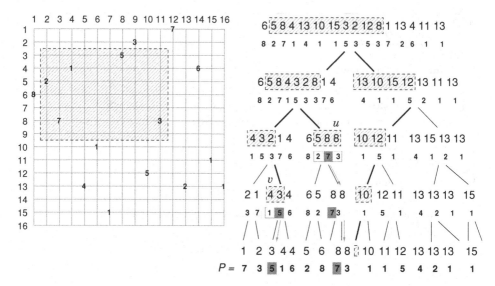

Figure 10.5. Solving top(2, 11, 3, 9, 2) on the grid of Figure 10.3, now with priorities associated with points (these are drawn in the grid as numbers in the positions of the points). The (virtual) arrays P_v are written as small bold numbers below the (also virtual) strings S_v. We show in gray the maximum priority in each of the nonempty maximal nodes that cover the query (v and u), and with arrows the way they are tracked down to the leaves, where the actual priorities are stored in array P.

(also conceptual) array P_v, in smaller bold numbers. Recall that we store B_v instead of S_v and the rMq data structure for P_v instead of P_v. At the bottom of the wavelet tree, we show the (actually stored) array P of the priorities.

Consider the query top(2, 11, 3, 9, 2), whose area is the same as that of Example 10.3. There are two relevant maximal nodes covering the y-coordinate range [3, 9]. Boxes with gray borders show the corresponding areas of the (conceptual) arrays P_v for these two nodes. The first, v, contains the priorities $P_v[1, 2] = \mathbf{1}, \mathbf{5}$, whereas the second, u, contains the priorities $P_u[2, 4] = \mathbf{2}, \mathbf{7}, \mathbf{3}$. On v, we compute $x_*^v = \mathsf{rMq}_{P_v}(1, 2) = 2$, which indicates that the maximum is at position 2. We track this position down until finding the priority $p^v = 5$ in array P on the bottom (the tracking process is shown with gray blocks and arrows). On u, we compute $x_*^u = \mathsf{rMq}_{P_u}(2, 4) = 3$, indicating that the maximum is at position 3. We track this point down until finding the priority $p^u = 7$. Since this is the highest priority, we report this point as the most important one in the two-dimensional range. Now we cut the range $P_u[2, 4]$ into two, $P_u[2, 2]$ and $P_u[4, 4]$, and insert them also in the set of candidates. The next largest one is $p^v = 5$, so this is reported as the second most important point and the query process is complete.

Time and Space

Let $q = y_2 - y_1 + 1$, as before. Recall from Section 10.1.2 that there are only $\mathcal{O}(\log q)$ maximal nodes covering the area, as there at most two per level and they have a height of at most $\lceil \log q \rceil$. After spending $\mathcal{O}(\log r)$ time to find those maximal nodes, we spend $\mathcal{O}(\log \log n)$ time to find each x_*^v value (this is the cost of our rMq implementation in Section 7.4.1) and then $\mathcal{O}(\log q)$ time to find the corresponding priority, p^v. We then repeat this process $2m$ times, twice each time we report an element and split its interval $[x_1^v, x_2^v]$ into two. The priority queue contains at most $2\log q + m$ elements, thus its operations cost $\mathcal{O}(\log m + \log\log q)$. The total cost is, therefore,

$$\mathcal{O}(\log r + (m + \log q)(\log q + \log m + \log\log n))$$

time. For example, for small m up to $\mathcal{O}(\log r)$, and disregarding loglogarithmic factors, the time is $\mathcal{O}(\log r \log q)$. For larger m, the time is $\mathcal{O}(m\log(qm))$.

The extra space needed by the priority queue is insignificant. Note that, if we let Q grow dynamically, we could proceed without knowing the value of m beforehand. We could just successively output the points with decreasing priority until desired.

On a grid of size $n \times r$, n points, and priorities in $[1, u]$, the structure requires $n(3\log r + \log u) + o(n\log r)$ bits, which is about twice the space needed to store the points and the priorities. This is due to the rMq structures we store at every level of the wavelet matrix. A way to trade this space for time is to store the rMq structures only every tth level. If we have to process a range $S_v[x_1, x_2]$ at a node without rMq structures, we split it into its two children, recursively until reaching nodes with rMq structures computed. Thus the (at most two) maximal nodes at distance $h < t$ to the next sampled level become 2^h nodes, which adds to a blowup factor of 2^t across the t consecutive non-sampled levels.

Then the space decreases to $n((1 + 2/t)\log r + \log u) + o(n\log r)$ bits, but the time becomes $\mathcal{O}(\log r + (m + (2^t/t)\log q)(\log q + \log m + t + \log\log n))$.[3] Therefore, this idea is advisable only for small t (which still produces significant space savings).

A related idea that works well in practice is to store rMq structures for all the nodes over some minimum height t. Maximal nodes below that level are solved by brute force: we scan the ranges $P_v[x_1, x_2]$, reaching P for each element and inserting it in the queue. Since the cost to reach P is only $\mathcal{O}(t)$, accessing contiguous positions in P_v is not so expensive, and the areas $[x_1, x_2]$ near the leaves are usually short, this is generally a good space/time tradeoff.

10.3.2 K^2-Trees

A different solution is possible by modifying the k^2-tree structure. At the root node, we take a point (x, y) with maximum priority p and *remove* it from the grid. The triple (x, y, p) is stored and associated with the root. Now we partition the grid into k^2 subgrids and proceed recursively, removing and separately storing a highest-priority point in each case. Note that, eventually, every point in the grid is associated with the triple of a k^2-tree node.

Example 10.10 *Figure 10.6 adds priorities to the grid of Figure 10.4, as numbers in the places of the points. Observe how the removal of the most important point of each quadrant alters the shape of the k^2-tree. In particular, this tree has no leaves at level*

---

[3] Here 2^t is divided by t because the query will contain at most $(\log q)/t$ levels with rMq structures, each of them contributing 2^t ranges to the final candidate set.

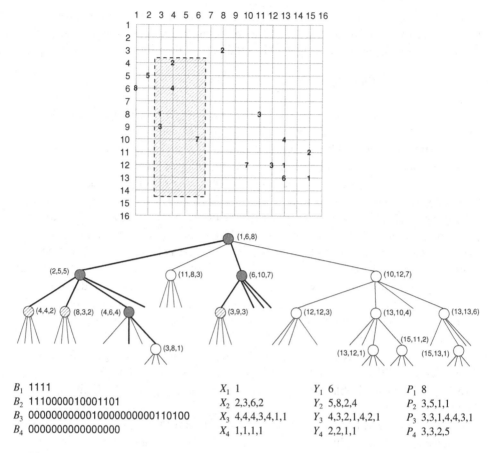

B_1 1111

X_1 1 Y_1 6 P_1 8

B_2 1110000010001101

X_2 2,3,6,2 Y_2 5,8,2,4 P_2 3,5,1,1

B_3 00000000000010000000000110100

X_3 4,4,4,3,4,1,1 Y_3 4,3,2,1,4,2,1 P_3 3,3,1,4,4,3,1

B_4 0000000000000000

X_4 1,1,1,1 Y_4 2,2,1,1 P_4 3,3,2,5

Figure 10.6. The grid of Figure 10.4, now with weighted points, and its k^2-tree based representation (a LOUDS bitvector separated by levels, and arrays of local x-coordinates, local y-coordinates, and differential priorities). We also illustrate the prioritized traversal for query top$(3, 6, 4, 14, 2)$. The processed nodes are grayed, while the hatched ones are inserted into the priority queue but not processed.

h. Note that each point is explicitly mentioned as a triple at some k^2-tree node. Grayed and shaded nodes, as well as the representation on the bottom, will be used later.

Succinct Representation

While the LOUDS representation of the k^2-tree topology reduces its size because of the removal of the explicit nodes, the heaviest part of the space is now in the explicit tuples (x, y, p) that are associated with each node. This can, however, be greatly reduced, because of the features of the k^2-tree.

Note that the k^2-tree now has exactly n nodes. Conceptually, we store arrays $X[1, n]$, $Y[1, n]$, and $P[1, n]$ for the x-coordinates, y-coordinates, and priorities p associated with the n nodes, in levelwise order. Therefore, if v is the identifier of a k^2-tree node in the LOUDS representation, then its tuple is $(X[v], Y[v], P[v])$.

Note that the $X[v]$ and $Y[v]$ values at level ℓ belong to a submatrix of size $(s/k^{\ell-1}) \times (s/k^{\ell-1})$, thus if we store their *local* coordinates, and separate X and Y into arrays X_ℓ

and Y_ℓ, one per level, then the local coordinates in the arrays of level ℓ require only $\log(s/k^{\ell-1})$ bits. We can easily track their global coordinate values as we descend by the k^2-tree.

To measure the effect of this reduction, consider the worst case where we have $(k^2)^{\ell-1}$ points at level ℓ, up to level $1 + \log_{k^2} n$, for n a power of k^2. The total space for one array (X or Y) is then

$$\sum_{\ell=1}^{1+\log_{k^2} n} (k^2)^{\ell-1} \log(s/k^{\ell-1}) = \sum_{\ell=0}^{\log_{k^2} n} (k^2)^\ell (\log s - \ell \log k) = \frac{k^2}{k^2-1} \frac{n \log \frac{s^2}{n}}{2} + \mathcal{O}(n)$$

bits.[4] When we add both X and Y, we obtain about the same space of the basic k^2-tree representation (Section 10.2). The LOUDS representation adds at most nk^2 bits, which can also be reduced to $\mathcal{O}(n \log k)$ by using sparse bitvectors (Section 4.4); this space component is also present in the basic k^2-tree. Again, the space decreases further if the points are clustered.

The case of the priorities is handled in a different way; recall Section 8.5.6. Since the p components of the tuples decrease as we go down in the tree, we store each priority component differentially with respect to its parent (except the root priority, which is stored as is). When we traverse the tree top-down, we can easily reconstruct the original value. Since the resulting numbers can be arbitrary, though we expect many of them to be small, we use a representation like direct access codes (Section 3.4.2) for P. It is a good idea to separate P by levels, into arrays P_ℓ, because the values could be smaller at deeper levels, and thus the direct access codes could be optimized differently for each level.

If the arrays X, Y, and P are separated by levels, it is convenient to separate the bitvector B into levels B_ℓ as well. In this way, a node v in level ℓ (that is, described at positions $B_\ell[k^2(v-1)+1, k^2 v]$) has its associated tuple at $(X_\ell[v], Y_\ell[v], P_\ell[v])$. The navigation toward children is still possible: the tth child of v exists iff $B_\ell[k^2(v-1) + t] = 1$, and if it exists, it is node $v' = \mathsf{rank}_1(B_\ell, k^2(v-1)+t)$ at level $\ell+1$.

Example 10.11 *Figure 10.6 shows the described representation on the bottom. For example, consider the tuple $(4, 6, 4)$, at level $\ell = 3$. The node corresponds to $v = 3$ in this level, which is represented at $B_\ell[k^2(v-1)+1, k^2 v] = B_3[9, 12]$. Here we see that it has only one child, the fourth. This child is $v' = \mathsf{rank}_1(B_3, 12) = 1$ at B_4, the one holding the point $(3, 8, 1)$.*

The tuple $(4, 6, 4)$ associated with v is represented at $(X_\ell[v], Y_\ell[v], P_\ell[v]) = (X_3[3], Y_3[3], P_3[3]) = (4, 2, 1)$. To interpret these data, we must consider that this k^2-tree node covers the third sub-quadrant of the first quadrant, that is, the area $[1, 4] \times [5, 8]$, thus we add the offset 0 to $X_3[3]$ and the offset 4 to $Y_3[3]$ to obtain the global point coordinates, $(4, 6)$. For the priority, the value 1 is relative to that of the parent, 5, thus the actual priority is $5 - 1 = 4$.

In practice, storing the cells $X_\ell[i]$ and $Y_\ell[i]$ together is more cache-friendly, because they will always be accessed together.

---

[4] We have used the identity $\sum_{\ell=0}^{t} \ell a^\ell = \frac{a^{t+1}((t+1)(a-1)-a)+a}{(a-1)^2}$.

Algorithm 10.7: Prioritized traversal for top on a k^2-tree. Uses operations *insert* and *extractMax* on priority queue Q.

---

1 **Proc** top$(G, x_1, x_2, y_1, y_2, m)$

   Input : An $s \times s$ grid G (seen as a k^2-tree, with s a power of k, in turn seen as
          arrays B_ℓ, X_ℓ, Y_ℓ, and P_ℓ), range $[x_1, x_2] \times [y_1, y_2]$, and value m.

   Output: Outputs m highest-priority points in $[x_1, x_2] \times [y_1, y_2]$.

2    $Q \leftarrow$ empty priority queue on tuples $(v, \ell, x, y, p, x_0, y_0, s)$, sorted by p

3    $insert(Q, (1, 1, \mathsf{access}(X_1, 1), \mathsf{access}(Y_1, 1), \mathsf{access}(P_1, 1), 0, 0, s))$

4   **while** $m > 0$ **and** Q *is not empty* **do**

5       $(v, \ell, x, y, p, x_0, y_0, s) \leftarrow extractMax(Q)$

6   **if** $x_1 \le x \le x_2$ **and** $y_1 \le y \le y_2$ **then**

7   **output** (x, y, p)

8          $m \leftarrow m - 1$

9   **if** $s > 1$ **then**

10         $l \leftarrow s/k$

11         $c_1 \leftarrow \lceil \max(x_1 - x_0, 1)/l \rceil$; $c_2 \leftarrow \lceil \min(x_2 - x_0, s)/l \rceil$

12         $r_1 \leftarrow \lceil \max(y_1 - y_0, 1)/l \rceil$; $r_2 \leftarrow \lceil \min(y_2 - y_0, s)/l \rceil$

13   **for** $r \leftarrow r_1$ **to** r_2 **do**

14   **for** $c \leftarrow c_1$ **to** c_2 **do**

15   **if** $\mathsf{access}(B_\ell, k^2(v-1) + (r-1)k + c) = 1$ **then**

16                  $v' \leftarrow \mathsf{rank}_1(B_\ell, k^2(v-1) + (r-1)k + c)$

17                  $p' \leftarrow p - \mathsf{access}(P_{\ell+1}, v')$

18                  $x' \leftarrow x_0 + \mathsf{access}(X_{\ell+1}, v')$

19                  $y' \leftarrow y_0 + \mathsf{access}(Y_{\ell+1}, v')$

20                  $x_0' \leftarrow x_0 + (c-1)l$; $y_0' \leftarrow y_0 + (r-1)l$

21                  $insert(Q, (v', \ell+1, x', y', p', x_0', y_0', l))$

Queries

On this structure, a query top(x_1, x_2, y_1, y_2, m) can be solved as follows. We initialize a max-priority queue Q where we insert the root node of the k^2-tree. Queue Q will store k^2-tree nodes, sorted by the priority p of their associated point (x, y, p).

Now we iteratively extract the first node, v (initially, this will be the root we have just inserted). If its associated point (x, y, p) falls within $[x_1, x_2] \times [y_1, y_2]$, we report it as the next highest-priority point in the query area. Now we insert in Q all the children of v with nonempty intersection with the area $[x_1, x_2] \times [y_1, y_2]$. As soon as we have reported m points, or if Q becomes empty because there are less than m points in the query area, we stop.

Algorithm 10.7 gives the details. While the process has no time guarantees (apart from the time to report all the points in the range), it works well in practice.

Example 10.12 *Figure 10.6 also illustrates the process to solve the query* top$(3, 6, 4, 14, 2)$. *The grayed nodes are those actually processed, whereas the hatched ones were inserted into Q but not processed.*

First, we insert the root node with its associated point $(x, y, p) = (1, 6, 8)$ *in* Q.
Then we start the iterative process. We extract the root and consider the point $(1, 6, 8)$.
Since it is outside the query area $[3, 6] \times [4, 14]$, *we discard it. Now we consider the 4*
children of the root, of which the first and the third intersect with the query range. Both
are then inserted into Q.

When we extract the maximum from Q, *we obtain the third child of the root, with*
associated point $(6, 10, 7)$. *This point is inside the query area, thus it is reported. All*
the 4 quadrants of this node intersect with the query area, but only the first child has
elements. This node (associated with point $(3, 9, 3)$*) is inserted into* Q.

We extract the next maximum from Q, *obtaining the first child of the root, associated*
with point $(2, 5, 5)$. *This element is outside the query area, so it is discarded. All the 4*
quadrants of this node intersect with the query area, so we insert into Q *its 3 existing*
children, associated with points $(4, 4, 2)$, $(8, 3, 2)$, *and* $(4, 6, 4)$.

When we extract the next maximum from Q, *we obtain the node associated with point*
$(4, 6, 4)$. *Since it is inside the query area, we report it and finish.*

Reducing Working Space

A potential problem with Algorithm 10.7 is that the space needed by the priority queue
Q is related to the time needed to solve the query. In particular, Q may become large
when we are forced to explore many nodes whose maximum points are promising but
are slightly outside of the query area. The only upper bound to the size of Q is given by
the time obtained in Section 10.2.1 for reporting all the points in the query area: it can
be proportional to the perimeter of the area plus the number of points in it. While good
secondary-memory implementations for priority queues exist, it is worth considering
a variant that uses only logarithmic extra space, even if it traverses more nodes.

Now we will store our best current results (up to m) in a min-priority queue R sorted
by priority. As long as $|R| < m$, every new element we find is inserted in R, but as
soon as $|R| = m$ we accept new elements only if their priority is larger than $min(R)$, its
minimum priority. Moreover, if we accept a new element when $|R| = m$, then the one
with minimum priority is ejected from R, to maintain its size at m.

With this queue, we perform the recursive traversal of Algorithm 10.5, pruned as follows: Before entering an area, we check if its maximum triple (x, y, p) is good enough
to be inserted in R. If it is not, we abandon the whole area because no other element
below the node can be relevant.

Note that this method may traverse more nodes than Algorithm 10.7. Early in the
process, we may explore areas that seem promising for the current results in R, but
later all the points the area inserted in R become ejected by heavier points found in
other areas. Instead, Algorithm 10.7 traverses the tree in an order that guarantees that
no such ultimately irrelevant areas will be processed. In exchange, the extra space is
now just the m tuples for R plus the $\mathcal{O}(\log_k s)$ words for the recursion, and the procedure
performs well in practice too (in addition, it might be faster because it handles a much
smaller priority queue). Algorithm 10.8 gives the details.

Example 10.13 *Consider again the query* top$(3, 6, 4, 14, 2)$ *on the* k^2*-tree of*
Figure 10.6, now with the recursive traversal. The root node is not in the area, so we
descend to its first and third children, which intersect with the query area. The triple
$(2, 5, 5)$ *at the first child of the root does not belong to the area either, but all of its*

Algorithm 10.8: Recursive traversal for top on a k^2-tree. Uses operations *insert*, *min*, and *extractMin* on priority queue R.

---

1 **Proc** top$(G, x_1, x_2, y_1, y_2, m)$

    Input : An $s \times s$ grid G (seen as a k^2-tree, with s a power of k, in turn seen as
                  arrays B_ℓ, X_ℓ, Y_ℓ, and P_ℓ), range $[x_1, x_2] \times [y_1, y_2]$, and value m.

    Output: Outputs m highest-priority points in $[x_1, x_2] \times [y_1, y_2]$.

2     $R \leftarrow$ empty priority queue on tuples (x, y, p) of size m, sorted by p

3     $top(1, 1, 2 \cdot \mathsf{access}(P_1, 1), x_1, x_2, y_1, y_2, 0, 0, s)$

4   **output** R

5 **Proc** $top(v, \ell, p, x_1, x_2, y_1, y_2, x_0, y_0, s)$

    Input : k^2-tree node v of level ℓ for sub-grid
              $[x_0 + 1, x_0 + s] \times [y_0 + 1, y_0 + s]$, with parent priority p, and
              nonempty range $[x_1, x_2] \times [y_1, y_2]$ intersecting the sub-grid.

    Output: Inserts in R the relevant sub-grid points in $[x_1, x_2] \times [y_1, y_2]$.

6     $p \leftarrow p - \mathsf{access}(P_\ell, v)$

7   **if** $|R| \geq m$ **and** $p \leq min(R)$ **then**

8   **return**

9     $x \leftarrow x_0 + \mathsf{access}(X_\ell, v)$

10     $y \leftarrow y_0 + \mathsf{access}(Y_\ell, v)$

11   **if** $x_1 \leq x \leq x_2$ **and** $y_1 \leq y \leq y_2$ **then**

12   **if** $|R| = m$ **then** $extractMin(R)$

13         $insert(R, (x, y, p))$

14   **if** $s > 1$ **then**

15         $l \leftarrow s/k$

16         $c_1 \leftarrow \lceil \max(x_1 - x_0, 1)/l \rceil$; $c_2 \leftarrow \lceil \min(x_2 - x_0, s)/l \rceil$

17         $r_1 \leftarrow \lceil \max(y_1 - y_0, 1)/l \rceil$; $r_2 \leftarrow \lceil \min(y_2 - y_0, s)/l \rceil$

18   **for** $r \leftarrow r_1$ **to** r_2 **do**

19   **for** $c \leftarrow c_1$ **to** c_2 **do**

20   **if** $\mathsf{access}(B_\ell, k^2(v - 1) + (r - 1)k + c) = 1$ **then**

21                     $v' \leftarrow \mathsf{rank}_1(B_\ell, k^2(v - 1) + (r - 1)k + c)$

22                     $x_0' \leftarrow x_0 + (c - 1)l$; $y_0' \leftarrow y_0 + (r - 1)l$

23                     $top(v', \ell + 1, p, x_1, x_2, y_1, y_2, x_0', y_0', l)$

---

children intersect with the area. The triples of the first and third children, $(4, 4, 2)$ and $(4, 6, 4)$, are inserted in R because they belong to the area. Thus our best answer up to now is $R = \langle (4, 6, 4), (4, 4, 2) \rangle$. The subtree rooted by the triple $(3, 8, 1)$ is not considered because its priority is already not good enough for our current R.

When we enter the third child of the root, the triple $(6, 10, 7)$ is inserted in R and it ejects $(4, 4, 2)$, so we reach $R = \langle (6, 10, 7), (4, 6, 4) \rangle$. The subtree rooted at the triple $(3, 9, 3)$ is discarded, because it is not good enough to get into R. As we have completed the (pruned) traversal, we output R and finish.

Note that, compared to the prioritized traversal of Example 10.12, we have pro-cessed the triple (4, 4, 2), *which was ultimately not part of the result.*

A way to traverse fewer nodes is to order the (up to k^2) recursive calls in line 23 of Algorithm 10.8 by decreasing priority. This only increases the recursion space to $\mathcal{O}(k^2 \log_k s)$ words.

Construction

The construction of this structure is not much different from that of the regular k^2-tree in Algorithm 9.7, now from a set of n points (x_i, y_i, p_i) (recalling that $E[p].u$ is the x-coordinate and $E[p].v$ is the y-coordinate). The main difference is that we have to scan each new range to process, in order to find the maximum priority, remove it, and append its data in the corresponding arrays X_ℓ, Y_ℓ, and P_ℓ. The values x_0 and y_0 are already stored in the queue, so computing the local coordinates is easy. To store differential priorities, we must include the p component of the parent node in the tuples. The construction complexity does not change.

10.4 Higher Dimensions

Up to now we have considered only two-dimensional grids. In many cases, grids of higher dimensions arise, in particular for databases storing multi-dimensional data cubes.

In two dimensions, wavelet trees require space close to the worst-case entropy of the data points and achieve time complexities close to the best possible ones. However, all the known data structures achieving polylogarithmic query times in dimension $d > 2$ require superlinear space (essentially, $\mathcal{O}(n \log^{d-1} n)$ bits). Thus wavelet trees are less interesting for higher dimensions, because they quickly become too large.

It is worth noting, however, that some restricted queries can be done in one extra dimension without blowing up the space. In particular, giving weights to points and looking for the heaviest points in a range can be interpreted as having a third dimension (the weight) and performing sorted range reporting in the area $[x_1, x_2] \times [y_1, y_2] \times [1, u]$. Thus we can handle ranges of the form $[x_1, x_2] \times [y_1, y_2] \times [1, z_2]$ and $[x_1, x_2] \times [y_1, y_2] \times [z_1, u]$ in logarithmic time and linear space, but not the general case $[x_1, x_2] \times [y_1, y_2] \times [z_1, z_2]$.

Quadtrees, instead, can be extended to d dimensions in a natural way without exceeding $\mathcal{O}(dn \log n)$ bits: each node halves the coordinate space across each dimension, then having 2^d children (for $d = 3$, this is known as an octree). The k^2-trees can be extended similarly to k^d-trees in d dimensions (not to be confused with kd-trees, see the references at the end of the chapter). They reach $\mathcal{O}\left(n \log \frac{s^d}{n} + dn \log k\right)$ bits, which is still linear space. The LOUDS representation and the query algorithms are completely analogous to k^2-trees. In exchange, these structures offer much weaker worst-case guarantees for range searches, as we have seen. For a query of side q, the time becomes $\mathcal{O}\left(q^{d-1} + (occ + 1) \cdot k^{d-1} \log_k s\right)$. While it worsens exponentially fast with d, the structure still performs reasonably well in low dimensions.

10.5 Applications

The applications of grids are countless, and extend beyond the most obvious ones of computational geometry and geographic information systems. In this section we present a small sample of those.

10.5.1 Dominating Points

A point (x, y) is said to *dominate* another point (x', y') if $x \le x'$ and $y \le y'$. A point is said to be *dominating* if it is not dominated by any other point. Finding dominating points on a grid is useful in many situations. For example, assume the x-coordinate measures the price of cars and the y-coordinate is their fuel consumption. Then a car is dominated by another that is cheaper and uses less fuel. A relevant query is then to find the dominating cars within some price range.

Another simple application is as follows: The x-coordinates of points are the time an event occurs, such as the measuring of the temperature in a region, and the y-coordinate is the measured value. If we want to report the historic minima (years that have been the coldest up to then), we have to retrieve the dominating points. We might also be interested in analyzing only a part of the grid, between years x_1 and x_2.

Sorted range reporting with wavelet trees provides an elegant solution to the problem of finding the dominating points in $[x_1, x_2] \times [y_1, y_2]$. Note that the leftmost point in the range must be a dominating one (recall that all the x-coordinates of points are different in a wavelet tree). Therefore, we find the leftmost point (x, y) in $[x_1, x_2] \times [y_1, y_2]$. Since this point dominates every other point in $[x, x_2] \times [y, y_2]$ and there are no other points in $[x_1, x] \times [y_1, y_2]$, we can now continue by finding the leftmost point (x', y') in $[x + 1, x_2] \times [y_1, y - 1]$, then the leftmost point in $[x' + 1, x_2] \times [y_1, y' - 1]$, and so on, until the remaining grid has no points. Using Algorithm 10.3, each dominating point is obtained in time $\mathcal{O}(\log r)$.

For this to work properly on wavelet trees, we must be cautious with the ties in x-coordinates. For range reporting, we have broken ties arbitrarily to build a grid with exactly one point per column. This time we must ensure that, in the case of a tie between (x, y) and (x, y'), the point with the lower y-coordinate is put to the left of the point with the higher y-coordinate.

If we need to use a definition of dominance where the larger y-coordinate dominates, we can modify the mapping accordingly. But if we need to perform both kinds of queries on the same structure, we may still use the order for the original definition and solve queries with the alternative definition. In this case, we make use of the bitvector B that maps the points: given the next leftmost point (x, y), we find its position in B with $p \leftarrow \mathsf{select}_0(B, x)$, then take the rightmost point that is mapped to the same x, $p' \leftarrow \mathsf{succ}_1(B, p) - 1$, and finally map it back to $x' \leftarrow x + p' - p$. We then find the rightmost point (x^*, y^*) in $[x, x'] \times [y_1, y_2]$, with a procedure analogous to $\mathsf{leftmost}$, report (x^*, y^*), and continue with $[x' + 1, x_2] \times [y^* + 1, y_2]$.

Example 10.14 *Consider the query range of Figure 10.3, this time to find the dominating points in $[2, 11] \times [3, 9]$. First we find the leftmost point, $(2, 5)$. Since this dominates the area $[2, 11] \times [5, 9]$ and there cannot be other points in $[2, 2] \times [3, 9]$, we* *now ask for the leftmost point in* $[3, 11] \times [3, 4]$. *The result is point* $(4, 4)$. *Now we ask for the leftmost point in* $[5, 11] \times [3, 3]$, *obtaining point* $(8, 3)$. *We are now done, since the remaining grid is empty (in general, we terminate when the grid has no points).*

10.5.2 Geographic Information Systems

We describe some possible applications of grid data structures to Geographic Information Systems (GIS). GIS need to handle large volumes of data and in many cases run on small devices such as cellphones, where the use of less memory to represent and transmit the data is important.

Map Services

Applications offering intelligent maps on the cellphone are now commonplace. The most basic service one expects is to display the map around the current location. Assume we have the intersections of the city stored as points in a grid. The streets connecting the intersections are stored in the form of a planar map, which adds at most $8n + o(n)$ bits to the grid data (recall Section 9.5.3). In addition we must store about $n \log n + o(n \log n)$ bits for a permutation that maps the points stored in the node order of the planar graph to the x-coordinate order in the grid, and vice versa.

Then displaying a window of the map around the current position requires a range reporting query to retrieve all the grid points within the window. We find the graph node v that corresponds to each retrieved point, and for each graph neighbor u of v, we find the grid point corresponding to u and draw a straight street segment between v and u (possibly clipped by the window if u falls outside of it).

Example 10.15 *Figure 10.7 shows how we display the streets of a city that intersect a window. It also shows that there may be streets that intersect the window, but whose endpoints are not captured by our range query.*

A solution to the problem illustrated in the example is to ensure that every street contains a node every d meters, even if the street is straight and has no intersections. Then, querying the range $[x_1 - d, x_2 + d] \times [y_1 - d, y_2 + d]$ is sufficient to capture all the street segments that intersect the window $[x_1, x_2] \times [y_1, y_2]$.

Facility Location

A typical query is to find the places in a neighborhood where some kind of facility exists, in some cases prioritized in some form. For example, consider a city where we set all the gas stations as points on a grid, and use as priority the price of the gas (giving higher priority to the lower price). Then queries like $\mathsf{top}(x_1, x_2, y_1, y_2, m)$ are useful for retrieving the m cheapest gas stations in a neighborhood.

A less obvious application is the problem of finding the facility closest to a point, for example, the closest drugstore. Distance can be measured with a complex function, such as the shortest street path considering traffic times. However, simple Manhattan distance (sum of the coordinate differences) or Euclidean distance give a rough approximation that is useful in obtaining a small set of reasonably close candidates, whose precise distances can then be evaluated one by one.

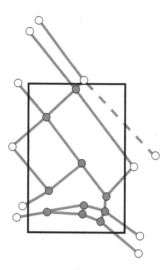

Figure 10.7. Displaying a window (enclosed by the black rectangle) of the city map of Figure 9.20. We retrieve the points that fall inside the window (grayed) using a range query, and then the neighbors of each using graph operations. Some of those fall outside the window (white nodes) but are still necessary to draw the street segments from the gray nodes. Note that there may be segments (like the dashed one) that intersect the window but whose endpoints fall outside.

Consider the problem of finding the m points closest to a query point (x, y), where the distance to (x', y') is measured as $|x - x'| + |y - y'|$ (Manhattan distance). We call this operation $\mathsf{closest}(x, y, m)$. We can use a technique similar to Algorithm 10.7. In this case the priority p for an area $[x_1, x_2] \times [y_1, y_2]$ is computed on the fly as $d_x + d_y$, where $d_x = x_1 - x$ if $x < x_1$, $x - x_2$ if $x > x_2$, and 0 otherwise, and d_y is computed analogously. This is a lower bound to the Manhattan distance between (x, y) and any point in $[x_1, x_2] \times [y_1, y_2]$. Therefore, the priority is not stored in the data structure, which becomes a simple k^2-tree (with no weighted points). A practical improvement is to favor smaller submatrices when they have the same priority in Q, as they are likely to yield points closer to the minimum distance.

Algorithm 10.9 gives the pseudocode. An alternative would have been to use successive range queries on larger and larger square areas centered on (x, y), stopping as soon as m points were found. A nice property of Algorithm 10.9 is that it processes exactly the same nodes that would be traversed if we knew the distance d to the mth closest point and issued a range reporting query on the area $[x - d, x + d] \times [y - d, y + d]$.

Example 10.16 *Consider finding the $m = 2$ points that are closest to $(x, y) = (8, 8)$ in the grid of Figure 10.4. The minimum distances to the four main submatrices are 0, 1, 1, and 2, respectively. These are inserted in Q. We then iteratively extract the node with the minimum distance to (x, y) and insert its submatrices, until finding the first m points. To avoid a tedious enumeration, the process is illustrated in Figure 10.8. The points finally found are $(11, 8)$ and $(6, 10)$.*

In Section 10.3.2 we considered the space problem posed by an uncontrolled growth of Q. It is possible to implement an analogous to Algorithm 10.8 as well and use no extra space at the expense of traversing slightly more nodes.

Algorithm 10.9: Procedure for closest on a k^2-tree.

---

1 **Proc** closest(G, x, y, m)

    Input : An $s \times s$ nonempty grid G (seen as k^2-tree T, with s a power of k),
             point (x, y), and value m.

    Output: Outputs m points closest to (x, y).

2   $Q \leftarrow \langle (1, 1, 0, 0, 0, s) \rangle$ (min-priority queue on tuples
    $(v, \ell, d, x_0, y_0, s)$, sorted by distance d and then by s)

3   **while** $m > 0$ **and** Q *is not empty* **do**

4     $(v, \ell, d, x_0, y_0, s) \leftarrow extractMin(Q)$

5   **if** $s = 1$ **then**

6   output $(x_0 + 1, y_0 + 1, d)$

7       $m \leftarrow m - 1$

8   **else**

9       $l \leftarrow s/k$

10       $c_1 \leftarrow \lceil \max(x_1 - x_0, 1)/l \rceil$; $c_2 \leftarrow \lceil \min(x_2 - x_0, s)/l \rceil$

11       $r_1 \leftarrow \lceil \max(y_1 - y_0, 1)/l \rceil$; $r_2 \leftarrow \lceil \min(y_2 - y_0, s)/l \rceil$

12   **for** $r \leftarrow r_1$ **to** r_2 **do**

13   **for** $c \leftarrow c_1$ **to** c_2 **do**

14   **if** childrenlabeled($T, v, (r - 1)k + c$) **then**

15             $v' \leftarrow$ labeledchild($T, v, (r - 1)k + c$)

16             $x'_0 \leftarrow x_0 + (c - 1)l$; $y'_0 \leftarrow y_0 + (r - 1)l$

17             $d' \leftarrow 0$

18   **if** $x \leq x'_0$ **then** $d' \leftarrow d' + x'_0 + 1 - x$

19   **else if** $x > x'_0 + l$ **then** $d' \leftarrow d' + x - x'_0 - l$

20   **if** $y \leq y'_0$ **then** $d' \leftarrow d' + y'_0 + 1 - y$

21   **else if** $y > y'_0 + l$ **then** $d' \leftarrow d' + y - y'_0 - l$

22             $insert(Q, (v', \ell + 1, d', x'_0, y'_0, l))$

Temporal Maps

Consider a two-dimensional grid representing a set of objects that evolve over time, for example, shops in a city that appear and disappear over the years. One possible representation is a k^3-tree, where time is taken as the third dimension, and we set a point at (x, y, t) if there was a shop at (x, y) in month t. Then, range search algorithms adapted to three dimensions can answer the query "Which shops existed in this neighborhood this last year?" (at least it can report their positions; we can obtain their names with another data structure associated with the 1s in the tree leaves).

Note, however, that we must avoid listing the same shop many times, if it was open for many consecutive months (as will usually be the case). This can be done by removing repeated names from the list, but it can represent a significant waste of time. It is also a waste of space, since a long-term shop is represented every month.

Another alternative is to represent the *events* of a shop appearing and disappearing. Then every shop will induce only 1 or 2 points in the grid. We should have

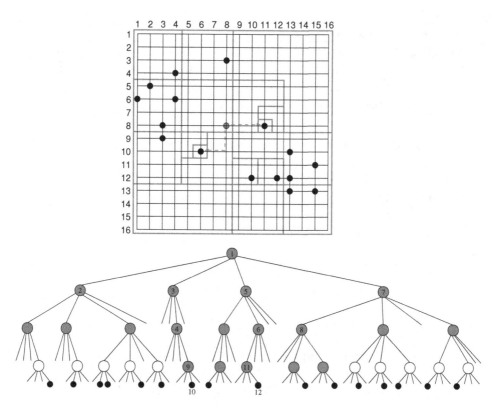

Figure 10.8. Solving query closest(8, 8, 2) on the k^2-tree of Figure 10.4. The grayed nodes are those included in Q at some moment, and the visited ones show their visit order. The regions of the grayed nodes are also enclosed in gray on the grid. The dashed arrows show the Manhattan distance to the two answers.

one three-dimensional grid for the appearing events and another for the disappearing events. We also need to store a set of *snapshots,* that is, two-dimensional grids containing all the shops that exist at times $t = d \cdot i$, for some sampling step d. Then, given a query $[x_1, x_2] \times [y_1, y_2] \times [t_1, t_2]$, we first collect all the points from the snapshot number $\lfloor t_1/d \rfloor$, in the range $[x_1, x_2] \times [y_1, y_2]$. We then collect all the appearing and all the disappearing events in $[x_1, x_2] \times [y_1, y_2] \times [\lfloor t_1/d \rfloor d + 1, t_1 - 1]$, so as to obtain the situation at date t_1. To this set of points, we add all the appearing events in $[x_1, x_2] \times [y_1, y_2] \times [t_1, t_2]$.

Raster Data

Imagine we want to represent large regions with some property (such as forests, lakes, and so on). We wish to use little space, taking advantage of large homogeneous submatrices, and at the same time allow for rapid visualization of any rectangular range (for example, for displaying a part of a large map). Assume, for concreteness, that the desired areas are seen as black cells and the others as white cells, and that we represent the black cells as points on a grid.

The basic k^2-tree is not a good structure for this purpose, because its space is associated with the total number of black cells in the image. It is possible, however, to design

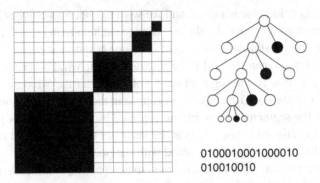

0100010001000010
010010010

Figure 10.9. A black and white image of 16×16 cells and its 2^2-tree representation using blocks for fully black and fully white sub-grids. The first bitvector represents the LOUDS topology, and the second indicates the color of the 0-bits in the inner nodes (0 for white and 1 for black).

a variant that does not recurse on areas that are all white (i.e., empty) or all black (i.e., full of points).

One alternative for representing this extended structure is to associate another bit with each 0 in the internal nodes, indicating the color (all white or all black) of the area that is not represented. Another alternative is to represent full areas by a 1-bit (as an internal node with children) with all k^2 0-bits as children. This is a combination that cannot arise on the basic k^2-tree, and thus it can be used to signal this case.

The first alternative spends 1 extra bit per full or empty area, whereas the second spends k^2 extra bits per full area. Which one is better depends on the amount of black points in the image. An advantage of the second alternative is that, if no significant black areas appear, it will cost nothing compared with a classical k^2-tree representation.

Example 10.17 *Figure 10.9 shows a toy image where the benefits of this representation are apparent. We choose the first of the two alternatives (indicating the color of the 0s in another bit array). The second alternative would have required more bits;* 0110 01100000 01100000 01100000 0010.

In both cases, a normal traversal for the points in an area $[x_1, x_2] \times [y_1, y_2]$ efficiently yields the information to display all the black and white cells. The space of this representation is proportional to the perimeters of the represented objects and not to their area.

The representation is also useful for bilevel images that contain large black and white areas. It can also be extended to three dimensions, where we can represent solid objects in a discrete space, spending space proportional to the size of the surfaces of the objects and not to their volume.

10.5.3 Object Visibility

Computing which objects are visible from a certain point is a routine activity in games and virtual reality. Let us consider first the simplest case of a one-dimensional "world" $[1, u]$, and a set of n one-dimensional segments $[a_i, b_i]$ in it, each of color c_i and at distance d_i from the observer. We wish to display a "window" $[x, y]$ of this world.

Closer segments occlude farther ones, and we wish to obtain as efficiently as possible the information on which color should we assign to each point in $[x, y]$. This is a simple model for horizontal visibility of objects of the same height, for example.

Note that, for a segment $[a_i, b_i]$ to be relevant to our window $[x, y]$, it must hold $a_i \leq y$ and $b_i \geq x$ (that is, the segment must not start after the window ends, nor end before the window starts). Therefore, if we represent the segments as points (b_i, a_i) on a grid of $u \times u$, the segments of interest are captured by a query $[x, u] \times [1, y]$. We can store the colors c_i aligned to the points at the leaves of the wavelet tree representation of the grid, so that they are easily retrieved with the points.

Moreover, we can use $-d_i$ as the priorities, so as to obtain first the elements that are not occluded by any other. Thus, let our first query be $\text{top}(x, u, 1, y, 1)$ and the result be the point (b_i, a_i). Then we color the area $[x, y] \cap [a_i, b_i] = [\max(x, a_i), \min(y, b_i)]$ (which is nonempty) with color c_i. Now, if $x < a_i$, we must still color the area $[x, a_i - 1]$, and if $b_i < y$, we must still color the area $[b_i + 1, y]$. Those 0, 1, or 2 areas are processed recursively, until we run out of areas to color or run out of segments relevant to each area. The cost on a wavelet tree is $\mathcal{O}(\log^2 u)$ per relevant segment colored in the window.

Example 10.18 *Figure 10.10 shows five segments in $[1, 10]$ and a visibility query on $[3, 8]$. The segments become weighted points on a 10×10 grid, and the visibility query is translated into the range query $[3, 10] \times [1, 8]$. Note how the segment with horizontal hatching falls outside the query. The rectangle retrieves the heaviest point, corresponding to the black segment. We then color the range $[7, 7]$ with black and recurse on the segments $[3, 6]$ and $[8, 8]$.*

The first segment translates into the query $[3, 10] \times [1, 6]$, which retrieves the diagonally hatched point as the heaviest one (i.e., closest to the observer). We assign its color to $[3, 6] \cap [5, 8] = [5, 6]$, and recurse on the segment $[3, 4]$. This translates into

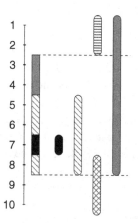
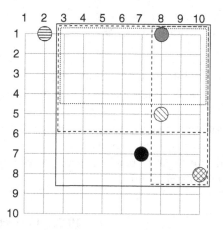

Figure 10.10. The structure for solving one-dimensional visibility. The "colored" segments $[a_i, b_i]$ are mapped to the grid as weighted points (b_i, a_i), and the query $[3, 8]$ becomes the range query $[3, 10] \times [1, 8]$. We enclose it in a black rectangle on the grid, and the subsequent queries in dashed and dotted rectangles. The final coloring is shown besides the scale on the left.

the range query $[3, 10] \times [1, 4]$, *which retrieves the gray point. Thus we color the range* $[3, 4] \cap [1, 8] = [3, 4]$ *with gray.*

On the other hand, the segment $[8, 8]$ *becomes the range query* $[8, 10] \times [1, 8]$, *which retrieves (again) the diagonally hatched point as the heaviest one. Thus we assign its color to the range* $[8, 8]$, *and finish.*

Note that the doubly hatched segment is not visible, even if it intersects with the range $[3, 8]$.

Let us now consider a two-dimensional world, where the objects are rectangles $[l_i, r_i] \times [t_i, b_i]$ with colors c_i and distances d_i, and the query is a rectangle $[x_1, x_2] \times [y_1, y_2]$. Then an object intersects with the window iff $l_i \leq x_2$, $r_i \geq x_1$, $t_i \leq y_2$, and $b_i \geq y_1$.

We can then represent the objects as points (l_i, r_i, t_i, b_i) with priorities $-d_i$ on a 4-dimensional grid, and use top queries on a k^4-tree. Our first query is $\mathsf{top}(1, x_2, x_1, u, 1, y_2, y_1, u, 1)$; let the result be (l_i, r_i, t_i, b_i). Then we assign color c_i to the nonempty area $[l_i, r_i] \times [t_i, b_i] \cap [x_1, x_2] \times [y_1, y_2]$. Now we must continue recursively in up to 4 areas: If $x_1 < l_i$, we color the area $[x_1, l_i - 1] \times [y_1, y_2]$; if $r_i < x_2$ we color the area $[r_i + 1, x_2] \times [y_1, y_2]$; if $y_1 < t_i$ we color the area $[\max(x_1, l_i + 1), \min(r_i - 1, x_2)] \times [y_1, t_i - 1]$; and if $b_i < y_2$ we color the area $[\max(x_1, l_i + 1), \min(r_i - 1, x_2)] \times [b_i + 1, y_2]$.

10.5.4 Position-Restricted Searches on Suffix Arrays

We introduced the suffix array in Section 8.5.3, as an array containing the permutation of the suffixes of a text $T[1, n]$ in lexicographic order. In the suffix array $A[1, n]$, the positions where a pattern string $P[1, m]$ appears are contiguous and can be determined in time $\mathcal{O}(m \log \log n)$ by adding a Patricia trie on the suffixes. The whole structure uses $n \log n + \mathcal{O}(n \log \sigma)$ bits, where σ is the alphabet size of T, and reports occ occurrences of P in total time $\mathcal{O}(m \log \log n + occ)$.

Imagine now that we are interested in the occurrences of P restricted to some text area $T[l, r]$. This could correspond to a sub-directory of files, to the documents produced during a time period, etc. The suffix array alone cannot carry out this search efficiently: We need first to find all the occurrences $A[s, e]$ of P in T, and then scan them one by one to collect those that belong to the range, $l \leq A[i] \leq r - m + 1$.

Let us define an $n \times n$ grid, and the n points $(i, A[i])$. This grid, implemented as a wavelet tree, takes $n \log n + o(n \log n)$ bits, very close to the space of the suffix array. Since the grid has exactly one point per column, no coordinate mapping is necessary. Now, once we determine the range $A[s, e]$ of the suffixes that start with P, we can find those that in addition lie within $T[l, r]$ by querying the range $[s, e] \times [l, r - m + 1]$ in the grid. We can determine in $\mathcal{O}(\log n)$ time the number of results (with $\mathsf{count}(s, e, l, r - m + 1)$), and report each such result also in time $\mathcal{O}(\log n)$ (with $\mathsf{report}(s, e, l, r - m + 1)$). By considering the more refined analysis in Section 10.1.2, the total time is $\mathcal{O}\left(m \log \log n + \log n + occ \log \frac{r-l}{occ}\right)$.

Example 10.19 *Figure 10.11 shows the same suffix array of Figure 8.20, now as a grid. We show how the search for the pattern* $P = \mathsf{a}$ *(which appears in* $A[s, e] = A[2, 6]$) *restricted to the interval* $T[l, r] = T[3, 9]$ *is mapped to a query on the grid range*

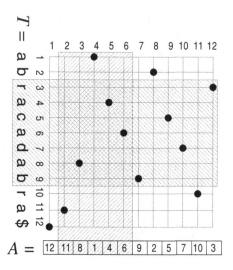

Figure 10.11. The suffix array of Figure 8.20, now regarded as a grid, and a position-restricted query for 'a' in $T[3, 9]$ seen as a range query $[2, 6] \times [3, 9]$.

$[2, 6] \times [3, 9]$, *finding* 3 *answers whose text positions correspond to the y-coordinate values of the points* (4, 6, *and* 8).

This grid representation can replace the suffix array, because it has sufficient information to compute $A[i]$ given i: the wavelet tree (actually, a wavelet matrix) can be regarded as the representation of A seen as a string on $[1, n]$ (Section 6.2), and thus it can retrieve $A[i]$ given i via an **access**(i) query, in time $\mathcal{O}(\log n)$. The Patricia tree search process involves $\mathcal{O}(m)$ accesses to A and $\mathcal{O}(m)$ labeled tree operations. Thus the total search time raises to $\mathcal{O}\left(m \log n + occ \log \frac{r-l}{occ}\right)$.

As an additional plus, using the fast reporting procedure *outputally* will report the points successively in text order. This cannot be done on a plain suffix array, unless we first extract all the positions and then sort them.

Imagine also that some passages of the texts are more important than others. For example, areas belonging to titles are more important than subtitles, those are more important than text bodies, and those are more important than footnotes. We can then associate priorities with the corresponding cells, and use **top**$(s, e, l, r - m + 1, f)$ queries to output the f most important occurrences of P within the given text ranges. Our algorithms on wavelet trees allow for an efficient solution to this sophisticated query.

10.5.5 Searching for Fuzzy Patterns

An extension of the problem of finding the occurrences of P in T is to allow some degree of flexibility in its occurrences. Some extensions of this kind are very hard, but in this section we will explore a couple of simple extensions that are handled well with a grid data structure.

The first one is to allow the pattern to have some positions $P[k] = \phi$, where the special symbol ϕ matches *any* character of Σ. These positions are called *wildcards*.

Wildcards are useful when we are unsure about the content of the pattern at some positions.

Let us focus on the case where we want to search for patterns $P[1, m]$ with a single wildcard at some position, $P[k] = \phi$. Apart from the suffix array $A[1, n]$ of T, we build its *prefix* array $A'[1, n]$, so that $A'[i]$ points to the ith prefix of T, $T[1, A'[i]]$, in lexicographic order of the *reversed* prefixes (we may assume, to build A', that a symbol $ precedes $T[1]$).

Now, the key property is that P (with $P[k] = \phi$) matches $T[i, i + m - 1]$ iff $P[1, k - 1]$ matches $T[i, i + k - 2]$ and $P[k + 1, m]$ matches $T[i + k, i + m - 1]$. This is equivalent to saying that $P[1, k - 1]$ matches the end of prefix $T[1, i + k - 2]$ and $P[k + 1, m]$ matches the beginning of suffix $T[i + k, n]$. Then if we run a search for $P[1, k - 1]^{rev}$ (i.e., $P[1, k - 1]$ read backwards) in the prefix array A', we will find the range $A'[s', e']$ of all the endpoints of prefixes of T that end with $P[1, k - 1]$, and if we run a search for $P[k + 1, m]$ in the suffix array A, we will find the range $A[s, e]$ of all the starting points of suffixes of T that start with $P[k + 1, m]$.

We will store a grid of size $[1, n] \times [1, n]$, with a point in (i, j) iff $A[i] = A'[j] + 2$. That is, the prefix of T ending at a position p is connected with the suffix of T starting at position $p + 2$ (we can add spurious points for the columns where $A[i] \in \{1, 2\}$ so as to have exactly one point per column). Therefore, if we find all the points (i, j) in the range $[s, e] \times [s', e']$ in this grid, we have all the positions $A'[j] - k + 2$ where P occurs in T. Using a wavelet tree for the grid, plus Patricia trees on the prefix and suffix arrays, we use $\mathcal{O}(n \log n)$ bits and find the occ occurrences of P in time $\mathcal{O}\left(m \log \log n + \log n + occ \log \frac{n}{occ}\right)$.

Example 10.20 *Figure 10.12 shows the prefix and suffix arrays of text $T =$ abracadabra$\$$, and the resulting ranges for the pattern $P =$ aϕa.*

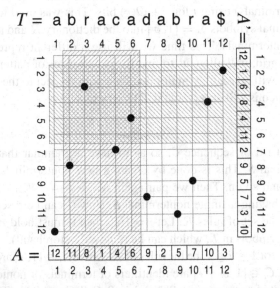

Figure 10.12. The suffix array A of Figure 8.20 and the corresponding prefix array A', with the grid that connects them to find patterns with one wildcard. We connect the positions (i, j) where $A[i] = A'[j] + 2$. The hatched areas correspond to the pattern $P =$ aϕa.

For example, the prefix array position $A'[3] = 6$ refers to the prefix abraca, *which precedes $A'[4] = 8$, which refers to* abracada, *because the reverse of the first,* acarba, *lexicographically precedes the reverse of the second,* adacarba.

As an example of the placement of points, there is a point at $(11, 4)$ because $A[11] = 10 = 8 + 2 = A'[4] + 2$.

Our pattern has the wildcard at $k = 2$, thus we search for $P[1, k-1]^{rev} = P[1]^{rev} =$ a *in A' and obtain $A'[s', e'] = A'[2, 6]$. We also search for $P[k+1, m] = P[3] =$* a *in A and obtain $A[s, e] = A[2, 6]$. Now the search for the grid range $[2, 6] \times [2, 6]$ returns the points $(3, 3)$ and $(6, 5)$. The former yields the occurrence starting at $A'[3] - k + 2 = 6$ (where P matches $T[6, 8] =$* ada*); the latter yields $A'[5] - k + 2 = 4$ (where P matches $T[4, 6] =$* aca*).*

The solution is easy to extend to searches with a fixed gap of wildcards, that is, $P[k, k+d-1] = \phi^d$: we just modify the grid definition so that we set a point in (i, j) if $A[i] = A'[j] + d + 1$. Note that, although the pattern and the position of the range of wildcards can be given at query time, the value of d is fixed at construction time.

Another application of the grid built for one wildcard is *approximate pattern matching* with one substitution error. That is, we want to find all the occurrences of P allowing at most one character to be changed at any position. This is useful, for example, to recover from typing or spelling errors, optical character recognition errors, experimental errors when sequencing DNA, etc. In this case, we take all the possible positions $k \in [1, m]$, and search for $P_k[1, m] = P[1, k-1] . \phi . P[k+1, m]$. One issue is that the *exact* occurrences of P will be reported m times.

10.5.6 Indexed Searching in Grammar-Compressed Text

In Section 8.5.2 we showed how to store a RePair dictionary $\mathcal{R}$ of r rules $A \to BC$ (defining r nonterminals) using $r \log r + \mathcal{O}(r)$ bits. This was used to compress a text $T[1, n]$ over terminal symbols $\Sigma = [1, \sigma]$ into the dictionary $\mathcal{R}$ and a sequence $\mathcal{C}$ over terminals and nonterminals. This time we will use a different representation which, with the use of a grid, will allow us to find the occurrences of patterns $P[1, m]$ in the text T. The space will be roughly multiplied by 4 with respect to the representation of Section 8.5.2, which is still acceptable if T is very repetitive.

Structure

First, we will get rid of sequence $\mathcal{C}$, so as to have a grammar that derives T from a single nonterminal S. This is done by creating new nonterminals $N_1 \to \mathcal{C}[1]\mathcal{C}[2]$, $N_2 \to \mathcal{C}[3]\mathcal{C}[4]$, and so on. Then we pair again $N'_1 \to N_1 N_2$, $N'_2 \to N_3 N_4$, and so on, recursively, until having a single nonterminal S. Now $\mathcal{C}$ can be discarded and all the information is in the set of rules $\mathcal{R}$. Let $r = |\mathcal{R}|$, then it must hold $r \geq \sigma - 1$ (unless there are unused symbols in T, which can be removed beforehand).

Let $A_i \to B_i C_i$, for $1 \leq i \leq r$, be the rules of $\mathcal{R}$, where $A_i \in [1, r]$ are the nonterminal identifiers and $B_i, C_i \in [1, \sigma + r]$ are identifiers of terminals or nonterminals. The set $\mathcal{R}$ will be represented as a sequence $R[1, 2r] = B_1 C_1 B_2 C_2 \ldots B_r C_r$. This sequence will in turn be represented using the technique of Section 6.1, which uses $2r \log(\sigma + r) + o(r \log r)$ bits, and supports select in constant time and access in time $\mathcal{O}(\log \log r)$.

In addition, we will store an $r \times r$ grid G where the rule $A_i \to B_i C_i$ will be stored as a point at coordinates (C_i, B_i). We will reserve the column C_i and the row B_i for the nonterminal A_i; there will be no other points in that column or that row.

The rows of the grid will be sorted in lexicographic order of the *reversed* strings to which the symbols B_i expand, and the columns will be sorted in lexicographic order of the (non-reversed) strings to which the symbols C_i expand. Non-terminal identifiers in $[1, r]$ will be assigned so that, if $A_i \to B_i C_i$ induces the (only) point at row j, then the identifier of nonterminal A_i is j.

Finally, we will store an array telling, for each nonterminal A_i, the length $\ell(A_i)$ of the string it expands to. The total space, considering the sequence R, the grid G, and the lengths ℓ, is $3r \log r + r \log n + o(r \log r)$ bits.

Example 10.21 *Figure 10.13 shows the grammar for the example text $T =$* abrabracadabrabra. *On the bottom we show the corresponding grid (the shades and grays will be used later).*

The strings on the rows are the expansions of the nonterminals B_i for all the rules $A_i \to B_i C_i$, whereas the strings on the columns are the expansions of the nonterminals

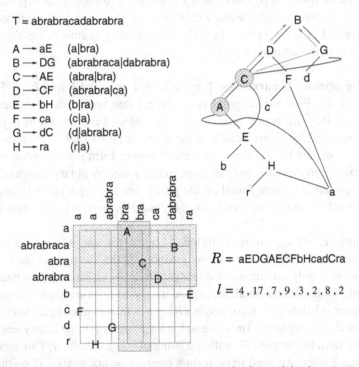

Figure 10.13. A grammar representation of the text $T =$ abrabracadabrabra. On the top left, the grammar (indicating, for legibility, the string each symbol expands to, divided into left and right part), with initial symbol B. On the top right, its representation as an acyclic graph (DAG). On the bottom, our representation, formed by the grid (on the left; the strings are shown only for legibility), the sequence R, and the array of lengths. The strings on the rows are the left-hand sides of the rules lexicographically sorted by their reverse; those on the columns are the right-hand sides lexicographically sorted. The shadows and grays illustrate Examples 10.22 and 10.23.

C_i. *Those strings are not actually stored. While the column strings are sorted in lexicographic order, those on the rows are sorted in lexicographic order of their reverse, for example, "abrabraca" comes before "abra" because it is lexicographically smaller when both are read backwards.*

The corresponding pair B_iC_i is then connected with the point that represents A_i. For example, the rule $\mathsf{A} \to \mathsf{aE}$ is shown as a point at row 1 and column 4, because 'a' is the first string in (reversed) lexicographic order, and E expands to 'bra', which is at position 4 in lexicographic order (note that there are 2 occurrences of 'bra'; we have broken ties arbitrarily). The names A to H have been given so that the labels in the grid increase with the rows (that is, $\mathsf{A} = 1$, $\mathsf{B} = 2$, etc.).

We also show the string R, which represents the right-hand sides of the rules, and the array ℓ of string lengths. For example, $\ell(1) = 4$ because A expands to 'abra', of length 4.

Searching

The main idea of the grid structure is that the occurrences of $P[1, m]$ in the nonterminals of the grammar are of two types: primary occurrences correspond to rules $A_i \to B_iC_i$ where P appears split into B_i and C_i, and secondary occurrences correspond to ancestors (in the grammar DAG) of nodes where primary or secondary occurrences appear. (The case $m = 1$ is an exception; here the only primary occurrence is the DAG leaf corresponding to the terminal $P[1]$.)

Finding the primary occurrences. For each $1 \le t < m$, cut P into $P_< = P[1, t]$ and $P_> = P[t + 1, m]$. Find the range of rows $[s_y, e_y]$ that finish with $P_<$; these form a range because they are sorted in lexicographic order of the reverse strings, and the range can be found by binary search of the reversed prefix of P, $P_<^{rev}$. Similarly, find the range of columns $[s_x, e_x]$ that start with $P_>$; these form a range because they are sorted in lexicographic order, and the range can be found by binary search of the suffix of P, $P_>$. Now all the points found on the grid range $[s_x, e_x] \times [s_y, e_y]$ correspond to the nonterminals A_i that rewrite as $A_i \to B_iC_i$, and P appears when we concatenate B_i with C_i.

The binary searches are done as follows. For the row range, we need to compare $P_<^{rev}$ with the reversed string of some row j. Since j is the identifier of the nonterminal $A \to BC$, we have only to compute $B = \mathsf{access}(R, 2j - 1)$. This can be a character or a nonterminal. If it is a nonterminal, we expand it right-to-left via recursive accesses to R. If the grammar is balanced (i.e., of height $\mathcal{O}(\log n)$), then extracting up to m characters at the end of B will require $\mathcal{O}((m + \log n) \log \log r)$ time. For the binary search on the columns, we need to compare $P_>$ with the string of some column j. This time, j is not the identifier. Rather, we need to perform a query $j' = \mathsf{access}(G, j)$ on the wavelet tree (regarding the grid G as a sequence of the row values of the points) to find the row j' of the only point in that column. Then j' is the identifier of the nonterminal $A \to BC$, and we want to expand C. Thus we compute $C = \mathsf{access}(R, 2j')$, and then expand its symbols recursively, left to right, until obtaining m symbols, analogously to the extraction of B.

Thus the m binary searches (for all the values of t) will require time $\mathcal{O}((m + \log n)m \log r \log \log r)$, which includes the time for the range searches on the grid. Extracting each resulting point will take $\mathcal{O}(\log r)$ time as well. The rows of the points extracted correspond to the nonterminals A.

From this part of the search we obtain a set of nonterminals A_i containing the primary occurrences of P. The offset where P appears in $A_i \to B_i C_i$, when we have split P into $P[1, t]$ and $P[t + 1, m]$, is $o_i = \ell(B_i) - t + 1$.

Example 10.22 *Let us search for* $P = $ abra *in Figure 10.13. We must try the splits* $t = 1$ ($P_< = $ a, $P_> = $ bra), $t = 2$ ($P_< = $ ab, $P_> = $ ra), *and* $t = 3$ ($P_< = $ abr, $P_> = $ a). *Of those, only the first split gives results. When we run the binary search for the range of row strings finishing with* $P_< = $ a, *we obtain* $[s_y, e_y] = [1, 4]$. *When we run the binary search for the range of column strings starting with* $P_> = $ bra, *we obtain* $[s_x, e_x] = [4, 5]$. *These ranges are hatched in different directions in the figure.*

Before continuing, let us see in detail how we access some row and some column strings for the binary search. To access the last $|P_<| = 1$ *characters of string* abra *at row* $j = 3$, *we compute* $B = $ access$(R, 2j - 1) = $ access$(R, 5) = $ A *to learn that we have to obtain the last symbol of nonterminal* A $= 1$. *Thus, we do* access$(R, 2 \cdot $ A$) = $ E *to learn that* A $\to$ XE *for some* X. *Thus we want the last symbol of* E $= 5$. *We do* access$(R, 2 \cdot $ E$) = $ H *to learn that* E $\to$ XH *for some* X, *and we want the last symbol of* H $= 8$. *Finally, we do* access$(R, 2 \cdot $ H$) = $ a, *and we have the answer we need. Now consider extracting the first* $|P_>| = 3$ *characters of the column string* bra *at position* $j = 5$. *With the query* $j' = $ access$(5) = 3$ *on the grid we obtain the nonterminal identifier. With* access$(R, 2j') = $ E *we learn that we need the first 3 characters of the expansion of* E $= 5$. *We do* access$(R, 2 \cdot $ E$ - 1) = $ b *to learn that* E $\to$ bX, *and thus have found the first of the 3 desired symbols. Since we need more, we find* X $= $ access$(R, 2 \cdot $ E$) = $ H, *so we need the first 2 symbols of* H $= 8$. *Those are found in* access$(R, 2 \cdot $ H$ - 1) = $ r *and* access$(R, 2 \cdot $ H$) = $ a, *thus we have found the desired string,* bra.

Let us continue with the search. We have found our desired range query $[s_x, e_x] \times [s_y, e_y] = [4, 5] \times [1, 4]$ *(doubly hatched in the figure). The range query returns points in 2 rows, 1 (i.e.,* A*) and 3 (i.e.,* C*). Both are highlighted on the top-right of the figure. In the first, the offset is* $o_1 = 1$, *since* A $\to$ aX *(because* access$(R, 2 \cdot $ A$ - 1) = $ a*) and thus* $o_1 = \ell(\text{a}) - t + 1 = 1 - 1 + 1 = 1$. *In the second, the offset is* $o_2 = 4$, *since* C $\to$ AX *(because* access$(R, 2 \cdot $ C$ - 1) = $ A*) and thus* $o_2 = \ell(\text{A}) - t + 1 = 4 - 1 + 1 = 4$.

Finding the secondary occurrences. For each A_i and offset o_i found, we have to track all the nonterminals that rewrite as A_i, directly or transitively, until reaching the initial symbol S, where the offset will be the position of P in T. Each time we reach S, a different position of P in T will be reported. To find the places where A_i is mentioned, we use **select** operations on R. We perform $\text{select}_{A_i}(R, j)$ for $j = 1, 2, \ldots$. For each $k = \text{select}_{A_i}(R, j)$, we compute $D = \lceil k/2 \rceil$, and then we know that $D \to A_i X$, for some X, if k is odd, or $D \to X A_i$ if k is even. In the first case, the offset stays at o_i, whereas in the second we must add $\ell(X)$ to it. Then we have to also track any occurrence of D

in R, and so on, until all the transitive mentions of A_i are processed. If the grammar is balanced, each occurrence of P is reported in time $\mathcal{O}(\log n \log \log r)$.

Example 10.23 *Let us continue Example 10.22 and find the secondary occurrences. We start from the first primary occurrence, in* A *with offset* $o_1 = 1$. *We find its only occurrence in* R *at* $k = \mathsf{select}_A(R, 1) = 5$, *which belongs to rule* $\lceil k/2 \rceil = 3 = $ C. *Since* k *is odd, we leave* $o_1 = 1$. *Now we find the occurrences of* C *in* R. *The first is* $k = \mathsf{select}_C(R, 1) = 7$, *which belongs to rule* $\lceil k/2 \rceil = 4 = $ D. *Since* k *is odd, we leave* $o_1 = 1$. *Then we find the only occurrence of* D *in* R, $k = \mathsf{select}_D(R, 1) = 3$, *which belongs to rule* $\lceil k/2 \rceil = 2 = $ B. *Since* k *is odd, we leave* $o_1 = 1$. *Finally, since* B *is the initial symbol of the grammar, we found the first occurrence of* P *in* T, *at* $T[o_1, o_1 + m - 1] = T[1, 4]$. *Note, at the top-right part of Figure 10.13, that we traversed the leftmost path of the grammar, from* A *upwards to* B *(shown with gray arrows).*

The second occurrence of C *in* R *is at* $k = \mathsf{select}_C(R, 2) = 14$, *which corresponds to rule* $\lceil k/2 \rceil = 7 = $ G. *Since* k *is even, we must update* $o_1 \leftarrow o_1 + \ell(\mathsf{access}(R, 13)) = 1 + \ell(\mathsf{d}) = 2$. *Now we find the only occurrence of* G *in* R, *at* $k = \mathsf{select}_G(R, 1) = 4$, *which corresponds to symbol* $\lceil k/2 \rceil = 2 = $ B. *Since* k *is even, we must update* $o_1 \leftarrow o_1 + \ell(\mathsf{access}(R, 3)) = 2 + \ell(\mathsf{D}) = 11$. *Since* B *is the root symbol, we found the occurrence of* P *that is at* $T[o_1, o_1 + m - 1] = T[11, 14]$. *Note that this corresponds to following the other path from* A *to* B, *where we move from* C *to* G.

The other 2 occurrences, at $T[4, 7]$ *and* $T[14, 17]$, *are found by tracking the occurrences of the other symbol found in the grid,* C. *Note that the paths we will traverse toward* B *are the same as before; however, this time we start from* $o_2 = 4$, *and thus the occurrences will be shifted by 3 positions.*

Overall, if the grammar is balanced, the cost to report occ occurrences of $P[1, m]$ in T is

$$\mathcal{O}((m + \log n)m \log r \log \log r + occ \log n \log \log r).$$

Algorithm 10.10 gives the pseudocode. We use the convention that, in R, the values in $[1, r]$ denote the nonterminal symbols, and values $R[j] > r$ denote the terminal symbol $R[j] - r$. For simplicity, we assume that $\ell[r + 1, r + \sigma] = 1$, giving the length of the terminal symbols in $[1, \sigma]$. Finally, we assume that **report** returns just the y-coordinates of the points in the grid.

Algorithm 10.10 also gives the procedure *extractleft*, which is used in the binary search of columns to extract a prefix of a given nonterminal. To compare $P_>$ with column j, we obtain the string *extractleft*$(\mathsf{access}(R, 2 \cdot \mathsf{access}(G, j)), |P_>|)$. To compare $P_<^{rev}$ with the reversed row j, we obtain the string *extractright*$(\mathsf{access}(R, 2j - 1), |P_<^{rev}|)$, where *extractright* is analogous to *extractleft*, except that it extracts from the right and in reverse order. In practice, it is more efficient to directly compare with the characters of P as we extract the symbols, so as to decide the lexicographical comparison as early as possible.

Finally, we can retrieve any $T[i, j]$ in time $\mathcal{O}((j - i + \log n) \log \log r)$, if the grammar is balanced, as follows. Start from the initial symbol $S \to BC$. If $\ell(B) \geq j$, then

---

Algorithm 10.10: Searching for P in a grammar-compressed text T.

---

1 **Proc** *search*(P)

    Input : Grammar-compressed text $T[1, n]$ (seen as a grid G, a sequence of
                rules $R[1, 2r]$, an array of lengths $\ell[1, r]$, and an initial symbol S),
                and search pattern $P[1, m]$.

    Output: Outputs the positions where P occurs in T.

2   **if** $m = 1$ **then** *secondaries*($r + P[1], 1$)

3   **else**

4   **for** $t \leftarrow 1$ **to** $m - 1$ **do**

5             $[s_x, e_x] \leftarrow$ binary search on the column strings for $P[t + 1, m]$

6             $[s_y, e_y] \leftarrow$ binary search on the reversed row strings for $P[1, t]^{rev}$

7   **for** $j \in$ report(G, s_x, e_x, s_y, e_y) **do** (reports y-coordinates)

8   *secondaries*($j, \ell[$access($R, 2j - 1$)$] - t + 1$)

9 **Proc** *secondaries*(A, *offs*)

    Input : A nonterminal A and the offset *offs* where P appears in it.

    Output: Outputs the occurrences of P in the initial grammar symbol S derived
                from this occurrence in A.

10   **if** $A = S$ **then** **output** *offs* (starting position of occurrence)

11   **else**

12   **for** $j \leftarrow 1$ **to** rank$_A(R, 2r)$ **do**

13             $k \leftarrow$ select$_A(R, j)$

14             $D \leftarrow \lceil k/2 \rceil$

15   *offs'* $\leftarrow$ *offs*

16   **if** k mod $2 = 0$ **then** *offs'* $\leftarrow$ *offs'* $+ \ell[$access($R, k - 1$)$]$

17   *secondaries*(D, *offs'*)

18 **Proc** *extractleft*(A, p)

    Input : A terminal or nonterminal A and a prefix length p.

    Output: Outputs the first p terminals of the expansion of A, or all if $p \geq \ell[A]$.

19   **if** $A > r$ **then** **output** $A - r$ (it is a terminal)

20   **else**

21         $B \leftarrow$ access($R, 2 \cdot A - 1$); *extractleft*(B, p)

22   **if** $p > \ell[B]$ **then**

23             $C \leftarrow$ access($R, 2 \cdot A$); *extractleft*($C, p - \ell[B]$)

---

continue recursively on B. If $\ell(B) < i$, then continue recursively on C with the range $[i - \ell(B), j - \ell(B)]$. If none of those conditions hold, enter recursively in both: first in B with the range $[i, \ell(B)]$ and then in C with the range $[1, j - \ell(B)]$. When reaching terminal nodes, output them.

10.6 Summary

A grid on c columns and r rows containing n points can be represented using wavelet matrices in $n \log \frac{cr}{n} + \mathcal{O}(n) + o(c + n \log r)$ bits, close to the worst-case entropy, so that the points on any rectangular area can be counted in $\mathcal{O}(\log r)$ time and reported in $\mathcal{O}(\log r)$ time each; faster reporting is possible if we want only the row values of the points. It is also possible to find the first point in a rectangle, in any direction, in time $\mathcal{O}(\log r)$. If the points have weights, then the space grows by a constant factor, but the m heaviest points in an area can be reported in time $\mathcal{O}((m + \log r)(\log r + \log m + \log \log n))$. The construction of the structure takes $\mathcal{O}(c + n \log n)$ time and $\mathcal{O}(c + n)$ bits of extra space on top of the array of point coordinates. Apart from its obvious geometric applications, this structure appears frequently in compact data structures for texts.

Another representation, based on k^2-trees, uses $\mathcal{O}\left(n \log \frac{rc}{n}\right)$ bits in the worst case. It can examine any cell and return any point in a rectangular area in time $\mathcal{O}(\log(rc))$, but the total time has an additive time penalty related to the perimeter of the query range. It can also handle points with weights with little space penalty, but the procedure to find the m heaviest points has no relevant time guarantees. K^2-trees perform well in practice when the points are clustered, in which case they take much less space than wavelet matrices and are competitive in time. They are also easily extended to other problems such as representing large areas full of points, higher-dimensional grids, and finding points closest to a query point. The k^2-tree can be built in time $\mathcal{O}(n \log(rc))$ and using no space apart from the input coordinates and the resulting compact structure.

10.7 Bibliographic Notes

Orthogonal range searching is a fundamental topic in Computer Science, for which there is a plethora of quality books and surveys on the topic (Preparata and Shamos, 1985; Agarwal and Erickson, 1999; de Berg *et al.*, 2008).

The technique of mapping real coordinates onto a discrete range dates back to Gabow *et al.* (1984).

Two dimensions. The range tree (Lueker, 1978; Bentley, 1979; Lee and Wong, 1980; Bentley, 1980) can be regarded as the predecessor of the wavelet trees used in computational geometry. It stores the points explicitly in each node, sorted by x-coordinate, and the tree partitions the y-coordinates. On an $n \times n$ grid storing n points, the range tree requires $\mathcal{O}\left(n \log^2 n\right)$ bits. It performs counting in time $\mathcal{O}\left(\log^2 n\right)$ (because it performs a binary search for the mapped range $[x_1, x_2]$ at each new node) and reports the *occ* points in a range in time $\mathcal{O}\left(\log^2 n + occ\right)$ (since it stores the points explicitly in every level). Willard (1985) avoided the multiple binary searches by making each coordinate point to its closest value in the next level. This reduced the counting time to $\mathcal{O}(\log n)$ and the reporting time to $\mathcal{O}(\log n + occ)$.

Chazelle (1988) can be regarded as the inventor of the wavelet tree in the computational geometry scenario. He modified the range trees to use bitvectors instead of representing the explicit points and replaced the binary searches (or Willard's pointers) by rank operations on those bitvectors (he used a rank technique similar to the simple one we described in Section 4.2.1, with $k = 1$). This reduced the space to $\mathcal{O}(n \log n)$ bits (that is, proportional to the worst-case entropy of the data) while keeping the counting time in $\mathcal{O}(\log n)$. Since reporting the points requires tracking them to the leaves, however, the reporting time raises to $\mathcal{O}((1 + occ) \log n)$, just like in our description. The only posterior improvement to Chazelle's wavelet trees was the reduction of their space to the asymptotically optimal $n \log n + o(n \log n)$ bits (Mäkinen and Navarro, 2007; Claude et al., 2015).

By some slight manipulation of wavelet trees (for example, increasing their arity), Chazelle (1988) obtained a linear-space variant using $\mathcal{O}(\frac{1}{\epsilon} n \log n)$ bits and reporting in time $\mathcal{O}(\log n + \frac{1}{\epsilon} occ \log^{\epsilon} n)$, for any constant $\epsilon > 0$. Chazelle (1988) and Overmars (1988) showed how to reduce the reporting time to as little as $\mathcal{O}(\log \log n + occ)$, but using up to $\mathcal{O}(n \log^2 n)$ bits.

The $\mathcal{O}(\log n)$ counting time we obtain with wavelet trees is close to optimal: it is not possible to count in less than $\Omega(\log n / \log \log n)$ time while using $\mathcal{O}(n \, \text{polylog} \, n)$ space (Pătraşcu, 2007). This optimal time was achieved within linear space by Jájá et al. (2004), and within the asymptotically optimal $n \log n + o(n \log n)$ bits by Bose et al. (2009), using a variant of multi-ary wavelet trees.

On the other hand, $\mathcal{O}(\log \log n + occ)$ is the best reporting time that can be achieved within $\mathcal{O}(n \, \text{polylog} \, n)$ space (Pătraşcu and Thorup, 2006; Chan et al., 2011). This time was reached using $\mathcal{O}(n \log^{1+\epsilon} n)$ bits of space (Alstrup et al., 2000), which is not known to be the minimum possible space to achieve optimal reporting time. Within linear space, the best reporting time achieved was $\mathcal{O}((1 + occ) \log^{\epsilon} n)$, by Chan et al. (2011) (they also achieve time $\mathcal{O}((1 + occ) \log \log n)$ within $\mathcal{O}(n \log n \log \log n)$ bits). Sorted range reporting can be carried out within the same space and time complexities (Nekrich and Navarro, 2012; Zhou, 2016).

Detailed explanations of several wavelet tree properties, useful for the more precise time and space analyses we presented, can be found in some recent articles (Gagie et al., 2012; Navarro, 2014). Procedures for sorted range reporting of various kinds on wavelet trees are described when using them to support binary relations (Barbay et al., 2013).

Related queries. Although our solutions are not much better for range emptiness than for counting, the former problem turns out to be easier. The $\Omega(\log \log n)$ time lower bound on the predecessor problem (Pătraşcu and Thorup, 2006) applies to range emptiness for any data structure with space $\mathcal{O}(n \, \text{polylog} \, n)$. This time has been reached within $\mathcal{O}(n \log n \log \log n)$ bits of space (Chan et al., 2011). Within linear space, it is possible to obtain $\mathcal{O}(\log^{\epsilon} n)$ time for any constant $\epsilon > 0$ (Chan et al., 2011). However, no time better than that for counting has been obtained within asymptotically optimal space.

Many other variants of the above problems have been studied, for example, considering query areas that are semi-infinite in some of the directions (which allows for lower complexities), that allow insertions/deletions of points, etc.

Quadtrees, k^2-trees, and similar structures. Brisaboa *et al.* (2014) introduced the k^2-tree as a technique to represent Web graphs in compact form. It can be seen as a compact representation of a region quadtree (Finkel and Bentley, 1974; Samet, 1984), more precisely the variant named MX-Quadtree (Wise and Franco, 1990; Samet, 2006). Our analysis of the time performance of k^2-trees is based on the so-called Quadtree Complexity Theorem (Klinger, 1971; Hunter and Steiglitz, 1979; Samet, 2006), which counts the number of nodes intersected by a line of length q.

The book by Samet (2006) covers many other data structures for spatial searching, in particular those that evenly partition the data points (like kd-trees) instead of evenly partitioning the space, like region quadtrees. Kd-trees (Bentley, 1975) also have poor worst-case search complexity ($\mathcal{O}(\sqrt{n} + occ)$) but work well in practice. The same worst-case complexity is obtained with point quadtrees, which evenly partition the data (Lee and Wong, 1977). Data-partitioning structures seem to be less attractive for a compact representation, because one is forced to represent coordinates explicitly without guarantees on their reduction at deeper levels.

Higher dimensions. Jájá *et al.* (2004) extended their counting to d dimensions in time $\mathcal{O}((\log n/\log\log n)^{d-1})$ using $\mathcal{O}(n\log^{d-1} n/(\log\log n)^{d-2})$ bits. In three dimensions, it is still possible to obtain the optimal reporting time $\mathcal{O}(\log\log n + occ)$ within $\mathcal{O}(n\log^{2+\epsilon} n)$ bits (Chan *et al.*, 2011). In $d \geq 4$ dimensions, this generalizes to time $\mathcal{O}(\log^{d-3} n\log\log n + occ)$ and $\mathcal{O}(n\log^{d+1} n)$ bits, or time $\mathcal{O}(\log^{d-3} n/(\log\log n)^{d-5} + occ)$ and $\mathcal{O}(n\log^{d-1+\epsilon} n)$ bits (Chan *et al.*, 2011).

In contrast, multidimensional kd-trees and point quadtrees require only linear space, $\mathcal{O}(dn\log n)$ bits, but their search complexity quickly worsens with the dimension, $\mathcal{O}(n^{(d-1)/d} + occ)$ (Lee and Wong, 1977), working well in practice only for low d. The search time of region quadtrees, as we have seen for $d = 2$, also has an additive factor of $\mathcal{O}(q^{d-1})$ for queries with side q.

A recent work (Okajima and Maruyama, 2015) shows how to obtain worst-case time $\mathcal{O}(n^{(d-2)/d}\log n + occ\log n)$, using $dn\log n + o(dn\log n)$ bits of space. The idea is to use one wavelet tree per coordinate but sort the sequence of points in *z-order*, whose sort key is formed by a number where the first bit of the d coordinates are concatenated, then the same for the second d bits, and so on. They show that a rectangle query can be decomposed into $\mathcal{O}(n^{(d-2)/d}\log n)$ one-dimensional intervals in z-order, each of which is intersected with some coordinate using the appropriate wavelet tree. Their experiments show that the structure can be an order of magnitude faster than kd-trees when the queries are not too selective, but their structure occupies around twice the kd-tree space (they store several accelerator structures to obtain that time performance). This has theoretical interest and is also promising in practice.

Prioritized reporting. The technique to add RMQ information to the wavelet tree levels to provide for prioritized reporting is described by Navarro *et al.* (2013), who also consider other scenarios where adding information to the wavelet tree is useful. They also describe an idea analogous to sorted range queries to obtain the dominating points. The idea to extract the heaviest points from the k^2-tree and explicitly represent them appears in Brisaboa *et al.* (2016) and can be regarded as a two-dimensional version of priority search trees (McCreight, 1985). They also show how to speed up counting on this structure by storing extra data. The prioritized and recursive traversals we used to find the m heaviest points on k^2-trees, as well as to find the m closest points, are instances of a more general technique to find nearest neighbors in spatial data structures, called best-fit and first-fit searching (Samet, 2006).

Applications to GIS. De Bernardo *et al.* (2013a,b) explored the use of k^2-trees in other scenarios, such as temporal maps, three-dimensional data, and raster data. Samet (2006) also mentions similar applications of quadtrees, for example, storing all the shortest paths in a planar graph in compact form (Sankaranarayanan *et al.*, 2009). Gagie *et al.* (2015) obtained further improvements on the k^2-trees that outperform the basic variant on sparse clustered grids.

A popular structure in GIS is the R-tree (Guttman, 1984; Manolopoulos *et al.*, 2005), which is specialized in handling rectangles. Brisaboa *et al.* (2013) made some improvements on static space-engineered variants of R-trees (Kim *et al.*, 2001) and showed that these outperform, in time and space, various extensions of wavelet trees to handle rectangles instead of points.

Applications to text. The use of grids for position-restricted search on suffix arrays was first mentioned by Mäkinen and Navarro (2007). The reporting time is dominated by that of the grid, so the linear-space improvements due to Chazelle (1988), for example, translate into faster range-reporting structures. The use of such a high space compared to the text size seems to be essential: Hon *et al.* (2012) showed that this problem cannot be solved in $\mathcal{O}((m + occ)\,\text{polylog}\,n)$ time within $\mathcal{O}(n \log \sigma)$ bits of space, unless a linear-space structure with polylogarithmic time is found for three-dimensional range reporting, which is unlikely (they evade the lower bound for sufficiently long patterns; the short patterns are the difficult ones). There is, on the other hand, some research on the use of more than $\mathcal{O}(n \log n)$ bits of space, which is not the focus of this book; the latest improvements are very recent (Biswas *et al.*, 2013; Bille and Gørtz, 2014). The use of grids to allow for wildcards on the patterns was first proposed by Amir *et al.* (2000) and Ferragina *et al.* (1999). Again, their performance is linked to that of the two-dimensional structure. Our index for grammar-based text indexing is simplified from the structures of Claude and Navarro (2010, 2012). Lewenstein (2013) offers a good survey of range search techniques applied to string matching.

Bibliography

Agarwal, P. K. and Erickson, J. (1999). Geometric range searching and its relatives. In *Advances in Discrete and Computational Geometry*, volume 223 of *Contemporary Mathematics*, pages 1–56. AMS Press.

Alstrup, S., Brodal, G., and Rauhe, T. (2000). New data structures for orthogonal range searching. In *Proc. 41st IEEE Symposium on Foundations of Computer Science (FOCS)*, pages 198–207.

Amir, A., Keselman, D., Landau, G. M., Lewenstein, M., Lewenstein, N., and Rodeh, M. (2000). Text indexing and dictionary matching with one error. *Journal of Algorithms*, 37(2), 309–325.

Barbay, J., Claude, F., and Navarro, G. (2013). Compact binary relation representations with rich functionality. *Information and Computation*, **232**, 19–37.

Bentley, J. L. (1975). Multidimensional binary search trees used for associative searching. *Communications of the ACM*, **18**(9), 509–517.

Bentley, J. L. (1979). Decomposable searching problems. *Information Processing Letters*, **8**(5), 244–251.

Bentley, J. L. (1980). Multidimensional divide-and-conquer. *Communications of the ACM*, **23**(4), 214–229.

Bille, P. and Gørtz, I. L. (2014). Substring range reporting. *Algorithmica*, **69**(2), 384–396.

Biswas, S., Ku, T.-H., Shah, R., and Thankachan, S. V. (2013). Position-restricted substring searching over small alphabets. In *Proc. 20th International Symposium on String Processing and Information Retrieval (SPIRE)*, LNCS 8214, pages 29–36.

Bose, P., He, M., Maheshwari, A., and Morin, P. (2009). Succinct orthogonal range search structures on a grid with applications to text indexing. In *Proc. 11th International Symposium on Algorithms and Data Structures (WADS)*, LNCS 5664, pages 98–109.

Brisaboa, N. R., Luaces, M., Navarro, G., and Seco, D. (2013). Space-efficient representations of rectangle datasets supporting orthogonal range querying. *Information Systems*, **35**(5), 635–655.

Brisaboa, N. R., Ladra, S., and Navarro, G. (2014). Compact representation of Web graphs with extended functionality. *Information Systems*, **39**(1), 152–174.

Brisaboa, N. R., de Bernardo, G., Konow, R., Navarro, G., and Seco, D. (2016). Aggregated 2D range queries on clustered points. *Information Systems*, **60**, 34–49.

Chan, T. M., Larsen, K. G., and Pătraşcu, M. (2011). Orthogonal range searching on the RAM, revisited. In *Proc. 27th ACM Symposium on Computational Geometry (SoCG)*, pages 1–10.

Chazelle, B. (1988). A functional approach to data structures and its use in multidimensional searching. *SIAM Journal on Computing*, **17**(3), 427–462.

Claude, F. and Navarro, G. (2010). Self-indexed grammar-based compression. *Fundamenta Informaticae*, **111**(3), 313–337.

Claude, F. and Navarro, G. (2012). Improved grammar-based compressed indexes. In *Proc. 19th International Symposium on String Processing and Information Retrieval (SPIRE)*, LNCS 7608, pages 180–192.

Claude, F., Navarro, G., and Ordóñez, A. (2015). The wavelet matrix: An efficient wavelet tree for large alphabets. *Information Systems*, **47**, 15–32.

de Berg, M., Cheong, O., van Kreveld, M., and Overmars, M. (2008). *Computational Geometry: Algorithms and Applications*. Springer-Verlag, 3rd edition.

de Bernardo, G., Brisaboa, N. R., Caro, D., and Rodríguez, M. A. (2013a). Compact data structures for temporal graphs. In *Proc. 23rd Data Compression Conference (DCC)*, page 477.

de Bernardo, G., Álvarez-García, S., Brisaboa, N. R., Navarro, G., and Pedreira, O. (2013b). Compact querieable representations of raster data. In *Proc. 20th International Symposium on String Processing and Information Retrieval (SPIRE)*, LNCS 8214, pages 96–108.

Ferragina, P., Muthukrishnan, S., and de Berg, M. (1999). Multi-method dispatching: A geometric approach with applications to string matching problems. In *Proc. 31st Annual ACM Symposium on Theory of Computing (STOC)*, pages 483–491.

Finkel, R. A. and Bentley, J. L. (1974). Quad Trees: A data structure for retrieval on composite keys. *Acta Informatica*, **4**, 1–9.

Gabow, H. N., Bentley, J. L., and Tarjan, R. E. (1984). Scaling and related techniques for geometry problems. In *Proc. 16th ACM Symposium on Theory of Computing (STOC)*, pages 135–143.

Gagie, T., Navarro, G., and Puglisi, S. J. (2012). New algorithms on wavelet trees and applications to information retrieval. *Theoretical Computer Science*, **426-427**, 25–41.

Gagie, T., González-Nova, J., Ladra, S., Navarro, G., and Seco, D. (2015). Faster compressed quadtrees. In *Proc. 25th Data Compression Conference (DCC)*, pages 93–102.

Guttman, A. (1984). R-trees: A dynamic index structure for spatial searching. In *Proc. ACM International Conference on Management of Data (SIGMOD)*, pages 47–57.

Hon, W.-K., Shah, R., Thankachan, S. V., and Vitter, J. S. (2012). On position restricted substring searching in succinct space. *Journal of Discrete Algorithms*, 17, 109–114.

Hunter, G. M. and Steiglitz, K. (1979). Operations on images using quad trees. *IEEE Transactions on Pattern Analysis and Machine Intelligence*, 1(2), 145–153.

Jájá, J., Mortensen, C. W., and Shi, Q. (2004). Space-efficient and fast algorithms for multidimensional dominance reporting and counting. In *Proc. 15th International Symposium on Algorithms and Computation (ISAAC)*, pages 558–568.

Kim, K., Cha, S. K., and Kwon, K. (2001). Optimizing multidimensional index trees for main memory access. *ACM SIGMOD Record*, 30(2), 139–150.

Klinger, A. (1971). Patterns and search statistics. In *Optimizing Methods in Statistics*, pages 303–337. Academic Press.

Lee, D. T. and Wong, C. K. (1977). Worst-case analysis for region and partial region searches in multidimensional binary search trees and balanced quad trees. *Acta Informatica*, 9, 23–29.

Lee, D. T. and Wong, C. K. (1980). Quintary trees: A file structure for multidimensional database systems. *ACM Transactions on Database Systems*, 5(3), 339–353.

Lewenstein, M. (2013). Orthogonal range searching for text indexing. In *Space-Efficient Data Structures, Streams, and Algorithms – Papers in Honor of J. Ian Munro on the Occasion of His 66th Birthday*, LNCS 8066, pages 267–302. Springer.

Lueker, G. S. (1978). A data structure for orthogonal range queries. In *Proc. 19th Annual Symposium on Foundations of Computer Science (FOCS)*, pages 28–34.

Mäkinen, V. and Navarro, G. (2007). Rank and select revisited and extended. *Theoretical Computer Science*, 387(3), 332–347.

Manolopoulos, Y., Nanopoulos, A., Papadopoulos, A. N., and Theodoridis, Y. (2005). *R-Trees: Theory and Applications*. Springer-Verlag.

McCreight, E. M. (1985). Priority search trees. *SIAM Journal on Computing*, 14(2), 257–276.

Navarro, G. (2014). Wavelet trees for all. *Journal of Discrete Algorithms*, 25, 2–20.

Navarro, G., Nekrich, Y., and Russo, L. M. S. (2013). Space-efficient data-analysis queries on grids. *Theoretical Computer Science*, 482, 60–72.

Nekrich, Y. and Navarro, G. (2012). Sorted range reporting. In *Proc. 13th Scandinavian Symposium on Algorithmic Theory (SWAT)*, LNCS 7357, pages 271–282.

Okajima, Y. and Maruyama, K. (2015). Faster linear-space orthogonal range searching in arbitrary dimensions. In *Proc. 17th Workshop on Algorithm Engineering and Experiments (ALENEX)*, pages 82–93.

Overmars, M. H. (1988). Efficient data structures for range searching on a grid. *Journal of Algorithms*, 9(2), 254–275.

Pătrașcu, M. (2007). Lower bounds for 2-dimensional range counting. In *Proc. 39th Annual ACM Symposium on Theory of Computing (STOC)*, pages 40–46.

Pătrașcu, M. and Thorup, M. (2006). Time-space trade-offs for predecessor search. In *Proc. 38th Annual ACM Symposium on Theory of Computing (STOC)*, pages 232–240.

Preparata, F. P. and Shamos, M. I. (1985). *Computational Geometry: An Introduction*. Springer.

Samet, H. (1984). The quadtree and related hierarchical data structures. *ACM Computing Surveys*, 16(2), 187–260.

Samet, H. (2006). *Foundations of Multidimensional and Metric Data Structures*. Morgan Kaufmann.

Sankaranarayanan, J., Samet, H., and Alborzi, H. (2009). Path oracles for spatial networks. *Proceedings of the VLDB Endowment*, 2(1), 1210–1221.

Willard, D. (1985). New data structures for orthogonal range queries. *SIAM Journal on Computing*, **14**(1), 232–253.

Wise, D. S. and Franco, J. (1990). Costs of quadtree representation of nondense matrices. *Journal of Parallel and Distributed Computing*, **9**(3), 282–296.

Zhou, G. (2016). Two-dimensional range successor in optimal time and almost linear space. *Information Processing Letters*, **116**(2), 171–174.

CHAPTER 11

Texts

A *text* $T[1, n]$ is an array of symbols over an alphabet $\Sigma = [1, \sigma]$. Although this is the same as a sequence in terms of data (see Chapter 6), texts support a very different set of operations, related to finding the occurrences of pattern strings $P[1, m]$ in T. We say that P *occurs* in T at position i if $T[i, i + m - 1] = P$. We will study two main text operations:

count(T, P): returns the number of positions where the string $P[1, m]$ occurs in $T[1, n]$, for any string P.

locate(T, P): returns the list of positions in T where the string $P[1, m]$ occurs, for any string P.

For technical convenience, we will assume that texts are terminated by the special symbol $T[n] = \$$, which is lexicographically smaller than all the others (in practice, we can interpret $\$ = 1$ and reserve the range $[2, \sigma]$ for the other symbols of T). The pattern, instead, is not terminated with $\$$.

We will also consider the case of *text collections* $\mathcal{T} = \{T^1, T^2, \ldots, T^\Delta\}$, which are sets of texts. Such a text collection will be represented as a single text $T[1, n] = T^1 \# T^2 \# \ldots T^\Delta \# \$$, where each text is terminated with another special symbol, #, distinct from $\$$ and also not present in the patterns P. Therefore, the occurrences of P in $\mathcal{T}$ correspond one-to-one to its occurrences in T. We will then focus only on single texts for the operations count and locate. The mapping between positions in T and positions in the corresponding texts T^d is easily carried out with a very sparse bitvector (Section 4.4) that marks the beginnings of the texts in T, using just $\mathcal{O}(\Delta w)$ bits.

The most widely used tool to support count and locate on a text $T[1, n]$ is the *suffix array*. We have anticipated this data structure in Sections 8.5.3 and 10.5.4, but this time we consider the basic version without Patricia trees on top of it: Consider the n suffixes of T of the form $T[i, n]$. The suffix array of T is then an array $A[1, n]$ where these n suffixes are listed in lexicographic order, identified by their starting position in T. Note that, because of the terminator $\$$, the lexicographic order between any two suffixes of T is well defined.

$$T = \text{a b r a c a d a b r a \$}$$

Figure 11.1. A suffix array of a text. The terminator, \$, is smaller than all the other characters. We show in gray the array cells pointing to the suffixes that start with $P = $ abra.

Example 11.1 *Figure 11.1 shows the suffix array $A[1, 12]$ for the text $T[1, 12] = $* abracadabra\$. *The grayed areas and the blocks in the text will be used later.*

The lexicographically smallest suffix is always $T[n] = $ \$, by definition, so it always holds $A[1] = n = 12$. The next smallest suffix starts at $A[2] = 11$, corresponding to $T[11, 12] = $ a\$. *The next one starts at $A[3] = 8$, corresponding to $T[8, 12] = $* abra\$, *and so on until the lexicographically largest suffix, starting at $A[12] = 3$ and corresponding to $T[3, 12] = $* racadabra\$.

The key property that makes suffix arrays useful for finding the occurrences of patterns $P[1, m]$ is that finding the occurrences of P in T is the same as finding the substrings of T that are equal to P. Since every substring is a prefix of some suffix, the problem is in turn the same as finding the suffixes of T that start with P. And since suffixes are lexicographically sorted in A, all the suffixes of T starting with P are listed in a contiguous area of A, such as $A[s, e]$. Thus, if we manage to find s and e, we have solved both problems: $\text{count}(T, P) = e - s + 1$ and $\text{locate}(T, P) = A[s, e]$.

Example 11.2 *All the starting positions of $P = $* abra *in the text T of Figure 11.1 are listed in the grayed range $A[3, 4] = \langle 8, 1\rangle$. The occurrences in T are enclosed in rectangles. Note that the positions $A[s], A[s + 1], \dots, A[e]$ are not listed in left-to-right order in T.*

In Section 8.5.3, we used a relatively complex labeled tree structure on top of A to find s and e in time $\mathcal{O}(m \log \log n)$. However, we can obtain reasonable time without adding those data structures: Since the suffixes of A are lexicographically sorted, we can look for s and e using binary searches. To find s, we search for the leftmost suffix $A[i]$ such that $T[A[i], A[i] + m - 1] \geq P$. To find e, we look for the rightmost suffix $A[i]$ such that $T[A[i], A[i] + m - 1] \leq P$. Since each lexicographic comparison in the binary search may involve comparing up to m symbols (that is, $P[1, m]$ with some $T[A[i], A[i] + m - 1]$), the cost of the binary search is $\mathcal{O}(m \log n)$.

While this slower solution does not require storing the Patricia tree, it still uses $n \log n$ bits for A plus the $n \log \sigma$ bits to represent T. Most of this chapter is about compact data structures that represent both T and A within space close to the entropy of T and still efficiently support operations count and locate, apart from recovering any desired substring of T. Interestingly, after the space reduction we will recover the good search time complexities we had with Patricia trees, and even less.

Since suffix arrays are permutations of $[1, n]$, one may think that $\log n! = n \log n - \mathcal{O}(n)$ bits is the best space we can hope for. However, not any permutation can be a suffix array. There are σ^n different texts of length n over alphabet $[1, \sigma]$, and therefore only σ^n of the $n!$ permutations of $[1, n]$ can be the suffix array of some text. Thus, it is not outright impossible to represent suffix arrays (and their corresponding texts) within $\log \sigma^n = n \log \sigma$ bits, and even less if T is compressible.

After we show how to compress suffix arrays, we will show how a more powerful data structure, the suffix tree, can be simulated with just $\mathcal{O}(n)$ bits on top of the suffix array. This suffix tree is, in addition, much more powerful than the simple structure described in Section 8.5.3.

11.1 Compressed Suffix Arrays

Since $A[1, n]$ is a permutation of $[1, n]$, we can also speak of its inverse, $A^{-1}[j]$. Note that $A^{-1}[j]$ is the position in A where the suffix $T[j, n]$ is mentioned. Equivalently, it is the position of $T[j, n]$ in the sorted list of the suffixes of T.

A key idea to compress the suffix array A is to switch our attention to a related permutation:

$$\Psi[i] = A^{-1}[(A[i] \bmod n) + 1].$$

This means that, if $A[i] = j$ refers to the suffix $T[j, n]$, then $i' = \Psi[i]$ is the position where $A[i'] = j + 1$ refers to the suffix $T[j + 1, n]$, that is, $A[\Psi[i]] = A[i] + 1$. The exception is for $A[1] = n$, where $\Psi[1]$ is the position i' such that $A[i'] = 1$.

Thus, if we have $A[i] = j$, then $A[\Psi[i]] = j + 1$, $A[\Psi[\Psi[i]]] = j + 2$, $A[\Psi[\Psi[\Psi[i]]]] = j + 3$, and so on, that is, $A[\Psi^k[i]] = j + k$. By iterating on Ψ, we virtually move forward in T.

Example 11.3 *Figure 11.2 shows the text T and suffix array A of Figure 11.1, and the corresponding arrays A^{-1} and Ψ. Suffix array positions are drawn slanted and text positions non-slanted. We show in gray the process of traversing $T[4, 6]$ by using Ψ. We start at $A[5] = 4$. Then $\Psi[5] = 9$ sends us to $A[9] = 5$, and $\Psi[9] = 6$ sends us to $A[6] = 6$.*

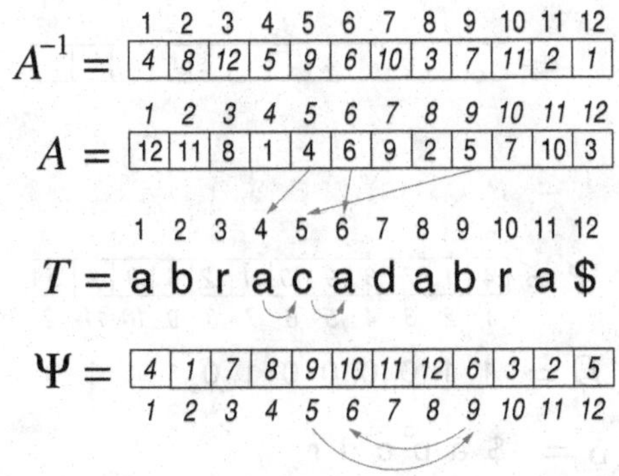

$$A^{-1} = \begin{array}{|c|c|c|c|c|c|c|c|c|c|c|c|} \hline 4 & 8 & 12 & 5 & 9 & 6 & 10 & 3 & 7 & 11 & 2 & 1 \\ \hline \end{array}$$

$$A = \begin{array}{|c|c|c|c|c|c|c|c|c|c|c|c|} \hline 12 & 11 & 8 & 1 & 4 & 6 & 9 & 2 & 5 & 7 & 10 & 3 \\ \hline \end{array}$$

$$T = \text{a b r a c a d a b r a \$}$$

$$\Psi = \begin{array}{|c|c|c|c|c|c|c|c|c|c|c|c|} \hline 4 & 1 & 7 & 8 & 9 & 10 & 11 & 12 & 6 & 3 & 2 & 5 \\ \hline \end{array}$$

Figure 11.2. Our example text T and suffix array A, and arrays A^{-1} and Ψ. The gray arrows illustrate how traversing the cells $A[\Psi^k[5]]$ virtually traverses the suffix $T[A[5], 12] = T[4, 12]$ left to right.

11.1.1 Replacing A with Ψ

Consider an additional bitvector $D[1, n]$, so that $D[i] = 1$ iff $i = 1$ or $T[A[i]] \neq T[A[i-1]]$. That is, D marks the positions where the suffixes in A change their first character. Consider also a short string $S[1, \sigma]$ containing all the distinct characters of T, in lexicographic order (we assume that not all the characters of $[1, \sigma]$ have to be present in T).

With these two structures, we can obtain the first symbol of any suffix given its suffix array position, that is, $T[A[i]] = S[\text{rank}(D, i)]$. Moreover, with the help of Ψ, we can obtain the whole suffix starting at $A[i]$, as follows:

$$T[A[i]] \quad \text{is} \quad S[\text{rank}(D, i)],$$

$$T[A[i] + 1] \quad \text{is} \quad S[\text{rank}(D, \Psi[i])],$$

$$T[A[i] + 2] \quad \text{is} \quad S[\text{rank}(D, \Psi[\Psi[i]])],$$

and so on. In general, $T[A[i] + k]$ is $S[\text{rank}(D, \Psi^k[i])]$.

Assume D supports constant-time rank (Chapter 4). Then, given i, we can obtain the substring $T[A[i], A[i] + m - 1]$ in time $\mathcal{O}(m)$. This is all we need to perform the comparisons of the binary searches that look for P in T. That is, we can find s and e in time $\mathcal{O}(m \log n)$, just as with the plain representation.

Example 11.4 *Figure 11.3 shows the structures we use for searching in our text: D, S, and Ψ. Arrays T and A are no longer necessary for the search. For example, the first comparison of the binary search reads the suffix pointed from $j = A[n/2] = A[6] = 6$. This is $T[6, n] = $* adabra$.

Note that we do not know j, the text position of the suffix we are reading. Yet we can still read the suffix if we know the suffix array position i that points to j. We start with $i = n/2 = 6$. We obtain $T[j] = S[\text{rank}(D, i)] = S[\text{rank}(D, 6)] = S[2] = $ a*. Now we compute $i' = \Psi[i] = 10$ and obtain $T[j + 1] = S[\text{rank}(D, i')] = S[\text{rank}(D, 10)] = S[5] = $* d*. Now we compute $i'' = \Psi[i'] = 3$ and obtain $T[j + 2] = S[\text{rank}(D, i'')] = S[\text{rank}(D, 3)] = S[2] = $* a*. Now we compute $i''' = \Psi[i''] = 7$ and obtain $T[j + 3] = S[\text{rank}(D, i''')] = S[\text{rank}(D, 7)] = S[3] = $* b*. Note that we are indeed obtaining the*

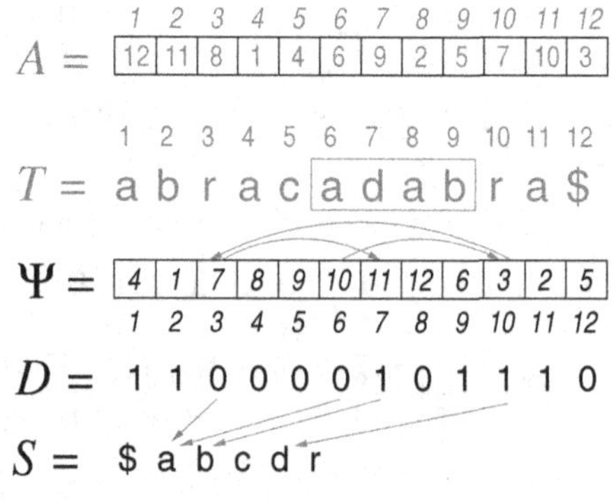

Figure 11.3. Our representation of the virtual elements T and A (in gray) using the explicit elements D, S, and Ψ (in black). The arrows illustrate the process to extract $T[A[6], A[6] + 3] = T[6, 9] = $ adab (in a rectangle).

Algorithm 11.1: Comparing P with $T[A[i], n]$ using Ψ.

Input : Text T and suffix array A (seen as structures Ψ, D, and S), pattern
$P[1, m]$, and position i of A to compare.

Output: Returns the result of the lexicographical comparison between P and
$T[A[i], A[i] + m - 1]$.

1 **for** $k \leftarrow 1$ **to** m **do**
2 $\quad$ $c \leftarrow S[\mathrm{rank}(D, i)]$
3 $\quad$ **if** $P[k] < c$ **then return** "$<$"
4 $\quad$ **if** $P[k] > c$ **then return** "$>$"
5 $\quad$ $i \leftarrow \Psi[i]$
6 **return** "$=$"

---

first characters of $T[6, n] =$ adabra$. *We continue this process as long as necessary to compare $T[6, n]$ with the search pattern P.*

Algorithm 11.1 shows how to compare P with the suffix of T pointed from $A[i]$. We are not using A or T anymore, but rather D, S, and Ψ. Assume we represent D as a compressed bitvector with constant-time rank support (Section 4.1.1) and S as a simple string. Then, since D contains at most σ 1s, it needs $\sigma \log \frac{n}{\sigma} + \mathcal{O}(\sigma) + o(n)$ bits. Added to the $\sigma \log \sigma$ bits required by a plain representation of S, we have $\sigma \log n + \mathcal{O}(\sigma) + o(n)$ bits for D and S.

Since Ψ is a permutation, however, its plain representation requires $n \log n$ bits, and thus the new representation gives almost no improvement compared to using the original arrays T and A. We show next, however, that Ψ can be significantly compressed, which makes this solution relevant.

11.1.2 Compressing Ψ

The key property that allows us to compress Ψ is that, within an area of A where the suffixes start with the same symbol, Ψ must be increasing. Let positions i and $i + 1$ be in the same area (so $i > 1$), and let $j = A[i]$ and $j' = A[i + 1]$. That is, it holds $T[j'] = T[A[i + 1]] = T[A[i]] = T[j]$. Since $A[i + 1]$ appears after $A[i]$, it must hold that $T[j', n] > T[j, n]$ in lexicographic order. But since $T[j'] = T[j]$, the first characters of both suffixes are equal, and the lexicographical comparison is decided by the tails of the suffixes. Therefore, it holds $T[j' + 1, n] > T[j + 1, n]$. Now, this means that value $j' + 1$ must appear to the right of value $j + 1$ in A. Since the position where $j' + 1$ appears in A is $A^{-1}[j' + 1] = A^{-1}[A[i + 1] + 1] = \Psi[i + 1]$, and the position where $j + 1$ appears in A is $A^{-1}[j + 1] = A^{-1}[A[i] + 1] = \Psi[i]$, this means that $\Psi[i + 1] > \Psi[i]$.

Example 11.5 *Consider $i = 4$ and $i + 1 = 5$ in Figure 11.2. These point to $T[A[i], n] = T[A[4], 12] = T[1, 12] =$* abracadabra$ *and $T[A[i + 1], n] = T[A[5], 12] = T[4, 12] =$* acadabra$, *respectively. Since $T[1, 12] < T[4, 12]$ in lexicographic order, that is,* abracadabra$ $<$ acadabra$, *and both start with* a, *it must be that*

bracadabra\$ < cadabra\$, *that is,* $T[2, 12] < T[5, 12]$. *Therefore,* $A^{-1}[2] = 8 <$
$9 = A^{-1}[5]$, *that is, 2 appears before 5 in A. But it is precisely* $\Psi[i] = \Psi[4] = 8$
that tells where $A[i] + 1 = A[4] + 1 = 2$ *is in A, and it is* $\Psi[i + 1] = \Psi[5] = 9$ *that*
tells where $A[i + 1] + 1 = A[5] + 1 = 5$ *is in A. Therefore,* $\Psi[i] = \Psi[4] = 8 < 9 =$
$\Psi[5] = \Psi[i + 1]$.

We can see that Ψ *is increasing in the areas of A that start with the same symbol:*
$\Psi[1] = \langle 4 \rangle$ *is the area of the* \$, $\Psi[2, 6] = \langle 1, 7, 8, 9, 10 \rangle$ *is the area of the* a, $\Psi[7, 8] =$
$\langle 11, 12 \rangle$ *is the area of the* b, $\Psi[9] = \langle 6 \rangle$ *is the area of the* c, $\Psi[10] = \langle 3 \rangle$ *is the area of*
the d, *and* $\Psi[11, 12] = \langle 2, 5 \rangle$ *is the area of the* r.

A way to take advantage of these increasing areas of Ψ is to cut it into σ increasing
arrays, $\Psi_c[1, n_c]$ for each $c \in \Sigma$ (where c appears n_c times in T), and represent each of
these increasing arrays with a structure that supports direct access to any position. One
pointer to each Ψ_c array, plus the storage of the last position $C[c]$ before Ψ_c starts in
Ψ, require just $\mathcal{O}(\sigma w)$ further bits and allow reducing any access to $\Psi[i]$ to an access
to $\Psi_c[i']$, where $c = S[\mathsf{rank}(D, i)]$ and $i' = i - C[c]$.[1]

Consider the use of, say, the δ-codes of Section 2.7 on the sequence of differ-
ences $x_1 = \Psi_c[1]$, $x_2 = \Psi_c[2] - \Psi_c[1]$, ..., $x_{n_c} = \Psi_c[n_c] - \Psi_c[n_c - 1]$. Since Ψ_c has
n_c increasing entries that go from 1 to n, the analysis of Section 2.8 shows that the total
number of bits needed by the δ-codes is $n_c \log \frac{n}{n_c} + \mathcal{O}\left(n_c \log \log \frac{n}{n_c} \right)$. Added over all
the σ arrays Ψ_c, this space is

$$\sum_{c \in \Sigma} n_c \log \frac{n}{n_c} + \mathcal{O}\left(n_c \log \log \frac{n}{n_c} \right) \leq n \mathcal{H}_0(T) + \mathcal{O}(n \log \mathcal{H}_0(T)),$$

where $\mathcal{H}_0(T) \leq \log \sigma$ is the zero-order empirical entropy of T (Section 2.3.2), and for
the $\mathcal{O}(\cdot)$-term we used Jensen's inequality as done in Section 2.9.

To provide direct access to any value $\Psi_c[i']$, we can use the sampled pointers and
partial sums technique of Sections 3.2.1 and 3.3. For example, in every $t = \Theta(\log n)$
positions of Ψ_c we store the sum of the previous differences, $\Psi_c[t \cdot r]$, and the position
where the next δ-code starts, each using $\Theta(\log n)$ bits. This requires $\mathcal{O}(n)$ bits for the
sampling. To access $\Psi_c[i']$, we take the nearest previous sample and decode up to t
δ-codes, adding them to obtain the final value. The access time to Ψ_c, and thus to Ψ, is
$\mathcal{O}(\log n)$.

Overall this solution requires at most $n \mathcal{H}_0(T) + \mathcal{O}(n \log \mathcal{H}_0(T) + n + \sigma w) =$
$n \mathcal{H}_0(T)(1 + o(1)) + \mathcal{O}(n + \sigma w)$ bits of space, and contains sufficient information to
compute s and e in time $\mathcal{O}(m \log^2 n)$.

Another alternative, with better space and time complexity, is to use the partial sums
solution of Section 4.5.1 to represent Ψ_c as the sums of the sequence $x_1, \ldots, x_{n_c}$. What
this does, essentially, is to mark the values $\Psi_c[i]$ in a bitvector $B_c[1, n]$, so that

$$B_c[\Psi_c[i]] = 1 \text{ for all } 1 \leq i \leq n_c,$$

and use the representation for very sparse bitvectors of Section 4.4. This computes any
$\Psi_c[i] = \mathsf{select}_1(B_c, i)$ in constant time and requires $n_c \log \frac{n}{n_c} + \mathcal{O}(n_c)$ bits. Overall this

---

[1] We use S for clarity. In practice we can avoid the use of S and store arrays $\Psi_{\mathsf{rank}(D, i)}$.

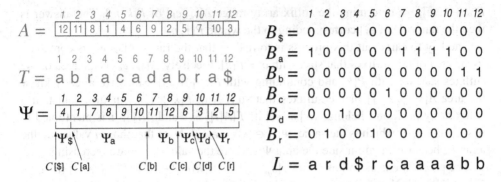

Figure 11.4. The representation of the Ψ_c structures (seen as ranges in Ψ) using bitvectors B_c, and the sequence L that represents all these B_c. Any element i in Ψ_c appears as $B_c[i] = 1$, and $L[i]$ is the only c such that $B_c[i] = 1$. Array C delimits the sub-arrays Ψ_c.

second solution uses $n\mathcal{H}_0(T) + \mathcal{O}(n + \sigma w)$ bits of space and computes s and e in time $\mathcal{O}(m \log n)$.

Example 11.6 *Figure 11.4 shows how Ψ is cut into the arrays Ψ_c and how these are represented with bitvectors B_c (disregard the final string L for now). The C array (also shown in the figure) contains $C[\$] = 0$, $C[\mathsf{a}] = 1$, $C[\mathsf{b}] = 6$, $C[\mathsf{c}] = 8$, $C[\mathsf{d}] = 9$, and $C[\mathsf{r}] = 10$. Then we have, for example, $\Psi_\mathsf{a}[4] = \mathsf{select}_1(B_\mathsf{a}, 4) = 9$.*

In Practice

The solution using bitvectors B_c is in theory preferable to the δ-codes–based solution. Whether this advantage translates to practice depends on the text T. In particular, the $\mathcal{O}(n)$-bits extra space term may be multiplied by a larger constant in the bitvectors than in the δ-codes. The δ-codes, in addition, may obtain space below $n\mathcal{H}_0(T)$ if the differences x_i are not uniformly distributed, which is indeed the case when the text has small high-order entropy $\mathcal{H}_k(T)$ (Section 2.4), as we show later in Section 11.3.4. Finally, although the δ-codes pose an $\mathcal{O}(\log n)$ extra factor in the time, this corresponds to scanning a contiguous memory area, which is cache-friendly. Other representations for the differences described in Section 2.7, such as γ-codes or PforDelta, although not giving the same space guarantees, may perform better in practice.

On the other hand, even if we achieve $\mathcal{O}(m \log n)$ search time, this is in practice worse than the $\mathcal{O}(m \log n)$ time of a binary search on a plain suffix array: while the latter requires $\mathcal{O}(\log n)$ accesses to arbitrary positions, each of which is followed by $\mathcal{O}(m)$ cache-friendly accesses to T, the former is made of $\mathcal{O}(m \log n)$ random accesses to Ψ. We explore next a technique to reduce this gap.

11.1.3 Backward Search

We can reduce the binary search time in practice with the so-called *backward search*. The idea is that we start with the suffix array range $A[s_m, e_m]$ of the single symbol $P[m] = P[m, m]$. Then, in general, knowing the suffix array range $A[s_{k+1}, e_{k+1}]$ of

$P[k + 1, m]$, we determine the suffix array range $A[s_k, e_k]$ of $P[k, m]$. The answer is then the range $A[s_1, e_1]$ corresponding to the whole $P[1, m]$.

The key to carry out this process is to realize that the range $A[s_k, e_k]$ is contained in the area of the suffixes that start with $c = P[k]$. Precisely, $A[s_k, e_k]$ is the area of the suffixes starting with $P[k]$ and continuing with $P[k + 1, m]$. Since we already know the area $A[s_{k+1}, e_{k+1}]$ of the suffixes that start with $P[k + 1, m]$, it turns out that a suffix array position i belongs to $[s_k, e_k]$ iff $T[A[i]] = c$ and $A[i] + 1$ is mentioned in $A[s_{k+1}, e_{k+1}]$, or which is the same, $\Psi[i] \in [s_{k+1}, e_{k+1}]$. Note that those i values define a range, because we are inside the area Ψ_c, where the values of Ψ are increasing.

The procedure is as follows. First, $[s_m, e_m] = [C[P[m]] + 1, C[P[m] + 1]]$ (assume $C[\sigma + 1] = n$). Now, given $[s_{k+1}, e_{k+1}]$, we obtain the range $[s_k, e_k]$ by a binary search on Ψ_c, where $c = P[k]$, for the range $\Psi_c[s'_k, e'_k]$ of the numbers i such that $\Psi_c[i] \in [s_{k+1}, e_{k+1}]$. Then $[s_k, e_k] = [C[c] + s'_k, C[c] + e'_k]$.

Example 11.7 *Consider backward searching for* $P =$ abra *in the structure of Figure 11.4. We start with* $[s_4, e_4] = [C[P[4]] + 1, C[P[4] + 1]] = [C[a] + 1, C[b]] = [2, 6]$*. Now, to compute* $[s_3, e_3]$*, we set* $c = P[3] =$ r *and run a binary search on* $\Psi_r[1, 2] = \langle 2, 5 \rangle$ *for the range of values contained in* $[s_4, e_4] = [2, 6]$*. The result is the range* $\Psi_r[1, 2] = \Psi[11, 12]$*, meaning that the suffixes in* $A[11, 12]$ *are those starting with* ra*.*

To compute $[s_2, e_2]$*, we set* $c = P[2] =$ b *and run a binary search on* $\Psi_b[1, 2] = \langle 11, 12 \rangle$ *for the range of values contained in* $[s_3, e_3] = [11, 12]$*. The result is the range* $\Psi_b[1, 2] = \Psi[7, 8]$*, meaning that the suffixes in* $A[7, 8]$ *are those starting with* bra*.*

Finally, to compute $[s_1, e_1]$*, we set* $c = P[1] =$ a *and run a binary search on* $\Psi_a[1, 5] = \langle 1, 7, 8, 9, 10 \rangle$ *for the range of values contained in* $[s_2, e_2] = [7, 8]$*. The result is the range* $\Psi_a[2, 3] = \Psi[3, 4]$*, meaning that the suffixes in* $A[3, 4]$ *are those starting with* abra*. Thus we have found* $A[s, e] = A[3, 4]$*.*

Algorithm 11.2 gives the pseudocode for backward search. The cost is again $\mathcal{O}(m \log n)$ accesses to Ψ, now formed by m steps, each of which involves two binary searches. While the initial positions accessed by the binary searches can be far away

---

Algorithm 11.2: Backward search on a compressed suffix array.

Input : Text T and suffix array A (seen as structures Ψ_c and array C) and pattern $P[1, m]$.

Output: Returns the range $[s, e]$ in A of the suffixes of T starting with P, or $\emptyset$ if P does not occur in T.

1 $[s, e] \leftarrow [C[P[m]] + 1, C[P[m] + 1]]$
2 **for** $k \leftarrow m - 1$ **downto** 1 **do**
3   **if** $s > e$ **then return** $\emptyset$
4     $c \leftarrow P[k]$
5     $[s', e'] \leftarrow$ binary search on Ψ_c for the range of numbers in $[s, e]$
6     $[s, e] \leftarrow [C[c] + s', C[c] + e']$
7 **return** $[s, e]$

from each other, the interval quickly converges to a small range, where the search is more cache-friendly. On the other hand, the normal search procedure on Ψ may access less than m symbols to decide a lexicographical comparison, whereas backward search always performs close to the worst case. In practice, however, backward search is usually faster.

The representation of Ψ_c based on sampling every $t = \Theta(\log n)$ positions is favored by the backward search: We can perform the binary search on the absolute samples first, and then complete the search between two samples in sequential form. Thus the backward search time is $\mathcal{O}(m \log n)$, even if we require $\mathcal{O}(\log n)$ time to access an individual Ψ value.

On the other hand, the representation of Ψ_c based on bitvectors B_c simplifies the backward search algorithm even further. Line 5 of Algorithm 11.2 can be written as

$$[s', e'] \leftarrow [\mathsf{rank}_1(B_c, s - 1) + 1, \mathsf{rank}_1(B_c, e)].$$

Example 11.8 *Consider the last paragraph in Example 11.7. Instead of a binary search on Ψ_a for the range of values contained in $[7, 8]$, we can just compute* $[\mathsf{rank}_1(B_\mathsf{a}, 7 - 1) + 1, \mathsf{rank}_1(B_\mathsf{a}, 8)] = [2, 3]$.

The cost of this rank operation is $\mathcal{O}\left(\log \frac{n}{n_c}\right)$ (see Section 4.4), which in the worst case can be as much as $\mathcal{O}(\log n)$ but can be much faster in practice. In particular, if the characters of P have the average frequency $n_c = n/\sigma$, then the cost of the backward search is $\mathcal{O}(m \log \sigma)$, asymptotically faster than the algorithm on plain suffix arrays and only outperformed by adding a Patricia tree on top of them.

11.1.4 Locating and Displaying

We have claimed that we replace T and A by Ψ and other structures (D and S for classical search, C for backward search). However, up to now we have shown only how to compute s and e. This is sufficient for answering $\mathsf{count}(T, P) = e - s + 1$, but not to answer $\mathsf{locate}(T, P)$ queries. For this query, we must be able to compute all the entries $A[i]$, for $s \le i \le e$. Furthermore, to replace T we must provide a mechanism to recover any desired substring $T[j, j + \ell - 1]$.

The mechanism used for locating is based on sampling T at regular intervals. We choose a sampling factor l and sample all the values of A that are a multiple of l, plus the value n (pointed from $A[1]$). We mark the sampled positions of A in a bitvector $B[1, n]$, that is, $B[i] = 1$ iff $i = 1$ or $A[i] \bmod l = 0$.

The sampled values of A are stored in a smaller array $A_S[1, \lceil n/l \rceil]$. More precisely, if $B[i] = 1$, then we store $A_S[\mathsf{rank}(B, i)] = A[i]$. Thus A_S requires $(n/l) \log n$ bits of space, and B requires $(n/l) \log l + \mathcal{O}(n/l) + o(n)$ further bits if represented in compressed form (Section 4.1.1). Together they add up to $\mathcal{O}((n/l) \log n) + o(n)$ bits.[2]

To compute $A[i]$, we proceed as follows. If $B[i] = 1$, then the answer is $A[i] = A_S[\mathsf{rank}(B, i)]$. Otherwise we compute $i' = \Psi[i]$. Now, if $B[i'] = 1$, then we know that $A[i'] = A_S[\mathsf{rank}(B, i')]$, and since $i' = \Psi[i]$, we have $A[i'] = A[i] + 1$. Therefore, in

---

[2] We store $A[i]$ for clarity, but we could store $A[i]/l$ instead, and then the total space would be $(n/l) \log n + \mathcal{O}(n/l) + o(n)$ bits.

Algorithm 11.3: Obtaining $A[i]$ on a compressed suffix array.

Input : Text T and suffix array A (seen as structures Ψ, B, and A_S) and position i of A.

Output: Returns $A[i]$.

1 $k \leftarrow 0$
2 **while** $\mathsf{access}(B, i) = 0$ **do**
3     $i \leftarrow \mathsf{read}(\Psi, i)$
4     $k \leftarrow k + 1$
5 **return** $A_S[\mathsf{rank}(B, i)] - k$

---

general, we compute $i_k = \Psi^k[i]$ iteratively until we find $B[i_k] = 1$ for some $k \geq 0$, and then it holds $A[i] = A[i_k] - k = A_S[\mathsf{rank}(B, i_k)] - k$. The cost to compute $A[i]$ is then at most l accesses to Ψ. For example, with constant-time access to Ψ we can choose $l = \Theta(\log n)$, which gives $\mathcal{O}(n)$ extra bits and $\mathcal{O}(\log n)$ time to compute any $A[i]$. Algorithm 11.3 summarizes the procedure.

Example 11.9 *Figure 11.5 (left) shows the sampling structures B and A_S for $l = 3$. The positions of A that contain multiples of l are $A[1] = 12$, $A[6] = 6$, $A[7] = 9$, and $A[12] = 3$. Those positions are set in B, and the sequence of values $\langle 12, 6, 9, 3 \rangle$ is stored in A_S.*

The figure also illustrates the process of computing $A[10]$. Since $B[10] = 0$, we jump to $\Psi[10] = 3$. Since $B[3] = 0$, we jump to $\Psi[3] = 7$. Since $B[7] = 1$, we know that $A[7] = A_S[\mathsf{rank}(B, 7)] = A_S[3] = 9$. Then, since $7 = \Psi^2[10]$, we have $A[10] = A[7] - 2 = 9 - 2 = 7$.

A similar process can be used to extract $T[j, j + \ell - 1]$. The main issue is how to determine $i = A^{-1}[j]$, since we have already seen that, with i, we can extract $T[A[i], A[i] + \ell - 1] = T[j, j + \ell - 1]$ via $\ell - 1$ applications of Ψ, as done when we simulated the classical binary search using Ψ. Here we should use the bitvector D and array S for maximum efficiency; otherwise we must run a binary search on C to emulate D.

$$A = \begin{array}{|c|c|c|c|c|c|c|c|c|c|c|c|} \hline 12 & 11 & 8 & 1 & 4 & 6 & 9 & 2 & 5 & 7 & 10 & 3 \\ \hline \end{array} \qquad T = \texttt{a b r a c a d a b r a \$}$$

$$B = \begin{array}{cccccccccccc} 1 & 0 & 0 & 0 & 0 & 1 & 1 & 0 & 0 & 0 & 0 & 1 \end{array}$$

$$A_S = \begin{array}{cccc} 12 & 6 & 9 & 3 \end{array} \qquad A_S^{-1} = \begin{array}{cccc} 12 & 6 & 7 & 1 \end{array}$$

$$\Psi = \begin{array}{|c|c|c|c|c|c|c|c|c|c|c|c|} \hline 4 & 1 & 7 & 8 & 9 & 10 & 11 & 12 & 6 & 3 & 2 & 5 \\ \hline \end{array}$$
$$\begin{array}{cccccccccccc} 1 & 2 & 3 & 4 & 5 & 6 & 7 & 8 & 9 & 10 & 11 & 12 \end{array}$$

$$\Psi = \begin{array}{|c|c|c|c|c|c|c|c|c|c|c|c|} \hline 4 & 1 & 7 & 8 & 9 & 10 & 11 & 12 & 6 & 3 & 2 & 5 \\ \hline \end{array}$$
$$\begin{array}{cccccccccccc} 1 & 2 & 3 & 4 & 5 & 6 & 7 & 8 & 9 & 10 & 11 & 12 \end{array}$$

Figure 11.5. The sampling structures B, A_S, and A_S^{-1}, associated with Ψ in our example. Structures A and T are virtual, and we show in black only their sampled positions (every 3rd position of T; their positions in A are marked in B). On the left, we illustrate the use of B, A_S, and Ψ to compute $A[10] = 7$. On the right, we use A_S^{-1} and Ψ to compute $A^{-1}[8] = 3$.

Algorithm 11.4: Displaying $T[j, j + \ell - 1]$ on a compressed suffix array.

Input : Text T (seen as structures Ψ, A_S^{-1}, D and S), sampling step l, and range
$\qquad$ $[j, j + \ell - 1]$ to display.
Output: Outputs $T[j, j + \ell - 1]$.

1 $j' \leftarrow \lfloor j/l \rfloor \cdot l$
2 **if** $j' = 0$ **then**
3 $\quad$ $j' \leftarrow 1$
4 $\quad$ $i \leftarrow \mathsf{read}(\Psi, 1)$

5 **else**
6 $\quad$ $i \leftarrow A_S^{-1}[j'/l]$

7 **for** $k \leftarrow j'$ **to** $j - 1$ **do**
8 $\quad$ $i \leftarrow \mathsf{read}(\Psi, i)$

9 **for** $k \leftarrow j$ **to** $j + \ell - 1$ **do**
10 $\quad$ **output** $S[\mathsf{rank}(D, i)]$
11 $\quad$ $i \leftarrow \mathsf{read}(\Psi, i)$

To compute $i = A^{-1}[j]$, we will use the same sampling step l (though we could use another) and store a sampled inverse suffix array, $A_S^{-1}[1, \lfloor n/l \rfloor]$, for the positions of T that are multiples of l, that is, $A_S^{-1}[j] = A^{-1}[j \cdot l]$ for all $1 \le j \le \lfloor n/l \rfloor$. Now, given j, we compute its rightmost preceding sample, $j' = \lfloor j/l \rfloor \cdot l$, and then know that $i' = A^{-1}[j'] = A_S^{-1}[j'/l]$ (an exception is $j' = 0$, in which case we set $j' = 1$ and have $i' = A^{-1}[j'] = A^{-1}[1] = \Psi[1]$). Finally, to compute $A^{-1}[j]$, we must apply Ψ $j - j'$ times over i', $i = \Psi^{j-j'}[i']$, so as to virtually advance from j' to j in T. Thus the overall cost is l applications of Ψ. For example, with constant-time access to Ψ, the whole process takes time $\mathcal{O}(l + \ell)$. With the value $l = \Theta(\log n)$, this is $\mathcal{O}(\ell + \log n)$ and the extra space is $\mathcal{O}(n)$ bits. Algorithm 11.4 summarizes the procedure.

Example 11.10 *Figure 11.5 (right) illustrates the computation of $A^{-1}[8]$. Since $l = 3$, the preceding sampled position in T is $j' = \lfloor 8/3 \rfloor \cdot 3 = 6$, whose inverse suffix array value is stored at $A_S^{-1}[6/3] = A_S^{-1}[2] = 6$. Thus we know that $i' = A^{-1}[6] = 6$. To determine $A^{-1}[8]$, we apply Ψ $8 - 6 = 2$ times on top of $i' = 6$, that is, $i = A^{-1}[8] = \Psi[\Psi[6]] = \Psi[10] = 3$.*

From position $i = 3$, we can use bitvector D and string S (see Figure 11.3) to compute $T[8] = S[\mathsf{rank}(D, 3)] = S[2] = \mathsf{a}$, $T[9] = S[\mathsf{rank}(D, \Psi[3])] = S[\mathsf{rank}(D, 7)] = S[3] = \mathsf{b}$, $T[10] = S[\mathsf{rank}(D, \Psi[\Psi[3]])] = S[\mathsf{rank}(D, 11)] = S[6] = \mathsf{r}$, and so on.

To conclude, a Ψ-based compressed suffix array on $T[1, n]$ can use $n\mathcal{H}_0(T) + \mathcal{O}(n + \sigma w)$ bits of space and support operation $\mathsf{count}(T, P[1, m])$ in time $\mathcal{O}(m \log n)$, and operation $\mathsf{locate}(T, P)$ in $\mathcal{O}(\log n)$ time per occurrence reported. It can display any text segment $T[j, j + \ell - 1]$ in time $\mathcal{O}(\ell + \log n)$, and can also compute any desired value $A[i]$ or $A^{-1}[j]$ in time $\mathcal{O}(\log n)$.

The reader may have noticed that Ψ is a permutation with at most σ increasing runs, and thus the representations we developed in Sections 5.3 and 6.4.1 should also yield space around $n\mathcal{H}_0(T)$. This is a fruitful path, which we explore in the next section from a slightly different angle.

11.2 The FM-Index

The FM-index builds on an alternative representation of the Ψ array, whose properties make it particularly interesting for relatively small alphabets. It represents Ψ with a sequence $L[1, n]$ on $[1, \sigma]$, defined as

$$L[i] = c \text{ such that } B_c[i] = 1$$

(note that there is only one c that qualifies for each i).

Example 11.11 *The bottom right of Figure 11.4 shows how the bitvectors B_c are represented by the single sequence $L[1, n]$.*

Observe that the situation is analogous to that of the beginning of Chapter 6, where we had a sequence $S[1, n]$ and attempted to represent it using σ bitvectors B_c, so that $\text{rank}_c/\text{select}_c$ operations on S were solved via operations $\text{rank}_1/\text{select}_1$ on bitvector B_c. This time we started with the bitvectors and now propose to replace them all with the sequence $L[1, n]$, which is the exact analogous of S in Chapter 6.

We mentioned that Algorithm 11.2 could be simplified by replacing the binary search of line 5 with a couple of rank operations on a bitvector B_c. If, instead of those bitvectors, we have a sequence representation (Chapter 6) for L, then we can replace $\text{rank}_1(B_c, p)$ by $\text{rank}_c(L, p)$. The result is Algorithm 11.5, a new backward search algorithm that uses only array C and sequence L.

Note that $L[1, n]$ contains the same characters of T in different order. That is, if c occurs n_c times in T, then $|\Psi_c| = n_c$, thus B_c has n_c 1s, and then L has n_c occurrences of c. Therefore, $\mathcal{H}_0(L) = \mathcal{H}_0(T)$ (recall Section 2.3.2). If we use a compressed wavelet tree for L (Section 6.2.4), then the total space of the FM-index is $n\mathcal{H}_0(T)(1 + o(1)) +$

Algorithm 11.5: Backward search on an FM-index.

> **Input** : Text T and suffix array A (seen as sequence L and array C) and pattern $P[1, m]$.
>
> **Output**: Returns the range $[s, e]$ in A of the suffixes of T starting with P, or $\emptyset$ if P does not occur in T.

1   $[s, e] \leftarrow [C[P[m]] + 1, C[P[m] + 1]]$
2   **for** $k \leftarrow m - 1$ **downto** 1 **do**
3   **if** $s > e$ **then return** $\emptyset$
4     $c \leftarrow P[k]$
5     $s \leftarrow C[c] + \text{rank}_c(L, s - 1) + 1$
6     $e \leftarrow C[c] + \text{rank}_c(L, e)$
7   **return** $[s, e]$

$o(n) + \mathcal{O}(\sigma w)$ bits and its backward search time is $\mathcal{O}(m \log \sigma)$, better than what we achieved when using Ψ.

For larger alphabets, we may consider the use of alphabet partitioning (Section 6.3). It raises the space only slightly, to $n\mathcal{H}_0(T)(1 + o(1)) + \mathcal{O}(n + \sigma w)$ bits, and in exchange the backward search is sped up to time $\mathcal{O}(m \log \log \sigma)$. This makes the FM-index counting faster than the Ψ-based suffix array for about the same space, both in theory and in practice. However, as we see soon, the FM-index is slower for the query locate.

Relation between L and A

We have shown that the sequence L, a permutation of T, is sufficient to emulate its suffix array. To understand what is L exactly, consider its definition, $L[i] = c$ such that $B_c[i] = 1$, that is, i appears in the range of Ψ_c. This is equivalent to saying that there exists one i' such that (a) i' is in the range of Ψ_c and (b) $\Psi[i'] = i$. Condition (a) is equivalent to $T[j'] = c$, where $j' = A[i']$. Condition (b) is equivalent to $A[i] = A[i'] + 1 = j' + 1$. In other words, $L[i] = c$ iff $T[A[i] - 1] = T[A[i']] = T[j'] = c$, or simply

$$L[i] = T[A[i] - 1]$$

(with the exception that $L[i] = T[n] = \$$ if $A[i] = 1$). That is, L can be obtained from A by taking the character preceding each suffix, in lexicographic order of the suffixes.

Example 11.12 *Consider again Figure 11.4. For example,* $L[3] = T[A[3] - 1] = T[7] = $ d.

Relation between L and Ψ

We can completely simulate array Ψ by using L. Consider $i' = \Psi[i]$, where i lies in the area of some Ψ_c; more precisely $\Psi[i] = \Psi_c[i_c]$, where $i_c = i - C[c]$. Since $\Psi_c[i_c] = \mathsf{select}_1(B_c, i_c) = \mathsf{select}_c(L, i_c)$, we have the identity $i' = \Psi[i] = \mathsf{select}_c(L, i - C[c])$. By taking rank_c on both sides, we have $\mathsf{rank}_c(L, i') = i - C[c]$, or which is the same,

$$i = \mathsf{LF}(i') = C[c] + \mathsf{rank}_c(L, i'), \text{ where } c = L[i'].$$

This function, which we have called $\mathsf{LF}(\cdot)$, is the inverse of Ψ: if $i' = \Psi[i]$, then $i = \mathsf{LF}(i')$. This means that function $\mathsf{LF}(\cdot)$ lets us virtually move backwards in T, just as we moved forwards with Ψ. The difference is that computing LF (or simulating Ψ) requires $\mathcal{O}(\log \sigma)$ or $\mathcal{O}(\log \log \sigma)$ time (depending on how we represent L), because we need access and rank (or select) on L. Instead, our direct representations of Ψ compute any entry $\Psi[i]$ in constant time, or $\mathcal{O}(\log n)$ cache-friendly time. This is why the FM-index is more advisable on smaller alphabets.

Example 11.13 *Consider again Figure 11.5. Let us now start at* $A[3] = 8$ *and move backwards in* T *using* LF. *First, we have* $c = L[3] = $ d *(see Figure 11.4) and thus* $\mathsf{LF}(3) = C[d] + \mathsf{rank}_d(L, 3) = 9 + 1 = 10$; *as expected,* $A[10] = 7 = A[3] - 1$. *Now we have* $c = L[10] = $ a *and thus* $\mathsf{LF}(10) = C[a] + \mathsf{rank}_a(L, 10) = 1 + 5 = 6$; *as expected,* $A[6] = 6 = A[3] - 2$.

Note that we are traversing the same cells as for locating in Example 11.10, but in the opposite direction.

Algorithm 11.6: Obtaining $A[i]$ on an FM-index.

Input : Text T and suffix array A (seen as structures C, L, B, and A_S) and
position i of A.
Output: Returns $A[i]$.

1 $k \leftarrow 0$
2 **while** access$(B, i) = 0$ **do**
3 | $c \leftarrow$ access(L, i)
4 | $i \leftarrow C[c] + \text{rank}_c(L, i)$
5 | $k \leftarrow k + 1$
6 **return** $A_S[\text{rank}(B, i)] + k$

Therefore, function LF enables exactly the same sampling mechanism we described
in Section 11.1.4, based on B, A_S, and A_S^{-1}. The details that have to change because LF
moves in T in the other direction are minimal; see Algorithms 11.6 and 11.7 (now we
assume that A_S samples the cells $A[i]$ where $A[i] \bmod l = 1$, thus $A_S^{-1}[j] = A^{-1}[j \cdot l + 1]$ for $j > 0$). Recall that the time to compute $A[i]$, $A^{-1}[j]$, and to display $T[j, j + \ell - 1]$, are now multiplied by the time to compute LF.

We have not yet explored, however, the most distinguishing characteristic of L,
which is that it paves the way to obtain high-order compression, instead of just $\mathcal{H}_0(T)$.
We explore this aspect in the next section.

Algorithm 11.7: Displaying $T[j, j + \ell - 1]$ on an FM-index.

Input : Text T (seen as structures C, L, and A_S^{-1}), sampling step l, and range
$[j, j + \ell - 1]$ to display.
Output: Outputs $T[j, j + \ell - 1]$ (in reverse order).

1 $j' \leftarrow \lceil (j + \ell - 1)/l \rceil \cdot l + 1$
2 **if** $j' > n$ **then**
3 | $j' \leftarrow n$
4 | $i \leftarrow 1$
5 **else**
6 | $i \leftarrow A_S^{-1}[(j' - 1)/l]$
7 **for** $k \leftarrow j'$ **downto** $j + \ell + 1$ **do**
8 | $c \leftarrow$ access(L, i)
9 | $i \leftarrow C[c] + \text{rank}_c(L, i)$
10 **for** $k \leftarrow j + \ell$ **downto** $j + 1$ **do**
11 | $c \leftarrow$ access(L, i)
12 | **output** c
13 | $i \leftarrow C[c] + \text{rank}_c(L, i)$

11.3 High-Order Compression

As said, using the string L to represent T and A, as done by the FM-index, makes it easy to reduce the space from $n\mathcal{H}_0(T)$ to $n\mathcal{H}_k(T)$, which can be significantly lower. To show this, we will study the origin of L from a completely different perspective.

11.3.1 The Burrows-Wheeler Transform

The Burrows-Wheeler Transform (BWT) of a text $T[1,n]$, called $T^{\mathsf{bwt}}[1,n]$, is a reversible permutation of the symbols of T. A graphical way to define it is to consider all the cyclic shifts of $T[1,n]$, that is, all the strings of the form $T[i,n] \,.\, T[1,i-1]$ for all $1 \le i \le n$. All these strings are then sorted lexicographically and written as the rows of a matrix $M[1,n][1,n]$. The last column of the matrix is T^{bwt}.

Note that sorting the cyclic shifts is equivalent to sorting the suffixes of T, since the terminator \$ defines any lexicographic comparison. Therefore, the rows $M[i]$ correspond to the suffixes of T. Since $M[i]$ contains the ith suffix in lexicographic order, it corresponds to the suffix that starts at $A[i]$, or equivalently, to the cyclic shift $T[A[i],n] \,.\, T[1,A[i]-1]$. Consequently, $T^{\mathsf{bwt}}[i]$, the last character of $M[i]$, is $T[A[i]-1]$ (or \$ if $A[i]=1$), that is, $T^{\mathsf{bwt}} = L$. In fact, the name L comes from being the "last" column of M. The first column, F, will also be relevant. Note that it contains the symbols of T in lexicographic order, and that the occurrences of each symbol c in F, if any, start at position $C[c]+1$.

Example 11.14 *Figure 11.6 shows the process to define the BWT of T =* abracadabra\$. *On the left we show all the cyclic shifts of T. On the right, we sorted them lexicographically. The last column is $L = T^{\mathsf{bwt}}$. In gray, we show how the ith row of matrix M is the ith suffix in lexicographic order, that is, the one starting at $A[i]$.*

T		A	F		L
a b r a c a d a b r a \$	1	12	\$	a b r a c a d a b r	a
b r a c a d a b r a \$ a	2	11	a	\$ a b r a c a d a b	r
r a c a d a b r a \$ a b	3	8	a	b r a \$ a b r a c a	d
a c a d a b r a \$ a b r	4	1	a	b r a c a d a b r a	\$
c a d a b r a \$ a b r a	5	4	a	c a d a b r a \$ a b	r
a d a b r a \$ a b r a c	6	6	a	d a b r a \$ a b r a	c
d a b r a \$ a b r a c a	7	9	b	r a \$ a b r a c a d	a
a b r a \$ a b r a c a d	8	2	b	r a c a d a b r a \$	a
b r a \$ a b r a c a d a	9	5	c	a d a b r a \$ a b r	a
r a \$ a b r a c a d a b	10	7	d	a b r a \$ a b r a c	a
a \$ a b r a c a d a b r	11	10	r	a \$ a b r a c a d a	b
\$ a b r a c a d a b r a	12	3	r	a c a d a b r a \$ a	b

Figure 11.6. On the left, the cyclic shifts of a text T. On the right, the matrix M formed by the sorted cyclic shifts. The last column is $L = T^{\mathsf{bwt}}$, and the first is F. In gray we show the relation with the suffix array A of T: the ith row of M contains $T[A[i],n] \,.\, T[1,A[i]-1]$.

To see that the BWT is reversible, consider that we know that $M[1][1] = \$ = T[n]$, therefore $M[1][n] = T[n-1] = L[1]$ gives the formula to compute $T[n-1]$. In general, assume we know that $M[i] = T[j+1, n] . T[1, j]$ (thus $M[i][n] = T[j] = L[i]$). We wish to find k such that $M[k] = T[j, n] . T[1, j-1]$. It must hold $F[k] = T[j] = L[i]$, thus k must be in the area of F corresponding to the symbol $c = L[i]$, but which of those is it? Recall that the rows of M are cyclic shifts of T. Thus, the rows starting with c are sorted by the text following that c in T, and the rows ending with c are also sorted by the text following that c in T. Then the rth c in L corresponds to the rth c in F, that is, $k = C[c] + \mathsf{rank}_c(L, i) = \mathsf{LF}(i)$. Now the meaning of the name LF is clear: it maps from positions in L to positions in F, the "last-to-first" mapping. See, for example, how the 'a's are sorted in F and L, in Figure 11.6.

Therefore, T is recovered by setting $T[n] = \$$, $i = 1$ and $j = n - 1$ and, repeatedly, setting $T[j] \leftarrow L[i]$, $i \leftarrow \mathsf{LF}(i)$, and $j \leftarrow j - 1$, until $j = 0$. Indeed, the mechanism to recover some $T[j, j + \ell - 1]$ with the FM-index is similar to this process, except that we start at some sampled text position slightly to the right of $T[j + \ell - 1]$.

The BWT was invented as a device for compression. The reason for this is made clear next.

11.3.2 High-Order Entropy

Let us return to the formula of the kth order entropy of a string T given in Section 2.4 (written slightly differently):

$$\mathcal{H}_k(T) = \sum_{S \in \Sigma^k} \frac{|T_S|}{n} \mathcal{H}_0(T_S) = \sum_{S \in \Sigma^k} \frac{n_S}{n} \sum_{c \in \Sigma} \frac{n_{Sc}}{n_S} \log \frac{n_S}{n_{Sc}} = \sum_{S \in \Sigma^k, c \in \Sigma} \frac{n_{Sc}}{n} \log \frac{n_S}{n_{Sc}},$$

where T_S is the string formed by all the characters following string S in T (in any order), $n_S = \mathsf{count}(T, S)$ is the number of occurrences of S in T, and similarly $n_{Sc} = \mathsf{count}(T, S . c) = \mathsf{count}(T_S, c)$. Note that $n_S = |T_S|$ except for $S = T[n-k+1, n]$, which is the last length-k string in T. In this case, $n_S = 1$ (because it is the only string containing \$) but $T_S = \varepsilon$. Still, we can also replace $|T_S|$ with n_S in the formula above in this case, because $|T_S| = 0$ and also $\sum_{c \in \Sigma} \frac{n_{Sc}}{n_S} \log \frac{n_S}{n_{Sc}} = 0$ (recall that we take $0 \log 0 = 0$).

Note also that it holds $\sum_{c \in \Sigma} n_{Sc} = |T_S|$ for all S. Therefore, $n_S = \sum_{c \in \Sigma} n_{Sc}$ except if $S = T[n-k+1, n]$, where $n_S = 1$ and $\sum_{c \in \Sigma} n_{Sc} = 0$. In this case, however, it holds $\log n_S = 0$. Thus, by separating the fractions into two logarithms, we have

$$n\mathcal{H}_k(T) = \sum_{S \in \Sigma^k, c \in \Sigma} n_{Sc} \log n_S - \sum_{S \in \Sigma^k, c \in \Sigma} n_{Sc} \log n_{Sc}$$

$$= \sum_{S \in \Sigma^k} n_S \log n_S - \sum_{S' \in \Sigma^{k+1}} n_{S'} \log n_{S'}.$$

Unlike the original formula for $\mathcal{H}_k(T)$, this new one is symmetric. That is, if we compute the kth order entropy of the reversed text, or equivalently, define T_S as the set of symbols in T that precede S (instead of following it), and assume that \$ precedes $T[1]$ instead of following it, we obtain the same formula. Note that the BWT regards T as being circular, that is, if we move backwards from $T[1]$, we arrive at $T[n]$.

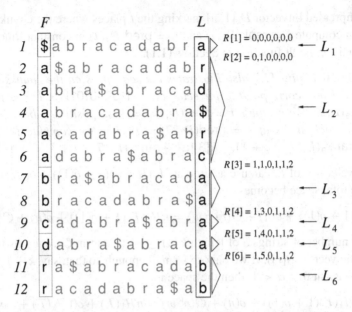

Figure 11.7. The FM-index construction achieving kth order entropy, for $k = 1$ in our example text, shown on the corresponding matrix M. Triangles indicate sequences built on the chunks L_r. The vectors $R[r]$ give the frequencies of the symbols $\langle \$, a, b, c, d, r \rangle$, in that order.

In other words, defining T_S as the set of symbols in T preceding or following S, if we place the symbol $\$$ appropriately, does not change $\mathcal{H}_k(T)$. We use the second definition (symbols preceding S) from now on.

Now regard M in Figure 11.6 again. Assume we choose k and cut M into t blocks $M[i_r, i_{r+1} - 1]$, where $1 = i_1 < i_2 < \ldots < i_t < i_{t+1} = n + 1$ are the rows where $M[i_r][1, k] \neq M[i_r - 1][1, k]$, for all $1 < r \leq t$. Then it holds that, for any $1 \leq r \leq t$, and choosing some convenient order for the symbols in T_S,

$$T_{S=M[i_r][1,k]} = L[i_r, i_{r+1} - 1],$$

that is, the symbols of L in the corresponding rows are the characters that precede the length-k prefix of the block of rows in M. Hence, by the formula of $\mathcal{H}_k(T)$, it is sufficient to compress each chunk $L_r = L[i_r, i_{r+1} - 1]$ to its zero-order entropy, to obtain total space $n\mathcal{H}_k(T)$.

Example 11.15 *Consider $k = 1$ in Figure 11.7 (the entries R will be used soon). The blocks are $L_1 = L[1, 1] = $ a, $L_2 = L[2, 6] = $ rd\$rc, $L_3 = L[7, 8] = $ aa, $L_4 = L[9] = $ a, $L_5 = L[10] = $ a, and $L_6 = L[11, 12] = $ bb. The zero-order entropies add up to $\frac{1}{12} \cdot \mathcal{H}_0(a) + \frac{5}{12} \cdot \mathcal{H}_0(rd\$rc) + \frac{2}{12} \cdot \mathcal{H}_0(aa) + \frac{1}{12} \cdot \mathcal{H}_0(a) + \frac{1}{12} \cdot \mathcal{H}_0(a) + \frac{2}{12} \cdot \mathcal{H}_0(bb) = \frac{5}{12} \cdot (3 \cdot \frac{1}{5} \log \frac{5}{1} + \frac{2}{5} \log \frac{5}{2}) \approx 0.80$. This is $\mathcal{H}_1(T)$, much smaller than $\mathcal{H}_0(T) \approx 2.28$.*

Therefore, if instead of using a single sequence for the whole L, we build a separate sequence for each chunk L_r, the total space becomes $n\mathcal{H}_k(T)$. The operations rank and access on L can then be replaced by operations on the chunks, if we have a table $R[r][1, \sigma]$ for each chunk r storing $R[r][c] = \text{rank}_c(L, i_r - 1)$. Then $\text{rank}_c(L, i) = R[r][c] + \text{rank}_c(L_r, i - i_r + 1)$, where i belongs to chunk L_r. We also need a compressed bitvector $D_k[1, n]$ marking the t places where the chunks begin, so that we can compute $r = \mathsf{rank}(D_k, i)$ and $i_r = \mathsf{pred}(D_k, i)$ in constant time (D_1 is the same D used for the Ψ function in Section 11.1).

Example 11.16 *Figure 11.7 also illustrates the sequences on the chunks L_r and the arrays $R[r]$. These correspond to bitvector $D_1 = $ 110000101110. For example, consider $\mathsf{rank}_a(L, 7)$. We compute $r = \mathsf{rank}(D_1, 7) = 3$, so position 7 belongs to chunk number 3, which starts at $i_r = \mathsf{pred}(D_1, 7) = 7$. Now we compute $\mathsf{rank}_a(L, 7) = R[r][a] + \mathsf{rank}_a(L_r, 7 - i_r + 1) = R[3][a] + \mathsf{rank}_a(L_3, 7 - 7 + 1) = 1 + 1 = 2$.*

The wavelet tree of L_r can use as little as $|L_r|\mathcal{H}_0(L_r)(1 + o(1)) + o(|L_r|) + \mathcal{O}(\sigma w)$ bits, so the total space becomes

$$n\mathcal{H}_k(T)(1 + o(1)) + o(n) + \mathcal{O}(t \cdot \sigma w) = n\mathcal{H}_k(T)(1 + o(1)) + o(n) + \mathcal{O}(\sigma^{k+1} w)$$

bits, as the number of strings S of length k is $t \le \sigma^k$ (the term $\mathcal{O}(t\sigma w)$ also counts the space for the vectors $R[r]$). If we choose k small enough so that, say, $k + 1 \le \alpha \log_\sigma n$ for some constant $0 < \alpha < 1$, then the space is

$$n\mathcal{H}_k(T)(1 + o(1)) + o(n) + \mathcal{O}(n^\alpha w) = n\mathcal{H}_k(T) + o((\mathcal{H}_k(T) + 1)n)$$

bits (here we are making the mild assumption $w = \mathcal{O}(\mathrm{polylog}\, n)$). Note, however, that to obtain larger k values, we need smaller alphabet sizes: already for $k = 1$ we need that $\sigma = o(\sqrt{n})$.

We must also consider the space for the sampled arrays A_S and A_S^{-1}, if they are used. For example, by choosing a sampling step of the form $\Theta(\log^{1+\epsilon} n / \log \sigma)$, for any constant $\epsilon > 0$, the total space is $n\mathcal{H}_k(T) + o(n \log \sigma)$ bits and the time to compute $A[i]$ and $A^{-1}[j]$ is $\mathcal{O}(\log^{1+\epsilon} n)$.

If, instead of wavelet trees, we use the alphabet-partitioned representation (Section 6.3), then the space increases by $\mathcal{O}(n)$ bits and the times to operate on any L_r decrease from $\mathcal{O}(\log \sigma)$ to $\mathcal{O}(\log \log \sigma)$. In practice, however, when $\mathcal{H}_k(T)$ is small, most chunks L_r have a low zero-order entropy $\mathcal{H}_0(L_r)$. That is, they contain a few distinct symbols, or at least a few symbols with high frequency. Hence, a Huffman-shaped wavelet tree (Section 6.2.4) is more space-efficient, and even more time-efficient, than the alphabet-partitioned representation, which is advisable only on large alphabets.

High-Order Compression without Partitioning

Partitioning L into chunks L_r involves a price: apart from finding the right contexts, at query time we must compute r using rank on D, i_r using pred on D, and also access the table $R[r]$.

Curiously we can also obtain high-order compression without any partitioning if we use the technique of Section 4.1.1 to represent the wavelet tree bitvectors B_v. Since the zero-order entropy of the bitvectors is made up from the sum of the zero-order entropies of small blocks of bits, the same analysis of Section 4.1.1 applied inside the area of each chunk L_r shows that these also add up to the sum of the zero-order entropies $|L_r|\mathcal{H}_0(L_r)$, that is, to $n\mathcal{H}_k(T)$. The result is also valid if we combine this compression with Huffman-shaped wavelet trees, which operate faster. Interestingly, the bound $n\mathcal{H}_k(T)(1 + o(1)) + o(n) + \mathcal{O}(\sigma^{k+1} w)$ now holds simultaneously for all k, not for a fixed k as before.

On the other hand, the bitvectors compressed with the technique of Section 4.1.1 are somewhat slower in practice than plain representations (note that we cannot obtain $n\mathcal{H}_k(T)$ bits by using plain bitvectors and a Huffman-shaped wavelet tree). Next we show how to obtain high-order compression with a simpler partitioning and using the faster uncompressed bitvectors.

11.3.3 Partitioning L into Uniform Chunks

Our discussion suggests that, unless we use specific compression methods like that of Section 4.1.1, we need to cut L into the correct chunks in order to obtain $n\mathcal{H}_k(T)$ bits of space. Surprisingly, we can cut L into chunks of equal length and still obtain the desired space. To understand why, let us start considering two strings X and Y, of lengths x and y, respectively. Let also x_c and y_c be the number of occurrences of symbol c in strings X and Y, respectively. We study how the zero-order entropy changes when we concatenate X and Y. Let us call

$$\mathcal{H}(x, y) = (x + y)\,\mathcal{H}\left(\frac{x}{x + y}\right) = x \log \frac{x + y}{x} + y \log \frac{x + y}{y} \leq x + y$$

(we are using the notation $\mathcal{H}(p)$ of Section 2.3). Then

$$|XY|\mathcal{H}_0(XY) = \sum_{c \in \Sigma}(x_c + y_c) \log \frac{x + y}{x_c + y_c}$$

$$= \sum_{c \in \Sigma}(x_c + y_c) \log(x + y) - \sum_{c \in \Sigma}(x_c + y_c) \log(x_c + y_c)$$

$$= (x + y) \log(x + y) - \sum_{c \in \Sigma}(x_c + y_c) \log(x_c + y_c),$$

and similarly we have

$$|X|\mathcal{H}_0(X) = x \log x - \sum_{c \in \Sigma} x_c \log x_c,$$

$$|Y|\mathcal{H}_0(Y) = y \log y - \sum_{c \in \Sigma} y_c \log y_c.$$

Therefore,

$$|XY|\mathcal{H}_0(XY) - |X|\mathcal{H}_0(X) - |Y|\mathcal{H}_0(Y)$$

$$= (x + y) \log(x + y) - \sum_{c \in \Sigma}(x_c + y_c) \log(x_c + y_c)$$

$$- x \log x + \sum_{c \in \Sigma} x_c \log x_c - y \log y + \sum_{c \in \Sigma} y_c \log y_c$$

$$= \mathcal{H}(x, y) - \sum_{c \in \Sigma} \mathcal{H}(x_c, y_c)$$

$$\leq \mathcal{H}(x, y) \leq x + y,$$

where it is also clear that

$$|XY|\mathcal{H}_0(XY) - |X|\mathcal{H}_0(X) - |Y|\mathcal{H}_0(Y) \geq 0,$$

as seen in Section 2.8 as an application of Jensen's inequality.

Now imagine that we start with our partitioning into chunks from Section 11.3.2, $L = L_1 . L_2 \ldots L_t$, which gives $\sum_{r=1}^{t} |L_r|\mathcal{H}_0(L_r) = n\mathcal{H}_k(T)$. Consider a second partitioning $L = Z_1 . Z_2 \ldots Z_{n/b}$ into chunks of fixed length b. We will convert one into the other and measure how the space changes. We start by adding to the first partitioning the cuts of the second, that is, we further partition some chunks L_r. By our argument above (Jensen's inequality), this does not increase $|L_r|\mathcal{H}_0(L_r)$. Now we remove the original cuts, which divide the chunks L_r (if they do not happen to be also cuts of some Z_i). By our calculation above, removing each cut from some chunk Z_i (that is, concatenating two strings X and Y) increases its entropy by at most $|Z_i| = b$ bits. Therefore, at the end, the total entropy can be at most $n\mathcal{H}_k(T) + b \cdot t \leq n\mathcal{H}_k(T) + b\sigma^k$.

Example 11.17 *Let us convert the partition $L = $ a . rd\$rc . aa . a . a . bb of Example 11.15 into a uniform partition with $b = 4$. It was shown that the entropy of this partition is $\mathcal{H}_1(T) \approx 0.8$. We first introduce cuts at multiples of 4, obtaining* a . rd\$. rc . aa . a . a . bb. *Since we cut* rd\$rc *into* rd\$. rc, *the entropy decreases, to about 0.563. Now we remove the original cuts, obtaining* ard\$. rcaa . aabb. *We showed that, since we removed 4 cuts, the entropy could increase by up to $\frac{1}{12} \cdot 4 \cdot b \approx$ 1.333. It increases a bit less in this case: joining* a . rd\$ *increases the total per-symbol entropy from 0.396 to 0.667; joining* rc . aa *increases it from 0.167 to 0.5; and joining* a . a . bb *increases it from 0 to 0.333. In total, the entropy increases from 0.563 to 1.5.*

We choose $b = \sigma w \log n$. This yields a total space of $n\mathcal{H}_k(T) + \sigma^{k+1} w \log n$ bits, which is $n\mathcal{H}_k(T) + o(n)$ if we choose $k + 1 \leq \alpha \log_\sigma n$ for any constant $0 < \alpha < 1$, under the same assumption $w = \mathcal{O}(\text{polylog } n)$ as before. In addition, the tables $R[r]$ have n/b rows, which add up to $(n/b)\sigma w = n/\log n = o(n)$ bits. Finally, since the new chunks are of length exactly b, we do not need the bitvector D to mark their beginnings; we simply compute $r = \lceil i/b \rceil$ and $i_r = (r-1)b + 1$. Adding the $o(n(\mathcal{H}_k(T) + 1))$ bits from the extra space of wavelet trees and samplings of A_S and A_S^{-1}, we reach $n\mathcal{H}_k(T) + o(n \log \sigma)$ bits as before.

11.3.4 High-Order Compression of Ψ

The same argument used for the FM-index can be used to show that Ψ can also be compressed to high-order entropy. Consider a particular context $S \in \Sigma^k$, and let $A[s_S, e_S]$ be the range of the suffixes that start with S. Then, for each $c \in \Sigma$, there is a contiguous region $\Psi_{c,S}$ inside Ψ_c such that $k \in \Psi_{c,S}$ iff $\Psi[k] \in [s_S, e_S]$. Note that $e_S - s_S + 1 = n_S$ and $|\Psi_{c,S}| = n_{cS}$, the number of occurrences of string $c . S$ in T.

Now consider a δ-encoding of the differential Ψ array. By fixing S and focusing on the values that belong to the ranges $\Psi_{c,S}$, and using the same reasoning of Section 11.1.2, we obtain

$$\sum_{c \in \Sigma} n_{cS} \log \frac{n_S}{n_{cS}} + \mathcal{O}\left(n_{cS} \log \log \frac{n_S}{n_{cS}} \right) \leq n_S \mathcal{H}_0(T_S) + \mathcal{O}(n_S \log \mathcal{H}_0(T_S))$$

bits, which added over all the contexts S gives $n\mathcal{H}_k(T) + \mathcal{O}(n\log\mathcal{H}_k(T)) + \mathcal{O}(\sigma^k\log n)$ bits. The last term comes from the σ^k transitions between contexts, whose differential value we cannot bound. For any $k \le \alpha\log_\sigma n$ and constant $0 < \alpha < 1$, the space in bits can be written as $n\mathcal{H}_k(T)(1 + o(1)) + \mathcal{O}(n)$, including samplings every $\log n$ positions for A_S and A_S^{-1}.

Therefore, a differential representation of Ψ, followed by a gap encoding like δ-codes, essentially reaches high-order entropy without further intervention. This is not the case if we represent the arrays Ψ_c with the bitvectors B_c, without any modification. Therefore, in texts where high-order entropy is significantly lower than zero-order entropy, the δ-encoded Ψ achieves less space than the use of bitvectors B_c.

11.4 Construction

The main challenge when building the structures in this section is the construction of the suffix array. Once we have $A[1, n]$ and $T[1, n]$, it is not hard to build the rest. We start with the suffix array construction and then consider its derived structures. We will also show how to build the compact structures directly, without building the suffix array as a (large) intermediate structure. This will be slower but enables indexing larger text collections.

11.4.1 Suffix Array Construction

In principle, A can be built by initializing $A[i] = i$ and then using any sorting algorithm, where the comparison between $A[i]$ and $A[j]$ is the lexicographic comparison of the suffixes $T[A[i], n]$ and $T[A[j], n]$. This is very simple to program and, depending on the sorting algorithm used, may take no extra space. We can use a simple Quick-Sort, or another algorithm more focused on sorting strings, such as RadixSort, 3-Way QuickSort, or combinations.

Using a general string sorting algorithm to build the suffix array may be fast enough, depending on the length of the prefixes shared by two suffixes. Say that the longest prefix shared by any two different suffixes $T[A[i], n]$ and $T[A[j], n]$ is ℓ. Then an algorithm using $\mathcal{O}(n\log n)$ string comparisons will require $\mathcal{O}(n\ell\log n)$ time, whereas RadixSort will require just $\mathcal{O}(n\ell)$ time.

In many text families, it is the case that $\ell = \mathcal{O}(\log n)$. For example, when the symbols are generated at random, even with a probability distribution that depends on the k previous symbols, for a constant k, it holds $\ell = \mathcal{O}(\log n)$ with high probability.[3] More generally, we say that those texts where the probability that two random suffixes coincide up to length l is $\mathcal{O}(\gamma^l)$ for some constant $0 < \gamma < 1$, are *typical*. On such a typical text, we have $\ell = \mathcal{O}(\log_{1/\gamma} n) = \mathcal{O}(\log n)$ with high probability, and any two random suffixes coincide only in their first $\mathcal{O}\left(\frac{1}{1-\gamma}\right) = \mathcal{O}(1)$ symbols. Therefore, on typical texts the suffix array can be built in $\mathcal{O}(n\log n)$ or $\mathcal{O}(n\log^2 n)$ time, depending on the

---

[3] That is, with probability tending to 1 as n tends to infinity.

string sorting algorithm used, and this is sufficiently good in practice. Many real-life text collections behave as typical texts and have a small ℓ.

Non-typical texts, however, do arise in real life as well. In applications where the text collection is formed by very similar documents, such as when indexing versions of documents, or sets of similar genomes, there are long repeated substrings in the text. When the text has long identical substrings, many suffixes share long prefixes and ℓ can be comparable to n. In this case, resorting to mere string sorting is impractical.

There are many suffix array construction algorithms that outperform the simple construction and work well for all kinds of texts. Somewhat surprisingly, the suffix array can be built in $\mathcal{O}(n)$ worst-case time, using just the space for T and A, and running fast in practice. The fastest algorithms, however, do not guarantee a good worst-case time. This is a broad topic that is not directly related to compact data structures, so we do not develop it further and provide instead a number of references and pointers to implementations at the end of the chapter.

Another reason not to insist on the construction of A is that we are more interested in building the final compact structures directly, as described next.

11.4.2 Building the BWT

Having T and A, we easily build the BWT $L[1, n]$ in linear time, since $L[i] = T[A[i] - 1]$ (taking $T[0] = \$$). However, we are building A, which uses $n \log n$ bits, as an intermediate structure to build L, which requires only $n \log \sigma$ bits.

A simple way to decrease the construction space is to build $A[1, n]$ by chunks of size b. Suppose that we determine which is the bth suffix of T, $T[A[b], n]$. Then we scan T and collect all the suffixes that are lexicographically smaller than $T[A[b], n]$ (including $T[A[b], n]$ itself). The b collected suffixes are then sorted using a string sorting algorithm. The result is the first chunk of A, $A[1, b]$, from where we can collect the first chunk of L, $L[1, b]$. Now we discard $A[1, b]$ and collect the suffixes that belong to the second chunk, larger than $T[A[b], n]$ and no larger than $T[A[2b], n]$, sort them to produce $A[b + 1, 2b]$, generate $L[b + 1, 2b]$, and so on.

In total, we need only $\mathcal{O}(b \log n)$ bits of space apart from T. The string L can be directly generated on disk if necessary, because is it produced left-to-right. Assuming we can collect the suffixes of each chunk in time $\mathcal{O}(tn)$ (for $t \leq \ell$), we need time $\mathcal{O}((n/b)(tn + b\ell))$ to build L if we use RadixSort. On a typical text, we have $\ell = \mathcal{O}(\log n)$ and $t = \mathcal{O}(1)$ with high probability (the latter is because we compare the dividing suffix with all the others in T). For example, with $b = n/ \log n$ and on a typical text, we need $\mathcal{O}(n)$ extra bits of space and build L in time $\mathcal{O}(n \log n)$.

Algorithm 11.8 shows the pseudocode. Note that it is not obvious how to find the dividing suffixes. Instead of those precise suffixes $T[A[kb], n]$, we use a procedure *genCut* to find a small set of short strings that, if used to limit chunks in A, guarantee that these are of size at most b.

To find those short limiting strings that approximate $T[A[kb], n]$, we can choose a small l value and establish that the chunks correspond to the suffixes starting with each distinct string of length l. On a typical text, we should choose $l = \mathcal{O}(\log(n/b))$ to have chunks of length $\mathcal{O}(b)$ (for $b = n/ \log n$, l is just $\mathcal{O}(\log \log n)$), but in practice some chunks may turn out to be much longer than others. A more sophisticated approach is

---

Algorithm 11.8: Building the BWT of a text T in compact space. The comparisons in line 6 must be carried out only up to the length of the *Cut* entry.

Input : Text $T[1, n]$ and maximum allowed chunk size b.
Output: Outputs $T^{\text{bwt}}[1, n]$.

1   Allocate array $A[1, b]$ of integers
2   $Cut[0, p] \leftarrow genCut(T, n, b)$ (Algorithm 11.9)
3   **for** $q \leftarrow 1$ **to** $p + 1$ **do**
4     $s \leftarrow 0$
5   **for** $j \leftarrow 1$ **to** n **do**
6   **if** $Cut[q - 1] < T[j, n] \leq Cut[q]$ **then**
7         $s \leftarrow s + 1$
8         $A[s] \leftarrow j$
9   Sort $A[1, s]$ using a string sorting algorithm
10   **for** $i \leftarrow 1$ **to** s **do**
11   **output** $T[A[i] - 1]$ (assuming $T[0] = \$$)

12   Free A and Cut

---

to start with $l = 1$, determine the chunk sizes, and recursively subdivide those that are longer than b. We also concatenate consecutive chunks if the result does not exceed the size b. This guarantees that we produce at most $2n/b$ chunks of length at most b, that is, just $2 \log n$ chunks for our choice of b.

Algorithm 11.9 shows the pseudocode. We generate in *Cut* a minimal set of prefixes, so that each prefix starts no more than b suffixes of T. The chunk lengths are stored in an array *Len*.[4] As we generate each new valid prefix, we merge its chunk with the previous, if possible. We cannot bound in advance the size to allocate for S, although it would not exceed $\mathcal{O}(\log n)$ on typical texts. We can start with this preliminary size and double it as needed.

To compute the total time of *genCut*, consider that further recursive calls of *expand* are made as long there are more than b suffixes starting with S, thus the tree of calls has at most n/b leaves. On a typical text, the average number of suffixes starting with a string S of length l is $n\,\mathcal{O}(\gamma^l)$, thus the average length of strings S starting less than b suffixes is $l = \log_{1/\gamma}(n/b) + \mathcal{O}(1)$. Then on average we perform $l(n/b)$ calls to *expand*, which is $\mathcal{O}(\log n \log \log n)$ for our choice of b. If *count* uses an $\mathcal{O}(n)$-time algorithm to find the occurrences of S in T, the total time is $\mathcal{O}(n \log n \log \log n)$ on typical texts. This can be reduced to $\mathcal{O}(n \log \log n)$ by performing an $\mathcal{O}(n)$-time multi-pattern search for all the strings S of the same length simultaneously.

Example 11.18 *For the text $T = $ abracadabra$\$$ and $b = 4$, the algorithm would generate the set Cut $= \{$ab, b, r$\}$. For $b = 3$, the algorithm would generate Cut $= \{$a$\$$, ac, b, d, r$\}$.*

---

[4] There will be an error of 1 in the predicted size of one of the chunks, because when the prefix string occurring at the end of T is expanded, that last occurrence is not counted. This is not problematic, of course.

Algorithm 11.9: Generating the partition of A for BWT construction.

---

1 **Proc** $genCut(T, n, b)$
  Input : Text $T[1, n]$ and chunk size b.
  Output: Returns the splitting strings $Cut[0, p]$.

2 | Allocate array $Cut[0, 2n/b]$ of strings and $Len[1, 2n/b]$ of integers
3 | Allocate string S
4 | $Cut[0] \leftarrow \varepsilon$
5 | $p \leftarrow expand(S, 0, 0)$
6 | Free Len and S
7 | **return** Cut reallocated to $[0, p]$

8 **Proc** $expand(S, k, p)$
  Input : String $S[1, k]$ and written position p.
  Output: Fills Cut and Len from $p + 1$ and returns new written position.

9 | $N \leftarrow count(S, k)$
10 | **for** $c \leftarrow 1$ **to** σ **do**
11 | $S[k + 1] \leftarrow c$
12 | **if** $N[c] \leq b$ **then**
13 | **if** $p = 0$ **or** $Len[p] + N[c] > b$ **then**
14 | $p \leftarrow p + 1$
15 | $Len[p] \leftarrow 0$
16 | $Cut[p] \leftarrow S[1, k + 1]$
17 | $Len[p] \leftarrow Len[p] + N[c]$
18 | **else** $p \leftarrow expand(S, k + 1, p)$
19 | Free N
20 | **return** p

21 **Proc** $count(S, k)$
  Input : String $S[1, k]$.
  Output: Returns the frequencies $N[1, \sigma]$ of the symbols following S in T.

22 | Allocate array $N[1, \sigma]$ of integers
23 | **for** $c \leftarrow 1$ **to** σ **do** $N[c] \leftarrow 0$
24 | **for** $j \leftarrow 1$ **to** $n - k$ **do**
25 | **if** $T[j, j + k - 1] = S$ **then** $N[T[j + k]] \leftarrow N[T[j + k]] + 1$
26 | **return** $N[1, \sigma]$

11.4.3 Building Ψ

Once $A[1, n]$ is built, we can build its inverse permutation $A^{-1}[1, n]$ and then build $\Psi[1, n]$ directly, in $\mathcal{O}(n)$ time. However, this takes $3n \log n$ bits to finally obtain a compressed representation of Ψ. Instead, the technique we gave in Section 11.4.2 to build the BWT can be extended to build the Ψ_c arrays directly in compressed form (and without materializing the string L).

We initialize the arrays Ψ_c, one per symbol $c \in \Sigma$. Now, each time we find the next value $L[i] = c$, we add the value i to Ψ_c. This can be immediately encoded differentially with respect to the previous value in Ψ_c, or can be sent to disk by chunks, or both. The only change we need is for line 11 of Algorithm 11.8 to say "**output** j to the stream of $\Psi_{T[A[i]-1]}$," where j counts the number of times line 11 has been executed.

11.5 Suffix Trees

In Section 8.5.3 we introduced simplified suffix trees as Patricia trees indexing all the suffixes of a text $T[1, n]$. These used $\mathcal{O}(n \log \sigma)$ bits on top of the suffix array. We showed how to search for patterns $P[1, m]$ in time $\mathcal{O}(m \log \log n)$, and we anticipated that actual suffix trees support more complex operations on T. In this section we show how to implement fully functional suffix trees within just $\mathcal{O}(n)$ bits on top of a compressed suffix array.

The compressed suffix tree structure for a text $T[1, n]$ over alphabet $[1, \sigma]$ is composed of three elements: (1) a compressed suffix array A on T; (2) the topology of the suffix tree; and (3) a *longest common prefix* array.

As for component (1), we have given various suffix array implementations in previous sections:

- Based on Ψ with δ-codes, using $n\mathcal{H}_k(T)(1 + o(1)) + \mathcal{O}(n)$ bits, counting in time $\mathcal{O}(m \log n)$, computing Ψ in time $\mathcal{O}(\log n)$, and A/A^{-1} in time $\mathcal{O}(\log^2 n)$.
- Based on Ψ with bitvectors B_c, using $n\mathcal{H}_0(T) + \mathcal{O}(n)$ bits, counting in time $\mathcal{O}(m \log n)$, computing Ψ in time $\mathcal{O}(1)$, and A/A^{-1} in time $\mathcal{O}(\log n)$.
- FM-index, using $n\mathcal{H}_k(T) + o(n \log \sigma)$ bits, counting in time $\mathcal{O}(m \log \sigma)$, computing LF in time $\mathcal{O}(\log \sigma)$, and A/A^{-1} in time $\mathcal{O}(\log^{1+\epsilon} n)$, for any constant $\epsilon > 0$. All these $\log \sigma$ times can be reduced to $\log \log \sigma$.

To keep the discussion general, we will say that the compressed suffix array uses $|CSA|$ bits, counts in time $\mathcal{O}(m t_P)$, computes Ψ or LF in time $\mathcal{O}(t_S)$, and computes any cell of A or A^{-1} in time $\mathcal{O}(t_A)$. Since $\Psi[i] = A^{-1}[A[i] + 1]$ and $LF(i) = A^{-1}[A[i] - 1]$, we may safely assume $t_S \leq t_A$.

For component (2), since the suffix tree has at most $2n$ nodes, the BP structure of Section 8.2 can represent it using at most $4n + o(n)$ bits, and offers all the functionality we will require in time as low as $\mathcal{O}(\log \log n)$.

The component (3) is described next, and then we will show the operations we support and how they are implemented. Finally, we will show how to represent component (3) using $2n + o(n)$ bits, so that the compressed suffix tree uses just $|CSA| + 6n + o(n)$ bits.

11.5.1 Longest Common Prefixes

Let $\mathsf{lcp}(X, Y)$ be the length of the longest common prefix between strings X and Y, that is, $\mathsf{lcp}(X, Y) = \max\{i, X[1, i] = Y[1, i]\}$. Then we define the *longest common prefix* array, $\mathsf{LCP}[2, n]$, as

$$\mathsf{LCP}[i] = \mathsf{lcp}(T[A[i], n], T[A[i-1], n]),$$

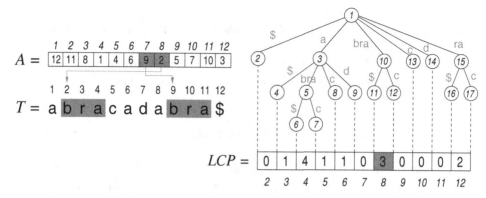

Figure 11.8. The suffix tree and array of $T =$ abracadabra$, showing the corresponding LCP array on the bottom. Edges that lead to leaves show only the first character of their string label (which extends until the terminator, $). The node numbers are given in preorder. Grayed blocks and arrows illustrate the meaning of LCP[8] = 3.

that is, the length of the prefix shared between the lexicographically ith and $(i-1)$th suffixes of T.

Example 11.19 *Figure 11.8 shows the same suffix tree of Figure 8.20 and its corresponding* LCP *array on the bottom. Then* LCP[8] = 3 *because the suffixes starting at* $A[8] = 2$ *and* $A[7] = 9$ *share a prefix of length 3,* $T[2, 4] = T[9, 11] =$ bra.

11.5.2 Suffix Tree Operations

The suffix tree operations can be classified as follows:

1. All the unlabeled ordinal tree operations of Table 8.1.
2. The labeled tree operations: childrenlabeled, labeledchild, and childlabel.
3. Operations that are specific of suffix trees:
   string(v), the string that labels the path from the root to node v.
   strdepth(v) = |string(v)|, the *string depth* of v.
   slink(v) = u such that, if string(v) = $c.X$, where $c \in \Sigma$ and $X \in \Sigma^*$, then string(u) = X. This is called the *suffix link* of v. For the root, we define slink(root()) = root().
   wlink(v, c) = u such that, if string(v) = X, then string(u) = $c.X$ (where $c \in \Sigma$). This is called the *Weiner link* of v by c. Unlike suffix links, a Weiner link may not lead to an explicit node, and may even not exist, as we explain soon.
4. Operations that depend mostly on the suffix array: compute $A[i]$ and $A^{-1}[j]$, extract $T[l, r]$, as well as the following ones:
   locus(P), the highest node v such that P is a prefix of string(v).
   count(v) = count(T, string(v)), given v.
   locate(v) = locate(T, string(v)), given v.

The last three operations enable the suffix tree as a device to perform pattern counting and locating: if $v =$ locus(P), then count(v) = count(T, P) and locate(v) =

locate(T, P), since the set of occurrences of P in T is the same set of occurrences of string(v) in T.

Example 11.20 *In the suffix tree of Figure 11.8, let* $v = 5$. *Then* string(v) = abra, strdepth(v) = 4, *and* slink(v) = u = 10, *since* string(u) = bra. *Conversely,* wlink(u, a) = v. *Instead,* wlink(u, d) *does not exist because* dbra *does not appear in* T, *and* wlink(v, d) *leads to the middle of the edge that goes to node 14 (whose edge label is* dabra\$, *whereas we were looking for the string* d . string(v) = dabra).

It holds v = locus(ab) = locus(abr) = locus(abra), *and these strings have the same set of occurrences in* T, $\{1, 8\}$. *Instead,* locus(a) = 3, *and* a *has a broader set of occurrences in* T, $\{1, 4, 6, 8, 11\}$.

The unlabeled tree operations can be directly solved on the tree topology, in time $\mathcal{O}(\log \log n)$ as explained. Let us now consider the others.

Operations That Depend on the Suffix Array

Operations $A[i]$ and $A^{-1}[j]$, as well as displaying any $T[l, r]$, are solved using just the compressed suffix array, the first two in time $\mathcal{O}(t_A)$ and the third in time $\mathcal{O}(t_A + (r - l + 1)t_S)$. The other operations, instead, require some help from the tree topology, as shown for some cases in Section 8.5.3.

First, locus(P) can be found by obtaining the range $A[s, e]$ of P, and then it holds locus(P) = lca(leafselect(s), leafselect(e)). This is easy to see from the definition of locus. We also obtain easily count(v) = leafnum(v) and locate(v) = $A[$leafrank(v), leafrank(v) + leafnum(v) − 1$]$ for any node v.

Obtaining the range $[s, e]$ (for locus) takes time $\mathcal{O}(m t_P)$. Obtaining each cell of A (for locate) takes time $\mathcal{O}(t_A)$. The additional tree operations cost $\mathcal{O}(\log \log n)$ time in all cases.

Example 11.21 *In Figure 11.8, we can search for* P = a, *obtaining the range* $A[2, 6]$. *Then* v = locus(P) = lca(leafselect(2), leafselect(6)) = lca(4, 9) = 3. *Then* P *has* count(v) = leafnum(v) = 5 *occurrences in* T, *and they are located in* $A[$leafrank(v), leafrank(v) + leafnum(v) − 1$]$ = $A[2, 6]$.

Computing string(v)

To access a specific symbol string(v)[i], we compute $T[A[$leafrank(v)$] + i − 1]$ with the mechanism provided by the compressed suffix array: we compute $S[$rank(D, $A^{-1}[A[$leafrank(v)$] + i − 1])]$ on a Ψ-based representation, or $L[A^{-1}[A[$leafrank(v)$] + i]]$ on an FM-index. This requires $\mathcal{O}(t_A + \log \log n)$ time.[5] If i is small, then a Ψ-based representation can instead compute $S[$rank(D, $\Psi^{i-1}[$leafrank(v)$])]$ in time $\mathcal{O}(i t_S + \log \log n)$, which may be faster.

To retrieve a substring of the form string(v)[i, j], we extract the text $T[A[$leafrank(v)$] + i − 1, A[$leafrank(v)$] + j − 1]$, in $\mathcal{O}(t_A + (j − i)t_S + \log \log n)$ time. Again, if i is small (and, in particular, if $i = 1$), we may rather prefer to iterate on Ψ to find the first position of the string, in time $\mathcal{O}(j t_S + \log \log n)$.

---

[5] Plus the time to access L in the FM-index, but since accessing L is involved in the computation of LF, we may assume it takes time $\mathcal{O}(t_S) = \mathcal{O}(t_A)$.

Example 11.22 *Consider again the suffix tree of Figure 11.8, and let $v = 5$. Then* $\mathsf{string}(v)[3] = T[A[\mathsf{leafrank}(v)] + 3 - 1] = T[A[3] + 2] = T[10] = \mathsf{r}$.

Computing $\mathsf{strdepth}(v)$

On an internal suffix tree node, operation $\mathsf{strdepth}(v)$ can be computed as $\mathsf{LCP}[i]$, where i is the first suffix of the second child of v, $i = \mathsf{leafrank}(\mathsf{child}(v, 2))$. Recall that all the internal suffix tree nodes have at least two children, and that the length of the prefix shared between the last suffix of $\mathsf{child}(v, t)$ and the first suffix of $\mathsf{child}(v, t + 1)$, for any t, is precisely $\mathsf{strdepth}(v)$.

In Section 11.5.3 we will show that the time to compute an LCP entry is $\mathcal{O}(t_A)$, so $\mathsf{strdepth}$ is computed in time $\mathcal{O}(t_A + \log \log n)$.

On leaves, string depths are computed differently. Since the leaf corresponding to $A[i]$ points to the suffix $T[A[i], n]$, its string depth can be computed as $n + 1 - A[\mathsf{leafrank}(v)]$, which also takes time $\mathcal{O}(t_A + \log \log n)$.

Example 11.23 *Consider again Figure 11.8. To find* $\mathsf{strdepth}(v)$ *for* $v = 3$, *we compute* $i = \mathsf{leafrank}(\mathsf{child}(v, 2)) = \mathsf{leafrank}(5) = 3$, *and then* $\mathsf{strdepth}(v) = \mathsf{LCP}[3] = 1$. *As another example, to find* $\mathsf{strdepth}(10)$, *we compute* $i = \mathsf{leafrank}(\mathsf{child}(10, 2)) = \mathsf{leafrank}(12) = 8$, *and then* $\mathsf{strdepth}(v) = \mathsf{LCP}[8] = 3$.

Now, let us compute $\mathsf{strdepth}(u)$ *for the leaf* $u = 12$. *This is* $n + 1 - A[\mathsf{leafrank}(12)] = 12 + 1 - A[8] = 11$, *which is correct since* $\mathsf{string}(12) = \mathsf{bracadabra\$}$.

Computing $\mathsf{slink}(v)$

For $v \neq \mathsf{root}()$, we compute $\mathsf{slink}(v)$ as follows. We obtain the leftmost and rightmost leaf offsets of v, $l = \mathsf{leafrank}(v)$ and $r = l + \mathsf{leafnum}(v) - 1$. Now it turns out that $\mathsf{slink}(v) = \mathsf{lca}(\mathsf{leafselect}(\Psi[l]), \mathsf{leafselect}(\Psi[r]))$, which can be computed in time $\mathcal{O}(t_S + \log \log n)$.

To see that the formula is correct, let v be an internal node and $\mathsf{string}(v) = c.X$ for $c \in \Sigma$ and $X \in \Sigma^*$. Then $T[A[l], n] = c.X.a\ldots$ and $T[A[r], n] = c.X.b\ldots$, for $a, b \in \Sigma$. Further, it must be $a \neq b$ because l and r descend by different children of v, and these are the first symbols on the edges toward those two children. Now, it holds $T[A[\Psi[l]], n] = X.a\ldots$ and $T[A[\Psi[r]], n] = X.b\ldots$. Since the two leaves $\mathsf{leafselect}(\Psi[l])$ and $\mathsf{leafselect}(\Psi[r])$ share exactly the prefix X, their lowest common ancestor must be the node u with $\mathsf{string}(u) = X$. Thus, $u = \mathsf{slink}(v)$. If, instead, v is a leaf, then the formula simplifies to $\mathsf{slink}(v) = \mathsf{leafselect}(\Psi[\mathsf{leafrank}(v)])$, which is easy to understand.

Example 11.24 *Figure 11.9 illustrates the way* $\mathsf{slink}(v)$ *is computed for the node* $v = 15$ *in our example suffix tree, which represents the string* ra *(a curved arrow goes from v to* $\mathsf{slink}(v)$*). First we find the leftmost and rightmost suffix array positions that descend from v, $l = \mathsf{leafrank}(v) = 11$ and $r = l + \mathsf{leafnum}(v) - 1 = 12$ (hatched). Now we compute* $\Psi[l] = \Psi[11] = 2$ *and* $\Psi[r] = \Psi[12] = 5$ *(hatched in the other direction). From those positions, we obtain the corresponding leaves,* $\mathsf{leafselect}(2) = 4$ *and* $\mathsf{leafselect}(5) = 8$. *Finally* $\mathsf{slink}(v) = \mathsf{lca}(4, 8) = 3$ *(marked with a bold circle), which represents the string* a.

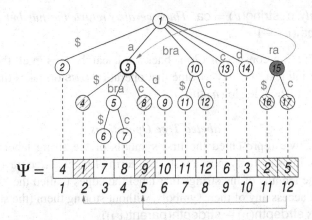

$$\Psi = \boxed{4}\,\boxed{1}\,\boxed{7}\,\boxed{8}\,\boxed{9}\,\boxed{10}\,\boxed{11}\,\boxed{12}\,\boxed{6}\,\boxed{3}\,\boxed{2}\,\boxed{5}$$

$$\qquad\ \ 1\ \ 2\ \ 3\ \ 4\ \ 5\ \ 6\ \ 7\ \ 8\ \ 9\ \ 10\ \ 11\ \ 12$$

Figure 11.9. Illustration of the way slink(15) = 3 is computed using Ψ and tree operations. We translate the range of node 15 using Ψ and then the lca of the translated range is slink(15). The operation wlink(3, r) = 15 follows the inverse process.

Now consider slink(3)*. Then* $l =$ leafrank(3) $= 2$ *and* $r = l +$ leafnum(3) $- 1 =$ 6*. We compute* $\Psi[2] = 1$ *and* $\Psi[6] = 10$*, which correspond to the nodes* 2 *and* 14*, and finally* lca(2, 14) $= 1$*, the root, which represents the empty string.*

If we are using an FM-index, we need to simulate $\Psi[i]$ to implement this operation. As shown in Section 11.2, it holds $\Psi[i] = \text{select}_c(L, i - C[c])$, where $c = S[\text{rank}(D, i)]$ (thus we must store D and S, but these require little space). Thus, we can compute $\Psi[i]$ in time $\mathcal{O}(t_S)$. In many cases we can instead build the FM-index on the reversed text T^{rev}, so that we can use the more direct LF function instead of simulating Ψ.

Computing wlink(v, c)

The area of A spanned by wlink(v, c) is that of the suffixes that start with c . string(v). Thus, if v spans the area $A[s, e] = A[\text{leafrank}(v), \text{leafrank}(v) + \text{leafnum}(v) - 1]$, we need to perform one backward search step from $[s, e]$, as in lines 5–6 of Algorithm 11.2 or 11.5. We will call this operation $[s, e] \leftarrow$ bwstep(s, e, c). If this operation returns $s > e$, then there is no Weiner link. Otherwise we obtain the node $u = \text{lca}(\text{leafselect}(s), \text{leafselect}(e))$. However, the actual answer may be in the edge that leads to u: If u is a leaf or strdepth(u) > strdepth(v) + 1, then string(u) starts with c . string(v) as desired, but it is longer. We return the pair (u, strdepth(v) + 1) to retain all the information.

Example 11.25 *Let us do the inverse of Example 11.24 (see also Figure 11.9). To find* wlink(u, r) *for* $u = 3$*, we compute* $[s, e] = [\text{leafrank}(u), \text{leafrank}(u) +$ leafnum(u) $- 1] = [2, 6]$*. Now we find* bwstep(2, 6, r) $= [11, 12]$*, which is the range in* A *of the suffixes that start with* r . string(u) $=$ ra*. Then we answer* lca(leafselect(11), leafselect(12)) $=$ lca(16, 17) $= 15 = v$*.*

If, instead, we attempted to compute wlink(u, b)*, we would have obtained the empty interval* bwstep(2, 6, b) $= [7, 6]$*, indicating that there is no answer.*

On the other hand, if we compute wlink(u, c)*, we obtain* bwstep(2, 6, c) $= [9, 9]$*, corresponding to node* 13*. However,* string(13) $=$ cadabra$*, whereas the string we* *sought was only* c.string(u) = ca. *Thus we also return the number of characters desired,* strdepth(u) + 1 = 2.

Since the counting consists of $\mathcal{O}(m)$ backward search steps in all the compressed suffix arrays of interest, we may assume that operation bwstep takes time $\mathcal{O}(t_P)$, and thus wlink takes $\mathcal{O}(t_P + \log\log n)$ time.

Labeled Tree Operations

In Section 8.5.3 we represented the first symbols of the string labels explicitly in $\mathcal{O}(n\log\sigma)$ bits, in order to support a restricted form of labeled tree traversal. Now we can compute the lengths of the strings that label the edges (called the "skips" in Section 8.5.3), and access any of their symbols, without storing them (the skip between v and its parent is strdepth(v) − strdepth(parent(v))).

Operations childrenlabeled(v, c) and labeledchild(v, c) can be implemented with a binary search on the children of v, looking for the child u such that string(u)[strdepth(v) + 1] = c. Since accessing individual positions of string(u) costs $\mathcal{O}(t_A + \log\log n)$ time, the binary search requires time $\mathcal{O}((t_A + \log\log n)\log\sigma)$. Finally, childlabel($u$) is found in $\mathcal{O}(t_A + \log\log n)$ time as string(u)[strdepth(parent(u)) + 1].

Example 11.26 *In Figure 11.8, let $u = 5$. Then the length of the string* bra *that leads to u from its parent $v =$* parent(u) = 3 *is calculated as* strdepth(u) − strdepth(v) = 4 − 1 = 3. *Moreover, u descends from v by the symbol* childlabel(u) = string(u)[strdepth(v) + 1] = string(u)[2] = b.

Now let us descend from v by the symbol b *(assuming we do not know u). We must run a binary search for* b *among the symbols of its children. Given that* strdepth(v) + 1 = 2, *those are* string(child(v, 1))[2] = string(4)[2] = $, string(child($v$, 2))[2] = string(5)[2] = b, string(child(v, 3))[2] = string(8)[2] = c, *and* string(child(v, 4))[2] = string(9)[2] = d.

Operation labeledchild is the most expensive one on compressed suffix trees. This makes it preferable to run pattern searches directly on the suffix array, as we have shown when computing locus(P), instead of descending from the root of the suffix tree. The former requires at most $\mathcal{O}(m\log n)$ time, whereas descending from the root takes at least $\mathcal{O}(m\log n\log\sigma)$ time.

Algorithm 11.10 summarizes the operations (except those that are solved directly on the tree topology or with A).

11.5.3 A Compact Representation

Now we show how to represent LCP[2, n] in $2n + o(n)$ bits, as promised. Let us define a permuted version of it, PLCP[1, $n − 1$]. This is simply the array LCP but in text order, that is, PLCP[j] = LCP[$A^{-1}[j]$] is the length of the prefix shared between $T[j, n]$ and the one lexicographically preceding it in T.

The array PLCP has an important property: for any j, PLCP[$j + 1$] ≥ PLCP[j] − 1. This is obvious if PLCP[j] = 0. Otherwise there is a suffix $T[j', n] < T[j, n]$ (in lexicographic order) that shares its first PLCP[j] ≥ 1 characters with $T[j, n]$, and thus

---

Algorithm 11.10: Computing the suffix tree operations that are not solved using only the tree topology or the compressed suffix array.

Input : Suffix tree on $T[1, n]$ (seen as a tree topology τ, a compressed suffix array A, and array LCP), pattern P, node $v \in \tau$, and symbol $c \in [1, \sigma]$.

1 **Proc** locus(P)
2    $[s, e] \leftarrow$ interval of A corresponding to P (Algorithm 11.2 or 11.5)
3   **return** lca(τ, leafselect(τ, s), leafselect(τ, e))

4 **Proc** count(v)
5   **return** leafnum(τ, v)

6 **Proc** locate(v)
7    $l \leftarrow$ leafrank(τ, v)
8   **return** $A[l, l + \text{leafnum}(\tau, v) - 1]$

9 **Proc** string(v, i) — *assuming* $1 \leq i \leq$ strdepth(v)
10   **return** $T[A[\text{leafrank}(\tau, v)] + i - 1]$ (the access to T is simulated)

11 **Proc** strdepth(v)
12   **if** isleaf(τ, v) **then return** $n + 1 - A[\text{leafrank}(\tau, v)]$
13   **return** LCP[leafrank(τ, child($\tau, v, 2$))]

14 **Proc** slink(v)
15   **if** $v = \text{root}(\tau)$ **then return** root(τ)
16    $l \leftarrow$ leafrank(τ, v); $r \leftarrow l + \text{leafnum}(\tau, v) - 1$
17   **return** lca(τ, leafselect($\tau, \Psi[l]$), leafselect($\tau, \Psi[r]$))
               (Ψ can also be simulated with the FM-index)

18 **Proc** wlink(v, c)
19    $s \leftarrow$ leafrank(τ, v); $e \leftarrow s + \text{leafnum}(\tau, v) - 1$
20    $[s, e] \leftarrow$ bwstep(s, e, c) (lines 5–6 of Algorithms 11.2 or 11.5)
21   **if** $s > e$ **then return** null
22    $u \leftarrow$ lca(τ, leafselect(τ, s), leafselect(τ, e))
23   **return** (u, strdepth(v) + 1)

24 **Proc** labeledchild(v, c)
25    $d \leftarrow$ strdepth(v) + 1
26    $u \leftarrow$ binary search for $u = $ child(τ, v, t) such that string(u, d) = c
27   **return** u (or null if there is no such u)

28 **Proc** childlabel(v) — *assuming* $v \neq \text{root}(\tau)$
29   **return** string(v, strdepth(parent(τ, v)) + 1)

$T[j' + 1, n]$ shares PLCP$[j] - 1$ characters with $T[j + 1, n] > T[j' + 1, n]$. Thus the suffix lexicographically preceding $T[j + 1, n]$, which shares the longest prefix with it among those lexicographically smaller than it, must share at least the first PLCP$[j] - 1$ characters.

This means that PLCP$[j] + 2j$ is a strictly increasing sequence, starting with PLCP$[1] + 2 \geq 0$ and ending with PLCP$[n - 1] + 2(n - 1) < 2n$ (because

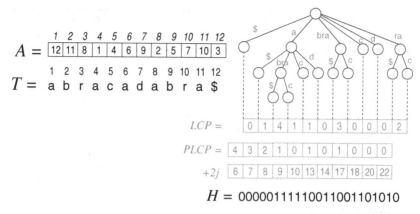

$H =$ 0000011111001100110101010

Figure 11.10. Compression of the LCP array. Array PLCP contains the same LCP values but in text order, not in suffix array order. The sequence PLCP$[j] + 2j$ is strictly increasing, and its values are marked in bitvector H.

$T[n-1, n]$ can share only one character with another suffix). Thus, we can represent PLCP$[j] + 2j$ using the technique of Section 4.5.1: use a bitvector $H[1, 2n-1]$ where we set to 1 the values PLCP$[j] + 2j$, and thus PLCP$[j] = \mathsf{select}_1(H, j) - 2j$ can be computed in constant time using $2n + o(n)$ bits (Section 4.3.3). With this, we can compute any cell LCP$[i] = $ PLCP$[A[i]]$ in time $\mathcal{O}(t_A)$.

Example 11.27 *Figure 11.10 shows how the LCP array of our example text is compressed. For example,* PLCP$[1] = 4$ *because* $T[1, n] = $ abracadabra$ *shares a prefix of length 4 with the suffix that lexicographically precedes it,* $T[8, n] = $ abra$. *Note that* PLCP$[j] + 2j$ *is strictly increasing, and thus its values can be marked in bitvector H, which is sufficient to represent* PLCP.

11.5.4 Construction

It is possible to build the suffix tree directly from T in $\mathcal{O}(n)$ time, and then compress it into the different components. As we are interested in using little space for construction, we consider a different path: we first build the compressed suffix array, then build the bitvector H that represents PLCP, and finally build the compressed tree topology.

Building H

We build PLCP as follows. For PLCP$[1]$, we compare $T[1, n]$ with $T[A[A^{-1}[1] - 1], n]$, symbol by symbol, until the prefixes differ. This comparison can be done with the compressed suffix array. Now we do the same for PLCP$[2]$. However, since we know that PLCP$[2] \geq $ PLCP$[1] - 1$, we start the comparison from offset $d = \max($PLCP$[1] - 1, 0)$, that is, we compare $T[2 + d, n]$ with $T[A[A^{-1}[2] - 1] + d, n]$. We continue in this way until computing all the values PLCP$[1, n-1]$. Since we perform PLCP$[j] - $ PLCP$[j-1] + \mathcal{O}(1)$ steps to compute PLCP$[j]$, the sum of the steps telescopes to $\mathcal{O}(n)$, and the total time is $\mathcal{O}(n\, t_A)$. Moreover, we can avoid generating the intermediate PLCP array, but rather fill the 1s in the bitvector H directly.

Building the Tree Topology

Once H is built, we can compute LCP values, which allows us to build the suffix tree topology. We traverse $A[1, n]$ from left to right and at step i add a new leaf at the right of the current suffix tree. The parent of this leaf must belong to the (current) rightmost path of the tree and have string depth LCP[i]. To do this efficiently, we maintain the internal nodes of the rightmost path in a stack with their string depths computed (with the root at the bottom), so for each new i we pop elements from the stack until the desired string depth (or less) is reached. If we find a node v in the stack with strdepth(v) = LCP[i], then the new leaf becomes the rightmost child of v (and the removed part of the stack no longer belongs to the rightmost path). Otherwise we find a node v with strdepth(v) < LCP[i] whose rightmost child u is a leaf or it satisfies strdepth(u) > LCP[i]. We must then create a node v' between v and u, with strdepth(v') = LCP[i], whose left child is u and whose right child is the new leaf.

Since we insert one element in the stack for each i, we add n elements overall, and thus we also remove at most n elements. Then the algorithm performs $\mathcal{O}(n)$ steps and its cost is $\mathcal{O}(n\, t_A)$.

Example 11.28 *Figure 11.11 shows the steps to build the tree topology from the* LCP *array of our example text. The numbers written on the rightmost path are the* strdepth *values stored in the stack. The inserted nodes are grayed. When we find a node v with* strdepth(v) = LCP[i], *we add 1 node, otherwise we add 2.*

In all but the most pathological cases, we can use $\mathcal{O}(n)$ extra bits of space in this construction by immediately compacting the subtrees that leave the rightmost path, into a sequence of parentheses. More precisely, let v be a node in the rightmost path, with children $x_1, \ldots, x_r$. Then x_r also belongs to the rightmost path. Let $P(x_i)$ be the BP representation of the subtree rooted at x_i. In the stack, node v stores strdepth(v) and a pointer to the concatenation $C(v) = P(x_1) \ldots P(x_{r-1})$. When the internal nodes $u_1, \ldots, u_k$ (from highest to lowest in the tree) are removed from the stack to add a new leaf z as the rightmost child of the parent v of u_1, we append $(\, C(u_1)\, (\, C(u_2) \ldots (\, C(u_k)\, (\,)\,)\,)^k$ to $C(v)$ (this is just $(\,)$ if $k = 0$). If, instead, $u_1, \ldots, u_k$ are removed from the stack to add a new internal node v' that is the parent of u_1 and z, then $C(v)$ does not change, and we set $C(v') \leftarrow (\, C(u_1)\, (\, C(u_2) \ldots (\, C(u_k)\, (\,)\,)\,)^k$.

Example 11.29 *In Figure 11.11, when we complete the processing of* LCP[4] = 4 *(bottom left frame), the root node stores $C(v_1) = (\,)$, the rightmost node at depth 2 stores $C(v_2) = (\,)$, and the rightmost node at depth 3 stores $C(v_3) = (\,)$. Now we process* LCP[5] = 1: *node v_3 leaves the stack, and a new leaf is added as the rightmost child of v_2. We then append $(\, C(v_3)\, (\,)\,) = (\,(\,)\,(\,)\,)$ to $C(v_2)$, which becomes $C(v_2) = (\,)\,(\,(\,)\,(\,)\,)$, as can be verified in the next frame.*

Therefore, only the nodes in the rightmost path of the suffix tree are maintained explicitly, whereas the rest of the nodes use $\mathcal{O}(n)$ bits: at most $2n$ parentheses are stored, but we need to allocate the new memory area for $C(v)$ before freeing the

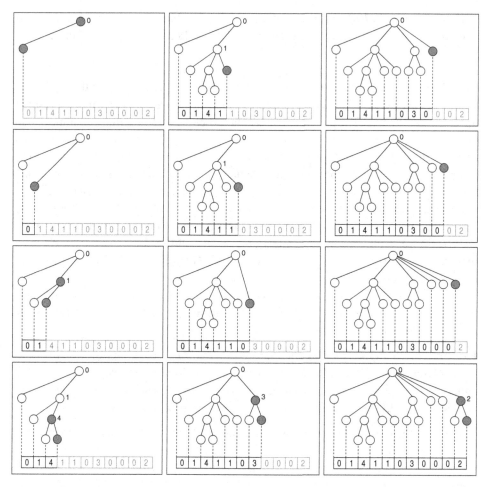

Figure 11.11. The steps of the generation of the tree topology from the LCP array. The process proceeds from left to right and top to bottom inside each column. The black part of LCP are the cells already processed, and the grayed nodes are those inserted at each step.

areas $C(u_i)$ that will be copied to it, so we may need up to $4n$ bits. On typical texts, the rightmost path is of length $\mathcal{O}(\log n)$, which adds only $\mathcal{O}(w \log n) = o(n)$ further bits.

The extra time due to successively copying the $C(v)$ areas can be split into two. On the one hand, all the new parentheses ' (' and ') ' that are written are proportional to the work done on the stack, which we have seen to be $\mathcal{O}(n)$. On the other hand, each existing parenthesis can be copied several times, but each time it is copied, it becomes part of the $C(v)$ sequence of a node v with smaller **strdepth**. Thus, on typical texts, the total number of parentheses copied is $\mathcal{O}(n \log n)$. Since they are copied in chunks of w bits, the total time is $\mathcal{O}(n)$ on typical texts. This is dominated by our previous $\mathcal{O}(n t_A)$ time.

Algorithm 11.11 details the construction of H and of the tree topology. We process a fake entry LCP$[n + 1] = 0$ at the end of *buildTree* to force the rightmost path to be compressed into the BP representation.

Algorithm 11.11: Building the suffix tree components. Uses operations *push*, *pop*, and *top* on stack R.

---

1 **Proc** *buildH*(A, T)

    Input : Suffix array $A[1, n]$ and text $T[1, n]$ (seen as a compressed suffix array).

    Output: Returns the bitvector $H[1, 2n - 1]$ representing PLCP.

2   Allocate bitvector $H[1, 2n - 1]$

3   **for** $i \leftarrow 1$ **to** $2n - 1$ **do** bitclear(H, i) (can be initialized wordwise)

4     $p \leftarrow 0$

5   **for** $j \leftarrow 1$ **to** $n - 1$ **do**

6         $d \leftarrow \max(p - 1, 0)$

7         $p \leftarrow d + \mathsf{lcp}(T[j + d, n], T[A[A^{-1}[j] - 1] + d, n])$

8   bitset$(H, p + 2j)$

9   **return** H

10 **Proc** *buildTree*(LCP)

    Input : Array LCP$[2, n]$ (already compressed).

    Output: Returns the BP representation of the suffix tree.

11   Allocate stack R of maximum size $1 + \max_{2 \le i \le n}$ LCP$[i]$

12     $push(R, \langle 0, \varepsilon \rangle)$ (R stores pairs $\langle \mathsf{strdepth}(v), C(v) \rangle$)

13   **for** $i \leftarrow 2$ **to** $n + 1$ **do**

14         $nC \leftarrow (\ )$ (allocate it and later reallocate as needed)

15   **if** $i \le n$ **then** $\ell \leftarrow$ LCP$[i]$ **else** $\ell \leftarrow 0$

16         $\langle d, C \rangle \leftarrow top(R)$

17   **while** $d > \ell$ **do**

18             $pop(R)$

19             $nC \leftarrow (\,.\,C\,.\,nC\,.\,)$

20   Free C

21             $\langle d, C \rangle \leftarrow top(R)$

22   **if** $d = \ell$ **then**

23   Append nC to C in $top(R)$ (reallocate C as needed)

24   Free nC

25   **else** $push(R, \langle \ell, nC \rangle)$

26     $\langle d, C \rangle \leftarrow top(R)$

27   Free R

28   **return** $(\,.\,C\,.\,)$

11.6 Applications

11.6.1 Finding Maximal Substrings of a Pattern

In Section 8.5.3 we sketched a couple of applications of suffix trees, which we can now address efficiently with the implementation described in this chapter. Now we present in more detail a bioinformatic problem that is solved well with suffix trees. Assume we have the suffix tree of a collection of genomes T. We then receive a short DNA sequence $P[1, m]$ and want to output all the maximal substrings of P that appear at least k times in T and are of length at least ℓ. Those substrings of P are likely to have biological significance.

It is easier to describe the algorithm on the *trie* of all the suffixes of T, where each edge is labeled by a single character. We will slide a variable-length window $[i, j]$ along P, and at the same time will know the trie node x corresponding to that window, that is, $P[i, j] = \text{string}(x)$. Initially, the window is $P[1, 0] = \varepsilon$ and $x = \text{root}()$. Each step has two phases. The *extension phase* increases j as much as possible, updating x accordingly, as long as $\text{leafnum}(x) \geq k$. When further extending the window is not possible, we report it if $j - i + 1 \geq \ell$ and switch to the *contraction phase*. In this phase, we increase i, updating x accordingly, until it becomes possible again to extend the window to the right. The total number of operations performed on the trie is $\mathcal{O}(m)$, because we advance either j or i at each step.

The actual algorithm is a bit more complicated because the suffix tree is a Patricia tree, not a trie, and then some trie nodes do not physically exist. Trie nodes will be represented by means of *virtual nodes* $x = \langle v, d, r \rangle$, where v is an actual suffix tree node, $d = \text{strdepth}(v)$ is maintained for efficiency, $x = \text{levelancestor}(v, r)$ in the trie, and there are no other suffix tree nodes between x and v (indeed, wlink delivers its answers as pairs $\langle v, d - r \rangle$).

Example 11.30 *Figure 11.12 shows the trie of the suffixes of our text $T = \text{abracadabra\$}$. The nodes that do not exist physically in the suffix tree are colored gray. Then, for example, we have that node $x = 5$ (now the preorder numbers refer to the trie of suffixes) is represented by the virtual node $\langle 7, 4, 2 \rangle$, whereas node $x = 20$, which exists in the suffix tree, is represented by $\langle 20, 2, 0 \rangle$. It holds $r = 0$ iff v appears in the suffix tree.*

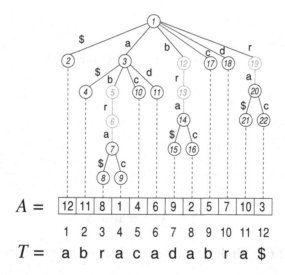

Figure 11.12. The trie of all the suffixes of a text T, showing in gray the nodes that do not exist physically in the suffix tree. We still omit the unary paths that descend from each leaf until the symbol $.

Algorithm 11.12: Finding the maximal intervals of P of length at least ℓ that occur at least k times in T.

Input : Suffix tree of text $T[1, n]$, pattern string $P[1, m]$, and parameters k and ℓ.
Output: Outputs all the maximal intervals of P of length at least ℓ that appear at least k times in T.

1   $x \leftarrow \langle \text{root}(), 0, 0 \rangle$
2   $[i, j] \leftarrow [1, 0]$
3   **while** $j < m$ **do**
4     $last\,j \leftarrow j$
5   **while** $j < m$ **do**
6       $y \leftarrow lchild(x, P[j + 1])$
7   **if** $y = \text{null}$ **or** $leafnum(y) < k$ **then**
8   **break**
9       $x \leftarrow y$
10       $j \leftarrow j + 1$
11   **if** $j > last\,j$ **and** $j - i + 1 \geq \ell$ **then**
12   output $[i, j]$
13     $x \leftarrow suflink(x)$
14     $i \leftarrow i + 1$
15   **if** $i > j$ **then**
16       $j \leftarrow i - 1$

Algorithm 11.12 gives the traversal procedure on those virtual nodes, using operations $lchild(x, c)$, $leafnum(y)$, and $suflink(x)$ to emulate the operations labeledchild(x, c), leafnum(y), and slink(x), respectively, on the trie.

Example 11.31 *We execute the traversal for the pattern* $P = $ cabraba, $k = 2$, *and* $\ell = 2$, *on the trie of Figure 11.12.*

We start with $[i, j] = [1, 0]$ *and* $x = 1$. *By letter* $P[j + 1] = $ c, *we descend to node* $y = lchild(x,$ c$) = 17$. *However, since* leafnum$(17) = 1 < 2 = k$, *we stop the extension phase. For the contraction phase, we set* $x = suflink(1) = 1$, $i = 2$, *and thus* $j = 1$.

Now we descend by letter $P[j + 1] = $ a, *reaching node* $y = 3$. *Since it has* leafnum$(3) = 5 \geq 2 = k$, *we set* $x = 3$ *and* $j = 2$. *We continue descending similarly to nodes* $x = 5$, $x = 6$, *and* $x = 7$, *ending with* $j = 5$. *Next we try to descend by* $P[j + 1] = $ b *and reach* $y = $ null, *so we stop the extension phase. Since* j *has changed and* $j - i + 1 = 4 \geq 2 = \ell$, *we output the maximal interval* $[i, j] = [2, 5]$.

Now, for the contraction phase, we set $x = suflink(7) = 14$ *and* $i = 3$. *We cannot descend by* $P[j + 1] = $ b. *We set again* $x = suflink(14) = 20$ *and* $i = 4$. *We still cannot descend by* $P[j + 1] = $ b. *Once more, we set* $x = suflink(20) = 3$ *and* $i = 5$.

Now we can descend by $P[j + 1] = $ b, *to node* $y = 5$. *Since* leafnum$(5) = 2 \geq 2 = k$, *we start the extension phase, setting* $x = y = 5$ *and* $j = 6$. *We try to descend from* $x = 5$ *by* $P[j + 1] = $ a, *but get* $y = $ null, *so we finish the extension phase. Since* j *has increased, we output the maximum interval* $[i, j] = [5, 6]$, *as its length is* $2 \geq 2 = \ell$.

Now we start contraction again. We set $x = suflink(5) = 12$ and $i = 6$, and try to descend by $P[j + 1] = $ a. As we fail, we set again $x = suflink(12) = 1$ and $i = 7$. Next we can descend by $P[j + 1] = $ a, to $y = 3$. Since leafnum(3) $= 5 \geq 2 = k$, we set $x = y = 3$ and $j = 7$. Now we stop the extension phase because $j = m = 7$. Although j has increased, we do not report the interval $[i, j] = [7, 7]$ because its length is $1 < 2 = \ell$.

At this point we stop because $j = m$. Overall we have reported the maximal intervals $P[2, 5] = $ abra and $P[5, 6] = $ ab.

Algorithm 11.13 shows how the operations *lchild*, *leafnum*, and *suflink* are implemented on the actual suffix tree. Note that, while the first two use a constant number of operations, *suflink* carries out an iteration in order to ensure that there are no physical nodes between slink(v) and its ancestor trie node at distance r. If there are physical nodes in between, slink(v) is replaced by the highest possible physical ancestor that describes the same virtual node using $r \geq 0$. We do this search iteratively, using parent, for simplicity, but we could do a binary search instead, using the tree operation levelancestor. Therefore, considering the cost of our compressed suffix arrays, the total time of our traversal algorithm is $\mathcal{O}(m \operatorname{polylog} n)$.

We leave, as an exercise to the reader, deriving an alternative solution that scans P right-to-left, using operations wlink and parent instead of labeledchild and slink. This variant can be more efficient in practice considering the cost to implement the suffix tree operations.

11.6.2 Labeled Trees Revisited

In Section 8.5.5 we combined a tree topology and a sequence of labels to enable an efficient representation of XML structures, so that the structure could be navigated efficiently. In this section we use an extension of the BWT concept (Section 11.3.1) to represent labeled trees. This arrangement supports a powerful operation called *subpath search*, which is analogous to pattern searching on texts: Given a sequence of labels, the subpath search operation finds all the paths in the tree labeled by such sequence.

Consider a labeled tree with n nodes, ℓ of which are leaves, and an alphabet of σ labels. We first transform it by adding a dummy leaf as the only child of each tree leaf. These dummy leaves have the special label '#'. We also add a special root, labeled '$', as the parent of the actual tree root. From now on we refer to the modified tree, which has $n + \ell + 1$ nodes, ℓ of which are leaves, and $\sigma + 2$ distinct labels. We then proceed as follows.

1. Traverse the tree in preorder and, for each internal node v, obtain a string by concatenating the labels of the nodes from v to the root.
2. Sort those strings lexicographically and stably (that is, respect the preorder when two strings are equal).
3. For each string corresponding to a path starting at node v, append the labels of the children of v, left to right, to a sequence L. Mark in a parallel bitvector B the first child of each node v with a 1.

Since every node except the root is a child of some other node, it is mentioned once in L, and thus L and B are of length $n + \ell$. String L has an alphabet of size $\sigma + 1$, since

---

Algorithm 11.13: Emulating operations on virtual suffix tree nodes.

---

1 **Proc** *lchild*($\langle v, d, r \rangle, c$)
    Input   : Virtual node $\langle v, d, r \rangle$ and character c.
    Output: Returns the virtual node obtained by descending from $\langle v, d, r \rangle$ by
             character c, or null if not possible.
2   **if** $r = 0$ **then**
3     $u = $ labeledchild(v, c)
4   **if** $u = $ null **then**
5   **return** null
6     $d' \leftarrow$ strdepth(u)
7   **return** $\langle u, d', d' - d - 1 \rangle$
8   **if** string($v, d - r + 1$) $= c$ **then**
9   **return** $\langle v, d, r - 1 \rangle$
10   **else return** null

11 **Proc** *leafnum*($\langle v, d, r \rangle$)
    Input   : Virtual node $\langle v, d, r \rangle$.
    Output: Returns the number of leaves below $\langle v, d, r \rangle$.
12   **return** leafnum(v)

13 **Proc** *suflink*($\langle v, d, r \rangle$)
    Input   : Virtual node $\langle v, d, r \rangle$.
    Output: Returns the virtual node obtained by going to the suffix link of
             $\langle v, d, r \rangle$.
14   $v \leftarrow$ slink(v)
15   $d \leftarrow d - 1$
16   **while** $r > 0$ **do**
17     $u \leftarrow$ parent(v)
18     $d' \leftarrow$ strdepth(u)
19   **if** $d' < d - r$ **then**
20   **break**
21     $v \leftarrow u$
22     $r \leftarrow r - (d - d')$
23     $d \leftarrow d'$
24   **return** $\langle v, d, r \rangle$

---

symbol '\$' does not appear in it. The number of 1s in B is $n + 1$, that is, one per internal node in the tree.

The tree is represented by the sequence L and the bitvector B, using $(n + \ell)(1 + \log(\sigma + 1))$ bits. By using a bitvector to remove the symbols '#' from L, the space can be reduced to $n \log \sigma + \mathcal{O}(n)$ bits. However, we will maintain the original representation for simplicity.

To carry out subpath searches, we also need a small array $C[0, \sigma + 1]$, so that $C[c]$ is the number of labels smaller than c in the tree. Label '$' is assumed to be 0, and label '#' is assumed to be $\sigma + 1$.

If we call $F[1, n + 1]$ the (virtual) array of the first symbols of all the sorted strings, then F, C, and L work more or less like in the BWT. The difference is that L is longer than F because L includes the ℓ leaves and F does not. Seen another way, F lists the internal nodes and L lists the children of internal nodes. Bitvector B is useful for performing the mapping, as it indicates where the sequences of children start.

Example 11.32 *Figure 11.13 shows how a labeled tree (on the left) is represented. The tree describes the structure of a chapter* C, *which has a title* T, *several sections* S, *and an optional appendix* A. *Each section usually has a title, and possibly other sections and figures* F. *Figures have a name* N.

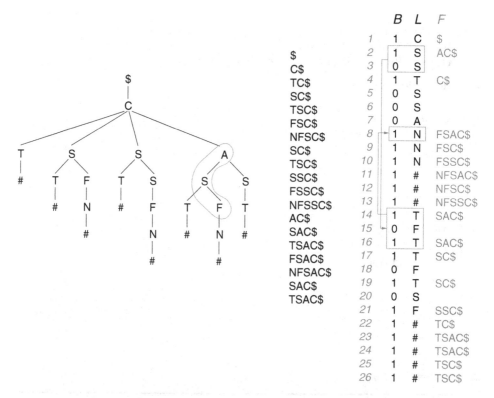

Figure 11.13. Representing an XML tree with a BWT-like structure. On the left, the tree (already extended with a spurious root labeled $ and leaves labeled #). In the middle, the set of node-to-root label sequences for all the internal nodes. On the right, the same strings sorted in lexicographic order (in gray; the first column is F), and with the sequence L of the labels of their children at their left (in black). Bitvector B distinguishes the first child label of each string. The final representation is formed by L and B. The gray squares and arrows illustrate the process to search for the upward paths labeled FSA, whose only occurrence in the tree is highlighted.

The original tree has $n = 18$ nodes, of which $\ell = 8$ are leaves, and $\sigma = 6$ labels. After adding the nodes labeled $ and #, the transformed tree has $n + \ell + 1 = 27$ nodes, of which $\ell = 8$ are leaves, and $\sigma + 2 = 8$ labels.

In the middle of the figure, we list the sequence of strings obtained by traversing the tree in preorder and listing all the sequences of labels starting at each internal node and reaching the root. On the right, in gray, we show the same set of strings, now lexicographically sorted. On the left of the sorted set, we list the children of each node in the sorted list. For example, the only node labeled A appears second in the list, and at that point we append the labels of its 2 children (both are S) to L. In B we set a 1 for the first child and a 0 for the rest (boxes and arrows will be used later).

Subpath Search

Assume we want to find the paths in the tree that read $P[1, m]$, in upward direction. The process is similar to the backward search described in Section 11.1.3. We will process P from $P[m]$ to $P[1]$. At step k, from m to 1, we will compute $L[s_k, e_k]$ such that all the paths that, read upwards, start with $P[k, m]$ are in the interval $[\mathsf{rank}(B, s_k), \mathsf{rank}(B, e_k)]$ of the array of the sorted strings.

We start with $s_m = \mathsf{select}(B, C[P[m]] + 1)$ and $e_m = \mathsf{select}(B, C[P[m] + 1] + 1) - 1$. Then, given $[s_{k+1}, e_{k+1}]$, we compute

$$s_k = \mathsf{select}(B, C[c] + \mathsf{rank}_c(L, s_{k+1} - 1) + 1),$$

$$e_k = \mathsf{select}(B, C[c] + \mathsf{rank}_c(L, e_{k+1}) + 1) - 1,$$

where $c = P[k]$. This works for the same reason as it does in the BWT: The occurrences of each symbol c are sorted by the same criterion in L and in F. At the end, the number of paths labeled P in the tree is $\mathsf{rank}(B, e_1) - \mathsf{rank}(B, s_1 - 1)$. Algorithm 11.14 details the subpath search process.

Example 11.33 *Consider the search for the upward path $P = \mathsf{FSA}$ in Figure 11.13, whose only occurrence is highlighted in the tree. This corresponds to finding figures in some section of the appendix. The values of array C are $C[\$] = 0$, $C[A] = 1$,*

Algorithm 11.14: Subpath search on BWT-like encoded labeled trees.

Input : A labeled tree (seen as sequence L, bitvector B, and array C) and pattern $P[1, m]$.

Output: Returns the range $[s, e]$, in the sorted array of upward path labels, of those starting with P, or $\emptyset$ if there is none.

1 $[s, e] \leftarrow [\mathsf{select}(B, C[P[m]] + 1), \mathsf{select}(B, C[P[m] + 1] + 1) - 1]$
2 **for** $k \leftarrow m - 1$ **downto** 1 **do**
3   **if** $s > e$ **then return** $\emptyset$
4     $c \leftarrow P[k]$
5     $s \leftarrow \mathsf{select}(B, C[c] + \mathsf{rank}_c(L, s - 1) + 1)$
6     $e \leftarrow \mathsf{select}(B, C[c] + \mathsf{rank}_c(L, e) + 1) - 1$

7 **return** $[\mathsf{rank}(B, s), \mathsf{rank}(B, e)]$

$C[C] = 2$, $C[F] = 3$, $C[N] = 6$, $C[S] = 9$, $C[T] = 14$, *and* $C[\#] = 19$. *We start with* $s_3 = \mathsf{select}(B, C[P[m]] + 1) = \mathsf{select}(B, C[A] + 1) = \mathsf{select}(B, 2) = 2$, *and* $e_3 = \mathsf{select}(B, C[P[m] + 1] + 1) - 1 = \mathsf{select}(B, C[C] + 1) - 1 = \mathsf{select}(B, 3) - 1 = 4 - 1 = 3$. *The corresponding range is shown in the figure with an open box containing* $L[s_3, e_3] = L[2, 3]$, *with arrows to the subsequent boxes we obtain for* $L[s_2, e_2]$ *and* $L[s_1, e_1]$.

Then we process $P[2] = \mathsf{S}$. *We compute* $s_2 = \mathsf{select}(B, C[\mathsf{S}] + \mathsf{rank}_\mathsf{S}(L, s_3 - 1) + 1) = \mathsf{select}(B, C[\mathsf{S}] + \mathsf{rank}_\mathsf{S}(L, 1) + 1) = \mathsf{select}(B, 10) = 14$, *and* $e_2 = \mathsf{select}(B, C[\mathsf{S}] + \mathsf{rank}_\mathsf{S}(L, e_3) + 1) - 1 = \mathsf{select}(B, C[\mathsf{S}] + \mathsf{rank}_\mathsf{S}(L, 3) + 1) - 1 = \mathsf{select}(B, 12) - 1 = 16$. *The range is then* $L[s_2, e_2] = L[14, 16]$.

Finally, we process $P[1] = \mathsf{F}$. *We compute* $s_1 = \mathsf{select}(B, C[\mathsf{F}] + \mathsf{rank}_\mathsf{F}(L, s_2 - 1) + 1) = \mathsf{select}(B, C[\mathsf{F}] + \mathsf{rank}_\mathsf{F}(L, 13) + 1) = \mathsf{select}(B, 4) = 8$, *and* $e_1 = \mathsf{select}(B, C[\mathsf{F}] + \mathsf{rank}_\mathsf{F}(L, e_2) + 1) - 1 = \mathsf{select}(B, C[\mathsf{F}] + \mathsf{rank}_\mathsf{F}(L, 16) + 1) - 1 = \mathsf{select}(B, 5) - 1 = 8$. *The final range is* $L[s_1, e_1] = L[8, 8]$.

The range of nodes is $[\mathsf{rank}(B, s_1), \mathsf{rank}(B, e_1)] = [4, 4]$, *corresponding to the 4th string in gray,* FSAC\$, *and the total number of nodes is* $4 - 4 + 1 = 1$.

Navigation

Apart from subpath search, a basic form of tree navigation is possible. Let us identify nodes by their position in F (therefore the range retrieved by a subpath search is also the range of the corresponding node identifiers).

Let v be the identifier of a tree node. Its k children are then written in $L[p, p + k - 1]$, where $p = \mathsf{select}(B, v)$ and $k = \mathsf{succ}(B, p + 1) - p$. Therefore, the identifier of the tth child of v is $v' = C[c] + \mathsf{rank}_c(L, p + t - 1)$, where $c = L[p + t - 1]$. We know that v is a leaf in the original tree when $L[p] = \#$. In those cases, the formula for the child should not be used.

We can also use rank and select in $L[p, p + k - 1]$ (or perhaps a linear scan, in practice) to identify the ith child with label c, if desired.

Analogously, to compute the parent of v, we first identify the label c of v as the one satisfying $C[c] < v \leq C[c + 1]$, then compute $p = \mathsf{select}_c(L, v - C[c])$, and finally the parent is $u = \mathsf{rank}(B, p)$. It is also possible to find out that v is the tth child of u, with $t = p - \mathsf{pred}(B, p) + 1$.

With a wavelet tree representation for L (Section 6.2), all these operations require time $\mathcal{O}(\log \sigma)$. This can be reduced to $\mathcal{O}(\log \log \sigma)$ by using a faster representation (Sections 6.1 or 6.3) and replacing the binary search on C by $\mathsf{rank}(D, v)$, where the compressed bitvector $D[1, n + 1]$ has a 1 at the first occurrence of each symbol in F.

Algorithm 11.15 details the supported operations. We can get rid of C, replacing $v - C[c]$ by $v - \mathsf{pred}(D, v) + 1$ in lines 8 and 22, and $C[c]$ by $\mathsf{select}(D, c) - 1$ elsewhere.

Example 11.34 *In Figure 11.13, the node labeled* C *has identifier 3, and the node labeled* A *has identifier* $v = 2$. *The children of* v *start in* L *at position* $p = \mathsf{select}(B, v) = 2$, *and they are* $k = \mathsf{succ}(B, 3) - 2 = 4 - 2 = 2$, *so their range is* $L[2, 3] = \mathsf{SS}$. *These are the labels of the two children of the node labeled* A. *To move to the second child,* $i = 2$, *we compute* $c = L[p + i - 1] = L[3] = \mathsf{S}$ *and then the child is* $v' = C[c] + \mathsf{rank}_c(L, p + i - 1) = C[\mathsf{S}] + \mathsf{rank}_\mathsf{S}(L, 3) = 9 + 2 = 11$.

Algorithm 11.15: Navigation on BWT-like encoded labeled trees.

Input : A labeled tree T (seen as sequence L, bitvector B, array C and bitvector D), node v (a position in F), symbol c, and index t.

1 **Proc** root(T)
2   **return** 1

3 **Proc** isleaf(T, v)
4     $p \leftarrow$ select(B, v)
5   **return** access(L, p) = #

6 **Proc** parent(T, v) — *assuming $v \neq 1$*
7     $c \leftarrow$ rank(D, v)
8     $p \leftarrow$ select$_c$($L, v - C[c]$)
9   **return** rank(B, p)

10 **Proc** nodemap(T, v)/nodeselect(T, v)
11   **return** v

12 **Proc** children(T, v)
13     $p \leftarrow$ select(B, v)
14   **if** access(L, p) = # **then return** 0
15   **return** succ($B, p + 1$) $- p$

16 **Proc** child(T, v, t) — *assuming $t \leq$ children(T, v)*
17     $p \leftarrow$ select(B, v)
18     $c \leftarrow$ access($L, p + t - 1$)
19   **return** $C[c] +$ rank$_c$($L, p + t - 1$)

20 **Proc** childrank(T, v) — *assuming $v \neq 1$*
21     $c \leftarrow$ rank(D, v)
22     $p \leftarrow$ select$_c$($L, v - C[c]$)
23   **return** $p -$ pred(B, p) $+ 1$

24 **Proc** childrenlabeled(T, v, c)
25     $p \leftarrow$ select(B, v)
26   **return** rank$_c$(L, succ($B, p + 1$) $- 1$) $-$ rank$_c$($L, p - 1$)

27 **Proc** labeledchild(T, v, c, t) — *assuming $t \leq$ childrenlabeled(T, v, c)*
28     $p \leftarrow$ select(B, v)
29   **return** $C[c] +$ rank$_c$($L, p - 1$) $+ t$

30 **Proc** childlabel(T, v) — *assuming $v \neq 1$*
31   **return** rank(D, v)

The eleventh sorted string (corresponding to the node $v' = 11$) is the second child of $v = 2$.

Analogously, let us compute the parent of $v' = 11$. Since $C[S] = 9 < v' \leq 14 = C[T]$, we have that the label of v' is $c = S$. Now, the parent of $v' = 11$ is rank(B, select$_S$($L, v - C[S]$)) = rank(B, select$_S$($L, 2$)) = rank($B, 3$) = 2 = v. *Furthermore, v' is the second child of v.*

Preorders

The node numbering induced by this representation may be inconvenient for other purposes, so one would like to have a way to compute preorder values from identifiers, and vice versa (i.e., **preorder** and **preorderselect**). This is similar to the sampling mechanism of the FM-index; see Section 11.2. We sample preorder values at regular intervals and use a bitvector aligned to F indicating which nodes are sampled. For sampled nodes, we store their preorder values in an array analogous to A_S, which is accessed using **rank** on that bitvector. Given a node v, we traverse the tree starting at v, in depth-first order using our navigation operations, until we find a sampled node. Then we read the preorder value of the sampled node and subtract the number of steps done until finding it.

For the inverse operation, we store the node identifiers of the same sampled nodes, now in preorder, in an array analogous to A_S^{-1}. Given a preorder value, we start from the previous sampled preorder value, whose node identifier is sampled, and perform the needed number of traversal operations on the tree until reaching the one with the desired preorder.

Operations **postorder** and **postorderselect** can be implemented analogously.

Tries Revisited

The data structure is useful for representing tries as well; recall Section 8.5.3. Tries represent a set of strings and support searches on the set; that is, given P, they can find whether or not P is in the set. With the BWT-like representation, we can do the same by looking for the subpath $\#P^{rev}\$$, where P^{rev} is P read in reverse direction. This search ensures that the path goes from the root to a leaf.

Tries can also carry out prefix searches, that is, list the strings of the set that are prefixed by P. In our representation, this is obtained by looking for the upward path $P^{rev}\$$. Moreover, we can also support suffix searches, that is, find all the strings in the set that end with P. This is obtained with a subpath search for $\#P^{rev}$, to ensure that the path ends in a leaf. Even more, by looking for just P^{rev}, we can find all the strings in the set that contain P as a substring. Suffix searches, and especially substring searches, are very difficult to implement with the representations of Section 8.5.3.

Note that for prefix and substring searches, our results are internal nodes, from which we must traverse toward the leaves to find the identifiers of the corresponding strings. These identifiers must be attached to the #s in L.

11.6.3 Document Retrieval

We have allowed our text to consist of the concatenation of the documents in a text collection, without changing the techniques to handle a single text. When we have a collection, however, there are other queries that might be of interest. These retrieve document identifiers instead of text positions.

The simplest of these operations is called *document listing*. Given a pattern $P[1, m]$, the goal is to output all the document identifiers where P appears. Of course, this can be done by first locating all the occurrences of P in T, then computing the document that contains each occurrence, and finally sorting and removing duplicates. Such an approach, however, requires obtaining all the *occ* occurrences of P, which may be many more than the *docc* distinct documents where P appears. We aim for a solution closer to the optimal time $\mathcal{O}(m + docc)$.

A solution using $\mathcal{O}(n \log n)$ bits is as follows. Build the (classical, not compressed) suffix tree of T, so that we can obtain the interval $A[s, e]$ of the occurrences starting with P. Build also the so-called *document array* of T, $D[1, n]$, so that $D[i]$ is the document identifier to which the suffix $T[A[i], n]$ belongs. Our goal is then to list the distinct values in $D[s, e]$.

To carry this out, we build a third array, $C[1, n]$, defined as

$$C[i] = \max \left(\{ j < i, D[j] = D[i] \} \cup \{0\} \right).$$

That is, $C[i]$ gives the rightmost position to the left of $D[i]$ where the value $D[i]$ has appeared, or zero if there is none.

The key property of array C is that the leftmost occurrence of each distinct document d in $D[s, e]$, say, $D[k] = d$, satisfies $C[k] < s$ (otherwise that would not be the leftmost occurrence of d in $D[s, e]$). Therefore, the distinct values in $D[s, e]$ can be found at the positions $k \in [s, e]$ where $C[k] < s$.

Now assume we build a range minimum query structure on C (Section 7.4.1). Then, if $k = \mathrm{rmq}_C(s, e)$ and $C[k] < s$, we report $D[k]$ as a distinct document and then continue recursively with the subintervals $[s, k - 1]$ and $[k + 1, e]$. If, in some subinterval $[i, j]$, it holds $C[\mathrm{rmq}_C(i, j)] \geq s$, then we know that no value in $[i, j]$ is smaller than s, and thus do not further consider this interval. Algorithm 11.16 shows the pseudocode.

This recursive calls form a tree of *docc* internal nodes, since every internal node reports a distinct value in $D[s, e]$. The leaves of the recursion tree, where the intervals

---

Algorithm 11.16: Document listing.

---

1 **Proc** *doclist*(T, P)
    Input : A text collection T (seen as its suffix tree, its document array D, its
              array C, and an rmq data structure on C) and pattern $P[1, m]$.
    Output: Outputs the distinct documents where P appears in the collection.

2     $[s, e] \leftarrow$ suffix array interval for P (found with the suffix tree)
3     $list(s, e, s)$

4 **Proc** *list*(i, j, s)
    Input : Interval $[i, j]$ and left endpoint of original interval $[s, e]$.
    Output: Outputs the documents whose first occurrence in $D[s, e]$ is in $D[i, j]$.

5   **if** $i > j$ **then return**
6     $k \leftarrow \mathrm{rmq}_C(i, j)$
7   **if** $C[k] \geq s$ **then return**
8   **output** $D[k]$
9     $list(i, k - 1, s)$
10    $list(k + 1, j, s)$

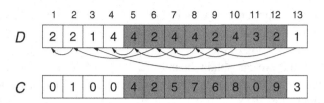

Figure 11.14. The structures for document listing. Array D contains the document where each suffix in A belongs, and C points to the previous occurrence of the same value in D (it is also shown as arrows on D). We show in gray the range [5, 12]. The leftmost positions k of the distinct values in $D[5, 12]$ are those where $C[k] < 5$.

$[i, j]$ are empty or do not have values smaller than s, are at most $docc + 1$. Therefore, the process carries out $\mathcal{O}(docc)$ steps.

Example 11.35 *Figure 11.14 shows a document array and its corresponding C array. Note that C can be interpreted as a set of linked lists on D, one per distinct document. Assume the search for P leads to the interval $[s, e] = [5, 12]$. Thus we wish to list all the distinct values in $D[5, 12]$.*

We start with $\mathsf{rmq}_C(5, 12) = 11$. Since $C[11] = 0 < 5 = s$, we report the document $D[11] = 3$ and continue recursively on the intervals $[5, 10]$ and $[12, 12]$.

On the left interval, we compute $\mathsf{rmq}_C(5, 10) = 6$, and since $C[6] = 2 < 5 = s$, we report the document $D[6] = 2$ and continue on the intervals $[5, 5]$ and $[7, 10]$.

On the interval $[5, 5]$, we compute $\mathsf{rmq}_C(5, 5) = 5$, and since $C[5] = 4 < 5 = s$, we report the document $D[5] = 4$. Both subintervals, $[5, 4]$ and $[6, 5]$, are empty, so we finish there.

On the interval $[7, 10]$, we compute $\mathsf{rmq}_C(7, 10) = 7$, but since $C[7] = 5 \geq 5 = s$, we have reported all the documents in $D[7, 10]$, and we stop. Similarly, we do not report any new document on the top right interval $[12, 12]$, since $C[12] = 9 \geq 5 = s$.

To implement this solution in little space, we replace each component by compact data structures. First, the suffix tree is replaced with a Ψ-based compressed suffix array using bitvectors B_c, which finds $[s, e]$ in time $\mathcal{O}(m \log n)$. Second, the array D is replaced by a bitvector $E[1, n]$ that marks the positions in T where new documents start. Thus, any cell $D[i]$ can be computed as $\mathsf{rank}(E, A[i])$ in time $\mathcal{O}(\log n)$, if we use $\mathcal{O}(n)$ bits for the suffix array sampling. Third, the rmq structure needs only $2n + o(n)$ bits and does not require access to C.

We still need access to C, however, in line 7 of Algorithm 11.16, to determine whether $C[k] \geq s$ or not. To get rid of C completely, we use another bitvector $V[1, \Delta]$, which has initially all 0s, and then we set $V[D[k]] \leftarrow 1$ every time we report a document $D[k]$ in line 8. Since we visit the left range (line 9) before the right range (line 10), we first find the leftmost occurrence of each document, that is, the only one where $C[k] < s$. Then it holds $C[k] \geq s$ iff $D[k]$ has already been reported, thus we can replace the condition in line 7 by $V[D[k]] = 1$. To reset V to all 0s before the next query, we use it as an initializable array (Section 3.4.1), or, if possible, we remember the values d output and reset $V[d] \leftarrow 0$ after running the query.

Overall we can use $n\mathcal{H}_0(T) + \mathcal{O}(n)$ bits of space, and carry out document listing in time $\mathcal{O}((m + docc)\log n)$. Other compressed suffix arrays yield slightly different space and time combinations.

Example 11.36 *Let us again run the query of Example 11.35, now using bitvector V. Initially, $V[d] = 0$ for all $1 \leq d \leq 4$.*

We start with $k = \mathsf{rmq}_C(5, 12) = 11$. Since $V[D[11]] = V[3] = 0$, we report the document $D[11] = 3$, set $V[3] \leftarrow 1$, and continue recursively on the intervals $[5, 10]$ and $[12, 12]$.

On the left interval, we compute $k = \mathsf{rmq}_C(5, 10) = 6$, and since $V[D[6]] = V[2] = 0$ we report the document $D[6] = 2$, set $V[2] \leftarrow 1$, and continue recursively on the intervals $[5, 5]$ and $[7, 10]$.

On the interval $[5, 5]$, we compute $k = \mathsf{rmq}_C(5, 5) = 5$, and since $V[D[5]] = V[4] = 0$, we report the document $D[5] = 4$, and set $V[4] \leftarrow 1$. Both subintervals, $[5, 4]$ and $[6, 5]$, are empty, so we finish there.

On the interval $[7, 10]$, we compute $k = \mathsf{rmq}_C(7, 10) = 7$, but since $V[D[7]] = V[4] = 1$, we have reported all the documents in $D[7, 10]$ and we stop. Similarly, we do not report any new document on the top right interval $[12, 12]$, since $V[D[12]] = V[2] = 1$.

11.6.4 XML Retrieval Revisited

In Section 8.5.5 we showed how labeled tree representations can support a subset of XPath, in particular queries related to structure. At that point, we warned that XPath contains conditions on the text content of the nodes, not only on their structure. We now complement the structural queries with the functionality provided in Section 11.6.3.

We see the text of each XML tree node as a different document. In XML each tree leaf, and each space between two siblings, may have text content. For simplicity, assume that text can appear only at tree leaves.[6] We then assume that the text of the ith leaf is the document number i. Now we build the document listing structure of Section 11.6.3 on those documents.

Consider a query like the one solved in Example 8.31. Here we are interested only in the books written by Donald Knuth that have not been returned to the library. We can then proceed as follows: (1) List all the document numbers (that is, leaf identifiers) where the string "Donald Knuth" appears in the text collection. (2) For each such tree leaf, move to its parent and check that the label of the parent node is author. (3) If so, perform the steps given in Example 8.31 on the corresponding book.

This scheme performs well if the string "Donald Knuth" does not appear frequently in the collection; otherwise a better strategy is to go book by book, check if the string under the author field is "Donald Knuth" (by extracting the text of the document), and in such case process the book.

The FM-index ability to count the number of occurrences of a string in the collection can be used as a hint to decide which of the two strategies to use. Database and text engines usually compute these kinds of statistics to design good query execution plans.

---

[6] Otherwise we may simply add fictitious leaves.

In our case, we prefer to know the number of *documents* where P appears, without listing them all. This is called document counting and can be solved using just $\mathcal{O}(n)$ bits; we give the proper references in the bibliography section.

11.7 Summary

A compressed suffix array can represent a text $T[1, n]$ over alphabet $[1, \sigma]$ within $n\mathcal{H}_0(T) + \mathcal{O}(n)$ bits of space. It counts the number of occurrences of any pattern $P[1, m]$ in time $\mathcal{O}(m \log n)$, and each occurrence position is then located in time $\mathcal{O}(\log n)$. Any substring $T[j, j + \ell - 1]$ is retrieved in time $\mathcal{O}(\ell + \log n)$. A second variant reduces the space to $n\mathcal{H}_k(T)(1 + o(1)) + \mathcal{O}(n)$ bits, for any $k \leq \alpha \log_\sigma n$ and any constant $0 < \alpha < 1$. It retains the counting time, but the others are multiplied by $\mathcal{O}(\log n)$. This factor, however, is not high in practice. A second family of structures, called FM-indexes, can use $n\mathcal{H}_k(T) + o(n \log \sigma)$ bits and count in time $\mathcal{O}(m \log \log \sigma)$. Locating each occurrence, however, takes $\mathcal{O}(\log^{1+\epsilon} n)$ time, for any constant $\epsilon > 0$, and extracting $T[l, r]$ takes time $\mathcal{O}(\ell \log \log \sigma + \log^{1+\epsilon} n)$.

The suffix tree requires $\mathcal{O}(n)$ bits on top of a compressed suffix array, and implements many other operations within similar times.

Compressed suffix arrays and trees can be built in $\mathcal{O}(n)$ time and $\mathcal{O}(n \log n)$ bits of space. On typical texts, compressed suffix arrays can be built in $\mathcal{O}(n \log n \log \log n)$ time and just $\mathcal{O}(n)$ extra bits on top of T and the final structure. Also, compressed suffix trees can be built on top of compressed suffix arrays using $\mathcal{O}(n)$ locating queries, and $\mathcal{O}(n)$ extra bits. More results on the construction in little space are given in the bibliographic discussion.

These tools are also useful in more sophisticated text-based applications, such as pattern mining, labeled trees and tries, document retrieval, and structured text collections.

11.8 Bibliographic Notes

Suffix arrays. The suffix array was invented independently by Gonnet *et al.* (1992) (who called them PAT arrays) and by Manber and Myers (1993); the terminology of the second group has prevailed. Apart from the $\mathcal{O}(m \log n)$ time algorithm based on binary search we have presented, Manber and Myers offered a more sophisticated one with time $\mathcal{O}(m + \log n)$. This required, however, storing $n \log n$ further bits.

Compressed suffix arrays. The Ψ function, and the first compressed suffix array based on it, was introduced in 2000 by Grossi and Vitter (2006) (recall that we give the best reference, not the earliest one). This structure was the first to use $\mathcal{O}(n \log \sigma)$ bits, which included the text itself. A variant of the structure was proposed by Rao (2002). Sadakane (2003) introduced and implemented the simplified Ψ-based structure we describe in the chapter. He used plain binary search in the beginning but later switched to backward search (Sadakane, 2002). He encoded Ψ differentially and achieved constant-time access, yet at the price of using $\mathcal{O}(n\mathcal{H}_0(T))$ bits of space. He also obtained $\mathcal{O}(\log^\epsilon n)$ time to compute $A[i]$ or $A^{-1}[j]$, but again using a hierarchy of

Ψ functions that multiplied the space by a constant. Our description is indeed closer to Sadakane's implementation, which has not been challenged until very recently (Huo *et al.*, 2014; Gog *et al.*, 2015).

The first structure achieving $n\mathcal{H}_k(T) + o(n\log\sigma)$ bits of space was also based on Ψ (Grossi *et al.*, 2003), with a more sophisticated storage arrangement (that included the invention of wavelet trees). Its counting time was $\mathcal{O}(m\log\sigma + \mathrm{polylog}\, n)$, so it was later superseded by FM-indexes. Experimental studies on its expected compression performance (Foschini *et al.*, 2006) confirmed that differential encoding was sufficient to obtain high-order compression of Ψ, with some sublinear penalty.

FM-indexes. The FM-index was introduced by Ferragina and Manzini (2005), also in 2000, together with the backward search concept. The original FM-index used $\mathcal{O}(n\mathcal{H}_k(T)) + o(n\log\sigma)$ bits and admitted only very small alphabets (constant-size, in theory). The version we describe, based on a sequence representation of T^{bwt}, reaches $n\mathcal{H}_k(T) + o(n\log\sigma)$ bits of space and handles arbitrary alphabets (Ferragina *et al.*, 2007). It uses the sampling mechanism we describe to compute $A[i]$ and $A^{-1}[j]$ (which is the same Sadakane actually implemented). Belazzougui and Navarro (2014) showed that the FM-index can use $n\mathcal{H}_k(T)(1 + o(1)) + \mathcal{O}(n)$ bits and count in time $\mathcal{O}(m)$, compute $A[i]$ and $A^{-1}[j]$ in time $\mathcal{O}(\log n)$, and retrieve $T[j, j + \ell - 1]$ in time $\mathcal{O}(\ell + \log n)$. The structure is complicated, however, and likely to pose a significant space overhead in the $\mathcal{O}(n)$ bits.

As we have shown in the chapter, the FM-index can be regarded as a particular encoding of the Ψ function. Later we also presented it as a direct construction on top of the Burrows-Wheeler Transform, which is the way the FM-index is usually described in the literature. Although the original article on the BWT is only a technical report (Burrows and Wheeler, 1994), today there is even a book dedicated to it (Adjeroh *et al.*, 2008).

Initially, the FM-index partitioned the string T^{bwt} into chunks, in a careful way, to obtain high-order compression. Ferragina *et al.* (2005) even devised an optimal partitioning method. Later Mäkinen and Navarro (2008) showed that using the compressed representation of Section 4.1.1 on the wavelet tree bitvectors was sufficient to obtain the same result, simultaneously for any k. Finally, Kärkkäinen and Puglisi (2011) showed that partitioning T^{bwt} into fixed-size blocks of a certain size was sufficient for the same purpose, without resorting to compressed bitvectors. This led to the most efficient FM-index in practice and is the method we describe to reach high-order compression. Its most recent and efficient implementation is by Gog *et al.* (2016).

A detailed survey of compressed suffix arrays (Navarro and Mäkinen, 2007) covers these and other variants we have omitted, and also shows why the differentially encoded Ψ of Sadakane achieves high-order entropy. Grossi (2011) offers a shorter, more recent survey, which also derives the FM-index from Ψ. Practical comparisons among compressed suffix arrays (Ferragina *et al.*, 2009a; González *et al.*, 2014) show that the main actors in practice are the indexes of Sadakane (2003) and of Ferragina *et al.* (2007) (whose best implementation is, as said, by Kärkkäinen and Puglisi). Experiments on the variant that offers $\mathcal{O}(\log\log\sigma)$ backward step time (Barbay *et al.*, 2014) showed that this variant is not significantly faster than the ones based on wavelet trees, even on large alphabets. New competitive FM-indexes are the result of recent improvements on compressed bitvectors (Kärkkäinen *et al.*, 2014; Huo *et al.*, 2015).

Lower bounds. Both in theory and in practice, compressed suffix arrays are competitive with classical ones for counting the occurrences but significantly slower for locating them. It turns out that the non-constant time to locate each occurrence is an intrinsic price for the compactness of these indexes. A lower bound (Chien *et al.*, 2015) states that any index able to locate the *occ* occurrences of patterns of length $m = \mathcal{O}(\log n)$ in time $\mathcal{O}(\text{polylog } n + occ)$ must use $\Omega(n \log n / \log \log n)$ bits in the worst case. Therefore, no compact index using $\mathcal{O}(n \log \sigma)$ bits can report each occurrence in constant time if σ is small, $\log \sigma = o(\log n / \log \log n)$.

Suffix array construction. Specific algorithms for string sorting are well reviewed, for example, in the book of Sedgewick and Wayne (2011). Szpankowski (1993) showed that texts generated from many reasonable probabilistic models behave in the way we defined as typical and have logarithmic lcp values with very high probability. The first non-trivial suffix array construction algorithm, by Manber and Myers (1993), obtained $\mathcal{O}(n \log n)$ worst-case time, and $\mathcal{O}(n \log \log n)$ on typical texts. Only in the year 2003, three almost simultaneous works showed how to build the suffix array in $\mathcal{O}(n)$ worst-case time (Ko and Aluru, 2005; Kim *et al.*, 2005; Kärkkäinen *et al.*, 2006). Puglisi *et al.* (2007) presented a complete (as of publication date) survey of suffix array construction algorithms. A more recent linear-time algorithm, *SA-DS* (Nong *et al.*, 2011), uses only the space for T and A plus $2n$ bits. They also introduce *SA-IS*, which is significantly faster and uses about the same space in practice (although it can use $n \log n + n$ extra bits in the worst case). *SA-IS* is relatively simple and is implemented in https://sites.google.com/site/yuta256/sais. Building on the ideas of Itoh and Tanaka (1999), Yuta Mori designed *DivSufSort*, which is to date the fastest algorithm in most cases (despite not being linear-time in the worst case) and uses almost no extra space. An informal but clear description of *DivSufSort* is available,[7] and the code can be downloaded from https://github.com/y-256/libdivsufsort. Mori also maintains up-to-date benchmarks comparing an exhaustive number of algorithms.[8] A very recent algorithm for construction on disk (Kärkkäinen *et al.*, 2015) yields an efficient parallel construction in memory that, with sufficient cores, is several times faster than *DivSufSort*. Yet it uses about $10n$ bytes.

When even the text does not fit in main memory, a fully secondary memory algorithm must be used to build the suffix array and LCP array. There are many efficient algorithms, both with optimal complexity (equivalent to sorting in secondary memory) and with higher complexity but competitive in practice (Crauser and Ferragina, 2002; Kärkkäinen *et al.*, 2006; Dementiev *et al.*, 2008; Ferragina *et al.*, 2012; Bingmann *et al.*, 2013; Kärkkäinen *et al.*, 2015; Kempa, 2015).

Compressed suffix array construction. Our direct BWT construction that does not use the $n \log n$ bits of the intermediate suffix array is a simplification of a stronger theoretical result by Kärkkäinen (2007). He obtains $\mathcal{O}(n)$ extra bits and $\mathcal{O}(n \log^2 n)$ time in the worst case, among other tradeoffs. He reports that the implementation is 2–3 times slower than a good suffix array construction algorithm, which seems to be a

---

[7] http://homepage3.nifty.com/wpage/software/itssort.txt.
[8] https://github.com/y-256/libdivsufsort/blob/wiki/SACA_Benchmarks.md.

reasonable price for building the BWT in little extra space. Okanohara and Sadakane (2009) showed how to build the BWT in $\mathcal{O}(n)$ time and using $\mathcal{O}(n \log \sigma \log \log_\sigma n)$ bits. On the other hand, Hon *et al.* (2009) built the BWT in $\mathcal{O}(n \log \log \sigma)$ time using $\mathcal{O}(n \log \sigma)$ bits. Both results have been recently superseded by Belazzougui (2015), who found an $\mathcal{O}(n)$ time construction using $\mathcal{O}(n \log \sigma)$ bits. Hon *et al.* (2007) managed to use compressed space, $\mathcal{O}(n(\mathcal{H}_0(T) + 1))$ bits but increasing the time to $\mathcal{O}(n \log n)$. As we have shown, it is very easy to build Ψ from T^{bwt}, or vice versa, in optimal time and no extra space apart from that of both compressed structures.

Deriving Ψ or T^{bwt} from the suffix array on disk via a few further secondary-memory sorts is also an easy exercise. Many of the on-disk suffix array construction algorithms can generate those compressed components directly.

Finally, we mentioned linear-time single- and multi-pattern string search algorithms. Those are classical and mentioned in many books (Navarro and Raffinot, 2002; Crochemore and Rytter, 2002).

Suffix trees. Suffix trees predate suffix arrays (Weiner, 1973), because the latter were designed as a space-economical version of the former. They can search for $P[1, m]$ in $\mathcal{O}(m)$ time and find many applications, from pure stringology to bioinformatics (Apostolico, 1985; Gusfield, 1997; Crochemore and Rytter, 2002). Suffix trees are built in $\mathcal{O}(n)$ time in main memory and in optimal time on secondary memory (Weiner, 1973; McCreight, 1976; Ukkonen, 1995; Farach-Colton *et al.*, 2000).

The methods we describe to build the LCP array from the suffix array, and to build the (uncompressed) suffix tree topology from the LCP array, are from Kasai *et al.* (2001). The LCP construction variant developed later by Kärkkäinen *et al.* (2009) is probably the fastest in practice. Some secondary memory algorithms have been proposed to build the suffix array and the LCP (Kärkkäinen *et al.*, 2006; Bingmann *et al.*, 2013; Kärkkäinen and Kempa, 2014; Kempa, 2015). The tree topology can then be built in one pass on disk over the LCP array using basically the same internal-memory algorithm.

Compressed suffix trees. Munro *et al.* (2001) described an early compact suffix tree data structure, but it still required $n \log n + \mathcal{O}(n)$ bits of space. In the chapter, we describe the compressed suffix tree of Sadakane (2007a), using our own tree topology representation. Later developments (Fischer *et al.*, 2009; Fischer, 2010; Russo *et al.*, 2011; Gog and Ohlebusch, 2013; Abeliuk *et al.*, 2013; Navarro and Russo, 2014; Ocker, 2015) struggled to reduce the $6n$ bits of extra space to $o(n)$, at the price of higher navigation times. Empirical comparisons (Gog, 2011; Gog and Ohlebusch, 2013; Abeliuk *et al.*, 2013) show that those developments offer relevant space/time tradeoffs, with the space going from as little as 4 to as much as 20 bits per symbol (text included) and time going from milliseconds to microseconds. Sadakane's structure is the fastest and largest in this group.

We presented simple construction algorithms, aiming at using the least possible extra space in practice. Our basic construction is a simplification of that of Hon *et al.* (2009), who used a theoretically stronger compressed suffix array and devised a way to build the suffix tree topology from the LCP array using $\mathcal{O}(n)$ bits in the worst case. They obtain $\mathcal{O}(n(\log \sigma + \log^\epsilon n))$ time and $\mathcal{O}(n \log \sigma)$ bits of space for any constant $\epsilon > 0$.

The recent linear-time BWT construction of Belazzougui (2015) can be extended to build all the compressed suffix tree components within randomized linear time and $\mathcal{O}(n \log \sigma)$ bits of space (Belazzougui, 2014). The topic has also been studied in depth from a more practical perspective (Ohlebusch and Gog, 2009; Sirén, 2010; Gog, 2011; Gog and Ohlebusch, 2013; Beller *et al.*, 2013).

Maximal substrings. The bioinformatic problem we describe for suffix trees is simple; Gusfield (1997) describes more advanced ones. On a classical suffix tree, the preferred way to find the suffix link of a virtual node is to reach it from an ancestor. This guarantees $\mathcal{O}(m)$ total time because the downward moves can be amortized. We preferred to go from a descendant because, with our level ancestor functionality, this adds only a logarithmic factor in an (unlikely) worst case, while in exchange moving up is significantly faster than moving down on a compressed suffix tree.

Labeled trees. The BWT-like representation of labeled trees we described was presented by Ferragina *et al.* (2009b), who called it XBW and implemented an application to index XML collections.

Document retrieval. The optimal-time document listing algorithm we described was presented by Muthukrishnan (2002). Sadakane (2007b) introduced the compact version, which we present using modern data structures for rmqs. Sadakane (2007b) also shows how to solve document counting queries in constant time given the suffix tree node, using only $\mathcal{O}(n)$ bits of extra space. Navarro (2014) recently wrote a survey on document retrieval problems and compact data structures for them.

The SXSI system (Arroyuelo *et al.*, 2015) combines a compact representation of the XML tree topology, a compact sequence representation of the labels, and a document retrieval system for the text contents. The way to handle documents is, however, more primitive than the ideas we presented.

Bibliography

Abeliuk, A., Cánovas, R., and Navarro, G. (2013). Practical compressed suffix trees. *Algorithms*, **6**(2), 319–351.

Adjeroh, D., Bell, T., and Mukherjee, A. (2008). *The Burrows-Wheeler Transform: Data Compression, Suffix Arrays, and Pattern Matching*. Springer.

Apostolico, A. (1985). The myriad virtues of subword trees. In *Combinatorial Algorithms on Words*, NATO ISI Series, pages 85–96. Springer-Verlag.

Arroyuelo, D., Claude, F., Maneth, S., Mäkinen, V., Navarro, G., Nguyễn, K., Sirén, J., and Välimäki, N. (2015). Fast in-memory XPath search using compressed indexes. *Software Practice and Experience*, **45**(3), 399–434.

Barbay, J., Claude, F., Gagie, T., Navarro, G., and Nekrich, Y. (2014). Efficient fully-compressed sequence representations. *Algorithmica*, **69**(1), 232–268.

Belazzougui, D. (2014). Linear time construction of compressed text indices in compact space. In *Proc. 46th ACM Symposium on Theory of Computing (STOC)*, pages 148–193.

Belazzougui, D. (2015). Linear time construction of compressed text indices in compact space. *CoRR*, **abs/1401.0936**. http://arxiv.org/abs/1401.0936v2.

Belazzougui, D. and Navarro, G. (2014). Alphabet-independent compressed text indexing. *ACM Transactions on Algorithms*, **10**(4), article 23.

Beller, T., Gog, S., Ohlebusch, E., and Schnattinger, T. (2013). Computing the longest common prefix array based on the Burrows-Wheeler transform. *Journal of Discrete Algorithms*, **18**, 22–31.

Bingmann, T., Fischer, J., and Osipov, V. (2013). Inducing suffix and lcp arrays in external memory. In *Proc. 15th Workshop on Algorithm Engineering and Experiments (ALENEX)*, pages 88–102.

Burrows, M. and Wheeler, D. (1994). A block sorting lossless data compression algorithm. Technical Report 124, Digital Equipment Corporation.

Chien, Y.-F., Hon, W.-K., Shah, R., Thankachan, S. V., and Vitter, J. S. (2015). Geometric BWT: compressed text indexing via sparse suffixes and range searching. *Algorithmica*, **71**(2), 258–278.

Crauser, A. and Ferragina, P. (2002). A theoretical and experimental study on the construction of suffix arrays in external memory. *Algorithmica*, **32**(1), 1–35.

Crochemore, M. and Rytter, W. (2002). *Jewels of Stringology*. World Scientific.

Dementiev, R., Kärkkäinen, J., Mehnert, J., and Sanders, P. (2008). Better external memory suffix array construction. *ACM Journal of Experimental Algorithmics*, **12**, article 3.4.

Farach-Colton, M., Ferragina, P., and Muthukrishnan, S. (2000). On the sorting-complexity of suffix tree construction. *Journal of the ACM*, **47**(6), 987–1011.

Ferragina, P. and Manzini, G. (2005). Indexing compressed texts. *Journal of the ACM*, **52**(4), 552–581.

Ferragina, P., Giancarlo, R., Manzini, G., and Sciortino, M. (2005). Boosting textual compression in optimal linear time. *Journal of the ACM*, **52**(4), 688–713.

Ferragina, P., Manzini, G., Mäkinen, V., and Navarro, G. (2007). Compressed representations of sequences and full-text indexes. *ACM Transactions on Algorithms*, **3**(2), article 20.

Ferragina, P., González, R., Navarro, G., and Venturini, R. (2009a). Compressed text indexes: From theory to practice. *ACM Journal of Experimental Algorithmics*, **13**, article 12.

Ferragina, P., Luccio, F., Manzini, G., and Muthukrishnan, S. (2009b). Compressing and indexing labeled trees, with applications. *Journal of the ACM*, **57**(1), article 4.

Ferragina, P., Gagie, T., and Manzini, G. (2012). Lightweight data indexing and compression in external memory. *Algorithmica*, **63**(3), 707–730.

Fischer, J. (2010). Wee LCP. *Information Processing Letters*, **110**, 317–320.

Fischer, J., Mäkinen, V., and Navarro, G. (2009). Faster entropy-bounded compressed suffix trees. *Theoretical Computer Science*, **410**(51), 5354–5364.

Foschini, L., Grossi, R., Gupta, A., and Vitter, J. S. (2006). When indexing equals compression: Experiments with compressing suffix arrays and applications. *ACM Transactions on Algorithms*, **2**(4), 611–639.

Gog, S. (2011). *Compressed Suffix Trees: Design, Construction, and Applications*. Ph.D. thesis, Ulm University, Germany.

Gog, S. and Ohlebusch, E. (2013). Compressed suffix trees: Efficient computation and storage of lcp-values. *ACM Journal of Experimental Algorithmics*, **18**, article 2.1.

Gog, S., Navarro, G., and Petri, M. (2015). Improved and extended locating functionality on compressed suffix arrays. *Journal of Discrete Algorithms*, **32**, 53–63.

Gog, S., Kärkkäinen, J., Kempa, D., Petri, M., and Puglisi, S. J. (2016). Faster, minuter. In *Proc. 26th Data Compression Conference (DCC)*, pages 53–62.

Gonnet, G., Baeza-Yates, R., and Snider, T. (1992). *Information Retrieval: Data Structures and Algorithms*, chapter 3: New indices for text: Pat trees and Pat arrays, pages 66–82. Prentice-Hall.

González, R., Navarro, G., and Ferrada, H. (2014). Locally compressed suffix arrays. *ACM Journal of Experimental Algorithmics*, **19**(1), article 1.

Grossi, R. (2011). A quick tour on suffix arrays and compressed suffix arrays. *Theoretical Computer Science*, **412**(27), 2964–2973.

Grossi, R. and Vitter, J. S. (2006). Compressed suffix arrays and suffix trees with applications to text indexing and string matching. *SIAM Journal on Computing*, **35**(2), 378–407.

Grossi, R., Gupta, A., and Vitter, J. S. (2003). High-order entropy-compressed text indexes. In *Proc. 14th Annual ACM-SIAM Symposium on Discrete Algorithms (SODA)*, pages 841–850.

Gusfield, D. (1997). *Algorithms on Strings, Trees and Sequences: Computer Science and Computational Biology*. Cambridge University Press.

Hon, W.-K., Lam, T.-W., Sadakane, K., Sung, W.-K., and Yiu, S.-M. (2007). A space and time efficient algorithm for constructing compressed suffix arrays. *Algorithmica*, **48**(1), 23–36.

Hon, W.-K., Sadakane, K., and Sung, W.-K. (2009). Breaking a time-and-space barrier in constructing full-text indices. *SIAM Journal on Computing*, **38**(6), 2162–2178.

Huo, H., Chen, L., Vitter, J. S., and Nekrich, Y. (2014). A practical implementation of compressed suffix arrays with applications to self-indexing. In *Proc. 24th Data Compression Conference (DCC)*, pages 292–301.

Huo, H., Chen, L., Zhao, H., Vitter, J. S., Nekrich, Y., and Yu, Q. (2015). A data-aware FM-index. In *Proc. 17th Workshop on Algorithm Engineering and Experiments (ALENEX)*, pages 10–23.

Itoh, H. and Tanaka, H. (1999). An efficient method for in memory construction of suffix arrays. In *Proc. 6th International Symposium on String Processing and Information Retrieval (SPIRE)*, pages 81–88.

Kärkkäinen, J. (2007). Fast BWT in small space by blockwise suffix sorting. *Theoretical Computer Science*, **387**(3), 249–257.

Kärkkäinen, J. and Kempa, D. (2014). LCP array construction in external memory. In *Proc. 13th International Symposium on Experimental Algorithms (SEA)*, LNCS 8504, pages 412–423.

Kärkkäinen, J. and Puglisi, S. J. (2011). Fixed block compression boosting in FM-indexes. In *Proc. 18th International Symposium on String Processing and Information Retrieval (SPIRE)*, LNCS 7024, pages 174–184.

Kärkkäinen, J., Sanders, P., and Burkhardt, S. (2006). Linear work suffix array construction. *Journal of the ACM*, **53**(6), 918–936.

Kärkkäinen, J., Manzini, G., and Puglisi, S. J. (2009). Permuted longest-common-prefix array. In *Proc. 20th Annual Symposium on Combinatorial Pattern Matching (CPM)*, LNCS 5577, pages 181–192.

Kärkkäinen, J., Kempa, D., and Puglisi, S. J. (2014). Hybrid compression of bitvectors for the FM-index. In *Proc. 24th Data Compression Conference (DCC)*, pages 302–311.

Kärkkäinen, J., Kempa, D., and Puglisi, S. J. (2015). Parallel external memory suffix sorting. In *Proc. 26th Annual Symposium on Combinatorial Pattern Matching (CPM)*, LNCS 9133, pages 329–342.

Kasai, T., Lee, G., Arimura, H., Arikawa, S., and Park, K. (2001). Linear-time longest-common-prefix computation in suffix arrays and its applications. In *Proc. 12th Annual Symposium on Combinatorial Pattern Matching (CPM)*, LNCS 2089, pages 181–192.

Kempa, D. (2015). *Efficient Construction of Fundamental Data Structures in Large-Scale Text Indexing*. Ph.D. thesis, University of Helsinki, Finland.

Kim, D. K., Sim, J. S., Park, H., and Park, K. (2005). Constructing suffix arrays in linear time. *Journal of Discrete Algorithms*, **3**(2–4), 126–142.

Ko, P. and Aluru, S. (2005). Space efficient linear time construction of suffix arrays. *Journal of Discrete Algorithms*, **3**(2–4), 143–156.

Mäkinen, V. and Navarro, G. (2008). Dynamic entropy-compressed sequences and full-text indexes. *ACM Transactions on Algorithms*, **4**(3), article 32.

Manber, U. and Myers, G. (1993). Suffix arrays: a new method for on-line string searches. *SIAM Journal on Computing*, **22**(5), 935–948.

McCreight, E. (1976). A space-economical suffix tree construction algorithm. *Journal of the ACM*, **23**(2), 262–272.

Munro, J. I., Raman, V., and Rao, S. S. (2001). Space efficient suffix trees. *Journal of Algorithms*, **39**(2), 205–222.

Muthukrishnan, S. (2002). Efficient algorithms for document retrieval problems. In *Proc. 13th Annual ACM-SIAM Symposium on Discrete Algorithms (SODA)*, pages 657–666.

Navarro, G. (2014). Spaces, trees and colors: The algorithmic landscape of document retrieval on sequences. *ACM Computing Surveys*, **46**(4), article 52.

Navarro, G. and Mäkinen, V. (2007). Compressed full-text indexes. *ACM Computing Surveys*, **39**(1), article 2.

Navarro, G. and Raffinot, M. (2002). *Flexible Pattern Matching in Strings*. Cambridge University Press.

Navarro, G. and Russo, L. M. S. (2014). Fast fully-compressed suffix trees. In *Proc. 24th Data Compression Conference (DCC)*, pages 283–291.

Nong, G., Zhang, S., and Chan, W. H. (2011). Two efficient algorithms for linear time suffix array construction. *IEEE Transactions on Computers*, **60**(10), 1471–1484.

Ocker, C. (2015). *Engineering Fully-Compressed Suffix Trees*. MSc thesis, Karlsruhe Institute of Technology, Germany.

Ohlebusch, E. and Gog, S. (2009). A compressed enhanced suffix array supporting fast string matching. In *Proc. 16th International Symposium on String Processing and Information Retrieval (SPIRE)*, LNCS 5721, pages 51–62.

Okanohara, D. and Sadakane, K. (2009). A linear-time Burrows-Wheeler transform using induced sorting. In *Proc. 16th International Symposium on String Processing and Information Retrieval (SPIRE)*, LNCS 5721, pages 90–101.

Puglisi, S. J., Smyth, W. F., and Turpin, A. (2007). A taxonomy of suffix array construction algorithms. *ACM Computing Surveys*, **39**(2), article 4.

Rao, S. S. (2002). Time-space trade-offs for compressed suffix arrays. *Information Processing Letters*, **82**(6), 307–311.

Russo, L. M. S., Navarro, G., and Oliveira, A. (2011). Fully-compressed suffix trees. *ACM Transactions on Algorithms*, **7**(4), article 53.

Sadakane, K. (2002). Succinct representations of *lcp* information and improvements in the compressed suffix arrays. In *Proc. 13th Annual ACM-SIAM Symposium on Discrete Algorithms (SODA)*, pages 225–232.

Sadakane, K. (2003). New text indexing functionalities of the compressed suffix arrays. *Journal of Algorithms*, **48**(2), 294–313.

Sadakane, K. (2007a). Compressed suffix trees with full functionality. *Theory of Computing Systems*, **41**(4), 589–607.

Sadakane, K. (2007b). Succinct data structures for flexible text retrieval systems. *Journal of Discrete Algorithms*, **5**, 12–22.

Sedgewick, R. and Wayne, K. (2011). *Algorithms*. Addison-Wesley, 4th edition.

Sirén, J. (2010). Sampled longest common prefix array. In *Proc. 21st Annual Symposium on Combinatorial Pattern Matching (CPM)*, LNCS 6129, pages 227–237.

Szpankowski, W. (1993). A generalized suffix tree and its (un)expected asymptotic behaviors. *SIAM Journal on Computiing*, **22**(6), 1176–1198.

Ukkonen, E. (1995). On-line construction of suffix trees. *Algorithmica*, **14**(3), 249–260.

Weiner, P. (1973). Linear pattern matching algorithm. In *Proc. 14th Annual IEEE Symposium on Switching and Automata Theory*, pages 1–11.

CHAPTER 12

Dynamic Structures

Throughout the book we have assumed that our compact data structures are static, that is, we build them once and they do not change anymore; we only support queries on them. In many cases the data are indeed static or change infrequently enough to allow us afford a periodic reconstruction of the data structures from scratch. In other cases, however, the data change frequently and reconstruction is unfeasible. This is the scenario we address in this chapter.

In many data types, supporting updates together with queries is intrinsically harder than the static case. For example, though we have seen that static bitvectors (Chapter 4), sequences (Chapter 6), and trees (Chapter 8) can support many operations in time $\mathcal{O}(\log \log n)$ or less, those operations require at least time $\Omega(\log n / \log \log n)$ when insertions and deletions of symbols (for bitvectors and sequences) or nodes (for trees) are allowed. In this chapter we will see practical techniques to turn those structures dynamic, with slowdown factors of typically $\mathcal{O}(w)$ compared to the base static representation. When n is large, $\mathcal{O}(w)$ becomes similar to $\mathcal{O}(\log n)$.

Dynamism usually allows one to build the data structures within their final compressed space, by successively inserting the elements. In general, however, this construction is significantly slower than the procedures we have seen throughout the book, although the latter typically use more space.

12.1 Bitvectors

Consider a bitvector $B[1, n]$, where in addition to the **access**, **rank**, and **select** operations described in Chapter 4, we support the following updates to B:

insert(B, i, b): inserts bit b between $B[i - 1]$ and $B[i]$, for $1 \le i \le n + 1$.
delete(B, i): deletes $B[i]$, for $1 \le i \le n$.

We show how to support both the query and the update operations in time $\mathcal{O}(w)$ while using $n + \mathcal{O}(n/w)$ bits of space, where n is the size of B at the time the operation is carried out. We later consider compression.

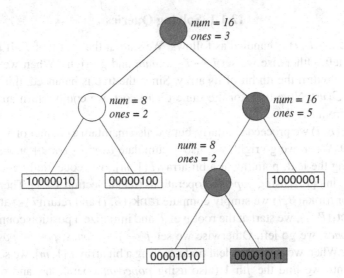

B = 10000010 00000100 00001010 00001011 10000001

Figure 12.1. The dynamic representation of a bitvector B (on the bottom). Internal nodes store the number of bits and number of 1s in their left subtree. Leaves point to chunks of bits. We show in gray the elements accessed to solve the queries of Example 12.2.

The data structure is a classical, pointer-based, balanced search tree T (an AVL or a Red-Black tree, for example), where the leaves point to arrays of $\Theta(w^2)$ bits (these bit arrays have no further structure). Each internal node v contains two fields: $v.num$ and $v.ones$ are the total number of bits and of 1s, respectively, stored at the leaves that descend from the *left child* of v. Leaves store, instead, the pointer $v.L$ to their bit array.

Example 12.1 *Figure 12.1 shows the dynamic representation of a bitvector. The bit arrays are of length 8 (although a range of lengths will be allowed). For example, the root node v indicates that its left child has $v.num = 16$ bits, of which $v.ones = 3$ are 1s. The grayed nodes will be used later.*

The extra space for the tree nodes is $\mathcal{O}(n/w)$ bits, since they store 2 counters and 2 pointers, using $4w$ bits, and there are $\mathcal{O}(n/w^2)$ nodes because each leaf stores $\Theta(w^2)$ bits. Therefore, the total space to store $B[1, n]$ in the dynamic structure is $n + \mathcal{O}(n/w)$ bits. We now describe how to carry out the query and update operations on this representation.

Bitvectors could be created empty, in which case the tree only has a single leaf with an empty bit array. The first internal node will be created when this array splits due to insertions, as we will see later. We maintain separately the length n of B. It may also be possible to provide an operation that takes a static bit array and builds a dynamic one, distributing it across $\Theta(n/w^2)$ leaves and internal nodes, and similarly an operation that turns a dynamic bitvector into static. Those are simple exercises we leave to the reader.

12.1.1 Solving Queries

A query access(B, i) is handled as follows. We start at the root v of T. If $i \leq v.num$, then we go left. Otherwise we set $i \leftarrow i - v.num$ and go right. When we arrive at a leaf node, we return the ith bit of its array. Since the tree is balanced, this takes time $\mathcal{O}(\log n) = \mathcal{O}(w)$. Note that, for the same $\mathcal{O}(w)$ cost, we could return any chunk of $\mathcal{O}(w^2)$ bits from B.

For rank$_1(B, i)$ we proceed similarly, but we also maintain a counter of 1s initialized as $ones \leftarrow 0$. When we go right, we also accumulate $ones \leftarrow ones + v.ones$. Finally, upon reaching the leaf, pointing at a bit array $L[1, m]$, we sequentially count in c the number of 1s in $L[1, i]$ using $popcount$ operations (recall Section 4.2.1). Then we return $ones + c$. For rank$_0(B, i)$ we simply compute rank$_1(B, i)$ and return $i - $ rank$_1(B, i)$.

For select$_1(B, j)$, we start at the root v of T and initialize a position counter $pos \leftarrow 0$. If $j \leq v.ones$, we go left. Otherwise we set $j \leftarrow j - v.ones$, $pos \leftarrow pos + v.num$, and go right. When we arrive at a leaf node, storing a bit array $L[1, m]$, we sequentially traverse L until we find the jth 1 (also using $popcount$ operations, and re-scanning bitwise the word where the answer lies). Say that the jth 1 is found at $L[p]$. Then we return $pos + p$.

Operation select$_0(B, j)$ proceeds similarly, except that instead of $v.ones$ in the internal nodes, we use $v.num - v.ones$, and in L we look for the jth 0.

Both rank and select operations spend $\mathcal{O}(\log n)$ time on the tree. Then, by computing $popcount$ on w-bit words in constant time, they spend $\mathcal{O}(w)$ time in the leaves. Algorithms 12.1 and 12.2 detail the query operations.

Example 12.2 *Consider again the bitvector of Figure 12.1. To carry out* access$(B, 30)$, *we traverse the grayed path of the tree. We start at the root node* v *with* $i = 30$. *Since* $i = 30 > 16 = v.num$, *we set* $i \leftarrow i - v.num = 30 - 16 = 14$ *and set* v *to the right child of the root. Since* $i = 14 \leq 16 = v.num$, *we set* v *to its left child. Since* $i = 14 > 8 = v.num$, *we set* $i \leftarrow i - v.num = 14 - 8 = 6$ *and go to the right child of* v. *This is the grayed leaf, where we answer* $v.L[i] = 00001011[6] = 0$.

To answer the query rank$_1(B, 30)$, *we traverse the same path but also maintain the variable "ones," initially set at* 0. *When we move from the root* v *to its right child, we set* $ones \leftarrow ones + v.ones = 0 + 3 = 3$. *When we go from the third internal node to its right child, we set* $ones \leftarrow ones + v.ones = 3 + 2 = 5$. *Finally, at the leaf* v, *we compute* $popcount(v.L[1, i]) = popcount(00001011[1, 6]) = 1$. *Thus the final answer is* $5 + 1 = 6$.

Let us now solve select$_1(B, j)$ *for* $j = 6$. *We start with variable* pos *set to* 0. *From the root* v, *we move to the right because* $j = 6 > 3 = v.ones$. *Thus, we update* $j \leftarrow j - v.ones = 6 - 3 = 3$, $pos \leftarrow pos + v.num = 0 + 16 = 16$, *and set* v *to the right child of the root. Since* $j = 3 \leq 5 = v.ones$, *we set* v *to its left child. Finally, since* $j = 3 > 2 = v.ones$, *we update* $j \leftarrow j - v.ones = 3 - 2 = 1$, $pos \leftarrow pos + v.num = 16 + 8 = 24$, *and set* v *to the grayed leaf. In* $v.L = 00001011$ *we find the first 1 (since* $j = 1$) *at position* $v.L[5]$. *Therefore, we answer* $24 + 5 = 29$.

12.1.2 Handling Updates

An operation insert(B, i, b) is carried out as follows. We traverse the tree as for access(B, i), starting at the root v. If $i \leq v.num$, we go left. In this case, we set

---

Algorithm 12.1: Answering access and rank queries on a dynamic bitvector. Children of internal nodes are pointed from fields *left* and *right*, and bit arrays of leaf nodes from field *L*.

---

1 **Proc** access(B, i)

    Input : Dynamic bitvector B (seen as tree T) and position i.

    Output: Returns $B[i]$.

2    $v \leftarrow T.root$

3   **while** v *is not a leaf* **do**

4   **if** $i \leq v.num$ **then**

5          $v \leftarrow v.left$

6   **else**

7          $i \leftarrow i - v.num$

8          $v \leftarrow v.right$

9   **return** bitread($v.L$, i)

10 **Proc** rank(B, i)

    Input : Dynamic bitvector B (seen as tree T) and position i.

    Output: Returns $\text{rank}_1(B, i)$.

11   $v \leftarrow T.root$

12   $ones \leftarrow 0$

13   **while** v *is not a leaf* **do**

14   **if** $i \leq v.num$ **then**

15         $v \leftarrow v.left$

16   **else**

17         $i \leftarrow i - v.num$

18         $ones \leftarrow ones + v.ones$

19         $v \leftarrow v.right$

20   **return** $ones + popcount(v.L[1, i])$

$v.num \leftarrow v.num + 1$ and, if $b = 1$, we also set $v.ones \leftarrow v.ones + 1$. If, instead, $i > v.num$, we set $i \leftarrow i - v.num$ and go right. When we arrive at a leaf node v, storing a bit array $v.L[1, \ell]$, we allocate a new memory area able to hold $\ell + 1$ bits, and write $v.L[1, i - 1] . b . v.L[i, \ell]$ to it. The old memory area is freed, and the new one becomes the bit array associated with the leaf. Note that ℓ is computed along the path to the leaf: it is initially $\ell \leftarrow n$, then it becomes $\ell \leftarrow v.num$ when we go left, or $\ell \leftarrow \ell - v.num$ when we go right.

An operation delete(B, i) is handled similarly, except that the fields $v.num$ and $v.ones$ are decremented instead of being incremented, and the new memory area contains $\ell - 1$ bits with content $v.L[1, i - 1] . v.L[i + 1, \ell]$.

Example 12.3 *Figure 12.2 shows the result of executing* insert(B, i, 1) *at* $i = 19$ *on the bitvector represented in Figure 12.1. The same grayed internal nodes are traversed. We start at the root* v. *Since* $i = 19 > 16 = v.num$, *we go right and set* $i \leftarrow i - v.num =$

Algorithm 12.2: Answering **select** queries on a dynamic bitvector. Children of internal nodes are pointed from fields *left* and *right*, and bit arrays of leaf nodes from field *L*.

---

1   **Proc** select$_1$(B, j)

     Input   : Dynamic bitvector B (seen as tree T) and index j.

     Output: Returns select$_1$(B, j).

2    $v \leftarrow T.root$

3    $pos \leftarrow 0$

4   **while** v *is not a leaf* **do**

5   **if** $j \leq v.ones$ **then**

6        $v \leftarrow v.left$

7   **else**

8        $j \leftarrow j - v.ones$

9        $pos \leftarrow pos + v.num$

10       $v \leftarrow v.right$

11    $p \leftarrow$ position of the jth 1 in v.L (using *popcount*)

12   **return** $pos + p$

13   **Proc** select$_0$(B, j)

     Input   : Dynamic bitvector B (seen as tree T) and index j.

     Output: Returns select$_0$(B, j).

14    $v \leftarrow T.root$

15    $pos \leftarrow 0$

16   **while** v *is not a leaf* **do**

17   **if** $j \leq v.num - v.ones$ **then**

18        $v \leftarrow v.left$

19   **else**

20        $j \leftarrow j - (v.num - v.ones)$

21        $pos \leftarrow pos + v.num$

22        $v \leftarrow v.right$

23    $p \leftarrow$ position of the jth 0 in v.L (using *popcount*)

24   **return** $pos + p$

$19 - 16 = 3$. *On the right child, we go left because* $i = 3 \leq 16 = v.num$. *Before going left, we set* $v.num \leftarrow v.num + 1 = 17$ *and, since we insert a* 1, *we also set* $v.ones \leftarrow v.ones + 1 = 6$. *On its left child (the lowest grayed node), it also holds* $i = 3 \leq 8 = v.num$, *thus we go left after setting* $v.num \leftarrow v.num + 1 = 9$ *and* $v.ones \leftarrow v.ones + 1 = 3$. *Finally, we arrive at the bit array of the leaf,* $v.L = $ 00001010, *where we insert the bit* 1 *at position* $i = 3$, *so* v.L *becomes* 001001010.

     It is a good exercise for the reader to repeat the query operations of Example 12.2 on the resulting bitvector, and also to run the query **delete**(B, 19), *which reverses the effect of this insertion.*

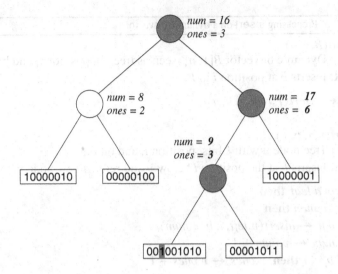

$B =$ 10000010 00000100 001001010 00001011 10000001

Figure 12.2. The structure of Figure 12.1 after **insert**$(B, 19, 1)$. Grayed internal nodes show the path to the leaf where the bit (in a grayed block) is inserted. The updated fields in internal nodes and the new bit are in bold.

In practice an integral number of computer words is allocated for the bit array of each leaf. When the number of bits grows from $k \cdot w$ to $k \cdot w + 1$ for some k, we reallocate a new memory area with one further computer word, that is, with enough space to hold $k \cdot w + w = \ell + w$ bits. Analogously, only when $2w$ allocated bits (that is, two computer words) are unused, we reallocate the leaf with *one* less computer word in size. Tracking whether the number of unused bits is between 0 and $w - 1$ or between w and $2w - 1$ requires storing one further bit in the leaves. Overall this technique increases the space usage only in $\mathcal{O}(n/w)$ bits and ensures that there is at most one memory allocation (which might be expensive) every w updates. Of course, if the memory allocator handles only multiples of t computer words, then we should replace w by $t \cdot w$ in these calculations. As a result, we perform one allocation every tw updates, and the space usage increases in $\mathcal{O}(nt/w)$ bits. Instead, we can retain $\mathcal{O}(n/w)$ extra bits and raise the time to $\mathcal{O}(tw)$ by using leaves of $\Theta(tw^2)$ bits, or use another space/time tradeoff. We will assume $t = 1$ in the sequel for simplicity.

Algorithm 12.3 details operation **insert**. Lines 14–20 handle leaf overflows, which are discussed next. The code for **delete** is deferred until we address leaf underflows, which will be more complicated.

Maintaining Bit Array Sizes

The remaining problem is that, to maintain the space and time performance, we must ensure that the size of the bit arrays at leaves is $\Theta(w^2)$. Let us say we allow them to hold less than $2w^2$ bits (we may multiply this limit by an integer constant in order to reduce extra space, yet the time to process a leaf increases). When a bit array reaches that size, it is cut into two, and a new internal node v is created with the two halves in its child leaves. We set $v.num$ to w^2 and $v.ones$ to the number of 1s in $v.left.L$. Then the

---

Algorithm 12.3: Processing insert on a dynamic bitvector.

---

1   **Proc** insert(B, i, b)

     Input : Dynamic bitvector $B[1, n]$ (seen as tree T), position i, and bit b.

     Output: Inserts b at position i in B.

2    $T.root \leftarrow insert(T.root, i, b, n)$

3   **Proc** $insert(v, i, b, \ell)$

     Input : Tree node v with ℓ bits, position i, and bit b.

     Output: Inserts b at the position i below v and returns new node v.

4   **if** v *is not a leaf* **then**

5   **if** $i \leq v.num$ **then**

6        $v.left \leftarrow insert(v.left, i, b, v.num)$

7        $v.num \leftarrow v.num + 1$

8   **if** $b = 1$ **then** $v.ones \leftarrow v.ones + 1$

9   **else**

10        $v.right \leftarrow insert(v.right, i - v.num, b, \ell - v.num)$

11   **else**

12   Reallocate $v.L$ (if necessary) to size $\ell + 1$

13   Insert bit b at $v.L[i]$, copying memory word-wise

14   **if** $\ell + 1 = 2w^2$ **then** (leaf overflow)

15   Split $v.L$ into two halves, at new leaves v_l and v_r

16   Convert v into an internal node

17        $v.left \leftarrow v_l$; $v.right \leftarrow v_r$

18        $v.num \leftarrow w^2$; $v.ones \leftarrow popcount(v_l.L[1, w^2])$

19   **if** v *needs a rotation* **then**

20   Carry out rotation (modifying v)

21   **return** v

---

tree may require rotations to recover its balance. In the case of a left-rotation , we start with v_1 and its right child v_2, and end with v_1 being the left child of v_2. In this case we must update the fields of v_2 as follows: $v_2.num \leftarrow v_2.num + v_1.num$ and $v_2.ones \leftarrow v_2.ones + v_1.ones$. A right-rotation is analogous: If we start with v_1 being the left child of v_2, we must correct $v_2.num \leftarrow v_2.num - v_1.num$ and $v_2.ones \leftarrow v_2.ones - v_1.ones$.

Example 12.4 *Figure 12.3 shows, on the left, the resulting tree after executing* insert($B, 25, 0$) *on the bitvector represented in Figure 12.2. Since the bit array size reached the maximum, assumed to be* 10 *in the example, it has been split and a new internal node (hatched) has been created. On the right of the figure, since the right child* v *of the root is unbalanced (under an AVL criterion) a right rotation is carried out. The other nodes involved in the rotation are grayed. Observe how the node* v, *which becomes the rightmost internal node, has its fields recomputed to* $v.num = 8$ *and* $v.ones = 3$.

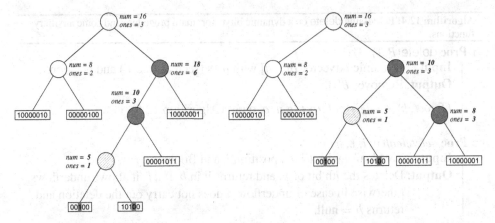

Figure 12.3. The structure of Figure 12.2 after a second insertion, insert(B, 25, 0). The leaf containing both inserted bits splits (left) and creates a (hatched) internal node, which then requires a rotation (right) that involves the grayed internal nodes. Note how the node fields change (in bold).

In the case of deletions, we forbid leaves to contain less than $w^2/2$ bits (unless the whole tree consists of a single leaf). When an underflow occurs at a leaf v, we try to obtain a bit from the preceding or following leaf, v'. If this is impossible because v' also has $w^2/2$ bits, we know that their union cannot overflow (it contains exactly $w^2 - 1$ bits; we allow up to $2w^2$). So we add the contents of v to those of v' and remove the leaf v.

Example 12.5 *Assume that a leaf must contain at least 5 bits. After several deletions in the tree on the right of Figure 12.3, we arrive at the tree on the left of Figure 12.4. Now the grayed leaf receives another deletion, which makes it underflow. But it takes a bit from its next leaf and its minimum allowed size is restored. The hatched leaf, instead, is merged with its previous leaf, as that one is too small to lend a bit. A rotation is needed after the merging of the leaves.*

Algorithms 12.4 and 12.5 give the details. We fix the underflowing leaf as we return from the recursion. This involves entering to another leaf again, but the underflow does

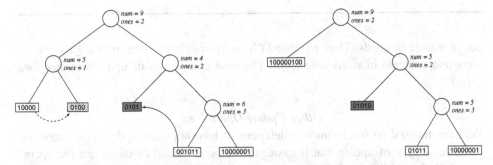

Figure 12.4. The structure of Figure 12.3 after several deletions and two underflow situations: the gray node is restored by borrowing a bit from the next leaf, whereas the hatched node is merged with its previous leaf.

Algorithm 12.4: Processing delete on a dynamic bitvector: main procedure and some auxiliary functions.

---

1 **Proc** delete(B, i)

   Input : Dynamic bitvector $B[1, n]$ with o 1s (seen as tree T) and position i.

   Output: Removes $B[i]$.

2    $\langle T.root, b \rangle \leftarrow delete(T.root, i, n, o, \textbf{true})$ (Algorithm 12.5)

3 **Proc** $deleteleaf(v, i, \ell, uf)$

   Input : Tree leaf v with ℓ bits, position i, and Boolean uf.

   Output: Deletes the ith bit of v, and returns it in b. If uf, it allows underflows, otherwise in case of underflow it does not carry out the deletion and returns $b = $ null.

4   **if** $\ell = w^2/2$ **and not** uf **then return** null

5    $b \leftarrow$ bitread($v.L, i$)

6   Remove bit $v.L[i]$, copying memory word-wise

7   Reallocate $v.L$ (if necessary) to size $\ell - 1$

8   **return** b

9 **Proc** $insw(v, i, \ell, C, s, o)$

   Input : Tree node v with ℓ bits, position i, and bit array $C[1, s]$ with o 1s.

   Output: Inserts C at the position i below v. Does not handle overflows.

10   **while** v *is not a leaf* **do**

11   **if** $i \leq v.num$ **then**

12          $v.num \leftarrow v.num + s$

13          $v.ones \leftarrow v.ones + o$

14          $\ell \leftarrow v.num$

15          $v \leftarrow v.left$

16   **else**

17          $\ell \leftarrow \ell - v.num$

18          $v \leftarrow v.right$

19   Reallocate $v.L$ (if necessary) to size $\ell + s$

20   Insert $C[1, s]$ at $v.L[i]$, copying memory word-wise

---

not propagate upwards. Thus we spend $\mathcal{O}(\log n)$ time in the tree, plus $\mathcal{O}(w)$ time to copy leaf contents in word-wise form. The time complexity of updates is therefore $\mathcal{O}(w)$.

Other Update Operations

We have focused on insertions and deletions of bits, but other update operations are possible. A type of update that is easier than insertions and deletions are the operations bitset and bitclear defined on bit arrays (Algorithm 3.1). If we define them on dynamic bitvectors, we need to traverse the tree T and update some counters, but no updates to the tree structure are necessary. Therefore, although they can be simulated

---

Algorithm 12.5: Processing delete on a dynamic bitvector: main recursive routine.

---

1 **Proc** $delete(v, i, \ell, o, uf)$

    Input : Tree node v, with ℓ bits and o 1s, position i, and Boolean uf.

    Output: Deletes the ith bit below v and returns $\langle v, b \rangle$, where v is the (possibly modified) pointer to v and b is the bit deleted. If uf, it handles underflows, otherwise in case of underflow it does not carry out the deletion and returns $b = $ null (and o is not used).

2   **if** v *is a leaf* **then return** $\langle v, deleteleaf(v, i, \ell, uf) \rangle$

3   **if** $i \le v.num$ **then**

4         $\langle v.left, b \rangle \leftarrow delete(v.left, i, v.num, v.ones, uf)$

5   **if** $b = $ null **then return** $\langle v, $ null$\rangle$

6   **if** $b = 1$ **then** $v.ones \leftarrow v.ones - 1$

7   **if** $v.num = w^2/2$ **then** (underflow, $v.left$ must be a leaf)

8             $\langle v.right, b' \rangle \leftarrow delete(v.right, 1, \ell - w^2/2, 0, \textbf{false})$

9   **if** $b' = $ null **then** (merge leaves)

10                 $v' \leftarrow insw(v.right, 1, \ell - w^2/2, v.left.L, w^2/2 - 1, v.ones)$

11   Free $v.left.L$, $v.left$, and v; **return** $\langle v', b \rangle$

12             $v.left \leftarrow insert(v.left, w^2/2, b', w^2/2 - 1)$

13   **if** $b' = 1$ **then** $v.ones \leftarrow v.ones + 1$

14   **else** $v.num \leftarrow v.num - 1$

15   **else**

16         $\langle v.right, b \rangle \leftarrow delete(v.right, i - v.num, \ell - v.num, o - v.ones, uf)$

17   **if** $b = $ null **then return** $\langle v, $ null$\rangle$

18   **if** $b = 1$ **then** $o \leftarrow o - 1$

19   **if** $\ell - v.num = w^2/2$ **then** (underflow, $v.right$ must be a leaf)

20             $\langle v.left, b' \rangle \leftarrow delete(v.left, v.num, v.num, 0, \textbf{false})$

21   **if** $b' = $ null **then** (merge leaves)

22                 $v' \leftarrow insw(v.left, v.num + 1, v.num, v.right.L, w^2/2 - 1, o - v.ones)$

23   Free $v.right.L$, $v.right$, and v; **return** $\langle v', b \rangle$

24             $v.right \leftarrow insert(v.right, 1, b', w^2/2 - 1)$

25         $v.num \leftarrow v.num - 1$

26   **if** $b' = 1$ **then** $v.ones \leftarrow v.ones - 1$

27   **if** v *needs a rotation* **then** Carry out rotation (modifying v)

28   **return** $\langle v, b \rangle$

---

by delete(B, i) followed by insert(B, i, b), the solution in Algorithm 12.6 is more efficient. Note that, if the only allowed update operations are bitset and bitclear, then the tree T needs not be dynamic; it might have a pointerless heap-like structure.

A slightly more complicated operation is to insert a chunk of $\mathcal{O}(w^2)$ bits in $B[i]$, insert($B, i, C[1, m]$). Let us consider the case $m \le 2w^2$; then we can repeat the process a constant number of times if necessary. By following the procedure of insert(B, i), we

---

Algorithm 12.6: Processing bitset and bitclear on a dynamic bitvector.

---

1 **Proc** bitset(B, i)

    Input : Dynamic bitvector B (seen as tree T) and position i.
    Output: Sets $B[i] \leftarrow 1$.

2     $bitset(T.root, i)$

3 **Proc** $bitset(v, i)$

    Input : Tree node v and position i.
    Output: Sets to 1 the ith bit below v, and returns if it changed.

4   **if** v *is not a leaf* **then**
5   **if** $i \leq v.num$ **then**
6             $flip \leftarrow bitset(v.left, i)$
7   **if** $flip$ **then** $v.ones \leftarrow v.ones + 1$
8   **return** $flip$
9   **else return** $bitset(v.right, i - v.num)$
10   **if** bitread($v.L, i$) $= 1$ **then return false**
11   bitset($v.L, i$) (Algorithm 3.1)
12   **return true**

13 **Proc** bitclear(B, i)

    Input : Dynamic bitvector B (seen as tree T) and position i.
    Output: Sets $B[i] \leftarrow 0$.

14     $bitclear(T.root, i)$

15 **Proc** $bitclear(v, i)$

    Input : Tree node v and position i.
    Output: Sets to 0 the ith bit below v, and returns if it changed.

16   **if** v *is not a leaf* **then**
17   **if** $i \leq v.num$ **then**
18             $flip \leftarrow bitclear(v.left, i)$
19   **if** $flip$ **then** $v.ones \leftarrow v.ones - 1$
20   **return** $flip$
21   **else return** $bitclear(v.right, i - v.num)$
22   **if** bitread($v.L, i$) $= 0$ **then return false**
23   bitclear($v.L, i$) (Algorithm 3.1)
24   **return true**

---

can reach a leaf and then insert the chunk at the correct position, by copying the data word-wise. If the leaf overflows, then we split it into two (which will be sufficient since it can contain at most $4w^2$ bits) and handle the split as usual. The total process takes $\mathcal{O}(w)$ time.

Deleting a chunk of $m \leq w^2/2$ bits starting at $B[i]$, $\mathsf{delete}_m(B, i)$, is similar but more cumbersome. First, we might have to delete bits from two leaves, both of which may underflow. The situation can be fixed by merging with neighboring leaves and then splitting if necessary, as in classical B-trees. All the process can be made $\mathcal{O}(w)$ time; we leave the details to the reader.

Other even more complex operations are to cut a bitvector into two, and to concatenate two bitvectors. It is possible to implement these operations in polylogarithmic time, by operating on a logarithmic number of nodes in T, but the details are more complicated. We give some pointers in the bibliographic section.

12.1.3 Compressed Bitvectors

It is possible to use the same dynamic technique on bitvectors compressed with the scheme of Section 4.1.1, which represents bit blocks of fixed size b using a variable-sized code (c, o). In this case, we write the block representations (c, o) consecutively in the leaves (first all the c and then all the o components).

Since now the bitvectors are compressed, a leaf representing $\Theta(w^2)$ bits may use less physical space. To maintain the time performance obtained on the plain bitvector representation, we keep the invariants on leaf sizes with respect to the number of bits represented, not the number of physical bits used. This still ensures that the tree pointers and the extra wasted space per leaf amount to only $\mathcal{O}(n/w)$ bits on top of the $n\mathcal{H}_0(B) + o(n)$ bits used by the static representation.

Since the blocks represent $b = \Theta(w)$ bits, each leaf will represent $\mathcal{O}(w)$ blocks. In order to process an **access**, **rank**, or **select** query, we traverse the $\mathcal{O}(w)$ class components (c) and need to decode only one component o, as explained in Section 4.1.1. Decoding this one component o also costs $\mathcal{O}(w)$ time.

The insertion or deletion of a bit in a block, however, requires decompressing, modifying, and recompressing all the blocks to the right of the insertion point. If we do this bitwise, updates require $\mathcal{O}(w^2)$ time. This can be reduced back to $\mathcal{O}(w)$ if we use the precomputed tables that encode and decode blocks in constant time described at the end of Section 4.1.1. We must choose a block size of the form $b = \Theta(w)$. This is a realistic assumption, because in most cases storing 2^b integers is acceptable for $b = w/2$ or $b = w/4$ (the table is same for all the bitvectors). For example, as recommended in Section 4.1.1, we may choose $b = 15$, so as to store $2^b = 32{,}768$ words.

Example 12.6 *Figure 12.5 (left) shows the same bitvector of Figure 12.1, but now the leaves represent the bit arrays with the (c, o) format of Section 4.1.1, for $b = 4$. For example, the grayed leaf encodes 0000 1010 as two blocks, the first of class 0 (i.e., zero bits set) and the second of class 2 (i.e., 2 bits set). Since class 2 is enumerated from $o = 0$ to $o = 5$ as 0011, 0101, 0110, 1001, 1010, and 1100, the blocks are $(0, 0)$ and $(2, 4)$. Note that the tree structure is identical; only the physical storage of the leaves changes.*

If we now perform the insertion of Figure 12.2 in that leaf, its contents change to $(1, 1)(2, 1)(0, 0)$, which represents 0010 0101 0000 (we know from the leaf size that

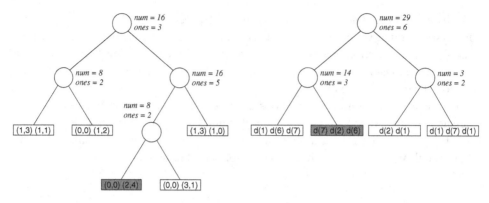

Figure 12.5. Two dynamic representations the same bitvector B of Figure 12.1. On the left, the pairs (c, o) of Section 4.1.1 for sparse bitvectors with $b = 4$. On the right, δ-codes (written as $d(i)$) for very sparse bitvectors.

only the first 9 bits are valid). Thus a single insertion may require rewriting the whole bit array in the leaf.

Very Sparse Bitvectors

When there are very few 1s, even the previous scheme may waste too much space. The entropy of a bitvector $B[1, n]$ with m 1s is $n\mathcal{H}_0(B) = m \log \frac{n}{m} + \mathcal{O}(m)$ (see the end of Section 2.3.1). If m is much smaller than n, the $\mathcal{O}(n/w)$ extra bits we spend may be much more than the entropy.

In this case we can represent the bit arrays of leaves by δ-coding the distance between consecutive 1s. A convenient invariant is now that the bit arrays of leaves contain $\Theta(w)$ 1s. The tree T is traversed in the same way, and the invariants on leaf sizes are maintained analogously as done with the basic format. Since every δ-code can be processed in constant time (see Section 2.7), we can handle leaves in $\mathcal{O}(w)$ time. We leave the details on how to process leaves for queries and updates as exercises to the reader; the code of **access**(B, i) is shown in Algorithm 12.7 as an example.

Example 12.7 *Figure 12.5 (right) shows the same bitvector of Figure 12.1, but now the leaves represent the bit arrays with the δ-codes of the distances between consecutive 1s (plus the distance from the beginning to the first 1). The bit sequence represented at each leaf always ends with a 1 (an extra 1 is appended at the end of B to avoid special cases). We use $d(i)$ to denote the δ-code of number i, which represents $0^{d(i)-1}$ 1. For example, the grayed leaf, containing $d(7)\,d(2)\,d(6)$, represents the bit array 000000101000001.*

*Note that the structure of the tree is different: we store one code per 1, and in this case we allow 2 to 3 codes per leaf. If we carry out **insert**$(B, 19, 1)$ as in Figure 12.2, then the codes in the leaf become $d(5)\,d(3)\,d(2)\,d(6)$ and the leaf overflows. Instead, if we did **insert**$(B, 19, 0)$, the codes would become $d(8)\,d(2)\,d(6)$ and their number stays the same.*

Algorithm 12.7: Answering access queries on a sparse dynamic bitvector. Children of internal nodes are pointed from fields *left* and *right*, and bit arrays of leaf nodes from field *L*. The bit array stores δ-codes.

---

1 **Proc access**(*B*, *i*)

    Input : Sparse dynamic bitvector *B* (seen as tree *T*) and position *i*.

    Output: Returns *B*[*i*].

2     $v \leftarrow T.root$

3   **while** *v* is *not a leaf* **do**

4   **if** $i \le v.num$ **then**

5             $v \leftarrow v.left$

6   **else**

7             $i \leftarrow i - v.num$

8             $v \leftarrow v.right$

9   **while** $i > 0$ **do**

10         $k \leftarrow$ decode next δ-encoded value

11         $i \leftarrow i - k$

12   **if** $i = 0$ **then return** 1

13   **else return** 0

With leaves holding $\Theta(w)$ 1s each, the tree is guaranteed to have $\mathcal{O}(m/w)$ nodes, and its space overhead is $\mathcal{O}(m)$ bits. The total space is then $m \log \frac{n}{m} + \mathcal{O}\left(m \log \log \frac{n}{m}\right) = n\mathcal{H}_0(B) + \mathcal{O}(n \log \mathcal{H}_0(B))$ bits (recall Sections 2.8 and 2.9), dominated by the space redundancy of the δ-codes. Note that the time to traverse the tree is $\mathcal{O}(\log m)$, so query and update times are dominated by the $\mathcal{O}(w)$ time spent on leaves, which is made up of fast cache-friendly accesses. Any other code from Section 2.7 can be used instead.

Note that the representation of Section 4.4 for very sparse bitvectors cannot be easily made dynamic, because the values of *m* (number of 1s) and *n* (bitvector length) change in each update, and that scheme uses $\log \frac{n}{m}$ to define the partition of the numbers into high and low parts.

12.2 Arrays and Partial Sums

In Chapter 3 we showed how to maintain an array $A[1, n]$ with cells of $\ell > 1$ bits using basically ℓn bits, while allowing constant time operations read(*A*, *i*). We also allowed modification of the content of cells in constant time, with operation write(*A*, *i*, *x*). The representation was obtained by writing the ℓ bits of each cell one after another in an array of computer words. It was not possible, however, to insert or delete cells in the array.

A simple extension of the bitvector representation of Section 12.1 enables inserting and deleting elements in the arrays and at the same time gives support for partial sums (Section 3.3). Let the leaves of *T* handle arrays of $\Theta((w/\ell)w)$ cells of ℓ bits. Then the extra space of the tree is $\mathcal{O}(n\ell/w) = o(n\ell)$ bits. Let the field $v.ones$ of internal nodes now store the sum of the cell values descending from the left child of v. Then the **access**, **rank**, and **select** algorithms for bitvectors become **read**, **sum**, and **search** algorithms for the array with partial sums. Only the leaves are handled differently.

On leaves, the operation **read** takes constant time, but **sum** and **search** require $\mathcal{O}((w/\ell)w)$ time to scan the array. If ℓ is significantly smaller than w, we may use techniques similar to popcounting (Section 4.2.1) to perform w/ℓ sums in a few operations and thus scan the array in $\mathcal{O}(w)$ time. For example, assume $w/\ell = 8$, and we have precomputed m1 $\leftarrow 0^\ell 1^\ell 0^\ell 1^\ell 0^\ell 1^\ell 0^\ell 1^\ell$, m2 $\leftarrow 0^{3\ell-2}1^{\ell+2}0^{3\ell-2}1^{\ell+2}$, and m3 $\leftarrow 0^{7\ell-3}1^{\ell+3}$. Then we can sum up the 8 consecutive cells of $1 = \ell > 1$ bits in a computer word L as follows, in C:

```c
v = (L & m1) + ((L >> 1) & m1);
v = (v + (v >> 2*1)) & m2;
return (v + (v >> 4*1)) & m3;
```

In fact, the number of operations grows as $\mathcal{O}(\log(w/\ell))$ with this technique, but this can be taken as a constant in practice (in theory, we can achieve constant time by using precomputed tables, but these are in most cases slower than a formula like the one above). Furthermore, modern processors have special instructions to add up a long sequence (128 or 256 bits) of ℓ-bit values, at least for some choices of ℓ.

Insertions and deletions of cells work essentially as for bitvectors. The main change is that, when inserting value x, we must set $v.ones \leftarrow v.ones + x$ every time we go to the left of v. Similarly, when we return from the deletion of a cell on the left child of v, which turned out to remove value x, we update $v.ones \leftarrow v.ones - x$.

Variable-Length Cells

In case of arrays with variable-length cells (Section 3.2), we can encode the values with, for example, δ-codes. The invariant, as with the very sparse bitvectors of Section 12.1.3, is that each leaf stores $\Theta(w)$ entries of A. The procedures are almost identical as for fixed cells, and the leaves can be scanned and updated by processing one δ-code at a time (this time, **read**(A, i) also needs to scan the leaf array). Then the operation times are $\mathcal{O}(w)$ and the extra space on top of the encoding is $\mathcal{O}(n)$ bits.

Example 12.8 *Figure 12.5 (right) can also be interpreted as the variable-length representation of array $A[1, 11] = \langle 0, 5, 6, 6, 1, 5, 1, 0, 0, 6, 0 \rangle$.*

Another approach would be, as in Section 4.5.1, to mark the sums of the array values in a sparse bitvector B. If we then use the dynamic very sparse bitvector representation of Section 12.1.3, what we obtain is precisely the sequence of δ-codes encoding the array values, as described in the previous paragraph. Thus both solutions boil down to the same in this case. A third solution, Elias-Fano codes (Section 3.4.3), becomes equivalent, in terms of time and space, to replacing δ-codes with γ-codes (Section 2.7).

12.3 Sequences

In Chapter 6 we covered static representations of sequences, which support the same access, rank, and select operations on bitvectors, now extended to a sequence $S[1, n]$ over an alphabet $[1, \sigma]$. From those representations, we focus on wavelet trees (Section 6.2) or wavelet matrices (Section 6.2.5), which build on bitvectors to obtain $\mathcal{O}(\log \sigma)$ time for the operations. There is no obvious way to make the representation based on permutations (Section 6.1) dynamic.

If we replace the bitvectors used in wavelet trees or matrices by their dynamic variant of Section 12.1, we automatically obtain a sequence representation where access, rank, and select queries are solved in $\mathcal{O}(w \log \sigma)$ time, and that uses $n \log \sigma + o(n \log \sigma)$ bits of space. If we use the compressed bitvectors of Section 12.1.3, the space becomes $n\mathcal{H}_0(S) + o(n \log \sigma)$ (recall Section 6.2.4). The other mechanism used in that section to obtain zero-order compression is Huffman-shaped wavelet trees. These do not carry over the dynamic scenario, since the Huffman shape may undergo significant changes (as well as the involved bitvectors) when frequencies are updated.

We will use the dynamic capabilities of the bitvectors to support insertions and deletions of symbols in S. We handle the following operations:

insert(S, i, c): inserts symbol c between $S[i - 1]$ and $S[i]$, for $1 \le i \le n + 1$.
delete(S, i): deletes $S[i]$, for $1 \le i \le n$.

To carry out insert(S, i, c) on a wavelet tree, we start with insert(B, i, x) on the root bitvector B, where $x = 0$ if $c \le \lceil \sigma/2 \rceil$ and $x = 1$ otherwise. Then we continue with $i \leftarrow \text{rank}_x(B, i)$, on the left child if $x = 0$ and on the right one if $x = 1$. Note that the computation of $\text{rank}_x(B, i)$ is carried out after we have inserted x in B. The successive values of x are obtained from c exactly as in static wavelet trees.

To implement delete(S, i) on a wavelet tree, we read $x \leftarrow \text{access}(B, i)$ and execute delete(B, i) on the root bitvector B. Now we compute $i \leftarrow \text{rank}_x(B, i - 1) + 1$ and continue recursively on the left child if $x = 0$ and on the right one if $x = 1$.

Algorithm 12.8 details the procedures. Some sequences of operations can be optimized into a single more general procedure, for example, an insert followed by a rank at the same position of $v.B$, or an access followed by a delete followed by a rank.

Example 12.9 *Figure 12.6 shows the changes that the bitvectors of a wavelet tree undergo upon symbol insertions and deletions. We start from the static wavelet tree of Figure 6.4, which represents the string $S =$ "to be or not to be, that is the question" (removing spaces and comma). We perform insert($S, 5, \text{t}$) (changing the first "be" to "bet") and then delete($S, 26$) (removing the last e).*

The grayed blocks show the bits that have been inserted in the bitvector upon the operation insert($S, 5, \text{t}$). For example, since $\text{t} = 11$ belongs to the second half of the alphabet $[1, \sigma] = [1, 12]$, we have $x = 1$ at the root. Thus we run insert($B, i, 1$) for $i = 5$ in the root bitvector. Now we update $i \leftarrow \text{rank}_1(B, 5) = 3$ and go to the right child of the root, which handles $S_{(7,12)}$. Since t belongs to the second half of $[7, 12]$, we set $x = 1$ again, run insert($B, 3, 1$) on this node, set $i \leftarrow \text{rank}_1(B, 3) = 2$, and move to the right child, the node handling $S_{(10,12)}$. Since t belongs to the first half of $[10, 12]$, we set $x = 0$, run insert($B, 2, 0$) on this node, set $i \leftarrow \text{rank}_0(B, 2) = 2$, and

---

Algorithm 12.8: Inserting and deleting symbols on a dynamic wavelet tree. The fields in the tree nodes are left child l, right child r, and dynamic bitvector B.

---

1 **Proc** insert(S, i, c)

> **Input** : Sequence S (seen as wavelet tree T), position i, and symbol c.
> **Output**: Inserts c at position i of S.

2    $v \leftarrow T.root$
3    $[a, b] \leftarrow [1, \sigma]$
4   **while** $v \neq$ null **do**
5   **if** $c \leq \lfloor (a + b)/2 \rfloor$ **then** $x \leftarrow 0$ **else** $x \leftarrow 1$
6   insert($v.B, i, x$)
7      $i \leftarrow$ rank$_x(v.B, i)$
8   **if** $x = 0$ **then**
9        $v \leftarrow v.l$
10        $b \leftarrow \lfloor (a + b)/2 \rfloor$
11   **else**
12        $v \leftarrow v.r$
13        $a \leftarrow \lfloor (a + b)/2 \rfloor + 1$

14 **Proc** delete(S, i)

> **Input** : Sequence S (seen as wavelet tree T) and position i.
> **Output**: Removes $S[i]$.

15    $v \leftarrow T.root$
16   **while** $v \neq$ null **do**
17      $x \leftarrow$ access($v.B, i$)
18   delete($v.B, i$)
19      $i \leftarrow$ rank$_x(v.B, i - 1) + 1$
20   **if** $x = 0$ **then** $v \leftarrow v.l$ **else** $v \leftarrow v.r$

---

move to the left child, which handles $S_{\langle 10,11 \rangle}$. *Finally, since* t *belongs to the second half of* [10, 11], *we run* insert($B, 2, 1$) *on this bitvector, and finish.*

The hatched blocks in the bitvectors indicate the positions that are going to be deleted to execute delete(S, i) *for* $i = 26$. *At the root, since* $x =$ access($B, 26$) $= 0$, *we run* delete($B, 26$), *compute* $i \leftarrow$ rank$_0(B, 25) + 1 = 11$, *and move to the left child of the root. The node handles* $S_{\langle 1,6 \rangle}$. *In this node we compute* $x =$ access($B, 11$) $= 0$, *so we run* delete($B, 11$), *compute* $i \leftarrow$ rank$_0(B, 10) + 1 = 7$, *and move to the left child. The new node handles* $S_{\langle 1,3 \rangle}$. *We compute* $x =$ access($B, 7$) $= 1$, *run* delete($B, 7$), *compute* $i \leftarrow$ rank$_1(B, 6) + 1 = 4$, *and move to the right child. Since this new node has no data, we finish.*

Updating a wavelet matrix is similar. To insert, we start performing insert(B_1, i, x), as done on the wavelet tree root. Then we continue with $i \leftarrow$ rank$_x(B_1, i)$, adding z_ℓ if $x = 1$. If $x = 0$, instead, we increase z_ℓ by 1. We then continue with the next level. To delete $S[i]$, we start with $x \leftarrow$ access(B_1, i) and run delete(B_1, i) as done

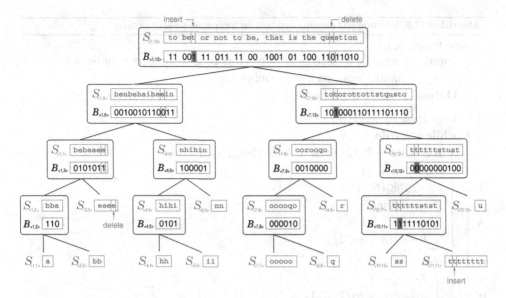

Figure 12.6. The wavelet tree of Figure 6.4 after running insert(S, 5, t), and marking the positions to carry out delete(S, 26). We show in gray the bits that were inserted in the first case, and hatch the bits that must be deleted in the second case. The involved symbols in the virtual strings S_v are enclosed in rectangles.

on the wavelet tree root. Then we update $i \leftarrow \mathsf{rank}_x(B_1, i-1) + 1$, adding z_ℓ if $x = 1$. Instead, if $x = 0$, we decrease z_ℓ by 1. We then continue with the next level.

Algorithm 12.9 gives the details. This time we use the alphabet limits $[a, b]$ to determine when to stop. Again, some optimizations are possible and left to the reader.

Just as for bitvectors, we can start with an empty sequence S or convert a static sequence into dynamic and vice versa. A dynamic representation of sequences and of wavelet trees yields dynamic variants of several other structures described from Chapter 6 onwards. The applications to graphs, grids, and texts will be described later in this chapter. Others, like binary relations, are left as an exercise to the reader.

12.4 Trees

Let us now consider the trees of Chapter 8. In addition to the query and navigation operations on static trees, we add two update operations:

insertchild(T, v, i, k): inserts a new ith child to node v, so that it becomes the parent of the current ith to $(i + k - 1)$th children, for $1 \le i \le \mathsf{children}(T, v) + 1$ and $0 \le k \le \mathsf{children}(T, v) + 1 - i$. It returns the identifier of the node inserted.
deletenode(T, v): deletes node v from T, so that its children now hang directly from the parent of v. Thus the root cannot be deleted (if it only has one child, the same effect can be obtained by deleting that child).

The operations are rather general. For example, insertchild($T, v, i, 0$) inserts a new leaf as the ith child of v. A leaf after all the current nodes is inserted with insertchild($T, v, \mathsf{children}(T, v) + 1, 0$). Instead, insertchild($T, v, i, 1$) inserts a new

---

Algorithm 12.9: Inserting and deleting symbols on a dynamic wavelet matrix.

---

1   **Proc** insert(S, i, c)

     Input : Sequence S (seen as the bitvectors B_ℓ and numbers z_ℓ of the wavelet matrix), position i, and symbol c.

     Output: Inserts c at position i of S.

2    $\ell \leftarrow 1; [a, b] \leftarrow [1, \sigma]$

3   **while** $a \neq b$ **do**

4   **if** $c \leq \lfloor (a + b)/2 \rfloor$ **then** $x \leftarrow 0$ **else** $x \leftarrow 1$

5   insert(B_ℓ, i, x)

6      $i \leftarrow \mathsf{rank}_x(B_\ell, i)$

7   **if** $x = 0$ **then**

8        $z_\ell \leftarrow z_\ell + 1$

9        $b \leftarrow \lfloor (a + b)/2 \rfloor$

10   **else**

11        $i \leftarrow z_\ell + i$

12        $a \leftarrow \lfloor (a + b)/2 \rfloor + 1$

13      $\ell \leftarrow \ell + 1$

14   **Proc** delete(S, i)

     Input : Sequence S (seen as the bitvectors B_ℓ and numbers z_ℓ of the wavelet matrix) and position i.

     Output: Removes $S[i]$.

15    $\ell \leftarrow 1; [a, b] \leftarrow [1, \sigma]$

16   **while** $a \neq b$ **do**

17      $x \leftarrow \mathsf{access}(B_\ell, i)$

18   delete(B_ℓ, i)

19      $i \leftarrow \mathsf{rank}_x(B_\ell, i - 1) + 1$

20   **if** $x = 0$ **then**

21        $z_\ell \leftarrow z_\ell - 1$

22        $b \leftarrow \lfloor (a + b)/2 \rfloor$

23   **else**

24        $i \leftarrow z_\ell + i$

25        $a \leftarrow \lfloor (a + b)/2 \rfloor + 1$

26      $\ell \leftarrow \ell + 1$

---

child that becomes the parent of a single node: the current ith child. Moreover, insertchild($T, v, 1, \mathsf{children}(T, v)$) inserts a new node between v and all its children (in particular, this can be used to indirectly insert a new root). Similarly, operation deletenode includes deleting leaves and unary nodes as special cases. Note that our dynamic trees cannot be empty, and therefore they can be created as one-node trees. Again, we will be able to easily convert between static and dynamic trees.

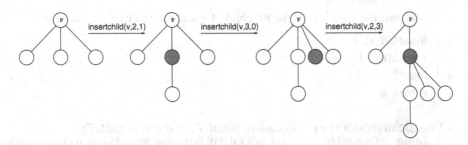

LOUDS 101110000   10111001000   1011110010000   101100111010000

BP   (()()())   (()(())())   (()(())()())   (()((())()()))

DFUDS (()((())))   (()((())()))   (()(((())())))   (()(())(((()())))

Figure 12.7. Insertion and deletion operations in a tree, with the corresponding representations at the top. We start with the leftmost tree and in each step insert the grayed node to obtain the next one. Similarly, we can start from the rightmost tree and interpret the previous tree as the result of deleting the grayed node.

Example 12.10 *Figure 12.7 shows the successive changes a tree undergoes as we apply various* **insertchild** *operations on it. The node that is added in each step is grayed. We can also read the sequence right to left, as the result of deleting the grayed node.*

By using the LOUDS representation on dynamic bitvectors, we will immediately obtain $O(w)$ time for all the query and navigation operations, while supporting insertion and deletion of leaves. The parenthesis-based representations BP and DFUDS will require more work to obtain dynamic range min-max trees (Section 7.1). In exchange, they will support more operations than LOUDS, including general **insertchild** and **deletenode** functionality, all in time $O(w)$.

We consider only insertion and deletion of individual nodes. Other operations that are easy on a pointer-based tree, like cutting out a whole subtree, or merging two trees into one, can also be carried out in polylogarithmic time, but are more complicated to implement. We provide some pointers at the end of the chapter.

A general note about mixing navigation and updates on trees is that updates change the positions of nodes in the bitvector or parentheses sequence, and we use those positions as node identifiers. If we are navigating the tree at the same time we are inserting nodes, we must be careful in adjusting the position of the current node upon insertions and deletions in the representation of the tree.

12.4.1 LOUDS Representation

This representation (Section 8.1) builds on **rank** and **select** operations on a single bitvector. Therefore, all the operations described for the static structure carry over a dynamic representation with an $O(w)$ time penalty factor, by using the plain bitvectors of Section 12.1. The tree can be initialized with one node, that is, with the bitvector **100** (recall that the LOUDS sequence includes a spurious **10** at the beginning).

Algorithm 12.10: Inserting and deleting leaves in a LOUDS representation.

---

1 **Proc** insertchild(T, v, i) — *assuming $i \leq$ children(T, v) $+ 1$*

    Input : Ordinal tree T (seen as LOUDS bitvector B), node v (a position in B)
           and index i.

    Output: Inserts a leaf as the ith child of v and returns its node identifier.

2   insert($B, v, 1$)

3     $u \leftarrow$ child(T, v, i)

4   insert($B, u, 0$)

5   **return** u

6 **Proc** deletenode(T, v) — *assuming* isleaf(T, v) *and* $v \neq$ root(T)

    Input : Ordinal tree T (seen as LOUDS bitvector B) and node v (a position in
           B).

    Output: Deletes leaf v.

7     $u \leftarrow$ select$_1$(B, rank$_0$($B, v - 1$))

8   delete(B, v)

9   delete(B, u)

Let us consider how to support updates. To execute insertchild($T, v, i, 0$) we must increase by 1 the arity of node v (by inserting a 1 at v) and then add a leaf node (a 0) at the corresponding position. This position is that of the current ith child of v. To delete a leaf v, the operation is the reverse: we compute its parent $u \leftarrow$ parent(T, v), and then delete $B[v]$ and $B[u]$ (in that order). Algorithm 12.10 shows the pseudocode, where insertchild($T, v, i, 0$) is called simply insertchild(T, v, i). Note that insertion works correctly even if $i =$ children(T, v) $+ 1$, and that in line 7 we have omitted the last step, involving pred$_0$, of the LOUDS parent formula, as it is unnecessary.

Operation insertchild(T, v, i, k) with $k \geq 1$, as well as the deletion of internal nodes, is not efficiently supported in the LOUDS representation, because those operations change the level (and thus the position in the bit array) of a potentially large number of nodes.

Example 12.11 *Consider the second tree of Figure 12.7. Its LOUDS representation is $B = 10111001000$, and $v =$ root() $= 3$. Then* insertchild($T, v, 3, 0$) = insertchild($T, 3, 3$) *inserts a 1 at $B[3]$, leaving it as $B = 101111001000$, and then inserts a 0 at $B[$child($T, v, 3$)$] = B[11]$, leaving $B = 10\underline{1}1110010\underline{0}00$. This is the LOUDS representation of the third tree of Figure 12.7.*

Consider now deleting the inserted leaf, $v = 11$. We compute $u \leftarrow$ parent(v) $= 3$. Now we execute delete($B, 11$), *leaving $B = 101111001000$, and finally* delete($B, 3$), *which leaves $B = 10111001000$, the LOUDS representation of the second tree of Figure 12.7. Instead of parent(v) $= 3$, line 7 of Algorithm 12.10 computes $u = 5$, which also leads us to delete a 1 from the description of parent(v) and obtains the same effect.*

Algorithm 12.11: Inserting and deleting leaves in a LOUDS cardinal tree.

---

1 **Proc** insertchild(T, v, l) — *assuming* **not** childrenlabeled(T, v, l)
　　Input : Cardinal tree T (seen as LOUDS bitvector B), node v, and label l.
　　Output: Inserts a leaf as the child labeled l of v, and returns its identifier.

2　　bitset($B, \sigma(v - 1) + l$)
3　　$u \leftarrow$ labeledchild(T, v, l)
4　　insert($B, \sigma(u - 1) + 1, 0^\sigma$)
5　　**return** u

6 **Proc** deletenode(T, v) — *assuming* isleaf(T, v) *and* $v \neq$ root(T)
　　Input : Cardinal tree T (seen as LOUDS bitvector B) and node v.
　　Output: Deletes leaf v.

7　　$p \leftarrow$ select$_1(B, v - 1)$
8　　delete$_\sigma(B, \sigma(v - 1) + 1)$
9　　bitclear(B, p)

Binary and Cardinal Trees

The LOUDS-based representation of binary and cardinal trees (Section 8.1.1) also builds on rank and select operations on bitvectors, and therefore can operate on dynamic bitvectors. Our compressed dynamic bitvectors can be used to reduce the size of cardinal trees of high arity. In the sequel we will treat binary trees as a particular case of cardinal trees, with arity $\sigma = 2$.

It is convenient to define operation insertchild(T, v, l), which inserts a leaf as the child of v labeled l, assuming that currently v has no such child. To implement insertchild(T, v, l) we use the extended operations defined at the end of Section 12.1.2: bitset($B, \sigma(v - 1) + l$) and then insert($B, \sigma(u - 1) + 1, 0^\sigma$), where $u =$ labeledchild(T, v, l). The reverse operation, to delete a leaf v, can be implemented by computing $u \leftarrow$ parent(T, v) and $l \leftarrow$ childlabel(T, v), and then executing delete$_\sigma(B, \sigma(v - 1) + 1)$ and bitclear($B, \sigma(u - 1) + l$).

Algorithm 12.11 gives the pseudocode. Line 7 simulates the parent and childlabel combination more efficiently. An initial tree with one node is created as bitvector 0^σ.

Example 12.12 *Figure 12.8 shows how the insertion of a node (grayed) in the binary tree ($\sigma = 2$) of Figure 8.3 is reflected on the tree representation (the top becomes the bottom bitvector). In turn, the deletion of the grayed node converts the bitvector on the bottom into the one on the top.*

The operation is insertchild($3, 1$). *We start setting $B[2(3 - 1) + 1] = B[5]$ to 1, indicating that this child now exists (the change is hatched in the bottom bitvector). We now insert the $\sigma = 2$ empty children of the new node, 00, at the position where the first ($l = 1$) child of $v = 3$ should be, $u \leftarrow$ labeledchild($3, 1$) $= 6$. We do insert($B, 2(6 - 1) + 1, 00$) $=$ insert($B, 11, 00$) and return the new node, 6. The result is the bitvector on the bottom.*

The reverse operation on this new tree, deletenode(v) *for $v = 6$, proceeds as follows. It finds the parent of v, $u \leftarrow$ parent(6) $= 3$, and the label by which v*

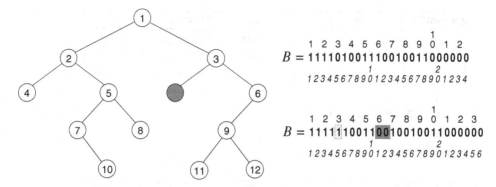

Figure 12.8. Insertion on a LOUDS-based binary tree. We insert the grayed node, which converts the bitvector B on top into that on the bottom. The corresponding inserted bits are those grayed, whereas the hatched bit is in the parent, which must now indicate that it has the grayed child. The deletion of the grayed node, in turn, converts the second bitvector into the first.

descends from u, $l \leftarrow$ childlabel$(6) = 1$. *Now it removes the description of the leaf* v, delete$_2(B, 2(6-1)+1) =$ delete$_2(B, 11)$, *and marks that the child labeled* l *of* u *does not exist anymore with* bitclear$(B, 2(3-1)+1) =$ bitclear$(B, 5)$. *The result is again the bitvector on the top.*

The operations therefore take $\mathcal{O}(w)$ time if $\sigma = \mathcal{O}(w^2)$. For larger σ, not only do the operations take more time, but also the space overhead of a plain representation of B makes the cardinal tree representation unattractive. In this case, a good alternative is to use a very sparse bitvector representation for B (Section 12.1.3). Then operation insert$(B, i, 0^\sigma)$ implies only finding the run $0^c 1$ where $B[i]$ belongs (as in Algorithm 12.7). This run is represented by the δ-code of c, which must then be replaced by the δ-code of $c + \sigma$. This can be done in $\mathcal{O}(w)$ time and does not even require tree rearrangements, because the number of 1s in the leaf does not change. To delete a leaf, similarly, we need to find the appropriate δ-code and decrease it by σ.

12.4.2 BP Representation

In a BP representation $B[1, 2n]$ (Section 8.2), the general node insertion operation insertchild(T, v, i, k) can be carried out by just adding a pair of parentheses at the right positions, say, opening at p and closing at q. Recall that opening parentheses are written as bits 1 and closing ones as 0s. This time, the navigation operations require a dynamic implementation of the range min-max trees of Section 7.1. We defer this to Section 12.4.4; for now we use close, child, and all the other navigation operations on the tree.

The opening parenthesis must be placed preceding the ith child, $p \leftarrow$ child(T, v, i). However, if $i =$ children$(T, v) + 1$ (to insert a child after the last current one), then p must be at the closing parenthesis of v, $p \leftarrow$ close(B, v). The position of q, similarly, must be that of the $(i + k)$th child of T, $q \leftarrow$ child$(T, v, i + k)$, but again, if $i + k =$ children$(T, v) + 1$, we must rather use $q \leftarrow$ close(B, v). Now we insert the pair in the right order: insert$(B, q, 0)$ and then insert$(B, p, 1)$. To run deletenode(T, v), we

---

Algorithm 12.12: Inserting and deleting nodes in a BP representation.

---

1 **Proc** insertchild(T, v, i, k) — *assuming* $i + k \leq$ children$(T, v) + 1$
   Input : Ordinal tree T (seen as BP bitvector B), node v (a position in B), and
            indexes i and k.
   Output: Inserts an ith child of v containing its ith to $(i + k - 1)$th current
            children, and returns its node identifier.
2   **if** $i \leq$ children(T, v) **then** $p \leftarrow$ child(T, v, i)
3   **else** $p \leftarrow$ close(B, v)
4   **if** $i + k \leq$ children(T, v) **then** $q \leftarrow$ child$(T, v, i + k)$
5   **else** $q \leftarrow$ close(B, v)
6   insert$(B, q, 0)$
7   insert$(B, p, 1)$
8   **return** p

9 **Proc** deletenode(T, v) — *assuming* $v \neq$ root(T)
   Input : Ordinal tree T (seen as BP bitvector B) and node v (a position in B).
   Output: Deletes node v.
10   delete$(B,$ close$(B, v))$
11   delete(B, v)

---

simply carry out delete$(B,$ close$(B, v))$ and then delete(B, v). A new tree with one node is created as the sequence ' $()$ '. Algorithm 12.12 gives the pseudocode.

Example 12.13 *The BP representation of the leftmost tree of Figure 12.7 is* $(()()())$, *and v is 1, the root. To execute* insertchild$(v, 2, 1)$, *which yields the second tree, we compute the positions of the opening and closing parentheses as $p \leftarrow$* child$(v, 2) = 4$ *and $q \leftarrow$* child$(v, 2 + 1) = 6$. *Now we perform* insert$(B, 6, 0)$ *and* insert$(B, 4, 1)$ *and obtain the sequence* $(()\underline{(()}())$, *which indeed represents the second subtree.*

Let us now perform insertchild$(v, 3, 0)$ *on the second subtree, to illustrate the case of a leaf insertion. This time we compute $p \leftarrow$* child$(v, 3) = 8$ *and also $q \leftarrow$* child$(v, 3 + 0) = 8$. *The insertions are both carried out at $B[8]$:* insert$(B, 8, 0)$ *and then* insert$(B, 8, 1)$. *The result,* $(()(())\underline{()}())$, *represents the third subtree.*

Finally, let us perform insertchild$(v, 2, 3)$ *on the third tree. We compute $p \leftarrow$* child$(v, 2) = 4$. *This time, since $2 + 3 = 5 > 4 =$* children(v), *we compute q in the other way: $q \leftarrow$* close$(B, v) = 12$. *We then carry out* insert$(B, 12, 0)$ *followed by* insert$(B, 4, 1)$. *The resulting sequence,* $(()\underline{((())()()})$, *represents the last subtree. We return the position $p = 4$ of the node inserted.*

As an example of a deletion, let us undo the last insertion: deletenode(4). *We simply run* delete$(B,$ close$(B, 4)) =$ delete$(B, 13)$ *and then* delete$(B, 4)$, *obtaining again the third tree.*

Binary Trees

The BP-based representation of binary trees seen in Section 8.2.1 can also be used in the dynamic scenario. A binary tree with only a root can be created as the string $(())$.

The update operations on the general tree can then be used to implement insertion and deletion of nodes in the binary tree. For example, if v has no left child, we can insert one with insert(B, $v + 1$, 0) followed by insert(B, $v + 1$, 1). But if v already has a left child u, these operations insert a new left child of v whose right child is u. To insert a new left child of v whose left child is u, instead, we do insert(B, close(B, v), 0) and then insert(B, $v + 1$, 1).

To insert a right child of v, we do $p \leftarrow$ close(B, v) and then insert(B, $p + 1$, 0) followed by insert(B, $p + 1$, 1). If v already had a right child u, this inserts a new right child whose right child is u. To insert a new right child of v whose left child is u, instead, we do insert(B, close(B, enclose(B, v)), 0) and then insert(B, $p + 1$, 1).

Deleting the parentheses at close(B, v) and v correctly removes leaves and unary nodes. The effect on a node with two children is not so interesting.

Example 12.14 *The BP-based representation of the binary tree of Figure 12.8 (without the gray node) is* ((((())(()()))())()((())())), *recall Figure 8.7. To insert the gray leaf as the left child of the node labeled 3 in Figure 12.8 (corresponding to the node labeled 8 in Figure 8.7, that is, the opening parenthesis at position $v = 16$ in the BP sequence), we do* insert(17, 0) *and then* insert(17, 1)*, obtaining* ((((())(()()))(_()_)((())())). *Now, to insert a right child to the node labeled 6 (corresponding to the node labeled 12 in Figure 8.7, that is, the position $v = 20$ in the new BP bitvector), we find $p \leftarrow$ close(20) = 27 and then do* insert(28, 0) *and* insert(28, 1)*, obtaining* ((((())(()()))()((())()_()_)).

12.4.3 DFUDS Representation

Updating a DFUDS representation (Section 8.3) is still reasonably simple, although not as much as BP. For operation insertchild(T, v, i, k), we first find the position where the child node must be inserted. As for BP, this is $p \leftarrow$ child(T, v, i) if $i \leq$ children(T, v). If $i =$ children(T, v) $+ 1$, instead, we must insert the node after the end of the subtree of v, $p \leftarrow$ fwdsearch(B, $v - 1$, -1) $+ 1$. Once p is found, we carry out insert(B, p, $1^k 0$) (which can be done in $\mathcal{O}(w)$ time if $k = \mathcal{O}(w^2)$, as we have seen) to signal that the next k siblings are now children of the inserted node p. Finally, we update the number of children of v: If $k = 0$ it gains a child, so we perform insert(B, v, 1), and if $k > 1$ it loses $k - 1$ children, so we perform delete$_{k-1}$(B, v).

To implement deletenode(T, v), we find the parent of v, $u \leftarrow$ parent(T, v), and the number of children of v, $k \leftarrow$ children(T, v). We now remove the representation of v, delete$_{k+1}$(B, v) and update the arity of the parent: We run delete(B, u) if $k = 0$ and insert(B, u, 1^{k-1}) if $k > 1$.

Algorithm 12.13 gives the pseudocode. Since the DFUDS sequence is always preceded by (( ), we create a tree with one node as the sequence (( )). A way to ensure $\mathcal{O}(w)$ time for all the operations is to encode every run of (one or more) opening or closing parentheses as a δ-code. This, however, increases the space to $\mathcal{O}(n)$ bits.

Example 12.15 *Let us now consider the DFUDS representation of the leftmost tree of Figure 12.7,* (()((()))), *and $v = 4$ is the root. Upon operation* insertchild(v, 2, 1)*, we compute $p \leftarrow$ child(v, 2) = 9. Now we insert '()' at B[9], to obtain* (()((())_()_)). *Since $k = 1$, this is the final representation of the second tree in the figure.*

Algorithm 12.13: Inserting and deleting nodes in a DFUDS representation.

---

1 **Proc** insertchild(T, v, i, k) — *assuming* $i + k \leq$ children(T, v) + 1

    Input : Ordinal tree T (seen as DFUDS bitvector B), node v (a position in B),
            and indexes i and k.

    Output: Inserts an ith child of v containing its ith to $(i + k - 1)$th children,
            and returns its node identifier.

2   **if** $i \leq$ children(T, v) **then** $p \leftarrow$ child(T, v, i)
3   **else** $p \leftarrow$ fwdsearch($B, v - 1, -1$) + 1
4   insert($B, p, 1^k 0$)
5   **if** $k = 0$ **then** insert($B, v, 1$)
6   **else if** $k > 1$ **then** delete$_{k-1}$(B, v)
7   **return** $p - k + 1$

8 **Proc** deletenode(T, v) — *assuming* $v \neq$ root(T)

    Input : Ordinal tree T (seen as DFUDS bitvector B) and node v (a position in
            B).

    Output: Deletes node v.

9     $u \leftarrow$ open($B, v - 1$)
10    $k \leftarrow$ children(T, v)
11   delete$_{k+1}$(B, v)
12   **if** $k = 0$ **then** delete(B, u)
13   **else if** $k > 1$ **then** insert($B, u, 1^{k-1}$)

Let us now execute insertchild($v, 4, 0$) *on the second subtree (the result will be the same as the* insertchild($v, 3, 0$) *operation that the figure illustrates). Since* $4 > 3 =$ children(v), *we compute* $p \leftarrow$ fwdsearch($B, v - 1, -1$) + 1 = 13. *Now we insert* $0 = $ ')' *at* $B[13]$. *Since* $k = 0$, *node* v *has gained a child, so we also run* insert($B, 4, 1$). *The result is* (()$\underline{(((()) ()))}$), *which represents the third tree.*

Finally, we run insertchild($v, 2, 3$) *on the third tree. We compute* $p \leftarrow$ child($v, 2$) = 10. *Then we carry out* insert($B, 10, 1110$), *and, since* $k > 1$, *we also run* delete$_{3-1}$(B, v), *because* v *has lost 2 children. The result,* (()$\underline{\_\_}$(())$\underline{((()())))}$, *represents the last subtree. We return the position* $p - k + 1 = 8$ *of the node inserted.*

Let us undo the last insertion with deletenode(v), *for* $v = 8$. *We find the parent of* v, $u \leftarrow$ parent(v) = 4 *and the number of children of* v, $k \leftarrow$ children(v) = 3. *Now we run* delete$_{3+1}$(B, v), *which removes the description of the node. Its children now automatically hang from its parent* u, *as soon as we update its number of children with* insert($B, u, 1^{3-1}$). *The result is again the DFUDS representation of the third tree.*

Cardinal Trees. Just as in Section 8.3.1, we can combine a DFUDS representation T with a bitvector $S[1, \sigma n]$ of preorder-aligned chunks of σ bits, in order to add DFUDS functionality to a cardinal tree representation. Bitvector S is initialized as 0^σ. To add a leaf child of v by label l (assuming it does not exist), we first find its preorder $p \leftarrow$ preorder(T, v) and the position where to insert the child among its siblings,

$r \leftarrow \mathsf{rank}_1(S, \sigma(p-1)+l) - \mathsf{rank}_1(S, \sigma(p-1))$. Now we insert the leaf in DFUDS with $u \leftarrow \mathsf{insertchild}(T, v, r+1, 0)$, marking that the label is l with $\mathsf{bitset}(S, \sigma(p-1)+l)$. Next we create the chunk for the created node u, with $q \leftarrow \mathsf{preorder}(T, u)$ and $\mathsf{insert}(S, \sigma(q-1)+1, 0^\sigma)$. We leave the deletion of a leaf as an exercise to the reader.

12.4.4 Dynamic Range Min-Max Trees

In Section 7.1 we introduced range min-max trees (rmM-trees) as a tool to support all the BP and DFUDS operations in $\mathcal{O}(\log n)$ time. Now we show how those complexities translate into the dynamic scenario.

The key idea is to replace the static complete binary tree by a dynamic balanced tree, such as an AVL or a Red-Black tree. Similarly to the structure for dynamic bitvectors (Section 12.1), each leaf of this tree will handle an array of $\Theta(w^2)$ parentheses (that is, bits). The nodes of the balanced tree (including leaves) will maintain the same fields e, m, M, and n of the static rmM-tree, and the internal ones will retain the fields *num* and *ones* used to provide rank and select on dynamic bitvectors (note that $v.e$, $v.m$, $v.M$, and $v.n$ refer to the node v itself, whereas $v.num$ and $v.ones$ still refer to the left child of v). The recursive formulas given for the rmM-tree construction (Section 7.1.1) can be used to recompute the fields of a node when a parenthesis is inserted or deleted at a descendant leaf, and upon tree rotations. Operations insert and delete for parentheses are then carried out exactly in the same way as dynamic bitvectors, but also taking care of recomputing the rmM-tree fields.

Algorithm 12.14 shows how the insertion method of Algorithm 12.3 is modified. Note that in line 26 we use $(w^2 + v_l.e)/2$ instead of computing $popcount(v_l.L[1, w^2])$, according to the formula for excess given at the beginning of Chapter 7. The extra field l, used to provide rank_{10} and select_{10} support (Section 7.1.4), can be maintained with a little more care than for *ones*; we leave it as an exercise to the reader.

The insertion and deletion time is $\mathcal{O}(w)$ plus the time spent for recomputing the fields e, m, M, and n on the leaves. The leaf can be sequentially scanned using the table C defined in the static version (see, for example, Algorithm 7.4). This time it is convenient to define C as processing chunks of $\Theta(w)$ parentheses, just as discussed for the tables of Section 12.1.3. If we do so, the scanning of a leaf also takes time $\mathcal{O}(w)$.

The navigation operations on the leaf arrays are also carried out using table C, in $\mathcal{O}(w)$ time. On the other hand, the operations on the tree require first descending using the field *num* to find the leaf where the operation must start (this was done directly in the static trees because blocks were of fixed size). Once the block has been scanned, we go upwards on the tree (by returning from the recursion that led us to the leaf), and at some point we go downwards again, to finally complete the operation by scanning another leaf. There are two downward scans, thus only $\mathcal{O}(\log n)$ tree nodes are processed.

Algorithms 12.15 and 12.16 give, as examples, the algorithms to compute fwdsearch and the minimum excess in a range. In fwdsearch, the recursive procedure considers various cases: In line 5, if the query starts from position 0, then we skip the whole subtree if field $v.m$ shows that the subtree does not contain the answer (this is essential to ensure that only two traversals are carried out on the tree). In line 7, if v is a leaf, the process is solved by scanning, exactly as in the static case. In line 9, if i starts on the right child of v, then the query is redirected there. In line 12, we

---

Algorithm 12.14: Inserting parentheses on a dynamic rmM-tree.

1 **Proc** insert(B, i, b)

    Input   : Dynamic parentheses sequence $B[1, n]$ (seen as rmM-tree R),
                position i, and parenthesis (bit) b.

    Output: Inserts b at position i of B.

2     $R.root \leftarrow insert(R.root, i, b, n)$

3 **Proc** *insert*(v, i, b, ℓ)

    Input   : Node v of the rmM-tree, covering ℓ leaves, position i, and
                parenthesis (bit) b.

    Output: Inserts b at the ith position below v and returns node v.

4   **if** *v is not a leaf* **then**

5   **if** $i \le v.num$ **then**

6             $v.num \leftarrow v.num + 1$

7   **if** $b = 1$ **then** $v.ones \leftarrow v.ones + 1$

8             $v.left \leftarrow insert(v.left, i, b, v.num)$

9   **else**

10            $v.right \leftarrow insert(v.right, i - v.num, b, \ell - v.num)$

11         $v.e \leftarrow v.left.e + v.right.e$

12         $v.m \leftarrow \min(v.left.m, v.left.e + v.right.m)$

13         $v.M \leftarrow \max(v.left.M, v.left.e + v.right.M)$

14   **if** $v.left.m < v.left.e + v.right.m$ **then** $v.n \leftarrow v.left.n$

15   **else if** $v.left.m > v.left.e + v.right.m$ **then** $v.n \leftarrow v.right.n$

16   **else** $v.n \leftarrow v.left.n + v.right.n$

17   **else**

18   Reallocate $v.L$ (if necessary) to size $\ell + 1$

19   Insert bit b at $v.L[i]$, copying memory word-wise

20   Recompute $v.e$, $v.m$, $v.M$, and $v.n$ sequentially on $v.L$

21   **if** $\ell + 1 = 2w^2$ **then** (leaf overflow)

22   Split $v.L$ into two halves, at new leaves v_l and v_r

23   Compute fields e, m, M, and n, for v_l and v_r, sequentially

24   Convert v into an internal node

25             $v.left \leftarrow v_l$; $v.right \leftarrow v_r$

26             $v.num \leftarrow w^2$; $v.ones \leftarrow (w^2 + v_l.e)/2$

27   **if** *v needs a rotation* **then**

28   Carry out rotation (modifying v and recomputing e, m, M, n)

29   **return** v

---

enter the left child, and if the answer is found inside, we return it. Finally, in line 15, we enter the right child after failing to find the answer in the left child. The logic of Algorithm 12.16 is simpler; the only delicate part is line 3, which ensures that whole subtrees are handled in constant time.

Algorithm 12.15: Computing fwdsearch(i, d) on a dynamic rmM-tree.

---

1 **Proc** fwdsearch(i, d)

    Input : Parentheses sequence of length n seen as a dynamic rmM-tree R, and parameters $i \geq 0$ and $d < 0$.

    Output: Returns fwdsearch(i, d).

2     $\langle d, j \rangle \leftarrow fwdsearch(R.root, i, d, n)$

3   **return** j

4 **Proc** $fwdsearch(v, i, d, \ell)$

    Input : Node v of the rmM-tree representing ℓ parentheses, a position $i \geq 0$ below v, and $d < 0$.

    Output: Returns $\langle d', j \rangle$. If $d' = d$, $j > i$ is the leftmost index below v with excess(j) = excess(i) + d. Otherwise d' is the excess from $i + 1$ to the end of v and j is the first position after v.

5   **if** $i = 0$ **and** $v.m > d$ **then**

6   **return** $\langle v.e, \ell + 1 \rangle$

7   **if** v *is a leaf* **then**

8   **return** $fwdblock(v.L[1, \ell], i, d)$ (Algorithm 7.4)

9   **if** $i \geq v.num$ **then**

10         $\langle d', j \rangle \leftarrow fwdsearch(v.right, i - v.num, d, \ell - v.num)$

11   **return** $\langle d', j + v.num \rangle$

12     $\langle d', j \rangle \leftarrow fwdsearch(v.left, i, d, v.num)$

13   **if** $d' = d$ **then**

14   **return** $\langle d, j \rangle$

15     $\langle d'', j \rangle \leftarrow fwdsearch(v.right, 0, d - d', \ell - v.num)$

16   **return** $\langle d' + d'', j + v.num \rangle$

Although we are storing the field e for simplicity, this is not necessary. Considering again the formula for the excess in the beginning of Chapter 7, we could replace $v.left.e$ by $2 \cdot v.ones - v.num$ in Algorithm 12.16. Instead, for Algorithm 12.15, which uses $v.e$, we should use a mechanism like the parameter ℓ, this time to maintain the total number of 1s below node v in a variable o. This is initially $n/2$, it becomes $v.ones$ on $v.left$ and $o - v.ones$ on $v.right$. Then we know that $v.e = 2 \cdot o - \ell$.

In total, the extra space is $\mathcal{O}(n/w)$ bits, and we carry out all the operations in time $\mathcal{O}(w)$. The only exception is the insertion or deletion of k parentheses in the DFUDS representation, which takes $\mathcal{O}(w + k/w)$ time.

Faster Navigation

When we carry out a tree traversal where the node v of each operation is the result of the previous one (say, consecutive **parent** operations from a leaf to the root), our interface requires finding the node again. This is not a problem in the static representation, because we arrive at the node in constant time; therefore we spend time $\mathcal{O}\big(\log |v' - v|\big)$

Algorithm 12.16: Computing the minimum excess in a dynamic rmM-tree.

Input : Parentheses sequence $B[1, n]$, seen as a dynamic rmM-tree R, and
parameters $1 \leq i \leq j \leq n$.
Output: Computes m, the minimum local excess in $B[i, j]$.

1   $m \leftarrow minexcess(R.root, i, j, n)$

2 **Proc** $minexcess(v, i, j, \ell)$
   Input : Node v of the rmM-tree representing a part $B[1, \ell]$ of the parentheses
   sequence, and positions $i \leq j$ below v.
   Output: Returns the minimum excess in $B[i, j]$.

3   **if** $i = 1$ **and** $j = \ell$ **then**
4    $\quad$ **return** $v.m$
5   **if** v *is a leaf* **then**
6    $\quad \langle m, d \rangle \leftarrow minblock(v.L[1, \ell], i, j)$ (Algorithm 7.7)
7    $\quad$ **return** m
8   **if** $j \leq v.num$ **then**
9    $\quad$ **return** $minexcess(v.left, i, j, v.num)$
10   **if** $i > v.num$ **then**
11   $\quad$ **return** $v.left.e + minexcess(v.right, i - v.num, j - v.num, \ell - v.num)$
12   $ml \leftarrow minexcess(v.left, i, v.num, v.num)$
13   $mr \leftarrow v.left.e + minexcess(v.right, 1, j - v.num, \ell - v.num)$
14   **return** $\min(ml, mr)$

---

to navigate from node v to v' (excluding the $\mathcal{O}(w)$ cost inside the leaves, which is cache-friendly). In the dynamic version, we spend anyway $\mathcal{O}(\log n)$ time to find v. For example, a depth-first traversal of the whole static tree requires $\mathcal{O}(n)$ time, whereas in the dynamic version it takes $\mathcal{O}(n \log n)$.

A way to get around this problem is to remember the leaf and offset corresponding to the resulting node; then we can start the next operation directly from there. If we provide T with parent pointers, we can also navigate from v to v' in time $\mathcal{O}(\log |v' - v|)$. The algorithms then become more similar to those of the static version. These we leave as an exercise to the reader.

12.4.5 Labeled Trees

The dynamic tree representations we described can be combined with a dynamic sequence representation from Section 12.3 to automatically obtain dynamic labeled trees; see Section 8.4. Then the queries that involve operating the sequence, in Algorithm 8.16, take time $\mathcal{O}(w \log \sigma)$. Update times are also multiplied by $\mathcal{O}(\log \sigma)$.

A generally better alternative is to represent the sequence as a dynamic array (Section 12.2), supporting only **insert**, **delete**, and **access**, in $\mathcal{O}(w)$ time (but accessing $\mathcal{O}(w^2 / \log \sigma)$ consecutive symbols within the same time; recall Section 12.1.1).

Using DFUDS, the operations in Algorithm 8.16 on a node with c children can then be carried out in time $\mathcal{O}(w + c \log \sigma / w^2)$, which is convenient in most cases (roughly, if $c < w^3$). Update times also improve to $\mathcal{O}(w)$ per change to the bitvector or parentheses sequence representing the tree topology.

12.5 Graphs and Grids

With the dynamic data structures we defined, we can immediately derive dynamic representations of graphs (Chapter 9) and grids (Chapter 10). The grid space will be fixed to $c \times r$, and we will perform range counting and reporting queries while also inserting and deleting points in the grid. The update operations are as follows:

insertpoint(G, x, y): inserts a new point at (x, y), for $1 \leq x \leq c$ and $1 \leq y \leq r$.
deletepoint(G, x, y): deletes a point (x, y), for $1 \leq x \leq c$ and $1 \leq y \leq r$.

We describe dynamic grids based on wavelet matrices and on k^2-trees. Note that the structures will handle simple points without weights. There is no obvious way to efficiently extend the techniques to handle weighted points to the dynamic case.

In terms of data structures, the sequence-based representation of Section 9.1.2 for general graphs can be regarded as a particular case of the grid representation based on wavelet matrices (Section 10.1). We used for graphs the faster sequence representation of Section 6.1, but it has no known efficient dynamic version. Similarly, the representation of Section 9.2 for clustered graphs builds on k^2-trees, and its queries are particular cases of those used for grids. Therefore, the results on the rest of this section apply to those graph representations as well. Note that inserting and deleting points in grids is equivalent to inserting and deleting edges in graphs, whereas the graph nodes remain fixed. On the other hand, no compact dynamic representation of planar graphs has been reported in the literature.

12.5.1 Dynamic Wavelet Matrices

In Section 12.3 we showed how to maintain dynamic wavelet matrices. We will use them just as in the static scenario of Section 10.1, but this time we will allow having more than one point with the same coordinates. With respect to the static scenario, we will have a time penalty factor of essentially $\mathcal{O}(w)$ for all the operations. This is not far from known lower bounds.

As in the static case, we have a bitvector $B[1, c + n] = 1\,0^{n_1} 1\,0^{n_2} \ldots 1\,0^{n_c}$ to indicate that there are n_i points with x-coordinate equal to i. This bitvector maps the x-coordinates to the interval $[1, n]$, and then a string $S[1, n]$ over alphabet $[1, r]$ represents the y-coordinates of the n points. Queries and results are mapped from the original $c \times r$ to the represented $n \times r$ grid and back, using **select** operations on B. By representing B as a dynamic bitvector (Section 12.1) and S as a wavelet matrix (Section 12.3), we use $c + n \log r + o(c + n \log r)$ bits and can carry out the counting method of Algorithm 10.1 in time $\mathcal{O}(w \log r)$, as well as reporting as in Algorithm 10.2 in time $\mathcal{O}(w \log r)$ per reported point. We can also find the leftmost point in a range (Algorithm 10.3) or the highest point in a range (Algorithm 10.4), also within time $\mathcal{O}(w \log r)$.

Algorithm 12.17: Inserting and deleting grid points using a wavelet matrix.

1 **Proc** insertpoint(G, x, y)
    Input : Grid G (seen as bitvector B and sequence S) and point (x, y).
    Output: Inserts (x, y) in G.
2     $p \leftarrow$ select$_1(B, x)$
3   insert($B, p + 1, 0$)
4   insert($S, p - x + 1, y$)

5 **Proc** deletepoint(G, x, y) — *assuming* $(x, y) \in G$
    Input : Grid G (seen as bitvector B and sequence S) and point (x, y).
    Output: Deletes (x, y) from G.
6     $p \leftarrow$ select$_1(B, x)$
7   delete($B, p + 1$)
8     $q \leftarrow$ select$_y(S, $rank$_y(S, p - x) + 1)$
9   delete(S, q)

Let us describe how the grid can be modified. To insert a new point (x, y), we find its x-coordinate in B, $p \leftarrow$ select$_1(B, x)$, insert a new 0 at $p + 1$, and then insert the y-coordinate at the appropriate position in S, $p - x + 1$. To delete point (x, y), we compute p as before and delete $B[p + 1]$. Now we must find it in S. Since we assume that point (x, y) exists, the leftmost y in S with column $\geq x$ must be at column x. We find it with $q \leftarrow$ select$_y(S, $rank$_y(S, p - x) + 1)$, and then remove $S[q]$. Note that if there are several points at the same (x, y) position, we delete one of them. If we do not assume that (x, y) exists in the grid, we must verify that $q \leq$ select$_1(x + 1) - (x + 1)$ before deleting $S[q]$.

Algorithm 12.17 shows the insertion and deletion algorithms. Both have time complexity $\mathcal{O}(w \log r)$. We can also find dominant points in this grid. However, since the points sharing the same x-coordinate are not sorted by y-coordinate, we must use a technique analogous to the one described at the end of Section 10.5.1, but looking for the highest or the lowest point, instead of the rightmost, between x and x'.

Example 12.16 *Figure 12.9 shows the same grid of Figure 10.4, now represented as a bitvector B and a sequence S. The current points are shown in gray. Let us now run* insertpoint($4, 9$). *First, we compute $p \leftarrow$* select$_1(B, 4) = 8$. *Then we insert the black 0, to mark that there is a new point at $x = 4$:* insert($B, 9, 0$) *now indicates that there are 3 such points. With p we now map the coordinate $x = 4$ to S: the points with $x = 4$, if any, start right after $p - x = 4$. Then we add the new point before the first one:* insert($S, 5, 9$) *inserts in S the black number 9 seen in the figure.*

Let us now run deletepoint($4, 9$) *to recover the original gray grid. We compute $p \leftarrow$* select$_1(B, 4) = 8$ *and then run* delete($B, p + 1$) = delete($B, 9$), *thus deleting the black 0 in B. We now must find some point with coordinate $y = 9$ in the range for $x = 4$ of S. Since the range starts after $p - x = 4$ and we assume such a point exists, it is correct to remove the first 9 in $S[5, n]$. Its position is found with $q \leftarrow$* select$_9(S, $rank$_9(S, 4) + 1) =$ select$_9(S, 2) = 5$. *We finish with* delete($S, 5$), *which removes the black 9 we inserted before.*

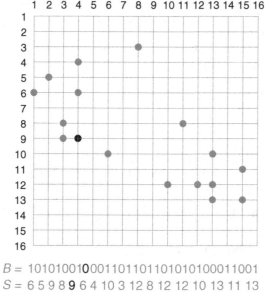

$B = 1010100\mathbf{1}0001101101101010100011001$

$S = 6\,5\,9\,8\,\mathbf{9}\,6\,4\,10\,3\,12\,8\,12\,12\,10\,13\,11\,13$

Figure 12.9. A grid represented as a bitvector B plus a sequence S, and the effect of inserting the (black) point $(4, 9)$ in it.

An extra feature of this representation is that we can insert new x-coordinates: $\mathsf{insert}(B, \mathsf{select}_1(B, x), 1)$, with $1 \leq x \leq c + 1$, inserts a new empty column right before coordinate x, shifting all the points at columns $\geq x$ one position to the right (with $x = c + 1$, we insert a new column at the end). Conversely, $\mathsf{delete}(B, \mathsf{select}_1(B, x))$, for $2 \leq x \leq c$, removes coordinate x and virtually moves the points with that coordinate to $x - 1$ (that is, it merges two columns in the grid). Both operations take time $\mathcal{O}(w)$. Unfortunately, we cannot do the same with rows (we can transpose the grid if we want the ability to insert/delete rows but not columns).

12.5.2 Dynamic k^2-Trees

The k^2-tree data structure described in Section 10.2 builds on LOUDS-based cardinal trees. Therefore, its dynamization is immediate. In particular, Algorithm 10.5 runs on the dynamic LOUDS representation of Section 12.4.1 with an $\mathcal{O}(w)$ slowdown factor. For inserting and deleting points, we simply traverse the path and add or remove the intermediate nodes as needed. Algorithm 12.18 shows the procedure. For simplicity we allow only square matrices of $s \times s$, with s a power of k, and a single point per cell.

Example 12.17 *Figure 12.10 shows the effect of inserting a point $(x, y) = (4, 11)$ on the grid of Figure 10.4, with $k = 2$. We start with $v \leftarrow \mathsf{root}() = 1$ and $l \leftarrow 16$. At the tree root, we set $l \leftarrow l/k = 8$, $c \leftarrow \lceil x/l \rceil = \lceil 4/8 \rceil = 1$ and $r \leftarrow \lceil y/l \rceil = \lceil 11/8 \rceil = 2$, meaning that the point to insert is in the third quadrant since $(r - 1)k + c = 3$. Since $\mathsf{childrenlabeled}(v, 3)$ is true, we do not need to insert the third child of the root. Now we move to this node, $v \leftarrow \mathsf{labeledchild}(v, 3) = 4$. We also map x and y to the submatrix of node v, $x \leftarrow x - (c - 1)l = 4$ and $y \leftarrow y - (r - 1)l = 3$.*

Algorithm 12.18: Inserting and deleting grid points using a k^2-tree.

---

1 **Proc** insertpoint(G, x, y) — *assuming* $(x, y) \notin G$

    Input : An $s \times s$ grid G (seen as a k^2-tree T, in turn seen as a LOUDS
              bitvector B) and point (x, y).

    Output: Inserts (x, y) in G.

2     $v \leftarrow \mathsf{root}(T)$

3     $l \leftarrow s$

4   **while** $l > k$ **do**

5       $l \leftarrow l/k$

6       $c \leftarrow \lceil x/l \rceil$; $r \leftarrow \lceil y/l \rceil$

7   **if not** $\mathsf{childrenlabeled}(T, v, (r-1)k + c)$ **then**

8         $v \leftarrow \mathsf{insertchild}(T, v, (r-1)k + c)$ (Algorithm 12.11, $\sigma = k^2$)

9   **else** $v \leftarrow \mathsf{labeledchild}(T, v, (r-1)k + c)$

10      $x \leftarrow x - (c-1)l$; $y \leftarrow y - (r-1)l$

11    $\mathsf{bitset}(B, k^2(v-1) + (y-1)k + x)$

12 **Proc** deletepoint(G, x, y) — *assumes* $(x, y) \in G$

    Input : An $s \times s$ grid G (seen as a k^2-tree T, in turn seen as a LOUDS
              bitvector B) and point (x, y).

    Output: Deletes (x, y) from G.

13    $delete(\mathsf{root}(T), x, y, s)$

14 **Proc** $delete(v, x, y, l)$

    Input : A node v of the k^2-tree representing an $l \times l$ grid, and a point (x, y)
              of the grid. The k^2-tree is represented with bitvector B using LOUDS.

    Output: Deletes (x, y) from the grid of v.

15   **if** $l = k$ **then**

16      $\mathsf{bitclear}(B, k^2(v-1) + (y-1)k + x)$

17   **else**

18      $l \leftarrow l/k$

19      $c \leftarrow \lceil x/l \rceil$; $r \leftarrow \lceil y/l \rceil$

20      $u \leftarrow \mathsf{labeledchild}(T, v, (r-1)k + c)$

21      $delete(u, x - (c-1)l, y - (r-1)l, l)$

22   **if** $\mathsf{isleaf}(T, u)$ **then**

23        $\mathsf{deletenode}(T, u)$ (Algorithm 12.11, $\sigma = k^2$)

In the third quadrant, we reduce again $l \leftarrow 4$ *and compute* $c \leftarrow 1$ *and* $r \leftarrow 1$, *meaning that* (x, y) *is in the first quadrant of* v. *Since* $\mathsf{childrenlabeled}(v, 1)$ *is true, the child exists and we move to it,* $v \leftarrow \mathsf{labeledchild}(v, 1) = 10$. *We map* x *and* y *to the submatrix of node* v, $x \leftarrow 4$ *and* $y \leftarrow 3$.

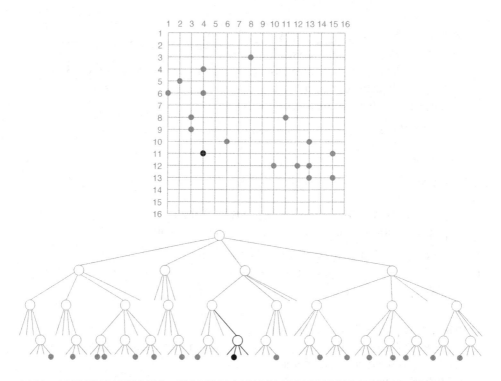

1111 1110001011001101 00010001110100010101100000111110111100
0001010001100001001000101000**0100**000100010001001000101000010001000

Figure 12.10. A grid represented graphically and as a k^2-tree, with the corresponding bitvector on the bottom. In black we show the effect of inserting a new point on the three representations.

In this sub-quadrant, we compute $l \leftarrow 2$, $c \leftarrow 2$ and $r \leftarrow 2$, meaning that (x, y) is in the fourth quadrant of v. Now **childrenlabeled**$(v, 4)$ is false (this operation, in Algorithm 8.4, inspects $B[40] = 0$, where B is as in Figure 10.4). This means that we have to insert the node where we want to descend. We perform **insertchild**$(v, 4)$. This sets $B[40] = 1$ and inserts **0000** at $B[85]$; see Algorithm 12.11. These are the 4 black bits in the second row of B; they are initially all zeros. Now we descend to the node just inserted, $v \leftarrow 22$, and map $x \leftarrow 2$ and $y \leftarrow 1$.

Finally, since $l = k$, we set the final bit, **bitset**$(B, k^2(v - 1) + (y - 1)k + x) =$ **bitset**$(B, 4 \cdot (22 - 1) + (1 - 1) \cdot 2 + 2) =$ **bitset**$(B, 86)$, setting the black 1 in the block we had inserted.

The deletion of the same point, **deletepoint**$(4, 11)$, carries out the reverse process. We start with $delete(1, 4, 11, 16)$, reducing $l \leftarrow 8$ and computing $c \leftarrow 1$ and $r \leftarrow 2$. We continue with $delete(4, 4, 3, 8)$. Now we compute $l \leftarrow 4$, $c \leftarrow 1$, and $r \leftarrow 1$, continuing with $delete(10, 4, 3, 4)$. We compute $l \leftarrow 2$, $c \leftarrow 2$, and $r \leftarrow 2$. We then continue with $delete(22, 2, 1, 2)$. Finally, since $l = k$, we carry out **bitclear**$(B, k^2(v - 1) + (y - 1)k + x) =$ **bitclear**$(B, 86)$, leaving the black bits of B again at **0000**.

Now we return from the recursion. After the call for $delete(22, 2, 1, 2)$, we ask if **isleaf**(22). Since its children are all zeros, v is a leaf and thus we remove it: **deletenode**(22) sets $B[40] = 0$ again and removes the 4 black bits at $B[85, 88]$. When *we return to the previous calls, the nodes are not yet leaves, so no further changes occur in the tree.*

12.6 Texts

Two data structures were introduced in Chapter 11 to handle text collections: the compressed suffix array based on the Ψ function, and the FM-index based on the BWT of the text. While the former consists of pointers within the suffix array, which undergo massive changes each time we insert or delete a suffix, the BWT can be maintained with the techniques seen in Section 12.3 to handle dynamic sequences. It is thus convenient to focus on FM-indexes.

Implementing a dynamic FM-index (Section 11.2) essentially requires maintaining the BWT of the concatenation $T[1, n]$ of the documents present in the collection. If we represent the bitvectors of the wavelet tree compressed as in Section 12.1.3, the space is $n\mathcal{H}_k(T) + o(n \log \sigma)$ bits, for any $k \leq \alpha \log_\sigma n$ and any constant $0 < \alpha < 1$ (recall Section 11.3.2). The times to count and locate will have an $\mathcal{O}(w)$ slowdown factor with respect to the static versions.

In a dynamic collection, we permit the following update operations:

insertdoc(T, D): inserts document $D[1, \ell]$ in the text collection represented by T. Returns a unique identifier for D.

deletedoc(T, a): deletes from T the document with identifier a.

12.6.1 Insertions

Let us first consider how the BWT of T, $L = T^{\mathsf{bwt}}$, and the vector $C[1, \sigma + 1]$ of the FM-index must be updated upon insertions. This is sufficient to support counting queries; the structures for locating will be considered later. For technical convenience our text T will not have the final terminator \$, just the document terminators #. This symbol will be interpreted as the value 1, and the regular symbols will be $[2, \sigma]$. Array C contains in $C[c]$ the number of occurrences of symbols $< c$ in T.

To insert $D[1, \ell]$, we first append (virtually) the symbol # at its end, so that $D[\ell + 1] = $ #. If there are Δ documents concatenated in T, then the first Δ suffixes of the suffix array $A[1, n]$ of $T[1, n]$ will point to the positions of those Δ symbols # in T. We can insert the # of D anywhere in $A[1, \Delta + 1]$ (it does not matter how those #s are ordered with respect to each other, because # is not used in the search patterns). Let us insert the suffix between $A[\Delta + 1]$ and $A[\Delta]$. To reflect this in the FM-index, we run insert($T^{\mathsf{bwt}}, \Delta + 1, D[\ell]$) and increase $C[c] \leftarrow C[c] + 1$ for all $c > D[\ell]$.

Now that we know the position $p = \Delta + 1$ of $D[\ell]$, we can compute the position to insert $D[\ell - 1]$ as

$$p \leftarrow \mathsf{LF}(p) + 1 = C[D[\ell]] + 1 + \mathsf{rank}_{D[\ell]}(T^{\mathsf{bwt}}, p)$$

(the reason for the "+1" is that we have not yet inserted the # in T^{bwt}, thus all the values in C are offset by 1). Then we run insert($T^{\mathsf{bwt}}, p, D[\ell - 1]$), increase $C[c] \leftarrow C[c] + 1$

for all $c > D[\ell - 1]$, and so on. When the moment to insert $D[0]$ comes, we actually insert # in T^{bwt}, and then we finish.

To carry out the updates to $C[1, \sigma + 1]$ efficiently, we represent it as a dynamic array C with partial sums (Section 12.2), so that $C[c]$ now stores the number of occurrences of c in T. Then, when inserting $D[j]$, we only have to increase $C[D[j]]$ by 1. In the formula for $\mathsf{LF}(p)$, instead of $C[c]$, we use $\mathsf{sum}(C, c - 1)$. Since C is small and does not undergo insertions or deletions, it can be represented with a simple heap-ordered array on all its σ cells. The operations on C then take $\mathcal{O}(\log \sigma)$ time.

Overall we can insert a new document $D[1, \ell]$ in the dynamic text collection in time $\mathcal{O}(\ell\, w \log \sigma)$, where the cost is dominated by the operations on the dynamic wavelet tree of T^{bwt}. Similarly, in time $\mathcal{O}(m\, w \log \sigma)$ we can carry out Algorithm 11.5 for finding the range $A[sp, ep]$ of a pattern $P[1, m]$.

12.6.2 Document Identifiers

Upon inserting a document, we must return a document identifier that does not change along insertions and deletions of other documents. Therefore, the value $\Delta + 1$ where $D[\ell]$ is inserted in T^{bwt}, for example, cannot be used, as it would change if a previous document $D'[1, \ell']$ is later deleted and its symbol $D'[\ell']$ is removed from $T^{\mathsf{bwt}}[1, \Delta]$. Instead, we will maintain one fixed memory cell for each document existing in T. The memory address a of the cell will be the document identifier. We will store some information on D in this memory address; the application can also attach any desired extra information (such as a file name, for example). The space for these cells is $\mathcal{O}(\Delta w)$ bits, which is insignificant unless there are many very short documents.

If the index has to be stored on disk for later use, the identifiers a can be changed by their corresponding positions $p \in [1, \Delta]$, and new identifiers can be obtained when the index is loaded again into main memory.

12.6.3 Samplings

In addition to T^{bwt} and C, the FM-index needs the samplings A_S and A_S^{-1}, plus the bitvector B, to carry out **locate** queries and display text contents. Since we handle a set of documents, it is natural that the positions are reported as pairs (a, j), meaning the position j within the document with identifier a. An important advantage of using this format directly is that insertions and deletions of other documents do not alter those local offsets j.

The bitvector $B[1, n]$ that signals the sampled suffix array positions will be maintained as a compressed dynamic bitvector (Section 12.1.3). While a dynamic array A_S storing the pairs (a, j) seems sufficient, we need a more involved structure so that we can also maintain A_S^{-1}. We will use two structures: A dynamic sequence A_I, over alphabet $[0, 2^w - 1]$ (implemented with a wavelet matrix, Section 12.5.1), will store the a components of the pairs (a, j), and a dynamic array A_a local to each document a will maintain the corresponding j components for document a.

When we insert $D[j - 1]$ at $T^{\mathsf{bwt}}[p]$, it means that $A[p]$ points to position j in D. We usually also insert a 0 at $B[p]$ to signal that $A[p]$ is not sampled. However, when j is of the form $t \cdot l + 1$, for a sampling step l, we instead insert a 1 in $B[p]$ and also insert the corresponding sample in A_S. This is done as follows. First, we insert a in $A_I[r]$, where $r = \mathsf{rank}(B, p)$. Second, we insert $t + 1 = (j - 1)/l + 1$ at $A_a[\mathsf{rank}_a(A_I, r)]$.

Thus, to compute a suffix array position $A[i]$, we carry out LF repeatedly over T^{bwt}, say, k times, until we reach a position i' where $B[i'] = 1$, just as in Algorithm 11.6. Now we return

- the document identifier $a = \mathsf{access}(A_I, r)$, for $r = \mathsf{rank}(B, i')$, and
- the offset $(A_a[\mathsf{rank}_a(A_I, r)] - 1) \cdot l + 1 + k$ within document a.

Note that we cannot abandon the correct document a while we iterate on LF, because the first position of each document is always sampled.

Array A_a is created empty when the insertion of the document a begins, and it can become static once the insertion terminates. Further, A_a is a permutation in $[1, \lceil \ell/l \rceil]$. When the insertion terminates and A_a becomes static, we create on it the representation of permutations given in Section 5.1. Then any cell of its inverse permutation A_a^{-1} can be computed in $\mathcal{O}(\log(\ell/l))$ time by using $\mathcal{O}(\ell/l)$ extra bits. All the information about A_a is stored in the memory cell allocated for a, as a field $a.A$.

The inverse permutation gives the desired support for A_S^{-1}: To recover the position in A of the suffix that points to offset $t \cdot l + 1$ in document a, we compute

$$\mathsf{select}(B, \mathsf{select}_a(A_I, A_a^{-1}(t + 1))).$$

This is sufficient to display any segment $D[i, j]$ of document $a = D[1, \ell]$, unless $j + 1$ is beyond the last sampled character. To cover this case, we also sample the position $D[\ell + 1]$, if it is not already of the form $\ell + 1 = t \cdot l + 1$. This will appear at the last cell of A_a^{-1}, and since $D[\ell]$ appears in $T^{\mathsf{bwt}}[1, \Delta]$, it will correspond to the first a in A_I (and thus to $A_a[1]$). We must store the length of document a in a field $a.\ell$ to know the position $A_a[1]$ corresponds to, since it may not be of the form $t \cdot l + 1$ like all the others.

Algorithm 12.19 shows the complete procedure to insert $D[1, \ell]$. In addition to the $\mathcal{O}(\ell w \log \sigma)$ time to update T^{bwt} and C, we spend time $\mathcal{O}\big((\ell/l)w^2\big)$ to update sequence A_I and array A_a. This is negligible if we use $l = \Theta(w^{1+\epsilon}/\log \sigma)$ for some constant $\epsilon > 0$, which is also convenient to make all the sampling structures use $\mathcal{O}((n/l)w) = o(n \log \sigma)$ bits.

Algorithm 12.20 gives the procedures for locating (i.e., computing $A[i]$) and displaying (i.e., extracting some $D[i, j]$). With our choice of l, the cost of $\mathcal{O}(w^2)$ incurred to operate A_I when locating and displaying is offset by the extra cost of $\mathcal{O}(l w \log \sigma) = \mathcal{O}(w^{2+\epsilon})$ spent in finding the sampled cell. Therefore, locating costs $\mathcal{O}(w^{2+\epsilon})$ time, whereas displaying $D[i, j]$ takes time $\mathcal{O}\big(w(w^{1+\epsilon} + (j - i)\log \sigma)\big)$.

Example 12.18 *Let us start with an empty collection and insert, as documents, the two most popular names of Example 8.22,* MARTINA *and* SOFIA. *Figure 12.11 shows how* T^{bwt} *evolves as we insert each symbol of* MARTINA# *(top left) and then each symbol of* SOFIA# *(top right), both in reverse order. On the bottom left, the figure shows the final state of the structures used for* locate, *for a sampling step of* $l = 3$.

Initially, T^{bwt}, *B, and A_I are empty,* $\Delta = n = 0$, *and the partial sums structure contains $C[c] = 0$ for all $c \in [1, \sigma]$. When we insert the first document, we allocate a memory cell, say, at address a, which will be the persistent identifier of document*

Algorithm 12.19: Inserting a document on a dynamic FM-index.

---

1 **Proc** insertdoc(T, D)

    Input : A text $T[1, n]$ representing Δ documents (seen as dynamic sequences T^{bwt} and A_I, dynamic bitvector B, and partial sums structure $C[1, \sigma]$, with # = 1), sampling step l, and a document $D[1, \ell]$.

    Output: Inserts D as a new document and returns its document identifier.

2   Allocate a record for D, let a be its memory address
3      $a.\ell \leftarrow \ell$
4   Create empty dynamic array $a.A$
5      $p \leftarrow \Delta + 1$
6   **for** $j \leftarrow \ell + 1$ **downto** 1 **do**
7   **if** $j > 1$ **then** $c \leftarrow D[j - 1]$ **else** $c \leftarrow$ #
8   insert(T^{bwt}, p, c)
9   write(C, c, read(C, c) + 1)
10   **if** $j = \ell + 1$ **or** $j \bmod l = 1$ **then**
11   insert($B, p, 1$)
12              $r \leftarrow$ rank(B, p)
13   insert(A_I, r, a)
14   insert($a.A$, rank$_a(A_I, r)$, $\lceil (j - 1)/l \rceil + 1$)
15   **else** insert($B, p, 0$)
16          $p \leftarrow$ sum($C, c - 1$) + 1 + rank$_c(T^{\mathsf{bwt}}, p$)
17   Make $a.A$ static and represent it as a permutation (Algorithm 5.2)
18      $n \leftarrow n + \ell + 1$
19      $\Delta \leftarrow \Delta + 1$
20   **return** a

$D[1, \ell] = D[1, 7] = $ MARTINA. *We also create an empty dynamic array A_a. We set $p \leftarrow \Delta + 1 = 1$ as the position where the last symbol of the document will be inserted in T^{bwt}.*

We now process the letters $D[j - 1]$ of document a, from $j = \ell + 1 = 8$ to $j = 1$. We first insert $c = D[j - 1] = D[7] = $ A at $T^{\mathsf{bwt}}[p]$, so $T^{\mathsf{bwt}} = $ A. We set $C[$A$] \leftarrow 1$. Since $j = \ell + 1$, this position is sampled, so we insert a 1 at $B[p]$ (then $B = $ 1), an 'a' at $A_I[r]$ for $r = $ rank(B, p) = 1 (then $A_I = a$), and $\lceil (8 - 1)/l \rceil + 1 = 4$ at $A_a[$rank$_a(A_I, r)] = A_a[1]$ (then $A_a = 4$). The sampled positions in this document are shown within a square in the figure (note that, if the position j is sampled, then the square encloses the symbol $D[j - 1]$). Finally, we compute the next insertion point, $p \leftarrow $ sum($C, $ A $- 1$) + 1 + rank$_A(T^{\mathsf{bwt}}, 1) = 0 + 1 + 1 = 2$.

Now $j = 7$ and we process $c = D[6] = $ N, which is inserted at $T^{\mathsf{bwt}}[p]$, so $T^{\mathsf{bwt}} = $ AN. We set $C[$N$] \leftarrow 1$. Since $j \bmod 3 = 1$, this position is also sampled, so we insert a 1 at $B[p]$ (then $B = $ 11), an 'a' at $A_I[r]$ for $r = $ rank(B, p) = 2 (then $A_I = a\,a$), and $(7 - 1)/3 + 1 = 3$ at $A_a[$rank$_a(A_I, r)] = A_a[2]$ (then $A_a = 4\,3$). Now we compute the next insertion point, $p \leftarrow $ sum($C, $ N $- 1$) + 1 + rank$_N(T^{\mathsf{bwt}}, 2) = 1 + 1 + 1 = 3$.

Algorithm 12.20: Locating and displaying on a dynamic FM-index.

1 **Proc** *locate*(A, i)

    Input : Suffix array $A[1, n]$ (seen as FM-index structures C, T^{bwt}, B, A_I, and
           cells a) and position i of A.

    Output: Returns $A[i]$ as a pair (document id, offset).

2    $k \leftarrow 0$

3   **while** $\mathsf{access}(B, i) = 0$ **do**

4       $c \leftarrow \mathsf{access}(T^{\mathsf{bwt}}, i)$

5       $i \leftarrow \mathsf{sum}(C, c - 1) + \mathsf{rank}_c(T^{\mathsf{bwt}}, i)$

6       $k \leftarrow k + 1$

7    $r \leftarrow \mathsf{rank}(B, i)$

8    $a \leftarrow \mathsf{access}(A_I, r)$

9    $j \leftarrow (a.A[\mathsf{rank}_a(A_I, r)] - 1) \cdot l + 1$

10   **if** $j > a.\ell$ **then** $j \leftarrow a.\ell + 1$ (last sample, can only occur if $k = 0$)

11   **return** $(a, j + k)$

12 **Proc** *display*(a, i, j)

    Input : Document D (seen as its identifier a) from a text T (seen as its
           FM-index structures C, T^{bwt}, B, A_I) and positions $i \le j$ of a.

    Output: Outputs $D[i, j]$ (in reverse order).

13   $j' \leftarrow \lceil j/l \rceil \cdot l + 1$

14   **if** $j' > a.\ell$ **then** (last sample)

15      $j' \leftarrow a.\ell + 1$

16      $p \leftarrow 1$

17   **else**

18      $p \leftarrow \mathsf{inverse}(a.A, (j' - 1)/l + 1)$ (Algorithm 5.1)

19   $p \leftarrow \mathsf{select}(B, \mathsf{select}_a(A_I, p))$

20   **for** $t \leftarrow j'$ **downto** $j + 2$ **do**

21      $c \leftarrow \mathsf{access}(T^{\mathsf{bwt}}, p)$

22      $p \leftarrow \mathsf{sum}(C, c - 1) + \mathsf{rank}_c(T^{\mathsf{bwt}}, p)$

23   **for** $t \leftarrow j + 1$ **downto** $i + 1$ **do**

24      $c \leftarrow \mathsf{access}(T^{\mathsf{bwt}}, p)$

25   **output** c

26      $p \leftarrow \mathsf{sum}(C, c - 1) + \mathsf{rank}_c(T^{\mathsf{bwt}}, p)$

The process continues as shown in the figure. When $j = 2$, it holds $p = 3$, and we insert $c = D[1] = \mathsf{M}$ at $T^{\mathsf{bwt}}[p]$, obtaining $T^{\mathsf{bwt}} = \mathsf{ANMTIAR}$, and set $C[\mathsf{M}] \leftarrow 1$. Since $j \bmod 3 = 2$, this position is not sampled, so we insert a 0 at $B[p]$ (then $B = \mathsf{1100001}$). We compute the next (and last) insertion point, $p \leftarrow \mathsf{sum}(C, \mathsf{M} - 1) + 1 + \mathsf{rank}_\mathsf{M}(T^{\mathsf{bwt}}, 3) = 3 + 1 + 1 = 5$.

Now $j = 1$ and then $c = \#$. We insert it at $T^{\mathsf{bwt}}[p]$, obtaining $T^{\mathsf{bwt}} = \mathsf{ANMT\#IAR}$, and set $C[\#] \leftarrow 1$. Since $j \bmod 3 = 1$, this position is sampled, so we insert a 1 at $B[p]$

insert A	A
insert N	AN
insert I	ANI
insert T	ANTI
insert R	ANTIR
insert A	ANTIAR
insert M	ANMTIAR
insert #	ANMT#IAR

insert A	AANMT#IAR
insert I	AANIMT#IAR
insert F	AANIMFT#IAR
insert O	AANIMOFT#IAR
insert S	AANIMOFT#ISAR
insert #	AANIMOFT#ISA#R

B	11100010100011
A_I	aba b a ba
A_a	4 3 1 2
A_b	3 2 1

delete 1	ANIMOFT#ISA#R
delete 2	AIMOFT#ISA#R
delete 8	AIMOFT#SA#R
delete 6	AIMOF#SA#R
delete 10	AIMOF#SA#
delete 8	AIMOF#S#
delete 3	AIOF#S#
delete 5	AIOFS#

Figure 12.11. The evolution of the BWT of a dynamic FM-index upon inserting document a = MARTINA (top left) and then b = SOFIA (top right), and finally deleting document a (bottom right). On the bottom left we show the values of B, A_I, A_a, and A_b (properly aligned to help interpreting them) after the insertion of the two documents. The sampled positions of a are shown inside squares in the BWT; those of b are shown inside rounded squares.

(then B = 11001001), an 'a' at $A_I[r]$ for r = rank(B, p) = 3 (then A_I = a a a a), and $(1 - 1)/3 + 1 = 1$ at $A_a[\text{rank}_a(A_I, r)] = A_a[3]$ (then A_a = 4 3 1 2).

The insertion has concluded. Array A_a = 4 3 1 2 is made static and preprocessed as a permutation. We set $n \leftarrow n + \ell + 1 = 8$ and $\Delta \leftarrow \Delta + 1 = 1$, and return the identifier a. The reader can verify that T^{bwt} is indeed the BWT of MARTINA# by following the static construction of Section 11.4.

Let us now briefly follow the insertion of the second document, $D[1, \ell] = D[1, 5] =$ SOFIA. We allocate a memory cell b for it, create an empty dynamic array A_b, and set $p \leftarrow \Delta + 1 = 2$ as the first insertion point. We then insert the $\ell = 5$ symbols of D backwards. Three of them ($j = 6$, $j = 4$, and $j = 1$) are sampled, thus we insert 3 'b's in A_I and elements 3 2 1 in A_b. The sampled positions of this document are shown inside squares of rounded corners. The final sequence is T^{bwt} = AANIMOFT#ISA#R, and the other structures are shown on the bottom left of the figure. Note that B marks the positions of the squares (with or without rounded corners), whereas A_I signals how the types of squares alternate in T^{bwt}.

12.6.4 Deletions

For deleting a document a representing $D[1, \ell]$, assume we know that $D[\ell]$ was inserted at $T^{\text{bwt}}[p]$. Then we compute $c \leftarrow T^{\text{bwt}}[p]$ and delete $T^{\text{bwt}}[p]$. Now we decrease $C[c]$ by 1 in the partial sums structure, compute the next position $p \leftarrow \text{sum}(C, c - 1) + \text{rank}_c(T^{\text{bwt}}, p - 1)$,[1] and continue until the character we remove is c = #. The other associated structures are also easily updated: upon deleting $T^{\text{bwt}}[p]$, we see if $B[p] = 1$.

---

[1] The value $\text{rank}_c(T^{\text{bwt}}, p)$ before deleting $T^{\text{bwt}}[p] = c$ corresponds to $\text{rank}_c(T^{\text{bwt}}, p - 1) + 1$ after the deletion. We do not add that 1, however, because we have removed symbol $D[\ell]$ from the area of the suffixes starting with # but we have not yet decreased $C[\#]$.

Algorithm 12.21: Deleting a document on a dynamic FM-index.

---

1 **Proc** deletedoc(T, a)

    Input : A text $T[1, n]$ representing Δ documents (seen as dynamic sequences T^{bwt} and A_I, dynamic bitvector B, and partial sums structure $C[1, \sigma]$, # = 1), and a document identifier a.

    Output: Deletes the document with identifier a.

2      $p \leftarrow \text{select}_a(A_I, 1)$

3      $c \leftarrow 2$ (or anything $\neq$ #)

4   **while** $c \neq$ # **do**

5          $c \leftarrow \text{access}(T^{\text{bwt}}, p)$

6          $\text{delete}(T^{\text{bwt}}, p)$

7          $\text{write}(C, c, \text{read}(C, c) - 1)$

8   **if** $\text{access}(B, p) = 1$ **then**

9              $\text{delete}(A_I, \text{rank}(B, p))$

10         $\text{delete}(B, p)$

11         $p \leftarrow \text{sum}(C, c - 1) + \text{rank}_c(T^{\text{bwt}}, p - 1)$

12     $n \leftarrow n - a.\ell - 1$

13     $\Delta \leftarrow \Delta - 1$

14   Free permutation $a.A$ and cell a

If it is, we delete $A_I[\text{rank}(B, p)]$. Then, in either case, we delete $B[p]$. At the end we delete the permutation A_a and free the memory cell a.

The value of p corresponding to $D[\ell]$ is easily found because we have sampled it in $A_a[1]$ (because it corresponds to the position of $D[\ell + 1] = $ #). Therefore, we can find p with $\text{select}(B, \text{select}_a(A_I, 1))$. Indeed, we do not need to run select on B, because we know that the first a in A_I is in $[1, \Delta]$, and $B[p] = 1$ for all $1 \leq p \leq \Delta$ since all the last positions are sampled.

Algorithm 12.21 gives the details. Overall we can delete document $D[1, \ell]$ in time $\mathcal{O}(\ell \, w \log \sigma)$, plus a less significant $\mathcal{O}((\ell/l)w^2)$ time needed to remove the corresponding cells in A_I.

Example 12.19 *The bottom right of Figure 12.11 shows the effect of deleting document a from the collection. We compute $p \leftarrow \text{select}_a(A_I, 1) = 1$, the initial deletion position (where $D[\ell]$ was inserted). We compute that last character, $c \leftarrow \text{access}(T^{\text{bwt}}, 1) = $ A, and delete $T^{\text{bwt}}[1]$, obtaining $T^{\text{bwt}} = $ ANIMOFT#ISA#R. We also decrease $C[A] \leftarrow C[A] - 1 = 3 - 1 = 2$. Since $B[1] = 1$, we delete $A_I[\text{rank}(B, 1)] = A_I[1]$, thus $A_I = b\,a\,b\,a\,b\,a$. We also delete $B[1]$, so $B = $ 1100010100011. Finally, we compute the next position to delete, $p \leftarrow \text{sum}(C, A - 1) + \text{rank}_A(T^{\text{bwt}}, 1 - 1) = 2 + 0 = 2$.*

Now we read $c \leftarrow \text{access}(T^{\text{bwt}}, 2) = $ N and delete $T^{\text{bwt}}[2]$, obtaining $T^{\text{bwt}} = $ AIMOFT#ISA#R. We also decrease $C[N] \leftarrow C[N] - 1 = 1 - 1 = 0$. Since $B[2] = 1$, we delete $A_I[\text{rank}(B, 2)] = A_I[2]$ (so $A_I = b\,b\,a\,b\,a$). Then we delete $B[2]$, obtaining $B = $ 100010100011. We now compute the next position to delete, $p \leftarrow \text{sum}(C, N - 1) + \text{rank}_N(T^{\text{bwt}}, 2 - 1) = 8 + 0 = 8$. The rest of the process can be followed in the figure, where the final value of T^{bwt} is the BWT of SOFIA#. The final values of the *locating structures are $B = 100101$ and $A_I = b\ b\ b$. The static structure A_a is freed and A_b is left unaltered.*

12.7 Memory Allocation

So far we have assumed that the language or the operating systems handles the allocation and deallocation of memory. This issue is of particular importance in compressed data structures, because general memory allocation systems may waste a significant percentage of memory: some may use up to twice the space that is actually allocated.

We can do better with our dynamic data structures, because our allocation patterns are particular: We have a set of fixed-size objects adding up to a negligible size, and another set of objects whose sizes belong to a small range of sizes. For example, in Section 12.1 a bitvector B that is represented using $|B|$ bits of space requires $\mathcal{O}(|B|/w^2)$ fixed-size internal tree nodes adding up to $\mathcal{O}(|B|/w)$ bits, and $\mathcal{O}(|B|/w^2)$ leaves of variable size, but always in $\mathcal{O}(w^2)$ bits. For example, plain bitvectors allocate leaves having from $w/2$ to $2w$ words. The situation is analogous with the arrays and partial sums of Section 12.2 and with the range min-max trees in Section 12.4.4. In the case of very sparse bitvectors with m 1s, there are $\mathcal{O}(m/w)$ internal nodes and leaves, the former adding up to $\mathcal{O}(m)$ bits. All the other dynamic structures in the chapter are built on top of these trees, or they are very small.

In this restricted scenario, we can largely reduce the memory allocation overhead. The internal node data can be allocated with the system-provided support, as their space overhead will still be of lower order and negligible in practice. We focus on how to handle the allocation of variable-size leaves.

Allocating Leaves

We maintain an independent memory allocator per distinct leaf size. The allocator for size s handles only leaves of s words (recall that we allocate integral amounts of words). Since the leaves have $\mathcal{O}(w)$ words, there are only $\mathcal{O}(w)$ different allocators. These allocators request memory from the system in fixed *chunks* of c words, which will accommodate up to $\lfloor c/s \rfloor$ leaves. Each allocator keeps track of only the *current* chunk $C_s[0, c-1]$, of which it has only used a prefix of p_s leaves. All the other chunks are fully used. When a new leaf of s words is allocated, the corresponding allocator returns the memory area $C_s[p_s \cdot s, p_s \cdot s + s - 1]$ (i.e., it returns a pointer to the position $C_s[p_s \cdot s]$), and increases p_s by 1. If, however, there is no space in C_s for the new leaf (i.e., $p_s \cdot s + s > c$), it requests a new chunk, which becomes C_s.

When a leaf with address x and of size s is freed (we always know the sizes of leaves), we take the last leaf in the current chunk, $C_s[(p_s - 1) \cdot s, p_s \cdot s - 1]$, *move* it to the freed space at $[x, x + s - 1]$, and decrease p_s by 1. Moving leaves is a nonstandard operation in classical memory allocation systems, because it requires modifying any existing pointer to $C_s[(p_s - 1) \cdot s]$, so that now it points to x. We can handle this with an indirection system: for each leaf we allocate a pointer at some memory address a, so that a never changes until we free the leaf. The application will point to a, not to the leaf data itself, and a will in turn point to the actual leaf content. Then we have to modify only the content of a when moving that leaf. The addresses a of the leaves stored in each chunk C_s are recorded at the end of the chunk (this wastes the last $\lfloor c/s \rfloor$

chunk words). Moving the leaf takes time $\mathcal{O}(s)$, which is proportional to the time of processing leaves in our applications.

When moving leaves it is possible that our current chunk becomes empty, in which case we return it to the memory manager and keep no current chunk. If a new leaf has to be allocated in this case, we request a new chunk to the system. If, instead, x is freed and we have no current chunk, we determine which is the chunk of x and make it our current chunk C_s. We then move the last leaf of C_s to position x so as to have a contiguous prefix of C_s in use. To determine the chunk of x, we may allocate an extra word per leaf, just behind its address, where the chunk address is stored. Thus we find the chunk address C_s at the memory position $x - 1$. Alternatively, if chunk addresses are aligned to multiples of c, we can simply compute $C_s = \lfloor x/c \rfloor \cdot c$.

Therefore, allocation can be done in $\mathcal{O}(1)$ time and deallocation in $\mathcal{O}(w)$ time, which does not affect the time complexities. The space wasted inside each chunk of c words is at most $s = \mathcal{O}(w)$ unused words at the end, plus $\mathcal{O}(c/s) = \mathcal{O}(c/w)$ words for managing the address indirection. In addition we can waste $\mathcal{O}(wc)$ words for the current chunks of each size, which may not be fully used. That is, if the data structure uses N words, the extra space is $\mathcal{O}((N/c)(w + c/w) + wc) = \mathcal{O}(Nw/c + N/w + wc)$ words. This is essentially $\mathcal{O}(N/w) = o(N)$ words if we choose $c = \Theta(w^2)$.

Allocating Chunks

We are left with the problem of allocating the chunks. Since these are all of the same size, we have reduced the problem of handling data segments of $\mathcal{O}(w)$ different sizes to a single size c. We need a single allocator for chunks.

One way to handle this problem is to choose a chunk size c that is particularly convenient for the system-supported allocation. Many of them round the requested space to the next multiple of a value or to the next power of 2. Thus, by choosing c appropriately we can avoid any overhead.

Another way to handle this problem is to have our allocator control most of the available main memory that is used for dynamic structures. Then we divide the memory into chunks of size c and use the first word of each free chunk to store a pointer to the next free chunk. That is, we have a list of free chunks (initially, all are free). Each time a chunk is allocated, we return the first element of the list. Each time a chunk is freed, we add it at the front of the list. Thus we easily handle chunk allocation and deallocation in constant time. The problem of this approach is that we are using all the memory all the time, which can be unfriendly to other software components.

If, instead, we want this memory area to grow and shrink as needed, we still can obtain constant amortized time (but some allocations and deallocations may require $\mathcal{O}(n)$ time). We maintain a single memory area for the chunks, whose size is doubled when it becomes full, or is halved when it becomes less than a quarter full. A compact prefix of the chunks in this area is used. Then the mechanism is similar to the operation for leaves inside a chunk: New allocated chunks are obtained by extending the prefix, and freed chunks are replaced by moving the last chunk of the prefix to occupy the hole. While moving a chunk costs $\mathcal{O}(c)$ time, any sequence of t operations can produce at most $\mathcal{O}(w + t/c)$ holes, and thus require $\mathcal{O}(wc + t)$ time.

The reallocation of the whole area also amounts to constant amortized time. Instead of doubling and halving, we can make the area grow and shrink by a factor of $1 + \alpha$, for some $0 < \alpha < 1$; the amortized time becomes $\mathcal{O}(1/\alpha)$.

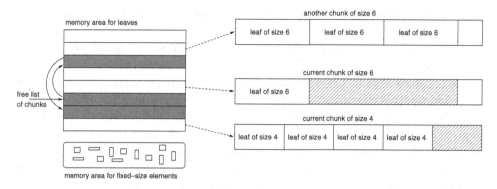

Figure 12.12. One of the layouts for memory allocation. The memory is divided into chunks, each of which contains a used prefix of leaves (the same size within a chunk). Free chunks are linked in a list. A small amount of extra memory is reserved for fixed-length elements.

A practical heuristic when deallocations are rare is to combine both schemes, that is, the area grows as needed but it never shrinks. We do not move chunks when they are freed. Instead, we maintain a list of free chunks and use them as the first choice for allocation. When there are no free chunks, we let the prefix (and, eventually, the area) grow. The same heuristic can be used inside chunks to avoid moving leaves, and thus indirection is not needed.

Example 12.20 *Figure 12.12 illustrates the case where we administer the dynamic memory with a linked list of free chunks, and leave a small extra space (of $\mathcal{O}(N/w)$ words) for the internal tree pointers and other small elements. The latter is managed by the general allocation system. The free chunks are grayed and linked to form a list. Some of the others are zoomed, to show two chunks holding leaves of 6 words (the current and another one) and one of 4 words (the current one). Only the current chunks have free space for more leaves (hatched). The non-current chunk of size 6 still has some wasted space because its size c is not a multiple of 6.*

12.8 Summary

Dynamic versions of the compact data structures for arrays, partial sums, bitvectors, sequences, trees, graphs, grids, texts, and others can be designed. They use the same asymptotic space of their static versions and support the same queries with an $\mathcal{O}(w)$ time penalty factor. Within the same time, they support basic update operations, such as inserting and deleting elements in arrays and partial sums, bits in bitvectors, symbols in sequences, nodes in trees, edges in graphs, points in grids, or documents in text collections.

12.9 Bibliographic Notes

Most of our $\mathcal{O}(w)$ slowdown factors in this chapter can be reduced to $\mathcal{O}(\log n)$ by using cells of $\Theta(w\lceil \log n \rceil)$ bits instead of $\Theta(w^2)$. We avoided this because one must then redefine the admissible leaf sizes whenever $\lceil \log n \rceil$ changes. While the problem can be managed in theory (Mäkinen and Navarro, 2008), the solution is cumbersome, and the slowdown factor is significant.

Arrays and partial sums. The problem of providing operations sum and search on a dynamic array $A[1, n]$ of ℓ-bit numbers, using $\ell n + o(\ell n)$ bits, has been studied for some time. Note that operation read can always be derived from sum. Raman *et al.* (2001) managed to support sum and write (that is, values can be updated but not inserted or deleted), in time $\mathcal{O}(\log_b n)$ and $\mathcal{O}(b)$, respectively, for any $\log n / \log \log n \leq b \leq n^\epsilon$ and any constant $0 < \epsilon < 1$. These times allow, for example, supporting both operations in time $\mathcal{O}(\log n / \log \log n)$, which is optimal even for $\ell = 1$ and in the amortized sense (Fredman and Saks, 1989).

Pătraşcu and Demaine (2006) showed that the time to support sum, search, and write must be $\Omega(\log n / \log(w/\delta))$ if the updates in write are limited to adding or subtracting δ-bit numbers to any cell. They give a structure matching these bounds. Note that their bound implies that any partial sums structure allowing insertions and deletions on ℓ-bit numbers requires time $\Omega(\log n / \log(w/\ell))$.

Hon *et al.* (2011) obtained $\mathcal{O}(\log_b n)$ time for sum and search, and $\mathcal{O}(b)$ time for write, for any $\log n / \log \log n \leq b \leq n$, as long as $\ell = \mathcal{O}(\log \log n)$. For general ℓ, instead, they proved that, if we have to use $\ell n + o(\ell n)$ bits of space, then search queries require $\Omega(\sqrt{\log n / \log \log n})$ time, independently of the update time (that is, this holds even for a static structure).

Raman *et al.* (2001) considered adding operations insert and delete to an array A, while supporting only query read (that is, a dynamic array with no partial sums). In this case, they also obtain $\mathcal{O}(\log n / \log \log n)$ time for the operations, which is again optimal (Fredman and Saks, 1989).

Mäkinen and Navarro (2008) obtained $\mathcal{O}(\log n)$ time for all the operations (sum, search, insert, delete), for any $\ell = \mathcal{O}(\log n)$. The solution described in the chapter is a simplification of their proposal. Navarro and Sadakane (2014) reduced the time to $\mathcal{O}(\log n / \log \log n)$ if only numbers up to $\mathcal{O}(\log n)$ are inserted and deleted and numbers in cells change by $\pm \mathcal{O}(\log n)$. Both results are optimal when $w = \Theta(\log n)$. The structures for arrays with variable-length cells (and very sparse bitvectors) we described are also inspired by these articles.

Bitvectors. When $\ell = 1$, the array with partial sums becomes a bitvector with rank and select support. Raman *et al.* (2001) showed how to support rank, select, and write in optimal time $\mathcal{O}(\log n / \log \log n)$ and $n + o(n)$ bits of space, but the update times were amortized. Hon *et al.* (2011) reached these times in the worst case, as we have seen.

Hon *et al.* (2011) also considered operations insert and delete, but their times were squared. Chan *et al.* (2007) recovered the optimal times for all the operations but using $\mathcal{O}(n)$ bits of space. Blandford and Blelloch (2004) made the first step toward compressing dynamic bitvectors. They obtained $\mathcal{O}(n\mathcal{H}_0(B))$ bits of space and $\mathcal{O}(\log n)$ time for all the operations. Mäkinen and Navarro (2008) reduced the space to $n\mathcal{H}_0(B) + o(n)$ bits, while maintaining the same times. The solution we describe for compressed bitvectors is a simplification of their structure. Finally, Navarro and Sadakane (2014) and He and Munro (2010) simultaneously obtained $n\mathcal{H}_0(B) + o(n)$ bits of space while supporting all the operations in the optimal time $\mathcal{O}(\log n / \log \log n)$. The former also show how to support extended operations, like cutting and joining bitvectors, in time $\mathcal{O}(w^{1+\epsilon})$.

We have not studied the techniques to decrease the time from $\mathcal{O}(\log n)$ to $\mathcal{O}(\log n / \log \log n)$ because they are generally complicated and unlikely to yield practical improvements. Klitzke and Nicholson (2016) implemented dynamic bitvectors with ad-hoc compression methods (such as using Lempel-Ziv on the leaves). Córdova and Navarro (2016) implemented the approach described in the chapter, ensuring asymptotically zero-order compression and obtaining competitive performance in practice.

Sequences. Mäkinen and Navarro (2008) combined wavelet trees and dynamic bitvectors as we have done in the chapter, obtaining $\mathcal{O}(\log n \log \sigma)$ time within $n\mathcal{H}_0(S) + o(n \log \sigma)$ bits. After several intermediate improvements (Lee and Park, 2009; González and Navarro, 2009), Navarro and Sadakane (2014) obtained time $\mathcal{O}((\log n / \log \log n)((1 + \log \sigma / \log \log n))$, the best possible with this approach, by using their faster dynamic bitvectors and multiary wavelet trees (Ferragina *et al.*, 2007).

Navarro and Nekrich (2014) showed that the time can be reduced sharply, to the optimal $\mathcal{O}(\log n / \log \log n)$, by avoiding the use of bitvector **rank** to move downwards in the wavelet tree. Their times for **insert** and **delete** are amortized, however. They can also obtain worst-case times, in which case those for **rank**, **insert**, and **delete** raise to $\mathcal{O}(\log n)$. After some improvements toward high-order compression (Grossi *et al.*,, 2013), Munro and Nekrich (2015) obtained $n\mathcal{H}_k(S) + o(n \log \sigma)$ bits and the optimal $\mathcal{O}(\log n / \log \log n)$ worst-case time for all the operations.

Despite the considerable complexity gap with the simple structures we describe in the chapter, we have omitted these more sophisticated solutions because they are much harder to implement. While the basic solution we present is indeed slow in practice (Córdova and Navarro, 2016), it is unclear if the theoretical improvements can actually be translated into practical speedups. The proposal of Munro and Nekrich (2015), however, introduces a new paradigm that is worth exploring: Instead of dynamic wavelet trees, they maintain static structures on substrings of S, plus one dynamic structure on a small subsequence. The dynamic structure needs not be compact and thus can be fast, whereas the other structures are static and thus are also fast.

Graphs and grids. The $\mathcal{O}(w^2)$ time we obtain for range counting on an $n \times n$ grid with n points is close to optimal, since a lower bound is $\Omega((\log n / \log \log n)^2)$ (Pătraşcu, 2007). Thus, while dynamic sequences can, at least in theory, operate much faster than the $\mathcal{O}(w \log \sigma)$ times we obtain, this is not the case of other structures that rely on dynamic wavelet trees or matrices, beyond their support for **rank** and **select** queries. He and Munro (2014) recently matched the lower bound, while using $\mathcal{O}(n \log n)$ bits.

The combination of k^2-trees and dynamic LOUDS we describe in the chapter has been shown to be practical (Brisaboa *et al.*, 2012).

Trees. The types of update operations we allow on trees were proposed by Chan *et al.* (2007). The updates needed to insert and delete nodes in the various tree representations are easily derived from the respective formats. In the case of LOUDS, the implementation using dynamic bitvectors is immediate. For the parentheses-based formats, our description is based on the simple proposal of Navarro and Sadakane (2014), which uses $2n + o(n)$ bits and obtains $\mathcal{O}(\log n)$ time for all the operations. They also present a more complex structure that reduces the time of some operations (open, close, parent, lca, leafrank, leafselect, insert, and delete) to $\mathcal{O}(\log n / \log \log n)$. For this reduction, they build on previous results by Chan *et al.* (2007), who also proved that the time $\mathcal{O}(\log n / \log \log n)$ is optimal for most relevant queries.

Previous works on dynamic trees support a restricted set of navigation operations (Raman and Rao, 2003; Farzan and Munro, 2011). Recent experimental results (Joannou and Raman, 2012), also considering limited functionality, show that the dynamic representation based on rmM-trees is practical and explore other interesting aspects such as the use of splay trees to speed up local traversals in the trees. They also introduce the idea of reaching in a direct way the node v where the operations start.

Navarro and Sadakane (2014) also explore more complex tree operations such as attaching and detaching subtrees, which are handled in $\mathcal{O}(w^{1+\epsilon})$ time.

There are not many works on succinct dynamic labeled trees, though one by Arroyuelo *et al.* (2016) obtains surprisingly low query times, $\mathcal{O}(\log \sigma / \log \log \sigma)$, and the same amortized update times. They take advantage of the limited tree arity (at most σ) to pack connected subtrees in memory blocks and use explicit pointers between blocks. Jansson *et al.* (2015) have recently presented another work on these lines.

Texts. The general model we have used to handle dynamic text collections is based on the work of Chan *et al.* (2007), as modified by Mäkinen and Navarro (2008). Chan *et al.* maintain both the Ψ function and the FM-index, so their space is not optimal. To dynamize Ψ, they maintain the bitvectors B_c described in Section 11.1.2, so they use $\mathcal{O}(\sigma n)$ bits of space, and inserting or deleting $D[1, \ell]$ costs $\mathcal{O}(\sigma \ell \log n)$ time. They could reach $\mathcal{O}(n \log \sigma)$ bits of space by compressing the bitvectors, but their update time is still linear in σ. In exchange, their counting time is $\mathcal{O}(m \log n)$ and their locating time with a sampling step l is $\mathcal{O}(l \log n)$. For deletions, they require presenting the text of the document $D[1, \ell]$ to be deleted, which is cumbersome.

Mäkinen and Navarro (2008) maintain only the FM-index, represented with a dynamic wavelet tree with compressed bitvectors, and then all the times are $\mathcal{O}(\log n \log \sigma)$ per step. They also show that the space is $n\mathcal{H}_k(T) + o(n \log \sigma)$ bits. They propose a mechanism of document identifiers similar to the one we described, so that deletion can be carried out by only exhibiting a document identifier. The only cost of this is the usually insignificant $\mathcal{O}(\Delta w)$ bits of space (which can be an issue only if we manage many very short documents). In the chapter we simplify their management of document identifiers and adapt an idea by Gog *et al.* (2015) to use inverse permutations for the sampling.

The successive improvements in the time to support queries on a dynamic sequence (Lee and Park, 2009; González and Navarro, 2009; Navarro and Sadakane, 2014; Navarro and Nekrich, 2014; Munro and Nekrich, 2015) directly impact the time complexity obtained for counting and locating, as well as for inserting and deleting documents. For example, with the fastest representations (Navarro and Nekrich, 2014; Munro and Nekrich, 2015), the counting time for $P[1, m]$ is $\mathcal{O}(m \log n / \log \log n)$, and the locating time with a sampling step l is $\mathcal{O}(l \log n / \log \log n)$.

A recent result by Munro *et al.* (2015) shows that data structures that handle sets of items, such as document collections, graphs (sets of edges), and binary relations (sets of pairs), can be made dynamic by following a general principle due to Bentley and Saxe (1980), which allows converting some static data structures into dynamic. The data are distributed across subcollections of doubling sizes, each of which is static except the smallest one, which receives the insertions. When the size of the smallest collection overflows, it is made static and placed in the next-size slot. If the slot is occupied by another collection (of that same size), both are merged and placed in the next slot, and so on. In the case of compact data structures, some care is needed to avoid using too much space at reconstruction time, to deamortize times if possible, and so on.

For the case of text collections, Munro *et al.* (2015) use a classical suffix tree on the smallest subcollection. They obtain $n\mathcal{H}_k(T) + o(n \log \sigma)$ bits of space, $\mathcal{O}(m \log \log n \log \log \sigma)$ counting time, $\mathcal{O}(l \log \log \sigma)$ locating time, $\mathcal{O}(\ell \log^\epsilon n)$ insertion time, and $\mathcal{O}(\ell(l + \log^\epsilon n))$ deletion time, for any constant $\epsilon > 0$ (a related idea was proposed for the FM-index (Ferragina and Manzini, 2005), but the results were not so good). While, as with other theoretical results, the practicality of this idea is yet to be established, the general approach is certainly interesting and may prove useful in practice. An important point it makes is that the complexities to maintain a dynamic text collection do not need to be tied with those to maintain a sequence supporting access, rank, and updates. For example, computing LF on a dynamic sequence costs $\Omega(\log n / \log \log n)$ time, but they handle it in time $\mathcal{O}(\log \log \sigma)$ with their approach (it is either done on a static sequence, or via a Weiner link on the suffix tree).

Chan *et al.* (2007) also showed how to maintain a compact dynamic suffix tree on a text collection, which we have omitted for simplicity. More recently, Russo *et al.* (2011) introduced a smaller dynamic compressed suffix tree.

Dynamic memory allocation. Depending on the runtime support, the space actually allocated might even double what the applications have requested. For example, the buddy memory system (Knowlton, 1965) allocates the power of 2 that follows the amount of memory requested. Current systems generally use a more sophisticated combination of methods that wastes less memory in practice (Mauerer, 2008). The classical buddy system requires $\mathcal{O}(\log n)$ time for allocation and deallocation. Demaine and Munro (1999) reduced this time to constant, amortized in the deallocations.

The scheme we have described is a variant of the one proposed by Munro (1986). It was recently implemented and tested (Klitzke and Nicholson, 2016; Córdova and Navarro, 2016), showing that the solution is practical and as fast as the system allocation. It uses almost no extra space on top of the raw data, whereas the system allocation uses up to 25% extra space. Klitzke and Nicholson (2016) obtained those results on dynamic bitvectors and also implemented a so-called *compressed RAM* (Jansson *et al.*, 2012; Grossi *et al.*, 2013), which maintains a memory area M of n words compressed to $n\mathcal{H}_k(M) + \mathcal{O}(\epsilon n w)$ bits while allowing reading cells in time $\mathcal{O}(1)$ and writing cells in time $\mathcal{O}(1/\epsilon)$ for any $\epsilon > 0$.

The structure that maintains a single memory area that grows and shrinks as needed is called an *extendible array*. Brodnik *et al.* (1999) showed practical ways to handle a set of extendible arrays of n memory cells in total, with only $\mathcal{O}(\sqrt{n})$ wasted extra cells and carrying out the operations in constant time. Raman and Rao (2003) obtained analogous results on the finer-grained case of arrays of *s* bits and without using an external memory allocator. Joannou and Raman (2011) and Katajainen (2016) studied experimentally various alternatives for implementing extendible arrays.

Bibliography

Arroyuelo, D., Davoodi, P., and Rao, S. S. (2016). Succinct dynamic cardinal trees. In *Algorithmica*, **74**(2), 742–777.

Bentley, J. L. and Saxe, J. B. (1980). Decomposable searching problems I: static-to-dynamic transformation. *Journal of Algorithms*, **1**(4), 301–358.

Blandford, D. and Blelloch, G. (2004). Compact representations of ordered sets. In *Proc. 15th Annual ACM-SIAM Symposium on Discrete Algorithms (SODA)*, pages 11–19.

Brisaboa, N. R., de Bernardo, G., and Navarro, G. (2012). Compressed dynamic binary relations. In *Proc. 22nd Data Compression Conference (DCC)*, pages 52–61.

Brodnik, A., Carlsson, S., Demaine, E. D., Munro, J. I., and Sedgewick, R. (1999). Resizable arrays in optimal time and space. In *Proc. 6th International Symposium on Algorithms and Data Structures (WADS)*, LNCS 1663, pages 37–48.

Chan, H.-L., Hon, W.-K., Lam, T.-W., and Sadakane, K. (2007). Compressed indexes for dynamic text collections. *ACM Transactions on Algorithms*, **3**(2), article 21.

Córdova, J. and Navarro, G. (2016). Practical dynamic entropy-compressed bitvectors with applications. In *Proc. 15th International Symposium on Experimental Algorithms (SEA)*, LNCS 9685, pages 105–117.

Demaine, E. D. and Munro, J. I. (1999). Fast allocation and deallocation with an improved buddy system. In *Proc. 19th Annual Conference on Foundations of Software Technology and Theoretical Computer Science (FSTTCS)*, LNCS 1738, pages 84–96.

Farzan, A. and Munro, J. I. (2011). Succinct representation of dynamic trees. *Theoretical Computer Science*, **412**(24), 2668–2678.

Ferragina, P. and Manzini, G. (2005). Indexing compressed texts. *Journal of the ACM*, **52**(4), 552–581.

Ferragina, P., Manzini, G., Mäkinen, V., and Navarro, G. (2007). Compressed representations of sequences and full-text indexes. *ACM Transactions on Algorithms*, **3**(2), article 20.

Fredman, M. and Saks, M. (1989). The cell probe complexity of dynamic data structures. In *Proc. 21st Annual ACM Symposium on Theory of Computing (STOC)*, pages 345–354.

Gog, S., Navarro, G., and Petri, M. (2015). Improved and extended locating functionality on compressed suffix arrays. *Journal of Discrete Algorithms*, **32**, 53–63.

González, R. and Navarro, G. (2009). Rank/select on dynamic compressed sequences and applications. *Theoretical Computer Science*, **410**, 4414–4422.

Grossi, R., Raman, R., Rao, S. S., and Venturini, R. (2013). Dynamic compressed strings with random access. In *Proc. 40th International Colloquium on Automata, Languages and Programming (ICALP)*, LNCS 7965, pages 504–515.

He, M. and Munro, J. I. (2010). Succinct representations of dynamic strings. In *Proc. 17th International Symposium on String Processing and Information Retrieval (SPIRE)*, LNCS 6393, pages 334–346.

He, M. and Munro, J. I. (2014). Space efficient data structures for dynamic orthogonal range counting. *Computational Geometry*, **47**(2), 268–281.

Hon, W.-K., Sadakane, K., and Sung, W.-K. (2011). Succinct data structures for searchable partial sums with optimal worst-case performance. *Theoretical Computer Science*, **412**(39), 5176–5186.

Jansson, J., Sadakane, K., and Sung, W.-K. (2012). CRAM: Compressed random access memory. In *Proc. 39th International Colloquium on Automata, Languages, and Programming (ICALP)*, LNCS 7391, pages 510–521.

Jansson, J., Sadakane, K., and Sung, W.-K. (2015). Linked dynamic tries with applications to LZ-compression in sublinear time and space. *Algorithmica*, **71**(4), 969–988.

Joannou, S. and Raman, R. (2011). An empirical evaluation of extendible arrays. In *Proc. 10th International Symposium on Experimental Algorithms (SEA)*, LNCS 6630, pages 447–458.

Joannou, S. and Raman, R. (2012). Dynamizing succinct tree representations. In *Proc. 11th International Symposium on Experimental Algorithms (SEA)*, LNCS 7276, pages 224–235.

Katajainen, J. (2016). Worst-case-efficient dynamic arrays in practice. In *Proc. 15th International Symposium on Experimental Algorithms (SEA)*, LNCS 9685, pages 167–183.

Klitzke, P. and Nicholson, P. K. (2016). A general framework for dynamic succinct and compressed data structures. In *Proc. 18th Workshop on Algorithm Engineering and Experiments (ALENEX)*, pages 160–173.

Knowlton, K. C. (1965). A fast storage allocator. *Communications of the ACM*, **8**(10), 623–625.

Lee, S. and Park, K. (2009). Dynamic rank/select structures with applications to run-length encoded texts. *Theoretical Computer Science*, **410**(43), 4402–4413.

Mäkinen, V. and Navarro, G. (2008). Dynamic entropy-compressed sequences and full-text indexes. *ACM Transactions on Algorithms*, **4**(3), article 32.

Mauerer, W. (2008). *Professional Linux Kernel Architecture*. Wrox Press.

Munro, J. I. (1986). An implicit data structure supporting insertion, deletion, and search in $O(\log n)$ time. *Journal of Computer and Systems Sciences*, **33**(1), 66–74.

Munro, J. I. and Nekrich, Y. (2015). Compressed data structures for dynamic sequences. In *Proc. 23rd Annual European Symposium on Algorithms (ESA)*, LNCS 9294, pages 891–902.

Munro, J. I., Nekrich, Y., and Vitter, J. S. (2015). Dynamic data structures for document collections and graphs. In *Proc. 34th ACM Symposium on Principles of Database Systems (PODS)*, pages 277–289.

Navarro, G. and Nekrich, Y. (2014). Optimal dynamic sequence representations. *SIAM Journal on Computing*, **43**(5), 1781–1806.

Navarro, G. and Sadakane, K. (2014). Fully-functional static and dynamic succinct trees. *ACM Transactions on Algorithms*, **10**(3), article 16.

Pătraşcu, M. (2007). Lower bounds for 2-dimensional range counting. In *Proc. 39th Annual ACM Symposium on Theory of Computing (STOC)*, pages 40–46.

Pătraşcu, M. and Demaine, E. D. (2006). Logarithmic lower bounds in the cell-probe model. *SIAM Journal on Computing*, **35**(4), 932–963.

Raman, R. and Rao, S. S. (2003). Succinct dynamic dictionaries and trees. In *Proc. 30th International Colloquium on Automata, Languages and Programming (ICALP)*, LNCS 2719, pages 357–368.

Raman, R., Raman, V., and Rao, S. S. (2001). Succinct dynamic data structures. In *Proc. 3rd International Symposium on Algorithms and Data Structures (WADS)*, pages 426–437.

Russo, L. M. S., Navarro, G., and Oliveira, A. (2011). Fully-compressed suffix trees. *ACM Transactions on Algorithms*, **7**(4), article 53.

CHAPTER 13

Recent Trends

Throughout the book we have covered a number of compact data structures that are well established and tested, and their basic aspects can be considered stable. This chapter is conceived as an epilogue, where we take a look to the future. We describe some recent trends that, while not mature or general enough to deserve a thorough treatment in the book, are certainly promising and likely to be the focus of intense research in the upcoming years. Therefore, the chapter may also serve to guide the readers looking for hot research topics. Its writing style is different from the other chapters, as we discuss the bibliography together with the main material.

First, we consider encoding data structures. These ensure only that a certain set of queries of interest can be answered; the actual data cannot be recovered. Encodings can offer significant space reductions with respect to the data entropy and are interesting because they have the potential to reach the minimum space needed just to answer the desired queries; nothing superfluous is stored. They also define a new concept of entropy, in terms not only of a universe of objects, but also of a set of queries posed on them. Encodings for a few problems exist already, but they are very recent and mostly in a theoretical stage.

Second, we consider repetitive document collections. Many of the largest text collections arising in applications these days are highly repetitive, and thus very compressible if one applies the right compression methods. The compact data structures we have seen, however, focus on statistical compression, which is insensitive to this kind of compressibility. New text indexes building on other compression principles are being designed, although they are generally slower than the classical ones and still do not reach the exact entropy bounds as current statistical methods do.

Finally, we consider secondary memory. Compact data structures use less space than classical ones and thus may fit in smaller and faster memories. However, they have generally less locality of reference, thus they are slower than classical structures when competing in the same level of the memory hierarchy. This is particularly relevant when the datasets are huge and the structures must operate on disk, where the space usage is not so important and locality of reference is crucial. In some cases compact data structures help speed up classical disk-based structures, whereas in others it can be proved that compactness imposes a steep price. While results exist in both directions, the whole scenario is not yet well understood.

13.1 Encoding Data Structures

In Section 7.4.1 we introduced a structure using only $2n + o(n)$ bits and answering range minimum queries $\mathsf{rmq}_A(i, j)$ on array $A[1, n]$, without accessing A at all. This means that, even if one cannot store every possible permutation array $A[1, n]$ in less than $n \log n$ bits, we need only $2n + o(n)$ bits to answer those particular queries on A. Sections 8.5.3 (autocompletion search), 8.5.7 (integer functions), 10.3.1 (weighted points), 11.6.3 (document retrieval), and 13.2.1 and 13.2.2 (Lempel-Ziv parsing and indexing) give examples where the contents of A itself are not relevant; we need only the results of rmq operations on it.

This idea opens the door to a new class of compact data structures called *encodings* (Raman, 2015). An encoding is a compact representation not of data (as a compressor would be), nor of a data type (with efficient access and support for some operations, as a compact data structure would be), but of an *abstract data type*. That is, an encoding grants access to the data only via a predefined set of queries, but the data are not accessible. Of course, some queries may be sufficient to recover the data (for example, we can reconstruct a bitvector $B[1, n]$ using only rank queries, $B[i] = \mathsf{rank}_1(B, i) - \mathsf{rank}_1(B, i - 1)$), and in this case an encoding supporting those queries cannot be smaller than the data entropy. However, in other cases, the allowed operations do not disclose sufficient information to reconstruct the data. For example, one cannot distinguish between $A[1, 4] = \langle 1, 3, 2, 4 \rangle$ and $A[1, 4] = \langle 1, 4, 2, 3 \rangle$ using queries $\mathsf{rmq}_A(i, j)$: both give exactly the same answers to all those queries. In those cases, the encoding may use less space than the smallest possible compact data structure.

13.1.1 Effective Entropy

An encoding problem is defined as a universe of objects $\mathcal{U}$ and a set of queries $\mathcal{Q}$. A first question about an encoding problem is which is the minimum space needed to answer those queries, independently of the time efficiency. A concept analogous to worst-case entropy (Section 2.1) is obtained by partitioning the set of the data objects $\mathcal{U}$ into equivalence classes. Two objects are in the same class iff they give the same answers to all the queries in $\mathcal{Q}$. Let $\mathcal{U}/\mathcal{Q}$ denote the set of the equivalence classes. The *effective entropy* (Golin *et al.*, 2016) of $\mathcal{U}$ under the set of queries $\mathcal{Q}$ is then

$$\mathcal{H}_{\text{eff}}(\mathcal{U}, \mathcal{Q}) = \log |\mathcal{U}/\mathcal{Q}|.$$

That is, $\mathcal{H}_{\text{eff}}$ is the minimum number of bits needed by an encoding that correctly answers all the queries in $\mathcal{Q}$. A representation using less than $\mathcal{H}_{\text{eff}}$ bits can distinguish less than $2^{\mathcal{H}_{\text{eff}}} = |\mathcal{U}/\mathcal{Q}|$ classes, and therefore it must use the same representation for two objects in $\mathcal{U}$ that are in different classes and thus should answer differently to some query.

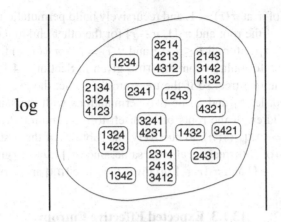

log

Figure 13.1. The effective entropy of permutations of [1, 4] with query rmq. The permutations are grouped according to their answers to every possible rmq, and the effective entropy is the number of groups.

Example 13.1 *Consider the set of permutations of* [1, 4], *where the only query of interest is* rmq. *The set* $\mathcal{U}$ *of* 4! = 24 *permutations is partitioned by the set of queries* $\mathcal{Q} = \{\text{rmq}(i, j), 1 \le i \le j \le 4\}$ *into the following classes:*

$$\mathcal{U}/\mathcal{Q} = \{\{1234\}, \{1243\}, \{1324, 1423\}, \{1342\}, \{1432\}, \{2134, 3124, 4123\},$$

$$\{2143, 3142, 4132\}, \{2314, 2413, 3412\}, \{2341\}, \{2431\},$$

$$\{3214, 4213, 4312\}, \{3241, 4231\}, \{3421\}, \{4321\}\}.$$

Thus, the effective entropy is $\mathcal{H}_{\text{eff}} = \log |\mathcal{U}/\mathcal{Q}| = \log 14 \approx 3.81$, *smaller than the entropy of* $\mathcal{U}$, $\mathcal{H}_{\text{wc}}(\mathcal{U}) = \log |\mathcal{U}| = \log 24 \approx 4.58$. *Figure 13.1 illustrates this concept.*

13.1.2 The Entropy of RMQs

Fischer and Heun (2011) showed that, in the case of permutation arrays $A[1, n]$ (and, in general, arrays with distinct elements) with operation rmq, the set $\mathcal{U}/\mathcal{Q}$ is isomorphic to the set of left-to-right minima trees on A (Section 7.4.1), or analogously, the set of Cartesian trees (Section 7.6). Therefore, its size is the nth Catalan number, $|\mathcal{U}/\mathcal{Q}| = \frac{1}{n+1}\binom{2n}{n} = 4^n/n^{3/2} \cdot \Theta(1)$ (recall Section 2.1), and thus $\mathcal{H}_{\text{eff}} = 2n - \mathcal{O}(\log n)$. Their structure using $2n + o(n)$ bits, analogous to the one we described in Section 7.4.1, is therefore optimal in size up to lower-order terms.

To prove the isomorphism, it is sufficient to show that (1) every permutation has a left-to-right minima tree and every ordinal tree is the left-to-right minima tree of some permutation; (2) two permutations have the same left-to-right minima trees iff they return the same answers to all queries rmq(i, j). If we prove this, then each left-to-right minima tree corresponds exactly to one equivalence class in $\mathcal{U}/\mathcal{Q}$.

For (1), the construction in Section 7.4.1 builds the left-to-right minima tree of any permutation. On the other hand, given an ordinal tree of $n + 1$ nodes, the root has postorder position $n + 1$ and let its first child have postorder position r. Then we can always build a permutation π whose left-to-right minima tree is that ordinal tree: We set the minimum of π at $\pi(r) = 1$, and recursively build permutations π_l on $[1, r - 1]$ for the first child of the root and $\pi_2[1, n - r]$ for the other children of the root. Then we set $\pi(i) = 1 + \pi_1(i)$ for all $1 \le i < r$ and $\pi(i) = r + \pi_2(i - r)$ for all $r < i \le n$.

To show (2), the formula to compute rmq given in Section 7.4.1 depends only on the left-to-right minima tree, so if the trees are the same, the answers are the same. On the other hand, let π_1 and π_2 be two permutations with the same rmq answers. Then the first children of the roots of both left-to-right minima trees are the same, $r = \mathrm{rmq}_{\pi_1}(1, n) = \mathrm{rmq}_{\pi_2}(1, n)$. Recursively, the subtrees of the first children and the other root children of both trees are also the same, since $\pi_1[1, r - 1]$ gives the same rmq answers as $\pi_2[1, r - 1]$ and $\pi_1[r + 1, n]$ gives the same rmq answers as $\pi_2[r + 1, n]$.

13.1.3 Expected Effective Entropy

We defined effective entropy analogously to the worst-case entropy of data sets. We can also combine the definition with object probabilities to give rise to more refined measures. Note that in Example 13.1 the different classes in $\mathcal{U}/\mathcal{Q}$ have different sizes. Then, if we assume that the objects in $\mathcal{U}$ are equally likely, we can refine the definition of effective entropy by considering the sizes of the classes. In this case, the lower bound on the space an encoding can achieve on average is called *expected effective entropy*:

$$\mathcal{H}(\mathcal{U}, \mathcal{Q}) = \sum_{C \in \mathcal{U}/\mathcal{Q}} \frac{|C|}{|\mathcal{U}|} \log \frac{|\mathcal{U}|}{|C|} \le \mathcal{H}_{\mathrm{eff}}(\mathcal{U}, \mathcal{Q}),$$

which is basically the Shannon entropy of the object classes, that is, the minimum average number of bits needed to encode the class of an object. For example, the value $\mathcal{H}(\mathcal{U}/\mathcal{Q})$ in the case of uniformly distributed permutations answering rmq is approximately $1.736\, n + \mathcal{O}(\log n)$ (Golin *et al.*, 2016). However, the best known encodings (which answer rmq in constant time) do not match this entropy; they use approximately $1.919\, n$ bits of space (Davoodi *et al.*, 2014). Still, this is less than the $2n + o(n)$ bits used by the best worst-case encoding.

Example 13.2 *In the classes of Figure 13.1, the expected effective entropy is* $\mathcal{H} = 4 \cdot \frac{3}{24} \log \frac{24}{3} + 2 \cdot \frac{2}{24} \log \frac{24}{2} + 8 \cdot \frac{1}{24} \log \frac{24}{1} \approx 3.63 < 3.81 \approx \mathcal{H}_{\mathrm{eff}}$.

13.1.4 Other Encoding Problems

The $2n$-bit encoding for rmq operations is the best known and most established result, but others have been studied. A particularly rich area are the encodings for various range queries on arrays $A[1, n]$ (Skala, 2013):

1. Fischer (2011) considered *previous/next smaller value* queries: given a position i, find the largest $j < i$ and the smallest $j > i$ such that $A[j] < A[i]$. They solved this problem in constant time with an encoding of $\log(3 + 2\sqrt{2})n + o(n) \approx 2.544n + o(n)$ bits. This size is optimal up to lower-order terms, and the encoding solves, in addition, rmqs on A in constant time. If the elements of A are all distinct, then the $2n$-bit Cartesian tree (Section 7.6) can answer these queries (j is i minus/plus the size of the subtree of the left/right child of i, minus/plus 1). If there are repeated

elements, we can still solve one of the two operations with $2n + o(n)$ bits: a parent operation on the left-to-right minima tree of Section 7.4.1 solves next smaller value queries, and an analogous right-to-left minima tree finds previous smaller values (Fischer *et al.*, 2009). In these two cases, the effective entropy is $2n - \mathcal{O}(\log n)$ bits, because the Cartesian tree can be reconstructed from the queries.

2. Recently, Nicholson and Raman (2015) showed that, when we do not mind if j is larger or smaller than i, and want only the j nearest to i such that $A[j] < A[i]$ (*nearest smaller value* queries), the effective entropy becomes much lower, $1.317n - \Theta(1)$ bits. They found an encoding using $1.694n + o(n)$ bits and constant time.

3. Gawrychowski and Nicholson (2015b) considered the case where we want the positions of the maximum and the minimum in $A[i, j]$ (*range min-max* queries). They showed that the effective entropy is $3n - \mathcal{O}(\text{polylog } n)$, and gave a structure using $3n + o(n)$ bits answering queries in constant time. Jo and Rao (2015) extended this encoding to various combinations of range minima/maxima and previous/next smaller/larger value problems, obtaining several upper bounds.

4. Davoodi *et al.* (2014) devised an encoding to find the positions of the maximum and second maximum (or minimum and second minimum) of $A[i, j]$ in constant time, using $3.272n + \mathcal{O}(\log n)$ bits of space. They proved that such a structure needs at least $2.656n - \mathcal{O}(\log n)$ bits.

5. Grossi *et al.* (2013) generalized the problem to *range top-k* queries, that is, finding the positions of the k largest elements in $A[i, j]$. They proved that the effective entropy is at least $n \log k - \mathcal{O}(n + k \log k)$ and devised a structure using $\mathcal{O}(n \log k)$ bits that answers queries in the optimal time $\mathcal{O}(k)$, for k fixed at indexing time.

6. Navarro *et al.* (2014) considered *range selection* queries: find the kth largest element in $A[i, j]$. The effective entropy of this problem is also at least $n \log k - \mathcal{O}(n + k \log k)$, and they found a structure using $\mathcal{O}(n \log k)$ bits that answers the query in time $\mathcal{O}(1 + \log k / \log \log n)$, which is optimal even if using $\mathcal{O}(n \text{ polylog } n)$ space (Jørgensen and Larsen, 2011). Here k can be given at query time, and the k in the space refers to the maximum k for which the structure can answer queries. They also generalized the previous result on top-k queries so that k can be given at query time.

7. Gawrychowski and Nicholson (2015b) found the precise constants for the effective entropy of range top-k and range selection queries: $n \log k + n(k + 1) \log(1 + 1/k) = n \log k + \Theta(n)$. For example, for $k = 2$ (that is, finding the maximum and second maximum), the exact lower bound is $(\log 2 + 3 \log \frac{3}{2})n \approx 2.755n$ bits. They also described an encoding reaching this space up to lower-order terms, but it does not support queries efficiently.

8. Gawrychowski and Nicholson (2015a) consider *range maximum sum* queries: This time $A[1, n]$ is an array of n numbers, positive and negative. Given a range $[i, j]$, we want to find the subrange $[i', j'] \subseteq [i, j]$ that maximizes $\sum_{k=i'}^{j'} A[k]$. They show that the effective entropy is $\approx 1.891n - \mathcal{O}(\log n)$, and provide an encoding using $\mathcal{O}(n)$ bits that answers the queries in constant time.

9. Navarro and Thankachan (2016) considered *range τ-majority* queries. A τ-majority in $A[i, j]$, for $0 < \tau < 1$, is an element that appears more than $\tau(j - i + 1)$ times in the range. The problem is then to return one position for each

τ-majority in a given range $A[i, j]$. They show that the effective entropy is $\Omega(n \log(1/\tau))$, and offer a structure using $\mathcal{O}(n \log(1/\tau))$ bits that answers queries in $\mathcal{O}\big((1/\tau) \log n \log \log_w(1/\tau)\big)$ time. When $1/\tau = \Theta(\text{polylog } n)$, they reach the optimal time $\mathcal{O}(1/\tau)$.

This line of development is apparently gaining momentum. Some queries have clear applications to data mining and other areas. For example, the encodings for top-k queries are useful to generalize the autocompletion searches described in Section 8.5.3 to the more natural case where the k most relevant autocompletions are offered to the user (and not only the first one). Even in those cases where applications are unclear, encodings are interesting theoretically, as they expand our understanding of the relation between space and time in compact data structures.

We finish this section with an example of a lower bound and of an encoding, both chosen for their simplicity.

A Lower Bound on Effective Entropy for Top-k Queries

Let us show that no encoding answering top-k queries may use less than $n \log k - \mathcal{O}(n + k \log k)$ bits (there are stronger lower bounds than this one (Gawrychowski and Nicholson, 2015b), but they require more complicated techniques). In many of these proofs, the idea is to encode a set of objects with worst-case entropy $\mathcal{H}_{\text{wc}}$, in such a way that they can then be decoded via the permitted queries on the encoding. Then the effective entropy of the encoding must be at least $\mathcal{H}_{\text{wc}}$.

In this case (Grossi *et al.*, 2013), we encode m permutations π_i on $[1, k]$ in an array $A[1, n]$, for $n = (m + 1)k$, and then decode the permutations using top-k queries on A. Since representing the m permutations requires at least $m \log k! = m(k \log k - \mathcal{O}(k)) = n \log k - \mathcal{O}(n + k \log k)$ bits in the worst case, an encoding able to recover them cannot use less space.

We will write each π_i in $A[(i - 1)k + 1, ik]$, shifted by $(i - 1)k$, that is, $A[(i - 1)k + j] = (i - 1)k + \pi_i(j)$ for all $1 \le j \le k$ and $1 \le i \le m$. The last cells are set to $A[mk + 1, n] = n$. Now, since all the numbers in $A[k + 1, 2k]$ are larger than those in $A[1, k]$, the top-k query on $A[1, k + 1]$ returns all the numbers except the minimum in $A[1, k]$. The query on $A[1, k + 2]$ returns all but the minimum and second minimum in $A[1, k]$, and so on. In this way we uncover the ordering of the values in $A[1, k]$ and thus π_1. We proceed similarly with π_2, performing top-k queries on $A[1, 2k + 1]$, $A[1, 2k + 2]$, and so on. Then we can recover all the permutations. Note that the lower bound holds even for the restricted queries of the form $A[1, j]$.

Example 13.3 *Let $k = 3$ and $m = 2$. We encode $\pi_1 = (3\,1\,2)$ and $\pi_2 = (1\,2\,3)$ in array A as follows:*

$$A[1, 9] = \langle 3, 1, 2, \ 4, 5, 6, \ 9, 9, 9 \rangle.$$

Then the top-3 positions in $A[1, 4]$ are 4, 1, and 3. This means that the minimum in $A[1, 3]$ is at $A[2]$, thus $\pi_1(2) = 1$. Now, the top-3 positions in $A[1, 5]$ are 5, 4, and 1. Thus $A[2]$ and $A[3]$ contain the two minima in $A[1, 3]$. Since we already know that $A[2]$ is the minimum, $A[3]$ must be the second minimum. Thus $\pi_1(3) = 2$. Finally, it can only be that $\pi_1(1) = 3$ and we have recovered $\pi_1 = (3\,1\,2)$.

We can similarly recover π_2: The top-3 positions of $A[1, 7]$ are 7, 6, and 5, so the minimum in $A[4, 6]$ is at $A[4]$, thus $\pi_2(1) = 1$. The top-3 positions of $A[1, 8]$ are 7, 8, and 6, so the second minimum is at $A[5]$. Thus $\pi_2(2) = 2$ and therefore $\pi_2(3) = 3$. We have also recovered $\pi_2 = (1\ 2\ 3)$.

An Encoding for τ-Majority Queries

Now we describe an encoding for τ-majority queries in an array $A[1, n]$ (Navarro and Thankachan, 2016). Let x be an array value. Let S_x be the set of all the (possibly overlapping) segments of A where x is a τ-majority. Then define bitvector $B_x[1, n]$ so that $B_x[i] = 1$ iff i belongs to some segment in S_x. Furthermore, let $M_x[1, \text{rank}(B_x, n)]$ be another bitvector aligned to the 1s in B_x, so that if $B_x[i] = 1$, then $M_x[\text{rank}(B_x, i)] = 1$ iff $A[i] = x$.

Example 13.4 *Let $A[1, 7] = \langle b, b, a, a, c, a, b \rangle$ and $\tau = 1/2$. Then, we have*

$$S_a = \{[2, 4], [2, 6], [3, 3], [3, 4], [3, 5], [3, 6], [3, 7], [4, 4], [4, 6], [6, 6]\},$$

$$S_b = \{[1, 1], [1, 2], [1, 3], [2, 2], [7, 7]\},$$

$$S_c = \{[5, 5]\}.$$

The corresponding bitvectors are as follows:

$$B_a = \langle 0\ 1\ 1\ 1\ 1\ 1\ 1 \rangle \quad B_b = \langle 1\ 1\ 1\ 0\ 0\ 0\ 1 \rangle \quad B_c = \langle 0\ 0\ 0\ 0\ 1\ 0\ 0 \rangle$$
$$M_a = \langle \ \ 0\ 1\ 1\ 0\ 1\ 0 \rangle \quad M_b = \langle 1\ 1\ 0 \qquad 1 \rangle \quad M_c = \langle \qquad 1 \ \ \rangle$$

Now, if x is a τ-majority in $A[i, j]$, then $[i, j] \in S_x$, and thus $B_x[i, j] = 1^{j-i+1}$. Furthermore, the interval $A[i, j]$ maps entirely to $M_x[i', j'] = M_x[\text{rank}(B_x, i), \text{rank}(B_x, j)]$, and therefore 1 is a τ-majority in $M_x[i', j']$. Note that both things can be established via rank queries on B_x and M_x. Conversely, if $B_x[i, j] = 1^{j-i+1}$ and 1 is a τ-majority in $M_x[i', j']$, then x is a τ-majority in $A[i, j]$. Therefore, A_x and M_x are sufficient to determine, in constant time, whether x is a τ-majority in any interval $A[i, j]$. In principle we could test each pair of bitvectors B_x and M_x to answer the query.

Moreover, if we find that x is a τ-majority in $A[i, j]$, we can recover all of its occurrences in $A[i, j]$: Each 1 in $M_x[p]$, $i' \le p \le j'$, is mapped back to $p + i - i'$, in the interval $[i, j]$.

Example 13.5 *In Example 13.4, we know that 'a' is a τ-majority in $A[i, j] = A[3, 6]$ because $B_a[3, 6] = 1111$ and 1 is a τ-majority in the range $M_a[i', j'] = M_a[\text{rank}(B_a, 3), \text{rank}(B_a, 6)] = M_a[2, 5] = 1101$. Each 1 in $M_a[2, 5]$ can be mapped back to a position in A, to tell where this majority appears in $A[1, 7]$. For example, the leftmost position is obtained by finding the first 1 in $M_a[i', j']$ with $p = \text{succ}(M_a, i') = \text{succ}(M_a, 2) = 2$, and then the position in A is $p + i - i' = 2 + 3 - 2 = 3$. Thus, the first occurrence of the τ-majority 'a' in $A[3, 6]$ is at $A[3]$.*

The problem is that there may be many different elements x, so the query time may be linear and bitvectors B_x and M_x may add up to quadratic space. However, if we consider the maximal runs of 1s in the bitvectors B_x, it turns out that all those runs can be merged on $\mathcal{O}((1/\tau) \log n)$ *coalesced* bitvectors B'_r, where each run $B_x[i, j] = 1^{j-i+1}$ is written in some $B'_r[i, j] = 1^{j-i+1}$ so that no two runs touch or overlap. Coalesced bitvectors M'_r

---

Algorithm 13.1: Reporting τ-majorities from an encoding.

Input : Array $A[1, n]$ (encoded as coalesced bitvectors B'_r and M'_r, for
              $1 \le r \le e$), parameter τ, and range $[i, j]$.
Output: Outputs the leftmost position of each distinct τ-majority in $A[i, j]$.

1 **for** $r \leftarrow 1$ **to** e **do**
2 $\quad$ $i' \leftarrow \mathsf{rank}(B'_r, i - 1) + 1$
3 $\quad$ $j' \leftarrow \mathsf{rank}(B'_r, j)$
4 $\quad$ **if** $j' - i' = j - i$ **then**
5 $\quad\quad$ $i'' \leftarrow \mathsf{rank}(M'_r, i' - 1) + 1$
6 $\quad\quad$ $j'' \leftarrow \mathsf{rank}(M'_r, j')$
7 $\quad\quad$ **if** $j'' - i'' + 1 > \tau \cdot (j - i + 1)$ **then**
8 $\quad\quad\quad$ $p \leftarrow \mathsf{succ}(M'_r, i')$
9 $\quad\quad\quad$ **output** $p + i - i'$

---

are built according to their corresponding bitvectors B'_r (each run in B'_r may correspond
to a different element x). Then we can store and query the coalesced bitvectors B'_r and
M'_r instead of the original ones B_x and M_x, and the query time becomes $\mathcal{O}((1/\tau) \log n)$.
Algorithm 13.1 shows the final pseudocode for queries.

Example 13.6 *In Example 13.4, we can coalesce all the runs in B_b and B_c into $B' = \langle 1\,1\,1\,0\,1\,0\,1 \rangle$, and correspondingly map M_b and M_c to $M' = \langle 1\,1\,0\,1\,1 \rangle$. We know that there is a τ-majority in $A[1, 3]$ because $B'[1, 3] = 111$ and 1 is a τ-majority in $M'[\mathsf{rank}(B', 1), \mathsf{rank}(B', 3)] = M'[1, 3] = 110$. We can still recover the positions of this τ-majority from M', but we no longer know which element it is (otherwise we could recover A via τ-majority queries on $A[i, i]$, and thus the encoding could not be smaller than the entropy of A).*

As for the space, it is shown that there are $\mathcal{O}(n/\tau)$ 1s across all the bitvectors B_x,
and the coalesced bitvectors add up to length $\mathcal{O}((n/\tau) \log n)$. Therefore, the technique
of Section 4.1.1 requires in total $\mathcal{O}((n/\tau) \log \log n)$ bits for representing all the bitvectors B'_r and M'_r. Reducing the space to the optimal $\mathcal{O}(n \log(1/\tau))$ bits requires more
technicalities (Navarro and Thankachan, 2016) and slightly increases the query time.

13.2 Repetitive Text Collections

Sequence databases formed by genomes of individuals of the same species (see, e.g.,
the 1000-genomes project),[1] versioned document collections such as Wikipedia,[2] and
software repositories storing a hierarchy of major and minor versions are examples of
document collections that consist of very similar documents. Recording the *edits* of
each version with respect to a previous one is a standard technique used in version

---

[1] http://www.1000genomes.org.
[2] http://www.wikipedia.org.

management systems to store and recover individual documents. However, it is more challenging to provide text search capabilities on such a compressed representation.

One could expect that actually storing all the documents and then applying the techniques of Chapter 11 would offer efficient searches within a space comparable to that of storing the edits, but this is not the case. The techniques studied in Chapter 11 exploit *statistical* compressibility and thus compress the collection to its zero-order or high-order empirical entropy (recall Chapter 2). This concept of entropy captures biased frequency distributions, or the predictability of the next symbol given k previous symbols, for a small k, but are blind to repetitiveness. Consider a statistically incompressible document $S[1, n]$ on $[1, \sigma]$ terminated in $S[n] = \# = 1$. Then it holds $n\mathcal{H}_k(S) \approx n \log \sigma$ for any small k. Now consider the text $T[1, tn] = S^t$, that is, T is formed by t consecutive copies of S. Clearly, one could compress $T[1, tn]$ to little more than $n \log \sigma$ bits, by storing S and then just indicating that it must be copied t times. However, if we attempt to use statistical compression, then the best space we can reach is $tn\mathcal{H}_k(T)$ bits, where

$$tn\mathcal{H}_k(T) = \sum_{C=s_1\dots s_k} |T_C|\, \mathcal{H}_0(T_C) = \sum_{C=s_1\dots s_k} t\, |S_C|\, \mathcal{H}_0(S_C) = tn\mathcal{H}_k(S) \approx tn \log \sigma,$$

where X_C is the string of the symbols following context C in X (see Section 2.4). For those contexts C that do not contain the separator #, that is, that do not cross from one copy of S to the next, it holds $T_C = (S_C)^t$, and thus $|T_C| = t\,|S_C|$ and $\mathcal{H}_0(T_C) = \mathcal{H}_0(S_C)$. For those contexts C that do contain #, say, $C[j] = \#$, it holds $S_C = \varepsilon$, but it also holds $\mathcal{H}_0(T_C) = 0$ because $T_C = S[k - j + 1]^{t-1}$. Thus the equality holds, and it means that the kth order compression of T cannot be better than compressing t separate copies of S (Kreft and Navarro, 2013).

13.2.1 Lempel-Ziv Compression

As we have seen, statistical compression does not capture repetitiveness, thus we need a different compression principle. A gold standard for repetitive texts is defined by Lempel-Ziv compression, more precisely the LZ76 compression method (Lempel and Ziv, 1976). In LZ76 the text is parsed into a sequence of phrases (we have already seen this concept in Section 8.5.4, for LZ78 compression). If we have already parsed $T[1, i]$, then the next phrase is the longest prefix of $T[i + 1, n]$ that has already appeared in $T[1, i]$, plus the symbol following that prefix.[3] Then, if the next phrase found is $T[i + 1, j] = T[i', j']\,.\,T[j]$, the LZ76 compression algorithm encodes the phrase as the triple $(i', j - i - 1, T[j])$, and continues parsing $T[j + 1, n]$.

If the LZ76 algorithm parses $T[1, n]$ into z phrases, then the output of the compressor has $\mathcal{O}(z \log n)$ bits. The value $z \log n$ is used as an entropy measure for repetitive text collections.[4]

Example 13.7 *Figure 13.2 shows the LZ76 parsing of the same text of Figure 8.21, into $z = 17$ phrases. At the top we show how the parsing cuts T into phrases. On the bottom*

---

[3] In the original formulation, they only require that the prefix starts in $T[1, i]$, so it can overlap $T[i + 1, n]$. Our definition is a variant (Farach and Thorup, 1995) used in the index we present later.

[4] Lempel and Ziv (1976) directly use z as the compressibility measure, but $z \log n$ connects more naturally with other entropy measures, as we will see shortly.

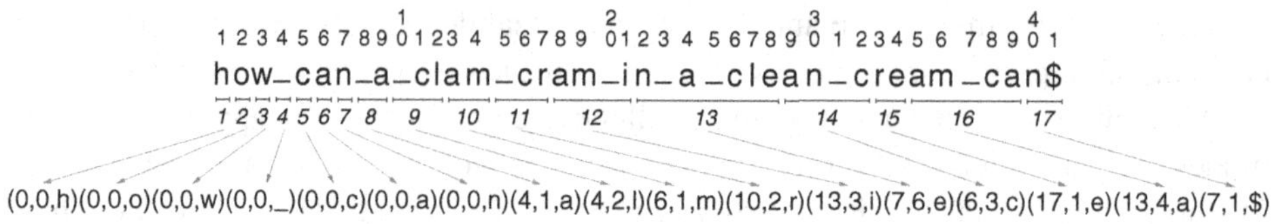

```
         1              2          3              4
1 2 3 4 5 6 7 8 9 0 1 2 3 4 5 6 7 8 9 0 1 2 3 4 5 6 7 8 9 0 1 2 3 4 5 6 7 8 9 0 1
how_can_a_clam_cram_in_a_clean_cream_can$
1 2 3 4 5 6 7 8  9  10  11   12      13     14   15    16      17
```

(0,0,h)(0,0,o)(0,0,w)(0,0,_)(0,0,c)(0,0,a)(0,0,n)(4,1,a)(4,2,l)(6,1,m)(10,2,r)(13,3,i)(7,6,e)(6,3,c)(17,1,e)(13,4,a)(7,1,$)

Figure 13.2. The LZ76 parsing of a text into $z = 17$ phrases. The space is shown as an underscore for legibility. Phrase numbers are in italics. On the bottom we show the Lempel-Ziv encoding of the text, with one triple per phrase.

we show the compressed file, where each phrase is coded as a triple. For example, the phrase number 13 corresponds to $T[22, 28] = $ n_a_cle, and is encoded as $(7, 6, e)$ because it is obtained by copying $T[7, 7 + 6 - 1] = $ n_a_cl and appending e.

Sometimes LZ76 is confused with LZ77 (Ziv and Lempel, 1977), a popular variant of LZ76 that restricts the length ℓ of the sliding window $T[i - \ell, i]$ from where the phrases can be copied. The triple can then be represented as $(i - j', j - i - 1, T[j])$ using $2 \log \ell + \log \sigma$ bits (particular implementations encode the triples in different ways; see, for example, Bell *et al.* (1990)). LZ77 is widely used for general-purpose compression, because it combines acceptable compression ratios with fast decompression. On typical texts, a window length like 2^{12} or 2^{15} is sufficient to spot long enough repetitions, and it simplifies finding and encoding the phrase. For repetitive collections, however, the original LZ76 is preferable, because in this case it is more likely to find long repetitions far away in the text. An implementation close in spirit to LZ76 is p7zip.[5]

LZ76 is also stronger than the LZ78 compression (Ziv and Lempel, 1978) we described in Section 8.5.4, because LZ78 can form phrases only by extending some previous phrase with a new symbol, whereas LZ76 can use any previous text substring. In exchange, as we have seen, the LZ78 parsing can be performed very efficiently with a trie of the current phrases.

Comparison with Statistical Entropy

All the Lempel-Ziv compressors converge, when n tends to infinity, to the Shannon entropy, both in the simple case of fixed-memory sources (recall Section 2.4) and in more general probabilistic processes (Lempel and Ziv, 1976; Ziv and Lempel, 1977, 1978; Sheinwald, 1994; Wyner and Ziv, 1994).

In terms of empirical entropy of finite texts, one can prove the following for *any* parsing that cuts T into z distinct phrases (which includes in particular the LZ76 and LZ78 parsings). First, it holds $z = \mathcal{O}(n/\log_\sigma n)$, which is easy to see by writing the z shortest possible distinct phrases whose lengths add up to n: σ phrases of length 1, σ^2 of length 2, and so on. This implies that $z \log n = \mathcal{O}(n \log \sigma)$. Second, it holds (Kosaraju and Manzini, 1999, Thm. A.4) that, for any k,

$$z \log z \leq n\mathcal{H}_k(T) + z(k \log \sigma + \log(n/z)) + \Theta(z),$$

---

[5] http://www.7-zip.org.

and therefore, by adding $z \log(n/z)$ in both sides,

$$z \log n \le n\mathcal{H}_k(T) + z(k \log \sigma + 2 \log(n/z)) + \Theta(z)$$

$$= n\mathcal{H}_k(T) + \mathcal{O}\left(\frac{n(k \log \sigma + \log\log_\sigma n + 1)}{\log_\sigma n} \right)$$

where in the last step we replaced z with $n/\log_\sigma n$ inside the $\mathcal{O}(\cdot)$ formula, because the formula was nondecreasing in z. Therefore, for $k = o(\log_\sigma n)$, it holds

$$z \log n \le n\mathcal{H}_k(T) + o(n \log \sigma).$$

This shows that both LZ76 and LZ78 converge to the kth order statistical entropy. The convergence is slow: The restriction on k can be seen as a condition for n to be large enough. In statistical compressors we had the weaker condition $k \le \alpha \log_\sigma n$ for any constant $0 < \alpha < 1$; recall Section 2.4. Thus, if a finite text T is compressible because of statistical reasons, then statistical compressors are generally more efficient than Lempel-Ziv compressors, as they reach $\mathcal{H}_k(T)$ sooner for any given k. Actually, in those kinds of texts, the indexes we described in Chapter 11 are more space-efficient than the Lempel-Ziv based indexes we are going to see in this section.

Performance on Repetitive Texts

The stronger nature of LZ76 compression shows up on repetitive texts. In those cases, LZ78 compression improves only mildly (note that it cannot produce less than $\sqrt{n}$ phrases, even in the text $T = a^n\$$). Instead, LZ76 compression can produce as little as $\log n$ phrases[6] and can be much better than statistical compression when the text is repetitive. In our example where $T = S^t$, even if the first copy of S turns out to be incompressible, all the others will be easily represented by referencing previous ones, thus $z = \mathcal{O}(n/\log_\sigma n) + \log t$ (the last $\log t$ triples are $(1, n, S[1])\,(2, 2n, S[2])\,(3, 4n, S[3]) \ldots$). Therefore, $z \log(tn)$ is much less than $tn\mathcal{H}_k(S) \approx tn \log \sigma$, and LZ76 succeeds where statistical compression failed.

Let us generalize this example to the case where T is formed by S and then $t - 1$ near-copies of it. Assume there are s edits (like symbol insertions, deletions, or substitutions) spread in the copies of S within $T[n + 1, tn]$. It is then easy to see that $z \le \mathcal{O}(n/\log_\sigma n) + t + s$; that is, the space grows proportionally to the number of edits. Of course, LZ76 does not only handle these restricted kinds of edits. Each new document that can be written as the concatenation of z' strings present anywhere in previous documents will be encoded in $\mathcal{O}(z' \log n)$ bits.

Efficient LZ76 Parsing

The LZ76 phrases can be found in linear time with the help of a suffix tree (Rodeh *et al.*, 1981), but this structure (Section 11.5) requires a lot of extra space, which hampers the parsing of large texts. Much recent research focuses on doing the LZ76 parsing in little time and memory space (Ohlebusch and Gog, 2011; Al-Hafeedh *et al.*, 2012; Kempa and Puglisi, 2013; Kärkkäinen *et al.*, 2013a,b; Goto and Bannai, 2013, 2014; Kärkkäinen *et al.*, 2014; Yamamoto *et al.*, 2014; Fischer *et al.*, 2015; Nishimoto *et al.*,

---

[6] If we consider the variant that allows the copied and new phrases overlap, it produces just 2 phrases on $T = a^n\$$: $(0, 0, a)\,(1, n - 1, \$)$.

Algorithm 13.2: Performing the LZ76 parsing of $T[1, n]$.

Input : A text $T[1, n]$.
Output: Outputs the z triples of the LZ76 parsing of T.

1   Reverse $T[1, n]$ to form $T^{rev}[1, n]$ (leave the $ at $T^{rev}[n]$)
2   Build the suffix array $A^r[1, n]$ of T^{rev}
3   Build the FM-index of A^r, as the sequence $L[1, n]$ and array $C[1, \sigma+1]$
4   Build the structure for range maximum queries on A^r, rMq_{A^r}
5   Free T^{rev} if desired
6   $i \leftarrow 0$
7   $p \leftarrow 1$ (to scan T with $L[p]$)
8   **while** $i < n$ **do**
9      $j \leftarrow i + 1$
10     $c \leftarrow L[p]$; $p \leftarrow \mathsf{LF}(p)$
11     $[sp, ep] \leftarrow [C[c] + 1, C[c + 1]]$
12     $i' \leftarrow 0$
13   **while** $j < n$ **and** $sp \le ep$ **and** $A^r[\mathsf{rMq}_{A^r}(sp, ep)] \ge n - i$ **do**
14        $i' \leftarrow n - A^r[\mathsf{rMq}_{A^r}(sp, ep)]$
15        $j \leftarrow j + 1$
16        $c \leftarrow L[p]$; $p \leftarrow \mathsf{LF}(p)$
17        $sp \leftarrow C[c] + \mathsf{rank}_c(L, sp - 1) + 1$
18        $ep \leftarrow C[c] + \mathsf{rank}_c(L, ep)$
19   **output** $(i' - (j - i - 1) + 1, j - i - 1, c)$
20     $i \leftarrow j$
21   Free A^r, L, C, and the structure for rMq_{A^r}

2015; Policriti and Prezza, 2016; Köppl and Sadakane, 2016). The last one, for example, obtains $\mathcal{O}(n \log \log \sigma)$ time and $\mathcal{O}(n \log \sigma)$ bits of space.

The version of the parsing we have defined, however, requires a different technique. One solution that runs in $\mathcal{O}(n \log \log \sigma)$ time and requires little more than a suffix array can be derived from algorithm CPS2 of Chen *et al.* (2008); see also Kreft and Navarro (2013). Build the suffix array A^r and the FM-index (Section 11.2) of the reversed text, $T^{rev}[1, n]$ (where we let $T^{rev}[n] = T[n] = \$$, elsewhere it holds $T^{rev}[i] = T[n - i]$). We use the permutation-based structure of Section 6.1 to represent the BWT in the FM-index. Build also a $2n$-bit range maximum query structure (Section 7.4.1) on the values of A^r. All these structures can be built in $\mathcal{O}(n)$ time.

Then the longest prefix of $T[i + 1, n]$ that appears in $T[1, i]$ can be found by successive backward search steps (Algorithm 11.5) for $T^{rev}[n - i - 1]$, $T^{rev}[n - i - 2, n - i - 1]$, $T^{rev}[n - i - 3, n - i - 1]$, and so on. We stop when $T^{rev}[n - j, n - i - 1]$ has an interval $A^r[sp, ep]$ that is empty or satisfies $A^r[\mathsf{rMq}_{A^r}(sp, ep)] < n - i$. Then no occurrence of $T^{rev}[n - j, n - i - 1]$ starts in $T^{rev}[n - i, n]$, or which is the same, no occurrence of $T[i + 1, j]$ ends in $T[1, i]$. This yields the new phrase $T[i + 1, j]$. Algorithm 13.2 shows the procedure.

Note that we need $n \log n + \mathcal{O}(n \log \sigma)$ bits to build the parsing. This could be reduced to $\mathcal{O}(n \log \sigma)$ by discarding A^r and using the locating ability of the FM-index, but then the time would raise to as much as $\mathcal{O}(n \log n)$.

13.2.2 Lempel-Ziv Indexing

Given the good performance of LZ76 at compressing repetitive texts, using it for developing indexes like those described in Chapter 11 is promising. One problem is that random access to arbitrary positions of the compressed text takes $\mathcal{O}(h)$ time in the worst case, where h is the length of the longest chain of references (that is, the text symbol $T[i]$ was copied from $T[i']$, but $T[i']$ was copied from $T[i'']$, and so on, h times, until the symbol is found explicitly in the third component of a triple).

Example 13.8 *To obtain $T[38] = \mathsf{c}$ from the LZ76 parsing of Figure 13.2, we start considering the triple $(13, 4, \mathsf{a})$, where $T[38]$ is contained with offset 4. Thus, we are redirected to extracting $T[13 - 1 + 4] = T[16]$. But $T[16]$ is contained in the phrase represented by the triple $(10, 2, \mathsf{r})$ with offset 2. Thus, we are redirected again, to $T[10 - 1 + 2] = T[11]$. Now the position is contained in the phrase represented by $(4, 2, \mathsf{l})$, with offset 2, and we are redirected once more, to $T[4 - 1 + 2] = T[5]$. Finally, $T[5]$ is in the phrase represented by the triple $(0, 0, \mathsf{c})$ with offset 1, thus we have $\mathsf{c} = T[5] = T[11] = T[16] = T[38]$. We required $h = 3$ steps in this worst-case example.*

Kreft and Navarro (2013) designed a text index based on LZ76 compression, which uses $3z \log n + \mathcal{O}(z \log \sigma) + o(n) \leq 3n\mathcal{H}_k(T) + o(n \log \sigma)$ bits of space (assuming $\log \sigma = o(\log n)$) and finds the occ occurrences of $P[1, m]$ in time $\mathcal{O}(m^2 h + m \log z + occ \log z)$. It can be regarded as a succinct representation of an earlier index (Kärkkäinen and Ukkonen, 1996). Next we describe a simplified version.

Much as in the grammar-based index we presented in Section 10.5.6, the occurrences are divided into primary (those crossing a phrase boundary) and secondary (those inside a phrase). We will also classify as primary an occurrence that ends at a phrase boundary. The key idea (Farach and Thorup, 1995) is that every secondary occurrence has been copied by the LZ76 parse from another place where there was a primary or an earlier secondary occurrence.

Finding Primary Occurrences

Primary occurrences are found with a two-dimensional structure similar to that of Section 10.5.6: For each phrase $T[i + 1, j]$ except the last one, we assign an x-coordinate to $T[i + 1, j]^{rev}$ and a y-coordinate to $T[j + 1, n]$, and set a point connecting both. Both coordinates are sorted in the lexicographic order of the strings they represent. Then any primary occurrence of P starting at position $j - k + 1$ inside some phrase $T[i + 1, j]$, for $1 \leq k \leq m$, will be found in the intersection of the lexicographic range of $P[1, k]^{rev}$ in the x-coordinates and the lexicographic range of $P[k + 1, m]$ in the y-coordinates. If $k = m$, $P[k + 1, m]$ is the whole range of y.

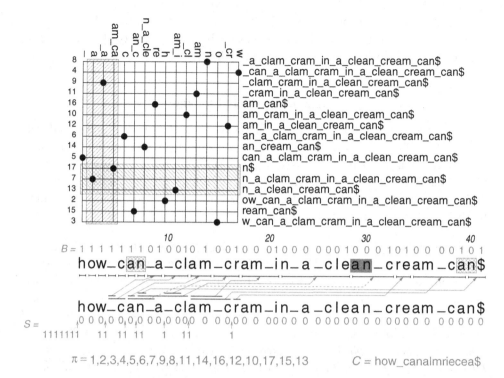

Figure 13.3. The LZ76-based index structure built on the text of Figure 13.2. The grid on the top connects phrases (in reverse order, as *x*-coordinates) with the suffix that follows them (as *y*-coordinates). Bitvector *B* marks phrase endings, and *S* marks where the sources start (1s) between text positions (0s). The mapping from phrases (1s in *B*) to their sources (1s in *S*) is given by π, and illustrated as gray arrows from sources to targets. String *C* contains the final symbols of phrases. The whole structure is then the grid, the values on the left of the grid, *B*, *S*, π, and *C*. Hatches, shadows, and dashed arrows illustrate the operations in Examples 13.9, 13.10, and 13.12.

Example 13.9 *Figure 13.3 shows the index for the text of Figure 13.2. Consider for now the grid on the top, where we have marked the ranges corresponding to the search for P = an and the value k = 1. The 2 primary occurrences are found as points in the grid, where we intersect the phrases ending in a with the phrase-aligned suffixes starting with n. The corresponding phrase numbers, 17 and 7, are found on the numbers written at the left of the grid. The alignment k = 2 does not produce further primary occurrences, as no phrase terminates with an.*

The grid takes $z \log z(1 + o(1))$ bits (Section 10.1), and other $z \log z$ bits are used to map the *y* coordinates to phrase numbers (as shown in the example). Thus, we have $2z \log z + o(z \log z) = 2z \log z + o(n \log \sigma)$ bits. For each *k*, the ranges of the partition of *P* are found by binary search. This requires a total of $\mathcal{O}(m \log z)$ string comparisons between parts of *P* and phrase-aligned substrings of *T*. In the binary search of the *y*-coordinates, the numbers we store map them to the phrase numbers from where the text must be extracted. For the *x*-coordinates, we can track the *y*-coordinate of the point on the grid (with a downward traversal on the wavelet matrix, in time $\mathcal{O}(\log z)$), obtain the phrase number *p*, and then we must extract a suffix of phrase

$p - 1$. We can extract each string in worst-case time $\mathcal{O}(mh)$, thus the total search time is $\mathcal{O}(m^2 h \log z + m \log^2 z + occ_p \log z)$, where the last component is the time used by the grid to report the occ_p primary occurrences. The actual solution (Kreft and Navarro, 2013) uses the Patricia trees described in Section 8.5.3 to reduce this time to $\mathcal{O}(m^2 h + m \log z + occ_p \log z)$, using $\mathcal{O}(z \log \sigma) = o(n \log \sigma)$ extra bits.

The device for converting phrase numbers to text positions is a bitvector $B[1, n]$ that marks the endpoints of phrases. Then $\mathsf{select}(B, p - 1) + 1 - k$ gives the starting point of a primary occurrence starting at phrase $p - 1$ and aligned at k (our grid finds the phrase number p). Since it has only z 1s, B can be represented in compressed form (Section 4.1.1) within $z \log(n/z) + \mathcal{O}(z) + o(n)$ bits. In practice, the representation using δ-codes described in Section 4.5.1 uses much less space in repetitive collections.

Example 13.10 *Bitvector $B[1, 41]$ is shown in gray, below the grid in Figure 13.3. We use it to find the text positions of the primary occurrences,* $\mathsf{select}(B, 17 - 1) + 1 - k = \mathsf{select}(B, 16) + 1 - 1 = 39$ *and* $\mathsf{select}(B, 7 - 1) + 1 - k = \mathsf{select}(B, 6) + 1 - 1 = 6$. *Thus the primary occurrences are at $T[6, 7]$ and $T[39, 40]$. They are shown hatched in Figure 13.3.*

Extracting Text

We also need a mechanism to describe the copying structure of the parsing, so that we can extract phrase prefixes or suffixes of length m in time $\mathcal{O}(mh)$. We use another bitvector, $S[1, n + z]$, that marks the beginnings of phrase *sources* (that is, the substrings that are copied to form each phrase). Since several sources can share the same starting point, S has one 0 per position in T (n 0s), and a 1 before the ith 0 per phrase source starting at position i (z 1s). The triples of the form $(0, 0, c)$ induce a 1 before the first 0. In addition, a permutation $\pi[1, z]$ maps the 1s of B to the 1s of S, and a string $C[1, z]$ stores the final symbols of the phrases. With these structures, it is easy to extract any $T[i]$ in time $\mathcal{O}(h)$.

Example 13.11 *Bitvector $S[1, 41 + 17] = S[1, 58]$, permutation $\pi[1, 17]$, and string $C[1, 17]$ are shown in gray at the bottom of Figure 13.3. To extract $T[38]$ as in Example 13.8, we see that $B[38] = 0$, so it is not represented in C. Its phrase number is* $\mathsf{rank}(B, 38 - 1) + 1 = 16$. *It has been copied from source number $\pi(16) = 15$, which starts at $T[\mathsf{select}(S, 15) - 15 + 1] = T[13]$. The offset of $T[38]$ within phrase 16 was $38 - \mathsf{pred}(B, 38 - 1) = 38 - 34 = 4$; therefore its text position in the source that starts at $T[13]$ is $T[13 - 1 + 4] = T[16]$. We then continue as in Example 13.8 until we have to extract $T[5]$, and since $B[5] = 1$, this symbol is found at $C[\mathsf{rank}(B, 5)] = C[5] = \mathsf{c}$.*

Represented in compressed form, S takes $z \log((n + z)/z) + \mathcal{O}(z) + o(n) = z \log(n/z) + \mathcal{O}(z) + o(n) = z \log(n/z) + o(n)$ bits. Permutation π takes $z \log z$ bits, and C takes $z \log \sigma = o(n \log \sigma)$ bits. Adding up all the spaces, we have the promised $3z \log z + 2z \log(n/z) + o(n \log \sigma) \leq 3z \log n + o(n \log \sigma)$ bits.

Finding the Secondary Occurrences

We still have to find the secondary occurrences. We enrich π with the structure of Section 5.1 to compute π^{-1} in $\mathcal{O}(\log z)$ time, using $\mathcal{O}(z) = o(n)$ additional bits. If a primary occurrence is at $T[i, i+m-1]$, we must find every source that covers $T[i, i+m-1]$, find its corresponding phrase using π^{-1}, and then locate the corresponding secondary occurrence within that phrase. That occurrence can in turn trigger other secondary occurrences.

Example 13.12 *The primary occurrences in Figure 13.3 were found at $T[6, 7]$ and $T[39, 40]$. There is a source covering $T[6, 7]$: the one with number 10. It starts at text position $\mathsf{select}(S, 10) - 10 + 1 = 6$. Its length is that of phrase number $\pi^{-1}(10) = 14$ (dashed arrow) minus 1, that is, $\mathsf{select}(B, 14) - \mathsf{select}(B, 13) - 1 = 32 - 28 - 1 = 3$, therefore the source covers $T[6, 6 + 3 - 1] = T[6, 8]$, which includes the primary occurrence at $T[6, 7]$. The offset of the occurrence inside source 10 is $6 - 6 = 0$, therefore its offset inside phrase 14 is also 0. Since phrase 14 starts at $\mathsf{select}(B, 14 - 1) + 1 = 29$, this secondary occurrence of $P = \mathsf{an}$ starts at $T[29 + 0] = T[29]$, and spans $T[29, 30]$. This is shown in gray in Figure 13.3. Since there are no further sources covering $T[6, 7]$, $T[29, 30]$, or $T[39, 40]$, we are done.*

We need an efficient way of finding all the sources covering an occurrence $T[i, i + m - 1]$. These are sources that start in $T[1, i]$ and end in $T[i + m - 1, n]$. One choice is to consider an array $E[1, z]$ with the *ending* positions of the sources marked in S, and store a range maximum query structure on E (Section 7.4.1; this uses only $2z + o(z) = o(n)$ bits). Then the entries that start in $T[1, i]$ are in $E[1, s]$, for $s = \mathsf{select}_0(S, i) - i$. We can thus run an algorithm similar to that of Section 11.6.3 to find all the values in $E[1, s]$ that are $\geq i + m - 1$, finding a new source covering $T[i, i + m - 1]$ in each step. Algorithm 13.3 gives the complete procedure for reporting each primary occurrence and its secondary ones. The extra time used to report all the occ_s secondary occurrences is $\mathcal{O}(occ_s \log z)$, dominated by the time to compute π^{-1}. This gives the total reporting complexity $\mathcal{O}(occ \log z)$.

By representing B and S as sparse bitvectors (Section 4.4), we retain our simplified complexity and the space becomes $3z \log n + o(z \log n)$ bits, which depends only logarithmically on n.

The index is shown to use less than 4% of the space of a plain representation of repetitive collections, much less than the indexes of Chapter 11 (Kreft and Navarro, 2013). Its search time is good for short patterns, yet it grows fast on longer ones, as expected from the search time complexity: The time is quadratic on m, and up to h steps are needed to extract each symbol.

Interestingly, there is no reason why this index should not work with the more general Lempel-Ziv parse that allows sources and phrases overlap. While in practice the difference is likely to be minimal, the more general parse can be produced more efficiently, as we have seen.

13.2.3 Faster and Larger Indexes

The most serious problem of Lempel-Ziv indexing is the $\mathcal{O}(mh)$ time to access a substring of length m of T, which impacts search time. Recent research aims at offering better access times. For example, block graphs (Gagie *et al.*, 2015a, 2014a) restrict the admissible phrases to be fixed blocks, of varying granularity. They can extract a substring in time $\mathcal{O}(m + \log n)$. The price is that they use $\mathcal{O}(z \log n \log(n/z))$ bits of space, which is superlinear in the LZ76 entropy. A more recent variant, called block

---

Algorithm 13.3: Reporting primary occurrence $T[i, i + m - 1]$ and its secondary occurrences, by calling *secondaries(i)*.

---

1 **Proc** *secondaries(i)*
    Input : Text $T[1, n]$ (seen as its LZ76-index components B, S, π, and rMq_E)
           and occurrence at $T[i, i + m - 1]$.
    Output: Reports $[i, i + m - 1]$ and all its secondary occurrences.
2   **output** $[i, i + m - 1]$
3     $second(1, \mathsf{select}_0(S, i) - i, i)$

4 **Proc** *second(q, s, i)*
    Input : Range $E[q, s]$ of sources and text position i.
    Output: Reports all the secondary occurrences of $T[i, i + m - 1]$ copied from
           the qth to the sth sources, and their further secondary occurrences.
5   **if** $q > s$ **then return**
6     $p \leftarrow \mathsf{rMq}_E(q, s)$
7     $t \leftarrow \pi^{-1}(p)$
8     $pi \leftarrow \mathsf{select}(S, p) - p + 1$
9     $ti \leftarrow \mathsf{select}(B, t - 1) + 1$
10    $\ell \leftarrow \mathsf{succ}(B, ti) - ti$
11   **if** $pi + \ell \geq i + m$ **then**
12        $secondaries(ti + i - pi)$
13        $second(q, p - 1, i)$
14        $second(p + 1, s, i)$

---

trees (Belazzougui *et al.*, 2015c), obtains time $\mathcal{O}\big((1 + m/\log_\sigma n)\log(n/z)\big)$. In another tradeoff, a block tree can occupy $\mathcal{O}\big(\frac{1}{\epsilon}(n\log\sigma)^\epsilon(z\log n)^{1-\epsilon}\big)$ bits, which is a weighted geometric mean between the uncompressed and the Lempel-Ziv compressed size, and extract a substring in time $\mathcal{O}\big(\frac{1}{\epsilon}(1 + m/\log_\sigma n)\big)$. They show that in practice block trees are much faster to access T than the grammars we described in Section 8.5.2, and use about the same space if the text is very repetitive. When the repetitiveness is milder, however, block trees are not so good.

Still, block graphs and trees do not yet support pattern searches. In the rest of this section we describe other more developed alternatives that have turned into text indexes for repetitive collections. All of them sacrifice the gold-standard $\mathcal{O}(z\log n)$-bit space provided by the LZ76 parsing in order to obtain lower search times.

Grammar-Based Indexing

Grammar compression, described in Section 8.5.2, converges to the statistical entropy of the text under very reasonable conditions (Kieffer and Yang, 2000), and they break it when the text is highly repetitive. However, finding the smallest grammar that represents $T[1, n]$ is NP-complete (Storer, 1977; Storer and Szymanski, 1982; Charikar *et al.*, 2005), and the size g (sum of the lengths of the right-hand sides of the rules) of the smallest grammar is never smaller than z, the number of LZ76 phrases of T (Rytter, 2003; Charikar *et al.*, 2005). Thus, grammar compression is never better than an LZ76 parsing. On the other hand, various approximations (Rytter, 2003; Charikar *et al.*, 2005; Sakamoto, 2005; Jez, 2015, 2016) produce grammars of size $g \leq z \log n$, and even $g \leq z \log(n/z)$. In practice, heuristics like Re-Pair (Larsson and Moffat, 2000) and Sequitur (Nevill-Manning *et al.*, 1994) perform very well. There is also some recent work on producing the grammars within little space (Maruyama *et al.*, 2012, 2013b).

A positive aspect of grammar compression over LZ76 is that any substring of length m of T can be accessed in time $\mathcal{O}(\log n + m/\log_\sigma n)$ from a grammar-compressed representation (Bille *et al.*, 2015; Belazzougui *et al.*, 2015a). This enables the development of indexes like the one we described in Section 10.5.6. A more sophisticated version (Claude and Navarro, 2012), uses $(3 + \epsilon)g \log n$ bits for any constant $\epsilon > 0$ and searches for $P[1, m]$ in time $\mathcal{O}(\frac{1}{\epsilon}m^2 \log\log_r n + (m + occ)\log n)$, where $r \leq g$ is the number of rules in the grammar. Note that the term h has disappeared from the time complexity.

Partial experiments on particular domains, however, suggest that grammar-based indexes are slightly larger and slower than the LZ76-index we have described (Claude *et al.*, 2010, 2016; Kreft and Navarro, 2013). However, the most optimized index (Claude and Navarro, 2012) is not yet implemented. Other indexes built on specific grammars and aimed at searching for long patterns (Maruyama *et al.*, 2013a) have been found to be generally inferior to FM-indexes on standard texts; however, they could perform better on repetitive collections.

LZ78

One may further weaken the compression method and use LZ78 (which corresponds to a restricted type of grammar). As we saw in Section 8.5.4, LZ78 compression enables access to any substring of length m of T in time $\mathcal{O}(m)$. Trie structures analogous to the one used in that section, plus a two-dimensional range search analogous to the one we described for the LZ76-based index, were used to develop various text indexes based on LZ78 compression (Navarro, 2004; Russo and Oliveira, 2008; Arroyuelo *et al.*, 2012). Although they can use as little as $(1 + \epsilon)n\mathcal{H}_k(T) + o(n \log \sigma)$ bits of space, they do not capture repetitiveness fast enough to be attractive on repetitive text collections. Instead, they are alternatives to the indexes studied in Chapter 11 for typical text collections. For example, an index using $(2 + \epsilon)n\mathcal{H}_k(T) + o(n \log \sigma)$ bits can perform searches in time $\mathcal{O}(\frac{1}{\epsilon}(m^2 + (m + occ)\log n))$. While this is still quadratic on m, the time per occurrence reported is lower in practice than in Chapter 11, so these indexes are faster on short patterns with many occurrences.

By using a different parsing or including an FM-index, the term $\mathcal{O}(m^2)$ can be removed from the time complexity (Ferragina and Manzini, 2005; Russo and Oliveira, 2008; Arroyuelo *et al.*, 2012), but the space becomes at least $(3 + \epsilon)n\mathcal{H}_k(T) + o(n \log \sigma)$ bits.

Kernelization

Combinations between grammar and Lempel-Ziv compression have been explored in an attempt to obtain the best from both. For example, by spending space slightly superlinear in the LZ76 entropy, $\mathcal{O}(z \log n \log\log z)$ bits, a search time of $\mathcal{O}(m^2 + (m + occ)\log\log n)$ can be obtained (Gagie *et al.*, 2012). This complexity is much better than that of indexes based on grammars or LZ78, and the penalty factor over the entropy is also generally better than $\mathcal{O}(\log(n/z))$. It is possible to improve the time even more, to $\mathcal{O}(m \log m + occ \log\log n)$ (Gagie *et al.*, 2014b), although the space becomes again $\mathcal{O}(z \log n \log(n/z))$ bits, as in grammar compression and block graphs/trees. These indexes are not yet implemented; experimental comparisons are needed to determine how acceptable the space is in practice, and if the better complexities turn into actual speedups.

The general idea in these indexes is to build a grammar-based structure that speeds up access on the prefixes and suffixes of phrases, which are the parts that need to be accessed when searching with a Lempel-Ziv based index. These are examples of a promising research direction called *kernelization*, which could lead to much faster indexes for repetitive text collections. The general idea is to extract, from a repetitive text, a small set of strings such that efficient searches are possible by fully indexing just those strings and storing a lightweight structure on the rest. Gagie and Puglisi (2015) offer a concise survey of the state of the art in kernelization.

Relative Lempel-Ziv

Another promising line is the so-called *Relative Lempel-Ziv*, in which a base text is stored in plain form and all the documents are compressed with LZ76, but only using phrases from the base text (Kuruppu *et al.*, 2010). This scheme allows for fast direct access (Deorowicz and Grabowski, 2011; Ferrada *et al.*, 2014) and can be combined with the ideas we described for LZ76 indexing (Gagie *et al.*, 2012; Do *et al.*, 2014) and even with suffix arrays and trees (Belazzougui *et al.*, 2014; Gagie *et al.*, 2015b). For example, with a base text of length n, it is possible to use $3n \log \sigma + \mathcal{O}(z \log n)$ bits and search for patterns in time $\mathcal{O}((m + occ) \log n)$. Other practical methods based on heuristics have been shown to work well in practice (Huang *et al.*, 2010; Yang *et al.*, 2013). A challenge of Relative Lempel-Ziv is to find an appropriate base text, for which techniques based on grammar compression have proved useful (Kuruppu *et al.*, 2011, 2012).

13.2.4 Compressed Suffix Arrays and Trees

All the indexes we have mentioned are indeed weaker than those based on suffix arrays and trees seen in Chapter 11. For example, most of them cannot directly count the number of times P appears in T. For this and other applications, having full suffix array and suffix tree functionality on repetitive text collections is of interest. This line has been pursued as well.

Compressed Suffix Arrays

Repetitiveness in a text collection does show up in its compressed suffix array and FM-index, but not in a way that is directly exploited by statistical compression. Repetitiveness induces long runs in function Ψ (Section 11.1) of the form $\Psi[k+1] = \Psi[k]+1$. This becomes a run of 1s when Ψ is differentially encoded. Therefore, run-length compression of the differential Ψ array yields much smaller representations. In the FM-index (Section 11.2), this effect shows up as long runs of equal symbols in T^{bwt}.

To see this, imagine a long string $X = a \cdot Y$ that appears in many places, starting at positions $p_1, p_2, \ldots, p_t$ in T. Those positions are contiguous in the suffix array A, say, $A[i, i+t-1] = \langle p_1, p_2, \ldots, p_t \rangle$. Then, the positions $p_1 + 1, p_2 + 1, \ldots, p_t + 1$ are also likely to appear contiguously in A, and in the same order (unless $b \cdot Y$ also appears in T, with $a \neq b$; then the position of Y may appear inserted somewhere in this second list). Say that $A[j, j+t-1] = \langle p_1 + 1, p_2 + 1, \ldots, p_t + 1 \rangle$. We then have

$\Psi[i] = j$, $\Psi[i + 1] = j + 1$, and so on until $\Psi[i + t - 1] = j + t - 1$. That is, we have a run $\Psi[i + k + 1] = \Psi[i + k] + 1$ for $0 \le k < t - 1$. The run appears analogously in the BWT: $T^{\text{bwt}}[j, j + t - 1] = a^t$. Note that, if X is long, then Y is likely to produce another run, and so on.

Example 13.13 *The Ψ array of the text $T = $ abracadabra\$, shown in Figure 11.2, has a long run $\Psi[3, 8] = \langle 7, 8, 9, 10, 11, 12 \rangle$. This is because the suffix array A contains a long part, $A[3, 8] = \langle 8, 1, 4, 6, 9, 2 \rangle$, that appears displaced by one unit in $A[7, 12] = \langle 9, 2, 5, 7, 10, 3 \rangle$ (note that the areas overlap).*

This long run is made of several smaller runs, and has a somewhat complex structure. On one hand, a repeated string $X = $ abra occurs $t = 2$ times, at positions $A[3, 4] = \langle 8, 1 \rangle$, string $Y = $ bra occurs at $A[7, 8] = \langle 9, 2 \rangle$, and string $Z = $ ra occurs at $A[11, 12] = \langle 10, 3 \rangle$. This explains the parts $\Psi[3, 4] = \langle 7, 8 \rangle$ and $\Psi[7, 8] = \langle 11, 12 \rangle$ of the run.

The first of those runs can be expanded to $\Psi[3, 6]$ by noticing that $A[3, 6] = \langle 8, 1, 4, 6 \rangle$ points to the suffixes abra\$, abracadabra\$, acadabra\$, and adabra\$, which stay together when we remove their leading a, thus $A[7, 10] = \langle 9, 2, 5, 7 \rangle$. Thus a run in Ψ is formed even if the suffixes are not of the form $a.Y$ for a single Y. By chance, this run continues with the second, $\Psi[7, 8]$.

In T^{bwt} (see L in Figure 11.4), the second run corresponds to $T^{\text{bwt}}[11, 12] = $ bb, and the first to $T^{\text{bwt}}[7, 10] = $ aaaa.

Mäkinen and Navarro (2005) showed that the number of runs in T is $\rho \le |T| \mathcal{H}_k(T) + \sigma^k$ for any k, and thus a run-length compression of Ψ or T^{bwt} is roughly upper bounded by the kth order statistical entropy of the text. On repetitive texts, this compression method outperforms statistical ones, but it is generally weaker than LZ76.[7] For example, if $T[1, tn] = S^t$, then Ψ is formed by $\rho = n$ runs of length t, and thus it can be represented in $\mathcal{O}(n \log(t\sigma))$ bits, much less than $tn \log \sigma$. However, if we spread s edits in T, each edit could destroy $\Theta(\sqrt{n})$ runs, because many suffixes may change their lexicographic position in the suffix array. This is shown in the following example by Mäkinen (2008).

Example 13.14 *The BWT of $T = SS$, where*
$$S = \text{abcde abcde acde acde ade adeae ae } \$, \textit{ is}$$
ee \$\$eeeeeeeeeeeeee aaaa bbbbaaaa ccccccccaaaa aadddddddddddaadd,
with $\rho = 11$ runs (we separate the parts of the BWT where the suffix array starts with each symbol). Now, if we insert f at $T[11]$ (right after the second abcde), the BWT becomes
ee \$\$eee<u>f</u>eeeeeeeeee aaaa bbb<u>a</u>aaa<u>b</u>ccccccccaaaa<u>c</u> aaddddddddddaadd<u>d</u> <u>e</u>,
where we have underlined the symbols moved or inserted. Thus, one insertion has created 6 new runs. We can increase this number by 1 for each new symbol we add to the alphabet, yet we need that $\sigma = \Omega(\sqrt{n})$.

On the other hand, if S is generated from a Markov source (Section 2.4), a random edit destroys only $\mathcal{O}(\log n)$ runs on average (Mäkinen et al., 2010). Thus, on average, we have that $\rho = \mathcal{O}(s \log n)$ and a run-length compression of Ψ uses

---

[7] There are some exceptions in extreme cases; for example in $T = a^n \$$ we have $z = \Theta(\log n)$ and $\rho = 2$. Still, recall that z is also 2 with the original LZ76 parsing that permits overlaps between source and target.

$\mathcal{O}((n + s \log n) \log(t\sigma))$ bits. Therefore, each edit increases the LZ76 entropy by at most $\log n$ bits, but it increases the size of a run-length compressed suffix array roughly by $\log^2 n$ bits on average.

Despite these drawbacks, run-length compression of Ψ or the BWT performs well in practice (below 10% of the text size on repetitive biological sequences (Mäkinen *et al.*, 2010)). It competes with grammar-compressed indexes, albeit LZ76 indexes are clearly smaller (Claude *et al.*, 2016). The main problem, however, is to compress the samples for locating and displaying (Section 11.1.4), as their number influences the performance of those operations. For example, storing one sample every w positions yields reasonable times, but it increases the space by 2 bits per symbol (i.e., 25% of the text size), much more than the 10% used by Ψ.

Sampling

Initial attempts to compress the samples did not perform well in practice (Mäkinen *et al.*, 2010). A more recent and promising workaround is to combine the run-length compressed Ψ or BWT with other structures whose sizes depend on the repetitiveness and that can locate the occurrences fast (Belazzougui *et al.*, 2015b). For example, using $\mathcal{O}((\rho + \rho^{rev} + z) \log n)$ bits, they report the *occ* occurrences of $P[1, m]$ in $\mathcal{O}(m \log z + occ(\log^\epsilon z + \log \log n))$ time for any constant $\epsilon > 0$, where ρ^{rev} is the number of runs in the BWT of T^{rev}. They obtain even faster reporting by combining a run-length compressed BWT with a CDAWG (Compact Directed Acyclic Word Graph) (Blumer *et al.*, 1987). A CDAWG is obtained by interpreting the suffix tree as an automaton that recognizes all the substrings of the text: all the suffix tree leaves are mapped to a single final state, and the resulting automaton is then minimized. The number of edges e of the CDAWG is never larger than the number of nodes in the suffix tree. Moreover, when the suffix tree has large repeated subtrees, minimization makes the CDAWG smaller as well. Still, the CDAWG is never smaller than $\max(z, \rho)$, so the space of their structure becomes dominated by the $\mathcal{O}(e \log n)$ bits of the CDAWG. In exchange, they report the occurrences in time $\mathcal{O}(m \log \log n + occ)$. Some preliminary studies toward implementing these combined structures have been made already (Belazzougui *et al.*, 2016).

Another relevant trend is the so-called suffix tree of an alignment (Na *et al.*, 2013b). They take a base sequence and index the others in the collection according to the way they align with the base sequence. On average, if we distribute s random edits and the base sequence is random text, the structure uses $\mathcal{O}((n + s \log n) \log n)$ bits. The search time is as with plain suffix trees, $\mathcal{O}(m + occ)$. A practical variant, called suffix array of an alignment (Na *et al.*, 2013a), is implemented and shown to be a promising alternative in practice.

Compressed Suffix Trees

Compressed suffix trees (Section 11.5) for repetitive text collections are built on top of run-length compressed suffix arrays or FM-indexes. The LCP array and the tree topology must also be compressed by means of exploiting repetitiveness.

As seen in Section 11.5.1, the LCP array can be represented with the bitvector $H[1, 2n - 1]$, which also has long runs if the text is repetitive. In various repetitive collections, the representation of H with the technique of Section 4.4.3, as suggested by Fischer *et al.* (2009), used only $0.4n$–$0.6n$ bits (Navarro and Ordóñez, 2016).

To see this, consider again our string $X = a.Y$ appearing at positions $A[i, i + t − 1] = \langle p_1, p_2, \ldots, p_t \rangle$ and $Y = b.Z$ at positions $A[j, j + t − 1] = \langle p_1 + 1, p_2 + 1, \ldots, p_t + 1 \rangle$. Then, for any $1 < k \leq t$, we have $\mathsf{PLCP}[p_k] = \mathsf{lcp}(T[p_{k−1}, n], T[p_k, n]) = 1 + \mathsf{lcp}(T[p_{k−1} + 1, n], T[p_k + 1, n]) = 1 + \mathsf{PLCP}[p_k + 1]$. Therefore, $\mathsf{PLCP}[p_k + 1] = \mathsf{PLCP}[p_k] − 1$. If in turn the occurrences of Z are contiguous in A, we also have $\mathsf{PLCP}[p_k + 2] = \mathsf{PLCP}[p_k] − 2$, and so on. If this continues r times, we have $\mathsf{PLCP}[p_k + \ell] = \mathsf{PLCP}[p_k] − \ell$ for all $1 \leq \ell \leq r$. This induces, for each $1 < k \leq t$, a run of r 1s in H, as all the bits at $\mathsf{PLCP}[p_k + \ell] + 2(p_k + \ell) = \mathsf{PLCP}[p_k] − \ell + 2(p_k + \ell) = \mathsf{PLCP}[p_k] + 2p_k + \ell$ are set. If the 1s are grouped in a few runs, then the 0s must be grouped too.

Example 13.15 *Consider the* LCP *array of* $T = \mathsf{abracadabra\$}$ *shown in Figure 11.10. Bitvector* $H[1, 23]$ *has only 11 runs. A particularly long one is* $H[6, 10] = 11111$. *It corresponds to* $X = \mathsf{abra}$, $Y = \mathsf{bra}$, *and* $Z = \mathsf{ra}$. *The range of* X *is* $A[3, 4] = \langle 8, 1 \rangle$, *that of* Y *is* $A[7, 8] = \langle 9, 2 \rangle$, *and that of* Z *is* $A[11, 12] = \langle 10, 3 \rangle$. *Then* $\mathsf{PLCP}[1] = \mathsf{lcp}(T[8, 12], T[1, 12]) = 4 = 1 + \mathsf{PLCP}[2]$ *and* $\mathsf{PLCP}[2] = \mathsf{lcp}(T[9, 12], T[2, 12]) = 3 = 1 + \mathsf{PLCP}[3]$. *Although the two occurrences of* Z *are not anymore contiguous if we remove their first symbol* r, *the sequence of* PLCP *values still keeps decreasing,* $\mathsf{PLCP}[4] = 1$ *and* $\mathsf{PLCP}[5] = 0$. *Thus* $\mathsf{PLCP}[j] + 2j = \langle 6, 7, 8, 9, 10 \rangle$ *if* $1 \leq j \leq 5$, *which yields the run in* $H[6, 10]$.

The tree topology contains large isomorphic structures when the collection is repetitive. Thus, its BP representation (Section 8.2) is a repetitive sequence, and it can be grammar-compressed. The balanced rmM-tree (Section 7.1) can be replaced with the grammar tree, and fields e, m, M, and n can be associated with nonterminals to support navigation (Bille *et al.*, 2015). In practice, instead of the maximum of $4n$ bits, the tree requires around $1.0n$–$1.5n$ bits on repetitive collections (Navarro and Ordóñez, 2016).

Example 13.16 *Consider the suffix tree of* $T = \mathsf{abracadabra\$}$ *shown in Figure 11.8. The tree topology contains various repeated substructures. These show up in its BP representation,*

$$(()(()(()())()())(()())()()(()())),$$

whose regularities can be captured, for example, with the grammar

$$A \rightarrow (()())$$
$$B \rightarrow A ()()$$
$$S \rightarrow (()(() B) B A),$$

where S *is the initial symbol.*

Applying all the reductions, the resulting suffix tree uses as little as $2.3n$–$3.2n$ bits, that is, 30%–40% of the text size.

An even smaller compressed suffix tree (Abeliuk *et al.*, 2013) omits the tree topology, and carries out the navigation using rmqs and next/previous smaller values (recall Section 13.1.4) on the LCP array (Fischer *et al.*, 2009). To speed up these queries, the differential LCP array ($\mathsf{LCP}'[2] = \mathsf{LCP}[2]$ and $\mathsf{LCP}'[i] = \mathsf{LCP}[i] − \mathsf{LCP}[i − 1]$ for

$i > 2$) is grammar-compressed and summary information is stored associated with the nonterminals of the grammar. The resulting suffix tree is indeed smaller (12%–25% of the text size), yet it is also several orders of magnitude slower.

The array LCP' is repetitive for the same reason Ψ has runs: if the positions of $X = a.Y$ appear in $A[i, i + t - 1] = \langle p_1, p_2, \ldots, p_t \rangle$ and the positions plus 1 appear in $A[j, j + t - 1] = \langle p_1 + 1, p_2 + 1, \ldots, p_t + 1 \rangle$, then $\mathsf{LCP}[i + k] = \mathsf{lcp}(T[p_{k+1}, n], T[p_k, n]) = 1 + \mathsf{lcp}(T[p_{k+1} + 1, n], T[p_k + 1, n]) = \mathsf{LCP}[j + k] + 1$, for all $1 \leq k < t$. Therefore, $\mathsf{LCP}'[i + 2, i + t - 1] = \mathsf{LCP}'[j + 2, j + t - 1]$.

Example 13.17 *Consider the* LCP *array of* $T = \mathsf{abracadabra\$}$ *in Figure 11.8. The differential* LCP *array is* $\mathsf{LCP}'[2, 12] = \langle 0, 1, 3, -3, 0, -1, 3, -3, 0, 0, 2 \rangle$. *It contains the repeated substring* $\langle 3, -3, 0 \rangle$, *corresponding to the long run* $\Psi[3, 6] = \langle 7, 8, 9, 10 \rangle$ *that starts with* a. *Then* $\mathsf{LCP}[4, 6] = \langle 4, 1, 1 \rangle$ *appears shifted in* $\mathsf{LCP}[8, 10] = \langle 3, 0, 0 \rangle$. *As a result, it holds* $\mathsf{LCP}'[5, 6] = \mathsf{LCP}'[9, 10] = \langle -3, 0 \rangle$ *(the repeated substring* $\langle 3, -3, 0 \rangle$ *is longer just by chance). The other run,* $\Psi[7, 8] = \langle 11, 12 \rangle$, *is too short for the effect to show up.*

The structure of Belazzougui *et al.* (2015b) for locating on suffix arrays can also be upgraded to a suffix tree, by storing the CDAWG of T and of its reverse. This allows them implement various relevant suffix tree operations in time $\mathcal{O}(\log \log n)$. This is another promising structure for repetitive text collections, although its practical relevance has not yet been established.

13.3 Secondary Memory

When a text is searched sequentially, compression improves not only space, but also locality of reference: scanning the uncompressed text $T[1, n]$ requires reading $(n \log \sigma)/w$ memory words, whereas we access only $n(H_0(T) + 1)/w$ words to scan the Huffman-compressed text (Section 2.6). When the text is on disk, the time savings are considerable.

The situation is different with compact data structures. In many cases, the space reduction comes at the cost of a lower locality of reference. For example, on a general tree, the subtree size of a node can be stored at the node itself, thus wasting space. In the balanced parenthesis representations of Section 8.2, we can compute the subtree size from the representation without the need to store it explicitly. However, this requires a close operation, which accesses a possibly remote memory address. Worse, consider the case of performing $\mathsf{access}(S, i)$ on a sequence S represented with a wavelet tree: It requires $\log \sigma$ remote memory accesses, compared to a single access if S is stored in plain form.

The lack of locality of reference is not a big problem when the reward for the reduced memory usage is to fit the data in a faster memory. However, when the data are large enough, even the compact data structures may have to reside on secondary memory. Disk devices strongly penalize low locality of reference, and on the other hand they are cheap enough to make space savings not so relevant. Therefore, the main interest in using compact data structures in secondary memory is to improve time performance under this cost model. This challenge is rarely considered in compact data structures.

The disk stores data in *pages* of D words (usually D is in the range of 1024 to 8192 words, thus $D = \omega(w)$ is a very reasonable theoretical assumption). All the data in a page are read together, and the cost to read the page is much higher than that of a sequential processing of D words in main memory. Further, in magnetic disks, reading consecutive pages is much cheaper than random pages, though this is not the case in solid-state drives. We will use a simple and general cost model for disk algorithms, which counts the number of disk pages read/written (Vitter, 2008); these are called "I/Os." When possible, we will count the exact number of I/Os instead of using $\mathcal{O}$-notation.

Just as for the example of compressed text scanning, the ability to fit more data within the same space may allow, with an appropriate design, a reduction in the number of pages read when traversing the data structures. However, the design principles may be different from those of main memory. In the sequel we consider some important cases where the good design of a compact data structure yields an advantage in the secondary memory scenario, and some other cases where reducing space can be proved to be counterproductive.

13.3.1 Bitvectors

Let us start with a simple problem. Consider the plain representation of a bitvector $B[1, n]$ providing constant-time rank support, as in Section 4.2.2. It takes one access to memory to perform access(B, i), and three to perform rank(B, i) queries. To reduce these to just one I/O on disk, we store B in $\lceil n/(Dw) \rceil$ consecutive disk pages (each page holds Dw bits). At the beginning of each page we store the cumulative rank$_1$ count up to the beginning of the page. These counters use only $nw/(Dw) = n/D = o(n/w)$ additional bits (much less in practice than the in-memory scheme) and allow us to solve rank queries with a single I/O.[8]

Operation select(B, j) is more complicated, but we can still handle it in 2–3 I/Os, in the same spirit of Section 4.3.3. First, a copy of the $\lceil n/(Dw) \rceil$ rank counters used above is stored, now compacted in an array $R[0, \lceil n/(Dw) \rceil]$, where $R[q] = \text{rank}_1(B, Dw \cdot q)$. This array uses n/D bits and spans $n/(D^2w)$ disk pages, fitting D entries per page. Now, given a parameter s, we store another array $S[0, \lfloor n/s \rfloor]$, where $S[d] = \lceil \text{select}_1(B, d \cdot s + 1)/(D^2w) \rceil$, that is, $S[d]$ is the disk page of R where the page of B containing the $(ds + 1)$th 1 is referenced.

Then, given j, the page of B to scan is found between the pages $S[d - 1]$ and $S[d]$ of R, for $d = \lceil (j - 1)/s \rceil$ (the last cell of each page where S is stored is repeated in the next page, to ensure that we access only one page of S). If $d = 0$ or $S[d] = S[d - 1]$, then we access the page $S[d]$ of R and perform a binary (or even sequential) search for the smallest q with $R[q] \geq j$. The answer is then in the qth page of B, which is finally scanned to complete the select operation. The process requires in total 3 I/Os.

If, instead, $S[d - 1] < S[d]$, then the same page of S stores the position of another file E where the s answers in that zone of S are directly stored, so we complete the

---

[8] Since we store a counter in the disk page, the free space left for data is slightly less, $Dw - w = (D - 1)w$ bits, so we should use $D - 1$ instead of D in the sequel. We omit this detail for simplicity.

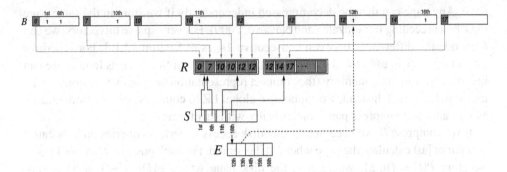

Figure 13.4. A bitvector B deployed on disk pages. The grayed blocks are the rank counters, also copied in array R (see the gray arrows). Array S points to the page in R referring to the page of B where every 5th 1 is (we show the precise position in the page of R, but the pointer just refers to the whole page). Array E stores all the 5 positions of the 1s when we cross pages in the array R. We show one explicit value, with a dashed arrow.

operation with 2 I/Os. It is sufficient to store only the first pointer to E in each page of S; the others can be deduced by scanning the page of S.

Example 13.18 *Figure 13.4 shows a part of a bitvector B stored on disk pages, and the corresponding arrays R, S, and E, with sampling $s = 5$ for* select. *To perform* access *or* rank *we simply access the corresponding page of B. For* $\text{select}_1(B, 10)$ *we compute $d = \lceil (10 - 1)/5 \rceil = 2$ and thus consider $S[2]$ and $S[1]$. Note that S points to pages, so $S[0] = S[1] = S[2] = 1$ point to the first page of R, whereas $S[3] = 2$ points to the second. Since $S[1] = S[2] = 1$, we read the first page of R and scan it to find the first $R[q] \geq 10$. This occurs for $R[2]$ (recall that R starts at 0), so we read the second page of B and find the 10th 1 (that is, the third in the page, because $10 - R[1] = 10 - 7 = 3$) in the position shown in the figure.*

If, instead, we want $\text{select}_1(B, 13)$, *we compute $d = \lceil (13 - 1)/5 \rceil = 3$ and then consider $S[3]$ and $S[2]$. Since $S[2] = 1 < 2 = S[3]$, they point to different pages of R, and we cannot afford to search between them (there could be a long range of pages between $S[2]$ and $S[3]$). But in this case we have stored the precise answers in E, from* $\text{select}_1(B, 12)$ *to* $\text{select}_1(B, 16)$. *The figure shows only the one we need.*

The total extra space is then n/D bits for the counters inside the pages, other n/D bits for R, nw/s bits for S, and at most other $sw \cdot n/(D^2 w) = sn/D^2$ bits for E, because it stores s entries every time $S[d]$ moves from a page of R to another, and there are $n/(D^2 w)$ pages in R. The extra space is minimized if we choose $s = D\sqrt{w}$, where it becomes $2n(1 + \sqrt{w})/D = o(n)$ bits. This is, for example, just 1.8% extra space if $w = 64$ and $D = 1024$.

Compressed Bitvectors

We can also store B in almost any compressed form on disk, as long as we are able to decompress any individual disk page without reading others. For example, we can use the compression scheme of Section 4.1.1 to obtain zero-order compression. We can also achieve kth order compression by using semi-static kth order modeling of the whole B (Section 2.4) together with arithmetic coding (Section 2.6.4) within each disk page. Any page can then be decompressed independently if we store in the same page the k bits preceding it (González and Navarro, 2009). For very sparse bitvectors, we can δ-encode the differences between consecutive 1s, as in Section 12.1.3. For repetitive bitvectors, we can use global grammar compression (Section 8.5.2), as long as we can keep the rules in main memory (the compact representation seen in that section may be useful in this case). Instead, we cannot use global LZ76 compression (Section 13.2.1), as we cannot decompress pages individually with this format.

If we compress B, we need one further disk access to perform queries on it, because we cannot just calculate the page where $B[i]$ is stored. For each position $Dw(t-1)+1$, we store $P[t] = (p, f)$, where p is the disk page where $B[Dw(t-1)+1]$ is represented, and f is the first position of B represented in page p. Array P occupies $2n/D = o(n)$ bits. To access $B[i]$, we compute $t = \lceil i/(Dw) \rceil$. Then if $i < P[t+1].f$ we read the page $P[t].p$ and decompress until recovering the bit number $i - P[t].f + 1$, which is $B[i]$. Otherwise we read the page $P[t+1].p$ and decompress until recovering the bit number $i - P[t+1].f + 1$ (we also let the disk pages where P is stored to overlap by one entry, to avoid reading two pages for $P[t]$ and $P[t+1]$).

In principle, it is not obvious that $B[i]$ can be only in page $P[t].p$ or in the next one, because some methods could obtain compression overall, but still expand some pages of B. We will ensure that no page of B is expanded by more than one bit (González and Navarro, 2009): If the compression method turns out to expand a page, then we store the page without compression. A bit is used to signal whether we use compression or not. Therefore, every page represents at least $Dw - 1$ bits. As a consequence, even if the bit $B[Dw(t-1)+1]$ is the last one represented in page $P[t].p$ and it turns out that $i = Dw(t-1) + Dw = Dwt$ is $Dw - 1$ positions ahead of $Dw(t-1) + 1$, it must still be represented in page $P[t+1].p$.[9]

Now array R stores the **rank** values up to the first position represented in each page, $R[q] = \text{rank}_1(B, P[q+1].f - 1)$, and array S is built according to R (that is, $S[d]$ is the disk page of R where the page containing $B[\text{select}_1(ds+1)]$ is referenced). The scheme operates in exactly the same way, and the number of I/Os is 2 for **access** and **rank** and 2–4 for **select** (we do not access B at all if $S[d-1] < S[d]$). With array P, the total space overhead is $(2\sqrt{w}+4)n/D$, which is below $0.02\,n$ for $w = 64$ and $D = 1024$.

If the bitvector has $m \ll n$ 1s, we may completely get rid of the $o(n)$ extra space. By storing the δ-encoded distances between consecutive 1s, the space is $m \log \frac{n}{m}(1 + o(1))$ bits, but we cannot use array P. Instead, we can find the desired block with a B-tree that maintains the first positions of B stored in each block and their corresponding **rank** counters. This adds $\mathcal{O}((m/D)w) = o(m)$ further bits of space, and the operations require $\mathcal{O}(\log_D m)$ I/Os.

Dynamic Bitvectors

The techniques of Section 12.1 to handle dynamic bitvectors are readily translated to disk. We replace the balanced binary tree with a B-tree of arity $\Theta(D)$ and deploy each leaf on a disk page. The usual B-tree mechanisms for handling page overflows

---

[9] Therefore, we could easily compress P, since $P[t].p \le P[t+1].p \le P[t].p + 1$, but P is already small and we aim at accessing only one disk page to read it.

and underflows are used. Each internal node stores two counters per child, indicating the number of bits and number of 1s inside the leaves descending from its leftward siblings. Then queries process each internal node in $\mathcal{O}(\log D)$ time and with one page read. Updates require $\mathcal{O}(D)$ time to update all the counters, but still one page read and one page write. All the operations and updates are then carried out in $\mathcal{O}(\log_D n)$ I/Os. Since we allocate full disk pages even if they are underutilized, the total space is up to 4 times the data size. However, this is less serious on disk. On the other hand, if we have M words available to store the first $\log_{D/2}(M/2)$ B-tree levels in main memory (since we use 2 counters per child), the I/Os are $\mathcal{O}(\log_D(n/M))$. For example, with $w = 32$ we need just 2 I/Os if we have $n = 2^{40}$ bits, $M = 2^{21}$ (i.e., 8 megabytes) of main memory, and $D = 2048$.

13.3.2 Sequences

Consider the wavelet tree representation of strings (Section 6.2), which requires $\mathcal{O}(\log \sigma)$ time to answer **access**, **rank**, or **select** queries. If we represent the wavelet tree with the disk-based bitvectors of Section 13.3.1, the cost of the operations will be $\mathcal{O}(\log \sigma)$ I/Os.

Instead, we extend the disk-based bitvectors to handle larger alphabets. We maintain the string $S[1, n]$ in plain form, in consecutive disk pages. Therefore, an **access**(S, i) operation is solved with one I/O, and we also access a substring very efficiently. Inside each disk page, we also store the σ **rank**$_c$ values up to the beginning of that page (similarly to the array R of Section 11.3.2). A **rank**$_c(S, i)$ query is then solved with one I/O, to access the page holding $S[i]$, read the **rank**$_c$ value stored in the page, and scan the symbols from the beginning of the page up to $S[i]$ to count the additional cs. This idea does not work so well in main memory, because we have to scan $\mathcal{O}(Dw/\log \sigma)$ symbols to complete the **rank**$_c$ calculation.

This scheme works if σ is not too large. It requires storing, for every disk page, σw bits with the **rank**$_c$ counters. Since there are $(D - \sigma)w$ useful bits left, the sequence S uses $p = n \log \sigma/((D - \sigma)w)$ pages, for a total of $pDw = n \log \sigma \cdot D/(D - \sigma)$ bits. For example, with a byte alphabet ($\sigma = 256$) the counters fit comfortably in a typical disk page, and the total space overhead goes from 33% if $D = 1024$ to about 3% if $D = 8192$. Slightly larger alphabets can be handled with 2 I/Os, by adding superblock counters and making the in-page counters relative, as in Section 4.2.2, or simply by storing the counters in another file.

To support **select**$_c(S, j)$ on small alphabets, we can use the solution of Section 13.3.1 for each symbol. There are p pages in S and thus p/D pages in R. Let n_c be the number of occurrences of c in S. Then the **select** structure for symbol c takes pw bits for the array R, $n_c w/s$ bits for the array we called S in that section, and at most $sw(p/D)$ for E. Added over all the symbols c, this gives $\sigma p(s/D + 1)w + nw/s$ bits, which is minimized for $s = \sqrt{nD/(\sigma p)}$, where the total extra space (considering the σpw extra bits for **rank**) is

$$2\left(\sqrt{\frac{n\sigma p}{D}}w + \sigma pw\right) = 2n\left(\sqrt{\frac{\sigma w \log \sigma}{D(D - \sigma)}} + \frac{\sigma \log \sigma}{D - \sigma}\right)$$

bits. This is around 77% extra space for $\sigma = 256$, $w = 64$, and $D = 1024$, and around 7.6% for $D = 8192$. So an alphabet of 256 symbols drives us close to the limit of what can be an acceptable extra space, depending on the disk page size D. A more general (and slower) solution for any alphabet size is described in Section 13.3.4.

Compression. Just as for bitvectors, we can store S in various compressed forms on the disk page, as long as we can decompress it locally. The penalty is, analogously to Section 13.3.1, pw further bits of space for the array P, and one extra I/O to determine the correct page.

Dynamism. A natural extension of the dynamic structure for bitvectors is to store $\sigma + 1$ counters per child in the internal nodes of the B-tree. This reduces their arity to $D/(\sigma + 1)$, and makes query and update times $\mathcal{O}(\log_{D/\sigma} n)$. Again, this is attractive only for small σ.

13.3.3 Trees

The tree representations we studied in Chapter 8 can be deployed on disk. LOUDS requires just bitvectors, which can be stored as in Section 13.3.1 to support each operation in a constant number of I/Os. For BP and DFUDS, we may consider an extension of rmM-trees (Section 7.1), where the leaves correspond to Dw parentheses stored in a disk page, and the rmM-tree is of arity $\Theta(D)$, like a B-tree. Then all the operations can be solved within $\mathcal{O}(\log_D n)$ I/Os, even in the dynamic case (Section 12.4.4).

These solutions are reasonable if we perform isolated operations that access random nodes of a tree, since in this case it is unavoidable to access at least one random disk page per access. However, most tree traversals are not random: many of them start from the root and move toward children or siblings, or start at a leaf and move toward parents. In this case, data organizations that pack close tree nodes together may significantly reduce the number of I/Os to complete a traversal.

The LOUDS, BP, and DFUDS representations are not local in this sense. They may need to access positions far away in the sequence when computing **child** or **parent** nodes (BP and DFUDS may stay within a single disk page when traversing a small subtree). Instead, ideas analogous to the tree covering (TC) representation we mentioned in Section 8.7 are promising. In this representation (Geary *et al.*, 2006; He *et al.*, 2012; Farzan and Munro, 2014), the trees are cut into blocks formed by connected subtrees. The same is done in some dynamic storage schemes for cardinal trees (Munro *et al.*, 2001; Jansson *et al.*, 2015; Arroyuelo *et al.*, 2016).

The connected subtrees are represented in compact form and pointers to other blocks are explicit. For example, we may use parentheses to represent the topology. Each leaf may be an actual tree leaf or may continue in another block. We store an array with the identifiers of the leaves that continue in another block, plus the corresponding pointers. If there are p pointers to blocks in total, their total space usage is $2pw$ bits.

To deploy the trees on disk, blocks can be identified with disk pages, and all the in-block operations can be done sequentially. The array of pointers of each block must be stored in its same page. If blocks contain $\Theta(Dw)$ nodes from $\mathcal{O}(1)$ different subtrees, then only $\mathcal{O}(n/(Dw))$ disk pages are needed for packing an n-node tree. Thus, p is also $\mathcal{O}(n/(Dw))$, since each page is pointed $\mathcal{O}(1)$ times, and the extra space for pointers

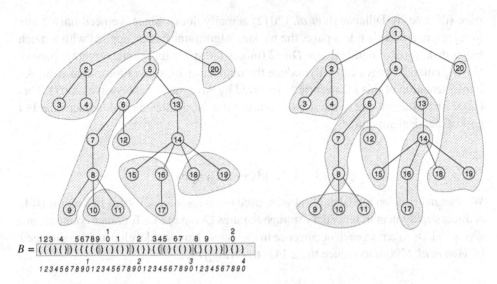

Figure 13.5. The BP (left) and a TC (right) packing of a tree, with a block size of 6 parentheses (left) and 3 nodes (right). The partition on the left is induced from the deployment on disk pages, putting the node in the page where its open parenthesis falls. On the right, the partitioning is explicit and optimized to ensure that at most 3 pages are read in any root-to-leaf traversal. In both cases we use 7 pages.

is just $2pw = \mathcal{O}(n/D) = o(n)$ bits. The only operations needed are in-page scans, and following pointers when moving to another disk page. On the other hand, it is harder to support operations such as subtree size without storing the data explicitly.

Example 13.19 *Figure 13.5 illustrates the packing into disk pages induced by the BP representation of the tree of Figure 8.4 (on the left, with 6 bits per page) and a possible TC representation (on the right, with 3 nodes per page). On the left we pack together the nodes whose opening parentheses are in the same disk page. Therefore, if we assume that at least this parenthesis must be accessed when the traversal reaches the node, then going from the root to node 17 requires accessing 4 disk pages. On the right, the packing is designed to ensure that any root-to-leaf traversal accesses at most 3 disk pages. We let some pages contain disconnected nodes to improve disk page utilization (but this increases the number of explicit pointers).*

Consider the subtree containing the root, on the right. The BP representation of its topology is $(()(()(()))())$, *with 4 leaves. All those continue in other blocks, thus its array of continuing leaves is* $\langle 1, 2, 3, 4 \rangle$ *and their pointers are* $\langle 2, 6, 14, 20 \rangle$ *(we use the node numbers as pointers for clarity). The BP representation of the subtree rooted at node 14 is* $(()(())()())$, *its continuing leaves are* $\langle 1, 3, 4 \rangle$, *and its pointers are* $\langle 15, 18, 19 \rangle$.

Therefore, the cost of a traversal is measured in terms of the number of explicit pointers that must be followed in the way, as they lead to another page. A TC partition can then be designed to minimize this number. Several partition methods have been proposed to minimize the cost of root-to-leaf or leaf-to-root traversals (Clark and Munro, 1996; Gil and Itai, 1999; Alstrup *et al.*, 2002; Hutchinson *et al.*, 2003; Brodal and Fagerberg, 2006; Dillabaugh *et al.*, 2012; Demaine *et al.*, 2015). We can combine any of these packing algorithms with a compact tree representation of the nodes in a page (the one by Dillabaugh *et al.* (2012) actually does). Since we need only 2 bits to represent a node inside a page, the packing algorithms can be applied with a much larger disk page, of nominal size $Dw/2$ (minus the space for pointers to other pages). Having enlarged pages can only reduce the number of I/Os in a root-to-leaf path. An implementation of this idea is briefly reported by Arroyuelo and Navarro (2007). This is our first example where the use of compact data structures on disk reduces the I/O cost of classical structures.

13.3.4 Grids and Graphs

Wavelet matrices on alphabet $[1, r]$ were used to represent $n \times r$ grids in Section 10.1. A direct deployment in secondary storage requires $\mathcal{O}(\log r)$ I/Os for range counting and $\mathcal{O}(\log r)$ I/Os to report each occurrence in the range. Now we develop an idea sketched by Hon *et al.* (2006) to reduce these I/Os to $\mathcal{O}(\log_D r)$.

Wavelet Matrices on Disk

We cannot directly apply the method of Section 13.3.2 to represent the wavelet matrix as a sequence, because in this case $\sigma = r$ is likely to be very large for that method, as we have seen. Instead, let us define a wavelet matrix of arity d, where in each level the alphabet is partitioned into d roughly equal parts. Then the wavelet matrix has $\log_d \sigma$ levels, and the sequence in each level takes $n \log d$ bits. Now we apply the representation of Section 13.3.2 on those sequences. The z_ℓ numbers of the wavelet matrix now become $d - 1$ values per level, which easily fit in main memory. Since we store dw bits for **rank** counters in each disk page of Dw bits, the wasted space is a factor of $d/(D - d)$ multiplying the raw data size. We can choose, for example, $d = \sqrt{D}$ to make this factor $\mathcal{O}(1/\sqrt{D})$, which is $o(1/\sqrt{w})$ and much smaller in practice, and still it holds $\log d = \Theta(\log D)$, which will be useful later.

This structure is equivalent to a multiary wavelet tree (Ferragina *et al.*, 2007). We can use it for representing a sequence $S[1, n]$ on an alphabet of any size σ, so that **access**, **rank**, and **select** are all carried out in $\mathcal{O}(\log_d \sigma) = \mathcal{O}(\log_D \sigma)$ I/Os. By compressing the sequences at each level as in Section 13.3.2, the space can be made $n\mathcal{H}_0(S) + o(n \log \sigma)$ bits.

To use the structure for representing an $n \times r$ grid, the counting and reporting procedures in Algorithms 10.1 and 10.2 must be slightly adapted. Sequences B_ℓ are not bitvectors anymore but have alphabet $[1, d]$. The range $[y_1, y_2]$ of the query may now span up to d subranges in the current node. Say that $[c_1, c_2] \subseteq [1, d]$ is the smallest range of symbols in a node that cover the range $[y_1, y_2]$, and that the points in this node correspond to the range $B_\ell[x_1, x_2]$. Then all the occurrences of $c_1 + 1, \ldots, c_2 - 1$ in $B_\ell[x_1, x_2]$ must be counted as results, because they are contained in the range of y-coordinates, and we must continue the counting recursively only on the children number c_1 and c_2. The computation of

$$\sum_{c=c_1+1}^{c_2-1} (\text{rank}_c(B_\ell, x_2) - \text{rank}_c(B_\ell, x_1 - 1))$$

Algorithm 13.4: Answering count with a wavelet matrix on disk. The only I/Os needed are explicit in line 9.

---

1 **Proc count**(G, x_1, x_2, y_1, y_2)

  Input : An $n \times r$ grid G (seen as a sequence S, in turn seen as the sequences
      B_ℓ on alphabet $[1, d]$ and values $z_\ell[1, d]$ of its multi-ary wavelet
      matrix), and range $[x_1, x_2] \times [y_1, y_2]$.

  Output: Returns count(G, x_1, x_2, y_1, y_2).

2 | **return** $count(x_1, x_2, y_1, y_2, 1, 1, r)$

3 **Proc** $count(x_1, x_2, y_1, y_2, \ell, a, b)$

  Input : Range $[x_1, x_2]$ of level ℓ, inside a segment of S_ℓ that represents
      symbols in $[a, b]$, and symbol range $[y_1, y_2]$.

  Output: Returns the number of symbols in $S_\ell[x_1, x_2]$ belonging to $[y_1, y_2]$.

4 | **if** $x_1 > x_2$ **then return** 0
5 | $m \leftarrow \lceil (b - a + 1)/d \rceil$
6 | $c_1 \leftarrow 1 + \max(0, \lfloor (y_1 - a)/m \rfloor)$
7 | $c_2 \leftarrow 1 + \min(d - 1, \lfloor (y_2 - a)/m \rfloor)$
8 | $t \leftarrow 0$
9 | Read the (at most two) disk pages where $B_\ell[x_1 - 1]$ and $B_\ell[x_2]$ lie
10 | **for** $c \leftarrow c_1$ **to** c_2 **do**
11 | $x_1' \leftarrow z_\ell[c] + \text{rank}_c(B_\ell, x_1 - 1) + 1$
12 | $x_2' \leftarrow z_\ell[c] + \text{rank}_c(B_\ell, x_2)$
13 | **if** $y_1 > a + (c - 1)m$ **or** $y_2 < \min(b, a + cm - 1)$ **then**
14 | $t \leftarrow t + count(x_1', x_2', y_1, y_2, \ell+1, a+(c-1)m, \min(b, a+cm-1))$
15 | **else** $t \leftarrow t + x_2' - x_1'$
16 | **return** t

---

can be done within 2 I/Os, as all the needed counters are stored in the pages of $B_\ell[x_1 - 1]$ and $B_\ell[x_2]$. The same argument given in the analysis of the query time in Section 10.1.1 applies to this case, showing that we perform at most two such operations per level. Therefore, the total counting time is $\mathcal{O}(\log_d r) = \mathcal{O}(\log_D r)$ I/Os, which is optimal even for one-dimensional range searches (Pătraşcu and Thorup, 2006; Vitter, 2008).

Algorithm 13.4 gives the details, where $z_\ell[c]$ is the number of symbols smaller than c in B_ℓ. The cth child of the node handling interval $[a, b]$ manages the subinterval $[a+(c-1)m, \min(b, a+cm-1)]$, for $m = \lceil (b-a+1)/d \rceil$.

Example 13.20 *Figure 13.6 shows the same grid of Figure 10.3 and the same query* $[2, 11] \times [3, 9]$, *but now with arity* $d = 4$ *on its wavelet tree. From the root, with string* $B_1 = 2221434113214134$ *we compute* $m = \lceil (b - a + 1)/d \rceil = \lceil (16 - 1 + 1)/4 \rceil = 4$ *and the extreme children* $c_1 = 1 + \max(0, \lfloor (y_1 - a)/m \rfloor) = 1$ *and* $c_2 = 1 + \min(d - 1, \lfloor (y_2 - a)/m \rfloor) = 3$, *so the fourth child is not considered. Since the second child is contained in the y-range of the query, we simply count its points in* $B_1[2, 11]$,

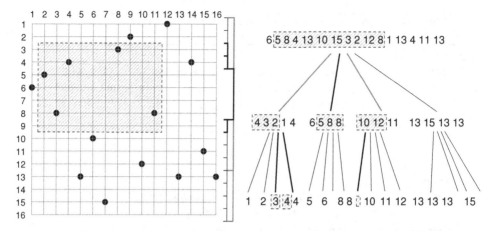

Figure 13.6. The same grid of Figure 10.3, now deployed on disk with a (toy) arity of $d = 4$, and the same query. The nodes reached by thick black edges are counted directly, whereas we enter recursively on those reached by thick gray edges. The corresponding y-ranges are shown on the right of the grid.

with $\mathsf{rank}_2(B_1, 11) - \mathsf{rank}_2(B_1, 2 - 1) = 4 - 1 = 3$. *Those are the points with y-coordinate range* $[5, 8]$ *inside the query:* $(2, 5)$, $(3, 8)$, *and* $(11, 8)$. *Instead, we must enter recursively in the first and third children, because they are not contained in the query y-range. We count* 2 *further points inside the first child,* $(8, 3)$ *and* $(4, 4)$, *and zero in the third.*

Reporting is similar: We must track each point downwards in order to find its y-coordinate. This requires $\log_d r$ operations on the sequences B_ℓ. To avoid the upward tracking of Section 10.1.2, we can store the x-coordinates redundantly aligned to the last level of the wavelet matrix.

Dynamism. If we use the dynamic sequences of Section 13.3.2 for the wavelet matrix levels, the grid allows for insertion and deletion of points (Section 12.5) in total time $\mathcal{O}\left(\log_d r \log_{D/d} n\right)$. This is also optimized for $d = \sqrt{D}$, giving $\mathcal{O}\left(\log_D r \log_D n\right)$ times.

Lower Bounds

Note that, while the counting time is optimal, the time to report occ occurrences is much worse than the optimal $\mathcal{O}(occ/D)$. This is not a consequence of a poor design, but an intrinsic cost of using linear space, that is, $\mathcal{O}(n)$ words. Subramanian and Ramaswamy (1995) proved that, in order to obtain $\mathcal{O}(\mathrm{polylog}_D n + occ/D)$ I/Os for range reporting in secondary memory, the data structure must use $\Omega(n \log n / \log \log_D n)$ words of space. For example, the index of Arge *et al.* (2005) uses the optimal $\mathcal{O}\left(\log_D n + occ/D\right)$ I/Os, but it requires superlinear space, $\mathcal{O}\left(n \log^2 n / \log \log n\right)$ words.

Reporting queries on grids is a well-known example where reducing space (even to linear) implies lower locality of reference and thus a higher query time, particularly on disk. Essentially, if the data are not replicated, then the points within a query range may be scattered along several areas of the disk, requiring many I/Os to collect them.

Linear-Size Grid Structures with Faster Reporting

The lower bound on the space applies to structures offering polylogarithmic worst-case time. Other linear-space structures with no such guarantees perform competitively for reporting in practice, even in high dimensions. For example, various popular disk-based structures for grids (Agarwal and Erickson, 1999) are analogous to the k^2-trees we studied in Section 10.2, but make special provisions to obtain $\mathcal{O}(occ/D)$ I/Os.

Static and dynamic k^2-trees can be directly deployed on disk using bitvectors. Now we describe a structure that also uses a regular space partitioning but it is not hierarchical, and show how compression helps reduce I/Os. Consider n points on an $s \times s$ grid. We cut it regularly into blocks of $b \times b$ cells, for $b = \sqrt{Dw}$. All the points of each block are written as a sparse bitvector (Section 4.4) of length b^2, so that if there are c points in the block, they require $c \log(b^2/c) + 2c$ bits (we do not need the rank/select structures on this bitvector, as we can easily visit its points in time $\mathcal{O}(c)$). The bits of a block require at most one disk page, but they may need much less. We concatenate the descriptions of the blocks in each row of blocks, left to right.

Given a query range of size $p \times q$, we would just need to find the $1 + \lceil q/b \rceil$ leftmost blocks that intersect the query range, and scan their points, continuing with the blocks to the right until we process the rightmost blocks that cover the query range. We can count the total number of I/Os in two parts: (1) The blocks that intersect the query range but are not contained in it; there are at most $2(p+q)/b + \mathcal{O}(1)$ of them and we spend at most one I/O on each. If we had stored the points as two coordinates in plain form, this would have been $2(p+q)/\sqrt{D/2} + \mathcal{O}(1)$. (2) The blocks totally contained in the query range, all of whose points are reported. If we stored the points in plain form, this would add $\mathcal{O}(occ/D)$ I/Os, but our compressed representation further speeds up this process. Let c_i be the number of points inside the ith block of this kind. Then the points take in total $\sum_i c_i \log(b^2/c_i) + 2c_i$ bits. Since the sum of all the involved block sizes is at most $p \cdot q$, the sum is in the worst case $occ \log(pq/occ) + 2occ$ by Jensen's inequality (Section 2.8, using $a_i = c_i$, $x_i = b^2/c_i$, and $f = \log$). As these bits are all contiguous, the I/Os for these blocks is $occ\,(\log(pq/occ) + 2)/Dw$.[10] Therefore, the total number of I/Os is

$$\frac{2(p+q)}{\sqrt{Dw}} + \frac{occ\,(\log(pq/occ) + 2)}{Dw} + \mathcal{O}(1),$$

where the improvement due to compression is clear.

We still have to store the $s^2/(Dw)$ pointers to disk pages for all the blocks. Of those, at most n are nonempty. We can pack on disk the pointers to nonempty blocks, in row-major order, and store them in a B-tree organized in this row-major order. Then we can easily find the pointers of the nonempty blocks closest to each of the $1 + \lceil q/b \rceil$ leftmost blocks covering the query range. These searches add $\mathcal{O}\big((1 + q/\sqrt{Dw})\log_D n)\big)$ I/Os to the time complexity.

This idea is analogous to a proposal by Grossi and Italiano (1999), who partition the data instead of the space to obtain $\mathcal{O}(\sqrt{n/D} + occ/D)$ I/Os within linear space. The topic of range search structures for secondary memory is wide; we refer the reader

---

[10] Actually, the blocks are packed along $1 + \lceil q/b \rceil$ rows, but the final block along each row was already counted as a block not contained in the query area.

to good books and surveys (Agarwal and Erickson, 1999; Arge, 2002; Samet, 2006; Vitter, 2008).

Graphs

Although structures for sequences, grids, and parentheses are useful for representing graphs compactly (see Chapter 9), secondary memory has not been a fertile field for compact graph representations. There are many very different graph problems, and each uses a different approach to access the graph, aiming in general at avoiding non-local memory accesses. A good initial reference for this topic is Vitter (2008, Chapter 10).

Of course, adjacency list compression techniques help reduce the number of I/Os used to read the neighbors of a node, but the other space reduction techniques we have seen tend to reduce locality (for example, the k^2-tree-like structure just seen takes $\mathcal{O}\left(n/\sqrt{Dw}\right)$ I/Os to extract a row or a column of the matrix, instead of the $\mathcal{O}(n/D)$ we would need with a plain adjacency list representation). Moreover, many of those algorithms modify the graph along the process, thus rendering static representations not very useful. As a positive example, Dillabaugh *et al.* (2016) obtained some initial results at representing planar graphs compactly on disk while supporting efficient path traversals.

In the so-called *semi-external* model, we assume that $n = \mathcal{O}(M)$, that is, we can store in memory a constant number of words per graph node. In this case many problems can be solved easily. For example, consider assigning a depth-first search (DFS) number to each node in a directed graph (Chiang *et al.*, 1995). We can maintain an array with the n DFS numbers (initially undefined) and push an initial node in a stack. At each step we pop the node at the top, number all its unknown neighbors, and push them in the stack. If the adjacency lists are stored contiguously, the I/O cost is $\mathcal{O}(n + e/D)$, and a compressed sequence representation helps reduce it further.

If n is too large for storing that array, one may proceed by passes. A hash table contains the distinct nodes that have been numbered. When this table gets full, we traverse all the adjacency lists removing every edge that points to those known nodes. Then the DFS numbers assigned are written to disk, the table is emptied in memory, and the DFS process is resumed (the stack is efficiently handled on disk). The total time is $\mathcal{O}(n + (n/M)e/D)$. Note that the graph is deleted along the process.

13.3.5 Texts

When a compressed text index (Chapter 11) does not fit in main memory, one might be tempted to simply store both the text $T[1, n]$ and its plain suffix array $A[1, n]$ on disk. This is not as rewarding as one might expect. Note that a binary search for the interval $A[sp, ep]$ of $P[1, m]$ involves $2 \log n$ I/Os to access suffix array positions, plus other $2 \log n$ I/Os to access the text positions $T[A[i], A[i] + m - 1]$ (let us assume for practicality that m is much smaller than D, so reading just one disk page of text usually suffices to obtain $T[A[i], A[i] + m - 1]$). The suffix array interval is narrowed at each step of the binary search, so when it is contained in one disk page, one further I/O brings all the desired cells into memory. Thus $2 \log(n/D)$ I/Os are sufficient on A. However, the number of text pages accessed is still $2 \log n$.

The search can be even less efficient if we deploy a compressed text index on disk. A forward search on Ψ requires $\mathcal{O}(m \log n)$ random accesses. A backward search on Ψ may access only $\mathcal{O}(m \log_D n)$ pages (Mäkinen et al., 2004). A backward search on the FM-index, if T^{bwt} is stored as suggested in Section 13.3.2, may require as little as $\mathcal{O}(m)$ I/Os (González and Navarro, 2009). For short patterns, this is significantly better than the $\mathcal{O}(\log n)$ I/Os required on a plain suffix array. Still, the cost is rather high.

Faster Counting

There have been several attempts to alleviate this problem, initially out of the scope of compact data structures. For example, one may sample the first suffix of each disk page of A and store an ℓ-length prefix of it in main memory (Baeza-Yates et al., 1996; Colussi and de Col, 1996). For $\ell = \mathcal{O}(\log n)$, the memory space usage can be as low as $(n/D)\ell \log \sigma = \mathcal{O}((n/D) \log n \log \sigma) = o(n \log \sigma)$ bits. Under reasonable probabilistic models (Szpankowski, 1993), the longest repeated substring in a text is of length $\mathcal{O}(\log n)$; therefore this value of ℓ is sufficient in the average case to make all the ℓ-length prefixes different. In any case, if the pattern length is $m \leq \ell$, then 2 suffix array pages, plus $2 \log D$ text pages, must be read to determine the interval $A[sp, ep]$. This is also the case if $m > \ell$ and all the ℓ-length prefixes are different. However, when prefixes longer than ℓ are shared between many suffixes, and $m > \ell$, the scheme may perform poorly.

A more sophisticated scheme to sample the suffixes and maintain suitable prefixes in main memory is LOF-SA (Sinha et al., 2008). LOF-SA chooses the maximal suffix tree nodes containing $\leq D$ leaves, and defines suffix array *blocks* as the ranges of leaves below those maximal nodes. A block may then contain up to D entries. A trie in main memory stores the top part of the suffix tree (up to the maximal nodes). If P occurs more than D times in T, then its search finishes inside the trie, and the answer $[sp, ep]$ is found directly in memory. Otherwise the search must continue inside a single suffix array block (1–2 pages on disk), and at most $2 \log D$ further text pages are read along the binary search on the suffix array block.

These $2 \log D$ accesses are reduced by storing, in this suffix array block, LCP values (Section 11.5.1) and some further symbols. Assume we scan the block left-to-right, and it holds $T[A[i], n] < P$ and $\mathsf{lcp}(P, T[A[i], n]) = r$. If $\mathsf{LCP}[i+1] = \mathsf{lcp}(T[A[i], n], T[A[i+1], n]) < r$, then P is not in T. Otherwise, if $\mathsf{LCP}[i+1] > r$, then we can move on to $i + 1$, as the invariant stays true. Only if $\mathsf{LCP}[i+1] = r$ we need to compare the symbols in $T[A[i+1] + r + 1, n]$.

The LOF-SA reduces the times of regularly sampled suffix arrays by half or more, although it increases the structure space to about $12n$ bytes and requires a significant amount of main memory (around 5% of the text size, in practice). The on-disk part of the structure was later reduced to about $7n$ bytes (Moffat et al., 2009), but the main memory usage was still a problem.

In a recent work (Gog et al., 2014) the LOF-SA is improved by a new arrangement called RoSA, which reduces the main memory space to about 1% of the text size and also reduces the disk space to about $2n$ bytes (in all cases, we are not counting the additional n bytes of the text itself). This work makes clever use of variants of the compact data structures we have seen in order to reduce disk times.

The idea used in RoSA to reduce the disk space comes from early works (Mäkinen, 2003; Mäkinen and Navarro, 2004, 2005) related to the discussion in Section 13.2.4. When the text has regularities, its suffix array has areas $A[i, i + t - 1]$ whose numbers appear shifted by 1 elsewhere, in $A[j, j + t - 1]$. This produces runs in Ψ and T^{bwt}. While the compression this idea yields on non-repetitive texts is mild, it is still useful in this scenario. Gog *et al.* (2014) cut $A[1, n]$ into blocks as in LOF-SA, and then detect full blocks $A[i, i']$ that appear (shifted by 1) inside another block $A[j, j']$. They then remove $A[i, i']$ and replace it with a reference (r, o, s), where r is the identifier of block $A[j, j']$, o is the offset of $A[i, i']$ inside $A[j, j']$, and $s = 1$ is the shift of its values. It might be that $A[j, j']$ appears in turn shifted by 1 inside another block $A[k, k']$, in which case both $A[i, i']$ and $A[j, j']$ are represented in terms of $A[k, k']$ (now the reference of $A[i, i']$ uses $s = 2$ as the shift value). Only the blocks that cannot be reduced in this way are explicitly represented.

Both the reduced and non-reduced blocks are represented as pointers to a content area on disk, with the corresponding s and o fields (these are zero for the non-reduced blocks). Then a single content area on disk may be pointed from several blocks. Blocks of just 1 suffix, however, are replaced by a direct pointer to the text, which is more efficient.

Example 13.21 *Figure 13.7 shows, on the left, the suffix array of* $T = $ abracadabra$, *and how it is split into blocks for* $D = 3$. *The sorted suffixes are shown on the right of the suffix array, and the boxes with black symbols correspond to the in-memory trie nodes. The suffix array blocks (shown on the suffix array) correspond to trie leaves, and to the maximal suffix tree nodes with at most D leaves.*

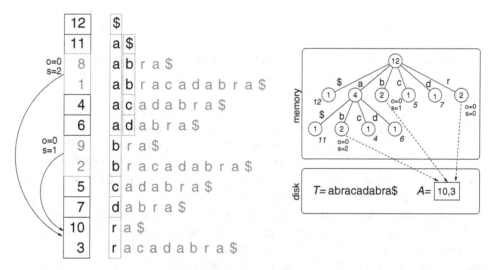

Figure 13.7. The scheme used by RoSA to reduce the suffix array space on disk. On the left we spot the repetitions (shifted by s) found on A that correspond to blocks. On the right, we show the in-memory trie (still in LOF-SA format) and the on-disk structures: the text T and some suffix array contents. The trie contains direct pointers to the text (in italics) for blocks of size 1, and (possibly shared) pointers to suffix array contents.

Two of the blocks, $A[3, 4] = \langle 8, 1 \rangle$ and $A[7, 8] = \langle 9, 2 \rangle$, can be reduced to $A[11, 12] = \langle 10, 3 \rangle$, because their entries are the same with a shift of $s = 2$ for $A[3, 4]$ and of $s = 1$ for $A[7, 8]$. Both offsets are $o = 0$.

On the right, we show the in-memory trie explicitly, with the suffix array range sizes inside the nodes. The leaves of size 1 point directly to the text (in italics). The others point to content areas on disk (only one in this example).

The space reduction in main memory is obtained by representing the LOF-SA trie as a reduced BWT (Section 11.3.1; recall strings F and L) of the reversed text. The text is reversed so that a backward search for the reverse pattern P^{rev} simulates a forward search for P in T. The BWT, L, can be reduced because we only need to simulate the traversal of trie nodes. The reduction chooses all the intervals $A^r[i, j]$ in the suffix array A^r of T^{rev} that represent trie nodes, and marks the positions i and $j + 1$ as 1s in a bitvector $bf[1, n]$. Those positions are then marked in a second bitvector $bl[1, n]$ using the LF mapping of the BWT of T^{rev}: $bl[l] = bf[LF(l)]$. That is, if a symbol $F[f]$ is marked in bf, then the same symbol is marked in bl at its position in $L[l]$ (where $f = LF(l)$). The reduced BWT, L', collects the BWT symbols at the positions where $bl[l] = 1$.

Example 13.22 *Figure 13.8 shows, on the right, the suffix array of $T^{rev} =$ arbadacarba\$ and its suffixes. On the suffixes, we mark with boxes the areas corresponding to the trie nodes. These were (see Figure 13.7) \$, a, b, c, d, r, a\$, ab, ac, and ad. Reversed, these correspond to the ranges in A^r for \$, a, b, c, d, r, \$a, ba, ca, and da. The positions i and $j + 1$ of each range $A^r[i, j]$ are marked in bf. For each mark $bf[f] = 1$ with $A^r[f] = p$, we mark the entry $bl[l] \leftarrow 1$ such that $A^r[l] = (p \mod n) + 1$. The reduced BWT is formed by the symbols of L whose bl entry is marked, in this case, $L' =$ abdc\$r.*

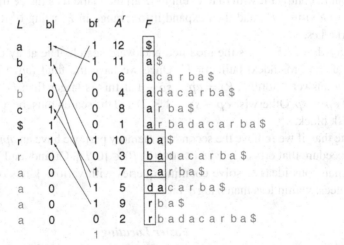

Figure 13.8. The scheme used by RoSA to reduce the trie space in memory. We mark in bf the limits of all the trie nodes in A^r and then project the 1s onto bl, at the position of L where the first symbol of the suffix (sequence F) is mapped. We then collect from L only the positions that are marked in bl.

Algorithm 13.5: Backward search on a reduced FM-index.

> **Input** : Trie nodes of T^{rev} and its suffix array A^r (seen as reduced sequence L',
> its array C', and bitvectors bf and bl) and pattern $P[1, m]$.
> **Output**: Returns the range $[sp, ep]$ in A^r of the trie of T^{rev} reached when
> searching for P, with $sp > ep$ if P does not occur in T^{rev}.

1 $[sp, ep] \leftarrow [1, n]$
2 **for** $k \leftarrow 1$ **to** m **do**
3 $\quad$ **if** $ep - sp + 1 \leq D$ **then return** $[sp, ep]$
4 $\quad$ $c \leftarrow P[k]$
5 $\quad$ $sp' \leftarrow \mathsf{rank}(\mathsf{bl}, sp - 1)$
6 $\quad$ $ep' \leftarrow \mathsf{rank}(\mathsf{bl}, ep)$
7 $\quad$ $sp'' \leftarrow \mathsf{rank}_c(L', sp')$
8 $\quad$ $ep'' \leftarrow \mathsf{rank}_c(L', ep')$
9 $\quad$ $sp \leftarrow \mathsf{select}(\mathsf{bf}, C'[c] + sp'' + 1)$
10 $\quad$ $ep \leftarrow \mathsf{select}(\mathsf{bf}, C'[c] + ep'' + 1) - 1$
11 **return** $[sp, ep]$

As long as we stay within the trie nodes, the FM-index backward search procedure (Algorithm 11.5) can be simulated on the reduced BWT and bitvectors bl and bf. The key property is that all the blocks are inside areas of A^r where the suffixes start with the same symbol c (in Example 13.22, there is exactly one block per symbol, but this is not always the case). In bf the 1s are sorted as in F, whereas in bl they are sorted as in L. Therefore, the occurrences of c in F are marked/unmarked in bf, and those in L are marked/unmarked in bl. As we saw in Section 11.3.1, those cs are in the same order in F and L. Therefore, to perform a backward step, we start from the current range in L, contract it with bl to count in L' all the marked cs inside the range, map the range to a virtual F', and then expand it to a range in F, using bf to account for the unmarked cs.

Algorithm 13.5 shows the modified backward search. The array C' refers to the C array of the FM-index, built for L'. Once we have the final range $[sp, ep]$, we can directly answer $\mathsf{count}(T, P) = ep - sp + 1$ if this is larger than D, and also answer zero if $ep > sp$. Otherwise $ep - sp + 1 \leq D$ and the search must be refined inside only one disk block.

Note that, if we remove the secondary memory part, we have an *approximate counting* procedure that errs only when $\mathsf{count}(T, P) \in [0, D]$. Orlandi and Venturini (2016) used analogous ideas to solve counting queries with various kinds of approximation guarantees, within less than $n \log \sigma$ bits.

Faster Locating

The locating procedure, that is, recovering the text positions $A[i]$ for $sp \leq i \leq ep$, where P appears in T, is also extremely non-local if we use suffix array sampling as in Chapter 11. Instead, if $A[1, n]$ is stored on disk, then at most $1 + \lceil (ep - sp)/D \rceil$ I/Os suffice. In RoSA, this may increase due to the suffix array division into blocks.

A different compression method for the suffix array can reduce this time, and make it even lower than on an uncompressed suffix array (González *et al.*, 2014). The idea is again to take advantage of the areas $A[i, i+t-1]$ and $A[j, j+t-1]$ that are shifted by a value of 1. If we represent A differentially, $A^d[1] = A[1]$ and $A^d[i+1] = A[i+1] - A[i]$, then in the case of the shifted areas it holds $A^d[i+1, i+t-1] = A^d[j+1, j+t-1]$. Those repetitions can then be reduced by grammar-compressing A^d (recall Section 8.5.2).

Example 13.23 *The suffix array of the text* $T = $ abracadabra$ *is shown in Figure 11.2. If we encode it differentially, we obtain*

$$A^d = \langle 12, -1, -3, -7, 3, 2, 3, -7, 3, 2, 3, -7 \rangle,$$

which has a long repetition $A^d[4, 8] = A^d[8, 12] = \langle -7, 3, 2, 3, -7 \rangle$ *related to the run* $\Psi[3, 8] = \langle 7, 8, 9, 10, 11, 12 \rangle$. *We can then grammar-compress* A^d *exploiting most of the repetition (not all, because its two occurrences overlap):*

$$A^d \rightarrow 12, -1, -3, X, X, -7$$
$$X \rightarrow -7, 3, 2, 3.$$

In practice, this method reduces the suffix array size by a factor of up to 4, depending on the compressibility of T. In a disk-based representation (González and Navarro, 2009), we store an absolute sample (i.e., the corresponding value of A) in the beginning of each disk page, and then a sequence of terminals and nonterminals representing a segment of A^d, until filling the disk page. The advantage of this representation is that more cells of A are stored inside a single disk page, and therefore the number $1 + \lceil (ep - sp)/D \rceil$ of I/Os to retrieve the positions of P decreases in practice.

The grammar rules, however, must be maintained in main memory to obtain that reduction in I/Os. We can stop the grammar generation process when the dictionary exceeds the main memory available, although stopping earlier will impact on the compression ratio. The compact grammar representation seen in Section 8.5.2 helps maintain larger grammars in memory, and thus improves the compression ratio and the I/O performance at locating.

Trie Structures on Disk

Another way to reduce the number of accesses of a binary search on a suffix array is to use the suffix tree structure. As we saw in Section 13.3.3, trees can be efficiently deployed on disk so that a root-to-leaf traversal reads the minimum possible number of disk pages. This was the key idea in an early structure by Clark and Munro (1996), which made 2–3 I/Os per query and used $4n$ to $5n$ bytes, plus the text.

Another trie-based solution is the String B-tree (Ferragina and Grossi, 1999), which can store a set of n strings within $\mathcal{O}(n)$ words on disk if it also has access to the strings. Therefore, it can store all the suffixes of $T[1, n]$ within this space. The idea is similar to that of the B-tree, so that $\Theta(D)$ strings are used inside internal nodes to guide the search toward the children. Those $\Theta(D)$ strings inside a single disk page are stored using a Patricia tree (Section 8.5.3), so that the space needed does not depend on their lengths. Then, at the end of the search, one must compare P again with some of the resulting suffixes to determine if it actually occurs in T. Na and Park (2004) further compacted the node representation, replacing the Patricia tree traversal by a linear scan over an array of branching symbols and LCPs.

The String B-tree searches in $\mathcal{O}(\log_D n)$ I/Os for counting (plus a term $\mathcal{O}(m/D)$ we have omitted everywhere for practicality) and $\mathcal{O}(occ/D)$ for locating, which is optimal. In practice, the structure performs just 2–3 I/Os per counting query. The space used by the structure on disk, however, is around $7n$ bytes plus the text. In exchange, the structure is more general, as it can maintain an arbitrary set of strings, and it is dynamic.

Geometric Structures

Note that, despite some heuristic reductions, the structures that can count with a few I/Os, and locate with $\mathcal{O}(occ/D)$ I/Os, use $\Theta(n \log n)$ bits of space. Instead, the compact structures using $\mathcal{O}(n \log \sigma)$ bits (Mäkinen *et al.*, 2004; González and Navarro, 2009), require at least m I/Os for searching, and $\mathcal{O}(occ)$ or more for locating. This separation is not accidental. Let us describe a disk-based index using $\mathcal{O}(n \log \sigma)$ bits, called the Geometric BWT (Chien *et al.*, 2015). The structure is useful to prove lower bounds on the disk performance of compact text indexes.

Let $d = \log_\sigma n$. The text $T[1, n]$ is cut into metasymbols of d symbols, forming a new text $T'[1, n/d]$ over an alphabet of size $\sigma^d = n$. The metasymbols respect the lexicographic order of the string of symbols they represent. Let $A'[1, n/d]$ be the suffix array of T'. Further, let y^{rev} be the metasymbol obtained by reading the $\log n$ bits of metasymbol y in reverse order. Now, define a grid on the points $(i, T'[A'[i] - 1]^{rev})$ such that $A'[i] > 1$, and build a String B-tree on the text $T'[1, n/d]$. This String B-tree uses $\mathcal{O}((n/d) \log n) = \mathcal{O}(n \log \sigma)$ bits. Similarly, the grid is of size $(n/d) \times n$ and has n/d points, thus it also fits in $\mathcal{O}(n \log \sigma)$ bits; recall Section 13.3.4.

Let us consider the search for patterns of length d or more (shorter ones are dealt with an ad hoc index). Each occurrence $T[i, i + m - 1]$ of $P[1, m]$ is said to be aligned at $k = (i - 1) \bmod d$. The occurrences of P aligned at $k = 0$ can be found directly in the String B-tree: We rewrite P as a sequence of metasymbols, $P'[1, \lceil m/d \rceil]$. If m is not a multiple of d, we create two patterns P_1 and P_2, by completing the last (incomplete) metasymbol with all 0s and all 1s, respectively. The String B-tree can then find the range $A'[sp_0, ep_0]$ corresponding to P' by searching for P_1 and P_2, in time $\mathcal{O}(\log_D n)$. Their positions in T' can then be found in time $\mathcal{O}(occ_0/D)$, where $occ_0 = ep_0 - sp_0 + 1$.

To find the occurrences aligned at $k > 0$, we cut $P = P_k^- \cdot P_k^+$, with $|P_k^-| = k$. We then proceed with P_k^+ on the String B-tree as before, this time only finding the range $A'[sp_k, ep_k]$ that corresponds to P_k^+, in $\mathcal{O}(\log_D n)$ time. On the other hand, P_k^- is reversed and completed with $d - k$ 0s and 1s to form metasymbols y_1 and y_2, respectively. Note that $[y_1, y_2]$ is the range of all the metasymbols that finish with P_k^-. Now, a range search for $[sp_k, ep_k] \times [y_1, y_2]$ gives all the positions $A'[i]$ that correspond to occurrences of P aligned at k. By using the secondary memory grid structure of Section 13.3.4, the time for the d queries adds up to $\mathcal{O}(\log_\sigma n \log_D n + occ \log_D n)$.

Example 13.24 *The Geometric BWT for $T = $ abrabracadabrabra\$, with $d = 3$, is shown in Figure 13.9: $T'[1, n/d] = T'[1, 6] = \langle abr \rangle \langle abr \rangle \langle aca \rangle \langle dab \rangle \langle rab \rangle \langle ra\$ \rangle$ is a text formed by triples, with suffix array $A' = \langle 1, 2, 3, 4, 6, 5 \rangle$. The y-coordinates of the grid correspond to all the possible triples, in lexicographic order (we only show the reverse triples that exist in T). The x-coordinates correspond to the positions of A'. For*

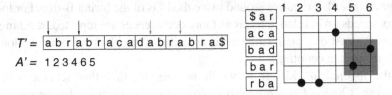

$T' =$ a b r a b r a c a d a b r a b r a $

$A' =$ 1 2 3 4 6 5

Figure 13.9. The Geometric BWT of $T =$ abrabracadabrabra$ with $d = 3$. On the left we show the text T' of the metasymbols and its suffix array A'. On the right we show the geometric structure associating each position $A[i]$ (x-coordinate) with the corresponding reversed symbol in the BWT of T' (y-coordinate). The occurrences of the search pattern $P =$ abra are shown with arrows on top of T', black for $k = 0$ and gray for $k = 2$. The grid area to find the occurrences with $k = 2$, $[5, 6] \times [3, 4]$, is also grayed.

example, there is a point at $(x = 6, y =$ bad$)$ *because* $T'[4] =$ dab $= y^{rev}$ *is followed by* $T'[A'[x], n/d] = T'[5, 6]$.

To search for $P =$ abra, *we try the different alignments. That for* $k = 0$ *looks for the suffixes prefixed by the range between* $P_1 = \langle$abr$\rangle \langle$a$\$\$\rangle$ *and* $P_2 = \langle$abr$\rangle \langle$a%%$\rangle$ *(assuming* % *is the largest symbol in the alphabet). The String B-tree finds the suffix array range* $A'[1, 2]$ *for it, thus we recover the positions* $T'[A'[1]] = T'[1]$, *corresponding to* $T[1]$, *and* $T'[A'[2]] = T'[2]$, *corresponding to* $T[4]$. *Those occurrences are shown with black arrows on top of* T'.

The other alignment that produces results is $k = 2$, *where* $P_2^- =$ ab *and* $P_2^+ =$ ra. *Pattern* P_2^- *yields the* y*-range of* ba*, where* * *stands for any character; the range spans* $[y_1, y_2] = [3, 4]$. *Pattern* P_2^+ *is expanded to the range* $[\langle$ra$\$\rangle, \langle$ra%$\rangle]$, *which is searched for in the String B-tree to yield the range* $A'[5, 6]$, *thus* $[sp_2, ep_2] = [5, 6]$. *Then the search in* $[sp_2, ep_2] \times [y_1, y_2]$ *(grayed in the figure) yields the points* $(6, 3)$ *and* $(5, 4)$. *The first one corresponds to* $T'[A'[6]] = T'[5]$ *with alignment* $k = 2$, *that is,* $T[(5 - 1) \cdot d + 1 - k] = T[11]$. *The second one corresponds to* $T'[A'[5]] = T'[6]$, *that is,* $T[(6 - 1) \cdot d + 1 - k] = T[14]$. *Those occurrences are shown with gray arrows on top of* T'.

Note that, compared with the larger secondary memory structures, the time per occurrence reported is particularly high. This can be converted into the optimal $\mathcal{O}(occ/D)$ for sufficiently long patterns (longer than about $\log^2 n$). However, for short patterns, Chien *et al.* (2015) show that the high cost per occurrence is a consequence of the index using only $\mathcal{O}(n \log \sigma)$ bits: Any disk-based index solving queries for patterns of length $m = \mathcal{O}(\log n)$ in $\mathcal{O}(\text{polylog}_D n / \log^2 n + occ/D)$ I/Os, must use $\Omega(n \log n / \log \log_D n)$ bits of space in the worst case. To prove the lower bound, they show that any grid can be seen as the Geometric BWT of some convenient text, so that range search problems on the grid can be expressed as text search problems. Known lower bounds on the former (Subramanian and Ramaswamy, 1995) then yield lower bounds on the latter.

Therefore, although we have seen that some space-reduction techniques yield a performance improvement, reducing the index space further involves a serious penalty in disk search performance.

On the other hand, the Geometric BWT has practical interest too. An implementation using K-d-trees (Chiu *et al.*, 2010) and tuned for $d = 4$ achieves roughly the same space of a plain suffix array (and around half the space of a String B-tree). For determining the range $A[sp, ep]$, it requires around twice the I/Os of the String B-tree. For locating, the index speeds up in relative terms as more occurrences are reported, reaching about 2–3 times the cost of a plain suffix array (recall that the plain suffix array alone does not perform well at counting).

On the theoretical side, it is worth mentioning that this scheme was modified to use $\mathcal{O}(n\mathcal{H}_k(T)) + o(n\log\sigma)$ bits, while increasing the search time to $\mathcal{O}\big((m/D + \log_\sigma n\log_D n)\log n + occ\log_D n\big)$ (Hon *et al.*, 2009). The idea is to keep metasymbols of $\log n$ bits, but now they may encode more than d symbols. Just as described at the end of Sections 13.3.1 and 13.3.2, they encode in each metasymbol the k preceding symbols and then use arithmetic encoding on as many new symbols as possible (González and Navarro, 2009). In practice, $\log n$ bits may be too short to encode the $k\log\sigma$ bits of the preceding symbols plus anything else, but instead the Huffman encoding of blocks (Section 4.1.2) may work well.

Bibliography

Abeliuk, A., Cánovas, R., and Navarro, G. (2013). Practical compressed suffix trees. *Algorithms*, **6**(2), 319–351.

Agarwal, P. K. and Erickson, J. (1999). Geometric range searching and its relatives. In *Advances in Discrete and Computational Geometry*, volume 223 of *Contemporary Mathematics*, pages 1–56. AMS Press.

Al-Hafeedh, A., Crochemore, M., Ilie, L., Kopylov, E., Smyth, W. F., Tischler, G., and Yusufu, M. (2012). A comparison of index-based Lempel-Ziv LZ77 factorization algorithms. *ACM Computing Surveys*, **45**(1), article 5.

Alstrup, S., Bender, M. A., Demaine, E. D., Farach-Colton, M., Munro, J. I., Rauhe, T., and Thorup, M. (2002). Efficient tree layout in a multilevel memory hierarchy. *CoRR*, **cs/0211010v2**. http://arxiv.org/abs/cs.DS/0211010.

Arge, L. (2002). External memory data structures. In *Handbook of Massive Data Sets*, chapter 9, pages 313–357. Kluwer Academic Publishers.

Arge, L., Brodal, G. S., Fagerberg, R., and Laustsen, M. (2005). Cache-oblivious planar orthogonal range searching and counting. In *Proc. 21st ACM Symposium on Computational Geometry (SoCG)*, pages 160–169.

Arroyuelo, D. and Navarro, G. (2007). A Lempel-Ziv text index on secondary storage. In *Proc. 18th Annual Symposium on Combinatorial Pattern Matching (CPM)*, LNCS 4580, pages 83–94.

Arroyuelo, D., Navarro, G., and Sadakane, K. (2012). Stronger Lempel-Ziv based compressed text indexing. *Algorithmica*, **62**(1), 54–101.

Arroyuelo, D., Davoodi, P., and Rao, S. S. (2016). Succinct dynamic cardinal trees. *Algorithmica*, **74**(2), 742–777.

Baeza-Yates, R., Barbosa, E. F., and Ziviani, N. (1996). Hierarchies of indices for text searching. *Information Systems*, **21**(6), 497–514.

Belazzougui, D., Gagie, T., Gog, S., Manzini, G., and Sirén, J. (2014). Relative FM-indexes. In *Proc. 21st International Symposium on String Processing and Information Retrieval (SPIRE)*, LNCS 8799, pages 52–64.

Belazzougui, D., Puglisi, S. J., and Tabei, Y. (2015a). Access, rank, select in grammar-compressed strings. In *Proc. 23rd Annual European Symposium on Algorithms (ESA)*, LNCS 9294, pages 142–154.

Belazzougui, D., Cunial, F., Gagie, T., Prezza, N., and Raffinot, M. (2016). Practical combinations of repetition-aware data structures. *CoRR*, **abs/1604.06002**. http://arxiv.org/abs/1604.06002.

Belazzougui, D., Cunial, F., Gagie, T., Prezza, N., and Raffinot, M. (2015b). Composite repetition-aware data structures. In *Proc. 26th Annual Symposium on Combinatorial Pattern Matching (CPM)*, LNCS 9133, pages 26–39.

Belazzougui, D., Gagie, T., Gawrychowski, P., Kärkkäinen, J., Ordóñez, A., Puglisi, S. J., and Tabei, Y. (2015c). Queries on LZ-bounded encodings. In *Proc. 25th Data Compression Conference (DCC)*, pages 83–92.

Bell, T. C., Cleary, J., and Witten, I. H. (1990). *Text Compression*. Prentice Hall.

Bille, P., Landau, G. M., Raman, R., Sadakane, K., Rao, S. S., and Weimann, O. (2015). Random access to grammar-compressed strings and trees. *SIAM Journal on Computing*, **44**(3), 513–539.

Blumer, A., Blumer, J., Haussler, D., McConnell, R. M., and Ehrenfeucht, A. (1987). Complete inverted files for efficient text retrieval and analysis. *Journal of the ACM*, **34**(3), 578–595.

Brodal, G. S. and Fagerberg, R. (2006). Cache-oblivious string dictionaries. In *Proc. 17th Annual ACM-SIAM Symposium on Discrete Algorithms (SODA)*, pages 581–590.

Charikar, M., Lehman, E., Liu, D., Panigrahy, R., Prabhakaran, M., Sahai, A., and Shelat, A. (2005). The smallest grammar problem. *IEEE Transactions on Information Theory*, **51**(7), 2554–2576.

Chen, G., Puglisi, S. J., and Smyth, W. F. (2008). Lempel-Ziv factorization using less time & space. *Mathematics in Computer Science*, **1**, 605–623.

Chiang, Y.-J., Goodrich, M. T., Grove, E. F., Tamassia, R., Vengroff, D. E., and Vitter, J. S. (1995). External-memory graph algorithms. In *Proc. 6th Annual ACM-SIAM Symposium on Discrete Algorithms (SODA)*, pages 139–149.

Chien, Y.-F., Hon, W.-K., Shah, R., Thankachan, S. V., and Vitter, J. S. (2015). Geometric BWT: compressed text indexing via sparse suffixes and range searching. *Algorithmica*, **71**(2), 258–278.

Chiu, S.-Y., Hon, W.-K., Shah, R., and Vitter, J. S. (2010). I/O-efficient compressed text indexes: From theory to practice. In *Proc. 20th Data Compression Conference (DCC)*, pages 426–434.

Clark, D. R. and Munro, J. I. (1996). Efficient suffix trees on secondary storage. In *Proc. 7th Annual ACM-SIAM Symposium on Discrete Algorithms (SODA)*, pages 383–391.

Claude, F. and Navarro, G. (2012). Improved grammar-based compressed indexes. In *Proc. 19th International Symposium on String Processing and Information Retrieval (SPIRE)*, LNCS 7608, pages 180–192.

Claude, F., Fariña, A., Martínez-Prieto, M., and Navarro, G. (2010). Compressed *q*-gram indexing for highly repetitive biological sequences. In *Proc. 10th IEEE Conference on Bioinformatics and Bioengineering (BIBE)*, pages 86–91.

Claude, F., Fariña, A., Martínez-Prieto, M., and Navarro, G. (2016). Universal indexes for highly repetitive document collections. *Information Systems*, **61**, 1–23.

Colussi, L. and de Col, A. (1996). A time and space efficient data structure for string searching on large texts. *Information Processing Letters*, **58**(5), 217–222.

Davoodi, P., Navarro, G., Raman, R., and Rao, S. S. (2014). Encoding range minima and range top-2 queries. *Philosophical Transactions of the Royal Society A*, **372**(20130131).

Demaine, E. D., Iacono, J., and Langerman, S. (2015). Worst-case optimal tree layout in external memory. *Algorithmica*, **72**(2), 369–378.

Deorowicz, S. and Grabowski, S. (2011). Robust relative compression of genomes with random access. *Bioinformatics*, **27**, 2979–2986.

Dillabaugh, C., He, M., and Maheshwari, A. (2012). Succinct and I/O efficient data structures for traversal in trees. *Algorithmica*, **63**(1–2), 201–223.

Dillabaugh, C., He, M., Maheshwari, A., and Zeh, N. (2016). I/O-efficient path traversal in succinct planar graphs. *Algorithmica*. Early view, DOI 10.1007/s00453-015-0086-7.

Do, H. H., Jansson, J., Sadakane, K., and Sung, W.-K. (2014). Fast relative Lempel-Ziv self-index for similar sequences. *Theoretical Computer Science*, **532**, 14–30.

Farach, M. and Thorup, M. (1995). String matching in Lempel-Ziv compressed strings. In *Proc. 27th ACM Symposium on Theory of Computing (STOC)*, pages 703–712.

Farzan, A. and Munro, J. I. (2014). A uniform paradigm to succinctly encode various families of trees. *Algorithmica*, **68**(1), 16–40.

Ferrada, H., Gagie, T., Gog, S., and Puglisi, S. J. (2014). Relative Lempel-Ziv with constant-time random access. In *Proc. 21st International Symposium on String Processing and Information Retrieval (SPIRE)*, LNCS 8799, pages 13–17.

Ferragina, P. and Grossi, R. (1999). The string B-tree: A new data structure for string search in external memory and its applications. *Journal of the ACM*, **46**(2), 236–280.

Ferragina, P. and Manzini, G. (2005). Indexing compressed texts. *Journal of the ACM*, **52**(4), 552–581.

Ferragina, P., Manzini, G., Mäkinen, V., and Navarro, G. (2007). Compressed representations of sequences and full-text indexes. *ACM Transactions on Algorithms*, **3**(2), article 20.

Fischer, J. (2011). Combined data structure for previous- and next-smaller-values. *Theoretical Computer Science*, **412**(22), 2451–2456.

Fischer, J. and Heun, V. (2011). Space-efficient preprocessing schemes for range minimum queries on static arrays. *SIAM Journal on Computing*, **40**(2), 465–492.

Fischer, J., Mäkinen, V., and Navarro, G. (2009). Faster entropy-bounded compressed suffix trees. *Theoretical Computer Science*, **410**(51), 5354–5364.

Fischer, J., I, T., and Köppl, D. (2015). Lempel Ziv computation in small space (LZ-CISS). In *Proc. 26th Annual Symposium on Combinatorial Pattern Matching (CPM)*, LNCS 9133, pages 172–184.

Gagie, T. and Puglisi, S. J. (2015). Searching and indexing genomic databases via kernelization. *Frontiers in Bioengineering and Biotechnology*, **3**(12).

Gagie, T., Gawrychowski, P., Kärkkäinen, J., Nekrich, Y., and Puglisi, S. J. (2012). A faster grammar-based self-index. In *Proc. 6th International Conference on Language and Automata Theory and Applications (LATA)*, LNCS 7183, pages 240–251.

Gagie, T., Hoobin, C., and Puglisi, S. J. (2014a). Block graphs in practice. In *Proc. 2nd International Conference on Algorithms for Big Data (ICABD)*, pages 30–36.

Gagie, T., Gawrychowski, P., Kärkkäinen, J., Nekrich, Y., and Puglisi, S. J. (2014b). LZ77-based self-indexing with faster pattern matching. In *Proc. 11th Latin American Theoretical Informatics Symposium (LATIN)*, LNCS 8392, pages 731–742.

Gagie, T., Gawrychowski, P., and Puglisi, S. J. (2015a). Approximate pattern matching in LZ77-compressed texts. *Journal of Discrete Algorithms*, **32**, 64–68.

Gagie, T., Navarro, G., Puglisi, S. J., and Sirén, J. (2015b). Relative compressed suffix trees. *CoRR*, **abs/1508.02550**. http://arxiv.org/abs/1508.02550.

Gawrychowski, P. and Nicholson, P. K. (2015a). Encodings of range maximum-sum segment queries and applications. In *Proc. 26th Annual Symposium on Combinatorial Pattern Matching (CPM)*, LNCS 9133, pages 196–206.

Gawrychowski, P. and Nicholson, P. K. (2015b). Optimal encodings for range top-k, selection, and min-max. In *Proc. 42nd International Colloquium on Automata, Languages, and Programming (ICALP), Part I*, LNCS 9134, pages 593–604.

Geary, R. F., Raman, R., and Raman, V. (2006). Succinct ordinal trees with level-ancestor queries. *ACM Transactions on Algorithms*, **2**(4), 510–534.

Gil, J. and Itai, A. (1999). How to pack trees. *Journal of Algorithms*, **32**(2), 108–132.

Gog, S., Moffat, A., Culpepper, J. S., Turpin, A., and Wirth, A. (2014). Large-scale pattern search using reduced-space on-disk suffix arrays. *IEEE Transactions on Knowledge and Data Engineering*, **26**(8), 1918–1931.

Golin, M. J., Iacono, J., Krizanc, D., Raman, R., Rao, S. S., and Shende, S. (2016). Encoding 2-D range maximum queries. *Theoretical Computer Science*, **609**, 316–327.

González, R. and Navarro, G. (2009). A compressed text index on secondary memory. *Journal of Combinatorial Mathematics and Combinatorial Computing*, **71**, 127–154.

González, R., Navarro, G., and Ferrada, H. (2014). Locally compressed suffix arrays. *ACM Journal of Experimental Algorithmics*, **19**(1), article 1.

Goto, K. and Bannai, H. (2013). Simpler and faster Lempel Ziv factorization. In *Proc. 23rd Data Compression Conference (DCC)*, pages 133–142.

Goto, K. and Bannai, H. (2014). Space efficient linear time Lempel-Ziv factorization for small alphabets. In *Proc. 24th Data Compression Conference (DCC)*, pages 163–172.

Grossi, R. and Italiano, G. F. (1999). Efficient cross-trees for external memory. In *External Memory Algorithms and Visualization*, DIMACS Series in Discrete Mathematics and Theoretical Computer Science. AMS Press.

Grossi, R., Iacono, J., Navarro, G., Raman, R., and Rao, S. S. (2013). Encodings for range selection and top-k queries. In *Proc. 21st Annual European Symposium on Algorithms (ESA)*, LNCS 8125, pages 553–564.

He, M., Munro, J. I., and Rao, S. S. (2012). Succinct ordinal trees based on tree covering. *ACM Transactions on Algorithms*, **8**(4), article 42.

Hon, W.-K., Shah, R., and Vitter, J. S. (2006). Ordered pattern matching: Towards full-text retrieval. Technical Report TR-06-008, Purdue University.

Hon, W.-K., Shah, R., Thankachan, S. V., and Vitter, J. S. (2009). On entropy-compressed text indexing in external memory. In *Proc. 16th International Symposium on String Processing and Information Retrieval (SPIRE)*, LNCS 5721, pages 75–89.

Huang, S., Lam, T. W., Sung, W.-K., Tam, S.-L., and Yiu, S.-M. (2010). Indexing similar DNA sequences. In *Proc. 6th International Conference on Algorithmic Aspects in Information and Management (AAIM)*, LNCS 6124, pages 180–190.

Hutchinson, D. A., Maheshwari, A., and Zeh, N. (2003). An external memory data structure for shortest path queries. *Discrete Applied Mathematics*, **126**, 55–82.

Jansson, J., Sadakane, K., and Sung, W.-K. (2015). Linked dynamic tries with applications to LZ-compression in sublinear time and space. *Algorithmica*, **71**(4), 969–988.

Jez, A. (2015). Approximation of grammar-based compression via recompression. *Theoretical Computer Science*, **592**, 115–134.

Jez, A. (2016). A really simple approximation of smallest grammar. *Theoretical Computer Science*, **616**, 141–150.

Jo, S. and Rao, S. S. (2015). Simultaneous encodings for range and next/previous larger/smaller value queries. In *Proc. 21st International Conference on Computing and Combinatorics (COCOON)*, LNCS 9198, pages 648–660.

Jørgensen, A. G. and Larsen, K. G. (2011). Range selection and median: Tight cell probe lower bounds and adaptive data structures. In *Proc. 22nd Annual ACM-SIAM Symposium on Discrete Algorithms (SODA)*, pages 805–813.

Kärkkäinen, J. and Ukkonen, E. (1996). Lempel-Ziv parsing and sublinear-size index structures for string matching. In *Proc. 3rd South American Workshop on String Processing (WSP)*, pages 141–155.

Kärkkäinen, J., Kempa, D., and Puglisi, S. J. (2013a). Lightweight Lempel-Ziv parsing. In *Proc. 12th International Symposium on Experimental Algorithms (SEA)*, pages 139–150.

Kärkkäinen, J., Kempa, D., and Puglisi, S. J. (2013b). Linear time Lempel-Ziv factorization: Simple, fast, small. In *Proc. 24th Annual Symposium on Combinatorial Pattern Matching (CPM)*, LNCS 7922, pages 189–200.

Kärkkäinen, J., Kempa, D., and Puglisi, S. J. (2014). Lempel-Ziv parsing in external memory. In *Proc. 24th Data Compression Conference (DCC)*, pages 153–162.

Kempa, D. and Puglisi, S. J. (2013). Lempel-Ziv factorization: Simple, fast, practical. In *Proc. 15th Workshop on Algorithm Engineering and Experiments (ALENEX)*, pages 103–112.

Kieffer, J. C. and Yang, E.-H. (2000). Grammar-based codes: A new class of universal lossless source codes. *IEEE Transactions on Information Theory*, **46**(3), 737–754.

Köppl, D. and Sadakane, K. (2016). Lempel-Ziv computation in compressed space (LZ-CICS). In *Proc. 26th Data Compression Conference (DCC)*, pages 3–12.

Kosaraju, S. R. and Manzini, G. (1999). Compression of low entropy strings with Lempel-Ziv algorithms. *SIAM Journal on Computing*, **29**(3), 893–911.

Kreft, S. and Navarro, G. (2013). On compressing and indexing repetitive sequences. *Theoretical Computer Science*, **483**, 115–133.

Kuruppu, S., Puglisi, S. J., and Zobel, J. (2010). Relative Lempel-Ziv compression of genomes for large-scale storage and retrieval. In *Proc. 17th International Symposium on String Processing and Information Retrieval (SPIRE)*, LNCS 6393, pages 201–206.

Kuruppu, S., Puglisi, S. J., and Zobel, J. (2011). Reference sequence construction for relative compression of genomes. In *Proc. 18th International Symposium on String Processing and Information Retrieval (SPIRE)*, LNCS 7024, pages 420–425.

Kuruppu, S., Beresford-Smith, B., Conway, T. C., and Zobel, J. (2012). Iterative dictionary construction for compression of large DNA data sets. *IEEE/ACM Transactions on Computational Biology and Bioinformatics*, **9**, 137–149.

Larsson, J. and Moffat, A. (2000). Off-line dictionary-based compression. *Proceedings of the IEEE*, **88**(11), 1722–1732.

Lempel, A. and Ziv, J. (1976). On the complexity of finite sequences. *IEEE Transactions on Information Theory*, **22**(1), 75–81.

Mäkinen, V. (2003). Compact suffix array – A space-efficient full-text index. *Fundamenta Informaticae*, **56**(1-2), 191–210.

Mäkinen, V. (2008). Personal communication.

Mäkinen, V. and Navarro, G. (2004). Compressed compact suffix arrays. In *Proc. 15th Annual Symposium on Combinatorial Pattern Matching (CPM)*, LNCS 3109, pages 420–433.

Mäkinen, V. and Navarro, G. (2005). Succinct suffix arrays based on run-length encoding. *Nordic Journal of Computing*, **12**(1), 40–66.

Mäkinen, V., Navarro, G., and Sadakane, K. (2004). Advantages of backward searching – efficient secondary memory and distributed implementation of compressed suffix arrays. In *Proc. 15th Annual International Symposium on Algorithms and Computation (ISAAC)*, LNCS 3341, pages 681–692.

Mäkinen, V., Navarro, G., Sirén, J., and Välimäki, N. (2010). Storage and retrieval of highly repetitive sequence collections. *Journal of Computational Biology*, **17**(3), 281–308.

Maruyama, S., Sakamoto, H., and Takeda, M. (2012). An online algorithm for lightweight grammar-based compression. *Algorithms*, **5**(2), 214–235.

Maruyama, S., Nakahara, M., Kishiue, N., and Sakamoto, H. (2013a). ESP-index: A compressed index based on edit-sensitive parsing. *Journal of Discrete Algorithms*, **18**, 100–112.

Maruyama, S., Tabei, Y., Sakamoto, H., and Sadakane, K. (2013b). Fully-online grammar compression. In *Proc. 20th International Symposium on String Processing and Information Retrieval (SPIRE)*, pages 218–229.

Moffat, A., Puglisi, S. J., and Sinha, R. (2009). Reducing space requirements for disk resident suffix arrays. In *Proc. 14th International Conference on Database Systems for Advanced Applications (DASFAA)*, pages 730–744.

Munro, J. I., Raman, V., and Storm, A. J. (2001). Representing dynamic binary trees succinctly. In *Proc. 12th Annual ACM-SIAM Symposium on Discrete Algorithm (SODA)*, pages 529–536.

Na, J. C. and Park, K. (2004). Simple implementation of String B-trees. In *Proc. 11th International Symposium on String Processing and Information Retrieval (SPIRE)*, LNCS 3246, pages 214–215.

Na, J. C., Park, H., Lee, S., Hong, M., Lecroq, T., Mouchard, L., and Park, K. (2013a). Suffix array of alignment: A practical index for similar data. In *Proc. 20th International Symposium on String Processing and Information Retrieval (SPIRE)*, LNCS 8214, pages 243–254.

Na, J. C., Park, H., Crochemore, M., Holub, J., Iliopoulos, C. S., Mouchard, L., and Park, K. (2013b). Suffix tree of alignment: An efficient index for similar data. In *Proc. 24th International Workshop on Combinatorial Algorithms (IWOCA)*, LNCS 8288, pages 337–348.

Navarro, G. (2004). Indexing text using the Ziv-Lempel trie. *Journal of Discrete Algorithms*, 2(1), 87–114.

Navarro, G. and Ordóñez, A. (2016). Faster compressed suffix trees for repetitive text collections. *Journal of Experimental Algorithmics*, 21(1), article 1.8.

Navarro, G. and Thankachan, S. V. (2016). Optimal encodings for range majority queries. *Algorithmica*, 74(3), 1082–1098.

Navarro, G., Raman, R., and Rao, S. S. (2014). Asymptotically optimal encodings for range selection. In *Proc. 34th Annual Conference on Foundations of Software Technology and Theoretical Computer Science (FSTTCS)*, pages 291–302.

Nevill-Manning, C., Witten, I., and Maulsby, D. (1994). Compression by induction of hierarchical grammars. In *Proc. 4th Data Compression Conference (DCC)*, pages 244–253.

Nicholson, P. K. and Raman, R. (2015). Encoding nearest largest values. In *Proc. 26th Annual Symposium on Combinatorial Pattern Matching (CPM)*, LNCS 9133, pages 385–395.

Nishimoto, T., I, T., Inenaga, S., Bannai, H., and Takeda, M. (2015). Dynamic index, LZ factorization, and LCE queries in compressed space. *CoRR*, **abs/1504.06954**. http://arxiv.org/abs/1504.06954.

Ohlebusch, E. and Gog, S. (2011). Lempel-Ziv factorization revisited. In *Proc. 22nd Annual Symposium on Combinatorial Pattern Matching (CPM)*, LNCS 6661, pages 15–26.

Orlandi, A. and Venturini, R. (2016). Space-efficient substring occurrence estimation. *Algorithmica*, 74(1), 65–90.

Pǎtraşcu, M. and Thorup, M. (2006). Time-space trade-offs for predecessor search. In *Proc. 38th Annual ACM Symposium on Theory of Computing (STOC)*, pages 232–240.

Policriti, A. and Prezza, N. (2016). Computing LZ77 in run-compressed space. In *Proc. 26th Data Compression Conference (DCC)*, pages 23–32.

Raman, R. (2015). Encoding data structures. In *Proc. 9th International Workshop on Algorithms and Computation (WALCOM)*, LNCS 8973, pages 1–7.

Rodeh, M., Pratt, V. R., and Even, S. (1981). Linear algorithm for data compression via string matching. *Journal of the ACM*, 28(1), 16–24.

Russo, L. M. S. and Oliveira, A. L. (2008). A compressed self-index using a Ziv-Lempel dictionary. *Information Retrieval*, 11(4), 359–388.

Rytter, W. (2003). Application of Lempel-Ziv factorization to the approximation of grammar-based compression. *Theoretical Computer Science*, 302(1–3), 211–222.

Sakamoto, H. (2005). A fully linear-time approximation algorithm for grammar-based compression. *Journal of Discrete Algorithms*, 3(2-4), 416–430.

Samet, H. (2006). *Foundations of Multidimensional and Metric Data Structures*. Morgan Kaufmann.

Sheinwald, D. (1994). On the Ziv-Lempel proof and related topics. *Proceedings of the IEEE*, **82**, 866–871.

Sinha, R., Puglisi, S. J., Moffat, A., and Turpin, A. (2008). Improving suffix array locality for fast pattern matching on disk. In *Proc. ACM International Conference on Management of Data (SIGMOD)*, pages 661–672.

Skala, M. (2013). Array range queries. In *Space-Efficient Data Structures, Streams, and Algorithms – Papers in Honor of J. Ian Munro on the Occasion of His 66th Birthday*, LNCS 8066, pages 333–350. Springer.

Storer, J. A. (1977). NP-completeness results concerning data compression. Technical Report 234, Department of Electrical Engineering and Computer Science, Princeton University.

Storer, J. A. and Szymanski, T. G. (1982). Data compression via textual substitution. *Journal of the ACM*, **29**(4), 928–951.

Subramanian, S. and Ramaswamy, S. (1995). The P-range tree: A new data structure for range searching in secondary memory. In *Proc. 6th Annual ACM-SIAM Symposium on Discrete Algorithms (SODA)*, pages 378–387.

Szpankowski, W. (1993). A generalized suffix tree and its (un)expected asymptotic behaviors. *SIAM Journal on Computing*, **22**(6), 1176–1198.

Vitter, J. S. (2008). *Algorithms and Data Structures for External Memory*. Now Publishers.

Wyner, A. and Ziv, J. (1994). The sliding-window Lempel-Ziv algorithm is asymptotically optimal. *Proceedings of the IEEE*, **82**, 872–877.

Yamamoto, J., I, T., Bannai, H., Inenaga, S., and Takeda, M. (2014). Faster compact on-line Lempel-Ziv factorization. In *Proc. 31st International Symposium on Theoretical Aspects of Computer Science (STACS)*, LIPIcs 25, pages 675–686.

Yang, X., Wang, B., Li, C., Wang, J., and Xie, X. (2013). Efficient direct search on compressed genomic data. In *Proc. 29th IEEE International Conference on Data Engineering (ICDE)*, pages 961–972.

Ziv, J. and Lempel, A. (1977). A universal algorithm for sequential data compression. *IEEE Transactions on Information Theory*, **23**(3), 337–343.

Ziv, J. and Lempel, A. (1978). Compression of individual sequences via variable length coding. *IEEE Transactions on Information Theory*, **24**(5), 530–536.

Index

Printed in the United States
by Baker & Taylor Publisher Services